NEW AMERICAN CROSSWORD PUZZLE DICTIONARY

NEW AMERICAN CROSSWORD PUZZLE DICTIONARY

EDITED BY

Albert and Loy Morehead

New Revised and Expanded Edition

Prepared by

Philip D. Morehead

A SIGNET BOOK

SIGNET
Published by the Penguin Group
Penguin Books USA Inc., 375 Hudson Street,
New York, New York 10014, U.S.A.
Penguin Books Ltd, 27 Wrights Lane,
London W8 5TZ, England
Penguin Books Australia Ltd, Ringwood,
Victoria, Australia
Penguin Books Canada Ltd, 10 Alcorn Avenue,
Toronto, Ontario, Canada M4V 3B2
Penguin Books (N.Z.) Ltd, 182–190 Wairau Road,
Auckland 10, New Zealand

Penguin Books Ltd, Registered Offices:
Harmondsworth, Middlesex, England

Published by Signet, an imprint of Dutton Signet,
a division of Penguin Books USA Inc.

New American Crossword Puzzle Dictionary
Edited by: Albert and Loy Morehead
Chief Compiler: Gerard Mosler
Staff: Philip D. Morehead
Earle Pitts
Beverly Bowers
John Hechtlinger
Ronald Moore

First Printing, November, 1967
First Printing, New Revised and Expanded Edition, December, 1986
13 12 11 10 9 8

Printed in the United States of America

PREFACE

The NEW AMERICAN CROSSWORD PUZZLE DICTIONARY was conceived by Albert H. Morehead, the well-known lexicographer and games expert, and compiled by a staff trained in the field, headed by Gerard Mosler. Mr. Morehead was a pioneer in the crossword puzzle field, having introduced the Cryptic (or Puns and Anagrams) type of puzzle to the United States, and his long experience editing dictionaries and encyclopedias made him uniquely qualified for the task.

As veteran crossword puzzle writer Jack Luzzatto wrote in the Introduction to the first edition: "This book is the finest aid available for solving crossword puzzles and other word games. It is the largest and most compendious book of its type, as a glance at the richness and range of the contents pages will reveal. So complete are the various categories that even a person who is not primarily interested in crosswords could put it to use as a handy reference guide in various fields. Special stress has been laid on the unusual words, exactly the ones that baffle most solvers. For the puzzle fan, this dictionary is the matchless source *par excellence,* a fount of information he cannot do without."

This new revision of Albert Morehead's classic has been thoroughly updated and designed to make finding the right answer easier than ever.

HOW TO USE THIS DICTIONARY

The user will get the most out of this dictionary if a few moments are spent becoming familiar with the wealth of information contained herein.

The dictionary is divided into three sections:

SECTION I lists definitions and key words with possible answers, the answers being arranged by length.

SECTION II contains listings of words under a variety of categories (user should consult the index of the section on page 245 and note the categories included).

SECTION III is a Word Locator for 2-, 3-, and 4-letter words, arranged in various alphabetical orders based on different letters in the words and clued by brief definitions.

Steps to Finding the Right Word

1) If the word you are looking for is a 2-, 3-, or 4-letter word, and you have any of the letters already, use Section III first. See instructions on page 352.

2) Look up the definition in Section I. Usually the best approach is to look up the principal word of the definition. For example, to find "quercine seed," look up "seed;" to find "Afr. antelope," look up "antelope."

3) See if the definition suggests one of the general categories contained in Section II:

The Bible	Literature
Chemical Elements	Mythology
Colors	Prefixes and Suffixes
Famous Names	Presidential Information
Foreign Words	Time Divisions—Calendars
Geography	Tribes, People, Natives
Heraldry	

A few moments taken to browse through this section will greatly increase the utility of it for the solver.

Cryptic Puzzles

For help in solving Cryptic or Puns and Anagrams puzzles, see the special section on p. 642.

Happy solving!

—*Philip D. Morehead*
Chicago, 1986

CONTENTS

SECTION I
Definitions and Answers

A

aa LAVA
Aaron's rod MULLEIN
abaca HEMP, LUPIS
abacus SOROBAN, SUANPAN
abalone ULLO, AWABI, ORMER, UHLLO, SEAEAR, EARSHELL
abandon MAROON, DISCARD
abandoned LORN, CORRUPT, DERELICT
abase(ment) LOWER, SHAME, MEIOSIS
abash COW, DAUNT, SHAME, HUMBLE
abatement LETUP
abbé MONK, PRIEST
abbess AMMA
abbey FLY, BADIA, ABADIA, PRIORY, NUNNERY
abbot ABBAS, COARB
abbreviations *use Word Locator, pp. 352–641*
abdicate RESIGN, RETIRE
abdomen BELLY, RUMEN, VENTER, VISCERA
abdominal HEMAL, CELIAC, COELIAC, VENTRAL
abduct PRESS, KIDNAP, SHANGHAI
abecedary TYRO, PRIMER
Abel's brother CAIN, SETH
Abelard's beloved ELOISE
abet EGG, FOMENT, INCITE
Abie's girl ROSE
abigail MAID
Abijah's son ASA
ability TALENT, CALIBER
abject BASE, VILE, MENIAL, SCURVY
abjure DENY, RECANT, REJECT
ablution SIDU, WASH, WUZU
abode DAR, HUT, NEST, HABITAT
abode of bliss EDEN, GOSHEN, ARCADIA
abode of dead AALU, AARU, ARALU, HADES, ORCUS, SHEOL
abolitionist LUNDY, STEVENS, GARRISON
abominable snowman YETI
aboriginal FIRST, BINGHI, NATIVE
abortion FAILURE, MISCARRIAGE
abound(ing) SNY, RIFE, SNEE, TEEM, SWARM
about (IN)RE, NEAR, SOME, ANENT, CIRCA
above OER, ATOP, OVER, UPON, SUPER, SUPRA
abrade RUB, FRET, CHAFE
Abraham's birthplace UR
Abraham's relative LOT, HARAN
abrasive BO(A)RT, EMERY, PUMICE, CORUNDUM
abridge RAZEE, CURTAIL, CONDENSE
abridgment DIGEST, PRECIS, EPITOME
abrogate ANNUL, CANCEL, RESCIND
abrupt CURT, RUDE, BLUNT, ICTIC
abrupt flexure GENU
Absalom's sister TAMAR
Absalom's slayer JOAB
abscond FLEE, ELOIN, ELOPE, ELOIGN, LEVANT
absent OFF, AWAY, AWOL, ABROAD
absolute FREE, VERY, ZERO, TOTAL, UTTER, CAPTAIN
absolve FREE, CLEAR, SHRIVE
absorb SOAK, SUCK, DRINK, IMBIBE, OCCLUDE
absorbed LOST, RAPT, SUNK
abstract ENS, BRIEF, ENTIA, COMPEND, EPITOME
abstruse ESOTERIC, ACROMATIC
abundance BOUNTY, GALORE, PLETHORA
abundant RIFE, AMPLE
abuse GALI, RAIL, GALEE, SNASH, REVILE, VIOLATE, MISTREAT
abut ADJOIN, BORDER
abutment ALETTE
abyss PIT, GULF, CHASM, VORAGO
Abyssinian *see* ETHIOPIAN
acacia SANT, SUNT, BABUL, GIDYA, KIKAR, MULGA, VEREK, VYALL, BABLAH, BABOOL, GIDGEA, GIDGEE, GIDYEA

academic MOOT, PEDANTIC
acadian CAJUN
accelerate REV, HASTEN, SPRINT
accent BLAS, TONE, ACUTE, ARSIS, GRAVE, ICTUS, BROGUE, STRESS, THESES
access ADIT, ENTRY, ENTREE
acclaim LAUD, ECLAT, PRAISE
acclivity SLANT, SLOPE, TALUS
accolade EMMY, TONY, AWARD, HONOR, OSCAR
accommodate FIT, LEND, FAVOR, LODGE, BILLET, OBLIGE
accomplish DO, EFFECT
accord with BEFIT
according to ALA, AUX, ALLA
accordingly ERGO, THUS, HENCE
accost HAIL, GREET, WAYLAY
account TAB, TOT, BILL, TALE, BATTEL
accounting term ITEM, ASSET, DEBIT, ENTRY, CREDIT, LEDGER
accountant CA, CPA, SIRCAR, AUDITOR
accouter GIRD, ARRAY, EQUIP
accumulate FUND, MASS, AMASS, HOARD, ACCRUE
accurate JUST, LEAL, NICE
accuse FRAME, DELATE, INDICT, REPORT
accustom ENURE, INURE
accustomed USED, WONT
ace JOT, ONE, TIP, AONE, TOPS, BASTO, PILOT
acerb SOUR, TART, BITTER
acetone ACETOL, KETONE
acetylene FOLAN, ETHINE, ETHYNE, TOLANE
ache YEN, PAIN, PANG, THROB
Achilles' slayer PARIS
acid KEEN, TART, AMINO, BORIC, OLEIC, NITRIC, OLEATE
acid radical ACYL, ANION, ACETYL
acidity ACOR
acknowledge NOD, OWN, AVOW, ADMIT, CONFESS
acme CAP, TIP, APEX, CREST, CLIMAX, HEYDAY
acolyte PATENER, THURIFER
acorn(s) MAST, OVEST, BELOTE, CAMATA
acquainted VERSANT
acquiesce CHIME, ASSENT
acquire WIN, GAIN, REAP
acrobat NAT, GYMNAST, TUMBLER, AERIALIST
acropolis CADMEA, CITADEL, LARISSA
across OER, OVER, TRAN(S)
acrostic AGLA, PUZZLE
act LAW, ACTU, BILL, DEED, FEAT, PLAY, WORK, ACTUS, EMOTE
action DEED, FIGHT, WORKS, AGENCY, PRAXIS, CONDUCT
action, put into ACTUATE
action word VERB
active BUSY, SPRY, AGILE, ALERT, BRISK, NIMBLE
actor HAM, DOER, MIME, AGENT, SERIO, MUMMER, PLAYER, STAGER, HISTRIO, THESPIAN, HISTRION
actors' group CAST, ACTRA, AFTRA, TROOP, EQUITY, TROUPE
actress DIVA, STAR, HEROINE, INGENUE, STARLET
actual REAL, TRUE, DEFACTO
actual, take as POSIT
actuate ROUSE, INCITE
acuate POINTED, SHARPEN
acuity WIT, EDGE
acute KEEN, SHARP, SHREWD
ad lib CASUAL, OFFHAND
adage SAW, DICT, MAXIM
adamant SET, FIRM, HARD
Adam's needle YUCCA
adapt SUIT, ADJUST, ATTUNE
add SUM, TOT, FOOT, TOTE, AFFIX, ANNEX, TOTAL, APPEND
adder *see* VIPER
addict(ion) FAN, BUFF, HOOK, USER, FIEND, HABIT, JUNKIE, MONKEY, DEVOTEE
addition(s) ELL, AFFIX, RIDER, ADDEND, ENCORE, ADDENDA, CODICIL
addle MIRE, MUDDLE
address HAIL, TACT, GREET, ACCOST, SPEECH
adenoids TONSILS
adept APT, EXPERT, VERSED
adequate DUE, FIT, MEET, AMPLE
adhere GLUE, HOLD, CLING, CLEAVE

adherent IST, ITE, AIDE, ALLY, VOTARY
adhesive TAR, GUM, GLUE, EPOXY, GLUEY, GUMMY, PASTE, CEMENT
adipose FAT, OBESE, SQUAB, SQUAT
adjective ADNOUN
adjourn DEFER, DELAY, SUSPEND, PROROGUE
adjust FIT, FIX, SET, TRIM, TRUE, ALIGN, ATTUNE, SETTLE
adjutant AIDE, STORK, ARGALA, HURGILA
adman BARKER, HUCKSTER
Admetus' wife ALCESTIS
admiral KING, SPEE, DEWEY, LEAHY, HALSEY, NELSON, NIMITZ, PORTER, FARRAGUT
admire ESTEEM, REVERE
admirer BEAU, SUITOR
admission PASS, CARD, ACCESS, ENTREE, TICKET
admonish URGE, WARN, CHIDE, EXHORT
admonisher MONITOR
ado FUSS, STIR, POTHER
adobe CLAY, BRICK
adolescence TEENS, YOUTH, NONAGE, PUBERTY
adolescent TEEN, MINOR, CALLOW, NUBILE, SUBDEB, PREBETIC, TEENAGER
adorn DECK, PINK, TRAP, BEGEM, DIGHT, BEDIZEN
adrift ASEA, LOST
adroit DEFT, HABILE
adulterate MIX, ALLOY, DEACON, DEBASE, DEFILE, DILUTE, CORRUPT
advance AID, ABET, LOAN, RAISE
advance guard VAN
advance slowly INCH, NOSE, CREEP
advantage BOT(E), EDGE, AVAIL, PROFIT, BENEFIT
advent COMING, ARRIVAL
adventure GEST, RISK, GESTE, DARING
advertiser SPONSOR
adventurer PICAROON
adventuress DEMIREP
advice LORE, REDE, AVISO
adviser EGERIA, MENTOR, NESTOR
advocate PRO, BACK, ANGEL, FAVOR, BACKER
Aegir's wife RAN
Aeneas' friend ACHATES
Aeneid poet VERGIL, VIRGIL
Aesir *see* NORSE GODS, *p. 320*
affair EVENT, LIAISON
affected FALLAL, BELOVED
affectionate FOND, DOTING
affirm AVER, AVOW, STATE, VOUCH, ASSERT, ATTEST
affirmative AY(E), YEA, YES, AMEN
affix PIN, JOIN, SEAL, STAMP
afflict(ion) AIL, PLY, TRY, VEX, WOE, HURT, ONUS, CURSE, DISTRESS
affluence EASE, FLOW, PLENTY, RICHES
affray RIOT, BRAWL, MELEE
Afghan DURANI
Afghan language PASHTO, PUSHTO; *see* IRANIAN
Afghan money PUL, ABBASI, AMANIA, AFGHANI
aficionado FAN, BUFF, DEVOTEE
aforesaid DITTO, PRIOR, SUPRA
aforethought PREPENSE
afraid RAD, ADRAD, REDDE
afreet GIANT; *see* DEMON
African language TIV, EFIK, EKOI, FULA, GOLA, KISSI, LIMBA, SERER, TEMNE, WOLOF, FULANI, IBIBIO, BALANTE; *see* BANTU, NIGER-CONGO, CUSHITIC, SEMITIC
African sectarian COPT, ABELITE
African tree IFE, BAKU, COLA, ODUM, ROKA, SHEA, ABURA, ADJAB, AFARA, BUMBO, DJAVE, IROKO, KHAYA, LIMBA, NARAS, NJAVE, OCHNA, POOLI, SASSY, UNONA, KORINA, MAFUR(R)A, TURTOSA, SASSWOOD; *see* TREE
Afrikaans TAAL
aft ABAFT, ASTERN
aftermath ROWEN, ARRISH, EDDISH, EDGREY
afterpiece, comic EXODE
aftersong EPODE
Agag slayer SAMUEL
again BIS, EFT, ANON, TWICE, ENCORE
against CON, ANTI, VERSUS
agalloch AGAR, AGGUR, ALOES, GAROC, TAMBAC

Agamemnon's kingdom MYCENAE
agate ONYX, ACHATE, MARBLE
agave ALOE, ISTLE, SISAL, SIZAL, MAGUEY, ZAPUPE
age ERA, ELD, EON, AERA, RIPEN, YEARS, SENESCE
age, of same COEVAL
aged OLD, ANILE, OLDEN, SENILE
agency ARM, CIA, FBI, FDA, FHA, FTC, HUD, ICC, IRS, NRA, NSA, OPA, DESK, DINT, NASA, WING; *see* U.N.
agent IST, SPY, AMIN, DOER, GMAN, TMAN, PROXY, WALLA, MEDIUM, WALLAH
agglomerate HEAP, LUMP, MASS, SLAG
aggravate NAG, TWIT, ENRAGE
agile LISH, SPRY, NIMBLE, LISSOME, SPRINGE
agitate FRET, STIR, CHURN, ROUSE
agitation GOG, FRET, STIR, DITHER, POTHER
aglow ALIT, RADIANT, SHINING
agnomen EPITHET, NICKNAME
agnostic ATHEOUS, INFIDEL, SKEPTIC, NESCIENT
ago SYNE, YORE, SINCE
agony WOE, PAIN, THROE
Agra tomb TAJ(MAHAL)
agree GEE, GIBE, JIBE, GRANT, TALLY, CONCUR
agreeable LIEF, AMENE, SUENT
agreement MISE, COVIN, IKRAR, ACCORD, CARTEL, ENTENTE
Agrippina's son NERO
Ahab's wife JEZEBEL
ai SLOTH
aid ABET, HELP, ASSIST, SUCCOR
Aida role AIDA, AMNERIS, RADAMES, RAMPHIS, AMONASRO
aim END, BUTT, ACIES, ETTLE, VISIE
air AER, ARIA, AURA, MIEN, TELE, TUNE, ETHER, OZONE, AERATE
air base, U.S. GUAM, OFFUT, SCOTT, ANDREWS, LANGLEY, LINDSEY, MAXWELL, KIRKLAND, RANDOLPH
air component NEON, ARGON, XENON, HELIUM, OXYGEN, KRYPTON, NITROGEN
air, pert. to AERO, AURAL
aircraft JET, MIG, GYRO, KITE, SHIP, SPAD, ZERO, STUKA, AVION, BLIMP, DRONE, PLANE, BOMBER, COPTER, AIRSHIP, BALLOON, GLIDER, BIPLANE, FIGHTER, MUSTANG, PROPJET, AEROSTAT, AIRPLANE, SPITFIRE, ZEPPELIN, AEROPLANE, DIRIGIBLE, MONOPLANE
aircraft carrier FLATTOP
aircraft part BAY, GUN, FLAP, HOOD, KEEL, NOSE, SKEW, TAIL, WING, STICK, STRUT, CABANE, ELEVON, RUDDER, AILERON, AIRFOIL, BLISTER, COWLING, NACELLE,
air-driven PNEUMATIC
airplane *see* AIRCRAFT
airplane shelter HANGAR
airport ORLY, OHARE, CROYDON, KENNEDY, PEARSON, SCUTTLE, SHANNON, HEATHROW, IDLEWILD, LAGUARDIA
airport part APRON, PYLON, STRIP, TOWER, HANGAR, RUNWAY, TARMAC
airship *see* AIRCRAFT
airtight HERMETIC
airy AERIAL, JAUNTY, ETHEREAL
ait ILE, EYOT, HOLM, ISLE(T)
Akan language TWI, TCHI, TSHI
akin SIB, AGNATE, COGNATE, GERMANE
Alabama information *see p. 308*
alameda MALL, WALK
alarm SOS, LARUM, PANIC, SIREN, TOCSIN
alas ACH, HEU, OCH, VAE, OIME, OHONE, OCHONE, OTOTOI
Alaska information *see p. 308*
Albanian dialect G(H)EG, TOSK
Albanian king ZOG(U)
Albanian money LEK, FRANC, QINTAR
albatross NELLY, GOONEY
Alberta information *see p. 306*
alcohol ETHAL, ETHYL, IDITE, IDITOL, TALITE
alcohol solid STERIN, STEROL

alcoholic SOT, WINY, BEERY, VINIC
Alcott heroine AMY, MEG, BETH
alcove BAY, NOOK, BOWER, NICHE, ORIEL, RECESS
alder ARN, ALISO, ALNUS
alderman BAILIE
ale *see* BEER
alembic STILL, RETORT
Alexander victory ISSUS, ARBELA
Alexander, wife of ROXANA
alga NORI, DASYA, FUCUS, ALARIA, DESMID, DIATOM
Algeria NUMIDIA
Algerian language ARABIC, BERBER
Algerian measure TARRI, TERMIN
Algerian money DINAR
Algerian weight UCKIA
Algiers district KASBA, CASBAH, KASBAH
Ali Baba's brother CASSIM
Ali Baba's password SESAME
alias AKA, ELSE, NAME, EPITHET, PENNAME
alibi PLEA, EXCUSE
alien GER, METIC, STRANGE
alienate WEAN, ESTRANGE
align TRAM, TRUE, DRESS, RANGE
alike AKIN, SAME, EQUAL
aliment *see* FOOD
Ali's descendants ALID(E)S
Ali's wife FATIMA
alkali LYE, REH, SODA, USAR
akaloid CERINE, CODEIN, ESERIN, THEINE, CAFFEIN, CODEINE, ESERINE, CAFFEINE
allay EASE, SLAKE, ASSUAGE, PALLIATE
allegiance FEALTY
allegory EMBLEM, APOLOG, ANAGOGE, PARABLE, APOLOGUE
allergy ATOPY
alley MIB, LOKE, WYND, TEWER
alliance EEC, AXIS, NATO, OASS, OPEC, ASEAN, SEATO, SHAPE, LEAGUE, ENTENTE
allice SHAD, ALEWIFE
allied AKIN, AGNATE, COGNATE
alligator *see* CROCODILE
alligator pear AVOCADO
allot DOLE, METE, CAVEL, GRANT
allotment *see* PORTION
allow LET, LOW, GRANT, ENDURE
allowance BOT(E), DOLE, ODDS, TARE, TRET, ARRAS, STINT, MARGIN
alloy LAY, PIG, AICH, ASEM, NIEL, TULA, BIDRI, BRASS, CALIN, DURAL, INVAR, STEEL, TERNE, VIDRY, ALBATA, ALNICO, ALUMEL, BIDERY, BIDREE, BILLON, BRONZE, GARBLE, LATTEN, NIELLO, OROIDE, PEWTER, SOLDER, TAMBAC, TEMPER, TOMBAC, AMALGAM, BABBITT, BIDDERY, DURIRON, ELINVAR, INCONEL, MIXTURE, PAKTONG, SPELTER, TOMBACK, TUTENAG, CALAMINE, CARBOLOY, ELECTRUM, HYPERNIK, NICHROME, PACKTONG, STELLITE
allspice PIMENTO
allude HINT, IMPLY, ADVERT
allure TICE, TOLE, TOLL, DECOY, TEMPT, ENTICE
allusion INKLING, INNUENDO
almond emulsion AMARIN, ORGEAT, AMARINE
almost NIGH, ANEAR, NEARLY
alms DOLE, CORBAN, MAUNDY, HANDOUT
alms chest ARCA, RELIQUARY
aloe substance ALOIN, PICRA
alone LORN, SOLA, SOLE, SOLO, SOLUS
aloof COOL, ABACK, REMOTE
alphabet ABC, OGAM, OGUM, OGHAM, SARADA, FUTHORC, CROSSROW
alphabet character RUNE
alphabets TEMA, LATIN, OGHAM, ONMUN, OSCAN, RUNIC, THERA, ATTICA, BRAHMI, CARIAN, HANKUL, LYDIAN, NASHKI, ARAMAIC, CHALCIS, MILETUS, MOABITE, PAHLAVI, PALMYRA, SABAEAN, UMBRIAN, CYRILLIC, ETRUSCAN, FALISCAN, LIBYANIC, SUMERIAN, CUNEIFORM,

GLAGOLITIC, PHOENICIAN; *see* GREEK, ARABIC, HEBREW, ENGLISH
Alps *see* MOUNTAINS
Alps pass *see* PASS
also EIK, EKE, PLUS, DITTO
altar ARA, BOMOS, HAIKAL, VEDIKA, CHANTRY
altar cloth PALL(A), DOSSAL, HAPLOMA
altar part BEMA, MENSA, GRADIN, RIDDEL, PISCINA, RETABLE, PREDELLA
alter GELD, VARY, MUTATE
alter ego SELF, FRIEND
alternate OTHER, WAVER, ROTATE, OSCILLATE
although EEN, ALBEIT
alula SQUAMA
alumni GRADS, PUPILS
always AYE, E(V)ER
amadou PUNK, TINDER
Amalekite king AGAG
amaryllis AGAVE, AMOLE, DAFFY, GUACO, JONQUIL, DAFFODIL, NARCISSUS
amateur TYRO, NOVICE, DABBLER
Amazon estuary PARA
Amazon queen ANTIOPE, HIPPOLYTA
Amazon tributary ICA, JARI, NAPO, PARA, PARU, JURUA, JUTAI, NEGRO, XINGU, MADEIRA
ambassador ELCHI, VAKIL, ELCHEE, LEGATE, NUNCIO
amber RESIN, LAMMER, SUCCIN, ELECTRUM, MEDREGAL
ambit SCOPE, SPHERE
amble PADNAG
ambush TRAP, BLIND, WAYLAY
amend ATONE, BEETE, REPAIR, REVISE
amendment RIDER, CODICIL
ament CHAT, CATKIN, CATTAIL, GOSLING
amerce FINE, MULCT, AFFEER
American GRINGO, YANK(EE)
American Indian *see* NATIVE AMERICAN
amide, pert. to AMIC
amino acid LYSIN, SERIN, VALIN, ALANIN, LYSINE, SERINE, VALINE, ALANINE, GLYCINE
Amish MENNONITE
amiss AWRY, AGLEY, ASTRAY
ammonia compound AMIN, AMIDE, AMINE
ammunition AMMO, AMMU, SHOT
amnesia FUGUE
Amos's friend ANDY
amount FECK, MISE, RISE, RATAL
amour-propre VANITY
ampersand AND, ALSO, PLUS
amphibian ANURA, ANURAN, APODA, CAUDATA, CAUDATE, COSTATA, URODELA, CAECILIA, SALIENTIA; *see* FROG, TOAD, SALAMANDER
amphitheater OVAL, ARENA, CAVEA, CIRQUE
ample WALLY, COPIOUS
amplify PAD, SWELL
amputate LOP, SEVER
amulet CHARM, SAFFI(E), FETISH, MERIAT, SCARAB, PERIAPT, TALISMAN
amuse DIVERT, REGALE, DELIGHT
anadem WREATH, CHAPLET, GARLAND
analyze ASSAY, PARSE, DISSECT
Anatolian language LUIAN, LUVIAN, LUWIAN, LYCIAN, LYDIAN, HITTITE
ancestor SIRE, MANU, ELDER, ATAVUS, BELSIRE
ancestral AVAL, AVITAL
anchor FIX, MOOR, AFFIX, KEDGE, DROGUE, GRAPNEL, KILLICK
anchor chain CABLE
anchor lifter DANDY, CAPSTAN
anchor part ARM, CAT, PEE, PALM, RING, TORE, CROWN, FLUKE, SHANK, TOROID
anchorite HERMIT, STYLITE
ancient OLD, AGED, EARLY, OLDEN, ARCHAIC, ARCHEAN
and PLUS, AMPERSAND
and so on ETC, USW
Andes *see* MOUNTAINS
Andes region PUNA, PUNO
andiron (FIRE)DOG, HESSIAN
Andorran language CATALAN
Andromeda's rescuer PERSEUS
Andy's friend AMOS
anecdote(s) ANA, TALE, STORY

anemic PALE, PALLID
anemone POLYP
anent (IN)RE, WITH, ABOUT, BESIDE
anesthetic GAS, DULL, ETHER, COCAIN, OPIATE, CHLORAL, DEMEROL, PROCAIN, STOVAIN, NOVOCAIN, XYLOCAIN, NOVOCAINE
angel MAH, EBLIS, SIJIL, URIEL, AZRAEL, BELIAL, CHERUB, SERAPH, SIJILL, ABADDON, GABRIEL, ISRAFIL, LUCIFER, MICHAEL, SAMMAEL
anger IRE, GALL, HUFF, RILE, ROIL, PIQUE, CHOLER
angle ELL, ZIG, AXIL, CANT, HADE, ARRIS, ELBOW, CORNER
Anglo-Saxon letter EDH, ETH, WEN, WYN, YOK, WYNN, YOGH
Anglo-Saxon money ORA
Anglo-Saxon official REEVE, GEREFA
Anglo-Saxon poem BEOWULF
Angolan language *see* BANTU
Angolan money ESCUDO, MACUTA, ANGOLAR, CENTAVO
angry MAD, HUFF, IRATE, RABID, WROTH, IREFUL, SNUFFY
anguish WOE, PAIN, AGONY
angular EDGY, ZIGZAG, POINTED
animal ZOON, BIPED, BEAST, BRUTE
animal cry ARF, BAY, HUM, LOW, MEW, MOO, TAP, YAP, BARK, BARR, BELL, BLAT, BRAY, GOWL, HISS, HOWL, JUCK, JUKE, MEWL, ROAR, YAUP, YAWL, YAWP, YELP, BLEAT, GROWL, GRUNT, MIAOU, MIAOW, NEIGH, SNARL, SNORT, WHINE, BALLOW, BOWWOW, SQUEAK, SQUEAL, WHINNY, TIRALEE; *see* BIRD
animal in literature JIP, MEG, APIS, BABE, BIMI, BRAN, CHIL, EGAN, GHAO, GRIP, MANG, MOTI, MYSA, NANA, RAMA, RANN, TYLO, BAMBI, BEVIS, DJALI, FADDA, GRANI, JUMBO, OSCAR, RUKSH, BAYARD, DAPPLE, FLOPIT, KATMIR, RAKUSH, ROLAND, WINNIE, ALBORAK, BAJARDO, BAVIECA, PEGASUS, RABICAN, REDWULL, XANTHUS, RABICANO, SLEIPNIR; *see* DOG
animal life BIOTA, FAUNA
animal, many-footed DECAPOD, HEXAPOD, OCTOPOD
animosity VENOM, ENMITY, HATRED, RANCOR
ankle, pert. to TARSAL, TALARIC
ankle(s) CUIT, HOCK, TALI, QUEET, TALUS, TARSI, TARSUS
annatto seeds ACHIOTE
anneal HEAT, TEMPER, TOUGHEN
annex ADD, ELL, APPEND
annihilate KILL, EFFACE, DESTROY
annotate GLOSE, GLOSS, GLOZE, COMMENT
annotation NOTE, RUBRIC, APOSTIL, EXEGESIS, FOOTNOTE
announce CERN, BRUIT, HERALD, STEVEN
announcement AD, BAN(S), BAN(NS), BLURB, NOTICE, GAZETTE, TIDINGS, BULLETIN
announcer DJ, MC, EMCEE, DEEJAY
annoy IRK, NAG, NOY, TRY, VEX, BORE, FASH, FIKE, GALL, HARRY, STURT, TEASE, MOLEST, PESTER
annual BOOK, MASS, PLANT, YEARLY, ETESIAN
annuity RENTE, PENSION, STIPEND, TONTINE
annul CASS, UNDO, VOID, ELIDE, ERASE, CANCEL, REVOKE
annular CYCLIC, RINGED
anoint OIL, ANELE, SALVE, BALSAM, CHRISM
anomalous ODD, ABERRANT
anon SOON, AGAIN, BEDEEN
ansa HANDLE
answer REPLY, RETORT, COMEBACK
answerable LIABLE
ant EMMET, KELEP, MAXIM, MINIM, NURSE, QUEEN, SAUBA, SLAVE, AMAZON, DRIVER, NEUTER, REDANT, WORKER, BULLDOG,

ERGATES, FORAGER, PISMIRE, REPLETE, ACULEATA
ant genus ATTA, ECITON, LASIUS, PONERA, FORMICA
antagonist FOE, ENEMY, RIVAL
ante PAY, POT, BLIND, KITTY, STAKE
anteater ANTBEAR, TAMANDU
antecedent(s) PRIOR, ANCESTRY
antelope, fabulous BAGWYN
antelope genus ORYX, KOBUS, OZANNA
antelopes DOE, GNU, KID, KOB, NIL, BUCK, DODA, GEMS, GUIB, KOBA, KUDU, ORYX, POKU, PUKU, TOPI, TORA, ADDAX, BAIRA, BEIRA, BEISA, BEKRA, BUBAL, CAAMA, CABRI, ELAND, ETAAC, GAMSE, GORAL, ISARD, IZARD, JAGLA, KAAMA, LICHI, NAGOR, NUNNI, ORIBI, PALLA, PASAN, SABLE, SAIGA, SASIN, TAKIN, TIANG, YAKIN, BAGWYN, BUBALE, CABREE, CABRIT, DIGDIG, DIKDIK, DUIKER, DUYKER, GOORAL, GRIMME, IMPALA, IMPOFO, KOKOON, KOODOO, KOUDOU, LECHWE, NAKONG, NILGAI, OUREBI, PALLAH, PASANG, POOKOO, PYGARG, REEBOK, RHEBOK, SASABY, SHAMMY, SHAMOY, BERENDO, BLAUBOK, BLESBOK, BUBALIS, CHAMOIS, CHIKARA, GEMSBOK, IMPALLA, NILGHAI, REDBUCK, SASSABI; *see* GAZELLE
antenna HORN, PALP, TOUCH, AERIAL, CERCUS, FEELER
antenna, end of CLAVA
anteroom HALL, FOYER, LOBBY
anthelion HALO, ANTISUN
anthem HYMN, MOTET, CANTATA
anther POLLEN, STAMEN
anthocyanin (O)ENIN
anthology ANA, CORPUS, GARLAND
antiaircraft FLA(C)K, ACKACK
antibiotic MYCIN, STREPTO, NEOMYCIN, PENICILLIN
antic DIDO, CAPER, PRANK
antidote SERUM, TOXIN, CACOON, EMETIC, REMEDY
antimacassar TIDY, DOILY
antimony KOH(O)L, SURMA, SOORMA
antiquated PASSE, ARCHAIC
antiquity ELD, YORE
antiseptic EGOL, BORAX, IODIN, IODOL, SALOL, CRECOL, IODINE, THYMOL
antitoxin SERA, SERUM, ANTIGEN
antler BEZ, DAG, BROW, HORN, SNAG, DAGUE, TRESTINE
antler parts TINE, PRONG, ROYAL, CROCHE, VELVET
anvil AMBOS, INCUS, STITH, TEEST, STITHY
anxiety HOE, CARE, FEAR, ANGOR, PANIC
any ALL, ARY, ONI, SOME
Apache chief MANGAS, COCHISE, GERONIMO, VICTORIO
Apache drink TISWIN
apart AROOM, ASIDE, ENISLED
apartment PAD, COOP, FLAT, ROOMS, SUITE, DINGLE, DUPLEX, STANZA
apartment house INSULA, TENEMENT
apathy ACEDIA, PHLEGM, TORPOR, DOLDRUMS
ape COPY, MIME, MOCK
ape genus PAN, SIMIA
apes MIAS, DREEL, DRILL, MAGOT, ORANG, PAPIO, PONGO, SATYR, WAWAH, APELET, BABOON, CHACMA, DOGAPE, GIBBON, MAIMON, MARTIN, MORMON, OURANG, PARROT, PONGIL, SIMIAN, WAUWAU, WOUWOU, HOOLOCK, MANDRILL, SIAMANG
aperture *see* OPENING
apex ACME, CUSP, APOGEE, CACUMEN
apex, belonging to APICAL
apex covering EPI
apex, rounded RETUSE
aphorism SAW, ADAGE, MAXIM, SUTRA, DICTUM, EPIGRAM
apiece PER, EACH
aplomb TACT, POISE, SURETY
Apocrypha *see p. 247*
apogee ACME, APEX, CLIMAX

Apollo birthplace **DELOS**
Apollo instrument **BOW, LYRE**
Apollo, pert. to **DELIAN**
apologue **MYTH, FABLE, ALLEGORY**
apoplexy **ESCA, STROKE**
apostate **RAT, RECREANT, RENEGADE, TURNCOAT**
apostle **NERI, REMI, ELIOT, ANSCAR, XAVIER, PATRICK, SCHOLAR, ULFILAS**
apostles of Christ **JOHN, JUDE, LEVI, JAMES, JUDAS, PETER, SIMON, ANDREW, CEPHAS, PHILIP, THOMAS, DIDYMUS, MATTHEW, ISCARIOT, MATTHIAS, THADDAEUS, BARTHOLOMEW**
apostolic manual **DIDACHE**
apothegm **SAW, AXIOM, ADAGE, DICTUM, SAYING**
appalling **AWFUL, TERRIBLE**
apparatus **GEAR, TOOL, DEVICE, GADGET**
apparel **GARB, RAIMENT**
apparent **OVERT, PLAIN, PATENT, EVIDENT, OBVIOUS**
apparition **GHOST, SHADE, SPECTER, REVENANT**
appealing **CATCHY, ATTRACTIVE**
appear **LOOM, KITHE**
appearance **AIR, MIEN, GUISE, PHASM, OSTENT**
append **ADD, AFFIX, ATTACH**
appendage **TAB, TAIL, CAUDA, RIDER, ADJUNCT**
appetite **ZEST, GUSTO, OREXIS**
appetite, abnormal **PICA, ASITIA, B(O)ULIMIA**
appetizer **CANAPE, APERITIF**
appetizing **SAVORY**
applaud **CLAP, LAUD, CHEER, EXTOL, PRAISE**
applauders **CLAQUE**
applause **OVATION, CLAPPING**
apple **CRAB, LOVE, POME, GOLDEN, PIPPIN, RUSSET, CODLING, COSTARD, WINESAP, PEARMAIN, DELICIOUS**
apple acid **MALIC**
apple product **ANONA, CIDER, POMACE**
apply **USE, RUBIN, APPOSE, IMPOSE, RELATE, PERTAIN**
appoint **SET, NAME, EQUIP, ORDAIN**
apportion **DEAL, DOLE, METE**
appraise **RATE, ASSAY, VALUE, ASSESS, EVALUE**
apprehend **NAB, FEAR, GRASP, GRIPE, INTUE, INTUIT**
apprentice **SNOB, TYRO, TRAINEE, NEOPHYTE**
approach **WAY, ADIT, (A)NEAR, ACCESS, IMPEND**
approbation **FAVOR, ASSENT, PRAISE, PLAUDIT**
appropriate **APT, MEET, ALLOT, USURP**
apron **BRAT, DICK, TIER, BARVEL, BISHOP, HOOVER, RUNWAY**
apropos **FIT, TIMELY, FITTING**
apt **FIT, PAT, DEFT, MEET, LIKELY, FITTING**
apteryx **MOA, KIWI, RATITE**
aptitude **BENT, GIFT, FLAIR, TALENT**
aquamarine **BLUE, BERYL**
aquarium **BOWL, TANK, GLOBE**
aqueduct **CANAL, CONDUIT**
aqueduct of Sylvius **ITER**
Arab **BROWN, GAMIN, HORSE, SEMITE, URCHIN**
Arabian *see also* **SAUDI ARABIAN**
Arabian chieftain **AMIR, EMIR, RAIS, REIS, AMEER, EMEER**
Arabian colony **ADEN**
Arabian lyric **G(H)AZEL**
Arabian measure **BARID, CUDDY, TEMAN, ZUDDA, FARSAKH, FARSANG, MARHALA, NUSFIAH**
Arabian measure (ancient) **DEN, SAA, FERK, KIST, CABDA, CAFIZ, MILLE, QASAB, ASSBAA, FEDDAN, GHALVA, QASABA, CAPHITE**
Arabian Nights characters **AGIB, AMINE, CANEM, FATIMA, HAROUN, SINBAD, ALADDIN, ALIBABA, BADOURA, HOUSSAIN, MORGIANA, SCHARIAH**
Arabian poet & romance **ANTAR(A)**
Arabian script **NESK(H)I**
Arabian tent village **DOUAR**
Arabian weight **BAHAR, CHEKI, KELLA, MAUND, TOMAN, MISKAL, BOKARD**
Arabian weight (ancient) **ROTL, NASCH, NEVAT, OCQUE, OUKIA**
Arabic alphabet **BA, FA, HA, RA, TA, YA, ZA, DAD, DAL,**

AYN, JIM, KAF, KHA, LAM, MIM, NUN, SAD, SIN, THA, WAW, ZAY, ALIF, DHAL, SHIN, GHAYN
arable LAINE, FERTILE, TILLABLE
arachnid ACERATA; *see* SPIDER, SCORPION, MITE, TICK, FLEA
arbiter UMPIRE, OVERMAN, REFEREE
arbitrary THETIC, DESPOTIC
arbor BOWER, RAMADA, PERGOLA
arboreal SYLVAN, DENDRAL
arcade LOGGIA, PORTICO, ARCATURE
arcadian RUSTIC, BUCOLIC
arcanum ELIXIR, SECRET, MYSTERY
arch COY, SLY, OGEE, CHIEF, HANCE, OGIVE, VAULT, IMPISH
archangel SATAN, URIEL, GABRIEL, MICHAEL, RAPHAEL
archbishop HATTO, ANSELM, BECKET, RAMSEY, CRANMER, PRIMATE
archer CLIM, CLYM, TELL, BOWER, CUPID
archery term BUTT, WAND, CLOUT
archetype IDEA, TYPE, IDEAL, MODEL, PATTERN
archfiend SATAN
architect ADAM, MEAD, WREN, MCKIM, BREUER, EIFFEL, KLENZE, PAXTON, WRIGHT, ALBERTI, BERNINI, GROPIUS, BRAMANTE, BULFINCH, SAARINEN, SULLIVAN
architectural feature ANTA, CYMA, SOCLE, FRIEZE, PLINTH
architecture, type of DORIC, GREEK, IONIC, LATIN, ROMAN, TUDOR, COPTIC, EMPIRE, FLORID, GOTHIC, LANCET, MOSLEM, NORMAN, ROCOCO, TUSCAN, BAUHAUS, BAROQUE, BOURBON, CLASSIC, MOORISH, RHENISH
arctic ICY, POLAR, GALOSH
ardor ELAN, FIRE, ZEAL, FERVOR
area TREF, TRACT, AREOLA, PURLIEU
arena BOWL, CAGE, OVAL, RING, RINK, SAND, TURF, DROME, LISTS, STADIUM
Argentine measure VARA, BRAZA, GALON, LEGUA, FENEGA, FRASCO, LASTRE, QUADRA, MANZANA
Argentine money PESO, CENTAVO
Argentine town AZUL
Argentine tree TALA, AJARI, AMBAY, TIMBO
Argentine weight LIBRA, QUINTAL
argonaut JASON, ACASTUS
Argos, princess of OANAE
argot *see* SLANG
argue MOOT, WORD, REBUT
argument AGON, FUSS, TIFF, WORDS, DEBATE, HASSLE, POLEMIC
aria AIR, SOLO; *see* SONG
arid DRY, VAPID, JEJUNE, STERILE
Aries RAM
arise MOUNT, REBEL, APPEAR
arista AWN, BEARD
aristocrat LORD, PEER, NOBLE
Aristotle's father AMYNTAS
Aristotle's home town STAGIRA
Aristotle's teacher PLATO
Aristotle's work ETHICS, ORGANON, POETICS
Arizona information *see p. 308*
ark ASYLUM, COFFER
ark landing place ARARAT
Arkansas information *see p. 000*
arm GIB, JIB, LIMB, EQUIP, GARDY, OXTER, BRANCH, PINION, FORTIFY, TENTACLE
arm of sea BAY, LOCH, FIRTH, FJORD, FRITH
arm, part of ULNA, ELBOW, OXTER, RADIUS, AXILLA, FOREARM, BRACHIUM
arm, pert. to BRACHIAL
armadillo APAR, PEBA, TATU, APARA, POYOU, TATOU, MATACO, PELUDO, DASYPUS, TATOUAY
armed band HOST, POSSE
armful LOCK, TAFFLE
armistice TRUCE
armor, arm & leg JAMB, CUISH, JAMBE, ARMLET, CUISSE, GREAVE, TUILLE, AILETTE, CHAUSSE, JAMBEAU, ROUNDEL, BRASSARD, BRASSART, GAUNTLET,

PALLETTE, PAULDRON, SABBATON, SOLLERET, VAMBRACE
armor bearer ARMIGER, CUSTREL
armor, body TACE, ACTON, CULET, TASSE, BYRNIE, CORIUM, LORICA, TASSET, TONLET, BROIGNE, HAUBERK, LAMBOYS, SURCOAT, DEMISUIT, DOSSIERE, GAMBESON, PANSIERE, PLASTRON
armor, full suit BARD, MAIL, WEED, BARDE, CUIRASS, PANOPLY, JAZERANT, PLACCATE
armor, head & neck COIF, HELM, ARMET, GALEA, VISOR, BEAVER, CAMAIL, CASQUE, GALERA, GORGET, HEAUME, HELMET, MORION, SALLET, SECRET, BASINET, GALERUM, GALERUS, (A)VENTAIL, BURGONET, CABASSET, GORGERIN
armor, horse POITREL, CHAMFRON, CRINIERE, CROUPIERE
arms *see* HERALDRY *p. 311*
army HERD, HERE, HOST, IMPI, LEGION, TROOPS, MILITARY
army division MORA, SQUAD, COHORT, LEGION, COMPANY, MANIPLE, PLATOON, INFANTRY, REGIMENT
army engineer SAPPER, SEABEE, PIONEER
aroid ARAD, ARUM, TARO, TANIA, KONJAK, TANIER
aroma AURA, NIDOR, SAVOR, BOUQUET
aromatic BALMY, SPICY, PIQUANT, PUNGENT
aromatic plant DILL, MACE, MINT, NARD, SAGE, ANISE, BASIL, CARUM, TANSY, GINSENG
aromatic substance TOLU, BUCCO, BUCHU, MYRRH, ARALIA, BALSAM
around NEAR, ABOUT, CIRCA
arouse FIRE, STIR, PIQUE, ACCITE
arquebus prop CROC
arraign PEACH, ACCUSE, INDICT, INDITE, IMPEACH
arrange FIX, PLAN, PLAT, ETTLE, SCORE, STAGE, DAIKER, DISPOSE
arrangement FILE, INDEX, TAXIS
arrangement, pert. to TACTIC
arrant BAD, UTTER, BRAZEN, VAGRANT
array DECK, ACIES, ADORN, PAREL, DEPLOY, APPAREL
arrears DEB(I)T
arrest NAB, HALT, SIST, STAY, PINCH, STUNT, COLLAR, DETAIN
arrive HENT, LAND, LIGHT
arrogance HUBRIS, HYBRIS
arrogant HIGH, LORDLY, UPPISH, CAVALIER
arrogate GRAB, CLAIM, USURP
arrow FLO, BARB, BOLT, DART, SELF, VIRE, FLANE, ROVER, SHAFT, SUMPIT(AN)
arrow case QUIVER
arrow maker BOWYER, FLETCHER
arrow part NOCK, PILE, STELE
arrow poison INEE, UPAS, URALI, ANTIAR, CURARE, WOORALI, WOORARA
arrowroot PIA, MUSA, ARARU, CANNA, TACCA, ARARAO, MARANTA, TAPIOCA
arrow-shaped BELOID
arroyo RUN, BAYOU, BROOK, CREEK, GULLY, HONDO
arsenic mixture SPEISS, ERINITE
arsonist PYRO, TORCH, FIREBUG
art ARS, WIT, WILE, KNACK, TRADE
art style *see* PAINTING
Artemis' victim ORION
artery WAY, AORTA, ATERIA, AVENUE, CAROTID; *see* VEIN
artful SLY, WILY, DOWNY, POLITIC
arthritis help ACTH, ASPIRIN(E), CORTISONE
Arthur's enemy MORDRED
Arthur's weapon RON, PRIDWIN, EXCALIBUR
Arthurian town AVALON, ASTOLAT, CAMELOT
artichoke CANADA, CYNARA, CHOROGI, GIRASOL
articulate JOIN, UTTER, VOCAL, JOINTED
artifice RUSE, CRAFT, DODGE, GUILE, TRICK, FINESSE

artificial FAKE, SHAM, FAKED, FALSE, PASTE, ERSATZ
artillery man GUN(NER), TOPECHEE
artist(e) DAB, ACTOR, ADEPT, BRUSH, ETCHER, FICTOR, SKETCHER; *see* PAINTER, SCULPTOR
artless NAIF, RUDE, NAIVE, SEELY, GAUCHE
arum ARAD, TARO, AROID, CALLA, STARCH
as QUA, LIKE, THUS, SINCE, WHILE
asafetida HING, LASER, FERULA, NARTHEX
asbestos ABISTON, AMIANTH
ascent RIST, UPGO, SLOPE, STEEP, STIPE
ascetic MUNI, YATI, YOGI, SADHU, YOGIN, ESSENE, HERMIT, AUSTERE, DERVISH
ascot TIE, SCARF, NECKTIE
ash(es) CHAR, SORB, ARTER, EMBER, ROWAN, VAREC, SINTER, WICKEN
ashen WAN, PALE, LIVID
ash fruit KEY, ROWAN, SAMARA
Asian HUN, SERE, THAI, TATAR, BURMAN, INDIAN, KOREAN, CHINESE
Asian plague CHOLERA
Asian tree ACLE, ASAK, ASOK, AUTE, DITA, KOZO, AEGLE, ASOKA, DURIO, MESUA, SIRIS, WAMPI, ZYLIA, NYSSA, MEDLAR, WAMPEE
aside OFF, APART, WHISPER
asinine INANE, SILLY, STUPID, IDIOTIC
ask SUE, THIG, FRAYN, SPEER, SPERE, ENTREAT
askew WRY, AGEE, ALOP, AWRY
asp URAEUS; *see* VIPER
aspect MIEN, SIDE, VULT, ANGLE, FACET, PHASE
aspen POPLAR, TREMBLE
asperse SKIT, SLUR, LIBEL, MALIGN, VILIFY, SLANDER
aspersion SLUR, INNUENDO
asphalt TAR, PITCH, BITUMEN
asphyxia APN(O)EA
aspire AIM, HOPE, COVET, CRAVE
ass DOLT, MOKE, BURRO, CUDDY, DICKY, JENNY, KIANG, KULAN, KYANG, NEDDY, CUDDIE, DICKEY, DONKEY, JENNET, KIYANG, KOULAN, ONAGER, QUAGGA, FUSSOCK, JACKASS, LONGEAR, ZEBRASS
assail PELT, BESET, MOLEST
Assamese dialect AO, KHAMI, LHOTA
assassin CAIN, THUG, SICARIAN
assault BLITZ, ONSET, SIEGE, STORM, BUFFET, THRUST
assay TRY, TEST, ANALYSIS
assaying cup TEST, CUPEL
assemblage BODY, HERD, LEVY, LEVEE, CAUCUS, THRONG; *see* BEVY
assemble MEET, HUDDLE, MUSTER, COLLECT
assembly HUI, BEVY, DIET, AGORA, COVEN, FORUM, GEMOT, PLENA, COVINE, GEMOTE, PLENUM, SABBAT, SESSION
assembly hall KIVA, ESTUFA
assembly, legislative DAIL, DUMA, RAAD, SEIM, SEJM, SEYM, YUAN, BOULE, JUNTA, CORTES, SENATE, COMMONS, KNESSET, LAGTING, RIGSDAG, RIKSDAG, CHAMBERS, CONGRESS, STORTING
assembly place PNYX, AGORA
assent NOD, AMEN, GRANT, ACCEDE
assert AFFY, AVER, POSIT, STATE, THREAP, THREEP
assess BOTE, IMPOSE; *see* TAX
assessor JUDGE, MUFTI, RATER
asset ESTATE, PROPERTY
assign ALLOT, CAVEL, REFER
assignment JOB, BEAT, DUTY, POST, TASK, ROUND
assimilate ABSORB, DIGEST
assist *see* AID
assistance ALMS, DOLE
assistant(s) AID, CAD, AIDE, CREW, HAND, STAFF, SECOND
assize WRIT, COURT, DECREE
associate MIX, MONK, MOOP, CRONY, HOBNOB, SOCIUS
association BOND, BUND, GILD, HONG, ARTEL, GUILD, HANSE, LODGE, UNION, CARTEL, CONGER, GRANGE

association football SOCCER
assortment FONT, BATCH, SUNDRIES
assuage CALM, EASE, ABATE, ALLAY, SLAKE
assume ENDUE, FEIGN, INFER, USURP, ARROGATE
assurance WORD, BRASS, APLOMB
assure PLEDGE, SICKER, WITTER
Assyria(n) ASSUR
Assyrian capital CALAH, KALAKH, NINEVEH
Assyrian ruler P(H)UL, SEMIRAMIS
aster DAISY; *see* FLOWER
astern AFT, BAFT, REAR, ABAFT
asteroid EROS, HEBE, IRIS, JUNO, CERES, FLORA, IRENE, METIS, VESTA, EGERIA, HYGEIA, ICARUS, PALLAS, PSYCHE, THETIS, ASTRAEA, EUNOMIA, FORTUNA, LUTETIA, MASSALIA, STARFISH
Astolat, Lily Maid ELAIN(E)
astound STUN, FERLY, SHOCK
astral SIDEREAL
astray LOST, AMISS
astringent ALUM, COTO, BORAL, STERN, CATECHU, STYPTIC(AL)
astrologer JOTI, JOSHI, JOTISI, CHALDEAN
astrology term APHETA, ALMUTEN, ANARETA
astronaut SEE, CARR, RIDE, GLENN, LAIKA, SCOTT, TITOV, WEITZ, WHITE, YOUNG, ALDRIN, BORMAN, CERNAN, CONRAD, COOPER, GIBSON, GORDON, LEONOV, LOVELL, SHIRRA, BASSETT, BLACKIE, BLUFORD, BREEZIE, COLLINS, CRIPPEN, GAGARIN, GRISSOM, KOMAROV, SHEPARD, SCHIRRA, YEGOROV, STAFFORD, ARMSTRONG, CARPENTER, COSMONAUT
astronaut term AOK, NOMINAL
astronomer BRAHE, HOYLE, JEANS, HALLEY, HUBBLE, KEPLER, NEWTON, GALILEO, PTOLOMY, COPERNICUS
astronomical URANIC
astronomical instrument ABA, ARMIL, SECTOR, ORRERY, SEXTANT
astronomical measure PARSEC, AZIMUTH
asunder APART, ATWAIN
asylum ARK, HOME, HAVEN, BEDLAM
atelier SHOP, STUDIO, WORKSHOP
atheist INFIDEL, AGNOSTIC
Athena epithet ALEA, ARELA, ERGANE, HIPPIA, PALLAS, MINERVA
Athena's shield (A)EGIS
Athenian ATTIC, METIC
Athenian ruler DRACO, ARCHON, CODRUS, CECROPS, THESEUS, PERICLES
athlete TURNER, GYMNAST
athletic event AGON, GAME, MEET, RACE, OLYMPICS
athwart OVER, AGAINST
Atlas BONE, MAPS, TITAN
atmosphere AURA, MAUVE, OZONE
atmospheric pressure, of BARIC
atom ISOBAR, ISOSTERE; *see* JOT
atom part ION, KAON, MUON, PION, MESON, BARYON, LEPTON, PHOTON, PROTON, NEUTRON, NUCLEUS, ELECTRON, NEUTRINO
atone ABY(E), EXPIATE, REDEEM
Atreus' slayer AEGISTHUS
attach FIX, PEND, AFFIX, APPEND
attaché case TASHIE
attached FOND, ADNATE, SESSILE
attack FIT, FRAY, RAID, BESET, BLITZ, BRASH, ONSET, SIEGE, SPASM, STRIKE
attar ITR, OIL, OTTO
attempt MIRD, OSSE, STAB, ESSAY, ETTLE, EFFORT
attendant(s) GILLY, SUITE, THANE, THEGN, TRAIN, VALET, DONZEL, GILLIE, VERGER
attention EAR, GAUM, HEED
attention sound PST, AHEM, PSST, COUGH
attentive WARY, TENTY, TENTIE
attenuate THIN, DILUTE, RAREFY
attest VOUCH, WITTEN, CERTIFY

attic LOFT, SOLAR, SOLER, DORMER, GARRET, TALLET, GRENIER
Attila HUN, ATLI, ETZEL
Attila's wife GUDRUN
attire *see* CLOTHING
attitudinize POSE, MINCE
attorney VAKIL, VAKEEL, ADVOCATE
attract DRAW, LURE
attraction DAHLIA, MAGNET
attribute OWE, TYPE, IMPUTE, ASCRIBE, FEATURE
attrition WEAR, GRIEF, REGRET
attune KEY, ADAPT, PITCH, ACCORD
auction CANT, ROUP, SALE, VEND, BRIDGE, HAMMER, VENDUE
audience EAR, PIT, EARING, PUBLIC, HEARING
audit SCAN, VERIFY, ACCOUNT
audition TRYOUT, HEARING
auditory OTIC, AURAL
auger BORE(R), GIMLET, WIMBLE
augment EKE, SWELL, VOWEL
augur BODE, SEER, AUSPEX
augury OMEN, PORTENT
August 1st LAMMAS
auk ALCA, POPE, URIA, ARRIE, MURRE, ROTCH, AUKLET, LUNGIE, MARROT, PUFFIN, ROTCHE, STRANY, DOVEKIE, GUILLEMOT
aunt TIA, TANTA, TANTE
aureate GOLDEN, ORNATE
aureole HALO, GLORY, NIMBUS
auric acid salt AURATE
auricle EAR, PINNA, ATRIUM
aurochs TUR, URUS, BISON
aurora EOS, DAWN
aurorian EOAN, ROSEATE
auspice EGIS, CARE, OMEN, AEGIS
auspicious BENIGN, DEXTER
Australian bird EMU, KOEL, COOEE, COOEY, GALAH, BROLGA, DRONGO
Australian cry COOEE, COOEY
Australian food KAI
Australian hut MIAM, MIMI, WURLY, GUNWA, MIAMIA, WURLEY
Australian money DOLLAR
Australian tree KARI, HAKEA, KARRI, NONDA, WILGA
Austrian language GERMAN, SLOVENE
Austrian measure FASS, FUSS, JOCH, MASS, MUTH, HALBE, LINIE, MEILE, METZE, PFIFF, PUNKT, ACHTEL, BECHER, KLAFTER, VIERTEL
Austrian money DUCAT, KRONE, FLORIN, HELLER, KREUZER, GROSCHEN, SCHILLING
Austrian weight MARK, SAUM, UNZE, DENAT, KARCH, PFUND, STEIN, PFENNIG, CENTNER
authentic REAL, TRUE, GENUINE, ORIGINAL
author POE, ANON, SAND, ZOLA, ALGER, CAPEK, DOYLE, GORKI, GRIMM, PAINE, STEIN, WOOLF, BUNYAN, FRANCE, HUDSON, IRVING, TAGORE, BENNETT, BOSWELL, KIPLING, ANDERSEN, ROUSSEAU, HEMINGWAY; *see* NOVELIST, POET, DRAMATIST, SHORT-STORY WRITER, ESSAYIST
authority RULE, SWAY, POWER, RIGHT, SAYSO
auto body style COUPE, SEDAN, TUDOR, WAGON, HARDTOP, HATCHBACK
auto court MOTEL
autobiography VITA, MEMOIRS
autocrat TSAR, MOGUL, TORSE, DESPOT
automaton GOLEM, ROBOT, ANDROID
automobile BUS, CAR, AUTO, DRAG, HACK, JEEP, TANK, TAXI, TRAM, WYNN, COACH, COUPE, LORRY, SEDAN, TRUCK, CAMION, HEARSE, JALOPY, JIGGER, JITNEY, LANDAU, TOURER, AUTOBUS, BERLINE, FLIVVER, JALLOPY, OMNIBUS, SCOOTER, SIDECAR, TAXICAB, TORPEDO, TRACTOR, TRAILER, TRAMCAR, TROLLEY, VOITURE, COUPELET, DUMPCART, MOTORBUS, MOTORCAB, MOTORCAR, ROADSTER, RUNABOUT, SUBURBAN, AMBULANCE, CABRIOLET, CHARABANC, LANDAULET, LIMOUSINE, BLACKMARIA, MOTORCYCLE
automobile, early REO, NASH,

EDSEL, HUDSON, MODELT, MAXWELL, PACKARD
automobile, inferior BOMB, CRATE, EDSEL, LEMON, WRECK, FLIVVER
automobile noise PING, RATTLE
automobile part BOOT, PLUG, TRIM, BRAKE, CHOKE, BONNET, BUMPER, CLUTCH, FENDER, STATOR, CHASSIS, STARTER, IGNITION; *see* VEHICLE
auxiliary verb MAY, SHALL
avalanche SLIDE, LA(U)WINE
avast STAY, STOP, CEASE
ave HAIL, FAREWELL
avenge VISIT, REQUITE, RETALIATE
avenger GOEL, NEMESIS
avenging spirit FURY, ALECTO, ERINYS, MAGAERA
avenue *see* STREET
average PAR, NORM, SOSO, MEDIAL
avert FEND, PARRY, SHEER, THWART
Avesta part YASNA, GATHAS, YASHTS, VENDIDAD, VISPERED
avifauna BIRDS, ORNIS
avocado COYO, PEAR, CHENIN, PERSEA
avocado sauce GUACAMOLE
avocation HOBBY, CALLING
avoid SHUN, EVADE, EVITE, ESCHEW
await PEND, STAY, TARRY
awake(n) (A)DAW, STIR, ALERT
award DSC, DSM, DSO, EMMY, MEED, OBIE, TONY, BONUS, GENIE, MEDAL, OSCAR, CONFER, LAUREL
aware HEP, RECK, WISE
away OFF, GONE, HYNE, HENCE, ABSENT
aweather, opposed to ALEE
awkward GAWKY, INEPT, CLUMSY, GAUCHE
awkward one LOUT, GALOOT, BUNGLER
awl BROD, DART, AUGER, ELSIN, BODKIN, STABBER
awn(ed) ILE, AVEL, BARB, ARISTA(TE)
awning TILT, CANOPY, SEMIAN, VELARIUM
awry CAM, AGEE, AJEE, AGLEY, GLEED
ax BILL, CELT, HACHE, ONCIN, FASCES, MACANA, POLEAX, BOUCHER, HALBERD, HATCHET, TWIBILL, FRANCISC, LOCHABER, PARTISAN, TOMAHAWK
axilla, pert. to ALA(R)
axiom MAXIM, TRUISM, APHORISM
axis, axle HUB, PIN, ARBOR, PIVOT
axis, pert. to AXILE
aye-aye LEMUR(OID)
Aztec hero(ine) NANA, NATA
Aztec temple TEOPAN, TEOCALLI
azure SKY, BLUE, CERULEAN

B

baal IDOL, MOLOCH
babble(r) BLAB, BLAT(E), HAVER, GLAVER, JABBER, HAVEREL
Babel DIN, SCHEME
Babel site SHINAR
baboon *see* APE
baboon-headed god HAPI, THOTH
babul GUM, GARAD, ACACIA
baby TOTO, WEAN, HUMOR
baby food PAP
Babylonia predecessor SUMER
Babylonian Adam ADAPA
Babylonian myth *see p. 319*
Babylonian numeral SAROS
baby's equip. BIB, DOLL, TALC, BOTTLE, DIAPER, RATTLE, TEETHER, LAYETTE
bacalao CODFISH, GROUPER
baccarat term COUP, BANCO, PUNTER, NATURAL
Bacchae, Bacchante M(A)ENAD
bacchanal ORGY, FEAST, REVELRY
bacchanal cry EVOE
bachelor AGAMIST, COELEBS
back AFT, AID, FRO, ABET, HIND, NOTA, REAR, NOTUM, STERN, DORSUM, TERGUM, ENDORSE, SPONSOR
back country BUSH, STICKS
back, lying on SUPINE
back, pert. to NOTAL, DORSAL, TERGAL
back, toward RETRAD, RETRAL
backbite SASS, MALIGN, VILIFY
backbone GRID, CHINE, NERVE, RIDGE; *see* SPINE

backer ANGEL, SPONSOR
backgammon TABLES, TRICTRAC
backtalk LIP, SASS, RETORT
bacon LARD, JAMON, PRIZE, SPECK, RASHER
Bacon work NOVUM, ORGANUM
bacteria GERM, AEROBE, COCCUS, VIBRIO, SARCINA
bacteriologist's wire OESE
bad ILL, EVIL, POOR, VILE
bad dream INCUBUS, NIGHTMARE
bad luck EVIL, MISHAP, AMBSACE
bad trip BUMMER
badge MON, PLAQUE, INSIGNE
badge, shoulder EPAULET
badger BAIT, FRET, BROCK, CHEVY, HECKLE, PESTER; *see* WEASEL
Badger State WI, WISCONSIN
badinage CHAFF, BANTER
baffle BALK, FOIL, POSE, ELUDE
bag NAB, SAC, CYST, GRIP, POKE, ASCUS, BOGUE, DILLI, POCKY, PURSE, CHAGUL, SACHET, MUSETTE, KNAPSACK, RETICULE
bag man PIPER
bag net FIKE, FYKE
bagatelle TRIFLE
baggage HUSSY, SAMAN, WENCH, DUNNAGE
baggage carrier PORTER, REDCAP
bagpipe music PIBROCH
bagpipe part LILL, DRONE, CHANTER
bagpipe player PIPER, SKIRLER
Bahaman aborigine LUCAYO, LUCAYAN
Bahrain money DINAR
bail BOND, HOOP, LADE, SURETY
bailiff REEVE, GEREFA
bait HANK, DECOY, SHRAP, BERLEY, CAPELIN
bait, drop DAB, DIB
bake FIRE, PARCH, ANNEAL, HARDEN
baker FLY, OST, OAST, OVEN, HORNERO
baking pit IMU, UMU, HUTCH
Balaam's steed ASS
balance ATRY, REST, POISE, SCALE, SANITY
balance of sentence PARISON
balance weight RIDER, BALLAST
balcony GALLERY, TERRACE
bald BARE, NAKED, HAIRLESS
Balder's killer HOD, HOTH, LOKI, HODER, HOTHR
baldness ACOMIA, ALOPECIA
bale EVIL, HARM, PACK, PYRE
balk COND, FOIL, REAR, REEST, IMPEDE
ball ORB, CLEW, GOLI, KNUR, PROM, TICE, DANCE, PINDA, PELLET
ball, hit LOB, BOWL, BUNT, SWAT
ballad LAI, LAY, DERRY
ballet dancer *see* DANCER
ballet term PAS, PLIE, JETE, COUPE, CHAINE, CHASSE, BOURREE, FOUETTE, POSITION, ARABESQUE
balloon part CAR, BASKET, GONDOLA, NACELLE
ballyhoo PLUG, TOUT, NOISE, PUFFERY
balm SALVE, BALSAM, ANODYNE
balmy MAD, SOFT, BLAND, SILLY, SWEET
Baltic language LATVIAN, LITHUANIAN; *see* FINNO-UGRIC
Baltimore heater LATROBE
balustrade PARAPET, RAILING
Bambi DEER
Bambi author SALTEN
bamboo, pickled shoots ACHAR
bamboozle FOOL, HOAX, CHEAT, HUMBUG, DECEIVE
ban BAR, TABOO, FORBID, INTERDICT
banal FLAT, CORNY, TRITE, TRIVIAL
banana FEI, MUSA, ENSETE, PLANTAIN
banana plant MUSA, ABACA, PESANG
band MOB, BELT, FESS, ZONA, COMBO, FACIA, PATTE, STRIA, CLAVUS, FASCIA, FILLET, LIGULA, RADULA, REGULA, TAENIA
bandleader DOC, RICH, SHAW, WEBB, WELK, BASIE, BLOCH, KRUPA, NORVO, SOUSA, DORSEY, HERMAN, KENTON, MILLER, OLIVER, VALLEE, WARING, CHORAGI, SPANIER, STRAUSS, GOODMAN; *see* CONDUCTOR
bandage SPICA, STUPE, LIGATE
bandit PAD, CACO, HOOD,

TORY, CATERAN, LADRONE, TULISAN
bane NEMESIS
banger LIE, SAUSAGE
Bangladesh language BENGALI
Bangladesh money TAKA
bangle ANKLET, CIRCLET
banish OUST, EXILE, EXPEL
bank BERM, BRAE, CAJA, DUNE, RELY, RIPA, BERME, DIGUE, SHORE
bank employee RUNNER, TELLER
bank, fishing HAAF
bank, pert. to RIPARIAN
bankbook PASSBOOK
banker BANYA, SARAF, MELLON, MORGAN, SHROFF
banknote BILL
bankroll WAD, ANGEL, BACKER, SPONSOR
bankrupt FAIL, BROKE, QUISBY
banner LABRUM; *see* FLAG
banquet DIFFA, JUNKET, REGALE, SPREAD
banter JOSH, TWIT, BORAK, CHAFF, ASTEISM
Bantu language ILA, FANG, LUBA, PEDI, SUTO, VILI, XOSA, ZULU, BEMBA, GANDA, KAMBA, KONGO, MAKUA, NGALA, RONGA, RUNDI, SOTHO, SWAZI, XHOSA, MBUNDU, NYANJA, RUANDA, SEPEDI, THONGA, TSWANA, KIKONGO, LINGALA, SWAHILI, FANGBULU, KIMBUNDU
banyan BUR(R)
baptize CHRISTEN; *see* NAME
bar FID, TIE, LOOP, RAIL, REIN, ROSE, SESS, SNIB, BETTY, BLOCK, BRIDE, DETER, ESTOP, INGOT, JIMMY, SHOAL, STEEK, BISTRO, HINDER, STRIPE, SALOON, TAVERN
bar, door RISP, STANG
barb JAG, NAG, FLUE, HARL, HERL, RAMUS, SPINE
Barbados native BIM
barbarian HUN, GOTH, ALIEN, VANDAL
Barbarossa FREDERICK
barbarous FELL, RUDE, CRUDE, CRUEL, ROUGH, BRUTAL, SAVAGE, HEATHEN
Barbary state ALGERIA, MOROCCO, TRIPOLI, TUNISIA
barber FISH, SHAVE, FIGARO, SHAVER, TONSOR, COMPOSER
bard SCOP, DRUID, RUNER, SCALD, SKALD, VATES, SAGAMAN, MINSTREL
bard of Avon SHAKESPEARE
bare BALD, NUDE, NAKED, STARK, STRIP
bargain DEAL, HUCK, KOOP, PRIG, TROG, DICKER, HAGGLE, HIGGLE, NIFFER, PALTER
barge HOY, PRAM, LUNGE, LURCH, PRAAM, SCOLD, SHREW
bark BAST, HIDE, RIND, ROSS, SKIN, BASTE, CORTEX; *see* ANIMAL CRY
bark, bitter NIEPA, NIOTA, QUININE, CINCHONA
bark, medicinal COTO, CASCA, MADAR, MUDAR, CANELLA
bark, mulberry KAPA, TA(P)PA
bark remover SPUD, ROSSER, SPUDDER
barker TOUT, PISTOL, SPIELER
barking LATRANT
barley BIG, BEER, BIGG, MALT, PTISAN, TISANE, TSAMBA
barm FOAM, YEAST
barn MEW, BYRE, AMBAR, LATHE, SKIPPER
Barnaby Rudge's raven GRIP
barnacle ACORN, BALANID
barometric line ISOBAR
barony HAN, FIEF
barrack(s) BILLET, CAN(N)ABA, BIVOUAC
barracuda SPET, BARRY, SENET, BECUNA, PICUDA, SENNET
barrel TUN, CADE, KNAG, TIERCE
barrel-maker COOPER, TUBBER, TUBMAN
barrel part LAG, BUNG, STAVE, GA(U)NTRY
barren DULL, GELD, SECK, DRAPE, EFFETE, HISTLE, STERILE
barren land REH, USAR, DESERT
barricade BAR, ABATIS, PALISADE
barrier DAM, PALE, TREBLE
barrister LAWYER, COUNSEL, ATTORNEY
barrow CART, KURGAN, TUMULUS
bartender MIXER, SKINKER, TAPSTER
barter MONG, SWAP, TROG, TROKE, NIFFER, TRAFFIC

base BAD, BAG, CAMP, VILE, CAITIFF, SERVILE
base, architectural DADO, SOCLE, PATTEN, PLINTH
base, attached by SESSILE
base on balls PASS, WALK
baseball league AMERICAN, NATIONAL
baseball managers and executives DARK, HOUK, MACK, MELE, FRICK, GRIMM, HANEY, KEANE, LOPEZ, TERRY, VEECK, ALSTON, BARROW, CRONIN, ECKERT, HARRIS, LANDIS, MARTIN, MCGRAW, RICKEY, RIGNEY, YAWKEY, ZIMMER, DRESSEN, HUGGINS, JOHNSON, STENGEL, BOUDREAU, COCHRANE, COMISKEY, DUROCHER, GRIFFITH
baseball player OTT, COBB, DEAN, FORD, FOXX, LYNN, MAYS, MIZE, RICE, ROSE, RUTH, WARD, AARON, ANSON, ARMAS, BAKER, BERRA, BOGGS, BROWN, CAREW, CAREY, DUFFY, EVERS, EWING, FABER, FLICK, GROVE, GWYNN, KEEFE, KELLY, KINER, LYONS, MARIS, PLANK, RIXEY, ROUSH, TERRY, VANCE, WALSH, WANER, WHEAT, WILLS, YOUNG, BENDER, CHANCE, CLARKE, DICKEY, FELLER, FRISCH, GALVIN, GEHRIG, GRIMES, GUIDRY, KALINN, KEELER, KOUFAX, LAJOIE, MANTLE, MANUSH, MUSIAL, PALMER, PARKER, SCHALK, SEAVER, SISLER, SNIDER, TINKER, WAGNER, WRIGHT, APPLING, BURKETT, CHESBRO, COLLINS, HORNSBY, HUBBELL, HUGGINS, JACKSON, JOHNSON, MADLOCK, NICHOLS, OROURKE, PENNOCK, RIZZUTO, SCHMIDT, SIMMONS, SPEAKER, TRAYNOR, WADDELL, WALLACE, BOUDREAU, CLEMENTE, COCHRANE, DIMAGGIO, DRYSDALE, ROBINSON, WILLIAMS
baseball team CUBS, METS, REDS, EXPOS, TWINS, ANGELS, ASTROS, BRAVES, GIANTS, PADRES, REDSOX, ROYALS, TIGERS, BREWERS, DODGERS, INDIANS, ORIOLES, PIRATES, RANGERS, YANKEES, BLUEJAYS, MARINERS, PHILLIES, WHITESOX, ATHLETICS, CARDINALS
baseball term BAG, ERA, HIT, OUT, RBI, BUNT, NINE, SACK, SAFE, SLAB, CATCH, FRAME, LINER, PITCH, PLATE, STEAL, STICK, RUBBER, SLUGGER
basement CELLAR
bashful COY, SHY, BLATE, HELOE, VERECUND
basic ROOT, PRIMARY, ESSENTIAL
basilica CANOPY, LATERAN
basin PAN, FONT, TALA, LAVER, STOUP, HOLLOW, LAVABO, LEKANE, MARINA, CUVETTE
basis FOND, AXIOM, PREMISE
bask SUN, APRICATE
basket PED, KISH, SKEP, DILLI, GRATE, MAUND, SERON, DOSSER, GABION, HAMPER, HOPPET, JICARA, KIPSEY, PEGALL, CRESSET, PANNIER
basket, fish CAUL, CAWL, KIPE, WEEL, CRAIL, CREEL
basket, fruit CABA(S), FRAIL, MOLLY, POTTLE, PUNNET, TAPNET
basket material RUSH, WOOD, OSIER, RAFFIA, RATTAN, SPLINT, WICKER, WILLOW
basket of coals CORB, CORF
basket, sports GOAL, CESTA
basketball inventor NAISMITH
basketball player CAGER, GUARD, CENTER, FORWARD, HOOPMAN, CAGESTER
basketball players BIRD, REED, COUSY, COWENS, ERVING, GERVIN, JABBAR, MALONE, MCADOO, PETTIT, RUSSELL, MARAVICH
basketball term NET, CAGE, FOUL, HOOP, LAYUP, WEAVE, BUCKET, DUNKER, FREEZE, JUMPER, DRIBBLE, KEYHOLE, PALMING, WALKING
basketry term RAND, OSIER, SLATH, SCALLOM

basketwork TEE, SLEW, WALE, SLA(R)TH
Basque WAIST, SCOTER, IBERIAN, BISCAYAN, EUSCARIAN
Basque game PELOTA
bass LOW, DEEP, VIOL, GRAVE, BASSO, DRONE, BURDEN, VIOLONE
bass (fish) ROCK, REDEYE, BARFISH
bast BARK, RAMIE, PHLOEM
baste DRAB, LARD, SLEW, CUDGEL
basto CARD, QUEEN
bat CLUB, HARPY, ALIPED, CUDGEL, RACKET, VAMPIRE
batfish DIABOLO
bathe LAVE, TOSH, CLEAN
bathhouse BAGNIO, CABANA
bathing suit TONGA, BIKINI, TRUNKS, MAILLOT
bath(s) BAIN, STEW, SAUNA, THERM(AE)
baton ROD, STICK, SCEPTER
batten RIB, REEPER
batter RAM, MAUL, PASTE, SLOPE
battering ram CORVUS, TEREBRA
battery CELL, PILE, PARAPET
battery term GRID, POST, CHARGER
battle COPE, FRAY, AFFRAY, HOSTING
battle cry ABU, ABOO, BANZAI
battle formation ACIES, HERSE, DEPLOY, PHALANX
battle hymn author HOWE, WARD, JULIA
battle site IVRY, JENA, STLO, ZAMA, ADOWA, ALAMO, BULGE, CRECY, IPSUS, ISSUS, MARNE, SEDAN, SOMME, VALMY, YPRES, ARBELA, BATAAN, CANNAE, CRESSY, SADOWA, SHILOH, VERDUN, DUNKIRK, MARENGO, PLATAEA, SALAMIS, BOSTOGNE, HASTINGS, SKAGERAK, WATERLOO, SKAGERRAK, TRAFALGAR; *see* CIVIL WAR
battlefield ARENA, CHAMP, SECTOR, TERRAIN, THEATER
battlement CRENEL, MERLON, PINION
battleship *see* SHIP
bauble TOY, GEWGAW, MAROTTE
Baucis' husband PHILEMON
Bavarian king LUDWIG
bawdy LEWD, OBSCENE, INDECENT
bawl *see* CRY
bay ISE, RED, VOE, COIL, COVE, KARA, BIGHT, CORAL, INLET, BISCAY, GALWAY, LAUREL, SAGAMI, TASMAN, UNGAVA, DONEGAL, SALERNO, THUNDER
Bay State MA, MASSACHUSETTS
bay window ORIEL
bazaar FAIR, SOOK, SOUK, AGORA, GINZA
beach PLAYA, SHORE, SHILLA, STRAND
beachcomber DRIFTER
beacon PIKE, FANAL, PHAROS
Beaconsfield DISRAELI
beads ROSARY, CHAPLET
beak NEB, NIB, TUTEL
beam RAY, SILE, CABER, GIRDER, LINTEL, RAFTER, TEMPLET, TEMPLATE
bean SOY, URD, LIMA, SOYA, MUNGO, PINTO, ADZUKI, LEGUME, HARICOT
bean curd TOFU
Beantown BOSTON
bear DUBB, URSA, BRUIN, YIELD, ENDURE, GRIZZLY, ICEBEAR, SUNBEAR
beard AWN, FUZZ, ARISTA, BARBET, GOATEE, SHADOW
bearer TOTER, SIRDAR
bearing AIR, MIEN, ORLE, PORT
beast LOUT, BRUTE
beast of burden OX, YAK, CAMEL, LLAMA; *see* ASS, HORSE
beastly VILE, FERAL, BRUTAL
beat LAM, TAN, CANE, DRUB, LACE, LASH, WELT, WHIP, PULSE, ROUND, CUDGEL, LARRUP, POMMEL, RHYTHM, SWINGE, SWITCH, THRASH, BELABOR; *see* TACK, ACCENT, DEFEAT
beater RAB, BATTEN
beau BLADE, FLAME, SWAIN
beauty parlor SALON
beauty treatment RUB, SET, WAVE, FACIAL, MUDPACK, MASSAGE

beaver CASTOR
beaver skin PLEW
Beaver State OR, OREGON
bêche-de-mer TREPANG
becket GROMMET
bed COT, KIP, BUNK, DOSS, DONGA, PALLET
bedclothes CASES, LINEN, SHEETS, PILLOWS, BLANKETS
bedlam RIOT, MELEE, UPROAR
Bedouin ARAB, RIFF, NOMAD, BERBER, RIFFIAN
bee DOR, BIKE, GYNE, HIVE, KING, DRONE, KARBI, MASON, QUEEN, BUMBEE, BUMBLE, KILLER, NEUTER, WORKER, ANDRENA, BUMBLER, BUMMLER, KOOTCHA, ACULEATA, HONEYBEE
bee genus APIS, APIDAE, BOMBUS, APOIDAE, TRIGONA
bee, pert. to APIAN
beech FAGUS, RAULI, ROBLE
beechnuts MAST
beehive SKEP, APIARY
beer ALE, BEER, BOCK, BREW, KVAS, MEAD, QUAS, SUDS, CHANG, KVASS, LAGER, POMBE, STOUT, PORTER, PANGASI, NEARBEER, METHEGLIN
beer ingredient HOPS, MALT, YEAST, BARLEY
Beethoven birthplace BONN
Beethoven opera FIDELIO
Beethoven sonata TEMPEST, ARCHDUKE, KREUTZER, PATHETIC
Beethoven symphony EROICA, PASTORAL
beetle DOR, BOUD, DOAR, DORE, DORR, GOGA, GOGO, IPID, POPE, TURK, BORER, CLOCK, FIDIA, GOGGA, HISPA, LYCID, MELOE, CHAFER, CLERID, CUCUYO, ELATER, GOLACH, GOLOCH, LAMIID, LARIID, LYCTID, MELOID, PICUDO, PIERID, PRUNER, PTINID, SAWYER, SCARAB, WEAVER, WEEVIL, BILLBUG, BUZZARD, CADELLE, CARABID, CARABUS, CUCUJID, DARDAOL, ELATRID, FIDDLER, FIREFLY, GIRDLER, GIRINID, GOLDBUG, GYRINID, HUMBUZZ, JUNEBUG, LADYBUG, LADYFLY, LAMPFLY, LUCANID, PTINOID, ROSEBUG, TUMBLER
beetle genus AMARA, LARIA, SAGRA, CLERUS, IPIDAE, LYCTUS, PTINUS, SILPHA, ADELOPS, AGRILUS, GYRINUS, LUCANUS, VEDALIA
before ERE, AFORE, PRIOR, EARLIER
beg SORN, CADGE, ENTREAT; *see* ASK
beget EAN, SIRE
Beggar's Opera author GAY
beggary WANT, PENURY
begin FANG, OPEN, ARISE
beginner TYRO, NOVICE, ROOKIE
beginning ALPHA, FRONT, ONSET, ORIGIN, INITIAL, NASCENT
begone OUT, VIA, SCAT, AROINT
beguile LURE, VAMP, WILE, WISE, COZEN
behave ACT, KEEP, DEPORT, COMPORT, CONDUCT
behest BID, ORDER, MANDATE
behind AFT, SLOW, ABAFT, AREAR, TARDY, ASTERN
behold LA, LO, SEE, ECCE, ESPY, VISE, VOILA
being(s) ENS, ESSE, LIFE, ENTIA, FRONT, HUMAN, ANTEAL, ENTITY
beldam(e) *see* HAG
Belgian FLEMING, WALLOON
Belgian language DUTCH, FRENCH, FLEMISH
Belgian measure AUNE, PIED, PERCHE
Belgian money BELGA, FRANC
Belgian weight LIVRE, CHARGE, CHARIOT
belief FAY, ISM, DOXY, CREDO, CREED, DEISM, DOGMA, FAITH, TENET, TROTH
believe DEEM, TROW
believer IST, DEIST, OMNIST
bell GONG, CODON, KNELL, TOCSIN, CAMPANA, CAMPANE, SQUILLA
bell set CHIME, CARILLON
bell town ADANO
belladonna ATROPIN, MANICON, ATROPINE
belle DEB, MAJA, PERI

Bellini opera NORMA, (I)PURITANI
belly RIFF, PLEON, THARM, PAUNCH, MIDRIFF
belong INHERE, PERTAIN
below NEATH, UNDER, SOTTO
belt OBI, LACE, SASH, ZONE, SMITE, CESTUS, CINGLE, CORDON, GIRDLE, BALDRIC(K), CEINTURE
bench BAR, PEW, BANC, DAIS, ZYGA, ZYGON, EXEDRA, SETTEE, THWART
bend BOW, NID, SAG, FLEX, KINK, LOUT, WARP, BULGE, CROOK, CURVE
beneath BELOW, UNDER, SOTTO
benedict GROOM
benediction SHEMA, BENISON
benefaction ALMS, BOON, GIFT
benefactor ANGEL, DONOR, PATRON, SPONSOR
benefice ANNAT, GLEBE
beneficial GOOD, SALUTARY
beneficiary HEIR, USER, DONEE, LEGATEE
benefit BOON, BOOT, AVAIL, PROFIT
benign SUAVE, GENIAL, GENTLE
Benin native FON
bent BIAS, HOOK, FLAIR, KNACK, TASTE
Beowulf's victim GRENDEL
bequest DOT, GIFT, DOWRY, LEGACY
berate JAW, WIG, CHEW, CHIDE, SCOLD, REVILE, CENSURE, CHEWOUT
bereave STRIP, WIDOW, DIVEST, DESPOIL
Berber MOOR, RIFF, HAMITE
Berber language RIF, DRAA, SIWI, KABYLE, LIBYAN, SHAWIA, TUAREG, ZENAGA, ZENETE, BERABER, GUANCHE, SAHARAN, TAMASHEK
bereft LORN, DEPRIVED
berg ICE, FLOE, BARROW
Berg opera LULU, WOZZECK
Bergen's dummy SNERD
berry PASA, BACCA, CUBEB, GRAPE, TOMATO, CURRANT, MADRONA; *see* FRUIT
berserk MAD, AMOK, ENRAGED
berth BED, JOB, BUNK, DOCK, SLIP, BILLET
beseech BEG, SUE, PRAY, ADJURE, APPEAL, OBTEST, ENTREAT
beset SIT, HARRY, OBSESS
besides AND, TOO, YET, ALSO, ELSE, INBY, OVER, THEN, EXCEPT
besiege BESET, OBSIDE, PESTER, PLAGUE
besmear DAUB, SOIL, TAINT
besom MOP, BROOM, HEATHER
bespangle STAR, STUD, ENSTAR
best ACME, AONE, BEAT, MOST, TOPS, CREAM, ELITE, CHOICE, OUTWIT, UTMOST
bet GO, POT, ANTE, PUNT, WAGE, HEDGE, STAKE, WAGER, MILIEU, PARLAY
bet, fail to pay WELCH, WELSH
betel SIRI, ARECA, BONGA, BUNGA, SIRIH
betray BLAB, SELL, SILE, TRAP, PEACH, SNARE, TRICK, REVEAL, SQUEAL
betrayer RAT, JUDAS, SEDUCER, TRAITOR
betroth AFFY, EARL, TOKEN, PLEDGE, PLIGHT
better TOP, (A)MEND, EMEND, REFORM
betting term ODDS, PUNT, TOUT, WAGER, BOOKIE, PARLAY
between AMELL, AMONG, INTER, MESNE
bevel CANT, EDGE, REAM, MITER, MITRE, SNAPE, ASLANT
beverage ADE, ALE, POP, TEA, BEER, SODA, WINE, CIDER, COCOA, MORAT, NEGUS, NECTAR, POSSET, LIQUOR, POTABLE; *see* DRINK
bevy NYE, HERD, PACK, WISP, BATCH, BROOD, CHARM, COVEY, DROVE, FLOCK, PLUMP, SIEGE, SKEIN, SUITE, SWARM, BAZAAR, COVERT, DESERT, FLIGHT, GAGGLE, MUSTER, SPRING
bewail CRY, WEY, WEEP, GRIEVE, LAMENT
beware SHUN, AVOID, ESCHEW
bewildered ASEA, DAZED, ADDLED, AMAZED
bewitch HEX, CHARM, ENAMOR, THRILL, ENCHANT, ENSORCEL
beyond BY, PAST, ULTRA, YONDER
bezel RIM, EDGE, SEAL, FACET, TEMPLET

Bhutan language NEPALI, DZONGKHA
bias PLY, BENT, CANT, SWAY, SLANT, SLOPE
biased person BIGOT
Bible BOOK, TEXT, WORD, WRIT, GOSPEL; *see also p. 246*
Bible version DOUAY, ITALA, TARGUM, HEXAPLA, REVISED, TYNDALE, VULGATE, PESHITTA, TETRAPLA, WYCLIFFE, KING JAMES
Biblical church workers LOIS, CHLOE, JULIA, LYDIA, PHEBE, RHODA, APPHIA, DORCAS, EUNICE, JOANNA, PERSIS, CLAUDIA, EUODIAS, SUSANNA, SAPPHIRA, SYNTYCHE, TRYPHENA, TRYPHOSA, PRISCILLA
Biblical information *see p. 246*
Biblical judges ELI, EHUD, ELON, JAIR, TOLA, ABDON, BARAK, IBZAN, GIDEON, SAMSON, SAMUEL, DEBORAH, OTHNIEL, SHAMGAR, JEPHTHAH, ABIMELECH
Biblical lands NOD, EDOM, ELAM, MOAB, SABA, EDREI, EKRON, JUDAH, MYSIA, PELLA, SUMER, ZOBAH, CANAAN, GOSHEN, TADMOR, LEBANON
Biblical money BEKA, MITE, BEKAH, SHEKEL, TALENT
Biblical mountains HOR, EBAL, NEBO, PEOR, SEIR, ZION, HOREB, MIZAR, SENIR, SINAI, TABOR, ARARAT, CARMEL, HERMON, PISGAH, THANACH
Biblical names AHI, BUZ, EVE, ABBA, ABDA, ADAM, AIAH, BELA, ERAN, ESLI, EZER, EZRI, HORI, IDDO, IRAM, ISUI, IVAH, LAEL, LEAH, MARA, NAUM, OBAL, OBIL, OREN, PUAH, REBA, SEBA, SHOA, SUAH, UCAL, ADLAI, AHBAN, AHLAI, ALVAN, BEZER, CUSHI, ETHAM, HADAD, HADID, HAGAB, HAGGI, HAMUL, ISHOD, ISHUI, JAPHO, JARAD, JERAH, KEDAR, LYCIA, MAHLI, REAIA, REUEL, SARID, SHEAL, SILAS, SIRAH, TALAH, TIRIA, UPHAZ, URIEL, ZABAD, ZAHAM, ZELAH
Biblical priests ELI, IRA, EZRA, AARON, ANNAS, URIAH, ZADOK, ELIJAH, JADDUA, JOIADA, JOSHUA, SAMUEL, ALCIMUS, ANANIAS, ELEAZAR, HILIKAH, JOHANAN, JOIAKIM, SERAIAH, ABIATHAR, CAIAPHAS, ELIASHIB, JEHOIADA
Biblical queens ABI, AZUBAH, ESTHER, NAAMAH, VASHTI, ZERUAH, ZIBIAH, AHINOAM, BERNICE, CANDACE, HAMUTAL, JEDIDAH, JERUSHA, JEZEBEL, MAACHAH, ZEBUDAH, ATHALIAH, DRUSILLA, NEHUSHTA, TAHPENES, BATHSHEBA
Biblical rulers OG, ASA, GOG, PUL, TOU, AGAG, AHAB, AHAZ, AMON, BERA, DOEG, ELAH, JEHU, NERO, OMRI, OREB, REBA, SAUL, AHIRA, BALAK, CYRUS, DAVID, HAMOR, HEROD, HIRAM, HOHAM, JABIN, JOASH, HOBAB, JORAM, MESHA, NADAB, PEKAH, PIRAM, REKEM, REZIN, REZON, SIHON, ZEBAH, ZIMRI, ABIJAH, ACHISH, ARETAS, BAASHA, CAESAR, DARIUS, HAZAEL, HEZION, HOSHEA, JOAHAZ, JOSIAH, JOSUAH, JOTHAM, LEMUEL, NAHASH, NECHOR, SARGON, SHINAB, SISERA, UZZIAH, AHAZIAH, AMAZIAH, JOHORAM, MENAHEM, PEKAIAH, SHALLUM, SHISHAK, SOLOMON, ATHALIA, HEZEKIAH, HYRCANUS, JEROBOAM, REHOBOAM, SHESHONK, ZEDEKIAH
Biblical sites UR, LUD, TOB, ARAM, EDEN, ELAH, ELIM, NAIN, SHUR, AENON, GEZER, HALAH, MOREH, NEGEB, OPHIR, PAHAN, SIRAH, AJALON, ATHLIT, BASHAN, BOZRAH, ENGEDI, HINNOM, KADESH, KIDRON, LAGASH, MASSAH, MIZPAH, SHARON, BAALBEK, CALVARY, GALILEE, CEHENNA, SHITTIM, BETHESDA
Biblical towns DAN, LUZ, NOB, ONO, CANA, ETAM, GATH,

GAZA, MAON, MARI, MYRA, TYRE, ZOAR, ACCAD, ARDER, BABEL, BARIS, BEREA, CALAH, DEBIR, DERBE, ELATH, ENDOR, ERECH, GEBAL, GERAR, GOLAN, HAZOR, JEBUS, JOPPA, PERGA, RESEN, SIDOM, SODOM, TROAS, ASHDOD, BETHEL, CYRENE, DOTHAN, EMMAUS, GADARA, GIBEAH, HEBRON, IBLEAM, KENATH, LIBNAH, MEDEBA, MIGDOL, PAPHOS, PISHON, RIBLAH, SARDIS, SHILOH, TARSUS, ANTIOCH, ASCALON, BABYLON, BEEROTH, BETHANY, CORINTH, EPHESUS, JERICHO, MEGIDDA, NINEVEH, ASHKALON, CAESAREA, NAZARETH, TIBERIAS

Biblical tribes DAN, GAD, KIR, LUD, CUSH, EDOM, LEVI, MOAB, PHUT, SHOA, UZAL, ASHER, DUMAH, EMIMS, JUDAH, LUBIM, MEDES, MINNI, ANAKIM, ARKITE, HAMITE, HIVITE, HORITE, JOSEPH, KENITE, LEVITE, REUBEN, SEMITE, SIMEON, SINITE, AMORITE, DINAITE, DODANIM, EDOMITE, HITTITE, MINAEAN, MITANNI, MOABITE, REPHAIM, RODANIM, SABAEAN, ZEBULUN, BENJAMIN, GADARINE, ISSACHAR, MIRARITE, NAPHTALI, NAZARITE, CANAANITE, SAMARITAN, SHELANITE

bicker SPAT, CAVIL, QUIBBLE

bicycle BIKE, TANDEM

bid ENJOIN, INVITE, TENDER; *see* BRIDGE

bier PYRE, TABUT, COFFIN, LITTER

bifurcation WYE, FORK, BRANCH

bight BAY, COVE, GULF, LOOP

bigot ZEALOT, FANATIC

bikini ATOLL, TONGA

bile GALL, VENOM, CHOLER, SPLEEN

bilk GYP, HOAX, CHEAT, TRICK

bill ACT, DUN, LAW, NEB, NIB, PEE, TAB, BEAK, CARD, MENU, NOTE, POSTER, TICKET, PLACARD

billet JOB, POST, BERTH, LODGE

billiards term CUE, BALK, BANK, KISS, POOL, REST, SPOT, CAROM, CHALK, MASSE

billow SEA, WAVE, SURGE, SWELL, ROLLER

bin ARK, CANCH, KENCH

bind WAP, LINK, TAPE, TILE, TRUSS, UNITE, COHERE, SECURE, SWATHE, CONFINE

binding YAPP

bingo KENO, LOTTO

biography LIFE, VITA, MEMOIR

biological BIOTIC(AL)

biological term GENE, RIMA

biologist *see* NOBEL

birch BIRK, CANE, FLOG, TREE, ALDER, STICK, BETULA

bird AVES, AVIS, IBIS, DIVER, ORNIS, TURCO, BARBET, DOPPER, GORLIN, HOOTER, NESTER, PEEPER, PULLUS, RAPTOR, SOARER, ANT BIRD, CHEEPER, CHIRPER, FLAPPER, FLOPPER, JACAMAR, MANAKIN, AVIFAUNA, FLAMINGO, LYREBIRD, TAPACOLO; *see* AUK, CRANE, CUCKOO, DOVE, DUCK, EAGLE, FALCON, FLYCATCHER, FOWL, GOATSUCKER, GOOSE, GULL, HAWK, HERON, HONEYEATER, HUMMINGBIRD, LOON, OWL, PARROT, PETREL, PHEASANT, PLOVER, RAIL, SANDPIPER, SONGBIRD

bird cry CAW, CRAW, HONK, PEEP, SING, CHEEP, CHIRM, CHIRP, CHUCK, CLUCK, QUACK, TWEET, CACKLE, GAGGLE, GOBBLE, SQUAWK, TRUMPET

bird, extinct MOA, DODO, MAMO

bird, flightless EMU, MOA, DODO, EMEU, KAGU, KIWI, RHEA, WEKA, DIDUS, NANDU, MOORUP, RAPHUS, APTERYX, OSTRICH, RATITE, WOODHEN, KIWIKIWI, NOTORNIS, CASSOWARY

bird, mythological ROC, RUKH, PH(O)ENIX, SIMORG(H), SIMURG(H)

bird of Juno PEACOCK

bird of Jupiter EAGLE

bird, pert. to AVIN, AVIAN, AVINE, OSCINE

bird, small TIT, TODY, WREN, BLUET, FINCH, PEWEE, PIPIT, SERIN, SYLPH, VIREO, TOMTIT
bird, talking CROW, MINA, MYNA, PARROT; *see* SONGBIRD
birdhouse COTE, NEST, AVIARY
birth ORIGIN, GENESIS, LYINGIN, DELIVERY, NATIVITY
birth, before PRENATAL, PREPARTUM
birth, by NE(E)
birth, of one's NATAL
birthday suit BUFF, NUDE, SKIN
birthmark MOLE, N(A)EVUS
birthstones *see p. 341*
bis AGAIN, TWICE, ENCORE, REPEAT
biscuit BUN, RUSK, PANAL, WAFER, PANTILE, RATAFIA
bishop ABBA, POPE, ALFIN, ARIUS, PONTIFF, PRELATE, PRIMATE
bishop's attire *see* VESTMENTS
bishop's seat SEE, APSE, BEMA, LAWN, DIOCESE
bistro BAR, PUB, TAVERN
bit ACE, FID, JOT, ORT, WEE, ATOM, IOTA, MITE, MOTE, PART, SNAP, WHIT, SPECK, MORSEL, SIPPET, PALLION
bite NIP, CHAM, CHEW, GNAW, SNAP, CHAMP, WHEAL, MORSEL
biting ACRID, CRISP, CAUSTIC, MORDANT
bitter AMAR, BILE, HATE, ACERB, ACRID, AIGRE
bittern KAKKAK; *see* HERON
bitterness RUE, ACOR, ATTER, MARAH, ACRIMONY
bitumen TAR, PITCH, ASPHALT
bivalve CLAM, MUSSEL, OYSTER
bizarre ODD, OUTRE, QUEER, DAEDAL, ODDISH
Bizet opera CARMEN
blab GOSSIP, TATTLE, PRATTLE
black DHU, JET, EBON, SABLE
black art MAGIC, SORCERY
black diamond COAL
black gold OIL
Black Sea EUXINE, PONTUS
blackbird MERL(E), LAZYBIRD; *see* CROW
blacken INK, SOOT, JAPAN, SHINE, DEFAME
blackguard GAMIN, KNAVE, VILIFY, VILLAIN
blackhead DUCK, PLUG, COMEDO, PIMPLE
blackheart CHERRY
blackjack MUG, COSH
blackout SKIT, FAINT
blacksmith LOHAR, SHOER, SMITHY, STITHY, FARRIER
blacksmith tool ANVIL, FORGE, HARDY, SWAGE, FULLER
blade BIT, OAR, EDGE, LEAF, TANG, DANDY, SPIRE, SWORD
blain SORE, BULLA, BLISTER
blame CHOP, ONUS, FAULT, GUILT, ODIUM, SNAPE, ASCRIBE, CENSURE
bland FLAT, MILD, SUAVE, URBANE
blandish COAX, CAJOLE, FLATTER, WHEEDLE
blanket BROT, COTTA, MANTA, QUILT, SHEET, CORONA, PONCHO, SERAPE, STROUD, TILPAH
blasé BORED, JADED
blast BUB, BANG, FLAW, GALE, ATTACK
blatant GLIB, GROSS, VOCAL, COARSE
blaze LOW, MARK, GLOW, FLARE
blazer JACKET
bleach BLANCH, CHLORE, WHITEN, ETIOLATE
bleak RAW, ABLET, DREAR(Y)
bleared INKY, DUSKY, RHEUMY
bleb BULLA, BUBBLE, BLISTER, PUSTULE
blemish FLAW, SLUR, TASH, AMPER, TACHE, BRUISE, MACULE, STIGMA
blench PALE, SHUN, AVOID, ELUDE, QUAIL, SHIRK, FLINCH, RECOIL
blenny POUT, GUNNEL, SHANNY, ROCKEEL
bless SAIN, BENSH, EXTOL, HALLOW, PRAISE, BEATIFY
blessed HOLY, SACRE, DIVINE, SACRED
blessing BOON, SAIN, GRACE, BENISON, BENEFICE
blight NIP, ROT, RUIN, RUST, SMUT, SOKA, MILDEW
blind SEEL, DECOY, SHADE, SHUTTER

blind alley IMPASSE, DEADEND, CULDESAC
blind, printing for BRAILLE
blindness CECITY, ANOPSIA
blink PINK, WINK, NICTATE, TWINKLE
bliss KEF, KIF, KEIF, KIEF, KIFF, HEAVEN, RAPTURE, ECSTASY
blissful HOLY, SEELY, ECSTATIC
blister BLEB, BLAIN, BLURE, BULLA(E)
blithe GAY, AIRY, JOVIAL
blizzard BURAN, PURGA
bloat SWELL, TUMEFY, DISTEND, INFLATE
bloated TUMID, TURGID
blob WEN, MASS, BLEMISH
bloc RING, CABAL, FACTION
block BAR, DAM, NOG, VOL, BITT, DOOK, FOIL, QUAD, CHECK, PERCH, DENTEL, DENTIL, HINDER, MUTULE, STYMIE
blockade BESIEGE, ISOLATE
blockhead ASS, OAF, MOKE, DUNCE, NINNY
blond(e) FAIR, FLAXEN, TOWHEAD
blood GORE, SERA, CRUOR, ICHOR, SERUM, PLASMA
blood emulsion CHYLE
blood, lack of AN(A)EMIA
blood money CRO, GALANAS
blood, pert. to H(A)EMAL, H(A)EMIC
blood poisoning PYEMIA
blood vessel *see* VEIN
bloodsucker FLEA, TICK, LEECH, VAMPIRE, PARASITE
bloody GORY, CURSED
bloom DOWN, PRIME, FLOWER, HEYDAY
Bloomsbury resident WOOLF, KEYNES
blooper SLIP, ERROR, LAPSE
blossom BLOOM, FLOWER
blot BLUR; *see* STAIN
blot out DELE(TE), EFFACE
blotch BLEB, BLAIN, BULLA, SPLAT, MACULA, MOTTLE
blouse TOP, MIDDY, CAMISA, GUIMPE, MIDDIE, SLIPON, CAMISOLE, PULLOVER, GARIBALDI
blow HIT, CONK, COUP, CRIG, DINT, GALE, HUFF, ONER, PANT, SWAT, WAFT, VAUNT, DISASTER
blow up EXPLODE, INFLATE
blowfish PUFFER
blubber CRY, FAT, WAIL, SPECK, LIPPER
blubber, strip FLENSE
bludgeon BAT, CLUB, MACE, BILLY
blue LOW, SAD, GLUM, DISMAL; *see p. 251*
Bluebeard's wife FATIMA
bluebird genus IRENA, SIALIA
bluebottle BLOWFLY
Bluegrass State KY, KENTUCKY
blue-pencil EDIT, CORRECT
blueprint MAP, PLAN, PLOT, DRAFT, TRACE
blues DUMPS, MEGRIMS, SADNESS, DOLDRUMS
bluff BRAG, CURT, HOAX, RUDE, CLIFF, STEEP, CRUSTY
blunder ERR, BULL, GAFF, SKEW, SLIP, BONER, BOTCH, ERROR, MISDO, BUNGLE
blunt DULL, RUDE, BLATE, GRUFF, OBTUND, OBTUSE, ASSUAGE
blush BLOOM, FLUSH, TINGE, MANTLE, REDDEN
bluster RANT, ROAR, BULLY, BRAVADO, SWAGGER
boa ABOMA, ANACONDA
board(s) EATS, LODGE, MEALS, PANEL, PLANK, STAGE, COUNCIL
board game *see* GAMES
boast BOG, GAB, BRAG, CROW, RAVE, GLOAT, PREEN, VAUNT, FLAUNT, BOMBAST, SWAGGER
boaster JINGO, BRAVADO, BRAGGART, RODOMONT
boastful air PARADO
boat *see* SHIP
boatman PHAON, CHARON
Boaz wife RUTH
bob DUCK, JERK, FLOAT, PENDANT, SHILLING
bobolink REEDBIRD, RICEBIRD
bode AUGUR, PORTEND, PRESAGE
bodice VEST, WAIST, BASQUE
body BOLE, BULK, FORM, KHET, LICH, MASS, RUPA, SOMA, STEM, TORSO, CORPSE, CORPUS, LICHAM, CADAVER, CARCASS
body motion, pert. to GESTIC
body of men ARMY, MASS, NAVY, CORPS, FORCE, POSSE

body part ARM, HIP, LEG, BACK, BONE, BUST, CELL, CHAP, DUCT, FOOT, HAND, HEAD, LIMB, LOIN, NECK, RUMP, SKIN, VEIN, ANKLE, BELLY, BLOOD, BOSOM, CHEST, KNEE, ELBOW, GLAND, GROIN, JOINT, LYMPH, NERVE, ORGAN, PENIS, SERUM, THIGH, TORSO, TRUNK, WAIST, WRIST, ANTRUM, ARMPIT, ARTERY, BREAST, DORSUM, FINGER, GULLET, HAUNCH, THORAX, ABDOMEN, PLECTRUM, SHOULDER, EPIDERMIS
body, pert. to SOMAL, SOMATIC
body segment SOMITE, MEROSOME, METAMERE, SOMATOME
bodyguard THANE
Boeotian capital THEBES
Boer language TAAL, AFRIKAANS
bog FEN, GOG, MIRE, MOOR, OOZE, QUAG, SYRT, MARSH, SWAMP, MORASS, SLOUGH
boggle JIB, SHY, BALK, ALARM, SCARE
bogus FAKE, SHAM, PHON(E)Y
Bohème character MIMI, MUSETTA, RODOLFO, MARCELLO
Bohème composer PUCCINI
bohemian ARTY, CZECH, GYPSY
boil STY, COCT, KYLE, RAGE, SORE, STEW, TEEM, BUBBLE, DECOCT, SEETHE, ESTUATE
boiler TANK, COPPER, RETORT, ALEMBIC, CALDRON
bold DERF, PERT, RASH, NERVY, BRAZEN, HEROIC, MALAPERT
bole DOSE, STEM, CRYPT, TRUNK
Boléro composer RAVEL
bolide METEOR, MISSILE
Bolivian language AYMARA, QUECHUA
Bolivian money CENTAVO, BOLIVIANO
boll POD, BULB, KNOB, ONION, SWELL
boll weevil PICUDO
Bolshevik RED, LENIN, TROTSKY
bolster AID, PROP, PILLOW
bolt BAR, PIN, LOCK, PAWL, SIFT, SLOT, ELOPE, FLASH, FASTEN, SCREEN, WINNOW
bolus CUD, CLOD, LUMP, MASS
bomb EGG, ABOMB, HBOMB, SHELL, ASHCAN, PETARD, GRENADE
bombard SHELL, STRAFE
bombardment RAFALE, BARRAGE
bombast ELA, GAS, RANT, BOAST, TUMOR, BLUSTER, FUSTIAN
bombastic TUMID, TURGID, FLOWERY, OROTUND, POMPOUS
bombyx ERI(A), MOTH
bond TIE, VOW, BAIL, DUTY, GLUE, YOKE, NEXUS, ESCROW, PLEDGE, VALENCE
bond(s)man ESNE, PEON, SERF, CHURL, HELOT, SLAVE, THRALL, VASSAL, VILLEIN
bond-stone PERPEND
bone OS, HIP, RIB, DENS, FANG, OSSA, ULNA, AMBON, AMBOS, ANCON, ANKLE, ANVIL, BLADE, CAPUT, COSTA, FEMUR, HYOID, ILIUM, INCUS, MALAR, MEROS, MOLAR, NASAL, PUBIS, RAMUS, SKULL, SPINE, TALUS, TEETH, TIBBY, TIBIA, TOOTH, VOMER, BICEPS, CANINE, CARPUS, COCCYX, CUBOID, CUSPID, CUTTER, DENTAL, DENTIN, DIPLOE, FIBULA, HALLUX, INSTEP, LUMBAR, MAGNUM, PELVIS, RACHIS, RADIUS, ROTULA, SACRUM, SPLINT, STAPES, TARSUS, ZYGOMA, BONELET, CARPAEL, COCHLEA, CRANIUM, DENTINE, ETHMOID, FRONTAL, GRINDER, HAMATUM, HIPBONE, HUMERUS, INCISOR, ISCHIUM, JAWBONE, JUGULUM, KNEECAP, KNUCKLE, LUNATUM, MALLEUS, MASTOID, MAXILLA, OSSELET, OSSICLE, OTOLITH, PATELLA, PHALANX, SCAPULA, SCIATIC, STERNUM, WORMIAN, BACKBONE, EYETOOTH, MANDIBLE, SHINBONE, VERTEBRA
bone, pert. to ULNAR, OSTEAL
boner FLUB, GOOF, SLIP

bonnet CAP, HOOD, LEGHORN
bonus TIP, MEED, AWARD, CUMSHAW, PREMIUM, PRESENT
bony HARD, LANK, LEAN, STIFF, OSSEOUS, SKELETAL
boo HISS, HOOT, JEER, RAZZ
boob ASS, DUNCE, NITWIT
booby LOSER, PRIZE, STUPID
boodle LOOT, SWAG, LOLLY
book MO, MS, LOG, MSS, VOL, HORA, OPUS, TOME, ALDUS, BIBLE, CODEX, DIARY, FOLIO, HORAE, LIBER, MANUAL, MISSAL, PRIMER, PSALTER
book part LEAF, PAGE, SPINE, JACKET
boom JIB, DRUM, ROAR, SPAR, SPRIT
boomerang KILEY, KYLIE, RECOIL, RESILE, BACKFIRE, RICOCHET
boon GAY, BENE, FAVOR, GRANT, JOVIAL
boor OAF, CARL, CLOD, LOUT, CHURL, CARLOT
boorish RUDE, GAWKY, VULGAR
boost ABET, KITE, LIFT, EXALT, HOIST
boot KICK, SHOE, SOCK, KAMIK, BOOTEE, BOOTIE, CRAKOW, MUCLUC, MUKLUK, PEDULE, BOTTINE, COTHURN, CRAKOWE, GAMBADO, HESSIAN, RECRUIT, TOPBOOT, BALMORAL, HALFBOOT, MUCKLUCK, NAPOLEON; *see* SHOE
booth SUQ, LOGE, SOOK, SOUK, CRAME, STALL
bootlick FAWN, TOADY, FLATTER
booty FANG, GAIN, LOOT PELF, PREY, SWAG
borax TINCAL
border HEM, MAT, TIP, ABUT, BRIM, LINE, RAND, BRINK, FLANK, FOREL, MARGE, SKIRT, VERGE, MARGIN, PURFLE, FLOROON
bore IRK, DRAG, TIDE, EAGRE, ENNUI, PRICK, PIERCE
boredom ENNUI, TEDIUM
borer AWL, BIT, AUGER, BEETLE, GIMLET, WIMBLE
born NE(E), NATE, NASCENT
Borneo native DYAK
borough BORG, BURG
borrow COPY, KICK, ADOPT, STEAL
borrowed stock BAER
bosh END, ROT, JOKE, POOH, TRIVIA, NONSENSE, RUBBISH
boss BAAS, KNOB, KNOP, STUD, UMBO, MASTER
Boston HUB, BACKBAY, BEANTOWN
Boston family CABOT, ELIOT, FILENE, LOWELL
botanical terms AXIL, NODE, SPUR, AMENT, HILUM, LOBED, OVATE, OVOID, RAPHE, SINUS, WHORL, ADNATE, CYMOSE, NODOSE, PILOSE, POLLEN, RACHIS, REPAND, RETUSE, RHAPHE, RUGOSE, SECUND, STIGMA, TERETE, BACCATE, CAUDATE, CILIATE, CLAVATE, CONNATE, CORDATE, CRENATE, CUNEATE, DENTATE, FALCATE, FOLIATE, GLOBOSE, HABITAT, HASTATE, HYALINE, INCISED, LABIATE, OBOVATE, OBOVOID, PALMATE, PELTATE, PILCATE, PINNATE, PLUMOSE, RADICLE, SEPTATE, SERRATE, SESSILE, SPICATE, SPINOSE, SPINULE, SULCATE, TERNATE, VALVATE, VEINLET, VILLOUS, VIRGATE
botanist RAY, BROWN, HALES, THOME, MENDEL, HELMONT, LINNAEUS, PRIESTLEY
botch MUX, FLUB, MESS, BUNGLE
bother AIL, FUSS, TODO, HARRY, TEASE, MEDDLE, MOLEST, PESTER
Botswana money RAND
bottle JUG, KIT, PIG, VIAL, CRUET, CRUSE, FLASK, PHIAL, CARAFE, CARBOY, FLAGON, MAGNUM, CANTEEN, COSTREL
bottom BED, BASE, LEES, SOLE, DREGS, FLOOR, NADIR, PLAYA, GROUND
bough(s) ARM, LIMB, TWIG, SHOOT, SPRIG, SHROUD, RAMAGE

boulevard DRIVE, AVENUE, CONCOURSE
bounce FIRE, LEAP, SACK, EJECT, VERVE, RECOIL, SPRING
bound HOP, DART, LOPE, SCUD, SKIM, LIMIT, STEND, DELIMIT
boundary LINE, MERE, METE, AMBIT, LIMIT
bounder CAD, CUB, RAKE, ROUE, SNOB
bounds AMBIT, COMPASS
bounty BOON, GIFT, MEED, BONUS, GRANT, PRIZE, LARGESS(E)
Bounty captain BLIGH
Bounty mate CHRISTIAN
bouquet ODOR, POSY, AROMA, POSEY, NOSEGAY
bourne GOAL, LIMIT, BROOK, STREAM
bout TURN, ESSAY, MATCH, ROUND, SETTO
bovine DULL, STOLID; *see* OX
bow ARC, NOD, ARCH, BEND, PROW, RODD, STEM, CURVE, DEFER, SALAM, STOOP, CURTSY, ONAGER, SALAAM, LONGBOW, QUARREL, ARBALEST, BALLISTA, CATAPULT, CROSSBOW, MANGONEL, TREBUCHET
bowed ARCATE, ARCUATE(D)
bowels PITY, RUTH, COLON
bower NOOK, ARBOR, KNAVE, ANCHOR, GROTTO
bowfin AMIA, LAWYER, DOGFISH, MUDFISH
bowl PAN, ARENA, BASIN, DEPAS, KITTY, MAZER, TANOA, ACERRA, BEAKER, CENSER, CHAWAN, THURIBLE
bowler HAT, DERBY, KEGLER
bowling BOCCIE, TENPINS, DUCKPINS, NINEPINS, SKITTLES
bowling term JACK, LANE, ALLEY, BREAK, FRAME, GREEN, SPARE, SPLIT, GUTTER, STRIKE, KINGPIN
box BIN, ARCA, BINN, CASE, CIST, CUFF, ETUI, INRO, LOGE, SEAT, SLAP, SLUG, SPAR, SWAT, TILL, CADDY, CAPSA, CHEST, CRATE, FIGHT, PUNCH, CASKET, COFFER, CAISSON, TRUMMEL, CANISTER
boxer DOG, FIGHTER, PUGILIST
boxers ALI, BAER, CLAY, HART, TATE, BURNS, DOKES, DURAN, ELLIS, LOUIS, HOLMES, LISTON, NORTON, SPINKS, TORRES, TUNNEY, CARNERA, CHARLES, CORBETT, DEMPSEY, FOREMAN, FRAZIER, FULLMER, GRIFFIN, JOHNSON, LAMOTTA, LEONARD, SHARKEY, WALCOTT, WILLARD, BRADDOCK, GRAZIANO, JEFFRIES, MARCIANO, ROBINSON, SULLIVAN, JOHANSSON, PATTERSON, SCHMELING
boxing RING, SAVATE
boxing, pert. to FISTIC
boxing term KO, JAB, REF, TKO, BELL, BOLO, BOUT, CARD, HOOK, KAYO, MATCH, ROUND, SETTO, CESTUS
boy BUB, LAD, TAD, TOT, GROOM, YOUTH, SHAVER; *see* MAN, MALE
boycott SHUN, BLACKBALL, BLACKLIST, OSTRACIZE
boyhood YOUTH, PUBERTY
boyish PUERILE
brace LEG, DUO, TWO, GIRD, PAIR, PROP, STAY, SHORE, TRUSS, CRUTCH, STIFFEN
brace and a half *see* THREE
bracer TONIC, STIMULANT
bracket CLASS, SHELF, STRUT, CORBEL, CONSOLE
bract GLUME, PALEA, PALET, SPADIX, SPATHE
brag CROW, RAVE, YELP, BOAST, PREEN, STRUT, VAPOR, VAUNT, SWAGGER
Brahma ATMAN
braid CUE, PLAT, TRIM, BREDE, INKLE, LACET, ORRIS, PLAIT, QUEUE, TRESS
brain, parts of GYRI, LOBE, PONS, ROOT, GYRUS, CORTEX, MEDULLA, CALLOSUM, CEREBRUM
brain term PAN, PIA, ALBA, DURA, HARN, ITER, LURA, OBEX, PYLA, TELA, UTAC
brake BUR(R), CURB, DRAG, BLOCK, BRUSH, DELAY
brake part DISK, DRUM, SHOE
branch ARM, BROG, FORK, LIMB, RAME, RAMUS, SPRIG, VIMEN, RAMIFY, RUNNER, STOLON

branched RAMAL, RAMATE, RAMOSE, RAMOUS, CLADOSE
branchia GILL
brand CHOP, FLAW, KIND, MARK, SEAR, LABEL, STAIN, STAMP, TAINT, STIGMA
brandish WIELD, FLAUNT, FLOURISH
brandy MARC, COGNAC; *see* LIQUOR
brash BOLD, HASTY, SAUCY
brass ALLOY, NERVE, OFFICER(S)
brat IMP, BANTLING
brave BOLD, DARE, DEFY, FACE, GAME, MANLY, STIFF, DARING, HEROIC, INDIAN
bravo BIS, OLE, RAH, THUG
brawl ROW, SHINDY; *see* FIGHT
brawny HARD, TOUGH, SINEWY
bray MIX, CRUSH, GRIND, HEEHAW
brazen PERT, NERVY, SASSY, CHEEKY
Brazil discoverer CABRAL
Brazilian aborigine ANDOA, CARIB
Brazilian measure MOIO, PASSO, TONEL, CUARTA, TAREFA; *see* PORTUGUESE MEASURE
Brazilian money REIS, CONTO, MILREIS, MOIDORE, CRUZEIRO
Brazilian tree APA, ANDA, ARACA, MURURE, WALLABA, ANDAASSU
Brazilian weight ONCA, LIBRA, ARROBA, OITAVA, ARRATEL, QUILATE, QUINTAL
breach GAP, RENT, RIFT, SLAP, CLEFT, CRACK, RUPTURE
bread BUN, CUSH, DIKA, LOAF, PAIN, PONE, ROLL, RUSK, BATCH, KISRA, MANNA, BREWIS, MATZOS, PANADA, SIPPET, MANCHET, MATZOTH
bread part RIND, CRUMB, CRUST
bread spread JAM, OLEO, JELLY, BUTTER
bread type RYE, AZYM, CORN, BLACK, CAROB, WHEAT, WHITE, BANANA, RAISIN
breadfruit KAJ, TERAP, JA(C)KFRUIT
break BOON, HINT, RUIN, SNAP, CRACK, HIATUS, RECESS, CAESURA, RUPTURE
breaker BILLOW, COMBER, ROLLER
break in STAVE, INITIATE
breakwater COB, DAM, DIKE, MOLE, PIER, QUAY, JETTY
bream TAI, CHAD, SCUP, PORGY, SHINER, SUNFISH
breast CHEST; *see* BODY
breastbone STERNUM
breastplate URIM, ARMOR, EPHOD, THORAX
breastwork FORT, REDAN, DICKEY, SCHERM, PARAPET, RAMPART
breath ANDE, HUFF, LIFE, PECH, PRANA, PNEUMA, HALITUS
breathe LIVE, PANT, PUFF, WHEEZE, RESPIRE
breather REST, BREAK, PAUSE
breathing GASP, RALE, PNEUMA, STRIDOR
breech BORE, BUTT, REAR, BLOCK
breechcloth MALO, CLOUT, GSTRING
breeches TREWS, BRITCHES, JODHPURS, TROUSERS
breed ILK, KIND, RACE, REAR, SIRE, BEGET, HATCH, RAISE, PROGENY
breeze AIR, AURA, FLAW, GUST, PIRR, STIR, WIND, ZEPHYR
breve MARK, NOTE, WRIT, BRIEF, MINIM, ORDER
brevet PATENT, LICENSE
breviary ORDO, DIGEST, PORTAS, COMPEND, EPITOME, PORTASS
brew MIX, PLOT, STEW, FOMENT, CONCOCT
brewer's material CORN, HOPS, MALT, YEAST, BARLEY
brewing GAAL, GAIL, GYLE, MALTING
bribe SOP, BAIT, SWAG, GRAFT, GRAVY, TEMPT, BOODLE, PAYOLA, SUBORN, DANEGELD
bric-a-brac CURIO, VERTU, VIRTU, BIBELOT
brick NOG, DOOK, MARL, ADOBE
brick carrier HOD
bricklayer MASON
bridal wreath SPIREA
bride KALLAH
Bridewell GAOL, JAIL, PRISON
bridge ARCH, LINK, PONS, PONT, SPAN, MAGAS, PONTOON
bridge part DECK, PIER, SHOE,

CABLE, CROWN, PYLON, TRUSS, HANGAR, CAISSON, TRESSEL, TRESTLE, SPANDREL
bridge (game) term BYE, LEG, SET, BOOK, DUCK, ECHO, JUMP, OPEN, SLAM, VOID, SHIFT, TRICK, DOUBLE, RUBBER, NOTRUMP; *see* CARD TERM
bridges ELSA, FORTH, MERIC, SANDO, SIGHS, STORY, TOWER, HOBART, HOWRAH, LONDON, MTHOPE, QUEBEC, RIALTO, VOULTE, BAYONNE, BIRECIC, MIAPIMI, NARROWS, OAKLAND, RAINBOW, SEVERIN, STJOHNS, VECCHIO, WESTEND, ARRABIDA, BROOKLYN, BURDEKIN, CORNWALL, DEERISLE, FORTPITT, HELLGATE, LONGVIEW, MACKINAC, MIRABEAU, TRANSBAY, WATERLOO, GOLDENGATE, TRIBOROUGH, VERRAZANO, WHITESTONE
bridle BIT, CURB, BRANK, CAPER, STRUT, BRANKS, PILLORY, SNAFFLE
brief CURT, PITHY, TERSE, CONCISE, LACONIC, SUMMARY
brigand BANDIT, LATRON
bright APT, GAY, GLEG, KEEN, NAIF, ANIME, LUCID, NITID, SHARP, SHINING
brightness NITOR, SHEEN, ACUMEN
brilliance ECLAT, LUSTER, GLITTER, ORIENCY
brilliant GEM, SIGNAL, DIAMOND, RADIANT
brim POKE, SKIRT; *see* EDGE
brine SEA, MAIN, SALT, BRACK, OCEAN, TEARS, PICKLE
bring FETCH, INCUR, COMMAND, CONDUCT
bring forth EAN, BEAR, YEAN, BEGET, HATCH
brink END, EVE, DITCH, MARGE, MARGIN
briny SALTY, SALINE
brisk LIVE, PERK, SPRY, YARE, ALERT, FLEET, KEDGE, PERKY, RAPID, SHARP, NIMBLE, CHEERY, ALLEGRO
bristle RIB, SETA, BRUSH, PREEN, PRIDE, SPINE, STRUT, CHAETA, PALPUS, RUFFLE
bristly HISPID, SETOSE
Britain UK, ALBION, BRITANNIA
British *see* ENGLISH
British Columbia information *see* p. 306
Brittany ARMORICA
brittle FROW, WEAK, CRISP, FRAIL, FROWY, FICKLE
broach AIR, AWL, VENT, BEGIN, RIMER, VOICE, LAUNCH, REAMER, PUBLISH
Broadway sign SRO
brogan BOOT, SHOE, STOGY
brogue *see* ACCENT
broil ROW, GRILL, MELEE, SCRAP, FRACAS, SCORCH
broker AGENT, FACTOR, JOBBER, SCHATCHEN
Bronx cheer RAZZ, RASPBERRY
bronze AES
brooch PIN, OUCH, CAMEO, CLASP, FIBULA, PECTORAL
brood FRY, NID, NYE, SIT, BEVY, MOPE, NEST, NIDE, COVEY, HATCH, LITTER
brook RUN, BEAR, BECK, RILL, ABIDE, CREEK, STAND, RILLET, RUNNEL
broom COW, MOP, SWAB, BESOM, HIRSE, WHISK
broth BROO, SOUP, BOUILLON, CONSOMME
brothel BAGNIO, BORDEL
brother FRA, PAL, SIB, MONK, BILLY, CADET, FRIAR, FELLOW, FRATER, SIBLING
brotherhood CLAN, SODALITY
brow TOP, BREE, EDGE, SNAP, CREST, RIDGE
browbeat BULLY, HECTOR
brown TAN, COOK, SEAR, TOAST, SUNTAN
browned TANNED, RISSOLE
browse BRUT, CROP, FEED, GRAZE, NIBBLE, PASTURE
bruise BRAY, DENT, HURT, MAUL, CRUSH, ICTUS, SHINER, CONTUSE, SQUEEZE
bruised HURT, LIVID, HUMBLE
bruit TELL, NOISE, RUMOR, HEARSAY
Brunhild relation ATLI, ASLAUG, SIGURD
brush TIP, FRAY, CLEAN, COPSE, FIGHT, FITCH, SCOPA(E)
brusque CURT, RUDE, BLUFF, BLUNT, GRUFF, TERSE, ABRUPT

brutal CRUEL, FERAL, CARNAL, COARSE, SAVAGE, BESTIAL
Brythonic CORNISH
bubble AIR, BEAD, BLEB, BOIL, BOLL, GLOB, BLAIN, CHEAT, SEETHE
buccaneer PIRATE, VIKING, CORSAIR, PICAROON
buck TOP, NOB, DUDE, STAG, TOFF, DANDY, SWELL, DOLLAR, RESIST
bucket SOE, TUB, BOWK, PAIL, STOP, SCOOP, SKEEL
Buckeye State OH, OHIO
buckle BLEND, TACH, WARP, CLASP, TACHE
bucolic IDYL, RURAL, RUSTIC, PASTORAL
bud GEM, IMP, CION, GERM, KNOP, BEGIN, GEMMA, GRAFT, SPROUT, BEGINNING
Buddha JATAKA, GAUTAMA
Buddha's wife AHALYA
buddy PAL, CHUM, PARTNER
budget BAG, PACK, PLAN, BUNCH, PACKET
buff SKIN, POLISH
buffalo ARNA, ARNEE, BISON; *see* OX
buffet BOX, SLAP, TOSS, SMITE
buffoon FOOL, JAPE, ZANY, ANTIC, CLOWN, DROLL, MIMER, ANDREW, JESTER
bug MITE; *see* INSECT
bugaboo GOGA, GOGO, JUMBO, MUMBO
bugbear OGRE, GOBLIN
bugle call TAPS, TATO(O), RETREAT, TANTARA, REVEILLE
build COOT, FORM, REAR, ERECT, RAISE
building ADOBE, TAPIA, INSULA, EDIFICE
building material WOOD, ADOBE, BRICK, STEEL, STONE, MORTAR, STUCCO, CONCRETE
building part BAY, ELL, ROOF, WING, ANNEX, ATTIC, QUOIN, CELLAR
bulb BUD, CORM, KNOB, LAMP, GLOBE, TUBER
Bulgarian measure KRINA, LEKHA
Bulgarian money LEV, LEW, DINAR, STOTINKA
Bulgarian ruler SIMEON, MARGARITA
Bulgarian weight OKA, OKE, TOVAR
bulge BAG, BUG, JUT, HUMP, KNOB, BLOAT, SWELL
bulging FULL, TUMID, CONVEX, GIBBOUS
bulk BODY, BOUK, MASS, GROSS, SHAPE, VOLUME
bull OX, COP, APIS, HAPI, SLIP, BOBBY, ERROR, PEELER, BLUNDER, SOLECISM
bulldoze COW, DIG, RAM, BULLY, FORCE, SCOOP, BROWBEAT
bullet BALL, SHOT, SLUG, DUMDUM, PELLET, TRACER
bullfight CORRIDA
bullfight cry OLE
bullfight term CAPA, COLETA, MULETA, VERONICA
bullfighter TORERO, MATADOR, PICADOR, TOREADOR
bullion BAR, MASS, INGOT, BILLOT
bull-like TAURINE
bullring ARENA
bull's-eye DAISY, TARGET
bully COW, BRAVO, SCARE, VAPOR, HECTOR, SHANNY
bulwark BAIL, FORT, SCONCE, BASTION, CITADEL, PARAPET, RAMPART
bum HOBO, IDLER, TRAMP
bump JOLT, OUST, COLLIDE
bumper BEADLE, BUNGLE, BLUNDER
bumpkin CLOD, HICK, LOUT, RUBE, YOKEL
bun JAG, WIG, CAKE, ROLL, STEM, TAIL, STALK
bunch LOT, BALE, TUFT, WISP, CROWD, FAGOT, SHEAF
bund DAM, DIKE, QUAY, LEAGUE
bundle BALE, BOLT, HANK, PACK, FADGE, FAGOT, SHEAF, PACKET
bung CORK, PLUG, SHIVE, STOPPER
bungle ERR, GOOF, BOTCH
bunk COT, BERTH, HOKUM, LODGE, SLEEP
bunker BIN, ABRI, CRIB, HAZARD, SANDHOLE
bunting FLAGS, TOWHEE, COWBIRD, ORTOLAN
buoy CAN, DAN, NUN, NUT, BELL, SPAR, FLOAT, LIGAN, RAISE

buoyancy FLO(A)TAGE
buoyant GAY, LIGHT, LILTING
burbot *see* COD
burden TAX, BIRN, CARE, CARK, LADE, LOAD, ONUS, CARGO, CUMBER, FARDEL
bureau DESK, CHEST, AGENCY, OFFICE, DRESSER
burgeon BUD, SHOOT, SPROUT
burglar's tool BAR, PICK, JIMMY
burial place AHU, LOW, GRAVE, BARROW, KURGAN, TUMULUS, CEMETERY, NECROPOLIS
buried HIDDEN, SUNKEN, IMBEDDED
burke MURDER, SUFFOCATE
burl KNOT, LUMP, PIMPLE
burlesque FARCE, REVUE, COMEDY, OVERDO, PARODY
burly BULKY, HUSKY, OBESE, STOUT
Burma chief BO(H), WUN, WOON
Burmese language *see* MON-KHMER, TIBETO-BURMAN
Burmese measure BYEE, SEIT, TENG
Burmese money PYA, KYAT
Burmese native WA, LAI, MON, CHIN, SHAN, KAREN, KACHIN
Burmese weight MOO, VIS, KYAT, VISS, TICAL, ABUCCO, PEIKTHA
burn ASH, CHAR, RILL, SERE, BROOK, CENSE, SCALD, SINGE, SCORCH, CONSUME, CREMATE
burner ETNA, ARGAND, BUNSEN
burning (A)FIRE, ARSON, CALID, EAGER, IRATE, ARDENT
burning bush WAHOO
burnisher *see* POLISHER
burr NUT, POD, HALO, RING, BRIAR, WHIRR, CIRCLE, CORONA
burrow DIG, HOLE, MINE, MOIL, ROOT, TUBE, NUZZLE, TUNNEL
burrowing animal MOLE GOPHER, MARMOT, SURICAT(E)
bursa SAC
burst POP, REND, ERUPT, REAVE, SPLIT, VOLLEY, EXPLODE
bury CACHE, EARTH, INTER, INURN, INHUME
bus JITNEY, AUTOCAR, OMNIBUS, CHARABANC
bus customer FARE, RIDER
bush TOD, BOSH, CLUMP, SHRUB, BOSCAGE
bush leagues MINORS
bushing PINTLE
bushy DUMOSE, DUMOUS
business FEAT, FIRM, GEAR, LINE, CHORE, CRAFT, STINT, TRADE, AFFAIR, ERRAND
buss DECK, KISS, DRESS, SMACK
bustard genus OTIS
bustle ADO, FISK, FUSS, TODO, HYPER, DITHER, FLURRY, POTHER
busybody SNOOP, MEDDLER, QUIDNUNC
but BAR, YET, MERE, ONLY, SAVE, STILL
butcher KILL, CUTUP, SLAUGHTER
butcher's tool GAFF, SKEWER, CLEAVER, GAMBREL
butchery CARNAGE, SHAMBLES, SLAUGHTER
butler SERVANT, SPENCER, STEWARD
butt RAM, TUP, BUNT, CASK, GOAD, PUSH, STUB, STUMP
butter GHI, GHEE, FULWA, MAHUA, BEURRE, PHULWA
butterfish POMFRET
butterfly ARGUS, COMMA, ELFIN, SATYR, WHITE, ZEBRA, APOLLO, COPPER, DANAID, URSULA, VIOLET, ADMIRAL, DANAINE, EMPEROR, JUNONIA, MONARCH, VANESSA, VICEROY, HESPERID, WANDERER
butterfly genus COLIAS, MORPHO, PIERIS, THECLA
buttery LARDER, PANTRY, SPENCE
button BUD, BOSS, HOOK, KNOB, KNOP, STUD, BADGE, OLIVE, FASTEN
button part SHANK
buttress PIER, PROP, STAY, OUTCAST
buyer CHAP, AGENT, EMPTOR, VENDEE
buzz HUM, WHIR(R); *see* SOUND
buzzard PERN, GLEDE; *see* HAWK
buzzer BEE, BELL, ALARM, HOWLER, SIGNAL
by AGO, PER, VIA, NEAR, PAST, WITH, ASIDE, CLOSE, BESIDE

by way of PER, VIA, THRU
bygone PAST, YORE, OLDEN, FORMER
bystander *see* SPECTATOR
byword PROVERB
Byzantine coin BESANT, BEZANT, BYZANT
Byzantine capital ISTANBUL, CONSTANTINOPLE

C

C mark CEDILLA
Caaba city MECCA
caama ASSE
cab HACK, TAXI, ARABA, HANSOM
cabal BLOC, PLOT, JUNTO, CLIQUE, INTRIGUE
cabbage COS, CHOU, COLE, KAIL, KALE, COLZA, KRAUT, SAVOY
cabin HUT, SHED, BERTH, CABAN, COACH, HOVEL, CABANA, SALOON, SHANTY
cabinet BUHL, BAHUT, BUREAU, CLOSET, ALMIRAH, ETAGERE, WHATNOT, MINISTRY
cabinet post DOE, DOT, HEW, HHS, HUD, ARMY, NAVY, LABOR, STATE, ENERGY, DEFENSE, JUSTICE, COMMERCE, INTERIOR, TREASURY
cable GUY, CORD, WIRE, COAXIAL, PAINTER
caboose CAB, CAR, HACK, GALLEY
cacao BROMA, COCKER
cache BURY, HIDE, STOW, STORE, TROVE, CONCEAL
cachet SEAL, STAMP, WAFER
cactus TUNA, NOPAL, CARDON, CEREUS, CHOLLA, MESCAL, MEZCAL, PEYOTE, CARDONA, OPUNTIA, SAGUARO
cactus fruit TUNA, SABRA, COCHAL
cad HEEL, KNAVE, BOUNDER
cadaver BODY, STIFF COR(P)SE, CARCASS
cadence LILT, PACE, TONE, CLOSE, METER, RHYTHM
cadet SON, PLEB(E), JUNIOR
cadge BEG, MOOCH, SPONGE
Cadiz GADES
Cadmus city THEBES
caduceus WAND, STAFF, SCEPTER
Caesar foe CASCA, BRUTUS, POMPEI, CASSIUS
Caesar relative ATIA, AURELIA
caesura REST, BREAK, PAUSE
cafe BISTRO, BARROOM, CABARET
caffeine THEIN, THEINA, THEINE
cage GIG, MEW, HUTCH
cagey SLY, CUNNING
cahoots LEAGUE, PARTNERS
caiman JACARE; *see* CROCODILE
Cain's brother ABEL, SETH
Cain's land NOD
Cain's victim ABEL
Caine captain QUEEG
caisson disease BENDS
caitiff BASE, MEAN, VILE
cajole COAX, PALP, CHEAT, DECOY, TEASE, BUTTER, ENTICE, BEGUILE, FLATTER, WHEEDLE
cake WIG, FARL, FLOE, PONE, WIGG, ANGEL, BATTY, SCONE, TORTE, WAFER, HARDEN, JUMBAL, JUMBLE, SPONGE
calamitous SAD, DIRE, EVIL, HAPLESS
calamity WOE, BLOW, WRACK, MISERY, DISASTER
calculate AIM, RATE, FRAME, TALLY, RECKON, COMPUTE
calculator LOG, TABLE, ABACUS
Calcutta measure KUNK, RAIK
Calcutta weight DHAN, PANK
caldron POT, BOILER, KETTLE
calendar LOG, ORDO, DIARY, DOCKET, ALMANAC, JOURNAL; *see p. 340*
calf BOB, DOGY, DOGIE, FATLING
calf, pert. to SURAL
calf meat VEAL
caliber BORE, GAUGE, METTLE, DIAMETER
calico SALLO(O)
California information *see p. 308*
caliph ALI, IMAM, OMAR, OTHMAN
calk NAP, COPY, STOP, CLOSE, CHINESE
call BAN, BID, DUB, CITE, NAME, SOOK, TERM, YELL, CLEPE, PHONE, ROUSE, TITLE, VISIT, ELICIT, INVITE, MUSTER, SUMMON; *see* CRY

call to prayer ADAN, AZAN

calla ARUM, LILY

called NAMED, STYLED, DUBBED, YCLEPT

caller GUEST, SUITOR, VISITOR

calligrapher PENMAN, SCRIBE

calling JOB, LINE, TRADE, METIER, (A)VOCATION

callous HARD, HORNY, TOUGH

callus CORN, CLAVUS

calm LOWN, LULL, ABATE, ALLAY, STILL, STOIC, PLACID, SERENE, PLACATE

calorie THERM(E)

calumet (PEACE)PIPE

calumniate BELIE, DEFAME, MALIGN, REVILE, VILIFY

calumny SLUR, ABUSE, LIBEL, SLANDER

Calvary GOLGOTHA

Calvinist BEREAN

calyx CUP, HUSK, SEPAL

cam COG, LOBE, CATCH, WIPER, TAPPET, TRIPPET

cambio coin(s) LIRA, LIRE

Cambodian language KHMER

Cambodian money RIEL

Cambria WALES

Cambridge college MIT, HARVARD

Cambridge exam TRIPOS

Cambridge student SIZAR, SIZER, OPTIME, WRANGLER

camel OONT, DELOUL, MEHARI, BACTRIAN

camel driver SARWAN

camel genus CAMELUS

camera BOX, SLR, PRESS, REFLEX, BROWNIE

camera equipment DOLLY, FLASH, FILTER, TRIPOD

camera part LENS, STOP, FINDER, SHUTTER, DIAPHRAGM

Cameroon language BANTU, SUDANIC

camp BOMA, POST, ETAPE, LAGER, TABOR, LAAGER, ZAREBA, BIVOUAC

camp, pert. to CASTRAL

camphor ALANT, APIOL, BORNEOL, MENTHOL

campus QUAD, FIELD

can JUG, MAY, TIN, JAIL, PRESERVE

Canadian CANUCK

Canadian information *see p. 306*

canal RIO, SOO, DUCT, ERIE, KIEL, SUEZ, ZANJA, MEATUS, PANAMA, STRAIT, CHANNEL, CONDUIT, WELLAND

canasta play MELD, FREEZE

cancel BLOT, DELE, VOID, ANNUL, ERASE, DELETE, EFFACE, REPEAL, REVOKE, POSTMARK

cancer CRAB, TUMOR, GROWTH

candid BLUNT, FRANK, NAIVE, HONEST, ARTLESS

candle DIP, WAX, TEST, TAPER, BOUGIE, CIERGE

candlenut tree AMA, KUKUI, BANKUL

candlestick CRUSIE, LAMPAD, LUSTRE, SCONCE, PRICKET, GIRANDOLE

candy DULCE, LOLLY, SWEET, TAFFY, BONBON, CIMBAL, COMFIT, DRAGEE, CONFECT, NOUGAT, CARAMEL, FONDANT, PRALINE, SWEETMEAT

cane FLAY, FLOG, WHIP, STEM, STICK, PUNISH, RATTAN, MALACCA

canine CUR, PUG, PUP, FANG, FICE, CUSPID; *see* DOG

Canio's wife NEDDA

canister CASE, CALIN

cannabis HEMP; *see* DRUG

cannon KRAG, ASPIC, DRAKE, MOYEN, SAKER, BERTHA, CULVER, FALCON, FOWLER, LICORN, MINNIE, MORTAR, POMPOM, TREPAN, BASTARD, BAZOOKA, BOMBARD, HACKBUT, LANTACA, LOMBARD, MOYENNE, ROBINET, TEREBRA, UNICORN, CULVERIN, HOWITZER

canny WARY, SHREWD

canoe *see* VESSEL

canon LAW, HYMN, LAUD, RULE, SONG, AXIOM, NODUS

canonical hours NONE, SEXT, LAUDS, PRIME, TIERCE, COMPLIN, ORTHROS, VESPERS

canopy SKY, COPE, DAIS, VAULT, TESTER, AWNING

cant *see* SLANG, TILT

cantata ORATORIO; *see* SONG

canteen PX, FLASK

canter RUN, PACE, RACK, WHINER

canticle ODE, HYMN, LAUD, SONG

canto AIR, FIT, PACE, FYTTE, PASSUS
canton STATE, QUARTER, DISTRICT
canvas DUCK, SAIL, TARP, TENT, TUKE, SCRIM, TEWKE, WIGAN
canvass POLL, SIFT, STUDY, SURVEY
canyon GAP, GULCH, CANADA
canyon mouth ABRA
cap LID, TAJ, TAM, TOP, COIF, CORK, KEPI, BERET, MUTCH, EXCEL, TUQUE, BARRET, BIGGIN, BONNET, CALPAC, COCKUP, MOBCAP, PILEUS, PINNER, CALOTTE, CALPACK, CHECHIA, COMMODE, FLANDAN, MONTERO, BALMORAL, BARRETTE, BIGGONET, SKULLCAP, YARMULKA; *see* HAT
capacity BENT, SIZE, KNACK, SKILL
cape ANN, COD, MAY, NES, RAS, COPE, FEAR, HORN, NAZE, NESS, ROBE, SCAW, SKAW, SABLE, BERTHA, DOLMAN, DOMINO, SONTAG, TIPPET, VISITE, HATTERAS, MANTILLA, PELERINE
Capek character ROBOT
Capek play RUR
caper HOP, DIDO, ROMP, ANTIC, FRISK, PRANK, GAMBOL, PRANCE, TITTUP
capital CITY, MAIN, BASIC, FATAL, STOCK, LETTER, PRIMAL; *see p. 285*
caprice FAD, KINK, WHIM, QUIRK, VAGARY, WHIMSEY
capsize UPEND, UPSET, OVERTURN
capstan DRUM, HOIST, LEVER
capsule POD, PILL, PEARL, THECA, CACHET, SHEATH
captain AHAB, RAIS, REIS, BLIGH, QUEEG, SOTNIK
captain's command TROOP, BATTERY, COMPANY
Captain's insignia EAGLE
caption TITLE, LEADER, LEGEND, HEADING
captious CROSS, TESTY, CARPING
captivate CHARM, ALLURE, ENAMOR, ENCHANT, ENSLAVE
capture BAG, COP, NAB, NET, PRIZE, SNARE ARREST
caput TOP, HEAD, DOOMED
car *see* CABIN, AUTOMOBILE
Caradoc BALA
caravan TREK, CAFILA, SAFARI
caravansary *see* INN
carbine *see* GUN
carbohydrate SUGAR, STARCH
carbon COAL, COKE, COPY, LEAD, SOOT
carbuncle RUBY, GARNET, PIMPLE, ANTHRAX
card ACE, PAM, SIX, TEN, TUM, TWO, WAG, COMB, DAME, FOUR, JACK, JASZ, KING, NINE, NOBS, SODA, TREY, BASTO, BOWER, DEUCE, HONOR, JOKER, KNAVE, MENEL, PEDRO, TAROC, TAROT, TEASE, ZENER, POSTAL, TAROCCO
card game GO, CAT, GIN, LOO, NAP, PAM, PIG, RUM, BRAG, FARO, FROG, GOLF, JASS, PICO, SKAT, SOLO, VINT, CINCH, FARGO, MACAO, MONTE, OHELL, OMBRE, PEDRO, PITCH, POKER, RUMMY, SAMBA, TAROT, WHIST, BOSTON, BRIDGE, ECARTE, EIGHTS, EUCHRE, FANTAN, GOBANG, GOFISH, HEARTS, MEMORY, PIQUET, POCHEN, ROUNCE, SLOUGH, AUTHORS, BARBUDI, BELOTTE, BEZIQUE, BOLIVIA, CANASTA, CASSINO, LOWBALL, MUGGINS, OLDMAID, PLAFOND, SEVENUP, CHOUETTE, CONQUIAN, CRAPETTE, CRIBBAGE, IDOUBTIT, JACKPOTS, MICHIGAN, NAPOLEON, OKLAHOMA, PATIENCE, PINOCHLE, POPEJOAN, PYRAMIDS, SIXTYSIX, SLAPJACK, ACEYDEUCY, BLACKJACK, FORTYFIVE, SOLITAIRE, TEAKETTLE, TWENTYONE
card, tarot SUN, FOOL, MOON, STAR, DEATH, DEVIL, TOWER, WORLD, ARCANA, HERMIT, LOVERS, CHARIOT, JUSTICE
card term BID, CAT, CUT, GIN, PIG, POT, DEAL, DECK, DROP, HAND, MELD, PACK, PASS, SUIT, VOLE, BLIND, BLITZ, CHECK, ENTRY, HONOR, KITTY, KNOCK, RAISE,

SMEAR, TRUMP, WIDOW, BRELAN, RENEGE, TENACE; *see* BRIDGE, CANASTA, POKER
cardinal ROY, CHIEF, LEGER, DATARY, RITTER, SHEHAN, CUSHING, MCGUIGAN, MCINTYRE, SPELLMAN
cardinal point EAST, WEST, NORTH, SOUTH
care CARK, HEED, RECK, TEND
careen TIP, YAW, CALK, CANT, HEEL, KEEL, LIST, TILT
career RUN, RUSH, CALLING, LIFEWORK, VOCATION
carefree GAY, BLITHE
careful WARY, CHARY, LEERY
careless LAX, LASH, RASH, CASUAL, REMISS
caress HUG, PET, CODDLE, COSSET, DANDLE, NUZZLE
cargo LAST, LOAD, GOODS, LADING, PORTAGE
caricature SKIT, FARCE, PARODY, TAKEOFF
caries DECAY
carmine RED, CRIMSON
carnage HAVOC, BLOODSHED
carnival FETE, FEAST, REVEL
carol LAY, NOEL; *see* SONG
caroler WAIT
carom SHOT, REBOUND, RICOCHET
Caron role GIGI
carousal ORGY, BINGE, REVEL, SPREE, JAMBOREE
carouse BIRLE, BOOZE, BOUSE
carp NAG, CAVIL, NIBBLE, CENSURE
carp(-like fish) ID, ASP, CHI, IDE, KOI, BLAY, CHUB, DACE, KIYI, ORFE, RUDD, SPOT, BLEAK, BREAM, GIBEL, GOBIO, HITCH, LOACH, MINIM, MINNY, PIRAI, ROACH, TENCH, CHEVIN, GOBIID, MAHSIR, MAHSUR, MINNOW, TAUTOG, FATHEAD, GOBIOID, GUAVINA, GUDGEON, MAHSEER, MORWONG, OLDWIFE, PINFISH, PINHEAD, FALLFISH
carpel LEAF, PISTIL, SOREMA
carpenter ANT, FRAMER, JOINER, WRIGHT
carpenter's tool AWL, SAW, ADZE, BEVEL, LEVEL, PLANE, CHISEL, HAMMER
carpet MAT, TAPET, TAPIS, TAPETE, DRUGGET; *see* RUG
carriage FLY, GIG, MIEN, PORT, SHAY, POISE, CALASH, MANNER; *see* VEHICLE
carrier HAMAL, PORTER, REDCAP
carrot DRIAS
carry LUG, BEAR, HOLD, RIDE, TOTE, FERRY, FETCH
carry off RAPE, ABDUCT
carry on WAGE, CAPER, CUTUP, CONDUCT
cart *see* VEHICLE
cartel PACT, POOL, TRUST
Carthage, of PUNIC
Carthage ruler DIDO, BARCA, HANNIBAL
cartilage GRISTLE
cartoon EPURE, DESIGN, SKETCH
cartoon character BC, HANS, JEFF, LUCY, MUTT, POGO, SHOE, ABNER, ANNIE, DONDI, FRITZ, HAGAR, JIGGS, LINUS, PLUTO, SLATS, ARCHIE, DENNIS, HERMAN, MICKEY, SLUGGS, BLONDIE, DAGWOOD, PEANUTS, GARFIELD
cartoonist LOW, REA, ARNO, BECK, CAPP, GRAY, HART, KING, NAST, BUELL, CRANE, DAVIS, DIRKS, GOULD, KELLY, KIRBY, SEGAR, STEIG, YOUNG, ADDAMS, CANIFF, DISNEY, FISHER, SCHULZ, SOGLOW, WALKER, FEIFFER, MAULDIN, MONTANA, THURBER, TRUDEAU, HERBLOCK
cartridge SHELL, CASING
carve SHAPE, CHISEL, INCISE, SCULPT
carving CAMEO, SCRIVE
casaba MELON, CANTALOUPE
case ETUI, INRO, ETWEE, FOREL, TRIAL, CARTON, DATIVE, FORELL, PETARD, SHEATH, ABLATIVE, GENITIVE, LOCATIVE, VOCATIVE
cash DUST, CLEAR, DARBY, HONOR, MONEY, SPECIE
cashier DROP, OUST, EXPEL, BURSAR, PURSER, TELLER
casing SHOE, COVER, LINER, SHEATH(ING)
casino TEN, TWO, PINK
cask KEG, TUB, TUN, VAT, BOSS, BUTT, CADE, RIER, BARECA, FIRKIN, TIERCE

cask part LAG, BILGE, CHIMB, CHIME
casket BOX, PYX, TYE, COFFIN, SHRINE
casserole STEW, RAGOUT
cassock SOUTANE; *see* VESTMENT
cast TOT, JILT, JUNK, MOLD, MOLT, SHED, SPEW, TINT, TOSS, FUSIL, SLING
cast aside ABANDON, DISCARD
castaway WAIF, MAROON, PARIAH, DERELICT
caste DOM, MAL, MEO, AHIR, GOLA, JATI, KORI, KULI, MAGI, MALI, PASI, RANK, TELI, CLASS, GRADE, SUDRA, VARNA, BANIAN, CHETTY, LOHANA, PARIAH, RAJPUT, VAISYA, BRAHMAN
caster VIAL, CRUET, PHIAL, WHEEL, HURLER, ROLLER
castigate BEAT, PUNISH, CENSURE, REPROVE, LAMBASTE
Castillian queen ISABELLA
castle ROOK, MORRO, CHATEAU, WINDSOR, ELSINORE, FORTRESS; *see* FORT
castle part KEEP, MOAT, TOWER, DONJON
castor HAT, BEAN, STAR, CRUET, BEAVER
Castor and Pollux TWINS, GEMINI, DIOSCURI
Castor's slayer IDAS
casual(s) LOAFERS, OFFHAND
casuarina TOA, AGOHO, AGOJO, BELAH, BELAR, HEOAK, BEEFWOOD
cat GIB, KIT, PUS, TAB, TOM, KITT, PUSS, FELID, KITTY, MEWER, MOGGY, PUSSY, QUEEN, TABBY, TOMMY, FELINE, GIBCAT, KITTEN, KITTIE, MEWLER, MOUSER, NEUTER, PURRER, PUSSIE, THOMAS, TOMCAT, LIONCEL
cat breed MAU, REX, MANX, KORAT, MANUL, TABBY, ANGOLA, ANGORA, BIRMAN, BOMBAY, OCICAT, SPHYNX, BOBTAIL, BURMESE, PERSIAN, SIAMESE, BALINESE, PARAGUAY, HIMALAYAN, SHORTHAIR, ABYSSINIAN
cat genus FELIS
cat, wild LEO, EYRA, LION, LYNX, PARD, PUMA, CHAUS, CHITA, OUNCE, TIGER, BOBCAT, CAFFER, CHETAH, COUGAR, JAGUAR, KAFFIR, LIONET, LUCERN, MARGAY, OCELOT, PARDAL, SERVAL, CARACAL, CHEETAH, GUEPARD, LEOPARD, LIBBARD, LIONESS, PANTHER, TIGRESS; *see* CIVET
catacomb TOMB, CRYPT, VAULT, LOCULUS
catafalque BIER, SCAFFOLD
catalog(ue) FILE, LIST, ROTA, CANON, INDEX, CENSUS, ROSTER
catapult HURL, ONAGER, BALISTA, PROJECT, BALLISTA, SCORPION
cataract CAST, LINN, FALLS, CALIGO, CASCADE
catarrh COLD, RHEUM
catcall BOO, RAZZ
catch KEP, NAB, NET, TRAP, GRAB, HAUL, HOOK, PAWL, SNAG, CLICK, INCUR, DETENT, ENTRAP, PELVIS, SNATCH, RATCHET
catchall BAG, BASKET, CLOSET
catchword CUE, SLOGAN, STARTER
category CASTE, CLASS, GENRE, GENUS, FAMILY, RUBRIC, SPECIES
cater FEED, PANDER, PURVEY, PROVIDE
caterpillar ERUCA, CANKER, LOOPER, WOUBIT, CUTWORM, WEBWORM, INCHWORM, SPANWORM; *see* MOTH, BUTTERFLY
catfish POUT, RAAD, WELS, BAGRE, DORAD, DORAS, HASSAR, TANDAN, ASPREDO, CANDIRU, FIDDLER, SILURID
catgut CORD, THARM, VIOLIN
Cathay CHINA
cathedral DOM, SOBOR, CHURCH, LATERAN, MINSTER
Catholic, Greek UNIAT(A)
catkin RAG, AMENT, SPIKE
catnip NEP, NIP, CATMINT
cat's-paw DUPE, GULL, TOOL, CULLY, STOOGE
cattle FAT, NOT, AVER, BOSS, BUCK, CALF, COWS, DOGY, KINE, NOWT, OXEN, QUEY, AIVER, ANGUS, CUSHA, DEVON, DOGIE, KERRY, PODDY, SANGA, SANGU,

SLINK, STEER, STIRK, STOCK, VACHE, ANKOLE, ANKOLI, AUROCS, BEEVES, CABREE, CALVER, CANNER, CATALO, DEXTER, DODDIE, HAWKEY, HAWKIE, HEIFER, JERSEY, MOILEY, MOOLEY, MULLEY, SUSSEX, VEALER, BERENDO, BIGHORN, BRAHMAN, BRAHMIN, CATTALO, GRASSER, SLINKER

cattle dealer DROVER, RANCHER

Caucasian language LAZ, UDI, ANDI, AVAR, ADIGHE, GEORGIAN

caucus POWWOW, MEETING

ca(u)ldron POT, RED, VAT, BOILER, KETTLE

cause AIM, END, ORIGIN

causeuse SOFA, TETEATETE

causeway DIKE, PATH, CAUSEY

caustic LYE, ALUM, LIME, ACRID, BITING, PHENOL, SEVERE, ERODENT, MORDANT, PUNGENT, PYROTIC

cauterize BURN, SEAR, BRAND

caution CARE, WARN, ADVICE

cautious SHY, WARY, CANNY, CHARY, FABIAN

cavalier PROUD, KNIGHT, HAUGHTY

Cavalleria character LOLA, ALFIO

cavalry TURM(A), HUSSARS, LANCERS

cavalry weapon LANCE, SABER

cavalryman ULAN, SOWAR, SPAHI, UHLAN, HUSSAR, SPAHEE, DRAGOON

cave(rn) DEN, GROT, LAIR, WEEM, ANTRE, CROFT, CRYPT, CAVITY, GROTTO, RECESS

cave explorer SPELUNKER

cave, inhabiting a SPEL(A)EAN

caveman TROGLODYTE

caviar ROE, IKRA

caviar fish STERLET, STURGEON

cavil CARP, HAFT, BICKER, CENSURE, QUIBBLE

cavity PIT, VUG, DENT, VOOG, VUGG, VUGH, DRUSE, FOSSA, GEODE, LUMEN, SINUS, ANTRUM, ATRIUM, POCKET

cavort DIDO, CAPER, PRANK

Cawdor, thane of MACBETH

cay REEF, ISLET

cayenne WHIST, CANARY, PEPPER, COPEPOD, CAPSICUM

cease HALT, QUIT, STAY, AVAST, PETER

Cecrop's city ATHENS

Cecrop's successor THESEUS

cede DEED, FORGO, GRANT, WAIVE, YIELD, ASSIGN

celebrity VIP, LION, NAME, STAR, ECLAT

celestial HOLY, DIVINE, URANIC, ANGELIC

cell EGG, KIL, GERM, KILL, GROUP, VAULT, SPORE, CYTODE, GAMETE, NEURON(E)

cell division SPIREM(E)

cell part LININ, ENERGID, NUCLEUS, PLASTID, VACUOLE

cella NAOS, SERDAB

celt AX, CHISEL

Celt IR, ITH, MIL, NAR, EBER, ERSE, GAEL, KELT, MANX, BRETON, MIDEDH

Celtic ERSE, MANX, WELSH, BRETON, GAELIC, KELTIC, CORNISH, GAULISH

Celtic lord TANIST

cement GLUE, LUTE, PASTE, PUTTY, MORTAR, SOLDER

cenobite NUN, MONK, FRIAR, ESSENE

cenoby ABBEY, PRIORY, CONVENT

censure FLAY, BLAME, CHIDE, KNOCK, SLATE, TARGE

census figure STAT

cent SOU, PENNY, COPPER

centaur CHIRON

center HUB, CORE, NAVE, FOCUS, HEART, PIVOT, NUCLEUS

center, away from DISTAL

center, toward ENTAD, MESIAL

centerpiece EPERGNE

central AXIAL, FOCAL, NUCLEAR, PIVOTAL

C. Amer. bird GUAN, JACU, SYLPH, TURCO, CONDOR

C. Amer. tree ULE, EBOE, AMATE

century plant PITA, AGAVE, MAGUEY

ceramic *see* CHINA

cerate WAX, LARD, SALVE

cereal BRAN, CORN, RICE, GRITS, GRUEL, MAIZE, WHEAT, FARINA, HOMINY, SECALE, OATMEAL

cerebrate THINK, PONDER, COGITATE

ceremony FORM, POMP, RITE, RITUAL
certain ONE, YEA, SURE, TRUE, FIXED
certificate SCRIP, STOCK, DIPLOMA, VOUCHER
certify OKAY, VOUCH, ATTEST, DEPOSE, EVINCE, LICENSE
cessation END, STAY, STOP, DEATH, PAUSE, DESITION
cesspool SINK, SUMP, SINKER
cetacean *see* WHALE, DOLPHIN
Ceylon SRILANKA
Ceylon native TODA, VEDDA(H)
Ceylon measure PARAH, AMUNAM
Ceylon money CENT, TANG, RUPEE
Ceylonese TAMIL
chafe RUB, VEX, FRET, FROT, GALL, ABRADE
chaff PUG, BRAN, HUSK, HULLS, TRASH, BANTER
chaffer SIEVE, DICKER, HAGGLE, HIGGLE
chaffinch CHINK, SPINK
chaffy SCALY, ACEROSE, PALEATE, TRIVIAL
chain FOB, TYE, GYVE, TORC, ALBERT, CATENA, FETTER, TETHER, TORQUE, MANACLE, SHACKLE
chair KAGO, SEAT, SEDAN, STOOL, ROCKER, SPEAKER
chair part RUNG, SPLAT
chalcedony ONYX, SARD, AGATE, CHERT, PRASE
Chaldean city UR
chalice AMA, CUP, BOWL, AMULA, CALIX, GRAIL
challenge DARE, DEFY, GAGE, CARTEL, QUESTION
chamber ODA, KIVA, ODAH, ROOM, CAMERA, LOCULUS
chamfer BEVEL, GROOVE, FLUTING
champ CHEW, MUNCH
champion ACE, BACK, HERO, VICTOR, ESPOUSE, PALADIN
chance HAP, LOT, FATE, LUCK, ODDS, RISK, OCCUR, HAZARD, KISMET, RANDOM, FORTUNE
chancel BEMA, JUBE
change COIN, FLUX, MUTA, VARY, ALTER, SHIFT, MODIFY, MUTATE, OBVERT
changeable FICKLE, PROTEAN, VARIANT
changeling ELF, OAF, DOLT, DUNCE, DOUBLE, RINGER
channel GAT, BAND, DIKE, DUCT, LEAF, PIPE, RACE, TUBE, CHUTE, FLUME, STRIA, ALVEUS, FURROW, GROOVE, GUTTER, MEDIUM, SLUICE, STRAIT, CONDUIT, STATION
Channel Islands measure CABOT
chant MELE, CRONE, INTONE, INTROIT, CANTICLE, RESPONSE
chanticleer COCK, ROOSTER
chantry ALTAR, CHAPEL, SHRINE
chaos NU, PO, NUN, PIE, APSU, KORE, MESS, VOID, ABYSS, BABEL, HAVOC
chaotic SNAFU
chap COVE, KIBE, CHINK, CRACK, KEREL, SPRAY
chapel CHOIR, BETHEL, CHANTRY, ORATORY, SISTINE
chaperon DUE(N)NA, ESCORT
chaplet ANADEM, FILLET, ROSARY, WREATH
Chaplin wife OONA
chapped KIBY, KIBED, SPLIT, CRACKED
char SEAR, SCORCH
character ROLE, RUNE, ETHOS, NEUME, REPUTE
charge FEE, COST, ONUS, DEBIT, ADJURE, INDICT
charger MOUNT, PLATE, STEED, PLATTER
chariot BIGA, RATH, WAIN, CURRE, ESSED, RATHA, ESSEDA, ESSEDE
charioteer HUR, JEHU, PILOT, AURIGA, DRIVER
charisma IT, GIFT, CHARM, POWER, APPEAL
charitable BENIGN, HUMANE
charity ALMS, DOLE, MERCY
charlatan FAKE(R), QUACK, EMPIRIC
Charlemagne's kin PEPIN, ORLANDO
charm MAGIC, AMULET, ENAMOR, ENCHANT, PERIAPT, SWASTIKA; *see* FETISH
chart MAP, PLAT, PLOT, GRAPH, TABLE, CHEMA, DIAGRAM, MERCATOR
charter LET, DEED, HIRE, RENT, GRANT, LEASE, PATENT

chary SHY, WARY, PRUDENT, CAUTIOUS
Charybdis, rock opposite SCYLLA
chasm GAP, GLUT, GULF, REFT, ABYSS, CLEFT, FLUME, GORGE, CREVAS, HIATUS, RAVINE
chassis BODY, FRAME, NACELLE
chaste PURE, MODEST, VESTAL
chasten ABASH, SMITE, HUMBLE
chastise TRIM, BLAME, SLATE, TAUNT, SWINGE, CENSURE
chasuble *see* VESTMENT
chat GAB, CHIN, COZE, TOVE, PRATE, CONFAB
chatelaine PIN, CLASP, BROOCH
chattel GOODS, SLAVE, EFFECTS
chatter GAB, GAS, YAP, BLAT, CLAP, PRATE, BABBLE, JABBER; *see* TALK
chatterer JAY, MAG, PIET
Chaucer inn TABARD
cheap VILE, PALTRY, SHODDY, SCHLOCK, NOMINAL
cheapskate MISER, PIKER, NIGGARD
cheat BAM, CON, FOB, FUB, GIP, GYP, BILK, CLIP, GULL, MUMP, SCAM, SWIZ, COZEN, GOUGE, RENIG, SHARK, SHARP, STING, WELCH, CHISEL, CONMAN, DIDDLE, RENEGE, SHARPER, SWINDLE
check NIP, TAB, CURB, REIN, STAY, BLOCK, STUNT, BRIDLE
checkered PIED, VAIR, PLAID, MOSAIC
checkers DAM(E)S, DRAUGHTS
checkers opening ALMA, DYKE, FIFE, CROSS, DENNY, KELSO, BOSTON, DUNDEE, NAILOR, BRISTOL
checkers term DAM, HUFF, KING, CROWN
checking block SPRAG
checkmate STOP, UNDO, BAFFLE, SCOTCH, STYMIE, THWART
cheek(s) CHAP, GALL, GENA, JAMP, JOLE, JOWL, BRASS, BUCCA, NERVE, SAUCE
cheek, pert. to GENAL, MALAR, BUCCAL
cheer OLE, RAH, CLAP, LAUD, ROOT, VIVA, BOOLA, BRAVO, ELATE, ENCORE, HOORAY, HURRAH, PRAISE, APPLAUD
cheerful GLEG, PERT, ROSY, JOLLY, PEART, BLITHE, HILARY
cheerless DRAB, GLUM, DREAR, DISMAL, DREARY, GLOOMY
cheese BLUE, BRIE, DICK, EDAM, CREAM, GOUDA, SWISS, DUNLOP, GRATIN, MYSOST, ROMANO, CHEDDAR, GRUYERE, RICOTTA, SAPSAGO, STILTON, BELPAESE, PARMESAN, TILSITER
cheesy CASEOUS
chemical compound ALUM, AMID, AMIN, AZIN, IMID, SALT, SODA, AMIDE, AMINE, AZINE, AZOLE, BORID, CERIA, ESTER, IMIDE, IMINE, NITER, NITRE, BORIDE, IODIDE, ISOMER, POTASH, ANATASE, DRYBONE, INOSITE, LEUCINE, METAMER, POTASSA, STEARATE
chemical element *see p. 249*
chemical radical BUTYL, ETHYL, TOLYL, METHYL, OXALYL, BENZOYL, CARBONYL
chemise SARK, SLIP, CYMAR, SHIFT
chemist HOFF, BOYLE, CURIE, KUHNE, STAHL, BECHER, COUPER, DALTON, KEKULE, LIEBIG, BUCHNER, FISCHER, HODGKIN, OSTWALD, PASTEUR, PAULING, AVOGADRO, MILLIKAN, ARRHENIUS, LAVOISIER, PRIESTLEY; *see* NOBEL
cherish PET, DOTE, PRIZE, ESTEEM, FOSTER, REVERE
cherry DUKE, FUJI, GEAN, MOREL, RUDDY, MORELL, CAPULIN, MARASCA, OXHEART, SIANGKI
chess term MATE, PIRC, CHECK, DEBUT, PRISE, CASTLE, FIDATE, GAMBIT, ENPRISE, JADOUBE
chessman KING, PAWN, ROOK, HORSE, PIECE, QUEEN, BISHOP, CASTLE, KNIGHT
chest ARK, ARCA, CASE, CIST, KIST, BAHUT, BOSOM, COFFER, LOCKER, THORAX
chestnut LING, RATA, LINGKO, MARRON
chevron RANK, ANGLE, STRIPE
chew BITE, CHAM, GNAW,

QUID, CHAMP, MUNCH, CHAVEL
chewink FINCH, TOWHEE
chic NATTY, NIFTY, DAPPER, MODISH, STYLISH
Chicago district LOOP
chicanery RUSE, WILE, CAVIL, INTRIGUE
chick pea BUB, GRAM, CHICH, CICER
chicken HEN, COCK, FRYER, LAYER, POULT, BROILER, ROASTER
chicken breed JAVA, BANTAM, SULTAN, LEGHORN, MINORCA
chicle GUM, LATEX
chicory ENDIVE, SUCCORY
chide RATE, SCOLD, BERATE, REPROVE
chief(tain) AGA, JAM, MIR, AMIR, ARCH, DATO, DATU, HEAD, JARL, MAIN, MORO, RAIS, RAJA, RANA, REIS, TYEE, YARL, ZAIM, ALDER, AMEER, DATTO, ELDER, FRIST, POMBO, PRIME, RAJAH, THANE, VITAL, ATAMAN, HETMAN, CAPITAL, SUPREME
chilblain KIBE, PERNIO
child(ren) FUB, KID, TAD, TOT, ARAB, BABE, BABY, BATA, BRAT, CHIT, TIKE, TYKE, BAIRN, GAMIN, CHILDE, INFANT, MOPPET, PROGENY
child, foster DALT, NORRY, NURRY
childish NAIVE, ASININE, PUERILE
childlike MEEK, NAIVE, DOCILE
Chilean measure VARA, LEGUA, LINEA, CUADRA, FANEGA
Chilean money PESO, COLON, LIBRA, CONDOR, ESCUDO, CENTAVO
Chilean tree ULMO, QUINA, MUERMO
chill ICE, NIP, AGUE, ALGOR, GELID, RIGOR, FREEZE, SHIVER
chilly ICY, RAW, COLD, COOL, ALGID, BLEAK, GELID
chime RIM, BELL, EDGE, AGREE, HARMONY
chimney LUM, FLUE, VENT, TEWEL
chimney piece PAREL, MANTEL
China CATHAY
china DELF(T), CERAMIC, DRESDEN, FAIENCE, CROCKERY, EGGSHELL; *see* PORCELAIN
chine SILK, CREST, RIDGE, SPINE
Chinese MAIO, SINO, SERIC, SINIC, CATAJA, JOHNNY, MONGOL, CATAJAN
Chinese aborigine MAN, YAO, MIAO, MANTZU
Chinese dialect WU, YI, MIN, AMOY, BUYI, TONG, HAKKA, FOOTOW, SWATOW, MANDARIN, CANTONESE, PEKINGESE
Chinese dynasty WU, HAN, SHU, SUI, WEI, CHIN, CHOU, HSIA, LIAO, MING, SUNG, TANG, YUAN, CHING, SHANG
Chinese factory HONG
Chinese language WA
Chinese measure HO, HU, LI, MU, PU, TU, FEN, TOU, CHIH, KISH, CHANG, CHING, SHENG
Chinese money LI, PU, CASH, CENT, TAEL, TIAO, YUAN
Chinese season CHIU, CHUN, HSIA, TUNG
Chinese society HUI, HOEY, TONG, BOXER
Chinese tree ICHO, KIRI, TUNG, LICHI, GINGKO, GINKGO, LITCHI
Chinese way TAO
Chinese weight LI, FEN, HAD, KIN, TAN, YIN, CHIN, MACE, SHIH, TAEL, CATTY, PICUL
chink BORE, RIFT, RIMA, RIME, CRACK, CRANNY
chinky RIMAL, RIMOSE, RIMOUS
chip BIT, NIG, NICK, CHECK, FLAKE, SPALL, GALLET, COUNTER
chipmunk CHIPPY, HACKEE
chipper SPRY, COCKY, PERKY
chirp PEW, PUE, PEEP, PIPE, CHEEP
chisel GAD, CELT, PARE, CHEAT, DROVE, SCULP, SLICK, POMMEL
chit IOU, INFANT, VOUCHER
chivy CRY, NAG, GAME, HUNT, CHASE, PURSUE
chock BLOCK, CLEAT, WEDGE
chocolate mixing stick MOLINET
chocolate powder PINOLE
choice OPT, AONE, PICK, RARE, CREAM, ELITE, PRIME,

OPTION, PICKED, SELECT, NOMINEE
choir singer CHORIST(ER); *see* SINGER
choir vestment COTTA, SURPLICE
choke DAM, GAG, CLOG, BURKE, WORRY, STIFLE
choler IRE, BILE, FURY, RAGE, ANGER, WRATH, SPLEEN
choleric FIERY, HUFFY, IRATE, TESTY
choose OPT, CULL, VOTE, ADOPT, ELECT, OPTATE, SELECT, DESTINE
chop AXE, HEW, LOP, CHIP, DICE, HACK, JOWL, CARVE, MINCE
chord TRIAD, TRINE, HARMONY
chore JOB, CHAR, DUTY, CHARE, STINT
chorus CHOIR, ACCORD, BURDEN, UNISON, REFRAIN
chorus girl CHORINE, ROCKETTE
Chosen COREA, KOREA
Christ's word on cross ELOI
christen NAME, CLEPE, BAPTIZE
Christian feast AGAPE
Christian Science founder EDDY
Christmas NOEL, XMAS, YULE(TIDE)
chromosome IDANT
chronicle ANNAL, DIARY, ANNALS, RECORD, ACCOUNT
chrysalis KELL, PUPA, NYMPH, COCOON, AURELIA
chrysanthemum MUM, KIKU, POMPOM, POMPON, ANEMONE, COSTMARY, FEVERFEW
chubby FAT, PLUMP, ROTUND
chuck FOOD, GRUB, HURL
chuckle CLUCK, CACKLE, GIGGLE, TITTER, CHORTLE
chunk GOB, WHANG, WHANK, GOBBET
chunky LUMPY, SQUAT, STOUT, STOCKY
church KIL, FANE, KIRK, TERA, CRYPT, SAMAJ, BETHEL, CHAPEL, MOSQUE, PAGODA, TEMPLE, MINSTER, MISSION, BASILICA, ECCLESIA, CATHEDRAL
church jurisdiction SEE, PARISH, DEANERY, DIOCESE
church leader ARIUS, PAPAS, ORIGEN, HIERARCH
Church of England ANGLICAN
church official ELDER, BEADLE, LECTOR, SEXTON, VERGER, SACRIST(AN); *see* CLERGY
church part NEF, PEW, APSE, BEMA, NAVE, ALTAR, BENCH, STALL, PARVIS, CHANCEL, ORATORY, STEEPLE, SACRISTY, TRANSEPT
church property GLEBE
Churchill relative SARAH, SOAMES
churchman DEAN, POPE, ABBOT, BISHOP, DEACON, PRIEST, RECTOR, PRELATE, PRIMATE, CARDINAL; *see* CLERGY
churl OAF, BOOR, CARL, LOUT, CEORL, KNAVE, VILLEIN
churlish DOUR, SOUR, SULKY, SURLY, SORDID, SULLEN
chute DUCT, FLUME, RAPIDS
ciborium PYX, CANOPY, COFFER
cider PERRY
Cid's horse BABIECA
Cid's sword COLADA
Cid's wife ISMENA
cigar ROPE, TOBY, CLARO, SEGAR, STOGY, CORONA, STOGIE, CHEROOT, CULEBRA, PANATELA
cigarette CIG, FAG, BIRI, CUBES, GASPER
cinch GRIP, BREEZE, FASTEN
cinder(s) ASH, SCAR, SLAG, ASHES, DROSS, EMBER, GLEED, SCORIA, CLINKER
cion BUD, GRAFT, SCION, SHOOT
Cipango JAPAN
cipher NIL, CODE, NULL, ZERO, AUGHT, OUGHT, NAUGHT
Circe's island AEAEA, AIAIA
Circe's kin MEDEA, AEETES
circle ORB, CIRC, DISK, EDDY, GIRD, HALO, HOOP, LOOP, NIMB, RING, GLOBE, RHOMB, CIRQUE, CLIQUE, CORDON, GIRDLE, ROTATE
circle part ARC, CHORD, CENTER, RADIUS, SECANT, SECTOR, SEGMENT, TANGENT
circuit LAP, TOUR, EYRE, ZONE, AMBIT, CYCLE, ORBIT, ROUTE, DETOUR
circuitous MAZY, DEVIOUS, SINUOUS
circular AD, BILL, ORBED, ROUND, ANNULAR, DISCOID

circulate BRUIT, DEFUSE, ROTATE, SPREAD
circumference GIRT, AMBIT, GIRTH, VERGE
circumlocution AMBAGE, VERBIAGE
circumspect WARY, CHARY, DISCREET
circumstance FACT, STATE, STRAIT, DETAIL, FACTOR, EPISODE
circus BIGTOP, CIRCLE, CIRQUE, CARNIVAL, COLISEUM
circus equipment NET, RING, TENT, TRAPEZE
circus post META
cirque CWM, CORRIE, RECESS, EROSION
cistern BAC, SAC, VAT, SUMP, WELL
citadel ARX, FORT, ALAMO, TOWER, CASTLE, FORTRESS
cite CALL, QUOTE, ADDUCE, MUSTER, SUBPOENA
cities, foreign *see p. 295*
cities, U.S. *see p. 292*
citizen CIT, VOTER, NATIVE, BURGHER, DENIZEN, OPPIDAN, RESIDENT
citron LIME, ETROG, LEMON, CEDRAT, ETHROG
city URBS, BURGH, POLIS, STADT
city division WARD, BOROUGH, DISTRICT
city, evil SODOM, BABYLON, GOMORRAH
City of Angels BANGKOK
City of Bridges BRUGES
City of Kings LIMA
City of Light PARIS
City of Seven Hills ROME
city of the dead NECROPOLIS
city, pert. to CIVIC, URBAN, MUNICIPAL
civet FOSSA, GALET, GENET, RASSE, ZIBET, BONDAR, MUSANG, PAGUMA, ZIBETH, NANDINE, PERFUME, VIVERRA; *see* CAT
civic LAY, CIVIL, SUAVE, URBAN, OPPIDAN, SECULAR
civil LAY, HEND, CIVIC, HENDE, SUAVE, POLITE, URBANE
Civil War battle SHILOH, BULLRUN, MALVERN, ANTIETAM
Civil War commander COX, LEE, HILL, HOOD, POLK, BANKS, BRAGG, BUELL, CANBY, CROOK, EARLY, EWELL, FLOYD, FOOTE, GRANT, LOGAN, MAURY, MEADE, MOSBY, PRICE, SYKES, BARRON, BUFORD, BUTLER, CUSTER, HOOKER, PORTER, SLOCUM, STUART, SUMNER, FORREST, JACKSON, PICKETT, MCCLELLAN
civilian clothes MUFTI, CIVVIES
civilization CULTURE
civilize POLISH, REFINE, EDUCATE
claim LIEN, EXACT, TITLE, USURP, ALLEGE, ARROGATE
clam MYA, RAZOR, MACTRA, QUAHOG, COQUINA, GEODUCK, GOEDUCK, MOLLUSK, QUAHAUG, QUOHAUG, SHIPWORM, LITTLENECK, CHERRYSTONE
clamor DIN, BERE, BUNK, NOISE, VOCAL
clamp BOLT, VICE, VISE, BRACE, CLASP, GLAND
clan GEN, OBE, SET, SIB, GENS, SEPT, SIOL, AYLLU, CASTE, GENOS, PHYLE, TRIBE, CLIQUE, FAMILY
clan, head of ALDER, THANE, TANIST
clandestine SLY, PRIVY, SECRET, FURTIVE
clang TONK, JANGLE, STROKE
clangor DIN, HUBBUB, UPROAR
clannish SECRET, TRIBAL
clap BLOW, APPLAUD
claret BLOOD, MEDOC, GRAVES, BORDEAUX, SAUTERNE
clarify FREE, CLEAR, RENDER, DEPURATE
clarinet PIBGORN, HORNPIPE, STOCKHORN, CHALUMEAU
clarinet register BREAK, THROAT, CLARINO, CLARION, CHALUMEAU
clarinet socket BIRN
clash JAR, COLLIDE, CONFLICT
clasp HUG, HASP, OUCH, TACH, CINCH, MORSE, TACHE, BUCKLE, ENFOLD, INFOLD
class ILK, CLAN, KIND, RACE, RANK, SORT, TYPE, CASTE, GENUS, ORDER, FAMILY,

GENERA, HEIMIN, SEMINAR, SPECIES
classical PURE, ATTIC, CHASTE
classification FILE, TAXIS, SYSTEM, CATEGORY
classify LIST, RANK, RATE, SORT, TYPE, GRADE, LABEL, ASSORT, TICKET, CATALOG
clatter DIN, RATTLE
clause PLANK, PROVISO
clavier PIANO, KEYBOARD
claw(s) HOOK, UNCI, CHELA, GRIFF, TALON, UNCUS, CHELAE, NIPPER, SCRAPE, UNGUIS, UNGULA
clay PUG, WAD, BOLE, LOAM, LUTE, TILE, ADOBE, ARGIL, BRICK, CRETA, LOESS, OCHER, OCHRE, TASCO, KAOLIN, SAGGAR, SAGGER, KAOLINE
clay bed GA(U)LT
clay layer SLOAM, SLOOM
clayey BOLAR, MALMY, LUTOSE
clean FAY, DUST, TRIM, BREAM, EMPTY, CHASTE, KOSHER
cleaner MOP, SOAP, BROOM, BRUSH, PURER, DUSTER, RAMROD, SCALER, VACUUM, SWEEPER
cleanse PURGE, PURIFY, DETERGE
clear FAY, NET, RID, FREE, LUCID, ACQUIT, AWEIGH, LIMPID, LUCENT, GRAPHIC
clearing SART, MILPA, ASSART
cleat KEVEL, PITON, SPIKE, STRIP, BATTEN, BOLLARD
cleave REND, RIVE, CLING, SPLIT, ADHERE, BISECT, SUNDER
cleaver FROE, FROW
cleft REFT, RIFT, RIMA, RIVA, CLOVEN, FORKED
clement MILD, LENIENT
clench GRIP, HOLD
Cleopatra's attendant IRAS
Cleopatra's lover ANTONY, CAESAR
Cleopatra's needle OBELISK
clergy ABBE, DEAN, CANON, CLERK, PADRE, PRIOR, RABBI, VICAR, CLERIC, CURATE, DIVINE, PARSON, PASTOR, PRIEST, RECTOR; *see* CHURCHMAN
clergy residence MANSE, RECTORY, VICARAGE, PARSONAGE
clerical collar RABATO
clerk AGENT, SCRIBE, TELLER
clever DEFT, HEND, CANNY, HENDE, SMART, ARTFUL, HABILE
clew CUE, BALL, HINT, SKEIN
click AGREE; *see* DETENT
cliff CRAG, KLIP, SCAR, BLUFF, CLEVE, SCARP
climax ACME, APEX, APOGEE, SUMMIT, ZENITH
climb SHIN, SOAR, GRIMP, SCALE, SPEEL, ASCENT, CLAMBER
climbing gear CLEAT, PITON, CRAMPON, CARABINER
clime REALM, TRACT, REGION
clinch HUG, GRIP, NAIL, CLAMP, RIVET, CLENCH
cling HANG, RELY, STICK, TRUST, ADHERE, COHERE
clip CUT, MOW, BARB, PARE, SNIP, TRIM, PRUNE, SHEAR, WHACK
clique SET, CLUB, GANG, RING, CABAL, JUNTO, COTERIE
cloaca PRIVY, SEWER
cloak HAP, CAPA, HIDE, MASK, PALL, WRAP, BLIND, CAPOT, CHOGA, MANTA, CAPOTE, JOSEPH, MANTLE, PONCHO, SARAPE, SERAPE, SHIELD, VISITE, PELISSE, CARDINAL, MANTILLA; *see* CAPE
clock NEF, BELL, DIAL, TIME, METER, TIMER, VERGE, WATCH
clock part DIAL, HAND, PAWL, CHIME, PEISE, DETENT, PALLET, PENDULUM
clod SOD, BOOR, DOLT, LOAM, LUMP, CLUMP, EARTH
clog(s) JAM, BALK, CURB, GETA, CHOKE, SABOT, CHOPIN, GALOSH, DAGGLE, PATTEN, CHOPINE
cloister CELL, STOA, ABBEY, CLOSE, FRIARY, PRIORY, CONVENT, NUNNERY
clone ancestor ORTET
clone member RAMET
close CAM, HUG, CALK, CODA, NEAR, NIGH, SEAL, SEAM, SEEL, SHUT, TAUT, DENSE, ESTOP, FINAL, MUGGY, STIVY, CHINSE, FINALE, STINGY, STUFFY, NIGGARD, OCCLUDE
close ranks SERRY

closet WC, EWRY, AMBRY, CUDDY, EWERY, LOCKER
closure LIEN, CLOSING, STOPPAGE
clot GEL, GOB, JELL, LUMP, MASS, CRUOR, THICKEN, COAGULATE
cloth BRIN, PATA, CRAPE, TAPET, CHEYNEY; *see* FABRIC
cloth, blemish in RIP, SNAG, TEAR, AMPER
clothe TOG, DECK, GARB, GIRD, VEST, ARRAY, DRAPE, ENDUE, INVEST
clothes stand RACK, TREE
clothing RIG, BRAT, DUDS, GARB, GEAR, RAGS, TOGS, ARRAY, BUREL, DICKY, DRESS, HABIT, KHAKI, LUNGI, SLOPS, SMOCK, ATTIRE, DICKEY, FINERY, KHAKEE, LUNGYI, OUTFIT, TIGHTS, APPAREL, CORSLET, COSTUME, HARNESS, NEGLIGE, PAISLEY, RAIMENT, REGALIA, ROMPERS, TOGGERY, VESTURE, CLEADING, CORSELET, FRIPPERY, NEGLIGEE, OVERALLS, PINAFORE; *see* VESTMENT, COAT, PANTS, SHIRT, SKIRT, DRESS, JACKET
clothing, historic CEST, HOOD, HUKE, PALL, CALOT, FROCK, PALLA, SCARF, SIMAR, STOCK, STOLA, STOLE, SYRMA, SYMAR, TALMA, TIARA, TUNIC, CESTUS, CHITON, CYCLAS, KIRTLE, MANTUA, PEPLOS, PILEUS, TABARD, TIPPET, TRIBON, ARISAID, CALOTTE, CAPUCHE, CHLAMYS, CUCULLA, DOUBLET, PAENULA, PALTOCK, SPENCER, SULTANE, SURCOAT, CINCTURE, GAMBESON, HIMATION, GABERDINE
clothing, native ABA, OBI, BAJU, HAIK, IZAR, KILT, MALO, MIND, SARI, SAYA, TOGA, BURKA, CABAN, CHOGA, CHOLI, DHOTI, GREGO, HAORI, JELAB, JEMMY, JIBBA, LUNGI, PAGNE, PAREU, PARKA, SAGUM, TOOSH, TREWS, ANORAK, BARVEL, BIETLE, BYRRUS, CABAAN, CANDYS, CHAMMA, DIRNDL, DOLMAN, HUIPIL, JELICK, JELLAB, JIBBAH, JIBBEH, JUBBAH, KAROSS, KIMONO, LUNGEE, MOOCHA, NETCHA, PONCHO, RAILLY, SARONG, TEMIAK, TOUSER, BURNOUS, CHUDDAH, CHUDDAR, CHUDDER, FILIBEG, GALABIA, SARAFAN, TABLIER, ZAMARRA
cloud(s) COMA, RACK, SCUD, SMUR, CIRRI, NUBIA, RACKS, VAPOR, CIRRUS, CUMULI, NEBULA, NIMBUS, STRATI, CUMULUS, STRATUS, NUBECULA
cloudy DIM, HAZY, FOGGY, FILMY, LOWERY, OVERCAST
clout BUMP, CUFF, NAIL, SLAP, SWAT, PATCH
cloven-footed FISSIPED
clover HAGI, HUBAM, MEDIC, SULLA, ALSIKE, LADINO
clown HOB, BOZO, GOFF, ZANY, PUNCH, JESTER, RUSTIC, BUFFOON
clownish GAWKY, LOUTISH
cloy CLOG, FILL, GLUT, PALL, SATE, GORGE, SATIATE, SURFEIT
club BAT, KIRI, MACE, MERE, PATU, POLT, BILLY, STAFF, STICK, WADDY, CUDGEL, LIBBET, MACANA, MARREE, NULLAH, TAIAHA, BLUDGEON, BLACKJACK, SHILLALAH, KNOBKERRIE
club, social USO, DOES, ELKS, TEAM, BRITH, LAMBS, LIONS, LODGE, MOOSE, ORDER, ZONTA, FRIARS, MASONS, ROTARY, KIWANIS, SOCIETY, SOROSIS, SORORITY
clubfoot TALIPED, TALIPES
club-shaped CLAVATE
clue CUE, TIP, HINT
clump CLOD, MOTT, TUFT, BUNCH, MOTTE, PATCH
clumsy AWK, GAUCHE, OAFISH, AWKWARD
clumsy person OX, OAF, BULL, SWAB, KLUTZ, LUMMOX
cluster NEP, CYME, TUFT, BUNCH, CLUMP, SORUS, SPRIG, ANADEM, RACEME
clutch GRIP, HOLD, GRASP
clutter JUMBLE, LITTER
coach BUS, FLY, STAGE, TUTOR, JARVEY, CARRIER, DILIGENCE; *see* HACK

coachman JEHU, WHIP, PILOT, DRIVER
coagulate GEL, SET, CAKE, CLOT, CURD, JELL, CURDLE, POSSET, CONGEAL
coagulant RENNET, STYPTIC
coal COB, JET, BASS, COKE, DUFF, SMUT, SWAD, EMBER, CARBON, CINDER, LIGNITE
coal box DAN, HOD, SCUTTLE
coal refuse ASH, COOM, CULM, SLAG, SMUT, SOOT, COOMB, CINDER, CLINKER
coal size EGG, NUT, PEA, STOVE
coalition AXIS, UNION, MERGER
coarse RUDE, CRASS, CRUDE, GROSS, RIBALD, VULGAR
coast RIPA, BEACH, GLIDE, SLIDE
coast, pert. to ORARIAN, LITTORAL, RIPARIAN
coaster BOB, LUGE, SLED, ROLLER (COASTER)
coat ABA, FUR, TOG, HAIR, HIDE, PELT, RIND, SKIN, WOOL, CLOAK, CRUST, GLAZE, LAYER, PLATE, TERNE, CAFTAN, COATEE, KAFTAN, PATINA, PELAGE, SURCOAT, SURTOUT, WRAPPER, MACKINAW, PINAFORE, GABARDINE, GABERDINE, INVERNESS, REDINGOTE; *see* OVERCOAT
coat part LAPEL, SKIRT, SLEEVE
coax COG, EGG, CANT, LURE, CAJOLE, ENTICE, WHEEDLE
cobble MEND, PAVE, BOTCH, PATCH
cobbler SOLER, SUTOR, SOUTER, CRISPIN
cobbler's tool AWL, LAST, ROZET
cobra NAG, HAJE, NAGA, MAMBA, RINGHALS; *see* VIPER
cobweb NET, TRAP, SNARE
cocaine COKE, DUST, SNOW
cocaine source COCA
cock TAP, HEAP, RICK, PRIME, FAUCET
cockade KNOT, ROSETTE
cockatoo ARARA, GALAH, CORELLA
cocker PET, CODDLE, FONDLE, PAMPER, SPANIEL
cockle GITH, KILN, OAST, SHELL
cockpit CAB, NOSE, ARENA, CABIN, NACELLE
cocktail BS, FIZZ, FLIP, GROG, PURL, SOUR, BRONX, DAISY, JULEP, NEGUS, PUNCH, SLING, SMASH, TODDY, BISHOP, CHASER, COOLER, EGGNOG, FRAPPE, GIBSON, GIMLET, POSSET, RICKEY, ROBROY, ROYALE, ZOMBIE, BACARDI, COBBLER, COLLINS, MARTINI, SIDECAR, STINGER, SWIZZLE, WASSAIL, DAIQUIRI, HIGHBALL, HOTTODDY, PINKLADY, SANGAREE, SPRITZER, ALEXANDER, CUBALIBRE, LAMBSWOOL, MANHATTAN, MARGARITA, PISCOSOUR
cocky PERT, PERKY, PROUD, JAUNTY
coconut COCO, PATE, COPRA, NARGIL, NOGGIN
coconut fiber COIR, KOIR, KYAR, COIRE
cocoon POD, CLEW, KELL
cod(-like fish) BIB, CUSK, GADE, HAKE, HAIK, LING, LOTA, POOR, POUT, TUSK, GADID, GADUS, SCROD, SPRAG, TORSK, BURBOT, GADOID, HADDIE, LAWYER, MURRAY, TOMCOD, WACHNA, BACALAO, BEARDIE, CODFISH, CODLING, DOGFISH, EELPOUT, HADDOCK, KEELING, POLLACK, POLLOCK, WHITING, STOCKFISH
cod, pert. to GADOID
code KEY, LAW, RULE, CODEX, CIPHER
codger CHURL, MISER, NIGGARD
codicil RIDER, SEQUEL, DIPLOMA
coerce COW, CURB, BULLY, FORCE, COMPEL
coffee MUD, RIO, JAVA, MOCHA, BRAZIL, SANTOS, SUMATRA, ESPRESSO
coffee cup FINJAN
coffee cup holder ZARF
coffee grind DRIP, FINE, PERC, SILEX, COARSE, VACUUM
coffee grinder MILL
coffeepot BIGGIN
coffer ARK, DAM, PYX, CHEST, CAISSON

cog CHEAT, CHUCK, TENON, TOOTH, WHEEDLE
cogitate CHEW, MULL, THINK
cognate AKIN, ALLIED, RELATED
cognizance KEN, HEED, NOTICE
cognizant HEP, ONTO, AWAKE, AWARE
cognomen NAME, EPITHET, SURNAME
coheir (CO)PARCENER
cohere BIND, CLING, STICK
coif CAP
coiffure HAIRDO
coign ANGLE, CORNER
coil ANSA, CLUE, CURL, LOOP, ROLL, WIND, HELIX, QUERL, TWINE, TWIST, WHORL
coin JOE, CASH, MINT, BRASS, INVENT, SPECIE, TALENT
coin box PYX, TILL, METER
coin edge NIG, (K)NURL
coin roll ROULEAU
coincide FIT, JIBE, AGREE, TALLY
colander SIEVE, BOLTER, STRAINER
cold ICY, RAW, ALGID, GELID, RHEUM, CORYZA, FRIGID, CATARRH
cold blood SANGFROID
cold sore HERPES
cole *see* CABBAGE
collaborator LAVAL, QUISLING
collar LEI, NAB, CANG, ETON, RING, RUFF, CATCH, FANON, ORALE, CANGUE, DICKY, BERTHA, CARCAN, CHOKER, DICKEY, GORGET, RABATO, REBATO, TORQUE, CARCANET
collation TEA, MEAL, REPAST, LUNCHEON
collect BAG, MASS, LEVY, AMASS, GLEAN, GARNER, PRAYER, SHEAVE, COMPILE
collection ANA, SET, CLAN, HEAP, MASS, RAFT, STACK, SYLVA, CORPUS, ROSARY, SORITE, DOSSIER, SORITES; *see* BEVY
collector's item CURIO, RARITY
colleen GIRL, LASS, MAID
college TOL, GUILD, LYCEE, BREVET, LYCEUM, NORMAL, ACADEMY, SEMINARY
college building GYM, LAB, DORM, FRAT
college class LECTURE, SEMINAR, TUTORIAL
college grounds LAWN, QUAD, CAMPUS
college nicknames DONS, ELIS, EPHS, NAVY, OWLS, RAMS, TARS, UTES, VOLS, ZIPS, BEARS, BULLS, DUKES, FORDS, HAWKS, HOYAS, IRISH, LIONS, LOBOS, MULES, AGGIES, AZTECS, BIGRED, BISONS, BRAVES, BRUINS, CADETS, EAGLES, EPHMEN, FLYERS, FRIARS, GATORS, ILLINI, JUMBOS, REBELS, REDMEN, SAXONS, TIGERS, TITANS, UCLANS, BADGERS, BEAVERS, BENGALS, BOBCATS, BONNIES, BRONCOS, BULLETS, COUGARS, COWBOYS, DRAGONS, FALCONS, GOPHERS, HUSKIES, INDIANS, KEYDETS, LARRIES, MAROONS, PIRATES, QUAKERS, ROCKETS, SOONERS, SPIDERS, TARTANS, TROJANS, VANDALS, VIKINGS, VIOLETS, BEARCATS, BUCKEYES, BULLDOGS, COLONELS, HOOSIERS, KINGSMEN, TARHEELS, WOLFPACK, WOLVERINES
college officer DON, DEAN, BEADLE, BURSAR, DOCENT, REGENT, PROCTOR, REGISTRAR
college student COED, SOPH, FROSH, PLEBE, JUNIOR, SENIOR, FRESHMAN, SOPHOMORE
college term QUARTER, SEMESTER, TRIMESTER
colleges COE, MIT, NYU, USC, VMI, VPI, CASE, DREW, DUKE, FENN, RICE, UCLA, YALE, BATES, BEREA, BROWN, CLARK, COLBY, DRAKE, DRURY, EMORY, LORAS, PRATT, RIDER, SMITH, TUFTS, AUSTIN, BAYLOR, BUTLER, CALVIN, DEPAUL, DEPAUW, DREXEL, FURMAN, GANNON, HARPUR, HOBART, HOWARD, HUNTER, LEHIGH, LOYOLA, MCGILL, MERCER, MORGAN, OLIVET, POMONA, PURDUE, TEMPLE, TULANE, UPSALA, VASSAR, WAGNER, XAVIER, ADELPHI, AMHERST, ANDREWS, ANTIOCH, BARNARD, BENTLEY,

BETHANY, BOWDOIN, BRADLEY, CHAPMAN, CITADEL, COLGATE, CORNELL, DENISON, FORDHAM, GONZAGA, GOUCHER, HAMPTON, HARVARD, HOFSTRA, LASALLE, MCMURRY, NEWCOMB, OBERLIN, PARSONS, RUTGERS, STJOHNS, SIMMONS, STETSON, STEVENS, SUFFOLK, TRINITY, WILLIAM, YESHIVA

collide BUMP, CRASH, CANNON, HURTLE
collier *see* MINER
colloid GEL, SOL
colloquialism IDIOM
collude PLOT, SCHEME, CONNIVE
Colombian weight SACO, CARGA, LIBRA, QUILATE, QUINTAL
Colombian money PESO, REAL, CONDOR, CENTAVO
colonel's command BRIGADE
colonel's insignia EAGLE
colonizer ANT, OECIST, SETTLER, PLANTER
colonnade STOA, PORTICO, TERRACE
color(s) DYE, HUE, FLAG, TINT, PAINT, SHADE, TINGE, BANNER, ENSIGN; *see p. 251*
color blindness DALTONISM
color, primary RED, BLUE, GREEN, INDIGO, ORANGE, VIOLET, YELLOW
color vehicle MAGILP, MEGILP
Colorado information *see p. 308*
Colorado tributary GILA, GREEN
colorful VIVID
coloring agent DYE, PIGMENT
colorist PAINTER
colorless WAN, DRAB, DULL, PALE, ASHEN, CLEAR, ALBINO, PALLID
Columbia US(A), AMERICA
Columbia river fish SALMON
Columbia tributary SNAKE, KOOTENAY
Columbus's captain PINZON
Columbus's place GENOA, PALOS
Columbus's ship NINA, PINTA, SANTAMARIA
Columbus's son DIEGO
column LAT, ANTA, FUST, DORIC, IONIC, STELE, TORSE, TORSO, PILLAR, PILASTER
column figure TELAMON, ATLANTES, CARYATID
column, ring of annulated BAGUE
Comanche SNAKE, PADUCA; *see p. 342*
comb CARD, RAKE, CREST, CURRY, RIDGE, TEASE
combat COPE, JOUST, SKIRMISH
combination CABAL, JUNTO, TRUST, UNION, CARTEL, LEAGUE, MERGER, FACTION
combine MIX, WED, JOIN, POOL, RING, BLEND, MARRY, CARTEL, SPLICE
combustible FIERY; *see* FUEL
come SUE, NEAR, (A)RISE, ENSUE, REACH, ACCRUE, ADVENE, ARRIVE
come about TACK, OCCUR, HAPPEN
come across PAYUP, DELIVER, DISCOVER
come around AGREE, ACCEPT, ASSENT
come back RECUR, RETURN
come by GET, GAIN, OBTAIN
come clean (CON)FESS
come forth JET, GUSH, SPEW, ISSUE, EMERGE, EMERSE, EMANATE
come in ENTER
come short MISS
come to TOTAL, AWAKE(N), REVIVE
come to grief FAIL, FALL
comeback ANSWER, RETORT, RIPOSTE, RECOVERY
comedian WAG, WIT, BUFF, ZANY, BUFFO, ANTIC, CLOWN, COMIC, JOKER, PANIC, JESTER, BUFFOON, FARCEUR
comedians MAY, COCA, HOPE, KAYE, MARX, WYNN, LAHR, SAHL, BENNY, BORGE, BURNS, CHASE, HARDY, LEWIS, PRYOR, SALES, ABBOTT, AKROYD, CAESAR, DRAPER, FIELDS, KEATON, KOVACS, LAUREL, LITTLE, LLOYD, MARTIN, RADNER, TOMLIN, WILSON, BELUSHI, BUTTONS, CHAPLIN, GLEASON, GROUCHO, HACKETT, NEWHART, RICKLES, SKELTON, VANDYKE, COSTELLO
comedy FARCE, HUMOR,

SATIRE, TRAVESTY, SLAPSTICK
comely FAIR, PRETTY, SEEMLY
come-on BAIT, LURE
comet's part COMA, HEAD, TAIL, TRAIN
comet's path ORBIT
comets ABE, FAYE, GALE, SEKI, TOBA, WILD, WOLF, AREND, BAADE, BIELA, BRAHE, ENCKE, IKEYA, KIRCH, KOPFF, MRKOS, SWIFT, WELLS, ALCOCK, BROOKS, COGGIA, DANIEL, DONATI, FINLAY, FORBES, HALLEY, HOLMES, LAHIRE, LEXELL, OLBERS, OTERMA, TEMPEL, TEWFIK, TUTTLE, ZIMMER, BARNARD, BRORSEN, DARREST, HUMASON, MECHAIN, PERRINE, STEARNS, BORRELLY, GRISCHOW, KOHOUTEK, WESTPHAL, MOREHOUSE
comfit *see* CANDY
comfort SOP, EASE, REPOSE, SOLACE, CONSOLE
comfortable COSH, COZY, SNUG, LITHE, PLEASING
comforter PUFF, QUILT, SCARF
comic(al) DROLL, FUNNY, ABSURD, RISIBLE; *see* COMEDIAN
comic strip *see* CARTOON
coming DUE, ADVENT, ARRIVAL
command BID, HEST, FIAT, ORDER, BEHEST, ENJOIN, DICTATE, MANDATE
commander AGA, CID, AGHA, CAID, QAID, SIRDAR, ALCAIDE
commandeer SEIZE, HIJACK
Commandments, Ten DECALOG(UE)
commando RAIDER
commence OPEN, BEGIN, START
commend KEN, LAUD, EXTOL, COMMIT
comment(ary) NOTE, ASIDE, GLOSS, GEMARA, POSTIL, REMARK, DESCANT, EXEGESIS, GLOSSARY, SCHOLION
commerce TRADE, BARTER, TRAFFIC
comminate BAN, CURSE, THREATEN
comminute MILL, CRUSH, GRIND
commiseration PITY, RUTH, EMPATHY
commission PROXY, BREVET, CHARGE, DEPUTE, ORDAIN
commit ASSIGN, CONSIGN, ENTRUST, INTRUST
committee GROUP, PANEL, JUNTA
commodious ROOMY, SPACIOUS
commodity WARE, GOODS, STAPLE, PRODUCT
common LOW, PLEB, JOINT, PLAIN, TRITE, USUAL, COARSE, MUTUAL, ORNERY, VULGAR, CURRENT, GENERAL, PLEBEIAN
commoner PLEB, PROLE, CITIZEN
commonplace BANAL, PROSY, TRITE, CLICHE, TRUISM, BROMIDE, HUMDRUM, PROSAIC
commotion ADO, CHOP, FUSS, STIR, TODO, FUROR, BUSTLE, HUBBUB, POTHER, WELTER
commune ANS, ATA, EDE, EPE, MIR, SHAR, IMPART, KOLHOZ, KIBBUTZ, KOLKHOZ, TOWNSHIP
communion HOST, MASS, SECT, HOUSEL, RAPPORT, VIATICUM, EUCHARIST
communion item AMA, PIX, PYX, HOST, FANON, PATEN, WAFER, EULOGIA
Communist leader TITO, HUSAK, DUBCEK; *see* RUSSIAN
Communist newspaper PRAVDA, WORKER, IZVESTIA
community MIR, TOWN, VILLAGE
compact BOND, ETUI, HARD, TRIG, DENSE, SOLID, CASTEL, VANITY, COVENANT
companion PAL, PEER, MATE, CRONY, ESCORT, SPOUSE, ACHATES, COMPEER, CONSORT, PARTNER
company CIE, LTD, BAND, BODY, FERE, FIRM, TROOP, TROUPE, BATTERY, PHALANX
comparative THAN, EQUAL, RELATIVE
compare EVEN, LIKEN, SEMBLE, COLLATE
comparison SIMILE, ANALOGY, PARABLE
compartment BAY, BIN, CELL, CABIN, SECTION

compass GYRO, AMBIT, GAMUT, SWEEP, ENCLOSE, TRAMMEL
compass part VANE, GIMBAL, BINNACLE
compass point NE, NW, SE, SW, ENE, ESE, NNE, NNW, SSE, SSW, WNW, WSW, RHUMB
compassion RUE, PITY, RUTH, GRACY, MERCY
compel MAKE, FORCE, IMPEL, COERCE
compendium BRIEF, DIGEST, PRECIS, SUMMARY, SYLLABUS
compensate PAY, ATONE, REPAY, TALLY
compensation UTU, BALM, REWARD, SALARY, REDRESS
compete VIE, COPE, MATCH, EMULATE
competent APT, SANE, ADEPT, CAPAX
competition FEIS, MATCH, STRIFE, RIVALRY
competitor VIER, RIVAL, OPPONENT
compile EDIT, SELECT, ARRANGE, COLLATE
compilation *see* COLLECTION
complacent SMUG, BLASE
complain CARP, FRET, FUSS, KICK, GRIPE, WHINE, GROUSE, REPINE, GRUMBLE
complaisant CIVIL, SUAVE, POLITE, AFFABLE, LENIENT
complement SET, UNIT
complete END, QUITE, TOTAL, UTTER, PLENARY
complex MAZE, MIXED, KNOTTY, NETWORK, TANGLED, MANIFOLD, SYNDROME, INTRICATE
complexion HUE, BLEE, TINT, TINGE
complicate INTORT, TANGLE, WORSEN, PERPLEX
complicated KNOTTY, COMPLEX, TANGLED
complication NODE, NODI, NODUS, SNARL
complicity COLLUSION
compliment LAUD, EXTOL, EULOGY
comply OBEY, ADAPT, ACCEDE
component PART, UNIT, FACTOR, ELEMENT, INTEGRAL
comport ACT, BEHAVE, DEMEAN, INVOLVE
composed COOL, QUIET, SOBER
composers ABT, ARNE, BACH, BERG, BOCK, CAGE, DUKE, FAIN, FOSS, IVES, KERN, LALO, ROME, WOLF, ADLER, ARLEN, AUBER, BALFE, BIZET, BLAKE, BLOCH, COHAN, DINDY, DUKAS, ELGAR, FRIML, GLUCK, GREEN, GRIEG, GROFE, GUIDO, HANDY, HAYDN, HOLST, IBERT, LEHAR, LISZT, LOEWE, LULLY, RAVEL, REGER, ROREM, SOUSA, STYNE, VERDI, WEBER, WEILL, BARBER, BARTOK, BERLIN, BOULEZ, BRAHMS, CARTER, CHOPIN, COWARD, DELIUS, DVORAK, FOSTER, FRANCK, GOUNOD, HANDEL, JOPLIN, LENNON, MAHLER, MOZART, PORTER, ROGERS, SCHUTZ, TAYLOR, WAGNER, WEBERN, ALBENIZ, BABBITT, BELLINI, BERLIOZ, BORODIN, BRITTEN, COPLAND, CORELLI, DEBUSSY, DEFALLA, DELIBES, HERBERT, JOSQUIN, LOESSER, MANCINI, MENOTTI, MILHAUD, POULENC, PUCCINI, PURCELL, RODGERS, ROMBERG, ROSSINI, SMETANA, STRAUSS, VIVALDI, YOUMANS, GERSHWIN, MASCAGNI, MASSENET, SCHUBERT, SONDHEIM, SIBELIUS, SULLIVAN, TELEMANN, BACHARACH, BERNSTEIN
composite COLLAGE, MONTAGE
composition NOME, OPUS, CENTO, ESSAY, PIECE, SCENA, THEME; *see* MUSIC
compositor TYPO, PRINTER
composure MIEN, POISE, QUIET, REPOSE, BALANCE
compound MIX, OLIO, AMIDE, OXIDE, FARRAGO, MIXTURE
comprehend GET, SEE, GRASP, LATCH, SENSE
compress PAD, STUPE, DIGEST, REDUCE, SHRINK, ABRIDGE, BANDAGE, CURTAIL, DEFLATE, PLEDGET, SQUEEZE, CONDENSE
comprise EMBODY, INCLUDE
compulsion FORCE, DURESS, STRESS
compulsory service DRAFT, ANGARY, ANGARIA, SLAVERY

compunction QUALM, REGRET, SCRUPLE
compute TALLY, TOTAL, ASSESS, FIGURE, RECKON
computer DEC, IBM, MAC, VAX, AMIGA, APPLE, ATARI, ENIAC, ANALOG, UNIVAC, DIGITAL
computer language ADA, LISP, LOGO, ALGOL, BASIC, COBOL, PASCAL, FORTRAN
computer term IO, BIT, CPU, DOS, LAN, RAM, ROM, BAUD, BLOS, BOOT, BYTE, CHIP, DATA, DISK, FILE, GIGO, PORT, UNIX, MODEM, BUFFER, CURSOR
comrade PAL, CHUM, BILLY, BUDDY, CRONY, TOVARICH
con ANTI, CHEAT, STUDY, VERSUS
concatenate JOIN, LINK, CHAIN, UNITE, CONNECT
concave DISHED, HOLLOW
concave molding SCOTIA
conceal WRY, MASK, PALM, VEIL, CACHE, CLOAK, ELOI(G)N
concealed INNER, PERDU, COVERT, LATENT, LARVATE
concede ADMIT, GRANT, YIELD
conceit FLAM, VANITY, EGOTISM
conceited person PRIG, SNOB, EGO(T)IST, PEACOCK
conceive PLAN, BRAIN, FRAME, IDEATE, IMAGINE
concentrate AIM, FIX, FOCUS, SYRUP, UNIFY, ELIXIR, DISTILL, ESSENCE, EXTRACT, CONDENSE
concentration camp *see* PRISON CAMP
conception IDEA, FANCY, IMAGE, NOTION
concern CARE, FIRM, SAKE, WORRY, AFFAIR, REGARD, RELATE
concerning RE, FOR, ANEN, INRE, ABOUT, ANEN(S)T
concert hall ODEON, ALBERT, FISHER, LYCEUM, MASSEY, ACADEMY, CARNEGIE
conch CHANK, SHELL, COCKLE, WINKLE
conciliate EASE, PACIFY, APPEASE, PLACATE
conciliatory GENTLE, IRENIC, WINNING
concise CURT, PITHY, TERSE
conclave CLOSET, MEETING
conclude REST, INFER, DEDUCE, FINISH, SETTLE, TERMINATE
conclusion END, CODA, FINIS, RESULT
conclusive FINAL, COGENT, TELLING
concoct MIX, BREW, COOK, HATCH
concord PACT, AMITY, RAPPORT
concordat TREATY, COMPACT, ENTENTE
concourse MALL, CROWD, THRONG
concrete HARD, REAL, BETON, ACTUAL, CEMENT, MORTAR
concur JIBE, AGREE, ASSENT
concussion SHOCK
condemn BAN, DOOM, FILE, BLAME, DECRY, CENSURE
condense CUT, DECOCT, DISTIL, SHRINK, DISTILL, COMPRESS
condescend DEIGN, FAVOR, STOOP
condiment SOY, CAPER, CHILI, CUMIN, CURRY, COMINO, HYSSOP, PEPPER, RELISH, CANELLA, CAYENNE, MUSTARD, PIMENTO, CAPSICUM, CARDAMOM, CARDAMON, CHARLOCK; *see* SEASONING, SPICE
condition IF, TERM, FACET, PHASE, PLIGHT, STATUS, PROVISO
condolence PITY
condone PARDON, FORGIVE
condor *see* VULTURE
conduce AID, LEND, TEND, EFFECT
conduct RUN, CONVEY, CONVOY, DEMEAN, ESCORT, MANAGE
conductor CAD, MUTI, WIRE, GUIDE, MEHTA, OZAWA, SOLTI, SZELL, ABBADO, BOULEZ, LEADER, WALTER, BEECHAM, CARRIER, KARAJAN, MAESTRO, ORMANDY, CICERONE, BERNSTEIN, LEINSDORF, SCHERCHEN, STOKOWSKI, TOSCANINI; *see* BANDLEADER
conduit ADIT, DUCT, MAIN, DRAIN, CHANNEL
cone COP, CONOID, CORNET,

FUNNEL, VOLCANO, STROBILE
cone-shaped CONIC, CONOID, CONICAL
coney DUPE, GULL, HARE, DAMAN, HYRAX, RABBIT
confection *see* CANDY
confederate REB, ALLY, REBEL, UNITE, ABETTOR, PARTNER; *see* CIVIL WAR
Confederate money BLUEBACK
Confederate president DAVIS
confederation BUND, UNION, LEAGUE
confer DUB, AWARD, ENDOW, BESTOW, PARLEY, CONSULT
conference SYNOD, CAUCUS, CONFAB, PALAVER
confess OWN, ADMIT, REVEAL, SHRIVE
confession CREDO, CREED, AVOWAL, SHRIFT
confessional BOOTH
confidant(e) CRONY, FRIEND
confide AFFY, TRUST, COMMIT, ENTRUST, INTRUST
confident SURE, SECURE, CERTAIN
confidential PRIVY, SECRET, ESOTERIC
confine BOX, DAM, HEM, PEN, CAGE, COOP, JAIL, CHECK, CRAMP, LIMIT, BORDER, INTERN
confined ILL, ABED, PENT
confirm RATIFY, VERIFY, ENDORSE
confiscate SEIZE, ESCHEAT, IMPOUND
conflict WAR, BOUT, FRAY, OPPOSE, STRIFE
conform FIT, ADAPT, COMPLY
confound FAZE, STUN, BAFFLE, NONPLUS
confront DEFY, FACE, BRAVE
Confucius work ANNALS, ICHING, CHUNCHIU
confuse ABASH, BEMUSE, FUDDLE, JUMBLE, FLUSTER, NONPLUS
confused ASEA, MUZZY, WESTY, ADDLED
confusion MESS, BABEL, CHAOS, SNAFU
confute REFUSE, DISPROVE
congeal GEL, SET, JELL, HARDEN, PECTIZE
congenital INBORN, INNATE, NATIVE
conger *see* EEL
Congo discoverer CAM, CAO
Congo language *see* BANTU
Congo tributary KASAI, UBANGI
congratulate LAUD, SALUTE, MACORIZE
congregation FOLD, FLOCK, PARISH, TEMPLE
congress MOD, DIET, DUMA, RADA, SETAN, MAILIS, SOVIET
conic section CIRCLE, ELLIPSE, PARABOLA, HYPERBOLA
conifer FIR, YEW, PINE, CEDAR, LARCH, SPRUCE
conjecture ETTLE, POSIT, THEORY, SURMISE
conjugal MARITAL, CONNUBIAL
conjunction AND, BUT, NOR, TIE, JOIN, THEN, ANDOR, SINCE, UNION
conjuncture CRISIS
conjure up EVOKE, INVOKE, SUMMON
conjurer MAGE, DOWSER, SHAMAN, VOODOO, WIZARD, EXORCIST, MAGICIAN
connect FIX, GLUE, JOIN, LINK, AFFIX, COUPLE
Connecticut college YALE, HARTT
Connecticut information *see p. 308*
connection BOND, LINK, NEXUS
connective tissue FASCIA, TENDON
connive ABET, CONSPIRE
connote MEAN, IMPLY
connubial MARITAL, CONJUGAL
conquer LICK, CRUSH, MASTER, SUBDUE
conqueror HERO, VICTOR
conscious WARE, AWAKE, AWARE, SENTIENT
conscript LEVY, DRAFT, MUSTER, DRAFTEE, RECRUIT
consecrate SAIN, BLESS, TABOO, ANOINT, HALLOW
consecrated OBLATE, SACRED
consensus ACCORD
consent AGREE, ACCEDE, COMPLY, CONCUR
consequence END, IMPORT, RESULT, SEQUEL, OUTCOME
consequently SO, ERGO, HENCE
conservative SAFE, TORY, DIEHARD, RIGHTIST
consider DEEM, MUSE, RATE, STUDY, TREAT, REFLECT

consideration HEED, PRICE, REASON
considering WHEN, SINCE
consign COMMIT, REMAND
consignee BROKER, FACTOR, RECEIVER
consignment CARGO
consistency DENSITY, HARMONY
consolation SOP, BOOBY, SOLACE
console CALM, BRACE, CHEER, CABINET, COMFORT
consolidate FUSE, KNIT, MERGE, COMBINE
consonant LENE, SURD, LENIS, ATONIC, DENTAL, FORTIS, SONANT, SPIRANT
consort MATE, SPOUSE, PARTNER
conspicuous OVERT, PATENT, SIGNAL, BLATANT, SALIENT
conspiracy COUP, CABAL, JUNTO, INTRIGUE
conspirator BRUTUS, FAWKES, CASSIUS, SABOTEUR
conspire PLOT, CABAL, SCHEME, COLLUDE, COMPLOT
constable COP, BULL, SLOP, BEADLE
constant FAST, LOYAL, STILL, STAUNCH
constellation ARA, ARGO, APUS, CRUX, GRUS, LYNX, URSA, VELA, CANIS, DRACO, HYDRA, INDUS, LEPUS, LUPUS, MALUS, MENSA, MUSCA, NORMA, ORION, PYXIS, ANTLIA, AQUILA, AURIGA, BOOTES, CAELUM, CARINA, CORVUS, CRATER, CYGNUS, DORADO, HYDRUS, OCTANS, PICTOR, PUPPIS, SCUTUM, TUCANA, VOLANS, CEPHEUS, COLUMBA, LACERTA, PEGASUS, PERSEUS, SAGITTA, SERPENS, SEXTANS
constellation, zodiac LEO, ARIES, LIBRA, VIRGO, CANCER, GEMINI, PISCES, TAURUS, SCORPIO, AQUARIUS, CAPRICORN, SAGITTARIUS
constitution CODE, HEALTH, MAKEUP, NATURE, CHARTER, IRONSIDES
constitutional WALK, BASIC, LEGAL, LAWFUL
constraint BOND, FORCE, DURESS
constrict CHOKE, CRAMP, NARROW, SHRINK, ASTRINGE
constrictor BOA, SPHINCTER
construct BUILD, ERECT, DEVISE
construction worker MASON, ROOFER, SEABEE, RIVETER
construe INFER, PARSE
consult CONFER
consume EAT, USE, BURN, WEAR, SPEND, WASTE
consummate END, SHEER, WHOLE, ARRANT, ACHIEVE
consumption USE, WASTE, PHTHISIS
contact ABUT, TOUCH, SYZYGY
contagion INFECTION
contagious CATCHING, INFECTIOUS
contain HOLD, CHECK, EMBODY, SUBSUME
container BAG, BOX, CAN, CUP, JAR, TIN, TUB, URN, VAT, CAGE, CASE, VASE, PHIAL, POUCH, BOTTLE, CARBOY, CARTON
contaminate SPOIL, SULLY, TAINT, DEFILE, POISON, POLLUTE
contemn SCORN, SPURN, DESPISE
contemplate BROOD, STUDY, THINK
contemporaneous COEVAL, CURRENT
contemporary COEVAL
contempt, show GECK, SCORN, SNEER, SNIFF, SNORT
contemptible LOW, BASE, MEAN, VILE, SORRY, ABJECT
contemptuous sound BAH, HISS, HOOT, PFUI, RAZZ, PHOOEY, CATCALL
contend VIE, WAR, COPE, DEAL, ARGUE, CLAIM, COMPETE
content GIST, SATED, REPLETE
contention FEUD, STRIFE, DISPUTE
contest WAR, AGON, BOUT, DUEL, FRAY, ARGUE, JOUST, ROLEO, AFFRAY, DEBATE, DISPUTE, TOURNEY
contiguous NEAR, ADJACENT, TOUCHING
continent NA, SA, AFR, EUR, AMER, ASIA, SOBER, AFRICA, CHASTE, AUSTRAL, EURASIA, LEMURIA, ATLANTIS, CASCADIA, ANTARCTICA

contingency CASE, EVENT, CHANCE
continue LAST, ENDURE, PERDURE
continued SERIAL, CHRONIC
contort WRAP, GNARL, TWIST
contour LINE, SHAPE, OUTLINE, PROFILE
contract DEAL, HIRE, KNIT, CATCH, INCUR, SHRINK
contraction EEN, EER, OER, TIS, AINT, CANT, ISNT, WONT, ARENT, MAYNT, SHANT
contradict DENY, BELIE, REBUT, IMPUGN, NEGATE, GAINSAY
contraption GISMO, GADGET, GIMMICK
contrary UNRULY, FROWARD, OPPOSED
contrast COMPARE
contribute GIVE, CHIPIN, DONATE
contribution TAX, ALMS, BOON, GIFT, TITHE, PRESENT
contrite SORRY, RUEFUL
contrivance PLANT, PLOT, DEVICE, GIMMICK
contrive PLOT, HATCH, DEVISE, MANAGE
control CURB, HANK, SWAY, CHECK, REIGN, STEER
controversial ERISTIC, POLEMIC(AL)
controversy DEBATE, DISPUTE
controvert DENY, REFUTE, GAINSAY
contusion BRUISE
conundrum POSER, ENIGMA, RIDDLE
convene SIT, MEET, CONVOKE
convenient HANDY, USEFUL
convent MATH, MUTH, ABBEY, NUNNERY, CLOISTER
conventional NOMIC, FORMAL, PROPER
converge MEET, FOCUS
conversant HEP, FAMILIAR
conversation DIALOG, PALAVER, CAUSERIE
convert GER, ALTER, ANSAR, PROSELYTE
convex ARCHED, GIBBOUS
convey BEAR, CEDE, CARRY, ASSIGN, TRANSFER
conveyance CAR, DEED, DEMISE, WAFTAGE
conveyor belt APRON
convict CON, LAG, FELON, LIFER, TERMER, CONDEMN
convince ASSURE, PERSUADE
convincing VALID, COGENT
convivial GAR, FESTAL, GENIAL
convocation SYNOD, COUNCIL, ASSEMBLY
convoke CALL, CONVENE, ASSEMBLE
convolution COIL, TWIST, WHORL
convoy PILOT, ESCORT, CONDUCT
convulsion FIT, SPASM, THROE
cony *see* CONEY
coo CURR, CHIRR, CHOUGH, MURMUR
cook CHEF, SHIR(R), MAGIRIST
cooking art CUISINE, MAGIRICS
cooking apparatus ETNA, OVEN, PLATE, RANGE, STOVE, ELEMENT, HIBACHI, HOTPLATE, MICROWAVE
cooking odor NIDOR
cooking term CUT, DIP, FRY, MIX, BAKE, BEAT, BOIL, BREE, CHOP, CUBE, DICE, DUST, FOLD, FRIT, HASH, LARD, MASH, MELT, PARE, ROLL, ROUX, SEAR, SHIR, SIFT, SOAK, STEW, STIR, WHIP, BASTE, BLEND, BROIL, BRUSH, CHILL, CREAM, FLAKE, FROST, GLACE, GLAZE, GRILL, GRIND, KNEAD, MINCE, PASTE, POACH, PUREE, ROAST, SAUTE, SCALD, SCORE, SHIRR, SIEVE, STEAM, STEEP, STOCK, TOAST, TRUSS, BLANCH, BRAISE, DREDGE, FILLET, FOLDIN, FRAPPE, MORTAR, PANFRY, PESTLE, REDUCE, SIMMER, SKEWER, GARNISH, PARBOIL, PREHEAT, SCALLOP, SPATULA, BARBECUE, JULIENNE, MARINATE, PANBROIL, STUFFING
cooking utensil PAN, POT, WOK, OLLA, KETTLE, SPIDER, TUREEN, GRIDDLE, SKILLET
cookout FRY, ROAST, BARBECUE
cool ICY, CALM, CHILL, GELID, NERVY, PLACID, COMPOSED
Coolidge Dam river GILA
cooling apparatus FAN, FRIDGE, FREEZER
coop MEW, PEN, STY, COTE, CASE, JAIL, HUTCH, ENCASE
cop BULL, FLIC, BOBBY, PEELER, GENDARME

copal ANIME, RESIN
Copenhagen park TIVOLI
copious LUSH, PROFUSE, REPLETE
copper CU, CENT, CUPRUM; *see* COP
copper alloy BRASS, BRONZE, OROIDE, RHEOTAN
Copperfield's kin DORA, AGNES, BETSY
copse BOSK, HOLT, COPPICE
Coptic clergyman AMBA, ANBA
copy APE, DRAFT, MODEL, CARBON, ECTYPE, ESTREAT
copyist SCRIBE, SCRIVENER
copyright PATENT
copyright violation PIRACY, PLAGIARY, PLAGIARISM
coquette FLIRT
coral POLYP, ZOOID, FUNGIA, PORITE, OCULINA, TUBIPORA, TUBIPORE
cord AEA, AGAL, LINE, RAIP, ROPE, WELT, HEDDLE, TENDON, TORSADE
cordage fiber *see* FIBER
Cordelia's kin LEAR, REGAN, GONERIL
cordial WARM, ARDENT; *see* LIQUEUR
core AME, GIST, NAVE, NIFE, PITH, HEART, NOWEL
Corinth BIMARIS
Corinthian general PISANDER
Corinthian king POLYBUS
cork FLOAT, SHIVE, BOBBER, STOPPLE
cormorant SHAG, DUIKER, DUYKER, GORMAW, PLOTUS, ANHINGA
corn SALT, MAIZE, CLAVUS, MEALIE
corn part COB, EAR, HUSK, SPIKE, STALK, STOVER, TASSEL, TUCKET
corner NOOK, TREE, ANGLE, HERNE, INGLE, NICHE
cornerstone COIN, COYN, COIGN, QUOIN, COIGNE
cornice DRIP, ASTRAGAL
Cornish prefix LAN, ROS, TRE
cornmeal MASA, SOFK, GRITS, SOFKI, HOMINY, SOFKEE
corny BANAL, MUSHY, TRITE
corolla PETAL(S), PERIANTH
corona CIGAR, FILLET, AUREOLA, AUREOLE, SCYPHUS
coronach DIRGE, THRENODY
coronet BURR, CROWN, TIARA, ANADEM, DIADEM
corporal NCO
corporate JOINT, COMMON, UNITED
corporeal HYLIC, BODILY, SOMATIC
corpse LICH, MUMMY, STIFF, CADAVER, CARCASS
corpulent BURLY, OBESE, PORTLY
corral PEN, STY, HERD, ATAJO, POUND
correct MEND, EDIT, OKAY, AMEND, EMEND, RIGHT, ADJUST, ARIGHT, REVISE, CHASTEN
correspond FIT, JIBE, AGREE, TALLY, WRITE
corridor HALL, AISLE, HALLWAY, PASSAGE(WAY)
corrode EAT, PIT, BURN, GNAW, RUST, DECAY, ERODE
corrosive ACID, CAUSTIC, MORDANT
corrupt VILE, SPOIL, VENAL, DEBASE, VITIATE
corsage WAIST, BODICE, BOUQUET
corsair PIRATE, PICAROON
corset BUSK, STAY(S)
cortege TRAIN, RETINUE
cortex BARK, RIND
corundum RUBY, EMERY, TOPAZ, AMETHYST, SAPPHIRE
corvine *see* CROW
Cosa Nostra MAFIA, FAMILY
cosmetic KOHL, HENNA, PAINT, ROUGE, CERUSE, MASCARA
cosmic order RITA
cosmonaut *see* ASTRONAUT
cosmos GLOBE, WORLD, UNIVERSE
Cossack RUSS, TURK, TATAR
Cossack regiment POLK, PULK
Cossack squadron SOTN(I)A
cosset PET, LAMB, CODDLE, FONDLE
cost LOSS, RATE, PRICE, CHARGE
Costa Rican measure FANEGA, CAJUELA
Costa Rican money COLON, CENTIMO
Costa Rican weight CAJA
costume RIG, GETUP; *see* CLOTHING

cot BED, CRIB
cote SHED, SHELTER
Côte d'Azur RIVIERA
coterie SET, JUNTO, CLIQUE
cottage BARI, CABIN, CHALET
cotton machine GIN, MULE, BALER, LINTER, WILLOW
cotton measure LEA, HANK
couch HIDE, LAIR, SOFA, DIVAN, SETTEE, DAVENPORT
cough HACK, TUSSIS
council FONO, SYNOD, WITAN, CABINET
councillor FAIPULE
counsel(or) REDE, WARN, CHIDE, LAWYER, MENTOR, NESTOR, PROCTOR
count TOT, EARL, GRAF, RELY, COMES, SCORE, TALLY, TOTAL, CENSUS, RECKON
Count of Monte Cristo DANTES
countenance ABET, FACE, VISAGE
counter BAR, CHIP, CHECK, SHELF, TOKEN, GEIGER, CONTEND
counterfeit FAKE, SHAM, BOGUS, FORGE, PHONY
counterirritant MOXA
countermand REVOKE, RESCIND
counterpart COPY, TWIN, DOUBLE, PENDANT, REPLICA
countersink REAM, BEVEL, CHAMFER
countertenor ALTO, FALSETTO
countless MYRIAD, INNUMERABLE
countries and capitals *see p. 285*
country LAND, PAIS, VALE, WILD, REALM, WEALD
country, pert. to RURAL, RUSTIC, AGRESTIC
countryman BOOR, SWAIN, RUSTIC, PATRIOT
county AMT, LAN, FLYKE, SHIRE, PARISH; *see p. 289*
county official SHERIFF
coup BLOW, FEAT, SCOOP, PUTSCH, STROKE
couple TWO, DYAD, PAIR, SPAN, BRACE, TWINS, GEMINI
coupled GEMEL, YOKED, WEDDED, GEMELED
couplet DISTICH
courage GRIT, GUTS, SAND, NERVE, PLUCK, SPUNK, VALOR, METTLE
courageous BOLD, BRAVE, DARING, HEROIC
courier GUIDE, ESTAFET(TE)
course LAP, LEG, WAY, ROAD, ROTE, SOUP, TACK, CYCLE, ROUTE, SALAD, TREND, ENTREE, DESSERT
course, school BOT, ENG, MED, ANAT, ARCH, BIOL, ECON, MATH, TRIG, ZOOL, PREMED
courser STEED
court(s) BAR, SUE, WOO, DARI, FORA, LEET, ROTA, YARD, CURIA, CURRY, DAIRO, FORUM, FAVOR, GEMOT, PATIO, GEMOTE, PALACE, PARVIS, PROBATE, TRIBUNAL
court action SUIT, TRIAL, APPEAL
court assistant EYRE, JURY, AMALA, AMLAH, CLERK, CRIER, MACER, BEADLE, ELISOR, BAILIFF, TALESMAN
court decision VERDICT
court order BOND, WRIT, ARRET, CITATION, MANDAMUS, SUBPOENA
court, pert. to AULIC
court president FOUD
court session ASSIZE, SITTING
courteous KIND, CIVIL, URBANE
courtesan THAIS, HETAERA
courtly HEND, AULIC, HENDE, ELEGANT
courtship SUIT, WOOING
couturier DIOR, PUCCI, RICCI, CARDIN, CHANEL, BALMAIN
cove CHAP, INLET, FELLOW; *see* BAY
covenant BOND, PACT, TREATY, PROMISE
cover(ing) CAP, LID, CEIL, COSY, HIDE, HUSK, PEEL, PELT, RIND, SEAL, SKIN, QUILT, PELAGE, SHEATH, TEGMEN, THATCH, SHEATHE, TEGUMEN
cover a bet FADE
covered AWASH, FLOODED
coverlet PALL, QUILT, THROW, AFGHAN, SPREAD
covert HIDDEN, SECRET
covet ENVY, PINE, CRAVE, YISSE
covetous GREEDY, ENVIOUS, JEALOUS
covey BEVY, BROOD, FLOCK
cow BOSSY, BULLY, DAUNT, BOVINE; *see* CATTLE
coward CUR, CRAVEN, CAITIFF, POLTROON

cowardly TIMID, CRAVEN, CHICKEN
cowboy GAUCHO, HERDER, LLANERO, PUNCHER, VAQUERO
cowboy movie OATER, WESTERN
cower QUAIL, CRINGE, SHRINK
cowfish TORO
cowl COUS, HOOD, AMICE
cowrie SHELL, WAMPUM
cowslip BLUEBELL, PRIMROSE
coxcomb FOP, NOB, DUPE, TOFF, DANDY, SWELL
coy ARCH, CHARY, DEMURE
coyote *see* WOLF
coypu NUTRIA
cozy SNUG, HOMEY, QUILT
crab UCA, MAIA, ZOEA, HIPPA, MAIAN, RACER, YABBY, ZOAEA, ZOOEA, BUSTER, CANCER, HERMIT, PARTAN, PEELER, SPRITE, YABBER, YABBIE, BUCKLER, FIDDLER, LIMULID, MUDCRAB, PANFISH, PEACRAB, SHEDDER, BLUECRAB, FROGCRAB, GRAPSOID, KINGCRAB, LADYCRAB, LANDCRAB, LIMULOID, OCHIDORE, OCYPODAN, RANINIAN
crab genus ANOMURA, GRAPSUS, LIMULUS, OCYPODE, CAMBARUS, PORTUNUS
crack CHAP, JOKE, KIBE, RIFT, SNAP, CHINK, CLEFT
cracker BISCUIT, SALTINE
crackle SNAP, SPUTTER, CREPITATE
cradle BED, CRIB, SLEE, CADRE, CRECHE, INFANCY
cradle song LULLABY
craft ART, TRADE, METIER, POLICE, TALENT
craftsman MASON, NAVVY, SMITH, WRIGHT, ARTISAN
crafty SLY, FOXY, WILY, ARTFUL, TRICKY
crag TOR, SCAR, ARETE, BRACK
crake CROW, RAIL, SORA
cram RAM, WAD, PACK, STUFF
cramp ART, KINK, SPASM, STITCH
crane JIB, COOT, GRUS, JENNY, SARUS, BROLGA, CHUNGA, CARIAMA, GOLIATH, LIMPKIN, SERIEMA, WHOOPER; *see* LIFTING
cranium SKULL
crank NUT, BEND, BRACE, WINCH, HANDLE, CAPRICE, CRACKPOT
cranky CROSS, TESTY, GROUCHY
cranny NOOK, CHINK, FISSURE
crash FAIL, BURST, CLOTH, LINEN, FAILURE
crasher INTRUDER
crass CRUDE, GROSS, COARSE, STUPID, VULGAR
crate BOX, CRADLE, ENCASE, HAMPER
crate maker CASER
crater PIT, CONE, LINNE, CAVITY, CALDERA
cravat TIE, ASCOT, SCARF
crave LONG, PINE, COVET, HANKER
craw MAW, CROP
crawl FAWN, INCH, CREEP, GROVEL
crayfish YABBY; *see* LOBSTER
crayon CHALK, PASTEL, PENCIL
craze FAD, RAGE, FUROR, MANIA, MADDEN
crazy REE, AMOK, DAFT, LOCO, LUNY, DAFFY, DOTTY, LOONY, MANIC, POTTY, WACKY
cream TOP, BEST, ECRU, ELITE
crease FOLD, RUCK, RUGA, SEAM, TUCK, CRIMP, STRIA
create MAKE, BEGET, PRODUCE
creator GOD, AUTHOR, DEMIURGE
creature BEING, MINION, WRETCH
credence FAITH, TRUST, BELIEF
credentials PAPERS, DIPLOMA, VOUCHER, CERTIFICATE
credit TICK, TRUST, IMPUTE, ASCRIBE
credit transfer GIRO
creditor DEBTEE, LENDER
creed NICENE; *see* BELIEF
creek GEO, GIO, RIA, RUN, KILL, VLEI, BAYOU
creep FAWN, INCH, CRAWL, TINGLE
creeper IVY, VINE, WORM, SNAKE
creeping REPENT, REPTANT
creepy EERIE, WEIRD, CRAWLY
cremate CALCINE
cremation SUTTEE
crescent(-shaped) CUSP, LUNE, MOON, LUNAR, LUNATE, LUNULA

cresset TORCH, LANTERN
crest TOP, TOR, COMB, PEAK, TUFT, ARETE, CROWN, RIDGE
crested PILEATE, CRISTATE(D)
Crete CANDIA
Cretan CANDIOT(E)
Cretan guardian TALOS
Cretan king MINOS
Cretan princess ARIADNE
crevice RIME, CLEFT, CRANNY
crew MEN, MOB, BAND, GANG, OARS, TEAM, HANDS
crib BIN, PONY, TROT, CRECHE
cribbage term GO, PEG, CRIB, NOBS, HEELS, LURCH
cricket GRIG, STOOL, INSECT
cricket term BAT, BYE, LEG, ONS, OFFS, OVER, SLIP, TICE, YORK, EDGER, MIDON, PITCH, BOWLER, CREASE, GOOGLY, WICKET, YORKER
crier HERALD, MUEZZIN
crime SIN, VICE, ARSON, FELONY, SIMONY
criminal FELON, NOCENT, CULPRIT, CONVICT
crimp FURL, FRIZ(Z), CREASE, GOFFER
crimson LAC, RED, CARMINE
cringe FAWN, COWER, QUAIL, WINCE
crinkle CRUMPLE
cripple(d) HALT, LAME, IMPAIR
crisis RUB, HEAD, PASS
crisp CURT, TERSE, BRITTLE
criterion NORM, TEST, CANON, STANDARD, TOUCHSTONE
critic BOOER, CARPER, CENSOR
critical NICE, ACUTE, EXACT, EXIGENT
criticism REVIEW, CENSURE, ZOILISM
criticize PAN, RAP, CARP, FLAY, CAVIL, ROAST, SLATE
critics SHAW, AUDEN, JAMES, PATER, DRYDEN
critique REVIEW
croak CAW, DIE, CROUP
Croatian SLAV, CROAT, SLOVENE
Croatian soldier PANDOUR
crochet KNIT
crochet stitch LOOP, CHAIN, PIQUE, TRICOT
crocodile GOA, CROC, GATOR, CAIMAN, CAYMAN, GAVIAL, JACARE, MUGGER, YACARE, ALLIGATOR
crocodile genus GAVIALIS
crocus IRIS
Croesus' land LYDIA
croft FARM, CRYPT, VAULT
cromlech DOLMEN
Cromwell NOLL, IRONSIDES
crone EWE, HAG, WITCH, BELDAM(E)
crony PAL, CHUM, MATE, BUDDY
crook BEND, HOOK, PEDA, CURVE, PEDUM, CROSIER, POTHOOK
crooked WRY, AGEE, AWRY, BENT, ASKEW, AKIMBO, CORRUPT
crooner BING, COMO, PERRY, CROSBY, MARTIN, SINATRA
crop(s) MAW, CRAW, RABI, REAP, ROWEN, GEBBIE, HARVEST
crop up ARISE, RECUR
croquet ROQUE
croquet term ARCH, HOOP, BISQUE, WICKET
crosier CROOK, STAFF
cross TAU, ANKH, CRUX, EDGY, ROOD, SPAN, IRATE, LATIN, TESTY, TRIAL, CELTIC, FYLFOT, POTENT, MALTESE, SALTIER, SALTIRE, SWASTIKA
cross out EX, CUT, DELE, CANCEL, DELETE
cross threads WEFT, WOOF
cross timber SPALE
crossbeam TRAVE, TREVE
crosspiece RUNG, CLEAT, EVENER
cross-stroke SERIF
crotch FORK, HOOK
crotchety ODD, QUEER, FITFUL
crouch COWER, SQUAT, STOOP
crouton SIPPET
crow DAW, KAE, CROW, ROOK, BOAST, CHOUGH, HOODIE, KOKAKO, JACKDAW, KOKAKOO
crowbar PRY, JIMMY
crowd JAM, MOB, CRAM, HERD, RUCK, CRAMP, PRESS, SERRY
crown BAY, CAP, TAJ, ATEF, PATE, POLL, CREST, TIARA, CORONA, DIADEM, CORONET, PSCHENT, CORONATE
Crown colony HONGKONG
crucial point CRUX, PIVOT, CRISIS
crucible CRUSET, RETORT

crucifix *see* CROSS
crude RAW, CRASS, COARSE
crude person BOOR, BEAST, BRUTE
cruel FELL, FERAL, SAVAGE, BESTIAL
cruet AMA, VIAL, CRUSE, CASTER, AMPULLA
cruise SAIL, COAST
cruising ASEA
crumb BIT, ORT, SCRAP
crumple RUCK, RUMPLE, SCRUNCH, WRINKLE
crunch CHEW, CRUSH, GRIND, MUNCH
cruor GRUME
crusade JAHAD, JIHAD, CAMPAIGN
crusader PILGRIM, TEMPLAR
crusader foe TURK, SALADIN, SARACEN
crush MASH, PRESS, SUBDUE
crust SCAB, SCALE, CORTEX
crustacean ALIMA, MYSID, MYSIS, SLATER, SOWBUG, SQUILL, ASELLUS, GRIBBLE, MACRURA, MYSIDAE, ONISCUS, PILLBUG, SQUILLA, COPEPODA, CUMACEAN, EPICARID, LERNAEAN; *see* LOBSTER, CRAB, SHRIMP, BARNACLE
crusty HARSH, SURLY
crutch PONY, PROP, SUPPORT
cry BOO, FAD, SOB, CALL, CROW, MEWL, MOAN, OYES, OYEZ, PULK, RAGE, RALE, ROAR, WAIL, WEEP, YELL, YOHO, COOEE, COOEY, GROAN, HALLO, HOLLA, HOLLO, LARUM, SHOUT, SNORE, TRILL, WHOOP, ALARUM, BOOHOO, CLAMOR, HALLOOA, HALLOO, HUBBUB, PLAINT, SCREAM, SCROOP, SHRIEK, SHRILL, SNIVEL, UPROAR, YOICKS, SCREECH, TALLYHO; *see* BIRDS, ANIMAL, SOUND
cry of approval BIS, BRAVO, HURRAH; *see* CHEER
cry of pain OW, OUCH, YELP
crypt TOMB, VAULT
cryptic OCCULT, SECRET, OBSCURE
crystal ICE, CLEAR, MACLE, DIAMOND
crystal gaze SCRY
cub FRY, PUP, COLT, LIONET
Cuban measure TAREA, CORDEL
Cuban tree JIQUE, JIQUI
cube DIE, DICE, NASIK, TESSERA, TESSELLA
cubicle CELL, NICHE, ALCOVE, CARREL
cubitus ULNA, FOREARM
Cuchulain kin LUG, EMER, CONNLA, SUALTAM, DECHTIRE
cuckoo ANI, MAD, KOEL, COOEE, CRAZY, KOKIL, COUCAL, KOKILA, LOURIE, MALKOHA, TOURACO, RAINBIRD
cucumber CUKE, PEPO, PEPINO, PICKLE, GHERKIN
cud CHEW, QUID, BOLUS, RUMEN
cuddle HUG, NESTLE, SNUGGLE
cuddy ASS, CLOSET, DONKEY, STUPID
cudgel BAT, CLUB, DRUB, BASTE, STAVE, TOWEL
cue NOD, ROD, TIP, HINT, TAIL, PRESA, SIGNAL
cuff SLAP, SMACK, BUFFET, POMMEL, MANACLE
cuff fastener TAB, LINK, STUD, BUTTON
cuirass ARMOR, BREASTPLATE
cuisine COOKERY, KITCHEN
cull DUPE, GLEAN, PLUCK, SELECT, WINNOW
culm STEM, SLACK, REFUSE
culmination ACME, APEX, AUGE, NOON, APOGEE, CLIMAX, VERTEX, ZENITH
culpable GUILTY, BLAMABLE
culprit FELON, OFFENDER
cult FAD, ISM, SECT, MANIA
cultivate EAR, HOE, FARM, PLOW, TILL, NURSE, HARROW, RATOON
cultivating tool HOE, PICK, RAKE, SPADE, HARROW
cultivation JUM, JOOM, TILTH
culture AGAR, POLISH, TILLAGE
culvert DRAIN, SEWER
cumbersome CLUMSY, UNWIELDY
cuneiform CUNEAL
cuneiform writing SUSIAN, ELAMITE, HITTITE
cunning ART, SLY, CUTE, FOXY, WILY, DEDAL, GUILE, ARTFUL, CALLID, CRAFTY, DAEDAL

cup AMA, DOP, TIG, TYG, LOTA, TASS, CALYX, CHARX, CRUSE, CUPEL, DEPAS, GODET, GRAIL, LOTAH, MAZER, COTULA, HOLMOS, NOGGIN, TROPHY
cupbearer HEBE, SAKI
Cupid DAN, AMOR, EROS, LOVE, PUTTO
Cupid sweetheart PSYCHE
cupola DOME, TURRET, LANTERN
cup-shaped PEZIZOID
cur MUT(T), FEIST, MONGREL
curare URALI, OORALI
curassow MITU
curator WARDEN
curb REIN, CHECK, BRIDLE, REPRESS
curd CRUD, CASEIN(E), CONGEAL
curdle SAM, POSSET, RENNET, CLABBER
cure TAN, CORN, HEAL, SMOKE; *see* REMEDY
cure-all ELIXIR, NOSTRUM, PANACEA
Curia court ROTA, SIGNATURA
curio VIRTU, BIBELOT
curiosity ODDITY, RARITY, WONDER
curious ODD, NOSY, SNOOPY
curl COIL, FEAK, FRIZ, KINK, TRESS, BERGER, RINGLET
curlew SNIPE, WHAUP, GODWIT
curling term HOG, TEE, HACK, PORT, SOOP, WICK, BESOM, HOUSE, BUTTON, PATLID, POTLID
curly UNDY, WAVY, KINKY, OUNDY
currency CHANGE; *see* MONEY
current AC, DC, EDDY, RIFE, TIDE, RAPID, COURSE, STREAM, PRESENT
current, ocean NINO, PERU, BLACK, NATAL, ALASKA, ARCTIC, KURILE, AGULHAS, MONSOON, OKHOTSK, OYASHIO, ALEUTIAN, BANGUELA, CANARIES, FALKLAND, HUMBOLDT, LABRADOR, TSUSHIMA
Currier's partner IVES
curry DRESS, GROOM, SPICE
curse HEX, OATH, REVILE, ANATHEM, MALISON, ANATHEMA
cursory HASTY, CASUAL
curt BLUNT, BRUSK, GRUFF, SQUAB, BRUSQUE
curtail LOP, PARE, REDUCE
curtain IRON, WALL, DRAPE, SCRIM, BAMBOO, SCREEN, VALANCE
curtain material LENO, GAUZE, NINON, SCRIM, TAPIS
curtsy DIP, SALAAM, SCRAPE
curve ARC, BOW, ESS, SNY, ARCH, BEND, HOOK, OGEE, CROOK, SINUS, ELLIPSE, PARABOLA
curve section ARC
curved NOWY, ADUNC, CONVEX, CONCAVE
cushion PAD, BOLSTER, HASSOCK
Cush's kin HAM, SEBA, NIMROD
Cushitic language AGAU, BEJA, GALA, GOFA, KAFA, ZALA, ALABA, AWIYA, BILIN, BURJI, GALLA, OMETO, QUARA, DARASA, HARURO, KHAMIR, QABENA, SIDAMO, SOMALI, WOLAMO, BASKETO, JANJERO, KAMBATTA, SAHOAFAR
cusp HORN, PEAK, POINT
cuss CURSE, SWEAR
custard apple ATES, ANNONA, SWEETSOP
custodian WARDEN, CURATOR, JANITOR
custody CARE, TRUST, CHARGE, DURANCE
custom(s) TAX, URE, CESS, DUTY, LEVY, TOLL, WONT, MORES, RITUS, SUNNA, USAGE, DASTUR, SUNNAH, TARIFF
customer CLIENT, PATRON
cut DOD, HEW, LOP, MOW, NIP, DICE, DOCK, FELL, GASH, HACK, KERF, REAP, SLIT, SNEE, SNIP, SNUB, TRIM, CARVE, SCARP, SEVER, SHEAR, SLASH, SLICE, SLISH, CLEAVE, ESCARP, LESION, TREPAN, ESCARPE
cut down RASEE, RAZEE
cut in half HALVE, BISECT, REDUCE, SECANT
cut of meat CHOP, LOIN, RIBS, RUMP, CHINE, CHUCK, FLANK, SHANK, STEAK, CUTLET, BRISKET, SIRLOIN, SHOULDER

cut off LOP, SNIP, ELIDE, ROACH
cutter SLED, SLOOP
cutting SCION, SHARP, SECANT, INCISAL, MORDANT
cutting tool AX, ADZ, AXE, BUR, DIE, HOB, SAW, SAX, ADZE, BOLO, BURIN, KNIFE, MOWER, RAZOR, CHASER, CHISEL, SCYTHE, SHEARS, SICKLE, MACHETE
cuttlefish SEPIA, SQUID, OCTOPUS
Cybele's consort ATYS, ATTIS
cycle BIKE, ROUND, SAROS
cyclone LOW, BAGUIO, TYPHOON
Cyclopes ARGES, BRONTES, POLYPHEMUS
Cyclops' defeater NOMAN, ODYSSEUS
cylinder INKER, BARREL, GAVION, PISTON, PLATEN
cyma GOLA, GULA, OGEE
cymbal(s) TAL, ZEL, PIATTI
Cymbelline's kin CLOTEN, IMOGEN
Cymric WELSH, BRETON
cynical SURLY, MOROSE, ASCETIC
cypress LAWN, CEDAR, GILIA
cyprinoid fish *see* CARP
Cyprus measure OKA, PIK, CASS, KOUZA, KARTOS, MEDIMNO
Cyprus weight OKA, MOOSA, KANTAR
cyst BAG, SAC, WEN, POUCH
czar IVAN, PAUL, BASIL, PETER, FEODOR, TYRANT, DICTATOR, NICHOLAS
Czechoslovak language CZECH, SLOVAK
Czechoslovak measure LAN, SAH, JITRO, KOREC, LATRO, LOKET, STRYCH
Czechoslovak money DUCAT, HALER, HELLER, KORUNA
Czechoslovak president BENES, MASARYK, NOVOTNY, SVOBODA

D

dab PAT, PECK, POKE, STAB, DIBBLE
dabbler DUFFER, AMATEUR, TRIFLER, SCIOLIST
dabchick GREBE, DIPPER
dad PA(PA), PATER, FATHER
Dadaist ARP, BALL, ERNST, GROSZ, TZARA, PICABIA, DUCHAMP
daddle FIST, HAND
dado DIE, BASE, SOLIDUM
Daedalus' son ICARUS
daffodil JONQUIL, NARCISSUS
daft CRAZY, SILLY, FOOLISH
Dagda relative BODB, ANGUS, BRIGIT, OENGUS
dagger CRIS, DIRK, KRIS, BALAS, BOWIE, KATAR, SKEAN, ANLACE, BODKIN, CREESE, STYLET, BAYONET, KHANJAR, PONIARD, STILETTO
Dahomean language *see* GUR
Dahomean native FON
daily ADAY, DIURNAL
dainty CATE, CHOICE, PETITE, TIDBIT, DELICACY
dairy LACTARIUM
dairy maid DEY(E)
dairy product MILK, CREAM, BUTTER, CHEESE
dais ESTRADE, ROSTRUM
daisy GOWAN, OXEYE, SHASTA, GERBERA, MARGUERITE
Dakota Terr. capital YANKTON
dale GLEN, VALE
dally LAG, TOY, DELAY
dam PEN, DIKE, SADD, SUDD, WAER, WEIR, GARTH, PARENT
damage MAR, HARM, HURT, IMPAIR
daman *see* CONEY
Damascus king ARETAS
dame LADY, MADAM, MATRON
damn DOOM, CURSE, CONDEMN
Damon's friend PYTHIAS
damp WET, DANK, MOIST
dams OAHE, GATUN, GORKY, KEBAN, WYMAN, BEKHME, BHAKRA, BUFORD, CONTRA, COUGAR, DEGRAY, FRIANT, BRANBY, HOOVER, KARIBA, KUROBE, MANGLA, MCNARY, NAVAHO, SAKUMA, SHASTA, SULTAN, VAIONT, WINSOR, WISHON, AHOKAN, BRIONES, CACHUMA, CARTERS, CASITAS, CICEROZ, CONCHAS, CURNERA, FONTANA, HIRAKUD, LUZZONE,

PACTOLA, PAHLEVI, SANFORD, SANLUIS, TRINITY, WATAUGA, BLUEMESA, COGSWELL, FORTPECK, GARRISON, KAKHOVKA, KINGSLEY, KREMASTA, MERRIMAN, OROVILLE, PINEFLAT, TERMINOS; *see* PLANT

damsel GIRL, MAIDEN

Danae lover ZEUS

Danae relative PERSEUS, ACRISIUS

dance BAL, HOP, BALL, PROM, PARTY, COTILL(I)ON

dance gear TUTU, TIGHTS, LEOTARD

dance step PAS; *see* BALLET

dance teacher MURRAY, ASTAIRE

dance type TAP, TOE, GOGO, BELLY, BALLET, FLAMENCO

dancer ALMA, ALME, ALMEH, KELLY, RASCH, SHAWN, BOLGER, CASTLE, GEISHA, GRAHAM, HOOFER, WIGMAN, ZORINA, ASTAIRE, CHORINE, DANSEUR, FONTEYN, NUREYEV, PAVLOVA, SHEARER, STDENIS, ULANOVA, DANSEUSE, FIGURANT, NIJINSKY, FIGURANTE, TALLCHIEF

dances HAY, HOP, JIG, HAKA, HORA, HULA, JOTA, JUBA, KOLO, POLO, REEL, SHAG, SIVA, BOREE, CONGA, CUECA, FLING, GALOP, GAVOT, GIGUE, LINDY, MAMBA, PAVAN, POLKA, RONDO, RUMBA, SAMBA, TANGO, TWIST, VALSE, VOLTA, WALTZ, ALTHEA, BALLET, BOLERO, BRANLE, CANCAN, CEBELL, DREHER, HORMOS, MAXIXE, MORRIS, NAUTCH, POLSKA, REDOWA, RHUMBA, SHIMMY, TRESCA, AURESCA, BOURREE, CANTICO, CHACCON, CHACONA, COURANT, CZARDAS, FORLANA, FOXTROT, FURIANT, FURLANA, GAVOTTA, GAVOTTE, HALLING, HOEDOWN, LANCERS, LAVOLTA, MAZURKA, MORISCO, ONESTEP, RAGTIME, ROMAIKA, SARDANA, SHUFFLE, TWOSTEP, ANGLAISE, BUNNYHOP, BUNNYHUG, CACHUCHA, CAKEWALK, CHACONNE, COTILLON, COURANTE, FANDANGO, GALLIARD, HABANERA, HORNPIPE, HULAHULA, LANCIERS, MATELOTE, RIGADOON, SARABAND

dandelion seed CYPSELA

dandruff SCURF

dandy FOP, BEAU, BUCK, DUDE, FINE, JAKE, TOFF, SWELL

Dane JUTLANDER

danger RISK, PERIL, HAZARD

danger signal SOS, ALARM

dangerous RISKY, PERILOUS

Daniel's companion MESHACH, ABEDNEGO, SHADRACH

Danish *see also* DENMARK

Danish measure FOD, MIL, POT, ALEN, FAVN, RODE, ALBUM, LINJE, TOMME, TONDE, ACHTEL, LANDMIL, OLTONDE, VIERTEL

Danish money ORE, KRONE, SKILLING

Danish weight ES, LOD, ORT, VOG, MARK, PUND, UNZE, KVINT, CENTNER, LISPUND, QUINTIN

dank WET, DAMP, HUMID, MOIST

Dante's muse BEATRICE

Danube DONAU, ISTER

Danube tributary INN, OLT, VAH, ENNS, HRON, ISAR, LECH, NAAB, PRUT, RABA, DRAVA, ILLER, ISKER, MARCH, NITRA, SIRET, TISZA

Danzig GDANSK

Daphne's father LADON

Daphne's lover CHLOE

dapper CHIC, NATTY, NIFTY

dapple(d) PIED, SPOT, FLECK

Dard SHINA, KAFIRI, KHOWAR, PISACA, KASHMIRI

Dardanus' brother IASION

dare DEFY, FACE, OSSE, RISK, BRAVE, VENTURE

daring BOLD, BRAVE, HARDY, INTREPID

dark EBON, DUSKY, MIRKY, MURKY, SWART, UNLIT, DISMAL, SOMBRE

Dark Continent AFRICA

darken DIM, BLACKEN, OBSCURE

darkness MIRK, MURK, GLOOM
darling PET, ROON, CHERI(E), ACUSHLA, ASTHORE
darn MEND, PATCH
dart BARB, BOLT, FLIT, ARROW, SCOOT, ELANCE
D'Artagnan friend ATHOS, ARAMIS, PORTHOS
Darwin ship BEAGLE
dash ELAN, LACE, TINGE, TOUCH, TRACE, VERVE, HURTLE, HYPHEN, SOUPCON
dashing GAY, BRAVE, SHOWY
dastard CAD, COWARD, CRAVEN
data FACTS, FIGURES
date IDES, NONE, COURT, NONES, TRYST, CALENDS, OUTMODE
date line on coin EXERGUE
dated OLD, PASSE
datum FACT
daub APPLY, SMEAR, PLASTER
daunt AWE, COW, DAW, AMATE
dauntless BRAVE, DARING, GALLANT
davenport SOFA, COUCH, SETTEE
David relative JESSE, TAMAR, ABSALOM, SOLOMON, BATHSHEBA
David victim URIAH, GOLIATH
davit SPAR, CRANE
daw *see* CROW
dawdle LAG, IDLE, POKE, DALLY
dawn DEW, EOS, SUNUP, AURORA
dawn, pert. to EOAN
Dawson's river YUKON
day YOM, DIES
day before EVE
daybreak DAWN, AURORA, SUNRISE
daydream FANCY, REVERIE
daze STUN, BEWILDER
dazzle STUN, BLIND, GLARE
de facto ACTUAL
de novo ANEW, AGAIN, AFRESH
dead FEY, FLAT, GONE, LATE, (A)MORT, INERT, NAPOO, EXPIRED
dead end IMPASSE, CULDESAC
Dead Sea fortress MASADA
dead tree(s) DRIKI, RAMPIKE
deaden DAMP, MUTE, NUMB
deadlock TIE, DRAW, IMPASSE
deadly MORT, FATAL, LETHAL, MORTAL
deadly sins ENVY, LUST, ANGER, PRIDE, SLOTH, GLUTTONY, COVETOUSNESS
deaf BARREN, MUFFLED
deal COPE, DOLE, GIVE, ALLOT, TRADE, HANDLE
dealer AGENT, COPER, HOUSE, BROKER, COOPER, CUTLER, DRAPER, MERCER, MONGER, TRADER, VINTNER
dean DECAN, DOYEN, ELDER, DOYENNE
dean, pert. to DECANAL
dear LOVED, COSTLY, VALUED
dearth WANT, FAMINE, DROUGHT, PAUCITY
death MORT, FINIS, DEMISE
death note MORT
death notice OBIT(UARY)
deathless IMMORTAL
deathwatch VIGIL
debacle ROUT, DISASTER
debar DENY, SHUT, STOP, DETER
debase ALLOY, LOWER, DEMEAN
debate AGON, MOOT, CANVASS
debauchee RAKE, ROUE, SATYR
debility ATONY, FRAILTY
debonair SUAVE, JAUNTY, ELEGANT
debris RUINS, SCREE, LITTER, JETSAM, FLOTSAM, RUBBISH
debt DUE, IOU, DUTY, ARREARS
decadence DECAY, DECLINE
decamp LAM, BOLT, ELOPE, SCRAM, LEVANT, VAMOSE, ABSCOND, VAMOOSE
decant DRAW, POUR, ELUTRIATE
decanter EWER, CROFT, CARAFE
decay BLET, CONK, CARIES, PUTREFY
deceased GONE, LATE, DEFUNCT
deceit SHAM, WILE, COVIN, FEINT, FRAUD, GUILE
deceitful SLY, WILY, ARTFUL
deceive BILK, DUPE, FLAM, GULL, SILE, COZEN, TRICK, GAMMON, HUMBUG, ILLUDE
deceiver LIAR, FAKER, TRAPAN, SHARPER, IMPOSTOR
decent MODEST, PROPER, SEEMLY

deception FAKE, HOAX, JAPE, RUSE, SHAM, WILE
deceptive VAGUE, HOLLOW, SERENIC
decide CERN, ELECT, RESOLVE
decimal TEN(TH), REPETEND
decimate KILL, SLAY, BURKE
decipher READ, SOLVE, DECODE
decision TKO, ARRET, DECREE, VERDICT, JUDGMENT, SENTENCE
deck PACK, POOP, ADORN, CARDS, DIZEN, ORLOP
declaim RANT, RAVE, ORATE, BLEEZE, BLOVIATE
declaration OATH, AVOWAL
Decl. of Independence signer LEE, HALL, HART, PACA, PENN, READ, ROSS, RUSH, ADAMS, CHASE, CLARK, FLOYD, GERRY, HEWES, LEWIS, LYNCH, PAINE, SMITH, STONE, WYTHE, CLYMER, ELLERY, HOOPER, MCKEAN, MORRIS, MORTON, NELSON, RODNEY, TAYLOR, WALTON, WILSON, BRAXTON, HANCOCK, HEYWARD, HOPKINS, SHERMAN, WHIPPLE, WOLCOTT, BARTLETT, FRANKLIN, GWINNETT, HARRISON, RUTLEDGE, STOCKTON, THORNTON, WILLIAMS, JEFFERSON, HOPKINSON, HUNTINGTON, WITHERSPOON
declare BID, AVER, AVOW, MELD, STATE, AVOUCH
decline DIP, EBB, FADE, SINK, DEMUR, DROOP, SLUMP, SPURN, TABES, REFUSE, SUBSIDE
declivity SCARP, SLANT, SLOPE, CALADE
decompose ROT, DECAY, SPOIL
decor SCENERY
decorate DECK, ADORN, BEDECK, MINIATE
decoration BADGE, PURFLE, RIBBON, TINSEL; *see* AWARD
decorous STAID, DEMURE, SEEMLY
decoy BAIT, LURE, TOLE, PLANT, CAPPER
decrease EBB, WANE, ABATE, LESSEN, RECEDE, DWINDLE
decree ACT, LAW, BULL, FIAT, WILL, WRIT, ARRET, CANON, EDICT, IRADE, UKASE, DICTUM, FIRMAN, MANDATE
decry BLAME, CENSURE, CONDEMN, DENOUNCE
dedicate DEVOTE, INSCRIBE
deduce DEEM, INFER, DERIVE
deduct BATE, FAIK, REBATE
deed(s) ACTA, CEDE, COUP, FACT, FAIT, FEAT, GEST(E), STROKE
deem HOLD, JUDGE, OPINE
deep LOW, SEA, BASS, DARK, WISE
deer DOE, ELK, ROE, AXIS, FAWN, HART, HIND, MAHA, MUSK, NAPU, PUDU, REIN, SIKA, SPAY, STAG, ADDRA, GEMUL, KAKUR, MARAL, RATWA, ROYAL, SPADO, CERVID, CHITAL, GUEMUL, RASCAL, SAMBAR, SAMBUR, THAMIN, WAPITI, BROCKET, CARIBOU, CERVOID, MUNTJAC, SAMBHUR, VENISON
deer genus RUSA, CERVUS, MAZAMA, MOSCHUS
deer meat VENISON
deer, pert. to DAMINE, CERVINE
deer pouch BELL
deer, small DEERLET, CHEVROTAIN
deer tail FLAG, SCUT
defame DECRY, LIBEL, MALIGN, VILIFY, SLANDER
default FAIL, MORA, WELCH
defeat BEST, FOIL, LIKE, MATE, ROUT, WORST, FAILURE
defect BUG, FLAW, SCOB, SNAG, DESERT
defective FAULTY, FLAWED, IMPERFECT
defective explosive DUD
defector RENEGADE, TURNCOAT
defendant REUS, CHAMPION
defense PLEA, ALIBI, PALISADE, SEPIMENT
defensible TENABLE
defer DELAY, YIELD, PUTOFF, RETARD, POSTPONE
deference FEALTY, HOMAGE, RESPECT
deficiency DEARTH, ULLAGE
deficiency disease DROPSY, SCURVY, RICKETS, BERIBERI, PELLAGRA
defile PASS, SOIL, SPOIL
define FIX, LIMIT, OUTLINE

definite EXACT, CERTAIN
deflect VEER, DIVERT, SWERVE
Defoe character MOLL, CRUSOE, FRIDAY
deform MAR, MAIM, WARP
defraud GYP, BILK, GULL, CHEAT, COZEN, CHOUSE
deft APT, ADROIT, CLEVER
defunct DEAD, GONE, EXTINCT
defy DARE, BEARD, FLOUT
degrade ABASE, LOWER, DEMEAN
degree(s) AB, BA, BS, CE, DD, EE, MD, ME, BAC, BFA, BSC, DDS, DSC, DVM, EDD, EST, LLB, LLD, MBA, NTH, PHD, RATE, STEP, BLITT, CLASS, LITTD, PITCH, RADIAN
dehydrate DRY, JERK, PARCH
Deianira's husband HERCULES
deign STOOP, CONDESCEND
Deiphobus' slayer MENELAUS
Deirdre's abductor NAISI
Deirdre's father PHELIM
deity GOD, NUMEN, GODDESS; *see p. 316*
dejected SAD, GLUM, DOWNCAST
Delaware information *see p. 308*
delay MORA, SLOW, WAIT, DEFER, MORAE, STALL, ARREST, DETAIN, LINGER
dele CANCEL, EXCISE, REMOVE
delegate AGENT, ENVOY, DEPUTY, LEGATE
delete DELE, ERASE, EXCISE, CANCEL
deletion DELE, APOCOPE, EXCISION
deliberate THINK, WEIGH, PONDER
Delibes work LAKME, COPPELIA
delicacy CATE, TIDBIT, FINESSE
delicious TASTY, LUSCIOUS
delight GLEE, AMUSE, CHARM, ELATE, MIRTH, REVEL
Delilah's lover SAMSON
delineate DRAW, LIMN, SKETCH
delinquency FAULT, FAILURE
delirious MAD, REE, RAVING
delirium tremens DTS, JIMJAMS
deliver RID, CEDE, FREE, SEND, UTTER, YIELD
dell DALE, GLEN, DINGLE
Delphi KASTRI
Delphic deity APOLLO, DIONYSUS
Delphic priestess PYTHIA
Delphic stone OMPHALOS
delude DUPE, FLAM, GULL, CHEAT, TRICK, DECEIVE
deluge FLOOD, SPATE, PLETHORA
delusion MOHA, MIRAGE, VISION
deluxe ELEGANT, ELABORATE, LUXURIOUS, SUMPTUOUS
delve DIG, DIP, GRUB, MINE, PROBE, SPADE
demand DUN, NEED, CLAIM, INSIST, SOLICIT
demeanor AIR, MIEN, CARRIAGE
demerit GIG, FAULT
demigod HERO, IDOL, SATYR
demise DEATH, BEQUEST, DECEASE
demodulate DETECT
demolish RASE, RAZE, RUIN, UNDO, LEVEL, WRECK
demon(s) ALP, DEV, IMP, JIN, NAT, AITU, ATUA, DEVA, JANN, JINN, MARA, OGRE, RAHU, WADE, AFRIT, ANITO, ASURA, DEUCE, FIEND, GENIE, GHOUL, JINNI, LAMIA, TROLL, ABIGOR, AFREET, AFRITE, DAEDAL, DAITYA, GOBLIN; *see* DEVIL
demonstrate SHOW, MARCH, PROVE, PICKET
Dempsey MAULER
demur WAVER, OBJECT, PROTEST
demure COY, MIM, SHY, PRIM, STAID
den CAVE, DIVE, LAIR, CAVEA, STUDY, CAVERN
denature ALTER, WEAKEN
denizen CITIZEN, HABITUE
Denmark THULE; *see also* DANISH
Denmark, rulers of CNUT, ERIK, GORM, KNUT, OLAF, SWEYN, CANUTE, MARGARET, VALDEMAR, WALDEMAR, CHRISTIAN, FREDERICK, MARGARETHE
denomination SECT, CLASS, SCHOOL
denote MEAN, IMPLY, PORTEND
denouement END, OUTCOME
denounce DECRY, ACCUSE, EXPOSE, CENSURE
dense DULL, CLOSE, CRASS, HEAVY, THICK, OBTUSE
dent NICK, NOTCH, EFFECT
dental ORAL, ODONTIC

dentine IVORY
dentist's tool BURR, DRILL, SCALER, FORCEPS
denture PLATE, TEETH, BRIDGE
denude BARE, STRIP
Denver AURARIA
deny ABJURE, DISOWN, NEGATE, REFUSE, GAINSAY
depart DIE, EXIT, VADE, SCRAM, BEGONE, DECAMP, VAMO(O)SE
department store MART, EMPORIUM
departure EXIT, EXODUS, HEGIRA, OUTGANG
depend LEAN, RELY, HINGE
dependent MINION, SPONGER, SUBJECT
depict DRAW, ETCH, LIMN, PORTRAY
depilate HUSK, PLUCK, SHAVE
depilatory RUSMA
deplete DRAIN, EMPTY, EXHAUST
deplore RUE, (BE)WAIL, GRIEVE
deport BAN, CARRY, EXILE, EXPEL, BANISH
depose AVER, OUST, UNSEAT
deposit BED, LODE, MARL, SILT, ARGOL, CACHE, DELTA, DREGS, GEEST, LOESS, PLACER, PLAQUE, SINTER, TARTAR, ALLUVIA, CALCULUS
depository SAFE, CACHE, DEPOT, VAULT
depot BASE, STATION, ENTREPOT
deprave CORRUPT, DEBAUCH, PERVERT, VITIATE
depredate ROB, LOOT, SPOIL
depress DENT, SINK, DAMPEN
depression COL, DIP, PIT, BLUES, DUMPS, ENNUI, FOVEA, GLOOM
deprived REFT, SHORN, BEREFT
depth DEEP, HOLE, ABYSS
depth charge ASHCAN
depth finder SONAR, SOUNDER
deputy AGENT, ENVOY, PROXY, VICAR, FACTOR
derange CRAZE, UPSET, DEMENT
derby EPSOM, BOWLER, KENTUCKY
derelict WAIF, SLACK, TRAMP, WRECK, ASTRAY, CASTAWAY
deride *see* MOCK
derision IRONY, SCORN, MOCKERY
derive DRAW, TRACE, DEDUCE
derrick RIG, CRANE, DAVIT, STEEVE
derrick part GIN, JIB, LEG, BEAM, BOOM, SPAR, PULLEY
dervish FAKIR, FAQ(U)IR
descendants GENS, SONS, ISSUE, (S)CIONS, PROGENY
descent BIRTH, SCARP, SLOPE
describe DRAW, DEPICT, RELATE, NARRATE
descry KEN, ESPY, BETRAY
Desdemona's attendant EMILIA
Desdemona's husband OTHELLO
desecrate ABUSE, POLLUTE
desert DUE, ERG, QUIT, WILD, LEAVE, WASTE, BARREN, ABANDON
Desert Fox, The ROMMEL
desert, pert. to EREMIC
desert vision MIRAGE
desert watering place OASIS
deserter RAT, AWOL, BOLTER, RUNAWAY, RECREANT, RENEGADE, TURNCOAT
deserts GOBI, THAR, DAHNA, NEFUD, SHAMO, ARUNTA, GIBSON, DAHAMA, LIBYAN, MOHAVE, NUBIAN, SAHARA, SYRIAN, ANNAFUD, ARABIAN, ATACAMA, ELHAMAD, KARAKUM, PAINTED, QARAQUM, SECHURA, COLORADO, KALAHARI, KIZILKUM, KYZYLKUM, MUYUNKUM, VIZCAINO
deserve EARN, RATE, MERIT
desiccated DRY, ARID, SERE
design AIM, END, PLAN, MOTIF, INTENT(ION)
designate ASSIGN, SELECT, APPOINT; *see* NAME
desire YEN, LUST, URGE, WANT, COVET, CRAVE, ASPIRE, LIBIDO
desirous FAIN, EAGER
desist STOP, CEASE, FORBEAR
desk AMBO, PULPIT, LECTERN, ROLLTOP, SECRETARY
desolate LORN, RAZE, SACK, BLEAK, DREARY
despicable LOW, BASE, MEAN
despise ABHOR, SPURN, CONTEMN
despoil ROB, STRIP, RAVAGE
despondent LOW, SAD, BLUE
despot CZAR, TSAR, TYRANT
dessert ICE, PIE, CAKE, TART, SWEET, AFTERS, MOUSSE, TRIFLE, SHERBET; *see* MENU

destination AIM, END, GOAL
destiny LOT, DOOM, EURE, FATE, KARMA, KISMET
destitute LORN, POOR, NEEDY
destroy RUIN, RASE, SACK, UNDO, WRECK
destroyed KAPUT
destructible FRAIL, FRAGILE
destruction STRY, TALA, HAVOC, STROY, WRACK
desuetude DISUSE
detach WEAN, SEVER, SUNDER
detail ITEM, NICETY, PATROL, ITEMIZE, SPECIFY
detain NAB, CHECK, DELAY, ARREST, INTERN
detect ESPY, NOSE, SPOT
detecting device RADAR, SONAR, DOWSER, FEELER, TENTACLE
detective TEC, DICK, BEAGLE, SLEUTH, TAILER, GUMSHOE, HAWKSHAW
detectives in literature SAM, CHAN, COOL, FELL, MAYO, MOTO, DUPIN, LUPIN, MASON, MCKEE, MORAN, NORTH, SAINT, SPADE, VANCE, WOLFE, CARTER, HAMMER, HOLMES, JUSTUS, MARPLE, POIROT, PORTER, SHAYNE, WIMSEY, CHARLES, FREEMAN, MACLAIN, MERLINI, RAFFLES, VALCOUR, FUMANCHU, WESTLAKE, MERRIVALE
detent DOG, PAWL, STOP, STUD, CATCH, CLICK, RATCHET
deter DETAIN, HINDER, PREVENT
detergent SOAP, SAPONIN, CLEANSER
deteriorate IMPAIR, WORSEN
determine FIX, JUDGE, DECIDE, RESOLVE
detest HATE, ABHOR, LOATHE, DESPISE
detonator CAP, SQUIB, EXPLODER
detour BYPASS, DEVIATION
detract DEROGATE, DISPARAGE
detritus SCREE, TALUS, DEBRIS
Deucalion relative HELLEN, PYRRHA, CLYMENE
devastate RAZE, SACK, WASTE
develop EVOLVE, MATURE, UNFOLD
Devi UMA, KALI, DURGA, GAURI, CHANDI, PARVATI, BHAIRAVI
Devi's consort SIVA
deviate ERR, YAW, HADE, WARP, SHIFT, STRAY, MUTATE, SWERVE, DIGRESS
device PLAN, PLOY, MOTTO, EMBLEM, IMPLEMENT
devil BENG, DULE, CHORT, DEUCE, EBLIS, HUGON, SATAN, AZAZEL, BELIAL, DICKENS, LUCIFER, SHAITAN, SHEITAN; *see* DEMON
devilfish RAY, MANTA
devise AIM, WILL, FRAME, SCHEME, CONCOCT
devoid EMPTY, VACANT LACKING
devotee FAN, IST, BUFF, BIGOT, VOTARY, ZEALOT
devotion ARDOR, PIETY, FEALTY, FERVOR, NOVENA
devour BOLT, WOLF, GORGE, CONSUME
devout HOLY, GODLY, PIOUS
dewlap FOLD, PALEA, WATTLE
dewy MOIST, RORAL, RORIC
dexterity ART, KNACK, FINESSE
dexterous APT, DEFT, HANDY, ADROIT
diabetic's medicine INSULIN
diabolic WICKED, IMPIOUS
diacritic BREVE, TILDE, ACCENT, MACRON, UMLAUT, DIERESIS
diadem *see* CROWN
diagonal BIAS, OBLIQUE
diagram PLAT, CHART, DRAFT, EPURE, SKETCH
dialect CANT, ARGOT, IDIOM, LINGO, JARGON, PATOIS
diameter BORE, MODULE, CALIBER
diamond GEM, ICE, BO(A)RT, RHOMB, CARBON, LOZENGE
diamond, famous HOPE, PITT, MATAN, DUDLEY, DUTOIT, HORNBY, KOLLUR, NASSAK, ORLOFF, PIGOTT, REGENT, CHAPADA, DEBEERS, EUGENIE, STEWART, TENNANT, TIFFANY, CULLINAN, KOHINOOR
diamondback RATTLER, TERRAPIN
Diana DELIA
Diana's parents LATONA, JUPITER

diaper DIDY, NAPKIN, NAPPIE
diaphanous THIN, SHEER
diaphragm, pert. to PHRENIC
diarist FRANK, PEPYS, BURNEY
diary LOG, RECORD, DAYBOOK, DIURNAL, JOURNAL
Diaspora GOLAH, GALUTH
diatribe SCREED, TIRADE, HARANGUE, JEREMIAD
dice CHOP, CUBE, MINCE
dice term COG, JOE, COME, DICK, FADE, MISS, NICK, ROLL, SICE, SISE, BONES, CRAPS, FIELD, POINT, SHOOT, BOXCAR, PHOEBE, AMBSACE, NATURAL
Dickens characters *see p. 315*
Dickens's pen name BOZ
dickey BIB, COLLAR, DONKEY, RUMBLE, VESTEE
dictator PERON, SULLA, CAESAR, DESPOT, FRANCO, HITLER, MIKADO, SHOGUN, STALIN, TYRANT, SALAZAR, TRUJILLO
dido ANTIC, CAPER, GAMBOL
Dido ELISSA
Dido relative ANNA, BELUS
Dido's lover AENEAS
die DOD, TAT, CUBE, DADO, SICCA, STAMP, EXPIRE, PERISH, TESSERA
diehard TORY, STUBBORN
diet BANT, FARE, REGIME(N), CONGRESS
differ VARY, DISSENT, DISAGREE
difference ODDS, EPACT, NUANCE
different OTHER, DIVERS, SUNDRY, DIVERSE
difficulty FIX, JAM, RUB, KNOT, NODE, PICKLE, SCRAPE, DILEMMA
diffident COY, SHY, MODEST
diffuse STREW, STROW, WORDY, PROLIX
dig JAB, GRUB, PION, DELVE
digest ABSORB, APERCU, PRECIS, EPITOME, PANDECT
digestive juice PAPAIN, PEPSIN, RENNIN
digging tool HOE, LOY, PICK, SPUD, SCOOP, SPADE, DREDGE, SHOVEL, MATTOCK
digit TOE, CIPHER, FINGER, INTEGER, NUMERAL
dignified LOFTY, NOBLE, SEDATE, STATELY
dike DITCH, JETTY, LEVEE
dilate SWELL, WIDEN, DISTEND
dilatory LAX, SLOW, TARDY, REMISS
dilemma FIX, JAM, PICKLE
dilettante AMATEUR, DABBLER
dill ANET, ANISE, FENNEL
dilute THIN, RAREFY, WEAKEN
dim FADE, BLEAR, DUSKY, FAINT
dimension SIZE, EXTENT, VOLUME, MEASURE, CAPACITY
diminish EBB, BATE, PLOY, SINK, WANE, ABATE, PETER, TAPER
diminutive suffix *see p. 333*
dingle DALE, DELL, GLEN
dingy DRAB, GRIMY, OURIE
dining room MESS, OECUS, SPENCE, CENACLE, REFECTORY
dinosaur SAURIAN; *see* LIZARD
dint DENT, MARK, FORCE
diocese *see* BISHOP'S SEAT
Dione children PELOPS, APHRODITE
Dionysus follower MAENAD
Dionysus parent ZEUS, SEMELE
Dioscuri ANAX, TWINS, ANACES, CASTOR, POLLUX
dip DAP, DIB, BAIL, DOPP, DUNK, LADE, DOUSE, MERSE
diplomacy TACT, FINESSE, PROTOCOL
diplomat ENVOY, CONSUL, LEGATE, NUNCIO, ATTACHE, EMISSARY, MINISTER, PROXENUS
dipper URSA, LADLE, SCOOP, SPOON, PIGGIN
Dirce's husband LYCUS
Dirce's victim ANTIOPE
dire FATAL, FUNEST, FEARFUL
direct AIM, CONN, OPEN, LEVEL, PILOT, POINT, STEER
direction *see* COMPASS POINT
director HEAD, LEADER, MANAGER
directory LIST, ORDO, BLUEBOOK, REGISTER
dirge KEEN, LINOS, LINUS, LAMENT, TRENTAL, THRENODY
dirigible *see* AIRCRAFT
dirk *see* DAGGER
dirt SOD, LOAM, SILT, SOIL, EARTH, FILTH, GRIME
dirty FOUL, DINGY, GRIMY, MUDDY

Dis HADES, ORCUS, PLUTO
disable SAP, LAME, MAIM, GRUEL
disadvantage DRAWBACK, HANDICAP, DETRIMENT, PREJUDICE
disagreeable MEAN, ORNERY
disagreement TIFF, FIGHT, SCRAP
disappear VANISH, EVANESCE
disavow DENY, DISOWN, RECANT
disbeliever THOMAS, ATHEIST, SKEPTIC
disburse PAY, SPEND, EXPEND
discard JUNK, MOLT, SCRAP, SLUFF, REJECT, ABANDON
discern KEN, DESCRY, DETECT
discernment TACT, ACUMEN
discharge DROP, EMIT, FIRE, OUST, SACK, EJECT, EXPEL
disciple CHELA, PUPIL, FOLLOWER; *see* APOSTLE
disciplinarian TYRANT, MARTINET
discipline DRILL, ORDER, FERULE
disclaim DENY, ABJURE, DISOWN
disclose BARE, EXPOSE, REVEAL
discolored DOTY, LIVID, USTULATE
discomfort MALAISE, DISTRESS
disconcert FAZE, ABASH, RATTLE
disconnect UNDO, SEVER, DETACH
disconsolate SAD, FORLORN
discontinue STOP, CEASE, DESIST, SUSPEND
discord JAR, ERIS, STRIFE
discount AGIO, BATTA, IGNORE, REBATE
discourage DAUNT, DETER, DAMPEN, DEJECT, DEPRIVE
discourse HOMILY, SERMON, DESCANT, PR(A)ELECT
discover (E)SPY, DISCERN, UNEARTH
discoverers OHM, DAVY, ERIC, KOCH, LEIF, SALK, BINET, CURIE, DAVYS, DEWAR, FERMI, FIELD, FREUD, GABOR, HENRY, HERTZ, SABIN, SIMON, DALTON, DARWIN, DOMAGK, EUCLID, HARVEY, HUYGENS, JENNER, KEPLER, MENDEL, NEWTON, PAVLOV, PLANCK, WALLIS, BANTING, CARLSON, EHRLICH, FARADAY, FLEMING, GALILEI, GALILEO, KENDALL, LINNAEUS, MOSELEY, PASTEUR, WAKSMAN, COLUMBUS, EINSTEIN, HERSCHEL, THOMPSON, DESCARTES; *see* EXPLORERS
discreet WARY, DEMURE, CAREFUL
discrepancy GAP, EPACT, VARIANCE
discrete DISTINCT, SEPARATE
discretion TACT, SKILL, JUDGMENT
discriminate SECERN, DISTINGUISH
discus DISK, QUOIT
discuss MOOT, TREAT, DEBATE, DILATE, DISSERT
discussion group FORUM, PANEL, SEMINAR
disdain SCORN, SPURN, DESPISE, CONTEMPT
disease MAL, MALADY, AILMENT, ILLNESS, DISORDER
disease carrier RAT, INSECT, TSETSE, VECTOR, MOSQUITO
disease, cause of GERM, VIRUS, MICROBE, BACILLUS, BACTERIA, PATHOGEN
disease, pert. to CLINIC, LOIMIC
diseases TB, FLU, POX, UTA, COLD, COMA, GOUT, PEST, PICA, VETA, YAWS, ZONA, ATAXY, BENDS, BUBAS, COLIC, COUGH, CROUP, FAINT, FAVUS, GLEET, LATAH, LEPRA, LYSSA, MANGE, MUMPS, NGANA, PALSY, PILES, POLIO, RHEUM, SHOCK, SPRUE, ABASIA, ABULIA, AINHUM, ALALIA, ALEXIA, ANEMIA, ANGINA, APHTHA, ASTHMA, ATAXIA, CANCER, CHOREA, CORYZA, COWPOX, CRAMPS, DENGUE, DROPSY, GRIPPE, HERNIA, NAGANA, OTITIS, PERTIS, PLAGUE, RABIES, SCURVY, SEPSIS, TETANY, THRUSH, TUSSIS, TYPHUS, UREMIA, ALLERGY, AMENTIA, AMNESIA, ANOPSIA, APHAGIA, APHASIA, APHONIA, ASTASIA, ATROPHY, CAISSON, CATARRH, CHOLERA, COLITIS, EMPYEMA, HICCUPS, ICTERUS, LEPROSY,

LOCKJAW, LUMBAGO, MALARIA, MEASLES, MYCOSIS, PARESIS, PODAGRA, PURPURA, RICKETS, ROSEOLA, RUBELLA, SYCOSIS, TERTIAN, TETANUS, TOXEMIA, TYPHOID, VARIOLA, VERTIGO, VIROSIS, ACIDOSIS, ADENOIDS, AKINESIA, ALASTRIM, ALLERGIA, ALOPECIA, ANOOPSIA, BERIBERI, BOTULISM, BURSITIS, CARDITIS, CORONARY, DEAFNESS, DIABETES, DIARRHEA, DIPLOPIA, DISCITIS, DIURESIS, EPILEPSY, ERYTHEMA, EXANTHEM, GANGRENE, HOOKWORM, INSOMNIA, JAUNDICE, LEUKEMIA, LORDOSIS, MIGRAINE, MYELITIS, MYOSITIS, MYXODEMA, NECROSIS, NEURITIS, OBTUSION, PELLAGRA, PHTHISIS, PINWORMS, PLEURISY, PRURITUS, PYORRHEA, RACHITIS, RHINITIS, RINGWORM, SCIATICA, SHINGLES, SMALLPOX, STENOSIS, SYPHILIS, TAPEWORM, TOXAEMIA, TRACHOMA, VITILIGO; *see* ANIMAL, PLANT, EYE, SKIN, DEFICIENCY

disembark LAND, DEPLANE, DETRAIN

disembowel GUT, DRAW, HULK

disencumber RID, FREE, DETACH

disengage FREE, PART, WEAN

disentangle CARD, FREE, UNDO, RAVEL

disfigure MAR, SCAR, DEFACE, DEFORM, MANGLE, UGLIFY

disgrace ABASE, ODIUM, SHEND, STIGMA, SCANDAL

disguise MASK, MUMM, SHAM

disgusting ODIOUS, FULSOME, HATEFUL

dish BOWL, LANX, COMAL, CRUSE, GRAIL, PATEN, PLATE, SERVE, VIAND, PATINA, SAUCER, TUREEN, VESSEL, CHARGER, COMPOTE, PLATTER, RAMEKIN, COMPOTIER; *see* MENU

dishabille NEGLIGEE

dishearten AMATE, DAUNT, DETER

dishevel MUSS, RUMPLE, TOUSLE

dishonor SHAME, DISGRACE, DISCREDIT

disinclined AVERSE, RELUCTANT

disinfectant IODIN, LYSOL, CRESOL, IODINE, PHENOL, CHLORINE, PEROXIDE

disintegrate DECAY, BREAKUP

disinter EXHUME, UNBURY, UNEARTH

disk ATEN, DIAL, PUCK, SPUT, PATEN, PLATE, WAFER, HARROW, RECORD, SEQUIN, PLATTER

dislike HATE, AVERSION, DISTASTE

dislocate SPLAY, LUXATE, DISJOINT, DISPLACE

dismal DRAB, DREAR(Y), SOMBRE

dismantle RAZE, STRIP, UNRIG

dismay FAZE, APPAL, DAUNT, APPALL

dismiss CAN, FIRE, OUST, DEMIT, REMUE, IGNORE, CASHIER

dismissal CONGE, OUSTER, REMOVAL

dismounted ALIT, DISLODGED

disorder MESS, DERAY, SNARL, JUMBLE, LITTER, CLUTTER

disown REJECT, DISAVOW, DISCLAIM

disparage *see* SLANDER

dispatch KILL, NOTE, POST, SEND, CABLE, HASTE, WASTE

dispel OUST, EJECT, BANISH, RUBOUT

dispensation RELEASE, EXEMPTION, PROVISION, ABSOLUTION

dispense DOLE, EXEMPT, FOREGO

disperse SPREAD, SCATTER

displaced person DP, EXILE, EVACUEE, REFUGEE

display AD, POST, SHEW, ARRAY, VAUNT, EVINCE, FLAUNT, OSTENT, PARADE, EXHIBIT

displease MIFF, ANGER, ANNOY, PIQUE, OFFEND, PROVOKE

displeasure ANGER, PIQUE

dispose (of) BIAS, SELL, DITCH, GROUP, PLACE, POSIT

disposed BENT, PRONE, READY, TENDING
dispossess OUST, EJECT, EVICT, DIVEST
disprove REBUT, NEGATE, REFUTE
disputatious ERISTIC, CONTENTIOUS
dispute CARP, FLITE, BICKER, DEBATE, HAGGLE, HIGGLE
disquiet FRET, UNEASE, ANXIETY
Disraeli novel SYBIL, TANCRED
disregard OMIT, WAIVE, IGNORE
disreputable SEAMY, SHADY
disrespectful RUDE, IMPOLITE
disseminate SOW, STREW, SPREAD
dissenter ANTI, HERETIC, SECTARY, RECUSANT
dissertation ESSAY, TRACT, SERMON, THESIS, TREATISE
dissimulate FEIGN, PRETEND
dissolute LEWD, LOOSE, RAKISH
dissolute person RAKE, ROUE
dissolve MELT, VANISH, DISBAND
dissonant ATONAL
distance meter ODOMETER
distant FAR, YON, AFAR, AWAY, ALOOF, BEYOND, REMOTE
distill BREW, DRIP, DECOCT
distilling device STILL, RETORT, ALEMBIC, MATRASS
distinct CLEAR, PLAIN, EVIDENT
distinction HONOR, PROMINENCE
distinguished FAMOUS, EMINENT
distort WARP, SLANT, TWIST, DEFORM
distraint NA(A)M, POIND
distress PAIN, AGONY, GRIEF, UPSET, ANGUISH, TROUBLE
distress signal SOS, ALARM, MAYDAY
distribute JOB, DEAL, DOLE, METE, ALLOT, RATION
district GAU, SOC, AREA, BELT, MIAO, PALE, SOKE, WARD, WICK, ZONE, FIELD, CANTON, SECTOR, CIRCUIT, DEMESNE, PRECINCT; *see p. 289*
distrust DOUBT, SUSPICION
disturb VEX, FAZE, ROIL, STATIC, HECKLE, MOLEST
disturbance ROW, RIOT, FRACAS, HUBBUB, TUMULT
ditch SAP, DIKE, FOSS, HOLL, JILT, MOAT, RINE, TAJO, DRAIN, FLUME, FOSSE, ZANJE, RELAIS, SLUICE, DISCARD
ditto TOO, ALSO, SAME, LIKEWISE
divagate STRAY, WANDER, DIGRESS
divan SOFA, COURT, CANAPE, LEEWAN, SALOON, SETTEE
dive DEN, DROP, FLIP, SPIN, SWAN, GAINER, HEADER, SALOON, BACKFLIP
diver's disease BENDS
diver's equipment TANK, CHUTE, SCUBA, AIRHOSE, SNORKEL, AQUALUNG, FLIPPERS, LIFELINE
diverge FORK, VARY, DEVIATE
diversion GAME, SPORT, PASTIME
divert AMUSE, PARRY, DECEIVE
divest BARE, DOFF, TIRL, STRIP, DENUDE, DEPRIVE
divide FORK, REND, RIVE, ALLOT, HALVE, BISECT, SUNDER, TRISECT
divided REFT, APART, CLEFT, SPLIT, PARTITE
dividend PLUM, BONUS, MELON, SHARE
divider BUNTON, MERIST, COMPASS
divination OMEN, SORS, AUGURY, SORTES, DOWSING
divination, pert. to FATIDIC
divine HOLY, SACRED, GODLIKE, SUPERNAL
divine being *see* GOD, GODDESS
Divine Comedy author DANTE
divine word GRACE, LOGOS
divining rod WAND, DOWSER
divinity GOD, JAH, IDOL, DEITY, NUMEN, YAHWE, ADONAI, ELOHIM, GODHEAD, JEHOVAH, THEOLOGY
diving equipment *see* DIVER
diving bird AUK, LOON, SMEW, GREBE, DUCKER
division HIEN, MEER, MERE, SECT, HSIEN, BUREAU, COHORT, EOGAEA, SCHISM, MITOSIS, SEGMENT, FRACTION
divorce GET(T), SPLIT, TALAK
divorce allowance ALIMONY, SUPPORT, PALIMONY
divulge BARE, TELL, REVEAL, DISCLOSE

Dixie(land) SOUTH
dizziness SCOTOMY, VERTIGO
dizziness, pert. to DINIC(AL)
dizzy GIDDY, SILLY, FOOLISH
dizzy, feel REEL
Djiboutan language ARABIC, FRENCH; *see* CUSHITIC
Dnieper tributary PSEL, SOZH, SULA, DESNA
do FARE, MAKE, CHEAT, PERFORM
do away with KILL, ABOLISH
do up WRAP
docile TAME, GENTLE, PLIANT
dock BOB, CUT, PEN, BANG, CLIP, FINE, LAND, PIER, QUAY, SLIP, BASIN, BERTH, JETTY, WHARF, DEDUCT
docket LABEL, AGENDA, CALENDAR
dockworker LUMPER, STEVEDORE
doctor MD, HAKIM, LEECH, MEDIC, QUACK, TREAT, HUKAMA, INTERN, MEDICO, TAMPER, CORONER, FALSIFY, INTERNE, SURGEON
doctrine ISM, CULT, RITE, SECT, CREED, DOGMA, MAXIM, TENET, CULTUS, THEORY
document PAPER, SCRIP, INSTRUMENT
document holder FILE, DOSSIER, HANAPER
doddering SENILE
dodge DUCK, EVADE, PARRY
Dodgers' old field EBBETTS
dodo FOGY, FOSSIL
doe *see* DEER
dog CUR, GYP, MUT, PUP, TOY, YAP, ALAN, BICK, FICE, FIST, FOOT, GARM, HUND, MUTT, RACH, TYKE, BITCH, BRACH, CANID, CANUS, CATCH, DOGGY, FEIST, POOCH, PUPPY, RACHE, SHOCK, TRACK, TRAIL, WHELP, ALAUND, ALAUNT, BANDOG, BARKER, BOWWOW, BUFFER, CUSSER, DOGGIE, FOLLOW, HUNTER, JOWLER, LAPDOG, MESSAN, MESSET, MESSIN, RANGER, RATTER, RUNNER, SEIZER, SLEUTH, THOOID, TOLLER, TOWSER, TUFTER, YAPPER, YAUPER, YAWPER, YELPER, COURSER, MONGREL, YAPSTER
dog breeds POM, PUG, ALCO, CHOW, DANE, GREW, LYAM, LYME, PEKE, PULI, SKYE, AKITA, BOXER, HOUND, HUSKY, MASTY, MERLE, AFGHAN, BASSET, BEAGLE, BRIARD, COCKER, COLLIE, COLPEO, KELPIE, LYCAON, POODLE, SALUKI, SAMOED, SAMOID, SCOTTY, SETTER, TALBOT, VIZSLA, BASENJI, BULLDOG, GRIFFON, HARRIER, MALTESE, MASTIFF, POINTER, SAMOYED, SCOTTIE, SHIHTZU, SPANIEL, TERRIER, WHIPPET, AIREDALE, BRITTANY, DOBERMAN, LABRADOR, PEKIN(G)ESE
dog chops FLEWS
dog, famous ASTA, CLEO, FALA, NEIL, TIGE, TOBY, YUKI, ARGUS, BELKA, BENJI, KELLY, LAIKA, LASSIE, RASCAL, CHECKERS, RINTINTIN
dog genus CUON, CYON, THOS, CANIS
dog, pert. to CANINE
dog star SIRIUS, PROCYON
dog, wild DIEB, DHOLE, DINGO, GUARA, PIDOG, AGUARA, COYDOG, JACKAL, KOLSON, KOLSUN, PYEDOG, AGOUARA; *see* WOLF
dogfish TOPE, BOWFIN, BURBOT, ROSSET
doghouse KENNEL
dogma ISM, CREED, DICTA, TENET, DOCTRINE
dogwood KOUSA, CORNEL, CORNUS, BUNCHBERRY
dole ALMS, METE, GRIEF, RELIEF
doleful SAD, DISMAL, MOURNFUL
doll TOY, MAMMET, MAUMET, PUPPET, MANIKIN
dollar BEAN, BILL, BUCK, TALER, WHEEL, SIMOLEON; *see* MONEY
dolly CART, TRUCK
dolphin SUSU, UNIE, BOUTO, DORADO, PALACH, PORPUS, SOOSOO, TURSIO, DELPHIN, NARWHAL, PELLOCK, PULLOCK, SNUFFER, GAIRFISH, NARWHALE, PORPOISE
dolphin genus INIA, PHOCAENA, TURSIOPS

dolt ASS, OAF, CLOD, COOT, LOUT, NUMP, DUNCE, NINNY, NUMPS
domain BOURN, REALM, BARONY, BOURNE, DEMENE, ESTATE, DEMESNE, BAILIWICK
dome PATE, ROOF, CONCHA, CUPOLA, THOLOS
domestic HOMY, MAID, TAME, HOMEY, LOCAL, NATIVE, SERVANT
domesticate TAME, BREAK, CIVILIZE
domineer BOSS, BULLY, HECTOR
dominate BOSS, RULE, CONTROL
Dominican FRIAR, JACOBIN
Dominican Republic measure ONA, TAREA
dominion SWAY, DUCHY, REALM, COLONY, EMPERY, PROVINCE
domino BONE, HOOD, MASK, AMICE, CLOAK
Don DUNA, TANAIS
Don Quixote author CERVANTES
Don Quixote's lady DULCINEA
Don Quixote's squire SANCHO
Don tributary CHIR, SOSNA, DONETS
donate GIVE, BESTOW, CONTRIBUTE
Donizetti opera LUCIA, ELIXIR, (DON)PASQUALE
donkey *see* ASS
doodad DINGUS, GADGET, GEWGAW
doodlesack BAGPIPE
doom FATE, RUIN, CONDEMN
doomed FATED, KAPUT
door GATE, TRAP, ENTRY, HATCH, INLET, JANUA, DINGLE, FUSUMA, PORTAL, POSTERN
door, god of JANUS
door part JAMB, KNOB, RAIL, SASH, SILL, LATCH, PANEL, STILE, ALETTE, CASING, LINTEL, MULLION
doorkeeper HASP, TILER, TYLER, PORTER, JANITOR, OSTIARY, CONCIERGE
dope INFO, DRUGS, DUMMY
Doris consort NEREUS
Doris offspring NEREID, THETIS
dormant INERT, ASLEEP, LATENT, TORPID
dormouse LOIR, LEROT
dorsal BACK, NOTAL, TERGAL
Dos Passos work USA
dose PILL, PO(R)TION
dosser DORSAL, PANNIER
dossier DATA, FILE, RECORD
dot IOTA, DOWER, DOWRY, SPECK, PERIOD, SPECKLE, STIPPLE
dote LIKE, ADORE, DRIVEL
doting FOND
dotted PIED, SEME, PINTO, PIEBALD
double KA, DUAL, TWIN, GEMEL, BINATE, DUPLEX
double-play trio EVERS, CHANCE, TINKER
double-reed instrument OBOE, SHALM, SHAWM, BASSOON, BOMBARD
doubloon ONZA
doubt SCRUPLE, DISTRUST
doubter THOMAS, SKEPTIC
dough DUFF, SPUD, MONEY, PASTE, BATTER
doughnut BAGEL, SINKER, BEIGNET, CRULLER, SIMBALL
doughty BOLD, BRAVE, VALIANT
dour SOUR, MOROSE, SULLEN
dove NUN, KUKU, LUPE, CULVER, CUSHAT, KUKUPA, POUTER, NAMAQUA, RINGDOVE
dovekie ALLE, ROTCH, ROTGE, ROTCHE; *see* AUK
dovetail FIT, JOIN(T), TENON
dowager WIDOW, MATRON
dowel PIN, COAK
dower DOS, DOWRY, ENDOW, ENDUE
down NAP, SAD, ALOW, DUNE, FUZZ, PILE, DUVET, EIDER, PRONATE
downcast SAD, GLOOMY, DEJECTED
downy PILAR, LANATE, VILLOUS
dowry DOS, DOT, GIFT, DOWER
doxology DOXA, KAINYN, KADDISH
doyen DEAN, SENIOR
doze NAP, DORM, CATNAP, DROWSE, SNOOZE
Dracula VAMPIRE
draft LEVY, SWIG, TASS, INDUCT, POTION, SKETCH, CONSCRIPT
drag LUG, TOW, TUG, HALE, HAUL, SNIG, BOTHER

dragnet WEB, TRAWL, TRAINEL
dragon ORC, KETU, RAHU, DRAKE, LADON, DUENNA, FAFNIR, WIVERN, BASILISK
dragon slayer CADMUS, GEORGE
drain SAP, SUMP, SEWER, CLOACA, CULVERT, DEPLETE, VITIATE
dram NIP, SLUG, DRAFT
drama NOH, AUTO, MIME, PLAY, STAGE, BUSKIN, KABUKI, NOGAKU
dramatic STAGY, VIVID, SCENIC
dramatic, be EMOTE
dramatist GAY, ASCH, HART, HUGO, INGE, RICE, SHAW, ALBEE, AUDEN, BEHAN, CAPEK, DUMAS, GOGOL, IBSEN, LEWIS, ODETS, SYNGE, YEATS, ZWEIG, BARRIE, BRECHT, DRYDEN, FERBER, GOETHE, HUGHES, JONSON, MOLNAR, OCASEY, ONEILL, RACINE, SARTRE, SENECA, STEELE, WILDER, ZINDEL, BAGNOLD, CHEKHOV, GILBERT, GOLDONI, JEFFERS, KAUFMAN, MARLOWE, MOLIERE, PLAUTUS, ROSTAND, SAROYAN, SHEPARD, TERENCE, WEBSTER, ANDERSON, ANNUNZIO, SCHILLER, SHERIDAN, SHERWOOD, VOLTAIRE, WILLIAMS, PIRANDELLO, STRINDBERG, SHAKESPEARE
drapery ARRAS, CANOPY, CURTAIN, VALANCE
drastic DIRE, SEVERE, EXTREME
Dravidian language KUI, TODA, TULU, GONDI, KHOND, MALTO, ORAON, TAMIL, BRAHUI, KODAGU, KURUKH, TELUGU, KANNADA, CANARESE, KANARESE, MALAYALAM
draw TIE, TOW, WIN, HALE, LIMN, TOLE, DEPICT, SIPHON
draw back WINCE, RESILE
draw forth EDUCE, DERIVE, ELICIT
draw tight BIND, COUL, FRAP
drawer(s) BIN, TILL, SHORTS
drawing room SALA, SALON, PARLOR
drawing tool CURVE, RULER, CRAYON, FUSAIN, PASTEL, PENCIL, TSQUARE
drawn TAUT, TENSE, TIRED, LENGTHY
dray VAN, CART, WAGON
dread AWE, FEAR, TERROR
dream MUSE, REVE, FANCY, VISION, FANTASY, REVERIE
dreary DREE, BLEAK, DISMAL, DREICH, DREIGH
dregs FAEX, LEES, MARC, SCUM, SILT, DRAFF, DROSS, MAGMA, SALIN, SORDES, VINASSE
drench SOAK, DOUSE, SOUSE
drenched WET, ASOP, DEWED
dress DAB, DUB, NIG, TAN, TAW, TOG, GOWN, SACK, BANIA, FROCK, SHIFT, TUNIC, PREEN, BANIAN, BANYAN, CAMISE, CLOTHE, CHEMISE, TEAGOWN; *see* CLOTHING
dresser CHEST, BUREAU, VANITY
dressing gown ROBE, KIMONO, NEGLIGE, WRAPPER, NEGLIGEE, PEIGNOIR
dressmaker MODISTE, COUTURIER(E), SEAMSTRESS
Dreyfus supporter ZOLA
dried SERE
dried food HAY, COPRA, JERKY, PRUNE, RAISIN, BILTONG, CHARQUI, PEM(M)ICAN
drift FLOAT, TENOR, TREND, COURSE, CURRENT
drill AWL, BORE, BURR, AUGER, TRAIN, GIMLET, PIERCE
drink ADE, BIB, AVA, LAP, NIP, NOG, PEG, POP, SIP, SOT, BOZA, COLA, GULP, KAVA, NIPA, SLUG, SODA, SWIG, TOPE, ASSAI, BOUSE, BUMBO, MORAT, NEGUS, NURSE, QUAFF, SWILL, TONIC, BRACER, CAUDLE, GUZZLE, IMBIBE, KUMISS, NECTAR, POSSET, PTISAN, TIPPLE; *see* BEVERAGE
drinker SOT, TOPER, BIBBER, TIPPLER, TOSSPOT
drinking horn RHYTON
drinking vessel *see* CUP, GLASS
drip LEAK, OOZE, SEEP, SILE, CREEP
drive LANE, RIDE, URGE, FORCE, IMPEL, MOTOR, STEER
drive back ROUT, REPEL, REPULSE
drive crazy CRAZE, MADDEN, DERANGE

drive in TAMP, HAMMER
drivel DOTE, DROOL, SLAVER
driver JEHU, WHIP, CABBY, HAMMER, SARWAN, CHAUFFEUR
drizzle RAIN, SMUR(R), MIZZLE
droll ODD, ZANY, WAGGISH
dromedary CAMEL, DELOUL, MEHARI
drone BEE, HUM, IDLER
drool DRIVEL, SLAVER, SLOBBER
droop LAG, SAG, WILT, SLOUCH
drop DAP, SIE, SYE, BEAD, DRIB, FALL, PLOP, SINK, GUTTA, MINIM, GLOBULE
drop in CALL, STOP, VISIT
dropsy EDEMA, HYDROPS
dross SCUM, SLAG, DREGS, SPRUE, SCORIA, SINTER, SULLAGE
drought SOKA, DEARTH, ARIDITY
drove HERD, PACK, RODE, ATAJO
drowse NAP, NOD, DOZE, DOVER
drub BEAT, CUDGEL, THRASH
drudge FAG, GRUB, HACK, MOIL, PLOT, TOIL, LABOR, SLAVE
drug KAT, KEF, KIF, LSD, POT, ACID, BANG, COCA, COKE, DOPE, DOSE, HASH, HEMP, JUNK, KHAT, KIEF, SINA, SNOW, ALOES, BENNY, BHANG, CRACK, GANJA, GRASS, HORSE, JALAP, MECON, OPIUM, SMACK, SPEED, SULFA, UPPER, COCAIN, CHARAS, DOWNER, FAGINE, HEROIN, OPIATE, REEFER, ANODYNE, COCAINE, HASHISH, CANNABIS, DILANTIN, METHADON, MORPHINE, NARCOTIC, MARIJUANA
drug reaction HIGH, TRIP
drug seller DEALER, PUSHER
drugget MAT, RUG, CARPET
drum DUB, BEAT, DRUB, REPEAT; *see* PERCUSSION
drum call DIAN, FLAM, RUFF, TATOO, RAPPEL, RUFFLE, TATTOO
drumstick LEG, TAMPON
drunk(ard) LIT, SOT, HIGH, LUSH, SOAK, WIND, POTTO, TOPER, BARFLY, BLOTTO, SOAKED, STONED, TIDDLY, TIPPLER, TOSSPOT
drupe TRYMA
dry SEC, ARID, BLOT, BRUT, SERE, WIPE, AREFY, SICCATE
dub NAME, TITLE, KNIGHT
dubious LEERY, SHADY, VAGUE
duck DIP, DODGE, EVADE, MERSE
ducklike ANATINE
ducks ANAS, COLK, COOT, DOGY, SKEW, TEAL, BUNTY, DILLY, DRAKE, EIDER, SCAUP, CANARD, DIPPER, GARROT, MARECA, QUANDY, SCOTER, ZUISIN, CANETON, DUNBIRD, GADWALE, GADWALL, GADWELL, MALLARD, OLDWIFE, PINTAIL, POCHARD, SAWBILL, SCOOTER, TWISTER, WIDGEON, BALDPATE, GARGANEY, OLDSQUAW, SHOVELER
duct VAS, FLUE, VASA, AORTA, CANAL, LEMNA, MAETUS, CONDUIT
dude FOP, DANDY, MACARONI
due FIT, HAK, DEBT, HAKH, OWED, REWARD, DESERTS, PAYABLE
duel TILT, JOUST, HOLMGANG
dugout ABRI, BANCA, FOXHOLE, PIRAGUA, PIROGUE
dukedom DUCHY
dull DRY, DUN, MAT, DRAB, LOGY, BLUNT, MATTE, PROSY, STOGY, TERNE, BORING, OBTUND, OBTUSE, PROSAIC
dullard OAF, BOOR, LOUT, DUNCE
dumb MUTE, SILENT
dun ASK, TAN, GRAY, MOUND, SWARTHY
dunce ASS, OAF, COOT, DOLT, DOPE, LOUT, BOBBY, FRONT, MORON, NINNY, PROXY, PONTIC
dupe BILK, CULL, GULL, HOAX, PAWN, COZEN, CULLY, SUCKER
duplicate COPY, STAT, TWIN, DOUBLE, REPEAT
duplicity FRAUD, DECEIT
durable TOUGH, STABLE, LASTING
duration SPAN, TERM, LENGTH
duress COERCION

during **WHILE, WITHIN, PENDING**
dusky **DIM, DARK, SWART(HY)**
dust **ASH, COOM, SOOT, BRISS, COOMB, STIVE, STOUR, POWDER**
Dutch *see* **NETHERLANDS**
Dutch Antilles **ARUBA**
Dutch dialect **TAAL, AFRIKAANS**
duty **CESS, LEVY, CHORE, DEVOIR, DHARMA, EXCISE, IMPOST, TARIFF, LASTAGE**
dwarf **ELF, FAY, NIX, URF, PIXY, PUCK, RUNT, SHEE, CRILE, GNOME, PIGMY, STUNT, TROLL, BANTAM, DROICH, DURGAN, MIDGET, SPRITE, MANIKIN**
dwarfs, seven **DOC, DOPEY, HAPPY, GRUMPY, SLEEPY, SNEEZY, BASHFUL**
dwell **BIDE, HARP, LIVE, STAY, STOP, LODGE**
dweller **TENANT, RESIDENT**
dwelling **HOME, ABODE, DOMICILE**
dwindle **EBB, ABATE, PETER**
dye **AAL, ANIL, TINT, WELD, WOAD, WOLD, AURIN, EOSIN, STAIN, TINGE, WOALD, ANATTA, ANATTO, ARCHIL, AURINE, EOSINE, MADDER, ORCHAL, ORCHIL, ANNATTA, ANNATTO, ANNOTTO, ARNATTO, ORSELLE**
dyeing method **BATIK**
dynamite inventor **NOBEL**
dynamo *see* **MOTOR**
dynasty **REALM, KINGDOM**; *see* **CHINESE**

E

each **PER, EVERY, APIECE**
eager **AGOG, AVID, FAIN, KEEN, YARE, ARDENT**
eagle **ERN(E), GIER, ETANA, HARPY, AQUILA**
eagre **BORE, WAVE**
ear **LUG, SPICA, SPIKE, HANDLE, SPICAE**
ear, part of **WAX, LOBE, AMBOS, ANVIL, CANAL, HELIX, INCUS, PINNA, SCALA, CONCHA, HAMMER, LOBULE, STAPES, TEGMEN, TRAGUS, AURICLE, CERUMEN, COCHLEA, EARDRUM, LOBULUS, MALLEUS, SACCULE, STIRRUP**
ear, pert. to **OTIC, AURAL, AURIC, LOBAR, BINOTIC, BINAURAL**
earache **OTALGY, OTALGIA**
earl **JARL, NOBLE(MAN)**
earlier **PRIOR, PREVIOUS**
earmark **SIGN, BRAND**
earn **EKE, WIN, GAIN, MERIT**
earnest **EAGER, ARDENT**
earnest money **ARLES, ARRHA, HANDSEL**
earnings **WAGES, PROFITS, SALARIES**
earth **ERD, GEO, BYON, CLAY, DIRT, LOAM, MARL, SOIL, GLEBE, TERRA**
earth, pert. to **GEAL, TERRENE**
earth surface **SIAL, SIMA, HORST, EPIGENE**
earthenware **POT, OLLA, DELFT, JASPER, CROCKERY, PORCELAIN**
earthly **MUNDANE, SECULAR, TEMPORAL**
earthquake **SEISM, TREMOR, TEMBLOR**
earthquake, pert. to **SEISMIC**
earthquake site **ASSAM, CUTCH, KANSU, QUITO, TOKYO, ALEPPO, ISCHIA, LISBON, MESSINA**
earthwork **DIKE, FORT, AGGER, MOUND, REDAN, RIDGE**
earthy **GROSS, COARSE, NATURAL**
ease **CALM, ALLAY, QUIET, RELIEF**
East **LEVANT, ORIENT, SUNRISE**
East European *see* **EUROPEAN**
East Indian language *see* **DRAVIDIAN**
East Indian shrub **SOLA, CUBEB, MADAR, MALOO, MUDAR, SOLAG, MUDDAR**
East Indian tree **BO, DAK, ENG, JAK, NIM, SAL, AMLA, ASAK, AULA, BIJA, DHAK, DILO, DUKU, JACK, KINO, NEEM, POON, TEAK, TOON, ACANA, DHAVA, DHAWA, KHAIR, KOKAN, LANSA, MAHUA, MELIA, MOHWA, NIEPA, PALAS, PIPAL, PULAS, ROHAN, ROHUN, SIRIS, SISSU, BANYAN, CACHOU,**

DEODAR, EMBLIC, LANSAT, LANSEH, SISSOO, CATECHU, MARGOSA, MASTTREE; *see* INDIAN TREE
east, pert. to EOAN, ASIAN
Easter PAAS, PACE, PASCH(A)
Easter, pert. to PASCHAL
eastern ASIATIC, ORIENTAL
easy FACILE, SIMPLE
easy job SNAP, CINCH, SINECURE
eat DIET, GNAW, RUST, ERODE, DEVOUR, INGEST
eat greedily LAB, BOLT, GULP, GORGE, RAVEN, RAVIN, GOBBLE, RAVINE
eatable EDIBLE, ESCULENT
eating away CAUSTIC, ERODENT
eating, pert. to DIETARY
eating place *see* RESTAURANT
ebb NEAP, SINK, WANE, RECEDE
eccentric ODD, CRANK, OUTRE, QUEER, MISFIT, UNICUM, ERRATIC
ecclesiastic CLERIC, PRIEST, PRELATE
ecclesiastical SACRED, CLERICAL, PRIESTLY
ecclesiastical hours *see* CANONICAL HOURS
ecclesiastical vestment *see* VESTMENT
echo APE, DITTO, ITERATE, RESOUND
éclat FAME, GLORY, RENOWN, SPLENDOR
eclipse DIM, DARKEN, OBSCURE, SURPASS
eclogue IDYL(L), PASTORAL
economical FRUGAL, THRIFTY
ecru TAN, BEIGE, YELLOW
ecstasy BLISS, RAPTURE
Ecuadorian language JIVAROAN, QUECHUAN
Ecuadorian measure CUADRA
Ecuadorian money SUCRE, CONDOR, CENTAVO
ecumenical council BASLE, LYONS, TRENT, NICAEA, VIENNE, EPHESUS, LATERAN, VATICAN
edacity GREED, VORACITY
eddo ROOT, TARO
eddy SWIRL, VORTEX
Eden's river GIHON, PISON
edge HEM, LIP, RIM, BRIM, ODDS, SILL, ARRIS, BRINK, MARGE, PICOT, RUCHE, SIDLE, VERGE, LABRUM, LIMBUS, SELVAGE
edgy TENSE, NERVOUS
edible EATABLE, ESCULENT
edict *see* DECREE
edit AMEND, EMEND, REDACT, REVISE, CORRECT
edition EXTRA, FIRST, ISSUE, STRIPE, BULLDOG, PRINTING
Edom ESAU, SEIR
Edomite noble UZ, BELA, IRAM, TEMAN
educated ERUDITE, LEARNED, LITERATE
educator HALL, KERR, MANN, DEWEY, ELIOT, JAMES, POUND, ROYCE, SETON, ANGELL, BASCOM, BUTLER, CONANT, GILMAN, HARPER, MATHER, PALMER, FLEXNER, FROEBEL, HOPKINS, NEILSON, PEABODY
educe EVOKE, INFER, ELICIT
eel GRIG, SNIG, ELVER, MORAY, CONGER, CUCHIA, FAUSEN, MUR(A)ENA; *see* LAMPREY
eel genus ANGUILLA
eelpout LING, BLENNY, BURBOT
eerie WEIRD, UNCANNY
efface ERASE, DELETE, EXPUNGE
effect ISSUE, RESULT, MEANING
effective COGENT, TELLING
effects GOODS, THINGS, PROPERTY
effeminate EPICENE, UNMANLY
effervesce FIZZ, FOAM, FROTH, AERATE, BUBBLE
effete ARID, JADED, SPENT, STERILE, DECADENT
effigy GUY, DOLL, ICON, IDOL, STATUE
effluvium AURA, FLATUS, MIASMA
effort DINT, ASSAY, NISUS, TRIAL, CONATUS
eft NEWT, LIZARD, TRITON
egg(s) NIT, OVA, ROE, OVUM, OVULE, CAVIAR
egg collector OOLOGIST
egg on GOAD, SPUR, URGE, INCITE
egg part YOLK, GLAIR, SHELL, WHITE, ALBUMEN, LATEBRA
egg-shaped OOID, OVAL, OVATE, OVOID, OVIFORM

egis SHIELD, AUSPICES
ego SELF, ATMAN, JIVATMA
egoism PRIDE, VANITY, CONCEIT
egregious GROSS, FLAGRANT
egress EXIT, OUTLET
egret *see* HERON
Egypt MIZRAIM
Egypt conqueror LYBIANS, NUBIANS, PTOLEMY, NAPOLEON
Egypt, pert. to COPTIC
Egyptian gods *see p. 318*
Egyptian language COPTIC; *see* ARABIC, HAMITIC
Egyptian measure PIK, RO(U)B, ABDAT, ARDEB, FARDE, KILAH, SAHME, AURURE, FEDDAN, KEDDAH, ROBHAN, DARIBAH, MALOUAH
Egyptian measure (ancient) KHET, THEB, CUBIT, ARTABA, SCHENE, CHORYOS
Egyptian money GIRSH, POUND, RIYAL, MEDINO, PIASTER, MILLIEME
Egyptian rulers TUT, FUAD, NIKI, PEPI, SETI, ABBAS, KHUFU, MENES, NECHO, ZOSER, AMASIS, AHMOSI, APRIES, CHEOPS, HATASU, HOPHRA, KAPHRE, NAGUIB, NASSER, RAMSES, SHISAK, SNEFRU, HARMHAB, OSORKON, PSAMTIK, PTOLEMY, SESHONK, THUTMOSE
Egyptian weights OKA, OKE, HEML, OKIA, ROTL, KERAT, UCKIA, KANTAR, QUINTAL
Egyptian weights (ancient) KAT, KET, KHAR, DEBEN, OKIEH
eider DOWN, DUCK
eidolon ICON, IDEAL, IMAGE
eighth note QUAVER
eight-sided figure OCTAGON
Eire ERIN, IRELAND
eject EMIT, OUST, SPEW, VOID, EVICT, SPURT, BOUNCE
eke ADD, IMP
El Salvador money COLON, CENTAVO
Elam capital SUSA, SHUSHAN
Elam's father SHEM
eland *see* ANTELOPE
elapse PASS, EXPIRE
elastic BUOYANT, SPRINGY, RESILIENT
elate EXALT, GLADDEN
elbow BEND, ANCON, ANGLE, CROWD, JOINT, NUDGE, JOSTLE
Electra kin ORESTES, AGAMEMNON
eld YORE
elder IVA, DEAN, PRIOR, SENIOR
eldest AINE(E), EIGNE, SENIOR
eldritch EERIE, WEIRD
elect OPT, CHOOSE, CHOSEN, SELECT
elector VOTER
electric particle (AN)ION, CATION, KATION
electric unit AMP, BEL, MHO, OHM, REL, DYNE, ELOD, PERM, VOLT, WATT, FARAD, HENRY, WEBER, AMPERE
electricity JUICE, POWER
electrify SHOCK, THRILL
electrode ANODE, CATHODE
electronic device IC, CHIP, DIODE, LASER, MASER, RESISTOR, CAPACITOR, TRANSISTOR
electronic tube TRIODE, PENTODE, TETRODE, KLYSTRON, MAGNETRON, THYRATRON
elegance GRACE, POLISH
elegant FINE, POSH, RICH, GENTEEL, REFINED, DIGNIFIED
elegy DIRGE, NENIA, LAMENT
element AIR, FIRE, RECT, PART, EARTH, WATER, FACTOR, ISOTOPE; *see p. 249*
elementary BASIC, PRIMAL, PRIMER, SIMPLE, PRIMARY
elephant COW, BULL, HINE, HATHI, JUMBO, ROGUE, TUSKER, LOXODON, PACHYDERM
elephant driver MAHOUT
elephant genus ELEPHAS
elevation MESA, MOUND, MOUNT, RIDEAU, PLATEAU
elevator CAGE, LIFT, HOIST, SPOUT, AIRFOIL
elf FAY, HOB, IMP, NIX, PERI, PIXY, PUCK, FAIRY, GNOME, NIXIE, OUPHE, PIXIE, GOBLIN, KOBOLD, SPRITE, BROWNIE, ERLKING
elfin FEY
elicit EDUCE, EVOKE, EXTRACT
elide DELE, OMIT, SLUR
Elijah ELIA, LIGE, ELIAS
elision SYNCOPE, OMISSION

elite PICK, CREAM
elixir RASA, SOMA, HAOMA, AMRITA, ARCANUM, PANACEA
Elizabeth I (GL)ORIANA
Elizabeth I parent ANNE, HENRY, BOLEYN
elliptic OVAL, OVATE, OBLONG
elk see DEER
ell WING, CUBIT
ellipse OVAL, CURVE
ellipsis SYNCOPE
elliptical OVAL, BRIEF, OVATE, OBLONG, CONCISE
elm ULMUS, W(H)AHOO
elm fruit KEY, SAMARA
elongated LINEAR, PROLATE
elope FLEE, ESCAPE, ABSCOND
eloquence ORATORY, RHETORIC
elude SHUN, DODGE, EVADE
elusive EELY, SLICK, SLIPPERY
Elysian HAPPY, BLISSFUL
emaciation TABES, WASTE, ATROPHY
emanation(s) AURA, BLAS, AURAE, NITON
emancipate FREE, MANUMIT, RELEASE
emancipator ABE, FREER, MOSES, LINCOLN
emasculate GELD, WEAKEN, CASTRATE
embalming fluid FORMALIN
embankment DAM, BUND, DIKE, DYKE, DIGUE, LEVEE, STAITHE
embark SHIP, BOARD
embarrass VEX, FAZE, ABASH
embassy MISSION, LEGATION
embassy official AIDE, ATTACHE
embellish DECK, GILD, PINK, ADORN, BEDECK, GARNISH
ember ASH, COAL, ISEL, IZLE, SPARK, CINDER, CLINKER
embezzle PECULATE, DEFALCATE
embitter FESTER, RANKLE
emblem BAR, FLAG, MACE, SIGN, BADGE, EAGLE, TOTEM, DESIGN, FASCES, SYMBOL, INSIGNE, INSIGNIA
embrace HUG, CLASP, ENARM, INARM, ACCEPT, CARESS, EMBODY, WELCOME
embrocation ARNICA, LINIMENT
embroider TAT, PURL, BREDE, COUCH, DECORATE
embroidery equipment CREWEL, TABORET, TAMBOUR
embroil MIXUP, MUDDLE
embryo CELL, GERM, FETUS
emend EDIT, ALTER, REVISE
emerald SMARAGD; *see* GEM
Emerald Isle ERIN, IRELAND
emerge RISE, ISSUE, EMANATE
emergency PASS, PINCH, CRISIS, CLUTCH, STRAIT, URGENCY
emery ABRASIVE, CORUNDUM
emetic IPECAC, MUSTARD
emigre(e) ALIEN, EXILE, REFUGEE
eminence FAME, HILL, NOTE, REPUTE
emirate AJMAN, DUBAI, QATAR, KUWAIT, BAHRAIN, FUJAIRA, SHARJAH, ABUDHABI
emissary SPY, AGENT, ENVOY, (DE)LEGATE
emit REEK, SHED, ERUCT, EXUDE
Emmentaler SWISS, GRUYERE
emmer SPELT, WHEAT
emotion ONDE, PATHOS, PASSION
emperor CZAR, TSAR, TZAR, AKBAR, MOGUL, TENNO, KAISER, MIKADO, PADISHAH
emphasis ICTUS, ACCENT, STRESS
empire RULE, SWAY, KINGDOM
Empire State NY, NEWYORK
employ USE, HIRE, PLACE, ENGAGE
employee(s) MAN, HAND, HELP, STAFF, WORKER, PERSONNEL
employer BOSS, JOSS, USER, HIRER
employment JOB, WORK, PLACE, TRADE
emporium MART, SHOP, STORE, MARKET
empress CZARINA
empty TOOM, VAIN, VOID, BLANK, DRAIN, INANE, DEVOID, VACANT, DEPLETE, VACUOUS, DEPLETED
emu RHEA, CASSOWARY; *see* BIRD
emulate APE, VIE, RIVAL, STRIVE
enact PASS, PERFORM, PORTRAY
enamelware LIMOGES, CLOISONNE
enamored FOND, SMITTEN
encamp TENT, PITCH, BIVOUAC
enchantress HAG, CIRCE, MEDEA, SIREN, WITCH

encircle HEM, ORB, GIRD, GIRT, EMBAY, ENVIRON
enclose MEW, PEN, CAGE, CASE, WRAP, FENCE, HEDGE, INCASE, CORRAL, ENCLAVE
enclosure STY, BAWN, COOP, YARD, ATAJO, SEKOS, CANCHA, CORRAL, STOCKADE
encomium ELOGE, PRAISE, EULOGY, TRIBUTE, PANEGYRIC
encore BIS, AGAIN, REPEAT
encounter MEET, BATTLE, ENGAGE
encourage EGG, ABET, URGE, BOOST, BRACE, ELATE, FOSTER
encroach IMPINGE, INFRINGE, TRESPASS
encumber LOAD, BURDEN, IMPEDE, SADDLE
end AIM, DIE, TIP, CODA, FINE, STUB, BOURN, FINIS, OMEGA, FINALE, INTENT, RESULT, THIRTY, REMNANT
end, tending to TELIC
endanger RISK, (IM)PERIL
endeavor AIM, TRY, VIE, ESSAY, NISUS
endive CHICORY, WITLOOF, ESCAROLE
endorse SIGN, RATIFY, SANCTION
endorsement VISA, VISE, BACKING
endow VEST, GRACE, BESTOW, INVEST
endowment BOON, DOWER, GRANT, TALENT, FELLOWSHIP
endue VEST, DOWER, DIGEST, INVEST
endurance STAMINA, FORTITUDE
endure BEAR, BIDE, DREE, LAST, WEAR, ABIDE, BROOK, PERSIST
enemy FOE, RIVAL, FOEMAN
energy PEP, VIM, ZIP, BENT, ERGAL, POWER, VIGOR, METTLE, POTENCY, STHENIA
energy, lack of ATONY, INERTIA
energy unit BTU, ERG, RAD, ERGON, JOULE, MEGERG
enervate SAP, DRAIN, WEAKEN
enforce COMPEL, IMPOSE
engage BOOK, HIRE, MESH, ENLIST, OCCUPY, RETAIN, BETROTH, CHARTER, AFFIANCE
engender SIRE, BEGET, BREED, PROMOTE, GENERATE
engine GIN, MOGUL, MOTOR, DIESEL, YARDER, MACHINE, TURBINE; *see* WEAPON
engine part PISTON; *see* MOTOR
engineer SAPPER, SEABEE
England ALBION
English LIMEY, SAXON, BRITISH, SILURES, SASSENACH
English alphabet AR, EF, EL, EM, EN, EX, WY, BEE, CEE, CUE, DEE, ESS, GEE, JAY, KAY, PEE, TEE, WYE, ZED, ZEE, AITCH, DOUBLEU
English measure PIN, COOM, PIPE, CHAIN, COOMB, COVER, JUGUM, FIRKIN, RUNLET, VIRGATE; *see* MEASURE
English money ANGEL, BODLE, CROWN, DRAKE, GROAT, PENNY, PLACK, POUND, BAWBEE, FLORIN, GUINEA, CAROLUS, JACOBUS, UNICORN, ATCHISON, FARTHING, SHILLING, HALFCROWN, SOVEREIGN; *see* MONEY
English ruler ANNE, EDWY, JOHN, EDRED, HENRY, JAMES, ALFRED, CANUTE, EDMUND, EDWARD, EGBERT, GEORGE, HAROLD, CHARLES, RICHARD, STEPHEN, WILLIAM, VICTORIA, ETHERLRED, ELIZABETH
English weight KIP, KEEL, BARGE, CLOVE, FAGOT, STONE, CENTAL, FIRKIN, POCKET
engrave ETCH, RIST, CARVE, CHASE, INFIX, CHISEL, INCISE, STIPPLE
engraver BLAKE, DURER, DAUMIER, HOGARTH, MANTEGNA
engraving, pert. to GLYPTIC
engraving tool BURIN, STYLE, MATTOIR
engrossed RAPT, ABSORBED
engulf WHELM, ABSORB, SWALLOW
enigma REBUS, PUZZLE, RIDDLE, SECRET, CONUNDRUM
enisle ISOLATE
enjoin BID, ORDER, FORBID
enjoy LIKE, RELISH
enjoyment ZEST, GUSTO, RELISH

enlarge REAM, DILATE, EXPAND, DISTEND
enlist JOIN, ENROLL, RECRUIT
enliven ELATE, ROUSE, ANIMATE
enmity ANIMUS, MALICE, RANCOR
ennead NINE
Enoch relative CAIN, IRAD, JARED
enormous HUGE, IMMENSE
Enos' father SETH
enough BAS, BUS, ENOW, AMPLE, BASTA
enrage IRK, ROIL, ANGER, MADDEN, INCENSE
enroll ENTER, ENLIST, IMPANEL, REGISTER
ensemble SUIT(E), COSTUME
ensign FLAG, BANNER, STANDARD
enslave ENTHRALL, SUBJUGATE
ensnare NET, WEB, LURE, BENET, DECOY, SNIGGLE
entangle MESH, SNARL, ENMESH, ENTRAP, RAFFLE
entente TREATY, CONCORD
enter LIST, ADMIT, ENROL, START, ENROLL, INSERT, RECORD
enterprise PROJECT, VENTURE, ENDEAVOR
entertain FETE, DIVERT, REGALE
entertainer(s) HOST, HETAERA, HETAIRA, HOSTESS, COURTESAN
enthrall ENSLAVE, CAPTIVATE
enthusiasm ESTRO; *see* ZEAL
enthusiast BUG, FAN, IST, BUFF, ADDICT, ZEALOT, DEVOTEE, FANATIC
entice BAIT, COAX, LURE, TOLE, COZEN, PIQUE, TEMPT, ALLURE, CAJOLE, INVEIGH
entire GAMUT, TOTAL, WHOLE, COMPLETE
entity ENS, BEING, ENTIA, ESSENCE
entomb BURY, INTER, INURN
entrails GUTS, OFFAL, BOWELS, UMBLES, VISCERA
entrance ADIT, DOOR, GATE, DEBUT, STILE, ACCESS, PORTAL, INGRESS
entreat BEG, PRAY, HALSE, PLEAD, ADJURE, HALSEN, SOLICIT
entry ITEM, NOTE, DEBIT, CREDIT, MINUTE
entwine WEAVE, ENLACE, WREATHE
enumerate LIST, TELL, TICK, COUNT, NUMBER
enunciate STATE, UTTER, DECLARE
enure HARDEN, ACCUSTOM
envelop WRAP, ENFOLD, INFOLD, INWRAP, SHROUD, SWADDLE
envelope POD, SACK, SHELL, SHEATH, CAPSULE, WRAPPER
environment MILIEU, PURLIEU
environs EXURBS, LOCALE, SETTING, SUBURBS, VICINITY, OUTSKIRTS
envy ONDE, COVET, SPITE, GRUDGE
enzyme ASE, FICIN, KINASE, LOTASE, MUTASE, OLEASE, PAPAIN, PEPSIN, RENNIN, ZYMASE, AMYLASE, MALTASE, PTYALIN, TRYPSIN, DIASTASE, INSULASE
eon ERA, OLAM, EPOCH
Eos DAWN, AURORA
epic EDDA, EPOS, POEM, SAGA, ENEID, ILIAD, AENEID, EPOPEE, HEROIC, BEOWULF, HOMERIC, ODYSSEY, KALEVALA, RAMAYANA, SAKUNTALA
epicure FRIAND, GOURMET, GOURMAND, SYBARITE
epicurean APICIAN
epidemic FLU, PEST, PLAGUE
episode EVENT, INCIDENT
epistle NOTE, LETTER, MISSIVE
epithet NAME, OATH, BYNAME, AGNOMEN
epitome BRIEF, DIGEST, SUMMARY, SYNOPSIS
epoch AGE, EON, ERA, BALA, ECCA, LIAS, MALM, MUAV, CHAZY, ERIAN, UINTA, ARENIG, KAIBAB, OOLITE, SERIES, FORMATION
equal ISO, TIE, EVEN, FERE, LIKE, MEET, PARI, PEER, TIED, ALIKE, MATCH, COMPEER
equality PAR(ITY), ISONOMY
equine *see* HORSE, ASS
equip FIT, RIG, GIRD, OUTFIT, ACCOUTRE
equipment RIG, GEAR, TACKLE
equitable FAIR, JUST, HONEST
equivocate EVADE, FENCE, HEDGE, PALTER

Er relative JUDAH, TAMAR
era AGE, CYCLE, EPOCH, GROUP, PERIOD, CENOZOIC, MESOZOIC, PALEOZOIC
eradicate RID, ROOT, ERASE, LEVEL, UPROOT, EPILATE
erase BLOT, DELE, CANCEL, DELETE, EFFACE
ere BEFORE, RATHER, SOONER
Erebus HADES
erect REAR, TALL, BUILD, RAISE
ergo HENCE, THEREFORE
Erin EIRE, IRELAND, HIBERNIA
Erinyes ALECTO, FURIES, MAGAERA, TISIPHONE
Eris DISCORD
Eris' relative ARES, NEMESIS
ermine FUR, STOAT, WEASEL
erode EAT, WEAR, CORRODE
Eros AMOR, LOVE, CUPID
erotic SEXY, BAWDY, AMATIVE, AMATORY, AMOROUS, PAPHIAN
err SIN, SLIP, STRAY, WANDER, MISTAKE
errand MISSION
error(s) BULL, TYPO, BONER, GAFFE, ERRATA, MISCUE, ERRATUM, SOLECISM
erse IRISH, SCOTS, GAELIC
erudite WISE, LEARNED, SCHOLARLY
erupt EMIT, BURST
Esau EDOM
Esau relative ADAH, ISAAC, JACOB
escapade DIDO, CAPER, PRANK
escape LAM, LEAK, ELUDE, EVADE, DECAMP, ABSCOND
eschew SHUN, FORGO, ABSTAIN
escort BEAU, USHER, CONVOY, DUENNA, SQUIRE, CONDUCT, RETINUE
esculent EDIBLE, EATABLE
escutcheon ARMS, CREST, SHIELD
Eskimo *see p. 342*
esophagus GULA, GULLET, WEASAND
esoteric INNER, ARCANE, MYSTIC, OCCULT
espalier LATTICE, TRELLIS, PALISADE
espouse ABET, ADOPT, MARRY
esprit MORALE, SPIRIT
essay TRY, TEST, CHRIA, PAPER, THEME, TRACT, THESIS, ATTEMPT, TREATISE
essayist LAMB, CAPEK, PATER, WOOLF, CATHER, IRVING, ORWELL, CARLYLE, EMERSON, THOREAU
essence ENS, GIST, PITH, RASA, ATTAR, BEING, SCENT, AMRITA, EXTRACT, PERFUME
essential MUST, BASAL, BASIC, VITAL
establish SET, BASE, FOUND, PROVE, SETTLE, VERIFY
estate ALOD, RANK, ALLOD, DAIRA, MANOR, TALUK, ASSETS, DOMAIN, LEGACY, HOLDING, ALLODIUM
esteem HONOR, PRIDE, PRIZE, ADMIRE, REPUTE, CHERISH
ester ETHER, ACETIN, IODIDE, OLEATE, STEARIN, SILICATE
estimate GAGE, METE, RATE, ASSAY, AUDIT, ASSESS, RECKON, APPRAISE
Estonian measure TUN, ELLE, LIIN, SULD, TOLL, FADEN, SAGENE
Estonian money SENT, KROON, ESTMARK
Estonian weight NAEL, PUUD
estrade DAIS
estrange WEAN, SPLIT, DIVERT, ALIENATE
estrus HEAT, FRENZY
estuary RIA, LOCH, PARA, FIORD, FIRTH, FJORD, FRITH, INLET, PLATA
étagère WHATNOT
etch CUT, SCORE, CHISEL, ENGRAVE
Eternal City ROME
eternity (A)EON, OLAM, INFINITY
ether SKY, ESTER, SPACE
ethereal AERY, AIRY, AERIAL, DELICATE, HEAVENLY
ethical MORAL, RIGHT, HONEST
Ethiopia CUSH, ABYSSINIA
Ethiopia, former capital MEROE
Ethiopian language GEEZ, GALLA, TIGRE; *see* SEMITIC
Ethiopian measure TAT, CUBA, KUBA
Ethiopian money BESA, GIRSH, TALARI, ASHRAFI
Ethiopian weight KASM, NATR, OKET, ALADA, NETER, WAKEA, WOGIET

ethnic FOLK, RACIAL
etiolate BLANCH, BLEACH, WHITEN
etiquette DECORUM, PROPRIETY
Etruscan god *see p. 331*
eucalyptus YATE, KARRI, JARRAH, MALLEE
eucharist *see* COMMUNION
eulogy PAIN, ELOGE, ENCOMIUM
Eumenides FURIES, ERINNYES
Europa's lover ZEUS
European BALT, DANE, FINN, LAPP, LETT, POLE, SERB, SLAV, CROAT, GREEK, SWEDE, SWISS, FRANK, SLOVAK
evacuate MOVE, VOID, EMPTY
evade BILK, FOIL, SHUN, AVOID, DODGE, ELUDE, PARRY, SHIRK, SHUNT, PALTER
evaluate GAGE, ASSAY, GAUGE, PRICE, ASSESS, APPRAISE
evanescent AIRY, FLEETING, EPHEMERAL, TRANSIENT
evangelist JOHN, LUKE, MARK, SMITH, GANTRY, GRAHAM, SUNDAY, APOSTLE, FALWELL, MATTHEW, ROBERTS, PREACHER, MCPHERSON, MISSIONARY
evaporate DRY, VANISH
eve DUSK, SUNDOWN, TWILIGHT
Eve relative ABEL, ADAM, CAIN, SETH
Eve tempter SERPENT
even SAME, FLUSH, LEVEL, PLANE, PLUMB, SQUARE, UNIFORM
evening DEN, DUSK, VESPER, GLOAMING
event AFFAIR, EPISODE, INCIDENT
ever AYE, EER, ALWAYS
Everest climber NORGAY, HILLARY, TENZING
Everglade State FL(A), FLORIDA
evergreen BOX, ATLE, BAGO, MORA, PIXY, TAWA, THEA, UPAS, WHIN, ATLEE, BIRMA, BOLDO, BOLDU, BUXUS, CATHA, CLOVE, ERICA, FURZE, GORSE, PIXIE, PYXIE, THUJA, TOYON, NUTMEG, CALABA, PEUMUS, SPRUCE, TOLLON, ARBUTUS, CONIFER
everlasting ETERN(E), OLAMIC, AGELONG, ETERNAL
every ALL, EACH
everyday DAILY, USUAL, COMMON
evict OUST, SACK, EXPEL
evidence SIGN, PROOF, TESTIMONY
evident CLEAR, PLAIN, PATENT, APPARENT, PALPABLE
evil MAL, BASE, HARM, MALA, VICE, VILE, WRONG, MALIGN
evil intent DOLUS, MALICE
evoke EDUCE, ELICIT, SUMMON
evolve (D)EDUCE, DERIVE, UNFOLD
ewe YOW, CRONE, THEAVE; *see* SHEEP
exacerbate IRE, IRK, ENRAGE, PROVOKE, IRRITATE
exact LEVY, BLEED, WREST, DEMAND, EXTORT, ESTREAT, LITERAL
exaggeration HYPERBOLE, EMBROIDERY
exalt ELATE, EXTOL, RAISE, DIGNIFY, ELEVATE
examination GRE, SAT, TAT, ORAL, QUIZ, TEST, AUDIT, PROBE, STUDY, TRIAL, BIOPSY, GREATS, TRIPOS, TRYOUT, AUTOPSY, CATECHISM
examine PRY, SPY, TRY, SCAN, CHECK, GRADE, APPOSE, PALPATE
example CASE, PINK, MODEL, SAMPLE, PARADIGM, SPECIMEN
exasperate IRK, TRY, VEX, RILE, ANGER, ANNOY, INFURIATE
excavate DIG, GRUB, MUCK, PION, SCOOP, DREDGE, UNEARTH
excavation PIT, HOLE, MINE, SHAFT, STOPE, HOLLOW
exceed CAP, BEST, PASS, EXCEL, OUTDO, BETTER
excellence CLASS, MERIT, VIRTU
excellent AONE, RARE, TOPS, PRIME, SUPER, DELUXE, SELECT, TIPTOP, WORTHY
except BAR, BUT, OMIT, SAVE, EXCLUDE
exceptional SPECIAL, UNUSUAL
excerpt QUOTE, EXTRACT, PASSAGE, CITATION
excess GLUT, EPACT, LUXUS, SPATE, NIMIETY, SURPLUS, PLETHORA

excessive UNDUE, INORDINATE
exchange PIT, SWAP, BANDY, TRADE, BARTER, BOURSE, MARKET, RIALTO, SWITCH
exchange medium SHOE, SYCEE, SCHUIT
exchequer FISC, FISK, TREASURY
excise TAX, DUTY, TOLL, REMOVE
excite ROIL, WHET, ELATE, ROUSE, AGITATE
excited AGOG, ASTIR, MANIC
excitement FURY, FUROR, FRENZY, FURORE, PASSION
exclaim CRY, SHOUT, EJACULATE
exclamation AH, BO, EH, HA, HI, MY, OH, OW, UM, ACH, AHA, AUG, BAH, BAM, BAW, BOH, FIE, FOH, GEE, GRR, HAH, HAW, HEM, HEP, HEU, HEY, HIC, HIP, HOI, HOO, HOY, HUH, OHO, OUF, PAH, PEW, POH, PST, PUE, SOH, TCH, TCK, TST, TUT, UGH, WEE, WHY, WOW, AHEM, AHEY, AITH, ALAS, ARAH, ARRA, BOOH, BOSH, CHUT, EGAD, EHEU, EVOE, GOSH, HEIN, HOCH, HUSH, NUTS, OUCH, PHEW, PHUT, PISH, PSHA, SOOK, TISH, TUSH, WHAM, WHEW, ALACK, ARRAH, BLIMY, FAUGH, HELLO, HEUCH, HEUGH, HURRA, HUZZA, PSHAW, UHHUH, ZOWIE, HURRAH, HURROO, OCHONE, OUTCRY; *see* CRY, OATH
exclude BAR, OMIT, DEBAR, DEPORT, BLACKBALL
exclusive ONLY, POSH, SOLE, SELECT, UNIQUE
excoriate FLAY, CHAFE, ABRADE
excrescence CORN, WART, STUD, GROWTH
excrete EGEST, EXUDE, EVACUATE
exculpate CLEAR, ACQUIT, ABSOLVE, EXONERATE
excursion TOUR, TREK, JAUNT, SALLY, JUNKET, OUTING
excuse PLEA, ALIBI, REMIT, ESSOIN(E)
execrate HATE, ABHOR, DETEST
execute DO, SIGN, LYNCH, SCRAG, ACHIEVE, PERFORM
executioner HANGMAN, HEADSMAN
exemplar COPY, MODEL, PATTERN
exempt EXON, FREE, IMMUNE
exemption GRACE, ESSOIN(E), IMPUNITY
exercise PLY, URE, TASK, DRILL, EXERT, NISUS, PRAXIS
exert STRAIN, EXERCISE
exhale EMIT, EXUDE
exhaust FAG, SAP, JADE, TIRE, DRAIN, SPEND, WASTE, DEPLETE
exhausted BEAT, DONE, WEAK, SPENT, WEARY, EFFETE
exhibit SHOW, SALON, DISPLAY, GALLERY
exhibition PARADE, PAGEANT, SPECTACLE
exhilarated GLAD, ELATED
exhort EGG, PROD, URGE, INCITE
exigency NEED
exigent URGENT, EXACTING, PRESSING
exiguous THIN, MEAGER, SLENDER
exile BANISH, DEPORT, EXPULSION
exist AM, BE, IS, ARE, LIVE, ENDURE, BREATHE
existence ENS, ESSE, BEING, CONDITION
existence, pert. to ONTAL, NOUMENAL
existentialist CAMUS, SARTRE
existing ALIVE, BEING, EXTANT
exit END, DEATH, LEAVE, DEMISE, DEPART, EGRESS
exodus FLIGHT, HEGIRA
Exodus author URIS
exonerate CLEAR, ACQUIT, ABSOLVE, EXCULPATE
exorbitant UNDUE, EXCESS, USURIOUS, EXCESSIVE
exotic ODD, ALIEN, FOREIGN, STRANGE
expand FLAN, SWELL, DILATE, DISTEND, INFLATE
expanse SEA, AREA, REACH, SCOPE, SWEEP, TRACT
expatriate EXILE, BANISH
expect HOPE, WAIT, WEEN, WISH, AWAIT
expedient FIT, PROPER, STOPGAP
expedite HIE, HURRY, SPEED, HASTEN, ADVANCE
expedition TREK, CHASE, JAUNT, QUEST, SAFARI, SHIKAR, CARAVAN, CRUSADE, SUFFARI

expel OUST, EJECT, EVICT, DEPORT
expend PAY, USE, WASTE, CONSUME
expense COST, PRICE, OUTLAY
experience FEEL, HAVE, LIVE, UNDERGO
experiment TRY, TEST, TRIAL
expert ACE, DEFT, ONER, WHIZ, ADEPT, CRACK
expiate ATONE, PURGE, SHRIVE
expire DIE, END, CEASE, PERISH
explain REDE, WISE, CLEAR, GLOSS, DEFINE
explicit CLEAR, LUCID, PRECISE, POSITIVE
explode POP, FIRE, BURST, DETONATE, FULMINATE
exploit CLIP, DEED, FEAT, GEST, MILK, TOUR, GESTE
explorer RAE, BYRD, PIKE, HEDIN, LEWIS, LOGAN, PERRY, SCOTT, BALBOA, CORTES, DELEON, DELONG, DESOTO, WILKES; *see* DISCOVERER
explosive CAP, TNT, AMMO, BOMB, MINE, PETN, SOUP, GAINE, FIERY, NITRO, TENSE, AMATOL, PETARD, TONITE, CORDITE, LIGNOSE, LYDDITE, DYNAMITE, MELINITE, PENT(H)RITE
exponent INDEX, ADVOCATE
export SHIP
expose AIR, BARE, REVEAL, UNMASK
exposition FAIR, SHOW, DISPLAY
expository EXEGETIC
expound REVEAL, EXPLAIN
express STATE, UTTER, EXPLICIT
expression MIEN, TERM, IDIOM, ASPECT, PHRASE, SAYING, ATTICISM, LOCUTION
expressive ELOQUENT
expulsion OUSTER, REMOVAL, EJECTION
exquisite FINE, ACUTE, CHOICE, PERFECT
extend EKE, JUT, LIE, REACH, RENEW, WIDEN, BEETLE, DEPLOY
extenuate EXCUSE, LESSEN, DIMINISH, PALLIATE
exterior ECTAL, OUTER, EXTRINSIC
exterminate DESTROY, ANNIHILATE
external OUTER, FOREIGN
extinct DEAD, DEFUNCT
extinct animal MOA, DODO, KIWI, MAMO, URUS, QUAGGA, MAMMOTH, DINOSAUR, MASTODON, STEGODON
extinguish DOUSE, DOWSE, QUELL, SNUFF, QUENCH, STIFLE, SMOTHER
extirpate DELE, RAZE, ROOT, STUB, UPROOT
extol LAUD, EXALT, PRAISE
extort MILK, BLEED, EXACT, WREST, WRING
extra ODD, OVER, PLUS, SUPE, SPARE, SUPER, INSERT, SURPLUS
extract ATAR, DRAW, OTTO, ATTAR, OTTAR, DISTIL, ELICIT, EVULSE, REMOVE, ESSENCE, ESTREAT, PERICOPE
extracts ANALECTA, ANALECTS
extraneous ALIEN, OUTER, EXOTIC
extraordinary UNCO, GREAT, REMARKABLE
extravagance ERA, WASTE
extravagant LUSH, OUTRE, PLUSH, FAROUT, LAVISH, ROCOCO, BAROQUE, PRODIGAL
extreme FINAL, ULTRA, SEVERE, DRASTIC, RADICAL
extremity END, TRIP, TOE, EDGE, FOOT, HAND, LIMB, POLE, TAIL
extricate FREE, RELEASE, LIBERATE
extrovert OUTGOING
extrude FORM, EJECT, EXPEL
exuberant LAVISH, PROFUSE
exudation GUM, LAC, SAP, AURA, PITCH, RESIN, SUDOR
exude EMIT, OOZE, REEK
exult CROW, GLORY, REJOICE
eye(s) EE, BUD, EEN, ORB, SEE, UTA, GLIM, HILA, OGLE, HILUM, LAMPS, OPTIC, SIGHT, STARE, OCULUS, PEEPER, STEMMA, VISION, OCELLUS
eye, black MOUSE, SHINER
eye infection *see* DISEASE
eye makeup KOH(O)L, LINER, SHADOW, MASCARA
eye, part of BREE, IRIS, LENS, UVEA, CILIA, ORBIT, PUPIL, CORNEA, EYELID, RETINA,

VISION, EYEBALL, EYEBROW, EYELASH
eye protector PATCH, VISOR, BLINDER, BLINKER, GOGGLES
eyeglass(es) LENS, SPECS, OCULAR, GOGGLES, MONOCLE, LORGNETTE, SPECTACLES
eyelet GROMMET, LOOPHOLE
eyot AIT, ILE, ISLE(T)
eyrie NEST

F

fable MYTH, YARN, APOLOG, LEGEND, PARABLE, ALLEGORY, APOLOGUE
fable author AESOP, GRIMM, BIDPAI, PILPAY, ANDERSEN
fabric MAT, NET, REP, TAT, WEB, ACCA, CRIN, DRAB, DUCK, FELT, GROS, HUCK, HUSI, IKAT, JEAN, JUSI, KELT, LACE, LAME, LAWN, LENO, LINT, MACO, MAUD, MESH, MULL, PILE, REPP, SABA, TAPA, ATLAS, BAIZE, BATIK, BEIGE, CHINE, CRAPE, CRASH, CREPE, DENIM, DOMET, DORIA, DRILL, FILET, GAUZE, GUNNY, KASHA, KHAKI, LACIS, LAINE, LINEN, LLAMA, MANTA, MOIRE, MUNGO, PANNE, PEKIN, PIQUE, PLAID, PLUSH, ROMAL, RUMAL, SATIN, SCRIM, SERGE, SUEDE, SURAH, SURAT, SWISS, TABBY, TAMIS, TERRY, TOILE, TULLE, TWEED, TWILL, UNION, VOILE, WIGAN, ALPACA, ARMURE, BATTIK, BEAVER, BOUCLE, BROCHE, BURLAP, CADDIS, CALICO, CAMACA, CAMLET, CANVAS, CHINTZ, COUTIL, COVERT, DAMASK, DIMITY, DOMETT, DOWLAS, EPONGE, ETOILE, FAILLE, FLEECE, FREIZE, GLORIA, KERSEY, LAMPAS, LINSEY, MADRAS, MALINE, MELTON, MERINO, MOHAIR, MOREEN, MUSLIN, OXFORD, PONGEE, POPLIN, RADIUM, RATINE, SAMITE, SATEEN, SAXONY, TAMISE, TARTAN, TISSUE, TRICOT, TUSSAH, VELOUR, VELURE, VELVET, VICUNA, WADMAL, WOOLEN, ZEPHYR, ALLOVER, BATISTE, BROCADE, BUCKRAM, BUNTING, GAMBRIC, CHALLIS, CHAMOIS, CHEVIOT, CHIFFON, COATING, DOESKIN, DRUGGET, DUVETYN, EPINGLE, ETAMINE, FLANNEL, FOULARD, FUSTIAN, GALATEA, GINGHAM, HABUTAI, HOLLAND, JACONET, MIXTURE, MOGADOR, NANKEEN, ORGANDY, ORGANZA, OTTOMAN, PAISLEY, PERCALE, SATINET, SILEXIA, STAMMEL, SUITING, TABINET, TAFFETA, TEXTILE, TICKING, TIFFANY, VEILING, VELOURS, WOOLLEN, WORSTED, BARATHEA, BIRDSEYE, BROCATEL, CASHMERE, CHAMBRAY, CHENILLE, CORDUROY, CRETONNE, DOMESTIC, DUNGAREE, DUVETINE, ESTAMENE, HOMESPUN, JACQUARD, LUSTRINE, MILANESE, MOGADORE, MOLESKIN, NAINSOOK, OILCLOTH, OSNABURG, PRUNELLA, SARSENET, SHANTUNG, SHEETING, SHIRTING, TAPESTRY, TARLATAN, TARLETAN, VALENCIA, WHIPCORD, ZIBELINE
fabric merchant DRAPER, MERCER
fabricate COIN, MAKE, ERECT, FEIGN, FORGE, DEVISE, SCHEME, CONCOCT
fabrication LIE, FAKE, FABLE, FICTION, FORGERY
fabulous MYTHICAL, LEGENDARY
façade FACE, FRONT
face MAP, MUG, PAN, DARE, DIAL, PHIZ, PUSS, FACET, REVET, SNOOT, FACADE, VISAGE, SURFACE
face card JACK, KING, HONOR, KNAVE, QUEEN, PICTURE
face downward PRONE, PRONATE
face, part of JAW, CHIN, EYES, NOSE, BEARD, CHEEK, DIMPLE
facet BEZEL, BEZIL, CULET, COLLET

facetious DROLL, WITTY, WAGGISH
face-to-face VISAVIS, TETEATETE
facile APT, DEFT, EASY, ADROIT
facility EASE, KNACK, MEANS
facsimile COPY, REPLICA, LIKENESS
fact(s) DATA, FAIT, FIAT, DATUM, FACTO, TRUTH
faction BLOC, SECT, SIDE, CABAL, JUNTO, CLIQUE
factor GENE, AGENT, BROKER
factory MILL, SHOP, PLANT, WORKSHOP
factual REAL, TRUE, ACTUAL
faculty BENT, KNACK, SENSE, TALENT
fad CRY, MODE, RAGE, CRAZE, FANCY, STYLE
fade DIE, DIM, PALE, WILT, WITHER
Faerie Queen author SPENSER
Faerie Queen character ATE, UNA, ALMA, TALUS, AMORET, DUESSA, ACRASIA
Fafnir brother REGIN
Fafnir slayer SIGURD, SIEGFRIED
fag RUMP, STUB, TIRE, EXHAUST
fagot TWIGS, BUNDLE, FASCINE
fail EBB, FLOP, LOSE, FLUNK
failing DEFECT, FOIBLE, WEAKNESS
failure DUD, BUST, FLOP, FIASCO
fain GLAD, EAGER, CONTENT
faineant LAZY, LOAFER, DONOTHING
faint DIM, FADE, WEAK, SWELT, SWOON, FEEBLE
fair JUST, MELA, SOSO, BAZAR, CLEAR, FERIA, BAZAAR, BLONDE, KERMIS, KERMESS
fair-lead WAPP
fairy ELF, FAY, MAB, NIZ, UNA, PERI, PIXY, PUCK, SHEE, VILA, VILY, DRYAD, NIXIE, PIXIE, SYLPH, TROLL, OBERON, SPRITE, TITANIA
fairy fort LIS(S), SHEE, SIDHE
faith CULT, DOXY, CREED, DOGMA, TENET, TROTH
faith, pert. to PISTIC
faithful LEAL, TRUE, LIEGE, LOYAL, STA(U)NCH
faithless FALSE, DISLOYAL
fake HOAX, SHAM, FEINT, FRAUD, PHON(E)Y, COUNTERFEIT
fakir YOGI, SWAMI, ASCETIC
falcon FALCO, HOBBY, SAKER, FANNER, JERKIN, KEELIE, LANNER, MERLIN, SHAHIN, KESTREL, SAKERET, SHAHEEN
falcon-headed god RA, MONT, HORUS, KHONS, MENTU
fall(s) LIN, SAG, SIN, DROP, LINN, PLAP, PLOP, SILE, SPILL, AUTUMN, PLUNGE, TOPPLE, CASCADE, CATARACT
fall back RECEDE, RETREAT
fall forward PITCH, TOPPLE
fall guy DUPE, PATSY, STOOGE
fall upon POUNCE, ASSAULT
fallacy IDOLA, IDOLUM, SOPHISM
falling sickness EPILEPSY, GRANDMAL
fallow IDLE, UNTILLED
false FAKE, SHAM, BOGUS, WRONG, PSEUDO, UNTRUE, SPURIOUS
false-hearted FICKLE
falsehood FIB, LIE, FLAM, FRAUD, CANARD
Falstaff's friend HAL, NYM, PETO, PISTOL
falter HAW, WAVER, DODDER, TOTTER
fame ECLAT, GLORY, HONOR, KUDOS, RENOWN, REPUTE
familiar BOLD, COSY, CLOSE, TRITE, VERSANT
family ILK, CLAN, GENS, LINE, SEPT, CINEL, GENOS, STOCK, TRIBE, STIRPS, LINEAGE
family, famous ESTE, ASTOR, DORIA, SOONG, DUPONT, MEDICI, KENNEDY, ROTHSCHILD, ROCKEFELLER
family tree LINE(AGE), PEDIGREE
famine DEARTH, HUNGER, SCARCITY
famous NOTED, EMINENT, RENOWNED
fan OGI, BUFF, PUNKA, FOMENT, PUNKAH, ROOTER, VOTARY, ZEALOT, DEVOTEE
fanatic NUT, BIGOT, JINGO, MANIC, RABID, MANIAC, ZEALOT, DEVOTEE, PARTISAN
fanciful QUAINT, WHIMSICAL, CAPRICIOUS
fancy IDEA, WHIM, QUIRK, SHINE, FOIBLE, IDEATE,

MEGRIM, NOTION, VAGARY, VISION, CAPRICE, CHIMERA, REVERIE, WHIMSEY
fang TUSK, BOOTY, TALON, TOOTH
fantastic QUEER, BIZARRE, FANCIFUL
far REMOTE, DISTANT
farce SKIT, EXODE, COMEDY, PARODY, MOCKERY, TRAVESTY
fare PAY, DIET, MENU, BOARD, TOKEN, THRIVE
farewell AVE, VALE, ADIEU, ADIOS, ANATH, CONGE, LEAVE, CONGEE
farinaceous MEALY, STARCHY
farinaceous food SAGO, SALEP
farm TILL, TORP, WERF, CROFT, HARAS, MAINS, RANCH, BARTON, CHACRA, KOLKHOZ, HACIENDA
farm building BARN, BYRE, SHED, SILO, STABLE, ONSTEAD
farm implement PLOW, BALER, FLAIL, HARROW, REAPER, TEDDER, COMBINE, TRACTOR
farm, pert. to VILLATIC
farmer MEO, HIND, RYOT, KULAK, SOWER, COTTER, TILLER, GRANGER
farmyard WERF, BARTON
faro term CASE, HOCK, SODA
farrow PIG, LITTER
fascia BAND, BELT, SASH, TAENIA
fascinate CHARM, ALLURE, BEWITCH, ENCHANT
Fascist RAS, NAZI, MUSSO, HITLER, FRANCO, FALANGIST, MUSSOLINI
fashion FAD, MOLD, MODE, RAGE, MODEL, SHAPE, STYLE, VOGUE, DESIGN
fashionable CHIC, SMART, STYLISH
fast LENT, APACE, EMBER, FLEET, CARENE, DHARNA, RAMADAN
fasten BOLT, GLUE, LOCK, NAIL, SEAL, SNIB, TACK, BELAY, RIVET, BATTEN
fastener NOG, NUT, PEG, PIN, BITT, BRAD, CLIP, HASP, HOOK, SNAP, STUD, CLAMP, CLEAT, DOWEL, STRAP, BUTTON, CLEVIS, COTTER, HALTER, STAPLE, ZIPPER
fastidious NICE, FUSSY, QUEASY, FINICAL, GOURMET, PRECISE
fat FOZY, LARD, LIPA, SUET, ADEPS, ELAIN, ESTER, OBESE, OLEIN, PUDGY, STOUT, ELAINE, GREASE, OLEINE, TALLOW, ADIPOSE, PINGUID, PORCINE, STEARIN(E)
fat, pert. to ADIPIC, ADIPOSE
fatal MORT, FERAL, DEADLY, FUNEST, LETHAL, MORTAL
fate LOT, DOOM, KARMA, KISMET
Fate(s) NONA, CLOTHO, DECUMA, MOIRAI, PARCAE, ATROPOS, LACHESIS
father ABU, POP, ABBA, ABOU, PAPA, PERE, SIRE, BEGET, PADRE, PATER
father, relating to AGNATE, PATERNAL
fathom DELVE, GRASP, PLUMP, PROBE, SOUND
fatigue FAG, SAP, BORE, JADE, TIRE, WEARY
Fatima relative ALI, ANNE, SEID, SAYID, FATIMID, MOHAMMED, BLUEBEARD
fatty OILY, GREASY, ADIPOSE
fatuous INANE, ASININE
faubourg SUBURB, BANLIEU
faucet TAP, COCK, SPIGOT, ROBINET
fault FLAW, CULPA, FOIBLE
faultfind NAG, CARP, CAVIL, KNOCK
faultfinder MOMUS, CRITIC
faulty BAD, FLAWED, PECCANT
faun SATYR, PANISK, SILENUS
Faust character HELEN, WAGNER, GRETCHEN, MARGARET
Faust writer GOETHE, GOUNOD
faux pas SLIP; *see* ERROR
favor BIAS, BOON, GRACE, TOKEN, OBLIGE, BENEFIT
favorite PET, HERO, IDOL, MINION
favoritism BIAS, NEPOTISM
fawn TOADY, CRINGE, GROVEL
fay *see* ELF, FAIRY
faze DAUNT, WORRY, DISTURB, DISCONCERT
FBI agent GMAN
FBI, former director HOOVER
fealty HOMAGE, LOYALTY
fear AWE, FUNK, DREAD, PHOBIA

fearful PAVID, TIMID, AFRAID, CRAVEN, TREPID
fearless BOLD, BRAVE, DARING, HEROIC, IMPAVID, INTREPID
feast FOY, MAS, FETE, LUAU, AGAPE, ARVAL, PURIM, REGALE, AHAAINA, BANQUET
feat ACT, DEED, STUNT, TRICK
feather(s) DOWN, HULU, TUFT, EIDER, PENNA, PINNA, PLUMA, QUILL, REMEX, PINION, PLUMAGE, REMIGES, TECTRIX
featherlike PINNATE, PLUMATE
feature STAR, MOTIF, TRAIT, ASPECT
Federalist author JAY, MADISON, HAMILTON
federate UNITE
federation UNION, LEAGUE, ALLIANCE
fee TIP, AGIO, DUES, FEOD, FIEF, TOKE, TOLL, CHARGE, RETAINER
feeble PUNY, WEAK, ANILE, DOTTY, DEBILE, FLABBY, INFIRM
feed OATS, AGIST, CATER, GRAZE, COSHER, FODDER, FORAGE
feedbox MANGER, TROUGH
feeding, forced GAVAGE
feel PALP, GROPE, SENSE, TOUCH
feeler PALP, BARBEL, PALPUS, TACTOR, PEDATE, ANTENNA, TENTACLE
feeling TOUCH, EMOTION, PASSION, SENSATION
feet, having PEDATE
feet, pert. to PEDAL, PODAL, PEDARY
feign ACT, FAKE, SHAM, PRETEND, SIMULATE, DISSEMBLE
feint MOCK, TRICK, PRETENSE
felicitous HAPPY, TIMELY
felid *see* CAT
feline CAT, SLY, WILY, CATTY
fell CUT, HEW, HIDE, PELT, SKIN, CRUEL, DEADLY, SAVAGE
fellow CAD, EGG, GUY, LAD, BOZO, CHAP, DICK, MATE, PEER, BLADE, CULLY, CHAPPY, CHAPPIE
fellowship SOCIETY, BONHOMIE, INTIMACY, SODALITY, COMMUNION
felon CON, OUTLAW, CULPRIT, CONVICT, WHITLOW, CRIMINAL
female SHE, MOM, SIS, AUNT, LADY, NIECE, MOTHER, SISTER, DISTAFF, FEMININE, DAUGHTER; *see* GIRL, WOMAN
female animal COW, DAM, DOE, DRI, EWE, GIN, HEN, NAK, PEN, REE, ROE, SHE, SOW, TEG, GILN, GYNE, HIND, JILL, MARE, NAGA, SLUT, URSA, ARNEE, BIDDY, BITCH, JENNY, TABBY, VIXEN, JENNET
fen BOG, MARSH, SWAMP, MORASS
fence HAHA, OXER, PARR, RAIL, FAGIN, HEDGE, STILE, HAWHAW, PALING, RADDLE, SCRIME, PALISADE
fence part PALE, POST, RAIL, STAKE, STILE, PALING, PICKET
fencer's cry HAI, HAY, SASA, TOUCHE, ENGARDE
fencing term PEL, BUTT, EPEE, FOIL, TUCK, VOLT, APPEL, CARTE, LUNGE, PARRY, PUNTO, SABER, SIXTE, SWORD, BUTTON, OCTAVE, QUARTE, QUINTE, RAPIER, REMISE, RIPOST, TIERCE, TOUCHE, ENGARDE, REPRISE, RIPOSTE, SECONDE, SEPTIME, PLASTROM
fend WARD, AVERT, PARRY
fennel HEMP, HERB, ANISE
Fenris' father LOKI
Fenris' slayer VIDAR
feral WILD, SAVAGE, UNTAMED
ferment BARM, FRET, ZYME, YEAST, LEAVEN
fermented drink ALE, BEER, MEAD, NIPA, SAKE, WINE, CIDER, KVASS, PERRY, KUMISS
fern NITO, BRAKE, NARDO, PITAU, PONGA, TODEA, NARDOO, BRACKEN, ELKHORN, WOODSIA, POLYPODY, STAGHORN
fern part SORI, FROND, SORUS, SPORE, CROSIER
ferocious FELL, WILD, FIERCE
Ferrara family ESTE
ferret PRY, SEARCH, WEASEL, POLECAT

ferry BAC, FORD, PONT
ferryman CHARON
fertile RICH, FECUND, FRUITFUL
fertilizer MARL, GUANO, MANURE, COMPOST
ferule ROD, RULER, STICK
fervor ZEAL, ZEST, ARDOR
festival ALE, BON, BUSK, FAIR, FETE, GALA, HOLI, MELA, PUJA, VOTA, DELIA, FERIA, HALOA, PURIM, SEDER, DEWALI, FIESTA, HOOLEE, KERMIS, OPALIA, PESACH, SUCCOS, KERMESS, SUKKOTH
festoon *see* GARLAND
fetid FOUL, OLID, RANK, FUSTY, PUTRID, RANCID, NOISOME
fetish OBI, JUJU, MOJO, OBIA, ZEME, ZEMI, ANITO, CHARM, OBEAH, TOTEM, GRIGRI, MASCOT, VOODOO
fetor STINK, MIASMA, STENCH
fetter CUFF, GYVE, IRON, HOBBLE, MANACLE, SHACKLE
fetus part CAUL, DOWN, LANUGO, CHORION
feud FIEF, FRAY, BROIL, AFFRAY, VENDETTA
feudal land FEOD, FEUD, FIEF, MANOR, DEMESNE, BENEFICE
feudal, opposed to AL(L)OD, AL(L)ODIUM
feudal payment HERIOT, RELIEF, TALLAGE, HEREGELD
feudal service AVERA
feudal tenant ESNE, LEUD, SERF, BORDER, COTTER, VASSAL, COTTIER, SOCAGER
fever AGUE, CAUMA, PYREXIA, TERTIANA
feverish HECTIC, FEBRILE, PYRETIC
few CURN, CURRAN
fez *see* CAP
fiber NOIL, STAPLE, STRANT, THREAD, NATURE
fiber plant ALOE, FLAX, HEMP, IXLE, SANA, SUNN, CAROA, ISTLE, IXTLE, RAMIE, SISAL, COTTON
fibers, man-made ARNEL, DYNEL, FIBRO, KODEL, LYCRA, NYLON, ORLON, RAYON, VELON, ARALAC, DACRON, DYNELO, LASTEX, TYCORA, VICARA, VINYON, ACETATE, ACRILAN, FORTREL, SARELON, SPANDEX, TREVIRA, CAPROLAN, CELANESE, FIBREFAX, FORTISAN, REVOLITE, REXENITE, FIBERGLAS, POLYESTER
fibers, natural BON, ADAD, BAST, COIR, ERUC, FERU, FLAX, HEMP, IMBE, JUTE, KEMP, MUGA, PIMA, PITA, RHEA, SILK, SUNN, TRAM, WOOL, AVACA, CAPOC, DATIL, FLOSS, ISTLE, IXTLE, KAPOK, KENAF, LISLE, OLONA, RAMIE, SISAL, TERAP, TWIST, AMBARY, ANGORA, COTTON, PEELER, RAFFIA, STAPLE, THREAD, ESPARTO, FILASSE, WHIPCORD
fickle ERRATIC, VOLATILE, INCONSTANT
fiction LIE, TALE, YARN, NOVEL, FIGMENT
fictitious BOGUS, FALSE, UNREAL, MYTHICAL, SPURIOUS
fiddle *see* STRING INSTRUMENT
fidgety NERVOUS, RESTIVE, RESTLESS
field LEA, ACRE, AGER, PADI, RAND, WONG, CROFT, GLEVE, RANGE, ROWEN, CAMPUS, DOMAIN, SPHERE, SAVANNA
field glass(es) BINOCLE, TELESCOPE, BINOCULARS
fiend *see* DEMON
fierce WILD, SAVAGE, VIOLENT
fiesta *see* FESTIVAL
fig BIT, FEG, FICO, FIGO, AMATE, BREBA, ELEME, ELEMI, FICUS, PIPAL, PIPUL, CARICA, PEEPAL, PEEPUL
fight BOUT, CLEM, DUEL, FEUD, FRAY, TILT, BRAWL, JOUST, MELEE, SCRAP, SETTO, AFFRAY, BARNEY, FRACAS, RUMPUS, RUCTION, SCUFFLE
fighter SPAD, ZERO, BOXER, WARRIOR, PUGILIST
figurative FLORID, ORNATE, FLOWERY, SYMBOLIC ALLEGORIC
figure of speech IRONY, TROPE, SIMILE, ZEUGMA, LITOTES, EPITROPE, METAPHOR, METONYMY, OXYMORON, HENDIADYS, HYPERBOLE
Fiji discoverer TASMAN
filament BRIN, DOWL, HAIR,

HARL, FIBER, HARLE, ELATER, FIBRIL, STRAND, TUNGSTEN
filbert HAZEL(NUT)
filch NIM, LIFT, PINCH, SWIPE
file RASP, CARLET, RECORD, DOSSIER, QUANNET
Filipino *see* PHILIPPINE
fill PAD, GLUT, SLATE, GORGE, STUFF
fillet ORLE, SNOOD, LISTER, REGULA, TAENIA
film BRAT, SCUM, XRAY, LAYER, MOVIE, CINEMA, PATINA, TALKIE, FEATURE
film term PAN, CLIP, REEL, SYNC, DOLLY, CREDIT, MOVIOLA
filter OOZE, SEEP, SIEVE, PURIFY, STRAIN
filth DIRT, MUCK, SMUT, GRIME
final LAST, TELIC, ULTIMATE
financial FISCAL, MONETARY
finch FINK, KATE, PAPE, JOREE, JUNCO, SERIN, SPINK, TARIN, TERIN, TWITE, BURION, CANARY, LINNET, ROLLER, SISKIN, TOWHEE, BUNTING, CHEWINK, ORTOLAN, REDPOLL, CARDINAL, GROSBEAK, HAWFINCH, LONGSPUR, SNOWBIRD, CROSSBILL
find DETECT, LOCATE, LIGHTON
fine CRO, LEVY, RARE, ABWAB, MULCT, AMERCE, IMPOST, MINUTE, SCONCE, GALANAS
Fingal relative MORNA, COMHAL, FERGUS, OSSIAN
Fingal's kingdom MORVEN
Fingal's sword LUNO
finger HOOF, DIGIT, INDEX, THUMB, PINKY, DACTYL, MEDIUS, POLLEX, THENAR, KNUCKLE, MINIMUS, POINTER
finger, part of NAIL, LUNULA, LUNULE, UNGUAL, UNGUIS, PHALANX
fingerprint ARCH, LOOP, WHORL
finial EPI, TEE, TOP, APEX
finicky FUSSY, DAINTY, PRISSY
finish END, WIN, SHOW, PLACE, ENDING, FINALE
finjan holder ZARF
Finland SUOMI
Finland, pert. to SUOMIC, SUOMISH
Finnish bath SAUNA
Finnish language *see* FINNO-UGRIC
Finnish measure KANNU, TUNNA, TUNLAND
Finnish money PENNI, MARKKA
Finno-Ugric language KOMI, LAPP, VEPS, KAREL, VOGUL, MAGYAR, OSTYAK, VOTYAK, ZYRIAN, FINNISH, LAPPISH, MORDVIN, PERMIAN, CHEREMIS, ESTONIAN, KARELIAN, LIVONIAN, HUNGARIAN
fir ABIES, SAPIN, BALSAM
fire AGNI, CHAR, ELAN, SACK, IGNIS, ANNEAL, IGNITE, KINDLE
fire god AGNI, ATAR, LOKI, SIVA, KAMA, VESTA, VULCAN
fire worshiper PARSE, GHEBER, PARSEE
firearm *see* GUN, RIFLE
fireman VAMP, STOKER
fireplace FOGON, GRATE, INGLE, HEARTH
fireplace part HOB, JAMB, SPIT, GRATE, JAMBE, SHELF, TONGS, FENDER, HEARTH, MANTEL, ANDIRON, FIREDOG, REREDOS
firewood LENA, FAGOT, BILLET, FAGGOT
fireworks CAP, BOMB, GERB(E), SQUIB, FIZGIG, PETARD, RIPRAP, ROCKET, SALUTE, TORPEDO
firm MUI, FAST, HARD, RIGID, TIGHT, STANCH, COMPANY, STAUNCH
firmament SKY, VAULT, WELKIN
firn ICE, NEVE, SNOW
first CHIEF, DEBUT, PRIME, PRIMAL, CAPITAL, INITIAL, ORIGINAL
firstborn AYNE, EIGNE
first-class ACE, AONE, TOPS, DELUXE, PALMARY
firth ARM, KYLE, FIORD, FJORD
fish FIN, ANGLE, DRAIL, TRAWL, TROLL, SEARCH
fish, cyprinoid *see* CARP
fish, fly for HARL, HERL, SEDGE, CAHILL, CLARET, HACKLE
fish, fossil DIPNOI, ELLOPS, DIPNOAN
fish, marine CUSK, HAKE, LING, SCUP, SHAD, GRUNT, SKATE, BLENNY, BONITO, TARPON

fish measure MEASE
fish sauce ALEC, GARUM
fish, small FRY, BRIT, DACE, SMELT, SPRAT, DARTER, MINNOW, SARDINE
fisherman EELER, SQUAM, ANGLER, NETTER, SEINER, WEIRER, PISCATOR,
fishes FRY, HAG, BARB, CAJI, GOBY, HUSS, LANT, MAPO, OPAH, RAUN, SAPO, SILE, TANG, CRAVO, HOUND, LANCE, MIDGE, SCROD, SKATE, TETRA, ANGLER, BICHIR, CARIBE, DORADO, MYXINE, POPEYE, REDFIN, REMORA, SLIMER, TAILER, WEEVER, AROWANA, CHALACO, FOXFISH, HAGFISH, JUGULAR, LOPHIID, MUDHAKE, PEGADOR, PIRHANA, POISSON, POMFRET, RATTAIL, SANDEEL, SURGEON, TELEOST, XIPHIAS, CHARACIN, DRAGONET, HUMANTIN, PIRARUCU, GRENADIER; *see* BARRACUDA, BASS, BLENNY, BOWFIN, CARP, CATFISH, COD, EEL, FLOUNDER, GAR, GROUPER, GUPPY, GURNARD, HERRING, MACKEREL, MINNOW, PERCH, PIKE, PUFFER, RAY, SALMON, SHARK, SILVERSIDES, STURGEON, TARPON, TROUT, WHITEFISH, WRASSE
fishhook FLY, GIG, BARB, GAFF, DRAIL, KIRBY, FIZGIG, SPROAT
fishing equipment BOB, NET, ROD, BUNT, FLEW, FLUE, FYKE, GAFF, GILL, HERL, PIRN, POLE, REEL, TROT, WEEL, WEIR, CREEL, DRAKE, FLOAT, NYMPH, QUILL, SEINE, SNELL, TRAWL, TROLL, BULTER, EELPOT, TACKLE, TONKIN, BOULTER, HARPOON, SPILLER, TRAMMEL
fissure RENT, RIFT, RIMA, RIME, SLIT, CHASM, CHINK, CLEFT, SULCUS
fist(s) NIEF, MITT, DUKES, NIEVE, MAULEY
fit APT, FAY, PET, HUFF, MESH, NEST, RIPE, SUIT, ADAPT, EQUIP, FADGE, SPELL, SPASM, OUTFIT, TANTRUM
five CEE, FIN, VEE, FIVER, PEDRO, MASHIE, PENTAD, QUINTET
Five Civilized Nations CREEK, CHOCTAW, CHEROKEE, SEMINOLE, CHICKASAW
Five Nations CAYUGA, MOHAWK, ONEIDA, SENECA, ONONDAGA
five-year period LUSTER, LUSTRUM
fix SET, MEND, FREEZE, REPAIR, SETTLE
fixation MANIA, OBSESSION
fixed-income person RENTIER
flaccid LAX, LIMP, FLABBY
flag ALEM, FANE, IRIS, JACK, SINK, BRUTE, ROGER, BANNER, BURGEE, COLORS, CORNET, ENSIGN, FANION, GUIDON, PENNON, BUNTING, PENNANT, BANDEROL, GONFALON, STANDARD, BANDEROLE
flag part FLY, FIELD, UNION, CANTON
flagellants ALBI
flagon EWER, STOUP, CARAFE
flagrant RANK, CRYING, GLARING, EGREGIOUS
flagstone SHALE, SLATE, PAVING
flail BEAT, THRESH
flake CHIP, RACK, FLECK, SCALE, SPALL, SPAWL, LAMINA
flank LEER, LISK, LOIN, SIDE
flap LAP, TAB, TAG, LOMA, SLAT, LAPPET, FLUTTER
flare FUSE, BLAZE, FUSEE, SPLAY, TORCH, SIGNAL
flash BOLT, LEVIN, SPEED, SPURT, DAZZLE
flashlight TORCH
flashy GAUDY, SHOWY, RAFFISH
flask OLPE, BETTY, CRUSE, GIRBA, FIASCO, FLACON, FLAGON, MATARA, CANTEEN, COSTREL, MATRASS
flat MOL, EVEN, BROKE, LEVEL, MOLLE, PLANE, STALE, SUITE, OBLATE, PLANATE
flatfish *see* RAY, FLOUNDER
flatten out CLAP, PLATTEN
flatter OIL, FAWN, PALP, TOADY, ADULATE
flatterer TOADY, SYCOPHANT
flattery OIL, BLARNEY, PALAVER

flavor GUST, LACE, TANG, AROMA, SAPOR, SAVOR, SEASON
flavorful SAPID
flavoring MINT, ANISE, ONION, TANSY, BURNET, CICELY, FENNEL, GINGER, BITTERS, EXTRACT, JUNIPER, SAFFRON, VANILLA, CINNAMON, ESTRAGON, GALANGAL, LAVENDER, LICORICE, TARRAGON, VANILLIN; *see* HERB, SPICE
flavorless FLAT, VAPID
flaw RIFT, BREAK, FAULT, DEFECT
flax TOW, FLIX, LINUM
flax, prepare RET
flaxlike TOWY
flea LOP, FLECH, FLECK, CHIGOE, JIGGER, PODURA, REDBUG, CHIGGER, PULICID
flea genus PULEX, DAPHNIA
Fledermaus character ADELE, FALKE, FRANK, ALFRED
flee LAM, RUN, BOLT, DECAMP, DESERT
fleece ABB, NAP, PILE, SKIN, WOOL, MULCT, SHEAR, SWINDLE
fleet FAST, NAVY, ARGOSY, ARMADA, ARMADO, FLOTILLA
flemish COIL; *see* DUTCH
flesh BODY, PULP; *see* MEAT
fleshy FAT, PULPY, CARNAL, SARCOUS
flexible LITHE, WITHY, LIMBER, LISSOM, PLIANT, SUPPLE, LISSOME, TENSILE
flier ACE, PILOT, PLUNGE
flight HOP, ROUT, EXODUS, HEGIRA, SCUTTLE, STAMPEDE; *see* BEVY
flight, put to ROUT
flighty BARMY, GIDDY, FRIVOLOUS
flimsy SLIM, FRAIL, SLIGHT
flinch SHY, QUAIL, BLENCH
fling CAST, DART, HURL
flint CHERT; *see* ROCK
flintlock FUSIL; *see* RIFLE
flip PERT, SNAP, TOSS
flippant BOLD, GLIB, PERT, SASSY, SAUCY, BRASSY
flirt FLIP, OGLE, WINK, COQUET
flit GAD, DART, SKIM
float BOB, BUOY, CORK, RAFT, SWIM, WAFT, DRIFT, PONTOON
floating AWASH, ADRIFT, NATANT
flock HERD, PACK, BROOD, DROVE, HORDE, SHOAL, SWARM, TROOP, HIRSEL; *see* BEVY
flog CAT, TROUNCE; *see* BEAT
flood SEA, BORE, TIDE, EAGRE, SPATE, DELUGE, FRESHET
floodgate CLOW, SLUICE
floor LEVEL, STORY, PLANCH, STOREY, ENTRESOL, MEZZANINE
flora and fauna BIOTA
Florence family MEDICI
florid ROSY, GAUDY, SHOWY, ORNATE
Florida fish BONACI, BONITO, TARPON, TETARD, GROUPER, SNAPPER, MACKEREL
Florida information *see p. 308*
Florida tree MABI, ACOMA, JOCUM, BUSTIC, JOCUMA
flotilla FLEET, ARMADA
Flotow opera MARTHA
flounder(-like fish) DAB, BUTT, SOLE, BRILL, FLUKE, WHIFF, WITCH, PLAICE, TURBOT, DABLOID, HALIBUT, PETRALE, TOPKNOT
flour AT(T)A, MEAL, FARINA, PINOLE
flourish WAX, FLAUNT, PARAPH, THRIVE, FANFARE, FUSTIAN, ROULADE, TANTARA, TANTIVY
flow RUN, FLUX, ISSUE, SPOUT
flower CYME, BLOOM, CREAM, ELITE, SPIKE, UMBEL, CORYMB, RACEME, BLOSSOM, PANICLE, THYRSUS; *see* FLOWERS
flower arrangement IKEBANA
flower part KNOT, STEM, AMENT, BRACT, CALYX, OVARY, OVULE, PETAL, SEPAL, STYLE, ANTHER, CARPEL, PISTIL, POLLEN, SPADIX, SPATHE, STAMEN, STIGMA, COROLLA, EPICARP, EXOCARP, PETIOLE, FILAMENT, PERICARP
flowers RUE, BETA, BIXA, BLOB, HOYA, INGA, LOTE, NAMA, POKE, POSY, ROSE, SANG, ULEX, WOAD, YAJE, YUCA,

ASPIC, ASTER, AVENS, BADAN, BLUET, BUGLE, CAJUN, CAMAS, CUMAY, DALEA, DWALE, GUAMA, HELIO, ILIMA, INULA, ISOTE, IZOTE, LAYIA, LUPIN, MESEM, MILLA, NANCE, ORACH, OXEYE, SEDUM, SOTOL, TULIP, ADONIS, AZALEA, CAMASH, CAMASS, COLEUS, COLIMA, COSMOS, DAHLIA, IBERIS, INDIGO, IPOMEA, JASMIN, KISSME, LUPINE, LYCIUM, NANCHE, ORACHE, ORPINE, OXALIS, SPIREA, SPURRY, SUMACH, TEASEL, THRIFT, VIOLET, ZINNIA, BEGONIA, BOUQUET, BOXWOOD, CAMPION, CASSAVA, FLYTRAP, FUCHSIA, GENTIAN, GINSENG, HEMLOCK, HENBANE, HONESTY, IPOMOEA, JASMINE, JUNIPER, LOBELIA, NOSEGAY, QUAMASH, RAGWEED, SOLANUM, SPIRAEA, SPURREY, VERBENA, BLUEBELL, CAMELLIA, FOXGLOVE, HAREBELL, HYACINTH, HYDROLEA, LOTEBUSH, MARIGOLD, POKEWEED, SATINPOD, TIDYTIPS

fluctuate VEER, WAVE(R), VIBRATE

flue DUCT, FUNNEL, CHIMNEY

fluent FREE, GLIB, FACILE, COPIOUS

fluff NAP, DOWN, FLOC, LINT, PUFF, FLOSS, PRIMP, MISCUE

fluid GAS, SAP, FLUX, SERUM, LIQUOR, PLASTIC

fluidity unit RHE

fluke BARB, HOOK, CLEEK

flume RACE, CHUTE, GORGE, SHUTE, SLUICE

flunky SNOB, GOFER, LACKEY, MENIAL

flurry ADO, STIR, GUST

flush GLOW, BLUSH, PLANE, DRENCH, LAVISH

flute GROOVE; *see* WIND INSTRUMENT

fluting PIPING, CHAMFER, GADROON

flutter FLAP, FLIP, FLIT, WAVE, HOVER, BUSTLE, QUIVER

fly DUN, GAD, KED, CLEG, GNAT, ZIMB, CLEGG, DRAKE, MIDGE, MUSCA, OXBOT, OXFLY, PERLA, SALLY, SEDGE, SERUT, STOUT, WHAME, ZABUB, ASILID, BEEFLY, BOTFLY, BREEZE, CADDIS, DOBSON, GADFLY, MIDGET, MUSCID, NITTER, PALMER, PERLID, PHORID, PUNKIE, SAWFLY, SEROOT, TSETSE, UJIFLY, BLOWFLY, CHALCID, CONOPID, CULICID, GALLFLY, GOUTFLY, HORNFLY, TIPULID, APPLEFLY, BEELOUSE, BIRDTICK, BLACKFLY, CRANEFLY, FRUITFLY, HORNTAIL, HOUSEFLY, ONIONFLY, PANORPID, STONEFLY, TATUKIRA; *see* FISH

fly genus PHORA, ASILUS, CEPHID, MUSCAE, TIPULA, DIOPSIS

fly, to DART, FLAP, FLIT, SCUD, SOAR, WHIR, WING, GLIDE, AVIATE

flycatcher PINA, PEWEE, PITTA, BECARD, PEEWEE, PHOEBE, PIPIRI, TYRANT, YETAPA, COTINGA, TOMFOOL, KINGBIRD, KINGTODY

flying saucer UFO

foam BARM, FIZZ, FUME, SCUM, SUDS, FROTH, SPUME

focus HUB, AXIS, CORE, CRUX, NUCLEUS

fodder HAY, GRAM, OATS, BARIT, FORGE, STRAW, VETCH, SILAGE, STOVER, ENSILAGE; *see* FORAGE

foe *see* ENEMY

fog RAG, HAZE, MIST, MURK, ROKE, SMOG, BEDIM, BRUME

foghorn SIREN(E)

foil BALK, EPEE, STUMP, BAFFLE, BANANA, DEFEAT, STOOGE

fold LAP, PEN, PLY, COTE, FAIL, FLAP, PLIE, RUGA, TUCK, CRIMP, DRAPE, FLOCK, PLAIT, PLEAT, PLICA, CREASE

foist FOB, PALM

folded RUGATE, PLICATE

foliage LEAFAGE, UMBRAGE

folk RACE, NATION, PEOPLE

folkway(s) MOS, MORES, CUSTOM(S)

follow DOG, HEEL, OBEY, TAIL, CHASE, ENSUE, HOUND, STALK, TRACE, TRAIL

follower IST, ITE, APER, BUFF, HEELER, VOTARY, ADHERENT
folly LUNACY, FATUITY
foment ABET, BREW, SPUR
fondness GRA, LOVE
font BOWL, TYPE, BASIN, LAVER, STOUP, ORIGIN, SOURCE, SPRING
food KAI, CHOW, DIET, EATS, FARE, GRUB, MENU, MESS, CATES, MANNA, SNACK, TABLE, AMRITA, FORAGE, PABLUM, TEREFA, TEREFE, VIANDS, ALIMENT, CUISINE, AMBROSIA, VICTUALS; *see* MENU
food fish COD, EEL, BASS, CARP, CERO, HAKE, LING, PIKE, SCUP, SHAD, SOLE, TUNA, HILSA, PERCH, SCROD, SMELT, SNOOK, TROUT, TUNNY, MULLET, PLAICE, ROBALO, SALMON, TURBOT, ALEWIFE, HALIBUT, HERRING, POMPANO, SARDINE, SNAPPER, MACKEREL
fool ASS, OAF, SAP, DOLT, JERK, RACA, SIMP, ZANY, CLOWN, DUMMY, DUNCE, NINNY, JESTER
foolish RASH, DAFT, ZANY, INANE, SILLY, HARISH, ASININE
foot PAD, PAW, PES, PUD, CHECK, IAMB, ARSIS, IONIC, TOTAL, DACTYL, IAMBIC, IAMBUS, ANAPEST, SPONDEE, TROCHEE, CHORIAMB, TRIBRACH
foot ailment CORN, WART, BUNION, CALLUS
foot part TOE, ARCH, HEEL, INCH, SOLE, VOLA, PELMA, INSTEP, TOENAIL
football RUGBY, RUGGER, SOCCER, BLADDER, PIGSKIN
football players and coaches OJ, GIP(PER), RAY, BELL, CARR, HEIN, MARA, OWEN, SIMS, BAUGH, BLOOD, BROWN, BUREN, CLARK, FOUTS, GUYON, HALAS, HEALY, HENRY, JONES, LAYNE, LYMAN, NEALE, STAGG, STARR, ALBERT, BLANDA, DORAIS, DUBLEY, FRIDGE, GRAHAM, GRANGE, HARRIS, HERBER, HESTON, HEWITT, HINGLE, HUGHES, HUTSON, ISBELL, LITTLE, MCAFEE, NESSER, NEVERS, PAYTON, ROCKNE, RODNEY, ROZIER, STRONG, THORPE, TITTLE, TURNER, UNITAS, WALKER, WARNER, ZUPPKE, BATTLES, CONERLY, EDWARDS, FOREMAN, GABRIEL, HORNUNG, HORWEEN, HUBBARD, LAMBEAU, LEEMANS, LUCKMAN, MAYNARD, MCNALLY, MONTANA, SIMPSON, STANTON, TRAFTON, CAMPBELL, STAUBACH
football teams JETS, RAMS, BEARS, BILLS, COLTS, LIONS, BROWNS, CHIEFS, EAGLES, GIANTS, OILERS, SAINTS
football term END, RUN, DOWN, KICK, PASS, PLAY, PUNT, BLOCK, GUARD, CENTER, ELEVEN, ONSIDE, SAFETY, TACKLE, LATERAL, OFFSIDE
footing TOEHOLD
footless APOD(AL)
footlike PEDATE
footman VALET, LACKEY, MENIAL, FLUNKEY
footnote GLOSS, APOSTIL, COMMENT
footnote marker OBELUS, ASTERISK
footpad HOOD, THUG, WHYO, BANDIT, BRIGAND
footstalk STRIG, PEDICEL
footstool MORA, CRICKET, HASSOCK, OTTOMAN, TABORET
fop BEAU, DUDE, DANDY, SWELL
forage ERS, GUAR, RAID, PROG, RAPE, GRASS, SULLA, ALSIKE, LUCERN, MARAUD, RUSSUD, ALFALFA, BERSEEM; *see* FODDER
foray RAID, SALLY, INROAD, MARAUD
forbear HOLD, CEASE, PAUSE, DESIST, ABSTAIN
forbid BAN, TABU, VETO, DEBAR, TABOO, ENJOIN
forbidden TABU, TREF, TABOO, T(E)REFA, ILLICIT
forbidden city LHASA, MECCA, PEKING
forbidding GRIM, STERN
force VIM, VIS, ARMY, BIOD, BIRR, DINT, ELOD, ODYL,

CORPS, DRIVE, IMPEL, POSSE, SINEW, VIGOR, COMPEL, DURESS, ENERGY, PANTOD
force, unit of DYNE, NEWTON, POUNDAL
forceps TONGS, PINCERS, NIPPERS
foreboding OMEN, PALL, AUGURY, PRESAGE
forecaster TOUT, TIPSTER, DOPESTER
forefather SIRE, ANCESTOR
forego DENY, WAIVE, RESIGN
forehead BROW, SINCIPUT
foreign words *see p. 264*
foreigner ALIEN, HAOLE, EMIGRE, GRINGO, OUTSIDER
foremost part BOW, VAN, ACRON, FRONT, LEADING
forerun SCOUT, HERALD, PIONEER, PRELUDE
foresee DIVINE, PREDICT
foreskin PREPUCE
forest GAPO, WOLD, ARDEN, COPSE, GROVE, GUBAT, SELVA, SILVA, TAIGA, WEALD, WOODS, SHERWOOD
forest, pert. to SILVAN, SYLVAN, NEMORAL
foretell BODE, SPAE, AUGUR, INSEE, PREDICT, PRESAGE
forever AKE, AYE, EER, ETERN(E)
forfeit KEN, FINE, LOSE, LAPSE, DEODAND
forge ANVIL, SHAPE, SMITHY, STITHY, FALSIFY, BLOOMERY, COUNTERFEIT
forgetfulness LETHE, AMNESIA, OBLIVION
forgive REMIT, EXCUSE, PARDON
forgiving CLEMENT, PLACABLE
fork DIG, PAY, PRONG, BRANCH, CROTCH, FURCATE, JUNCTION
forked BIFID, CLEFT, ZIGZAG, FURCATE, LITUATE
forlorn BEREFT
form MOLD, RUPA, BLANK, EIDOS, MODEL, RITUAL, TAILLE
form, pert. to MODAL
formal BALL, PRIM, PROM, STIFF, DISTANT
formalism PUNCTILIO
formality FORMULA, REDTAPE, CEREMONY, PROTOCOL, PROPRIETY
formation FILE, LINE, BIOME, HERSE, ORDER, COLUMN ECHELON
former(ly) EX, NEE, ERST, ONCE, PRIOR, QUONDAM
former days ELD, PAST, YORE
formless ARUPA
Formosa TAIWAN
formula LAW, LURRY, MANTRA, RECIPE
Forseti's father BALDER
Forseti palace GLITNIR
fort DIX, DUN, ORD, PAH, COTA, DOON, KEEP, KNOX, KOTA, POST, COTTA, HENRY, CASTLE, DONJON, SCONCE, SUMTER, ALCAZAR, CITADEL, BASTILLE, MARTELLO
forthwith NOW, ANON, (EFT)SOON
fortification LIS(S), REDAN, TALUS, ABATIS, BASTION, RAMPART, RAVELIN, REDOUBT
fortuitous CHANCE
fortunate SRI, ROSY, SHRI, BLEST, FAUST, SHREE, DEXTER
fortune HAP, LOT, BAHI, FATE, TYCHE, RICHES, WEALTH
fortune-teller SEER, AUGUR, GYPSY, SIBYL, ORACLE, PALMIST, SPAEMAN, HARUSPEX
forum *see* ASSEMBLY
forward BOLD, SEND, SHIP, AHEAD, BRAZEN, TRANSMIT
fossil DOLITE, PINITE, CRINITE, CALAMITE, DINOSAUR
foster REAR, CHERISH, PROMOTE
foul RANK, VILE, NASTY, FILTHY
foulmouthed PROFANE
foul-smelling OLID, FETID, REEKY, NOISOME
found SET, CAST, BASE, MOLD, ENDOW
foundation BED, BASE, BASIS, CORSET, GIRDLE, RIPRAP, BEDROCK
foundling WAIF, EPPIE
fountain JET, FONS, FONT, SYKE, WELL, BIMINI, SOURCE, SPRING
Four H, meaning HEAD, HANDS, HEART, HEALTH

Four Horsemen WAR, DEATH, FAMINE, LAYDEN, MILLER, CROWLEY, PESTILENCE, STUHLDREHER
fourscore EIGHTY
fowl HEN, COCK, DUCK, GUAN, JACU, KEET, MITU, RYPE, BIDDY, CAPON, KOKLA, LOWAN, MALEO, BANTAM, BRAHMA, BRAMAH, GROUSE, HOUDAN, LEIPOA, PIGEON, PULLET, SULTAN, TURKEY, CHICKEN, DORKING, GALEENY, GOBBLER, LEGHORN, MEGAPOD, MOORHEN, PEACOCK, CURASSOW, PHEASANT, PARTRIDGE, PTARMIGAN
fowl genus CRAX, PIPILE, ORTALUS, RASORES
fox TOD, KIT, ASSE, CAAMA, SWIFT, VIXEN, ZERDA, BAGMAN, CORSAC, FENNEC, LOWRIE, RENARD
fox genus VULPES
foxy SLY, WILY, CRAFTY, VULPINE
fracas *see* FIGHT
fraction PART, SCRAP, MOIETY, ALIQUOT, DECIMAL, SEGMENT
fractious UNRULY, PEEVISH
fragile FRAIL, BRITTLE
fragment ANA, BIT, ORT, SNIP, WISP, SCRAP, SHARD, SHERD
fragrant BALMY, OLENT, SWEET, SCENTED, AROMATIC
frailty SIN, FLAW, FAULT, FOIBLE
frame(work) RACK, SESS, CADRE, HERSE, TRUSS, TENTER, CHASSIS, STENTER, TABORET, TRESSEL, TRESTLE
France GAUL; *see* FRENCH
franchise SOC, SOKE, VOTE, LICENSE
frank BLUNT, NAIVE, EXEMPT
Frankenstein author SHELLEY
frankfurter HOTDOG, WIENER
frankincense THUS, OLIBANUM
Frankish king PEPIN, CLOVIS, CHARLEMAGNE
Frankish vassal LEUD, LITUS
Franks, pert. to SALIC
fraud CON, FAKE, HOAX, JAPE, RUSE, SHAM, BUNCO, COVIN, COZENAGE
fraught BESET, LADEN
fray CHAFE, RAVEL; *see* FIGHT
freak WHIM, QUIRK, CAPRICE
freckle LENTIGO
free RID, CLEAR, LOOSE, EXEMPT, GRATIS, LOOSEN, MANUMIT
freedman LAET, LATIN, THANE
free-for-all CLEM, FRAY, MELEE, SETTO, RUMBLE
freeman CEORL, CHURL, THANE, THEGN, VILLEIN
freeze ICE, NIP, CHILL, GELATE, CONGEAL
freight CARGO, LADING
French GALLIC, ROMANCE
French leader BLUM, COTY, HUGH, AURIOL, CARNOT, DOUMER, LEBRUN, PETAIN, PHILIP, THIERS, DEGAULLE, MACMAHON, POINCARE, POMPIDOU, DOUMERGUE, MITTERAND
French measure POT, LIEUE, LIGNE, MINOT, PINTE, ARPENT, HEMINE, PERCHE, CHOPINE, POISSON
French money ECU, SOL, SOU, AGNEL, FRANC, LIARD, LOUIS, OBOLE, BESANT, CENTIME, SOLIDUS, NAPOLEON
French native BRETON, GASCON, NORMAN
French Revolution leader MARAT, CLOOTS, DANTON, HEBERT
French Revolution month *see p. 340*
French royal family CAPET, VALOIS, BOURBON, CAROLINGIAN
French ruler ODO, HUGH, EUDES, HENRY, LOUIS, CHARLES; *see* FRANKISH
French weight GROS, MARC, ONCE, LIVRE, TONNE
French words *see p. 265*
frenzy AMOK, FUROR, MANIA
frequent OFT, HAUNT, HABITUAL
fresh RAW, FLIP, PERT, BRISK, NOVEL, SASSY, SPICK, VIVID
freshet FLOOD, SPATE
freshman FROSH, PLEBE, NOVICE
fret FUSS, STEW, CHAFE, WORRY
Frey's home ALFHEIM
Frey's wife GERDA
Freya relative FREY, ODIN, NJORD

friar FRA, MONK, TUCK, ABBOT, FRATER, LISTER, SERVITE
Friday source FRIGGA
friend AMI, AMY, DOG, PAL, AMIE, CHUM, KITH, MATE, AMIGO, BUDDY, CRONY, DAMON, QUAKER, ACHATES, PYTHIAS
friendship AMITY, COMITY
Frigg relative VE, ODIN, FULLA, BALDER
fright(en) AWE, FLEY, FUNK, GAST, ALARM, PANIC, SCARE
frightful GRIM, SCARY, FEARFUL, GHASTLY
frigid ICY, COLD, FORMAL, GLACIAL
frill RUFF, JABOT, RUCHE, RUFFLE, FALBALA, FLOUNCE, FURBELOW
fringe EDGE, LOMA, THRUM, BORDER, TASSEL
frisk CAPER, FROLIC, GAMBOL, SEARCH, TITTUP
frivolous PETTY, SILLY, TRIVIAL
frog RANA, FROSH, FROSK, PEEPER, AGLOSSA, HYLIDAE, PADDOCK, TADPOLE, BULLFROG, FERREIRO, LINGUATA; *see* TOAD
frolic DIDO, LARK, PLAY, CAPER, SPORT, SPREE
front VAN, FACE, FORE, DUMMY, FACADE, STOOGE, OBVERSE
frontal METOPIC
frontiersman CODY, EARP, BOONE, BOWIE, CLARK, LOGAN, CARSON, CROCKETT, HICKOK
frost ICE, HOAR, RIME
froth FOAM, SCUM, SUDS, SPUME, YEAST, LATHER
frown LOUR, LOWER, SCOWL, GLOWER, GRIMACE
frozen ICY, FRORE, GELID, GLACE, FRAPPE
frozen dessert ICE, FRAPPE, MOUSSE, SORBET, SHERBET, SPUMONI
frugal CHARY, SPARE, THRIFTY
fruit NUT, CONE, CROP, PEPO, POME, AKENE, BERRY, DRUPE, GOURD, YIELD, ACHENE, AECIUM, LEGUME, LOMENT, NUTLET, PROFIT, TELIUM, DESSERT, ETAERIO, SILICLE, SILIQUE, SYNCARP, UTRICLE; *see* FRUITS
fruitcake SIMNEL
fruitless VAIN, BARREN, STERILE
fruits FIG, HAW, HIP, DATE, LIME, PAPA, PEAR, PLUME, POME, SLOE, SORB, ACORN, AKALA, AKELA, ANANA, ANISE, ANONA, APPLE, BAUNO, BETEL, CATES, CEDRA, COPEI, CUBEB, CUPAY, CUPEY, ETROG, GOBBE, GOURD, GRAPE, GUAVA, JAMBO, LEMON, LUFFA, MANGO, MELON, MORUS, NGAIO, OLIVE, OSAGE, PAPAW, PEACH, RIMAS, ANNONA, BANANA, BAOBAB, CEDRAT, CHERRY, CITRON, CITRUS, COFFEA, COLANE, DURIAN, ETHROG, JUJUBE, LOOFAH, LOQUAT, MEDLAR, ORANGE, PAPAIA, PAPAYA, PAWPAW, PEPPER, QUINCE, SAMARA, SQUASH, TERFEZ, TOMATO, APRICOT, AVOCADO, CARAWAY, CEDRATE, COCONUT, CUMQUAT, KUMQUAT, PUMPKIN, SOLANUM, TANGELO
frustrate DASH, FOIL, SCOTCH, THWART
fry SAUTE, FRIZZ(LE)
fuel GAS, LOG, OIL, CHIP, COAL, COKE, PEAT, PEET, WOOD, BRIQUET, CHARCOAL, KEROSENE
fugitive MAROON, ESCAPEE, RUNAWAY
fugue part DUX, COMES, PEDAL, THEME, ANSWER, STRETTO
full SATED, OROTUND, PLENARY, REPLETE
fullness PLENUM, SATIETY, SURFEIT, PLETHORA
Fulton's steamboat CLERMONT
fumble DROP, FLUB, GROPE, BUNGLE
fume FRET, RAGE, RAVE, REEK, SMELL, SMOKE
function ACT, USE, DUTY, ROLE, SINE, WORK, COSINE, TANGENT
fund STOCK, STORE, SUPPLY
fundamental BASAL, BASIC, VITAL, PRIMAL, RADICAL
funeral BURIAL, EXEQUIES
funeral director MORTICIAN

fungus BUNT, KNOT, MOLD, PUFF, PUNK, RUST, SMUT, WART, ERGOT, FOMES, IRPEX, MOREL, MOULD, MUCOR, PHOMA, PORIA, UREDO, VALSA, VERPA, YEAST, AGARIC, AMADOU, CAEOMA, FUMAGO, MILDEW, ZYTHIA, AMANITA, BLEWITS, BOLETUS, STEREUM, TRUFFLE; *see* MUSHROOM
funnies *see* CARTOON
funny ODD, COMIC, DROLL
fur CAT, DOG, FOX, KID, BEAR, CALF, FLIX, GOAT, HAIR, HARE, LAMB, LYNX, MINK, MOLE, PELT, PLEW, PONY, SEAL, SKIN, VAIR, WOLF, CIVET, FITCH, GENET, KOALA, LLAMA, OTTER, PAHMI, PANDA, SABLE, SHEEP, SKUNK, ALPACA, BADGER, BEAVER, DESMAN, ERMINE, FISHER, JACKAL, JAGUAR, MARMOT, MARTEN, MONKEY, NUTRIA, OCELOT, PELAGE, PELTRY, RABBIT, SUSLIK, VICUNA, WEASEL, WOMBAT, CARACAL, CHEETAH, CRIMMER, FITCHEW, GUANACO, HAMSTER, KARAKUL, KRIMMER, LEOPARD, MINIVER, MUSKRAT, OPOSSUM, RACCOON, WALLABY
Furies *see* ERINYES
furnace part TUE, BOSH, FAULD, GRATE, TEWEL, TUYERE
furnish CATER, ENDOW, EQUIP, PLENISH
furnishings RIG, GEAR, DECOR
furor ADO, RAGE, FRENZY
furrow RUT, PLOW, RILL, SEAM, CHASE, DRILL, RILLE, STRIA, GROOVE, SULCUS, TRENCH
furrowed RIVOSE, RUTTED
further AID, AND, TOO, YET, ABET, MORE
furtive SLY, WARY, SNEAKY
fury IRE, RAGE, WRATH
fuse FRIT, WELD, MERGE, SMELT, ANNEAL, SOLDER
fuss ADO, FIKE, STIR, TODO, PREEN, BUSTLE, FANTOD, FIDGET, POTHER
fussy PRISSY, FINICAL
futile VAIN, OTIOSE, USELESS
fylfot SWASTIKA

G

gab CHAT, MOUTH, PRATE
gable PINION, AILERON
Gabon language FRENCH; *see* BANTU
gad ROAM, ROVE, PROWL
Gad relative ERI, ARELI, ASHER, HAGGI, JACOB, ZILPAH
gadget GISMO, DINGUS, DOODAD, JIGGER, JIMJAM
gadoid *see* COD
Gaea relative CHAOS, URANUS
Gael(ic) CELT, ERSE, MANX, SCOT, IRISH, CELTIC, KELTIC, SCOTCH, GADHELIC, GOIDELIC
gaff HOAX, HOOK, SP(E)AR, FLEECE, GAMBLE
gag QUIP, CHOKE, RETCH, MUFFLE
gage PAWN, PLUM, GLOVE, WAGER
gain GET, NET, WIN, EARN, LUCRE, PROFIT
gainsay DENY, IMPUGN, REFUTE
gait RUN, LOPE, PACE, RACK, TROT, VOLT, WALK, AMBIT, AMBLE, CANTER, GALLOP, SHAMBLE
gaiters SPATS, PUTTEES, LEGGINGS
Galahad relative ELAINE, LANCELOT
Galatea's lover ACIS, PYGMALION
gale GUST, WIND, BLAST, STORM
Galilee town CANA, NAZARETH
gall VEX, BILE, FRET, RANCOR
galleon CARAC(K), CARRACK; *see* VESSEL
gallery POY, LOFT, ALURE, SALON, ARCADE, LOGGIA, PIAZZA, PUBLIC, SOLLAR, VERANDA
galley AESC, BARGE, PROOF, BIREME, DRUDGE, DROMOND, KITCHEN, TRIREME
gallic FRENCH, GAULISH
gallinaceous RASORIAL; *see* FOWL
gallop RUN, LOPE, PELT, AUBIN, TANTIVY

gallows NOOSE, GIBBET, YARDARM
Gambian language WOLOF, MANDINKA
Gambian money DALASI
gambler DICER, SHARK, SHARP, SHILL, BETTOR, PUNTER, TINHORN, SHILLABER
gambling assistant TOUT, RAKER, DEALER, CROUPIER
gambling game DICE, FARO, KENO, PICO, BINGO, MONTE, POKER, STUSS, BACCARAT, ROULETTE, BLACKJACK
gambling house RENO, CASINO, MONACO, LASVEGAS
gambol DIDO, ROMP, CAPER, FRISK, FROLIC, CURVET
game FUN, BOLD, LAME, LUDI, SPORT, FROLIC, CONTEST, PASTIME, WILLING
game bird DUCK, GUAN, RAIL, QUAIL, SNIPE, GROUSE, PLOVER, PHEASANT, PARTRIDGE
game fish BASS, CERO, SCAD, TUNA, SARGO, TROUT, BONITO, MARLIN, SALMON, TARPON
game piece DIE, PIN, MAN, BALL, TILE, TOKEN, DOMINO, COUNTER
gamekeeper RANGER, WARDEN
games GO, COB, TAG, TAW, PIG, DIBS, DICE, FARO, HOGO, KENO, LUDO, MALL, MILL, POOL, WARI, BINGO, CHESS, CRAPS, DARTS, HALMA, JACKS, LOTTO, SALVO, SHOGI, STUSS, BOCCIE, CRAMBO, GHOSTS, HAZARD, MAJONG, MERELS, POSSUM, TIVOLI, BIRLING, HANGMAN, MAHJONG, MANCALA, MARBLES, PACHISI, SNOOKER, ANAGRAMS, BACCARAT, CHARADES, CHECKERS, DOMINOES, DRAUGHTS, LEAPFROG, MAHJONGG, MONOPOLY, PALLMALL, ROULETTE, SCRABBLE, BAGATELLE, HOPSCOTCH, PARCHEESI, TITTATTOE, BACKGAMMON, BATTLESHIP, CATEGORIES, POSTOFFICE; *see* CARD GAMES, SPORTS
Gandhi title MAHATMA
gang BAND, CREW, RING, CABAL
Ganges tributary SON, GOGRA, GUNTI, GANDAK
gangster MUG, GOON, HOOD, THUG, WHYO, YEGG, TOUGH, GORILLA, HOODLUM, MAFIOSO, TORPEDO
gangway RAMP, AISLE, PLANK
gannet SULA, BOOBY, GOOSE, SOLAN, MARGOT
ganoid fish *see* GAR, BOWFIN, STURGEON
Ganymede relative ILUS, TROS
gap GULF, M(E)USE, MUSET, SHARD, BREACH, HIATUS, LACUNA
gape GAWK, OGLE, YAWN, OSCITATE
gar(-like fish) IHI, BALAO, SAURY, BELONE, BONACI, GARFISH, GARPIKE, HALFBEAK
garage MEW, CARPORT
garb *see* CLOTHING
garbage OFFAL, SWILL, TRASH, MIDDEN, REFUSE
garden EDEN, PLOT, ARBOR, GARTH, PATCH, HERBARY, OLITORY, ORCHARD
Garden City CHICAGO
garden tool HOE, HOSE, RAKE, SPADE, DIBBLE, TROWEL
garland LEI, ANADEM, FILLET, WREATH, CHAPLET, FESTOON
garlic MOLY, RAMSON
garment ROBING; *see* CLOTHING
garnish DECK, LARD, TRIM, BEDECK, RELISH
garret LOFT, ATTIC, SOLER
garrison POST, PRESIDIO
gas BRAG, DAMP, DRUG, FUEL, NEON, EXAN, ARGON, ETHER, ETHYL, FREON, OXANE, RADON, XENON, ARSINE, BUTANE, FLATUS, HELIUM, KETONE, ETHANE, PETROL, BENZENE, KRYPTON, METHANE, PROPANE, STIBINE, FLUORINE, PHOSGENE
gasoline NAPALM, PETROL(EUM)
gasp PANT, WHEEZE
gastropod *see* SNAIL
gate BAB, SPRUE; *see* DOOR
gateway DAR, PYLON, TORAN, TORII, SLUICE, TORANA
Gath hero GOLIATH
gather LEK, CULL, AMASS, GLEAN, PLAIT, SHEVE, SHIRR,

GARNER, MUSTER, SHEAVE, COLLATE
gaudy SHOWY, FLASHY, GARISH, TAWDRY
Gaulish people REMI, CELTS, BELGAE, SEQUANI
gaunt SICKLY, HAGGARD; *see* LEAN
gauze LENO, CREPE, LISSE, MARLI, TULLE, BAREGE, TISSUE, CHIFFON
Gawain relative LOT, GARETH, GAHERIS, MORDRED, AGRAVAIN
gay AIRY, HAPPY, JOLLY, MERRY, RIANT, JOCUND, LIVELY
gaze GAWK, OGLE, PEER, STARE
gazelle *see* ANTELOPE
Gdansk DANZIG
gear CAM, COG, KIT, GARB, DUFFEL, PINION, TACKLE
gelastic RISIBLE
gelatin AGAR, ASPIC, COLLIN, COLLOID
gem ICE, JET, JADE, ONYX, OPAL, RUBY, SARD, AGATE, AMBER, BALAS, BERYL, CAMEO, PEARL, PRASE, TOPAZ, GARNET, IOLITE, JASPER, LIGURE, MUFFIN, PLASMA, PYROPE, SCARAB, SPINEL, BURMITE, DIAMOND, EMERALD, PERIDOT, HEMATITE, SAPPHIRE; *see* JEWEL, STONE
gem face BEZEL, CULET, FACET, TABLE
gem setting OUCH, PAVE, BEZEL, CHATON
Gem State ID, IDAHO
Gemini TWINS, CASTOR, POLLUX
gender SEX, BEGET, NEUTER
genealogy TREE, LINAGE, DESCENT, LINEAGE, PEDIGREE
general USUAL, COMMON, PANDEMIC, INCLUSIVE, UNIVERSAL
generals BOR, GRANT, ANDERS, PATTON, BRADLEY, SHERMAN, PERSHING, SHERIDAN, MACARTHUR; *see* CIVIL WAR
generator DYNAMO
genie *see* DEMON
Genoese family DORIA
Genoese money JANE
gentile GOY, PAGAN, HEATHEN
gentle MILD, SOFT, TAME, BALMY, DOCILE, PLACID
gentlemen SER, SIR, BABU, TOFF, BABOO, SENOR, GALLANT, YOUNKER
genus *see* CLASS
geode VUG, VOOG, VUGG, VUGH, DRUSE, CAVITY, NODULE
geographer KANT, MELA, VAREN, VIDAL, BUACHE, CLUVEL, RITTER, STRABO, THALES, APIANUS, BRUNHES, MUNSTER, PTOLEMY, HUMBOLDT, MERCATOR
geological division ERA, EPOCH, PERIOD, SERIES, SYSTEM
geological epoch BALA, CULM, LIAS, MALM, MOINE, DOGGER, EOCENE, MIOCENE, HOLOCENE, PLIOCENE
geological era AZOIC, ARCHEAN, CENOZOIC, MESOZOIC, ALGONKIAN, PALEOZOIC
geological formation IONE, TERRANE, TERRENE
geological period PERMIAN, CAMBRIAN, DEVONIAN, JURASSIC, SILURIAN, TERTIARY, TRIASSIC, QUATERNARY
geologist HUXLEY, STRABO
geometric figure CUBE, CUSP, RHOMB, CIRCLE, OBLONG, SQUARE, TRIGON, ELLIPSE, POLYGON
geometric solid CONE, CUBE, LUNE, PRISM, SPHERE, PYRAMID, CYLINDER
geometrician EUCLID, THALES
geometry term PI, LOCI, SINE, CHORD, LOCUS, SECANT, VERSOR, TANGENT, THEOREM
Georgia information *see p. 308*
geranium RUTA
Gerda's husband FREY
germ BUG, SPORE, VIRUS, MICROBE, BACTERIA; *see* SEED
germ-free ASEPTIC, ANTISEPTIC
German HUN, BOCHE, JERRY, KRAUT, ALMAIN, TEUTON; *see p. 269*
German measure AAM, FASS, FUSS, STAB, ZOLL, EIMER, FUDER, KANNE, KETTE,

MAASS, MASSEL, MORGEN, STRICH, KLAFTER, SCHEFFEL
German money MARK, T(H)ALER, PFENNIG, BLAFFERT
German rulers OTTO, EBERT, ALBERT, CONRAD, HITLER, JOSEPH, RUDOLF, FRANCIS, LEOPOLD, LOTHAIR, RUDOLPH, THERESA, CONRADIN, MATTHIAS
German weight LOT, PFUND, STEIN, CENTNER
German words *see p. 269*
germane APT, AKIN, FITTING, RELEVANT, PERTINENT
Germanic language TAAL, DUTCH, DANISH, GERMAN, GOTHIC, ENGLISH, FAROESE, FLEMISH, FRISIAN, SWEDISH, YIDDISH, FRANKISH, TEUTONIC, AFRIKAANS, ICELANDIC, NORWEGIAN, SCANDINAVIAN
Gestapo chief HIMMLER
gesture NOD, MIME, WAVE, TOKEN, ACTION, MOTION
get EARN, GAIN, ATTAIN, OBTAIN, SECURE
get out! SCAT, SHOO, SCRAM, SKIDOO, VAMOSE, SKIDDOO, VAMOOSE
get well HEAL, RECOVER
Ghanian language *see* KWA, GUR
Ghanian money CEDI
Ghanian native EWE, FANTI, ASHANTI
ghastly LURID, PALLID, MACABRE
ghost KER, BHUT, HANT, JUBA, WAFF, LARVA, LEMUR, MANES, SHADE, SPOOK, UMBRA, CASPER, SHADOW, WRAITH, EIDOLON, PHANTOM, SPECTER; *see* SPIRIT
giant(ess) ANAK, BANA, ETEN, LOKI, SUKR, YMIR, BALOR, GYGES, JUMBO, TITAN, BESTLA, BUNYAN, FAFNIR, CYCLOPS, GOLIATH, MAMMOTH, TITANIC
giant killer JACK, DAVID, APOLLO
gibbon *see* APE
gibe RIB, JEER, FLEER, TAUNT
Gibson garnish ONION
gift DOW, SOP, TIP, ALMS, BOON, DOLE, ENAM, BONUS, LEGACY, TALENT, HANDSEL
gig JOB, NAP, WHIM, CHAISE
Gil Blas author LESAGE
Gilbert and Sullivan operetta MIKADO, PIRATES, IOLANTHE, PATIENCE, PINAFORE
gild DORE, ENRICH, AUREATE
gill GUT, BROOK, WATTLE
gin SLOE, TRAP, RUMMY, SNARE, SCHNAP(P)S
gipsy *see* GYPSY
giraffe *see* RUMINANT
girder BEAM, TBAR, IBEAM, TRUSS
girdle OBI, CEST, SASH, CESTUS, CINGLE, CORSET; *see* ENCLOSE
girl SIS, CHIT, DAME, JILL, LASS, MAID, MINX, MISS, BELLE, FRAIL, SKIRT, DAMSEL, HOYDEN, MAIDEN, TOMBOY, COLLEEN; *see* WOMAN, FEMALE
gist NUB, CORE, CRUX, PITH, POINT, KERNEL, ESSENCE
give GIE, BESTOW, CONFER, DONATE
give up CEDE, QUIT, YIELD, RENOUNCE, SURRENDER
gizzard CRAW, THROAT, STOMACH
glacial deposit AS, OS, ASAR, KAME, OSAR, PAHA, ESCAR, ESKAR, ESKER, PLACER, MORAINE
glacial ice FIRN, NEVE, SERAC
glaciation stage CARY, GUNZ, RISS, WURM, ACHEN, IOWAN, SAALE, ELSTER, MINDEL, MANKATO, VALDERS
glacier ICECAP, PIEDMONT
glacier, facing a STOSS
gladiator trainer LANISTA
gladly FAIN, LIEF, READILY
glance SCAN, SKIM, APERCU
gland GLANS, THYMUS, CAROTID, PAROTID, THYROID, EXOCRINE, PANCREAS, PROSTATE, ENDOCRINE, HOLOCRINE, LYMPHATIC, MEROCRINE, PITUITARY
gland, edible RIS, NOIX
gland secretion BILE, GALL, SALIVA, CHALONE, AUTACOID; *see* HORMONE
glass CALX, FRIT, LENX, PANE, PONY, FRITT, SMALT, UVIOL, CULLET, GOBLET, MIRROR, RUMMER, STRASS, CRYSTAL,

LALIQUE, OPALINE, PARISON, SNIFTER, TUMBLER, OBSIDIAN
glass ingredient FRIT, LIME, SAND, SODA, ALKALI, POTASH, SILICA, ZAFFIR
glasses *see* EYEGLASSES
glassmaker GLAZIER
glassmaker's rod PONTY, PUNTY, PONTIL
glassy VITRIC, CRYSTAL, HYALINE
Glaucus' father MINOS, SISYPHUS
Glaucus' slayer AJAX
gleam GLINT, GLOZE, GLISTEN
glib OILY, BLAND, FACILE
glide SKI, SKID, SKIM, SKIP, SLIP, SKATE, SLIDE, SASHAY
gloat EXULT
globe ORB, BALL, CLEW, EARTH, SPHERE
globule BEAD, BLOB, DROP
gloom MURK, BLUES, DUMPS
gloomy WAN, DARK, DOUR, ADUSK, FERAL, DREAR(Y), MOROSE
glorify LAUD, EXALT, EXTOL
gloss SHEEN, EXCUSE, EXEGESIS
glossary CLAVIS, LEXICON
glossy GLIB, GLACE, NITID, SLICK
glottal stop STOD, CATCH, STOSS
glove MITT, CESTUS, SLIPON
glove shape TRANK
glow BLAZE, EXCEL, RUTILATE
glowing ARDENT, CANDENT, LAMBENT
Gluck opera ORFEO, ARMIDA
glucoside GEIN, RUTIN, ESTEVIN
glue AGAR, PASTE, MUCILAGE
glut CLOY, SATE, GORGE, STUFF, SURFEIT
glutton HELLUO, CORMORANT
gnarl NUR, KNUR, NURR, SNAG, GROWL, KNURR
gnat MIDGE; *see* FLY
gnaw BITE, CHEW, FRET, ERODE, NIBBLE, CORRODE, TORMENT
gnome *see* ELF
gnu KOKOON; *see* ANTELOPE
go DIE, GAE, MOVE, QUIT, STIR, SUIT, LEAVE
go astray ERR, SIN, ABERRATE
goad EGG, GAD, PROD, SPUR, URGE, ANKUS, PRICK, STICK
goal AIM, META, POST, TAPE, BOURN, THULE, BOURNE
goat KID, TUR, IBEX, TAHR, TEGG, THAR, BILLY, NANNY, PASAN, ANGORA, CAPRID, JHARAL, PASANG, MARKHOR
goat genus CAPRA
goatish CAPRINE, HIRCINE
goatsucker PISK, POTOO, BULLBAT, OILBIRD, GUACHARO, NIGHTJAR, POORWILL, NIGHTHAWK, WHIPPOORWILL
Gobi Desert SHAMO, HANHAI
goblet TASS, BOCAL, HANAP, CHALICE; *see* GLASS
goblin NIS, BHUT, POOK, PUCA, PUCK, NISSE; *see* ELF
god(s) DI, DEI, DII, DEUS, IDOL, DEITY, TOTEM, PARAGON; *see p. 316*
God IAM, JAH, JHVH, YHVH, ALLAH, ADONAI, ELOHIM, YAHWEH, JEHOVAH
god, false BAAL, DAGON, BAALIM, MAMMON, MOLOCH
goddess DEA, STAR(LET); *see* GRACES, NORNS, HORAE
godfather PADRINO, SPONSOR
Goethe character FAUST, MIGNON, WERTHER
Goethe's city WEIMAR
goiter STRUMA
gold AU, ORO, SOL, CYME, GILT, AURUM, ORMOLU
gold coin LION, LIRA, OBAN, ANGEL, DARIC, DUCAT, EAGLE, KRONE, LOUIS, MOHUR, OBANG, SCUDO, TOMAN, GUINEA, PISTOLE, DOUBLOON, IMPERIAL
golden AURIC, DURRY, AUREATE
golden apple character IDUN, ATLAS, LADON, PARIS, HESPERID, APHRODITE
golden fleece character JASON, MEDEA, AEETES, ARGONAUT
Golden State CA, CALIFORNIA
golf club IRON, WOOD, CLEEK, SPOON, WEDGE, DRIVER, MASHIE, PUTTER, BRASSIE, MIDIRON, NIBLICK
golf term LIE, PAR, PUT, TEE, TOE, BAFF, BONE, CHIP, FORE, HOOK, LOFT, NOSE, PUTT,

TRAP, BOGEY, DIVOT, EAGLE, LINKS, PITCH, ROUGH, SLICE, BIRDIE, BISQUE, DORMIE, HAZARD, SCLAFF, STANCE, FAIRWAY, MULLIGAN

golfer BOLT, TEER, BOROS, FLOYD, HOGAN, JONES, RAWLS, SNEAD, STACY, CASPER, DUBBER, OUIMET, PALMER, PLAYER, WATSON, YANCEY, LITTLER, MANGRUM, NICHOLS, SANDERS, STADLER, TREVINO, VENTURI, NICKLAUS, ZAHARIAS

Golgotha CALVARY

Goliath's home GATH

Goliath slayer DAVID

gone AGO, OUT, PAST, YORE

Goneril relative LEAR, REGAN, ALBANY, CORDELIA

gong TAM(TAM)

good BON, MORAL, PUCKA, PUKKA, SOUND, VALID

good-bye AVE, CIAO, TATA, ADIEU, ALOHA, SOLONG, FAREWELL

goods FEE, BONA, STOCK, WARES, WRACK, FREIGHT

goods in sea LAGAN, LIGAN, JETSAM, LAGEND, FLOTSAM

goof ERR, BONER, BLUNDER

goose NENE, WAVY, BRANT, CHAJA, SOLAN, GANDER, GREYLAG, GRAYLAG, SCREAMER

goose egg ZERO

goose genus CHEN, ANSER

Gopher State MN, MINNESOTA

gore CRUOR, INSET, GUSSET; *see* STAB

gorge CLOY, GLUT, CHASM, FLUME, GULLY, KLOOF, STRID, TANGI, CANYON, CLOUGH, RAVINE

Gorgon MEDUSA, STHENO, EURYALE, JEZEBEL

Gorgon parents CETO, PHORCYS

gorilla GOON, THUG, BRUTE; *see* APES

gospel JOHN, LUKE, MARK, TRUTH, EVANGEL, MATTHEW, EVANGILE, SYNOPTIC

gossip CAT, EME, GUP, DIRT, TALE, ONDIT, CLAVER, NORATE, TATTLE

Goth BERIG, EURIC, ALARIC, FILIMER, RODERICK, LEOVIGILD, THEODORIC

gouge ROUT, CHEAT, FRAUD, SWINDLE

goulash STEW, RAGOUT, MULLIGAN

Gounod opera FAUST, ROMEO

gourd PEPO; *see* FRUITS

gout BLOB, GOUT, CULVERT, PODAGRA

govern CURB, RULE, BRIDLE, DIRECT

governess NANNY, TUTOR, DUENNA

government SWAY, STATE, POLITY, REGIME(N), DOMINION

government control REGIE

governor BEY, DEY, VALI, WALI, PASHA, PILOT, TUPAN, DYNAST, EPARCH, REGENT, SATRAP, SHERIF, SHOGUN, TUCHUN, TYCOON, VAIVOD, VOIVOD, KHEDIVE, SHEREEF, VICEROY, VOIVODE, HOSPODAR, REGULATOR

grace TACT, ADORN, CHARM, FAVOR, MERCY, PARDON

graceful FEAT, GENT, GAINLY, SVELTE, SYLPHIC

Graces AGLAIA, THALIA, CHARITES, EUPHROSYNE

grade MARK, RANK, RATE, SORT, STEP, CLASS, LEVEL, SLANT

Graeae ENYO, DEINO, PEMPHREDO

graft IMP, CION, SLIP, BRIBE, CLAVE, SCION, SHOOT, KICKBACK, BAKSHEESH

grail AMA, CUP, CHALICE, SANGREAL

grain BIT, BRAN, DURA, MEAL, MILO, SAMP, SEED, DOORA, DOURA, DURRA, GRIST, SPECK, WHEAT, DHURRA, HEGARI, TEMPER; *see* CEREAL

grammatical term MODE, MOOD, PARSE, TELIC, ACTIVE, COPULA, FINITE, GENDER, ARTICLE, JUSSIVE, PASSIVE, SUBJECT, SYNESIS, PARADIGM, PARTICLE, PREDICATE, SYLLEPSIS; *see* CASE, TENSE

granary BIN, CRIB, GOLA, GUNJ, SILO, GUNGE, JAGIR, GRANGE, JAGEER, JAGHIR

grandchild OY(E)

grandparental AVAL

grant CEDE, ENAM, MISE, AWARD, PATENT, REMISE, CHARTER, SUBSIDY

grantor DONOR
grape UVA, BACO, UGNI, GAMAY, PINOT, SIRAH, TOKAY, VITIS, MALAGA, MUSCAT, MUSKAT, RAISIN, WAMPEE, CATAWBA, CONCORD, FURMINT, MALMSEY, CABERNET, DOLCETTO, GRENACHE, MALVASIA, NEBBIOLO, PALOMINO, PROSECCO, RIESLING, RULANDER, SEMILLON, SYLVANER, SAUVIGNON, ZINFANDEL, CHARDONNAY
grape disease ESCA, APOPLEXY
grape syrup DIBS, MUST, SAPA, STUM
grapefruit POMELO, SHADDOCK
grapelike UVAL
graphite KISH, LEAD, PLUMBAGO
grasp HENT, EREPT, SEIZE
grass HAY, POA, ALFA, CANE, ICHU, JAVA, LAWN, ADLAI, ADLAY, ALANG, AVENA, BROME, COGON, OTATE, STIPA, BAMBOO, DARNEL, FESCUE, ESPARTO, TIMOTHY; *see* CEREAL
grasshopper CAGN, DRUM, GRIG, WETA, BRUKE, RACER, ROACH, STICK, CHANGA, EARWIG, EMPUSA, LOCUST, MANTID, MANTIS, PHASMA, BLATTID, CATYDID, CRACKET, CRICKET, DRUMMER, GRYLLID, KATYDID, KNOCKER, MANTOID, PROPHET, STICKBUG
grasshopper genus BLATTA, GRYLLUS
grassland LEA, MEAD, VELD, PAMPA, RANGE, SWARD, VELDT, PASTURE, PRAIRIE, SAVANNA
grate JAR, RASP, CHARK, CREAK, GRIDE, ABRADE, IRRITATE
gratify SATE, PLEASE, ARRIDE
gratinate BROWN, CRISP
grating GRID, RASP, GRILL, RASPY, GRILLE, HOARSE, LATTICE
gratuity FEE, TIP, BOON, VAIL, PILON, CUMSHA(W), BAKSHEESH
grave DULL, ETCH, CARVE, FOSSE, MOUND, SOBER, STAID, SUANT, BARROW, SEDATE, SOMBER; *see* TOMB
graveclothes SHROUD, CEREMENT
gravel OS, ESKER, BEACH, GEEST, BALLAST
gravestone SLAB, STELA, STELE, MARKER, STELAE, STELAI
gravy JUS, SAUCE, PROFIT
gray DULL, HOAR, ASHEN, HOARY; *see p. 251*
graze RUB, FEED, NICK, AGIST, TOUCH, BROWSE, GLANCE
grease OIL, LARD, MORT, SUET, BRIBE, AXUNGE
greasewood CHICO, ORACHE, CHAMISO, HOPSAGE
great BARO, SUPER, AUGUST, MICKLE
Great Lake ERIE, HURON, ONTARIO, MICHIGAN, SUPERIOR
great number LAC, HEAP, HOST, LAKH, GALAXY, LEGION
Great White Way BROADWAY
grebe FINFOOT, PYGOPOD, DABCHICK, DIDAPPER
Greece ELLAS, ACHAEA, ACHAIA, ATTICA, HELLAS
greed AVARICE, AVIDITY, EDACITY, CUPIDITY
greedy GRIPPLE, COVETOUS, ESURIENT
Greek ATTIC, ARGIVE, AEOLIAN, GRECIAN, HELLENE, HELLENIC
Greek alphabet MU, NU, PI, XI, CHI, ETA, PHI, PSI, RHO, TAU, BETA, IOTA, ZETA, ALPHA, DELTA, GAMMA, KAPPA, OMEGA, SIGMA, THETA, LAMBDA, EPSILON, OMICRON, UPSILON
Greek dialect AEOLIC, ATTIC, DORIC, IONIC, KOINE, MINOAN, AEOLIAN, CYPRIAN, CYPRIOT, BOEOTIAN, MYCENEAN
Greek measure PIK, ACAENA, BACHEL, BARILE, COTULA, GRAMME, KOILON, PALAME, STADION, STREMMA
Greek measure (ancient) BEMA, POUS, CHOUS, PYGON, DICHAS, ACAENA, ORGYIA, AMPHORA, STADIUM
Greek money OBOL, LEPTON, STATER, DRACHMA

Greek weight MNA, OKA, MINA, LITRA, DRAMME, OBULUS, STATER, DRACHMA
Greek weight (ancient) DIOBOL, CHALCON
green RAW, VERD, LEAFY, CALLOW, VERDANT; *see p. 251*
Green Mountain State VT, VERMONT
greenhorn TYRO, IKONA, ROOKIE
Greenland settlement ETAH
greeting AVE, HAIL, ALOHA, HELLO, NETOP, ACCOIL, CURTSY, SALUTE
grief WOE, DOLE, TEEN, DOLOR, MISERY
Grieg hero(ine) ASE, GYNT, PEER
grievance BEEF, GRIPE, SCORE, GRAVAMEN
grill GRID, QUIZ, RACK, BROIL, TAVERN, GRATING
grim SET, DOUR, MACABRE
grimace MOW, MOUE, MOWE, POUT, FLEER, SCOWL, SMIRK, MURGEON
grime DIRT, SMUT, SOOT, COLLY, FILTH
grind BRAY, CHEW, CRAM, GRIT, MILL, WHET, CRUSH, GNASH
grinder GRIT, HONE, MANO, MILL, MOLAR, TOOTH, METATE, MORTAR, MULLER, PESTLE
grippe FLU, COLD
grit SAND, NERVE, PLUCK, GRAVEL
grits KASHA, HOMINY
grommet RING, LOOP, BECKET, EYELET
groom PAGE, SAIS, SICE, SYCE, CURRY, TRAIN, OSTLER, EQUERRY, HOSTLER, BENEDICT
groove RUT, CHASE, CROZE, FLUTE, SCARF, STRIA, RABBET, RAGGLE, SULCUS
grooved LIRATE, STRIATE
grope FEEL, PROBE, FUMBLE
gross RANK, CRASS, CRUDE, VULGAR, GLARING
grotesque ODD, FREAK, GOTHIC, BIZARRE
grotto *see* CAVE
ground SET, LAND, SOIL, BASIS, FOUND, TERRAIN
groundhog MARMOT, WOODCHUCK
group ERA, NYE, BAND, BLOC, BODY, CREW, TEAM, CADRE, CLASS, CORPS, FLEET, GENUS, CLAQUE, MUSTER, PHYLUM, DIORAMA; *see* BEVY
grouper GAG, CONY, HIND, MERO, CONEY, GUASA, SCAMP, AGUAJI, BONACI, CHERNA, GROPER, HAPUKU, WARSAW, GOURAMI, SEABASS, WHAPUKU
grouse *see* PHEASANT
grove HOLT, TOPE, COPSE, NEMUS
grovel FAWN, WORM, COWER
grow WAX, BREED, RAISE, ACCRUE, MATURE, SPROUT, THRIVE
growing out ENATE
growl YAR, GIRN, GNAR, GURL, YARR, SNARL, GRUMBLE
grown ADULT, MATURE
growth WEN, CORN, MOLE, WART, POLYP, TUMOR, CANCER, CLAVUS
grub DIG, EATS, LARVA, ASSART
grudge ENVY, PIQUE, SPITE
gruel ATOLE, BURGOO, CAUDLE, LOBLOLLY
gruesome GRIM, GRISLY, MACABRE
gruff RUDE, HARSH, SURLY
grumble HONE, GRIPE, GROWL, GROUCH, MUTTER
grunt RONCO, SNORT; *see* SNAPPER
guarantee BOND, CAGE, AVAIL, SURETY, WARRANT, SCHOLIUM
guard TILE(R), WATCH, BANTAY, CONVOY, FENDER, GHAFIR, PATROL, PICKET, SENTRY, SHIELD, DRABANT, OSTIARY
guardhouse BRIG, HOOSEGOW
guardian ARGUS, CUSTOS, WARDEN, CURATOR, TRUSTEE, TUTELAR, CERBERUS
Guatemalan money PESO, QUETZAL
Gudrun's husband ATLI, HELGI, HERWIG, SIGURD, SIEGFRIED
guerrilla(s) MAQUI, REBEL, MAQUIS, CHETNIK, FEDAYEE, PARTISAN
guess THEORY, SURMISE

guest CALLER, VISITOR
guide KEY, PIR, CLEW, LEAD, PILOT, SCOUT, STEER, CONVOY, LEADER, SHIKARI, CICERONE, SHIKAREE
guidebook ORDO, BAEDEKER, MICHELIN, VADEMECUM
Guidonian note UT, ARE, ELA, BEMI, BEFA, ELAMI, CEFAUT, FEFAUT, ALAMIRE, CESOLFA, DELASOL, DESOLRE, GAMMAUT
guild HUI, TONG, HANSE, LIANA, EPIPHYTE, PARASITE
guilt SIN, CRIME, CULPA
guilty NOCENT, CULPABLE
Guinea language FANG, CRIOLO; *see* MANDE
Guinea weight AKEY, PISO, UZAN, BENDA, SERON
Guinevere's husband ARTHUR
Guinevere's lover LANCELOT
guise FORM, MIEN, SHAPE, ASPECT
guitar *see* STRING INSTRUMENT
gulch GULLY, ARROYO, CANYON, COULEE, RAVINE
gulf MORO, ABYSS, ALBAY, BIGHT, CHASM, DAVAO, DULCE, SAROS, TONKIN
gull COB, MEW, COBB, DUPE, SKUA, CHEAT, CULLY, PEWIT, BONXIE, HOODIE, JAEGER, PEEWIT, TEASER, ICEGULL,
gull genus XEMA, LARID
gullet MAW, CRAW, FAUCES, SWALLOW
gulls, pert. to LARINE
gully SIKE, WADI, DONGA, ARROYO, NULLAH
gum AMRA, KINO, CAROB, LATEX, LOBAN, MATTI, MYRRH, TUART, XYLAN, ACACIA, ACACIN, BALATA, CHICLE, GHATTI, KARAYA, TUPELO, WATTLE, ACACINE
gumbo OCRA, OKRA, SOUP
gums, pert. to ULETIC, GINGIVAL
gun DAG, GAT, ROD, BREN, COLT, HAIK, HAKE, IRON, ROER, STEN, BARIL, BETSY, LUGER, MAXIM, MINIE, RIFLE, BARKER, CHASER, DRAGON, HEATER, JEZAIL, JINGAL, MAGNUM, MAUSER, MUSKET, PISTOL, ROSCOE, TUPERA, BARETTA, BULLDOG, CARBINE, DUNGEON, GATLING, SHOTGUN, FIRELOCK, PISTOLET, TROMBONE
gun part NAB, PIN, BEAD, BOLT, BORE, BUTT, COCK, LOCK, GOMER, SIGHT, STOCK, BARREL, BREECH, HAMMER, CHAMBER, TRIGGER, CYLINDER, MAGAZINE
gunfire SALVO, RAFALE, VOLLEY, BROADSIDE, FUSILLADE
gunpowder TEA, NITER
Gunther relative HAGEN, GUTRUNE, BRYNHILDE, GRIMHILDE
Gur language GURMA, MOSSI, BARIBA, SENUFO, DAGBANE, DAGOMBA, GURUNSI
gurgle BICKER, BURBLE
gurnard(-like fish) TUB, ELLECK, BATFISH, TUBFISH, VOLADOR
gush FLOW, RUSH, SPOUT, SPURT
gust FLAW, RUSH, BLAST, SQUALL
gusto ELAN, ZEST, PALATE, RELISH
gut GULLY, INTESTINE
gutta SOH, DROP, SIAK, MINIM
gutter SLUM, DITCH, CULLIS, TROUGH
guttural HUSKY, VELAR
guy rope STAY, VANG
gym feat KIP(P), CROSS, LEVER, SCALE
gymnast SZABO, CONNOR, RETTON, TURNER, VIDMAR, ACROBAT, ATHLETE, GAYLORD, TUMBLER, COMENICI
gypsum YESO, GESSO
gypsy ROM, RYE, CALE, CALO, CHAI, CHAL, RANI, ROMI, APTAL, CAIRD, NOMAD, ROMNI, GITANO, ROAMER, ROMANY, SELUNG, TSIGANE, BOHEMIAN

H

H-shaped ZYGAL
habile APT, ABLE, CLEVER
habit RUT, GARB, MODE, WONT, USAGE, COSTUME
habitual USUAL, COMMON, WONTED

habituate USE, DRILL, ENURE, INURE, ADDICT, FREQUENT
habitué USER, REGULAR
hack CAB, NAG, CHOP, GASH, GRUB, TAXI, COUGH, DEVIL, DRUDGE, WRITER, MATTOCK
hackneyed WORN, BANAL, STALE, STOCK, TRITE
Hades DIS, ARALU, ORCUS, PLUTO, EREBUS, TARTARUS; *see* HELL
Hades relative RHEA, ZEUS, CRONUS, POSEIDON, PERSEPHONE
hag FURY, CRONE, HARPY, SHREW, VECKE, VIXEN, BELDAM, VIRAGO, HARRIDAN
haggard WAN, DRAWN, GAUNT
haggle PRIG, CAVIL, PALTER, BARGAIN, CHAFFER, QUIBBLE
hail AVE, AHOY, POUR, AVAST, SLEET, SALUTE, GRAUPEL
Hailey novel HOTEL, AIRPORT
hair FUR, MOP, NAP, DOWN, FUZZ, LOCK, PILE, POLL, SHAG, CRINE, ROACH, TRESS, LANUGO, THATCH
hair fastener PIN, CLIP, BODKIN, HAIRPIN, BARRETTE
hair, fix SET, COIF, PERM, WAVE, RINSE, MARCEL, SHINGLE
hair product COMB, BRUSH, HENNA, RINSE, CURLER, POMADE, SHAMPOO
hair, remove BOB, TRIM, (D)EPILATE
hair shirt CILICE
hairdresser BARBER, FRISEUR, COIFFEUR, COIFFEUSE
hairless BALD, PELON, GLABROUS
hairpiece RAT, WIG, FALL, ROLL, PERUKE, TOUPEE
hairy PILAR, COMATE, COMOSE, PILOSE, CILIATE, CRINITE, HIRSUTE, VILLOSE, VILLOUS, CRINATED
Haitian language CREOLE
Haitian money FRANC, GOURDE
Haitian ruler ESTIME, DUVALIER, MAGLOIRE
halberd GLAIVE, GISARME
Halévy opera (LA)JUIVE
half DEMI, HEMI, SEMI, MOIETY
half-breed MULE, GRIFF, METIS, GRIFFE, LADINO, MESTEE, MUSTEE, MESTIZO, METISSE, MULATTO
half-moon ARC, LUNE(TTE), CRESCENT
half note MINIM
halibut *see* FLATFISH
hall(s) AULA, DORM, SAAL, XYST, ATRIA, FOYER, ODEON, XYSTUS
hallucinogen LSD, ACID, CAAPI, PEYOTE, MESCALINE
halo AURA, NIMB, BROUGH, CORONA, NIMBUS, AUREOLA, AUREOLE
halogen IODINE, BROMINE, ASTATINE, CHLORINE, FLUORINE
halt HOLD, LAME, LIMP, STEM, STOP, CEASE, HOBBLE
ham EMOTE, GAMMON, RASHER, OVERACT
Ham relative CUSH, PHUT, CANAAN
Hamite AFAR, GALLA, TIBBU, BERBER, TUAREG, DANAKIL, GUANCHE
Hamitic language *see* BERBER, CUSHITIC
hamlet MIR, BURG, DORP, TREF, ALDEA, THORP, CLACHAN
Hamlet relative CLAUDIUS, GERTRUDE
Hamlet site DENMARK, ELSINORE
Hamlet's friend HORATIO
Hamlet's girlfriend OPHELIA
Hamlet's slayer LAERTES
hammer BEAT, MAUL, POUND, BEETLE, FULLER, MALLET, OLIVER, PLEXOR, SLEDGE
hammer part CLAW, HEAD, PEEN, POLL
hamper PED, CRAMP, MAUND, FETTER, HINDER, IMPEDE, TRAMMEL; *see* BASKET
Hampshire HANTS
hand PUD, DEAL, MANO, NEAF, NIEF, MANUS, NIEVE, SCRIPT, LABORER, APPLAUSE
hand, part of FIST, LOOF, PALM, VOLA, FINGER, THENAR
hand, pert. to VOLAR, CHIRAL, MANUAL, THENAR
handbag CABA, PURSE, CLUTCH
handbill FLYER, DODGER, LEAFLET
handcuff DARBY, FETTER, NIPPERS, MANACLE

Handel work CAESAR, MESSIAH, ORLANDO, RINALDO
handicap ODDS, RACE, HINDER
handkerchief HANKIE, SUDARY, FOULARD, SUDARIUM, VERNICLE, VERONICA
handle EAR, LUG, PAW, ANSA, BOOL, DEAL, HAFT, HANK, HILT, TOTE, HELVE, SNATH, SNEAD, SWIPE, TREAT, SNATHE
handled DEALT, ANSATE, PALMED
handsome BRAW, COMELY, LIBERAL
handstone MANO
handwriting on the wall MENE, TEKEL, UPHARSIN
handy DEFT, ADROIT, HABILE
hang PEND, LOLL, DRAPE, DROOP, HOVER, DANGLE, IMPEND
hanger-on LEECH, TOADY, HEELER, PARASITE
hangnail WHITLOW
hank RAN, COIL, LOOP, SKEIN
Hannibal conqueror SCIPIO
Hannibal's father BARCA, HAMILCAR
haphazard CASUAL, RANDOM
happen FARE, OCCUR, BEFALL, BETIDE, CHANCE
happy COSH, FAUST, BLITHE
harangue RANT, ORATE, SPIEL, SCREED, TIRADE, DIATRIBE
harass NAG, BAIT, JADE, RIDE, BESET, HECKLE, PESTER
harbor BAY, COVE, PIER, PORT, HAVEN, HITHE, CONCEAL
hard STERN, FLINTY, STEELY, ADAMANT, ARDUOUS, CALLOUS, PETROUS
harden GEL, SET, KERN, ENURE, INURE, STEEL, TEMPER, INDURATE
hardtack TOMMY, PANTILE
hardwood ASH, ELM, OAK, IPIL, TEAK, BEECH, BIRCH, EBONY, MAPLE, HICKORY, MAHOGANY
Hardy character JUDE, TESS
hare genus LEPUS, PEDETES
hare(-like rodents) BUN, WAT, BAWD, CONY, HARE, PIKA, BUNNY, CUTTY, DAMAN, HYRAX, LAPIN, DASSIE, MALKIN, MAUKIN, RABBIT, TAPETI, FLEMISH, LEPORID, LEVERET, RATHARE
harem ODA, SERAI, ZENANA, SERAGLIO
hark HEAR, HEED, LIST, ATTEND, LISTEN
harm MAR, BALE, BANE, DERE, HURT, DAMAGE, INJURE, SCATHE
harmful ILL, NOXAL, NOCENT, BANEFUL, NOISOME, NOXIOUS
harmful influence NOXA, UPAS
harmonize SET, AGREE, BLEND, ATTUNE
harmony KEY, CHIME, COSMOS, UNISON, CONCORD
harness RIG, GEAR, TAME, ARMOR, EQUIP, GRAITH, INSPAN
harness part BIT, TUG, HAME, REIN, BLIND, TRACE, BILLET, BRIDLE, COLLAR, HALTER, TERRET, CRUPPER
Harpies AELLO, CELAENO, OCYPETE, PODARGE
harquebus support CROC
harrow CHIP, DRAG, TILL
harsh DURE, ACERB, CRUEL, STERN, COARSE, RASPING
hart *see* DEER
hartebeest *see* ANTELOPE
harvest CROP, KIRN, RABI, REAP, RABBI, YIELD, GARNER
harvest machine *see* FARM
hash CHOP, MINCE, BUNGLE
hassle FRAY, MELEE, RUCKUS
hassock TUT, PESS, TUFT, STOOL
hasten HIE, SCAMP, SPEED
hasty pudding HASH, MUSH, SEPON, SUP(P)AWN
hat DIP, FEZ, LID, TAM, BAKU, CADY, COIF, FELT, FLAT, KADY, KATY, TILE, TOPI, BENJY, BENNY, BERET, BOXER, BUSBY, CADDY, DERBY, DICER, GIBUS, MILAN, SQUAM, STRAW, TERAI, TOPEE, TOQUE, BEAVER, BOATER, BONNET, BOWLER, CASTOR, CLAQUE, CLOCHE, COCKUP, FEDORA, PANAMA, RAFFIA, SAILOR, SCONCE, SLOUCH, TOPHAT, TOPPER, TRILBY, BANDEAU, BRIMMER, CAUBEEN, CHAPEAU, HOMBURG, LEGHORN, PETASOS,

PETASUS, PILLBOX, PORKPIE, SALACOT, SALAKOT, SUNDOWN, TARBUSH, TRICORN, BEARSKIN, CAPELINE, OPERAHAT, SOMBRERO, TARBOOSH, TARBOUSH, SOUWESTER; *see* HEADWEAR, CAP

hatch DEVISE, CONCOCT

hatchet AX(E), MOGO, TOMAHAWK

hate DOSA, MISO, ABHOR, ODIUM, MALICE, RANCOR, AVERSION

Hatfield foe MCCOY

haul LUG, TOW, TUG, DRAG, HALE, SWAG, BOOTY, BOUSE, TRICE

haunch HIP, BUTTOCK

haunt DEN, DIVE, NEST, SPOOK, OBSESS, PURLIEU

haven LEE, PORT, HITHE, ASYLUM, REFUGE

Hawaiian bird IO, OO, IIWI, KOAE, MAMO, OMAO, OOAA, PALILA

Hawaiian fish AHI, AKU, AWA, ULUA, AKULE

Hawaiian information *see p. 308*

Hawaiian language *see* POLYNESIAN

Hawaiian tree KOA, AULU, NAIO, OHIA, AALII, LEHUA, ILIAHI

hawk GOS, IOA, IWA, EYAS, KAHU, KITE, ASTUR, FALCON, OSPREY, SHIKRA, TERCEL, FRIGATE, GOSHAWK, HAGGARD, HARRIER, KESTREL, MANOWAR, TIERCEL, CARACARA; *see* BUZZARD

hawk genus IO, BUTEO, PANDION, ACCIPITER

hawker ROWEN, CADGER, COSTER, PEDLAR, CHAPMAN, PEDDLER, HUCKSTER

Hawkeye State IA, IOWA

hawthorn HAW, MAY, A(I)GLET

hay CHAFF, CLOVER, ALFALFA, TIMOTHY

haystack COB, MOW, COIL, GOAF, PIKE, RICK

hazard DARE, RISK, PERIL, STAKE

haze FOG, FILM, GLIN, MIST, PALL, SMOG, BRUME

hazel A(I)GLET

head NOB, NUT, TOP, VAN, BEAN, CONK, LEAD, PASH, PATE, POLL, TETE, CAPUT, CHIEF, FRONT, SKULL, CAPITA, MAZARD, NODDLE, NOGGIN, NOODLE, CRANIUM

head, membrane covering CAUL, OMENTUM

head, part of EAR, EYE, JAW, FACE, HAIR, JOWL, NOSE, BRAIN, CHEEK, CROWN, FRONS, INION, MOUTH, NARES, SCALP, SINUS, BASION, BREGMA, MENTUM, OCULUS, THORAX, THROAT, VERTEX, EYEBROW, EYELASH, OCCIPUT, ANTINION, CALVARIA, FOREHEAD, SINCIPUT

headache MEGRIM, MIGRAINE

headland RAS, CAPE, NAZE, NESS, BLUFF

headman BOSS, CHIEF, HETMAN, INDUNA, SACHEM

headquarters HQ, BASE, SEAT

headstrong RASH, WAYWARD

headwear BOW, AGAL, POUF, TIAR, CROWN, MITER, MITRE, SHAKO, SNOOD, TIARA, DIADEM, FILLET, HENNIN, TURBAN, WIMPLE, HAVELOCK, HEADGEAR, STEPHANE; *see* HAT, CAP, HOOD

healthy HALE, SANE, SOUND

heap COB, PILE, RAFF, RAFT, AMASS, MOUND, STACK, CONGERIES

hearing OYER, PROBE, TRIAL, INQUEST, AUDIENCE

hearken HEAR, HEED, HIST, LIST, ATTEND, LISTEN

heart COR(E), GIST, PITH, BOSOM, BREAST, CARDIA, TICKER

heart disease ANGINA, CARDITIS, CORONARY

heartburn PYROSIS

hearth LING, INGLE, FIRESIDE

heart-shaped CORDATE, CARDIOID

heat RUT, WARM, ZEAL, ARDOR, CALOR, CAUMA, FEVER, TEPOR, ESTRUS

heat unit BTU, THERM, CALORIE

heater ETNA, OVEN, STOVE, BUNSEN, PISTOL

heath BENT, GRIG, LING, MOOR, PIPE, BESOM, ERICA, GORSE, BRUYERE, HEATHER

heathen PAGAN, PAYNIM, INFIDEL
heave CAST, KECK, FLING, SCEND, SWELL, VOMIT
heaven SKY, CIEL, EDEN, SION, ZION, URANO, WELKIN, VALHALLA
heavenly DIVINE, EDENIC, URANIC, ANGELIC, SERAPHIC, SUPERNAL
heavenly being AFA, ANGEL, CHERUB, SERAPH(IM)
heavenly body SUN, MOON, STAR, COMET, METEOR, PLANET, ASTEROID
heavy DENSE, INERT, GRAVE, LADEN, LEADEN, WEIGHTY
Hebrew alphabet HE, PE, AIN, MEM, NUN, SIN, TAV, TAW, VAU, WAW, ALEF, AYIN, BETH, CAPH, ELEF, KAPH, KOPH, QOPH, RESH, SADE, SHIN, TETH, YODH, ALEPH, CHETH, GIMEL, ZAYIN, DALETH, LAMEDH, SAMEKH
Hebrew marginal note KRI, QRI, KERE, KERI, QERE, Q(U)ERI
Hebrew measure CAB, KAB, HIN, KOR, LOG, BATH, EPHA, EZBA, OMER, REED, SEAH, CUBIT, EPHAH, HOMER
Hebrew month *see p. 340*
Hebrew weight MINA, BEKA, REBA, BEKAH, REBAH, SHEKEL
heckle BAIT, ANNOY, TAUNT, NEEDLE
Hector relative PRIAM, HECUBA, ANDROMACHE
Hecuba relative PARIS, PRIAM, HECTOR, TROILUS, CASSANDRA
hedge HEM, REW, ROW, BOMA, WAVER, RADDLE
heed MIND, NOTE, OBEY, RECK
heel CAD, CALX, OBEY, CAREEN
height ACME, PITCH, CLIMAX, SUMMIT, STATURE
heir HERES, SCION, HAERES, HERITOR, LEGATEE, PARCENER, INHERITOR
Helen relative LEDA, DORUS, MENELAUS
Helen's abductor PARIS
Helen's suitor AJAX, PARIS
helical TORSE, SPIRAL
hell PIT, ABYSS, SHEOL, NARAKA, TOPHET, ABADDON, AVERNUS, GEHENNA, INFERNO; *see* HADES
helmet ARMET, CASQUE, HEAUME, MORION, SALADE, SALLET, BASINET, BURGONET
helmet-shaped GALEATE
helmsman COX(ON), PILOT, TILLER, STEERER, COXSWAIN
Héloise husband ABELARD
help ABET, TIDE, STAFF, REMEDY, SECOND, SUCCOR
helper AIDE, ASSIST(ER)
Helvetic SWISS
hem in BESET, FENCE, INVEST
hemp IFE, SUN, TOW, PITA, SUNN, ABACA, BHANG, DAGGA, GANJA, GUNJA, MURVA, SISAL, SIZAL, CHARAS, GANJAH, GUNJAH, MOORVA
hen LAYER, PULLET, SITTER, POULARD
hence OFF, AWAY, ERGO, THEN
henpeck NAG, DOMINEER
Henry VIII's wives ANNE, JANE, PARR, ARAGON, BOLEYN, CLEVES, HOWARD, SEYMOUR, CATHERINE
herald CRIER, USHER, BLAZON
heraldry *see p. 311*
herb genus AMMI, GEUM, SIUM, AJUGA, APIUM, CICER, SEDUM
herbs IVA, NEP, NIP, RUE, ALOE, ANET, ARUM, BALM, BENE, BUNK, COLE, COUS, DILL, GOBO, KERS, LEEK, MEUM, MOLY, MUSA, RAPE, RUTA, SAGE, WORT, ANISE, BASIL, BENNE, BENNI, BLITE, CARUM, CLARY, CRESS, DRIAS, ERUCA, GALAX, RHOEO, SARAH, SEDGE, TANSY, THYME, YERBA, ALLIUM, ARNICA, BORAGE, CATNIP, CELERY, COLEUS, ENDIVE, GINGER, POTATO, QUINOA, SALVIA, SAVORY, SESAME, TOMATO, TURNIP, YARROW, ALECOST, BONESET, BURDOCK, CARAWAY, CHERVIL, CHICORY, GINSENG, MILFOIL, MUGWORT, PAPAVER, PARSLEY, PARSNIP, POTHERB, SALSIFY, SHALLOT, SPINACH, VERBENA, WITLOOF, ACHILLEA, ANGELICA, COSTMARY, ESCHALOT, SAMPHIRE, TURMERIC, VERONICA; *see* PEA, BEAN, ASTER, CARROT

herb, mythical MOLY
Hercules feat IOLE, HYDRA, HESIONE
Hercules relatives ZEUS, ALCMENE
herd GAM, MOB, POD, CAV(V)Y, DROVE, FLACK, SHOAL, CAVIYA, CORRAL, MANADA, REMUDA, SOUNDER
herdsman SENN, COWBOY, DROVER, GAUCHO, VACHER, VAQUERO, RANCHERO
hereditary factor DNA, GEN, RNA, GENE
heretic PERVERT, DISSENTER
heretofore ERST, ERENOW, QUONDAM
Hermes relative PAN, MAIA, ZEUS
hermit SANTON, ASCETIC, EREMITE, RECLUSE, STYLITE, ANCHORITE
hero IDOL, LEAD, LION, STAR, DEMIGOD, PALADIN, CHAMPION
Hero's lover LEANDER
Herodias relative HEROD, SALOME, ANTIPAS
heroic EPIC(AL), GALLANT, VALIANT
heroic poem *see* EPIC
heroin SNOW, HORSE, SMACK
heron QUA, HERN, SOCO, EGRET, GUARA, HERNE, QUAWK, UMBER, KOTUKU, BITTERN, SQUACCO, BOATBILL, SHOEBILL, SHOEBIRD, UMBRETTE, HAMMERKOP; *see* GANNET
heron genus ARDEA
herring(-like fish) BANG, BRIT, SHAD, ALLIS, ALOSA, BRITT, CHIRO, CISCO, DORAB, HILSA, MARAY, MATIE, SMELT, SPRAT, ALLICE, BUNKER, GARVIE, TWAITE, ALEWIFE, ANCHOVY, BUGFISH, BUGHEAD, CLUPEID, LONGJAW, MOONEYE, SARDINE, MENHADEN, PILCHARD
hesitate HAW, HEM, DEMUR, WAVER, FALTER, TEETER
hex JINX, SPELL, WITCH, HOODOO
hiatus COL, GAP, BREAK, CHASM, LACUNA
hibiscus HAU, BOLA, PURAU, MAHAGUA, MAJAGUA, BALIBAGO
hick RUBE, YOKEL, HAYSEED
hidden INNER, PERDU, ARCANE, COVERT, LATENT
hide(s) KIP, FELL, MASK, PELT, SKIN, VEIL, CACHE, JUFTI, SCREEN
hideous UGLY, SCABROUS, REPULSIVE
high ALT, DEAR, ALOFT, DRUNK
highest point APEX, PEAK, APOGEE, FINIAL, VERTEX, ZENITH
highlander GAEL, SCOT, TARTAN
high-strung TENSE, NERVOUS
highway ITER, PIKE, AVENUE, FREEWAY
highwayman PAD, BRIGAND, LADRONE, HIJACKER
hike BOOST, TRAMP, DECAMP
hill COP, KOP, TOR, BRAE, BULT, DAGH, DENE, DOWN, DUNE, HOLT, KAME, KNAP, LOMA, MESA, PAHA, RATH, TUMP, BUTTE, KNOLL, KOPJE, MORRO, MOUND, COPPLE, CUESTA, LOMITA, TERTRE
hilt HAFT, HELVE, HANDLE
Himalayan country NEPAL, TIBET, BHUTAN, SIKKIM
Himalayas *see* MOUNTAINS
hind BACK, REAR; *see* DEER
hinder BALK, DETER, HAMPER
Hindu SER, BABU, JAIN, SEIK, SIKH, JAINA, TAMIL, GENTOO
Hindu mythology *see p. 321*
hinge AXIS, BUTT, JOINT, PIVOT
hint CUE, TIP, CLEW, CLUE, IMPLY, INKLE, ALLUDE
hip COXA, ILIA, HAUNCH, HUCKLE
hire LET, RENT, LEASE, ENGAGE, SALARY, CHARTER
hired labor TOGT
historian ANTIQUARY, ARCHIVIST
historians LOT, BEDE, HUME, KNOX, LIVY, MORE, STOW, ADAMS, BACON, BEARD, CANTU, NEPOS, PARIS, PLINY, RANKE, RENAN, SEGUR, SKENE, STEIN, CAMDEN, DAUNOU, FROUDE, GIBBON, MIGNET, MOTLEY, OSGOOD, STUBBS, WILSON, BOSSUET,

BOSWELL, CARLYLE, LELEWEL, PSELLUS, SALLUST, TACITUS, TOYNBEE, HERODOTUS
history CLIO, LORE, ANNALS, RECORD, MEMOIR
hit BOP, CUFF, SLUG, SOCK, CLOUT, SMITE, LARRUP, POMMEL
hitch TUG, LIMP, SNAG, HOBBLE
Hitler's wife EVA, BRAUN
Hittite ancestor HETH, (K)HATTI
hive(s) GUM, SKEP, SWARM, UREDO, APIARY
hoard SAVE, AMASS, CACHE, STASH
hoarder ANT, MISER, NIGGARD
hoarfrost RAG, RIME
hoax BAM, GULL, RUSE, SHAM, SPOOF, CANARD, HUMBUG
hobby FAD, PASTIME, AVOCATION
hobgoblin IMP, BOGY, PUCK, BOGEY, SPRITE, BUGBEAR
hobo STIFF, TRAMP, VAGRANT
hock HAM, HOX, PAWN, GAMBREL
hockey HURLEY, SHINNY, HURLING
hockey player ORR, HULL, CLARKE, ICEMAN, LAFLEUR, RICHARD, ESPOSITO, GRETZKEY
hockey team JETS, BLUES, KINGS, BRUINS, FLAMES, FLYERS, OILERS, SABRES, CANUCKS, RANGERS, WHALERS
hockey term CAGE, PUCK, BULLY, CAMAN, ICING, GOALIE, CAMMOCK, FACEOFF
hodgepodge HASH, MESS, OLIO, OLLA, CENTO, MEDLEY, FARRAGO
hogwash SWILL, REFUSE, BALONEY
hoist DROP, JACK, LIFT, REAR, HEAVE, SLING
hold BITE, GRIP, STAY, AVAST, BELAY, HATCH, THINK, DETAIN
holder DOP(P), OWNER, TENANT
holding SEAT, TENURE
hold EYE, PIT, BORE, DENT, GEAT, GIME, LILL, PORE, SCYE, SLOT, VOID, SPRUE, SIPAPU
holiday(s) TET, XMAS, FERIA, FERIE, EASTER, FIESTA, RECESS, NONLEDAY
Holland *see* NETHERLANDS
hollow PIT, DENT, GORE, GULF, HOWE, BIGHT, FALSE, FOVEA, SCOOP, DIMPLE
holly ASSI, HOLM, ILEX, MATE, ACEBO, DAHOON, YAUPON, CASSINA, CASSINE
Hollywood street VINE, SUNSET
Holmes author DOYLE
Holy City KIEV, ROME, ZION, LHASA, MECCA, MEDINA, BENARES, HARDWAR, VARANASI, JERUSALEM
holy man SADH, FAKIR, SADHU
home NEST, ABODE, ASTRE, HEARTH, HABITAT
Homer work ILIAD, ODYSSEY
homestead TOFT, MESSUAGE
Honduran measure VARA, MILLA, TERCIA
Honduran money CENTAVO, LEMPIRA
hone WHET, STROP, SHARPEN
honest TRUE, FRANK, SINCERE, UPRIGHT
honey MEL, DEAR, MELL, DARLING
honey drink MEAD, MORAT, PIMENT
honeycombed FAVOSE, RIDDLED
honeyeater OO, IAO, IHI, BEAR, MOHO, MAOMAO, BELLBIRD
honor ACE, TEN, JACK, KING, QUEEN, CREDIT, ESTEEM, DIGNITY
hood HOW, COWL, BIGGIN, CALASH, CAMAIL, CAPOTE, SURTOUT; *see* GANGSTER
hoodoo HEX, JINX, JYNX, JONAH
hoof CLEE, UNGUIS, UNGULA
hook GAFF, CLEEK, CRAMPON, HAMULUS
hooked ADUNC, HAMUS, GAFFED, HAMATE, HAMOSE, CLEEKED, FALCATE, ADUNCOUS, AQUILINE, FALCATED
hoopoe UPUPA
Hoosier State IN(D), INDIANA
hope LONG, SPES, ASPIRE
hopscotch stone PEEVER
Hora DIKE, EIRENE, EUNOMIA
horde PACK, DROVE, SWARM, THRONG
horizon SKYLINE, AZIMUTH

horizontal FLUSH, PLANE, PRONE
horizontal timber LINTEL
hormone ESTRIOL, ESTRONE, GASTRIN, INSULIN, THEELIN, ANDROGEN, ESTROGEN, LIPOCAIC, SECRETIN, ADRENALIN, CORTISONE, ESTRADIOL, PROGESTIN, PROLACTIN, THYROXINE
horn DAG, CUSP, BUGLE, CORNU, FRENCH, PRONG, ANTLER, BASSET, RHYTON, SHOFAR, ENGLISH
horn tissue SCUR, KERATIN
hornbill TOCK, HOMRAI
hornet VESPID; *see* WASP
hornless NOT, MULEY, POLEY, DODDIE, MULLEY, POLLED, ACEROUS
horrible DIRE, GRIM, GRISLY
horse BLOCK, FRAME, TRESTLE
horse(s) BAY, COB, CUT, DUN, GEE, JEE, NAG, RIP, TIT, YAD, ARAB, BARB, COBB, COLT, FOAL, GOER, GRAY, GREY, HACK, HOSS, JADE, MOKE, NAIG, PRAD, PROD, ROAN, RUCK, SIRE, STUD, TURK, YABU, YADE, YAUD, ARABY, BIDET, BRONC, CAPLE, CAPUL, DUMMY, EQUID, FILLY, HAIRY, HOBBY, LOPER, MILER, MOUNT, NEDDY, PACER, PINTO, RACER, ROGUE, SHIER, SHIRE, SHYER, STEED, STIFF, TACKY, WALER, AMBLER, BOLTER, BRONCO, CABBER, CAYUSE, CHEVAL, COOSER, CURTAL, DAPPLE, DOBBIN, DRIVER, ENTIRE, EQUINE, FENCER, FILLER, GANGER, GARRAN, GARRON, GEEGEE, GLEYDE, HUNTER, JENNET, JUMPER, KEFFEL, LADINO, LEADER, MAIDEN, MORGAN, ORLOFF, OUTLAW, PADNAG, PELTER, PLATER, ROARER, ROUNCY, RUNNER, SAVAGE, SORREL, TACKEY, TARPAN, TRACER, VANNER, ARABIAN, BARBARY, BELGIAN, BOBTAIL, BRONCHO, CAVALLO, CHARGER, CLIPPER, COACHER, COURSER, DRAFTER, FLEMISH, GELDING, HACKNEY, MUSTANG, NEIGHER, PIEBALD, PRANCER, SADDLER, SPANKER, SUFFOLK, SUMPTER, WHEELER, ZEBROID, ZEBRULA; *see* RACEHORSE
horse, command to GEE, HAW, HUP, WHOA, GIDDAP
horse disease LOCO, FRUSH, SURRA, HEAVES, LAMPAS, NAGANA, SPAVIN, SURRAH, THRUSH, DOURINE, LAMPERS, QUITTOR, MALANDERS
horse genus EQUUS
horse part FROG, HOCK, HOOF, FRUSH, SHANK, CANNON, GASKIN, INSTEP, STIFLE, CORONET, FETLOCK, PASTERN
horseman RIDER, GAUCHO, JOCKEY
horsemanship MANEGE
horseshoeing frame TRAVE
Horus parent ISIS, OSIRIS
hose SOCK(S), ANKLET, BOOTEE, BOOTIE, MOGGAN, HOSIERY, STOCKING(S)
hospital attendant RN, AIDE, NURSE, INTERN(E), ORDERLY, THERAPIST
host PYX, ARMY, HORDE, PATEN, WAFER, LEGION, THRONG
hostility ANIMUS, ENMITY, ILLWILL
hot FIERY, SULTRY, PEPPERY, THERMAL
hot iron CAUTER(Y)
hotel INN, LODGE, HOSTEL
hound *see* DOG
house ECO, HUT, CASA, COTE, HOME, IGLU, ROOF, ABODE, BAHAY, IGLOO, TEMPE, TUPEK, VILLA, CASINO, GAZEBO, MAISON, COTTAGE, MANSION
household FAMILY, MENAGE
hovel HUT, HUTCH, SHACK
hover FLIT, WAVER, FLUTTER
hoyden ROMP, TOMBOY
hub NAVE, BOSTON, CENTER
hubbub ADO, DIN, STIR, TODO, TUMULT, UPROAR
hue CRY, COLOR, SHADE, TINGE
huge VAST, ENORM, GIANT
Huguenot leader CONDE, ADRETS, MORNAY, COLIGNY
hull POD, HUSK, CALYX, SHUCK

human HOMO, SOUL, WIGHT, MORTAL, ADAMITE
humble MEEK, ABASE, DEMEAN, MODEST, SUBMISS
humbug BOSH, FLAM, HOAX, FRAUD, GAMMON
humid DANK, MOIST, SULTRY
hummingbird CARIB, SYLPH, TOPAZ, HERMIT, HUMMER, COLIBRI, JACOBIN, PUFFLEG, SNOWCAP, WARRIOR, COQUETTE
hummingbird genus SAPPHO
humor FUN, WIT, BABY, MOOD, WHIM, CATER, LYMPH, PHLEGM
humorist ADE, NYE, WAG, WIT, COBB, NASH, ADAMS, ALLEN, BAKER, TWAIN, ROGERS, THURBER, BENCHLEY
humpbacked GIBBOUS
Hun ATLI, BOCHE, ETZEL, ATTILA, GERMAN, VANDAL
hundred HECTO, CENTUM
Hungarian MAGYAR
Hungarian language *see* FINNO-UGRIC
Hungarian leader KUN, DOBI, NAGY, KADAR, KAROLYI
Hungarian measure HOLD, JOCH, YOKZ, METZE
Hungarian money GARA, PENGO, FILLER
hunger YEN, CLEM, ITCH, PINE, ACORIA
hunt TRAP, POACH, STALK, TRAIL, FERRET, SHIKAR
hunter JAGER, ORION, JAEGER, NIMROD, SHIKARI, TRAPPER
huntress DIANA, SKADI, ARTEMIS, ATALANTA
hurl TOSS, FLING, PITCH
hurry HIE, DASH, TEAR, HASTE, SESSA, HASTEN
hurt MAR, ACHE, DERE, HARM, PAIN, IMPAIR, LESION
hurtful NOCENT, MALEFIC, NOISOME
husband GROOM, OLDMAN, SANNUP, GOODMAN; *see* SPOUSE
husband's brother LEVIR
husbandry THRIFT, TILLAGE, GEOPONICS
hush (H)SH, CALM, ALLAY, SHUSH
husk BRAN, HULL, LEAM, SHUCK
hut COT, BARI, COTE, ISBA, MIAM, MIMI, SHAD, SKEO, CABIN, HOGAN, HOVEL, JACAL, SHACK, TOLDO, LEANTO, MIAMIA
hutch BIN, PEN, COOP, CHEST, WARREN
hybrid CROSS, MIXED, MONGREL
Hyde's other half JEKYLL
hydrate SLAKE
hydrocarbon TOLAN, BUTANE, CYMENE, MELENE, ETHANE, OCTANE, PINENE, METHANE, PROPANE, RETENE, TERPENE, TOLUENE
hydroelectric *see* PLANT
hydrogen compound IMINE, HYDRIDE
hymn ODE, SONG, PSALM
hyperbole ELA, AUXESIS
Hyperion relative GE, EOS, HELIOS, SELENE, URANUS
hypnotic state COMA, TRANCE
hypocrisy CANT, DECEIT, PRETENSE
hysteria FIT, PANIC, FRENZY

I

I EGO, IOTA, SELF
Iago's wife EMILIA
ibex *see* GOAT
Ibsen character ASE, GYNT, NORA, PEER, EKDAL, HEDDA, ROSMER, ELLIDA
ice BERG, FIRN, FLOE, GRUE, NEVE, SISH, BRASH, FROST, LOLLY, SERAC, BISQUE, PAYOLA, SHERBET
ice mass PAN, BERG, CALF, FLOE, PACK, GLACIER, GROWLER, ICEBERG
iced GELID, GLACE, FRAPPE, FROSTED
Icelandic measure FET, ALIN, LINA, FERFET, POTTUR, FERALIN, FERMILA, OLTUNNA
Icelandic money AURAR, EYRIR, KRONA
icon *see* IMAGE
icy COLD, GELID, FRIGID, GLACIAL
id EGO, PSYCHE
Idaho information *see p. 308*
idea EIDOS, FANCY, NOTION, SCHEME, INKLING

ideal HERO, IDOL, MODEL, PARAGON, PERFECT, UTOPIAN
ideal state ICARIA, OCEANA, UTOPIA, EREWHON
identical ONE, SAME, TWIN, ALIKE
ideology ISM, DOGMA, THEORY
idiocy AMENTIA, ANOESIA
idiom CANT, ARGOT, DIALECT, LOCUTION, PARLANCE
idiot OAF, AMENT, MORON, CRETIN
idle OFF, LAZE, LAZY, LOAF, GAMMER, LOITER, OTIANT, OTIOSE; *see* INERT
idleness SLOTH
idler SPIV, DRONE, SLACKER
idol LION, ZEMI, PAGOD, FETISH, IDOLON, IDOLUM, PAGODA, SYMBOL, TERAPH, EIDOLON
idyl ECLOGUE, PASTORAL
if not ELSE, NISI, UNLESS
ignorance TAMAS, NESCIENCE
iguana *see* LIZARD
Iliad author HOMER
Iliad character AJAX, HELEN, NESTOR, PRIAM, HECTOR, CALCHAS, STENTOR, ULYSSES, ACHILLES
ilk SORT, KIND, STRIPE
ill ABED, EVIL, UNWELL, WICKED
ill will SPITE, VENOM, ANIMUS, MALICE, RANCOR
illegal ILLICIT, UNLAWFUL
Illinois information *see p. 308*
illusion TULLE, MIRAGE, CHIMERA, FANTASY
illustrator DORE, DUFY, SENDAK, CHAGALL, ROCKWELL, BEARDSLEY
image FORM, ICON, IKON, SIGIL, EFFIGY, RECEPT, STATUE, REPLICA; *see* IDOL
imaginary UNREAL, FICTIVE
imagine WIS, WEEN, IDEATE, SURMISE
imbecile FOOL, AMENT, ANILE, MORON, CRETIN, DOTARD, FATUOUS
imbibe BIB, SIP, GULP, DRINK
imbue TINCT, TINGE, INFUSE, INGRAIN, INSPIRE, PERVADE
imitate APE, ECHO, MIME, MIMIC
imitation COPY, SHAM, APISM, BOGUS, MIMESIS, MIMICRY
immature RAW, GREEN, CALLOW, NEANIC, UNRIPE, PUERILE
immediately NOW, PDQ, ANON, STAT, PRESTO, PRONTO, PROMPTLY
immense HUGE, VAST(Y)
immerse DIP, DUCK, DUNK, DOUSE, STEEP, ENGROSS
immigrant ALIEN, METIC, GRIFFIN, WETBACK
immodest BOLD, BRAZEN, FORWARD
immunizing substance SERUM, HAPTEN, TOXOID, HAPTENE, VACCINE
imp *see* ELF, DEMON
impact JAR, BRUNT, FORCE, SHOCK
impair MAR, HARM, SPOIL, DAMAGE, VITIATE
impale FIX, GORE, SPIT, SPEAR
impasse CULDESAC, DEADLOCK
impassive STOIC, PLACID, STOLID
impeach IMPUGN, INDICT, ACCUSE
impede BLOCK, ESTOP, HAMPER, STYMIE, THWART
impediment DRAG, CHECK, HITCH, BARRIER, OBSTACLE
impending IMMINENT
imperial REGAL, MAJESTIC
impertinent FLIP, PERT, RUDE, SASSY, SAUCY, MALAPERT
implant FIX, ROOT, GRAFT, ENROOT, ENGRAFT, INSPIRE, INSTILL
implement KIT, TOOL, EQUIP, DEVICE, ENFORCE, UTENSIL
implicit TACIT, INNATE, DEDUCED, INHERENT
imply HINT, MEAN, CONNOTE
impolite RUDE
import DRIFT, TENOR, INTENT
impose FOB, LAY, LEVY, PALM, FOIST, ENTAIL, IMPUTE, OBTRUDE
impost *see* TAX
impostor SHAM, FAKER, FRAUD, PHONY, QUACK, PHONEY, RINGER, CHARLATAN
impound POIND
impress DENT, LEVY, MARK, DRAFT, PRINT, STAMP
imprison CAGE, JAIL, QUAD, IMMURE, CONFINE
imprisonment LIMBO, DURESS, DURANCE

impromptu ADLIB, OFFHAND, EXTEMPORE
improve AMEND, EMEND, REVISE
improvise PONG, VAMP, ADLIB, INVENT, CONTRIVE
impudence LIP, GALL, BRASS, CHEEK, NERVE
impudent BOLD, FLIP, PERT, BRASH, FRESH, SAUCY
impulse SPUR, URGE, WHIM, NISUS, MOTIVE, IMPETUS
impulsive RASH, SNAP, IMPETUOUS
impute (A)RET, IMPOSE, ASCRIBE
in addition AND, TOO, ALSO, PLUS, BESIDES, FURTHER
in case IF, LEST
in fact TRULY, INDEED, DEFACTO
in favor FOR, PRO
in love GAGA, SMITTEN
in person LIVE
in spite of MAUGRE, DESPITE
inactive LATENT, STATIC, DORMANT, FAINEANT; *see* IDLE, INERT
inadequate SCANT(Y), UNEQUAL
inane VOID, SILLY, VAPID
inanimate DEAD, INERT, LIFELESS
inarticulate DUMB, MUTE, APHONIC
inborn INNATE, NATIVE, CONNATE, INHERENT
Inca QUECHUAN
Inca conqueror PIZARRO
Inca ruler HUASCAR, ATAHUALPA
incantation CHARM, SPELL, PRAYER, CANTRAP, CANTRIP
incense GUM, JOSS, MATTI, MYRRH, SPICE, ENRAGE, STACTE, OLIBANUM
incentive SPUR, MOTIVE, IMPULSE
incident EVENT, EPISODE
incidental MINOR, CASUAL, CHANCE
incidentally OBITER, APROPOS
incinerate BURN, (IN)CREMATE
incision CUT, GASH, SLIT, NOTCH
incisive ACUTE, SHARP, BITING
incite EGG, ABET, GOAD, PROD, SPUR, URGE, IMPEL, ROUSE, FOMENT, SUBORN
inclination BEND, BENT, BIAS, GRADE, SLANT, TASTE, LEANING
incline CANT, LEAN, RAMP, TEND, TILT, SLOPE, TREND, VERGE, DEVIATE
inclined APT, SKEW, PRONE
inclusive BROAD, GENERIC
income PAY, WAGE, RENTE, SALARY, USANCE, ANNUITY, PENSION, STIPEND
inconstant FICKLE, MUTABLE, VOLATILE, CAPRICIOUS
increase EKE, WAX, RISE, ACCRUE, DILATE, STEPUP, GREATEN
incubate BROOD, HATCH, CONCOCT
incubus DEMON, SPIRIT, NIGHTMARE
inculcate IMBUE, INSTIL
incursion RAID, FORAY, INROAD
indecent LEWD, RACY, RISQUE, OBSCENE, IMMODEST
indeed ARU, WIS, AROO, IWIS, AROON, REALLY, VERILY
indefinite DIM, HAZY, LOOSE, VAGUE
indefinite amount ANY, FEW, SOME
indentation NICK, CRENA, DINGE, NOTCH, CRENAE, MARGIN, CRENELET
index PIP, FIST, MARK, TABLE, GNOMON, POINTER
Indian, American *see* NATIVE AMERICAN
Indian language KHASI; *see* INDIC, DRAVIDIAN, MUNDA
Indian leader ASOKA, NEHRU, GANDHI, SHASTRI
Indian measure GUZ, JOW, KOS, BEGA, HATH, JAOB, KOSS, BIGHA, COVID, CROSA, DRONA, GARCE, HASTA, GEERAH, MUSHTI, UNGLEE
Indian money DAM, LAC, PIE, ANNA, DAWM, FELS, HOON, LAKH, PICE, TARA, CRORE, FANAM, MOHUR, RUPEE, PAGODA
Indian tree BEL, DAR, AMRA, BAEL, ANJAN, ARUSA, DADAP, HOGPLUM; *see* EAST INDIAN, WEST INDIAN
Indian weight SER, DHAN, PALA, PICE, RATI, TOLA, ADPAO, BAHAR, MAUND, RATTI, CHITTAK

Indiana information *see p. 308*
Indic language PALI, BHILI, ORIYA, VEDIC, NEPALI, PAHARI, SANSKRIT, SINHALESE, RAJASTHANI
indicate BODE, MARK, NOTE
indicator DIAL, SIGN, VANE, ARROW, GAUGE, POINTER, REGISTER
indict PEACH, ACCUSE, ARRAIGN, IMPEACH
indifference APATHY, LETHARGY
indifferent COLD, COOL, SOSO, BLASE, STOIC, NEUTRAL, STOICAL
indigenous INNATE, NATIVE, EDAPHIC, ENDEMIC
indigent POOR, NEEDY, DESTITUTE
indignity INSULT, SLIGHT, AFFRONT
indite PEN, WRITE, (IN)SCRIBE
individual ONE, BION, SELF, SOLE, BEING
Indochina LAOS, BURMA, MALAYA, VIETNAM, CAMBODIA, THAILAND
Indo-European ARYA(N)
Indo-European language *see* CELTIC, GERMANIC, ITALIC, SLAVIC, IRANIAN, INDIC
indolent LAZY, SORN, OTIOSE, SUPINE, TORPID, LISTLESS
Indonesian language *see* PACIFIC ISLANDS
Indonesian measure BOUW, KILAN, TAKAR, GANTANG, TJENKAL
Indonesian money RUPIAH
Indonesian weight TJI, HOEN, TALI, WANG, PICUL, REAAL, KOJANG, KULACK
induce LEAD, URGE, REASON
inductance unit HENRY
indulge PET, CODDLE, PAMPER, PETTLE, GRATIFY
inebriate SOT, TIGHT, TIPSY, TOPER, SQUIFFY, INTOXICATE
inept CLUMSY, AWKWARD
inert DEAD, DULL, AMORT, LATENT, SUPINE
inexperienced LAY, RAW, GREEN, NAIVE, CALLOW
infamy ODIUM, SHAME, VILLAINY
infant TOT, BABE, BRAT, CHIT, WEAN, BAIRN, CHRISOM, PAPOOSE
infantryman ASKAR, ZOUAVE, DOGFACE, CHASSEUR, DOUGHBOY
infatuate BESOT, CHARM, ENAMOR
infection STREP, TAINT
inference SURMISE, ILLATION
inferior LOW, POOR, LOWER, MINOR, PETTY, SHODDY
Inferno author DANTE
infidel PAGAN, KAFFIR, ATHEIST, HEATHEN, HERETIC, SARACEN
infinite VAST, BOUNDLESS
infinity OLAM, ANATA
infirm ANILE, SENILE, DECREPIT
inflame FAN, RILE, INCITE, IGNITE, MADDEN, RANKLE
inflammable PICEOUS
inflammable substance PUNK, AMADOU, TINDER
inflammation STY, ITIS, CROUP, RUBOR, ANGINA, GARGET, IRITIS, OMITIS, QUINSY, ULITIS, CATARRH, COLITIS, ILEITIS, PINKEYE, UVEITIS, CYSTITIS, MASTITIS, PLHEGMON
inflated GASSY, TUMID, BLOATED
inflexible GRIM, IRON, RIGID, STARK, DOGGED, ADAMANT
inflict DEAL, WREAK, IMPOSE
inflorescence CYME, AMENT, WHORL, RACEME, SPADIX
influence PULL, SWAY, CLOUT, IMPEL, AFFECT, INDUCE, WEIGHT
influenza FLU, GRIP, CORYZA, GRIPPE, CATARRH
inform RAT, SING, DELATE, SQUEAL, APPRIZE
information DATA, DOPE, ITEM, LORE, NEWS, AVISO, DOSSIER
informed HEP, HIP, AWARE
informer SPY, FINK, NARK, STOOL, PIGEON, SNITCH, DELATOR
infusion TEA, WORT, TISANE, TINCTURE
ingot BAR, PIG, SHOE, SYCEE
inhabitant CIT, ITE, INMATE, CITIZEN, DENIZEN, RESIDENT
inhale SNIFF, BREATHE, INSPIRE
inherent BASIC, INBORN, INNATE
inheritance LEGACY, BEQUEST, HERITAGE, PATRIMONY

inheritor *see* HEIR
inhibit BAR, ENJOIN, REPRESS
inhuman FELL, SAVAGE, BRUTAL, BESTIAL
initial(s) CIPHER, MONOGRAM
initiate HAZE, OPEN, BEGIN, EPOPT, FOUND, START, EPOPTA, INDUCT
injection HYPO, SHOT, ENEMA, SYRETTE
injure MAR, HARM, LAME, MAIM, TEEN, IMPAIR, SCATHE
injury ILL, TEEN, TORT, WOUND, LESION, MAYHEM, TRAUMA
inlaid work BUHL, MOSAIC, NIELLO, TARSIA
inlet BAY, RIA, VOE, ZEE, COVE, BAYOU, BIGHT, FIORD, SLOUGH
inn KHAN, FONDA, HOTEL, LODGE, MOTEL, SERAI, HOSTEL, IMARET, POSADA, TABARD, TAVERN, AUBERGE, HOSPICE, LOCANDA, CHOULTRY, HOSTELRY
innards *see* ENTRAILS
innate INBORN, NATIVE, NATURAL
inner BEN, ENTAL, ESOTERIC
innkeeper HOST, PADRONE, BONIFACE, PUBLICAN
innocence BLUET, NAIVETE
inquire ASK, SNOOP
insane MAD, LUNY, BATTY, CRAZY, DOTTY, LOON(E)Y
insanity FOLIE, MANIA, LUNACY, AMENTIA, MADNESS, VESANIA, DEMENTIA
inscribe MARK, WRITE, ENGRAVE
inscription RUNE, ENVOY, LEGEND, EPITAPH, EXERGUE, GRAFFITO
insect IMAGO, NYMPH, HUMMER, AURELIA, CREEPER, FISHMOTH, CHILOPOD, DIPLOPOD, FIREBRAT, LACEWING, MILLEPED, MYRIAPOD, PAUROPOD, DRAGONFLY, SILVERFISH; *see* BEETLE, BEE, FLY, MOSQUITO, WASP, ANT, BUTTERFLY, MOTH, BUG, LOUSE, GRASSHOPPER
insect body part COXA, PALP, ACRON, CLAVA, NOTUM, FEELER, LABIUM, PALPUS, STEMMA, THORAX, OCELLUS
insect stage EGG, PUPA, IMAGO, LARVA, NYMPH, REDIA, COCOON, INSTAR, PREPUPA, SUBIMAGO
inseminate SOW, (IM)PLANT
insert GODET, IMMIT, INLAY, INSET, PANEL
insidious SLY, ARCH, CUNNING
insight KEN, ACUMEN
insignia BADGE, MEDAL, EMBLEM
insignificant PUNY, PETTY, PALTRY, TRIVIAL
insipid DRY, DULL, FLAT, PROSY, JEJUNE
inspect SCAN, AUDIT, OVERSEE
inspire IMBUE, EXCITE, INHALE
install INDUCT, INVEST, ORDAIN, INSTATE
instant POP, WINK, JIFFY, TRICE
instead ELSE, LIEU, RATHER
instigate EGG, ABET, SPUR, CAUSE, INCITE, PROMPT, SUBORN, PROVOKE
instinct BENT, GIFT, KNACK, TALENT
instruct BRIEF, COACH, EDIFY, TEACH, IMPART, EDUCATE
instruction LESSON, COUNSEL, TUITION
instructor COACH, LECTOR, LECTURER; *see* TEACHER
instrument DEED, WILL, AGENT, MEANS, MEDIA, ORGAN, AGENCY, DEVICE, GADGET, MEDIUM, DOCUMENT; *see* STRING, WIND, BRASS, PERCUSSION
insulate (EN)ISLE, ISOLATE
insulation MICA, TAPE, ASBESTOS, CAULKING, ROCKWOOL, ISOLATION
insult CAG, FIG, SLUR, RUFFLE, AFFRONT
insurance type AUTO, FIRE, LIFE, TERM, THEFT, HEALTH, ANNUITY, FLOATER, MEDICAL, NOFAULT, TONTINE, ACCIDENT, BURGLARY, HOSPITAL, PROPERTY, COLLISION, LIABILITY
insurgent REBEL, RISER, RIOTER, UPSTART, MUTINEER
insurrection MUTINY, REVOLT
integer NORM, DIGIT, FIGURE

intellect MIND, NOUS, INWIT, MAHAT, SENSE, NOESIS, REASON
intellectual MENTAL, NOETIC, EGGHEAD
intend AIM, TRY, MEAN, ETTLE, SUPPOSE, INTEREST
inter BURY, INURN, ENTOMB, INHUME
intercede PLEAD, MEDIATE
interdict BAN, BAR, VETO, TABOO, ENJOIN, PROSCRIBE
interest WEAL, PIQUE, SHARE, BEHALF, MOTIVE, USANCE
interference HUM, MUSH, RAIN, SNOW, BLOOM, FLARE, GHOST, NOISE, STATIC
interim DIASTEM; *see* INTERVAL
interjection *see* EXCLAMATION
interlude JIG, BREAK, PAUSE, VERSET, INTERIM, ENTRACTE
intermediate MESNE, MEDIAN, MIDDLE
intermission STOP, BREAK, PAUSE, RECESS, INTERVAL
intermittent FITFUL, RECURRENT, SPASMODIC
internal INNER, INWARD
interpret READ, REDE, RENDER, EXPOUND, CONSTRUE
interpreter EXEGETE, LATINER, DRAGOMAN, LING(UI)STER
interrogative HOW, WHO, WHY, WHAT, WHEN, WHERE
interruption BREAK, OUTAGE
intersect CUT, MEET, CROSS, DECUSSATE
interstice PORE, CHINK, STOMA, AREOLA, AREOLE, SPIRACLE
intertwine KNIT, LACE, WEAVE, ENLACE, PLEACH
interval GAP, REST, BREAK, LAPSE, HIATUS, LACUNA, CAESURA, INTERIM
intervening MESNE, BETWEEN
interweave MAT, PLA(I)T, PLASH, TWINE, RADDLE
intestine GUT, BOWEL, COLON, BOWELS, ENTRAILS
intimidate AWE, COW, ABASH, BULLY, DAUNT, COERCE, BUFFALO
intolerant BIASED, NARROW, BIGOTED
intone CHANT, CROON, RECITE
intoxicated *see* DRUNK
intricate MAZY, D(A)EDAL, KNOTTY, TRICKY, COMPLEX, GORDIAN
intrigue WILE, AMOUR, CABAL, AFFAIR, BRIGUE, SCHEME
introduce IMMIT, USHER, BROACH, INSERT, LAUNCH, PRESENT
introduction PROEM, ISAGOGE, PREFACE, PRELUDE, PREAMBLE, FOREWORD
intrude CRASH, BUTTIN, MEDDLE, TRESPASS
intuition HUNCH, INSIGHT
inundation *see* FLOOD
invade RAID, VIOLATE
invalid NULL, SICK, VOID, FALSE, INFIRM, SICKLY, DISABLED
inveigh RAIL, CENSURE
inveigle COAX, LURE, ENTICE
invent COIN, FORGE, DEVISE
inventor BELL, BENZ, COLT, DAVY, HOWE, IVES, LAND, LONG, OTIS, SWAN, TAIT, WATT, YALE, BAIRD, FITCH, HYATT, MORSE, NOBEL, OHAIN, TESLA, BUNSEN, DIESEL, DURYEA, EDISON, FULTON, GEIGER, KEPLER, MAIZEL, MERCER, NEWTON, PASCAL, SPERRY, WANKEL, WRIGHT, BABBAGE, BRAILLE, CARRIER, CURTISS, DAIMLER, DAVINCI, EASTMAN, FARADAY, GATLING, GODDARD, LAENNEC, MARCONI, PULLMAN, REAUMUR, SIEMENS, SPRAGUE, WHITNEY, BERLINER, BESSEMER, BUSHNELL, DAGUERRE, MERCATOR, DEFOREST, FRANKLIN, GILLETTE, GOODYEAR, LANGMUIR, ROENTGEN, SIKORSKY, WATERMAN, GUTENBERG
inventory LIST, STOCK, STORE
invest ENDOW, ENDUE, INDUE, CLOTHE, ORDAIN
investigate PROBE, INDAGATE
inveterate CHRONIC, HABITUAL
invigorate BRACE, ANIMATE
invite ASK, BID, SUE, SOLICIT
involve LAP, COIL, ENTAIL, EMBROIL, INCLUDE
iodine source KELP
iota *see* JOT

Iowa information *see p. 308*
ipecac source EVEA
Iran ELAM, PERSIA
Iranian languages FARSI, GALCHA, PASHTO, PUSHTO, TADJIK, TAJIKI, AVESTAN, BALUCHI, KURDISH, OSSETIC, PAHLAVI, PERSIAN, SOGDIAN
Iranian measure GUZ, MOU, ZAR, MANSION
Iranian money PUL, KRAN, LARI, POUL, RIAL, DARIC, DINAR, MOHUR, SHAHI, TOMAN, ASHRAFI, PAHLEVI
Iranian weight ZAR, DRAM, DUNG, SANG, ABBAS, DINAR, MAUND, BATMAN, GANDUM, KARWAR, NAKHOD, ABBASSI
Iraqi language ARABIC; *see* IRANIAN
Iraqi measure MISHARA
Iraqi money DINAR
irascible HOT, EDGY, BRASH, TESTY, TOUCHY
irate MAD, ANGRY, WROTH, PIQUED
Ireland, Irish EIRE, ERIN, ERSE, IRENA, EIRANN, HIBERNIA
iris FLAG, GLAD, IRID, IXIA, CROCI, SEDGE, CROCUS, FREESIA, GLADDON, GLADIOLUS
Irish kingdom MEATH, ULSTER, MUNSTER, CONNACHT, LEINSTER
Irish language GAELIC
Irish measure BANDLE, FATHMUR
Irish money RAP, PENCE, POUND, SHILLING
Irish party SINNFEIN
Irishman PAT, AIRE, CELT, HARP, MICK, PADDY, TEAGUE, MILESIAN, HIBERNIAN
irk IRE, VEX, ANNOY, CHAFE, NETTLE, IRRITATE
iron STEEL, FERRUM, MANGLE, MASHIE, FERRITE
iron, pert. to FERRIC, FERROUS
irons *see* FETTER
irony SATIRE, SARCASM
irrational INANE, ABSURD
irrational number SURD
irregular WILD, EROSE, ATYPIC, FITFUL, SPOTTY, UNEVEN, ERRATIC
irritate IRE, IRK, VEX, GALL, RILE, CHAFE, HECTOR, NEEDLE, NETTLE, RANKLE, PROVOKE
Ishmael PARIAH, OUTCAST
isinglass AGAR, MICA, KANTEN
Isis relative HORUS, OSIRIS
Islamic *see* MOHAMMEDAN
island AIT, CAY, ILE, KEY, EYOT, HOLM, ILOT, ISLE, ISLA, REEF, ATOLL, ISLET, ISOLA, INSULA; *see p. 300*
island, pert. to INSULAR
isolate DETACH, ENISLE, IMMURE
Isolde's lover TRISTAN, TRISTRAM
Israel ZION, JACOB, CANAAN, PALESTINE
Israeli money MIL, POUND, PRUTA
Israelite JEW, SION, ZION, HEBREW
Israelite king *see* BIBLICAL RULERS
issue DOLE, EMIT, FLUX, METE, ENSUE, EGRESS, PROGENY
isthmus KRA, BALK, NECK, STRAIT
Italian LATIN, ROMAN, PICENE, SABINE, TUSCAN
Italian family ASTI, ESTE, CENCI, DORIA, DONATI, MEDICI
Italian measure CANNA, PALMO, PUNTO, STAIO, MIGLIO, MOGGIO, RUBBIO, TAVOLA, BRACCIO
Italian money LIRA, LIRE, SCUDO, SOLDO, ZECHIN(O)
Italian weight ONCIA, DENARO, GANDUM, LIBBRA, OTTAVA
Italian words *see p. 268*
Italic languages LADIN, LATIN, OSCAN, CREOLE, FRENCH, CATALAN, ITALIAN, ROMANCE, ROMANIC, ROMANSH, SPANISH, FRIULIAN, UMBRIAN, VENETIC, FALISCAN, RUMANIAN, PROVENCAL, ROUMANIAN, SARDINIAN, PORTUGUESE
itch RIFF, URGE, CRAVE, MANGE, PSORA, ECZEMA, SCABIES, PRURITUS
item UNIT, DATUM, ENTRY, DETAIL, AGENDUM
ivory TUSH, TUSK, DENTINE
Ivory Coast language *see* KWA, GUR, MANDE

ivy VINE, CLIMBER, CREEPER
Ivy League college ELI, PENN, YALE, BROWN, CORNELL, HARVARD, COLUMBIA, DARTMOUTH, PRINCETON

J

jab DIG, BLOW, POKE, PUNCH
Jabberwocky word WABE, MIMSY, SLITHY, UFFISH, VORPAL, BRILLIG
jack NOB, PAM, MULE, NOBS, BOWER, HOIST, KNAVE, OPENER, RABBIT, TINKER
jackal DIEB, THOS; *see* DOG
jackal-headed god ANUBIS
jacket TUX, BAJU, ETON, JUMP, JUPE, PEEL, RIND, SACK, SKIN, BADJU, BANIA, GREGO, PARKA, POLKA, WAMUS, ANORAK, BADJOO, BANIAN, BANYAN, BLAZER, BOLERO, CASING, GANSEY, REEFER, SACQUE, TUXEDO, WAMMUS, WARMUS, BEDGOWN, DOUBLET, NORFOLK, PALETOT, PEACOAT, SPENCER, SURCOAT, WRAPPER, CAMISOLE, CARDIGAN, JAQUETTE, MACKINAW; *see* COAT
Jacob relative *see p. 248*
jagged ZAG, ZIG, CLEFT, EROSE, RAGGED, SERRATE(D)
jaguar *see* CAT
jai alai PELOTA
jai alai term BLE, CESTA, QUANTE, REBOTE, FRONTON
jail CAN, JUG, PEN, BRIG, CAGE, CELL, COOP, GAOL, QUOD, STIR, TANK, CLINK, POKEY, COOLER, LOCKUP
jailer SCREW, GAOLER, WARDEN, TURNKEY
Jakarta BATAVIA
jam FIX, MESS, CRUSH, CONSERVE
jangle JAR, CLANG, CLASH, BICKER
janitor SUPER, PORTER, SEXTON
Japan(ese) AINO, AINU, NIPPON, CIPANGO
Japanese-American ISSEI, KIBEI, NISEI, SANSEI
Japanese measure BU, GO, JO, MO, RI, SE, TO, BOO, CHO, RIN, SHO, SUN, TAN, HIRO, KOKU, SHAKU, TSUBO
Japanese money BU, RIN, SEN, YEN, OBAN, TEMPO, ICHIBU, ITZEBU
Japanese painting school KANO, TOSA, SHIJO, SESSHU, UKIYOE
Japanese ruler JIMMU, JUNGO, KEIKI, MEIJI, SAIWA, TENNO, MIKADO, NAGAKO, TAISHO
Japanese tree G(O)UMI, KIAKI, KEYAKI
Japanese weight MO, FUN, KIN, RIN, SHI, KATI, KWAN, NIYO, MOMME, PICUL
Japanese writing KANA
jar JUG, URN, EWER, JOLT, OLLA, BANGA, CADUS, CLASH, CROCK, CRUSE, STEAN, STEEN, DOLIUM, GOGLET, HYDRIA, KALPIS, PELIKE, AMPHORA, TERRINE; *see* VASE
jargon CANT, ARGOT, IDIOM, LINGO, PATTER; *see* SLANG
Jason relative AESON, MEDEA
Jason's ship ARGO
jaunty CHIC, PERK, COCKY, PERKY, SHOWY, DAPPER, MODISH, RAKISH, SPRUCE
Javanese language KAVI, KAWI, SAS(S)AK
Javanese measure PAAL
javelin JERID, JEREED; *see* SPEAR
jaw MAW, CHAP, JOWL, MAXILLA, MANDIBLE
jaw, pert. to GNATHIC
Jayhawk State KS, KANSAS
jazz BOP, RAG, JIVE, BEBOP, SWING, RAGTIME
jeans LEVIS, DENIMS
jeer *see* MOCK
Jehovah *see* GOD
jejune DRY, ARID, FLAT, STALE, BARREN, INSIPID
Jekyll's other half HYDE
jelly JAM, ASPIC, CANDY, GUAVA, PECTIN
jellyfish JELLY, QUARL, EPHYRA, MEDUSA, ACALEPH, AURELIA, MEDUSAN, SUNFISH, ACALEPHE
jeremiad LAMENT, TIRADE
jerk YANK, DUMMY, HITCH, TWITCH
Jerusalem SION, ZION
jest MOT, JAPE, JIBE, QUIP

jester GOLIARD; *see* BUFFOON
Jesuit founder LOYOLA
Jesus LAMB, AGNUS, LOGOS, CHRIST, SAVIO(U)R, REDEEMER
jet EBON, BLACK, RAVEN, SABRE, SPOUT, STREAM
jet engine JATO, ATHODYD
jetty DOCK, MOLE, PIER, QUAY, WHARF, STARLING
Jew HEBREW, SEMITE, ISRAELITE
jewel BIJOU, LOUPE, PRIZE, TRINKET; *see* GEM
jewelry, mock LOGIE, PASTE, STRASS
Jewish JUDAIC; *see* HEBREW, ISRAELI
Jezebel relative AHAB
jib BALK, BOOM, SPAR
jinx HEX, JONAH, HOODOO
jitters CREEPS, NERVES, DITHERS, JIMJAMS
jittery EDGY, JUMPY, HECTIC
Joan of Arc PUCELLE
Joan of Arc birthplace DOMREMY
Job's comforters ELIHU, BILDAD, ZOPHAR, ELIPHAZ
Jocasta relative LAIUS, OEDIPUS
jocund GAY, MERRY, JOYFUL
jog HOD, TROT, DUNCH, NUDGE, REMIND
John IAN, EOAN, EOIN, HANS, IVAN, SEAN
join MELD, WELD, YOKE, MERGE, MITER, MITRE, UNITE, ATTACH, ENLIST, RABBET, SPLICE
joint COXA, DUAL, GENU, KNEE, LINK, NODE, SEAM, ELBOW, HINGE, NEXUS, SCARF, SPALD, SPAUL, TENON, WRIST, SPAULD, ARTHRON
joke GAG, KID, MOT, PUN, RIB, JAPE, JEST, JOSH, QUIP, TWIT, SALLY, TEASE
joker DOR, WAG, WIT, CARD, CLOWN, PUNSTER, JESTER, BUFFOON, FARCEUR
jolly YAWL, MERRY, JOCUND
jolt JAR, JERK, SHOCK, JOUNCE
Jordanian money DINAR
Joseph relative MARY, JACOB, RACHEL
jostle JOG, MAUL, ELBOW, BUFFET, HUSTLE
jot ACE, BUT, IOTA, MITE, MOTE, NOTE, WHIT, TITTLE
journal LOG, DIARY, PAPER, RECORD, DIURNAL, TRUNNION
journalist BOK, DANA, HOWE, OCHS, PYLE, REID, RICE, RIIS, WEED, ADAMS, BROUN, DAVIS, GRADY, HERSH, NOYES, SWOPE, WHITE, BIERCE, BOWLES, CURTIS, FINLEY, GODKIN, HARVEY, HEARST, RUNYON, GREELEY, MCCLURE, MENCKEN, NEWSMAN, BRISBANE, REPORTER
journey EYRE, HIKE, ITER, RIDE, TOUR, TREK, TRIP, JAUNT, JUNKET, TRAVEL, VOYAGE, ODYSSEY
joust BOUT, TILT, TOURNEY
joy GLEE, ZEST, BLISS, MIRTH, DELIGHT, RAPTURE
joyous GAY, GLAD, MERRY, RIANT, BLITHE, ELATED, FESTAL
Judean notable HEROD, PILATE
judge(s) TRY, UMP, CADI, CAZI, CAZY, DEEM, DOOM, FOUD, KADI, KAZI, KAZY, RATE, HAKIM, JUDEX, MINOS, AEACUS, CRITIC, PUISNE, UMPIRE, ALCALDE, ARBITER, REFEREE; *see* JURIST
judgment DOOM, VIEW, ARRET, AWARD, VERDICT, DECISION
jug EWER, LOTA, OLPE, TOBY, BUIRE, LOTAH, FLAGON, LOCKUP, PITCHER
juice JUS, SAP, MUST, RHOB, SAPA, STUM, SURA
Juliet relative TYBALT, CAPULET
Juliet's fiancé PARIS
Juliet's lover ROMEO
jumble PI, MIX, PIE, HASH, MESS, OLIO, MEDLEY, FARRAGO
jump HOP, JERK, LEAP, SKIP, BOUND, VAULT
juncture SEAM, JOINT, SUTURE
Jungle Book author KIPLING
Jungle Book character AKELA, MOWGLI
junior FILS, CADET, PUISNE
juniper CADE, GORSE, R(A)ETEM, SAVIN(E)
Juno, Jupiter *see p. 317*
jurisdiction SOC, SOKE, VENUE
jurist KEY, ELEN, HAND, GAIUS, NIZER, SOLON,

DARROW, ERSKIN, HOLMES, LANDIS, SIRICA, CARDOZO, SAVIGNY; *see* JUSTICE
jury PANEL, PETIT, GRAND, VENIRE
just DUE, FAIR, MORAL, BARELY
justice, chief JAY, TAFT, CHASE, STONE, TANEY, WAITE, WHITE, FULLER, HUGHES, VINSON, WARREN, MARSHALL
jut BULGE, PROJECT, PROTRUDE
jute DESI, HEMP, DAISEE
jute fabric MAT, GUNNY, BURLAP, SACKING

K

kaiser WILHELM
kale *see* CABBAGE
kangaroo ROO, JOEY, BOOMER, WALLABY, PADEMELON
kangaroo bear KOALA
Kashmiri language *see* DARD
kayak CANOE, UMIAK, OOMIA(C)K
keel FIN, LIST, TILT, CAREEN, CARINA, RUDDLE
keen GARE, GLEG, TART, WAIL, ACRID, ACUTE, DIRGE, EAGER, SHARP, SNELL, ASTUTE
keenness EDGE, ZEST, ACIES, ARDOR
keep SAVE, TEND, RETAIN, CUSTODY; *see* FORT
keeper NAB, TILER, MAHOUT, RANGER, CURATOR; *see* JAILER
keepsake RELIC, TOKEN, MEMENTO
keg TUN, VAT, CADE, CASK, FIRKIN, BREAKER, GROWLER
Kenya language SWAHILI
kerchief CURCH, SCARF, BANDANA, BABUSHKA
kernel NUT, PIT, CORE, GIST, PITH, SEED
kettle BILLY, CALDRON, POTHOLE, CAULDRON
kettledrum *see* PERCUSSION
key CAY, CLUE, CODE, ISLE, PONY, DITAL, ISLET, PITCH, CLAVIS, COTTER, SPLINE, TAPPER, TONALITY
key part BIT, BOW, PIN, WEB, LOOP, STEM, COLLAR
Keystone State PA, PENN(SYLVANIA)
khan AGA, ALI, INN, CHAM, PRINCE
Khoisan BUSHMAN, HOTTENTOT
kick BOOT, HACK, PUNT, RECOIL
kid LAD, RIB, JOSH, SUEDE, TEASE, BANTER, (Y)EARLING
kidnap ABDUCT, RAVISH, SNATCH, SHANGHAI
kidneys, pert. to RENAL, NEPHRIC
kill PREY, SLAY, VETO, CANCEL, MURDER
killer BRAVO, SLAYER, ASSASSIN
kiln OST, LEER, LEHR, OAST, OVEN, TILER(Y)
kin SIB(S), FOLKS, FAMILY
kind ILK, TYPE, GENOS, GENRE, GENUS, SEELY, BENIGN, GENIAL, GENTLE, SPECIES
kindle TIND, WHET, SPUNK, IGNITE
kindness BOON, GRACE, LENITY
kindred KIN, SIB, AKIN, KITH, COGNATE
king REX, REY, ROI, KRAL, SOPHY, REGULUS, PADISHAH
King Arthur *see* ARTHURIAN
king, pert. to REG(N)AL
kingdom REALM, DOMAIN, EMPIRE, MONARCHY
kingfisher TODY, HALCYON, KOOKABURRA
kingfisher genus ALCEDO, DACELO
kinship NASAB, ENATION, AFFINITY, AGNATION
kismet DOOM, FATE, DESTINY
kiss BUSS, PECK, SMACK, CARESS, OSCULATE
kit LOT, SET, TUB, GEAR, PACK, BUCKET, OUTFIT
kitchen GALLEY, COOKERY, CUISINE, SCULLERY
kitchen fixture OVEN, SINK, RANGE, STOVE, FRIDGE, ICEBOX
kitchen utensil CORER, DICER, LADLE, MIXER, RICER, SCOOP, SIEVE, BEATER, FUNNEL, GRATER, JUICER, OPENER, PEELER, SPATULA, COLANDER; *see* COOKING

kite GLEAN, GLEDE, PUTTOCK
kite genus ELANUS, MILVUS
kitty POT, ANTE, POOL, WIDOW
knack FEAT, HANG, FLAIR, TALENT
knave NOB, PAM, JACK, NOBS, BOWER, CHURL, LOREL, LOSEL, ROGUE, SCAMP
knead ELT, MALAX, PETRIE, MASSAGE
knee GENU, HOCK
knee part DIB, HOCK, ROTULA, PATELLA, HAMSTRING
knife DAH, DOW, SNY, ULU, BOLO, CHIV, DIRK, KRIS, SHIV, SNEE, STAB, BLADE, BOWIE, CHIVE, FLEAM, BARLOW, BETRAY, BODKIN, CARVER, CATLIN, LANCET, CATLING, STILETTO; *see* DAGGER
knife cover SHEATH, SCABBARD
knife part HAFT, TANG
knight(s) DUB, SIR, BEVIS, EQUES, RITTER, EQUITES, PALADIN, TEMPLAR, BANNERET; *see p. 331*
knitting term PURL, SLEY, GAUGE, STITCH
knob NUB, BOSS, KNOP, NODE, STUD, UMBO, KNURL, FINIAL, NUBBLE
knobbed NODAL, NODOSE, TOROSE
knock down DECK, FLOOR
knockout KO, TKO, BASH, KAYO
knoll KNAP, TOFT, MOUND, HUMMOCK
knot NEP, BEND, BURL, KNAR, KNOR, KNUR, LOOP, LUMP, MILE, NODE, NODI, NOIL, REEF, SNAG, GNARL, HITCH, KNAUR, KNURL, MOUSE, NODUS, AMORET, GRANNY, TREFOIL, BOWLINE
knot, remove ENODATE, UNRAVEL
know DEN, WIS, WOT, WIST, INTUIT
knowing HIP, ONTO, WISE, SCIENT, GNOSTIC
knowledge KEN, KITH, LORE, OLOGY, NOESIS, WISDOM, SCIENTIA
Koran chapter SURA(H)
Korea CHOSEN
Korean leader KWON, PARK, RHEE, SUNG
Korean money WON, CHON, HWAN
kosher, opposite of TREF(A)
Kubla Khan river ALPH
Kwa language GA, EDO, EWE, FON, IBO, KRU, AGNI, AKAN, NUPE, BASSA, GREBO, YORUBA

L

label TAG, FILLET, INFULA, LAPPET, PASTER, STICKER
labor *see* WORK
labor leader GREEN, HOFFA, LEWIS, MEANY, QUILL, REUTHER, PETRILLO
labor union AFL, CIO, ELA, ILA, ITA, IWW, UAW, ARTEL, GUILD, ILGWU, LOCAL, AFLCIO
laboratory utensil RETORT, ALEMBIC, CRUCIBLE, TESTTUBE
laborer ESNE, HAND, HELP, PEON, TOTY, NAVVY, PROLE, COOLIE, FELLAH, SEGGON, TOILER, BRACERO
labyrinth MAZE
lace BEAT, LASH, ADORN, AGLET, BRAID, CLUNY, FILET, GRILL, LACIS, ORRIS, SNARE, AIGLET, EDGING, GRILLE, ALENCON, GUIPURE, MACRAME, MALINES, TATTING, FILIGREE
lace, make TAT
lacerate RIP, TEAR, LANIATE
lack NEED, WANT, DEARTH, FAMINE, DEFICIT, SCARCITY
lackey FLUNKY, FOOTMAN
lacking SHY, SHORT, DEVOID
laconic CURT, TERSE, CONCISE
lacquer JAPAN, ENAMEL, VARNISH
ladder STY, STEE, SCALE, POMPIER
ladder part RUNG, STEP, ROUND, SPOKE, STAVE, RUNDLE
lading CARGO
ladle DIP, BAIL, GEAT, SCOOP, SHANK, DIPPER
lady BIBI, BURD, DAME, BEEBEE; *see* MADAM
Lady of the Lake ELLEN, NIMUE, VIVIAN

Laertes relative OPHELIA, ULYSSES, POLONIUS
lag DRAG, DALLY, TARRY
lagoon HAFF, LIMAN
lair DEN, CAVE, HAUNT, COVERT
Laius relative JOCASTA, OEDIPUS
lake LOCH, MERE, SHAT, TARN, LOUGH, SHOTT, LAGOON, SALINA
Lake George HORICON
Lake State MI, MICHIGAN
Lakes REE, SEG, VAN, ZUG, BAFA, BIWA, CHAD, COMO, DEBO, ERIE, ISEO, KIVU, MEAD, TAAL, TANA, THUN, ABAYA, AMMER, AMPER, ASNEN, ATLIN, ATTER, BAKER, BALAH, BELOE, CADDO, CHANY, ELTON, ENARE, GARDA, GARRY, ILMEN, INARI, JUNIN, KYOGA, LANAO, LEMAN, MERIN, MINTO, MIRIM, MWERU, NIRIZ, NYASA, ONEGA, PETEN, POOPO, PSKOV, TAHOE, TAUPO, TSANA, TUMBA, URMIA, ACHKEL, ALAKUL, ALBANO, ALBERT, ANNECY, APOPKA, BABINE, BAIKAL, DONNER, IAZBAL, KHANKA, LADOGA, MAGADI, ONEIDA, PEIPUS, RUDOLF, SALTON, SIMCOE, VANERN, ATITLAN, BALATON, BALKASH, DUBAWNT, ILIAMNA, KOKONOR, NIPIGON, TEXCOCO, TORRENS, MANITOBA, TITICACA, VICTORIA; *see* GREAT LAKE
Lakshmi consort VISHNU
lama MONK, DALAI, TESHU
lamb (Y)EAN; *see* SHEEP
lame HALT, FEEBLE, INFIRM, CRIPPLE, DISABLE
Lamech relative ADAH, NOAH, JABAL, JUBAL
lament RUE, WEY, HONE, KEEN, MOAN, PINE, WAIL, DIRGE, BEWAIL, GRIEVE, REPINE
lamentation LINOS, TANGI, PLAINT, PLANGOR
lamina *see* LAYER
lamp DAVY, GLIM, ARGAND, CRUSIE, GEORDIE, LAMPION, LUCERNE, LUCIGEN
lamp part WICK, BURNER, CHIMNEY, CRESSET
lamp, waving of ARATI
lampoon SKIT, SQUIB, PARODY, SATIRE, TAKEOFF
lamprey RAMPER; *see* EEL
lance OPEN, SLASH, SPEAR, PIERCE, JAVELIN
Lancelot beloved ELAINE, GUINEVERE
lancer U(H)LAN, HUSSAR
lancet *see* KNIFE
land ALOD, DOAB, DUAB, FELI, GISH, GORE, MULK, ODAL, UDAL, ARADA, ARADO, ARDER, GLEBE, SOLUM, TILTH, TRACT, VELDT, WEALD, ALIGHT, ASSART, DEBARK, STEPPE, TUNDRA, PRAIRIE, ALODIUM
land, barren GALL, WASTE, DESERT
land measure *see* MEASURE
land, pert. to AGRARIAN, GEOPONIC
landholder THANE, THEGN, ZAMINDAR
landing KEY, DOCK, GHAT, PIER, QUAI, QUAY, GHAUT, JETTY, LEVEE, WHARF
landlord HOST, LAIRD, OWNER, LEASER, BONIFACE, INNKEEPER
landmark COPA, MERE, CAIRN, MEITH, SENAL
landscape VISTA, SURVEY, PAYSAGE, SCENERY
lane PATH, WYND, ALLEY
language IDIOM, TONGUE, DIALECT, DICTION, PARLANCE
language, artificial RO, IDO, VOLAPUK, ESPERANTO
language families GUR, IJO, KWA, AINU, CHAD, DARD, THAI, TUPI, ARYAN, BANTU, GREEK, HATSA, INDIC, KAREN, MANDE, MUNDA, TAMIL, TATAR, YAKUT, AFGHAN, ALTAIC, ARABIC, BALTIC, BASQUE, BERBER, CELTIC, GILYAK, ITALIC, KOREAN, PAPUAN, SLAVIC, TELUGA, TURKIC, URALIC,
languish FLAG, PINE, WASTE
languor KEF, KAIF, KEEF, KIEF, KIFF, BLUES, ENNUI, TORPOR
lanky LEAN, GANGLY, SLENDER
lantern LAMP, LOUVER, CRESSET
lanyard CORD, ROPE, THONG

Laomedon kingdom TROY
Laomedon relative ILUS, PRIAM
Laotian language LAO
Laotian money AT(T), KIP
lapel FLAP REVER(S)
lapse ERR, SIN(K), VENALITY; see INTERVAL
larch genus LARIX
large FULL, AMPLE, GREAT, DECUMAN, OUTSIZE
lariat LAZO, ROPE, LASSO, NOOSE, REATA, RIATA
lariat eye HONDA, HONDO(O)
lark SPREE, FROLIC; see SONGBIRD
lark genus ALAUDA
larva BOT(T), CRAB, GRUB, MAWK, SLUG, TURK, REDIA, VELUM, CADDIS, GENTLE, MAGGOT, TUSSAH, WABBLE, WARBLE, CADDICE, CADELLE, CODWORM, FLYBLOW, PLANULA, PLUTEUS, WIGGLER, CERCARIA, GLOWWORM, NAUPLIUS, PEARSLUG, TORNARIA, WRIGGLER; see WORM
lascivious LEWD, WANTON
lash FLOG, KNUT, WALE, YERK, QUIRT, WHALE; see WHIP
lasso see LARIAT
last END, DURE, FINAL, OMEGA, ENDURE, FINALE
last but one PENULT
Last Mohican UNCAS
Last Supper C(O)ENA; see COMMUNION
latch(ing) BELAY, SNECK, LASKET
late NEO, NEW, DEAD, SERO, TARDY, RECENT
latent HIDDEN, DORMANT
lath SLAT, SPALE, SPLINT
lather FOAM, SCUM, SUDS, FROTH, SPUME, FRENZY
Latin words see p. 270
Latona relative DIANA, APOLLO
Latter-Day Saint MORMON
lattice BOWER, GRILLE, SCREEN, TRELLIS, CANCELLI
Latvian LETT(IC), LETTISH
Latvian measure KANNE, STOOF, KULMET
Latvian money LAT, RUBLIS, SANTIMS, KAPEIKA
laud EXTOL, PRAISE
laugh(s) HOWL, ROAR, FLEER, CACKLE, GUFFAW, GIGGLE, TITTER, CHORTLE, SNICKER
laughable see COMIC
laughing RIANT, RIDENT
laughter, pert. to GELASTIC
launch SEND, LANCE, PROPEL; see SHIP
laundry equipment IRON, SOAP, DRIER, BLEACH, MANGLE, WASHER
laurel ANIBA, CASSY, WICKY, DAPHNE, CAJEPUT, CASSYTHA
lava AA, ASH, BOMB, MAGMA, COULEE, LATITE, SCORIA, TAXITE, LAPILLUS
lavatory BOWL, BASIN, LAVABO, RESTROOM
law ACT, FAS, JUS, LEX, ADAT, CODE, JURE, RULE, TORA, CANON, DROIT, EDICT, SALIC, TORAH, TALION, TALMUD, DECALOG, STATUTE, DECALOGUE
law, pert. to LEGAL, FORENSIC
lawful LEGAL, LICIT, ENNOMIC
lawgiver DRACO, SOLON, MINOS, MOSES
lawmaker see LEGISLATOR
lawn PLOT, GLADE, SWARD, BATISTE, CAMBRIC
lawyer JURIST, LEGIST, PORTIA, COUNSEL, ADVOCATE, ATTORNEY, BARRISTER, COUNSELOR, SOLICITOR
laxative APERIENT, CATHARTIC, PURGATIVE
lay BET, LAIC, DITTY, PLACE, BALLAD, LAICAL, ASCRIBE, SECULAR
lay up HEAP, HOARD, STORE
layer PLY, COAT, TIER, CORTEX, LAMINA, PATINA, STRATA, VENEER, PROVINE, STRATUM
lazy (one) BUM, LUSK, DRONE, IDLER, LOAFER, OTIOSE
lea MEAD, SWARD, MEADOW, PASTURE
lead WAD, HEAD, PILOT, PLUMB, PRESA, GALENA, SINKER, SOLDER, PLUMBUM, PRECENT
leader DUX, VAN, DUCE, CHIEF, GUIDE, SNELL, CANTOR, FUHRER, CAUDILLO
leading VAN, CHIEF, FORE(MOST)
leaf OLA, OLE, FOIL, OLAY, OLLA, PAGE, BRACT, FOLIO, FROND, SEPAL, SHEET,

LAMINA, SPATHE, LAMELLA, TENDRIL
leaf part PEN, RIB, VEIN, BLADE, STOMA, MIDRIB, STIPEL, PETIOLE, STIPULE, STOMATA
leaflet FLYER, PINNA, TRACT
leafy FOLIOSE
league BLOC, BUND, PACT, HANSE, COMBINE, ENTENTE
Leah relative LEVI, JACOB, JUDAH, LABAN, RACHEL, REUBEN, SIMEON
leak OOZE, SEEP, SPILL
lean BONY, LANK, GAUNT, LANKY, SPARE, SCRAWNY
lean-to SHED, LINTER
Leander's lover HERO
leap LOUP, LOWP, SKIP, FRISK, LUNGE, SALTO, STEND, VAULT, CURVET
Lear relative REGAN, GONERIL, CORDELIA
learn CON, STUDY, MEMORIZE
learned ERUDITE, LETTERED, LITERATE
learned person *see* SAGE
learning KEN, LORE, WISDOM
lease LET, HIRE, RENT, CONVEY, DEMISE, CHARTER
leash CURB, JESS, LUNE, LYAM
leather ELK, KID, BOCK, CALF, NAPA, ROAN, YUFT, ALUTA, JUFTI, MOCHA, SUEDE, BULGAR, LEVANT, OXHIDE, SKIVER, VELLUM, CANEPIN, CHAMOIS, COWHIDE, MOROCCO, SHAGREEN
leather, convert into TAN, TAW
leave EXIT, PAGE, QUIT, WILL, ADIEU, CONGE, EXEAT, VACATE, FURLOUGH
leaven BARM, ZYME, YEAST
leavings ORTS, CHAFF, DRAFF, DREGS, RESIDUE; *see* REFUSE
Lebanese language ARABIC
Lebanese money POUND, PIASTER
lectern AMBO, DESK, PULPIT
Leda's child HELEN, CASTOR, POLLUX
Leda's lover SWAN, ZEUS
ledge CAY, BERM, LODE, REEF, SILL, APRON, BERME, SHELF
ledger item ASSET, DEBIT, ENTRY, CREDIT
leech SAIL, TOADY, PARASITE
lees DRAF, DREGS, DROSS, MOTHER
left KAY, PORT, WENT, LARBOARD
left-hand (page) LEVO, VERSO
leftist LIBERAL, RADICAL
leftover ORT, SCRAP, MORSEL, REMNANT
leg GAM, PEG, PIN, GAMB, LIMB, GAMMON
leg part CRUS, KNEE, SHIN, ANKLE, SHANK; *see* BONE
leg, pert. to SURAL, CRURAL
legacy GIFT, WILL, BEQUEST
legal LEAL, JURAL, LICIT, VALID, LAWFUL
legal action RES, CASE, SUIT, LAWSUIT, LITIGATION
legal term ACTA, BILL, LIEN, MORA, PLEA, TORT, WRIT, DROIT, VENUE, APPEAL, CAVEAT, DELICT, SEIZIN, SUMMONS, DEMURRER, SUBPOENA
legate ENVOY, NUNCIO
legation EMBASSY, MISSION
legend MYTH, SAGA, FABLE, MOTTO, CAPTION, FICTION
legging COCKER, COGGER, GAITER, PUTTEE, GAMBADO
legislator DRACO, MINOS, MOSES, SOLON, DEPUTY, SENATOR
legislature *see* ASSEMBLY
legitimate REAL, LEGAL, LICIT, VALID, GENUINE
legume PEA, POD, BEAN, GUAR, PULSE, LOMENT, SOYBEAN
legwear CHAPS, SHAPS, SPATS, GARTER, GAMASHES, SUSPENDERS; *see* PANTS, LEGGING
leisure EASE, REST, TOOM, OTIUM, REPOSE
lemur LORI, MAKI, VARI, AVAHI, INDRI, KOKAM, LORIS, POTTO, SIFAC, ADAPID, AYEAYE, COLUGO, MACACO, MOHOLI, SIFAKA, LEMURID, TARSIER
lemur genus ADAPIS, INDRIS
Lena tributary ALDAN, VITIM
length EXTENT; *see* MEASURE
lengthy LONG, PROLIX
lenient GENTLE, CLEMENT
lens ADON, GLASS, TORIC, CONVEX, CONCAVE, MENISCUS
Leoncavallo opera ZAZA, BOHEME, PAGLIACCI
leopard PANTHER; *see* CAT

leotard TIGHTS
leper LAZAR, PARIAH, OUTCAST
Lesage novel (GIL)BLAS
Lesbos poet ARION, SAPPHO, ALCAEUS, LESCHES
lessee RENTER, TENANT
lessen BATE, FADE, THIN, ABATE, MINIFY, REDUCE, MITIGATE
lesson LECTURE, EXERCISE
let ALLOW, PERMIT; *see* LEASE
let it stand STET
let up EASE, ABATE, RELAX
lethal *see* FATAL
lethargy COMA, SOPOR, APATHY, STUPOR, TORPOR, INERTIA, LANGUOR
Leto relative COEUS, DIANA, APOLLO, ARTEMIS
letter BULL, LINE, MEMO, NOTE, RUNE, BRIEF, DEMIT, BILLET, PARAPH, UNCIAL, CAPITAL, EPISTLE, MISSIVE; *see* ALPHABET
letter, Anglo-Saxon EDH, ETH, WEN, THORN
lettuce COS, BIBB, SALAD, ENDIVE, ICEBERG, ROMAINE
levee DURBAR; *see* EMBANKMENT, LANDING
level AIM, EVEN, RASE, RAZE, FLUSH, GRADE, PLANE, STEADY
lever BAR, PRY, CANT, PEVY, CRANK, PEAVY, PEDAL, PRIZE, TAPPET
Levi relative JACOB, GERSHON, KOHATA, MERARI
levy DRAFT, MUSTER; *see* TAX
lewd CADGY, LUSTFUL, INDECENT
Lhasa palace POTALA
liable APT, BOUND, EXPOSED, SUBJECT
liar FIBBER, ANANIAS, WERNARD
libel DEFAME, SLANDER, ROORBACK
liberal BROAD, GENEROUS, TOLERANT
liberate FREE, REDEEM, MANUMIT
Liberian language *see* KWA, MANDE
libertine RAKE, ROUE, DEBAUCHEE
Libyan measure PIK(E), BOZZE, JABIA, MATTARO
license GRANT, PATENT
lichen USNEA, ARCHIL, ORCHIL, EVERNIA, LUNGWORT
lichen derivative ARCHIL, LITMUS, PERSIS, CUDBEAR
lick LAP, FLOG, WHIP, THRASH
lid CAP, TOP, COVER, OPERCULUM
lie FIB, LIGE, INHERE, FICTION
lie in wait LURK, SKULK
Liechtenstein money FRANC, RAPPEN
lieutenant LUFF, LOOEY, LOOIE, JEMADAR, SHAVETAIL
lieutenant's command PLATOON
life VIE, BIOS, DAYS, VITA, ANIMA, BIOTA, CAREER
life, pert. to VITAL, BIOTIC(AL)
life preserver DONUT, MAEWEST
life principle JIVA, ATMAN, PRANA
lifeless DEAD, FLAT, AMORT, AZOIC, INERT, DEFUNCT, EXTINCT
lift(ed) HEFT, HOVE, PERK, EXALT, HEAVE, HOIST, RAISE, STEAL, ELEVATOR
lifting engine RAM, JACK, CRANE, DAVIT, HOIST, JENNY, NORIA, SAKIEH, SHADOFF
ligament BOND, DESMO, TAENIA
light ARC, AIRY, GLIM, HALO, LAND, LUNT, NEON, FANAL, FLARE, FLASH, KLEIG, LASER, LEGER, MATCH, TAPER, TORCH, CANDLE, CORONA, IGNITE, ILLUME, NIMBUS, SCONCE, CRESSET; *see* LAMP, LANTERN
light unit LUX, PYR, PHOT, LUMEN, CARCEL, HEFNER
lighter HOY, SCOW, SPILL
light-headed DIZZY, GIDDY
lighthearted GAY, CAREFREE
lighthouse PHARE, PHAROS
lightning BOLT, LAIT, FLASH, LEVIN, FIREBALL, WILDFIRE
ligulate LORATE
like AKIN, ENJOY, RELISH, COGNATE
likely APT, PRONE, SEEMLY
likeness ICON, GUISE, IMAGE, EFFIGY, ANALOGY
likewise ITEM, DITTO, BESIDES
liking FANCY, TASTE, FONDNESS

lilac PRIM, MAUVE, PRIVET, SYRINGA, PIPETREE
lily LIS, ALOE, ARUM, SEGO, CALLA, DATIL, HOSTA, LOTUS, TUCKY, TULIP, WOKAS, YUCCA, DAGGER, GUNKIA, SMILAX, BAYONET, HYACINTH
lily maid of Astolat ELAINE
limb ARM, FIN, LEG, WING, BOUGH, BRANCH, MEMBER
limber LITHE, SUPPLE, PLIABLE
lime CALX, CITRUS, LINDEN
limestone CAEN, CALP, LIAS, MALM, TUFA, CHALK, OOLITE
limit EDGE, PALE, SPAN, TERM, BOURN, STENT, STINT, BORDER, BOURNE, CONFINE
limp HALT, FLABBY, FLIMSY
Lincoln assassin BOOTH
linden LIN, LIME, LIND, LINN, TEIL, TILIA, BASSWOOD
line CUE, DRY, ROW, WAD, CORD, EDGE, FILE, RANK, TROT, AGONE, CERIF, QUEUE, SERIF, SNELL, STEAN, STRIA, CERIPH, CORDON, EARING, PATTER, SECANT, STEENE, STRIAE, VECTOR, MARLINE
lineage STEM, BLOOD, STOCK, STRAIN, DESCENT, PEDIGREE; *see* FAMILY
linen LAWN, CRASH, SCRIM, TOILE, BYSSUS, DAMASK, DOWLAS, NAPERY, SHEETS, BATISTE, CAMBRIC, DRABBET, HOLLAND, LINGERIE
linen measure CUT, HEER
lines, marked by RULED, STRIATE(D)
linger LAG, DALLY, DWELL, TARRY, DAWDLE, LOITER
lingerie *see* UNDERWEAR
lingo *see* JARGON
lining GASKET, BUSHING, DOUBLURE, WAINSCOT
link(s) YOKE, CHAIN, NEXUS, COPULA, COUPLE, COURSE, CONJOIN, CONNECT, CATENA(T)E
lint TENT, FUZZ, FLUFF
lion LEO, ARIEL, SIMBA; *see* CAT
lion-headed god(dess) SEKHMET, NEFERTUM
lip RIM, EDGE, SASS, LABIUM
lip ornament LABRET, PELELE
lip, pert. to LABIAL
liquefied FUSIL(E), POTATE
liquefy RUN, FUSE, MELT, THAW
liqueur ANIS, MARC, RAKI, AURUM, CACAO, CREME, NOYAU, PEACH, SNAPS, ANANAS, BANANA, CASSIS, CHERRY, FRAISE, GENEPI, KIRSCH, KUMMEL, MENTHE, MISTRA, PERNOD, POUSSE, SNAPPS, STREGA, CORDIAL, CURACAO, NOYEAUX, PARFAIT, RATAFIA, SLOEGIN, ABSINTHE, ANISETTE, AMARETTO, PRUNELLE, SCHNAPPS, TIAMARIA; *see* LIQUORS
liquid measure *see* MEASURE
liquidate KILL, PURGE, SETTLE, AMORTIZE
liquor, bad BOUSE, BOWSE, SLIPSLOP
liquors GIN, RUM, RYE, BENO, TIFF, KEFIR, PISCO, VODKA, ARRACK, BRANDY, COGNAC, GENEPI, KUMISS, MASTIC, MESCAL, PULQUE, SCOTCH, WHISKY, YVETTE, AQUAVIT, BACARDI, BOURBON, DAMIANA, QUETSCH, RASPAIL, TEQUILA, WHISKEY, ADVOCAAT, ARMAGNAC, CALVADOS, CLEANRUM, DRAMBUIE, APPLEJACK, SLIVOVITZ; *see* BEER, DRINK, LIQUEUR
lissome LITHE, NIMBLE, SVELTE
list TIP, ALBE, CANT, CAST, HARK, HEEL, LEAN, LEET, PLOW, ROTA, TILT, ALBUM, INDEX, PANEL, SLATE, TABLE, AGENDA, CAREEN, ROSTER, TARIFF, CATALOG, REGISTER
listen BUG, HARK, HEAR, HEED, HIST, OBEY, HARKEN, EAVESDROP
listener BUGGER, AUDITOR
listlessness *see* APATHY
litany EKTENE, ROGATION
literal EXACT, STRICT, VERBAL, PROSAIC, VIRTUAL, EXPLICIT
literature, characters in *see p. 313*
lithe AGILE, PLIANT, SUPPLE, SVELTE, LISSOME, FLEXIBLE
lithograph PRINT, CHROMO
lithographer REDON, BONNARD, HOKUSAI, KOLLWITZ

Lithuanian money LIT(AS), MARKA, RUBLE, CENTAS, FENNIG, OSTMARK
litter BIER, BROOD, CABIN, MULCH, FARROW
little SMA, WEE, POCO, PUNY, PETIT, MINUTE, PALTRY
Little Corporal NAPOLEON
Little Russia UKRAINE
liturgy MASS, RITE, RITUAL
litus SERF, COLONUS
live ARE, DWELL, EXIST, QUICK, RESIDE, TEEMING
livelihood KEEP, BREAD, LIVING, MEANS, SUPPORT
lively VIR, KEEN, PERK, PERT, SPRY, VIVO, YARE, AGILE, BRISK, CANTY, DESTO, PEART, PERKY, VIVID, NIMBLE, ANIMATO
lively person GRIG, DYNAMO
liver, pert. to HEPATIC
livid WAN, BLAE, PALE, ASHEN
lixivium LYE, LEACH
lizard DAB, ADDA, DABB, GILA, SEPS, TEJU, URAN, ANOLE, ANOLI, GECKO, GUANO, SKINK, SWIFT, TOKAY, VARAN, WARAL, AGAMID, ANGUID, HARDIM, IGUANA, LACERT, LEGUAN, MOLOCH, WORREL, WORRAL, ZONURE, ANOLIAN, CHEECHA, IGUANID, MONITOR, SAURIAN, SCINCID, TARENTE, AGAMIDAE, ANGUIDAE, BASILISK, HELODERM, IGUANOID, MOKOMOKO, MOSASAUR, SCORPION, BLOWWORM, WHIPTAIL, CHAMELEON; *see* SALAMANDER
lizard genus UTA, AGAMA, DRACO, SEKKO, AMEIVA, ANGUIS, ANOLIS, MABUYA, EUMECES, GEKKOTA, IGUANID, LACERTA, PYGOPUS, TEIIDAE, VARANUS, ZONURID, ZONURUS, LACERATE, LYGOSOMA
lizardlike SAURIAN
llama LAMA, PACO, ALPACA, VICUNA, GUANACO
load CARK, LADE, ONUS, CARGO
loaf BAP, CAKE, IDLE, LOLL, MIKE, LOITER, LOUNGE
loam MARL, MALM, LOESS, REGUR
loath AVERSE, RELUCTANT
lobby HALL, FOYER ANTEROOM, VESTIBULE
lobster DAD, ERYON, HOMARD, CRAWDAD, CRAWFISH, CRAYFISH
lobster genus ASTACUS, MACRURA
local CHAPTER, EDAPHIC, TOPICAL
locale SITE, SCENE, VENUE
locality AREA, SPOT, ZONE, LOCUS, PLACED, PURLIEU
lock JAG, TAG, CURL, FRIB, HASP, TRESS, COTTER, DETENT, RINGLET
lock part BOLT, WARD, STUMP, TUMBLER, CYLINDER
lockjaw TETANUS, TRISMUS
locks, Panama Canal GATUN
locomotive DOLLY, DUMMY, MOGUL, TEXAS, BIGBOY, DINKEY, MIKADO, PACIFIC, PRAIRIE, SANTAFE, SWITCHER; *see* TRAIN
locust *see* GRASSHOPPER
lode LEAD, REEF, VEIN, LEDGE, RIDER, SCRIN
lodestar POLARIS
lodge BOARD, CABIN, ROOST, BILLET, QUARTER; *see* TENT
lodger ROOMER, TRANSIENT
loft LOB, ATTIC, GARRET, GALLERY, MANSARD
log DIARY, RECORD, TIMBER
logarithm unit BEL, MANTISSA
loge BOX, BOOTH, STALL
loggia ARCADE, PORTICO
logic term LEMMA, PONENT, SALTUS, ORGANON, PREMISS, SORITES, SUMPTION, SUBALTERN
logroller BIRLER, DECKER
Lohengrin's bride ELSA
loincloth MALO, MARO, DHOTI, LUNGI, PAGNE, DHOOTI
loiter POKE, SAUNTER; *see* LINGER
Loki relative HEL(A), VALI, NERVE, SIGYN, FENRIS
Loki's victim BALDER
London AGUSTA
London quarter SOHO, ADELPHI, CHELSEA, MAYFAIR, HOLBORN, LAMBETH, BELGRAVIA
London street BOND, BAKER, FLEET, STRAND

Lone Ranger's companion TONTO
Lone Ranger's horse SILVER
Lone Star State TX, TEXAS
long YEN, ACHE, PANT, PINE, COVET, CRAVE, YEARN, ASPIRE, HANKER, PROLIX
long ago ELD, YORE(TIME)
long live VIVA, VIVE, EVVIVA
longshoreman DOCKER, LUMPER, STEVEDORE
look CON, EYE, KEN, PRY, SEE, GAZE, HIST, LEER, MIEN, OGLE, PEEK, PEEP, PEER, PORE, SCAN, SKEW, VIEW, ASPECT, GANDER, GLANCE
lookout WORRY, CONNER; *see* GUARD
loom TOOL, WEAVE, APPEAR, VESSEL
loom part LAM, BEAM, CAAM, MAIL, PIRN, REED, SHED, SLEY, WARP, WEFT, EASER, GRIFF, HEALD, BATTEN, HEDDLE, LINGOE, PICKER, ROLLER, TEMPLE, HARNESS, SHUTTLE, TREADLE
loon LOWN, DIVER, WABBY, PYGOPOD; *see* GREBE
loon genus GAVIA
loop EYE, ANSA, PURL, BIGHT, BRIDE, HONDA, NOOSE, PICOT, TERRY, PARRAL, PARREL, CIRCUIT, GROMMET
loophole M(E)USE, PRETEXT
loose(n) LAX, EASE, LEWD, LIMP, UNDO, BAGGY, RELAX, UNTIE, REMISS, WANTON
loot SACK, BOOTY, RIFLE, SPOIL(S), PLUNDER, RANSACK
lop POLL, SNED, SNIP, PRUNE, SNATHE
lopsided ALOP, ALIST, ASKEW
loquacious GLIB, WINDY, VOLUBLE
loquat MEDLAR, NISPERO
lord MAR, KAAN, KAUN, KAWN, KHAN, PEER, LAIRD, LIEGE, PALATINE; *see* NOBLE
Lord's Supper *see* COMMUNION
lore LARE, WISDOM
lose AMIT, FAIL, MISS, FORFEIT
lost ASEA, GONE, (A)STRAY, MISLAID
lot HAP, DOOM, FATE, SCAD, SLEW, SLUE, SHARE, HAZARD, PARCEL, DESTINY
Lot relative MOAB, HARAN, GARETH, GAWAIN, MILCAH, WAHELA
lotion *see* OINTMENT
lottery BINGO, LOTTO, RAFFLE, DRAWING, NUMBERS, TOMBOLA
lotus *see* LILY
loud FORTE, SHOWY, VULGAR
loudness unit DB, PHON, SONE, DECIBEL
loudspeaker CONE, WOOFER, MONITOR, TWEETER
Louisiana information *see p. 308*
Louisiana native CAJUN, CAIJAN, CREOLE, ACADIAN
lounge LAZE, LOLL, SOFA, DIVAN, LOBBY, SETTEE, RECLINE
louse NIT, RAT, CRUMB, COOTIE, PALMER, PSOCID, COLLIER, MORPION, PSOCINE
lout HOB, OAF, BOOR, GAWK, YAHOO
louver SLAT, SLIT, TRANSOM, ABATVENT
love GRA, LOO, WOO, DEAR, DOAT, DOTE, AMOR, ZEAL, ZERO, ADORE, AMOUR, ENAMOR, DARLING
lover JO, BEAU, FLAME, LEMAN, ROMEO, SPARK, SWAIN, MINION, AMORIST, GALLANT, PARAMOUR
loving FOND, DOTING, EROTIC, AMATIVE, AMATORY, AMOROUS
low BAS, MOO, BASE, BLUE, ORRA, VILE, HUMBLE, MENIAL
lower DIP, LOOM, LOUR, VAIL, ABASE, SCOWL, DEBASE, GLOWER, NETHER
lowest point NADIR, PERIGEE
lowly MEEK, HUMBLE
lox OXYGEN, SALMON
loyal LEAL, TRUE, STA(U)NCH
loyalty TROTH, HOMAGE, PIETAS
lozenge RHOMB, CACHOU, JUJUBE, MASCLE, PASTIL, ROTULA, TROCHE, DIAMOND, PASTI(L)LE
lubricate OIL, LUBE, GREASE
luck LOT, CESS, CHANCE, HAZARD
luck, bad JINX, DEUCE
luck, pert. to ALEATORY
lucky stroke FLUKE
Lucretia's rapist SEXTUS
ludicrous COMIC, ABSURD, RISIBLE

luggage BAGS, TRAPS, BAGGAGE
lukewarm TEPID
lull CALM, HUSH, RESPITE
Lumber State ME, MAINE
lumberman LOGGER, SAWYER, TOPPER, GIRDLER
lump NUB, WAD, BURL, CLOD, CLOT, NODE, SWAD, TUMOR
lunatic CRAZY, INSANE, MADMAN
luncheon TIFFIN, UNDERN
lunchroom CAFE, DINER, EATERY, COUNTER
lung sound RALE, BRUIT, RATTLE
lurch JOLL, ROLL, SWAB, PITCH, CAREEN
lure BAIT, SPOON, ENTICE, MINNOW, SEDUCE, PLUNKER, SPINNER, WIGGLER
lurid WAN, PALE, GARISH
lurk HIDE, PROWL, SKULK, SNEAK
luster GLAZE, GLOSS, SHEEN, SCHILLER
lusterless DIM, MAT(TE)
lustrous NAIF, NITID, SILKY
lusty BURLY, BRAWNY, ROBUST
lute CLAY, SEAL; *see* STRING INSTRUMENT
luxuriant LUSH, RANK, LAVISH, ORNATE, FERTILE
luxuriate BASK, THRIVE, WALLOW
Lydian language ANATOLIC
Lydian ruler ARDYS, GYGES, CROESUS, OMPHALE
lynx BOBCAT; *see* CAT
lyric(al) ODE, ALBA, MELIC; *see* POEM
lyricist CAHN, HART, KAHN, DAVID, DIETZ, DUBIN, GREEN, COMDEN, FIELDS, MERCER, YELLEN, DESYLVA, GILBERT, HARBURG, HEYWARD, GERSHWIN, HAMMERSTEIN
Lysander's lover HERMIA

M

macabre LURID, WEIRD, GHASTLY
Macao money AVO, PATACA
macaroni ZITI, DANDY, DITALI, FORATI, STELLE, FUSILLI, GNOCCHI; *see* PASTA
Macbeth character ANGUS, BANQUO, DUNCAN, HECATE, LENNOX, MACDUFF
mace CLUB, STAFF, SCEPTRE
mace-bearer BEDEL, MACER, BEDELL
macerate VEX, PINE; *see* SOAK
Macheath's wife POLLY
Machiavellian WILY, ASTUTE
machine RIG, TOOL, DRILL, LATHE, MOTOR, PARTY, ROBOT, DEVICE, ENGINE, GADGET, AUTOMATON
machine part CAM, COG, GIB, HUB, AXLE, GEAR, PAWL, ROTOR
mackerel(-like fish) AKU, CERO, PETO, TUNA, TUNNY, WAHOO, BONITA, BONITO, CHEBOG, ESPADA, GASCON, MARLIN, SAUREL, SIERRA, TINKER, CAVALLA, ESCOLAR, ESPADON, GEELBEC, OILFISH, PINTADO, VOLADOR, ALBACORE, KINGFISH, SAILFISH, SKIPJACK
mackerel, young SPIKE, TINKER, BLINKER
mad SORE, IRATE, RABID, INSANE
Madagascar language MALAGASY
madam MUM, DONA, FRAU, MAAM, DONNA, MILADY, SENORA
Madame Butterfly writer BELASCO, PUCCINI
madder RUBIA, GARANCE, MUNJEET
madhouse BABEL, ASYLUM, BEDLAM
madness *see* INSANITY
madrigal GLEE, SONG
magazine PULP, DEPOT, SLICK, STORE, GLOSSY, JOURNAL
maggot *see* LARVA
Magi CASPAR, GASPAR, MELCHIOR, BALTHASAR
magic OBI, JADU, JUJU, MAYA, RUNE, GOETY, JADOO, OBEAH, GOETIC, HOODOO, VOODOO, CONJURY, GRAMARY(E)
magic word PRESTO, SESAME
magician MAGE, MAGI, CIRCE, MAGUS, WITCH, MAGIAN, MERLIN, SHAMAN, WIZARD, HOUDINI, WARLOCK

Maginot line, opp. to LIMES, WESTWALL, SIEGFRIED
magistrate AG(H)A, CADI, DOGE, FOUD, EDILE, EPHOR, JUDGE, MAYOR, AEDILE, ARCHON, BAILIE, CENSOR, CONSUL, PRETOR, SYNDIC, PRAETOR, PREFECT, TRIBUNE; *see* JUDGE
magnate COB, VIP, MOGUL, NABOB, SHOGUN, TYCOON
magnet ALNICO, LODESTONE
magnetic MESMERIC
magnetic unit WEBER, MAXWELL
magnifying glass LOUPE
magnolia YULAN
Magnolia State MS, MISS(ISSIPPI)
magpie MAG, PIE(T), CISSA, MADGE, SIRGANG
magpie genus PICA
mahatma ARHAT, GANDHI, ARAHAT
mahogany SIPO, TOON, CAOBA, NARRA
Maia relative ATLAS, HERMES, PLEIONE
maid AMA, IYA, AMAH, AYAH, EYAH, BONNE, WENCH, SLAVEY, ABIGAIL, ANCILLA, MATRANEE
maiden NEW, LASS, MISS, FIRST, MISSY, DAMSEL, LASSIE, VIRGIN, COLLEEN
maidenhead HYMEN
mail DA(U)K, DAWK, POST, SEND, ARMOR
maim MAR, LAME, MANGLE, SCOTCH, CRIPPLE
main DUCT, MIGHT, VITAL
Maine information *see p. 308*
maintain AVOW, HOLD, KEEP, CLAIM, UPHOLD, PRESERVE
majestic GRAND, AUGUST, STATELY
Major Barbara author SHAW
major's insignia OAKLEAF
majordomo BUTLER, STEWARD, SENESCHAL
majority AGE, MOST, SENIORITY
make DO, FORM, MOLD, FORCE
makeshift STOPGAP, EXPEDIENT
makeup BLUSH, ROUGE, FORMAT, LAYOUT, POWDER, SHADOW, MASCARA, LIPSTICK
malaria QUARTAN, PALUDISM
Malawi language CHICHEWA
Malawi money KWACHA
Malayan language JAKUN, MALAY, SAKAI
Malayan money ORA, TRA(H), RINGGIT, TAMPANG
Malaysian state KEDAH, PERAK, SABAH, JOHORE, PAHANG, PENANG, PERLIS
Maldivian language DIVEHI
male HIM, MACHO, MANLY, VIRILE; *see* MAN, BOY
male animal *see specific animal*
Mali language FRENCH, BAMBARA; *see* GUR
malice PIQUE, SPITE, VENOM, GRUDGE, RANCOR, SPLEEN
malign ABUSE, LIBEL, DEFAME, VILIFY, ASPERSE, BANEFUL
malignant EVIL, HEINOUS, VICIOUS
mall ALLEE, AVENUE, PROMENADE
malleable SOFT, DOCILE, DUCTILE, TENSILE
mallet TUP, MADGE, GAVEL, BEETLE; *see* HAMMER
mallow HOCK, OKRA, MALVA, ALTHEA, COTTON, ALTHAEA, GARANCE, HOLLYHOCK
malt drink *see* BEER
Maltese measure SALM(A)
mammals, aquatic OTTER, DESMAN, DUGONG, MANATI, RYTINA, SEACOW, YUNGAN, COWFISH, MANATEE, SEALION, HALICORE, PINNIPED, SIRENIAN; *see* WHALE, WALRUS, DOLPHIN, SEAL
man HOMO, BIPED, HUMAN, SAHIB, STAFF, VALET, HOMBRE, FORTIFY, SERVANT; *see* MALE
man, elderly DODO, FOGY, CRONE, CODGER, DOTARD, GAFFER, GEEZER, NESTOR, SENIOR
man, handsome FOP, BEAU, ADONIS, APOLLO
man of brass TALOS
Man Without a Country NOLAN
manage TEND, DIGHT, WANGLE
manageable RULY, TAME, YARE, DOCILE, WIELDY
manager AGENT, GERENT, GRIEVE, SYNDIC, STEWARD, OPERATOR, IMPRESARIO

mandarin's home YAMEN, YAMUN
Mande language VAI, KONO, LOMA, MANO, SUSU, DYULA, MENDE, KPELLE, BAMBARA, MALINKE
mane JUBA, SHAG, BRUSH, STUBBLE
maned CRINED, JUBATE
manger BIN, CRIB, CRATCH, CRECHE, TROUGH
mangle IRON, MAIM, MAUL, GARBLE, CALENDAR
mangrove BACAO, BACAUAN
mangy SCABBY, SCURVY, SQUALID
Manhattan *see* NEW YORK
Manhattan buyer MINUIT
mania FAD, CRAZE, FRENZY
manifest SHOW, OVERT, ARRANT, ATTEST, EVINCE, PATENT
man(n)ikin DWARF, MODEL
maniple FANO(N), FANUM, ORALE
Manitoba information *see p. 306*
Manitoba rebel RIEL, LOUIS
manly MACHO, VIRILE
mannequin *see* MANIKIN
manner(s) AIR, AURA, MIEN, MODE, WONT, MORES, METHOD
manor ESTATE, DEMESNE
mansard ATTIC, GARRET
mansion DOME, MANOR, VILLA
mantel LEDGE, LINTEL
mantle *see* CLOAK
manual training SLOID, SLOYD
manure DUNG, MUCK, GUANO, ORDURE
manuscript(s) MS(S), CODEX, FOLIO, SCRIPT, SCROLL, CODICES
Manxman CELT, GAEL
many LOT, GOBS, LOTS, LOADS, MAINT, REAMS, SCADS, MYRIAD
many-colored PIED, MOTLEY, RAINBOW
Mao's successor HUA
map(s) PLAT, ATLAS, CHART, GRAPH, INSET
maple genus ACER
mar SCAR, DEFACE, BLEMISH
marauder HUN, VITI, RAIDER, VANDAL
marble(s) MIB, MIG, TAW, ALAY, DUCK, MARL, MIGG, AGGIE, ALLEY, RANCE, RANSE, MARMOR, RINGER, CARRARA, CIPOLIN, SHOOTER
Marceau character BIP
march king SOUSA
mare YAUD; *see* HORSE
margin HEM, RIM, EDGE, RAND, BRINK, LIMIT, BORDER
Marianas discoverer MAGELLAN
marigold CRAZ(E)Y
marijuana POT, HEMP, JOINT, ROACH, REEFER; *see* DRUG
marina DOCK, BASIN, HARBOR
marine JOLLY, NAVAL, GYRENE, OCEANIC, PELAGIC
marine organism SALPA, BUGULA, PEDATA, PLOIMA, SEAFAN, ACTINIA, BRYOZOA, CRINOID, ROTIFER, TREPANG, VELELLA, PHORONIS; *see* CORAL
mark SCAR, BRAND, STAIN, STAMP, TALLY, STIGMA, SYMBOL, STIGMATA
mark, diacritical TIL, BREVE, PRIME, TILDE, ACCENT, MACRON, UMLAUT, CEDILLA, DIERESIS
mark, printers' DELE, STET, CARET
mark, reference FIST, HAND, STAR, INDEX, OBELI, DAGGER, DIESIS, OBELUS, OBELISK, POINTER, SECTION, ASTERISK, ASTERISM
Mark's wife ISOLDE
marker(s) DAN, TAB, CHIP, META, PYLON, STELA, STELE, SCORER, STELAE, STELAI, COUNTER
market SUQ, FORA, GUNJ, MART, SELL, SOOK, SOUK, VEND, AGORA, BAZAR, FORUM, GUNGE, PASAR, TRONE, BAZAAR, RIALTO, EMPORIUM
marksman SNIPER, HAWKEYE
Marley's partner SCROOGE
marriage OTA, MUTA, NUPTIALS
marriage, absence of AGAMY
marriage notice BAN(NS)
marriage settlement DOS, DOT(E), MAHR, DOW(E)RY
marriageable NUBILE
married WED, COVERT
marrow CORE, PITH, KEEST, LOVER, SPOUSE, MEDULLA

marry WED, WIVE, HITCH, ESPOUSE
Mars, pert. to AREAN, MARTIAN
Marseillaise composer (DE)LISLE
marsh BOG, FEN, MIRE, MOOR, MOSS, QUAG, SLUE, LERNA, LIMAN, PINSK, SWALE, MORASS, MUSKE OR MUSKEG, PRIPET, SALINA, MAREMMA, PONTINE
marsh bird COOT, RAIL, SORA, SNIPE, STILT, BITTERN
marsh fever HELODES
marsh gas METHANE
marshall NEY, FOCH, ARRAY, PETAIN, ROMMEL, ARRANGE
marshy PALUDAL, PALUDINE
marsupial JOEY, BILBI, BILBY, COALA, FLIER, FLYER, KOALA, QUICA, SELVA, SILVA, TAPOA, TUNGO, YABBI, YAPOK, BOOMER, CUSCUS, JERBOA, NUMBAT, POSSUM, WOMBAT, YAPOCK, DASYURE, OPOSSUM, WALLABY, ANTEATER, COESCOES, FORESTER, KANGAROO, WALLAROO, BANDICOOT, PADEMELON, PETAURIST, PHALANGER, PHILANDER, THYLACINE
marsupial genus MARMOSA, DASYURUS, MACROPUS, TARSIPES, DIDELPHIS
mart EMPORIUM
marten SABLE, FISHER
martini garnish LEMON, OLIVE, ONION
marvel WONDER, MIRACLE, PRODIGY
Marx brothers CHICO, GUMMO, HARPO, ZEPPO, GROUCHO
Maryland information *see p. 308*
mask LOUP, VISOR, DOMINO, SCREEN
masker MUMMER
mason *see* STONECUTTER
masquerade MUM(M), MASQUE, RIDOTTO, DISGUISE
mass GOB, WAD, BULK, BOLUS, TUMOR, GATHER, MATTER
Mass part PAX, CREDO, KYRIE, GLORIA, GOSPEL, LAVABO, COLLECT, EPISTLE, GRADUAL, INTROIT, PREFACE, SANCTUS, SECRETA, FRACTION
Massachusetts information *see p. 308*
massacre POGROM, CARNAGE
massage RUB, KNEAD
Massenet opera MANON, THAIS, SAPPHO, WERTHER
mast *see* SHIP PART
master BOY, BAAS, BOSS, LORD, RULE, EMCEE, LEARN, SUBDUE, CAPTAIN; *see* TEACHER
master, pert. to a HERILE
mastery GRIP, SWAY, CONTROL
masticate GUM, CHAW, CHEW
mat PAD, RUG, YAPA, BANIG, DOILY, SNARL, MATRIX, PETATE
matador TORERO, TOREADOR
match FIT, PEER, FUSEE, MARRY, TALLY, VESTA, LUCIFER
matchmaker BROKER, SHADCHAN
mate FERE, MATCH, FELLOW, SPOUSE
material STUFF; *see* FABRIC
mathematical term PI, LOG, COSH, SECH, SINE, SINH, SURD, TANH, NABLA, RADIX, RATIO, COSINE, RADIAN, SCALAR, TENSOR, VECTOR, VESSOR, FACIEND, FACIENT, OPERAND, CONSTANT, QUADRANT, VARIABLE
mathematician BOOLE, EULER, GAUSS, VIETA, EUCLID, FERMAT, KELVIN, NAPIER, NEWTON, PASCAL, WIENER, ALKASHI, CARROLL, CREMONA, HUYGENS, LAPLACE, PTOLEMY, RUSSELL, VERNIER, ALBIRUNI, EINSTEIN, LEIBNITZ, DESCARTES
mathematics, branch of TRIG, CONICS, ALGEBRA, CALCULUS, GEOMETRY, ARITHMETIC
matrix CAST, MOLD, WOMB, GANGUE
matter PUS, RES, HYLE, PITH, IMPORT
mattress TICK, FUTON, PALLET
mature AGE, DUE, RIPE, ADULT, RIPEN, MELLOW, PAYABLE
maudlin MUSHY, TEARY
Maugham play RAIN
maul PAW, CLUB, MANGLE
mawkish SOPPY, CLOYING
maxim SAW, ADAGE, AXIOM, GNOME, MORAL, MOTTO, CLICHE, TRUISM, PROVERB

May Day SOS, BELTANE, BEALTINE
maze LABYRINTH
McGuffey book READER
meadow LEA, LAWN, MEAD, VEGA, HAUGH
meager LEAN, PUNY, SCANT, LENTEN, SCANTY, SPARSE
meal ATA, TEA, ATTA, BRAN, CENA, MASA, BEVER, FLOUR, LUNCH, DINNER, FARINA, PINOLA, PINOLE, REPAST
mean(s) LOW, BASE, AGENT, IMPLY, AVENUE, INTEND, MEDIUM, METHOD, SCURVY, WEALTH
meander ROAM, WANDER, RAMBLE
meaning SENSE, TENOR, DESIGN
meaning, pert. to LITERAL, SEMANTIC
meantime WHILST; *see* INTERVAL
measles ROSEOLA, RUBELLA, RUBEOLA
measure GAGE, METE, PAGE, SCAN, GAUGE, EXTENT
measure, metric ARE, KILO, LITER, METER, HECTARE, CENTIARE, DECALITER, DECAMETER, DECILITER, DECIMETER, KILOLITER, KILOMETER, CENTILITER, CENTIMETER, HECTOLITER, HECTOMETER, MILLIMETER
measure, U.S. & British *(for other countries see specific entry)* CUT, ELL, LEA, ROD, TUN, ACRE, BOLT, BUTT, CORD, DRAM, DRUM, FOOT, HAND, HANK, HEER, INCH, IRON, LINE, LINK, MILE, NAIL, PACE, PALM, PECK, PINT, PIPE, POLE, ROOD, SPAN, YARD, YOKE, BLOCK, BODGE, CHAIN, DIGIT, LABOR, MINIM, OUNCE, PERCH, PRIME, QUART, SKEIN, BARREL, BASKET, BUSHEL, FATHOM, GALLON, LEAGUE, SECOND, THREAD, FURLONG, SECTION, HOGSHEAD
measuring device LOG, ROD, DIAL, POLE, RULE, TAPE, CHAIN, CLOCK, GAUGE, RULER, STADIA, CALIPER, SEXTANT, TRANSIT, DIPSTICK
meat BEEF, LAMB, MEAL, PORK, VEAL, FLESH, TRIPE, KERNEL, MUTTON, VENISON; *see* CUT, MENU
meat on skewer CABOB, KABOB, KEBAB, SHAS(H)LIK
meatless LENTEN, MAIGRE, VEGETARIAN
mechanics STATICS, DYNAMICS, KINETICS, WORKINGS
meddle PRY, MELL, SNOOP, TAMPER
meddlesome CURIOUS, OFFICIOUS
Medea relative JASON, AEETES
media TV, FILM, MOVIE, PRESS, PRINT, RADIO, TELEVISION
median PAR, MEAN, MESAL, MESNE, MESIAL, AVERAGE
medical IATRIC, CURATIVE
medical group AMA
medicinal plant AGAR, ALOE, HERB, ANISE, JALAP, ORRIS, SENNA, TANSY, ARNICA, COHOSH, CROTON, IPECAC, GINSENG
medicine man PEAI, PIAY, BASIR, KAHUNA, PIACHE, SHAMAN, ANGEKOK
mediocre SOSO, AVERAGE
meditate MULL, MUSE, PONDER
medium MEAN(S), AGENCY, PSYCHIC; *see* MEDIA
medley OLIO, FARRAGO, MELANGE, PASTICCIO, POTPOURRI
Medusa relative STHENO, EURYALE
Medusa's slayer PERSEUS
meek TAME, HUMBLE, MODEST
meet(ing) GAM, DATE, FACE, RALLY, SYNOD, TRYST, CAUCUS, INDABA, SEANCE, SEEMLY, SESSION, SEMINAR
Meistersinger SACHS
melancholy BLUE(S), DOLOR, DREAR, MISERY, RUEFUL
Meleager relative ALTHEA, OENEUS
melee *see* FIGHT
mellow RIPE, SOFT, RIPEN, SOFTEN, MATURE
melodious ARIOSE, ARIOSO, DULCET, TUNEFUL
melody AIR, SONG, TUNE, MELOS, STRAIN, MELISMA
melon PEPO, CASABA, HONEYDEW, CANTALOUP(E)

melt RUN, FUSE, FUZE, SWALE, SWEAL, RENDER, CLARIFY
Melville work OMOO, TYPEE, MOBYDICK
member LIMB, PART, FELLOW
membrane PIA, WEB, CAUL, FILM, TELA, VELA, MATER, VELUM
memento RELIC, TOKEN, KEEPSAKE
Memnon slayer ACHILLES
memorandum CHIT, NOTE, BRIEF, MINUTE
memorial RIP, XAT, CA(I)RN, TROPHY, EPITAPH
memory loss AMNESIA
memory, pert. to MNESIC, MNEMONIC
mend FIX, DARN, HEAL, KNIT, PATCH, COBBLE, RELINE
mender TINKER, COBBLER
mendicant DANDI, DANDY, FAKIR, FRIAR, BEGGAR, FAKEER
Menelaus relative HELEN, ATREUS, HERMIONE, AGAMEMNON
menial *see* SERVANT
Menlo Park inventor EDISON
Mennonite sect AMISH, WISLER
Menotti opera AMAHL, CONSUL, MEDIUM, TELEPHONE
mental PHRENIC
mention CITE, NAME, REFER
menu BILL, CARTE
menu items and terms AME, BAP, BUN, JAM, KAI, PIE, POI, AGAR, BABA, CAKE, CHOU, FLAN, PATE, ROTI, SABA, SOUP, TART, ASADO, ASPIC, AUJUS, BOMBE, BROSE, BROTH, CABOB, CANIN, COUPE, CREPE, DURRY, DOUGH, FILET, GRAVY, GUMBO, KABOB, LACTO, PASTA, PATTY, PILAF, PILAU, PILAW, PIZZA, PIZZE, PUREE, SALAD, SALMI, SCONE, STALK, STEAK, TORTE, WAFER, BATTER, BISQUE, BLINIS, BONBON, BORSCH, BORSHT, BOUDIN, CANAPE, CATSUP, COLLOP, CREOLE, CUSCUS, CUTLET, ECLAIR, ENTREE, FLAMBE, FONDUE, GATEAU, GIBLET, HAGGIS, KNODEL, KUCHEN, MOUSSE, MUFFIN, NOUGAT, OMELET, PANADA, PANADE, PASTRY, POSOLE, SPONGE, SUNDAE, TAMALE, TIDBIT, TONGUE, TRIFLE, ALAKING, ALAMODE, BEIGNET, BLINTZE, BRIOCHE, CASSATA, CHOWDER, COMPOTE, CROUTON, CUPCAKE, DESSERT, DEVILED, FILLING, FLAMAND, FONDANT, GARBURE, GNOCCHI, KETCHUP, LASAGNE, PANCAKE, PARFAIT, PEASOUP, POLENTA, POPOVER, PRALINE, PUDDING, RAREBIT, RAVIOLI, RISOTTO, RISSOLE, SAVARIN, SHERBET, SOUFFLE, SPUMONI, TIMBALE, TRUFFLE, ZAKUSKA, APERITIF, AUBEURRE, AUGRATIN, CONSOMME, DEVILLED, ESPRESSO, FLAMANDE
mercenary VENAL, HESSIAN, ARMATOLI, HIRELING
merchant SETH, COSTER, DEALER, MONGER, SUTLER, TRADER, VENDOR, PEDDLER
Merchant of Venice character GOBBO, TUBAL, PORTIA, ANTONIO, JESSICA, SHYLOCK
mercy PITY, RUTH, LENITY
mere FEN, LAKE, POOL, MARSH
merge WED, FUSE, BLEND
Mérimée story CARMEN
merit EARN, MEED, WORTH
merry GAY, JOLLY, JOCOSE
Merry Andrew CLOWN, JESTER
Merry Widow composer LEHAR
Merry Wives character NYM, FORD, CAIUS, FENTON, PISTOL, FALSTAFF
merry-go-round CAROUSEL, WHIRLIGIG, WHIRLYGIG
mesa BUTTE, PLATEAU
mescal AGAVE, MAGUEY, PEYOTE, PEYOTL
Mesopotamia IRAK, IRAQ
mess CHOW, BOTCH, BUNGLE
messenger PAGE, ENVOY, HERALD, HERMES, NUNCIO, COURIER, MERCURY, EMISSARY
Messiah composer HANDEL
metal TIN, GOLD, IRON, LEAD, STEEL, COPPER, BRONZE, SILVER, ALUMINUM; *see* MINERAL, ALLOY
metallic TINNY
metallic element *see p. 249*

metalworker SMITH, VULCAN, WELDER, RIVETER
metalworking tool DIE, ANVIL, DRILL, LATHE, SWAGE, TONGS
Metamorphoses author OVID
metaphor TROPE, SIMILE
meteor LYRID, URSID, BOLIDE, CYGNID, LEONID, PISCID, TAURID, AQUARID, ARIETID, GEMINID, ORIONID, PERSEID, DRACONID, VIRGINID
meteorite HOBA, LUCE, LOKET, AIGLE, SIENA, WESTON, ELBOGEN, HATFORD, ORGUEIL, TEKTITE, TUNGUSKA
meter RHYTHM, CADENCE
method WAY, MODE, PLAN, ORDER, SCHEME, SYSTEM
Methodism founder WESLEY
Metis relative ZEUS, TETHYS
metric *see* MEASURE, WEIGHT
mettle PLUCK, SPUNK, SPIRIT
mew BARN, SHED, GARAGE, STABLES
Mexican AZTEC, CHICANO
Mexican measure VARA, BARIL, CARGA, JARRA, LABOR, LEGUA, LINEA, SITIO, FANEGA, PULGADA
Mexican money PESO, REAL, TLAC, CLACO, TLACO, AZTECA, CENTAVO
Mexican president GIL, DIAZ, ORDAZ, ALEMAN, CALLES, HUERTA, JUAREZ, MADERO, MADRID, MATEOS
Mexican tree AMAPA, DRAGO, EBANO, GUAYULE, MESQUIT(E)
Mexican weight ONZA, CARGA, LIBRA, MARCO, ADARME, ARROBA, OCHAVA, TERCIO
mezzanine ENTRESOL
Michelangelo work DAVID, PIETA
Michigan information *see p.* 308
microbe(s) GERM, VIRUS, BACTERIA
microspores POLLEN
middle HUB, MESAL, MESNE, CENTER, CENTRY, MEDIAL, MESIAL, CENTRAL
middle, toward the MES(I)AD
Middle East IRAN, IRAQ, BURMA, EGYPT, INDIA, SYRIA, ISRAEL, JORDAN, PERSIA, LEBANON
midget RUNT, DWARF, PIGMY, PYGMY
midship, off ABEAM
midshipman MIDDY, REEFER
Midsummer Night's Dream character PUCK, SNOUT, HERMIA, OBERON, QUINCE, THISBE, TITANIA
midwife DHAI, GAMP, GRANNY, HEBAMME, PARTERA
mien GUISE, POISE, OSTENT
mighty FELL, POTENT, VALIANT, PUISSANT
mignonette DYER, WELD, RESEDA
migration TREK, EXODUS
migratory worker JOAD, OKIE, ARKIE, BRACERO, WETBACK
Mikado character KOKO, YUMYUM, POOHBAH, NANKIPOO
Mikado's court DAIRI
Milan opera house (LA)SCALA
mild MOY, SHY, MEEK, SOFT, BLAND, PLACID
mildew MOLD, MUST, MOULD, BLIGHT
mile, nautical KNOT
milieu ENVIRON, AMBIANCE
military MARTIAL, WARLIKE
military leaders COX, LEE, NEY, ORD, CLAY, FOCH, GAGE, HAIG, HOWE, KNOX, PIKE, SAXE, SIMS, ALLEN, BANKS, BRAGG, BUELL, CLARK, DAYAN, DEWEY, DRAKE, EARLY, GRANT, JONES, LEAHY, MEADE, MILNE, MURAT, PERRY, WOLFE, ABRAMS, ARNOLD, CUSTER, GORDON, HALSEY, HODGES, JOFFRE, MOLTKE, NELSON, NIMITZ, PATTON, PETAIN, PICKEN, PUTNAM, RAEDER, ROMMEL, SPAATZ, STUART, SUMTER, ZHUKOV, BRADLEY, DECATUR, FORREST, HOUSTON, JACKSON, SHERMAN, TIRPITZ, BLUECHER, BURGOYNE, BURNSIDE, CROCKETT, FARRAGUT, JELLICOE, JOHNSTON, LAWRENCE, MARSHALL, MONTCALM, MITCHELL, NAPOLEON, PERSHING, SCHUYLER, SHERIDAN, STILWELL, MACARTHUR; *see* GENERALS, CIVIL WAR
military unit CADRE, SQUAD, COMPANY, PLATOON,

DIVISION, REGIMENT, BATTALION, DETACHMENT
milk LAC, CURD, SKYR, TYRE, BLEED, LEBAN, LEBEN, TAYIR, KUMISS, CLABBER, LACTOSE
milk part CURD, WHEY, SERUM, CASEIN, PLASMA
milk, pert. to LACTIC, LACTEAL
Milky Way GALAXY
mill (K)NURL, QUERN, ARRASTRA
millet CUMBU, MILIUM; *see* GRASS
millimeter, 1000th part MICRON
millisecond SIGMA
millstone support RYND
millwheel part AWE, LADE
Milne character POOH, ROBIN
mimic APE(R), MIMA, MIME, SHAM, QUASI, PSEUDO
mince DICE, SHRED, SIMPER
mind CARE, HEED, OBEY, NOUS, RECK, SOUL, TEND, WITS
mind, pert. to MENTAL, PHRENIC
mine PIT, SAP, LODE, VEIN, STOPE, QUARRY
miner SAPPER, COLLIER, SANDHOG
mineral ORE, WAD, COAL, MICA, PACO, TALC, YESO, BORAX, EMERY, FLINT, GESSO, TRONA, ACMITE, ADULAR, ALBITE, AUGITE, BARITE, BARYTE, BLENDE, DIPYRE, EMERIL, GALENA, GYPSUM, HELVIN, HUMITE, LATITE, MORLOP, PINITE, PLASMA, PYRITE, QUARTZ, RUTILE, SALITE, SMIRIS, SPHENE, SPINEL, SYLVIN, ZIRCON, ALTAITE, ALUMITE, ALUNITE, APATITE, ASPHALT, BARYTES, BAUXITE, BIOTITE, BITUMEN, BOGIRON, BORNITE, CALCITE, CELSIAN, CRYSTAL, CUPRITE, CYANITE, DANAITE, DESMINE, EDENITE, EPIDOTE, FAHLERZ,GAHLORE, DELSPAR, GAHNITE, GEDRITE, GLIMMER, HELVINE, HELVITE, HESSITE, INYOITE, JADEITE, JARGOON, KERNITE, KYANITE, LAURITE, MARTITE, MEEKITE, ORTHITE, PETZITE, RASPITE, REALGAR, SENAITE, SYLVINE, SYLVITE, THORITE, THULITE, TILEORE, ULEXITE, URALITE, WOLFRAM, WOODTIN, ZINCITE, ZOISITE, ZUNYITE, ADULARIA, ALKINITE, ALLANITE, ANDESINE, ANKERITE, ASBESTOS, ASPHALTE, AUTUNITE, BEAUXITE, BORACITE, BRONZITE, BROOKITE, CHLORITE, CHROMITE, CINNABAR, CORUNDUM, CROCOITE, CRYOLITE, DANALITE, DATOLITE, DIALLAGE, DIASPORE, DIOPSIDE, DOLOMITE, ELEOLITE, EMBOLITE, EPSOMITE, FELDSPAR, FLUORITE, ORPIMENT, PLUMBAGO, PYROXENE, ROCKMILK, SANIDINE, SARDONYX, STILBITE, SUNSTONE; *see* ROCK, STONE
minim DASH, DROP, MITE
mining term GOB, LOB, NOG, TUB, ADIT, DAMP, GOAF, PILE, SUMP, WHIM, WHIN, ASTEL, HUTCH, RESUE, SPRAG, STOPE, STULL, STULM, WINZE, SOLLAR
mining tool GAD, DAVY, SPAD, STEIL, JUMPER, TREPAN, MANDREL, MANDRIL
minister AID, CATER, VIZI(E)R, PREMIER; *see* CLERGY
mink VISON, KOLINSKY
Minnesota information *see p. 308*
Minnesotan GOPHER
minor PETTY, LESSER, UNDERAGE
minority NONAGE, PUPILAGE
Minos relative ARIADNE, PHAEDRA, PASIPHAE
minstrel BARD, SCOP, ARIOI, RIMER, RUNER, SKALD, GLEEMAN, GOLIARD, JONGLEUR
mint BALM, COIN, SAGE, BASIL, CLARY, FRESH, STAMP, THYME, CATNIP, HYSSOP, INVENT, SAVORY, DITTANY, POTHERB
minute(s) WEE, ACTA, MEMO, TINY, SMALL, DETAIL, RECORD
miracle ANOMY, MARVEL, WONDER
miracle site CANA, FATIMA, LOURDES
mire *see* MUD

Miriam relative AARON, AMRAM, MOSES
mirror GLASS, CRYSTAL, REFLECT, SPECULUM
miscarriage ABORTION
miscellany *see* MEDLEY
mischief HOB, DIDO, HAVOC, PRANK, WRACK, CANTRIP
miser CHURL, HUNKS, NABAL, MARNER, NIGGARD, SCROOGE
miserly TIGHT, STINGY, NIGGARD
misery AGONY, DOLOR, CHAGRIN
misgiving DOUBT, SCRUPLE
Mishnah section ABOT, MOED, ABOTH, NASHIM, ZERAIM, NEZIKIN, PERAKIM, SEDARIM
misprint(s) TYPO, ERRATA
misrepresent BELIE, GARBLE
miss FAIL, ESCAPE; *see* GIRL
missile BALL, BOLA, BOLT, BOMB, DART, SHOT, SLUG, GRAPE, KILEY, SHAFT, SHELL, ATLATL, BULLET, DUMDUM, PELLET, WOMERA, GRENADE, OUTCAST, TORPEDO, SHRAPNEL, BOOMERANG, PROJECTILE; *see* ROCKET
missile site SILO
missing AWOL, LOST, TRUANT
mission ERRAND, CALLING, EMBASSY, CONSULATE
Mississippi information *see p. 308*
Mississippi river tributaries RED, IOWA, OHIO, ROCK, BLACK, WHITE, ARKANSAS, CHIPPEWA, ILLINOIS, MISSOURI, WISCONSIN
Missouri information *see p. 308*
mist FOG, RAG, HAZE, SMOG, SMUR, BRUME, MISLE, VAPOR, SEREIN
mistake(s) BULL, GOOF, SLIP, TYPO, BONER, LAPSE, BARNEY, ERRATA, BLOOPER, ERRATUM
mister DON, PAN, SIR, BABU, HERR, MIAN, SIRE, BABOO, SAHEB, SAHIB, SENOR, SIGNOR, MONSIEUR; *see* TITLE
mistress DAME, PARAMOUR
mite ATOM, IOTA, MOTE, ATOMY, ACARI(NA); *see* TICK
mitigate EASE, ABATE, ALLAY, TEMPER, ASSUAGE
mix STIR, TEER, ADDLE, KNEAD, GARBLE, MINGLE, SCRAMBLE
mixture HASH, MONG, OLIO, MAGMA, MEDLEY, MELANGE
moat FOSS, DITCH, FOSSE, GRAFF
mob ROUT, RUCK, BOODLE, RABBLE, THRONG, CANAILLE, RIFFRAFF
mobile FLUID, FLEXIBLE
Moby Dick author MELVILLE
Moby Dick character PIP, AHAB, STUBB, ISHMAEL, QUEEQUEG, STARBUCK
Moby Dick ship PEQUOD
moccasin LARRIGAN
mock GIBE, JAPE, JEER, JIBE, RAZZ, FLEER, FLOUT, SCOFF, SPOOF, TAUNT, DERIDE
mockingbird MOCKER
mode FAD, FLAIR, STYLE, VOGUE
mode, musical MAJOR, MINOR, DORIAN, IONIAN, LYDIAN, AEOLIAN, LOCRIAN, PHRYGIAN
model SIT, NORM, POSE, TYPE, IDEAL, SITTER, MANIKIN, PARAGON, MANNIKIN, PARADIGM, MANNEQUIN
moderate COOL, ABATE, SOBER, LESSEN, SOFTEN, STEADY, TEMPER
modern NEO, LATE, NOVEL
modest SHY, MEEK, DEMURE
modify VARY, ALTER, AMEND, EMEND, REVISE, TEMPER
modish CHIC, STYLISH
Mogul emperor AKBAR, BABAR, BABER, BABUR, JEHAN
Mohammed relative ALI, ABBAS, AISHA, AMINA, SAUDA, AYESHA, FATIMA, JINNAH, KADIJA, ZAYNAB
Mohammed's birthplace MECCA
Mohammed's burial place MEDINA
Mohammed's descendant SAID, SEID, SAYID, SHERIF
Mohammed's supporters ANSAR
Mohammedan(ism) HANIF, ISLAM, MOSLEM, ISLAMIC, ISLAMITE
Mohammedan feast day ASHURA
Mohammedan principle IJMA
Moirae *see* FATES
moist DAMP, DANK, DEWY, UVID, HUMID
moisten MOIL, SOAK, BEDEW, DAMPEN

molasses TREACLE, TRIACLE
mold CAST, MUST, KNEAD, MATRIX, MILDEW, PATTERN
molding CYMA, GULA, OGEE, TORI, CONGE, OVOLI, OVOLO, SPLAY, TORUS, FILLET, LISTEL, REGLET, REGULA, SCOTIA, CAVETTO, ECHINUS, REEDING, ASTRAGAL
molding edge AR(R)IS
moldy FUSTY, MUSTY
mole PIER, QUAY, JETTY, NEVUS, TALPA, TAUPE
molecule part ION, ATOM, ANION
molest VEX, FRET, ANNOY, CHAFE
Molière character ALCESTE, TARTUFFE
mollusk PIPI, SLUG, BORER, CHANK, CONCH, COWRY, DORIS, HARPA, PINNA, AEOLID, CASSIS, CHITON, CLIONE, COCKLE, COWRIE, DOLIUM, JINGLE, LIMPET, NUCULA, PHOLAS, PURPLE, PYRULA, TEREDO, TETHYS, TRITON, VOLUTA, VOLUTE, ASTARTE, BIVALVE, BLUBBER, DECAPOD, ETHERIA, NUCULID, PANDORA, POLYPOD, SCALLOP, SCYLLAE, SPIRULA, TELLINA, TEREBRA, TONEROA, TOXIFER, TROCHID, TROCHUS, VELIGER, APLYSIAS, ARKSHELL, CASSIDID, GEOPHILA, NAUTILUS, UNIVALVE, VERMETID; *see* SNAIL, CLAM, MUSSEL, ABALONE, JELLYFISH, OCTOPUS, OYSTER, SLUG
mollusk genus MUREX, OLIVA, VENUS, AEOLIS, PECTEN, GLAUCUS, VELUTINA, VERMETUS
Molnar play LILIOM
molt MEW, CAST, SHED
molten rock *see* LAVA
moment JIFF(Y), TRICE, IMPORT
Mona Lisa artist (DA)VINCI, LEONARDO
Monaco dynasty GRIMALDI
monad ATOM, UNIT, ENTITY
monarch RULER, CALIPH, SULTAN; *see* KING, QUEEN, EMPEROR, EMPRESS
monastery MATH, TERA, ABBEY, RIBAT, TEKKE, TEKYA, CENOBY, FRIARY, MANDRA, PRIORY, VIHARA, NUNNERY, LAMASERY
monetary FISCAL, NUMMARY, FINANCIAL, PECUNIARY
money *(see specific countries for currencies)* BIT, BOB, FIN, RED, CASH, COIN, CUSH, GELT, KALE, LARI, MOSS, PELF, PLUM, QUID, ULLO, COWRY, DEUCE, DOUGH, FIVER, GRAND, GRIGS, LARIN, LUCRE, SEWAN, UHLLO, COWRIE, MAZUMA, MONKEY, SEAWAN, SPENSE, TANNER, TENDER, TENNER, WAMPUM, CENTURY, LETTUCE, SAWBUCK, SHEKELS, TWOBITS
money box ARCA, SAFE, TILL, COFFER, DRAWER, REGISTER
money market BOURSE, EXCHANGE
moneylender USURER, MAHAJAN, SHYLOCK
Mongol HU, ELEUT, KALKA, TATAR, BURIAT, BURYAT, KALMU(C)K, KHALKHA
Mongolian money TUGRIK
Mongolic language KALKA, BURYAT, KHALKHA, KHALKA, KALMUCK, MONGOLIAN
mongoose URVA, MANGUE
mongrel CUR, MUT(T), HYBRID
monk FRA, ABBE, LAMA, SUFI, ABBOT, ARHAT, BONZE, FAKIR, FRIAR, LOHAN, PRIOR, ARAHAT, BHIKKY, PONGYI, SANTON, CALOYER, DERVISH, TALAPOIN
monk settlement SCETE, SKETE
monkey KRA, PUG, BRUH, DOUC, KAGA, MAHA, MICO, MONA, MONK, MONO, SAKI, TITI, ARABA, DEBID, JACKO, JOCKO, MUNGA, PATAS, RESUS, SAJOU, TOQUE, YARKE, BANDAR, COAITA, COUXIA, COUXIO, GRIVET, GUENON, HOWLER, LANGUR, MACACO, MACHIN, MARTIN, NISNAS, PINCHE, RHESUS, RILAWA, SAGOIN, SIMIAN, SIMPAI, TEETEE, VERVET, YARKEE, COLOBIN, GUARIBA, MACAQUE, NOSEAPE, ROLOWAY, SAPAJOU,

STENTOR, TAMARIN, WISTITI; *see* APE
monkey genus AOTUS, CEBUS, MIDAS, ATELES, GALAGO, MACACA, COLOBUS, MACACUS, SAIMIRI
monkey puzzle PINON
Mon-Khmer language WA, MON, JAKUN, KHASI, KHMER, SAKAI, PALAUNG, CAMBODIAN
monkshood ATIS, ACONITE
monogram CIPHER
monolith MENHIR, OBELISK
monopoly POOL, TRUST, CARTEL
monotonous FLAT, TEDIOUS, TIRESOME
monster GILA, GOUL, GOWL, OGRE, BRUTE, GHOUL, HYDRA, RAHAB, TERAS, ELLOPS, KRAKEN, GRENDEL; *see p. 331*
Montague enemy CAPULET
Montana information *see p. 308*
Montenegro money PARA, FLORIN, PERPERA
Montezuma's captor CORTEZ
month ULT, INST, ULTIMO, INSTANT; *see p. 340*
monument CARN, LECH, CAIRN, STELE, TABUT, DOLMEN, MENHIR, RECORD, SHRINE, CENOTAPH, CROMLECH
mooch BEG, CADGE
mood VEIN, HUMOR, TEMPER
moody SULKY, MOROSE
moon GAZE, LUNA, CRESCENT; *see* SATELLITE
moon, pert. to LUNAR, SELENIC
moon phase NEW, FULL, GIBBOUS
moon valley RILL, CLEFT, RILLE
moon's age EPACT
moor FEN, HEATH, LANDE, MUSLIM
mooring place DOCK, PORT, SLIP, BERTH, HARBOR, MARINA
Moorish MORISCO, MORESQUE, MORISCAN, MAURESQUE
moose genus ALCES
moot MEETING, DEBATABLE
mop SWAB, SWOB, MERKIN, SCOVEL
moral MAXIM, RIGHT, ETHICAL
morass *see* MARSH
mordant ACID, ACRID, EROSIVE, CORROSIVE
more BIS, PIU, TOO, PLUS, EXTRA, ENCORE, EXCESS
More's island UTOPIA
Mormon SMITH, YOUNG, DANITE
morning MATIN, UMAGA, MATINAL; *see* DAWN
morning glory KOALI, IPOM(O)EA, BINDWEED
Moroccan money OKIA, RIAL, DIRHAM
Moroccan weight ROTL, GERBE, KINTAR
moron AMENT, IDIOT
morose BLUE, DOUR, GLUM, GRUM, SOUR, SURLY
morsel BIT, ORT, SOP, BITE, SCRAP
mortal MAN, HUMAN, FATAL, DEADLY, LETHAL
mortar COMPO, CANNON, CO(E)HORN
mortgage LIEN, PLEDGE, WADSET
mortuary MORGUE, CHARNEL
mosaic MUSIVE, TESSERA
Mosaic law TORA(H)
mosaic materials TILE, SMALTO, TESSERA
Moses relative AARON, JETHRO, MIRIAM, ZIPPORAH
Moses' spies CALEB, NAHBI, GADDIEL
Moslem *see* MOHAMMEDAN
mosque JAMI, OMAR, MASJID
mosque part MIHRAB, MIMBAR, MINARET
mosquito genus AEDES, CULEX
moss BRYUM, MNIUM, MUSCI
moth PUG, MOCH, SLUG, EGGAR, EGGER, MICRO, PLUME, SWIFT, WITCH, BOGUNG, BOMBYX, BUGONG, CODLIN, COSSID, DAGGER, ERMINE, HERALD, IOMOTH, LAPPET, MILLER, PSYCHE, QUAKER, RUSTIC, SPHINX, TINEAN, TINEID, TUSSAH, TUSSER, ARCTIID, BAGWORM, BEEMOTH, BUDWORM, CODLING, CRAMBID, DRINKER, FOOTMAN, PSYCHID, PUGMOTH, PYRALID, TINEOID, TORTRIX, TUSSOCK, TUSSORE, URANIID, WAXMOTH, YAMAMAI, ARMYWORM,

BOLLWORM, FORESTER, HAWKMOTH, LUNAMOTH, PLUTELLA, SILKWORM
moth genus TINEA, ARCTIA, PLUSIA, AGROTIS, ATTACUS, CRAMBUS, JUGATAE, PYRALIS
mother DAM, AMMA, MATER, ABBESS; *see* DREGS
mother-of-pearl NACRE
motion, pert. to MOTIVE, KINETIC
motion picture *see* MOVIE
motion, producing MOTILE, MOTIFIC
motionless INERT, STILL
motive SPUR, CAUSE, THEME, REASON, SPRING, IMPULSE
motmot MOMOT, ROLLER, KIROMBO
motor ENGINE, TURBINE
motor part CAM, COIL, GEAR, ROTOR, STATOR, CAPACITOR
mottled PIED, ROEY, PINTO, DAPPLED, PIEBALD
motto ADAGE, MAXIM, BYWORD, SLOGAN, CATCHWORD
mound AHU, TEE, DENE, HUMP, TELL, TERP, TUMP, KNOLL, BARROW, TUMULUS
Mount of Olives OLIVET
Mount Vesuvius city POMPEII
mountain KAF, GAE, BERG, SIERRA
mountain range ALPS, HARZ, URAL, ALTAI, ATLAS, OZARK, ELBURZ, KUNLUN, POCONO, VOSGES, ZAGROS, ROCKIES, SUDETES, CAUCASUS, HIMALAYA, PYRENEES, APENNINES, DOLOMITES
mountains ABU, ALP, API, DOM, ERZ, HOR, IDA, OMI, AGUA, ALAI, BEAR, BONA, COOK, GUNA, HENG, HOOD, JAJA, JURA, KIBO, KING, MANA, MERU, MIDI, NEBO, DETA, OSSA, RIGI, TODI, TORO, VISO, WOOD, YALE, ZUPO, ALTAR, ALTYN, ARBER, ATHOS, BAKER, BLANC, BROAD, CACHI, CENIS, CORNO, EIFEL, EIGER, ELGON, EOLUS, EVANS, GUYOT, HEKLA, HOREB, HUILA, KABRU, KAMET, KENYA, LAUDO, LEONE, LOGAN, LONGS, POTRA, SEGUR, TABOR, TAHAN, USHBA, WALSH, ALADAG, ALATAU, AMPATO, ANADIR, ARARAT, BAIKAL, BANDAI, BLANCA, CARMEL, CARNIC, CONDOR, ELBRUS, EREBUS, GRAIAN, HERMON, JUNCAL, KAILAS, KAZBEK, MAKALU, MERAPI, OLIVET, ORTLER, PELION, PISSIS, ROBSON, SAHAMA, SHASTA, STEELE, TAGANA, TAUNUS, TRISUL, ALBERES, ANTHONY, BERNINA, DAPSANG, EVEREST, FORAKER, HELICON, MUZTAGH, NILGIRI, OROHENA, PALOMAR, RAINIER, SEMENOV, COROPUNA, DEMAVEND, FUJIYAMA, ILLIMANI, JUNGFRAU, MCKINLEY, WRANGELL, ACONCAGUA, ANNAPURNA, MANDADEVI, PIKESPEAK, TUPUNGATO, CHIMBORAZO, MATTERHORN
mountebank QUACK, EMPIRIC
mourn RUE, SIGH, WAIL, WEEP, BEWAIL, GRIEVE, LAMENT
mourner MUTE, WEEPER, PENITENT
mouse VOLE; *see* RODENT
mouth(s) GOB, MUN, ORA, ABRA, BOCA, LADE, BOCCA, CODON, DELTA, FRITH, INLET, STOMA, VOICE, ESTUARY
mouth part GUM, LIP, TOOTH, UVULA, VELUM, LABIUM, PALATE, RICTUS, TONGUE, GINGIVA, OMPHALOS, UNDERLIP, UPPERLIP
mouthful GOBBET
mouthpiece BOCAL
mouthward ORAD
move GO, LEAD, PUSH, WALK, BUDGE, IMPEL, AFFECT
move sidewise EDGE, SLUE, SIDLE
move slowly EDGE, INCH, WORM
move to and fro WAG, FLAP, SWAY
movement MOTO, MUDGE, TAXIS, TEMPO, THEME, RHYTHM
movie FILM, FLICK, CINEMA, TALKIE, CARTOON, MUSICAL, QUICKIE, WESTERN, NEWSREEL, MELODRAMA

movie process TODDAO, CINERAMA
mow DESS, GOAF, LOFT, MATH
Mozart cataloguer KO(E)CHEL
Mozart opera FIGARO, (MAGIC)FLUTE, (DON)GIOVANNI
mud MIRE, MUCK, OOZE, SILT, SLOB, SALSE, SLIME, SLUDGE
muddle MESS, SOSS, ADDLE, SNAFU, EMBROIL
muddy ROILY, SLIMY, TURBID,
muffin COB, GEM, POPOVER
mug NOG, JACK, PUSS, TOBY, STEIN, NOGGIN
mulberry FUSTIC, MURREY, SYCAMINE
mulct FINE, AMERCE, PUNISH
mule MARE, HINNY
mull THINK, PONDER
multitude MOB, HOST, HORDE, GALAXY, LEGION, MYRIAD
Munda language HO, ASURI, JUANG, KORKU, KORWA, GADABA, KHARIA, SAVARA, MUNDARI, SANTALI, KHERWARI
mundane COSMIC, EARTHLY, TERRENE, WORLDLY, TEMPORAL
murder BURKE, HOMICIDE
murder fine CRO, MURDRUM, BLOODWIT(E)
murmur HUM, CURR, PURR, MUTTER
muscle BEEF, DURA, TELA, THEW, BRAWN, PSOAS, SINEW, TENDO, TENIA, TERES, BICEPS, FLEXOR, LACERT, RECTUS, SOLEUS, TAENIA, TENDON, TENSOR, VASTUS, CANINUS, DELTOID, DILATOR, ERECTOR, GLUTEUS, ILIACUS, LEVATOR, MIDRIFF, NASALIS, TRICEPS, ABDUCTOR, ADDUCTOR, EXTENSOR, LIGAMENT, MENTALIS, MUSCULUS, PALMARIS, PECTORAL, PERONEUS, RISORIUS, SCALENUS, SERRATUS, SPINALIS, SPLENIUS, DEPRESSOR, DIAPHRAGM, MASSETTER, SARTORIUS, SPHINCTER, TRAPEZIUS
musclelike MYOID
muscular BURLY, THEWY, TOROSE
muse MULL, REVE, PONDER
Muses CLIO, ERATO, THALIA, URANIA, EUTERPE, CALLIOPE, POLYMNIA, MELPOMENE, TERPSICHORE
museum RYKS, TATE, CLUNY, FIELD, FREER, GETTY, PITTI, PRADO, LOUVRE, UFFIZI, GALLERY, CLOISTERS, HERMITAGE
mush PAP, SAMP, SEPON, ATOLE, SUPAWN; *see* PORRIDGE
mushroom CEPE, MOREL, AGARIC
music HARMONY
music hall GAFF, BIJOU, EMPIRE, PALACE, ALHAMBRA, COLISEUM, WINDMILL, PALLADIUM, HIPPODROME
musical direction VIF, PIU, RIT, ADUE, ARCO, FINE, LENT, LOCO, MENO, MOTO, ZART, ANIME, DOLCE, FORTE, GRAVE, INNIG, LARGO, LENTO, MESTO, MOLTO, MOSSO, OSSIA, PIANO, SECCO, SEGUE, TACET, TARDO, ADAGIO, ARIOSO, ATEMPO, BELEBT, COMODO, DACAPO, GIUSTO, MASSIG, MUNTER, PRESTO, RUBATO, SUBITO, TENUTO, VELOCE, VIVACE, AGITATO, ALLEGRO, ALSEGNO, AMABILE, AMOROSO, ANDANTE, ANIMATO, ATTACCA, CALANDO, CONBRIO, CONMOTO, DETACHE, DOLENTE, GIOCOSO, GIOIOSO, LANGSAM, LEBHAFT, MARCATO, MARTELE, MORENDO, PORTATO, STRETTO, COLLEGNO, CONANIMA, CONFUOCO, GRAZIOSO, LEGGIERO, MAESTOSO, MARZIALE, MODERATO, PARLANDO, PIUMOSSO, RITENUTO, SPICCATO, STACCATO, UNACORDA
musical form CODA, OPUS, RAGA, TEMA, TRIO, CANON, CATCH, ETUDE, FUGUE, MARCH, OCTET, OPERA, REVUE, ROUND, SUITE, STUCK, TROLL, MINUET, POLSKA, SONATA, VERSET, BRAVURA, CADENZA, CONCERT, FANFARE,

MUSETTE, MUSICAL, PARTITA, PIBROCH, PRELUDE, RECITAL, REQUIEM, ROMANCE, SCHERZO, SESTOLE, TOCCATA, BERCEUSE, CONCERTO, DUETTINO, FANTASIA, NOCTURNE, NOTTURNO, OPERETTA, ORATORIO, OVERTURE, PASTORAL, RHAPSODY, SERENADE, SERENATA, SESTOLET, SONATINA, SYMPHONY, TONEPOEM; *see* SONG, DANCE

musical group DUO, BAND, SOLO, TRIO, CHOIR, NONET, OCTET, CHORUS, SEPTET, SEXTET, KAPELLE, QUARTET, QUINTET, ORCHESTRA

musical instrument *see* STRING, WIND, BRASS, PERCUSSION

musical part ALTO, BASS, BASSO, CANTO, MEZZO, TENOR, SOPRANO, BARITONE, BARYTONE, CONTRALTO

musical play CATS, HAIR, MAME, MONA, SARI, ANNIE, EVITA, FANNY, OHKAY, SALLY, SUNNY, CANCAN, EILEEN, GREASE, KISMET, CABARET, CANDIDE, FIREFLY, JUBILEE, MAYTIME, NEWMOON, PALJOEY, ROBERTA, CAROUSEL, OKLAHOMA, SHOWBOAT

musical term ALT, BIS, BAR, DOT, DUR, JUG, KEY, PES, TER, TIE, ADUE, CLEF, FLAT, FUSA, HOLD, MOLL, RAGA, REST, ROOT, SLUR, TAKT, TONE, ANCUS, BRACE, BREVE, CHORD, CLOSE, DUPLE, EPODE, FUSEE, GAMUT, GRACE, GUIDA, KLANG, LONGA, MAXIM, METER, MINIM, MOTIF, NEUMA, NEUME, PAUSE, PEDAL, PIENA, PIENO, PITCH, PRESA, SCALE, SCORE, SHAKE, SHARP, SOLFA, SPACE, STAFF, STAVE, TEMPO, TONIC, TRIAD, TRILL, TROPE, VIRGA, BURDEN, CLIVIS, DEGREE, DITONE, ENCORE, GROUND, HOCKET, MELODY, MOTIVE, OCTAVE, PARODY, PHRASE, PLAGAL, PNEUMA, QUAVER, RELISH, RENVOI, RHYTHM, SERIAL, TACTUS, TIERCE, TIMBRE, TRIPLE, UNISON, BARLINE, CADENCE, CLUSTER, FERMATA, HARMONY, INCIPIT, KEYNOTE, MEASURE, MEDIANT, MELISMA, MORDENT, NATURAL, ORISCUS, PODATUS, PRESSUS, PUNCTUM, PUNCTUS, RIPIENO, ROULADE, SALICUS, SIXFOUR, SOLFEGE, SYNCOPE, TREMOLO, TRIPLET, TRITONE, VIBRATO, ARPEGGIO, CROTCHET, DIAPASON, DYNAMICS, HALFNOTE, MODALITY, NOTATION, SEMIFUSA, SEMITONE; *see* MODE, NOTE

musician BARD, WAIT, FIFER, JUBAL, LUTER, PIPER, AULETE, BUGLER, CORNET, HARPER, LEADER, LUTIST, MUSICO, OBOIST, VIOLER, CELLIST, DRUMMER, DUBADUB, FIDDLER, GAMBIST, HARPIST, HORNIST, MAESTRO, ORPHEUS, PIANIST, SOLOIST, VIOLIST, COMPOSER, CYMBALER, DUETTIST, FLAUTIST, GRIDDLER, LUTANIST, MELODIST, MINSTREL, ORGANIST, STRUMMER, THRUMMER, TWANGLER, VIRTUOSO, CONDUCTOR, CORNETIST, TIMPANIST, TRUMPETER, VIOLINIST; *see* SINGER

musket CULVERIN; *see* GUN

musketeer ATHOS, ARAMIS, PORTHOS, DARTAGNAN

muslin MULL, BATISTE, ORGANDY

mussel UNIO, NAIAD, MUCKET, MUSCLE, MYTILID, MYTILUS, UNIONID, DEERHORN

Mussolini (IL)DUCE

must MA(U)N, MOLD, SAPA, STUM

mustard RUNCH, CHARLOCK

musty FETID, FUSTY, MOLDY

mute MUM, LENE, SURD, MUFFLE

mutilate MAIM, GARBLE, MANGLE

mutt CUR, MONGREL; *see* DOG

Mutt's friend JEFF

mutual JOINT, COMMON
myrtle AUSU, PENDA
mysterious ARCANE, OCCULT, CRYPTIC, ESOTERIC
mystery RUNE, ARCANA, ENIGMA, ARCANUM, WHODUNIT, SACRAMENT
mystic SUFI, COVERT, OCCULT, SUFIST, TAOIST, CABALIC, ESOTERIC
myth SAGA, FABLE, LEGEND, FICTION
mythology *see p. 316*

N

nab NAIL, NICK, ARREST, SNATCH
nadir DEPTHS
nag SHREW, BADGER, HECTOR, HENPECK; *see* HORSE
naiad NYMPH, OREAD
nail(s) HOB, BRAD, CLAW, SPAD, STUD, TACK, CLOUT, SPRIG, TALON, TENTER, UNGUES, UNGUIS, UNGULA(E); *see* NAB
naïve CANDID, SIMPLE, ARTLESS
naked BARE, NUDE, INVALID
name DUB, NOUN, ONYM, TERM, ALIAS, CLEPE, NOMEN, TITLE, EPONYM, AGNOMEN, CACONYM, ENTITLE, EPITHET, MONIKER, COGNOMEN, NOMINATE
name, female ADA, ANN, ECA, IDA, INA, MAE, ANNE, ALMA, ANNE, DORA, ETTA, KATE, LISA, LOLA, MARY, NORA, VERA, ANITA, CELIA, DAISY, ELENA, FANNY, IRENE, SALLY
name, male ABE, ELI, IAN, IRA, PAT, ADAM, ALAN, AMOS, CARL, DANA, DION, EMIL, ENOS, ERIC, EVAN, EZRA, HANS, JACK, JAKE, JOEL, JOHN, JUDE, LEON, LUKE, MARK, NEIL, OTTO, OWEN, PAUL, BASIL, HIRAM, HOMER, ALBERT, DONALD, GEORGE, OLIVER, STEVEN, WARREN, CHARLES
named YCLEPT, YCLEPED
nameless ANONYMOUS
namely VIZ, SCIL, TOWIT, SCILICET, VIDELICET
names, famous *see p. 255*
Naomi relative RUTH
naos CELLA
nap DOZE, WINK, DROWSE, SIESTA, SNOOZE
nap, coarse GIG, RAS, PILE, SHAG, TEASEL, TEASLE, TEAZEL, TEAZLE
nape NUCHA, SCRUFF, NIDDICK
napkin BIB, DIDIE, DIAPER
Napoleon relative ELIZA, JEROME, LUCIEN, CAROLINE, JOSEPHINE
Napoleon's isle ELBA, CORSICA, HELENA
narcotic *see* DRUG
narrate SPIN, RELATE, RECOUNT
narrative SAGA, STORY, ACCOUNT
narrow ANGUST, LINEAL, STRAIT
narrow-minded PETTY, BIASED, BIGOTED
nasal NARIAL, NARINE, RHINAL
nation STATE, PEOPLE, COUNTRY
native ITE, RAW, SON, TAO, BORN, NATAL, INBORN, INNATE, DENIZEN, ENDEMIC, INDIGENE; *see p. 342*
native American INDIAN, AMERIND
native American (Indian) chief INCA, TYEE, SACHEM, CACIQUE, CAZIQUE, SAGAMORE
native American (Indian) languages COOS, EYAK, KAMI, POMO, YUKI, ZUNI, AYMAR, CARIB, HAIDA, KAROK, KIOWA, MAYAN, OTOMI, TAINO, WASHO, WIYOT, YUCHI, YUMAN, YUROK, ARAWAK, AYMARA, MIXTEC, NAVAJO, SHASTA, SIOUAN, TANOAN, CADDOAN, CARIBAN, CHINOOK, KERESAN, NAHUATL, QUECHUA, QUICHUA, TLINGIT, ACHOMAWI, KOOTENAI, PENUTIAN, SALISHAN, WAKASHAN, ARAWAKAN, ALGONQUI(A)N, IROQUOIAN, TSIMSHIAH; *see p. 342 (names of languages and tribes are often the same)*

native American (Indian) money **PEAG(E), PIMAN, WAMPUM**
native American (Indian) tribes *see p. 342*
natty **CHIC, TRIM, SHARP, SMART, SPRUCE**
natural **RAW, BORN, INNATE, NATIVE**
naturalist **GRAY, MUIR, SARS, BEEBE, BREHM, LINNE, PLINY, AKELEY, CARVER, DARWIN, FRESIA, JORDAN, MENDEL, ANDREWS, ANIMIST, AUDUBON, BURBANK, DEVRIES, LAMARCK, LINDLEY, THOREAU, BOTANIST, LINNAEUS, BIOLOGIST**
nature **ILK, TYPE, OUSIA, ESSENCE**
nausea **PALL, QUALM, WAMBLE, DISGUST**
nautical **NAVAL, MARINE, TARRISH, MARITIME**
nautical equipment **HELM, SONAR, NIGGER, TOGGLE, CAPSTAN, COMPASS, GRAPNEL, PELORUS, SEXTANT, BINNACLE**; *see* **ROPE**
nautical term **AHOY, ALOW, ATRY, OHOY, ABAFT, ABEAM, AFORE, AVAST**
Nautilus captain **NEMO**
Navaho **DINE**
navigate **SAIL, PILOT, STEER**
navigation aid **BUOY, LORAN, RADAR, SONAR**
navigator **COOK, DIAS, ERIC, GAMA, KEIF, ROSS, CABOT, DRAKE, BAFFIN, BERING, DAGAMA, HUDSON, TASMAN, RALEIGH**
navy **FLEET, ARMADA, FLOTILLA, SQUADRON**
near **DEAR, NIGH, ABOUT, CLOSE**
nearsighted **MYOPIC, PURBLIND**
nearsighted person **MYOPE**
neat **PRIM, TIDY, TOSH, TRIG, TRIM, NATTY, SOIGNE, SPRUCE**
Nebraska information *see p. 308*
necessitate **COMPEL, ENTAIL**
neck **PET, KISS, NUCHA, NUQUE, SPOON, CERVIX, COLLUM, SCRUFF, STRAIT, ISTHMUS**
necklace **CARCAN, CHOKER, STRAND, TORQUE, BALDRIC, RIVIERE, SAUTOIR, CARCANET**
neckwear **BIB, BOA, BOW, TIE, RUFF, ASCOT, JABOT, BOWTIE, CARCAN, CHOKER, COLLAR, CRAVAT, TUCKER, NECKTIE, CARCANET, PEIGNOIR**
need **LACK, WANT, PENURY, STRAIT, REQUIRE, STRAITS**
needle **SEW, GOAD, HYPO, PROD, BODKIN, HECKLE, STYLUS, OBELISK**
needlefish **GAR, PIPEFISH**
needle-shaped **ACUATE, ACERATE, ACEROSE, ACICULAR, SPICULAR**
needlework **SEWING, SAMPLER, EMBROIDERY, PETITPOINT**
needy **POOR, INDIGENT, DESTITUTE**
ne'er-do-well **LOSEL**
negative **NEY, NIX, NON, NOT, NEIN, NYET, MINUS**
negative pole **CATHODE**
neglect **OMIT, SHIRK, FORGET, SLIGHT, DEFAULT**
negligent **LAX, SLACK, REMISS**
negotiate **PARLE, TREAT, PARLEY, BARGAIN**
Negro **IBO, KRU, IGBO, KROO, BANTU, BLACK, HAUSA, ETHIOP, HAUSSA, HUBSHI, NUBIAN, YORUBA**
nemesis **BANE, AVENGER**
Nepalese language **NEWARI**; *see* **INDIC**
Nepalese money **MOHAR, RUPEE**
nephew **NEVE, VASU, NEPOTE**
Neptune relative **MEDUSA, TRITON**
nerve **GALL, PLUCK, COURAGE**
nerve cell **NEURON**
nerve-cell process **AXON(E), NEURITE, DENDRITE**
nerve layer(s) **ALVEI, ALVEUS**
nerves **TENIA, VAGUS, MYELON, TAENIA, GANGLION**
nervous **EDGY, TENSE, JITTERY, SKITTISH**
nest **DEN, NID, AERY, EYRY, DRAY, DREY, NIDE, NIDI, AERIE, NIDUS**
nestle **CUDDLE, NUZZLE, SNUGGLE**
nestling **EYAS, POULT, SQUAB**
net **FYKE, CLEAR, LACIS, SEINE, SNARE, STENT, TRAWL, FILLET, SAGENE, RETICLE, SPILLER**
Netherlands **DUTCH, HOLLAND**
Netherlands leaders **JONG, NASSAU, JULIANA, ZIJLSTRA**

Netherlands measure **EL, AAM, AUM, KAN, KOP, ZAK, DUIM, VOET, MUDDE, ROEDE, STOOP, BUNDER, MAATJE, MUTSJE, STREEP, SCHEPEL**
Netherlands money **DOIT, OORD, FLORIN, GULDEN, STIVER, DAALDER, GUILDER**
Netherlands weights **ONS, LOOD, POND, GREIN, KORREL, WICHTJE**
netlike **MESHY, RETIARY**
nettle **BUR, IRK, VEX, FRET**
network **WEB, MESH, RETE, RETIA, PLEXUS**
neuter **NEUTRAL, SEXLESS**
Nevada information *see p. 308*
new **LATE, NOVEL, MODERN, RECENT, NEOTERIC, ORIGINAL**
New Englander **YANKEE**
New Hampshire, New Jersey, New Mexico, New York information *see p. 308*
New Mexico **CIBOLA**
New Mexico artists' colony **TAOS**
New Testament *see p. 247*
New York City **GOTHAM, BIGAPPLE**
New York City borough **BRONX, QUEENS, BROOKLYN, RICHMOND, MANHATTAN**
New York City street **WALL, BOWERY, BROADWAY**
New Zealand bird **KEA, MOA, TUI, HUIA, KAKI, KIWI, WEKA**
New Zealand language **MAORI**
New Zealand tree **KI, TI, AKE, AUTE, KARO, KOPI, MAHO, MAKO, MIRO, PUKA, RATA, RIMU, TAWA, TORO, TORU, TUTU, WHAU, HINAU, KAURI, MAHOE, MAIRE, MAPAU, MAPOU, TOWAI, AKEAKE, KAMAHI, KARAKA, TARATA, TOTARA, MAKOMAKO**
Newfoundland information *see p. 306*
news **WORD, REPORT, TIDINGS**
news agency **AP, UP, INS, UPI, TASS, ANETA, DOMEI, REUTERS**
newspaper **DAILY, SHEET, GAZETTE, JOURNAL, TABLOID**
newsperson **CUB, REPORTER, COLUMNIST, JOURNALIST**
newstand **KIOSK**
newt *see* **SALAMANDER**
next **PROCHAIN, PROCHEIN**
nib **BEAK, BILL, POINT**
nibble **GNAW, KNAB, KNAP**
Nicaraguan measure **SUERTE, ESTAJAL, MANZANA**
Nicaraguan money **CENTAVO, CORDOBA**
niche *see* **NOOK**
nick **DENT, NOTCH, TALLY**
nickle **JITNEY**
nickname **MONI(C)KER, SO(U)BRIQUET**
nicotinic acid **NIACIN**
nifty **SMART, CLASSY, STYLISH**
Niger language **HAUSA, DJERMA, SONGHAI**
Niger-Congo language **IJO**; *see* **GUR, KWA, MANDE**
Nigerian language **IBO, HAUSA, YORUBA**; *see* **KWA**
Nigerian money **NAIRA**
niggard(ly) **MISER, PIKER, STINGY**
night **EVE, NOX, NYX, NATT, NOTT, DEATH**
nightcap **HOW, COWL, BIGGIN**
nightingale **BULBUL, PHILOMEL**
nightmare **ALP, MARA, INCUBUS**
Nile **ABBAI**
Nile tributary **SOBAT, ATBARA, KAGERA**
Nilotic language **LUO, LWO, ALUR, BARI, NUER, TESO, DINKA, LANGO, MASAI, NANDI, ACHOLI**
nimble **SPRY, AGILE, LISSOM, SUPPLE, VOLANT, LISSOME**
nimbus **HALO, AURA, GLORIA, AUREOLA**
Niobe relative **PELOPS, AMPHION, TANTALUS**
nip **BITE, PECK, DRINK**
nipple **DUG, PAP, TEAT, PAPILLA**
nitrogen **AZO(TE)**
nitwit **BOOB, FOOL, IDIOT, BOOBY**
no **NAE, NAW, NAY, NIX, NOPE**
Noah, pert. to **NOETIC, NOACHIAN**
Noah relative **HAM, ARAM, SHEM, LAMECH, JAPHETH**
Nobel chemistry prize **HAHN, HOFF, KLUG, KUHN, TODD, UREY, ADLER, ASTON, BOSCH, BROWN, CURIE, DEBYE, DIELS, FLORY, FUKUI,**

HABER, LIBBY, NATTA, PREGL, SOFFY, SYNGE, TAUBE, BAEYER, CALVIN, HARDEN, HEVESY, KARRER, LELOIR, MARTIN, NERNST, PERUTZ, RAMSAY, SANGER, SUMNER, WERNER, WITTIG, OSTWALD, PAULING

Nobel economics prize ARROW, HICKS, KLEIN, LEWIS, OHLIN, SIMON, STONE, TOBIN, DEBREU, FRISCH, MYRDAL, KUZNETS, SCHULTZ, STIGLER, SAMUELSON

Nobel literature prize BOLL, BUCK, GIDE, MANN, SHAW, AGNON, BUNIN, CAMUS, ELIOT, HESSE, HEYSE, LEGER, LEWIS, SACHS, WHITE, YEATS, ANDRIC, BELLOW, DUGARD, ELYTIS, EUCKEN, FRANCE, HAMSUN, JENSEN, NERUDA, ONEILL, SARTRE, TAGORE, UNDSET, BECKETT, BERGSON, CENETTI, KIPLING, MARQUEZ, MAURIAC, ROLLAND, FAULKNER, CHURCHILL, HEMINGWAY, PASTERNAK, SHOLOKHOV, STEINBECK

Nobel medicine prize DAM, CORI, DALE, HESS, HILL, KATZ, KOCH, ROSS, ROUS, VANE, ARBER, BLOCK, BOVET, CAJAL, CHAIN, CRICK, DOISY, GOLGI, HENCH, HUBEL, JACOB, KREBS, KROGH, LOEWI, LURIA, LWOFF, LYNEN, MINOT, MONIZ, MONOD, OCHOA, SMITH, SNELL, TATUM, TEMIN, YALOW, ADRIAN, BARANY, BEADLE, BEKESY, BORDET, BURNET, CARREL, CLAUDE, DOMAGK, ECCLES, ENDERS, FINSEN, FLOREY, GASSER, HUXLEY, KOCHER, KOSSEL, MORGAN, MULLER, MURPHY, PAVLOV, PORTER, RICHET, SPERRY, WATSON, WELLER, WIESEL, FLEMING, HOPKINS, ERLANGER, MEYERHOF

Nobel peace prize IRC, ORR, THO, HULL, KING, MOTT, PIRE, ROOT, SATO, TUTU, ASSER, BAJER, BALCH, BEGIN, DAWES, FRIED, GOBAT, LAMAS, LANGE, PASSY, SADAT, ADDAMS, ANGELL, BRANDT, BRIAND, BUNCHE, BUTLER, CASSIN, CREMER, DUNANT, MONETA, MYRDAL, NANSEN, QUIDDE, UNICEF, WALESA, WILSON, THERESA, ESQUIVEL, SAKHAROV

Nobel physics prize LEE, BOHR, BORN, HESS, LAUE, RABI, RYLE, TAMM, TING, WIEN, YANG, BASOV, BETHE, BLOCH, BOTHE, BRAGG, BRAUN, CURIE, DALEN, DIRAC, FERMI, FITCH, FRANK, GABOR, HERTZ, KUSCH, MAYER, PAULI, RAMAN, SEGRE, STARK, STERN, BARKLA, CRONIN, FRANCK, GLASER, JENSEN, LANDAU, LENARD, PERRIN, PLANCK, POWELL, TOWNES, WALTON, WIGNER, WILSON, YUKAWA, ZEEMAN, MARCONI, EINSTEIN, ROENTGEN

noble DON, DUC, SIR, DOGE, DUKE, EARL, GRAF, JARL, KAMI, KUGE, LADY, LORD, PEER, BARIN, BARON, COUNT, MURZA, THANE, DAIMIO, MILADY, RITTER, YONKER, DUCHESS, GRANDEE, HIDALGO, MARQUIS, PEERESS, BARONESS, CONTESSA, COUNTESS, MARQUISE, VISCOUNT

nod BOW, BECK, WINK, DROWSE

Nod, west of EDEN

nodding NUTANT, ANNUENT

node KNOB, KNOT, KNUR(L)

noise DIN, BABEL, BRUIT, CLAMOR, HUBBUB, RACKET

noisome FETID, NOXIOUS

nomad ARAB, GYPSY, BEDOUIN, SARACEN, SCENITE

nominal PAR, TOKEN, TITULAR

nonbeliever PAGAN, ATHEIST, INFIDEL, AGNOSTIC

noncommissioned officer CPL, NCO, CORPORAL, SERGEANT

nonconformist REBEL, BEATNIK, HERETIC, SECTARY, RECUSANT

nonentity NIL, CIPHER, NULITY

nongypsy GAJO

non-Jew(s) GOI, GOY(IM), GENTILE

non-Mohammedan RAIA, RAYAH, GIAOUR, KAFFIR, ZENDIK

nonpareil ONER, NONSUCH, PARAGON, NONESUCH, PEERLESS

nonplus STUMP, PUZZLE, CONFOUND
nonprofessional LAY, LAIC
nonsense ROT, BLAH, PISH, POOH, HOOEY, TRIPE, DRIVEL, TWADDLE, FLUMMERY, FOLDEROL, MALARKEY
nonsense creature GOOP, SMOO, GOLUK, SHMOO, SNARK, BOOJUM
noodles MEIN, FARFEL, FERFEL, LAKSHEN; *see* PASTA
nook WRO, CANT, COVE, HERNE, NICHE, ALCOVE, CRANNY, RECESS
noose LOOP, LEASH, HALTER
normal USUAL, AVERAGE, TYPICAL
Norse gods AESIR; *see p. 320*
north(ern) POLAR, ARTIC, BOREAL
North Carolina, North Dakota information *see p. 308*
North Pole discoverer PEARY
North Star POLARIS, LODESTAR
Norway, rulers of ERIC, INGE, OLAF, OLAV, OSCAR, HAAKON, HAROLD, MAGNUS, SIGURD, SVERRE, CHRISTIAN
Norwegian language LAPP, RIKSMAAL, LANDSMAAL
Norwegian measure FOT, MAL, ALEN, MAAL, SKIEPPE
Norwegian money ORE, KRONE
Norwegian weight LOD, MARK, PUND
nose NEB, PUG, BEAK, NASUS, SCENT, SNIFF, SNOOP, MUZZLE
nose part NARE, VOMER, SEPTUM
nose type PUG, SNUB, ROMAN, NASUTE, SIMOUS, AQUILINE
nostrils, of NARIC, NARIAL, NARINE
notch DENT, DINT, KERF, NICK, NOCK, CRENA, SCORE, CRENAE
notched CRENATE, SERRATE(D)
note IOU, CHIT, LOAN, MEMO, BILLET, POSTIL, RENOWN, APOSTIL, SCHOLIUM, APOSTILLE; *see* SCALE
nothing NIL, NIX, NUL(L), ZERO, NIHIL, CIPHER, NAUGHT, TRIFLE
notice SEE, CITE, HEED, MARK, REGARD, REVIEW, DISCERN
notion BEE, IDEA, VIEW, WHIM, CURIO, FANCY
notorious ARRANT, INFAMOUS
notwithstanding THO, YET
noun APTOTE, GERUND, VERBAL
nourish FEED, FOSTER, SUCCOR
nourishing ALMA, RICH, ALIBLE
nourishment FOOD, MANNA, ALIMENT, PABULUM, NUTRI(M)ENT
Nova Scotia ACADIA; *see p. 306*
novel RARE, RECENT, FICTION
novelist LEE, AGEE, ASCH, BUCK, FORD, GIDE, GREY, HUGO, JONG, MANN, SAND, WOUK, ZOLA, BENET, CAMUS, CRANE, DEFOE, DUMAS, ELIOT, HARDY, HARTE, HENRY, HESSE, JAMES, JOYCE, KAFKA, LEWIS, MILNE, OHARA, SCOTT, STAEL, STOWE, SWIFT, TWAIN, VERNE, WAUGH, WELLS, WELTY, WOLFE, WYLIE, ZWEIG, ALCOTT, AUSTEN, BALZAC, BARRIE, BELLOW, BRONTE, CATHER, CONRAD, COOPER, DAUDET, FERBER, GOETHE, HERSEY, HOLMES, IRVING, KRANTZ, LESAGE, LONDON, MAILER, MILLER, ORWELL, PORTER, PROUST, STERNE, STYRON, UPDIKE, WARREN, BELLAMY, CLEMENS, COLETTE, DICKENS, DREISER, FORSTER, MALAMUD, MALRAUX, MAUGHAM, ROLLAND, SAROYAN, TOLSTOI, TOLSTOY, WHARTON, ANNUNZIO, FAULKNER, FIELDING, FLAUBERT, FORESTER, LAGERLOF, LAWRENCE, MELVILLE, MEREDITH, MICHENER, RABELAIS, SALINGER, SINCLAIR, TROLLOPE, TURGENEV; *see* NOBEL
novelty FAD, NEWNESS, CURIOSITY
novice TYRO, ROOKIE, ACOLYTE, AMATEUR, BEGINNER
now NOO, HERE, EXTANT, PRONTO, PRESENT
noxious NOCENT, HARMFUL, NOISOME, MEPHITIC
nozzle ROSE, VENT, GIANT, TUYERE
nub GIST, KNOT, LUMP
nucleus CORE, GERM, CADRE, KERNEL

nude BARE, NAKED
nudge JOG, GOAD, KNUB, POKE, PROD
nudist ADAMITE
nuisance BORE, PEST, PLAGUE
nullify UNDO, VETO, VOID, CANCEL, NEGATE, REPEAL, ABROGATE
number LAC, LAKH, TEEN, SURD, UNIT, COUNT, DIGIT, STEEN, CIPHER, FIGURE, SCALAR, ALIQUOT, AMOUNT, COMPUTE, INTEGER
numerous LOTS, MANY, SCADS, GALORE, MYRIAD, MANIFOLD, MULTIPLE
nun CLARE, ABBESS, SISTER, MINORESS, VOTARESS
nunnery *see* CONVENT
nurse AMA, IYA, AMAH, AYAH, BABA, EYAH, FEED, REAR, TEND, BONNE, NANNY, FOSTER, SUCKLE, LACTATE, NUTRICE
nursery CRECHE, HOTHOUSE
nursery rhyme characters DAW, DUN, COLE, JACK, JILL, JUDY, POLT, ROSE, TROT, WREN, COLIN, GILES, JENNY, KITTY, MOREY, POLLY, PUNCH, SIMON, SPRAT, TAFFY, BOGGEN, BOPEEP, FOSTER, GRIGGS, GRUNDY, HORNER, JENNIE, MACKEY, MUFFET, PORGIE, SPRATT, TONSEY, TUCKER, WARLEY, WILLIE, WINKIE, BLUEBEN, BOLDERO, FAUSTUS, FINIKIN, HUBBARD, SHAFTOE, TERENCE, DAMETROY, ETTICOAT, FLINDERS, KINGCOLE, TOMTHUMB, BETTYBLUE, DANDYPRAT, MCDIDDLER, REDBREAST, TOMMYTROT
nut KOLA, PILI, ACORN, BETEL, LICHI, PECAN, PINON, ALMOND, BRAZIL, CASHEW, LICHEE, WALNUT, HICKORY
nut(s), pert. to NUCAL
Nutmeg State CT, CONN(ECTICUT)
nutria COYPU
nutritional TROPHIC
nymph MAIA, NAIS, DRYAD, HOURI, LARVA, NAIAD, NIXIE, OREAD, SYLPH, KELPIE, NEREID, ONDINE, UNDINE, OCEANID

O

oaf BOOR, DOLT, GAWK, LOUT, RUBE, BUMPKIN
oak CORK, HOLM, ILEX, EMORY, ROBLE, ROBUR, CERRIS, ENCINA, DURMAST, QUERCUS
oak fruit MAST, ACORN, CAMATA, BELLOTE
oakum, seal with CA(U)LK
oar ROW, BLADE, ROWER, SCULL, SWEEP, PADDLE, PROPEL
oar holder LOCK, THOLE, ROWLOCK
oar part LOOM, PALM, PEEL
oarsman ROWER, STROKE
oasis OJO, WADI, WADY, SPRING
oat AVENA, HAVER; *see* CEREAL
oath BAN, ODS, VOW, AITH, DARN, DANG, DRAT, EGAD, GOSH, HECK, LAWK, OONS, BEDAD, BEGAD, CURSE, LAWKS, ZOOKS, CRIKEY, CRIPES, SBLOOD, ZOUNDS, SERMENT; *see* CRY, EXCLAMATION
obedient DOCILE, COMPLIANT
obeisance CONGEE, HOMAGE, DEFERENCE; *see* BOW
obelisk NEEDLE, MONOLITH
Oberon's messenger PUCK
Oberon's wife TITANIA
obese PUDGY, PURSY, PORTLY, PYKNIC, ADIPOSE, LIPAROUS
obey MIND, HEED, COMPLY
obi *see* SASH
object AIM, CARP, KICK, MIND, CAVIL, DEMUR
object of art CURIO, BIBELOT
objection CAVIL, SCRUPLE
objective AIM, GOAL, TARGET, PURPOSE, DETACHED
objects, biblical URIM, THUMMIM
obligation IOU, TIE, BOND, DEBT, DUTY, MUST, ONUS
oblique AWRY, CANT, ASKEW, SLANT, BEVEL, SLOPT, ASLANT
obliterate RAZE, ANNUL, EFFACE; *see* ERASE
oblivion LETHE, LIMBO, NIRVANA

oboe *see* WIND INSTRUMENT
obscene LEWD, GROSS, COARSE, SMUTTY, INDECENT
obscure DIM, FOG, DARK, BEDIM, CLOUD, LOWLY, MURKY, VAGUE, DARKEN, DARKLE, OCCULT, CRYPTIC, ECLIPSE, OVERSILE
obsequies WAKE, RITES, FUNERAL
observance CUSTOM, PRACTICE
observant ALERT, PERCEPTIVE
observatory HALE, LICK, DUNLAP, HOOKER, YERKES, AGASSIZ, CORDOBA, PALOMAR
observe MARK, NOTE, OBEY, ABIDE, BEHOLD, REMARK, MENTION
obsess HAUNT, PREOCCUPY
obsession MANIA, IDEEFIXE
obsolete PASSE, ARCHAIC, DISUSED, OUTMODED
obstacle SNAG, HITCH, HURDLE, BARRIER
obstinate SET, HARD, MULISH, RENITENT, STUBBORN
obstruct DIT, CLOG, DITT, FOIL
obtain FANG, SECURE
obtuse DULL, DENSE
obvious OVERT, PLAIN, EVIDENT
occasion SELE, NONCE, MOTIVE
occasional ODD, ORRA, ANTRIN, SPORADIC
occidental PONENT, HESPERIAN
occult HIDDEN, MYSTIC, SECRET
occultism MAGIC, CABALA
occupant RENTEE, TENANT, RESIDENT, INCUMBENT
occupation JOB, CALL, WORK, CRAFT, TRADE, METIER
occupy EMPLOY, ENGAGE, ENGROSS
occur APPEAR, BETIDE, HAPPEN
ocean DEEP, MAIN, BRINE, ARCTIC, INDIAN, PACIFIC, ATLANTIC, ANTARCTIC; *see* SEA
oceanic DIPS(E)Y, MARINE, PELAGIC
octave UTAS, UTIS
Octavia's husband ANTHONY
octopus POLYP, POULP(E), SCUTTLE
octopus genus POLYPUS
odd AWK, RUM, ORRA, DROLL, QUEER, RUMMY, AZYGO(U)S
odd-job man JACK, JOEY, SWAMPER
Odin relative VE, BOR, TIU, TYR, FRIA, GRID, JORD, SIGI, THOR, VILI, FRIGG, BALDER
odious HATEFUL, HEINOUS
odor FUME, NOSE, REEK, AROMA, FETOR, FUMET, NIDOR, SCENT
odorless AOSMIC
Odysseus *see* ULYSSES
Odyssey author HOMER
Oedipus relative LAIUS, ISMENE, JOCASTA, ANTIGONE, ETEOCLES
off AGEE, AWAY, WRONG, SKEWED
offend CAG, SIN, VEX, MIFF, CHAFE, PIQUE, INSULT, NETTLE, AFFRONT, OUTRAGE
offense SIN, MALA, TORT, CRIME, DELIT, MALUM, WRONG, DELICT, FELONY, INSULT, UMBRAGE
offer BID, TENDER, PROFFER, PROPOSE
offering GIFT, TRIBUTE, OBLATION
offhand ADLIB, CASUAL, CAVALIER, INFORMAL, EXTEMPORE
office DUTY, POST, BUREAU, FUNCTION, POSITION
officer COP, ENS, NEO, EXON, DEWAN, DIWAN, MACER, AVENER, BAILIE, BEADLE, DEPUTY, LICTOR, PARNAS, TINDAL, BAILIFF, SHERIFF, CONSTABLE
officer, military NCO, SGT, MATE, MAJOR, ATAMAN, CORNET, ENSIGN, HETMAN, SIRDAR, YOEMAN, ADMIRAL, CAPTAIN, COLONEL, GENERAL, MARSHAL, NAVARCH, PROVOST, CORPORAL, SERGEANT, CENTURION, COMMANDER, COMMODORE, SUBALTERN, LIEUTENANT
official KUAN, KWAN, EDILE, HAJIB, AEDILE, SATRAP, TRIBUNE
offset BALANCE, COMPENSATE
offshoot CION, SLIP, SPUR, SCION, BRANCH
offspring HEIR, CHILD, ISSUE, PROGENY
Ohio information *see p. 308*

oil BAY, BEN, FAT, HOP, RUE, TIL, BALM, CADE, CHIA, GHEE, LARD, LUBE, MACE, NARD, OLEO, TUNG, ATTAR, BENNE, BRIBE, BUCHU, IRONE, KAPOK, MADIA, OLEUM, ORRIS, SEBUM, TANSY, TUNNY, ACEITE, AJOWAN, ANOINT, ASARUM, BALSAM, CARAPA, CASSIA, CASTOR, CETENE, COSTUS, CURCAS, LOTION, NEROLI, SAFROL, ARACHIS, LINSEED, PERILLA, RAVISON; *see* FAT, GAS
oil, pert. to OLEIC
oilskin SLICKER
oily FATTY, SLICK, GREASY
ointment BALM, NARD, SALVE, CARRON, CERATE, POMADE, UNGUENT, VASELINE
OK, okay RIGHT, ROGER
Oklahoma information *see p. 308*
old ELD, AGED, AULD, GRAY, WORN, ANILE, HOARY, SENILE, ELDERLY, OGYGIAN
old hand VET, EXPERT, VETERAN
old maid SPINSTER
old sod ERIN, IRELAND
Old Testament *see p. 246*
old times ELD, YORE, QUONDAM
old woman HAG, CRONE, BELDAM, GAMMER
old-fashioned DATED, FUSTY, PASSE, SQUARE
Oliver Twist character *see p. 315*
Olympic site (summer) ROME, PARIS, SEOUL, TOKYO, ATHENS, BERLIN, LONDON, MOSCOW, MUNICH, ANTWERP, HELSINKI, MONTREAL
Olympic site (winter) OSLO, CALGARY, CORTINA, CHAMONIX, GRENOBLE, SARAJEVO, STMORITZ
Oman language ARABIC; *see* INDIC
Oman money GAJ, GOZ, GHAZI, MAHMUDI
omen AUSPICE; *see* PRESAGE
ominous GRAVE, SINISTER
omission APOCOPE, DEFAULT, ELISION, SYNCOPE
omit DELE, PASS, SKIP, ELIDE, DELETE, SLIGHT, NEGLECT
once ANES; *see* FORMER
one ACE, AIN, UNI, MONO, UNIT
onesided BIASED, PARTIAL
onion CIVE, LEEK, CHIVE, CIBO(U)L, SHALLOT, ESCHALOT, SCALLION
onion genus ALLIUM
only BUT, LONE, MERE, SAVE, SOLE, SIMPLY
onset START, ATTACK, ASSAULT
Ontario information *see p. 306*
onyx NICOLO; *see* CHALCEDONY
ooze LEAK, SEEP, SEIP, SIPE, SYPE, EXUD(AT)E
open AJAR, AGAPE, OVERT, UNTIE, BROACH, HONEST, PATENT, PUBLIC, VACANT
opening BUR, GAP, BOLE, BORE, BURR, HOLE, PORE, RIFT, RIMA, SLIT, SLOT, VENT, CLEFT, SINUS, STOMA, CAVITY, EYELET, GAMBIT, HIATUS, MEATUS, FORAMEN, ORIFICE, STOMATA
opera hat GIBUS, TOPPER
opera house MET, (LA)SCALA
operate RUN, WORK, MANAGE
Ophelia relative LAERTES, POLONIUS
Ophelia's love HAMLET
opinion DOOM, DOXY, CREDO, TENET, NOTION, JUDGMENT
opium derivative HEROIN, CODEINE, MORPHINE
opium source POPPY
opossum *see* MARSUPIAL
opponent FOE, ANTI, RIVAL
opportune APT, TIMELY, APROPOS
opportunity HENT; *see* CHANCE
oppose DEFY, IMPUGN, OPPUGN
opposite ANTI, POLAR, CONTRA, COUNTER, CONTRARY, CONVERSE, ANTIPODAL
opprobrium ODIUM, INFAMY, OBLOQUY
optical illusion MIRAGE
optical instrument PRISM, ALIDAD(E), BINOCULAR, PERISCOPE, TELESCOPE, MICROSCOPE
optimistic ROSY, HOPEFUL, ROSEATE, SANGUINE
option CHOICE, ELECTIVE
oracle SEER, AUGUR, DELOS, SIBYL, DELPHI, SPHINX, DELPHOS

oral PAROL, ALOUD, VOCAL, PAROLE, SPOKEN, VERBAL
orange MOCK, CHINO, HEDGE, NAVEL, OSAGE, MANDARIN, VALENCIA, TANGERINE
orangutan *see* APE
orator CATO, OTIS, BRYAN, HENRY, CICERO, LYSIAS, RHETOR, CUSHING, EVERETT
oratory CHAPEL, CHANTRY
orbit PATH, AMBIT, CYCLE, CIRCUIT
orbit point APSIS, APOGEE, PERIGEE
orchestra PIT, BAND, PARQUET
orchestrate SCORE
orchid DISA, FAHAM, SALEB, SALEP, SATYR, VANDA, POGONIA
ordain ENACT, FROCK, DECREE
ordeal TRIAL, CRUCIBLE
order BID, LINE, FIAT, WRIT, ALINE, ARRAY, EDICT, LODGE, EUTAXY, SYSTEM
order of merit AVIZ, BATH, VASA, CROWN, SWORD, ALBERT, CHRIST, STOLAF, LEOPOLD, STLOUIS
ordinance LAW, CANON, ASSIZE
ordinary USUAL, COMMON, AVERAGE; *see* TAVERN
ordnance GUNS, ARMOR, ARTILLERY
ore *see* MINERAL
Oregon information *see p. 308*
Orestes relative ELECTRA, HERMIONE, AGAMEMNON
organ CALLIOPE
organ, body COR, LUNG, MAZA, NEER, TEAT, WOMB, BOWEL, CALYX, CECUM, COLON, HEART, HEPAR, ILEUM, LIVER, MAMMA, METRA, OVARY, BOWELS, CAECUM, CARDIA, CARPUS, KIDNEY, LARYNX, PLEURA, RECTUM, SPLEEN, TONSIL, UTERUS, VISCUS, BLADDER, JEJUNUM, PHARYNX, PYLORUS, SIGMOID, STOMACH, TRACHEA, VISCERA, APPENDIX, BRONCHUS, DUODENUM, ENTRAILS, PANCREAS, PLACENTA, TONSILLA, ESOPHAGUS, INTESTINE, VENTRICLE
organ control KNOB, STUD, PEDAL, PISTON, TABLET, COUPLER, DRAWKNOB
organ division ECHO, SOLO, ALTAR, CHOIR, GREAT, PEDAL, SWELL, CHANCEL, GALLERY, ANTIPHONAL
organ part BOX, PIPE, WIND, ACTION, PALLET, ROLLER, SLIDER, CONSOLE, SHUTTER, TRACKER
organ stop SEXT, TERZ, GAMBE, NASAT, QUINT, DOLCAN, GEDEKT, MIXTUR, MONTRE, NASARD, SCHARF, TIERCE, BOURDON, CELESTA, LARIGOT, MELODIA, MIXTURE, POSAUNE, RANKETT, SUBBASS, TREMOLO, BOMBARDE, DIAPASON, DULCIANA, GEMSHORN, PRESTANT, REGISTER, KRUMMHORN, NACHTHORN, PRINCIPAL, UNDAMARIS, WALDFLOTE
organic INHERENT, FUNDAMENTAL
organism BODY, AMEBA, MONAD, MONAS, ZOOID, AMOEBA
organization CLUB, CADRE, MORIM, SETUP, OUTFIT, SOCIETY
orgy BASH, BINGE, CAROUSAL
oriental ASIAN, EASTER, ORTIVE, EASTERN, LEVANTINE
orifice LURA, PORE, MOUTH, STOMA, OSTIOLE
origin BUD, GERM, SEED, OUTSET, SOURCE, GENESIS
original FRESH, FONTAL, UNIQUE, PRISTINE
original sin ADAM
oriole PIROL, LORIOT
oriole genus CACICUS, ICTERUS
ornament EPI, BOSS, DECK, FRET, OUCH, STUD, DECOR, GUTTA, SPANG, AMULET, BEDECK, EMBOSS, FINIAL, SCROLL, EPAULET, SPANGLE, EPAULETTE
ornate SHOWY, FLORID, BAROQUE
ornery MULISH, STUBBORN
Orpheus' wife EURYDICE
oscine *see* SONGBIRD
Osiris relative NUT, SET, ATEF, ISIS, HORUS, ANUBIS
ostentation POMP, ECLAT, GLOSS, STRUT, PARADE, DISPLAY
ostracize BAR, BANISH, EXCLUDE

Ostrogoth *see* GOTH
Otello composer VERDI, ROSSINI
Othello's ensign IAGO
otic AURAL, AUDITORY
otter *see* MAMMALS, AQUATIC
ottoman POUF, TURK, HASSOCK
Ottoman court PORTE
ouch CLASP, BROOCH
oust EVICT, BOUNCE, CASHIER
out UIT, AWAY, EXIT, FORTH, PASSE, EGRESS
out of date PASSE, STALE, DEMODE
out-and-out RANK, SHEER, ARRANT
outbreak RASH, EMEUTE, BOUTADE
outburst FLARE, SPATE, STORM
outcast (Y)ETA, EXILE, HAGAR, LEPER, NOLAN, RONIN, PARIAH, ISHMAEL, CHANDALA
outcry GAFF, HUBBUB, POTHER
outer ECTAL, FOREIGN
outfit KIT, FIG, GRAB, GEAR, SUIT, UNIT, GETUP, EQUIP, REGALIA, CAPARISON
outhouse PRIVY
outlandish ALIEN, OUTRE, EXOTIC
outlaw BAN, RONIN, BANDIT, DESPERADO
outlet VENT, EGRESS, SOCKET
outline SHAPE, TRACE, SCHEMA, SKETCH, CONTOUR, PROFILE, SUMMARY, SILHOUETTE
outlook SCOPE, VISTA, PURVIEW
outmoded DATED, PASSE, DESUETE
output YIELD, PRODUCTION
outrage ABUSE, AFFRONT, INJURY, INSULT, OFFENSE
outrigger PRAU, PROA; *see* VESSEL
outspoken BLUNT, FRANK, CANDID
outward ECTAD, EXTRINSIC
outwit EUCHRE, OUTSMART
outwork TENAIL, LUNETTE, RAVELIN
oven IMU, OON, UMU, KILN, LEER, LEHR, OAST, TILER, HIBACHI
over OER, ATOP, DONE, SURPLUS
overact HAM, EMOTE, OUTDO
overcoat BENJY, BENNY, CAPOT(E), RAGLAN, ULSTER, PALETOT, SPENCER, SURTOUT, BENJAMIN, BALMACAAN, GREATCOAT
overcome DEFEAT, MASTER, SUBDUE
overdue ARREAR, REMISS, UNPAID
overflow DEBORD, SURPLUS; *see* FLOOD
overhang LOOM, EAVES, BEETLE
overhead ALOFT, COSTS, UPKEEP
overlay LAP, CEIL
overlook OMIT, SKIP, IGNORE, REVIEW, SURVEY, CONDONE
overseer CORK, BAILIFF, CAPORAL, STEWARD
overshoe ARCTIC, GALOSH, PATTEN, RUBBER
overtake PASS, CATCH
overthrow DEPOSE, TOPPLE, UNSEAT, REVERSE
overture ADVANCE, PRELUDE
overweight OBESE
owing DUE, UNPAID, PAYABLE
owl LULU, RURU, MADGE, OWLET, PADGE, BOOBOOK, HOWLET, HULLET, MOPOKE, WOOLERT, MOREPORK
owl genus BUBO, TYTO, KETUPA, NYCTEA
own HAVE, CONFESS, POSSESS
ox YAK, ANOA, BUCK, BUFF, BULL, CALF, DOGY, GAUR, MOIL, NEAT, OUSE, QUEY, TORO, URUS, ZEBU, BISON, BOBBY, BOSSY, CAURE, DOGIE, GAYAL, GYALL, STEER, BANTIN, BHARAL, BOVOID, BUFFLE, BURHEL, HUMLIE, NAHOOR, SARLAK, SARLYK, TAURUS, WISENT, AUROCHS, BANTENG, BUFFALO, BULLOCK, BURRHEL, TAURINE
ox genus BOS, OVIBOS
oxide CALX
oxidize RUST, CALCINE
oxygen OXID(E), OZONE
oyster SPAT, CHAMA, ANOMIA, HUITRE, SHARPER, SPONDYL
oyster bed material CULCH, CU(L)TCH
oyster farm PARK, CLAIRE
Oz author BAUM
Oz character EM, PIP, OZMA, TOTO, GLINDA, DOROTHY

P

pace RATE, STEP, TEMPO; *see* GAIT
pachyderm HIPPO, RHINO, ELEPHANT
pacific CALM, (E)IRENIC
Pacific discoverer BALBOA
Pacific islands language BUGI, MORO, AKLAN, BATAK, BIKOL, MALAY, MAORI, BISAYA, CEBUAN, HANTIK, IGOROT, MANGAR, TAGALA, BISAYAN, CEBUANO, ILOCANO, TAGALOG, VISAYAN, ACHINESE, BALINESE, BUGINESE, JAVANESE, HAWAIIAN, MADURESE, MALAGASY, PAMPANGA, PAMPANGO, PAMPANGAN, SUNDANESE, HILIGAYNON, INDONESIAN, MELANESIAN, POLYNESIAN, SAMARLEYTE
pacify *see* CALM
pack RAM, WAD, CRAM, DECK, STOW, TAMP, DEACON, STEEVE, SUMPTER
pack animal ASS, MULE, BURRO, CAMEL, LLAMA, DONKEY, JACKASS, SUMPTER
package BALE, FADGE, CEROON, PARCEL, ROBBIN, SEROON
packing LUTE, OAKUM, GASKET, SPONGE, EXCELSIOR
pact TREATY, COMPACT, ENTENTE, COVENANT, CONCORDAT
pad MAT, WASE, TRAMP, DABBER, TABLET, CUSHION
paddle *see* OAR
Paduan family CARRARA
pagan ETHNIC, PAYNIM, HEATHEN
page FOLIO, RECTO, VERSO, RUBRIC, BELLHOP
pageant POMP, SHOW, PARADE
Pagliacci character BEPPO, CANIO, NEDDA, TONIO, SILVIO
pagoda TA, PON, TAA
pail COG, SOE, BOULK, COGUE, SKEEL, STOOP, STOUP, PIGGIN
pain ACHE, PANG, AGONY, THROE
painkiller COCA, OPIATE, ANODYNE; *see* ANESTHETIC
painlessness APONIA
paint FARD, LIMN, FUCUS, ROUGE, STAIN, DEPICT, PARGET, MINIATE, PIGMENT, STIPPLE
painter ARP, RAY, HALS, CARR, COLE, DALI, DORE, DUFY, GOYA, GRIS, HALS, KENT, KLEE, MARC, MIRO, RENI, WOOD, BOSCH, COROT, CURRY, DAVID, DEGAS, DURER, ERNST, GORKY, HICKS, HOMER, LEGER, LIPPI, LOUIS, MANET, MARIN, MONET, MOSES, MUNCH, PEALE, RYDER, SARTO, STEEN, SULLY, VINCI, WATTS, WYETH, ANDREA, BENTON, BRAQUE, CATLIN, CHURCH, COPLEY, EAKINS, GIOTTO, HASSAM, HOPPER, INGRES, INNESS, LEBRUN, MILLET, MOREAU, PISANO, RENOIR, RIBERA, RIVERA, RUBENS, SEURAT, SISLEY, STUART, TANGUY, TITIAN, WARHOL, BELLOWS, BONHEUR, BONNARD, BOUCHER, BRUEGEL, CEZANNE, CHAGALL, CHARDIN, COURBET, DAUMIER, DAVINCI, DUCHAMP, ELGRECO, GAUGUIN, HOGARTH, HOLBEIN, MATISSE, MURILLO, PICASSO, POLLOCK, POUSSIN, RAPHAEL, ROUAULT, SARGENT, UTRILLO, VANDYCK, VANEYCK, VANGOGH, VERMEER, WATTEAU, ANGELICO, BREUGHEL, COREGGIO, MANTEGNA, MONDRIAN, PISSARRO, REYNOLDS, ROUSSEAU, RUYSDAEL, VERONESE, WHISTLER, CONSTABLE, CORREGGIO, FRAGONARD, KANDINSKY, REMBRANDT
painting OIL; *see* PICTURE
painting equipment BRUSH, EASEL, CANVAS, PALLET, ROLLER, PALETTE, SPATULA, TABORET, MAHLSTICK, MAULSTICK
painting medium OIL, CASEIN, TEMPERA, ENCAUSTIC
painting method SECCO, FRESCO, GOUACHE, GRISAILLE

painting style OP, POP, DADA, GENRE, CUBIST, ROCOCO, BAROQUE, CLASSIC, DADAIST, FAUVISM, IMPASTO, ABSTRACT, FUTURIST, IDEALIST, GRISAILLE, REALISTIC
pair DUO, DIAD, DUAD, DUET, DYAD, MATE, SPAN, TEAM, YOKE, BRACE
paired TWIN, GEMEL, MATED, JUGATE, TEAMED, MATCHED
Pakistani language URDU, HINDI, BENGALI, PUNJABI
Pakistani money ANNA, PICE, RUPEE
Pakistani statesman AYUB, MIRZA, JINNAH
pal CHUM, MATE, CRONY, CULLY
palace COURT, MANSION
palatable SAPID, TASTY
palate UVULA, VELUM
palaver CHAT, TALK, PARLEY, CHATTER, FLATTER
pale WAN, ASHY, ASHEN, MEALY, PASTY, DOUGHY, PALLID, PALLOR, PASTEL, SALLOW
Palestine ERETS, CANAAN, ISRAEL
Palestine district GAZA, HAIFA, LYDDA, PERAEA, GALILEE, SAMARIA, JERUSALEM
palindrome ERE, EVE, TAT, BOOB, NOON, KAYAK, MADAM, REFER
palisade HURDIS, ESPALIER
Pallas ATHENA, MINERVA
pallid WAN, PALE, SALLOW
palm LOOF, VOLA, KUDOS, THENAR, CONCEAL
palm juice SURA
palm off FOB, FOIST
palm tree DOM, KOU, ATAP, BURI, COCO, NIPA, PAUM, SAGO, DOUM, ARECA, ASSAI, ATTAP, BONGA, BONGO, BUNGA, COCOA, COCOS, CYCAS, DATIL, HOWEA, INAJA, JAGUA, NIKAU, PALMA, RATAN, SABAL, TUCUM, UNAMO, YAGUA, YARAY, ARENGA, ASSAHY, GEBANG, GOMUTI, GRIGRI, GRUGRU, PACAYA, RAFFIA, RATTAN, TUCUMA, COCONUT, PIASABA, PIASAVA, TALIPOT, COCOANUT, DOOMPALM, PIASSABA, PIASSAVA
palpable EVIDENT, MANIFEST
palpitation TIRL, THROB, PALMUS
paltry MEAN, POOR, CHEAP, PETTY, SMALL
pamper PET, SPOIL, CODDLE, COSHER, COSSET, FONDLE
pamphlet CHAP, TRACT, BROCHURE, CHAPBOOK
pan RIB, SUMP, BASIN, ROAST; *see* COOKING
panacea CURE, ELIXIR, CUREALL
panache APLOMB, SWAGGER
Panama DARIEN
Panaman money CENT, BALBOA
Panaman tree COPA, YAYA, CA(U)TIVO
pander PIMP, PROCURER
panel JURY, PANE, PLAQUE, VENIRE
pang ACHE, RACK, THROE
Panhandle State WV(A)
panic FEAR, FRAY, FUNK, TERROR
panorama VIEW, SCAPE, VISTA
panpipe ANTARA, SYRINX
Pan's lover ECHO, SYRINX
pant GASP, HUFF, PUFF, YEARN
panther COUGAR, JAGUAR, LEOPARD
pantry AMBRY, EWERY, LARDER, SPENCE, BUTTERY
pants JEANS, SLACKS, TIGHTS, BLOOMERS, BREECHES, KNICKERS, TROUSERS, PLUSFOURS
Papal palace VATICAN
paper BOND, TAPA, CREPE, ESSAY, KRAFT, MANILA, PAPIER, PELURE, TISSUE, VELLUM, PAPYRUS, DOCUMENT
paper folding ORIGAMI
paper, imperfect CASSE, SALLE, RETREE
paper measure REAM, QUIRE, BUNDLE
paper size DEMY, POST, POTT, ATLAS, CROWN, FOLIO, ROYAL, EMPEROR, ELEPHANT, FOOLSCAP, IMPERIAL
par NORMAL, AVERAGE
parade ARRAY, MARCH, STRUT, FLAUNT, PAGEANT
paradise EDEN, JODO, ZION, HEAVEN, UTOPIA, ELYSIUM, NIRVANA, SHANGRILA

Paradise Lost author MILTON
paradiselike EDENIC, ELYSIAN
paragon TYPE, IDEAL, MODEL, EXEMPLAR, NONESUCH
paragraph ITEM, CLAUSE, PILCROW
Paraguayan langauge GUARANI
Paraguayan measure PIE, LINE, LINO, VARA, LEGUA, CORDEL, CUADRA
Paraguayan money CENTIMO, GUARANI
parallelogram RHOMB(US), RHOMBOID
paralysis PALSY, POLIO, PLEGIA, PARESIS
paramour LEMAN, LOVER, SWAIN
Parana tributary IVAI, PARDO, TIETE, VERDE, SALADO
parasite BINE, FLEA, MITE, PEGA, TRYP, APHID, LEECH, TOADY, FAWNER, REMORA, SPONGE
Parcae *see* FATES
parcel LOT, METE, PLAT, ALLOT, BUNDLE, PACKET
parch DRY, SEAR, SCORCH, TORREFY, TORRIFY
parchment FOR(R)EL, VELLUM
parchment roll PELL, SCROLL
pardon MERCY, REMIT, ASSOIL, AMNESTY, CONDONE
pare CUT, PEEL, SKIVE, WHITTLE
parent DAM, SIRE, MATER, PATER, MOTHER, FATHER
Paris relative PRIAM, HECUBA, OENONE
Paris section BOIS, CITE, PASSY, AUTEUIL, NEUILLY
parish head PASTOR, RECTOR
park COMMON, PRATER
park, national ZION, PLATT, ACADIA, LASSEN, SHILOH, BIGBEND, GLACIER, OLYMPIC, SEQUOIA, ANTIETAM, CARLSBAD, CHALMETE, COLONIAL, MANASSAS, PEARIDGE, SARATOGA, WINDCAVE, YOSEMITE, HALEAKALA, MESAVERDE
parley CONFER, POWWOW, PALAVER, PARLANCE
parliament *see* ASSEMBLY
parliament report HANSARD
parlor SALA, SALON, LOCUTORY
parochial NARROW, PROVINCIAL
parody SATIRE, BURLESQUE
paroxysm FIT, AGONY, SPASM
parrot KEA, ECHO, JAKO, KAKA, LORY, VASA, MACAW, MIMIC, POLLY, BUDGIE, KAKAPO, REPEAT, LORILET, ROSELLA, BUDGIGAR, COCKATOO, LORIKEET, LOVEBIRD, PARAKEET, POPINJAY
parrot genus ARA
parry FEND, WARD, FENCE, REPLY, DEFLECT
Parsifal character KUNDRY, AMFORTAS, KLINGSOR
parsimonious CLOSE, FRUGAL, STINGY, MISERLY
parsley LOVAGE
parson(age) *see* CLERGY
part ROLE, SOME, BREAK, PIECE, SEVER, CLEAVE, SECTOR, SUNDER, ELEMENT
part of speech NOUN, VERB, ADVERB, PRONOUN, ADJECTIVE, CONJUNCTION, PREPOSITION, INTERJECTION
Parthenon site ACROPOLIS
particle BIT, AFFIX, GRAIN, MESON, PALEA, MESOTRON, RAMENTUM; *see* ATOM, JOT
particular ODD, ITEM, FUSSY, UNIQUE
partisan ZEALOT, ADHERENT
partition SEPTA, SEPTUM
partner ALLY, MATE, SPOUSE
partnership HUI, HOEY, CAHOOT
partridge KYAH, TITAR, CHUKAR, CHUKOR, REDLEG, SEESEE, FRANCOLIN
party TEA, BASH, GALA, PROM, SECT, STAG, CIRCLE, CLIQUE, SOCIAL, SOIREE, SHINDIG
parvenu SNOB, CLIMBER, UPSTART
Pasiphaë's husband MINOS
pass COL, DIE, GAP, BYGO, FADE, GHAT, HAND, OMIT, SKIP, ELIDE, ENACT, GHAUT, LAPSE, REEVE, RELAY, DEFILE, ELAPSE, TICKET, SKITTER
pass, mountain APO, CISA, FUTA, BOLAN, GIOVI, MAIPO, BURZIL, CHUMBI, DARYAL, KHYBER, SHIPKA, ARLBERG, BRENNER, MAMISON, PESCARA, SIMPLON, SOMPORT, SPLUGEN, MONTCENIS

passageway GAT, GUT, ADIT, DUCT, EXIT, HALL, ITER, AISLE, ALURE, CANAL, SLYPE, STOPE, STULM, ARCADE, CLAUSE, EGRESS, TRANSIT
passenger FARE, RIDER
passion LUST, RAGA, ZEAL
Passover PASCH, SEDAR, SEDER, PASCHA
password PAROLE, SHIBBOLETH
past AGO, GONE, OVER, BYGONE
pasta ZITI, DITALI, MELONE, RIGATI, FUSILLI, GNOCCHI, MAFALDE, MEZZANI, PASTINA, RAVIOLI, ROTELLE, BUCATINI, LINGUINI, SPAGHETTI; *see* NOODLES, MACARONI
paste PAP, BOND, GLUE, STRASS
pastel TINT, WOAD, CRAYON
paste-up DUMMY, COLLAGE
pastime HOBBY, DIVERSION
pastor *see* CLERGY
pastoral IDYL, RURAL, RUSTIC, BUCOLIC, IDYLLIC
pastry PIE, TART, CRUST, TORTE, ECLAIR, STRUDEL
pasture ING, LEA, HEAF, HOGA, AGIST, SHIELING
pat APT, DAB, FIT, TAP, GLIB
patch DARN, MEND, BODGE, CLOUT
patchwork CENTO, MEDLEY, MOSAIC, MONTAGE
patella ROTULA, KNEEPAN
paten ARCA, DISC, ARCAE
patent BERAT, TITLE, LICENSE
path BERM, LOCUS, ORBIT, CASAUN, RODDIN(G)
patient CASE, STOIC, INVALID
patois CANT, ARGOT, JARGON
patriarch DAN, GAD, HAM, REU, CAIN, EBER, ENOS, ESAU, HETH, IRAD, LEVI, NASI, NOAH, SETH, SHEM, SIRE, ASHER, ELDER, ENOCH, ISAAC, JACOB, JARED, JUDAH, KENAN, NAHOR, PATER, PELEG, SERUG, TERAH, CAINAN, CANAAN, JOKTAN, JOSEPH, LAMECH, REUBEN, SIMEON, ABRAHAM, ISHMAEL, JAPHETH, ZEBULUN, ARPHAXAD, BENJAMIN, ISSACHAR, MAHALEEL, MEHUJAEL, NAPHTALI, METHUSAEL, METHUSELAH
patriot HALE, OTIS, ALLEN, REVERE
patriotic group DAR, SAR
patron ANGEL, SAINT, CLIENT, SPONSOR
patron saint ELMO, IVES, LUKE, OLAF, DENIS, GILES, JAMES, PETER, GEORGE, CRISPIN, PATRICK
patronage EGIS, WING, AEGIS, FAVOR, AUSPICES
pattern NORM, SETT, TYPE, IDEAL, MODEL, DAMIER, FORMAT, PARAGON, STENCIL
Paul's birthplace TARSUS
Paul's companion SILAS, SOPATER
pause LULL, REST, SELAH, TRUCE, C(A)ESURA, RESPITE
pave TILE, COBBLE, ASPHALT
pavilion TELD, TENT, KIOSK, GAZEBO, MARQUEE
paving material TAR(MAC), ASPHALT, MACADAM, CONCRETE
paving stone FLAG, SETT, PAVER
paw PUD, FOOT, GAUM
pawl DETENT, PALLET, RATCHET
pawn GAGE, HOCK, WAGER, PIGNUS, PLEDGE, HOSTAGE
pay FEE, TIP, ANTE, WAGE, REMIT, SPEND, DEFRAY, REWARD, STIPEND
paymaster BUXY, BAKSHI, PURSER
payment CRO, FEE, CENS, ERIC, KIST, SCOT, ANNAT, LABOLA, REBATE
pea DAL, TUR, DHAL, ARHAR, CICER, DHOLL, PISUR
peace PAX, LISS, GRITH, IRENE, SHALOM, NIRVANA
peaceful IRENIC, HALCYON
Peach State GA, GEORGIA
peacock PAON, PAVO, PAWN
peak ALP, BEN, TOR, ACME, APEX, CUSP, PITON, CLIMAX, SUMMIT, ZENITH
peanut MANI, GOOBER, EARTHNUT
pear BOSC, ANJOU, NOPAL, PYRUS, COMICE, SECKEL, SICKLE
pearl GEM, NACRE, ONION, OLIVET
pearlweed SAGINA
peasant TAO, CARL, PEON,

RYOT, CEORL, CHURL, KULAK, RAYAT, COOLIE, COTTAR, COTTER, FELLAH, MUZHIK, TILLER, PAISANO
peat MOOR, TURF, TURBARY
pebble JACK, SCREE
peck DAB, NIP, KISS, KNIP
peculiar ODD, QUEER, UNUSUAL
pedal LEVER, CELESTE, TREADLE
peddle HAWK, SELL, TOUT, VEND, TRANT
peddler HAWKER; *see* MERCHANT
pedestal BASE, GAINE
pedestal part DADO, ORLO, SOCLE, PLINTH, SURBASE
pedigree LINE, RACE, STOCK, FAMILY, STRAIN
peduncle STEM, SCAPE, STALK, STIPES
peek PEEP, PEER, GLANCE
peel BARK, FLAY, HARL, PARE, RIND, SKIN, SKIVE
peep PULE, SKEG, CHEEP, DEKKO
peep show RAREE
Peeping Tom VOYEUR
peer FERE, GAZE, PEEK, PEEP, FEERE, RIVAL; *see* NOBLE
Peer Gynt relative ASE, SOLVEIG
Peer Gynt writer GRIEG, IBSEN
peevish GRUFF, TESTY, TOUCHY
peg LEG, NOB, TEE, KNAG, DOWEL, THOLE, TRENAIL, TRUNNEL, TREENAIL
Pegasus' mother MEDUSA
Peleus relative AEACUS, TELAMON, ACHILLES, ANTIGONE
pelican KOAE, DARTER, SNAKEBIRD
Pelican State LA, LOUISIANA
pellet GOLI, PALLION
pellucid CLEAR, LIMPID, LUCENT
pelota *see* JAI ALAI
pelt FELL, HIDE, SKIN, STONE; *see* FUR, LEATHER
pelvic ILIAC, PUBIC
pen STY, COTE, JAIL, SWAN, KRAAL, QUILL, STYLE, CORRAL, INDITE, SCRIPT
pen names *see p. 260*
pen point NEB, NIB
penalty CAIN, FINE, FORFEIT
penchant TASTE, LIKING, LEANING
pendant BOB, FOB, LOP, LOCKET
penetrate BORE, ENTER, IMBUE, IMPALE, PIERCE
penguin GENTOO
peninsula ANN, ACTE, EYRE, KOLA, KRIM, BANKS, GASPE, ITALY, KATAR, MALAY, MOREA, QATAR, SINAI, ARABIA, AVALON, BALKAN, BATAAN, BONDOC, CRIMEA, IBERIA, ISTRIA, JUTLAND, KOWLOON, MALACCA, LABRADOR, MELVILLE, KAMCHATKA
penmanship HAND, SCRIPT
pennant WHIP, BURGEE, PENCEL, PENNON
Pennsylvania information *see p. 308*
penny CENT, GROAT, COPPER
Pentateuch LAW, TORA(H); *see p. 246*
peony PIN(E)Y, MOUTAN
people MEN, MOB, CLAN, FOLK, ONES, RACE, VOLK, CROWD, DEMOS, GENTE, DAOINE, NATION, RABBLE
pep VIM, VERVE, VIGOR, GINGER
pepper AWA, CAVA, IKMO, ITMO, KAVA, SIRI, BETEL, CHILE, CHILI, CAYENNE, PAPRIKA, PIMENTO, KAVAKAVA
Pequod captain AHAB
Pequod owner PELEG, BILDAD
Pequod sailor *see* MOBY DICK
per VIA, EACH, APIECE
perceive SPOT, SENSE, DESCRY
perception EAR, ESP, TACT, GRASP, ACUMEN, NOESIS
perch ROD, SIT, AERIE, ROOST
perch(-like fish) AWA, BAR, RAM, TAI, BOCE, DRUM, JOCU, LORO, MOKI, PEGA, POGY, RUFF, SAMA, SCAD, SCUP, SISI, ULUA, ACARA, BETTA, BOGUE, BOLTI, BOLTY, BREAM, BULTI, CABIO, CHOPA, COBIA, JUREL, LAUIA, MOLET, MUGIL, MUSKY, PARGO, PERCA, PORGY, RONCO, SARGO, SNOOK, WIRRA, XUREL, ANABAS, APOGON, ARCHER, BESUGO, CARANX, CREOLE, CROCUS, CUBERA,

DARTER, DENTEX, DORADO, GERRES, HUSSAR, LAWYER, LOUVAR, MAIGER, MAIGRE, MEAGER, MEAGRE, MULLET, MULLID, NATIVE, PAGRUS, PERCID, REMORA, ROBALO, ROMERO, RUNNER, SALELE, SAUGER, SCARUS, SHINER, SPARID, TAMURE, WIRRAH, ZINGEL, ALFIONA, BARBUDO, BASSLET, BURRITO, CARAPUS, CAVALLY, CHROMIC, CRAPPIE, CROAKER, DOURADE, DOURADO, GOURAMI, GUAPENA, JEWFISH, LABROID, MOJARRA, OLDWIFE, PICAREL, PIGFISH, POMPANO, REDLING, SEABASS, SERRANO, SILLAGO, SPAROID, SUNFISH, TOMTATE, TOTOABA, TOTUAVA, VIAJACA, WALLEYE, WAREHOU, WHITING, MILKFISH, TREVALLY; *see* BASS, GROUPER

percolate OOZE, SEEP, EXUDE, LEACH, FILTER

percussion instrument ZEL, BELL, DRUM, GONG, TAAR, TOPH, TRAP, BELLS, BONES, BONGO, CHIME, DAIRA, DRONE, GRAND, PIANO, PUNGI, SARON, TABOR, TOMBE, TRAPS, ZANZE, CYMBAL, KETTLE, MARACA, NAGARA, PIATTI, RAPPEL, SPINET, TABRET, TAMTAM, TIMBAL, TOMTOM, TYMPAN, ANACARA, BOMBARD, CELESTA, CLAVIAL, CYMBALS, MANDORE, MARIMBA, PIANINO, PIANOLA, SISTRUM, TABORET, TIMBREL, TIMPANI, TIMPANO, TYMPANO, UPRIGHT, CARILLON, CASTANET, CLAPPERS, CROTALUM, LAPIDEON, MELODION, PIANETTE, TABOURIN, TRIANGLE, ZAMBOMBA, XYLOPHONE

perfect IDEAL, MODEL, FLAWLESS

perfidious FALSE, DISLOYAL

perforate BORE, DRILL, PRICK, PIERCE, RIDDLE, TREPAN

performer DOER, ACTOR, AGENT, SHINE, ARTIST, PLAYER, SINGER, ARTISTE

perfume ATAR, MUSK, OTTO, AROMA, ATTAR, CENSE, PASTIL, SACHET, BOUQUET

perfume source ATAR, MUSK, ATTAR, IRONE, MYRRH, ORRIS, CASTOR, IONONE, SAFROL, BERGAMOT

perhaps HAPLY, MAYBE, MAYHAP

Pericles' mistress ASPASIA

peril RISK, DANGER, HAZARD

period AGE, DOT, EON, ERA, SPAN, TERM, TIME, CYCLE, STAGE, SYSTEM; *see* GEOLOGICAL

periodic CYCLIC, ETESIAN

peripheral DISTAL, EXTERNAL

periphery EDGE, AMBIT, LIMIT

periwinkle WINK, VINCA, DOG(S)BANE

permanent FIXED, LASTING

permeate IMBUE, DIFFUSE, PERVADE

permit LET, VISA, ALLOW, EXEAT, CEDULA, SANCTION

Peron's wife EVA, EVITA

perpetual CHRONIC, CONSTANT

perplex ELUDE, STUMP, BAFFLE, CONFUSE, MYSTIFY, NONPLUS, BEWILDER

persecute HARASS, OPPRESS

Persephone relative HADES, DEMETER, ZAGREUS

Perseus' mother DANAE

Persia IRAN

Persian LUR, MEDE, IRANI; *see* IRANIAN

Persian ruler SHAH, CYRUS, DARIUS, SULTAN, XERXES

persist LAST, PLOD, ENDURE

personable COMELY, HANDSOME

personage VIP, NIBS, BIGWIG

personality EGO, SELF

personnel CREW, HANDS, SQUAD, STAFF, STABLE, TROUPE

perspiration DEW, SUDOR, SWEAT

persuade COAX, URGE, INDUCE

pert FLIP, SASSY, SAUCY

pertinent APT, FIT, ANENT, GERMANE, RELEVANT

perturb ALARM, HARASS, RUFFLE

peruse CON, SCAN, STUDY, SURVEY, SCRUTINIZE

Peruvian language AYMARA, QUECHUA

Peruvian measure TOPO, GALON

Peruvian money SOL, LIBRA, DINERO, PESETA
pervade IMBRUE, PERFUSE, PERMEATE
pervert WARP, TWIST, DISTORT
pest NAG, BANE, CURSE, PLAGUE, SCOURGE, NUISANCE
pester NAG, ANNOY, TEASE, BADGER, HARASS, HECTOR
pestle BRAY, PILUM, BEETLE, MULLER, PISTIL
pestle companion MORTAR
pet CADE, NECK, PIQUE, CODDLE, COSSET, FONDLE
Peter Pan author BARRIE
Peter Pan character HOOK, NANA, SMEE, WENDY, TINKER(BELL)
petiole STEM, STALK, STIPE
petition SUE, PLEA, SUIT, APPEAL
Petrarch's love LAURA
petrel GONY, TITI, MOLLY, NELLY, PRION, FORMEL, FULMAR, GOONEY, TEETEE, PINTADO, STINKER, JOHNDOWN, ALBATROSS, MALLEMUCK, MOLLEMUCK, MOLLYHAWK
petrol *see* GAS
petroleum derivative COKE, PITCH, BUTANE, ASPHALT, BENZINE, BITUMEN, NAPHTHA
Petruchio's wife KAT(IE)
petticoat SLIP, CRINOLINE
petty MEAN, SMALL, TRIVIAL, INFERIOR, PICAYUNE
peyote CACTUS, MESCAL
phantom(s) EIDOLA, EIDOLON
pharaoh *see* EGYPTIAN
phase FACET, STAGE, ASPECT, INSTAR
pheasant ARGUS, CHEER, KALIJ, MONAL, HOAZIN, KALEEJ, MINAUL, MONAUL, MOONAL, PUKRAS, HOATZIN, KALEEGE, MOONAUL
Philemon's wife BAUCIS
philippic SCREED, TIRADE, HARANGUE, JOBATION
Philippine language PILIPINO; *see* PACIFIC ISLANDS
Philippine leader ROXAS, AQUINO, GARCIA, OSMENA, MARCOS, QUIRINO
Philippine measure LOAN, BRAZA, CABAN, CHUPA, GANTA, APATAN, BALITA, QUINON
Philippine tree DAO, IBA, ACLE, BOGO, IFIL, IPIL, ABILO, ALMON, ANILO, BAYOG, BAYOK, BETIS, DANLI, GUIJO, LAUAN, LIGAS, YACAL, ABILAO, ANILAO, ANILAU, DANGLIN
Philippine weight FARDO, PICUL, PUNTO, LACHSA, QUILATE
philosopher HUME, JOAD, KANT, MOTI, ZENO, BACON, BRUNO, BUBER, COMTE, CYNIC, EDMAN, HEGEL, JAMES, LOCKE, PLATO, HUXLEY, LAOTZE, PASCAL, PEIRCE, SARTRE, SENECA, THALES, BENTHAM, BERGSON, DIDEROT, HUSSERL, LEIBNIZ, RUSSELL, SKEPTIC, SPENCER, SPINOZA, ZETETIC, AVERROES, BERKELEY, FICHTEAN, SOCRATES, SPENGLER
philosopher's stone ELIXIR
philosophy YOGA, EGOISM, MONISM, ATOMISM, REALISM, SENSISM, SOPHISM, THOMISM, HEDONISM, IDEALISM, PSYCHISM, SOMATISM, STOICISM, VITALISM, CASUISTRY
phlegmatic COOL, DULL, SLUGGISH
phloem BARK, BAST, TISSUE
phone *see* TELEPHONE
phonetic system IPA, ROMIC
phonograph PLAYER, VICTROLA
phony *see* FAKE
photo(s) MUG, PIC, PIX, SHOT, SNAP, STAT
photography equipment FILM, HYPO, FIXER, TONER, REDUCER, DEVELOPER
phrase CLAUSE, LOCUTION
physic *see* LAXATIVE
physical SOMAL, SOMATIC
physician DOC, CURER, LEECH, MEDIC, DOCTOR, SURGEON, INTERNIST
physicians ERB, MAYO, PARE, POTT, REED, RUSK, SALK, GALEN, HADEN, OSLER, PAGET, SABIN, SPOCK, CARREL, COLLES, DOOLEY, FINLAY, FINSEN, HALLER, HARVEY, JENNER, LISTER, MESMER, MORTON, PARRAN, PERERA, RHAZES; *see* NOBEL

physicists OHM, ABBE, HAHN, MACH, BOYLE, CURIE, ERMAN, FERMI, ROSSI, VOLTA, AMPERE, BUNSEN, TELLER; *see* NOBEL
physics branch OPTICS, STATICS, DYNAMICS, KINETICS, ACOUSTICS, MECHANICS
pianist ANDA, HESS, NERO, ARRAU, GOULD, KEMPF, ROSEN, BUSONI, CURZON, ITURBI, LEVANT, SERKIN, CLIBURN, HOFMANN, RICHTER, SOLOMON, HOROWITZ, LHEVINNE, PACHMANN
piano SPINET; *see* PERCUSSION
piazza ARCADE, SQUARE, VERANDA
picayune *see* PETTY
pick CULL, ELITE, GLEAN, PLUCK, NIBBLE, SELECT, PLECTRUM
picket PALE, STAKE, TETHER
pickle ALEC, CORN, CURE, ACHAR, BRINE, SOUSE, GHERKIN
pickpocket DIP, WIRE, DIPPER
picnic JUNKET, OUTING, COOKOUT, CLAMBAKE
Picnic author INGE
picture ICON, MURAL, CANVAS, DEPICT, FRESCO, EPITOME, MONTAGE, PROFILE, TABLEAU; *see* PHOTO
picturesque QUAINT, IDYLLIC
pidgin language SABIR, JARGON, CHINOOK, BECHEDEMER
pie PASTY, HUMBLE, COBBLER
piebald PIED, PINTO, CALICO
piece BIT, CHIP, PART, SLICE, CANTLE, COLLOP; *see* GUN
piece out EKE, CANTLE
pier COB, ANTA, COBB, PILASTER, BUTTRESS; *see* LANDING
pierce GORE, STAB, GOUGE, GRIDE, LANCE, THIRL
pig HOG, SOW, MOLD, SLOB, INGOT, SHOAT; *see* SWINE
pigeon NUN, GOURA, TURBIT, FANTAIL, INFORMER; *see* DOVE
pigeon genus COLUMBA
pigment *see p. 251*
pigment-forming substance DOPA
pigtail CUE, PLAIT, QUEUE, COLETA
pike GED, ESOX, GEDD, JACK, LUCE, MUSKIE, ZANDER
pilaster ANTA, ALETTE
pile NAP, RICK, HOARD, STACK
pile driver RAM, TUP, OLIVER, FISTUCA
pilfer FILCH, STEAL, SWIPE
pilgrim HADJI, PALMER, MIGRANT, PIONEER
pilgrimage HADJ, QUEST, CRUSADE
pilgrim's garb IHRAM
Pilgrim's Progress author BUNYAN
pill DOSE, GOLI, BOLUS, PELLET
pillage *see* PLUNDER
pillar LAT, JAMB, PIER, PROP, HERMA, NEWEL, SHAFT, STELE, OBELISK, PILASTER
pillory CANG, JOUG, YOKE, BRANK, STOCK, TRONE, BRANKS, CANGUE
pillow COD, BOLSTER
pilot GUIDE, STEER, AVIATOR
pilotless aircraft DRONE, GLIDER
pimple POCK, PAPULE, PUSTULE
pin FID, NOG, ACUS, TIGE, AGLET, DOWEL, RIVET, THOLE, BROOCH, COTTER, FIBULA, PINTLE, SKEWER, SKITTLE
pinafore TIER, APRON
pincer(s) CLAW, TONGS, FORCEPS, NIPPERS, TWEEZER(S)
pinch NIP, DASH, CRAMP, PUGIL, TWEAK, ARREST, STRAIT
pinched URLED, CHITTY
pine FADE, FLAG, MOPE, YEARN
pine tree IE, CHIL, CHIR, HALA, IEIE, MIRO, PINO, BUNYA, KAORI, KAURI, MATAI, MATSU, OCOTE, PINON, VACOA, COWRIE, KAURIE, KAWRIE, TARWOOD, CHIRPINE, CHEERPINE
Pine Tree State ME, MAINE
pineapple NANA, PITA, ANANA(S)
pink PIERCE, SCALLOP; *see p. 251*
pinnacle EPI, APEX, SERAC, ZENITH
pinniped SEAL, WALRUS

pinochle term DIX, BETE, MELD, KITTY, WIDOW
pinto PIEBALD, MOTTLED
pious GODLY, DEVOUT, SACRED
pip ACE, HIT, ROUP, SEED, SPOT
pipe HUB, TEE, FIFE, FLUE, NUBB, REED, TUBE, BRIAR, BRIER, RISER, STRAW, DUDEEN, HOOKAH, CALUMET, CONDUIT, NARGILE
pipelike TUBATE
piquant RACY, SHARP, ZESTY
pique PEEVE, STING, NETTLE
piquet term PIC, CAPOT, REPIC, RUBICON, SINKING
pirate KIDD, ANSON, DRAKE, ROVER, MORGAN, VIKING, BRIGAND, CORNISH, CORSAIR, PICAROON, PRIVATEER
pistol *see* GUN
pit HOLE, MINE, POCK, SEED, SUMP, ABYSS, FOSSA, FOVEA, LACUNA
pitch REEL, TONE, FLING, TOSS, CURVE, LURCH, RESIN, SPIEL, TWIRL, PATTER, SLIDER, BITUMEN
pitcher *see* JUG, BASEBALL
pith JET, NUB, GIST, PULP
pithy CORKY, MEATY, TERSE
pitted ETCHED, STONED, FOVEATE
pity RUTH, MERCY
pixy *see* ELF
placard BILL, POST(ER), AFFICHE
place(s) JOB, SET, LIEU, LOCI, RANK, SEAT, SPOT, LOCUS, NICHE, POSIT, SCENE, SITUS, STEAD, VENUE, ASSIGN, LOCALE, STATUS
placid CALM, SUANT, HALCYON
plagiarize CRIB, LIFT, PIRATE
plague *see* PEST, PESTER
plaid MAUD, TARTAN
plain CHOL, EVEN, MERE, VELD, WOLD, BLUNT, CAMPO, CLEAR, HEATH, LLANO, PAMPA, VELDT, WEALD, CHASTE, HOMELY, STEPPE, TUNDRA, EVIDENT, LOWLAND, PRAIRIE, SAVANNA
plait PLY, MESH, PLEX, BRAID
plan PLOT, ETTLE, INTEND
plane FLAT, LEVEL, SURFACE; *see* AIRCRAFT
planet MARS, EARTH, PLUTO, VENUS, SATURN, URANUS, JUPITER, MERCURY, NEPTUNE
planetarium ORRERY
plank DECK, SLATE, TICKET
plant(s) SOW, MILL, FLORA, INSERT, FACTORY
plant disease BLET, BUNT, CURL, ESCA, GALL, RUST, SMUT, ERGOT, SCALD, AECIUM, BLIGHT, FUNGUS, ERINOSE, STIPPEN
plant, hydroelectric GURI, ROSS, ASWAN, NUREK, SWIFT, ASSUAN, BRATSK, DALLES, FURNAS, HOOVER, INGURI, BOULDER, KUIBYSHEV, VOLGOGRAD; *see* DAM
plantation HOLT, FINCA, YERBAL, BOWERY, HACIENDA
plaster ADOBE, GESSO, SMEAR, PARGET, STUCCO
plastic BUNA, UREA, ALKYD, FURAN, NYLON, VINYL, CASEIN, FURANE, LIGNIN, LUCITE, ACETATE, ACRYLIC, FICTILE, FORMICA, NITRATE, PLIABLE, POLYMER, TERPENE, BAKELITE, PHENOLIC, RESINOID, SYNTHETIC
plate DOD, GRID, SLAB, PATEN, SCUTE, DISCUS, TAGGER
plateau MESA, PLAT, PUNA, KAR(R)OO, PARAMO
platform BEMA, DAIS, KANG, DOLLY, SOLEA, STAGE, PERRON, SOLLAR, SOLLER, ESTRADE, ROSTRUM
Plato work CRITO, PHAEDO, REPUBLIC
Plato's idea EIDE, EIDOS
Plato's teacher SOCRATES
platter ASHET, SALVER, TRENCHER
play ACT, DRAMA, ENACT, FARCE, SCOPE, SPIEL, SPORT, COMEDY, MASQUE, MIRACLE, MYSTERY, PAGEANT, TRAGEDY
play part ACT, BIT, ROLE, EXODE, SCENA, SCENE, EXODOS, EXODUS, FINALE, STANZA, WALKON, CURTAIN
player(s) DUB, HAM, CAST, DIVA, MIME, STAR, ACTOR,

SHINE, MUMMER, ACTRESS, TROUPER, THESPIAN
playful FRISKY, SPORTIVE
playground equipment GYM, SLIDE, SWING, TEETER
plaything TOY, PAWN, BAUBLE
plaza MARKET, PIAZZA, SQUARE
plea ABATER, DEMURRER, ENTREATY
plead SUE, PRESS, ENTREAT
pleasant LEPID, GENIAL, AMIABLE
please SUIT, FANCY, ARRIDE
pleated PLISSE, PLICATE, SHIRRED
pledge VAS, VOW, BOND, GAGE, OATH, PAWN, SWEAR, TOAST, TROTH, ENGAGE
Pleiades MAIA, MEROPE, ALCYONE, CELAENO, ELECTRA, STEROPE, TAYGETA
plenty LOADS, ENOUGH, UBERTY
pliable WAXY, LITHE, PLIANT, SUPPLE, PLASTIC
plight VOW, GAGE, PLEDGE, SCRAPE, DILEMMA
plinth BASE, ORLO
plod SLOG, TRUDGE
plot LOT, SITE, CABAL, SCHEME, CONSPIRE, SCENARIO
plover OXEYE, PRINE, SANDY, SNIPE, STILT, TIRMA, CURLEW, DIKKOP, DRIVER, GODWIT, HAGDON, JACANA, MARLIN, TURNIX, WILLET, CAPELLA, COURSER, DOTTREL, DOWITCH, LAPWING, TATTLER, WIMBREL, DOTTEREL, KILLDEER, WHIMBREL, DOWITCHER
plover genus LIMOSA, TOTANUS
plow ROVE, TILL, FURROW
plow part SOLE, SHARE, SLADE, COLTER, CLEVIS, SHEATH
ploy MANEUVER, STRATEGY
pluck GRIT, SAND, SPUNK, STRUM, SNATCH, TWEEZE
plug BOTT, BUNG, CORK, QUID, BOOST, CAULK, SPILE, PLATER, TAMPON, STOPPER
plum SLA, GAGE, JOBO, SLOE, DUHAT, ISLAY, JAMAN, PRUNE, DAMSON, ORLEANS
plume EGRET, PREEN, AIGRET, PANACHE
plump FUBSY, CHUBBY, ROTUND
plunder ROB, LOOT, PREY, SACK, BOOTY, RAVEN, RAVIN, REAVE, RIFLE, SPOIL, STRIP, MARAUD, PILFER, RAPINE, RAVAGE, RAVINE, PILLAGE, RANSACK
plunge DIP, DIVE, DUNK, DOUSE
Pluto relative OPS, CERES, SATURN, JUPITER, NEPTUNE, PROSERPINA
Po tributary ADDA, DORA, OGLIO, MINCIO, TANARO, TICINO
poach SHIRR, STEAL, TRESPASS
pock *see* PIMPLE
pocket FOB, SAC, LODE, POCHE, CAVITY, CULDESAC
pocketbook PURSE, WALLET
pod(s) GAM, ARIL, BOLL, OKRA, PIPI, CAROB, SHUCK, HARICOT
podium DAIS, FOOT, LECTERN
Poe work RAVEN, GOLDBUG
poem DIT, LAI, LAY, ODE, DUAN, IDYL, CANTO, ELEGY, EPODE, IDYLL, POESY, PSALM, RUNES, VERSE, AMHRAN, BALLAD, ODELET, SONNET, BUCOLIC, ECLOGUE, GEORGIC, VIRELAY, RONDEAU, TRIOLET; *see* EPIC, VERSE
poet BARD, SCOP, ODIST, RIMER, SCALD, SKALD, MYRIST, METRIST
poet laureate KAY, PYE, ROWE, TATE, LEWIS, AUSTIN, CIBBER, DANIEL, DRYDEN, EUSDEN, JONSON, WARTON, BERNARD, BRIDGES, CHAUCER, SKELTON, SOUTHEY, SPENSER, BETJEMAN, DAVENANT, SHADWELL, MASEFIELD, TENNYSON, WORDSWORTH
poets GAY, KEY, POE, GRAY, NASH, OVID, POPE, AIKEN, AUDEN, BENET, BLAKE, BURNS, BYRON, CRANE, DANTE, DONNE, ELIOT, FROST, GUEST, HARDY, HARTE, HEINE, HESSE, IBSEN, JOYCE, KEATS, MOORE, POUND, RILEY, RILKE, SCOTT, TASSO, WILDE, YEATS, ARNOLD, BRECHT, COWPER,

DRYDEN, GOETHE, HOLMES, HORACE, HUGHES, JONSON, KILMER, LOWELL, MILLAY, MILTON, MUSSET, NERUDA, PARKER, PINDAR, SAPPHO, TAGORE, THOMAS, VILLON, VIRGIL, ARIOSTO, CHAUCER, EMERSON, GAUTIER, GILBERT, HERRICK, HOUSMAN, JEFFERS, KHAYYAM, KIPLING, LINDSAY, MARLOWE, MASTERS, MISTRAL, PUSHKIN, RIMBAUD, RONSARD, ROSTAND, SHELLEY, SPENSER, WHITMAN, ANNUNZIO, BROWNING, CUMMINGS, MALLARME, MELVILLE, MEREDITH, PETRARCH, ROSSETTI, SANDBURG, SCHILLER, STENDHAL, TEASDALE, TENNYSON, VOLTAIRE, WHITTIER; *see* NOVELIST, AUTHOR, DRAMATIST

poi source TARO

poignant KEEN, MOVING, TOUCHING

point ACE, DOT, END, JOT, ORD, TIP, BARB, GOAL, NODE, SPIT, PUNTA, PUNTO

pointed TERSE, ACUATE, OGIVAL

pointer ROD, YAD, CLUE, HAND, WAND, FESCUE, GNOMON

pointless INANE, SENSELESS

poise HOVER, APLOMB, BEARING

poison BANE, BISH, HEMP, INEE, LOCO, UPAS, ATTER, SUMAC, TAINT, TOXIN, URALI, URARE, URARI, VENOM, CONINE, CURARE, CURARI, DATURA, MESCAL, ARSENIC, CYANIDE

poisonous TOXIC, NOCUOUS, VENOMOUS, VIRULENT

poke JAB, JOG, PROD, NUDGE, DAWDLE

poker term BUG, CAT, DOG, PAT, POT, SEE, ANTE, DRAW, FULL, FOLD, HOLE, PAIR, RUNT, STAY, STUD, BLAZE, FLASH, FLUSH, KITTY, RAISE, SKEET, TIGER, KICKER, KILTER, PELTER, PIGEON, BOBTAIL

pokeweed POCAN, SCOKE, GARGET

pole PEW, AXIS, MAST, PUNT, CABER, QUANT, SPRIT, STILT, THILL

pole to pole AX(I)AL

polecat FITCH, SKUNK, FERRET, FITCHET, FOU(L)MART

police CID, FBI, MVD, NKVD, OGPU, SURETE, GESTAPO

police officer MP, COP, BULL, DICK, FUZZ, NARC, ZARP, BOBBY, MATRON, PEELER, REDCAP, OFFICER, TROOPER

polio vaccine inventor SALK, SABIN

polish WAX, BUFF, GLAZE, GRACE, SHEEN, SHINE, BURNISH, FURBISH, LEVIGATE

Polish measure CAL, MILA, MORG, LINJA, MORGA, SAZEN, STOPA, WIOKA, CWIERC, KORZEC, KWARTA, LOKIEC, GARNIEC

Polish money DUCAT, GROSZ, MARKA, ZLOTY, FENNIG, HALERZ

Polish weight LUT, FUNT, UNCYA, KAMIAN, SKRUPUL

polished SLEEK, GLOSSY, URBANE, ELEGANT

polisher BUFF, EMERY, RABAT, BUFFER, CROCUS, PUMICE

polite CIVIL, URBANE, GENTEEL, GRACIOUS, COURTEOUS

politician HEELER, CONNIVER

poll HEAD, SURVEY, CANVASS

pollster ROPER, GALLUP, HARRIS

pollute SOIL, TAINT, DEFILE

Polonius relative LAERTES, OPHELIA

polygon *see* GEOMETRIC

Polynesian language MAORI, SAMOAN, TONGAN, HAWAIIAN, TAHITIAN; *see* PACIFIC ISLANDS

polyp HYDRA, GORGONIA

Pompeia's husband CAESAR

pompous TUMID, TURGID, BOMBASTIC

pond LUM, TARN, LOCHAN

ponder MULL, PORE, WEIGH, REFLECT, RUMINATE

pontiff POPE, BISHOP, PONTIFEX

pony NAG, TAT, CAVY, CRIB, DRAM, TATT, TROT, NAGGY, PONEY, TATOO, WELSH, EXMOOR, SHELTY, TANGUN, TATTOO, SHELTIE

pool DIB, DUB, CARR, LINN, LLYN, MERE, TARN, KITTY, LAGOON, PUDDLE; *see* BILLIARDS
poor NEEDY, SEELY, INFERIOR
Pope PAPACY, PONTIFF
Popes LEO, JOHN, PAUL, PIUS, CONON, DONUS, FELIX, GAIUS, LANDO, LINUS, PETER, RATTI, SOTER, URBAN, ADRIAN, AGATHO, ALBERT, ANGELO, FABIAN, JULIUS, LUCIUS, MARCUS, MARTIN, PHILIP, SIXTUS, VICTOR, ANTEROS, CLEMENT, DAMASUS, GREGORY, HYGINUS, MARINUS, MONTINI, PACELLI, PASCHAL, ROMANUS, SERGIUS, STEPHEN, URSINUS, ZOSIMUS, JOHNPAUL, RONCALLI
Popeye character BLUTO, OLIVE
poplar ASP, ABELE, ALAMO, ASPEN, BALSAM
poppy MAW, PAPAVER, CREAMCUPS
pops conductor KUNZEL, FIEDLER, WILLIAMS
populace HOIPOLLOI; *see* PEOPLE
popular COMMON, DEMOTIC, FAMILIAR, PLEBEIAN
porcelain KO, MING, CHINA, DERBY, IMARI, MURRA, SPODE, SEVRES, CELADON, FAIENCE, LIMOGES, MEISSEN, GOMBROON; *see* POTTERY
porch STOA, LANAI, STOOP, PARVIS, PIAZZA, GALILEE, PORTICO, VERANDA(H)
porcupine(-like rodent) CAVY, DEGU, AGUTI, CAVIA, COYPU, PORKY, AGOUTI, AGOUTY, APEREA, COYPOU, NUTRIA
pore(s) STOMA, PONDER, FORAMEN, OSTIOLE, STOMATA
pork PIG, HOG, LARDO(O)N; *see* CUT
porpoise SEAHOG, DOLPHIN, HOGFISH
porridge POB, MUSH, POBS, SAMP, ATOLE, BROSE, GROUT, GRUEL, POLENTA, POTTAGE
port LARBOARD; *see* HARBOR
portend, portent *see* PRESAGE
porter AKABO, HAMAL, TAMEN, COOLIE, DARWAN, KHAMAL, REDCAP, BELLBOY, BELLMAN, CARGADOR; *see* BEER
Portia relative BASSANIO
Portia's maid NERISSA
Portia's suitor ARAGON, MOROCCO
portico STOA, XYST, ARCADE, PARVIS, XYSTUS, NARTHEX
portion BIT, DOT, LOT, DOLE, METE, QUOTA, RATION
portray DRAW, LIMN, DEPICT
Portugal LUSITANIA
Portuguese measure PE, BOTA, MEIO, PIPA, VARA, ALMUD, BRACA, FANGA, GEIRA, LEGOA, LINHA, MILHA, PALMO, ALMUDE, COVADO, OITAVA, QUARTO, FERRADO, SELAMIN
Portuguese money REIS, CONTO, DOBRA, DINERO, ESCUDO, TOSTAO, CENTAVO, CRUSADO, MOIDORE, JOHANNES
Portuguese weight GRAO; *see* BRAZILIAN
pose SIT, MIEN, FEIGN, MODEL
Poseidon relative ZEUS, HADES, CRONUS, TRITON, ANTAEUS, PEGASUS
position STAND, STANCE, UBIETY; *see* PLACE
positive PLUS, SURE, ACTUAL, THETIC
positive pole ANODE
possible FEASIBLE, PROBABLE, POTENTIAL
possibly HAPLY, MAYBE, PERHAPS
post DAK, JOB, BITT, CAMP, JAMB, MAIL, NEWEL, STAKE, COLUMN, PILLAR, BOLLARD, CAPSTAN
poster BILL, AFFICHE, PLACARD
posterior HIND, REAR, DORSAL, RETRAL, BUTTOCK(S)
postmark CACHET, INDICIA
postpone DEFER, TABLE, SHELVE
postulate AXIOM, CLAIM, POSIT, ASSUME, PREMISE
posture MIEN, STANCE
pot LOTA, CRUSE, KITTY, LOTAH, ALUDEL, PIPKIN
potassium ALUM, NITER, GROUGH, KALITE, POTASH, MURIATE

potato YAM, CHAT, SPUD, TATER, TATIE, TUBER, BATATA
potent COGENT, MIGHTY, STRONG
potential LATENT, POSSIBLE
potion DOSE, PHILTER, NEPENTHE
potter's tool KICK, PALLET, LATHE, THROW, WHEEL
pottery CHUN, KUAN, TING, TUNG, YUEH, DELFT, LEEDS, BASALT, CROUCH, JASPER, FAIENCE, GOMBROON, WEDGWOOD; *see* PORCELAIN
pottery, pert. to CERAMIC, FICTILE
pouch POD, SAC(K), BURSA, SPORRAN
pouch-shaped SACCATE
poultry *see* FOWL
poultry disease PIP, POX, ROUP, GAPES
pound BRAY, DRUB, QUID, TAMP, TUND, THUMP, BRUISE
pour GUSH, RAIN, SPEW, TEEM, DECANT, LIBATE
pout FRET, MOPE, MOUE, SULK, GRIMACE
poverty NEED, WANT, PENURY
powder ABIR, DUST, TALC, PICRA, ROUGE, POUNCE, PUMICE
powdery DUSTY, FRIABLE
power OD, VIS, DINT, MANA, ODYL, SWAY, FORCE, MIGHT
powerful POTENT, PUISSANT
powwow INDABA, PARLEY, COUNCIL, MEETING
practical UTILE, PRAGMATIC
practice DRILL, HABIT, USAGE, PRAXIS, EXERCISE, REHEARSE
Prairie State IL, ILLINOIS
praise LAUD, TOUT, ECLAT, ELOGE, EXALT, EXTOL, KUDOS, EULOGY
prance CAPER, CAVORT
prank DIDO, ANTIC, CAPER, CURVET, MISCHIEF
prate GAB, YAP, BUKH, BUKK
pray BEG, ORA, SUE, DAVEN, APPEAL, BESEECH
prayer AVE, BEAD, BENE, PLEA, SUIT, ALENU, CREDO, GRACE, MATIN, SALAT, LITANY, NOVENA, ORISON, VESPER, ROGATION
prayer book ORDO, MISSAL, PORTAS, PRIMER, PORTASS, BREVIARY
prayer place IDGAH
prayer stick BAHO, PAHO, BAHOO
praying figure ORANT
preacher *see* EVANGELIST, CLERGY
precept(s) CODE, DICTA, TENET
precipice CRAG, LINN, PALI
precipitate RASH, HASTY, SUDDEN
precipitation DEW, HAIL, MIST, RAIN, SNOW, SLEET
precise TIDY, EXACT, RIGID, FORMAL, STRICT
preclude IMPEDE; *see* PREVENT
preconceive IDEATE, SCHEME
predicament FIX, JAM, PASS, SPOT, SCRAPE, STRAIT, DILEMMA, STRAITS
predict BODE, AUGUR, WEIRD, DIVINE, FORECAST, FORETELL
predisposed PRONE, BIASED
preen PLUME, PRIMP, PRINK
prefer PICK, FANCY, FAVOR
prefixes *see p. 331*
prejudice HARM, BIAS
prelate INGE, POPE, ABBOT, BISHOP, PONTIFF, PRIMATE, CARDINAL
prelude INTRO, PROEM, OVERTURE
premise LEMMA, POSTULATE
premium AGIO, BONUS
preoccupy ABSORB, OBSESS
prepare FIT, EDIT, GIRD, PAVE, ADAPT, EQUIP, REDACT
preposition TO, FOR, OUT, FROM, INTO, ONTO, UNTO, UPON, WITH, AFTER
prerogative RIGHT, PRIVILEGE
presage BODE, OMEN, SIGN, AUGUR, TOKEN, AUGURY, HERALD, OSTENT, PORTEND, PORTENT
prescribe DIRECT, ORDAIN, OUTLAW
prescribed THETIC
present BOON, GIFT, GIVE, NONCE, TODAY, BESTOW, DONATE, TENDER
presently NOW, ANON, ENOW, SOON, SHORTLY
preserve CAN, JAM, TIN, CORN, CURE, KEEP, FREEZE
president assassinated KENNEDY, LINCOLN, GARFIELD, MCKINLEY

presidential assassin BOOTH, OSWALD, GUITEAU, CZOLGOSZ
presidential information *see p. 336*
presidential nickname ABE, CAL, FDR, IKE, JFK, LBJ, JACK, JIMMY, TEDDY
press CRAM, IRON, TAMP, SERRY, STAMP, WEDGE
press agent FLACK, PUBLICIST
pressing URGENT, EXIGENT
pressure DURESS, STRESS
pressure unit BARAD, BARIE, PASCAL
pretend FAKE, FEIGN, ALLEGE, PROFESS, SIMULATE
pretender QUACK, ASPIRANT, IMPOSTOR, SCIOLIST
pretense(s) AIRS, RUSE, FEINT
pretentious SIDY, TAWDRY, POMPOUS
pretext ALIBI, EXCUSE
pretty FAIR, BONNY, COMELY, MIGNON(NE)
prevail WIN, SWAY, OBTAIN
prevalent RIFE, EXTANT, RAMPANT
prevent BAR, BALK, STOP, AVERT, DEBAR, DETER, ESTOP, THWART, PRECLUDE, FORESTALL
prey PRIZE, RAVIN, QUARRY
Priam relative PARIS, HECTOR, TROILUS, LAOMEDON, CASSANDRA
Priam's kingdom TROY
price COST, FARE, RATE, TOLL
prick GOAD, SPUR, URGE, STING
prickle BUR(R), SETA, SPINE, ACANTHA, ACULEUS, SPICULA
pride VANITY, CONCEIT
priest ELI, FRA, LAMA, MUST, PAPA, ABUNA, DRUID, MOBED, SARIP, FLAMEN, SHAMAN, CALCHAS, PANDITA; *see* CLERGY, BIBLICAL PRIESTS
priestess AUGE, ENTUM, VESTAL
priesthood MAGI, SALII
prim DEMURE, MODEST, PRISSY
primate BISHOP; *see* APE, MONKEY
primeval OLD, EARLY, NATIVE, PRISTINE
primp PREEN, PRINK, PRUNE
primrose GLAUX, OXLIP, COWSLIP, PRIMULA, AURICULA
prince RAS, IMAM, KHAM, KNEZ, RANA, IMAUM, NAWAB, DAUPHIN, GAEKWAR, ATHELING
princess RANI, BEGUM, RANEE
princewood CYP
principle YIN, YANG, BASIS, LOGOS, PRANA, TENET, PRECEPT, DOCTRINE; *see* MAXIM
print ETCHING, PUBLISH
printer DAY, FUST, TORY, TYPO, PRESS, SHORT, CAXTON, JENSON, THOMAS, NUTHEAD, PLANTIN, BRADFORD, FRANKLIN, GUTENBERG
printing tools and terms EM, EN, PI, BED, CUT, FAT, FLY, JOB, LAY, LOW, MAT, OUT, PIE, SET, SUB, BANK, BITE, BODY, CASE, COPY, DELE, DRAG, DRAW, FACE, FEET, FIST, FONT, FORM, KERN, LEAD, LEAN, LINE, NICK, QUAD, RACK, RISE, ROLL, RULE, SLIP, SLUG, SLUR, SORT, STEM, STET, TAKE, TYPE, ALLEY, BELLY, BLOCK, BOXIN, BRACE, CARET, CHASE, COLON, COMMA, CUTIN, DUMMY, DWELL, FRAME, HORSE, INSET, PLATE, POINT, PROOF, QUOIN, RUNIN, SERIF, SETUP, SHAKE, SHANK, SHEET, SPACE, STAND, STICK, STONE, TITLE, TOKEN, ACCENT, BATTER, BEARER, BODKIN, BRAYER, CANCEL, CASTER, CERIPH, CHAPEL, CLICHE, COCKUP, DABBER, DAGGER, DELETE, DIESIS, DOCTOR, DOUBLE, EMBOSS, FINGER, GALLEY, IMPOSE, INDENT, ITALIC, LEADER, LETTER, LOCKUP, MACKLE, MAKEUP, MARGIN, MATRIX, MATTER, NIPPER, OFFCUT, OFFSET, PICKUP, PLATEN, POSTER, REGLET, REVISE, ROLLER, ROUNCE, SETOFF, THIRTY, TYMPAN, BASTARD, CLICKER, COLLATE, COMPOSE, COUNTER, FRISKET, GAGEPIN, GRIPPER,

HEADING, HELLBOX, IMPRINT, JOBWORK, JUSTIFY, MEASURE, MORTISE, MOVABLE, OPENING, OVERLAY, OVERRUN, PACKING, PINMARK, PLANNER, QUADRAT, REPRINT
prior FORMER, EARLIER, ANTERIOR
prison *see* JAIL
prison camp GULAG, BELSEN, DACHAU, STALAG, AUSCHWITZ
private PFC, PVT, SECRET, INTIMATE, PERSONAL
privateer *see* PIRATE
privilege OCTROI, PATENT, CHARTER, LICENSE, FRANCHISE
privy JAKES, PRIVY, STOOL, CLOACA, TOILET, OUTHOUSE
prize PRY, TERN; *see* AWARD
probable BELIKE, LIKELY
probe SOUND, STYLET, INQUEST
problem NUT, CRUX, POSER
proboscis NEB, NOSE, SNOUT, TRUNK, ANTLIA
proceed WEND, ISSUE, PRESS
proceedings ACTA, ACTS, ACTION
proceeds YIELD, INCOME, PRODUCE, PROFITS
procession FILE, TRAIN, PARADE, CORTEGE, RETINUE
proclaim CRY, KNELL, VOICE, HERALD, DECLARE
proclamation BAN(N)S, EDICT, NOTICE
proctor AGENT, PROXY, MONITOR
prod EDD, GOAD, POKE
prodigal LAVISH, WASTREL, GENEROUS
prodigy MARVEL, MIRACLE, PORTENT
produce BEGET, CAUSE, YIELD, APPORT, CREATE, INWORK, ENGENDER, GENERATE
product OPUS, EFFECT, RESULT
profane NOA, DEFILE, VIOLATE
profession ART, JOB, CALL, LINE, CRAFT, TRADE, AVOWAL, CAREER, METIER, CALLING, PURSUIT, VOCATION
proficiency SKILL, APTITUDE
profit NET, BOOT, GAIN, VAIL, AVAIL, BENEFIT
profit-taker PERNOR
profitable FAT, UTILE, PAYING, USEFUL, GAINFUL, LUCRATIVE
profound DEEP, SOLEMN, ABSTRUSE
profuse LUSH, LAVISH, PRODIGAL
progenitor SIRE, PARENT
progeny SEED, ISSUE, SCION
program AGENDA, OUTLINE, SCHEDULE, SYLLABUS
prohibit BAN, (DE)BAR, TABOO
prohibited TABOO, ILLICIT
prohibition VETO, EMBARGO
project JUT, IDEA, SCHEME
projectile SHELL, BULLET, ROCKET, MISSILE, TORPEDO
projecting piece ARM, RIM, FLANGE, TENDON
projection CAM, EAR, HOB, BARB, HOBB, KNOP, LOBE, SNAG, BULGE, LEDGE, PRONG, SHELF, SOCLE
prolific FECUND, FERTILE
promenade MALL, PRADO, MARINA, PASEAR, ALAMEDA
Prometheus' gift FIRE
prominent CHIEF, SALIENT
promise IOU, (A)VOW, NOTE, OATH, WORD, PAROLE, PLEDGE
Promised Land ZION, CANAAN
promontory TOR, CAPE, NASE, NAZE, NESS, NOUP, SKAW, SPIT
promote AID, ABET, FOSTER, ADVANCE
prompt CUE, SOON, URGE, YARE
prone APT, SUPINE, PROSTRATE
prong NIB, PEG, FANG, TINE, TOOTH, ANTLER
pronoun IT, HER, HIM, HIS, ONE, OUR, SHE, YOU, HERS, MINE, OURS, THAT, THEE, THEM, THEY, THIS, THOU, YOUR, THEIR, THESE, THINE, THOSE
pronounce BURR, SLUR, STRESS
pronunciation mark *see* MARK
proof SAFE, REPRO, TRIAL, GALLEY, REVISE, EVIDENCE
proofreader's mark *see* MARK
prop GIB, HOLD, STAY, BRACE, RANGE, CRUTCH, BOLSTER
propel PEG, DRIVE, LAUNCH
propeller BLADE, ROTOR, SCREW
proper DUE, FIT, JUST, MEET, RIGHT

properly APTLY, FEATLY
property ALOD, DHAN, LAND, ASSET, GOODS, LANDS, ESTATE, WEALTH, CHATTEL, ALLODIUM, HOLDINGS
property, hold on LIEN
property, receiver of ALIENEE
prophesy FORETELL; *see* PRESAGE
prophet SEER, AUGUR, VATES, ORACLE
prophet, Biblical AMOS, JEHU, JOEL, HOSEA, JONAH, MICAH, MOSES, NAHUM, DANIEL, ELIJAH, ELISHA, ISAIAH, NATHAN, SAMUEL, OBADIAH, MALACHI, JEREMIAH, HABAKKUK, ZECHARIAH, ZEPHANIAH
prophetess SIBYL, PYTHIA(N), SEERESS, CASSANDRA, PYTHONESS
prophetic VATIC, MANTIC, FATIDIC, VATICAL, ORACULAR, FATIDICAL
proportion RATE, QUOTA, RATIO
proposition(s) LEMMA, OFFER, PORISM, THESES, THESIS, PREMISE, THEOREM
proprietor OWNER, PATROON
prosaic DULL, LITERAL
proscribe BAN, FORBID, OUTLAW
prosecute SUE, INTEND, LITIGATE
proselyte *see* CONVERT
Proserpina's husband PLUTO
prospect HOPE, MINE, VISTA
prosper BATTEN, THRIVE, FLOURISH
prosperity HAP, SONS, WEAL, SONSE, WEALTH, WELFARE
Prospero's servant ARIEL
prosperous PALMY, WEALTHY
prostitute TART, TRAMP, TRULL, WHORE, CHIPPY, HARLOT, TROLLOP
prostrate BOW, FELL, PRONE, REPENT, SUPINE
protagonist HERO, STAR, RIVAL
protection LEE, EGIS, WING, AEGIS, APRON, SHELTER
protection right MUND, GRITH
protégé(e) WARD, CLIENT, DISCIPLE
protein ZEIN, ABRIN, MUCIN, RICIN, CASEIN, FIBRIN, GLOBIN, GLUTIN, HISTON, ALBUMIN, GLIADIN, HISTONE, HORDEIN, PEPTIDE, PEPTONE, GLOBULIN, GLUTELIN, PROLAMIN
protest OBJECT, SQUAWK, DISSENT
Protestant MORMON, BAPTIST, LUTHERAN, METHODIST
protozoan MONAD, LOBOSA, EUGLENA, PROTIST, STENTOR, HELIOZOA, ORBULINA, SUCTORIA
protrude JUT, BEETLE, PROJECT
protuberance JAG, NUB, HUMP, KNOB, KNOT, LOVE, NODE, UMBO, WART, GNARL, INION, KNURL, TORUS
protuberant STRUT, TOROSE
proud VAIN, ARROGANT
prove EVINCE, DERAIGN
proverb *see* MAXIM
provide CATER, ENDOW, ENDUE, AFFORD, PURVEY, FURNISH
provided IF, BODEN, SOBEIT
provident FRUGAL, PRUDENT, THRIFTY
provincial LOCAL, RUSTIC, NARROW
provisioner SUTLER, VICTUALER, VIVANDIER
provisions CATES, ANNONA, LARDER
proviso SALVO, CLAUSE
provoke IRE, RILE, ROIL, ANGER, ANNOY, PEEVE, PIQUE, NEEDLE, NETTLE
prow BOW, PROA, STEM
prowl LURK, SNEAK, STEAL
proxy AGENT, DEPUTY, DELEGATE
prudent SAGE, WISE, CHARY
prudish COY, NICE, DEMURE
prune LOP, SNED, TRIM, PREEN
pry JIMMY, LEVER, PRIZE, SNOOP
psalm(s) LAUD(S), HALLEL, PRAISE, VENITE, CANTATE, CANTICLE, MISERERE
pseudonym NOM, ALIAS, ANANYM, ANONYM, PENNAME, SOBRIQUET; *see. p. 260*
psyche MIND, PNEUMA, SPIRIT
Psyche's lover CUPID
psychiatrist JUNG, RANK, REIK, WARD, ADLER, BINET, BRILL, FREUD, JAMES, JANET, WUNDT, BREUER, HORNEY,

MESMER, SHRINK, ANALYST, CHARCOT, ALIENIST
pub *see* TAVERN
public KUNG, OPEN, CIVIC, KNOWN, OVERT, COMMON
publication BOOK, ISSUE, PAPER, EDITION, JOURNAL, MAGAZINE, NEWSPAPER
publicize AIR, PLUG, PUFF, TOUT
publish AIR, EDIT, VENT, ISSUE, PRINT, BLAZON, DELATE, REVEAL, SPREAD
publisher OCHS, FIELDS, HEARST, MERRIAM, SULZBERGER
Puccini opera MANON, TOSCA, (LA)BOHEME, TURANDOT, BUTTERFLY
pudding HOY, DUFF, SAGO, CUSTARD
puddle POOL, MUDDY, PLASH, WALLOW, PLASHET, LOBLOLLY
Puerto Rican governor MUNOZ, ALBERTO, SANCHEZ, MAYAGUEZ
puff FLAM, RISE, WAFF, BLURB, ELATE, SWELL
puffer LIJA, MOLA, BLOWER, CHAPIN, DIODON, MOLOID, TAMBOR, BOXFISH, BURFISH, COWFISH, CUCKOLD, OLDWIFE, BLUEGILL, BURRFISH, TRUNKFISH
pull TOW, TUG, DRAG, HALE, YANK, BOISE, PLUCK, WRENCH
pulley WHEEL, SHEAVE, TACKLE
pulp PAP, PITH, RAPE, CHYME, SLIME, POMACE
pulpit AMBO, BEMA, MIMBAR, ROSTRUM
pulsate BEAT, THROB, LIBRATE
pulverize BRAY, MILL, MULL, CRUSH, GRIND, POUND, POWDER, ATOMIZE
pump DRAW, QUIZ, INFLATE
punch JAB, BLOW, BORE, POKE, DOUSE, PASTE, STAMP, MATTOIR, PRITCHEL
Punch and Judy dog TOBY
punctual PROMPT
punctuation mark DOT, DASH, BRACE, CARET, COLON, COMMA, POINT, SLANT, HYPHEN, PARENS, PERIOD, QUOTES, BRACKET, LEADERS, SOLIDUS, VIRGULE, ELLIPSIS, GUILLEMET, SEMICOLON
puncture PRICK, PIERCE
pungent TEZ, TART, SHARP, SPICY, TANGY, PIQUANT
punish FINE, FRAP, AMERCE, CHASTEN, SCOURGE
punishment WRACK, FERULE, PENALTY
punishment, pert. to PENAL
punk HOODLUM; *see* TINDER
punt KENT, QUANT, GAMBLE
puny TINY, WEAK, FRAIL, SLIGHT
pupil GLENE; *see* STUDENT
puppet DOLL, TOOL, KUKLA, OLLIE, EFFIGY, MAUMET
pure MERE, NEAT, PUTE, SHEER, CHASTE, VIRGIN
purgative *see* LAXATIVE
purify PURGE, FILTER, REFINE
purport FECK, GIST, TENOR
purpose AIM, END, GOAL, SAKE, ARTHA, INTENT, MEANING
purposive TELIC
purse BAG, CLUTCH, PUCKER
pursue DOG, HUNT, TAIL, CHASE, HOUND, STALK, TRAIL, FOLLOW
pursy PUDGY, PUFFY, STOUT
pus MATTER, SANIES
push PING, PROD, BOOST, NUDGE
pustule *see* PIMPLE
put aside DAFF
put away BANK, CACHE, STORE
put off DOFF, HAFT, DEFER, STALL
put on DON, ADORN, FEIGN, STAGE, PRODUCE
put out FIRE, OUST, SACK, DOUSE, EJECT, EVICT, SNUFF
put up with BEAR, ENDURE, TOLERATE
puzzle(s) CRUX, POSE, AMAZE, POSER, REBUS, BAFFLE, CRUCES, ENIGMA, RIDDLE, MYSTIFY, NONPLUS, TANGRAM
Pygmalion author SHAW
pygmy RUNT, ATOMY, MINIM; *see* DWARF
Pylades' friend ORESTES
pyramid CONE, KHUFU, CHEOPS, KHAFRE, MENKAURE
Pyramus' lover THISBE
pyromaniac FIREBUG, ARSONIST
Pythias' friend DAMON

Q

QED word ERAT, QUOD
quack CROCUS, HUMBUG, IMPOSTOR, SANGRADO, CHARLATAN
quadrant ARC, HENRY, FOURTH
quadrate AGREE, SQUARE, QUARTER
quadrille DANCE, LANCERS
quadruped BEAST, ANIMAL, MAMMAL
quaff *see* DRINK
quagmire BOG, FEN, MORASS, SLOUGH
quail LOWA, COLIN, COWER, WINCE, BLENCH, BOBWHITE
quail genus COLINUS
quaint DROLL, CURIOUS
quake SHAKE, QUIVER, SHIVER, TREMOR, TEMBLOR, TREMBLE
Quaker FOX, HICKS, FRIEND
quaking ASPEN, TREMOR, TREPID
qualify FIT, PASS, ADAPT, EQUIP, LIMIT, ENTITLE, PREPARE
quality GUNA, GRADE, RAJAS, TAMAS, TRAIT, METTLE, SATTVA, TIMBRE, CALIBER
qualm DEMUR, NAUSEA, SCRUPLE
quandary FIX, STRAIT, DILEMMA
quantity DOSE, SIZE, GRIST, AMOUNT, EXTENT
quarrel SPAT, BICKER, BRABBLE, DISPUTE, RUCTION; *see* FIGHT
quarry PIT, GAME, MINE, PREY, EXCAVATION
quarter COIN, LODGE, MERCY, BILLET, TWOBITS, DISTRICT
quarter note CROTCHET
quarter of year RAITH
quarters DIGS, ETAPE, BILLET, BIVOUAC, COMMONS
quartz *see* MINERAL
quash CASS, VOID, ANNUL, QUELL, CASSARE, SQUELCH
quaternion TETRAD
quaver SHAKE, TRILL, EIGHTH
quay *see* LANDING
Quebec information *see p. 306*
queen ENA, MAB, ANNE, BESS, DIDO, HERA, MARY, SATI, BASTA, BEGUM, ELENA, MARIE, BEEGUM, ORIANA, REGINA, EMPRESS, VICTORIA
queen of Sheba BALKIS
queenly REG(IN)AL
queer ODD, DROLL, FUNNY, QUAINT, CURIOUS, UNUSUAL
quell CALM, CRUSH, QUASH, QUIET, SPRING
quench ALLAY, DOUSE, SLAKE, STIFLE
question ASK, NUT, POSE, QUIZ, GRILL, ISSUE, POINT, POSER, QUERY
questionable MOOT, FISHY, SHADY, SUSPECT
quetzal TROGON
queue CUE, FILE, PIGTAIL
quibble PUN, CARP, CAVIL, EVADE, SOPHISM
quick FAST, LISH, LIVE, YARE, AGILE, ALIVE, FLEET, RAPID, SWIFT, TOSTO, ACTIVE, PRESTO, PROMPT, SNAPPY
quickly ANON, CITO, APACE, PRESTO, PRONTO, INSTANTER
quicksand SYRT, MORASS, SYRTIS
quid CUD, FID, WAD, CHAW, CHEW
quiescent LATENT, DORMANT
quiet MUM, PST, TST, TUT, CALM, HUSH, LULL, ALLAY, STILL, SMOOTH
quill(s) COP, PEN, REMEX, SPINA, SPINE, CALAMI
quilt DUVET, EIDER, CADDOW
quinine KINA, QUINA
quintessence GIST, PITH, ELIXIR
quirk KINK, WHIM, TWIST, ODDITY
quirt WHIP, ROMAL
quit STOP, RESIGN, RETIRE
quivering *see* QUAKING
Quixote *see* DON QUIXOTE
quixotic FANCIFUL, ROMANTIC, CHIVALROUS
quiz EXAM, TEST, PROBE
quoits JUKSKEI
quoits term HOB, MOT, TEE, SKEI, DISCUS
quorum PLENUM, COMPANY, MAJORITY
quota SHARE, RATION
quotation CHRIA, CITAL, EXCERPT, EXTRACT
quote CITE, ADDUCE

R

Ra consort MUT
rabbi GAON, AMORA, HAKAM
rabbit *see* HARE
rabble SCUM, RAFF, DREGS, CANAILLE, RIFFRAFF; *see* MOB, PEOPLE
rabble-rouser AGITATOR, DEMAGOGUE
rabies LYSSA
raccoon(-like mammal) COON, COATI, PANDA, NARICA, RACOON, TELEDU
racoon genus NASAU
race HIE, DASH, LADE, LINE, BREED, DERBY, FLUME, RELAY, SPRINT, STIRPS, CONTEST, LINEAGE, REGATTA, PEDIGREE
race, pert. to ETHNIC
racecourse LAP, OVAL, RING, TURF, ASCOT, BOWIE, DOWNS, EPSOM, TRACK, HIALEAH, JAMAICA, PIMLICO, AQUEDUCT, SARATOGA
racehorse PACER, MAIDEN, MUDDER, PLATER, TROTTER
racehorses ZEV, NOOR, ALSAB, ARMED, KELSO, OMAHA, PAVOT, SWAPS, ALTHEA, BUSHER, GUNBOW, NASHUA, PONDER, STYMIE, ASSAULT, MANOWAR, NEEDLES, SHUTOUT, TOMFOOL, ALLALONG, BIMELICH, CITATION, CHARRYBACK, CHALLEDON, DETERMINE, KAUAIKING, SIRBARTON, STAGEHAND, WHIRLAWAY, SECRETARIAT
Rachel relative LEAH, JACOB, LABAN, JOSEPH, BENJAMIN
racing driver FOYT, HILL, SNEVA, UNSER, MEARS, ANDRETTI
racing term LAP, WIN, CARD, FORM, LANE, SHOW, TAPE, PLACE, PURSE, PYLON, SILKS, FINISH, STAKES, STRETCH, HANDICAP
rack GIN, FRAME, TORMENT
racket BAT, DIN, GAME, BABEL
racy SPICY, RISQUE, PIQUANT
Radames' love AIDA
radar term BLIP, RACON, SCOPE, RADOME, SHORAN
radiant ASHINE, LUMINOUS
radiation unit RAD, ROENTGEN
radical RED, REBEL, ULTRA, LEFTIST, LEFTWING; *see* ROOT
radio SET, CRYSTAL, WIRELESS
radioactive element NITON, RADON, CURIUM, IONIUM, RADIUM, THORON, ACTINON, FERMIUM, THORIUM, URANIUM, ACTINIUM, ASTATINE, FRANCIUM, NOBELIUM
radioactivity unit DPM, DPS, REM, REP, CURIE, HALFLIFE
radium discoverer CURIE
radius RAY, RANGE, SPOKE, SWEEP
raffish LOW, TAWDRY, VULGAR
raffle DRAW(ING), LOTTERY
raft MOKI, BALSA, FLOAT
rag MOCK, TEASE, SHRED, TATTER
rage FAD, FUME, FURY, RAMP, RANT, RESE, FUROR, STORM, VOGUE, TANTRUM
ragged ROUGH, FRAYED, SHABBY
ragout STEW, SALMI, GOULASH, HARICOT, MULLIGAN
raid FORAY, ONSET, INROAD, MARAUD, RAZZIA, COMMANDO
rail BAR, RANT, FENCE, SCOLD, REVILE, SEPTUM
rails KORA, MOHO, SORA, WEKA, CRAKE, MUDHEN, COULAN, MOORHEN, TIKLING, WATERCOCK
railing FENCE, GRATE, PARAPET
railroad car VAN, FLAT, TANK, BUGGY, COACH, DINER, BOXCAR, DINGHY, REEFER, SMOKER, TENDER, CABOOSE, FLATCAR, GONDOLA, PULLMAN, RATTLER, SLEEPER, WAGONLIT
railroad term TIE, CROW, FROG, SPUR, YARD, CHAIR, FLARE, FUSEE, GAUGE, SHUNT, GANTLET, SLEEPER, CROSSTIE, HIGHBALL, PEDESTAL, SEMAPHORE
railroader RAIL, GUARD, BRAKIE, PORTER, FIREMAN,

BAKEHEAD, ENGINEER, YARDMAN, MOTORMAN, CONDUCTOR
raiment *see* CLOTHING
rain DAB, HAIL, MIST, POUR, TEEM, BRASH, MISLE, SLEET, SPATE, FLURRY, MIZZLE, SEREIN, SHOWER, DRIZZLE, TORRENT
rain, pert. to HYETAL, PLUVIAL
rainbow ARC, IRIS
rainbow, pert. to IRID(I)AL
raincoat MACK, PONCHO, OILSKIN, SLICKER, OILSKINS
rainy MISTY, SHOWERY, PLUVIOUS
raise GROW, HIKE, REAR, BREED, ERECT, HOIST
raisin LEXIA, CURRANT
rake COMB, ROUE, SLANT, PEPPER, SCRAPE, STRAFE, ENFILADE, LOTHARIO, LIBERTINE
rally MEET, REVIVE, RESURGE
ram TUP, BUTT, TAMP, ARIES, STUFF, WETHER
ram-headed god AMON, KHNUM
ramble GAD, ROVE, SAUNTER
ramp RAGE, APRON, CLIMB, SLOPE, ROADWAY
rampart AGGER, REDAN, VALLUM, PARAPET, RAVELIN
ranch HACIENDA, ESTANCIA, PLANTATION
rancid RANK, FETID, SMELLY
rancor SPITE, VENOM, MALICE
random CASUAL, CHANCE, DESULTORY, HAPHAZARD
range AREA, ROAM, DRIFT, GAMUT, ORBIT, SCOPE, SIERRA; *see* MOUNTAIN
Rangoon measure LAH, DAIN, TAUN
rank ROW, RATE, TIER, ARRANT, DEGREE, RANCID, STATUS
rankle GALL, FESTER, IRRITATE
ransack RIFLE, PILLAGE, RUMMAGE
ransom CLAIM, REDEEM, RESCUE
rant RAIL, RAVE, BLUSTER
rap BOP, BOX, CUFF, THUMP, WHACK, THWACK
rape NAVET, RAVISH, ASSAULT, VIOLATE
rapid FLEET, QUICK, SWIFT
rapids CHUTE, DELLS, DALLES
rapidly APACE, SKELP
rapture BLISS, ECSTASY
rascal CAD, IMP, ROGUE, SCAMP, VARLET, SCOUNDREL
rash POX, HASTY, HIVES, UNWISE, SCABIES; *see* SKIN
rasp FILE, GRATE, SCRAPE
rat SCAB, STOOL, GNAWER, VERMIN
rat(-like rodent) LOIR, MOLE, PACA, TANA, VOLE, WANT, GUNDI, LABBA, LEROT, METAD, MOUDY, MOUSE, MOUSY, RANNY, SHREW, ZEMMI, ZEMNI, ZOKOR, GERBIL, JERBOA, MOUSEY, MYGALE, RATTAN, RATTON, HAMSTER, LEMMING, MUSKRAT, POTOROO, SANDRAT, SONDELI
rat genus MUS, GLIS, SOREX, ZAPUS, GEOMYS, MYODES, MYOXUS, TUPAIA
ratchet *see* DETENT
rate TAX, AGIO, CESS, BATTA, ASSESS, ESTIMATE
rather ERE, SOONER, INSTEAD
ratify BIND, SEAL, SIGN, APPROVE
rating MARK, RANK, GRADE, SCORE
ratio RATE, QUOTA, DEGREE
ration DOLE, METE, SHARE, ALLOWANCE
rational SANE, LUCID, SOUND
rationalize THOB, REASON
rattan CANE, PALM, SEGA
rattle RALE, CLATTER, CONFUSE
raucous HARSH, HOARSE, STRIDENT
ravage RAZE, SACK, DESPOIL
Ravel work BOLERO, DAPHNIS
raveling LINT
raven GRIP, CORBIE, DEVOUR
Raven author POE
ravine GAP, DALE, LINN, WADI, WADY, DONGA, GORGE, GULCH, GULLY, ARROYO, NULLAH
raw DAMP, SORE, BAWDY, BLEAK, GREEN, UNRIPE
ray BEAM, BETA, ALPHA, ANODE, CANAL, GAMMA, GLEAM, LASER, COSMIC, LENARD, ACTINIC, CATHODE
ray(-like fish) SKATE, MANTA, ROKER, BATOID, OBISPO, BATFISH, COWNOSE,

FIDDLER, PRISTIS, TORPEDO, STINGRAY, DEVILFISH
ray genus RAJA, MOBULA
rayon ACETATE, VISCOSE, CELANESE
rays, pert. to RADIAL
raze LEVEL, DEMOLISH
re ABOUT, ANENT
reach GAIN, ATTAIN, EXTENT, STRETCH
reactance measure OHM
reaction TAXIS, REFLEX, TROPISM, RESPONSE
reactionary TORY, BIRCHER, DIEHARD, RIGHTIST, MISONEIST, RIGHTWING
read SCAN, PERUSE, PRELECT, CONSTRUE, DECIPHER
read, inability to ALEXIA
reader LECTOR, PRIMER, ANAGNOST
reading KRI, KERE, KERI, LECTION
ready RIPE, YARE, HANDY
real thing(s) ENTIA, MCCOY
really ARU, QUITE, INDEED
realm REICH, DOMAIN, SPHERE
reap CUT, GARNER, SICKLE, HARVEST
reaping tool SCYTHE, SICKLE, TWIBIL(L)
rear(ing) AFT, BREED, ERECT, NURSE, STEND, STERN, PESADE, ARRIERE, DERRIERE
rear, to the (AB)AFT, ASTERN
reason(ing) NOUS, ARGUE, LOGIC, SENSE, MOTIVE, APRIORI
reason, deprive of DEMENT
rebel DEFY, RISE, MUTINY, RESIST, REVOLT
rebellion MUTINY, PUTSCH, REVOLT, SEDITION
rebound DAP, ECHO, CAROM, BOUNCE, RESILE, RICOCHET
rebuff SLAP, SNUB, SPURN, CENSURE, HIGHHAT
rebuke SLAP, CENSURE, REPROVE
recalcitrant WAYWARD, PERVERSE, RENITENT
recant ABJURE, RETRACT
recede EBB, REGRESS, RETREAT
receiver FENCE, RADIO, BAILEE, TRUSTEE
recent NEO, NEW, LATE, NOVEL, MODERN, NEOTERIC
receptacle BIN, BOX, CAN, POT, URN, CASE, FONT, PAIL, TRAY, BASIN, CRATE, ACERRA, BASKET, BUCKET, HAMPER, VESSEL
reception FETE, LEVEE, SALON, DURBAR, SOIREE, ACCUEIL
recess BAY, APSE, NOOK, NICHE, INTERVAL; *see* CUBICLE
recession SLUMP, SETBACK, DOWNTURN
recipient HEIR, DONEE
recital ACCOUNT, CONCERT, MUSICALE
recite SCAN, QUOTE, RECOUNT
reckless MAD, RASH, MADCAP, WANTON, RAMSTAM
reckon ARET, COUNT, GUESS, TALLY, IMPUTE, COMPUTE
reclaim RENEW, REDEEM, REFORM
recline LIE, LEAN, LOLL, COUCH, LOUNGE
recluse HERMIT, ASCETIC, EREMITE, ANCHORET, SOLITARY
recognize OWN, AVOW, ADMIT, GRANT, IDENTIFY, REALIZE
recoil SHY, KICK, COWER, QUAIL, WINCE, RESILE, SHRINK, KICKBACK, RICOCHET
recommend TOUT, ADVISE, COUNSEL
recompense PAY, WAGE, REPAY; *see* REWARD
reconcile ATONE, HARMONIZE
reconnaissance RECCO, RECON, ESPIAL, SURVEY
reconnoiter SPY, SCAN, SCOUT
record CD, LP, LOG, TAB, ACTA, DISC, DISK, FILE, LIST, NOTE, ROLL, TAPE, DIARY, ENTER, ENTRY, FASTI, AGENDA, ANNALS, DOCKET, ENROLL, MINUTE, BLOTTER, DOSSIER, HANSARD, PLATTER, REGISTER
recording DISC, DISK, TAPE, WIRE, PLATTER
recount TELL, RELATE
recover RALLY, SALVE, RECOUP
recovery TROVER, SALVAGE
recreant BASE, FALSE, CRAVEN
recreation SPORT, PASTIME
recruit BOOT, LEVY, DRAFT, RALLY, ENLIST, INDUCT, MUSTER, ROOKIE, DRAFTEE, ENLISTEE, CONSCRIPT
rectifier DIODE

rectify REMEDY, SALVAGE; *see* CORRECT
rector *see* CLERGY
Red Desert NEFUD, ANNAFUD
red dye root CHAY, CHOY
redact EDIT, DRAFT, REVISE
redeem FREE, ATONE, RANSOM
Redeemer GOEL, SAVIOR, MESSIAH, SAVIOUR
reduce DIET, PARE, REEF, SLIM, THIN, SLASH, DERATE, LESSEN, SHRINK, CURTAIL
reduction CUTBACK, MEIOSIS
redwood SEQUOIA
reed instrument *see* WIND INSTRUMENT
reef BAR, CAY, KAY, KEY, ATOLL, LEDGE, SHOAL, SANDBAR
reek FUG, FUME, SMELL
reel PIRN, SPIN, SWAY, TEETER, TOTTER
reeve BAILIFF, STEWARD, OVERSEER
refer CITE, HARP, ADVERT, ALLUDE, ASCRIBE, PERTAIN
referee JUDGE, UMPIRE, ARBITER, OVERMAN
refine PURIFY, CLARIFY, IMPROVE
reflection ECHO, SLUR, GLARE, IMAGE, MUSING
refractor LENS, PRISM, TELESCOPE
refrain BOB, FALA, LALA, DERRY, BURDEN, DESIST, LUDDEN, ABSTAIN, FORBEAR
refrigerator COOLER, ICEBOX, FREEZER
refuge ARK, HAVEN, ASYLUM, HARBOR, SANCTUM, SHELTER
refugee EMIGRE, ESCAPEE, FUGITIVE
refuse COT, POB, COOM, BALK, DENY, LEES, MARC, SCUM, SLAG, COOMB, DRAFF, DROSS, OFFAL, SCRAP, TRASH, RECUSE, SCORIA, RUBBISH
refute REBUT, DISPROVE
regal ROYAL, KINGLY, QUEENLY, STATELY
regale FETE, FEAST, BANQUET
regalia FINERY, INSIGNIA
Regan relative LEAR, GONERIL, CORDELIA
regard GAZE, ESTEEM, RESPECT, CONSIDER
regarding *see* CONCERNING
regimen DIET, RULE, DRILL
regiment ALAI, POLK, PULK, COSSACK
region AREA, BELT, ZONE, CLIME, LOCALE, SECTOR, CLIMATE, PURLIEU
register *see* RECORD
regret RUE, REPENT, DEPLORE
regular STEADY, ORDERLY, UNIFORM
rehearse DRILL, RECITE, PRACTICE
reign RAJ, RULE, SWAY, TERM, GOVERN, REGIME
reign, pert. to REGNAL, REGNANT
reinforce FORTIFY, BUTTRESS
reinstate REVEST, RESTORE
reiterate *see* REPEAT
reject JILT, SPURN, REBUFF, REPULSE
rejoice GLORY, DELIGHT
rejoinder REPLY, ANSWER, RETORT
relapse REVERT, BACKSLIDE
relate REFER, DETAIL, RECITE, NARRATE, PERTAIN, RECOUNT
related (A)KIN, ENATE, AGNATE, ENATIC, GERMAN, COGNATE, GERMANE
relation KIN, SIB, KITH, RATIO, REGARD
relative EME, KIN, SIB, AUNT, ENATE, INLAW, NIECE, AGNATE, PARENT, KINDRED, KINSMAN, SIBLING
relative pronoun WHO, THAT, WHAT, WHICH
relax(ing) EASE, LOOSEN, RELENT, SOFTEN, DETENTE, SLACKEN
relay RACE, AGENT, SERVO, SHIFT, REMUDA, REMOUNT
release LOOSE, REMISE, PUBLISH
relegate EXILE, ASSIGN, BANISH, CONSIGN
relent THAW, MODIFY, SOFTEN
relevant APT, GERMAN, APROPOS, GERMANE
relic CURIO, TOKEN, MEMENTO, VESTIGE
relief AID, BAS, DOLE, FRET, REDRESS
religion CULT, CREED, FAITH, HINDU, ISLAM, PIETY, SHINTO, TAOISM, JUDAISM,

SIKHISM, BUDDHISM, CHRISTIANITY
religious leaders FOX, HUS, EDDY, HUSS, KNOX, BARTH, BOOTH, BUBER, MOODY, PEALE, SMITH, YOUNG, ABBOTT, BECKET, BIDDLE, BUDDHA, CALVIN, COTTON, GRAHAM, LAOTZU, LOYOLA, LUTHER, MATHER, SUNDAY, WESLEY, WOLSEY, AQUINAS, BEECHER, BRUNNER, EDWARDS, FALWELL, NIEBUHR, ROBERTS, RUSSELL, SEABURY, TILLICH, TYNDALL, ZWINGLI, GARRISON, IGNATIUS, MOHAMMED, MUHAMMAD, TALMADGE, WILLIAMS, WYCLIFFE, MCPHERSON
religious order JESUIT, MARIST, TEMPLAR, DOMINICAN, FRANCISCAN
relinquish CEDE, QUIT, DEMIT, WAIVE, YIELD, RESIGN
reliquary APSE, ARCA(E), CHEST, CASKET, SHRINE, MEMORIA
relish DASH, TANG, ZEST, ACHAR, GUSTO, SAVOR; *see* CONDIMENT
reluctant LO(A)TH, AVERSE
rely BANK, LEAN, COUNT, DEPEND
remainder REAR, REST, ARREAR, RESIDUE, UNITATE
remains RUINS, TRACES, CORPSE, CADAVER, VESTIGES
remark MOT, CRACK, SALLY, OBSERVE
remedy FIX, SOP, BALM, CURE, BALSAM, ELIXIR, PHYSIC, CUREALL, NOSTRUM, PANACEA, PLACEBO, ANTIDOTE
remember RECALL, REMIND, RECOLLECT
remiss LAX, SLACK, DILATORY
remit ABATE, RELAX, LESSEN
remnant END, ORT, REST, SHRED, RESIDUE; *see* DREGS
remote (A)FAR, ALOOF, DISTANT
remove GUT, DOFF, OUST, ELOIN, CANCEL, DELETE, DEPOSE, DISBAR, ELOIGN(E), IMPEACH
remunerate PAY, REWARD, RECOMPENSE
Remus brother ROMULUS
renal NEPHRI(TI)C
rend RIVE, TEAR, WREST
render RIVE, DEPICT, CLARIFY, DELIVER, PERFORM, TRANSLATE
rendezvous DATE, TRYST
renegade TRAITOR, APOSTATE; *see* DESERTER
renew RESUME, REFRESH, RESTORE
renounce RENAY, ABJURE, REJECT, RENEGE, ABDICATE, ABNEGATE
renown NOTE, PRESTIGE; *see* FAME
rent LET, RIP, HIRE, TEAR, TORN, LEASE, SPLIT, AVENGE
repair IMP, DARN, MEND
repartee QUIP, SALLY, BANTER, RETORT, RIPOST(E)
repast MEAL, LUNCH, SNACK, TIFFIN, COLLATION, REFECTION
repay MEED, REFUND, REQUITE
repeal ANNUL, REVOKE, RESCIND
repeat BIS, DIN(G), ECHO, HARP, RAME, SEGNO, ENCORE, ITERATE, REPRISE, REITERATE
repel PARRY, REBUFF, REJECT
repent RUE, GRIEVE, CREEPING
repetition ROTE, PLOCE, ENCORE, MERISM, ANAPHORA
replace RESTORE, SUPPLANT
replete FULL, RIFE, SATED, GORGED
reply ANSWER, REJOIN, RETORT
report POP, BANG, FAME, BRUIT, ONDIT, CAHIER, HANSARD, BULLETIN
reporter *see* NEWSPERSON
repose EASE, REST, CONFIDE
repository SAFE, CHEST, VAULT
represent ENACT, DEPICT, PORTRAY, DESCRIBE
representative AGENT, ENVOY, PROXY, DEPUTY, FACTOR, LEGATE, NUNCIO, DELEGATE
repress CHECK, CRUSH, QUELL, SUBDUE
reprieve GRACE, DESPITE
reprimand BAWL, SCOLD, REPROVE
reprisal MARQUE, REVENGE
reproach RACA, RATE, BLAME, TAUNT, BERATE, CENSURE

reproductive body EGG, SPERM, GAMETE
reprove FLAY, SCOLD, BERATE, CENSURE
reptile HISSER, SAURIA, CRAWLER, CREEPER, DIAPSID, LORICATA, LORICATE, SQUAMATA; *see* TURTLE, SNAKE, VIPER, CROCODILE, LIZARD
reptiles, pert. to SAURIAN, OPHIDIAN, VIPERINE
Republic author PLATO
Republican Party GOP
repudiate DENY, DISOWN, RECANT
repulse REPEL, REBUFF
repulsive UGLY, ODIOUS, FULSOME
reputation NAME, IZZAT, ESTEEM; *see* FAME
request ASK, PLEA, BESEECH, ROGATION
requirement NEED, REQUISITE
rescind ANNUL, CANCEL, RECALL, REPEAL
rescue FREE, SAVE, RANSOM
research STUDY, INQUIRY
resemblance IMAGE, LIKENESS
resentment CHOLER, RANCOR, DUDGEON, UMBRAGE
reserve FUND, STOCK, STORE, BACKLOG, NESTEGG
reservoir SUMP, STORE, CENOTE, CISTERN
residence ABODE, DOMICILE
resident CIT, ITE, INMATE, INTERN, TENANT, CITIZEN, INTERNE
residue ASH, SLAG, DREGS, WASTE
resign QUIT, DEMIT, ABANDON
resin ALK, GUM, LAC, ALKYD, AMBER, ANIME, COPAL, ELEMI, GUGAL, JALAP, KAURI, MYRRH, PITCH, BALSAM, DAMMAR, ESERIN, MASTIC, STORAX, BURMITE, CAMBOGE, EXUDATE, GALIPOT, CAMBOGE, LADANUM, ELECTRUM, GALLIPOT, LABDANUM, SANDARAC
resist DEFY, FEND, OPPOSE
resolute FIXED, DOGGED
resort SPA, USE, REFER, ASYLUM
resound BOOM, ECHO, PEAL, RING
resource(s) FUNDS, MEANS, ASSETS, DEVICE, CAPITAL
respect HONOR, ESTEEM, REVERE
respite LULL; *see* INTERVAL
respond ACT, FEEL, RISE, REACT
responsibility DUTY, ONUS
rest LIE, SIT, EASE, LEAN, PAUSE, PERCH, GAFFLE, REPOSE, SIESTA, CAESURA, SURPLUS
restaurant SPA, CAFE, DINER, GRILL, BISTRO, BUFFET, EATERY, ONEARM, AUTOMAT, BEANERY, PIZZERIA
restaurant employee CHEF, COOK, BUSBOY, WAITER, MAITRED, WAITRESS
resthouse *see* INN
restive BALKY, MULISH, UNEASY, UNRULY, SKITTISH
restless NERVOUS, RESTIVE
restorative TONIC, BRACER, ANODYNE
restore FIX, HEAL, STET, REVIVE
restrain CURB, REIN, STAY, CHECK, DETER, STINT, ENJOIN, TETHER
restrict CRAMP, LIMIT, CENSOR, COERCE, CONFINE
restricted INSULAR, EXCLUSIVE
result ISSUE, UPSHOT, OUTCOME
resume RENEW, PRECIS, SUMMARY, ABSTRACT
retain HIRE, KEEP, SAVE, EMPLOY
retaliate REPAY, REQUITE
retaliation TALION, REPRISAL
retard BRAKE, CHECK, STUNT; *see* DELAY
retch GAG, KECK, VOMIT
retina part ROD, CONE, FOVEA, MACULA
retinue COURT, MEINY, STAFF, SUITE, TRAIN, ESCORT, STABLE, CORTEGE
retire(d) ABED, QUIT, RECEDE, EMERITUS
retiring SHY, MODEST, RESERVED
retort QUIP, VIAL, SALLY, RIPOST, ALEMBIC, RIPOSTE, REPARTEE
retouch PATCH, DOCTOR
retract DISOWN, RECANT, DISAVOW

retreat DEN, NEST, NOOK, RECEDE, RETIRAL; *see* REFUGE
retribution NEMESIS, REVENGE
retrieve REGAIN, RECOVER, RESTORE
retrograde EBB, LAPSE, RECEDE, RELAPSE, RETREAT, REVERSE
return(s) RECUR, VOTES, YIELD, ANSWER, PROFIT, REVERT, RIPOST, RESTORE, RIPOSTE, EXCHANGE
returning REDIENT
reveal AIR, BARE, EXPOSE, IMPART, UNVEIL, DIVULGE
reveille DIAN, LEVET
revelry ORGY, DEBAUCH
revenge TALION, REQUITE, VENDETTA
revenue ANNAT, RENTAL, INCOME, ANNATES
reverberate ECHO, BOUNCE, REECHO, RESOUND
reverberating REBOANT(IC)
reverie DREAM, MUSING, FANTASY
reverse VERSO, REVOKE, SETBACK, OPPOSITE, TRANSPOSE
reversion ATAVISM, ESCHEAT
review PARADE, REVISE, SURVEY, JOURNAL, CRITIQUE
revile RAIL, DEBASE, VILIFY
revise EDIT, AMEND, REDACT, UPDATE
revive RALLY, RESURGE
revoke ADEEM, RENEGE, REPEAL
revolt RISE, REBEL, MUTINY, DISGUST, NAUSEATE
revolution REV, RPM, COUP, GYRE, TURN, CYCLE
revolutionist LENIN, MARAT, ANARCH, CASTRO, FENIAN, PESTEL, SETTIMO
revolve BIRL, PIRL, ROLL, SPIN, TURN, TWIRL, WHIRL, CIRCLE, GYRATE, ROTATE
reward CUP, TIP, UTU, PRIZE, GUERDON; *see* AWARD
Rhea relative GE, GAEA, HERA, ZEUS, HADES, CRONOS, URANUS, DEMETER, POSEIDON
Rhine tributary ILL, AARE, ERFT, LAHN, MAIN, NAHE, RUHR, SIEG, LIPPE, NECKAR, MOSELLE
rhinoceros BADAK, BORELE, KEITLOA
Rhode Island information *see p. 308*
Rhodes statue COLOSSUS
rheumatism LUMBAGO
Rhodesia ZIMBABWE
rhyme VERSE, CRAMBO
rhythm BEAT, LILT, TIME, METRE, PULSE, SWING, CADENCE
rib KID, COSTA, RIDGE, TEASE
ribbed WALED, COSTATE
ribbon TENE, COQUE, CORDON, FILLET, LISERE
ribs, pert. to COSTAL, COSTATE
rice BORO, SELA, ARROZ, CHITS, DARAC, PADDY, PALAY
rice dish PILAF, RISOTTO
rich OPULENT, WEALTHY, AFFLUENT
rich person HAVE, DIVES, MIDAS, NABOR, NAWAB, PLUTO, CROESUS
ricochet SKIP, CAROM, REBOUND
rid FREE, REAM, CLEAR, PURGE
riddle REE, SIFT, REBUS, PEPPER, LOGOGRIPH; *see* PUZZLE
rider FARE, CLAUSE, JOCKEY
ridge(s) BILO, GYRI, KAME, KEEL, OSAR, RAND, SPUR, WALE, WELT, ARETE, CREST, ESKER, LANDE, OESAR, PARMA, RAPHE, SERRA, SPINE, STRIA, CARINA, CUESTA, RIDEAU, SIERRA
ridicule GUY, PAN, TWIT, MOMUS, BANTER; *see* MOCK
rifle STRIP, DESPOIL; *see* GUN
rift GAP, RENT, CLEFT, BREACH, SCHISM, FISSURE
rig FIT, CART, GEAR, EQUIP, TACKLE
rigging part MAST, ROPE, SAIL, SPAR, YARD, CHAIN, SHROUD
right CLAIM, DROIT, RECTO, TITLE, DEXTER, LICENSE, REDRESS
right-handed DEXTRAL
rigid SET, FIRM, HARD, STIFF
Rigoletto character BORSA, GILDA, CEPRANO, MARULLO
Rigoletto composer VERDI
rigorous STERN, STRUT, SEVERE
rim LIP, EDGE, ORLE, BRINK, CHIMB, CHIME, CHINE, FELLY, SOMMA, VERGE, FELLOE, FLANGE

rind HULL, HUSK, PEEL, SKIN, SHELL
ring(s) CRIC, HOOP, LOOP, PEAL, TOLL, ARENA, CLINK, KNELL, LUNET, CIRCLE, GASKET, GINNAL, SIGNET, TERRET, TERRIT, CIRCLET, ANNULET, GROMMET
Ring character ERDA, LOGE, MIME, HAGEN, WOTAN, FAFNER, FASOLT, FRICKA, HUNDING, ALBERICH, SIEGMUND, SIEGFRIED, SIEGLINDE, BRUNNHILDE
Ring composer WAGNER
ring part CHATON; *see* SETTING
ring-shaped ANNULAR, CIRCINATE
riot MELEE, EMEUTE, UPROAR
rip REND, RIVE, TEAR, SPLIT
ripe(n) AUGUST; *see* MATURE
riposte RETORT, THRUST
ripple LAP, PURL, RIFF, WAVE, RIFFLE, WAVELET
rise SOAR, REBEL, ASCENT
risible DROLL, GELASTIC
risk DARE, PERIL, CHANCE, HAZARD, VENTURE
risqué RACY, OFFCOLOR
rite(s) PAX, CULT, FORM, AGAPE, SACRA, ABDEST, LITANY, NOVENA, RITUAL, LITURGY, CEREMONY; *see* SACRAMENT
rival FOE, EQUAL, OPPONENT
river REE, RIO, BAHR, ILOG; *see p. 303*
river, Biblical ULAI, ARNON, DRACO, HABOR, JABBOK, JORDAN, KISHON, TIGRIS
river mouth BOCA, LADE, DELTA, ESTUARY
river, pert. to a AMNIC
river, underworld STYX, LETHE, ACHERON, COCYTUS, PHLEGETHON
riverbank, of a RIPARIAN
riverbed WADI, WADY, CHANNEL
Riviera city NICE, CANNES
rivulet RILL, BROOK, RUNNEL
road RTE, VIA, WAY, DRUN, ITER, LANE, PATH, PIKE, AGGER, ROUTE, TARMAC, FREEWAY, HIGHWAY, PARKWAY, THRUWAY, AUTOBAHN, SPEEDWAY, EXPRESSWAY
road, pert. to VIATIC(AL)
roam *see* WANDER
roar BELLOW; *see* NOISE, CRY
roast PAN, PARCH, BANTER, CALCINE
rob REAVE, RIFLE, FLEECE
robber YEGG, THIEF, BANDIT, DACOIT, BRIGAND, CATELAN
robe PALL; *see* DRESS
robin RUDDOCK
Robin Hood friend TUCK, WILL, MARIAN
Robinson Crusoe author DEFOE
Robinson Crusoe man FRIDAY
robot GOLEM, AUTOMATON
robots, play about RUR
robust HALE, LUSTY, STOUT, WALLY
rock CRAG, LAVA, REEL, SIMA, SWAY, TUFA, TUFF, WHIN, CHALK, CHERT, CLINT, CRETA, SHALE, SHIST, SLATE, TALUS, APLITE, BASALT, DACITE, GNEISS, MARBLE, SCHIST, SCYLLA, TOTTER, DIORITE, GRANITE, HAPLITE, LIMESTONE; *see* MINERAL, STONE
rock salt EMOL, AMOLE, HALITE
rocket ABM, ABLE, BABY, FROG, GIRD, ICBM, IRBM, JUNO, MIRV, MRBM, NIKE, SARK, SCUD, SEGO, SERB, SKUA, THOR, ZEUS, AGENA, ATLAS, DELTA, GENIE, GOLEM, KOMET, LANCE, MIRAK, SASIN, SCARP, SCOUT, SKEAN, TITAN, ARIANE, CRUISE, EUROPA, FALCON, GEMINI, ROHINI, SANDAL, SATURN, SAVAGE, SAWFLY, SPRINT, BULLPUP, CENTAUR, DIAMANT, JUPITER, POLARIS, SADDLER, SAPWOOD, SKYLARK, SPARROW, SPARTAN, TERRIER, VICTORY, CENTAURE, CORPORAL, LACROSSE, HOUNDDOG, PERSHING, POSEIDON, REDSTONE, VANGUARD, MINUTEMAN, BLACKARROW, HONESTJOHN, LITTLEJOHN, SIDEWINDER
rockfish BASS, REINA, RASHER, TAMBOR, STRIPER, BOCACCIO
rocky SHAKY, CRAGGY
rod BAR, CUE, AXLE, CANE, POLE, SPIT, WAND, OSIER,

PERCH, STAFF, FERULE, TOGGLE; *see* GUN
rodent GNAWER; *see* HARE, RAT, SQUIRREL, PORCUPINE
roe OVA, MILT, SPAWN, CAVIAR
rogue CAD, IMP, WAG, SCUM, KNAVE, SCAMP, PICARO, RASCAL, VARLET, CAITIFF, HELLION, SHARPER
roguish SLY, ARCH, PAWKY
roister BRAG, REVEL, SPREE
Roland companion OLIVER
Roland foe GAN, GANO, GANELON, FERRAGUS
Roland's horn OLIVANT
role BIT, LEAD, PART, HEAVY, WALKON, INGENUE, FUNCTION
roll BAP, BUN, ROB, WAD, BOLT, FURL, LIST, ROTA, TOSS, BAGEL, BIALY, SLATE, ROSTER, SCROLL, TATTOO, CAROTTE
roller *see* WHEEL
Roman LATIN, ITALIAN, QUIRITE
Roman gods *see p. 317*
Roman hill CAELIAN, VIMINAL, AVENTINE, PALATINE, QUIRINAL, ESQUILINE, CAPITOLINE
Roman measure PES, JUGA, URNA, ACTUS, CLIMA, CUBIT, UNCIA, CULEUS, DOLIUM, GRAOUS, MODIUS, PALMUS, PASSUS, SALTUS, VERSUS, CYATHUS, DIGITUS
Roman money AS, AES, SEMIS, DINDER, SOLIDUS, DENARIUS, SESTERCE
Roman, prominent NERO, NUMA, OTHO, GALBA, NERVA, SULLA, TITUS, DECIUS, GALLUS, JULIAN, JULIUS, SCIPIO, TRAJAN, HADRIAN, SEVERUS, AUGUSTUS, CALIGULA, CLAUDIUS, COMMODUS, DOMITIAN, PERTINAX, TIBERIUS
Roman weight AS, BES, LIBRA, UNCIA, DUELLA, SEXTULA, SOLIDUS
romance WOO, GEST, COURT, FABLE, GESTE, AFFAIR, FICTION
Romance language *see* ITALIC
romance-teller ANTERI
Romanian money BAN, LEI, LEU, LEY
Rome conqueror ALARIC, GAISERIC
Rome founder REMUS, ROMULUS
Romeo and Juliet character *see p. 314*
romp PLAY, FROLIC
Romulus' brother/victim REMUS
rood CRUCIFIX; *see* CROSS
roof HIP, CURB, FISH, HOWE, GABLE, PRATT, WARREN, GAMBREL, MANSARD, KINGPOST, QUEENPOST; *see* DOME
roof part EAVE, CLEAT, JOIST, RIDGE, SPRAG, STRUT, TRUSS, FILLET, PURLIN, RAFTER, VALLEY
roofing RAG, TILE, SLATE, THATCH, PANTILE, SHINGLE
rook CROW, CHEAT, CASTLE
room ALA, DEN, EWRY, LOFT, PLAT, SALA, ATRIA, EWERY, OECUS, PLATT, SPACE, ATRIUM, CHAMBER, ROTUNDA
roost SIT, NEST, LIGHT, PERCH, ALIGHT, GARRET
rooster, young COCKEREL
root BASE, EDDO, ETYM, GRUB, STEM, TARO, IMBED, ORRIS, RADIX, TUBER, WATAP, ETYMON, FIBRIL, MANIOC, RADISH, RAMSON, SENEGA, CASSAVA, GINSENG, RADICAL, RHATANY; *see* CHEER
rootlet RADICEL, RADICLE
roots YAM, BEET, CHAY, CHOY, EDDO, GABE, GABI, JUCA, KALO, TARO, YAMP, YUCA, CHAYA, CHOYA, RAMPS, TANIA, TANYA, YAMPA, ARALIA, CARDON, CARROT, CASAVA, GINGER, RADISH, TANIER, TANNIA, TANYAH, TURNIP, CARDOON, CASSAVA, PARSNIP, RAMPION, RHUBARB, SALSIFY
rope CORD, JEFF, LAZO, BIGHT, BRACE, LASSO, LONGE, REATA, REEVE, RIATA, LARIAT, TETHER, CORDAGE, MARLINE
rope fiber *see* FIBER
rope, nautical FOX, TYE, FAST, LIFT, SPAN, STAY, TACK,

VANG, WAPP, BRAIL, EARING, GASKET, HAWSER, RATLIN, SENNIT, SHROUD, LANIARD, LANYARD, PAINTER, RATLINE, SNOTTER
Rosamunda's king ALBOIN
rosary BEADS, CHAPLET, BEADROLL
rosary bead AVE, GAUD(Y)
rose GUL, GEUM, ROSA, DRYAS, DEWDROP, RAMBLER, SPIRAEA, HAWTHORN
rose of Sharon ALTHEA
rosewood MOLOMPI
rosolic acid AURIN(E)
Rossini opera BARBER, OTELLO
rostrum DAIS, PROW, PULPIT
rot RET, DECAY, SPOIL, PUTREFY
rotate *see* REVOLVE
rotating piece CAM, AXIS, AXLE, REEL, ARBOR, ROTOR, WHEEL, BOBBIN, DASHER, MANDREL, SPINDLE
rotten RANK, FETIC, PUTRID
roué *see* RAKE
rough CURT, RUDE, BUMPY, CRUDE, GRUFF, HARSH, HILLY, COARSE, HUBBLY, RUGGED, UNEVEN
roughness LIPPER
roulette term BAS, NOIR, PAIR, PASSE, ROUGE, IMPAIR, MILIEU
round ROTA, ORBED, CYCLE, SALVO, PERIOD, ROTULA, ROTUND, GLOBATE, GLOBOID
Round Table *see p. 331*
roundabout AMBAGE, DETOUR, DEVIOUS, CIRCUITOUS
roundup RODEO
rouse STIR, WAKEN, BESTIR
rout MOB, FLIGHT, DEBACLE
route WAY, COURSE, ITINERARY
routine RUT, ROTE, WONT
rove *see* WANDER
row OAR, RANK, TIER, FILE, LINE, SCULL; *see* FIGHT
rowdy BHOY, THUG, RUFFIAN
rowlock THOLE, PUPPET
Roxane's lover CYRANO
Roy Rogers's horse TRIGGER
Roy Rogers's wife (DALE) EVANS
royal REGAL, AUGUST, KINGLY, QUEENLY, IMPERIAL
royalty FEE, ALII
rub BUFF, CHAFE, SHINE, ABRADE, SCRAPE, BURNISH
Rubáiyát author OMAR, KHAYYAM
rubber GUM, PARA, BUTYL, CEARA, LATEX, CAUCHO, ERASER, GALOSH, EBONITE, ELASTIC, GUAYULE
rubbish ROT, JUNK, GULCH, DROSS, SCREE, STENT, DEBRIS, NONSENSE; *see* REFUSE
ruby SARD, BALAS, SARDIUS
rudder HELM, TILLER
ruddy RED, ROSY, SANGUINE
rude GRUFF, HARSH, ROUGH, COARSE, RUGGED
rudiment ABC, GERM, ANLAGE
rue RUTA, REGRET, DEPLORE
ruff REE(VE), RUCHE, TRUMP, COLLAR, FRAISE, TIPPET
ruffer NAPPER
ruffian THUG, BULLY, HOOLIGAN
ruffle MUSS, SHIR, CRIMP, FRILL, RUCHE, SHIRR, PUCKER
rug AGRA, BAKU, KUBA, CHILA, HERAT, KAZAK, KILIM, KULAH, LADIK, MECCA, MELAS, MELES, MOSUL, NAMDA, NUMDA, SARUK, SENNA, SUMAK, TAPET, TEKKE, USHAK, YOMUD, YORUK, AFGHAN, GELEEM, HERATI, KASHAN, KIRMAN, MOGHAN, NAMMAD, OUSHAK, RUNNER, SAROUK, SHIRAZ, TADRIZ, WILTON, BERGAMA, BERGAMO, BOKHARA, DERBEND, DRUGGET, FERAHAN, GIORDES, GUENDJE, HAMADAN, INGRAIN, ISFAHAN, SHIRVAN, AKHISSAR, BRUSSELS, CAGESTAN, FERAGHAN, GHIORDES, KABISTAN, KARABAGH, LESGHIAN, SERABEND, ANATOLIAN, AXMINSTER, BROADLOOM, CAUCASIAN, KHOROSSAN, KURDISTAN, SAMARKAND
rugby term TRY, MARK, FIVES, PITCH, SCRUM, TOUCH, NOSIDE, TACKLE, HEELING, KNOCKON, SCRUMMAGE
ruin DOOM, HAVOC, WRACK, DEBRIS, DESTROY

rule LAW, CODE, NORM, CANON, HABIT, PRECEPT, DOMINEER; *see* REIGN
ruler CZAR, KING, SHAH, TSAR, CALIF, MPRET, NEGUS, NIZAM, CALIPH, FERULE, KAISER, SULTAN, CZARINA, TSARINA, MONARCH, SULTANA
Rumanian *see* ROMANIAN
rumen CUD, PAUNCH, STOMACH
ruminant COW, YAK, DEER, GOAT, BISON, CAMEL, LLAMA, SHEEP, ALPACA, GIRAFFE, ANTELOPE
ruminate CHEW, MULL, PONDER
rumor FAMA, BRUIT, ONDIT, GOSSIP, NORATE, REPORT, HEARSAY
rump CROUP, BREECH, BUTTOCKS
rumple MUSS, TOUSLE, DISHEVEL
run HIE, FLOW, LEAK, SCUD, BROOK, ELOPE, PANIC, SPRINT, OPERATE
run across MEET, ENCOUNTER
run aground MOOR, BEACH, STRAND
run in ARREST, INSERT
rung STEP, SPOKE, STAVE, RUNDLE
runner BLADE, MILER, RACER, SCARF, STOLO(N), COURIER
runway RAMP, CHUTE, STRIP, TRAIL, TARMAC, AIRSTRIP
rural RUSTIC, BUCOLIC, GEORGIC, AGRARIAN, PASTORAL
ruse DODGE, TRICK, ARTIFICE
rush HASTE, HURRY, ONSET, SPATE, SPEED, SPURT, SURGE, HASTEN, HURTLE
Russia(n) RED, SOVIET, MUSCOVY
Russian language *see* SLAVIC, CAUCASIAN
Russian measure FUT, LOF, DUIM, FASS, STOF, OSMIN, STOOF, VERST, ARSHIN, CHARKA, PALETZ, SAGENE, TCHAST, ARCHINE, GARNETZ, TOTCHKA
Russian money ALTIN, KOPEK, RUBLE, KOPECK, POLTINA, IMPERIAL
Russian, prominent IVAN, LVOV, PAUL, BASIL, FEDOR, LENIN, PETER, ALEXIS, STALIN, MICHAEL, MOLOTOV, ROMANOV, TROTSKY, BREZHNEV, BULGANIN, KERENSKY, MALENKOV, ANDROPOV, NICHOLAS, ALEXANDER, CATHERINE, CHERNENKO, ELIZABETH, GORBACHEV, KHRUSHCHEV
Russian weight LOT, PUD, DOLA, FUNT, POOD, KAMIAN
rust AERUGO, CORRODE, OXIDIZE, VERDIGRIS
Rustam relative ZAL, SOHRAB, RUDABAH
rustic BOOR, CARL, HICK, RUBE, CARLE, RURAL, SWAIN, YOKAL, SYLVAN, YEOMAN, BUCOLIC, PEASANT, AGRESTIC
rustler ABACTOR, ABIGEUS
rut HEAT, TRACK, FURROW, GROOVE
Ruth relative BOAZ, OBED, NAOMI, EILEEN, MAHLON
Rwandan language FRENCH, SWAHILI
rye ERGOT, DARNEL; *see* CEREAL, GYPSY

S

S-shaped SIGMATE, SIGMOID
saber (Y)ATAGHAN; *see* SWORD
sac POD, CYST, ASCUS, BURSA, VENTER
saccharine source TAR
sack BAG, LOOT, GUNNY, POUCH, RAVAGE, PLUNDER
sacking JUTE, GUNNY, BURLAP
sacrament MASS, RITE, BAPTISM, PENANCE, UNCTION, EUCHARIST, MATRIMONY, COMMUNION, CONFIRMATION
sacred HOLY, PIOUS, HALLOWED, INVIOLATE, SACROSANCT
sacred object ICON, ZOGO, RELIC
sacred place ALTIS, ABATON, HIERON, SHRINE
sacrifice IMMOLATE, LIBATION, OBLATION, OFFERING
sacrificial offering HIERA, SPHAGION

sacrificial rite SOMA
sacrilegious IMPIOUS, PROFANE
sad BAD, BLUE, MESTO, DISMAL, DOLENT, TRISTE
saddle APAREJO, PILLION
saddle part PAD, HORN, CINCH, GIRTH, MANTA, PANEL, SKIRT, CANTLE, CORONA, JOCKEY, LATIGO, PANNEL, POMMEL, GAMBADO, STIRRUP, SUBADERO
saddlebag ALFORJA
sadness DOLOR, PATHOS
safari TREK, CARAVAN, EXPEDITION
safe SOUND, VAULT, COFFER, SECURE, STRONGBOX
safe-conduct PASS, COWLE, PASSPORT
safekeeping CUSTODY, STORAGE
safety pin CLASP, FIBULA
sag SINK, WILT, DROOP, DECLINE
saga MYTH; *see* EPIC
sagacious WISE, ASTUTE, SAPIENT, PERCEPTIVE
sage SOLON, NESTOR; *see* SCHOLAR
Sagebrush State NV, NEV(ADA)
sail JIB, LUG, KITE, LUFF, VELA, GLIDE, ROYAL, CRUISE, LATEEN, MIZZEN, SPANKER
sail part TIE, BUNT, CLEW, FOOT, HEAD, IRON, LIFT, REEF, WHIP, YOKE, HORSE, LEECH, SHEET, EARING, CRINGLE, BUNTLINE
sailboat *see* SHIP
sailor GOB, TAR, SALT, LASCAR, MARINE, SEABEE, SEADOG, SEAMAN, MARINER, MATELOT
saint ST, PIR, STE, HOLY, ALBAN, ALVAR, ARHAT, CANONIZE; *see* PATRON
St. Andrew's cross SALTIRE
St. Anthony's cross TAU
St. Elmo's fire HELENA, CORPOSANT
St. Francis's birthplace ASSISI
St. Nicholas SANTA
St. Vitus' dance CHOREA
saintly HOLY, PURE, PIOUS
sake END, CAUSE, BENEFIT
salad SLAW, GREENS, SALLET, LETTUCE
salamander ASK, EFT, OLM, NEWT, ASKER, SIREN, TWEEG, TRITON, AXOLOTL, CAUDATA, DOGFISH, PROTEUS, URODELA, AMPHIUMA, MUDDEVIL, MUDPUPPY, NECTURUS, TRITURUS, WATERDOG, HELLBENDER; *see* LIZARD
salary PAY, SCREW, WAGES, STIPEND, EARNINGS
sale SELLOUT; *see* AUCTION
salesman AGENT, CLERK, VENDOR, DRUMMER
saline BRACK, SALTY, BRACKISH
saliva SPIT, RHEUM, SPITTLE
saliva, pert. to SIALIC
sallow OSIER, PASTY, WILLOW
sally QUIP, RAID, ERUPT, FORAY, SORTIE, RIPOSTE
salmon(-like fish) AYU, LAX, CHUM, COHO, DORE, JACK, KELT, KETA, MASU, PENK, PIKE, PINK, CISCO, COHOE, HADDO, HOLIA, HUCHO, LENOK, SMELT, SUEUR, UMBRA, ALEVIN, BAGGIT, CAPLIN, CHIVEY, HUCHEN, INANGA, KIPPER, SAMLET, AULOPID, CAPELAN, CAPELIN, CHINOOK, GWYNIAD, HOUTING, ICEFISH, OOLACAN, QUINNAT, REDFISH, SKEGGER, SOCKEYE, UMBRINE, CAPELING, EULACHAN, GRAYLING, GRYNIARD, LOOSEJAW, PICKEREL, MUDMINNOW, VIPERFISH; *see* PIKE, TROUT
salmon, young PARR, SMOLT, GRILSE
Salome relative HEROD(IAS)
salon HALL, LEVEE, PARLOR, GALLERY
saloon BAR, DIVE, SEDAN; *see* TAVERN
salt SAL, NACL, BORAX, BRINE, SOUSE, HALITE; *see* SAILOR
salt factory SALTERN, SALTERY
salt, pert. to HALOID, SALINE
salt pond LICK, CHOTT, SHOTT, SALINA
saltpeter NITER, NITRE
salty RACY, BRACK, BRINY, SPICY
salutation AVE, HAIL, ALOH, TOAST, ACHARA, SALAAM, SHALOM
salute BOW, DIP, TIP, HAIL, GREET, SALVO

Salvation Army founder BOOTH
salve BALM, ANOINT, CERATE, LOTION, UNGUENT, OINTMENT
salvia CHIA, SAGE, CLARY
salvo SHOT, BURST, ROUND, PROVISO
same ILK, IDEM, DITTO
Samoyed language TAVGI, YURAK, KAMASIN, YENISEI
sample POLL, MODEL, TASTE, SWATCH, PATTERN
Samson deathplace GAZA
Samson's lover DELILAH
Samuel relative JOEL, ABIAH, HANNAH
Samuel's victim AGAG
sanctify BLESS, HALLOW, PURIFY
sanction BAN, AMEN, FIAT, OKAY, ASSENT, FIRMAN, RATIFY
sanctuary BEMA, FANE, NAOS, BAMAH, HAVEN, ADYTUM, REFUGE, SHRINE
sand GRIT, PAAR, BEACH, GRAVEL
sand hill(s) AREG, DENE, DUNE
sandal CALIGA, PATTEN, FLIPFLOP, GUARACHE, HUARACHE, HUARACHO
sandalwood ALGUM, ALMUG, SANTAL
sandbar *see* REEF
sandpiper KNOT, QUIS, RUFF, STIB, REEVE, STINT, TEREK, AVOCET, DUNLIN, OXLING, REDLEG, TEETER, BROWNIE, TATTLER, WOODHEN, PEETWEET, WOODCOCK
sandpiper genus TRINGA
sandstone GRIT, WACKE, ARKOSE
sandstorm SAMUM, HABOOB, SAMIEL, SIMOOM
sandwich BLT, HERO, HO(A)GIE, GRINDER, POORBOY, TORPEDO, SUBMARINE
sandy GRITTY, ARENOSE, SABULOUS
sane LUCID, SOBER, RATIONAL
sang-froid COOL, POISE
sanguinary GORY, BLOODY
sanguine RUDDY, ARDENT, BLOODY, CONFIDENT
sanitary CLEAN, HYGIENIC
Sanskrit PALI, URDU, HINDI, VEDIC, ORIYA, BIHARI, LAHNDA, NEPALI, ROMANY, SINDHI, BENGALI, KONKANI, MARATHI, PUNJABI, ASSAMESE, GUJARATI, PRAKRITS, SINGHALESE; *see* INDIC
sap DIG, COSH, FOOL, DRAIN, DUMMY, FLUID, JUICE, WEAKEN
sapodilla ACANA, CHICO, MAMEY, BUSTIC, MAMMEE, SAPOTA, SAPOTE
sapor GUSTO, SAVOR, TASTE
Sappho's island LESBOS
Saracen ARAB, MOOR, MOSLEM
Sarah relative ISAAC, ABRAHAM
Sarah's handmaid HAGAR
sarcasm IRONY, JEERS, SATIRE
sarcastic IRONIC, CAUSTIC, MORDANT, SATIRIC
sardine PILCHARD
Sarpedon relative ZEUS, MINOS, EUROPA
sash OBI, BAND, CASING, GIRDLE
Saskatchewan information *see p. 306*
Satan ABADDON, AHRIMAN, APOLLYON, MEPHISTO; *see* DEVIL
satellite, artificial ECS, OTS, ANIK, AZUR, ECHO, GOES, KIKU, LUNA, MARS, SAGE, SPOT, ZOND, AEROS, ARIEL, BLOCK, EKRAN, LUNIK, MIDAS, RELAY, SAMOS, SOYUZ, TAIYO, TIROS, TRIAD, UHURU, COSMOS, FERRET, METEOR, NIMBUS, PALAPA, POLYOT, RADUGA, SATCOM, SEASAT, SKYNET, SYNCOM, WESTAR, COMSTAR, BIGBIRD, COURIER, GLOBCOM, LANDSAT, MOLNIYA, NAVSTAR, PEGASUS, SOUNDER, SPUTNIK, TELSTAR, TRANSIT, GORIZONT, PROSPERO, EARLYBIRD, DISCOVERER, INTERCOSMOS; *see* SPACECRAFT
satellites of Jupiter IO, PAN, HERA, LEDA, CARME, ELARA, HADES, METIS, THEBE, EUROPA, HESTIA, SINOPE, ANANICE, DEMETER, HIMALIA, LYSITHEA, ADRASTEA, AMALTHEA, CALLISTO, GANYMEDE, PASIPHAE, POSEIDON

satellites of Mars DEIMOS, PHOBOS
satellites of Neptune NEREID, TRITON
satellites of Saturn RHEA, DIONE, JANUS, MIMAS, TITAN, PHOEBE, TETHYS, CALYPSO, IAPETUS, TELESTO, HYPERION, ENCELADUS
satellites of Uranus ARIEL, OBERON, MIRANDA, TITANIA, UMBRIEL
satiate *see* CLOY
satire IRONY, RIDICULE
satirical WRY, IRONIC, CAUSTIC
satirist POPE, SWIFT, BUTLER, HORACE, LUCIAN, OLDHAM, BOILEAU, JUVENAL, MOLIERE, FIELDING, LUCILIUS, VOLTAIRE
satisfaction CRO, UTU, AMENDS
satisfy MEET, SERVE, FULFIL(L)
saturate SOP, SOAK, IMBUE, STEEP, DRENCH, SEETHE
Saturday source SATURN
Saturn relative OPS, CYBELE, JUPITER
saturnine GLUM, GRAVE, GLOOMY, MOROSE
satyr FAUN, PANISC, SILENUS
sauce SOY, ALEC, CHILI, CURRY, GARUM, MELBA, CATSUP, GANSEL, MORNAY, KETCHUP, MARENGO, SOUBISE, SUPREME, TABASCO, TARTARE, VELOUTE, BARBECUE, BECHAMEL, DRESSING, MARINARA, MATELOTE, MEUNIERE, REMOLADE, BEARNAISE, MACEDOINE, REMOULADE, WORCESTER
saucy PERT, BRASH, IMPUDENT
Saudi-Arabian *see also* ARABIAN
Saudi-Arabian money POUND, RIYAL
Saudi-Arabian ruler FAHD, SAUD, FAISAL, KHALID, IBNSAUD
Saudi relative NER, KISH, ABIEL, JONATHAN
saunter AMBLE, STROLL, LOITER
sausage FRANK, WURST, HOTDOG, SALAMI, WIENER, BOLOGNA, PUDDING, SAVELOW, CERVELAT
savage FELL, FERAL, YAHOO
savant *see* SCHOLAR
save BUT, HOARD, LAYBY, SPARE, STINT, REDEEM, RESCUE
saving(s) ESTATE, EXCEPT, FRUGAL
savory SAPID, SIPID, TASTY, YUMMY, PIQUANT
saw RIB, ADAGE, EDGER, MAXIM, MOTTO, SERRA, COPING, SAYING, TREPAN, CROSSCUT
sawhorse TRESTLE
sawlike part(s) SERRA(E)
Saxon ruler ALFRED, EGBERT, EDWARD, HAROLD
say MOUTH, SPEAK, UTTER, VOICE, DECLARE
saying(s) DIT, MOT, REDE, LOGIA, AGRAPHA; *see* MAXIM
scab CRUST, MANGE, ESCHAR, BLACKLEG
scabbard CASE, SHEATH, PILCHER
scaffold GIBBET, RIGGER, GALLOWS, STAGING
scale PALE, CLIMB, GAMUT, PALEA, PALET, TRONE, LAMINA, SQUAMA, BALANCE
scale, notes of DI, DO, FA, FI, LA, LE, LI, ME, MI, RA, RE, RI, SE, SI, TE, TI, UT, DOH, SOH, SOL, RAY, MESE, NETE, MESON, TRITE; *see* GUIDONIAN NOTE
scallop PINK, QUIN, CRENA
scallop genus PECTEN
scalloped WAVY, CRENATE
scalpel LANCET, BISTOURY
scaly SCURFY, SCUTATE, TEGULAR
scamp IMP, RASCAL, SCALAWAG
scan READ, SKIM, SURVEY
scandal ODIUM, SHAME, IGNOMINY
scandalize DECRY, SHOCK, OFFEND
Scandinavian ROS, RUS, DANE, FINN, GEAT, LAPP, NORSE, SWEDE, VIKING, NORSEMAN; *see* GERMANIC, FINNO-UGRIC
scant MEAGER, SKIMPY, SLIGHT, SPARSE
scapegoat BUTT, PATSY, VICTIM
scar ARR, MAR(K), CATFACE, CICATRIX
scarab AMULET, BEETLE

scarce(ly) **VIX, RARE, BARELY**
scarcity **LACK, DEARTH, PAUCITY**
scare **ALARM, DAUNT, TERRIFY**
scarecrow **MALKIN, MAUKIN, MAWKIN, MAULKIN**
scarf **BOA, TIE, ASCOT, BARBE, FANON, FICHU, NUBIA, ORALE, STOCK, STOLE, THROW, CRAVAT, BANDANA, DOPATTA, MUFFLER, BANDANNA, KERCHIEF, MANTILLA;** *see* **SHAWL**
Scarlett O'Hara's home **TARA**
scarlike **ULOID**
scatter **SOW, TED, ROUT, SCOAD, STREW, DISPEL, LITTER**
scattered **SEME, DIFFUSE, SPORADIC**
scenario **SCRIPT, LIBRETTO**
scene **SITE, VIEW, SCAPE, VISTA, LOCALE, TABLEAU**
scene of action **ARENA, SPHERE**
scenery **DROPS, FLATS, VISTA, DIORAMA**
scent **AURA, DRAG, FOIL, NOSE, TRAIL;** *see* **ODOR**
scented **OLENT, SPICY, AROMATIC, PERFUMED, REDOLENT**
scepter **MACE, STAFF, TRIDENT**
schedule **LIST, PLAN, SLATE, AGENDA, CALENDAR**
scheme **PLAN, PLOT, CABAL, CHART, SYSTEM, PROJECT**
schism **SPLIT, CLIQUE, DISCORD, FACTION**
scholar **ULEMA, PANDIT, PEDANT, PUNDIT, SAVANT, HARMONIST**
scholarly **ERUDITE, LEARNED, STUDIOUS**
scholarship **BURSE, BURSARY, STIPEND, ERUDITION**
school **GAM, POD, TOL, PREP, SECT, ECOLE, LYCEE, SHOAL, LYCEUM, MANEGE, ACADEMY, COLLEGE**
school grounds **QUAD, CAMPUS**
science **OLOGY, SKILL, TECHNICS**
scientist **SAVANT, CHEMIST, BOTANIST, BIOLOGIST, PHYSICIST**
scion **BUD, SON, HEIR, GRAFT, SHOOT, SPRIG**
scoff **CARP, GIBE, GIRD, JEER, JIBE, RAIL, SNEER, TAUNT**
scold **JAW, NAG, CARP, FLAY, RAIL, RATE, CHIDE, HARPY, SHREW, REVILE, VIRAGO**
scone **FARL, SKON, FARLE**
scoop **BEAT, LADLE, DREDGE**
scope **AREA, SPAN, AMBIT, RANGE, EXTENT**
scorch **BURN, CHAR, SEAR, SERE, PARCH, SINGE, BLISTER**
score **TD, HIT, RUN, TAB, DEBT, GOAL, TICK, CHALK, NOTCH, POINT, TALLY, BASKET, GROOVE, SAFETY, TWENTY, TOUCHDOWN**
scoria *see* **DROSS, LAVA**
scorn **GECK, SCOFF, SCOUT, SPURN, CONTEMN, DISDAIN**
scorpion **ONAGER, CATAPULT;** *see* **LIZARD**
scorpion fish **BLOB, SKIL, POGGE, REINA, VIUVA, BESHOW, COTTID, TAMBOR, BERGYLT, CORSAIR, COTTOID, POACHER, SCULPIN, SKIPPER**
scotch **CUT, GASH, CHOCK, CRUSH, SCORE, FRUGAL, STINGY**
Scotland **ALBA, ECOSSE, SCOTIA**
Scottish dialect **LALLANS**
Scottish measure **BOLL, LIPPY, FIRLOT, CHALDER**
Scottish money **DEMY, LION, BAUBEE, BAWBEE**
Scottish ruler **MARY, BRUCE, EDGAR, JAMES, BALIOL, DUNCAN, ROBERT, STUART, MACBETH, MALCOLM**
Scottish weight **BOLL, DROP, TRONE**
scoundrel **CAD, KNAVE, ROGUE, SCAMP, VARLET, VILLAIN**
scour **FLUSH, PURGE, SCRUB, POLISH**
scourge **BANE, FLOG, LASH, WHIP, PLAGUE**
scout unit **DEN, PACK, TROOP, PATROL**
scow **BARGE, LIGHTER**
scowl **LOUR, FROWN, (G)LOWER**
scrabble **CRAWL, CREEP, DOODLE, SCRAWL, SCRATCH**
scrap **ORT, RAZE, MAMMOCK;** *see* **BIT, FIGHT**
scrape **GALL, RAKE, RASP, GRAZE, ABRADE, DREDGE, SCUFFLE**

scrapings RAMENTA, SHAVINGS
scratch MAR, RIT, RASP, SCRAPE
scream SHRIEK, SCREECH; *see* CRY
screed *see* DIATRIBE
screen BLIND, PAVIS, SHADE, SHOJI, TATTY, BONNET, PURDAH, SHIELD, REREDOS, PARAVENT; *see* SIEVE
scribe CLERK, NOTARY, PENMAN, COPYIST
scrimp SAVE, SKIMP, STINT, ECONOMIZE
script BOOK, RONDE, SERTA, LIBRETTO
scripture VEDA, AGAMA, BIBLE, KORAN, SRUTI, SUTRA, TORAH, AVESTA, GEMARA, GRANTH, MASORA, MISHNA, PURANA, SMRITI, TALMUD, TANTRA, ALCORAN, HAGGADA, HALAKAH, MASORAH, MIDRASH, MISHNAH
scroll LIST, ROLL, VOLUTE
Scrooge associate MARLEY, CRATCHIT
scrub MEAN, BRUSH, SCOUR
scruff FILM, NAPE, NUQUE
scrupulous NICE, EXACT, PRECISE
scrutinize CON, EYE, SCAN, PROBE, INSPECT
scuffle FRAY, BRAWL, MELEE, TUSSLE
sculptor ARP, MIRO, DEGAS, MOORE, MYRON, RODIN, WATTS, CALDER, CANOVA, FRENCH, GIOTTO, MILLES, PISANO, BARLACH, BERNINI, BORGLUM, CELLINI, DAVINCI, EPSTEIN, MAILLOL, PHIDIAS, PICASSO, ZADKINE, BRANCUSI, DAVIDSON, GHIBERTI, GIRARDON, LIPCHITZ, DONATELLO, SANSOVINO, GIACOMETTI
sculptor's equipment CHISEL, GRAVER, CALIPER, GRADINE, SPATULA, ARMATURE
sculpture BUST, GRAVE, RELIEF, STATUE, CARVING, BASRELIEF
scum *see* DROSS
scuttle HOD, SINK, SWAMP
Scylla relative NISUS, CRATAIS, PHORCYS
sea RED, ZEE, ARAL, BAHR, DEAD, DEEP, MAIN, MARE, ROSS, SULU, SURF, BRINE, CORAL, OCEAN, AEGEAN, IONIAN, SAGAMI, SCOTIA, CASPIAN, ADRIATIC
sea, of the NAVAL, MARINE, OCEANIC, PELAGIC, MARITIME, NAUTICAL
seabird AUK, ERN, MEW, ERNE, GULL, SHAG, SKUA, TERN, NODDY, SCAUP, SOLAN, FULMAR, GANNET, PETREL, PUFFIN, SCOTER, CORMORANT
sea-ear ABALONE
seafarer *see* SAILOR
seal BULLA, SIGIL, CACHET, SIGNET
seal genus PHOCA, PHOCIDAE, PHOCINAE
seal, pert. to PHOCINE
seals WIG, SEAL, MATKA, OTARY, SWILE, URSAL, URSUK, USSUK, UTSUK, BEATER, DOTARD, JACKET, MAKLAK, MATKAH, OTARIA, PHOCID, FURSEAL, OTARIAN, OTARINE, PHOCOID, SADDLER, SEALION, SEALKIE
seam BED, DART, JOIN, LODE, VEIN, SUTURE
seaman *see* SAILOR
seamark BUOY, MEITH, BEACON, PHAROS
seance SESSION, SITTING
sear DRY, CHAR, PARCH, SCORCH, WITHER
search COMB, DELVE, DOWSE, FRISK, GROPE, QUEST, FERRET, FORAGE, RANSACK, RUMMAGE
season(s) AGE, CORN, CURE, FALL, SALT, SELE, HORAE, INURE, SPICE, AUTUMN, FLAVOR, SPRING, SUMMER, TEMPER, WINTER; *see p. 341*
season, church LENT, ADVENT, EASTER, TRINITY, EPIPHANY, ASCENSION, CHRISTMAS, PENTECOST
seasonings BAY, SALT, CHIVE, THYME, BURNET, CELERY, GARLIC, LOVAGE, CARAWAY, CHERVIL, COWSLIP, DITTANY, FIGWORT, OREGANO, PIGNOLI, MARJORAM, ORIGANUM, SERPOLET; *see* SPICE, HERB, CONDIMENT

seat(s) PEW, BANC, POST, ASANA, BENCH, CHAIR, SELLA, CURULE, HOWDAH, PEWAGE, SEDILE, SETTEE, SEDILIA
seaweed AGAR, KELP, LIMU, NORI, DULSE, FUCUS, LAVER, VAREC, WRACK, TANGLE, VARECH, AMANORI, ROCKWEED, SARGASSO
Seb relative SET, SHU, ISIS, OSIRIS, TEFNUT
seclude IMMURE, ISOLATE
second ABET, JIFFY, TRICE, MOMENT
secondary BYE, LESS, MINOR
secondhand USED, WORN
secret PRIVY, COVERT, LATENT, MYSTIC, OCCULT; *see* MYSTERY
secret society KKK, EGBO, PORO, TONG, MAF(F)IA, CAMORRA, BLACKHAND
secretion GUM, SAP, BILE, LAAP, LERP, MUSK, LAARP, LATEX, MUCUS, SWEAT, SALIVA, AUTACOID
sect CULT, WING, PARTY, FACTION
section LEG, AREA, ZONE, STAGE, SECTOR, QUARTER, SEGMENT
secular LAY, CIVIL, TEMPORAL
secure FIX, FAST, MOOR, SAFE, SURE, BELAY, RIVET, ANCHOR, FASTEN, STABLE
security GRITH, STOCK, PLEDGE; *see* SURETY
sedan LITTER
sedate GRAVE, SOBER, SERIOUS
sedative AMYTAL, OPIATE, ANODYNE, BROMIDE, DEMEROL, LUMINAL, BARBITAL, GOOFBALL, NARCOTIC, NEMBUTAL
sediment LEES, SILT, DRAFF, DREGS, LOESS, MAGMA, SLUDGE, SILTAGE
sedition MUTINY, REVOLT, RISING
see EYE, (E)SPY, VIDE, DESCRY, DIOCESE, DISCERN
seed NUT, PIP, PIT, SOW, GERM, MILT, OVULE, SEMEN, SPERM, SPORE, KERNEL, NUCULE, NUTLET, PIPPIN, PYRENE
seed coat BUR, ARIL, BURR, HULL, HUSK, TESTA, TEGMEN, TESTAE, TEGUMEN
seedless (plant) FERN, AGAMOUS
seeds TARE, ANISE, BENNE, CACAO, COCOA, CUMIN, PANGI, PINON, PULSE, SIEVA, SITAO, COWPEA, CUMMIN, FENNEL, KANARI, LEGUME, LENTIL, PEANUT, SESAME, CARAWAY, HARICOT, MUSTARD; *see* BEAN, NUT
seeming LIKE, QUASI, LIKELY
seemly FIT, MEET, RIGHT, PROPER
seep OOZE, DRAIN, EXUDE, LEACH
seer SIBYL, ARUSPEX, PROPHET
seesaw FLAP, TILT, TEETER, BASCULE
seethe BOIL, BUBBLE, SIMMER, FERMENT
segment ARC, PART, TORE, SECTOR, SOMITE, TELSON
segmental TORIC
seine NET, TRAWL, SAGENE
seize NAB, GRAB, HENT, GRASP, REAVE, USURP, ARREST, COLLAR
select OPT, CULL, PICK, WALE, CREAM, ELITE
Selene parent THEA, HYPERION
self EGO, SEITY, ENTITY
self-confidence POISE, APLOMB
self-defense JUDO, KARATE, JUJITSU
self-esteem PRIDE, EGOISM, VANITY, CONCEIT
self-love NARC(ISS)ISM
self-righteous SMUG, PHARISAIC
sell HAWK, VEND, SCALP, MARKET, PEDDLE, RETAIL, AUCTION
semblance COPY, MIEN, FEINT, GUISE, IMAGE
Semele relative INO, AGAVE, CADMUS, DIONYSUS, HARMONIA
Semele's lover ZEUS
Semite JEW, ARAB, HEBREW
Semitic language GEEZ, NUZI, GAFAT, MAHRI, PUNIC, TIGRE, ARABIC, GURAGE, HARARI, HEBREW, QARAWI, SYRIAC, ARAMAIC, AMHARIC, EDOMITE, MALTESE, MINAEAN, MOABITE, SABAEAN, SOKOTRI, AKKADIAN, AMMONITE, ASSYRIAN, ETHIOPIC, LIHYANIC, MANDAEAN,

SAFAITIC, SHKHAURI, TALMUDIC, THAMUDIC, TIGRINYA, UGARITIC, CANAANITE, HARRANIAN, PHOENICIAN
senate CURIA, CHAMBER, COUNCIL
senator SOLON
send EMIT, SHIP, ROUTE, FORWARD
send back REMIT, REMAND, RETURN
Senegalese language *see* WEST-ATLANTIC
senility DOTAGE, CADUCITY
senior AINE, DEAN, ELDER
sensation FEELING, PERCEPTION
sense ESP, FEEL, FLAIR, SIGHT, SMELL, TASTE, TOUCH, ACUMEN, INTUIT, HEARING
senseless MAD, INANE, ABSURD, FUTILE, STUPID, WANTON
sensible SANE, WISE, SOBER
sensitive SORE, TENDER, TOUCHY
sentence RAP, DOOM, TERM, DECISION
sentence part VERB, CLAUSE, PHRASE, SUBJECT, PREDICATE
sentimental GUSHY, SOPPY, MAWKISH, ROMANTIC
sentimentality MUSH, BATHOS
sentinel VIGIL, SENTRY, VEDETTE
separate SIFT, SORT, APART, SPLIT, DETACH, DIVIDE, SECERN, ISOLATE
separation SCHISM, AVULSION, DIVORCE, APARTHEID
sepulcher *see* TOMB
sequel EFFECT, UPSHOT
sequence SCALE, TIERCE; *see* SERIES
sequester ENISLE, ISOLATE, CLOISTER
sequin SPANGLE, ZECCHIN(O)
seraglio HAREM, SERAI, ZENANA
serene CALM, IRENIC, PLACID
serf NEIF, LITUS, NEIFE, COLONA, COLONUS; *see* BONDMAN
sergeant NCO, SARGE, TOPKICK
serially SERIATIM
series SET, CHAIN, GAMUT, CATENA, FLIGHT, STRING
serious GRAVE, SOBER, EARNEST
sermon HOMILY, KHUTBAH, LECTURE, REPROOF
serpent SEPT, APEPI, ELOPS; *see* SNAKE, VIPER
serpent worship OPHISM
serpentine OPHITE, OPHIOID, SINUOUS, OPHIDIAN
servant BOY, GYP, MAN, BATA, PAGE, ALILA, GILLY, HAMAL, VALET, BUTLER, FERASH, FLUNKY, GARCON, GILLIE, LACKEY, MENIAL, POTBOY, POTMAN, GOSSOON; *see* MAID
server TRAY, SALVER, WAITER
service USE, MASS, RITE(S), DEVOIR
serviceman/woman GI, VET, WAC, WAVE; *see* SAILOR, SOLDIER, SPAR, WREN
serviette NAPKIN
servile ABJECT, MENIAL, FAWNING, SLAVISH
servitude *see* SLAVERY
sesame TIL, BENE, TEEL, BENNE, BENNI, SEMSEM
set FIX, GEL, JELL, BATCH, MOUNT, CLIQUE, HARDEN, COTERIE
set aside DEFER, DISCARD, REJECT
set off EXPLODE, DETONATE
setback UPSET, RELAPSE, REVERSE
Seth relative EVE, ABEL, ADAM, CAIN, ENOS
setting PAVE, BEZEL, MOUNT, SCENE, CHATON, MILIEU
settled ALIT, FIXED, VESTED
settlement COLONY, PAYMENT
settler BOOMER, SOONER, PIONEER, COLONIST
seven HEPTAD, PLEIAD, SEPTET, SEPTUOR, SEPTETTE
Seven Sisters *see* PLEIADES
Seven Wonders ZEUS, PHAROS, RHODES, EPHESUS, COLOSSUS, PYRAMIDS
sever CUT, LOP, REND, RIVE
severe CRUEL, HARSH, STRICT
sew HEM, FELL, TACK, STITCH, SUTURE
sewing terms HEM, TAT, BIND, FELL, KNIT, PURL, RUIN, SEAM, TACK, WHIP, BASTE, QUILT, RENTER, CROCHET
sexes, common to both UNISEX, EPICENE
sexton SHAMAS, SHAMES, SHAMMASH, SACRISTAN
sexual GAMIC, CARNAL, EROTIC

Seychelles langauge **CREOLE**
shabby **WORN, DOWDY, MANGY, SEEDY, RAGGED, SCURVY**
shabby woman **DOWD, SLUT, DOWDY, FRUMP, SLAVEN, SLATTERN**
shack **HUT, SHED, HOVEL SHANTY**
shackle **BOND, IRON;** *see* **CHAIN**
shad **ALLIS, ALOSA, ALEWIFE**
shade **HUE, TINT, TINGE, VISOR, NUANCE, SCREEN**
shade tree **ASH, ELM, LIN(DEN)**
shadow **CLOUD, SHADE, UMBRA;** *see* **GHOST, TRAIL**
shaft **AXIS, FLUE, FUST, POLE, ARBOR, ARROW, SCAPE, SPIRE, STELE, THILL, COLUMN, PILLAR, SPINDLE**
shaggy **BUSHY, NAPPY, HIRSUTE**
shake **JAR, JOLT, ROCK, NIDGE, QUIVER, UNNERVE, VIBRATE**
Shakespeare relative **ANNE, JOHN, EDMUND, HAMNET, JUDITH, SUSANNA**
Shakespearean character *see p. 314*
Shakespearean theater **GLOBE**
sham **FAKE, HOAX, MOCK, FEIGN**
shame **FIE, ABASH, MORTIFY**
shameless **BRASH, BRAZEN**
shank(s) **GAM, CRUS, GAMB, SHIN, CRURA**
shape **FORM, MOLD, GUISE, TAILLE, CONTOUR, FASHION**
share **CUT, LOT, PART, DIVVY, STAKE, PORTION**
shark **GATA, HAYE, JAWS, MAKO, TOPE, PUPPY, RHINA, TOPER, GALEID, GALEUS, ISURUS, LAMNID, REQUIN, ACRODUS, DOGFISH, ISUROID, PLACOID, RATFISH, REQUIEM, SAWFISH, TIBURON, GREATWHITE, HAMMERHEAD**
sharp **GLEG, KEEN, ACERB, ACUTE, CHEAT, EDGED, ACUATE**
sharpen **HONE, WHET, GRIND, STROP**
sharpshooter **JAGER, SNIPER, MARKSMAN**
shave **PARE, PLANE, SLICE, SCRAPE**
shawl **MAUD, WRAP, LAMBA, MANTA, PATTU, TALIS, TALIT, PATTOO, TALITH, TALLIS, TALLIT, PAISLEY, TALLITH;** *see* **SCARF**
sheaf **BALE, GERB, GAVEL, BUNDLE**
shear **SHAVE, FLEECE;** *see* **CLIP**
sheath **OCREA, DRESS, SHOCK, THECA, SPATHE, CAPSULE, SCABBARD**
shed **COTE, DOFF, EMIT, MOLT, MOULT, HANGAR, LEANTO**
sheep **EWE, HOG, MUG, NOT, OWE, PET, RAM, SHA, TEG, TUP, YOW, AGNI, ARUI, BUCK, CADE, DOWN, HOGG, LAMB, LONK, MUGS, SHIP, TEGG, AGNUS, ANGUS, ARGAL, AUDAD, BRAXY, CRONE, DUMBA, HEDER, PODDY, URIAL, AGNEAU, AOUDAD, ARGALI, BARHAL, BHARAL, NAHOOR, OORIAL, ROMNEY, SHEDER, THEAVE, WASTER, WEDDER, WETHER, WOOLIE, WOOLLY, BLEATER, CARACUL, CHEVIOT, CHILVER, DELAINE, EANLING, KARAKUL, LAMBKIN, LINCOLN, MOUFLON, MUFFLON, ROSELLA**
sheep disease **COE, GID, SHAB, STURDY, SCRAPIE**
sheep genus **BOS, OVIS**
sheepfold **PEN, REE, COTE, KRAAL, REEVE**
sheeplike **MEEK, OVINE**
sheepskin **BOCK, BOND, ROAN, BASIL, SKIVER, DIPLOMA**
sheepwalk **SLAIT**
sheer **VEER, UTTER, SWERVE**
shelf **BERM(E), LEDGE, GRADIN, LEDGER, MANTEL, RETABLE**
shell **BOMB, BURR, LIMA, SHOT, SKIN, CONCH, HARPA, MUREX, SHUCK, CONCHA, GONKER, TUNICA, BOMBARD**
shell money **PEAG, COWRY, PEAGE, SEWAN, COWRIE, SEAWAN, WAMPUM, SEAWANT**
shellac **LAC, RESIN, VARNISH**
shellfish *see* **MOLLUSK, CRUSTACEAN**
shelter **LEE, COTE, BIELD, SHEAL, SCREEN;** *see* **REFUGE**
sheltered **ALEE**
Shem descendant **SEMITE**

Shem relative HAM, LUD, ARAM, ELAM, NOAH, NAAMAH, JAPHETH
shepherd TEND, PASTOR, CORYDON, DAPHNIS, THYRSIS
sherbet ICE, SORBET
sheriff REEVE, ELISOR, SHRIEVE
Sherlock Holmes author DOYLE
Sherlock Holmes's friend WATSON
Shetlands measure URE, MARKLAND
shield ECU, AEGIS, MULGA, PAVIS, PELTA, SCUTE, TARGE, SCUTUM, TARGET, BUCKLER, CLIPEUS, ROTELLA, ROUNDEL, HIELAMAN
shield-shaped PELTATE, SCUTATE, CLYPEATE
shift GANG, GYBE, JIBE, VEER, DODGE, SHUNT, SWITCH, CHEMISE, DEVIATE
shilly-shally HEDGE, WAVER
shine GLEAM, POLISH, RADIATE
shingle(s) FLIP, SHIM, ZONA, BEACH, FACIA, HERPES
ship SEND, FORWARD; *see* WARSHIP, VESSEL
ship crew ABLE, HAND, MATE, BUNGS, COOPER, PURSER, STOKER, YEOMAN, STEWARD
ship, famous ARGO, FRAM, GJOA, NINA, AOTEA, ARAWA, CAINE, MAINE, PINTA, BOUNTY, TAINUI, OREGON, ARIZONA, HOROUTA, MATATUA, MONITOR, OLYMPIA, PELICAN, REVENGE, SQUALUS, TITANIC, BISMARCK, BONHOMME, CLERMONT, ENDEAVOR, GRAFSPEE, HALFMOON, HARTFORD, MERRIMAC, MISSOURI, SAVANNAH, TAKITUNU, YORKTOWN, LUSITANIA, MAYFLOWER, BIRKENHEAD, GOLDENHIND, SANTAMARIA
ship officer BOSN, MATE, PIPES, MASTER, PURSER, CAPTAIN, SKIPPER, BOATSWAIN
ship, part of AFT, BOW, BOX, FID, NEF, RIB, RUN, SNY, BACK, BEAK, BIBB, BITT, BOOM, BRIG, DECK, DOCK, GAFF, HEAD, HELM, HOLD, HULK, HULL, JACK, KEEL, LOOF, MAST, NOSE, POLE, POOP, PORT, PROW, RAIL, SKAG, SKEG, SPAR, SPIR, STEM, YARD, BILGE, BOWER, CABIN, DAVIT, HATCH, HAWSE, KEVEL, ORLOP, SALON, SNAPE, SPRIT, STERN, WAIST, BRIDGE, BUNKER, CANVAS, GALLEY, GUNNEL, ISLAND, RUDDER, STEEVE, STRAKE, TILLER, BOLLARD, BULWARK, BUMPKIN, COUNTER, FORETOP, FUTTOCK, GANGWAY, GUNWALE, JIBSTAY, KEELSON, KILLICK, KNUCKLE, MAINTOP, SCUPPER, SCUTTLE, SNORKEL, SPANKER, SPIRKET, TOPMAST, YARDARM, STEERAGE, PROMENADE
ship, sailing CAT, GIG, HOY, BARK, BRIG, BUSS, DHOW, DONI, JUNK, KOFF, PINK, PRAM, SAIC, SAIL, SNOW, TODE, TOUP, TROW, YAWL, ZULU, BARGE, BATEL, BOLIA, CASCO, DANDY, DHONI, DRAKE, FOIST, KETCH, PINKY, PRAAM, RASEE, RAZEE, SETEE, SHARP, SLOOP, SMACK, TJALK, XEBEC, YANKY, ZABRA, ARGOSY, BAIDAR, BARQUE, BAWLEY, BILALO, BOLIAH, BORLEY, BOUTRE, CAIQUE, CANGIA, CARVEL, DINGHY, DOGGER, DROMON, GALIOT, GAYYOU, HOGGIE, HOLCAD, HOOKER, LANCHA, LORCHA, LUGGER, MISTIC, PRAHAM, PULWAR, SAILER, SAMBUK, SAMPAN, SANDAL, SCAFFY, SETTEE, SHIBAR, SKAFFY, TARTAN, TOSHER, TRANKY, BIRLING, BUMBOAT, CARVEL, CATBOAT, GALLEON, GALLIOT, PATAMAR, PIRAGUA, POLACCA, SHALLOP, DAHABEAH, SCHOONER, CARAVELLE; *see* WARSHIP, VESSEL
shirk FUNK, DODGE, EVADE, SOLDIER, MALINGER, GOLDBRICK
shirt TOB, SARK, TOBE, BANIA, DICKY, BANIAN, BANYAN, CAMISA, CAMISE, DICKEY, JERSEY, CHEMISE, PULLOVER
shiver GRUE, SHAKE, SHUDDER

shoal REEF, DRAVE, HORDE, RIFFLE
shoal-water deposit CULM
shock JOLT, STUN, APPAL, BRUNT, APPALL, IMPACT, TRAUMA
shod CALCED
shoe CACK, GETA, MULE, PUMP, ROMEO, SABOT, STOGA, STOGY, ANKLET, BROGAN, BROGUE, CALIGA, CRAKOW, GAITER, OXFORD, SLIPON, STEPIN, STOGIE, BLUCHER, CHOPINE, CRAKOWE, SNEAKER, BALMORAL, COLONIAL, POULAINE
shoe part HEEL, LAST, RAND, SOLE, VAMP, WELT, EYELET, INSOLE, LACING, TOEBOY, UPPERS
shoemaker SNOB, SUTOR, BOTCHER, COBBLER, CRISPIN
shoemaker's equipment LAST, TREE, ELS(H)IN, LINGEL, LINGLE
shoes S(C)HOON, TALARIA
shoot BAG, BUD, UDO, BINE, CHIT, CION, FIRE, LIMB, TWIG, GEMMA, SCION, SNIPE, SPRIG, STOLO, TURIO, VIMEN, RATOON, STOLON, TILLER, TURION
shooting match TIR, SHOOT, SKEET
shooting star *see* METEOR
shop MART, STORE, TRADE, ATELIER, FACTORY, TABERNA, BOUTIQUE
shore PROP, RIPA, COAST, WARTH, RIVAGE, STRAND
shore bird SORA, SNIPE, STILT, WADER, AVOCET, CURLEW; *see* RAIL, SANDPIPER, PLOVER
short CURT, PUDGY, TERSE, SCANTY, STUBBY, LACONIC
short story writer POE, BABEL, GOGOL, HARTE, HENRY, KAFKA, STEAD, BIERCE, PARKER, PORTER, RUNYON, SINGER, CHEKHOV, LARDNER, MALAMUD, PUSHKIN, CHEEVER, ALEICHEM, TURGENEV, (DE)MAUPASSANT
short-winded PURSE, WHEEZY
shortage LACK, NEED, DEFICIT
shorten LOP, CROP, DELE, DOCK, ELIDE, ABRIDGE
shorthand GREGG, PITMAN, STENOTYPE
shorts TRUNKS, DRAWERS
shot TRY, DOSE, FLECKED
shoulder BERM, EPAULE, SCAPULA
shoulder, of the ALAR, SCAPULAR
shout CALL, ROAR, YELL; *see* CRY
shove JOG, BUNT, PUSH, NUDGE, JOSTLE
shovel VAN, PEEL, SCOOP, SPADE
show LEGIT, RAREE, DISPLAY, EXPOSE
Show Boat captain ANDY
Show Boat writer KERN, FERBER
showcase ETALAGE, VITRINE
shower SKEW, SPATE, SPRAY; *see* RAIN
showy LOUD, GAUDY, GARISH
shrew ERD, KATE, HARPY, VIXEN, TARTAR, VIRAGO, XANTIPPE
shrewd SLY, ARCH, CAGY, FOXY, WILY, CANNY, PAWKY, ASTUTE
shrike DRONGO, LANIUS, MINIVET, TRILLER
shrill PIPY, ACUTE, SKIRL, ARGUTE, PIPING
shrimp CARID, PRAWN, ARTEMIA, CARIDEAN, CARIDOID, CREVETTE
shrimp genus CARIDA
shrine ARK, PIR, NAOS, TOMB, TOPE, ALTAR, STUPA, CHASSE, DAGOBA, DARGAH, DURGAH, FATIMA, SAMOAH, CHAITYA, LOURDES, MARTYRY, FERETORY, RELIQUARY
shrink COWER, QUAIL, WIZEN, SHRIVEL, CONTRACT
shrivel CURL, WIZEN, WITHER
Shropshire SALOP
shroud PALL, VEIL, SHEET, SCREEN, CEREMENT
shrub(s) TOD, AKIA, BUSH, CADE, GOAI, INGA, ITEA, PELU, WHIN, ALDER, CHICO, ELDER, FURZE, GORSE, HENNA, LILAC, SALAL, SAVIN, SUMAC, URENA, ABELIA, BONSAI, FRUTEX, JASMIN, KOWHAI, LAUREL, BOSCAGE, LANTANA; *see* EVERGREEN, ACACIA, TREES

shuck POD, HUSK, SHELL
shudder *see* SHIVER
shuffle MIX, RIFFLE, SHAMBLE
shun AVOID, DODGE, EVADE
shunt VEER, SHIFT, DIVERT, SWITCH
shut up DAM, (S)HUSH, IMMURE, SILENCE
shutter BLIND, SHADE, PERSIENNE
shuttle PIRN, SPOOL, BOBBIN
shuttle, space ATLANTIS, COLUMBIA, DISCOVERY, CHALLENGER, ENTERPRISE
shy COY, JIB, MIM, BALK, SKIT, CHARY, START, RECOIL, BASHFUL
Shylock's daughter JESSICA
Siam *see* THAILAND
Siberian VOGUL, SAMOYED
sibilant PSST, HISSING
sibyl *see* SEER
sick ILL, ABED, AILING
sickle-shaped FALCATE
Siddhartha BUDDHA, GAUTAMA
side AGREE, FACET, FLANK, LATUS, ASPECT
side, pert. to COSTAL, LATERAL
sidereal ASTRAL, STARRY
sidestep AVOID, EVADE, SKIRT
sidetrack AVERT, SHUNT, DIVERT
sidewise ASKEW, ASLANT, ASKANCE
sidle CANT, CRAB, SKEW, SKIRT
siege, lay BESET, INVEST
Siegfried SIGURD
Seigfried's mother SIEGLINDE
Siegfried's slayer HAGEN
Siegried's sword BALMUNG
Sierra Leone language TEMNE; *see* MANDE
sieve BOLT, LAUN, SIFT, PUREE, BOLTER, RIDDLE, SIFTER, GRIZZLY; *see* STRAINER
sift LUE, REE, SIE, BOLT, RIDDLE, SCREEN, WINNOW
sigh SOB, MOAN, SOUF, SOUGH
sight AIM, KEN, BEAD, ESPY, SCENE, VISTA
sight, pert. to OCULAR, VISUAL
Sigmund relative SIGNY, SIGURD, HJORDIS, VOLSUNG
sign MARK, OMEN, PLUS, RUNE, SEIN, BADGE, MINUS, PRESA, SEGNO, TOKEN, PORTENT
sign, pert. to SEMIC
signal CUE, PST, TAP, BUZZ, ALARM, FLARE, FUSEE, SIREN, BEACON, CURFEW, ENSIGN, MOTION, BLINKER, CHAMADE, FOGHORN
signature HAND, PARAPH, SCROLL
signet SEAL, SIGIL
signify BODE, IMPLY, DENOTE
Sigurd relative REGIN, GUDRUN, SIGMUND
Sigurd's victim FAFNIR
Silas Marner author ELIOT
silence GAG, PAX, MUM, CALM, HUSH, LULL, MUTE, REST, TACE
silent MUM, GLUM, MUTE, TACET, TACIT
silhouette OUTLINE, PROFILE
silica MICA, SILEX, QUARTZ
silk thread BAVE, TRAM, FLOSS, TRAME, SLEAVE, TUSSAH, TUSSER, TUSSORE
silkworm ERI, BOMBYX, TUSSORE
silkworm disease UJI
silly DAFFY, INANE, ASININE, PUERILE
silver COINS, SYCEE, ARGENT, SILLER, STERLING
Silver State NV, NEV(ADA)
silversides GUPPY, KILLY, PLATY, LUCINA, GRUNION, GULARIC, MAYFISH
similar AKIN, LIKE, ALIKE
simper MINCE, SMIRK, TEEHEE
simple EASY, MERE, PLAIN, SILLY, ARTLESS
simpleton DAW, BOOB, COOT, DUPE, GAUP, GOWK, GUMP, BOOBY, GOOSE, NITWIT
simulate ACT, APE, MOCK, SHAM, FEIGN, AFFECT, INVENT
sin ERR, EVIL, SLIP, VICE, ERROR, INIQUITY, TRESPASS; *see* DEADLY
since AGO, YET, SYNE, HENCE
sincere OPEN, FRANK, CANDID, HONEST, EARNEST
sinewy ROPY, WIRY, TOUGH, BRAWNY
sinful EVIL, WICKED, IMMORAL, PECCANT
sing HUM, LILT, TELL, CAROL, CHANT, CHIRP, CROON, JODEL, TROLL, SQUEAL, WARBLE

Singapore language MALAY, TAMIL, CHINESE
singer ALMA, ALME, ALTO, BARD, BASS, DIVA, WAIT, ALMAH, ALMEH, MEZZO, TENOR, VOICE, CANTOR, MUSICO, CAROLER, CHANTER, CHORIST, CROONER, GLEEMAN, SOPRANO, WARBLER, YODELER, BARITONE, BARYTONE, CHANTEUR, MELODIST, MINSTREL, SONGSTER, VOCALIST, CHORISTER, CHANTEUSE, CONTRALTO; *see* MUSICIAN, SONGBIRD
singer, famous ALDA, BORI, LIND, PONS, CALVE, GIGLI, GLUCK, LANZA, LUCCA, MELBA, PATTI, PINZA, PRICE, RUFFO, CALLAS, CARUSO, ONEGIN, TAUBER, DOMINGO, LEHMANN, NILSSON, STEVENS, TEBALDI, TIBBETT, TRAUBEL, PAVAROTTI, SUTHERLAND
single ACE, ONE, LONE, MONO, ONLY, SOLO, UNAL, ALONE, UNWED
singular ODD, QUEER, UNIQUE, CURIOUS
sinister EVIL, LEFT, OMINOUS
sink SAG, BOWL, FAIL, FLAG, BASIN, DOLINA
sinning ERRANT, PECCANT
sinuous WAVY, SNAKY, SPIRAL
sir *see* TITLE
siren CIRCE, LURLEI, LORELEI
sirocco *see* WIND
sisal *see* HEMP
Sisera's killer JAEL
sister NUN, SIB, SIS, NURSE, SOROR
Sisyphus relative AEOLUS, MEROPE, CORINTH
sit POSE, BROOD, PERCH, ROOST
site SEAT, SCENE, LOCATION
sitting POSE, CLUTCH, SEANCE, SEDENT, ASTRIDE, SESSION
situation JOB, CASE, POST, SITE, STATE, PLIGHT
Siva relative UMA, DEVI, KALI, MAYA, SATI, DURGA, GAURI, AMBIKA, SKANDA, BHAVANI, PARVATI
six HEXAD, SENARY, SESTET, SEXTET
Six, Les AURIC, DUREY, MILHAUD, POULENC, HONEGGER, TAILLEFERRE
sizing GLUE, GLAZE, SEALER
sizzle HISS, FRIZZ(LE)
skein RAP, WEB, HANK, HASP, MESH, SLEAVE
skeleton ATOMY, BONES, CADRE, CORAL, FRAME, SPONGE
skeptic CYNIC, LUCIAN, PYRRHO, THOMAS, AGNOSTIC, APORETIC
sketch DRAW, LIMN, SKIT, DOODLE, DRAWING, OUTLINE, ESQUISSE
skewer PIN, SPIT, TRUSS, SKIVER
ski part TIP, HEEL, SOLE, GAMBER, SHOVEL
ski term INRUN, MOGUL, SCHUSS, SLALOM, CHRISTY, VORLAGE, PASSGANG, SITZMARK, SNOWPLOW, TELEMARK
skid SLEW, SLIP, VEER, SLIDE
skill ART, GIFT, TALENT, FINESSE
skillet *see* COOKING
skillful ABLE, DEFT, ADEPT, ADROIT, DAEDAL, HABILE, SCIENT
skim DART, FLIT, SCUD, SCUM
skimpy SCANT, FRUGAL, STINGY
skin FUR, BARK, COAT, FELL, FLAY, HIDE, PELT, CUTIS, DERMA, STRIP, CORIUM
skin, pert. to DERMAL, DERMIC
skinny LEAN, THIN, SCRAGGY
skip DAP, FLIT, OMIT, CAPER, ELIDE, SALTO, SPRING
skipper RAIS, REIS, MASTER, CAPTAIN
skirmish TILT; *see* FIGHT
skirt JUPE, SAYA, JUPON, PAREU, TUNIC, BASQUE, PANIER, PEPLUM, DIRNDL, PANNIER, CRINOLINE, HOOPSKIRT, OVERSKIRT, PETTICOAT
skit JIBE, CAPER, NUMBER, PARODY, SKETCH
skittish JUMPY, NERVOUS
skittle(s) PIN, BOWLS, NINEPINS
skulk LURK, PROWL, SLINK
skull part INION, BREGMA, GONION, LAMBDA, NASION, CRANIUM, DACRYON,

PTERION, CALVARIA, BRAINPAN
skull, pert. to INIAL, CRANIAL
skullcap COIF, BEANIE, PILEUS, CALOTTE, YARMULKE, ZUCCHETTO
skunk TELEDU, POLECAT, MEPHITIS
sky COPE, TIEN, AZUR, LANGI, VAULT, WELKIN
slab DALLE, STELE, TABLET
slack LAX, IDLE, LAZE, REMISS
slacker SPIV, TRUANT, SHIRKER
slag *see* DROSS, LAVA
slake QUENCH, SATISFY
slam RAP, BANG, SHUT, VOLE
slander SLUR, DECRY, LIBEL, MALIGN, REVILE, ASPERSE, CALUMNY
slang CANT, JIVE, ARGOT, FLASH, LINGO, JARGON, PATOIS, DIALECT
slant BIAS, ANGLE; *see* SLOPE
slanted AWRY, SKEW, ASKEW, SKEWY, RAKISH
slap BIFF, CUFF, SNUB, SWAT
slash DAB, JAG, GASH, SLISH
slat(s) LATH, STAVE, STRIP, BATTEN, LOUVER, SPLINE
slate TILE, DOCKET, TABLET; *see* LIST
slaughter POGROM, CARNAGE, KILLING, MASSACRE
slaughterhouse ABATTOIR, BUTCHERY, KNACKERY, SHAMBLES
Slav POLE, SERB, SORB, WEND, CROAT, CZECH, VENED, BULGAR, SLOVAK
slave DASI, ESNE, ALIPIN, MAROON, THRALL; *see* BONDMAN
Slavic language CZECH, POLISH, SLOVAC, RUSSIAN, SERBIAN, SLOVENE, SORBIAN, WENDISH, POLABIAN, BULGARIAN, KASHUBIAN, UKRAINIAN, MACEDONIAN, BYELORUSSIAN
sled LUGE, PUNG, HURDLE, SLEDGE, SLEIGH, COASTER, TRAVOIS; *see* VEHICLE
sleek SLICK, GLOSSY, SMOOTH
sleep NAP, NOD, DOSS, DOZE, WINK, SOPOR, DROWSE, SIESTA, SNOOZE
sleeping car PULLMAN
sleeping sickness NAGANA
sleepy DROWSY, OSCITANT, SOMNOLENT
sleeve ARM, GIGOT, DOLMAN
sleigh *see* SLED
slender LANK, LEAN, SLIM, THIN, LITHE, REEDY, SVELT, SLIGHT
slenderize REDUCE
sleuth *see* DETECTIVE
slice CUT, COLP, GASH, SLAB, LAYER, CANTLE, COLLOP, FLITCH, RASHER
slick OILY, SLEEK, CLEVER
slide SKID, SLUE, CHUTE
slight CUT, SLIM, SLUR, SNUB, FAINT, SCANT, SPURN
slim THIN, SMALL, SLIGHT, SVELTE
slime MUCK, OOZE, SLUDGE
sling CAST, FLING
slip ERR, BULL, DOCK, BONER, LAPSE, ERROR, GAFFE, GLIDE, ELAPSE, CUTTING, SOLECISM
slipper MULE, ROMEO, BOOTEE, BOOTIE, CRAKOW, JULIET, PINSON, CHINELA, CHINELE, CRAKOWE, BABOUCHE
slippery SLY, EELY, SLIMY, SHIFTY, ELUSIVE
slit GASH, SLASH
sliver SPLINTER
slob CLOD, LUMMOX, SLOVEN
slogan MOTTO, SHIBBOLETH
slope TIP, BRAE, CANT, HADE, KEEL, RAKE, RAMP, RISE, TILT, BEVEL, SCRAP, SPLAY, TALUS, ESCARP, GLACIS, VERSANT, GRADIENT
sloth AI, UNAU, BHALU, INDOLENCE
sloth genus BRUTA
slough BOG, MIRE, MOLT, SHED, BAYOU, INLET, MARSH, SWAMP
slow POKY, LARGO, LENTO, ADAGIO, ANDANTE, LARGHETTO
sludge MUD, MIRE, OOZE, SLUSH
slug SWAT, LIMAX, BULLET, ELYSIA, GEOPHILA
sluggard DRONE, IDLER, LOAFER
sluggish LOGY, POKY, DOPEY, TORPID
sluice CLOW, GATE, GOUT, FLUME, SASSE, SEWER
slum GHETTO

slumber SLEEP, REPOSE
slump SAG, SINK, DECLINE
slur ELIDE, STAIN, SULLY, STIGMA
slush POSH, SLOSH, SLEECH
slut HUSSY, QUEAN, SLATTERN
sly ARCH, FOXY, SLEE, WILY, CAGEY, SLOAN, ARTFUL, ASTUTE, CRAFTY, SHREWD, CUNNING
smack BUSS, KISS, SLAP, GUSTO, SAVOR
small LIL, WEE, PUNY, TINY, DINKY, ELFIN, PETIT, PETTY, TEENY, BANTAM, MINUTE, PETITE
small amount DRAM, PINCH, MODICUM; *see* BIT, JOT
smallpox VARIOLA
smart CHIC, POSH, TRIG, NATTY, STING, CLEVER, DAPPER
smash DASH, BREAK, CRUSH, SHATTER
smear DAUB; *see* STAIN
smell *see* ODOR
smelly *see* FETID
smile GRIN, FLEER, SMIRK, SIMPER
smirch DIRTY, STAIN, SULLY
smirk GRIN, LEER, SNEER, SIMPER
smite HIT, STRIKE, AFFLICT
smith MIME, FORGER, VULCAN
smock FROCK, CAMISE, GABERDINE
smoke CURE, FLOC, FUME, LUNT, REEK, SMOG, SMAZE
smokeless powder FILITE
smoky FUMID, REEKY, SOOTY, FUMOSE
smooth EVEN, GLIB, IRON, LENE, SAND, GLOSS, GRIND, LEVEL, PREEN, SLICK, SUAVE, GLASSY
smother CHOKE, STIFLE, STRANGLE
smudge BLOT, SMEAR, BLACKEN
snack BITE, NOSH, BEVER, CANAPE, MORSEL, TIFFIN
snag TEAR, HITCH, TOOTH
snail CONE, CONUS, DRILL, HELIX, MITRA, OLIVA, PHYSA, THAIS, TURBO, WHELK, CERION, DODMAN, NATICA, WINKLE, RISSOID, VALVATA, VERTIGO, VITRINA, DOGWHELK, EARSNAIL, GEOPHILA, JANTHINA, NERITINA, SOLARIUM, TOPSHELL, PERIWINKLE
snail genus NERITA, LYMNAEA, PURPURA
snake ASP, BOA, BOM, NAG, BOID, NAGA, ABOMA, ADDER, BITIS, COBRA, CRIBO, KRAIT, MAMBA, RACER, BONGAR, DIPSAS, DRAGON, ELAPID, ILYSIA, KARAIT, KERRIL, PYTHON, BOKADAM, CAMOODI, ELAPINE, HAGWORM, LANGAHA, PRESTER, RATTLER, REPTILE, SANDBOA, SERPENT, TREEBOA, VIPERID, ANACONDA, BUNGARUM, CASCABEL, CASCAVEL, COLUBRID, EGGEATER, MICRURUS, OPHIDIAN, RATSNAKE, RINGHALS, COACHWHIP, CORNSNAKE, HETERODON, KINGCOBRA, KINGSNAKE, MILKSNAKE, MOLESNAKE, ROUGHTAIL, WARTSNAKE, WHIPSNAKE; *see* VIPER
snake genus NAJA, ELAPS, BOIDAE, CAUSUS, NATRIX, COLUBER, OPHIDIA, BUNGARUS, COLUBRID, CROTALUS, ELAPIDAE, ELAPINAE, SERPENTES
snake, pert. to OPHIC
snakebite aid GUACO, CEDRON
snake-haired woman *see* GORGON
snap BITE, KNAP, COOKY, FLICK, FILLIP, SIMPLE
snap up SNUP
snapper TAMURE
snappish EDGY, CROSS, TESTY, UNCIVIL
snappy BRISK, SHARP
snare GIN, NET, WEB, LURE, TRAP, BENET, DECOY, SPRINGE
snarl GIRN, GNAR, GNARL, GNARR, GROWL, TANGLE
snatch NAB, GRAB, EREPT, FILCH, CLUTCH, PILFER
sneak LURK, SKULK, SLINK, STEAL
sneer *see* MOCK
snide SLY, MEAN
sniff SCENT, SNORT

snip CLIP, PIECE, SHEAR
snob PRIG, BRAHMIN, PARVENU
snood NET, SNELL, FILLET
snoop PRY, LURK, SKULK
snoring STERTOR
snort SNIFF, SNUFF
snout BEAK, NOSE, SERRA, MUZZLE, PROBOSCIS
snow SNA, FIRN, NEVE, PASH, SLEET, COCAINE
snowy NIVAL, NIVEOUS
snub CUT, SCORN, REBUFF, SLIGHT
snuff SNIFF, SNORT, RAPPEE
snuffbox bean CACOON
snug COSY, COZY, TAUT, TRIG, WARM
snuggle HUG, CUDDLE, NESTLE
so SAE, SIC, ERGO, THUS, TRUE, VERY, HENCE
so be it AMEN
soak RET, SOG, SOP, SOUSE, STEEP, FLEECE
soap SAPO, SUDS, AMOLE, CASTILE, DETERGENT
soap vine GOGO
soapstone TALC
sober GRAVE, STAID, SEDATE
sobriquet ALIAS, NICKNAME
social TEA, CIVIC, CIVIL
Socialist DEBS, MARX, OWEN, SHAW, CABET, ENGELS, JAURES, THOMAS, FOURIER, PROUDHON, SUNYATSEN, SAINTSIMON
society *see* ASSOCIATION
sock(s) HOSE, ANKLET, WALLOP
socket PAN, MORTISE
Socrates' poison HEMLOCK
Socrates' pupil PLATO, PHAEDO
Socrates' wife XANTIPPE
sod DIRT, PEAT, TURF, EARTH, GLEBE, SWARD
sodden WET, SOGGY, POACHY, SOAKED
sodium SAL(T), SODA, NITER, NITRE, TRONA, NATRON
sofa COUCH, DIVAN, SQUAB, CANAPE, SETTEE, SETTLE
soft LOW, EASY, WAXY, PIANO
soft drink ADE, POP, COLA, SODA, SODAPOP
soft shoulder BERM(E)
soften BATE, MUTE, LENIFY, MELLOW, RELENT, MOLLIFY; *see* MELT
soft-soap CAJOLE, BLARNEY, FLATTER(Y)

Sohrab relative *see* RUSTAM
soil SOD, LOAM, MARL, DIRTY, GOMBO, HUMUS, LOESS, DEFILE, PEDOCAL
solder FUSE, BRAZE, ROSIN
soldier GI, ROK, VET, KERN, ANZAC, ASKAR, CADET, CROAT, JAGER, KERNE, POILU, NIZAM, REDIF, SEPOY, TOMMY, UHLAN, ATKINS, GALOOT, JAEGER, LANCER, ZOUAVE, DOGFACE, PANDOUR, SADSACK, BUCKSKIN; *see* MERCENARY
sole LONE, ONLY, VOLA, SLADE; *see* FLOUNDER
sole, of the PLANTAR
solemn GRAVE, FORMAL, SOMBER
solicit ASK, BEG, BID, FRUM, PLEA, TOUT, URGE, COURT, PLEAD, CANVASS
solid FIRM, HARD, DENSE, MASSY, COMPACT; *see* GEOMETRIC
solidify OSSIFY, PETRIFY; *see* CONGEAL
solitaire KLONDIKE, CANFIELD, PATIENCE
solitary (A)LONE, SINGLE, REMOTE
Solomon relative DAVID
solution strength TITER, TITRE
solve UNFOLD, UNRAVEL
solvent WATER, CUMENE, GLYCOL, KETONE, PHENOL, ACETONE, ALCOHOL, ANILINE, BENZENE, DIOXANE, LIGROIN, FURFURAL, GLYCEROL
Somalian measure CABA, JARAT, TABAL, JUCHART
Somalian money BESA, SOMALO
somber DARK, MURKY, DISMAL, GLOOMY
son BAR, MAC, FILS, FITZ, HEIR, CADET, SCION, ABSALOM, DAUPHIN, PROGENY
sonar ASDIC
son-in-law GENER
song AIR, LAY, ODE, UTA, ARIA, DITE, FADO, GLEE, HYMN, LEED, LIED, MASS, MELE, NOEL, PEAN, TUNE, BAROL, BLUES, CHANT, DERRY, DIRGE, DITTY, DOINA, ELEGY, LYRIC,

MATIN, MELOS, MOTET, PAEAN, PSALM, THEME, ANTHEM, ARIOSO, AUBADE, BALLAD, CHANTY, CHAUNT, CHORAL, LIEDER, STROUD, CANCION, CANTATA, CANZONE, CHANCON, CHANSON, CHANTEY, CHORALE, DESCANT, LULLABY, WASSAIL, ANTIPHON, CANTICLE, CAVATINA, CORONACH, FOLKSONG, MADRIGAL, PARTSONG, SERENADE; *see* MUSICAL FORM

songbird JAY, POE, TIT, TUI, CHAT, IIWI, KOKO, LARK, POPE, QUIT, WREN, CUTIA, CUTTY, MAVIS, PIPIT, ROBIN, VANGA, VIREO, IFRITA, SISKIN, VERDIN, WITTOL, BABBLER, BUSHTIT, CATBIRD, COWBIRD, GRACKLE, KINGLET, MAYBIRD, POEBIRD, SKYLARK, SUNBIRD, TANAGER, TIMALIA, TITLARK, TRILLER, WAGTAIL, WAXWING, BOATTAIL, NUTHATCH, REDSTART, THRASHER, TITMOUSE, WHINCHAT; *see* CROW, FINCH, ORIOLE, SHRIKE, SPARROW, STARLING, SWALLOW, TANAGER, THRUSH, WARBLER, WEAVERBIRD

songbird genus LOXIA, ANTHUS, OSCINE, CAPELLA, MIMIDAE

songlike LYRIC, MELIC, ARIOSE

sonship FILIETY

soon ANON, ENOW, TITE, EARLY, PRONTO

sooner ERE(R), RATHER

Sooner State OK, OKLAHOMA

soot COOM, DIRT, SMUT, SOTE, COLLY, GRIME, BISTER,

soothe CALM, LULL, ALLAY, SALVE

soothing DULCIT, ANODYNE, LENITIVE

soothsayer SPAER, AUSPEX, DIVINE, ORACLE, PYTHON, PALMIST, (H)ARUSPEX; *see* ORACLE

sop SOAK, BRIBE, MORSEL

sophisticate SPOIL, DEBASE, CORRUPT

sophisticated HEP, HIP, BLASE, COMPLEX, REFINED

Sophocles character ELECTRA, OEDIPUS

soprano TREBLE; *see* SINGER

sorcerer *see* WIZARD

sorceress USHA, CIRCE, LAMIA, SIREN, WITCH

sorcery *see* MAGIC

sordid BASE, MEAN, VILE, SEAMY

sore SAIR, ANGRY, LESION

sorghum MILO, KAFIR, SORGO, IMPHEE, KAFFIR, SORGHO; *see* GRAIN

sorrow RUE, WOE, DOLOR, LAMENT, REMORSE

sorry SAD, POOR, PALTRY, CONTRITE, PENITENT

sort ILK, CULL, KIND, SIFT, TYPE, GRADE, TRIAGE

sorter GRADER, STAPLER

sortie *see* SALLY

sortilege LOT; *see* MAGIC

sot BLOAT, RUMMY, SOUSE, TOPER

soul AME, ATMA, ANIMA, ATMAN, PRANA, PNEUMA, PSYCHE, JIVATMA

sound FIRM, HALE, TRIG, AUDIO, INLET, PLUMB, SOLID, VALID, FATHOM, STRAIT

sound, pert. to SONIC, SONANT

sounding device SONAR, SONDE

soundless MUTE, SILENT, ASONANT

sounds DIN, POP, POW, RAP, ZAP, ZIP, BANG, BIRR, BONG, BOOM, BUST, BUZZ, CHUG, CLAP, CLOP, DING, DONG, ECHO, FIZZ, FLOP, GLUG, GOWL, LISP, PEAL, PING, PUFF, PURL, RING, ROLL, SIGH, SLAM, TALK, TANG, THUD, TICK, TINK, TOLL, TONE, TOOT, TUCK, TUNE, WHAM, WHOP, YARR, ALARM, BINGO, BLARE, BLAST, CLANG, CLANK CLICK, CLINK, CLOOP, CLUMP, CLUNK, CRACK, CREAK, CRUMP, DRONE, FLUMP, GLUCK, GRIDE, KNELL, MUSIC, NOISE, PLASH, PLUMP, SKIRL, SMACK, SOUGH, SWISH, TROIT, TWANG, TWEET, VOICE, WHACK, WHANG,

WHIRR, WOOSH, ACCENT, BUBBLE, CRUNCH, FIZZLE, JANGLE, JINGLE, MELODY, MUFFLE, MURMUR, MUTTER, NICKER, PATTER, RATTLE, REPORT, RUSTLE, SIZZLE, SPEECH, SPLASH, SPLISH, SQUISH, TATTOO, TIMBRE, TINGLE, TINKLE, WHOOSH, CADENCE, CLANGOR, CLATTER, DUBADUB, PITAPAT, RATATAT, RUBADUB, SONANCY, STRIDOR, TWITTER, WHISTLE; *see* CRY, ANIMAL, BIRD

soup BISK, STEW, BROTH, GUMBO, PUREE, BISQUE, BURGOO, POTAGE, CHOWDER, POTTAGE, BOUILLON, CONSOMME

soupçon BIT, HINT, TRACE, SUSPICION

sour WRY, ACID, TART, ACERB, ACRID, ACIDIC, BLEEZE, ACETOSE

source FONT, ROOT, ORIGIN, SPRING

South SUR, DIXIE, AUSTER

So. African BOER, AFRIKANER

So. African language AFRIKAANS; *see* BANTU

So. African leader SMUTS, HERTZOG, VORSTER

So. African measure MUID, MOREN, SCHEPEL

So. African money CENT, POND, RAND, FLORIN, DAALDER

So. American tree COCA, CUCA, MORA, TOLU, VERA, BALSA, CACAO, CAROB, CEBIL, CEIBO, COUMA, HEVEA, SORVA, TENIO, UMIRI, UMIRY, BOMBAX, ASSEGAI

So. American tribe *see p. 344*

South Carolina, South Dakota information *see p. 308*

southern AUSTRAL

souvenir RELIC, MEMENTO, KEEPSAKE

sovereign QUID, SKIV, IMPERIAL; *see* MONARCH

sovereignty SWAY, EMPERY, DYNASTY, DOMINION

soviet COUNCIL

Soviet republic *see p. 287*

sow SOO, SEED, PLANT, SCATTER; *see* SWINE

soybean, product MISO, TOFU

spa *see* SPRING

space GAP, LORA, LORE, ROOM, AREOLA, AREOLE, HIATUS, METOPE

space, pert. to SPATIAL

spacecraft MARS, APOLLO, COSMOS, GEMINI, PROTON, RANGER, SKYLAB, VENERA, VIKING, MARINER, MERCURY, PEGASUS, PIONEER, PROGNOZ, SPUTNIK, VOSKHOD, VOYAGER, ELEKTRON, EXPLORER, PROGRESS, SPACELAB, SURVEYOR, VANGUARD, FRIENDSHIP; *see* ROCKET, SATELLITE

spaceman *see* ASTRONAUT

spacious VAST, LARGE, ROOMY

spade DIG, LOY, CARD, SPUD, SHOVEL

spaghetti *see* PASTA

Spain, Spaniard DIEGO, IBERIA(N), CASTILIAN

Spain, language of BASQUE, CATALAN, GALICIAN

span ARCH, PAIR, TEAM, YOKE, BRIDGE

Spanish dialect ASTURIAN, ARAGONESE, CASTILIAN, ANDALUSIAN

Spanish hero (EL)CID

Spanish kingdom LEON, ARAGON, CASTILE

Spanish measure BUTT, CODO, COPA, DEDO, MOYO, VARA, ALMUD, BRAZA, CAHIZ, LEGUA, LINEA, MEDIO, PALMO, SESMA, ARROBA, CUARTA, ESTADO, FANEGA, RACION, YUGADA, CANTARA, CELEMIN, ESTADEL, PULGADA

Spanish money PESO, REAL, PESETA, ALFONSO, CENTIMO, PISTOLE

Spanish weight ONZA, LIBRA, MARCO, TOMIN, ADARME, ARROBA, DINERO, OCHAVA

Spanish words *see p. 264*

spar BOX, BOOM, GAFF, MAST, YARD, SPRIT; *see* FIGHT

spare LEAN, THIN, EXTRA, GAUNT, LENTEN, MEAGER

spark WOO, BEAU, COURT, KINDLE, SCINTILLA

spark producer FLINT
sparkle FLASH, GLEAM, GLISTEN, GLITTER, CORUSCATE
sparrow DONEY, CHIPPY, CHIPPIE, DUNNOCK, RICEBIRD
sparse MEAGER, SCANTY
Spartan king AGIS, LEONIDAS, MENELAUS, TYNDAREUS
spasm FIT, TIC, CRAMP, ICTUS, THROE, CHOREA, CLONUS
spat ROW, TIFF, GAITER, DISPUTE
spate FLOOD, DELUGE, DOWNPOUR
spatial AREAL
spatula KNIFE, TROWEL, SPREADER
spawn OVA, ROE, EGGS, REDD, BEGET, PRODUCE
speak SAY, LISP, ORATE, UTTER, VOICE, ARTICULATE
speak, inability to ALALIA, MUTISM, APHASIA
speaker AUDIO, ORATOR, RHETOR, LOCUTOR
spear GIG, DART, FRAM, GAFF, GORE, PIKE, ACLYS, BLADE, LANCE, ONCIN, PILUM, SHAFT, SHOOT, VOUGE, ATLATL, ERAMEA, GIDGEE, GLAIVE, PIERCE, ASSAGAI, ASSEGAI, BAYONET, BOURDON, HARPOON, JAVELIN, LEISTER, TRIDENT, VERUTUM, GAVELOCK
spear thrower ATLATL, WOMERA
spear-shaped HASTATE
special KHAS, RARE, KHASS, UNIQUE, UNUSUAL
specie CASH, COIN, MONEY
species *see* CLASS
specific PRECISE, CONCRETE, DEFINITE
specimen SLIDE, SAMPLE, SWATCH
speck BIT, DOT, FLAW, MOTE, FLECK, PARTICLE
spectacle DRAMA, PAGEANT
spectacles *see* EYEGLASSES
spectator OBSERVER, ONLOOKER
specter BOG(E)Y, GHOST, SHADE, SPOOK, SPIRIT, SPRITE, WRAITH, EIDOLON, PHANTOM
speech SPIEL, SERMON, LECTURE, ORATION, PARLANCE
speech art ORATORY, RHETORIC
speech defect LISP, ALOGIA, STAMMER, STUTTER, LALLATION
speechless MUM, DUMB, MUTE, SURD, APHASIC, APHEMIC, APHONIC
speed HIE, RUN, PACE, RACE, TEAR, HASTE, TEMPO, HASTEN
speedy APACE, QUICK, RAPID, SWIFT, PROMPT
spell HEX, JYNX, HOODOO, TRANCE
spend LAVISH, DISBURSE
spendthrift ROUNDER, WASTREL, PRODIGAL
spent WORN, TIRED, EFFETE, FAGGED
sphere ORB, GLOBE, ORBIT, SCOPE, RONDULE
spice DASH, MACE, MULL, TANG, CLOVE, CUBEB, GUSTO, CASSIA, NUTMEG, SEASON, STACTE, ALLSPICE; *see* HERB, SEASONING, CONDIMENT
spice ball FAG(G)OT
spicule TOXA, OXEA, ACTINE
spicy RACY, FIERY, RISQUE, PUNGENT, AROMATIC
spider COP, TRIVET, GRIDDLE, SKILLET, ARACHNID
spider fluid ARANEIN
spider genus LYCOSA, ARGIOPE, ATTIDAE, PHOLCUS, ARANEIDA, ULOBORUS
spiders ARAIN, ATTID, ARRAND, KATIPO, MYGALE, ARANEID, LYCOSID, MYGALID, PHOLCID, PHRYNID, ATTERCOP, ETTERCAP, LONGLEGS, ORBITELE, SOLIFUGE, SOLPUGID, THOMISID, ULOBORID, WANDERER, TARANTULA
spigot PLUG, SPILE; *see* FAUCET
spike DAG, EAR, GAD, BROB, TINE, SPICA, ANTLER, IMPALE
spiked TINED, SPICATE
spile TAP, BUNG, PLUG, SPOUT, SPIGOT
spill SHED, SLOP, TUMBLE
spin BIRL, EDDY, REEL, RIDE, TWIRL, WHIRL, ROTATE
spinach ORACH, GREENS, ORACHE

spinal RACHIAL, RACHIDIAN
spinal cord MYELON
spindle COP, AXIS, AXLE, HASP, ARBOR, QUILL, MANDREL
spine AXIS, AXON, SETA, ARETE, CHINE, QUILL, THORN, CHAETA, NEEDLE, RACHIS, VERTEBRA
spinet PIANO, UPRIGHT, VIRGINAL
spinning machine MULE, JENNY, CHARK(H)A, THROSTLE
spinning term FLYER, WHORL, BOBBIN, ROVING, WHARVE, DISTAFF, SPINDLE, TREADLE, TRAVELER
spiny HISPID, THORNY, PRICKLY
spiral(s) HELIX, VOLUTE, HELICAL, HELICES, HELICOID, SCROLLED
spire SHAFT, STALK, FLECHE, STEEPLE; *see* TOWER
spirit FAY, JIN, ELAN, JINN, SOUL, ZEMI, AGIEL, ARIEL, DEMON, DEVIL, GEIST, GENIE, GENII, HUACA, JINNI, KELPY, LARES, METAL, DAEMON, ELIXIR, ESPRIT, JINNEE, KELPIE, MANITO, MORALE, UNDINE, YAKSHA, BANSHEE, BANSHIE, KATCINA, LEMURES, MANITOU; *see* GHOST
spirited EAGER, LUSTY, LIVELY, SPUNKY
spit EMIT, SHOAL, IMPALE, SALIVA, SKEWER
spite VENOM, MALICE, RANCOR, SPLEEN
splash LAP, DAUB, PURL, SWASH, SPARGE, SP(L)ATTER
spleen IRE, GALL, MILT, SPITE
splendid GRAND, AUREATE
splendor POMP, ECLAT, SHEEN, LUSTER, GRANDEUR
splenic MILTY, LIENAL
splice WED, JOIN(T), UNITE
splinter SPILL, SHIVER, SLIVER, FLINDER
split TEAR, RIFT, BURST, CLEAVE, SCHISM; *see* SUNDER
split hairs CAVIL, QUIBBLE
splotch BLOT, STAIN, SPLASH
spoil(s) MAR, PET, ROT, LOOT, SOUR, UNDO, BOOTY, BOTCH, DECAY, TAINT, CODDLE
spoked RADIAL
spoken ORAL, ALOUD, PAROL(E), VIVAVOCE
sponge MUMP, SWAB, ASCON, CADGE, ERASE, MOOCH, ASCULA, LEUCON
sponge spicule OXEA, TOXA, ACTINE
sponsor ANGEL, PATRON, SURETY
sponsorship (A)EGIS, AUSPICES
spoof FOOL, HOAX, JOKE
spooky EERIE, WEIRD, SPECTRAL
spool COP, PIRN, REEL, WHORL, BOBBIN, WHARVE
spoon PET, NECK, LADLE, SCOOP
sporadic DESULTORY, OCCASIONAL
spore(s) SORI, SORUX, ZYGOTE
spore case(s) ASCI, ASCUS, THECA
spore fruit AECIA, TELIA, AECIUM, TELIUM
sport RUX, ROMP, WEAR, FROLIC, GAMBOL, PASTIME
sport field GRID, OVAL, RINK, COURT, GREEN, LINKS, TRACK, COURSE, GROUND, DIAMOND, GRIDIRON; *see* ARENA
sports JUDO, POLO, POOL, BANDY, BOWLS, CATCH, DARTS, FIVES, RUGBY, TRACK, BOXING, DISCUS, DIVING, HOCKEY, KARATE, PELOTA, QUOITS, RACING, SHINNY, SKIING, SOCCER, SQUASH, TENNIS, BOWLING, CRICKET, CROQUET, CURLING, FENCING, FISHING, HUNTING, JAIALAI, JOGGING, PALLONE, RUNNING, SHOTPUT, SKATING, SNOOKER, TENPINS, TILTING, BASEBALL, BOLOBALL, FOOTBALL, HANDBALL, HURDLING, LACROSSE, NINEPINS, PALLMALL, PINGPONG, ROUNDERS, SKITTLES, SOFTBALL, SWIMMING, TUGOFWAR, BADMINTON, BILLIARDS, ICEHOCKEY, STICKBALL, WATERBALL, WATERPOLO, WRESTLING, BASKETBALL, DECKTENNIS, GYMNASTICS,

HORSESHOES, ICESKATING, LAWNTENNIS, VOLLEYBALL, TABLETENNIS
spot PIP, ESPY, FLAW, SMUT, MACLE, NEVUS, DETECT, MACULA, SMUTCH, TILAKA, OCELLUS
spotted PIED, PINTO, MACLED, NOTATE, DAPPLED, PIEBALD, SKEWBALD
spouse MATE, CONSORT, PARTNER; *see* HUSBAND, WIFE
spout JET, GUSH, SPILE, FAUCET, NOZZLE
spray FOAM, SCUD, SURF, SPRIG, SPUME, LIPPER, ATOMIZE
spread FAN, TED, OLEO, BRUIT, RANCH, RIVET, SCOPE, STREW, DEPLOY, GOSSIP, NORATE
spree BAT, BOUT, BUST, LARK, TOOT, BINGE, DRUNK, BENDER, FROLIC, CAROUSAL
sprig BRAD, HEIR, TWIG, SCION
sprightly TID, PERT, AGILE, ALERT, BRISK, PEART, BLITHE
spring(s) AIN, EMS, SPA, BATH, COIL, FONT, KELD, SEEP, STEM, BADEN, BOUND, BUXTON, GEYSER, RECOIL, RESILE, BALNEUM, THERMAE, CASTALIA, SARATOGA
spring, pert. to FONTAL, VERNAL
springboard BATULE
springlike VERNAL
sprinkle DEG, SOW, SPRAY, MOTTLE, SPARGE, DREDGE, SCATTER
sprite *see* ELF, SPIRIT
sprout BUD, CHIT, GROW, SCION
spruce TRIG, TRIM, NATTY, PICEA, YEDDO, DAPPER
spry AGILE, BRISK, NIMBLE
spume FOAM, SCUM, FROTH
spunk PLUCK, METTLE; *see* TINDER
spur GAFF, GOAD, ROWEL, CALCAR, GRIFFE
spurious FAKE, BOGUS, FALSE
spurn KICK, SCORN, REJECT
spurt JET, GUSH, SQUIRT
spy ABEL, BOND, GOLD, HALE, HARI, KEEK, PEEK, PEER, ANDRE, FUCHS, PINTO, SNOOP, ARNOLD, CAVELL, SMILEY, SOBELL, MATAHARI
squabble ROW, SPAT, HASSLE, DISPUTE, QUARREL
squalid MANGY, NASTY, SORDID
squall GALE, GUST; *see* WIND
squama ALULA, TEGULA, CALYPTER
squander WASTE, DISSIPATE
square EVEN, FAIR, PLAZA, TALLY
squash PEPO, CRUSH, QUELL, CUSHAW, CYMLING, FLATTEN, PUMPKIN, SCALLOP, SQUELCH, ZUCCHINI
squat DUMPY, FUBSY, PUDGY, CROUCH
squaw MAHALA, MAHALY
squeamish HELOE, QUEASY, FINICAL
squid CALAMAR, INKFISH, CALAMARY
squirrel(-like rodent) BUN, BOBAC, SISEL, XERUS, BEAVER, BOBACK, CHIPPY, GOPHER, MARMOT, SUSLIK, TAGUAN, TALPID, ASSAPAN, CHIPPIE
squirrel genus XERUS, TAMIAS
squirt *see* SPURT
stab GORE, PINK, IMPALE, PIERCE, SKEWER
stabilizer GYRO, BALLAST
stable MEW, BARN, BYRE, SOLID, STALL, STEADY, PADDOCK, CONSTANT
stableman GROOM, AVENER, OSTLER, CURRIER, HOSTLER
stack FLUE, PILE, RICK, CHIMNEY, SCINTLE
stadium STANDS; *see* ARENA
staff ROD, MACE, ANKUS, BATON, CROOK, PEDUM, SQUAD, VERGE, BASTON, CUDGEL, CROSIER, RETINUE, SCEPTER, THYRSUS, CADUCEUS
stag BUCK, DEER, HART, MALE, POLLARD; *see* DEER
stage DAIS, PHASE, PRODUCE, PLATFORM; *see* THEATER
stage direction EXIT, ENTER, MANET, EXEUNT, SENNET
stage equipment RAG, TAB, DROP, FLAT, FOOT, OLEO,

PROP, SPOT, CLOTH, FLOAT, TEASER, CURTAIN, FLIPPER
stage names *see p. 261*
stage part DOCK, GRID, LOFT, WING, APRON, FLIES, SKENE, BOARDS, SKENAI, PAREDUS, COULISSE, GRIDIRON, PLATFORM, PROSCENIUM
stagehand GRIP, CHIPS, FLYMAN, GAFFER, JUICER, PITMAN, CALLBOY, BESTBOY, SCENIST
stagger REEL, STOT, LURCH, WAMBLE
staggering AREEL
stagnation STASIS
staid SOBER, SEDATE, STEADY
stain DYE, BLOT, SPOT, TINT, TASH, SULLY, TAINT, SMIRCH, SMUDGE, SMUTCH, STIGMA
stair term RUN, RISE, NEWEL, RISER, TREAD, FLIGHT, NOSING, LANDING
stake PEL, POT, ANTE, PALE, POST, SPILE, WAGER, PALING, PALISADE
stakelike PALAR
stale BANAL, MUSTY, PASSE, TRITE, EFFETE, RANCID
stalemate TIE, DRAW, IMPASSE, DEADLOCK
stalk(s) CULM, STEM, SCAPE, STIPE, CAULIS, RATOON, PEDICEL, PEDICLE, PETIOLE
stall PEW, CRIB, LOGE, STOG, BOOTH, DELAY, NICHE, STABLE
stallion STUD, STEED, ENTIRE, MORGAN
stamina ENDURANCE
stammer HAW, HEM, FAFFLE, STUTTER
stamp DIE, CHOP, SEAL, BRAND, SIGIL, CACHET, EMBOSS, PESTLE, IMPRINT
stanch DAM, FIRM LEAL, STEM
stand BASE, RISE, ZARF, ABIDE, BOOTH, EASEL, STALL, CASTER, ENDURE, TEAPOY, TRIPOD, TRIVET, TABORET
standard PAR, NORM, TOUG, TYPE, CANON, IDEAL, MODEL, NORMA, TITER, LABARUM; *see* FLAG
standing RANK, ERECT, STATIC, STATUS, PRESTIGE
stanza STEV, ENVOY, STAVE, DISTICH, STROPHE, RUBAIYAT
star COR, NOVA, ASTER, STELLA, ASTERISK; *see* STARS
star cluster GALAXY, SPIRAL, ASTERISM, MILKYWAY, PLEIADES
starch AMYL, ARUM, SAGO, SALEP, FARINA, MANIOC, CASSAVA, STIFFEN
stare GAPE, GAZE, OGLE, GLARE
stark BLEAK, BARREN, DESOLATE
starlike ASTRAL, STARRY, ASTROSE, STELLAR, SIDEREAL, STELLATE
starling HUIA, MINO, MYNA(H), PASTOR
starry STELLAR, SIDEREAL
stars SUN, YED, ADIB, ALYA, ATIK, AZHA, BEID, CAPH, DURH, ENIF, IZAR, JUGA, KAUS, KEID, KIDS, MAIA, MIRA, NAOS, PHAD, SADR, SALM, SKAT, UNUK, VEGA, WEGA, WEZN, ACRAB, ACRUX, AGENA, ALCOR, ALGOL, ALKES, ANCHA, ARKAB, ARNEB, ATLAS, BAHAM, BIHAM, CHARA, CUJAM, CURSA, DABIG, DELTA, DENEB, DIFDA, DUBHE, ERRAI, FURUD, GEMMA, HAMAL, HOMAN, KIFFA, MATAR, MEDIA, MERAK, MIRAC, MIRAK, MIZAR, NIHAL, NUNKI, PHACD, PHAET, RIGEL, SABIK, SAIPH, SPICA, TANIA, WEZEN, ZOSMA, ACAMAR, ADHARA, ALBALI, ALGEDI, ALHENA, ALIOTH, ALKAID, ALMACH, ALNASI, ALTAIR, ALTAIS, ALTARF, ALUDRA, ANCHAT, ARIDED, BOTEIN, CASTOR, DHENEB, ELNATH, ETAMIN, GIENAH, HYADES, KOCHAB, LESATH, MARFIK, MARKAB, MEGREZ, MEISSA, MENKAR, MANKIB, MERKEB, MEROPE, MIRACH, MIRFAK, MURZIN, NEKKAR, PHECDA, PLEIAD, POLLUX, PROPUS, SCHEAT, SIRIUS, SMYRNA, THUBAN, YILDUN, ZANIAH, ZAURAK
start SHY, ONSET, ROUSE, SHOCK, LAUNCH

startle SCARE, SHOCK
starvation FAMINE, INEDIA
stash HIDE, CACHE, HOARD
state AVER, AVOW, ETAT, MOOD, CLAIM, ESTRE, TUATH, ALLEGE, FETTLE, NATION, POLITY, STATUS
statehouse CAPITOL
stately GRAND, REGAL, AUGUST, MAJESTIC
statement BILL, EDICT, DICTUM, PRECIS, ASSERTION
statesman GENRO
statesmen DAY, FOX, ITO, EDEN, BLOM, CATO, CLAY, FISH, GREY, MEIR, PEEL, PITT, ROOT, TITO, TOJO, BENES, BEVIN, CABOT, CIANO, DAWES, HENRY, LODGE, MARAT, NENNI, NITTI, SMUTS, SPAAK, THANT, TISZA, ATTLEE, BRIAND, BUELOW, BUNCHE, CAVOUR, CICERO, CURZON, DANTON, DULLES, ERHARD, FOUCHE, GEORGE, HORTHY, HUGHES, LYTTON, PELHAM, ACHESON, ASQUITH, BALDWIN, BALFOUR, BULLITT, CALHOUN, CLAYTON, COLBERT, HERRIOT, KELLOGG, KOSSUTH, LANSING, MASARYK, MAZARIN, PULASKI, REYNAUD, SALAZAR, STANLEY, STIMSON, TROTZKY, WALPOLE, ADENAUER, BISMARCK, BREZHNEV, BUKHARIN, CROMWELL, DISRAELI, DOLLFUSS, GAMBETTA, HAMILTON, LITVINOV, MIRABEAU, POTEMKIN, RATHENAU, STANHOPE, BENGURION, CHURCHILL, GORBACHEV, KISSINGER, PILSUDSKI, RICHELIEU, ROOSEVELT
static *see* INTERFERENCE
station POST, RANK, DEPOT, PLACE, TERMINAL, TERMINUS
stationary FIXED, STILL, STATIC, STABILE
statue ICON, ORANT, TORSO, EFFIGY, XOANON, ACROLITH, FIGURINE
status RANK, STANDING, CONDITION
statute ACT, LAW, ORDINANCE
stave LAG, BASH, RUNG, STAP
stave off FEND, WARD, AVERT
stay BAR, PROP, STOP, TACK, ABIDE, CHECK, TARRY, LINGER
staylace AGLET
stead LIEU, PLACE
steady BEAU, EVEN, FIXED, STABLE, CONSTANT, UNIFORM
steak CHUCK, FILET, ROUND, TBONE, MINUTE, SIRLOIN
steal COP, NIM, ROB, BONE, CRIB, GLOM, HOOK, LIFT, LOOT, FLICH, HEIST, PINCH, POACH, SWIPE, PILFER, RUSTLE, SNATCH, SNITCH, BARGAIN
steam OAM, FUME, MIST, STUFA, VAPOR
steamboat PACKET
steep RET, SOP, BOWK, SOAK, IMBUE, SHEER, ABRUPT
steeple SPIRE, TOWER, BELFRY, TURRET, MINARET
steer YAW, COND, CONN, HELM, LUFF, GUIDE, PILOT
steering mechanism HELM, WHEEL, RUDDER, TILLER
steersman COX, PILOT, COXSWAIN
stellar ASTRAL, STARRY
stem BASE, BINE, CANE, CORM, CULM, PROW, RISE, ARISE, SHAFT, STALK, STIPE, STRAW, TUBER, DERIVE; *see* ROOT
stench *see* ODOR
step(s) PAS, GAIT, PACE, GRADE, PHASE, STAIR, STILE, TREAD, CHASSE, GRADIN, STRIDE
stern AFT, DOUR, GRIM, REAR, HARSH, AUSTERE
stevedore LOADER, LUMPER, PACKER, STOWER
stew FRET, FUME, HASH, OLIO, OLLA, CURRY, BURGOO, RAGOUT, HARICOT, POTTAGE, TERRINE, COUSCOUS
steward REEVE, FACTOR, DAPIFER, KHANSAMAH
stick(s) BAR, BAT, GAD, BRIN, CANE, GLUE, POGO, WAND, BATON, CAMAN, FAGOT,

PASTE, STILT, ADHERE, CLEAVE, COHERE, MUNDLE; *see* STAFF
sticker BURR, SEAL, LABEL, POSER, THORN
stickler PURIST, TAPIST
sticky GOOEY, GUMMY, TACKY
stiff PRIM, RIGID, CORPSE, FORMAL, WOODEN
stifle CHOKE, MUFFLE, SCOTCH, SUPPRESS
stigma *see* STAIN
still BUT, YET, CALM, COSH, INERT, PLACID, RETORT, WITHAL, ALEMBIC
stimulant THEIN, TONIC, COFFEE, THEINE, CAFFEIN, AMMONIA, CAFFEINE
stimulate FAN, FIRE, GOAD, SPUR, WHET, ELATE, ROUSE
stimulus GOAD, SPUR, DRIVE, STING, MOTIVE
sting BARB, BITE, PRICK, SMART
stinger ANT, GNAT, WASP, HORNET
stingy MEAN, CLOSE, SKIMPY, MISERLY
stink *see* ODOR
stint DUTY, TASK, CHORE, SKIMP, SCRIMP, SKINCH
stipend PAY, WAGE, ANNAT, SALARY, PENSION, PREBEND
stir ADO, FUSS, RILE, ROIL, TODO, BUDGE, INCITE; *see* JAIL
stitch SEW, TACK, TUCK, BASTE, CRICK, SUTURE
stoat ERMINE, WEASEL
stock RACE, BREED, GOODS, HOARD, STORE, STIRPS, PLENISH
stock exchange CURB, BOURSE, MARKET
stockade PEN, BOMA, ETAPE, CORRAL, BULWARK
stockings HOSE, NYLONS, HOSIERY
stocky STUB, DUMPY, PLUMP, SQUAT, CHUNKY
stoic ZENO, SENECA, PATIENT, SPARTAN
stoker TEASER, FIREMAN
stole SCARF, ORARION, FILCHED
stolen property HAUL, LOOT, PELF, SWAG, MANNER, MAINOUR
stolid DULL, HEAVY, OBTUSE, WOODEN, PHLEGMATIC
stomach CRAW, BELLY, RUMEN, TRIPE, OMASUM, VENTER
stone GEM, PIT, FLAG, SEED, GEODE, HERMA, LAPIS, STEAN, STEEN, TABLE, ASHLAR, PEBBLE, CALLAIS, DORNICK, ROSETTA, LAPIDATE, LAPILLUS; *see* ROCK, MINERAL
stone heap AHU, KARN, CAIRN(E)
stone, precious LASK, OPAL, RUBY, BAHIA, DORJE, LASKE, RUBIN, VAJRA, ADAMAS, LASQUE, LIGURE, TABLET, ANTHRAX, BRIOLET, CATSEYE, DIAMOND, EMERALD, JACINTH, PRASINE, RUBELET, SMARAGD, HYACINTH, SAPPHIRE
stone, semiprecious JADE, BERYL, LAPIS, MACLE, TOPAZ, GARNET, IOLITE, QUARTZ, SPINEL, ZIRCON, AXINITE, EUCLASE, GIRASOL, HYALITE, KUNZITE, OLIVINE, OVALINE, PERIDOT, TURCOIS, TURKOIS, AMETHYST, ESSONITE, GIRASOLE, MELANITE, NEPHRITE, SODALITE, TURQUOISE
stone, woman turned to NIOBE
stonecutter MASON, LAPICIDE
stonecutter's tool SAX, HAWK, SEAX, DROVE, GAVEL, BANKER, BROACH, CHISEL, BOASTER
stonelike LITHOID
stoneware GRES
stooge FOIL, TOOL, PAWN, DUMMY
stool STUMP, TABOURET, FOOTSTOOL
stool pigeon RAT, SPY, NARK, INFORMER
stoop BOW, BEND, DEIGN, PORCH, VERANDA(H)
stop DAM, END, BALK, CONK, PLUG, QUIT, REST, STEM, WHOA, AVAST, BELAY, CLOSE, PAUSE, STALL, ARREST, DESIST; *see* ORGAN

stopgap EXPEDIENT, MAKESHIFT
stoppage JAM, HALT, STASIS, CLOTURE
stopper WAD, BUNG, CORK, PLUG, SPILE, TAMPION
store PX, COOP, MART, POST, CACHE, HOARD, STOCK, ENSILE, SUPPLY, CANTEEN, GROCERY, SUTLERY
storehouse BARN, GOLA, SILO, DEPOT, ETAPE, ARSENAL, GRANARY, MAGAZINE
storeroom CELLAR, CLOSET, LARDER, PANTRY, BUTTERY
stork JABIRU, MAGUARI, MARABOU, ADJUTANT
stork genus CICONIA
storm BURA, FUME, FURY, GALE, RAGE, RANT, RAVE, BURAN, ORAGE, SAMIEL, SIMOON, KHAMSIN, SHAITAN, TEMPEST, TORNADO, TYPHOON
stormy petrel ASSILAG
story EPIC, GEST, LORE, REDE, SAGA, TALE, YARN, CONTE, FABLE, GESTE, NOVEL, LEGEND
stout FAT, BURLY, HUSKY, PORTLY, STANCH, STOCKY; *see* BEER
stove ETNA, RANGE, COCKLE
stow PACK, STORE, STEEVE
Stowe character EVA, TOM, SIMON, TOPSY, LEGREE
strafe RAKE, CENSURE
straight AROW, JUST, PURE, RIGHT, DIRECT, HONEST
strain TAX, LINE, TIRE, EXERT, STOCK, EFFORT, PURIFY, LINEAGE, TENSION
strainer SILE, SIEVE, STRUM, TAMIS, TAMMY, SCREEN, COLANDER
strait BASS, NECK, MENAI, NARROW, TORRES, CHANNEL, EVRIPOS, MALACCA, MESSINA, MACKINAC, MAGELLAN, GIBRALTAR
strand PLY, BEACH, FIBER, SHORE, THREAD
strange ODD, RARE, UNCO, FREMD, OUTRE, WEIRD, EXOTIC
stranger ALIEN, FOREIGNER
strangle CHOKE, GARROT, SCRAG, STIFLE, GARROTTE, THROTTLE
strap JESS, REIN, LEASH, THONG, HALTER, LATIGO
strap-shaped LORATE, LIGULATE
strass GLASS, PASTE
stratagem COUP, PLOY, RUSE, WILE, SCHEME, TACTIC, TREPAN
stratum BED, SEAM, LAYER, FOLIUM
Strauss work SALOME, ARIADNE, DONJUAN, ELEKTRA, FLEDERMAUS
Stravinsky work RITE, FIREBIRD, PETROUCHKA, PULCINELLA
straw CHAFF, HAULM, FESCUE
stray ERR, GAD, WAIF, DOGIE, RAMBLE, DEVIATE
streak ROE, LINE, VEIN, STRIA, TRAIT, STRIAE
streaky LINY, ROWY, LACED
stream AAR, RIO, RUN, FLOW, RILL, SIKE, BOURN, BROOK, RIVER, ARROYO, RUNNEL
streamer FLAG, BANNER, PENNANT
street RII, RIO, RUE, VIA, WAY, CALLE, ARTERY, AVENUE
streetcar TRAM, TROLL(E)Y
strength MAIN, FORCE, MIGHT, VIGOR, POTENCY
stress ARSIS, ICTUS, ACCENT, STRAIN, TENSION
stretch EKE, STENT, TRACT, SPREAD, DISTEND
stretched out CRANED, PROLATE
stretcher LITTER, (S)TENTER
strew SOW, SPREAD, SCATTER
strict NICE, EXACT, STERN, SEVERE, AUSTERE
stride GAIT, PACE, STEP
strident HARSH, SHRILL, GRATING
strife WAR, FEUD, STASIS, DISCORD, STRUGGLE
strike BAT, RAP, BAFF, CONK, PELT, PUTT, SLAP, SLUG, SOCK, SWAT, WHAM, CLOUT, SMITE, WHACK, LARRUP, PELTER, POMMEL, BOYCOTT, WALKOUT
strikebreaker *see* SCAB
string CORD, LACE, LINE, TWINE, CATGUT
string instrument GUE, KIT, UKE, ARPA, ASOR, BINA, CRUT, GIGA, GORA, HARP, KOTO, LUTE, LYRE, ROTE, TURR, VINA, VIOL, AMATI,

BANJO, CANUN, CELLO, CROOD, CROWD, CRWTH, GAMBA, GEIGE, GORAH, GOURA, GRAND, GUDOK, GUIGE, GUMBE, GUMBY, GUSLA, JAMON, KITAR, NABLA, NANGA, NEBEL, PIANO, REBAB, REBEC, ROCTA, RUANA, SAROD, SITAR, STRAD, TARAU, TIPLE, VIOLA, VOYAL, VOYOL, CATGUT, CHELYS, CITOLE, FIDDLE, GOUSLE, GUITAR, KISSAR, KITTAR, REBECK, RIBIBE, SABECA, SANCHO, SANTIR, SATTAR, SPINET, TYMPAN, URHEEN, VIELLE, VIOLIN, ZITHER, BANDORE, CEMBALO, CHROTTA, CITHARA, CITTERN, CLAVIAL, CLAVIER, CREMONA, GITTERN, KANTELE, MANDOLA, PANDORA, PANDORE, PIANINO, PIANOLA, SAMBUKE, SAMISEN, SARANGI, SARINDA, THEORBO, UKULELE, UPRIGHT, VIHUELA, ARCHLUTE, AUTOHARP, BARITONE, BELLHARP, CLAVICIN, DULCIMER, JEWSHARP, MANDOLIN, PIANETTE, POCHETTE, PSALTERY, VIRGINAL, ZIMBALON, BALALAIKA, MONOCHORD

strip BARE, FLAY, LATH, LIST, PEEL, SLAT, SWATH, BATTEN, DIVEST, FILLET, FLENSE, SPLINE, STRAKE, DISROBE, UNDRESS

stripe BAND, STREAK, CHEVRON

striped VITTATE, STRIATED

stripling LAD, SPRIG, YOUTH

stripper ECDYSIAST

strive VIE, LABOR, STRAIN

stroke FIT, BAFF, COUP, FEAT, ICTUS, CARESS, FONDLE

stroll ROVE, TURN, WALK, JAUNT, MEANDER, SAUNTER

strong FERE, HALE, GAMY, BRAWNY, COGENT, MADURO, ROBUST, VIRILE, PUISSANT

strong point FORTE

strong-arm man GOON, THUG, BOUNCER

strongbox SAFE, VAULT, COFFER

stronghold *see* FORT

strongly AMAIN

strongman ATLAS, TITAN, SAMSON, TARZAN, SAMPSON, HERCULES

strophe STANZA

structure FRAME, EDIFICE

struggle COPE, MELEE, PENIEL, STRIFE, CONFLICT, FLOUNDER

strum PLUCK, THRUM, FINGER

strut BRACE, SUPPORT, SWAGGER

stub BUTT, SNAG, GUARD, STUMP

stubborn DOGGED, MULISH, ORNERY, WILLFUL

stud BOSS, KNOB, NAIL, STALLION

student COED, TYRO, AGGIE, ELEVE, PLEBE, PUPIL, ECOLIER, LEARNER, MONITOR, SCHOLAR, DISCIPLE

studio ATELIER, WORKSHOP

study CON, DEN, BONE, CRAM, PORE, READ, PONDER, EXAMINE

study group CLASS, SEMINAR

stuff PAD, RAM, CRAM, GORGE

stuffing WAD, FARCE, KAPOK, DRESSING

stum MUST, JUICE, RENEW

stumble STOT, TRIP, BLUNDER

stump BUTT, SNAG, STUB, PUZZLE

stun DAZE, SHOCK, ASTOUND

stunt FEAT, DWARF, TRICK

stupefy DAZE, DOPE, MAZE, NUMB, STUN, BESOT

stupid DUMB, CRASS, DENSE, DOPEY, OBTUSE, GLAIKIT

stupid person ASS, OAF, CLOD, COOT, DODO, DOLT, LOON, LOUT, LOWN, MOKE, DUMMY, DUNCE, GOOSE

stupor COMA, SOPOR, TORPOR

sturdy GID, HARDY, STOUT, WALLY, ROBUST

sturgeon HUSO, ELOPS, BELUGA, GANOID, HAUSEN, KALUGA, BELOUGA, STERLET, PADDLEFISH

Stuyvesant's estate BOWERY

style FAD, TON, CHIC, MODE, NAME, GENRE, VOGUE

stylish CHIC, TONY, NOBBY, CLASSY, MODISH

stymie BALK, FOIL, IMPEDE
styptic ALUM, AMADOU, ASTRINGENT
suave SMOOTH, URBANE, GRACIOUS
subdue BEAT, CRUSH, QUELL, WORST, DEFEAT, MASTER
subject NOUN, TEXT, LIEGE, PRONE, THEME, TOPIC, VASSAL
sublime LOFTY, NOBLE, EXALTED
submarine UBOAT, PIGBOAT, NAUTILUS
submerge DIVE, SINK, PLUNGE
submissive MEEK, TAME, DOCILE
submit BOW, OBEY, PROPOSE
subordinate AIDE, SECOND, HIRELING, MYRMIDON
subside EBB, SINK, WANE, ABATE
subsidy AID, GRANT, SUPPORT
subsist FARE, LIVE, EXIST
substance GIST, PITH, MEANS, STUFF, WEALTH, ESSENCE
substantiate VERIFY, BOLSTER, CONFIRM, WARRANT
substitute VICE, PROXY, DEPUTY, ERSATZ, STANDIN, SUPPLANT
subterfuge DODGE, SHIFT, EVASION
subtle SLY, DEEP, WILY, ARTFUL, CUNNING, PROFOUND
subtract *see* DEDUCT
suburb ENVIRON, FAUBOURG
subvert RUIN, UPSET, CORRUPT
subway BMT, IND, IRT, BART, TUBE, METRO, UNDERGROUND
succeed WIN, ENSUE, FOLLOW, THRIVE, PROSPER, FLOURISH
success HIT, LUCK, ARTHA
successive(ly) AROW, SERIATE
succinct BRIEF, PITHY, TERSE, CONCISE, LACONIC
succumb DIE, YIELD, SUBMIT
Sudan language EFE, MADI, MORU, LENDU; *see* GUR, MANDE
sudden HASTY, ABRUPT
sue WOO, COURT, APPEAL, ENTREAT, LITIGATE
suet FAT, LARD, TALLOW
suffer LET, BEAR, BIDE, CLEM, DREE, PERMIT, STARVE
suffixes *see p. 333*
suffocate CHOKE, STIFLE, SMOTHER, ASPHYXIATE
suffrage VOTE, BALLOT, FRANCHISE
suffragist MILL, BROWN, BECKER, BRIGHT, ANTHONY, BLOOMER, STANTON
sugar GUR, OSE, CANE, BIOSE, HEXOSE, KETOSE, PANELA, GLUCOSE, LACTOSE, MALTOSE, MANNOSE, PANOCHA, SUCROSE, DEXTROSE
sugar cane disease ILIAU
sugar-molasses, mixture MELADA
sugar source SAP, BEET, CANE, CORN, MILK, FRUIT, GRAPE, MAPLE
sugar substitute ASPARTAME, CYCLAMATE, SACCHARIN
suggest HINT, IMPLY, PROPOSE, INTIMATE, INSINUATE
suicide SUTTEE, SEPPUKU, FELODESE, HARAKIRI
suit FIT, ADAPT, HABIT, PETITION, GABARDINE
suit (cards) CUPS, CLUBS, WANDS, EAGLES, HEARTS, ROYALS, SPADES, SWORDS, DIAMONDS, PENTACLES
suitable APT, FIT, MEET, PROPER, FITTING
suitcase *see* BAG
suite FLAT, SERIES, RETINUE
suitor BEAU, SWAIN, WOOER
sulk PET, MOPE, POUT, GROUCH
sullen DOUR, GLUM, GRUFF, POUTY, SURLY, SULKY, TESTY, MOPING, MOROSE, BALEFUL
sultan MURAD, SELIM
sultanate OMAN, MAHRA, KUWAIT, MUSCAT
sultry HOT, CLOSE, HUMID, MUGGY, EROTIC, TORRID
sum ADD, TOT(AL), AMOUNT
sumac RHUS, YEARA, SUMACH
Sumerian dialect EMESAL
summary GIST, BRIEF, RECAP, DIGEST, PRECIS, RESUME
summer, pert. to ESTIVAL
summerhouse CASINO, COTTAGE
summit(s) CAP, DOD, ACME, APEX, KNAP, PEAK, CREST, APICES

summon(s) BID, CALL, CITE, PAGE, SIST, WRIT, CLEPE, EVOKE, KNELL, BECKON, SUBPOENA
sump PIT, WELL, DRAIN
sumptuous RICH, GRAND, LAVISH
sun SOL, TITAN, HELIOS, PHOEBUS
Sun King LOUIS
sun, pert. to SOLAR, HELIACAL
sunder REND, RIVE, SEVER, SPLIT, CLEAVE, DIVIDE
sundry DIVERS, VARIOUS
sunflower GUMWEED, MARIGOLD
Sunflower State KS, KAN(SAS)
sundial part STYLE, GNOMON
sunrise DAWN, AURORA
sunroom(s) SOLARIA, SOLARIUM
sunshade VISOR, AWNING, PARASOL
Sunshine State FL(A), FLORIDA
sunspot(s) UMBRA, FACULA, MACULA, FRECKLE, PENUMBRA(E)
superb RICH, NOBLE, LORDLY, ELEGANT, MAJESTIC
superfluous EXTRA, DETROP, FUTILE, COPIOUS, EXCESSIVE
superior BOSS, BETTER
superlative ULTRA, SUPREME
Superman birthplace KRYPTON
Superman character KENT, LOIS
supernatural MAGIC, OCCULT, UNEARTHLY
supernatural power MANA, NGAI, MAGIC, WAKAN, ORENDA
supersede REPLACE, SUCCEED, SUPPLANT
superstition, object of FETICH, FETISH, TALISMAN
supple AGILE, LITHE, LIMBER, PLIANT, LISSOME
supplement ADD, EKE, APPENDIX
supplication PLEA, SUIT, PRAYER, ENTREATY
supply CATER, EQUIP, RELAY, STOCK, ENDOW, BACKLOG
support FID, LEG, PEG, ABET, BACK, BASE, PROP, STAY, BRACE, PILLAR, SECOND, TRIPOD, UNIPOD
suppose WIS, TROW, WEEN, GUESS, OPINE, ASSUME, RECKON, IMAGINE, SURMISE
suppress BAN, CHECK, QUASH, QUELL, STIFLE, SMOTHER
supreme CHIEF, FINAL, ULTIMATE
sure FIRM, SAFE, SECURE, STABLE
surety VAS, BAIL, BOND, GAGE, HOSTAGE, MAINPRISE
surf SEA, FOAM, SPRAY, SWELL
surface NAP, FACE(T), NAPPE, VENEER, AIRFOIL, EXTERIOR
surfeit *see* CLOY
surfeited BLASE, SATED, REPLETE
surge PUSH, RISE, ROLL, HEAVE, PITCH, SWELL, BILLOW
surgeon MEDICO, DOCTOR, SAWBONES
surgical tools and terms BUR, HYPO, SPUD, SWAB, AMPUL, CLAMP, FLEAM, LANCE, PROBE, SETON, SNARE, STAFF, STUPE, STYLE, SWATH, BILABE, BOUGIE, CATLIN, DOSSIL, GARROT, GORGET, LANCET, MATRIX, NEEDLE, PROBER, SCALER, SPLINT, STILET, STYLET, SUTURE, SWATHE, TAMPON, TREPAN, TROCAR, TWEEZE, VELTIS, XYSTER, ABLATOR, AMPOULE, AMPULLA, CANNULA, CATLING, CAUTERY, CURETTE, EJECTOR, FORCEPS, LEVATOR, MANDREL, MANDRIN, PIPETTE, PLEDGET, PLESSOR, PLUGGER, PLUNGER, SCALPEL, SPATULA, SYRINGE, TRACTOR, TRILABE, TROCHAR, BISTOURY, CATHETER, CROTCHET, DENTAGRA, ECRASEUR, ELEVATOR, EXPLORER, FORCIPES, SPECULUM, SQUEEZER, TENACULA
Suriname language DUTCH, SRANAN, TAKITAKI
surly *see* SULLEN
surmise GUESS, INFER, OPINE
surpass CAP, TOP, BEST, EXCEL, OUTDO, ECLIPSE
surplus EXTRA, EXCESS, OVERAGE

surprise JOLT, AMAZE, ASTOUND
surrender CEDE, YIELD, REMISE, RESIGN, CESSION, DEDITION
surrogate LOCUM, DEPUTY, REGENT
surround GIRD, RING, BESET, INARM, AMBUSH, INVEST, ENCLOSE, ENVELOP
survey MAP, PLOT, POLL, SCAN, REVIEW, CANVASS
surveying instrument ROD, LEVEL, STADIA, ALIDADE, CALIPER, TRANSIT, VERNIER
surveyor's assistant RODMAN, LINEMAN
suspect THINK, IMAGINE, PRESUME, SURMISE
suspend BAR, HAND, STAY, DEFER, DISBAR, ADJOURN
suspended PENDENT, PENSILE
suspenders BRACES, GALLOWS, GALLUSES
suspension DELAY, STOPPAGE
suspicion HINT, HUNCH, TRACE, INKLING
sustained (SOS)TENUTO
sustenance FOOD, BREAD, MANNA
suture SEW, SEAM, RAPHE
swab MOP, WIPE, MALKIN
swaddle WRAP, SWATHE
swag LOOT, SWAY, BOOTY, LURCH
swain LOVER, SUITOR, GALLANT
swallow EAT, BOLT, GULP, ABSORB, INGEST, MARTIN, MARTLET, HIRUNDINE
swamp SLOO, SLUE, VLEI, TAIGA, TERAI; *see* MARSH
swan COB, PEN, CYGNET
swan genus OLOR, CYGNUS
swap TRADE, BARTER, EXCHANGE
swarm BEVY, HIVE, NEST, TEEM, CROWD, HORDE
swarthy DUN, DARK, DUSKY
swastika FYLFOT
sway YAW, REEL, ROCK, ROLL, RULE, WAVER
Swaziland language SISWATI
Swaziland money LILANGENI
swear VOW, AVER, AVOW, CURSE, AFFIRM, DEPONE, DEPOSE, PLEDGE
sweat OOZE, EXUDE, SUDOR
sweater GANSEY, JERSEY, SLIPON, CARDIGAN, PULLOVER
Sweden, rulers of CARL, INGE, JOHN, JOHAN, OSCAR, SWEYN, BIRGER, CHARLES, ADOLPHUS, GUSTAVUS, MARGARET, CHRISTIAN, CHRISTINA, FREDERICK
Swedish measure AM, ALN, FOT, REF, TUM, FAMN, FODER, KANNA, KAPPE, LINJE, NYMIL, SPANN, TUNNA, JUMFRU, KOLLAST, TUNLAND, OXHUVUD
Swedish money ORE, DALER, KRONA, RIGSDALER
Swedish weight ASS, ORT, PUND, STEN, UNTZ, NYLAST, LISPUND
sweep DRAG, DUST, RAKE, RANGE, SWATH, TRAIL
sweet HONEY, DULCET, SUGARY; *see* CANDY
sweet potato YAM, BATATA, CAMOTE, OCARINA
sweetbread RIS, THYMUS, PANCREAS
sweetheart JO, GRA, BEAU, JILL, LASS, FLAME, LEMAN, LOVER, POPSY, FIANCE, LASSIE, STEADY, SUITOR, FIANCEE, VALENTINE
sweetmeat *see* CANDY
swell PUFF, SURF, WAVE, BULGE, HEAVE, DILATE
swelling STY, WEN, BUBO, GALL, LUMP, NODE, PUFF, BLAIN, EDEMA, POLYP, GOITER, STRUMA, POLYPUS, HEMATOMA
swerve SHY, VEER, SHEER, CAREEN
swift CRAN, FAST, FLIT, FLEET, SWIFTLET
swift genus APUS
swiftly APACE
swig GULP, DRAFT, DRINK
swill SLOP, QUAFF, GARBAGE
swimming NATANT
swimsuit *see* BATHING SUIT
swindle(r) CON, SKIN, BUNCO, TREPAN; *see* CHEAT
swine HOG, PIG, SOW, APER, BOAR, GALT, GILT, PORK, RUNT, SUID, YILT, DUROC, ESSEX, GRICE, PIGGY, SHOAT, SHOTE, SHOTT, SNORK, SUINA, COCHON, GUSSIE, JABALI, JAVALI,

PIGGIE, PIGLET, PORKER, PORKET, TITMAN, GRUNTER, PECCARY, ROASTER, SNORKER, SUFFOLK, SUIDIAN
swine feeding PANNAGE
swine fever ROUGET
swine genus SUS
swine, pert. to PORCINE
swing HANG, JAZZ, JIVE, SWAY, DANGLE, SWITCH, BRANDISH
swinish PORCINE, SUILLINE
swipe LIFT, LEVER, STEAL, HANDLE, PILFER
swirl CURL, EDDY, GORCE, GURGE, TWIST, WHORL
Swiss, Switzerland LADIN, SUISSE, HELVETIA
Swiss language LADIN, ROMANS(C)H
Swiss measure POT, AUNE, FUSS, IMMI, MUID, PIED, SAUM, ZOLL, LIEUE, MAASS, POUCE, SCHUH, STAAB, TOISE, PERCHE, SETIER, KLAFTER, VIERTEL
Swiss money BATZ, FRANC, RAPPE, CENTIME
Swiss patriot TELL
switch TWIG, SHUNT, TOGGLE
swollen TUMID, BOLLEN, EDEMIC, TOROSE, TURGID, TURGENT
swoon SWEB, FAINT, SYNCOPE
swoop POUNCE, DESCEND
sword GRAM, ASCALON, ASKELON, BALMUNG, EXCALIBUR
sword part POMMEL
swords SAX, BOLO, CHIV, EPEE, FALX, FOIL, KRIS, PATA, SEAX, TUCK, BILBO, BRAND, CATAN, DIEGO, ESTOC, KUKRI, SABER, ANDREW, BANCAL, BARONG, DUSACK, FLORET, GLAIVE, KATANA, KHANDA, MACANA, PARANG, RAPIER, SPATHA, TOLEDO, VERDUN, WAFTER, CUTLASS, ESPADON, ESTOQUE, FERRARA, MACHETE, SLASHER, YASHMAC, BASELARD, CLAYMORE, DAMASCUS, FALCHION, SCHLAGER, SCIMITAR, YATAGHAN, SCHIAVONE
sword-shaped ENSATE, XIPHOID, ENSIFORM, GLADIATE
sycamore PLANE, PLATAN(E)
sycophant LEECH, TOADY, FLUNKY, YESMAN
syllable MORA, ARSIS, MORAE, TONIC, PENULT, SONANT, THESIS, ULTIMA
sylvan SHADY, WOODY, WOODED
symbolic figure ZOA
symmetry GRACE, BALANCE, HARMONY
sympathetic TENDER, CONGENIAL
sympathy ACCORD, AFFINITY, COMPASSION
symphony movement FINALE, MENUET, MINUET, SCHERZO, MINUETTO
symptom SIGN, WARNING, PRODROME
synagogue SHUL; *see* TEMPLE
synagogue officer PARNAS(S), SHAM(M)AS, SHAM(M)ASH
syncope FAINT, SWOON, ELISION
syndicate JUDGE, COMBINE
synod COUNCIL, ASSEMBLY
synopsis GIST, DIGEST, RESUME, SUMMARY, ABSTRACT
synthetic ARTIFICIAL; *see* FABRIC
syphilis POX, LUES
syphilis test HAHN
Syrian measure MAKUK, GARAVA
Syrian weight COLA
syrup GORGEAT, SORGHUM, TREACLE, MOLASSES
system ISM, CODE, METHOD, REGIME(N)

T

T-shaped TAU
tab PAN, BILL, FLAP, CHECK, LABEL
tabby CAT, MOREEN, TAFFETA, BRINDLED
tabernacle PYX, TENT, AMBRY, NICHE, CHURCH, TEMPLE
table PYE, FARE, DEFER, SHELVE, VANITY, CREDENCE, POUDREUSE; *see* LIST, STAND
tableland MESA, PLAT, PUNA, KAROO, PLATEAU

tablet PAD, BRED, PILL, SLAB, FACIA, SLATE, STELE, TROCHE
taboo, opposed to NOA
tacit SILENT, IMPLIED, UNSPOKEN
taciturn BRIEF, LACONIC, RETICENT, SATURNINE
tack BEAT, BUSK, JIBE, BASTE, ZIGZAG, SECURE; *see* NAIL
tackle CAT, GUN, GEAR, JEERS, LUFF, GRASP, GARNET, OUTFIT, RUNNER
tacky DOWDY, SEEDY, SHABBY
tact FINESSE, DIPLOMACY
tactic(s) PLOY, MANEUVER, STRATEGY
tactless RUDE, GAUCHE, IMPOLITE
tad TOT, TYKE, GAMIN, URCHIN
tag A(I)GLET, APPEND
tail BUN, FUD, TAG, BUNT, CODA, HIND, SCUT, CAUDA, QUEUE, TRAIL, VERSO, FOLLOW, WREATH
tail, pert. to CAUDAL, CAUDATE
tailless ACAUDAL, ANUROUS
tailor FIT, SARTOR, CLOTHIER
tailor's equipment HAM, GOOSE, NEEDLE, THREAD, SADIRON, THIMBLE
taint ROT, STAIN, SULLY, INFECT, BLEMISH, POLLUTE
Taiwan FORMOSA
Taj Mahal builder JAHAN, JEHAN
Taj Mahal location AGRA
take NAB, GRAB, STEAL, USURP
take away ADEEM, HEAVE, REVOKE
take care HEED, MIND, BEWARE
take off DOFF, FLEE, LEAVE, MIMIC, PARODY
take out DELE, ELIDE, EXPUNGE
take place OCCUR, HAPPEN
talc POWDER, AGALITE, STEATITE, SOAPSTONE
tale LAI, REDE, GESTE, LEGEND; *see* STORY
talent ART, DOWER, FLAIR, FORTE, KNACK, GENIUS, FACULTY
talisman *see* CHARM
talk GAB, GAS, JAW, YAK, BLAB, CHAT, KNAP, RANT, RAVE, SASS, CRACK, ORATE, PRATE, SPEAK, SPIEL, PARLEY, PATTER, YABBER, LECTURE, PALAVER, HARANGUE
tall HIGH, LOFTY
tallow FAT, SUET, STEARN
tally JIBE, MATCH, NOTCH, SCORE
Talmud part GEMARA, MISHNAH
talon FANG, SPUR, STOCK, HALLUX, ZIPPER; *see* NAIL
tamarack LARCH
tambourine *see* PERCUSSION
tame FLAT, BREAK, DOCILE, SUBDUE, INSIPID
tamp PUG, RAM, PACK, POUND
tamper GAFF, MEDDLE, TRIFLE
tan DUN, TAW, BUFF, ECRU, FLOG, ROSS, BEIGE
tang NIP, ZEST, SAVOR, STING
tangent ADJACENT, TOUCHING
tangible TACTILE, PALPABLE
Tangiers measure KULA, MUDD
tangle MAT, FOUL, KNOT, SHAG, SNARL, SLEAVE, EMBROIL
tank VAT, BASIN, OILER, CISTERN
tankard MUG, STEIN; *see* GOBLET
Tantalus relative ZEUS, NIOBE, PELOPS
tantrum (CAT)FIT, CONNIPTION
Taoism founder LAOTSE, LAOTZE
tap DRAFT, DECANT; *see* SPIGOT, TAVERN
taper WANE; *see* CANDLE
tapered CONOID, SPIRED, TERETE
tapestry ARRAS, TAPIS, BAYEUX, DORSAL, DOSSER, GOBELIN
tapeworm T(A)ENIA, CESTODE, CESTOID
tapioca source SALEP, CASAVA, MANIOC, CASSAVA, MANIHOT
tapir (D)ANTA
tar GOB, BREA, PITCH, MALTHA; *see* SAILOR

tardy LATE, REMISS, DILATORY
tare WEED, VETCH
target AIM, BUTT, MARK, BULLSEYE, OBJECTIVE
tariff TAX, DUTY, LEVY, LIST, RATE
tarnish SOIL, STAIN, SULLY
tarot *see* CARD
tarpon ELOPS, OXEYE, SABALO, TARPUM, BONEFISH
tarry LAG, BIDE, STAY, WAIT, DALLY, DAWDLE, LOITER
tarsus HOCK, ANKLE, SHANK
tart ACID, FLAN, KEEN, ACERB, ACRID, HUSSY, SAUCY
tartan PLAID
tartar ARGAL, ARGOL, TARTRE
task PENSUM; *see* CHORE
tassel TUFT, TERCEL, ZIZITH
taste SIP, SUP, TANG, SAVOR, SNACK, DEGUST, FLAVOR, LIKING, PALATE
tasteless FLAT, CRUDE, STALE, VAPID, GAUCHE
tasty *see* SAVORY
tatter RAG, TAG, SCRAP, SHRED
tattle BLAB, PEACH, GOSSIP
tattooing MOKO
taunt JEER, MOCK, TWIT, SCOFF, SNEER, NEEDLE
taut EDGY, SNUG, TRIG, RIGID, STIFF, TENSE, TIGHT, NERVOUS
tavern BAR, INN, PUB, TAP, KHAN, TAMBO, BARROOM, BISTRO, CANTINA, SALOON, TAPROOM
tawdry GAUDY, FLASHY, SLEAZY
tawny DUSKY, SWART, RUBIATE
tax CRO, FEE, CESS, DUTY, GELD, LEVY, SCAT, SCOT, SESS, TIRE, TOLL, LIKIN, RATAL, SCATT, STENT, TITHE, ABKARI, ANNALE, ASSESS, AVANIA, CUSTOM, EXCISE, HIDAGE, IMPOST, INCOME, OCTROI, TAILLE, TARIFF, ANNATES, SCUTAGE, TALLAGE, TRIBUTE
tax collector IRS, OCTROI
taxi CAB, HACK, ARABA, HANSOM
tea CHA, KAT, QAT, TAY, CHAA, KHAT, MATE, TCHA, TSIA, BOHEA, CONGO, DIRCA, HYSON, LEDUM, OOPAK, PEKOE, YERBA, CONGOU, KEEMUN, OOLONG, OOPACK, OSWEGO, PTISAN, TISANE, CAMBRIC, LAPSANG, SOUCHONG
teacake LUNN, SCON(E)
teach DRILL, TUTOR, INSTRUCT
teacher DON, RAB, REB, ALIM, GURU, PROF, MOLLA, MULLA, RABBI, TUTOR, DOCENT, MASTER, MENTOR, MOLLAH, MULLAH, PUNDIT, PEDAGOG, PRECEPTOR, PROFESSOR, INSTRUCTOR
teachers' org. NEA
team RIG, CREW, FIVE, GANG, NINE, PAIR, SPAN, YOKE, ELEVEN, STRING, TANDEM
teamster CARTER, DRIVER
teapot KETTLE, SAMOVAR
teapot cover COS(E)Y
tear JAG, RIP, BEAD, REND, RENT, TATTER, DIVULSE
tearful MOIST, MAUDLIN
tease KID, RIB, COMB, JOSH, RIDE, TWIT, BOTHER, NEEDLE
tedious BORING, DREARY, HUMDRUM
tedium ENNUI, BOREDOM, MONOTONY
teem POUR, SWARM, ABOUND
teeter SWAY, SEESAW, WOBBLE
teeth *see* TOOTH
teeth, false PLATE, DENTURE
Telamon relative AJAX, AEACUS, PELEUS
telegraph part BUG, KEY, ANVIL, TAPPER, TICKER
telegraph signal DAH, DIT, DOT, DASH
telegraphic speed unit BAUD
telegram WIRE, CABLE, MESSAGE
telephone CALL, DIAL, RING, PHONE
telephone term TRUNK, CENTRAL
telescope TUBE, GLASS, BINOCLE
television TV, TELLY, VIDEO
television term SCAN, ADDER, MIXER, RELAY, PICKUP,

SCREEN, SIGNAL, ENCODER, VIDICON, ORTHICON, SCOPHONY, TELECAST, TELEVISE, KINESCOPE
tell OWN, IMPART, DIVULGE; *see* RELATE
Tell's home URI
teller POTDAR, CAMBIST; *see* CASHIER
temerity GALL, CHEEK, NERVE
temper PET, NEAL, HUMOR, ANNEAL, DANDER, TANTRUM
temperament MOOD, GEMUT
temperate MILD, SOBER, MODERATE
Tempest character ARIEL, CALIBAN, PROSPERO
temple TAA, VAT, WAT, FANE, MOSK, NOAS, RATH, CELLA, HUACA, KIACK, KOVIL, RATHA, MOSQUE, PAGODA, TEOCALLI, SYNAGOGUE
temple part NAOS, CELLA, TORII, ADYTUM, PRONAOS, SANCTUM
temporary ACTING, INTERIM, STOPGAP
tempt *see* ENTICE
temptress *see* SIREN
ten DECA(D), DENARY
Ten Commandments DECALOG(UE)
ten thousand MYRIAD
tenacity PLUCK, OBSTINACY
tenancy SOCAGE, TENURE
tenant SAER, INMATE, LESSEE, RENTER, CROFTER, RESIDENT
tend CARE, SERVE, MANAGE, INCLINE
tendency BENT, TENOR, TREND
tender SOFT, SORE, OFFER, GENTLE
tendon CORD, THEW, SINEW, LEADER
tendril BINE, CURL, SPRIG, CAPREOL
tenement FLAT, HOUSE, ROOKERY
tenet DOGMA, MAXIM, PRECEPT
Tennessee information *see* *p. 308*
tennis players FRY, ARTH, ASHE, BETZ, BORG, HARD, HART, HOAD, HUNT, KING, LUTZ, NOAH, WARD, WILLS, BUDGE, BUENO, COOKE, COURT, EVERT, FALES, KODES, LAVER, LENDL, LLOYD, MOODY, OSUNA, PERRY, RIGGS, ROCHE, SEARS, SMITH, VILAS, VINES, WILLS, AUSTIN, BECKER, BOWREY, BROUGH, BROWNE, CASALS, COCHET, COOPER, DROBNY, DUPONT, EBBERN, FRASER, GIBSON, GIMENO, JACOBS, JAEGER, KRAMER, LARNED, LARSEN, LIZANA, MARBLE, MULLOY, MURRAY, PARKER, RICHEY, SEGURA, SEIXAS, STOLLE, SUSMAN, SUTTON, TILDEN, WRIGHT, ALLISON, BARTZEN, BASSETT, CONNORS, EMERSON, LACOSTE, MALLORY, MCENROE, NASTASE, NUTHALL, OSBORNE, RALSTON, SANTANA, SEDGMAN, SHRIVER, TALBERT, TRABERT, WALLACH, GONZALES, WILANDER, GOOLAGONG
tennis term AD, ACE, BAT, BYE, CUT, LET, LOB, SET, CHOP, GAME, LOBB, LOVE, TOSS, VASS, ALLEY, COURT, DEUCE, DRIVE, FAULT, LINER, MATCH, RALLY, SLICE, SMASH, BISQUE, RACKET, STROKE, VOLLEY, DOUBLES, SINGLES, SERVICE
Tennyson character ENID, MAUD, ISOLT, ELAINE
tenon COG, COAK, TUSK
tenor GIST, DRIFT, TREND; *see* SINGER
tense FLEX, PAST, AORIST, FUTURE, PERFECT, PRESENT, PRETERIT, PLUPERFECT; *see* TAUT
tension STRAIN, STRESS
tent PAWL, TIPI, WITU, YURT, TEPEE, TUPEK, YURTA, BIGTOP, ENCAMP, PUPTENT, WIGWAM, KIBITKA, MARQUEE, PAVILION
tent dweller GYPSY, KEDAR, NOMAD, YURUK, INDIAN, BEDOUIN, SCENITE

tentacle PALP, FEELER, ANTENNA
tenth part DECI, TITHE
tentmaker OMAR, KHAYYAM
tenuous RARE, FLIMSY, SLENDER
tenure TERM, INCUMBENCY
ten-year period DECADE, DECENNIAL, DECENNIUM
termination END, CLOSE, EXPIRY
tepee LODGE, WIGWAM, WICKIUP
term DUB, CALL, NAME, TENURE
termagant *see* SHREW
terminal END, ANODE, DEPOT, FINAL, LIMIT, CATHODE
termite NASUTE, TERMES, WHITEANT
tern KIP, RIXY, NODDY, PEARL, SCRAY(E), STERNA, MEDRICK, SKIMMER
terrace TIER, PATIO, GALLERY, PLATEAU, PORTICO
terrestrial GEAL, EARTHLY, MUNDANE, TERRENE, WORLDLY
terrible DIRE, AWFUL, SEVERE
terrier FOX, BULL, SKYE, CAIRN, BOSTON, SCOTCH, AIREDALE
terrify ALARM, APPAL, DAUNT, APPALL, DISMAY
territory REALM, DOMAIN, ENCLAVE, TERRENE, BAILIWICK
terror FEAR, DREAD, PANIC
terrorist GOON, THUG, APACHE, ALARMIST, NIHILIST
terse *see* BRIEF
tessellated INLAID, MOSAIC
test BOSE, EXAM, QUIZ, ASSAY, TEMPT, TRIAL, DRYRUN, TRYOUT, EXAMINE
testify AVER, AVOW, DEPOSE
testy TOUCHY, PEEVISH, PEPPERY
tether LEASH, LONGE, LARIAT
Teuton GOTH, GERMAN
Texas information *see p. 308*
textile *see* FABRIC
texture NAP, WEB, WALE, WOOF, GRAIN, WEAVE, FABRIC
Thackeray character BECKY, ESMOND
Thai SHAN, SIAMESE
Thai language LAO, AHOM, SHAN, CHUANG, KHAMTI, ZHUANG, SIAMESE
Thai measure WA, KEN, NIU, RAI, SAT, SEN, SOK, WAH, YOT, KEUP, NGAN, TANG, KWIEN, TANAN
Thai money AT(T), BAHT, FUANG, TICAL, PYNUNG, SALUNG, SATANG
Thai weight PAI, BAHT, HAPH, KLAM, KLOM, CHANG, COYAN, FUANG, PICUL, TICAL, SALUNG, SOMPAY, TAMLUNG
Thaïs writer FRANCE, MASSENET
Thames estuary NORE
thane MACBETH
thank REQUITE
that is IE, VIZ, IDEST, NAMELY
thaw MELT, SOFTEN, DISSOLVE
theater GAFF, ODEA, SWAN, DRAMA, GLOBE, HOUSE, LEGIT, ODEON, ODEUM, OPERA, STAGE, FARNESE, BROADWAY, THEATRON
theater group BMI, ANTA, ASCAP, EQUITY, HABIMA
theater part BOX, PIT, LOGE, AISLE, CAVEA, FRONT, SCENE, STAGE, STALL, CIRCLE, PODIUM, BALCONY, DIAZOMA, GALLERY, PARTERRE
theater sign SRO, MARQUEE
theatrical STAGY, POMPOUS, HISTRIONIC
Theban ruler CREON, OEDIPUS
Thebes founder CADMUS
theft LARCENY, ROBBERY
theme TEMA, MOTIF, TOPIC, STRAIN, LEITMOTIF
then POI, ANON, NEXT
theologians *see* RELIGIOUS LEADERS
theoretical TITULAR, ABSTRACT, ACADEMIC, PLATONIC
theory ISM, NOTION, DOCTRINE
there AT, YON, THEN, TOWARD, YONDER

therefore ARGO, ERGO, ARGAL, HENCE, SINCE, WHENCE
thermal unit BTU, DEGREE, CALORIE
thesaurus ROGET, LEXICON, TREASURY
thesis ESSAY, THEORY, TREATISE
Thetis relative PELEUS, ACHILLES
thick FAT, CRASS, DENSE, STUPID
thicket TOD, BOSK, BUSH, RONE, SHAW, BRAKE, COPSE, JUNGLE, BOSCAGE, SPINNEY, TUSSOCK
thick-lipped BLOBBER, LABROSE
thief CHOR, PRIG, GANEF, GANOF, GONOF, PIKER, SANSI, KLEPTO, BURGLAR, FILCHER, LURCHER
thigh, of the FEMORAL
thin LANK, LEAN, RARE, REEDY, SHEER, SPARE, DILUTE, PAPERY, RAREFY, SPARSE, TENUOUS
thing(s) RES, CHOSE, MATTER
think WIS, DEEM, MULL, MUSE, TROW, WEEN, OPINE, IDEATE, REASON, RECKON
Thinker sculptor RODIN
third TIERCE, TERNARY
thirst-producing DIPSETIC
thirsty (A)DRY, ARID, PARCHED
thirty, series of TRENTAL
Thisbe's lover PYRAMUS
thistle BURR, KUSUM, DINDLE, SAFFLOWER
thither YON(D), THERE, YONDER
Thomas opera HAMLET, MIGNON
thong RIEM, BRAIL, KNOUT, QUIRT, ROMAL, STRAP
Thor relative SIF, ULL, ODIN, ULLR
thorn BARB, BRIAR, BRIER, SPINE, NETTLE
thorn apple METEL, DATURA
thorny BRAMBLY, SPINATE, SPINOSE
thorough ABSOLUTE, COMPLETE
thoroughfare WAY, AVENUE, STREET
thousand MIL(LE)
thousand years CHILIAD, MILLIAD, MILLENNIUM

thrall *see* BONDMAN
thrash WALE, YERK, BLESS, WHALE, TROUNCE; *see* BEAT
thread CLEW, CLUE, CORD, PURL, TRAM, WARP, WEFT, FIBER, FILUM, LISLE, REEVE, TENOR, TWINE, STAMEN, RETICLE
threadbare SEEDY, STALE, TRITE, RAGGED, SHABBY
threadlike FILAR, FILATE, FILOSE, NEMALINE
threat OMEN, MENACE, WARNING
three TER, DREI, TERN, TRIO, LEASH, THRIN, TRIAD, TIERCE
threefold TRINE, TERNAL, TREBLE, TERNARY, TERNATE
threnody DIRGE, REQUIEM
threshold EVE, SILL, LIMEN
thrifty FRUGAL, SAVING, MISERLY, SPARING
thrill KICK, STIR, TIRL, EXCITE
thrive WAX, BOOM, ADDLE, BATTEN, PROSPER, SUCCEED, FLOURISH
throat MAW, CRAG, GORGE, FAUCES, GULLET, WEASAND
throat, pert. to (JU)GULAR, GUTTURAL
throb BEAT, PUMP, POUND, PULSATE
throe PANG, RACK, AGONY, SPASM
throne ASANA, GADDI, GADHI, MUSNUD
throng HOST, CROWD, HORDE, PRESS
throttle GAG, CHOKE, SCRAG
through PER, VIA, DONE
throw CAST, HURL, KEST, TOSS, WRAP, FLING, HEAVE, PITCH
thrush OMAO, KAMAO, MAVIS, OUSEL, OUZEL, ROBIN, SHAMA, VEERY, DIPPER, MISSEL, MISTLE, REDWING, BELLBIRD
thrush genus TURDUS, CINCLUS
thrust JAB, JUT, BUTT, DART, FOIN, STAB, TILT, IMPEL,

LUNGE, ONSET, SHOVE, DARTLE, EXSERT
thug GOON, HOOD, TOUGH, GORILLA, HOODLUM
thumb DIGIT, POLLEX, THENAR
thunder CLAP, PEAL, ROLL, RUMBLE
thurible CENSER
Thursday source THOR
thus SIC, YET, ERGO
thwart *see* BAFFLE
thyroid disorder GOITER
tiara CROWN, DIADEM, CORONET
Tibeto-Burman language LAI, MRU, BODO, GARO, NAGA, LIMBU, MURMI, KACHIN, LEPCHA, LUSHEI, NEWARI, BURMESE, TIBETAN
tick MARK, ACARI, ARGAS, CHECK, PIQUE, ACARID, CREDIT, IXODID, TAMPAN, ACARIDA, ACARINA, ARGASID, IXODIAN, CARAPATO, IXODIDAE; *see* MITE
ticket PASS, LABEL, SLATE, BALLOT, DOCKET
tickle AMUSE, EXCITE, TINGLE
tidal flow EBB, BORE, NEAP, EAGRE, FLOOD
tidbit GOSSIP, MORSEL, KICKSHAW
tide FLOW, NEAP, SURF, TIME, FLOOD, SURGE
tidings NEWS, GOSPEL, EVANGEL
tidy NEAT, REDO, TRIG, TRIM, KEMPT, SPRUCE
tie BEAM, BIND, BOND, LASH, MOOR, TACH, NEXUS, TACHE, TRUSS, LIGATE, SLEEPER; *see* NECKWEAR
tier BANK, RANK, LAYER
tight TIPSY, STINGY; *see* TAUT
tighten FRAP, LACE, TAUTEN
tights LEOTARD
tightwad *see* MISER
Tigris tributary ZAB, DIYALA
tile FAVI, FAVUS, KASHI, IMBREX, TEGULA, PANTILE, TESSERA
till CASH, PLOW, CULTIVATE
tiller HELM, FARMER, PLOWMAN
tilt TIP, CANT, HEEL, LEAN, LIST, JOUST, SLANT, CAREEN
timber LOG, BEAM, BIBB, BITT, LOGS, KEVEL, BATTEN, CAMBER, STUMPAGE
timber rot DOAT, DOTE
time AGE, ELD, EON, ERA, EVE, AEON, BEAT, DATE, YORE, EPOCH, TEMPI, TEMPO, TENSE; *see p. 340*
time being NONCE
time, pert. to ERAL, TEMPORAL
timepiece CLOCK, WATCH, SUNDIAL, HOURGLASS
timid SHY, PAVID, TREPID
tin CAN, COAT, STANNUM
tin, pert. to STANNIC, STANNOUS
tinamou MACUCA, YNAMBU
tincture DYE, TINT; *see p. 251*
tinder PUNK, AMADOU
tine FANG, SNAG, TYND, PRONG, SPIKE, ANTLER
tinfoil TAIN
tinge DYE, DASH, IMBUE, TAINT, TOUCH, TRACE
tingle DIRL, THIRL, DINDLE, THRILL
Tinker's teammate EVERS, CHANCE
tinkle TING, CHINK, DINGLE
tint DYE, HUE, SHADE, STAIN, TINGE; *see p. 251*
tiny WEE, MINUTE, PETITE
tip CUE, END, APEX, KNAP, VERTEX; *see* GRATUITY, TILT
tipster TOUT(ER), INSIDER
tipsy *see* DRUNK
tirade SPATE; *see* DIATRIBE
tire FAG, BORE, CLOY, JADE, PNEU, WEARY, STRAKE, RETREAD
tire part RIM, SHOE, SIPE, TUBE, TREAD, CASING
tiresome DULL, BORING, TEDIOUS
tissue WEB, BAST, MESH, TELA, FIBER, FASCIA, PHLOEM
Titania's spouse OBERON
Titans *see p. 317*

Titans' parents GE, GAEA, URANUS
tithe LEVY, TEIND, TENTH, TIEND
title MR, MS, SR, AGA, ALI, AYA, BEY, DOM, MME, MRS, PAN, RAS, SIR, SRI, VON, AGHA, BABA, COJA, DAME, EARL, EMIR, GRAP, HERR, HOJA, KHAN, LORD, MAAM, MISS, NAME, PANI, SIDI, TERM, TUAN, AGBAR, DONNA, EMEER, GHAZI, MADAM, MOLLA, MULLA, NAWAB, PACHA, PASHA, PRINZ, SAYID, SHREE, BASHAW, PANOIT, SAIYID, SAYYID, SHERIF, CAPTION, HEADING, HUZOOR, SHEREFF; *see* NOBLE
titmouse *see* SONGBIRD
titter LAUGH, GIGGLE, SNICKER
to wit NAMELY, SCILICET
toad AGUA, BUFO, HYLA, PIPA, TOADY, ALYTES, ANURAN, HOPTOAD, PADDOCK, LINGUATA, TREETOAD
toadstool *see* MUSHROOM
toady FAWN, FLUNKY, LACKEY, TRUCKLE
toast LEEP, BREDE, BROWN, MELBA, SALUD, SANTE, SKOAL, CHEERS, PROSIT, SALUTE, SIPPET, SLAINTE
tobacco CAPA, CHAW, PLUG, QUID, SANA, SHAG, WEED, SCREW, SNUFF, BURLEY, RAPPEE, VUELTA, CAPORAL, LATAKIA, ORONOCO, PERIQUE, UPPOWOC
tobacco ash DOTTEL, DOTTLE
tocsin BELL, GONG, ALARM
to-do ADO, FUSS, STIR
toe DIGIT, SLANT, HALLUX, MINIMUS
toff DUDE, SWELL
tog(s) *see* CLOTHING
Togo language FRENCH; *see* KWA
toil PEAL, RING, KNEEL; *see* TAX
toilet WC, JOHN, PRIVY
toilet water BAYRUM, COLOGNE, LAVENDER
token FARE, SIGN, SLUG, BADGE, SCRIP, EMBLEM, PLEDGE
Tokyo (Y)EDO
Tokyo district GINZA, AKADAKA, YOSHIWARA
tolerable SOSO, MIDDLING, PASSABLE
tolerance STAMINA, PATIENCE
tolerate BEAR, BROOK, STAND, SUFFER
toll DUE, FEE, TAX, DUTY, RATE, PEAL, RING, KNELL
tomb CIST, MOLE, CRYPT, TABUT, VAULT, BARROW, DOKHMA, MASTABA, OSSUARY, TUMULUS, CISTVAEN, CROMLECH; *see* SHRINE
tomboy ROMP, HOIDEN, HOYDEN
tomorrow MANANA
tone KEY, TEAN, PITCH, TIMBRE
Tonga money PAANGA
tongue TAB, CHIB, FLAP, NEAP, TANG, IDIOM, GLOSSA, LINGUA, CLAPPER
tongue, pert. to APICAL, GLOSSAL
tonic ALOE, TANSY, BRACER, ELIXIR, FILLIP, PICKUP, CHIRATA, ROBORANT
too ALSO, OVERLY, BESIDES
tool(s) DUPE, GEAR, MEANS, DEVICE, GADGET, UTENSIL
tooth COG, GAM, FANG, TINE, TUSH, TUSK, IVORY, MOLAR, PRONG, CANINE, CUSPID, WISDOM, INCISOR, BICUSPID
tooth incrustation PLAQUE, TARTAR
tooth part GUM, NECK, PULP, ROOT, CROWN, NERVE, DENTIN, ENAMEL, CEMENTUM
toothed DENTATE, SERRATE
toothless EDENTATE
top AI, ACE, CAP, EPI, LIP, ACME, APEX, FINIAL, VERTEX, ZENITH
toper SOT, DRUNK, RUMMY, SOUSE
topknot TUFT, CREST, ONKOS, PANACHE
topminnow GUPPY, MOLLY, MOLLIE, HELLERI, PUPFISH, RIVULUS, GAMBUSIA, KILLIFISH, SWORDTAIL

torch LINK, LUNT, MUSSAL, CRESSET, FLAMBEAU
torment BAIT, BANE, AGONY, ANNOY, HARRY, TEASE, ORDEAL
torn REFT, RENT, RIVEN, SPLIT
tornado FUNNEL, CYCLONE, TWISTER, WHIRLWIND
Toronto YORK, HOGTOWN
torpid DULL, NUMB, INERT
torrent RUSH, FLOOD, SPATE
torrid ARID, ARDENT, SULTRY
torso BODY, TRUNK
tortoise *see* TURTLE
torture FLAY, RACK, GARBLE, MARTYR, STRAPPADO
Tory DIEHARD, LOYALIST
Tosca character MARIO, SCARPIA
Tosca writer SARDOU, PUCCINI
toss LOB, CAST, FLIP, TAVE, BANDY, FLING, PITCH, THROW, BUFFET
total SUM, ENTIRE, DESTROY
totem EPONYM
totem pole XAT
totter ROCK, SHAKE, STAGGER
toucan TOCO, ARACARI
touch TIG, ABUT, DASH, FEEL, PALP, GRAZE, CONTACT, IMPINGE
touch, pert. to HAPTIC, TACTIC, TACTILE, TACTUAL
touching RE, ANENT, TANGENT
touchwood *see* TINDER
touchy SORE, TESTY, IRRITABLE
tough WIRY, BULLY, CHEWY, HARDY, ROWDY, WITHY, STURDY
toupee *see* HAIRPIECE
tour EYRE, TRIP, SHIFT, SAFARI, VOYAGE, CIRCUIT
tournament TILT, JOUST, MATCH
tousle MUSS, RUMPLE, DISHEVEL
tow DRAW, PULL, FLAX, HARDS, HURDS
toward ECTAD, ENTAD, FACING
towel WIPE, DIAPER, NAPKIN
tower TOR, EDAR, TOPE, BABEL, PYLON, STUPA, BELFRY, DONJON, GAZEBO, GOPURA, PAGODA, RONDEL, DIKARA, DIKHRA, TURRET, VIMANA, MINARET, SIKHARA, TORRION, MARTELLO, CAMPANILE; *see* SPIRE, WATCHTOWER
town(ship) BURG, DEME, STAD, VILL, BAYAN, BURGH, MACHI, STADT; *see* VILLAGE
town, of a CIVIC, URBAN, OPPIDAN
toy DALLY, BAUBLE, FONDLE, GEWGAW; *see* TRIFLE
trace HINT, TANG, TINGE, ENGRAM, SKETCH, SOUPCON, VESTIGE
track RUT, RAIL, SLOT, SPUR, TURF, WAKE, RAILS, SCENT, SPOOR, TRAIL, COURSE
tracker TAIL, PUGGI, HUNTER
tractor CAT, MULE, SEMI
trade BANDY; *see* BARTER, PROFESSION, SELL
trademark LOGO, MARK, BRAND
trader MONGER; *see* MERCHANT
trading post PX, CANTEEN
trading site PIT, MART, *see* MARKET, RIALTO, CANTEEN
tradition LORE, USAGE, CUSTOM
traduce SLUR, LIBEL, DEFAME, MALIGN, SMEAR
Trafalgar victor NELSON
traffic TRADE, BUSINESS, COMMERCE
tragic SAD, FATAL, PATHETIC
trail DOG, HEEL, TAIL, HOUND, TRACE, FOLLOW, SHADOW; *see* TRACK
train TUBE, COACH, DRILL, FLIER, LOCAL, EXPRESS, FREIGHT, LIMITED, SHUTTLE, SPECIAL, INSTRUCT, MANIFEST, FREIGHTER, PASSENGER; *see* RETINUE
trainer COACH, HANDLER
traitor RAT, JUDAS, LAVAL, ARNOLD, PAUKER, PETAIN, RAKOSI, BETRAYER, CHAMBERS, QUISLING, TURNCOAT

trajectory ARC, PATH, CURVE
tramp BUM, HIKE, HOBO, TRAIPSE, VAGRANT
trample CHAMP, POACH, TREAD
trance DAZE, LUPA, SOPOR, SPELL
tranquilize CALM, PACIFY, SEDATE, SOOTHE
tranquilizer DOWNER, LIBRIUM, ATARAXIC, SEDATIVE
transaction DEAL, SALE
transcend TOP, PASS, EXCEL
transfer CEDE, DEED, DECAL, GRANT, CONVEY, DEMISE, DEPUTE
transferer ALIENOR
transfix PIN, IMPALE, PIERCE
transform ALTER, CHANGE, CONVERT
transit, mass BUS, TRAIN, JITNEY, SUBWAY, TROLLEY
transgress SIN, INFRACT, VIOLATE
transient FLEETING, EPHEMERAL, TEMPORARY
transition FLUX, CHANGE, PASSAGE
translate DECODE, RENDER, INTERPRET
transom SLAT, TRAVE, LINTEL, LOUVER
transparent CLEAR, LUCID, SHEER, LIMPID, HYALINE
transport CARRY, CONVEY, RAPTURE
trap GIN, NET, TIPE, WEIR, SNARE, AMBUSH, ENSNARE
trapdoor DROP, HATCH
trapshooting term SKEET, PIGEON
trash JUNK, RAFF, WASTE, REFUSE
travel TOUR, TREK, WEND
travel, pert. to VIATIC
traveler VIATOR, PILGRIM, TOURIST, WAYFARER, ITINERANT
Traviata character FLORA, ALFREDO, VIOLETTA
Traviata composer VERDI
tray HOD, TILL, SALVER, SERVER, COASTER
treachery DECEIT, PERFIDY, BETRAYAL
tread PAD, STEP, TIRE, VOLT, SNEAK, TRAMPLE
treadle LEVER, PEDAL, CHALAZA
treason PERFIDY, BETRAYAL, SEDITION
treasure ROON, CACHE, HOARD, TROVE, CHERISH
Treasure State MT, MONT(ANA)
treasurer BURSAR, FISCAL, PURSER, BOUCHER
treasury FISC, FISK, BURSE, VAULT, BURSARY, COFFERS
treasury agent(s) TMAN, TMEN
treat USE, DEAL, DOSE, DOCTOR, REGALE, DELIGHT
treatise ESSAY, SUMMA, TRACT, THESIS, MONOGRAPH
treatment CARE, USAGE, HANDLING
tree POLE, POST, STAKE, WOODS, CORNER, TIMBER, BOSCAGE, GALLOWS, SAPLING, SEEDLING; *see* FOREST
tree, pert. to SYLVAN, ARBOREAL
trees APA, IFE, INA, KOU, ULE, ACER, AKEE, BREA, CHIA, DITA, DOON, HULE, ILEX, KAKI, OHIA, RATA, TITI, ACKEE, ASANA, BALSA, CAROB, LEHUA, MALUS, MANIU, NARRA, NOGAL, OCHNA, PADUS, POLAK, SALAL, SIMAL, TOONA, UNONA, ALMOND, LOCUST, WALNUT, QUASSIA, SOLANUM, TAMARIX, WALLABA; *see* EVERGREEN, PALM, PINE, OAK, TROPICAL, POPLAR, ACACIA
trellis ARBOR, LATTICE, PERGOLA, ESPALIER
tremble QUAKE, DIDDER, DODDER
tremolo TRILL, QUAVER, VIBRATO
tremulous ASPEN, TREPID, QUAVERY
trench *see* DITCH
trenchant KEEN, ACUTE, SHARP
trend BENT, DRIFT, TENOR
trespass SIN, POACH, INVADE, TROVER, INTRUDE, ENCROACH
tress CURL, LOCK, BRAID, PLAIT, RINGLET

trestle BRIDGE, VIADUCT
triad TRIO, TRINARY, TRINITY
trial CASE, SUIT, ASSIZE, ORDEAL, HEARING, INQUEST, INQUIRY, LAWSUIT; *see* TEST
triangle GORE, DELTA, GUSSET, OBTUSE, TRIGON, SCALENE
triangle part LEG, BASE, SIDE, HYPOTENUSE
tribe CLAN, GENS, RACE, GROUP; *see* BIBLICAL TRIBES; *see p. 342*
tribulation WOE, TRIAL, MISERY, DISTRESS
tribunal BAR, ROTA, BENCH, COURT, FORUM
tribute KUDOS, EULOGY, HOMAGE, CARATCH; *see* TAX
trick FOB, FUB, DIDO, DUPE, FLAM, GAWD, GULL, HOAX, JAPE, JEST, NICK, RUSE, WILE, DODGE, STUNT, GAMBIT, TREPAN, FICELLE, FLIMFLAM
trickle DRIP, SEEP
tricks won BOOK, NULL, SLAM, CAPOT, NULLO
trident SPEAR, LEISTER
Trieste measure ORNA, ORNE
trifle TOY, DOIT, FICO, DALLY, FLIRT, NIGGLE, PALTER
trigonometric function SINE, COSINE, SECANT, (CO)TANGENT
trill ROLL, SHAKE, WARBLE, MORDENT, TIRALEE
trim CUT, LOP, DOCK, TRIG, ADORN, PREEN, PRUNE, SHEAR, SHRAG, SVELTE
trimmed SNOD, SHORN, ADORNED
trimming(s) GIMP, FLOTS, RUCHE, BURLET, GUIPURE, RUCHING
trinity THREE, TRIAD, TRINE
trinket GAUD, BIJOU, GEWGAW, BIBELOT
trip ERR, FALL, SLIP, TOUR, VOYAGE, STUMBLE
triple TRI, TREBLE
triplet(s) TRIN(E), TERCET, TREBLE
tripod CAT, STAND, SPIDER, TRIVET
Tristram's beloved ISOLT, ISEULT, ISOLDE
trite DULL, HACK, BANAL, CORNY, INANE, STALE, JEJUNE
triumph EXULT, SUCCESS, VICTORY
trivet SPIDER, TRIPOD
trivial PETTY, COMMON, PALTRY
trivium LOGIC, GRAMMAR, RHETORIC
troche PASTIL, ROTULA, LOZENGE, PASTIL(L)E
trogon QUETZAL, TOCORORO
Troilus lover CRESSIDA
Troilus relative PRIAM, APOLLO, HECUBA
Trojan ILIAN, DARDAN
Trojan hero ENEAS, PARIS, AENEAS, AGENOR, DARDAN, HECTOR
Trojan king PRIAM
troll *see* DWARF
trolley TRAM, STREETCAR
trombone SACKBUT; *see* WIND INSTRUMENT
troops MEN, ARMY, FORCES
trophy CUP, PALM, MEDAL, SCALP, LAUREL
tropical fish OPAH, GUASA, SARGO, ROBALO, SALEMA, MOJARRA
tropical tree AKEE, BITO, EBON, GUAO, HURA, KOKO, MABA, MAHO, PALM, SIDA, ACAPU, ANATO, ANONA, ARJAN, ARJUN, BALSA, BARIA, BONGO, CEIBA, CHICO, DALLI, EBONY, GUAMA, GUAVA, ICACO, ICICA, IXORA, KOKKO, LEHUA, MAHOE, MARIA, PACAY, QUIRA, ROBLE, SAMAN, SERON, SIRIS, TREMA, URUCU, VITEX, ZAMAN, ZORRO, ACAJOU, ANATTO, ANNONA, BANANA, BANYAN, BAOBAB, BRAZIL, CASHEW, COLIMA, KUMBUK, LEBBEK, PAPAYA, SAPOTA, ZAMANG, ANNATTO, AVOCADO, SANDBOX, CINCHONA, TAMARIND, TAMARISK
trot JOG, PACE, PONY, AMBLE, DANCE
troubadour POET, JONGLEUR, MINSTREL
trouble(s) ADO, AIL, WOE, FASH, ILLS, PAINS, WORRY, EFFORT, MOLEST

troublemaker IMP, HELLION, AGITATOR
trough HOD, BOSH, TRUG, BASIN, GUTTER, MANGER, STRAKE; *see* CHANNEL
trounce BEAT, FLOG, THRASH
trousers CHAPS, JEANS, PANTS, SLOPS, TREWS, SLACKS, PEGTOPS, BREECHES
trout CHAR, KELT, CHARR, LONGE, SEWEN, SEWIN, SIWIN, SPROD, TOGUE, TROUT, TRUFF, QUASKY, TAIMEN, OQUASSA
trowel DARBY, FLOAT, PLANE
Troy ILIUM, ILLION, WEIGHT
Troy, pert. to ILIAC, ILIAN, TROJAN
truant TRONE, LAGGARD, SHIRKER, TRIVANT, VAGRANT
truck VAN, LORRY, TRADE, BARTER, CAMION, PICKUP; *see* VEHICLE
truculent CRUEL, DEADLY, VITRIOLIC
trudge PACE, PLOD, SLOG
true LEAL, VERY, RIGHT, GERMANE
truism ADAGE, AXIOM, PLATITUDE
truly YEA, QUITE, SOOTH, INDEED, REALLY
trump TOP, RUFF, OUTDO, PEACH
trumpet HORN, BUGLE, BUCCINA, CLARION; *see* WIND INSTRUMENT
trumpet call SENNET, SINNET, TUCKET, CHAMADE, FANFARE, FLOURISH, REVEILLE
trundle CART, ROLL, RULL, CASTER
trunk BOLE, CABER, CHEST, TORSO, LOCKER, PROBOSCIS
truss BIND, PROP, BRACE
trust RELY, TROW, CARTEL, CUSTODY, MONOPOLY
truth TAO, UNA, FACT, FEALTY, VERITY
truth drug PENTOTHAL
truthful CANDID, HONEST, VERIDIC(AL)
try TAX, SHOT, TEST, CRACK, ESSAY, ETTLE, STRIVE, ATTEMPT
tryout TEST, TRIAL, AUDITION
tryst DATE, MEETING, RENDEZVOUS
tub KID, KIT, SOE, COWL, GAAL, GYLE, KNAP, KNOP, KEEVE, SKEEL, KEELER, HOGSHEAD; *see* VAT
tuba *see* WIND INSTRUMENT
tube DUCT, HOSE, PIPE, PIPET, SIPPER, SUBWAY, BURETTE, PIPETTE, SNORKEL
tuber OCA, YAM, EDDO, TARO, TRUB, JALAP, SALEB, SALEP, POTATO, TRUFFLE
tuberculosis PTHISIS, CONSUMPTION
tuck LAP, FOLD, HIDE, PLEAT, RUCHE
Tuesday source TIUTIV, TIW
tuft COMA, CLUMP, CREST
tug TOW, DRAG, DRAW, HAUL, JERK, PULL, YANK
tumble FALL, SPIN, TRIP
tumor OMA, WEN, YAW, CYST, MORO, GUMMA, MYOMA, GLIOMA, LIPOMA, ANGIOMA, FIBROMA, NEUROMA, OSTEOMA, OSTEOME, SARCOMA, HEMATOMA, MELANOMA
tumult DIN, RIOT, BABEL, LURRY, UPROAR
tuna PEAR, TUNNY, OPUNTIA
tune AIR, ARIA, MELODY
Tungusic language GOLDI, LAMUT, MANCHU, TUNGUS
tunic JAMA(H), CHITON, MANTLE
Tunisian measure SAA(H), UEBA, CAFIZ, WHIBA
Tunisian money DINAR
Tunisian weight ROTL, ARTEL, ICKIA, KANTAR
tunnel TUBE, CENIS, TANNA, BURROW, NOOSAC, MOFFAT, SEVERN, ARLBERG, CASCADE, HOLLAND, LINCOLN, SIMPLON
tunnel term ADIT, SHAFT, SLOPE, STOPE, RISING, HEADING, SINKING
turban LUNG(Y)I, MANDIL, MUNDIL
turbid MURKY, ROILY, ROILED
turbulent STORMY, AGITATED
turf SOD, PEAT, DIVOT, SWARD
turgid TOROSE, BLOATED, SWOLLEN

Turk TA(R)TAR, OSMANLI, OTTOMAN
Turkic language KAZAK, TATAR, UZBEK, YAKUT, KAZAKH, KIRGIZ, UIGHUR, BASHKIR, CHUVASH, KIRGHIZ, TURKISH, TURKMEN, TURKOMAN
Turkish government PORTE
Turkish leader BAYAR, INONU, KEMAL, SUNAY, DEMIREL
Turkish measure PIK, HATT, KHAT, ZIRA, ALMUD, BERRI, DONUM, KILEH, ARSHIN, DJERIB, FORTIN, PARMAK
Turkish money LIRA, PARA, ALTUN, ASPER, MAHBUB, SEQUIN, ALTILIK, BESHLIK, PIASTER, ZECCHINO
Turkish ruler KHAN, CALIPH, SULTAN
Turkish weight OKA, OKE, KILE, ROTL, CEQUI, CHEKE, KERAT, KILEH, BATMAN, DIRHAM, KANTAR, MISKAL, YUSDRUM
turmoil HURLY, BUSTLE, WELTER
turn HAW, BEND, BENT, GYRE, VEER, VERT, SPIN, EVERT, HINGE, PIVOT, SHUNT, VERTE, VOLTI, WHIRL, DETOUR, REVERT, ROTATE; *see* VEER
turn down VETO, SPURN, REJECT, DECLINE
turncoat BOLTER, TRAITOR, APOSTATE, RENEGADE
turnip NEEP, SWEDE
turpentine derivative ROSIN, PINENE, TERPENE
turpentine resin ALK, GAL(L)IPOT
turret CUPOLA, BARTIZAN
turtle EMYD, ARRAU, COOTER, EMYDEA, GOPHER, JURARA, SLIDER, ATHECAE, PAINTED, SNAPPER, TURTLET, ARCHELON, EMYDIDAE, HAWKBILL, MATAMATA, TERRAPIN, TORTOISE
turtle delicacy CALIPEE, CALIPASH
turtle genus EMYS, CHELYS, CARETTA, CHELONE, TESTUDO, TRIGNYX, CHELONIA, CHELYDRA, EMYDINAE, TERRAPENE
tusk FANG, IVORY, RAZOR
tussle FIGHT, GRAPPLE, SCUFFLE, WRESTLE
tutor TUTE, COACH, MENTOR
twaddle ROT, JARGON, CHATTER, FUSTIAN, PRATTLE
Twelfth Night character FESTE, VIOLA, ORSINO, MALVOLIO
twenty CORGE, SCORE
twenty-fourth part CARAT, KARAT
twice BIS, ENCORE
twig SLIP, SCION, SHOOT, SPRIG, WITHE, BRANCH
twigs, made of VIRGAL, WATTLED
twilight EVE, DUSK, GLOAM, EVENTIDE, GLOAMING
twin ENG, CHANG, GEMEL
twin crystal MACLE
twine COIL, HEMP, WIND, TWIST
twinge QUALM, TWITCH, SCRUPLE
twinkle WINK, GLEAM, GLINT
twist FEAK, FOIL, KINK, SKEW, SLUB, WARP, GNARL, GRIND, WRICK, INTORT, SQUIRM, CONTORT
twisted (A)WRY, SKEW, KINKY, TORSE, TORTILE
twister *see* WHIRLWIND
twit JEER, JIBE, SCOFF, TEASE
twitch TIC, JERK, TWEAK
two DUO, PAIR, BRACE, TWINS
twofold DUAL, TWIN, BINAL, BINARY
two-footed BIPED(AL)
two-month period BIMESTER
two-spot DEUCE
tycoon BARON, MOGUL, NABOB, SHOGUN, GRANDEE
type ILK, FONT, KIND, NORM, SORT, BRAND, BREED, CLASS, GENRE, MODEL, SPECIES
type part BODY, FACE, FEET, KERN, NECK, NICK, STEM, BEARD, SERIF, SHANK, GROOVE, COUNTER, SHOULDER
type size PICA, AGATE, CANON, ELITE, PEARL, MINION, PRIMER, BREVIER, DIAMOND, ENGLISH, PARAGON
typeface PIE, HESS, NEWS, AGATE, BEMBO, GOUDY,

IONIC, ROMAN, RONDE, RUNIC, TIMES, VOGUE, BODONI, BULMER, CASLON, COCHIN, FUTURA, GOTHIC, ITALIC, SCRIPT, STYMIE, CENTURY, CURSIVE, GRANJON, CLOISTER, GARAMOND, SANSERIF
typewriter part KEY, TAB, SHIFT, PLATEN, ROLLER, SPACER, CARRIAGE, TABULATOR
tyrant NERO, CAESAR, DESPOT
Tyre royalty DIDO, HIRAM
tyro NOVICE, NEOPHYTE

U

Ugandan language LUO, LUGANDA, SWAHILI
Ugandan leader AMIN, OBOTE
ugly PLAIN, HOMELY, HIDEOUS
ukase EDICT, DECREE
Ukrainian money GRIVNA, SCHAGIV
ulcer SORE, CANKER, CHANCRE
ultimate FINAL, EVENTUAL, FARTHEST
Ulysses author JOYCE
Ulysses' dog ARGUS
Ulysses' friend MENTOR
Ulysses' realm ITHACA
Ulysses relative LAERTES, PENELOPE, TELEMACHUS
umbrella GAMP, CHUTE, SHADE, CHATTA, PARASOL
umpire REF, UMP, JUDGE, ARBITER, DAYSMAN, REFEREE
U.N. agency FAO, ILO, IMF, IMO, ITU, UPU, WHO, WMO, GATT, IAEA, IBRD, ICAO, IFAO, WIPO, UNESCO
U.N. Sec'y-General LIE, THANT, CUELLAR, WALDHEIM
unaccented ATONIC
unadorned BALD, NAKED, STARK, CHASTE
unaffected NAIVE, SIMPLE, NATURAL
unaspirated LENE
unattached FREE, SINGLE, VAGILE
unbeliever GIAOUR, DOUBTER, SKEPTIC, AGNOSTIC; *see* HEATHEN, INFIDEL
unbroken WHOLE, INTACT
uncanny UNCO, EERIE, WEIRD
uncertain SHAKY, VAGUE, DUBIOUS
uncle EAM, EME, OOM, SAM, YEME, DUTCH, NUNKA, NUNKS, NUNKY, REMUS
Uncle Tom's Cabin *see* STOWE
unclean TREF, VILE, DIRTY, TREFA, FILTHY, IMMUND, LEPROUS
unclothe TIRL, STRIP, DIVEST
uncommon ODD, RARE, EXOTIC, SPECIAL, UNUSUAL
unconscious state COMA, FAINT, SWOON, TRANCE, SYNCOPE, NARCOSIS
uncouth RUDE, GAUCHE, VULGAR
uncouth person CAD, BOOR, LOUT, YAHOO, CODGER, GALOOT
uncovered BARE, NUDE, NAKED, EXPOSED
unctuous OILY, SMUG, SLEEK, SUAVE, GREASY, PINGUID
under SUB, ALOW, SOUS, BELOW, INFRA, NEATH, SOTTO, NETHER
undergo DREE, ENDURE, SUFFER
undergraduate FROSH, PLEBE, JUNIOR, FRESHMAN, SOPHOMORE
underhanded SLY, DERN, COVERT, SECRET, CLANDESTINE
underling AIDE, SLAVE, SUBALTERN
undermine SAP, ERODE, WEAKEN, SUBVERT
undershirt(s) *see* UNDERWEAR
undersong TIERCE
understand DIG, KEN, GRASP, SAVVY, PERCEIVE
understanding KEN, NOUS, SENSE, ACCORD, ENTENTE
understudy SUB, COVER, SECOND, APPRENTICE, SUBSTITUTE
undertaking PROJECT, VENTURE
underwear BRA, JUMP, SLIP, CYMAR, JUMPS, SIMAR, SMOCK, STAYS, BRIEFS, BUSTLE, CAMISA, CAMISE, CORSET, GIRDLE, LINDER, UNDIES, BANDEAU, CHEMISE, DESSOUS,

DRAWERS, GSTRING, PANTIES, STAMMEL, STEPINS, TEDDIES, CAMISOLE, CORSELET, KNICKERS, LINGERIE, SCANTIES, BRASSIERE, LOINCLOTH
underworld *see* HADES, HELL
undeveloped BARREN, EMBRYO, LATENT
undress STRIP, DISHABILLE
undulate WAVE, RIPPLE, PULSATE
undulation WAVE, TREMOLO
unearth DIGUP, EXHUME, DISCLOSE
uneasiness QUALMS, UNREST, ANXIETY, MALAISE
uneven ODD, EROSE, HUBBLY, RAGGED, SPOTTY
unfailing SURE, CERTAIN
unfair FOUL, BIASED, PARTIAL
unfair move FOUL, FULK
unfaithful UNTRUE, DISLOYAL
unfavorable ILL, ADVERSE, CONTRARY
unfeeling NUMB, CRUEL, CALLOUS
unfold OPEN, DEPLOY, EVOLVE, REVEAL, UNFURL
unfortunate HAPLESS, LUCKLESS
unfriendly COLD, HOSTILE, INIMICAL
ungainly GAWKY, STIFF, CLUMSY
unguent BALM, NARD, CRATE, SALVE, CEROMA, CHRISM, POMADE
ungula *see* CLAW, HOOF
unhappy SAD, BLUE, DIRE, MOROSE
unhealthy MORBID, SICKLY
unholy WICKED, IMPIOUS, PROFANE
unicorn LIN, MONOCEROS
uniform EVEN, FLAT, FLOT, HABIT, LIVERY, STEADY
union AFL, CIO, HUI, ILA, ITA, TWU, UAW, UMW, BLOC, BOND, ARTEL, GUILD, HANSE, ILGWU, FUSION, LEAGUE, MERGER
unique (thing) LONE, ONER, SOLE
unit ONE, ITEM, PIECE
unite MIX, WED, ALLY, FUSE, JOIN, KNIT, MELD, WELD, YOKE, BLEND, MERGE, RABET
United Kingdom *see* ENGLAND
United Nations *see* U.N.
United States *see* U.S.
universal COSMIC, GLOBAL, CATHOLIC, ECLECTIC, ECUMENIC, PANDEMIC
universe LOKA, WORLD, COSMOS
university *see* COLLEGE
unjust BIASED, UNFAIR, PARTIAL
unkeeled RATITE
unkempt MESSY, SHABBY, UNTIDY
unknown IGNOTE, INCOGNITO
unless BUT, LEST, NISI, SAVE, EXCEPT
unlock OPEN, SOLVE, DECODE, REVEAL
unlucky HAPLESS, INFAUST
unmarried SOLE, UNWED, SINGLE, CELIBATE
unmarried state AGAMY, CELIBACY
unoccupied IDLE, EMPTY, VACANT
unpaid DUE, OWING
unplowed strip HADE
unpredictable ERRATIC, WAYWARD
unprofitable SECK, BARREN
unravel FEAZE, SOLVE, TEASE
unrefined RAW, CRASS, CRUDE, COARSE, EARTHY
unrest FERMENT, DISQUIET, AGITATION
unruly RESTIVE, FRACTIOUS
unseen LATENT, INVISIBLE
unskilled RAW, INEPT, AWKWARD
unsparing LAVISH, LIBERAL
unspoken MUTE, TACIT, SILENT, APHONIC
unstable FICKLE, LABILE, ASTATIC, ERRATIC
unsuitable INAPT, UNFIT, WRONG
untamed WILD, FERAL, FERINE
untidy DOWDY, MESSY, SLOPPY
until HENT, TILL, WHEN
untilled FALLOW
untouched VIRGIN, PRISTINE
untrue FALSE, DISLOYAL, UNFAITHFUL
unusual OUTRE, EXOTIC, STRANGE
unwilling LO(A)TH, AVERSE
unwilling, be NILL
unwise FOOLISH, UNSOUND, IMPOLITIC

unworldly NAIVE, WEIRD, SPIRITUAL
unworthy VILE, UNFIT, INDIGN
unyielding FAST, FIRM, GRIM, STANCH, ADAMANT
Upanishad ISHA
upbraid CHIDE, SCOLD, REBUKE
upon EPI, SUR, ATOP, ONTO, OVER
upright FAIR, JUST, TRUE, ERECT
uprising COUP, (E)MEUTE, PUTSCH, REVOLT
uproar ADO, DIN, RIOT, BABEL, HUBBUB, RACKET, RUCKUS
upset TOPPLE, CAPSIZE
upstart SNOB, PARVENU
up-to-date MODERN, TOPICAL
Uranus relative GE, GAEA, RHEA, SATURN, TITANS
urban CIVIC, OPPIDAN
urbane SUAVE, SMOOTH, POLISHED
urchin IMP, TAD, ARAB, GAMIN, ECHINUS, MUDLARK
urge EGG, PLY, YEN, ABET, COAX, GOAD, LUST, PROD, SPUR, IMPEL
urial SHA
urticaria RASH, HIVES, UREDO
Uruguayan measure CUADRA, SUERTE
urus TUR, AUROCHS
U.S. measures *see* MEASURE
U.S. money CENT, DIME, MILL, EAGLE, PENNY, DOLLAR, NICKEL, QUARTER; *see* MONEY
U.S. state information *see p. 308*
use APPLY, EXERT, INURE, WASTE, CUSTOM, EMPLOY, FUNCTION
used WORN, SPENT, SECONDHAND
useless IDLE, NULL, VOID, FUTILE, OTIOSE, INUTILE
usual NORMAL, WONTED, HABITUAL
usurp SEIZE, ASSUME
Utah information *see p. 308*
uterus WOMB, MATRIX
Utopian IDEAL, EDENIC, QUIXOTIC, IDEALISTIC
utter BID, SAY, RANK, VENT, SHEER, SPEAK, STARK, TOTAL, COMPLETE
utterly FULLY, QUITE, STARK

V

vacant VOID, BLANK, DEVOID
vacation REST, RESPITE, HOLIDAY
vacillate REEL, WAVER, SEESAW, TEETER, HESITATE
vacuous EMPTY, INANE, HOLLOW
vacuum VOID, CAVITY, HOLLOW
vacuum, opposite of PLENUM
vagabond BUM, VAG, HOBO, LOREL, SHIRK, TRAMP, RODNEY, TRUANT, WAFFIE, VAGRANT; *see* WANDERER
vagary WHIM, FANCY, CAPRICE
vagrant SPIV, CAIRD; *see* VAGABOND
vague DIM, HAZY, OBSCURE
vain IDLE, SMUG, EMPTY, VAPID, FUTILE
valance PELMET, PALMETTE
vale ADIEU; *see* VALLEY
valet *see* SERVANT
valiant BRAVE, WIGHT, INTREPID, STALWART
valid SOUND, COGENT, DEJURE
valise BAG, ETUI, GRIP, SATCHEL
valley DALE, DELL, GLEN, RILL, VAAL, VALE, WADI, WADY, ATRIO, COOMB, DHOON, GLADE, KLOOF, NEMEA, RILLE, SWALE, TEMPE, BOLSON, COULEE, DINGLE, HOLLOW, STRATH, GEHENNA
value RATE, PRIZE, REGARD, APPRAISE
valve CUSP, DAMPER, POPPET, VENTIL, VALVULA; *see* FAUCET
vamp FLIRT, UPPER, SEDUCE
vampire BAT, GHOUL, LAMIA, DRACULA
van FORE, LORRY, TRUCK
vandal HUN, GOTH, TEUTON
vanish FADE, SINK, EVANESCE
vanity AIRS, PRIDE, EGOISM, CONCEIT, EGOTISM, VAINGLORY
vantage point COIGN(E)
vapid INANE, STALE, JEJUNE

vapor ATMO, BRAG, FUME, HAZE, MIST, REEK, ROKE, BRUME, CLOUD, STEAM, CONTRAIL
Varangians ROS
variable FICKLE, SHIFTY, MUTABLE, PROTEAN
variation SHADE, CHANGE, NUANCE, LECTION
variegated PIED, SHOT, PINTO, CALICO, DAPPLE, MOTLEY
variety KIND, SORT, TYPE, CLASS, GENUS, SPECIES
various SUNDRY, DIVERSE, SEVERAL
varlet CAD, PAGE, CHURL, KNAVE
varnish TUNG, GLOSS, JAPAN, SHELLAC(K)
varnish ingredient LAC, COPAL, ELEMI, RESIN
vary ALTER, CHANGE, DEPART
vase URN, ASKOS, DINOS, DIOTA, ECHEA, TAZZA, DEINOS, PELIKE, SITULA, AMPHORA, ECHEION, POTICHE
vassal LIEGE; *see* BONDMAN
vast COSMIC, OCEANIC, IMMENSE
vat BAC, TUN, KEIR, KIER, KIVE, TANK, KEEVE, CISTERN
vault ARCH, DOME, LEAP, SAFE, BOUND, CRYPT, CURVET
Vedic dialect PALI
veer SHY, YAW, SKEW, SLUE, SWAY, TURN, SHEER, SHIFT, SWERVE
vegetable PEA, SOY, BEAN, BEET, CORN, KALE, LEEK, OCRA, OKRA, OKRO, BENDY, CHARD, ONION, PEASE, ROOTS, SABZI, CARROT, LEGUME, POTATO, CABBAGE, HARICOT, LETTUCE, SOYBEAN, SPINACH
vegetation FLORA, VERDURE
vehement HOT, KEEN, AMAIN, ARDENT, FERVENT
vehicle FORM, AGENT, STYLE, MEDIUM, DILUENT, CONVEYANCE
vehicle(s) FLY, GIG, RIG, RUT, ARBA, BIGA, BIKE, BUTT, BYKE, CART, CHAY, DRAG, DRAY, DUKE, EKKA, GOAT, HACK, LUGE, MAIL, PLOW, PRAM, PUTT, RATH, SADO, SHAY, TEAM, TODE, TRAP, WAIN, ARABA, BANDY, BRAKE, BREAK, BRETT, CYCLE, DANDY, DILLY, DOLLY, ESSED, GURRY, HURLY, JERRY, JUTKA, RATHA, SADOO, STAGE, SULKY, TONGA, WAGON, BARROW, BERLIN, CALASH, CALESA, CHAISE, CHARET, CISIUM, DENNET, DROSKY, ESSEDA, ESSEDE, FIACRE, GHARRI, GHARRY, GOCART, HANSOM, HEARSE, HERDIC, JINGLE, JINKER, KOSONG, LANDAU, LIMBER, RECKLA, SAFETY, SHOFUL, SPIDER, SURREY, TANDEM, TELEGA, TROIKA, BICYCLE, BOUNDER, BRITZKA, CAISSON, CALECHE, CARAVAN, CARIOLE, CAROCHE, CARRETA, CHARIOT, CONCORD, CROYDON, DOGCART, DOSADOS, DROSHKY, FOURGON, GONDOLA, GROWLER, HACKERY, HACKNEY, KIBITKA, MORFREY, PHAETON, RICKSHA, SCOOTER, TALLYHO, TARTANA, TILBURY, TRICYCLE, TRUCKLE, TUMBLER, TUMBREL, TUMBRIL, TURNOUT, UNICORN, VETTURA, VISAVIS, VOITURE, VOLANTE; *see* AUTOMOBILE
vehicle on runners BOB, SKI, PULE, PUNG, SLED, PALKI, PULKA, SKATE, TRAIN, CUTTER, HURDLE, JAMPAN, JUMPER, PALKEE, SLEDGE, SLEIGH, BOBSLED, COASTER, GODEVIL, TRAVOIS, SNOWSHOE, TOBOGGAN, TRAVOISE, BOBSLEIGH
vehicle part BOX, CAM, FAN, RIM, AXLE, GEAR, HOOD, PLUG, SHOE, TIRE, TUBE, BRAKE, MOTOR, PEDAL, REINS, SHAFT, SPOKE, THILL, WHEEL, WIPER, BONNET, BUMPER, CLUTCH, ENGINE, INTAKE, PILLAR, PISTON, RUMBLE, SADDLE, SPRING,

BATTERY, CHASSIS, EXHAUST, MAGNETO, MUFFLER, STARTER, TONNEAU, CYLINDER, FLYWHEEL, IGNITION, MUDGUARD, OILGAUGE, RADIATOR, SPROCKET, THROTTLE, GEARSHIFT, HANDLEBAR, SPARKPLUG; *see* AUTOMOBILE
vehicle, portable JUAN, KAGO, DANDI, DANDY, DOOLI, SEDAN, DOOLEY, DOOLIE, HOWDAH, KURUMA, LITTER, TELEGA, TOMJON, TONJON, CACOLET, NORIMON, SKILIFT, MUNCHEEL, PALANKEEN, PALANQUIN, STRETCHER
veil CAUL, VELUM, YASMAK, MUFFLER, YASHMAK
vein VENA, DRIFT, TENOR, DUCTUS, VENULA, ARTERIA, JUGULAR, VENACAVA; *see* LODE
velocity RATE, SPEED, RAPIDITY
velvet PANNE, VELOUR
venal SORDID, CORRUPT, SELFISH
vendetta FEUD
vendor *see* MERCHANT
veneer LAC, BURL, LAYER, ENAMEL, POLISH, OVERLAY
venerable OLD, AGED, HOAR, SAGE, HOARY
veneration AWE, DULIA, ESTEEM, LATRIA, RESPECT
Venetian blind JALOUSIE
Venetian district RIALTO
Venetian money BETSO, BEZZO
Venezuelan leader LEONI, CALDERA
Venezuelan money REAL, MEDIO, FUERTE, BOLIVAR, CENTIMO, MOROCOTA
vengeance TALION, WANION, REPRISAL
venom BANE, GALL, SPITE, POISON
vent BUNG, FLUE, ISSUE, EGRESS
ventral HEMAD, HEMAL, STERNAL
venture DARE, RISK, FLING, FLYER, HAZARD
Venus ISHTAR, ASTARTE, APHRODITE
Venus, island of MELOS
Venus' beloved ADONIS
Venus' son AMOR, CUPID
veranda PYAL, PATIO, LOGGIA; *see* PORCH
verbal ORAL, VOCAL, SPOKEN
verbose WINDY, WORDY, PROLIX, DIFFUSE
verdant GREEN
Verdi opera AIDA, BALLO, ERNANI, OTELLO, MACBETH, NABUCCO, DONCARLO, FALSTAFF, TRAVIATA, RIGOLETTO, TROVATORE
verdict FINDING, DECISION, JUDGMENT
verdure GREENS, FOLIAGE
verge EDGE, TRIM, BRINK, MARGE, BORDER
verify TEST, AUDIT, PROVE, ATTEST, CONFIRM
verily YEA, AMEN, CERTES, INDEED, REALLY
verity AXIOM, TRUTH, REALITY
vermin PEST, VARMINT
Vermont information *see p. 308*
Verne character NEMO
vernier NONIUS
versatile DEFT, MOBILE, TALENTED
verse RANN, STICH; *see* POEM
verse form IAMB, DACTYL, DIPODY, OCTAVE, PANTUN, ANAPEST, COUPLET, DIMETER, DISTICH, SESTINA, SPONDEE, TRISEME, TROCHEE, VIRELAY, ANAPAEST, QUATRAIN
vertical ERECT, PLUMB, UPRIGHT
vertically APEAK
vertigo DINUS, MEGRIM, SCOTOMY
vesicle SAC, BLEB, CYST, BULLA, CAVITY, BLISTER, UTRICLE
vessel AMA, CUP, JAR, JUG, MUG, PAN, POT, TUB, TUN, URN, VAT, BOWL, CASK, ETNA, FONT, LOTA, OLLA, TANK, VASE, AMULA, BASIN, BOCAL, FLASK, GLASS, GOURD, LOTAH, STEIN, AFTABA, BOTTLE, CRATER, PATERA, DECANTER; *see also* SHIP, WARSHIP
vessel, engine-driven TUG, AVISO, OILER, OOLAK,

QBOAT, SHOUT, DROGER, LAUNCH, PADDLE, PONTIN, PUFFER, TENDER, CANALER, COASTER, COLLIER, DREDGER, DRIFTER, DROGHER, LIGHTER, PINNACE, STEAMER, TOWBOAT, CANNALLER, INDIAMAN, CABLESHIP, GUARDSHIP, LIGHTSHIP, MOTORBOAT, PILOTBOAT, POWERBOAT, SPEEDBOAT, STEAMBOAT, STEAMSHIP

vessel, general **TOW, BOAT, HULK, KEEL, MAIL, MARD, MARN, NAVY, CRAFT, FERRY, FLEET, LINER, PRORE, RACER, YACHT, ARMADA, CUTTER, MARINE, PACKET, SEALER, SLAVER, TANKER, TONNER, WHALER, PONTOON, VEDETTE, DERELICT, FLOTILLA, LIFEBOAT, CANALBOAT, FERRYBOAT, FREIGHTER, PRIVATEER, TRANSPORT, WHALESHIP**

vessel, oared **BEC, BUM, COG, GIG, ACON, DINK, DORY, GUFA, KUFA, MULE, OARS, PAHI, PLAT, PRAH, PRAO, PRAU, PROA, PUNT, RAFT, SCOW, WAKA, ACCON, BALSA, BANCA, BARIS, BIDAR, BIRCH, BUNGO, CANOE, COBLE, DINGY, DONGA, DUNGA, FLOAT, FUNNY, GOOFA, JOLLY, KAYAK, KELEK, MOSES, PRAHU, PUNGY, SCULL, SHELL, SKIFF, UMIAK, VINTA, WAAPA, BAIDAK, BALLAM, BAROTO, BATEAU, BIREME, BUGEYE, CAYUCA, CAYUCO, CORIAL, DINGEY, DUGOUT, GALLEY, GOUPHA, JANGAR, KUPHAR, LERRET, NUGGAR, OOMIAK, OUMIAC, PITPAN, PUNGEY, RANDAN, ROBROY, SEXERN, TORPID, UMIACK, WHERRY, ALMADIA, ALMADIE, BIDARKA, BUCKEYE, CASCARA, CORACLE, CURRACH, CURRAGH, CURRANE, DROMOND, FOUROAR, GONDOLA, JANGADA, LAKATOI, MASOOLA, PAIROAR, PIROGUE, SCULLER, SKIPPET, TRIREME, UNIREME**

vest **ENDOW, GILET, CLOTHE, LINDER, VESTEE, EMPOWER**

vestal **PURE, CHASTE, SACRED**

vestibule **HALL, FOYER, LOBBY**

vestige **RELIC, SHRED, TRACE, SHADOW, REMNANT, SURVIVAL**

vestment, ecclesiastic **ALB(A), COPE, COWL, AMICE, COTTA, EPHOD, FANON, FROCK, MITER, MITRE, ORALE, PHANO, RABAT, RABBI, SIMAR, STOCK, STOLE, ALMUCE, CASULA, CHIMER, GUIMPE, PILEUS, ROCHET, PLANET, TIPPET, VAKASS, BERETTA, BIRETTA, BUSKINS, CAPUCHE, CASSOCK, CHIMERE, CHRISOM, CHRYSOM, CUCULLA, MANIPLE, MOZETTA, ORARION, ORARIUM, PALLIUM, PLANETA, SOUTANE, TUNICLE, ZIMARRA, BERRETTA, CAPUCHIN, CHASUBLE, DALMATIC, MOZZETTA, SCAPULAR, SURPLICE**

vestry **CHAPEL, SACRISTY**

vetch **ERS, AKRA, TARE, FITCH**

veteran **STAGER, TROUPER, OLDTIMER**

vetiver **BENA, CUSCUS**

veto **DENY, FORBID, KIBOSH, NAYSAY**

vex **IRK, CARK, FASH, GALL, RILE, ROIL, HARRY, NETTLE**

viand(s) *see* **FOOD**

vibrate **TIRL, DINDLE, JIGGLE, QUAVER, QUIVER, THRILL, TREMBLE**

vibration **TREMOLO, FREMITUS**

vicar *see* **CLERGY**

vice **SIN, STEAD, PIACLE**

viceroy **NAWAB, EXARCH, REGENT**

Vichy premier **LAVAL**

vicinity **AREA, ENVIRONS**

vicious **BAD, EVIL, MEAN, CRUEL, SINFUL, WICKED**

victim **DUPE, FISH, GULL, MARK, PREY, CULLY, MARTYR, CATSPAW, FALLGUY**

victory NIKE, PALM, ROUT, LAUREL
victory cry ABU, ABOO
victual(s) *see* FOOD
vie COPE, RIVAL, STRIVE, COMPETE, CONTEND
Vietnamese leader KY, DIEM, DONG, MINH, KHANH, THIEU
Vietnamese measure LY, GON, MAU, NGU, QUO, SAO, TAO, SHITA, THUOC, TRUONG
Vietnamese money DONG, PIASTER
Vietnamese weight TA, CAN, BINH, DONG
view EYE, OGLE, SCENE, VISTA, OBJECT, OPINION
vigilant WARY, ALERT, AWAKE
vigor VIR, STAMINA; *see* ENERGY, FORCE
vigorous HALE, HARDY, ROBUST
viking ERIC, LEIF, OLAF, ROLLO, ROVER, PIRATE
vile LOW, BASE, MEAN, CHEAP, ABJECT, SORDID, VULGAR
vilify ABUSE, MALIGN, REVILE
village GAV, REW, KAIK, MURA, STAD, VILL, CASAL, DESSA, KAIKA, KRAAL, BUSTEE, CASALE, PUEBLO, RANCHO, CLACHAN; *see* HAMLET
villain BOOR, HEAVY, KNAVE, ROGUE, BADDIE, LEGREE
villein *see* SERF
vim PEP, ZIP, VIGOR, ENERGY
vindictive SPITEFUL, MALICIOUS
vine AKA, HOP, IVY, IYO, PEA, BINE, GRAPE, LIANA, COWAGE, LABLAB, CLIMBER, COWHAGE, CREEPER, WISTERIA
vinegar EISEL, ACETUM, ALEGAR, EISELL
vinegar, pert. to ACETIC
vineyard CLOS, COTE, CHATEAU
violate ABUSE, INJURE, RAVISH, INFRACT, ENCROACH
violence FURY, RAGE, ASSAULT
violent WILD, RABID, RAVING
violet PANSY, VIOLA, KISSME, PENSEE; *see p. 251*
violin *see* STRING INSTRUMENT
violin maker AMATI, CREMONA, GUARNERI, STRADIVARI
violinist AUER, ELMAN, STERN, YSAYE, HEIFETZ, MENUHIN, PERLMAN, SZIGETI, GRUMIAUX, KREISLER, KREUTZER, MILSTEIN, OISTRAKH, PAGANINI
viper BITIS, DABOIA, DABOYA, JESSUR, HOGNOSE, BONETAIL, CERASTES, JARARACA, LACHESIS, MOCCASIN, PITVIPER, PUFFADDER, FERDELANCE; *see* SNAKE
viper genus ECHIS, BOTHROPS
virago VIXEN, AMAZON, HELLCAT
Virgil poem (A)ENEID
Virgil's hero(ine) DIDO, (A)ENEAS
virgin PURE, PIETA, CHASTE, VESTAL, MADONNA
Virginia information *see p. 308*
virgule COMMA, SOLIDUS
virile MACHO, MANLY, MASCULINE
virtue MERIT, QUALITY, CHASTITY
virtues, cardinal HOPE, FAITH, CHARITY, JUSTICE, PRUDENCE, FORTITUDE, TEMPERANCE
virulent RABID, DEADLY, NOXIOUS
virus GERM, VENOM, VACCINE, PATHOGEN
visage ASPECT; *see* FACE
viscera GUTS, VITALS, INNARDS
viscous LIMY, ROPY, SIZY, GLUEY, SLIMY, STICKY
Vishnu incarnation RAMA, KRSNA, BUDDHA, KALKIN
Vishnu relative SRI, INDRA, LAKSHMI, RUKMINI
visible CLEAR, PATENT, EVIDENT
Visigoth *see* GOTH
vision DREAM, GHOST, PHANTOM
visionary FEY, AIRY, IDEAL, DREAMY, UNREAL, UTOPIAN
visit GAM, SEE, CALL, STAY, HAUNT, SOJOURN
visitor GUEST, CALLER, COMPANY
visor BRIM, SHADE, VIZARD

vista VIEW, SCENE, OUTLOOK, SCENERY, PANORAMA
visual OCULAR, OPTICAL
vital LIVING, MORTAL, ESSENTIAL
vital energy HORME
vitality SAP; *see* ENERGY
vitalize VIVIFY, ANIMATE
vitamin BIOTIN, CITRIN, FLAVIN, NIACIN, ADERMIN, ANEURIN, CHOLINE, TORULIN, THIAMINE
vitiate VOID, SPOIL, TAINT, DEFILE, IMPAIR
vitrify BAKE, FUSE, GLAZE
vitriolic SHARP, BITING, CAUSTIC
vitriols SORY, SULFATE
vituperate ABUSE, SCOLD, BERATE, REVILE, STRAFE
vivacity BRIO, DASH, ELAN; *see* ENERGY
vivid LIVE, CLEAR, LUCID, BRIGHT, GRAPHIC
vixen *see* FOX, VIRAGO
vocabulary ARGOT, JARGON, LEXICON, GLOSSARY
vocal ORAL, TONIC, SONANT, VERBAL, VOICED; *see* SONG
vocation ART, TRADE, CAREER, METIER, OFFICE, CALLING, MISSION
vociferous NOISY, BLATANT
vogue TON, MODE, FAVOR, USAGE, CUSTOM, FASHION
voice SAY, VOX, EMIT, VOCE, VOTE, SOUND, TONGUE; *see* SINGER
voice, pert. to ORAL, VOCAL, PHONETIC
voiced TONIC, SONANT, VIBRANT
voiceless MUTE, SURD, SILENT, ASONANT, SPIRATE
void NUL(L), SPACE, VACANT, VACATE, VACUUM, INVALID; *see* ANNUL
volatile BIRD, FICKLE, MUTABLE
volcanic ejection MOYA, TUFF, BELCH, SALSE, PUMICE; *see* LAVA
volcano ASO, AWU, USU, ETNA, FOGO, FUJI, GEDE, NASU, POAS, SIAU, TAAL, AETNA, AGUNG, ASAMA, ASKJA, AZUMA, BALBI, BATUR, FUEGO, GEDEH, HEKLA, IRAZU, KELUD, KISKA, MANAM, MAYON, OSIMA, PASTO, PELEE, RAUNG, AJUSCO, AKUTAN, ALCEDO, AMBRYM, ANTUCO, ARAYAT, ARENAL, BIGBEN, CHOKAI, COLIMA, DOMUYO, DUKONO, EREBUS, HUDSON, IZALCO, KARKAR, KATMAI, KRAFLA, LASSEN, LLAIMA, LOPEVI, MARAPI, MAZAMA, MERAPI, ONTAKE, OSORNO, PACAYA, PAVLOF, PURACE, SANGAY, SEGUAM, SEMERU, SLAMET, TELICA, TIATIA, TOLIMA, ATITLAN, GARELOI, ILIAMNA, KILAUEA, LANGILA, OMETEPE, REDOUBT, TAMBORA, TRIDENT, KRAKATAO, KRAKATAU, MAUNALOA, RINDJANI, VESUVIUS
Volga tributary OKA, KAMA, SURA, MOLOGA, SAMARA
volition WILL, OPTION, CONATION
volley BURST, SALVO, DISCHARGE
Voltaire AROUET
Voltaire work ZADIG, ZAIRE, ALZIRE, CANDIDE
voluble GLIB, FLUENT
volume BULK, MASS, RANGE, CUBAGE, LOUDNESS; *see* BOOK
voluptuous SENSUAL, SENSUOUS
vomit PUKE, SPEW, BELCH, REJECT
vomiting EMESIS
voodoo HEX, OBI, JINX, OBEAH, VODUN
voodoo deity ZOMBI
voracious EDACIOUS, RAVENOUS
vortex EDDY, GYRE, MAELSTROM
vote AYE, NAY, NOD, YEA, POLL, ELECT, PROXY, STRAW, BALLOT, PLACET
vouch AVER, AFFIRM, ATTEST
voucher CHIT, NOTE, STUB
vouchsafe DEIGN, GRANT, STOOP, YIELD, BESTOW, CONCEDE
vow OATH, PLEDGE, PROMISE
voyage TREK, TRIP, CRUISE, SAFARI, VOYAGE, JOURNEY
Vulcan relative JUNO, MAIA, CUPID, VENUS

vulgar LOW, MEAN, RUDE, COARSE, BOORISH
vulnerable LIABLE, SUSCEPTIBLE
vulture URUBU, CONDOR

W

wacky FEY, MAD, ODD, SCREWY
wad CRAM, LUMP, STUFF, BUNDLE
wade FORD, SLOG, PLODGE
wading bird IBIS, RAIL, SORA, CRANE, EGRET, HERON, SNIPE, STORK, UMBER, AVOCET, CURLEW, JACANA, JABIRU, GRALLAE, FLAMINGO
wafer DISK, HOST, OBLEY, LAMINA, TROCHE
waft GUST, WAIF, CARRY, FLOAT
wag WAVE, SHAKE, WIGGLE; *see* JOKER
wage(s) FEE, PAY, UTU, HIRE, BATTA, SALARY, STIPEND
wager RISK, HAZARD; *see* BET
Wagner opera RING, RIENZI, TRISTAN, WALKURE, PARSIFAL, LOHENGRIN, SIEGFRIED
Wagner relative MINNA, COSIMA, WIELAND, WOLFGANG
Wagnerian role ELSA, ERDA, SENTA, ISOLDE, RIENZI, TRISTAN; *see* RING
wagon CART, TRAM, WAIN, TELEGA, TUMBREL
wagon part NEAP, POLE, BLADE, THILL, CLEVIS
waif ARAB, GAMIN, STRAY, URCHIN, MUDLARK, FOUNDLING
wail HOWL, KEEN, WAUL, MOURN, LAMENT, ULULATE
waist GIRTH, BODICE, HALTER, MIDRIFF; *see* BLOUSE
wait BIDE, STAY, TARRY
wait on TEND, CATER, SERVE
waiter/waitress CARHOP, GARCON, SALVER, HOSTESS, STEWARD
waive CEDE, DEFER, FOREGO
wake STIR, AWAKE, ROUSE, VIGIL, WAKEN, WATCH, TRACK, AROUSE, AWAKEN, KINDLE
wakeful VIGILANT, WATCHFUL
Walden author THOREAU
wale RIB, WELT, WHEAL
Wales CYMRU, CAMBRIA
walk HIKE, LIMP, MALL, PACE, PAUP, PLOD, SLOG, STEP, STOA, AMBLE, MARCH, MINCE, STRUT, TRAMP, LUMBER, STROLL, WADDLE, ALAMEDA, LAMBETH, SAUNTER, SWAGGER
walking stick CANE, STAFF, WADDY
wall MUR(E), LEVEE, SEPTA, SPINA, ESCARP, PARIES, SEPTUM, BARRIER, PARAPET, RAMPART
wall covering ARRAS, PAINT, PAPER, TAPESTRY
wall piece DADO, PANEL, TEMPLET, TEMPLATE, WAINSCOT
wallet PURSE, SCRIP, BILLFOLD
wallop LAM, BEAT, BLOW, SMITE
wallow REVEL, GROVEL, WELTER
walnut *see* NUT
walrus MORSE, SEACOW, UNICORN, WALTRON, ODOBENUS
walrus genus BRUTA
wampum PEAG(E), MONEY, SE(A)WAN, ROANOKE
wan ASHY, PALE, ASHEN, WAXEN, PALLID, SALLOW, SICKLY
wand ROD, MACE, BATON, WITHE, WATTLE, SCEPTER
wander ERR, GAD, HAAK, HAIK, HAKE, MOON, ROAM, ROVE, RANGE, STRAY, DIGRESS, MEANDER
wanderer WAIF, GYPSY, NOMAD, ROVER, STRAY, PALMER, VIATOR, BEDOUIN, MIGRANT, SCENITE, ITINERANT; *see* VAGABOND
wandering ERRANT, TRUANT, NOMADIC, ODYSSEY, BOHEMIAN, VAGABOND
wane EBB, ABATE, SUBSIDE
wangle FINAGLE, WHEEDLE
want NEED, CRAVE, YEARN, DEARTH, PENURY, POVERTY

wanton LEWD, WILD, LOOSE
wapiti *see* DEER
war(fare) BOER, WEER, CIVIL, FIGHT, JEHAD, JIHAD, PUNIC, BALKAN, GALLIC, STRIFE, CRIMEAN, CRUSADE, SAMNITE, CONFLICT, HOSTILITY
War and Peace author TOLSTOI
war cry ALALA, AMORT, WHOOP, BANZAI, WARISON, GERONIMO
war, pert. to MARTIAL
warble YODEL; *see* SING
warbler HOODIE, MUFFET, CREEPER, WHITETHROAT
warbler genus SYLVIA, SEIURUS
ward FEND, AVERT, REPEL, PARRY, CUSTODY, PROTEGE(E)
warden GUARD, RANGER, GUARDIAN
wardrobe CHEST, PRESS, CLOSET
warehouse DEPOT, ETAPE, BODEGA, GODOWN, ARSENAL, ENTREPOT
warlike MARTIAL, MILITANT
warlock *see* WITCH, MAGICIAN
warm BEEK, HEAT, BALMY, CALID, TEPID, ARDENT, REHEAT
warn FLAG, ADVISE, SIGNAL, CAUTION, PREVISE, ADMONISH
warning OMEN, ALARM, ALERT, CAVEAT, PORTENT
warp BIAS, CRAM, SILT, BUCKLE, CONTORT, DISTORT
warp term ABB, DENT, LOOM, REED, LEASE, RAVEL, THRUM, EVENER, RADDLE, ROLLER, STAMEN
warplane *see* AIRCRAFT
warrant(s) WRIT, BERAT, PLEVIN
warren HUTCH
warrior TOA, IMPI, SINGH, SPAHI, AMAZON, SANNUP, COSSACK, HESSIAN, SAMURAI; *see* SOLDIER
warship LST, RAM, SUB, BOYER, SCOUT, UBOAT, ANDREW, CARACK, CHASER, PTBOAT, CARRACK, CARRIER, CORSAIR, CRUISER, FLATTOP, FRIGATE, GUNBOAT, LANTCHA, MONITOR, SNORKEL, CORVETTE, FIRESHIP, FLAGSHIP, GALLEASS, GALLIASS, IRONCLAD, MANOFWAR, BOMBARDER, DESTROYER, EAGLEBOAT, FIRSTRATE, MINELAYER, SUBMARINE
wart WEN, TUMOR, VERRUCA
wary CAG(E)Y, CANNY, CHARY
wash LAVE, LOSH, SWAB, BATHE, ELUTE, LEACH, RINSE, SWILL, ARROYO, COULEE, LAUNDER
washings ELUATE
Washington (state) information *see p. 308*
wasp BIKE, MASON, SPHEX, WAPSE, WHAMP, WOPSE, DAUBER, DIGGER, HORNET, VESPID, CYNIPID, EUMENID, MASARID, MUDWASP, MUTILLA, VESPINA, ACULEATA, SANDWASP
wasp genus VESPA, BEMBEX, BEMBIX, TIPHIA, EUMENES
waste GNAW, IDLE, LOSS, SCUM, CHAFF, DECAY, DREGS, DROSS, BARREN, REFUSE, ATROPHY, FRITTER, GARBAGE, EFFLUVIUM
waste allowance TRET
waste fiber NOIL
waste silk KNUB, FRISON
waste time IDLE, LOAF, DAWDLE, FIDDLE, FRIBBLE, SOLDIER
wasteful WASTREL, PRODIGAL
wasteland MOOR, HEATH, DESERT, WASTREL
watch EYE, SEE, SPY, GLOM, MIND, TEND, GUARD, VIGIL, DIGITAL, ANALOG(UE)
watch part DIAL, HAND, PAWL, STEM, STUD, BEZEL, CLICK, CROWN, JEWEL, DETENT, PALLET, CRYSTAL
watchdog GARM, BANDOG, MASTIFF, CERBERUS
watchful ALERT, AWAKE, CAUTIOUS
watchman ARGUS, GUARD, SENTRY, SERENO, VEDETTE, CHOKIDAR
watchtower ATALAYA, MIRADOR, BARBICAN
watchword MOTTO, SLOGAN, PASSWORD, SHIBBOLETH

water EAU, AQUA, BROO, EAUX, RAIN, HTWOO, DILUTE, HYDROL, IRRIGATE, SPRINKLE
water bird ERN, COOT, GULL, IBIS, LOON, RAIL, SWAN, TERN, BRANT, CRANE, EGRET, HERON, OUSEL, STILT, AVOCET, JACANA, PELICAN
water boy BHISTI, BHEESTY, BHEESTIE
water buffalo ARNA, ARNEE, CARABAO
water chestnut LING, TRAPA, CALTROP
water, living in LOTIC, AQUATIC, LENITIC
water surface RYME
watercolor GOUACHE, TEMPERA, AQUARELLE
watercourse RIA, FLUX, LADE, RACE, BROOK, CREEK, GULLY, NULLA, RIVER, NULLAH, RAVINE, STREAM
waterfall LIN, LYN, FOSS, LINN, TWIN, ANGEL, BOWEN, DETTI, FORCE, KEGON, SAULT, TOWER, FINCHA, GUAIRA, HANDOL, HELENA, HOWICK, IGUAZU, MARINA, NARADA, RIBBON, TUGELA, VERNAL, VETTIS, VORING, YUDAKI, CASCADE, CAUVERY, GASTEIN, GOLLING, HANDEGG, IGUASSU, KALAMBO, NIAGARA, PASSAIC, RUACANA, CATARACT, VICTORIA, YOSEMITE, HORSESHOE
watering place WELL, OASIS; *see* SPRING
waterless DRY, ARID, ANHYDROUS
water-raising device WHIM, WHIN, NORIA, SWEEP, TABUT, SHADUF, TABOOT, SHADOOF
watershed BASIN, CRISIS, DIVIDE
waterway CANAL, RIVER, STRAIT, STREAM, CHANNEL
waterwheel NORIA, SAKIA, PADDLE, SAKIEH, TURBINE
watery THIN, SOGGY, WASHY, SEROUS, AQUEOUS
wattle GILL, DEWLAP, LAPPET
wave FLY, WAFT, BECKON, COMBER, RIPPLE, ROLLER, BREAKER; *see* BILLOW
waver SWAY, FALTER, TEETER
wavy ONDY, UNDE, UNDY, CRISP, NEBULE, REPAND, UNDATE, UNDOSE
wax CERE, CODE, GROW, PELA, CERIN, CEROMA, CERESIN
wax, pert. to CERAL
way TAO, VIA, ITER, LANE, MODE, ROAD, WONT, HABIT, MEANS, ROUTE
way out EXIT, EGRESS
wayfarer VIATOR, TRAVELER
wayside rest PARAO
weak WAN, FLAT, PUNY, FAINT, FRAIL, DEBILE, EFFETE, FEEBLE, INFIRM
weaken SAP, DILUTE, LABEFY, VITIATE, ENERVATE, ENFEEBLE
weakling PULER, SISSY, SOFTIE
weakness ATONY, FOIBLE, ACRATIA, FRAILTY
wealth PELF, LUCRE, ASSETS, MAMMON, CAPITAL, FORTUNE, OPULENCE, AFFLUENCE
wealthy LUSH, FLUSH, HEELED, MONEYED, OPULENT; *see* RICH
weapon ARM(E), ARMS; *see* GUN, KNIFE, SPEAR, SWORD, CANON
wear DON, USE, FRAY, CHAFE, ERODE, ABRADE, CORRODE
wearisome DREE, DULL, DREICH
weary FAG, BORE, JADE, TIRE, TUCKER
weasel(-like mammals) FOIN, MINK, PATE, VARE, BROCK, FITCH, HURON, OTTER, PAHMI, PEKAN, RATEL, SABLE, SKUNK, STOAT, TAYRA, ZORIL, BADGER, BAUSON, BRAIRO, ERMINE, FERRET, FISHER, GALERA, GRISON, MARTEN, WEASEL, FITCHET, GLUTTON, MINIVER, POLECAT, SANDPIG, ZORILLA, BRAIREAU, CARCAJOU, KOLINSKY, MUISHOND
weasel genus GULO, LATAX, LUTRA, MELES, MARTES, MYDAUS, ENHYDRA, ICTONYX, MUSTELA, TAXIDEA, MEPHITIS

weather term FOG, HOT, ICY, THI, WET, COLD, FAIR, HAIL, RAIN, SMOG, SNOW, WARM, CHILL, FOGGY, FROST, HUMID, SLEET, SMAZE, THERM, WINDY, CHILLY, CLOUDY, DEGREE, ISOBAR, STORMY, DROUGHT, HUMIDITY, ISOTHERM, OVERCAST
weathercock FANE, VANE, GIROUETTE
weave KNIT, LOOM, BRAID, PLAIT, PLASH, PLEACH, ENTWINE
weaver WEBSTER
weaverbird NUN, BAYA, TAHA, VEUVE, OXBIRD, WHIDAH, WHYDAH, WAXBILL
weaverbird genus QUELEA
weaving term COP, LAY, UNI, SLEY, WOOF, LATHE, LEASE, LISSE, RAVEL, BOBBIN, LAPETT; *see* LOOM
web NET, TELA, GOSSAMER
web, pert. to TELAR(Y), RETIARY
web-footed bird DUCK, LOON, SWAN, GOOSE, AVOCET, GANNET, PELICAN, PENGUIN, ALBATROSS, CORMORANT
Weber opera OBERON, (DER)FREISCHUTZ
wed MATE, WIVE, MARRY, MERGE, UNITE, ESPOUSE
wedding HYMEN, ESPOUSAL, MARRIAGE, NUPTIALS
wedge CAM, JAM, FROE, FROW, GLUT, GORE, SHIM, CHOCK, COIGN, QUOIN, SPRAG, COTTER, CUNEUS, GUSSET
wedge-shaped CUNEATE
Wednesday source WODEN
weed HOE, CULL, DOCK, PEST, TARE, COUCH, JIMSON, QUITCH, SPURRY, CHARLOCK, DANDELION
week OUK, SENNET, HEBDOMAD, SENNIGHT
weep ORP, SOB, BAWL, BOHO(O), BOOHOO, LAMENT, BLUBBER; *see* CRY
weevil *see* BEETLE
weft WOFT, WOOF
weighing device *see* SCALE
weight BOB, TOD, HEFT, LOAD, NAIL, PARI, TRON, TROY, CLOVE, PEISE, TRONE, VALUE
weight, metric TON, GRAM, KILO, QUINTAL, KILOGRAM, MILLIGRAM
weight, pert. to BARIC
weight, U.S. & British (*for other countries see specific entry*) CWT, KEG, KIP, TON, DRAM, CARAT, OUNCE, POUND, BARREL, CENTAL
weight system TROY, METRIC, AVOIRDUPOIS
weir DAM, TRAP, GARTH
weird ODO, EERY, UNCO, EERIE, SPOOKY, UNCANNY, ELDRITCH
welcome HAIL, GREET, ACCOIL
weld SEAM, JOINT, SOLDER
welfare WEAL, BENEFIT
well AIN, BIEN, FONT, HALE, SOUND, SPRING, FOUNTAIN
well curb PUTEAL
well done EUGE, BRAVO, BULLY
well known NOTED, FAMOUS, FAMILIAR, RENOWNED
well lining STEEN
well read VERSED, LEARNED, LITERATE
Welsh CYMRY, KYMRY, TAFFY, CYMRIC, KYMRIC, CAMBRIAN
welt LASH, WALE, STRIP
wen CYST, MOLE, CLYER, TALPA
wench DOXY, HUSSY; *see* MAID
wend PASS, SORB, MEANDER
werewolf LOUPGAROU, LYCANTHROPE
West African tree AKEE, ODUM, ACKEE, IROKO
West-Atlantic language GOLA, KISSI, LIMBA, SERER, TEMNE, WOLOF, BALANTE
West Indian music CALYPSO
West Indian tree MABI, ACANA, GENIP, GINEP, YACCA, BALATA, PIMENTO, ALLSPICE; *see* INDIAN
West Point mascot MULE
West Pointer PLEB, CADET, PLEBE, YEARLING
West Virginia information *see p. 308*
western OATER, OCCIDENTAL
wet RET, SOP, WAT, ASOP, DAMP, DANK, SOAK, MOIST, SOPPING
wetback PEON, BRACERO
whack BEAT, SLAP, SMACK

whale FLOG, THRASH
whale(s) ORC, SEI, CETE, ORCA, KRENG, OTARY, POGGY, SCRAG, SPERM, BALEEN, BELUGA, BLOWER, FINNER, GIBBAR, KILLER, BOWHEAD, FINBACK, FINFISH, GRAMPUS, MARSOON, RIPSACK, RORQUAL, SPOUTER, ZIPHIAN, BALAENID, CACHALOT, HUMPBACK, MOBYDICK, MUTILATE, LEVIATHAN
whale genus HUSE, HUSO, BALAENA, ORCINUS, ZALOPHUS
whale hunter AHAB
whale sound MEW, BARK, SONG, CLICK, WHINE, SQUEAL, CHIRRUP, WHISTLE
whalebone BALEEN
whales, pert. to CETIC, CETACEAN
wharf *see* LANDING
whatnot OMNIUM, CABINET, ETAGERE
wheat SUJI, SUJEE, DURUM, EMMER, SPELT, EINKORN, POULARD
wheat disease BUNT, RUST, SMUT, ERGOT
wheedle COG, COAX, CAJOLE, WANGLE
wheel(s) DISK, HELM, ROLL, ROTA, SPIN, NORIA, ROWEL, CASTER, GYRATE, PULLEY, ROTATE, SHEAVE, SPROCKET
wheel part CAM, HOB, HUB, RIM, AXLE, NAVE, TIRE, ARBOR, FELLY, SPOKE, FLANGE, STRAKE
wheeze GAG, GASP, RALE
whelp PUP(PY), YOUTH
whereas SINCE, SEEING, INASMUCH
wherewithal MEANS, RESOURCES
whet HONE, GRIND, SHARPEN
whetstone RIP, BUHR, HONE
whey SERA, SERUM, WHIG
whiff GUST, PUFF, WAFT, SMELL
while WHEN, ALBEIT, DAWDLE
whim FAD, TOY, KINK, FREAK, HUMOR, NOTION, CAPRICE
whimper KEEN, WHINE; *see* CRY
whinny FURZY, HINNY, NEIGH

whip CROP, FLOG, PLET, AZOTE, KNOUT, QUIRT, CHICOTE, KURBASH; *see* BEAT
whip mark WALE, WEAL, STRIPE
whipsocket SNEAD
whirl REEL, SPIN, GYRATE
whirlpool EDDY, WEEL, WIEL, GURGE, SWIRL, VORTEX, MAELSTROM
whirlwind EDDY, CYCLONE, TORNADO, TWISTER
whiskers BEARD, CHOPS, GOATEE, VIBRISSA, MUSTACHE, SIDEBURN(S)
whiskey HOOCH, POTEEN, ROTGUT, POTHEEN, FIREWATER; *see* LIQUOR
whisper HINT, ASIDE, TUTEL, MURMUR, BREATHE
whist term MORT, SLAM, SOLO, VOLE, GRAND, MISERE
whistle CALL, FUTE, PIPE, TOOT, SIREN, TOOTLE, CATCALL
whit DOIT; *see* BIT
white BAWN, LABAN, CHALKY
white man BUCKRA, GRINGO, CACHILA, PALEFACE
whitefish CISCO, POWAN, POLLAN, POLLEN, INCONNU, LAVARET, VENDACE, TULLIBEE
whiten BLANCH, BLEACH, ETIOLATE
whitewash CLEAR, GLOSS, PARGET
Whittier heroine MAUD, MOLL(Y)
whiz HUM, PIRR, WHIR
whole TOTO, SOUND, TOTAL, UNCUT, ENTIRE, INTACT
wholesale GROSS, MASSIVE
wick SNAST, SNUFF, SNASTE
wicked *see* EVIL
wickerwork RA(T)TAN
wicket ARCH, GATE, HOOP, STUMP, INNING, WINDOW
wide VAST, AMPLE, BROAD, LARGE
widespread RIFE, RAMPANT, PREVALENT
widgeon *see* DUCK
widow SKAT, RELICT, SUTTEE
widow's share MITE, T(I)ERCE
width BREADTH, LATITUDE
wife RIB, FEME, FERE, FRAU, FROW, UXOR, BRIDE,

FEMME, SQUAW, MATRON, MISSUS; *see* SPOUSE
wife's property DOS
wifely UXORIAL
wig MAT, RUG, BUSBY, DIVOT, DOILY, JASEY, PERUKE, TOUPEE, PERIWIG, RAMIL(L)IE
wigwam TIPI, TE(E)PEE, WICKIUP
wild FERAL, RABID, FERINE
Wild West show RODEO
wildcat *see* CAT
wile ART, LURE, RUSE, TRICK, DECEIT
will WISH, BEHEST, DESIRE, CONATION, VELLEITY, VOLITION, TESTAMENT
will beneficiary DEVISEE
will maker DEVISOR
willful WAYWARD, STUBBORN, OBSTINATE
willing BAIN
willingly FAIN, LIEF, READILY
willow ITEA, EDDER, OSIER, SALIX, WITHY
wilt FADE, COWER, DROOP, WITHER
wily SLY, FOXY, SUBTLE
wimble AUGER, GIMLET
wimple GORGET, WIMLUNGE
wince SHY, FLINCH, RECOIL
winch CRANK, HOIST, WINDLASS
wind AFER, BISE, BORA, GALE, GUST, KONA, PUNA, PUNO, FOEHN, LESTE, NOTUS, SIROC, TRADE, TWINE, TWIST, AUSTER, BOREAS, BREATH, BUSTER, DUSTER, FLATUS, FLURRY, KAMSIN, SAMIEL, SARSAR, SHAMAL, SHIMAL, SIMOOM, SIMOON, SOLANO, ZEPHYR, CYCLONE, ETESIAN, GREGALE, KHAMSIN, MISTRAL, MONSOON, PAMPERO, SIROCCO, TEMPEST
wind indicator COCK, CONE, SOCK, VANE, SLEEVE
wind instrument OAT, ALTO, BEME, BEEN, FIFE, HORN, LURE, OBOE, PIPE, REED, SANG, TUBA, ZINK, AULOS, BUGLE, CHENG, CODON, CORNO, FLUTE, KAZOO, ORGAN, REGAL, SHAWM, SHENG, TRUMP, ZINKE, ATABAL, CLARIN, CORNET, LITUUS, POMMER, SHOFAR, SYRINX, TRIBON, TROMBA, ALTHORN, ANKLONG, ANKLUNG, BAGPIPE, BASSOON, BUCCINA, CLARION, DIAULOS, HAUTBOY, HELICON, MUSETTE, OCARINA, PANPIPE, PIBCORN, PIBGORN, PICCOLO, RACKETT, SACKBUT, SAXHORN, SERPENT, SHOPHAR, TRUMPET, BARITONE, CALLIOPE, CLARINET, CROMORNE, MELODEON, NEHILOTH, PANPIPES, POSTHORN, RECORDER, SOURDINE, TROMBONE
windborne AEOLIAN
windfall BOON, BONANZA
winding MAZY, AMBAGE, TORTUOUS
winding sheet SHROUD, CEREMENT
windlass REEL, WHIM, WHIN, CRANK, WINCH, CAPSTAN
windmill part AWE, CAP, CURB, SAIL, VANE
window SASH, ORIEL, OXEYE, DORMER, LUCARNE, ROUNDEL, TRANSOM, SKYLIGHT
window part CAME, PANE, SASH, SILL, MUNTIN, LEADING, MULLION, TRANSOM
window setter GLAZIER
windpipe WEASAND, TRACHEA
windstorm BURA(N), SQUALL, TORNADO, TWISTER, TYPHOON
Windy City CHICAGO
wine CRU, RED, SEC, VIN, BRUT, CUIT, CUTE, DOUX, MUST, GRAVE, WHITE, NATURAL
wine(s) AHR, AYL, ASTI, BUAL, GIRO, HOCK, NAHE, PORT, ROSE, SACK, SAKE, SAKI, SEKT, ANJOU, BADEN, BLANC, BYRRH, CAPRI, CORVO, FIXIN, MACON, MEDOC, PFALZ, PICON, RIOJA, ROUGE, SOAVE, TAVEL, TINTA, TOKAY, TRIER, XERES, YQUEM, ZUCCO, ALBANA, ALBANO, ALELLA, ALSACE, ARBOIS, AUSONE, BAROLO, BARSAC, BEAUNE, CANARY,

CHINON, CLARET, GRAVES, LILLET, MALAGA, MASDEU, MONICA, MUSCAT, PATRAS, PERNOD, PINEAU, RUFINA, SAUMUR, SHERRY, SPANNA, VOLNAY, YVORNE, BANYULS, CALDARO, CATAWBA, CHABLIS, CHIANTI, CREMANT, DAGORED, EPERNAY, FALERNO, FLANKEN, FLEURIE, INFERNO, MADEIRA, MALMSEY, MARGAUX, MARSALA, MAYWINE, MOSCATO, MOSELLE, OLOROSO, ORVIETO, PASSITO, POMEROL, POMMARD, REDWINE, SEEWEIN, SERCIAL, SEYSSEL, VERDISO, VESUVIO, VINGRIS, VOUVRAY, ALEATICO, ALSATIAN, BORDEAUX, BURGUNDY, CABERNET, CALVADOS, CHABLAIS, COLDDUCK, CORONATA, DUBONNET, FRASCATI, GRENACHE, MUSCADET, MUSCATEL, PIESPORT, RHEINGAU, RIESLING, RUBYPORT, SANCERRE, SAUTERNE, SYLVANER, TOURAINE, VERMOUTH; *see* LIQUOR

wine disorder CASSE

wine drink *see* DRINK

wine, pert. to VINIC, VINOUS

wine term DRY, SEC, BRUT, BODY, SEVE, VINT, FLINTY, BOUQUET

wine with honey MULSE

wineglass TULIP, RUMMER

wing ALA, ELL, ALAE, ALULA, ANNEX, PENNA, PINNA, ALETTE, PINION, ELYTRON, TEGMINA, TEGUMEN

wing part FLAP, FLANK, AILERON

wing, pert. to ALAR

winged AILE, ALAR, ALATE

winged deity EROS, NIKE, CUPID

winged figure IDOLON, IDOLUM, EIDOLON

winged fruit SAMARA

wing-footed ALIPED

wingless APTERAL, DEALATE(D)

wink BAT, FLICKER, NICTATE

Winnie the Pooh author MILNE

Winter's Tale character DION, MOPSA, DORCAS, LEONTES

wintry ARCTIC, BOREAL, BRUMAL, HIEMAL, HYEMAL, HIBERNAL

wipe RUB, SWAB, ERASE, EFFACE

wipe out KILL, ERASE, REMOVE, ELIMINATE, ERADICATE

wire CORD, LEAD, LINE, LITZ, CABLE, CIRCUIT, RETICLE

Wisconsin information *see p. 308*

wisdom WIT, LORE, GNOSIS

wise man MAGI, SAGE, MAGUS, SOLON, WITAN, GASPAR, MENTOR, NESTOR, PANDIT, SAVANT, MAHATMA, SOLOMON

wish HOPE, WANT, DESIRE

wishy-washy WEAK, INSIPID

wisp TAIT, TATE, TUFT, WASE

wisteria FUJI

wit WAG, HUMOR, IRONY, ESPRIT

witch HAG, HEX, BRUJA, CIRCE, CRONE, ENDOR, HECAT, LAMIA, BELDAM, DUESSA, HECATE, LILITH, ACRASIA, BELDAME, CARLINE, WARLOCK

witch city ENDOR, SALEM

witch doctor BRUJO, GOOFER, SHAMAN, WIZARD

witchcraft *see* SORCERY

withdraw QUIT, WEAN, RETIRE, SECEDE, RETREAT, RETRACT

wither FADE, SERE, WILT, WIZEN, SHRIVEL

withhold DENY, KEEP, REFUSE

without SANS, MINUS, OUTSIDE

witness SEE, TESTE, ATTEST, DEPONENT, ONLOOKER

witticism *see* JOKE

wizard *see* MAGICIAN

Wodehouse character JEEVES

woe BANE, DOLOR, MISERY

wolf LOBO, CHANCO, COYOTE, THOOID; *see* DOG

wolf genus CANIS

wolfish LUPINE, THOOID, RAVENOUS

Wolverine State MI, MICH(IGAN)

woman SHE, PERI, BELLE, HOURI, MENAD, VIXEN, MAENAD, PARAMOUR; *see* HAG, MADAM, WIFE, FEMALE

womb WAME, BELLY, MATRIX, UTERUS, VENTER
Wonder State AR, ARK(ANSAS)
wont HABIT, USAGE, CUSTOM
woo *see* COURT
wood(s) ASH, ELM, GUM, OAK, YEW, LANA, BALSA, BIRCH, CAHUY, CEDAR, EBONY, KOKRA, MAPLE, NARRA, ALERCE, CHERRY, LUMBER, TIMBER, WALNUT, CHESTNUT, MAHOGANY, ROSEWOOD, SYCAMORE; *see* FOREST, GOLF
wood, bend in SNY
wood measure CORD, FATHOM
wood, piece of DEAL, LATH, SLAT, BOARD, PLANK, SPRAG, STAVE, BILLET
woodchuck MARMOT, WEJACK
wooded BOSKY, SYLVAN
wooden STIFF, TREEN, STOLID
woodpecker KATE, PICULE, YAFFLE, FLICKER, LOGCOCK, PICULET, WITWALL, WRYNECK
woodpecker genus JYNX, PICI
woodwind *see* WIND INSTRUMENT
woodworking tool ADZ, AWL, ADZE, FROE, FROW
woody TREEN, SYLVAN, XYLOID, LIGNEUS
woof ABB, WEFT, TEXTURE
wool DOWN, GARE, HAIR, YARN, FLOCK, FLEECE, FLOCCUS; *see* FIBER, FABRIC
wool cluster NEP
wool measure HEER
wool package FADGE
wool variety ALPACA, ANGORA, MERINO, VIRGIN, CHALLIS
woolly FLEECY, LANATE, LANOSE
word TERM, LOGOS, PAROL, RHEMA, PAROLE, PLEDGE, ANAGRAM
words TEXT, LYRICS
wordy PROLIX, DIFFUSE, TEDIOUS
work FAG, JOB, PLY, MOIL, OPUS, TOIL, CHARE, CHORE, ERGON, GRIND, LABOR, SLAVE, STINT, POTTER, TRAVAIL
work out SOLVE, EXERCISE
work unit ERG(ON), KILERG
workman ARRY, CREW, HAND, PEON, ROTO, VOLK, CAGER, ARTISAN, OPERANT, OPERATOR
workshop LAB, MILL, PLANT, STUDIO, ATELIER, FACTORY
world LOKA, EARTH, GLOBE, COSMOS, MANKIND, UNIVERSE
World War battle *see* BATTLE
World War I group AEF, BEF, AMEX
World War II area CBI, ETO, MTO
worldly LAY, LAIC, CARNAL, MORTAL, MUNDANE, SECULAR
World's Fair sites GHENT, OSAKA, PARIS, LONDON, VIENNA, CHICAGO, NEWYORK, SEATTLE, BRUSSELS, MONTREAL, VANCOUVER
worldwide *see* UNIVERSAL
worm LOA, NAID, NAIS, WORM, APODA, BORER, FLUKE, LEECH, ANOPLA, APODAN, CADDIS, ENOPLA, EUNICE, NEREIS, PALOLO, PEDATA, PLOIMA, SEAFAN, SYLLID, ANNELID, ASCARID, ASCARIS, CARBORA, ENOPLAN, EUNICID, FILARIA, GORDIUS, LINGULA, PINWORM, SABELLA, SAGITTA, SANGSUE, SERPULA, ANNELIDA, ANNELOID, ANNULATA, ANNULATE, BDELLOID, CLEPSINE, HELMINTH, NEMATODA, NEMATODE, NEMATOID, SABELLID, SEAMOUSE, TUBEWORM, TUBICOLA
worm, to INCH, CRAWL, CREEP, SINUATE
worm track NEREITE
worn (out) USED, EROSE, JADED, SPENT, EFFETE, MAGGED, SHABBY, ATTRITE
worry RUX, CARE, FRET, STEW, DISTRESS; *see* VEX
worship PUJA, ADORE, DULIA, HOMAGE, LATRIA, REVERE, RITUAL
worst BEAT, BEST, ROUT
worsted cloth SERGE, ETAMINE, GABARDINE
worth MERIT, VALUE, IMPORT

worthless BAFF, RACA, PALTRY, TRASHY, NUGATORY
wound VULN, LESION, TRAUMA
wrangle ROW, SPAR, SPAT, BICKER, HAGGLE, HASSLE
wrap LAP, FURL, SWATHE, SWADDLE; *see* SHAWL, CLOAK
wrapper TILLOT, ENVELOPE
wrasse BOLLAN, CUNNER, TAPIRO, CHOGSET, HOGFISH
wrath *see* ANGER
wreath ORLE, TORSE, INFULA, CIRCLET; *see* GARLAND
wreckage FLOTSAM
wrench TWIST, MONKEY, SPRAIN, SPANNER, STILLSON
wrest JERK, REND, YANK, PLUCK, TWIST, WRING, ELICIT
wrestle TUSSLE, GRAPPLE; *see* FIGHT
wrestling SUMO
wrestling term PIN, CHIP, FALL, HANK, HIPE, HYPE, LOCK, MARE, CLICK, HITCH, NELSON, BACKHEEL, CHANCERY, SCISSORS, GRAPEVINE
wretch KNAVE, ROGUE, CAITIFF
wriggling EELY
wring TWIST, WREST, WRENCH, EXTRACT, SQUEEZE
wrinkle RUCK, RUGA, SEAM, ANGLE, RUGAE, PIMPLE
wrinkled RUGOSE, RUGOUS
wrist CARPUS
wrist guard BRACE
writ CAPE, BREVE, TALES, CAPIAS, ELEGIT, VENIRE, PRECIPE, PROCESS, SUMMONS, MANDAMUS, PRAECIPE, SUBPOENA
write PEN, NOTE, FRAME, INDITE, NOTATE, SCRAWL, SCRIVE
writer CLERK, PENMAN, PROSER, SCRIBE, COPYIST; *see* AUTHOR, POET, NOVELIST, DRAMATIST
writhe TWIST, SQUIRM, CONTORT
writing instrument PEN, BRUSH, CHALK, PLUME, QUILL, STYLE, PENCIL, STYLUS, SNORKEL, BALLPOINT
wrong(s) MALA, TORT, MALUM
wrongdoer FELON, SINNER, CULPRIT, CRIMINAL
wrongful UNFAIR, UNJUST
wryneck WHIPLASH, TORTICOLLIS
Wyoming information *see p. 308*

X

Xanthippe's husband SOCRATES
X ray ROENTGEN, TOMOGRAPH
X-shaped XED, CHIASMAL, CRUCIATE
xylophone GAMELAN, MARIMBA, GAMELANG, GIGELIRA, STICCADO, VIBRAHARP

Y

Y('s) WYE, YOK, WIES, YOGH
yacht *see* VESSEL
yacht basin MARINA
yahoo LOUT, BRUTE, SAVAGE
yak SARLAK, SARLYK
Yale ELI
Yalta conference member STALIN, CHURCHILL, ROOSEVELT
yam HOI, UBE, UBI, UVE, UVI, KAAWI
yammer WAIL, WHIMPER, COMPLAIN
yang, opposite of YIN
yank JERK, TWIST
yap *see* CRY
yard QUAD, SPAR, GARTH, PATIO
yarn ABB, FOX, GARN, KNOP, SLUB, INKLE, THRUM, CREWEL, SPINEL, THREAD; *see* STORY, FIBER
yarn count TYPP
yarn measure COP, LEA, RAP, CLEW, CLUE, HANK, HEER, SKEIN
yaw GAPE, LURCH, STEER, SWERVE
yawn GAPE, OSCITATE
year ANNO, HAAB

year type LEAP, LUNAR, SOLAR, FISCAL, CALENDAR, SIDEREAL, TROPICAL
yearbook ANNUAL, ALMANAC
yearly ANNUAL, ETESIAN, PERANNUM
yearn ACHE, FLAG, PINE, COVET, CRAVE, HANKER
yeast LOB, BARM, BEES, KOJI, LEAVEN, ANAMITE, FERMENT
yell GOWL, HOWL, YOWL; *see* CRY
yellow ocher SIL
yellowish SALLOW, XANTHIC, LUTESCENT; *see p. 251*
yelp YAP, YIP, KIYI, YAUP, YAWP, YOUP
Yemen money RIAL, DINAR, RIYAL
yes AY, OK, AYE, YEA, YEP, YEAH
yet BUT, SOFAR, STILL, THOUGH, HOWEVER
yew genus TAXUS
yield BOW, NET, BEND, CEDE, GIVE, WAIVE, COMPLY, RETURN, FURNISH, PRODUCE
yoga HATHA, JNANA, KARMA, BHAKTI
yoga trance DHYANA, DHARANA, SAMADHI
yogi JNANI, SWAMI; *see* ASCETIC
yoke CANG, JOIN, LINK, TEAM, CANGUE, COUPLE, INSPAN, HARNESS
yoke part BOW, RIEM, SKEY, OXBOW, RIEMPIE
yokel OAF, HICK, RUBE, BUMPKIN
yolk YELLOW, VITELLUS
young RAW, FRESH, GREEN, JUVENILE, YOUTHFUL
young animal(s) (*see also specific animal*) CUB, KID, KIT, PUP, CALF, COLT, FOAL, GILT, JOEY, STOT, BROOD, FILLY, PUPPY, SHOAT, WHELP, LITTER, SUCKLING, YEARLING
young bird (*see also specific bird*) EYAS, CHICK, POULT, EAGLET, CHEEPER, FLAPPER, NESTLING, SQUEAKER, FLEDGLING
young fish (*see also specific fish*) FRY, FINGERLING
youngster TEEN, MINOR, GOSSOON, TEENAGER; *see* BOY, CHILD, GIRL
youth LAD, TEEN, CHIEL, MINOR, SHAVER, TEENAGER
youthful BOYISH, CALLOW, NEANIC, GIRLISH, PUERILE
Yseult *see* ISOLDE
yucca PITA, DATIL
Yugoslav language *see* SLAVIC
Yugoslav measure OKA, RIF, AKOV, RALO, DONUM, KHVAT, LANAZ, PALAZ, STOPA, RALICA, MOTYKA
Yugoslav money PARA, DINAR
Yugoslav premier BROZ, TITO
Yugoslav weight TOVAR, WAGON, DRAMMA, SATLIJK
Yukon Territory information *see p. 306*

Z

Zaire CONGO
Zaire money ZAIRE
Zal relative *see* RUSTAM
Zambia language *see* BANTU
Zambia money KWACHA
Zanzibar weight GISLA
zeal ELAN, ZEST, ARDOR, GUSTO, VERVE, FERVOR, RELISH
zealot *see* FAN, FANATIC
zealous AVID, EAGER, ARDENT, FERVID, EARNEST, FERVENT
zebra DAUW, ZEBRASS, ZEBROID, ZEBRULA
zenith ACME, PEAK, HEYDAY
zenith, opposite of NADIR
Zeno follower STOIC
zeppelin *see* AIRCRAFT
zero *see* CIPHER
zest TANG; *see* ZEAL
Zeus epithet AMMON, SOTER, TELEIOS
Zeus relative *see p. 317, 325*
zigzag TACK, CRANK(LE)
Zilpah relative GAD, ASHER
zinc BLENDE, SPELTER, TUTENAG
zip PEP, TANG, VIGOR, STINGO
zipper TALON
zodiac signs *see* CONSTELLATION
Zola novel NANA, REVE, TERRE, VERITE, DEBACLE, GERMINAL
zone BELT, CLIME, TRACT
zoo MENAGERIE
Zoroastrian PARSI, PARSEE, MASDAIST

SECTION II
Categories

THE BIBLE

BOOKS OF THE OLD TESTAMENT

King James Version	*Abbr.*	*Douay Version*	*Abbr.*
1. GENESIS	GEN	GENESIS	GEN
2. EXODUS	EX(OD)	EXODUS	EX(OD)
3. LEVITICUS	LEV(IT)	LEVITICUS	LEV(IT)
4. NUMBERS	NUM(B)	NUMBERS	NUM(B)
5. DEUTERONOMY	DEUT	DEUTERONOMY	DEUT
6. JOSHUA	JOS(H)	JOSUE	JOS
7. JUDGES	JUD(G)	JUDGES	JUD(G)
8. RUTH		RUTH	
9. SAMUEL I	SAM(L)	KINGS I	KI, KGS
10. SAMUEL II	SAM(L)	KINGS II	KI, KGS
11. KINGS I	KI, KGS	KINGS III	KI, KGS
12. KINGS II	KI, KGS	KINGS IV	KI, KGS
13. CHRONICLES I	CHRON	PARALIPOMENON I	PAR
14. CHRONICLES II	CHRON	PARALIPOMENON II	PAR
15. EZRA	EZ(R)	ESDRAS I	ESD
16. NEHEMIAH	NEH	ESDRAS II	ESD
17. ESTHER	ES(TH)	ESTHER	ES(TH)
18. JOB		JOB	
19. PSALMS	PS(A)	PSALMS	PS(A)
20. PROVERBS	PROV	PROVERBS	PROV
21. ECCLESIASTES	ECCL(ES)	ECCLESIASTES	ECCL(ES)
22. SONG OF SOLOMON	S OF SOL	CANTICLE OF CANTICLES	CANT
23. ISAIAH	IS(A)	ISAIAS	IS(A)
24. JEREMIAH	JER	JEREMIAS	JER
25. LAMENTATIONS	LAM	LAMENTATIONS	LAM
26. EZEKIEL	EZEK	EZECHIEL	EZECH
27. DANIEL	DAN(L)	DANIEL	DAN(L)
28. HOSEA	HOS	OSEE	
29. JOEL	JL, JO	JOEL	JL, JO
30. AMOS		AMOS	
31. OBADIAH	OB(AD)	ABDIAS	
32. JONAH		JONAS	
33. MICAH	MIC	MICHEAS	MICH
34. NAHUM	NAH	NAHUM	NAH
35. HABAKKUK	HAB	HABACUC	HAB
36. ZEPHANIAH	ZEPH	SOPHONIAS	SOPH
37. HAGGAI	HAG	AGGEUS	AGG
38. ZECHARIAH	ZECH	ZACHARIAS	ZACH
39. MALACHI	MAL	MALACHIAS	MAL

THE APOCRYPHA

TOBIT	WISDOM*
BARUCH*	SUSANNA
ESDRAS I, II	MACHABEES I, II*
ESDRAS III, IV*	ECCLESIASTICUS*
ESTHER*	BEL AND THE DRAGON
JUDITH*	PRAYER OF MANASSES
SIRACH	SUSANNA AND THE ELDERS
TOBIAS	SONG OF THE THREE CHILDREN

* Indicates books in Douay Version

BOOKS OF THE NEW TESTAMENT

	Abbr.		*Abbr.*
MATTHEW	MAT(T)	TIMOTHY I	TIM
MARK		TIMOTHY II	TIM
LUKE		TITUS	TIT
JOHN		PHILEMON	PHIL(EM)
THE ACTS	ACTS	HEBREWS	HEB(R)
ROMANS	ROM	JAMES	JA(S)
CORINTHIANS I	COR	PETER I	PET
CORINTHIANS II	COR	PETER II	PET
GALATIANS	GAL	JOHN I	
EPHESIANS	EPH(ES)	JOHN II	
PHILIPPIANS	PHIL	JOHN III	
COLOSSIANS	COL(OSS)	JUDE	
THESSALONIANS I	THESS	REVELATION	REV
THESSALONIANS II	THESS		

Note: All names as given above are also used in the Douay Version with the exception of Revelation, therein named APOCALYPSE (APOC).

FAMILY RELATIONS

Father	*Offspring*	*Father*	*Offspring*
ELI	Hophni, Phinehas	JONA	Peter
HAM	Cush, Phut	KISH	Saul
JOB	Jemima, Kezia	LEVI	Gershon, Jochebed
NER	Abner	NOAH	Ham, Shem, Japheth
NUN	Joshua	OBED	Jesse
ADAM	Abel, Cain, Seth	SAUL	Jonathan, Merab, Michal
AHAB	Athaliah	SEIR	Timna
AHAZ	Helekiah	SETH	Enos
AMON	Josiah	SHEM	Aram, Eber
ARAM	Mash	SODI	Gaddiel
BOAZ	Obed	AARON	Nadab, Adihu, Eleazar, Ithamar
BUZI	Ezekiel		
CAIN	Enoch	ABIEL	Kish, Ner
CUSH	Nimrod	AMRAM	Aaron, Moses, Miriam
EBER	Peleg, Joktan	ASHER	Ara
ELON	Bashemath, Adah	BEERI	Judith
ESAU	Korah, Anah	CALEB	Achsah

Father	*Offspring*
DAVID	Solomon, Tamar, Absalom, Amnon, Adonijah, Ithream, Maacah
ELIAM	Bathsheba
ENOCH	Methuselah, Irad
HARAN	Lot, Milcah, Ischa
HEBER	Shuah
HEROD	Antipas
ISAAC	Jacob, Esau
ITHRA	Amasa
JACOB	Dan, Gad, Levi, Asher, Dinah, Judah, Joseph, Reuben, Simeon, Zebulun, Benjamin, Issachar, Naphtali
JAMES	Jude
JARED	Enoch
JESSE	David, Abigail
JOASH	Gideon
JONAS	Peter
JUDAH	Er
LABAN	Leah, Rachel
MOSES	Gershom, Eliezer
NAHOR	Terah, Maacah, Huz
SERUG	Nahor
SIMON	Judas
TERAH	Haran, Abraham
ADAIAH	Jedidah
GILEAD	Jephthah
JETHRO	Zipporah
JOKTAN	Obal, Ebal
JOSEPH	Manasseh, Ephraim; Jesus, James, Jude
LAMECH	Noah, Naamah, Jabal, Jubal, Tubalcain
MACHIR	Gilead
MANOAH	Samson
PHAREZ	Tamar
SALMON	Boaz
SAMUEL	Abiah
TALMAI	Maacah
ABRAHAM	Isaac, Ishmael
ABSALOM	Maacah
DIBLAIM	Gomer
ELKANAH	Samuel
ETHBAAL	Jezebel
ISHMAEL	Massa
SHAPHAT	Elisha
SOLOMON	Rehoboam
ZEBEDEE	James, John
ALPHAEUS	James
HERODIAS	Salome
JEREMIAH	Hamutal
REHOBOAM	Abija
ZECHARIAH	Abi
METHUSELAH	Lamech

Mother	*Offspring*
ABI	Hezekiah
EVE	Abel, Cain, Seth
ADAH	Jabal, Jubal
ANNA	Mary
JAEL	Shua
LEAH	Levi, Dinah, Judah, Reuben, Simeon, Zebulun, Issachar
LOIS	Eunice
MARY	Jesus; James, Joses
RUTH	Obed
ABIAH	Ashur
EGLAH	Ithream
HAGAR	Ishmael
NAOMI	Mahlon; Chilion
RAHAB	Boaz
SARAH	Isaac
TAMAR	Pharez
TIMNA	Amalek
ABITAL	Shephatiah
BILHAH	Dan, Naphtali
EUNICE	Timothy
HANNAH	Samuel
JUDITH	Korah
MAACAH	Asa; Absalom; Abijah
MILCAH	Haran; Rebekah, Huz
NAAMAH	Rehoboam
RACHEL	Joseph, Benjamin
SALOME	James, John
TALMAI	Maachah, Absalom
ZERUAH	Jeroboam
ZIBIAH	Joash
ZILLAH	Naamah
ZILPAH	Gad, Asher
ABIGAIL	Amasa
AHINOAM	Jonathan, Amnon, Merab, Michal
HAMUTAL	Zedekiah
JEDIDAH	Josiah
JEZEBEL	Athaliah, Jehoram
REBECAH	Esau, Jacob
REBEKAH	Leah, Rachel
ZERUIAH	Joab, Asahel, Abishai
ATHALIAH	Ahaziah
JOCHEBED	Moses, Aaron, Miriam
ZIPPORAH	Gershom, Eliezer
BATHSHEBA	Solomon

Wife	*Husband*
ABI	Ahaz
ADAH	Lamech; Esau
ANAH	Esau
JAEL	Heber
LEAH	Jacob
MARY	Joseph, Cleophas

Wife	*Husband*	*Wife*	*Husband*
RUTH	Mahlon; Boaz	**VASHTI**	Ahasuerus
ABIAH	Hezron	**ZERESH**	Haman
EGLAH	David	**ZIBIAH**	Ahaziah
EPHAH	Caleb	**ZILLAH**	Lemech
GOMER	Hosea	**ZILPAH**	Jacob
HAGAR	Abraham	**ABIGAIL**	Nabal; David; Ithra
HELAH	Ashur	**ABIHAIL**	Rehoboam
MERAB	Adriel	**AHINOAM**	Saul; David
NAOMI	Elimelech	**ASENATH**	Joseph
ORPAH	Chilion	**CLAUDIA**	Pilate
RAHAB	Salmon	**DEBORAH**	Lapidoth
SARAH	Abraham	**HAGGITH**	David
SARAI	Abram	**HAMUTAL**	Josiah
TAMAR	Er, Onan, Judah	**JEDIDAH**	Amon
ABITAL	David	**JEZEBEL**	Ahab
AZUBAH	Asa; Caleb	**KETURAH**	Abraham
BILHAH	Jacob	**REBEKAH**	Isaac
ESTHER	Ahasuerus	**ELISHEBA**	Aaron
HANNAH	Elkanah	**HADASSAH**	= **ESTHER**
JUDITH	Esau	**HERODIAS**	Herod
MAACAH	David; Rehoboam	**JOCHEBED**	Amram
MICHAL	Phalti; David	**SAPPHIRA**	Ananias
MILCAH	Nahor	**ZIPPORAH**	Moses
MIRIAM	Hur	**BASHEMATH**	Esau
RACHEL	Jacob	**BATHSHEBA**	Uriah; David
RIZPAH	Saul	**AHOLIBAMAH**	Esau
SALOME	Zebedee		

CHEMICAL ELEMENTS

Element	*No.*	*Symbol*	*Type*[1]	*Group*	*Source*
TIN	50	Sn	M		cassiterite
GOLD	79	Au	M		sylvanite
IRON	26	Fe	M		hematite
LEAD	82	Pb	M		galena
NEON	10	Ne	G		atmosphere
ZINC	30	Zn	M		sphalerite
ARGON	18	Ar or A	G		atmosphere
BORON	5	B	N		borax
*RADON	86	Rn	G		radium
XENON	54	Xe	G		atmosphere
BARIUM	56	Ba	M	alkaline-earth	barite
CARBON	6	C	N		graphite
CERIUM	58	Ce	M	lanthanide	monazite
CESIUM	55	Cs	M		pollucite
COBALT	27	Co	M		smaltite
COPPER	29	Cu	M		cuprite
*CURIUM	96	Cm	M	actinide	plutonium
ERBIUM	68	Er	M	lanthanide	gadolinite
HELIUM	2	He	G		natural gas

*radioactive element
[1]M = metallic, N = nonmetallic, G = gaseous

Element	*No.*	*Symbol*	*Type*[1]	*Group*	*Source*
INDIUM	49	In	M		sphalerite
IODINE	53	I	N	halogen	Chile saltpeter
NICKEL	28	Ni	M		nickelite
OSMIUM	76	Os	M		iridosmine
OXYGEN	8	O	G		atmosphere
*RADIUM	88	Ra	M	alkaline-earth	pitchblende
SILVER	47	Ag	M		argentite
SODIUM	11	Na	M		Chile saltpeter
SULFUR	16	S	N		limestone
ARSENIC	33	As	M		orpiment
BISMUTH	83	Bi	M		bismite
BROMINE	35	Br	N	halogen	sea water
CADMIUM	48	Cd	M		zinc ores
CALCIUM	20	Ca	M	alkaline-earth	gypsum
*FERMIUM	100	Fm	M	actinide	plutonium
GALLIUM	31	Ga	M		bauxite
HAFNIUM	72	Hf	M		zircon
HOLMIUM	67	Ho	M	lanthanide	gadolinite
IRIDIUM	77	Ir	M		iridosmine
KRYPTON	36	Kr	G		atmosphere
LITHIUM	3	Li	M		spodumene
MERCURY	80	Hg	M		cinnabar
NIOBIUM	41	Nb	M		columbite
RHENIUM	75	Re	M		molybdenite
RHODIUM	45	Rh	M		platinum ores
SILICON	14	Si	N		silica
SULPHUR					= SULFUR
TERBIUM	65	Tb	M	lanthanide	monazite
*THORIUM	90	Th	M	actinide	thorite
THULIUM	69	Tm	M	lanthanide	rare earth
*URANIUM	92	U	M	actinide	pitchblende
WOLFRAM		W			= TUNGSTEN
YTTRIUM	39	Y	M		rare earth
*ACTINIUM	89	Ac	M	actinide	pitchblende
ALUMINUM	13	Al	M		bauxite
ANTIMONY	51	Sb	M		stibnite
*ASTATINE	85	At	N	halogen	bismuth
CHLORINE	17	Cl	N	halogen	salt
CHROMIUM	24	Cr	M		chromite
EUROPIUM	63	Eu	M	lanthanide	monazite
FLUORINE	9	F	N	halogen	fluorite
*FRANCIUM	87	Fr	M		actinium
HYDROGEN	1	H	G		atmosphere
LUTETIUM	71	Lu	M	lanthanide	rare earth
NITROGEN	7	N	N		sodium nitrate
*NOBELIUM	102	No	M	actinide	curium
PLATINUM	78	Pt	M		alluvial
*POLONIUM	84	Po	M		pitchblende
RUBIDIUM	37	Rb	M		pollucite
SAMARIUM	62	Sm	M	lanthanide	monazite
SCANDIUM	21	Sc	M		monazite
SELENIUM	34	Se	N		clausthalite
TANTALUM	73	Ta	M		tantalite
THALLIUM	81	Tl	M		crookesite
TITANIUM	22	Ti	M		rutile
TUNGSTEN	74	W	M		scheelite

Element	*No.*	*Symbol*	*Type*[1]	*Group*	*Source*
VANADIUM	23	V	M		vanadinite
*AMERICIUM	95	Am	M	actinide	uranium
*BERKELIUM	97	Bk	M	actinide	americium
BERYLLIUM	4	Be	M	alkaline-earth	beryl
COLUMBIUM		Cb			= NIOBIUM
GERMANIUM	32	Ge	M		germanite
LANTHANUM	57	La	M		rare earth
MAGNESIUM	12	Mg	M	alkaline-earth	magnesite
MANGANESE	25	Mn	M		pyrolusite
NEODYMIUM	60	Nd	M	lanthanide	monazite
*NEPTUNIUM	93	Np	M	actinide	uranium
PALLADIUM	46	Pd	M		gold ores
*PLUTONIUM	94	Pu	M	actinide	pitchblende
POTASSIUM	19	K	M		potassium chloride
RUTHENIUM	44	Ru	M		iridosmine
STRONTIUM	38	Sr	M	alkaline-earth	celestite
TELLURIUM	52	Te	M		sylvanite
YTTERBIUM	70	Yb	M	lanthanide	rare earth
ZIRCONIUM	40	Zr	M		zircon
DYSPROSIUM	66	Dy	M	lanthanide	rare earth
GADOLINIUM	64	Gd	M	lanthanide	gadolinite
*LAWRENCIUM	103	Lw	M	actinide	artificial
MOLYBDENUM	42	Mo	M		molybdenite
PHOSPHORUS	15	P	N		apatite
*PROMETHIUM	61	Pm	M	lanthanide	rare earth
*TECHNETIUM	43	Tc	M		uranium
*CALIFORNIUM	98	Cf	M	actinide	curium
*EINSTEINIUM	99	Es or E	M	actinide	plutonium
*MENDELEVIUM	101	Md or Mv	M	actinide	einsteinium
PRASEODYMIUM	59	Pr	M	lanthanide	rare earth
*PROTACTINIUM	91	Pa	M	actinide	uranium

COLORS

ASH	gray	**SKY**	blue
BAT	gray	**TAN**	red/yellow
BAY	brown	**TEA**	yellow/green
DOE	red/yellow		
DUN	red/yellow	**BARK**	red/yellow
FOX	brown	**BICE**	blue/green
IVY	green	**BLUE**	
JET	black	**BOLE**	red/yellow
OAK	brown	**BRAN**	red/yellow
RAT	yellow	**BUFF**	yellow/red
RED		**CLAY**	yellow/red

CORK	brown
CORN	red/yellow
CUBA	brown
CYAN	blue
DEER	brown
DORE	yellow
DOVE	blue/gray
DRAB	brown
DUNE	red/yellow
DUSK	blue/red
DUST	red/yellow
EBON	black
ECRU	red/yellow
FAON	brown
FAWN	brown
FLAX	red/yellow
FLEA	red
GOLD	
GOYA	red
GRAY	
GULL	gray
HEBE	red
HOAR	gray
HOPI	brown
IRON	gray
JADE	green
LAKE	red
LAMA	brown
LAVA	yellow/red
LEAD	gray
LIME	yellow/red
MESA	brown
MILK	white
MOSS	green
MUSK	yellow/red
NAVY	blue
NILE	blue/green
NUDE	red/yellow
OPAL	(varies)
PINK	
PLUM	blue/red
PUCE	red
PURI	yellow
ROAN	yellow/red
ROSE	red
RUBY	red
RUST	red/yellow
SAGE	green
SAND	red/yellow
SAXE	blue
SEAL	brown
SIAM	brown
TEAK	brown
WINE	red
ZINC	blue/red
ACIER	gray
ACORN	red/yellow
AGATE	red/yellow

ALOMA	yellow/red
AMBER	yellow/red
ASHEN	gray
AZTEC	yellow/red
AZURE	blue
BAPHE	red
BEIGE	red/yellow
BERYL	blue[green
BLOND	yellow/red
BLUET	blue
BRICK	red/yellow
BROWN	
CACAO	red/yellow
CADET	blue
CAMEL	brown
CAMEO	(varies)
CEDAR	yellow/red
CEDRE	green
CHING	blue
COCOA	brown
CONGO	brown
CORAL	red
CREAM	red/yellow
DELFT	blue
DURRY	yellow
EMAIL	green/blue
EMBER	yellow/red
FAIRY	green
FLAME	red
FLESH	red/yellow
GREEN	
GYPSY	brown
HAZEL	brown
HENNA	brown
HOARY	gray
IVORY	white/yellow
KHAKI	brown
LEMON	yellow
LILAC	blue/red
LIVER	brown
MAIZE	yellow/red
MAPLE	red/yellow
MAUVE	blue/red
MELON	red/yellow
METAL	gray/blue
MOCHA	brown
MOUSE	gray
MUMMY	brown
NEGRO	brown
NIKKO	blue
OCHER	yellow
OLIVE	gray
PABLO	brown
PANSY	blue/red
PEACH	red/yellow
PEARL	gray/blue
PERSE	blue
PLOMB	gray
POPPY	red

PRUNE	blue/red
PUTTY	yellow/red
RAVEN	black
ROUGE	red
SABLE	black
SEDGE	brown
SEPIA	brown
SIENA	red
SIRUP	red/yellow
SLATE	blue/red
SMALT	blue
SNUFF	brown
SPRAY	blue/green
STEEL	gray
STRAW	red/yellow
SUDAN	red/yellow
SUEDE	brown
TAUPE	yellow
TAWNY	brown
TENNE	brown
TIVER	red
TOTEM	red/yellow
TWINE	red/yellow
UMBER	brown
VENUS	green

ACACIA	yellow
ACAJOU	brown
AFGHAN	yellow/red
ALESAN	red/yellow
ARGENT	white
AUBURN	red
AUTUMN	red/yellow
BEAVER	brown
BISTER	brown
BISTRE	brown
BRONZE	brown
CANARY	yellow
CANDID	white
CANNON	yellow/gray
CARROT	red/yellow
CASTOR	red/yellow
CERISE	red
CHERRY	red
CITRON	yellow
CLARET	red
COBALT	green/blue
COCHIN	brown
COFFEE	brown
CONDOR	brown
COPPER	brown
CYANIC	blue
DAHLIA	blue/red
DAMASK	red
DAMSON	blue/red
ERMINE	white
ESKIMO	brown
EVEQUE	blue/red
FALLOW	yellow
FUSTIC	yellow/red
GARNET	red
HATHOR	blue
HAVANA	brown
HUNTER	green
INDIGO	red/blue
JASPER	yellow/green
LIERRE	green
MADDER	blue/red
MALLOW	blue/red
MANILA	yellow/red
MARINE	blue
MAROON	brown
MASCOT	blue/red
MASTIC	yellow/red
MIKADO	red/yellow
MIMOSA	yellow
MINIUM	red
MODENA	blue/red
MOUSSE	green
MURREY	red
MYRTLE	green
NUTRIA	red/yellow
ONDINE	yellow/green
ORANGE	
ORCHID	blue/red
ORIENT	blue
ORIOLE	red/yellow
PAWNEE	red/yellow
PENSEE	blue/red
PONGEE	yellow/red
PURPLE	
PURREE	yellow
QUAKER	gray
RADDLE	red
RAISIN	blue/red
RESEDA	green
RUBRIC	red
RUDDLE	red/yellow
RUSSET	brown
SALMON	red/yellow
SEASAN	red/yellow
SEVRES	blue
SHRIMP	red
SIENNA	brown
SIERRA	red
SILVER	gray
SORREL	brown
STUCCO	red/yellow
SULFUR	yellow
SULTAN	red
TIFFIN	brown
TITIAN	red
TOMATO	red
TUSCAN	red
TYRIAN	blue/red
VESTAL	red/blue
VIOLET	
WALNUT	brown

YELLOW	
ZENITH	blue
ADMIRAL	blue
ANEMONE	red/blue
ANNATTO	red/yellow
ANTIQUE	red/yellow
APRICOT	red/yellow
ARDOISE	red/blue
BEGONIA	red
BISCUIT	red/yellow
BITUMEN	brown
CALDRON	red
CARAIBE	brown
CARMINE	red
CELADON	green
CELESTE	blue
CHAMOIS	red/yellow
CITRINE	yellow
CORBEAU	green
CRIMSON	red
EMERALD	yellow/green
FEUILLE	brown
FILBERT	brown
FIREFLY	yellow/red
FUCHSIA	red
GAMBOGE	red/yellow
GLAIEUL	red
GOBELIN	blue
GRANITE	red
GRIZZLE	gray
HEATHER	blue/red
JONQUIL	yellow
LEATHER	red/yellow
LOBSTER	red/yellow
LOGWOOD	blue
MAGENTA	red/blue
MALABAR	brown
MASCARA	red
MATELOT	blue
MERMAID	yellow/green
MESANGE	green/blue
MUSTARD	red/yellow
NACARAT	red
OAKWOOD	brown
OLDWOOD	red
OPHELIA	red/blue
OXBLOOD	yellow/red
PEACOCK	blue
PERIDOT	green
PIMENTO	red
PONCEAU	red
PRAIRIE	yellow/red
PRALINE	brown
PRASINE	green
ROSEATE	red
SAFFRON	yellow
SCARLET	red
SERPENT	green/yellow
TANBARK	brown
TEAROSE	yellow/red
THISTLE	blue/red
TILLEUL	green
TOBACCO	brown
TUSSORE	red
ABSINTHE	green
ALDERNEY	red/yellow
ALGERIAN	brown
BISMARCK	red/yellow
BORDEAUX	red
BRUNDORE	black/green
CAFENOIR	brown
CAPUCINE	yellow
CARDINAL	red
CERULEAN	blue
CHASSEUR	green
CHAUDRON	brown
CHESTNUT	brown
CINNABAR	red
CREVETTE	red
EMINENCE	blue/red
FUCHSINE	red
GENDARME	blue
GERANIUM	yellow/red
GLOWWORM	green/yellow
GUNMETAL	gray
HYACINTH	blue/red
LAVENDER	blue/red
MAHOGANY	brown
MANDARIN	red/orange
MARIGOLD	orange
MAUVETTE	blue/red
MAZARINE	blue
MOSSROSE	red
MULBERRY	red
MUSHROOM	brown
NOISETTE	brown
PALMETTO	yellow/green
PARAKEET	green
PERROCHE	green
PRIMROSE	red/yellow
RAWUMBER	brown
ROSEWOOD	red/yellow
SAPPHIRE	blue
SAUTERNE	red/yellow
SHAMROCK	green
TERRAPIN	brown
VIRIDIAN	yellow/green
WEDGWOOD	blue
WISTERIA	blue/red

FAMOUS NAMES

FIRST AND LAST NAMES

Abbott	BUD
Abner	LIL
Aldo	RAY
Allen	MEL
Alfonso	DON
Annabel	LEE
Arden	EVE
Ayres	LEW
Baba	ALI
Beerbohm	MAX
Ben	HUR
Blas	GIL
Bloch	RAY
Bolger	RAY
Brynner	YUL
Calloway	CAB
Carney	ART
Carson	KIT
Chaney	LON
Charisse	CYD
Cliburn	VAN
Doris	DAY
Dorothy	DIX
Durocher	LEO, LIP
Eddie	FOY
Gehrig	LOU
Gershwin	IRA
Gould	JAY
Gray	ASA
Hammarskjold	DAG
Hogan	BEN
Houston	SAM
Hur	BEN
Hus	JAN
Jan	HUS
Jonson	BEN
Khan	AGA, ALI
Linkletter	ART
Louis	JOE
Lowell	AMY
Lupino	IDA
Masaryk	JAN
Mel	OTT
Myrna	LOY
Neal	DOW
Novak	KIM
Ott	MEL
Paine	TOM
Peerce	JAN
Rayburn	SAM
Rogers	ROY
Rohmer	SAX
Rutledge	ANN
Saud	IBN
Sawyer	TOM
Schmeling	MAX
Silvers	SID
Snead	SAM
Stout	REX
Sumac	YMA
Tolstoy	LEO
Torme	MEL
Trygve	LIE
Turpin	BEN
Uncle	SAM
Vermeer	JAN
Wallach	ELI
Whitney	ELI
Wray	FAY
Yutang	LIN
Aaron	BURR, HANK
Acheson	DEAN
Adam	BEDE
Adams	JOHN
Addams	JANE
Alan	ALDA
Alden	JOHN
Alexander	HAIG, POPE
Alfred	LUNT
Ali	KHAN
Allen	FRED
Allyson	JUNE
Aly	KHAN
André	GIDE
Anita	LOOS
Anna	HELD
Anthony	EDEN
Antony	MARK
Arnaz	DESI
Artemus	WARD
Asa	GRAY
Austen	JANE
Autry	GENE
Babe	RUTH
Baez	JOAN
Bagnold	ENID
Bartok	BELA
Bede	ADAM
Bennett	CERF
Bernard	SHAW
Berra	YOGI
Bert	LAHR
Billy	ROSE
Blum	LEON
Bogarde	DIRK
Boleyn	ANNE
Bonheur	ROSA
Bradley	OMAR
Broz	TITO
Buffalo Bill	CODY
Burl	IVES
Captain	AHAB, NEMO
Carnegie	DALE
Cassius	CLAY
Catherine	PARR
Chagall	MARC
Chaplin	OONA
Chase	ILKA
Chico	MARX
Christian	DIOR
Christie	ANNA
Conde	NAST
Connie	MACK
Cooper	GARY
Crockett	DAVY
Coward	NOEL
Craig	RICE
Dean	RUSK
De La Roche	MAZO
Descartes	RENE
Dewey	JOHN
Disney	WALT
Dizzy	DEAN
Dorian	GRAY
Dow	NEAL
Drury	LANE
Dudevant	SAND
Eartha	KITT
Edouard	LALO
Eleanora	DUSE
Elia	LAMB
Elias	HOWE
Elihu	ROOT, YALE
Ellington	DUKE
Elmer	RICE
Elton	JOHN
Emile	ZOLA
Emily	POST
En-Lai	CHOU
Ericson	LEIF
Ernie	PYLE
Eugene	DEBS
Eyre	JANE
Evans	DALE
Fay	WRAY
Ferber	EDNA
Flanders	MOLL
Frances	ALDA

Frans	**HALS**
Fritz	**LANG**
Gagarin	**YURI**
George	**SAND**
Geste	**BEAU**
Gil	**BLAS**
Goldberg	**RUBE**
Goldie	**HAWN**
Goriot	**PERE**
Gray	**ZANE**
Grey	**JANE**
Guido	**RENI**
Guthrie	**ARLO**
Hamsun	**KNUT**
Harlow	**JEAN**
Harold	**UREY**
Harpo	**MARX**
Hart	**MOSS**
Harte	**BRET**
Hayworth	**RITA**
Held	**ANNA**
Helmer	**NORA**
Hendrix	**JIMI**
Henry	**CLAY, FORD**
Heyerdahl	**THOR**
Hopkins	**MARK**
Horace	**MANN**
Horne	**LENA**
Huey	**LONG**
Hugo	**WOLF**
Ibn	**SAUD**
Immanuel	**KANT**
Italo	**TAJO**
Iturbi	**JOSE**
Jacob	**RIIS**
Jane	**EYRE, GREY**
Jenny	**LIND**
Jerome	**KERN**
Joan	**BAEZ**
Johnny	**CASH**
Jonas	**SALK**
Karl	**MARX**
Kalman	**IMRE**
Karenina	**ANNA**
Klee	**PAUL**
Khachaturian	**ARAM**
Khayyam	**OMAR**
Kreuger	**IVAR**
Lahr	**BERT**
Lardner	**RING**
Laurel	**STAN**
Lawrence	**WELK**
Lazarus	**EMMA**
Leon	**BLUM**
Lillian	**GISH**
Lily	**PONS**
Long	**HUEY**
Louis	**RIEL**
Lugosi	**BELA**

Mamie	**DOUD**
Marco	**POLO**
Margaret	**ROSE**
Marquette	**PERE**
Marx	**KARL**
Mary	**TODD**
Mata	**HARI**
Maxwell	**ELSA**
Meitner	**LISE**
Mondrian	**PIET**
Montez	**LOLA**
Moss	**HART**
Mostel	**ZERO**
Muni	**PAUL**
Musial	**STAN**
Nathan	**HALE**
Niels	**BOHR**
O'Casey	**SEAN**
Ogden	**NASH**
Pacelli	**PIUS**
Paul	**ANKA, KLEE, MUNI**
Pavlova	**ANNA**
Perry	**COMO**
Peter	**ARNO**
Phileas	**FOGG**
Pinza	**EZIO**
Pons	**LILY**
Porter	**COLE**
Pound	**EZRA**
Rockwell	**KENT**
Roger	**MUDD**
Rogers	**WILL**
Rusk	**DEAN**
Ruth	**BABE**
Saarinen	**EERO**
Sally	**LUNN**
Salvador	**DALI**
Schipa	**TITO**
Schulberg	**BUDD**
Shalom	**ASCH**
Sibelius	**JEAN**
Squire	**CASS**
Stern	**ISAAC**
Steven	**RISE**
Stravinsky	**IGOR**
Syngman	**RHEE**
The Red	**ERIC**
Thomas	**MANN**
Tilden	**BILL**
Tito	**BROZ**
Tunney	**GENE**
Tweed	**BOSS**
Ty	**COBB**
Tyler	**JOHN**
Uriah	**HEEP**
Vannevar	**BUSH**
Vincent van	**GOGH**
Walter	**REED**

Warburg	**OTTO**
Warren	**EARL**
Waugh	**ALEC**
Webster	**NOAH**
Weill	**KURT**
Whiteman	**PAUL**
Wiley	**POST**
Willard	**EMMA**
Zane	**GRAY**
Zebulon	**PIKE**
Zeppo	**MARX**

Abigail	**SMITH**
Adams	**MAUDE**
Adelina	**PATTI**
Al(fred)	**SMITH**
Albert	**CAMUS**
Alec	**WAUGH**
Alessandro	**VOLTA**
Alexandre	**DUMAS**
Alighieri	**DANTE**
Allen	**ETHAN, STEVE, WOODY**
Alma	**GLUCK**
Al Rashin	**HARUN**
Amundsen	**ROALD**
Anthony	**QUINN, SUSAN**
Arden	**ENOCH**
Arsene	**LUPIN**
Arthur	**BOYLE**
Ataturk	**KEMAL**
Auguste	**RODIN**
Bailey	**PEARL**
Barkley	**ALBEN**
Barrymore	**ETHEL**
Barton	**CLARK**
Basie	**COUNT**
Beau	**GESTE**
Becky	**SHARP**
Ben	**HOGAN**
Benedetto	**CROCE**
Beniamino	**GIGLI**
Benjamin	**SPOCK**
Bergson	**HENRI**
Berling	**GOSTA**
Bernhardt	**SARAH**
Berry	**CHUCK**
Bette	**DAVIS**
Bolivar	**SIMON**
Booth	**EDWIN**
Boss	**TWEED**
Boswell	**JAMES**
Brahe	**TYCHO**
Brendan	**BEHAN**
Bret	**HARTE**
Brigham	**YOUNG**
Bruce	**CABOT**
Buchanan	**JAMES**

Buck PEARL
Bunche RALPH
Capek KAREL
Carnera PRIMO
Carpenter SCOTT
Carroll LEWIS
Casals PABLO
Castle IRENE
Cather WILLA
Channing CAROL
Chase CHEVY
Chauncey DEPEW
Chekhov ANTON
Chou ENLAI
Chuck BERRY
Clark GABLE
Claude MONET
Clay HENRY
Como PERRY
Cooper ALICE
Copland AARON
Count BASIE
Cox WALLY
Daniel BOONE, DEFOE
Davis BETTE
Dean DIZZY
De l'Enclos NINON
De Leon PONCE
Desi ARNAZ
De Valera EAMON
Dickinson EMILY
Dionne MARIE, OLIVA
Dodsworth BRENT
Doone LORNA
Doud MAMIE
Dvorak ANTON
Edouard MANET
Edvard GREIG
Edward ELGAR
Edwin BOOTH
Edyie GORME
Elbridge GERRY
Ellery QUEEN
Emmet KELLY
Enoch ARDEN
Enrico FERMI
Ethan ALLEN, FROME
Eve CURIE
Evita PERON
Ezra POUND
Farlay MOWAT
Ferde GROFE
Fibber MCGEE
Field CYRUS
Ford EDSEL, HENRY
Francis BACON, DRAKE
Franck CESAR
Franz LEHAR, LISZT

Franz KAFKA
Frome ETHAN
Fulton SHEEN
Gabler HEDDA
Gantry ELMER
Garbo GRETA
Gene AUTRY
George LLOYD
Georges BIZET
Gertrude STEIN
Gherman TITOV
Gide ANDRE
Giordano BRUNO
Goldoni CARLO
Goodman BENNY
Gorky MAXIM
Gorme EDYIE
Graham BILLY
Green HETTY
Greta GARBO
Grofe FERDE
Giuseppe VERDI
Guitry SACHA
Hals FRANS
Hank AARON
Hanks NANCY
Harold ICKES
Hayes HELEN
Heep URIAH
Heinrich HEINE
Helen HAYES
Henrik IBSEN
Hetty GREEN
Hitler ADOLF
Horatio ALGER
Houdini HARRY
Howe ELIAS
Ichabod CRANE
Ilka CHASE
Janos KADAR
James JESSE, JOYCE
Jawaharial NEHRU
Jay GOULD
Jean P. MARAT
Jefferson DAVIS
Jesse JAMES
John ADAMS, ALDEN, BROWN, DEWEY, ELTON, SMITH, TYLER
John Philip SOUSA
Jonathan SWIFT
Joplin JANIS
Jose GRECO
Joyce JAMES
Juan PERON
Jules VERNE
June HAVOC
Kadar JANOS

Kafka FRANZ
Karel CAPEK
Kazantzakis NIKOS
Keller HELEN
Kim NOVAK
Kreisler FRITZ
Koussevitzky SERGE
Kurt WEILL
Lagerlof SELMA
Lane DRURY
Lanza MARIO
Lawes LEWIS
Legree SIMON
Lehar FRANZ
Lehmann LOTTE
Lena HORNE
Lescaut MANON
Levant OSCAR
Lewis LAWES
Lil ABNER
Liszt FRANZ
Loos ANITA
Lonigan STUDS
Lorna DOONE
Loy MYRNA
Lunn SALLY
Maksim GORKI
Manuel de FALLA
Marie CURIE
Marner SILAS
Mario LANZA
Marx CHICO, HARPO, ZEPPO
Maude ADAMS
Maurice RAVEL
Maurois ANDRE
Maxim GORKI
Mel ALLEN, TORME
Meriwether LEWIS
Merman ETHEL
Miller GLENN
Milton BERLE
Minuit PETER
Mitchell MARIA
Monroe JAMES
Morini ERICA
Nancy HANKS
Nash OGDEN
Nation CARRY
Nero WOLFE
Newton ISAAC
Nikola TESLA
Nikolai LENIN
Onegin EUGEN
Orlando LASSO
Oscar WILDE
Pancho VILLA
Pasternak BORIS
Pasteur LOUIS

Patrick	**HENRY**
Pauling	**LINUS**
Perry	**MASON**
Philo	**VANCE**
Picasso	**PABLO**
Pierre	**CURIE**
Pirandello	**LUIGI**
Polo	**MARCO**
Post	**EMILY**
Priscilla	**ALDEN**
Pyle	**ERNIE**
Rainer	**RILKE**
Ralph	**NADER**
Reni	**GUIDO**
Rex	**STOUT**
Rhodes	**CECIL**
Rice	**CRAIG, ELMER**
Rickenbacker	**EDDIE**
Rivera	**DIEGO**
Rockne	**KNUTE**
Root	**ELIHU**
Rose	**BILLY**
Rosenblum	**MAXIE**
Rubinstein	**ANTON, ARTUR**
Runyon	**DAMON**
Salk	**JONAS**
Salmon	**CHASE**
Sam	**UNCLE**
Samuel	**MORSE, PEPYS**
Sancho	**PANZA**
Sharp	**BECKY**
Shaw	**ARTIE**
Sigmund	**FREUD**
Sinclair	**LEWIS, UPTON**
Sklodowska	**CURIE**
Sonja	**HENIE**
Standish	**MILES**
Stengel	**CASEY**
Stephen	**CRANE**
Stevenson	**ADLAI**
Sunday	**BILLY**
Tajo	**ITALO**
Tamburlaine	**TIMUR**
Tarkington	**BOOTH**
Templar	**SIMON**
Thatcher	**BECKY**
Thomas	**WOLFE, MOORE**
Thomas	**HARDY, DYLAN**
Tom	**PAINE**
Torquato	**TASSO**
Truman	**HARRY**
Tycho	**BRAHE**
Varden	**DOLLY**
Victor	**BORGE**
Virginia	**WOOLF**
Vladimir	**LENIN**
Walter	**BRUNO**
Walton	**IZAAK**
Welles	**ORSON**
Werner von	**BRAUN**
Wharton	**EDITH**
Wilde	**OSCAR**
William Butler	**YEATS**
Winslow	**HOMER**
Xavier	**CUGAT**
Yale	**ELIHU**
Yogi	**BERRA**
Zola	**EMILE**

Albertus	**MAGNUS**
Aldous	**HUXLEY**
Alexis	**CARREL**
Ambrose	**BIERCE**
Anatole	**FRANCE**
Angelo	**GIOTTO**
Anne	**BOLEYN**
Anton	**DVORAK**
Arrhenius	**SVANTE**
Bacall	**LAUREN**
Balzac	**HONORE**
Barrymore	**LIONEL**
Beatrice	**LILLIE**
Bela	**BARTOK**
Bell	**CURRER**
Ben	**JONSON, TURPIN**
Benedict	**ARNOLD**
Berlin	**IRVING**
Berlioz	**HECTOR**
Bernard	**BARUCH**
Bess	**TRUMAN**
Bill	**TILDEN**
Billy	**SUNDAY, GRAHAM**
Blaise	**PASCAL**
Boone	**DANIEL**
Breughel	**PIETER**
Bruno	**WALTER**
Burbank	**LUTHER**
Carnegie	**ANDREW**
Carrel	**ALEXIS**
Carry	**NATION**
Caruso	**ENRICO**
Castle	**VERNON**
Cecil	**RHODES**
Cesar	**FRANCK**
Cesare	**BORGIA**
Charlotte	**BRONTE, CORDAY**
Christie	**AGATHA**
Clara	**BARTON**
Clarence	**DARROW**
Cleveland	**GROVER**
Clement	**ATTLEE**
Cole	**PORTER**
Collins	**WILKIE**
Conrad	**JOSEPH**
Coolidge	**CALVIN**
Custis	**MARTHA**
Damon	**RUNYON**
Dantes	**EDMOND**
Debs	**EUGENE**
Defoe	**DANIEL**
Diego	**RIVERA**
Dionne	**CECILE, EMILIE**
Dodger	**ARTFUL**
Dolly	**VARDEN**
Donatello	**DONATO**
Dostoevsky	**FEODOR**
Dreyfus	**ALFRED**
Dylan	**THOMAS**
Eamon de	**VALERA**
Earhart	**AMELIA**
Edgar	**HOOVER**
Edmond	**DANTES**
Edna	**FERBER**
Einstein	**ALBERT**
Eleanor	**STEBER**
Elgar	**EDWARD**
Elmer	**GANTRY**
Emily	**BRONTE**
Enrico	**CARUSO**
Erhard	**LUDWIG**
Eric	**AMBLER, THERED**
Erica	**MORINI**
Eugen	**ONEGIN**
Eugene	**ONEILL**
Ferenc	**MOLNAR**
Fermi	**ENRICO**
Franklin	**PIERCE**
Frederic	**CHOPIN**
Gary	**COOPER**
Gene	**TUNNEY**
Glenn	**JOHN**
Giotto	**ANGELO**
Graham	**GREENE, MARTHA**
Gray	**DORIAN**
Greeley	**HORACE**
Gregor	**MENDEL**
Grissom	**VIRGIL**
Hale	**NATHAN**
Harding	**WARREN**
Harry S.	**TRUMAN**
Hedda	**GABLER**
Helen	**KELLER**
Henry	**HUDSON**
Hemingway	**ERNEST**
Hercule	**POIROT**
Herbert	**HOOVER, VICTOR**
Hernando	**CORTES, DESOTO**
Honoré	**BALZAC**

Horatio	**NELSON**
Hugo	**VICTOR**
Humphrey	**HUBERT,**
	BOGART
Huxley	**ALDOUS**
Ignazio	**SILONE**
Imre	**KALMAN**
Irene	**CASTLE**
Irving	**BERLIN**
Isadora	**DUNCAN**
Isaac	**NEWTON**
Izaak	**WALTON**
Jack	**LONDON**
Jackson	**ANDREW**
Jane	**ADDAMS,**
	AUSTEN
Janis	**JOPLIN**
Jean	**HARLOW**
Jim	**NABORS**
Johannes	**BRAHMS,**
	KEPLER
Johnson	**ANDREW,**
	LYNDON
Jose	**ITURBI**
Josef	**STALIN**
Kern	**JEROME**
Knut	**HAMSUN**
Knute	**ROCKNE**
Kodaly	**ZOLTAN**
Lauren	**BACALL**
Lloyd	**GEORGE**
Lombroso	**CESARE**
Lorenzo de	**MEDICI**
Lucrezia	**BORGIA**
Ludwig	**ERHARD**
Lupin	**ARSENE**
Mack	**CONNIE**
Mahler	**GUSTAV**
Mailer	**NORMAN**
Mann	**HORACE,**
	THOMAS
Mantle	**MICKEY**
Marcel	**PROUST**
Marilyn	**MONROE**
Martha	**CUSTIS,**
	GRAHAM
Martin	**LUTHER**
Mascagni	**PIETRO**
Melville	**HERMAN**
Mendel	**GREGOR**
Menuhin	**YEHUDI**
Mickey	**MANTLE**
Mohandas	**GANDHI**
Mowat	**FARLAY**
Mussolini	**BENITO**
Nielsson	**BIRGIT**
Noel	**COWARD**
Nora	**HELMER**
Norman	**MAILER**
O Henry	**PORTER**
Orson	**WELLES**
Orville	**WRIGHT**
Pablo	**CASALS**
Paganini	**NICOLO**
Panza	**SANCHO**
Pascal	**BLAISE**
Père	**GORIOT**
Ponce	**DELEON**
Priscilla	**MULLEN**
Proust	**MARCEL**
Pulitzer	**JOSEPH**
Ralph	**BUNCHE**
Richard	**WAGNER**
Robinson	**CRUSOE**
Rolland	**ROMAIN**
Rudy	**VALLEE**
Sax	**ROHMER**
Schweitzer	**ALBERT**
Silas	**MARNER**
Sigrid	**UNDSET**
Simon	**LEGREE**
Skelton	**MARTHA**
Spengler	**OSWALD**
Spinoza	**BARUCH**
Stalin	**JOSEPH**
Strachey	**LYTTON**
Streisand	**BARBRA**
Sumner	**WELLES**
Tebaldi	**RENATA**
Thomas	**HOBBES**
Thornton	**WILDER**
Todd	**DOLLEY**
Toqueville	**ALEXIS**
Toscanini	**ARTURO**
Ulanova	**GALINA**
Undset	**SIGRID**
Urey	**HAROLD**
Van Buren	**MARTIN**
Vecelli	**TITIAN**
Vernon	**CASTLE**
Villa	**PANCHO**
Waksman	**SELMAN**
Walt	**DISNEY**
Webster	**DANIEL**
Will	**ROGERS**
Wolfe	**THOMAS**
Wright	**WILBUR**
Zanuck	**DARRYL**
Zoltan	**KODALY**
Aleksei	**KOSYGIN**
Amelia	**EARHART**
Andrew	**JACKSON,**
	JOHNSON
Anna	**PAVLOVA**
Arthur	**CHESTER**
Baldwin	**STANLEY**
Benvenuto	**CELLINI**
Bierce	**AMBROSE**
Caldwell	**ERSKINE**
Carlo	**GOLDONI**
Carroll	**DODGSON**
Casey	**STENGEL**
Chamberlain	**NEVILLE**
Dionne	**ANNETTE**
Dodgson	**CARROLL**
Dolly	**MADISON**
Eden	**ANTHONY**
Fillmore	**MILLARD**
Flagstad	**KIRSTEN**
France	**ANATOLE**
Galina	**ULANOVA**
Gian-Carlo	**MENOTTI**
Giacomo	**PUCCINI**
Guglielmo	**MARCONI**
Henri	**BERGSON**
Hoover	**HERBERT**
Horace	**GREELEY**
Hull	**CORDELL**
Kemal	**ATATURK**
Laurence	**OLIVIER**
Leif	**ERICSON**
Leonardo	**DAVINCI**
Lillian	**RUSSELL**
Louis	**PASTEUR**
Luther	**BURBANK**
Macchiavelli	**NICCOLO**
Marc	**CHAGALL**
Mark	**ANTHONY**
Mark Twain	**CLEMENS**
Omar	**BRADLEY**
Pablo	**PICASSO**
Pike	**ZEBULON**
Pius	**PACELLI**
Primo	**CARNERA**
Priscilla	**MULLINS**
Prosper	**MERIMEE**
Rembrandt	**VANRIJN**
Ring	**LARDNER**
Rosa	**BONHEUR**
Russell	**LILLIAN**
Simon	**BOLIVAR**
	TEMPLAR
Smith	**ABIGAIL**
Susan	**ANTHONY**
Taylor	**ZACHARY**
Titov	**GHERMAN**
Van Gogh	**VINCENT**
Victor	**HERBERT**
Von Braun	**WERNHER**
Walter	**RALEIGH**
Ward	**ARTEMUS**
Warren	**HARDING**
Wendell	**WILLKIE**
Willkie	**WENDELL**
Yuri	**GAGARIN**
Young	**BRIGHAM**

MIDDLE NAMES

Nasr—Din	**ED**
Abd—Krim	**EL**
John—Passos	**DOS**
Katherine—Porter	**ANN**
Louisa—Alcott	**MAY**
Mao—Tung	**TSE**
Mary—Evans	**ANN**
Sun—Sen	**YAT**
Chester—Arthur	**ALAN**
Claudia—Taylor	**ALTA**
Ermanno—Ferrari	**WOLF**
Francis—Coppola	**FORD**
Henry—Beecher	**WARD**
James—Polk	**KNOX**
Jean—Sartre	**PAUL**
John—Jones	**PAUL**
Julia—Howe	**WARD**
Peter—Hayes	**LIND**
William—Benet	**ROSE**
Arthur—Doyle	**CONAN**
Charles—Hughes	**EVANS**
Clare—Luce	**BOOTH**
David—George	**LLOYD**
Erich—Remarque	**MARIA**
Dwight—Eisenhower	**DAVID**
Francis—Key	**SCOTT**
Herbert—Hoover	**CLARK**
Henry—Lodge	**CABOT**
Helen—Moody	**WILLS**
Henry—Thoreau	**DAVID**
James—Garfield	**ABRAM**
John—Astor	**JACOB**
John—Garner	**NANCE**
Peter—Tchaikovsky	**ILICH**
Ralph—Emerson	**WALDO**
Richard—Lee	**HENRY**
William—Harrison	**HENRY**
Alexander—Bell	**GRAHAM**
Anne—Lindbergh	**MORROW**
Charles—Reilly	**NELSON**
Edward—Lytton	**BULWER**
Franklin—Roosevelt	**DELANO**
Franz—Haydn	**JOSEPH**
Gaius—Caesar	**JULIUS**
Herbert—Wells	**GEORGE**
John—Adams	**QUINCY**
John—Booth	**WILKES**
John—Coolidge	**CALVIN**
John—Dulles	**FOSTER**
John—Mill	**STUART**
John—Sousa	**PHILIP**
Leslie—Hope	**TOWNES**
Lyndon—Johnson	**BAINES**
Mamie—Doud	**GENEVA**
Nicholas—Butler	**MURRAY**
Nicolas—Korsakov	**RIMSKY**
Paul—White	**DUDLEY**
Percy—Shelley	**BYSSHE**
Samuel—Coleridge	**TAYLOR**
Steven—Cleveland	**GROVER**
William—Bryant	**CULLEN**
William—Porter	**SYDNEY**
William—Taft	**HOWARD**
William—Yeats	**BUTLER**
Dante—Rossetti	**GABRIEL**
Elizabeth—Browning	**BARRETT**
Erle—Gardner	**STANLEY**
George—Shaw	**BERNARD**
Harriet—Stowe	**BEECHER**
Hubert—Humphrey	**HORATIO**
John—Curry	**STEUART**
John—Rockefeller	**DAVISON**
Marcus—Cicero	**TULLIUS**
Mary—Rinehart	**ROBERTS**
Norman—Peale	**VINCENT**
Oliver—Holmes	**WENDELL**
Pierre—Trudeau	**ELLIOT**
Thomas—Eliot	**STEARNS**
Wolfgang—Mozart	**AMADEUS**
James—Cooper	**FENIMORE**
Johann—Goethe	**WOLFGANG**
John—Morgan	**PIERPONT**
John—North	**RINGLING**
Richard—Sheridan	**BRINSLEY**
William—Bryan	**JENNINGS**
William—Sherman	**TECUMSEH**

PEN NAMES

BOZ	Dickens
ELIA	Lamb
SAKI	Monroe
OUIDA	de la Ramée
O HENRY	Porter
VOLTAIRE	Arouet
MARK TWAIN	Clemens
S S VAN DINE	Wright
NANCY BOYD	Millay
CURRER BELL	Brontë
GEORGE SAND	Dudevant
PIERRE LOTI	Viaud

ALICE TOKLAS	Stein	LEWIS CARROLL	Dodgson
ARTEMUS WARD	Browne	ANATOLE FRANCE	Thibault
GEORGE ELIOT	Evans	PETROLEUM V NASBY	Locke

ORIGINAL NAMES OF CELEBRITIES

BY STAGE NAME

Stage Name	*Given Name*
DAY, Doris	Doris von Kappelhoff
DEE, Sandra	Alexandra Zuck
LEE, Peggy	Norma Egstrom
ALDA, Alan	Alphonso D'Abruzzo
CHER	Cherilyn Sarkisian
FOXX, Redd	John Sanford
JOHN, Elton	Reginald Dwight
WOOD, Natalie	Natasha Gurdin
ALLEN, Woody	Allen Konigsberg
BENNY, Jack	Benjamin Kubelsky
BLAKE, Robert	Michael Gubitosi
BORGE, Victor	Borge Rosenbaum
BURNS, George	Nathan Birnbaum
CAINE, Michael	Maurice Micklewhit
DEREK, Bo	Cathleen Collins
GARBO, Greta	Greta Gustafsson
GRANT, Cary	Archibald Leach
JONES, Tom	Thomas Woodward
LANZA, Mario	Alfredo Cocozza
LEIGH, Janet	Jeanette Morrison
LEWIS, Jerry	Joseph Levitch
LOREN, Sophia	Sophia Scicoloni
LORRE, Peter	Laszio Lowenstein
MOORE, Garry	Thomas Morfit
PARKS, Bert	Bert Jacobson
SHEEN, Martin	Ramon Estevez
SILLS, Beverly	Belle Silverman
STARR, Ringo	Richard Starkey
WAYNE, John	Marion Morrison
WYMAN, Jane	Sarah Jane Fulks
BACALL, Lauren	Betty Joan Perske
COOPER, Alice	Vincent Furnier
COSELL, Howard	Howard Cohen
CURTIS, Tony	Bernard Schwartz
DENVER, John	Henry John Deutschend
FIELDS, W. C.	Will Claude Dukenfield
GARNER, James	James Baumgardner
HOLDEN, William	William Beedle
HUDSON, Rock	Roy Scherer, Jr.
HUNTER, Kim	Janet Cole
KEATON, Diane	Diane Hall
LAUREL, Stan	Arthur Jefferson
MALDEN, Karl	Malden Sekulovich
MARTIN, Dean	Dino Crocetti
MARTIN, Tony	Alvin Morris
MERMAN, Ethel	Ethel Zimmerman

Stage Name	*Given Name*
MONROE, Marilyn	Norma Jean Mortenson
MONROE, Marilyn	Norma Jean Baker
OBRIAN, Hugh	Hugh Krampke
RIVERS, Joan	Joan Sandra Molinsky
ROGERS, Ginger	Virginia McMath
ROGERS, Roy	Leonard Slye
ROONEY, Mickey	Joe Yule, Jr.
SHARIF, Omar	Michael Shalhoub
THOMAS, Danny	Amos Jacobs
TUCKER, Sophie	Sophia Kalish
WILDER, Gene	Jerome Silberman
ASTAIRE, Fred	Frederick Austerlitz
BENNETT, Tony	Anthony Benedetto
BUTTONS, Red	Aaron Chwatt
GARLAND, Judy	Frances Gumm
GRANGER, Stewart	James Stewart
HOUDINI, Harry	Ehrich Weiss
JOURDAN, Louis	Louis Gendre
MONTAND, Yves	Ivo Levi
PALANCE, Jack	Walter Palanuik
SOTHERN, Ann	Harriette Lake
STEVENS, Connie	Concetta Ingolia
CHARISSE, Cyd	Tula Finklea
CRAWFORD, Joan	Lucille LeSueur
HAYWORTH, Rita	Margarita Cansino
LAWRENCE, Steve	Sidney Leibowitz
MACLAINE, Shirley	Shirley Beaty
PICKFORD, Mary	Gladys Smith
STANWYCK, Barbara	Ruby Stevens
FAIRBANKS, Douglas	Douglas Ullman
MANSFIELD, Jayne	Vera Jane Palmer

BY GIVEN NAME

Given Name	*Stage Name*
COLE, Janet	Kim Hunter
GUMM, Frances	Judy Garland
HALL, Diane	Diane Keaton
LAKE, Harriette	Ann Sothern
LEVI, Ivo	Yves Montand
SLYE, Leonard	Roy Rogers
YULE, Joe, Jr.	Mickey Rooney
ZUCK, Alexandra	Sandra Dee
BAKER, Norma Jean	Marilyn Monroe
BEATY, Shirley	Shirley MacLaine
FULKS, Sarah Jane	Jane Wyman
LEACH, Archibald	Cary Grant
COHEN, Howard	Howard Cosell
SMITH, Gladys	Mary Pickford
WEISS, Ehrich	Harry Houdini

Given Name	*Stage Name*
BEEDLE, William	William Holden
CHWATT, Aaron	Red Buttons
DWIGHT, Reginald	Elton John
GENDRE, Louis	Louis Jourdan
GURDIN, Natasha	Natalie Wood
JACOBS, Amos	Danny Thomas
KALISH, Sophia	Sophie Tucker
MCMATH, Virginia	Ginger Rogers
MORFIT, Thomas	Garry Moore
MORRIS, Alvin	Tony Martin
PALMER, Vera Jane	Jayne Mansfield
PERSKE, Betty Joan	Lauren Bacall
ULLMAN, Douglas	Douglas Fairbanks
CANSINO, Margarita	Rita Hayworth
COCOZZA, Alfredo	Mario Lanza
COLLINS, Cathleen	Bo Derek
EGSTROM, Norma	Peggy Lee
ESTEVEZ, Ramon	Martin Sheen
FINKLEA, Tula	Cyd Charisse
FURNIER, Vincent	Alice Cooper
INGOLIA, Concetta	Connie Stevens
KRAMPKE, Hugh	Hugh O'Brian
LESUEUR, Lucille	Joan Crawford
LEVITCH, Joseph	Jerry Lewis
SANFORD, John	Redd Foxx
SCHERER, Roy Jr.	Rock Hudson
STARKEY, Richard	Ringo Starr
STEVENS, Ruby	Barbara Stanwyck
STEWART, James	Stewart Granger
BIRNBAUM, Nathan	George Burns
CROCETTI, Dino	Dean Martin
DABRUZZO, Alphonso	Alan Alda
GUBITOSI, Michael	Robert Blake
JACOBSON, Bert	Bert Parks
KUBELSKY, Benjamin	Jack Benny
MOLINSKY, Joan Sandra	Joan Rivers
MORRISON, Jeanette	Janet Leigh
MORRISON, Marion	John Wayne
SCHWARTZ, Bernard	Tony Curtis
PALANUIK, Walter	Jack Palance
SHALHOUB, Michael	Omar Sharif
WOODWARD, Thomas	Tom Jones
BENEDETTO, Anthony	Tony Bennett
JEFFERSON, Arthur	Stan Laurel
LEIBOWITZ, Sidney	Steve Lawrence
MORTENSON, Norma Jean	Marilyn Monroe
ROSENBAUM, Borge	Victor Borge
SARKISIAN, Cherilyn	Cher
SCICOLONI, Sophia	Sophia Loren
SILBERMAN, Jerome	Gene Wilder
SILVERMAN, Belle	Beverly Sills
ZIMMERMAN, Ethel	Ethel Merman

FOREIGN WORDS

ALPHABETICAL BY FOREIGN WORD

SPANISH

ACA hither, here
AHI there
AJO garlic
AMO master, owner
ANO year
ASI thus
DAR give
DEL of the
HOY today
IDA departure
LEY law
MAS more
MUY very
OJO eye
OLE bravo
ORO gold
OSO bear
POR because of, by, for, through
REY king
RIA estuary, inlet
RIO river
RON rum
SER be(ing)
SUR south
TIA aunt
TIO uncle
VER see
VEZ time, turn

ABAD abbot
ACTO event, lawsuit
AGUA water
ALBO white
ALLA there
ALLI there
ALMA soul
ALMO sweetheart
ALTO high, loud
AMAR to love
AQUI here
ASAR to annoy, roast
ASNO ass, donkey
ASTA horn, mast, spear
AYER yesterday
AZUL blue
BAJO low, short, under
BANO bath
BESO kiss
BOCA mouth
BOLA ball
CADA each
CAJA box, cash
CAMA bed
CAPA cape
CARA face, façade
CARO dear
CASA home, house
CERA wax
CIMA peak, summit, top
CODO elbow
COMO as, like, why, how?
COSA thing
DAMA lady, mistress
DEDO finger, toe
DIOS God
EDED age
ELLO it
ENTE being
ESTE east
FRIO cold
GATO cat, jack
HABA bean, kernel
HIJA daughter
HIJO child, son
JEFE chief
JUEZ judge
LADO direction, room, side
LAGO lake
LOMA hill
MALO bad, evil, poor
MANO hand
MESA table
MONO monkey
NINA girl, young
NINO boy, child, young
OBRA construction; repairs; work
OCIO idleness, leisure; pastime
OIDO ear
ONDA wave
PASO gait, step, pace
PATO duck, drake
PAVO turkey
PELO hair, nap
PEON laborer
PERO but
PICO beak, point
POCO few, little
REJA grate, grille, lattice
RICO rich
ROJO red
ROPA clothes, dry-goods
ROTO broken, ragged
SALA hall, living room, parlor
SANO healthy, sound
SITO located, situated
SOGA cord, rope
SOLO only
TAJO cut
TODO all, every, whole
TORO bull
TRAS after, behind
VACA cow
VEGA meadow, plain

ACASO chance, maybe, perhaps
ACERA sidewalk
ADIOS good-bye
ALDEA village
AMIGO friend
ANIMO soul, spirit, will
ANTES before, formerly
ATRAS back, behind
BAHIA bay
BARBA beard, chin
BARCA boat
BARCO boat
BELLO beautiful
CABRA goat
CALDO broth
CALOR heat, warmth
CANON canyon
CARNE meat
CARTA letter
CHICA girl, lass
CHICO child, little, small
CHITO hush
CIELO heaven, sky
CUICO cop

DIOSA goddess
DOLER ache, grieve, hurt
DONDE where
DUENA landlady
DUENO landlord, master
ENANO little
ESTAR be
ESTIO summer
FALDA dress, skirt, foothill
FINCA plantation, property, real estate
FONDA inn, restaurant
FRESA strawberry
FUEGO fire
GALLO cock
GENTE folks, people, troops
HABLA language
HASTA until
HUEVO egg
JUEGO game, play
LETRA letter
LUEGO soon, then
MADRE mother
MATAR kill
MERCA purchase
MONJA nun
MOSCA fly
MUJER woman
NADAR float, swim
NAVIO ship, vessel
NEGRA black
NOCHE night
NORTE north
NUEVO new

OESTE west
PADRE father
PAMPA prairie
PERRO dog
PLATA silver
PLATO plate
POBRE poor
PRESO convict, prisoner
RATON mouse
REATA lasso
RECIO strong
REINA queen
SENAL landmark, mark, sign, token, trace
SENOR gentleman, master, mister, sir
SILLA chair
TABLE table
TANTO so much
TARDE afternoon, evening, late
TENER have
TESTA head
TOMAR have
UNICO only
VELOZ quick, agile
ZORRO fox

ABADIA abbey
ALERTA watchword
ALTEZA Highness
ALTURA height
ARROYO creek, stream
BARATO cheap
BLANCO white

BODEGA (wine) cellar, grocery store
CABEZA head
CALIDO warm
CAMBIO change, exchange (rate)
CAMISA shirt
CIUDAD city
COCINA kitchen
COMIDA dinner, meal, food
CORREO mail, post office
CUANDO when
DUENNA chaperon
ESPOSA wife
ESPOSO husband
GITANO gypsy, tricky
GRANDE large
GUERRA conflict, war
HOMBRE man
INGLES English
LADRON robber, thief
MANANA morning
PAGADO paid
PALOMA dove, pigeon
PASADO past
POSADA inn
PRENSA press
RESERO cowboy, herdsman
SENORA lady, madam, Mrs.
TARDIO late

FRENCH

AME soul
AMI friend
ANE ass, donkey
BAL ball (dance)
BAS low, stocking
BLE corn, wheat
BON good
CAS case, circumstance, event
COL mountains pass, neck
COU neck
CRU crude, raw, vineyard
DES since
DIT said, spoken

DOS back
DUC duke
EAU water
EST east, is
ETE summer
FER iron
FEU fire, heat
FIL thread
FOI credit, faith, honor
FOU fool(ish)
GRE wish, liking, will
ICI here
ILE island
JEU game, sport
JUS gravy, juice

LIS lily
MAL evil, ill(ness), sickness
MER sea
MUR wall
NEE born
NEZ nose
NOM fame, name, noun
NON no
OIE goose
OUI yes
PEU few, little
PIS worse
PLI fold, wrinkle, habit

RIZ rice
ROI king
SEC dry
SEL salt
SUD south
SUR on, over, upon, sure
SUS upon
TEL such
TIR fire, shooting
UNI level, united
VIF lively
VIN wine

ABAS down with
ABBE abbot
ABRI dugout, shelter
ACTE act
AIGU sharp
AILE wing(ed)
AINE elder
AISE comfort, ease
AMER bitter
AMIE friend
ANGE angel
ANSE handle
ARME weapon
AUBE dawn
AVEC with
AVIS opinion, warning
AZUR blue
BAIN bath
BANC bench
BEBE baby
BETE beast, stupid
BIEN well
BLEU blue
BOIS wood
BRAS arm
BRUN brown
CHER dear, expensive
CHEZ among, with, in, at home with
CHOU cabbage
CHUT hush!
CIEL heaven, sky
CLOU nail
COUT cost
CUIR leather
DANS in
DEFI defiance
DEJA already
DELA beyond
DIEU God
DORE gilded, gilt, golden
DOUX gentle, soft, sweet
DRAP cloth
EGAL equal
ETAT state
ETRE be(ing)
FAIM hunger
FAIT deed
FAUX false
FILS son
FLIC cop
FOIS time
GANT glove
GARE beware, station
GENS people
GRAS fat
GRIS gray
HAUT high
HEIN exclamation
HIER yesterday
HORS out
IDEE idea
IVRE drunk
JEUX games
JOUR day
JUGE judge
JUPE petticoat, skirt
LAIT milk
LIER tie
LIRE read
LORS then
LOUP half mask, wolf
MAIN hand
MAIS but
MARI husband
MERE mother
MIDI noon
MIEL honey
MONT mountain
MOUE grimace
NEUF new
NOIR black
NORD north
NUIT night
OBUS shell
OEIL eye
OEUF egg
ONDE wave
OSER dare
OTER doff, remove
PAIN bread
PAIX peace
PAYS country, land, nation
PEAU skin
PERE father
PEUR fear
PIED foot
PIRE worse
PONT bridge
PRES almost, near
PRET ready
PRIX cost, price, prize
PUIS then
RECU receipt
REVE dream
RIEN nothing
RIRE laugh
ROTI roast
ROUX red
SANS without
SCIE saw
SEUL alone
SOIE silk
SOIF thirst
SOIN care
SOIR evening
SOIT agreed!
SOUS under
TANT so much
TARD late
TETE head
TOIT roof
TOUS all, every
TOUT all, any, every, whole
TRES very
VELO bicycle
VERT green
VITE quick
VOIR see
VRAI true
YEUX eyes

ACHAT purchase
ADIEU farewell
AIMER to love
AINSI thus
ALLEE avenue
ALLER go
ALORS then
AMANT lover
AMOUR love
APRES after
ARBRE tree
ARGOT slang
ARRET arrest, pause
ASSEZ enough
AUSSI also
AUTRE other
AVANT before, forward
AVARE miser
AVION airplane
AVOIR have
BAGUE ring

BIERE	beer
BLANC	white
BOEUF	beef
BOIRE	to drink
BONNE	maid, nurse
BRUIT	fame, noise, reputation
CARRE	square
CHAUD	hot, warm
CHERE	dear
CHERI	dear
CHIEN	dog
COMME	like
COMTE	count, earl
DETTE	debt, obligation
DOIGT	finger
DROIT	law, right, straight
ECOLE	school
ELEVE	pupil
EMAIL	enamel
ENCRE	ink
ENFER	hell
ENFIN	finally
ENTRE	among, between
ETAGE	floor
FAUTE	error, fault, lack
FILLE	daughter
FLEUR	flower
FRAIS	fresh
FRERE	brother
FROID	cold
GAFFE	blunder
GRAND	large
HELAS	alas
HEURE	hour
HIVER	winter
HOMME	man
JAIME	I love
JAUNE	yellow
JEUNE	young
JOLIE	pretty
LACHE	coward(ly)
LAPIN	rabbit
LEGER	light, slight
LIVRE	book
LOUER	to hire, to rent
LOURD	heavy
LYCEE	school
MAIRE	mayor
MAMAN	mamma
MARIE	bridegroom
MARIN	marine, sailor
MATIN	morning
MELER	mix
MERCI	thanks
METRO	subway
MIEUX	better
MOINS	less
MONDE	world
MUSEE	museum
NEIGE	snow
NEUVE	new
NUAGE	cloud
ONCLE	uncle
ORAGE	storm
OUEST	west
OUTRE	bizarre
PARMI	amid
PEINE	pain, penalty, trouble
PETIT	small
PLAGE	beach
PLEIN	full
PLUIE	rain
POCHE	pocket
POIDS	weight
POILU	soldier
POIRE	pear
POSTE	mail
POULE	chicken
PRISE	capture
QUAND	when
REINE	queen
RENTE	annuity, income
REPAS	meal
REVER	to dream
RICHE	rich
ROSEE	dew
ROUGE	red
SALLE	hall, room
SALUT	cheers, greeting, safety
SANTE	health
SAVON	soap
SELON	according
SOEUR	sister
SOMME	sum
SORTE	kind, manner, sort
TABLE	table
TANTE	aunt
TASSE	cup
TENIR	hold, possess
TERRE	earth, land, world
TOMBE	grave
VACHE	cow
VERRE	glass
VOICI	here
VOILA	there!
AFFAME	hungry
AGNEAU	lamb
AMENDE	penalty, reparation
AMITIE	friendship
AUTOUR	around
AVENIR	future
BAISER	to kiss
BAISSE	fall of stocks
BERGER	shepherd
BEURRE	butter
BOURSE	stock exchange
CACHOT	dungeon, prison
CADEAU	gift
CAHIER	blank book, copy book
CAREME	Lent
CARNET	notebook
CHAISE	chair
CHEVAL	horse
CLOCHE	bell
DABORD	at first
DETROP	too much, superfluous
DIABLE	devil
DOUANE	customs
ECRIRE	write
EGLISE	church
ENCORE	again
ENFANT	child
ETOILE	star
FAUSSE	false
FIACRE	carriage
FRAISE	strawberry
GAREDE	beware
GATEAU	cake
GAUCHE	awkward, clumsy, left
GUERRE	war
HAUSSE	rise of prices
LANGUE	language, tongue
MAISON	home, house
MARIEE	bride
MEUBLE	furniture
MOEURS	customs
MONTRE	watch
MOUCHE	fly
MOUTON	sheep
NAVIRE	ship
NOMBRE	number
OCTROI	concession, toll
OUVERT	open

PAREIL	equal
PARLER	speak
PATOIS	dialect, lingo
PAUVRE	poor
PENSEE	thought
ROUSSE	red
SAISON	season
SAVOIR	know, understand
SOIGNE	well groomed
SOLDAT	soldier
SOLEIL	sun
SOURIS	mouse
SURETE	police bureau, safety, security
TRENTE	thirty

ITALIAN

AVO	grandfather
BUE	ox
CON	against, with
DIO	God
ETA	age
GIU	below, down
IVI	there
MAI	always, ever, never
OCA	goose, simpleton
ORA	duration, hour, now, time
OVE	where
PIU	many, more
QUA	here
QUI	here
SUD	south
ZIA	aunt
ZIO	uncle

AGRO	sour
ALBA	dawn
ARTE	art
ASSI	much
ATTO	act, deed
BENE	well
BERE	drink, swallow
CAPO	head
CARA	dear
CARO	dear
CERA	wax
CIMA	mountain peak, summit
CODA	end, tail
COSA	matter, thing
COSI	so, thus
DONO	gift, talent
DOPO	after
ECCO	lo!
ESTE	east
FEDE	confidence, faith
GELO	frost, ice
GESU	Jesus
GIRO	tour
GITA	tour
IERI	yesterday
LAGO	lake
LATO	side
LUME	light
MANO	hand
MELA	apple
NASO	nose
NAVE	ship
NERO	black
NORD	north
ODIO	hatred
OGGI	today
OGNI	each, every
PELO	hair
POCO	few, little, thin
POMO	apple
RIVA	shore
SALA	hall
SEDE	seat
SERA	afternoon, evening, night
SETE	thirst
SITO	situated
UOMO	husband, man
UOVO	egg
VEDO	I see
VERO	real, true
VISO	face
VOCE	voice

ABITO	dress
ACQUA	water
ADDIO	farewell, good-bye
ALTRO	other
AMARE	to love
AMICA	friend
AMICO	friend
AMORE	love
ANIMA	soul, spirit
ASINO	ass, donkey
ASTRO	star
AVERE	get, have
BABBO	dad
BACIO	kiss
BARBA	beard
BASTA	enough
BIRRA	beer
BOCCA	mouth
BOLLO	stamp
BUONO	good
CAFFE	café
CALLE	street
CAMPO	camp, field
CARTA	paper
CASSA	chest
CIELO	heaven, sky
CITTA	city, town
CONTO	account
CORSA	course, race
CORSO	street
DETTO	said
DONNA	lady
DONNE	women
DUOMO	cathedral
ESTRO	ardor
FATTO	done
FERIA	holiday
FERRO	iron
FESTA	feast, holiday
FORCA	fork
FORZA	force, power, strength
FRATE	monk
GAMBA	leg
GATTA	cat
GROSS	large
ISOLA	isle
LADRO	thief
LEGGE	law
LEGNO	wood
LESSO	boiled
LETTO	bed
MADRE	mother
MENTE	mind
MOLTO	many, much, very
MONDO	world
NOTTE	night
OVEST	west
PADRE	father
PALLA	ball
PASTA	dough
PASTO	meal
PELLE	skin
PONTE	bridge
PORTA	door, gate
PORTO	harbor
PREGO	please
PUNTO	not at all

RETTO straight
RICCO rich
ROSSO red
SALSA sauce
SARTO tailor
SCUSA excuse
SEDIA chair
SEGNO sign
SENZA without
SONNO sleep
SOTTO under
SPADA sword
SPOSA bride, spouse
SPOSO spouse
TANTO so much
TARDO late
TERGO back
TESTA head
TORRE tower
TORTO twisted, wrong
TUTTI all
TUTTO all

ADESSO now
ALBERO tree
ALLORA then
AMANTE lover
ANCORA yet
APERTO open
AVANTI forward
BIANCO white
CANALE canal
CASALE hamlet, village
CHIAVE key
DACAPO again, from the beginning
DENARO money
DESTRO right
DOGANA custom house
DOMANI tomorrow
ESSERE be(ing)
ESTERO foreign
FIGLIA daughter
FIGLIO son
GIORNO day
GRANDE large
GRAZIE thanks
GROSSO large
MARITO husband
MONETA money
NIENTE nothing
POVERO poor
QUANDO when, how much
REGINA queen
SCARPA shoe
SIGNOR gentleman
STELLA star
STESSO same, self
STRADA road
TAVOLA table
VALUTA value

GERMAN

AAL eel
ABT abbot
ACH alas
AHN ancestor
ALS as, than
ARM poor
AUF of, on, upon
AUS from, of, out of
BEI about, among, at, with
EIS ice
ENG narrow
IST is
KUH cow
MIT with
NAH near
NEU new
NIE never
OHR ear
OST east
SUD south
TAL valley
TOR gate
TOT dead
UHR clock, watch
UND and
VON from, of
VOR before
WEG path, way
WIE how
ZUG train

ABER but
ADEL nobility
ALLE all
ALTE age, old
ARZT doctor
AUGE eye
AULA hall
BART beard
BAUM tree
BEIN lag
BETT bed
BIER beer
BILD figure, image, picture
BLAU blue
BLUT blood
BROT bread
BUCH book
BUND band, league, bundle
DAME lady, woman
DANN then
DENN for, then, then
DIEB thief
DING thing
DOCH still, yet
DORF village
DORT there, yonder
ECHT genuine, pure, real
EDEL noble
EHER first
ENTE duck
ERDE earth
ESEL ass
ETWA about, nearly, perhaps
FAUL dirty, foul, lazy
FEIN elegant, fine
FLUG flight
FRAU lady, wife, woman
FREI free
FRUH early
GABE gift
GANZ all
GAST visitor
GELD cash, coin, money
GERN gladly, willingly
GOTT God, lord
GRAF count, earl, nobleman
HAAR hair
HALS neck
HAUS house, residence
HEIM home
HERR gentleman, lord, sir
HERZ heart
HIER here
HOCH high, tall, viva! (salute)
HUHN chicken
HUND dog
JEDE every
JENE that

KALT cold
KLUG clever
LIED air, song, tune
LUFT air
MEER sea
MEHR more
MORD murder
NACH after, behind
NEIN no
NEUE new
NOCH besides, yet
NORD north
OBEN above, top
OBER upper
OBST fruit
ODER or
OHNE without
PAAR couple, pair
RAUM room, space
REDE language, speech
RUHE calm, peace, repose, rest
RUHM glory
SAAL hall, room
SEHR greatly, much, very
SEIN be(ing)
SIEG triumph, victory
SOHN son
SPAT late
TIEF deep
TURM tower
UBER above, over
UFER bank, shore
VIEL much
VOLK nation, people, race
VOLL full
WAHR genuine, real, true
WEIB wife, woman
WEIL because
WEIT distant, far, wide
WELT humanity, society, world
WENN if, when
WEST west
WIRT host
WOHL well

ABEND evening
ALLES everything
ANDER different, else
ANGST fear
APFEL apple
BEIDE both
BESEN broom
BITTE please, request
BLITZ lightning
BRAUT bride
BRIEF letter
DAHER hence
DAMEN ladies
DANKE thanks
DURCH across, through
DURST thirst
EINST once
EISEN iron
ESSEN eat
GABEL fork
GASSE alley, lane, path, street
GATTE husband, spouse
GEBEN give
GEHEN go, move, walk
GEIST mind, soul, spirit
HABEN have
HAFEN harbor, haven
HEUTE today
IMMER always
INSEL island
JAGER hunter
KLEIN little, small
KREUZ cross
KRIEG strife, war
LEDER leather
LESEN read
LEUTE people, persons
LIEBE affection, love
NACHT night
NEBEN beside
NEUER new
NEUES new
NICHT not
ONKEL uncle

OSTEN east, Orient
PREIS cost, prize
PROST cheers!
REGEN rain
REICH empire, rich
SEELE soul
SONNE sun
SPIEL game, play
STAAT state
STADT city, town
STAHL steel
STUHL chair
SUDEN south
TAFEL table
TANTE aunt
TISCH table
UNTEN below, beneath
UNTER below, beneath
VATER father
WAGEN carriage, dare, to
WARUM why
WENIG few, little

ARBEIT labor, toil, work
BILLIG cheap
BRUDER brother
EINMAL once
FRAUEN ladies
GATTEN wife
GLOCKE bell
HERREN gentleman
HIMMEL heaven, sky
LOFFEL spoon
MESSER knife
MITTAG noon
MORGEN morning, tomorrow
MUTTER mother
NORDEN north
PROSIT cheers!
SCHNEE snow
SCHULE school
SELBST self
SOLDAT soldier
TELLER plate
WESTEN west
WIEDER again
WISSEN know(ledge)

LATIN

AES copper
AMO I love
ARA altar, pyre
ARS art, trade

ARX citadel, fortress
AUT either, or
BIS twice
COR heart

CUM with
DEA goddess
DEI gods
DUX leader

EST	is
FAS	lawful, divine law
HEU	alas
IBI	there
IRA	anger, wrath
JUS	law
LAC	milk
LEX	law
MOS	custom, will
NON	not
ORA	edge, shore, pray
PAX	peace
PES	foot
QUA	as
RES	thing
REX	king
SED	but
TER	three times
UBI	where
VAE	alas
VAS	pledge, vessel
VIR	husband, man
VIS	force, power, strength

ACTU	thing done
ACUS	needle, pin
AGER	field
AGNI	lambs
AGRI	fields
ALIA	other
ALII	others
ALTA	high
AMAS	you love
AMAT	he loves
ANNO	in the year
ANTE	before
AQUA	water
AVES	birds
AVIS	bird
AVUS	grandfather
BENE	well
BONA	property
CAVE	beware
CENA	dinner, supper
CITO	soon
DIEM	day
DIES	day(s)
DIXI	I have spoken
ECCE	behold!, lo!
EHEU	alas
ERAT	was
ESSE	be(ing)
GENU	knee
HORA	hour
IBID	at the same place
IDEM	same
ITER	road
LANA	wool
LAUS	praise
MARE	sea
MENS	mind
MONS	mountain
NEMO	nobody
NISI	except, unless
NOTA	note, observe!
NUNC	now
OVUM	egg
PARS	part
PONS	bridge
POST	after
PUER	boy, child
RATA	proportion, share
REUS	culprit, defendant
SINE	without
SORS	lot, prophecy
SPES	hope
TACE	hush!
TOTO	(in) all
URBS	city
UXOR	wife
VADE	go away!
VIDE	see!
VITA	life
VOLA	palm (hand)

ABBAS	abbot
ACIES	battle line, keenness
ACTES	edge
ACTUS	thing done
AEGER	sick
AGNUS	lamb
ALIUD	another thing
ALIUS	other
AMICA	friend
ANIMA	air, wind, soul
ANNUS	year
ANTEA	before
ASTRA	stars
AURUM	gold
BEATA	blessed, happy
BONUM	good
CALIX	cup, goblet
CAUDA	tail
CIBUS	fodder, food
CIRCA	about
COENA	supper
COPIA	abundance, plenty
CULPA	error, fault, negligence
DIVUS	divine
DOLUS	deceit, fraud
FIDES	confidence, faith, trust
FILIA	daughter
FRONS	brow, forehead
GALEA	helmet
IDEST	that is
IGNIS	fire
INTRA	within
JANUA	door
JUXTA	nearby
LATUS	broad, wide, side
LENIS	gentle, smooth, soft
LIBER	book
LOCUS	place
MALUM	evil
MALUS	bad, wicked
MANET	it remains
MISSA	Mass, the
MODUS	form, method
NEFAS	sinful, unlawful
NIHIL	nothing
NOMEN	name
OBSTA	resist!
OMNIA	all
OMNIS	all
OTIUM	ease, leisure
PECUS	cattle, flock, herd
PORTA	door, gate
QUARE	why
QUOAD	as far as
REGES	kings
RETRO	backward, behind
RITUS	rite, usage
SANUS	healthy, sound
SOLUS	alone, only
SUPER	above, over, upon, more
TERRA	earth, ground, land
TOTUM	all
TRANS	across, over
VENIA	pardon
VINUM	sour, wine

ACHAIA	Greece
AESTAS	summer
ALITER	otherwise
AMICUS	friend
BEATUS	blessed, happy

BELLUM	war
CIRCUM	around
DEXTER	right
DOCTUS	learned, well-informed
EMPTIO	buying
FEMINA	woman
FERRUM	iron
FILIUS	son
FURTUM	theft
IGITUR	therefore
ITERUM	again
LAPSUS	error, gliding, sliding
MAGNUS	great
PARTIM	partly
PATRIA	fatherland
PISCES	fishes
PISCIS	fish
PRIMUM	first
PRIMUS	first
REGINA	queen
REGNUM	authority, kingdom, tyranny
SEMPER	always
SERVUS	servant, slave
SORTES	lots

ALPHABETICAL BY DEFINITION

SPANISH

aunt	**TIA**
be(ing)	**SER**
bear	**OSO**
because of	**POR**
bravo	**OLE**
by	**POR**
departure	**IDA**
estuary	**RIA**
eye	**OJO**
for	**POR**
garlic	**AJO**
give	**DAR**
gold	**ORO**
hither, here	**ACA**
inlet	**RIA**
king	**REY**
law	**LEY**
master	**AMO**
more	**MAS**
of the	**DEL**
owner	**AMO**
river	**RIO**
rum	**RON**
see	**VER**
south	**SUR**
there	**AHI**
through	**POR**
thus	**ASI**
time	**VEZ**
today	**HOY**
turn	**VEZ**
uncle	**TIO**
very	**MUY**
year	**ANO**
abbot	**ABAD**
after	**TRAS**
age	**EDAD**
all	**TODO**
annoy	**ASAR**
as	**COMO**
ass	**ASNO**
bad	**MALO**
ball	**BOLA**
bath	**BANO**
beak	**PICO**
bean	**HABA**
bed	**CAMA**
behind	**TRAS**
being	**ENTE**
blue	**AZUL**
box	**CAJA**
boy	**NINO**
broken	**ROTO**
bull	**TORO**
but	**PERO**
cape	**CAPA**
cash	**CAJA**
cat	**GATO**
chief	**JEFE**
child	**NINO, HIJO**
clothes	**ROPA**
cold	**FRIO**
construction	**OBRA**
cord	**SOGA**
cow	**VAGA**
cut	**TAJO**
daughter	**HIJA**
dear	**CARO**
direction	**LADO**
donkey	**ASNO**
drygoods	**ROPA**
duck, drake	**PATO**
each	**CADA**
ear	**OIDO**
east	**ESTE**
elbow	**CODO**
event	**ACTO**
every	**TODO**
evil	**MALO**
face, façade	**CARA**
few	**POCO**
finger	**DEDO**
gait	**PASO**
girl	**NINA**
God	**DIOS**
grate, grille	**REJA**
hair	**PELO**
hall	**SALA**
hand	**MANO**
healthy	**SANO**
here	**AQUI**
high	**ALTO**
hill	**LOMA**
home	**CASA**
horn	**ASTA**
house	**CASA**
how?	**COMO**
idleness	**OCIO**
it	**ELLO**
jack	**GATO**
judge	**JUEZ**
kernel	**HABA**
kiss	**BESO**
laborer	**PEON**
lady	**DAMA**
lake	**LAGO**
lattice	**REJA**
lawsuit	**ACTO**
leisure	**OCIO**
like	**COMO**
little	**POCO**
living room	**SALA**
located	**SITO**
loud	**ALTO**
love, to	**AMAR**
low	**BAJO**
mast	**ASTA**
meadow	**VEGA**
mistress	**DAMA**
monkey	**MONO**
mouth	**BOCA**
nap	**PELO**
only	**SOLO**
pace	**PASO**
parlor	**SALA**

pastime	OCIO
peak	CIMA
peak	PICO
plain	VEGA
point	PICO
poor	MALO
ragged	ROTO
red	ROJO
repairs	OBRA
rich	RICO
roast, to	ASAR
room	LADO
rope	SOGA
short	BAJO
side	LADO
situated	SITO
son	HIJO
soul	ALMA
sound	SANO
spear	ASTA
step	PASO
summit	CIMA
sweetheart	ALMO
table	MESA
there	ALLA, ALLI
thing	COSA
toe	DEDO
top	CIMA
turkey	PAVO
under	BAJO
water	AGUA
wave	ONDA
wax	CERA
white	ALBO
whole	TODO
why	COMO
work	OBRA
yesterday	AYER
young	NINA, NINO

ache	DOLER
afternoon	TARDE
agile	VELOZ
back	ATRAS
bay	BAHIA
be	ESTAR
beard	BARBA
beautiful	BELLO
before	ANTES
behind	ATRAS
black	NEGRA
boat	BARCA, BARCO
broth	CALDO
canyon	CANON
chair	SILLA
chance	ACASO
child	CHICO
chin	BARBA
cock	GALLO
convict	PRESO
cop	CUICO
dog	PERRO
dress	FALDA
egg	HUEVO
evening	TARDE
father	PADRE
fire	FUEGO
float	NADAR
fly	MOSCA
folks	GENTE
foothill	FALDA
formerly	ANTES
fox	ZORRO
friend	AMIGO, AMIGA
game	JUEGO
gentleman	SENOR
girl	CHICA
goat	CABRA
goddess	DIOSA
good-bye	ADIOS
grieve	DOLER
have	TENER, TOMAR
head	TESTA
heat	CALOR
heaven	CIELO
hurt	DOLER
hush	CHITO
inn	FONDA
kill	MATAR
landlady	DUENA
landlord	DUENO
landmark	SENAL
language	HABLA
lass	CHICA
lasso	REATA
late	TARDE
letter	CARTA, LETRA
little	CHICO, ENANO
mark	SENAL
master	SENOR, DUENO
maybe	ACASO
meat	CARNE
mister	SENOR
mother	MADRE
mouse	RATON
new	NUEVO
night	NOCHE
north	NORTE
nun	MONJA
only	UNICO
people	GENTE
perhaps	ACASO
plantation	FINCA
plate	PLATO
play	JUEGO
poor	POBRE
prairie	PAMPA
prisoner	PRESO
property	FINCA
purchase	MERCA
queen	REINA
quick	VELOZ
real estate	FINCA
restaurant	FONDA
ship	NAVIO
sidewalk	ACERA
sign	SENAL
silver	PLATA
sir	SENOR
skirt	FALDA
sky	CIELO
small	CHICO
so much	TANTO
soon	LUEGO
soul, spirit	ANIMO
strawberry	FRESA
strong	RECIO
summer	ESTIO
swim	NADAR
table	TABLA
then	LUEGO
token, trace	SENAL
troops	GENTE
until	HASTA
vessel	NAVIO
village	ALDEA
warmth	CALOR
west	OESTE
where	DONDE
will	ANIMO
woman	MUJER

abbey	ABADIA
cellar	BODEGA
change	CAMBIO
chaperon	DUENNA
cheap	BARATO
city	CIUDAD
conflict	GUERRA
cowboy	RESERO
creek	ARROYO
dinner	COMIDA
dove	PALOMA
English	INGLES
exchange (rate)	CAMBIO
food	COMIDO
grocery store	BODEGA
gypsy	GITANO
head	CABEZA
height	ALTURA
herdsman	RESERO
Highness	ALTEZA
husband	ESPOSO
inn	POSADA
kitchen	COCINA
lady	SENORA

large	GRANDE
late	TARDIO
madam	SENORA
mail	CORREO
man	HOMBRE
meal	COMIDA
morning	MANANA
Mrs.	SENORA
paid	PAGADO
past	PASADO
pigeon	PALOMA
post office	CORREO
press	PRENSA
robber	LADRON
shirt	CAMISA
stream	ARROYO
thief	LADRON
tricky	GITANO
war	GUERRA
warm	CALIDO
watchword	ALERTA
when	CUANDO
white	BLANCO
wife	ESPOSA
winecellar	BODEGA

FRENCH

ass	ANE
back	DOS
ball (dance)	BAL
born	NEE
case	CAS
circumstance	CAS
corn	BLE
credit	FOI
crude	CRU
donkey	ANE
dry	SEC
duke	DUC
east	EST
event	CAS
evil	MAL
faith	FOI
fame	NOM
few	PEU
fire	FEU, TIR
fold	PLI
fool(ish)	FOU
friend	AMI
game	JEU
good	BON
goose	OIE
gravy	JUS
habit	PLI
heat	FEU
here	ICI
honor	FOI
ill, illness	MAL
iron	FER
is	EST
island	ILE
juice	JUS
king	ROI
level	UNI
liking	GRE
lily	LIS
little	PEU
lively	VIF
low	BAS
mt. pass	COL
name	NOM
neck	COL, COU
no	NON
nose	NEZ
noun	NOM
on, over	SUR
raw	CRU
rice	RIZ
said	DIT
salt	SEL
sea	MER
shooting	TIR
sickness	MAL
since	DES
soul	AME
south	SUD
spoken	DIT
sport	JEU
stocking	BAS
such	TEL
summer	ETE
sure	SUR
thread	FIL
united	UNI
upon	SUR, SUS
vineyard	CRU
wall	MUR
water	EAU
wheat	BLE
will	GRE
wine	VIN
wish	GRE
worse	PIS
wrinkle	PLI
yes	OUI

abbot	ABBE
act	ACTE
agreed!	SOIT
all	TOUS, TOUT
alone	SEUL
almost	PRES
already	DEJA
among	CHEZ
angel	ANGE
any	TOUT
arm	BRAS
at home with	CHEZ
baby	BEBE
bath	BAIN
beast	BETE
be(ing)	ETRE
bench	BANC
beware	GARE
beyond	DELA
bicycle	VELO
bitter	AMER
black	NOIR
blue	AZUR, BLEU
bread	PAIN
bridge	PONT
brown	BRUN
but	MAIS
cabbage	CHOU
care	SOIN
cloth	DRAP
comfort	AISE
cop	FLIC
cost	COUT, PRIX
country	PAYS
dare	OSER
dawn	AUBE
day	JOUR
dear	CHER
deed	FAIT
defiance	DEFI
doff	OTER
down with	ABAS
dream	REVE
drunk	IVRE
dugout	ABRI
ease	AISE
egg	OEUF
elder	AINE
equal	EGAL
evening	SOIR
every	TOUS, TOUT
exclamation	HEIN
expensive	CHER
eye	OEIL
eyes	YEUX
false	FAUX
fat	GRAS
father	PERE
fear	PEUR
foot	PIED
friend	AMIE
games	JEUX

gentle **DOUX**
gilded, gilt **DORE**
glove **GANT**
God **DIEU**
golden **DORE**
gray **GRIS**
green **VERT**
grimace **MOUE**
half mask **LOUP**
hand **MAIN**
handle **ANSE**
head **TETE**
heaven **CIEL**
high **HAUT**
honey **MIEL**
hunger **FAIM**
husband **MARI**
hush! **CHUT**
idea **IDEE**
in **CHEZ, DANS**
judge **JUGE**
land **PAYS**
late **TARD**
laugh **RIRE**
leather **CUIR**
milk **LAIT**
mother **MERE**
mountain **MONT**
nail **CLOU**
nation **PAYS**
near **PRES**
new **NEUF**
night **NUIT**
noon **MIDI**
north **NORD**
nothing **RIEN**
opinion **AVIS**
out **HORS**
peace **PAIX**
people **GENS**
petticoat **JUPE**
pretty **JOLI**
price, prize **PRIX**
quick **VITE**
read **LIRE**
ready **PRET**
receipt **RECU**
red **ROUX**
remove **OTER**
roast **ROTI**
roof **TOIT**
saw **SCIE**
see **VOIR**
sharp **AIGU**
shell **OBUS**
shelter **ABRI**
silk **SOIE**
skin **PEAU**
skirt **JUPE**
sky **CIEL**
soft **DOUX**
so much **TANT**
son **FILS**
state **ETAT**
station **GARE**
stupid **BETE**
sweet **DOUX**
then **LORS, PUIS**
thirst **SOIF**
tie **LIER**
time **FOIS**
true **VRAI**
under **SOUS**
very **TRES**
warning **AVIS**
wave **ONDE**
weapon **ARME**
well **BIEN**
whole **TOUT**
wing(ed) **AILE**
with **AVEC, CHEZ**
without **SANS**
wolf **LOUP**
wood **BOIS**
worse **PIRE**
yesterday **HIER**

according **SELON**
after **APRES**
airplane **AVION**
alas **HELAS**
also **AUSSI**
amid **PARMI**
among **ENTRE**
annuity **RENTE**
arrest **ARRET**
aunt **TANTE**
avenue **ALLEE**
beach **PLAGE**
beef **BOEUF**
beer **BIERE**
before **AVANT**
better **MIEUX**
between **ENTRE**
bizarre **OUTRE**
blunder **GAFFE**
book **LIVRE**
bridegroom **MARIE**
brother **FRERE**
capture **PRISE**
cheers **SALUT**
chicken **POULE**
cloud **NUAGE**
cold **FROID**
count **COMTE**
cow **VACHE**
coward(ly) **LACHE**
cup **TASSE**
daughter **FILLE**
dear **CHERE, CHERI**
debt **DETTE**
dew **ROSEE**
dog **CHIEN**
dream, to **REVER**
drink, to **BOIRE**
earl **COMTE**
earth **TERRE**
enamel **EMAIL**
enough **ASSEZ**
error **FAUTE**
fame **BRUIT**
farewell **ADIEU**
fault **FAUTE**
finally **ENFIN**
finger **DOIGT**
floor **ETAGE**
flower **FLEUR**
forward **AVANT**
fresh **FRAIS**
full **PLEIN**
glass **VERRE**
go **ALLER**
grave **TOMBE**
greeting **SALUT**
hall **SALLE**
have **AVOIR**
health **SANTE**
heavy **LOURD**
hell **ENFER**
here **VOICI**
hire **LOUER**
hold **TENIR**
hot **CHAUD**
hour **HEURE**
I love **JAIME**
income **RENTE**
ink **ENCRE**
kind **SORTE**
lack **FAUTE**
land **TERRE**
large **GRAND**
law **DROIT**
less **MOINS**
light **LEGER**
like **COMME**
love **AMOUR**
love, to **AIMER**
lover **AMANT**
maid **BONNE**
mail **POSTE**
mamma **MAMAN**
man **HOMME**
manner **SORTE**
marine **MARIN**
mayor **MAIRE**
meal **REPAS**
miser **AVARE**

mix MELER
morning MATIN
museum MUSEE
new NEUVE
noise BRUIT
nurse BONNE
obligation DETTE
other AUTRE
pain PEINE
pause ARRET
pear POIRE
penalty PEINE
pocket POCHE
possess TENIR
pupil ELEVE
purchase ACHAT
queen REINE
rabbit LAPIN
rain PLUIE
red ROUGE
rent, to LOUER
reputation BRUIT
rich RICHE
right DROIT
ring BAGUE
room SALLE
safety SALUT
sailor MARIN
school ECOLE, LYCEE
sister SOEUR
slang ARGOT
slight LEGER
small PETIT
snow NEIGE
soap SAVON
soldier POILU
sort SORTE
square CARRE
storm ORAGE
straight DROIT
subway METRO
sum SOMME
table TABLE
thanks MERCI
then ALORS
there! VOILA
thus AINSI
tree ARBRE
trouble PEINE
uncle ONCLE
warm CHAUD
weight POIDS
west OUEST
when QUAND
white BLANC
winter HIVER
world MONDE, TERRE
yellow JAUNE
young JEUNE

again ENCORE
around AUTOUR
at first DABORD
awkward GAUCHE
bell CLOCHE
beware GAREDE
blank book CAHIER
bride MARIEE
butter BEURRE
cake GATEAU
carriage FIACRE
chair CHAISE
child ENFANT
church EGLISE
clumsy GAUCHE
concession OCTROI
copybook CAHIER
customs DOUANE, MOEURS
devil DIABLE
dialect PATOIS
dungeon CACHOT
equal PAREIL
fall of stocks BAISSE
false FAUSSE
fly MOUCHE
friendship AMITIE
furniture MEUBLE
future AVENIR
gift CADEAU
home MAISON
horse CHEVAL
house MAISON
hungry AFFAME
kiss BAISER
know SAVOIR
lamb AGNEAU
language LANGUE
left GAUCHE
Lent CAREME
lingo PATOIS
mouse SOURIS
notebook CARNET
number NOMBRE
open OUVERT
penalty AMENDE
police bureau SURETE
poor PAUVRE
prison CACHOT
red ROUSSE
reparation AMENDE
rise of prices HAUSSE
safety SURETE
season SAISON
security SURETE
sheep MOUTON
shepherd BERGER
ship NAVIRE
soldier SOLDAT
speak PARLER
star ETOILE
stock exchange BOURSE
strawberry FRAISE
sun SOLEIL
superfluous DETROP
thirty TRENTE
thought PENSEE
toll OCTROI
tongue LANGUE
too much DETROP
understand SAVOIR
war GUERRE
watch MONTRE
well-groomed SOIGNE
write ECRIRE

ITALIAN

against CON
age ETA
always MAI
aunt ZIA
below, down GIU
duration ORA
ever MAI
God DIO
goose OCA
grandfather AVO
here QUA, QUI
hour ORA
many, more PIU
never MAI
now ORA
ox BUE
simpleton OCA
south SUD
there IVI
time ORA
uncle ZIO
where OVE
with CON

act ATTO
after DOPO
afternoon SERA
apple MELA, POMO
art ARTE
black NERO
confidence FEDE
dawn ALBA
dear CARA, CARO

deed	ATTO
drink, to	BERE
each	OGNI
east	ESTE
egg	UOVO
end	CODA
evening	SERA
every	OGNI
face	VISO
faith	FEDE
few	POCO
frost	GELO
gift	DONO
hair	PELO
hall	SALA
hand	MANO
hatred	ODIO
head	CAPO
husband	UOMO
ice	GELO
I see	VEDO
Jesus	GESU
lake	LAGO
light	LUME
little	POCO
lo!	ECCO
man	UOMO
matter	COSA
mountain peak	CIMA
night	SERA
north	NORD
nose	NASO
real	VERO
seat	SEDE
ship	NAVE
shore	RIVA
side	LATO
situated	SITO
so	COSI
sour	AGRO
summit	CIMA
swallow	BERE
tail	CODA
talent	DONO
thin	POCO
thing	COSA
thirst	SETE
thus	COSI
today	OGGI
tour	GIRO, GITA
true	VERO
voice	VOCE
wax	CERA
well	BENE
yesterday	IERI

account	CONTO
all	TUTTI, TUTTO
ardor	ESTRO
ass	ASINO
back	TERGO
ball	PALLA
beard	BARBA
bed	LETTO
beer	BIRRA
boiled	LESSO
bride	SPOSA
bridge	PONTE
café	CAFFE
camp	CAMPO
cat	GATTA
cathedral	DUOMO
chair	SEDIA
chest	CASSA
city	CITTA
course	CORSA
dad	BABBO
done	FATTO
donkey	ASINO
door	PORTA
dough	PASTA
dress	ABITO
enough	BASTA
excuse	SCUSA
farewell	ADDIO
father	PADRE
feast	FESTA
field	CAMPO
force	FORZA
fork	FORCA
friend	AMICA, AMICO
gate	PORTA
get	AVERE
good	BUONO
good-bye	ADDIO
harbor	PORTO
have	AVERE
head	TESTA
heaven	CIELO
holiday	FERIA, FESTA
iron	FERRO
isle	ISOLA
kiss	BACIO
lady	DONNA
late	TARDO
law	LEGGE
leg	GAMBA
love	AMORE
love, to	AMARE
many	MOLTO
meal	PASTO
mind	MENTE
monk	FRATE
mother	MADRE
mouth	BOCCA
much	ASSAI, MOLTO
night	NOTTE
not at all	PUNTO
other	ALTRO
paper	CARTA
please	PREGO
power	FORZA
race	CORSA
red	ROSSO
rich	RICCO
said	DETTO
sauce	SALSA
sign	SEGNO
skin	PELLE
sky	CIELO
sleep	SONNO
so much	TANTO
soul, spirit	ANIMA
spouse	SPOSA, SPOSO
stamp	BOLLO
star	ASTRO
straight	RETTO
street	CALLE, CORSO
strength	FORZA
sword	SPADA
tailor	SARTO
thief	LADRO
tower	TORRE
town	CITTA
twisted	TORTO
under	SOTTO
very	MOLTO
water	ACQUA
west	OVEST
without	SENZA
woman	DONNA
women	DONNE
wood	LEGNO
world	MONDO
wrong	TORTO

again	DACAPO
be(ing)	ESSERE
canal	CANALE
custom house	DOGANA
daughter	FIGLIA
day	GIORNO
foreign	ESTERO
forward	AVANTI
from the beginning	DACAPO
gentleman	SIGNOR
hamlet	CASALE
how much	QUANTO
husband	MARITO
key	CHIAVE
large	GROSSO, GRANDE
lover	AMANTE
money	DENARO, MONETA
nothing	NIENTE

now	ADESSO
open	APERTO
poor	POVERO
queen	REGINA
right	DESTRO
road	STRADA
same, self	STESSO
shoe	SCARPA
son	FIGLIO
star	STELLA
table	TAVOLA
thanks	GRAZIE
then	ALLORA
tomorrow	DOMANI
tree	ALBERO
value	VALUTA
village	CASALE
when	QUANDO
white	BIANCO
yet	ANCORA

GERMAN

abbot	ABT
about	BEI
alas	ACH
among	BEI
ancestor	AHN
and	UND
as	ALS
at	BEI
before	VOR
clock	UHR
cow	KUH
dead	TOT
ear	OHR
east	OST
eel	AAL
from	AUS, VON
gate	TOR
how	WIE
ice	EIS
is	IST
narrow	ENG
near	NAH
never	NIE
new	NEU
of	AUF, AUS, VON
on	AUF
out of	AUS
path	WEG
poor	ARM
south	SUD
than	ALS
train	ZUG
upon	AUF
valley	TAL
watch	UHR
way	WEG
with	BEI, MIT

about	ETWA
above	OBEN, UBER
after	NACH
age	ALTE
air	LIED, LUFT
all	ALLE, GANZ
ass	ESEL
band	BUND
bank	UFER
beard	BART
because	WEIL
bed	BETT
beer	BIER
behind	NACH
be(ing)	SEIN
besides	NOCH
blood	BLUT
blue	BLAU
book	BUCH
bread	BROT
bundle	BUND
but	ABER
calm	RUHE
cash	GELD
chicken	HUHN
clever	KLUG
coin	GELD
cold	KALT
count	GRAF
couple	PAAR
deep	TIEF
dirty	FAUL
distant	WEIT
doctor	ARZT
dog	HUND
duck	ENTE
earl	GRAF
early	FRUH
earth	ERDE
elegant	FEIN
every	JEDE
eye	AUGE
far	WEIT
figure	BILD
fine	FEIN
first	EHER
flight	FLUG
for	DENN
foul	FAUL
free	FREI
fruit	OBST
full	VOLL
gentleman	HERR
genuine	ECHT, WAHR
gift	GABE
gladly	GERN
glory	RUHM
God	GOTT
greatly	SEHR
hair	HAAR
hall	AULA, SAAL
heart	HERZ
here	HIER
high	HOCH
home	HEIM
host	WIRT
house	HAUS
humanity	WELT
if	WENN
image	BILD
lady	DAME, FRAU
language	REDE
late	SPAT
lazy	FAUL
league	BUND
leg	BEIN
lord	GOTT, HERR
man	MANN
many	VIEL
mind	SINN
mister	HERR
money	GELD
more	MEHR
much	SEHR, VIEL
murder	MORD
nation	VOLK
nearly	ETWA
neck	HALS
new	NEUE
no	NEIN
nobility	ADEL
noble	EDEL
nobleman	GRAF
north	NORD
old	ALTE
or	ODER
over	UBER
pair	PAAR
peace	RUHE
people	VOLK
perhaps	ETWA
picture	BILD
pure	ECHT
race	VOLK
real	ECHT, WAHR
repose	RUHE
residence	HAUS
rest	RUHE
room	RAUM, SAAL

sea **MEER**
shore **UFER**
sir **HERR**
society **WELT**
son **SOHN**
song **LIED**
space **RAUM**
speech **REDE**
still **DOCH**
tall **HOCH**
than **DENN**
that **JENE**
then **DANN, DENN**
there **DORT**
thief **DIEB**
thing **DING**
top **OBEN**
tower **TURM**
tree **BAUM**
triumph **SIEG**
true **WAHR**
tune **LIED**
upper **OBER**
very **SEHR**
victory **SIEG**
village **DORF**
visitor **GAST**
viva! (salute) **HOCH**
well **WOHL**
west **WEST**
when **WENN**
wide **WEIT**
wife **FRAU, WEIB**
willingly **GERN**
without **OHNE**
woman **DAME, FRAU, WEIB**
world **WELT**
yet **DOCH, NOCH**
yonder **DORT**

across **DURCH**
affection **LIEBE**
alley **GASSE**
always **IMMER**
apple **APFEL**
aunt **TANTE**
below, beneath **UNTER, UNTEN**
beside **NEBEN**
both **BEIDE**
bride **BRAUT**
broom **BESEN**
carriage **WAGEN**
chair **STUHL**
cheers! **PROST**
city **STADT**
cost **PREIS**
cross **KREUZ**
dare, to **WAGEN**
different **ANDER**
east **OSTEN**
eat **ESSEN**
else **ANDER**
empire **REICH**
evening **ABEND**
everything **ALLES**
father **VATER**
fear **ANGST**
few **WENIG**
fork **GABEL**
game **SPIEL**
give **GEBEN**
go **GEHEN**
harbor **HAFEN**
have **HABEN**
haven **HAFEN**
hence **DAHER**
hunter **JAGER**
husband **GATTE**
iron **EISEN**
island **INSEL**
ladies **DAMEN**
lane **GASSE**
leather **LEDER**
letter **BRIEF**
lightning **BLITZ**
little **KLEIN, WENIG**
love **LIEBE**
mind **GEIST**
move **GEHEN**
new **NEUER, NEUES**
night **NACHT**
not **NICHT**
once **EINST**
orient **OSTEN**
path **GASSE**
play **SPIEL**
people **LEUTE**
persons **LEUTE**
play **SPIEL**
please **BITTE**
price **PREIS**
rain **REGEN**
read **LESEN**
request **BITTE**
rich **REICH**
small **KLEIN**
soul **GEIST, SEELE**
south **SUDEN**
spirit **GEIST**
spouse **GATTE**
state **STAAT**
steel **STAHL**
street **GASSE**
strife **KRIEG**
sun **SONNE**
table **TAFEL, TISCH**
thanks **DANKE**
thirst **DURST**
through **DURCH**
today **HEUTE**
town **STADT**
uncle **ONKEL**
walk **GEHEN**
war **KRIEG**
why **WARUM**

again **WIEDER**
bell **GLOCKE**
brother **BRUDER**
cheap **BILLIG**
cheers! **PROSIT**
gentlemen **HERREN**
heaven **HIMMEL**
knife **MESSER**
know(ledge) **WISSEN**
labor **ARBEIT**
ladies **FRAUEN**
morning **MORGEN**
mother **MUTTER**
noon **MITTAG**
north **NORDEN**
once **EINMAL**
plate **TELLER**
school **SCHULE**
self **SELBST**
sky **HIMMEL**
snow **SCHNEE**
soldier **SOLDAT**
spoon **LOFFEL**
toil **ARBEIT**
tomorrow **MORGEN**
west **WESTEN**
wife **GATTIN**
work **ARBEIT**

LATIN

alas **HEU, VAE**
altar **ARA**
anger **IRA**
art **ARS**
as **QUA**
bronze **AES**
but **SED**
citadel **ARX**
copper **AES**
custom **MOS**
divine law **FAS**
edge **ORA**

either	**AUT**
foot	**PES**
force	**VIS**
fortress	**ARX**
goddess	**DEA**
gods	**DEI**
heart	**COR**
husband	**VIR**
I love	**AMO**
is	**EST**
king	**REX**
law	**JUS, LEX**
lawful	**FAS**
leader	**DUX**
man	**VIR**
milk	**LAC**
not	**NON**
or	**AUT**
peace	**PAX**
pledge	**VAS**
power	**VIS**
pray	**ORA**
pyre	**ARA**
shore	**ORA**
strength	**VIS**
there	**IBI**
thing	**RES**
three times	**TER**
trade	**ARS**
twice	**BIS**
vessel	**VAS**
where	**UBI**
will	**MOS**
with	**CUM**
wrath	**IRA**

after	**POST**
alas	**EHEU**
all	**TOTO**
at the same place	**IBID**
before	**ANTE**
behold!	**ECCE**
be(ing)	**ESSE**
beware	**CAVE**
bird	**AVIS**
birds	**AVES**
boy	**PUER**
bridge	**PONS**
child	**PUER**
city	**URBS**
culprit	**REUS**
day	**DIEM**
day(s)	**DIES**
defendant	**REUS**
dinner	**CENA**
egg	**OVUM**
except	**NISI**
field	**AGER**
fields	**AGRI**

go away!	**VADE**
grandfather	**AVUS**
he loves	**AMAT**
high	**ALTA**
hope	**SPES**
hour	**HORA**
hush!	**TACE**
I have spoken	**DIXI**
in all	**TOTO**
in the year	**ANNO**
knee	**GENU**
lambs	**AGNI**
life	**VITA**
lo!	**ECCE**
lot	**SORS**
mind	**MENS**
mountain	**MONS**
needle	**ACUS**
nobody	**NEMO**
note	**NOTA**
now	**NUNC**
observe!	**NOTA**
other	**ALIA**
others	**ALII**
palm: hand	**VOLA**
part	**PARS**
pin	**ACUS**
praise	**LAUS**
property	**BONA**
prophecy	**SORS**
proportion	**RATA**
road	**ITER**
same	**IDEM**
sea	**MARE**
see!	**VIDE**
share	**RATA**
soon	**CITO**
supper	**CENA**
thing done	**ACTU**
unless	**NISI**
was	**ERAT**
water	**AQUA**
well	**BENE**
wife	**UXOR**
without	**SINE**
wool	**LANA**
you love	**AMAS**

abbot	**ABBAS**
about	**CIRCA**
above	**SUPER**
abundance	**COPIA**
across	**TRANS**
air	**ANIMA**
all	**TOTUM**
all	**OMNIA, OMNIS**
alone	**SOLUS**
another thing	**ALIUD**
as far as	**QUOAD**

backward	**RETRO**
bad	**MALUS**
battle line	**ACIES**
before	**ANTEA**
behind	**RETRO**
blessed	**BEATA**
book	**LIBER**
broad	**LATUS**
brow	**FRONS**
cattle	**PECUS**
confidence	**FIDES**
cup	**CALIX**
daughter	**FILIA**
deceit	**DOLUS**
divine	**DIVUS**
door	**JANUA, PORTA**
earth	**TERRA**
ease	**OTIUM**
edge	**ACTES**
error	**CULPA**
evil	**MALUM**
faith	**FIDES**
fault	**CULPA**
fire	**IGNIS**
flock	**PECUS**
fodder, food	**CIBUS**
forehead	**FRONS**
form	**MODUS**
fraud	**DOLUS**
friend	**AMICA**
gate	**PORTA**
gentle	**LENIS**
goblet	**CALIX**
gold	**AURUM**
good	**BONUM**
ground	**TERRA**
happy	**BEATA**
healthy	**SANUS**
helmet	**GALEA**
herd	**PECUS**
keenness	**ACIES**
kings	**REGES**
lamb	**AGNUS**
land	**TERRA**
leisure	**OTIUM**
mass, the	**MISSA**
method	**MODUS**
more	**SUPER**
name	**NOMEN**
near by	**JUXTA**
negligence	**CULPA**
nothing	**NIHIL**
only	**SOLUS**
other	**ALIUS**
over	**SUPER, TRANS**
pardon	**VENIA**
place	**LOCUS**
plenty	**COPIA**
remains, it	**MANET**

resist!	OBSTA
rite	RITUS
sick	AEGER
side	LATUS
sinful	NEFAS
smooth	LENIS
soft	LENIS
soul	ANIMA
sound	SANUS
sour	VINUM
stars	ASTRA
supper	COENA
tail	CAUDA
that is	IDEST
thing done	ACTUS
trust	FIDES
unlawful	NEFAS
upon	SUPER
usage	RITUS
why	QUARE
wicked	MALUS
wide	LATUS
wind	ANIMA
wine	VINUM
within	INTRA
year	ANNUS

again	ITERUM
always	SEMPER
around	CIRCUM
authority	REGNUM
blessed	BEATUS
buying	EMPTIO
error	LAPSUS
fatherland	PATRIA
first	PRIMUM, PRIMUS
fish	PISCIS
fishes	PISCES
friend	AMICUS
gliding	LAPSUS
great	MAGNUS
Greece	ACHAIA
happy	BEATUS
iron	FERRUM
kingdom	REGNUM
learned	DOCTUS
lots	SORTES
otherwise	ALITER
partly	PARTIM
queen	REGINA
right	DEXTER
servant, slave	SERVUS
sliding	LAPSUS
son	FILIUS
summer	AESTAS
theft	FURTUM
therefore	IGITUR
tyranny	REGNUM
war	BELLUM
well-informed	DOCTUS
woman	FEMINA

ARTICLES, PRONOUNS, POSSESSIVES, AND NUMERALS IN FIVE LANGUAGES

ARTICLES

Spanish	*French*	*Italian*	*German*	
EL	AU	I	DAS	EINEN
LA	DU	IL	DEM	EINER
LO	LA	LA	DEN	EINES
UN	LE	LE	DER	
LAS	UN	LO	DES	
LOS	AUX	UN	DIE	
UNA	DES	GLI	EIN	
UNAS	LES	UNA	EINE	
UNOS	UNE	UNO	EINEM	

PRONOUNS AND POSSESSIVES

Spanish

EL	TE	MIA*	VOS
LA	TI	MIO*	ALGO
LE	TU*	MIS*	CADA
LO	YO	NOS	CUAL
ME	ESA	QUE	CUYA
MI*	ESE	SUS*	CUYO
OS	ESO	TAL	ELLA
SE	LAS	TUS*	ELLO
SI	LES	UNA	ESAS
SU*	LOS	UNO	ESOS

*Indicates possessive pronouns or adjectives

ESTA
ESTE
ESTO
MIAS*
MIOS*
NADA
SUYA*
SUYO*
TUYA*
TUYO*
UNAS
UNOS
ALGUN
AQUEL
CUYAS
CUYOS
ELLAS
ELLOS
ESTAS
ESTOS
NADIE
USTED
QUIEN
SUYAS*
SUYOS*
TALES
TUYAS*
TUYOS*
ALGUNA
ALGUNO
CUALES
NINGUN
ALGUIEN
ALGUNAS
ALGUNOS
AQUELLA
AQUELLO
NINGUNA
NINGUNO
NUESTRA*
NUESTRO*
QUIENES
USTEDES
VUESTRA*
VUESTRO*

French

Y
CA
CE
EN
IL
JE
LA
LE
MA*
ME
ON
OU
SA*
SE
TA*
TE
TU
CES
CET
EUX
ILS
LES
LUI
MES*
MOI
MON*
NOS*
NUL
QUE
QUI
SES*
SOI
SON*
TEL
TES*
TOI
TON*
VOS*
CECI
CELA
CEUX
DONT
ELLE
LEUR*
MIEN*
NOUS
QUEL
QUOI
RIEN
SIEN*
TELS
TIEN*
VOUS
AUCUN
CELLE
CELUI
CETTE
ELLES
LEURS*
MIENS*
NOTRE*
NULLE
QUELS
SIENS*
TELLE
TIENS*
VOTRE*
AUCUNE
AUTRUI
CELLES
CHACUN
LEQUEL
MIENNE*
NOTRES*
QUELLE
SIENNE*
TELLES
TIENNE*
VOTRES*
CHACUNE
MIENNES*
QUELLES
SIENNES*
TIENNES*

Italian

CI
IO
LA
LE
LI
LO
ME
MI
NE
SE
SI
TE
TI
TU
VI
CHE
CHI
CIO
CUI
GLI
LEI
LUI
MIA*
MIE*
MIO*
NOI
SUA*
SUE*
SUO*
TAL
TUA*
TUE*
TUO*
VOI
EGLI
ELLA
ESSA
ESSE
ESSI
ESSO
LORO*
MIEI*
QUAL
QUEL
SUOI*
TALE
TALI
TUOI*
COLEI
COLUI
NIUNO
NULLA
QUALE
QUALI
ALCUNA
ALCUNE
ALCUNI
ALCUNO
ALTRUI
COLORO
COSTEI
COSTUI
NIENTE
NOSTRA*
NOSTRE*
NOSTRI*
NOSTRO*
OGNUNA
OGNUNO
QUEGLI
QUELLA
QUELLE
QUELLI
QUELLO
QUESTA
QUESTE

QUESTI
QUESTO
VOSTRA*
VOSTRE*
VOSTRI*
VOSTRO*
COSTORO
NESSUNA
NESSUNO
QUALCHE

German

DU
ER
ES
DAS
DEM
DEN
DER
DIE
ICH
IHM
IHN
IHR*
MAN
MIR
SIE
UNS
WAS
WEM
WEN
WER
WES
WIR
DEIN*
DICH
DIES
EUCH
EUER*
EURE*
IHRE*
JEDE
JENE
KEIN
MICH
MEIN*
SEIN*
SICH
DEINE*
DENEN
DEREN
DERER
DIESE
ETWAS
EUERE*
EUREM*
EUREN*
EURER*
EURES*
IHNEN
IHREM*
IHREN*
IHRER*
IHRES*
JEDEM
JEDEN
JEDER
JEDES
JENEM
JENEN
JENER
JENES
KEINE
MEINE*
SEINE*
UNSER*
DEINEM*
DEINEN*
DEINER*
DEINES*
DESSEN
DIESEM
DIESEN
DIESER
DIESES
EUEREM*
EUEREN*
EUERER*
EUERES*
JEMAND
KEINEM
KEINEN
KEINER
KEINES
MEINEM*
MEINEN*
MEINER*
MEINES*
NICHTS
SEINEM*
SEINEN*
SEINER*
SEINES*
UNSERE*
WELCHE
WESSEN
JEMANDS
NIEMAND
UNSEREM*
UNSEREN*
UNSERER*
UNSERES*
WELCHEM
WELCHEN
WELCHER
WELCHES

Latin

EA
EI
EO
HI
ID
IS
ME
SE
TE
TU
CUI
EAE
EAM
EAS
EGO
EIS
EOS
EUM
HAC
HAE
HAS
HIC
HIS
HOC
HOS
MEA*
MEI*
MEO*
NOS
QUA
QUI
QUO
SUA*
SUI*
SUO*
TOS*
TUA*
TUI*
TUO*
VOS
EIUS
HAEC
HANC
HUIC
HUNC
IDEM
ILLA
ILLE
ILLI
ILLO
IPSA
IPSE
IPSI
IPSO
ISTA
ISTE
ISTI
ISTO
MEAE*
MEAM*
MEAS*
MEIS*
MEOS*
MEUM*
MEUS*
MIHI
QUAE
QUAM
QUAS
QUEM
QUID
QUIS
QUOD
QUOS
SIBI
SUAE*
SUAM*
SUAS*
SUIS*
SUOS*
SUUM*
SUUS*
TIBI
TUAE*
TUAM*
TUAS*
TUIS*
TUUM*
TUUS*
CUIUS
EADEM
EARUM
EIDEM
EODEM
EORUM
HARUM

HORUM
HUIUS
ILLAE
ILLAM
ILLAS
ILLIS
ILLOS
ILLUD
ILLUM
IPSAE
IPSAM
IPSAS
IPSIS
IPSOS
IPSUM
ISTAE
ISTAM
ISTAS
ISTIS
ISTOS
ISTUD
ISTUM
NOBIS
VOBIS
ALICUI
ALIQUA
ALIQUI
ALIQUO
CUIDAM
CUIQUE
EAEDEM
EANDEM
EASDEM
EISDEM
EOSDEM
EUNDEM
ILLIUS
IPSIUS
ISTIUS
MEARUM*
MEORUM*
NOSTER*
NOSTRA*
NOSTRI*
NOSTRO*
QUADAM
QUARUM
QUIBUS
QUIDAM
QUIQUE
QUOQUE
QUOQUO
QUORUM
SUARUM*
SUORUM*
TUARUM*
TUORUM*
VESTER*
VESTRA*
VESTRI*
VESTRO*
ALIQUAE
ALIQUAM
ALIQUAS
ALIQUEM
ALIQUID
ALIQUIS
ALIQUOD
ALIQUOS
CUIQUAM
EIUSDEM
ILLARUM
ILLORUM
IPSARUM
IPSORUM
ISTARUM
ISTORUM
NOSTRAE*
NOSTRAM*
NOSTRAS*
NOSTRIS*
NOSTROS*
NOSTRUM*
QUAEDAM
QUAEQUE
QUANDAM
QUASDAM
QUASQUE
QUEMQUE
QUENDAM
QUIDDAM
QUIDQUE
QUISQUE
QUOQUAM
QUOSDAM
QUOSQUE
VESTRAE*
VESTRAM*
VESTRAS*
VESTRIS*
VESTROS*
VESTRUM*

NUMERALS

	Spanish	*French*	*Italian*	*German*	*Latin*
1	UNO	UN	UNO	EINS	UNUS
2	DOS	DEUX	DUE	ZWEI	DUO
3	TRES	TROIS	TRE	DREI	TRES
4	CUATRO	QUATRE	QUATTRO	VIER	QUATTUOR
5	CINCO	CINQ	CINQUE	FUNF	QUINQUE
6	SEIS	SIX	SEI	SECHS	SEX
7	SIETE	SEPT	SETTE	SIEBEN	SEPTEM
8	OCHO	HUIT	OTTO	ACHT	OCTO
9	NUEVE	NEUF	NOVE	NEUN	NOVEM
10	DIEZ	DIX	DIECI	ZEHN	DECEM
11	ONCE	ONZE	UNDICI	ELF	UNDECIM
12	DOZE	DOUZE	DODICI	ZWOLF	DUODECIM
20	VEINTE	VINGT	VENTI	ZWANZIG	VIGINTI
30	TREINTA	TRENTE	TRENTA	DREISSIG	TRIGINTA
40	CUA- RENTA	QUARANTE	QUARANTA	VIERZIG	QUADRA- GINTA
50	CIN- CUENTA	CINQUANTE	CINQUANTA	FUNFZIG	QUINQUA- GINTA
60	SESENTA	SOIXANTE	SESSANTA	SECHZIG	SEXAGINTA
70	SETENTA	SOIXANTE- DIX	SETTANTA	SIEBZIG	SEPTUA- GINTA
80	OCHENTA	QUATRE- VINGT	OTTANTA	ACHTZIG	OCTOGINTA
90	NOVENTA	QUATRE- VINGTDIX	NOVANTA	NEUNZIG	NONAGINTA
100	CIENTO	CENT	CENTO	HUNDERT	CENTUM
1000	MIL	MILLE	MILLE	TAUSEND	MILLE

GEOGRAPHY

COUNTRIES AND CAPITALS

CAR	Bangui
UAE	Abu Dhabi
UAR	=EGYPT

CHAD	Ndjamena
CUBA	Havana
FIJI	Suva
IRAK	=IRAQ
IRAN	Teh(e)ran
IRAQ	Baghdad
LAOS	Vientiane
MALI	Bamako
OMAN	Muscat
PERU	Lima
SIAM	=THAILAND
TOGO	Lome
USSR	Moscow

BENIN	Porto-Novo
BURMA	Rangoon
CHILE	Santiago
CHINA	Peking (Beijing)
CHINA	Taipei
CONGO	Brazzaville
EGYPT	Cairo
GABON	Libreville
GHANA	Accra
HAITI	Port-au-Prince
INDIA	New Delhi
ITALY	Rome
JAPAN	Tokyo
KENYA	Nairobi
KOREA	Seoul
KOREA	Pyongyang
LIBYA	Tripoli
MALTA	Valletta
NAURU	Yaren
NEPAL	Kathmandu
NIGER	Niamey
PAPUA	Port Moresby
QATAR	Doha
SPAIN	Madrid
SUDAN	Khartoum
SYRIA	Damascus
TONGA	Nuku'alofa
WALES	Cardiff
YEMEN	Aden
YEMEN	Sana
ZAIRE	Kinshasa

ANGOLA	Luanda
BELIZE	Belmopan
BHUTAN	Tashi-chho (Thimphu)
BRAZIL	Brasilia
BRUNEI	Bandar Seri Begawan
CANADA	Ottawa
CEYLON	=SRI LANKA
CYPRUS	Nicosia
FRANCE	Paris
GAMBIA	Banjul
GREECE	Athens
GUINEA	Conakry
GUINEA	Malabo
GUYANA	Georgetown
ISRAEL	Jerusalem
JORDAN	Amman
KUWAIT	Kuwait (City)
MALAWI	Lilongwe
MEXICO	Mexico City
MONACO	Monaco
NORWAY	Oslo
PANAMA	Panama (City)
POLAND	Warsaw
RWANDA	Kigali
SWEDEN	Stockholm
TOBAGO	Port of Spain
TURKEY	Ankara
TUVALU	Funafuti
UGANDA	Kampala
ZAMBIA	Lusaka

ALBANIA	Tirana
ALGERIA	Algiers
ANDORRA	Andorra la Vella
ANTIGUA	St. John's
AUSTRIA	Vienna
BAHAMAS	Nassau
BAHRAIN	Manama
BARBUDA	St. John's
BELGIUM	Brussels
BOLIVIA	La Paz, Sucre
BRITAIN	London
BURUNDI	Bujumbura
COMOROS	Moroni
DAHOMEY	=BENIN
DENMARK	Copenhagen
ECUADOR	Quito
ENGLAND	London
FINLAND	Helsinki
GERMANY	Bonn
GERMANY	East Berlin
GRENADA	St. George's
HOLLAND	=NETHERLANDS
HUNGARY	Budapest
ICELAND	Reykjavik
IRELAND	Dublin

JAMAICA	Kingston
LEBANON	Beirut
LESOTHO	Maseru
LIBERIA	Monrovia
MALDIVE (ISLANDS)	Male
MOROCCO	Rabat
NIGERIA	Lagos
ROMANIA	Bucharest
SAOTOME	Sao Tome
SENEGAL	Dakar
SOLOMON (ISLANDS)	Honiara
SOMALIA	Mogadishu
STKITTS	**=STCHRISTOPHER**
TRUCIAL (STATES)	**=UAE**
TUNISIA	Tunis
URUGAY	Montevideo
VANUATU	Vila
VATICAN	Vatican City
VIETNAM	Hanoi

BARBADOS	Bridgetown
BOTSWANA	Gaborone
BULGARIA	Sofia
CAMBODIA	Phnom Penh
CAMEROON	Yaounde
COLOMBIA	Bogota
DJIBOUTI	Djibouti
DOMINICA	Roseau
ETHIOPIA	Addis Ababa
HONDURAS	Tegucigalpa
KIRIBATI	Tarawa
MALAGASY	**=MADAGASCAR**
MALAYSIA	Kuala Lumpur
MONGOLIA	Ulan Bator (Ulaan Baatar)
PAKISTAN	Islamabad
PARAGUAY	Asunción
PORTUGAL	Lisbon
RHODESIA	**=ZIMBABWE**
SCOTLAND	Edinburgh
SRILANKA	Colombo
TANZANIA	Dar-es-Salaam
THAILAND	Bangkok
TRINIDAD	Port-of-Spain
ZIMBABWE	Harare

ARGENTINA	Buenos Aires
AUSTRALIA	Canberra
CAPEVERDE	Prala
COSTARICA	San Jose
DOMINICAN (REPUBLIC)	Santo Domingo

GREENLAND	**=KALAALLITNUNAAT**
GUATEMALA	Guatemala City
INDONESIA	(D)jakarta
KAMPUCHEA	**=CAMBODIA**
MAURITIUS	Port Louis
NICARAGUA	Managua
SANMARINO	San Marino
SINGAPORE	Singapore
SWAZILAND	Mbabane
VENEZUELA	Caracas

BANGLADESH	Dacca
ELSALVADOR	San Salvador
IVORYCOAST	Abidjan
LUXEMBOURG	Luxembourg
MADAGASCAR	Antananarivo
MAURITANIA	Nouakchott
MOZAMBIQUE	Maputo
NEWZEALAND	Wellington
SEYCHELLES	Victoria
SAINTLUCIA	Castries
TANGANYIKA	**=TANZANIA**
UPPERVOLTA	Ouagadougou
YUGOSLAVIA	Belgrade

AFGHANISTAN	Kabul
NETHERLANDS	Amsterdam, The Hague
PHILIPPINES	Manila, Quezon City
SAUDIARABIA	Riad (Riyadh)
SIERRALEONE	Freetown
SOUTHAFRICA	Capetown, Pretoria, Bloemfontein
SWITZERLAND	Bern(e)

GREATBRITAIN	London
GUINEABISSAU	Bissau
SAINTVINCENT	Kingstown
UNITEDSTATES	Washington
WESTERNSAMOA	Apia
LIECHTENSTEIN	Vaduz
STCHRISTOPHER	Basseterre
UNITEDKINGDOM	London

CZECHOSLOVAKIA	Prague (Praha)
KALAALLITNUNAAT	Nuuk (Gothab)
NORTHERNIRELAND	Belfast

UNION OF SOVIET SOCIALIST REPUBLICS

UZBEK S.S.R.	Tashkent	ESTONIAN S.S.R.	Tallinn
KAZAKH S.S.R	Alma-Ata	GEORGIAN S.S.R.	Tbilisi (Tiflis)
KIRGHIZ S.S.R.	Frunze	MOLDAVIAN S.S.R.	Kishinev
LATVIAN S.S.R.	Riga	UKRAINIAN S.S.R.	Kiev
RUSSIAN S.F.S.R.	Moscow	AZERBAIJAN S.S.R.	Baku
TADZHIK S.S.R.	Dushanbe	LITHUANIAN S.S.R.	Vilnius (Vilna)
TURKMEN S.S.R.	Ashkhabad	BYELORUSSIAN S.S.R.	Minsk
ARMENIAN S.S.R.	Erevan		

OTHER COUNTRIES OF EUROPE, ANCIENT AND MODERN

FORMER INDEPENDENT COUNTRIES OF MEDIEVAL AND MODERN TIMES

LEON	PSKOV	MODENA	SERBIA
BADEN	SAVOY	NAPLES	SICILY
GENOA	ARAGON	NASSAU	VENICE
HESSE	BOSNIA	RUSSIA	ARMENIA
PARMA	LATVIA	SAXONY	BATAVIA
BAVARIA	NAVARRE	LOMBARDY	OLDENBERG
BOHEMIA	PRUSSIA	MOLDAVIA	POMERANIA
CASTILE	SILESIA	PIEDMONT	SCHLESWIG
ESTONIA	TUSCANY	RUTHENIA	WALLACHIA
GALICIA	UKRAINE	SLAVONIA	BESSARABIA
GEORGIA	VENETIA	SLOVENIA	MONTENEGRO
GRANADA	ANATOLIA	CIRCASSIA	WESTPHALIA
HANOVER	ESTHONIA	DARMSTADT	BYELORUSSIA
LIVONIA	HANNOVER	KURDISTAN	MESOPOTAMIA
MORAVIA	HOLSTEIN	LITHUANIA	MECKLENBERG

ANCIENT COUNTRIES OF BRITISH ISLES

KENT	MERCIA	DANELAW	PICTLAND
ESSEX	SCOTIA	IRELAND	EASTANGLIA
WALES	SUSSEX	DALRIADA	NORTHUMBRIA
ANGLIA	WESSEX	HIBERNIA	

COUNTRIES, REGIONS, AND CITIES OF ANCIENT ROMAN TIMES

GAUL	ALBANIA	PICENUM	HELVETIA
DACIA	BAETICA	POMPEII	HIBERNIA
GADES	BELGICA	SALONAE	MASSILIA
HIPPO	BRITAIN	SAMNIUM	PANNONIA
NARBO	CORDUBA	SCANDIA	SARDINIA
UTICA	CORSICA	TOLETUM	SARGOSSA
APULIA	ETRURIA	VENETIA	SARMATIA
ARABIA	GALICIA	BRUTTIUM	AQUITANIA
GALLIA	GERMANY	CAESAREA	BRITANNIA
IBERIA	LIGURIA	CALABRIA	CALEDONIA
ISTRIA	LUCANIA	CAMPANIA	ILLYRICUM
LATIUM	LUTETIA	CARTHAGE	LONDINIUM
MOESIA	MESSANA	DALMATIA	LUSITANIA
RAETIA	NORICUM	EBORACUM	PALESTINE
SICILY	NUMIDIA	GERMANIA	MAURETANIA
UMBRIA	ODESSUS		

ANCIENT GREEK AND EASTERN STATES AND CITIES

COS
IOS
ACTE
ARIA
CEOS
CIUS
CYME
DIAM
DURA
ELAM
ELIS
ELON
GAZA
ICUS
LATO
PISA
SIND
SOLI
SUSA
TEOS
TYRE
AEGAE
AENIS
AENUS
ARGOS
ASINE
BARCA
CARIA
CHIOS
DELOS
DORIS
GOLGI
ILIUM
IONIA
IPSUS
ISSUS
LAMIA
LEROS
LIBYA
LYDIA
MALIS
MEDIA
MELOS
MYSIA
NAXOS
NEMEA
PAROS
PELLA
PYDNA
PYLOS
RAGAE
SAMOS
SIDON
SYENE
SYRIA
TEGEA
TELOS
TEMPE
TENOS
THERA
TROAS
TYANA
ZIDON
ABDERA
ABYDUS
ACHAEA
AMASIA
ANAPHE
ANCORE
ANCYRA
ANDROS
APAMEA
ARBELA
ATHENS
ATTICA
CARDIA
CAUNUS
CITIUM
CNIDUS
CORONE
CUNAXA
CURIUM
CYRENE
DELPHI
DODONA
EPIRUS
EUBOEA
HYDREA
ICARIA
IMBROS
ITHACA
LEMNOS
LESBOS
LEUCAS
LINDUS
LISSUS
LOCRIS
MEGARA
MYLASA
MYRINE
PAPHOS
PARIUM
PATALA
PATRAE
PERSIA
PHASIS
PHERAE
PONTUS
PRIENE
RHODES
SAGALA
SARDES
SCIONE
SCYROS
SESTUS
SICYON
SINOPE
SKUDRA
SMYRNA
SPARTA
TARSUS
TAXILA
THASOS
THEBES
THRACE
TIRYNS
TYRONE
ZEUGMA
AETOLIA
AMATHUS
AMORGOS
AMYCLAE
ANTIOCH
ARCADIA
ARGOLIS
ARMENIA
ARSINOE
ASSYRIA
BABYLON
BACTRIA
BISITUN
BOEOTIA
CALYDON
CAMIRUS
CERYNIA
CHALCIS
CILICIA
CIMILOS
CLEONAE
CNOSSUS
CORCYRA
CORINTH
CYDONIA
CYNURIA
CYTHERA
DECELEA
ELEUSIS
EPHESUS
ERETRIA
GANDARA
GORDIUM
GORTYNA
IALYSUS
IDALIUM
LACONIA
LARISSA
LEUCTRA
MACEDON
MARONEA
MEMPHIS
MESSENE
METHONE
MILETUS
MYCENAE
MYCONOS
NISIBIS
NISYROS
OLYMPIA
PAEONIA
PAGASAE
PALLENE
PALMYRA
PARTHIA
PHOCAEA
PHRYGIA
PIRAEUS
PISIDIA
PRAESUS
SALAMIS
SAMARIA
SCYTHIA
SIPHNOS
STAGIRA
SUSIANA
TANAGRA
TENEDOS
THERMUM
TRALLAS
TROEZEN
XANTHUS
ACANTHUS
AMBRACIA
AMPHISSA
BERENICE
BITHYNIA
CALYMNOS
CARMANIA
CARPASIA
COLOPHON
DAMASCUS
ECBATANA
ERYTHRAE
GANDHARA
GEDROSIA
HYRCANIA
LAPETHUS
MAGNESIA
MARATHON
MARGIANA
MESSENIA
MYTILENE
OLYNTHUS
PELUSIUM
PERGAMUM

PHASELIS
PHILIPPI
PRIANSUS
SELENCIA
SERIPHOS
SITHONIA
SOGDIANA
TAMASSUS
THESSALY
TRAPEZUM
ZARIASPA
ACARNANIA
ARACHOSIA
BABYLONIA
BUCEPHALA
CALCHEDON
CARPATHOS
CHAERONEA
CHORASMIA
CTESIPHON
DASCYLIUM
DOLOPIANS
DRANGIANA
EPIDAURUS
JERUSALEM
MARACANDA
MESAMBRIA
NAUCRATIS
NICOMEDIA
PHARSALUS
PHOENICIA
PTOLOMAIS
THAPSACUS
ALEXANDRIA
CAPPADOCIA
CHALCIDICE
PERSEPOLIS
SAMOTHRACE
THERMOPYLAE

DEPARTMENTS, COMMUNES, PROVINCES, STATES, DISTRICTS, REGIONS, COUNTIES, CANTONS, COLONIES, POSSESSIONS

AIN	France
AKI	Japan
ANS	Belgium
AYR	Scotland
EDE	Netherlands
ELY	England
EPE	Netherlands
GOA	India
MOL	Belgium
PAU	France
RIF	Morocco
URI	Switzerland
VAR	France
ZUG	Switzerland
BAGO	Philippines
BAIA	Brazil
BIEL	Switzerland
BIRR	Ireland
BOGO	Philippines
BUTE	Scotland
CHUR	Switzerland
COMO	Italy
DOAB	India
ELIS	Greece
ENNA	Italy
ESTE	Italy
EURE	France
FANO	Italy
FARS	Iran
FIFE	Scotland
GAZA	Israel
GEEL	Belgium
GHOR	Afghanistan
HAUD	Ethiopia
ISSY	France
JAEN	Spain
JIND	India
KAFA	Ethiopia
KENT	England
LAON	France
LARA	Venezuela
LEON	Spain
LUGO	Italy, Spain
MAYO	Ireland
MONS	Belgium
NAGA	Philippines
NEJD	Saudi Arabia
OUDH	India
PARA	Brazil
PEGU	Burma
RAND	South Africa
REWA	India
RIFF	Morocco
RUHR	Germany
SAAR	France
SIND	India
SULU	Philippines
SWAT	Pakistan
VAUD	Switzerland
VICH	Spain
VIMY	France
AALST	Belgium
AARAU	Switzerland
ACQUI	Italy
ADIRA	Italy
AGRIA	Italy
AKYAB	Burma
ALAVA	Spain
ALBAY	Philippines
ALGAU	Germany
ALORA	Spain
ALOST	Belgium
ALWAR	India
ALWUR	India
AMAPA	Brazil
AMARA	Iran
ANGRI	Italy
ANGUL	India

ANGUS	Scotland
ANJOU	France
ANNAM	Vietnam
AONIA	Greece
ARGAO	Philippines
ARLON	Belgium
ASOLO	Italy
ASSAM	India
ASSEN	Netherlands
ASWAN	Egypt
AUBIN	France
AUTUN	France
AVILA	Spain
BADEN	Germany
BAENA	Spain
BAHIA	Brazil
BAMRA	India
BALKH	Afghanistan
BANAT	Yugoslavia
BANAT	Romania
BANFF	Canada
BEHAR	India
BENIN	Nigeria
BERAR	India
BERKS	England
BIHAR	India
BLYTH	England
BORNU	Nigeria
BOURG	France
BRAGA	Portugal
BREDA	Netherlands
BUCKS	England
CAPIZ	Philippines
CAPRI	Italy
CAVAN	Ireland
CEARA	Brazil
CHACO	South America
CHIAI	China
CLARE	Ireland
COORG	India
CUNEO	Italy
DELFT	Netherlands
DERBY	England
DEVON	England
DORIS	Greece
ESSEX	England
EUPEN	Belgium
EUTIN	Germany
EVERE	Belgium
EVORA	Portugal
FORLI	Italy
GALLA	Ethiopia
GANDO	Nigeria
GOIAS	Brazil
GOUDA	Netherlands
HANTS	England
HEJAZ	Saudi Arabia
HERAT	Afghanistan
HESSE	Germany
HONAN	China
HOPEH	China
HOPEI	China
HUNAN	China
HUNZA	India
HUPEH	China
IMOLA	Italy
IONIA	Greece
JEHOL	China
JHIND	India
KAFFA	Ethiopia
KALAT	Pakistan
KANSU	China
KEDAH	Malaysia
KERRY	Ireland
KIRIN	China
KUTCH	India
LECCE	Italy
LIPPE	Germany
LOUTH	Ireland
LUCCA	Italy
LUXOR	Egypt
MASSA	Italy
MEATH	Ireland
MEDOC	France
MONZA	Italy
NAIRN	Scotland
NATAL	South Africa
NEGEB	Israel
NEGEV	Israel
NUBIA	Sudan
PAVIA	Italy
PERAK	Malaysia
PIAUI	Brazil
POOLE	England
SAVOY	France
SIENA	Italy
SINDH	India
SLIGO	Ireland
SORIA	Spain
TERNI	Italy
TIGRE	Ethiopia
TIROL	Austria
TYROL	Austria
UDINE	Italy
WALES	United Kingdom
WILTS	England

AARGAU	Switzerland
ACADIA	Canada
ACHAEA	Greece
ALCAMO	Italy
ALCIRA	Spain
ALIAGA	Philippines
ALLGAU	Germany
ALMELO	Netherlands
ALPHEN	Netherlands
ALSACE	France
AMHARA	Ethiopia

ANCASH	Peru
ANDRIA	Italy
ANGELN	Germany
ANGOLA	Portugal
ANHALT	Germany
ANTRIM	Ireland
AOMORI	Japan
APULIA	Italy
ARAGON	Spain
ARAKAN	Burma
ARAUCO	Chile
ARCADY	Greece
AREZZO	Italy
ARMAGH	Ireland
ASHTON	England
ASSISI	Italy
ATHOLE	Scotland
ATTICA	Greece
BAYBAY	Philippines
BENGAL	India
BOSNIA	Yugoslavia
BRUGGE	Belgium
CARCAR	Philippines
CHAHAR	China
CHIHLI	China
COCHIN	India
CORATO	Italy
DORSET	England
EMILIA	Italy
EMPOLI	Italy
FUKIEN	China
FULHAM	England
GILGIT	India
GLARUS	Switzerland
GUIANA	South America
HAZARA	Pakistan
KARROO	South Africa
KUWAIT	Asia
LATIUM	Italy
MODENA	Italy
OAXACA	Mexico
OLDHAM	England
ORISSA	India
PAHANG	Malaysia
PAMIRS	Asia
PERLIS	Malaysia
PRIPET	USSR
PANJAB	India
PUNJAB	India
RAGUSA	Italy
SAXONY	Germany
SERBIA	Yugoslavia
SHANSI	China
SHARON	Israel
SHENSI	China
SIKKIM	India
SONORA	Mexico
STYRIA	Austria
SURREY	England
SUSSEX	England
SWABIA	Germany
TERUEL	Spain
THRACE	Greece
UMBRIA	Italy
VALAIS	Switzerland
VENDEE	France
YUNNAN	China

ALBERTA	Canada
ALMADEN	Spain
ALMANSA	Spain
ANDENNE	Belgium
ARCADIA	Greece
ASHANTI	Ghana
BAVARIA	Germany
BOEOTIA	Greece
BOHEMIA	Yugoslavia
BRABANT	Belgium
CASTILE	Spain
CHELSEA	England
CROATIA	Yugoslavia
DURANGO	Mexico
GALICIA	Poland, Spain
GASCONY	France
GWALIOR	India
HOLBORN	England
JALISCO	Mexico
KARELIA	USSR
LAMBETH	England
LAPLAND	Sweden
LIVONIA	Latvia
MASURIA	Poland
MORAVIA	Czechoslovakia
MORELOS	Mexico
NAVARRA	Spain
ORIENTE	Cuba
RIVIERA	France
SARAWAK	Indonesia
SIBERIA	Asia
SINALAO	Mexico
SITSANG	Tibet
SURINAM	South America
TABASCO	Mexico
TESCHEN	Poland
THURGAU	Switzerland

CITIES—UNITED STATES

ADA	Ohio
AJO	Ariz.
AVA	Mo.
ELY	Minn.
OLA	Ark.
OPP	Ala.
ROY	Ut.
RYE	N.Y.
WAR	W.Va.
AIEA	Haw.
ALMA	Mich.
ARCO	Id.
ARMA	Kan.
AYER	Mass.
BATH	Me.
BUHL	Id.
DALE	Pa.
DORA	Ala.
DUNN	N.C.
DUPO	Ill.
EDNA	Tex.
ELKO	Nev.
ELMA	N.Y.
ELOY	Ariz.
ENID	Okla.
ERIE	Pa.
GARY	Ind.
HAYS	Kan.
HILO	Haw.
HOLT	Mich.
HUGO	Okla.
IOLA	Kan.
KENT	Ohio
LEHI	Ut.
LIMA	Ohio
LODI	N.J.
LYNN	Mass.
MART	Tex.
MAUD	Okla.
MENA	Ark.
MESA	Ariz.
MILO	Me.
MORA	Minn.
NAPA	Cal.
OMAK	Wash.
OREM	Ut.
PANA	Ill.
RENO	Nev.
RUSK	Tex.
RUTH	Nev.
RYAN	Okla.
SACO	Me.
SPUR	Tex.

TAMA	Ia.
TROY	N.Y.
WACO	Tex.
WARE	Mass.
WEIR	Kan.
WRAY	Col.
YORK	Pa.
YUMA	Ariz.
ZION	Ill.
AIKEN	S.C.
AKRON	Ohio
ALAMO	Tex.
ALBIA	Ia.
ALCOA	Tenn.
ALICE	Tex.
ALTON	Ill.
ANOKA	Minn.
ASPEN	Col.
BARRE	Vt.
BEREA	Ohio
BLAIR	Neb.
BOISE*	Ida.
BOONE	Ia.
BRONX	N.Y.
BRYAN	Tex.
BUTTE	Mont.
CAMAS	Wash.
CANEY	Kan.
CAREY	Ohio
CARMI	Ill.
CASEY	Ill.
CAYCE	S.C.
CHICO	Cal.
CHINO	Cal.
CLARE	Mich.
CLYDE	Ohio
COCOA	Fla.
COLBY	Kan.
CORRY	Pa.
CREWE	Va.
CUERO	Tex.
DANIA	Fla.
DEPEW	N.Y.
DERRY	N.H.
DIXON	Ill.
DONNA	Tex.
DOVER*	Del.
EATON	Ohio
EDINA	Minn.
ELDON	Mo.
ELGIN	Ill.
ENNIS	Tex.
ERWIN	Tenn.

FARGO	N.D.
FLINT	Mich.
FLORA	Ill.
GALAX	Va.
GALVA	Ill.
GREER	S.C.
HAVRE	Mont.
HOBBS	N.M.
HOUMA	La.
ILION	N.Y.
IONIA	Mich.
IRWIN	Pa.
ISLIP	N.Y.
KAPAA	Haw.
KEENE	N.H.
KELSO	Wash.
LADUE	Mo.
LAMAR	Col.
LIHUE	Haw.
LOGAN	Ut.
MACON	Ga.
MIAMI	Fla.
MINGO	Ohio
MINOT	N.D.
NAMPA	Id.
NILES	Ill.
OCALA	Fla.
OLNEY	Ill.
OMAHA	Neb.
ONAWA	Ia.
ORONO	Me.
OSSEO	Minn.
OWEGO	N.Y.
PAMPA	Tex.
PAOLA	Kan.
PAOLI	Pa.
PARMA	Ohio
PASCO	Wash.
PECOS	Tex.
PEKIN	Ill.
PELLA	Ia.
PHARR	Tex.
PIQUA	Ohio
PRATT	Kan.
PROVO	Ut.
PRYOR	Okla.
RATON	N.M.
RAYNE	La.
RIPON	Wis.
ROLFE	Ia.
ROLLA	Mo.
ROTAN	Tex.
SALEM*	Ore.
SANDY	Ut.

*Indicates state capital

SAYRE Pa.
SELMA Ala.
STOWE Pa., Vt.
TAMPA Fla.
TEMPE Ariz.
TOMAH Wis.
TULSA Okla.
TYLER Tex.
UKIAH Cal.
UTICA N.Y.
VISTA Cal.
WAHOO Neb.
WELCH W.Va.
WYLIE Tex.
WYNNE Ark.
XENIA Ohio

ADRIAN Mich.
AGAWAM Mass.
ALBANY* N.Y.
ALGONA Ia.
ANTIGO Wis.
AUBURN N.Y.
AURORA Ill.
AUSTIN* Tex.
BANGOR Me.
BARTOW Fla.
BELOIT Wis.
BENTON Ark.
BETHEL Pa.
BILOXI Miss.
BONHAM Tex.
BORGER Tex.
BOSTON* Mass.
BREWER Me.
BUFORD Ga.
BUNKIE La.
BURNET Tex.
CAMDEN N.J.
CANTON Ohio
CASPER Wyo.
CELINA Ohio
CICERO Ill.
CLOVIS N.M.
COHOES N.Y.
COLTON Cal.
CONROE Tex.
CONWAY Ark.
CORBIN Ky.
CORONA Cal.
COSCOB Conn.
COVINA Cal.
CRESCO Ia.
CUDAHY Wis.
DALLAS Tex.
DALTON Ga.
DARIEN Conn.
DAWSON Ga.
DAYTON Ohio
DEKALB Ill.
DELAND Fla.
DELANO Cal.
DEMING N.M.
DENVER* Col.
DEPERE Wis.
DESOTO Mo.
DEXTER Mo.
DILLON S.C.
DOLTON Ill.
DOWNEY Cal.
DRACUT Mass.
DUBOIS Pa.
DULUTH Minn.
EASTON Pa.
ECORSE Mich.
ELDORA Ia.
ELKTON Md.
ELMIRA N.Y.
ELRENO Okla.
ELWOOD Ind.
ELYRIA Ohio
EMMAUS Pa.
EPPING N.H.
EUCLID Ohio
EUGENE Ore.
EUNICE La.
EUREKA Cal.
EUSTIS Fla.
EXETER N.H.
FRESNO Cal.
GALENA Ill.
GALION Ohio
GERING Neb.
GIRARD Ohio
GOLDEN Col.
GORHAM Me.
GRETNA La.
GROTON Conn.
HAMDEN Conn.
HARLAN Ky.
HELENA* Mont.
HINTON W.Va.
HOBART Ind.
IDABEL Okla.
ITHACA N.Y.
JASPER Ala.
JOLIET Ill.
JOPLIN Mo.
JUNEAU* Alas.
KENTON Ohio
KEOKUK Ia.
KOKOMO Ind.
LAREDO Tex.
LAUREL Miss.
LAWTON Okla.
LEMARS Ia.
LENNOX Cal.
LENOIR N.C.
LINDEN N.J.
LOMITA Cal.
LORAIN Ohio
LOWELL Mass.
MCADOO Pa.
MCCOMB Miss.
MACOMB Ill.
MADERA Cal.
MALDEN Mass.
MARION Ind., Ohio
MERCED Cal.
MILTON Mass.
MOBILE Ala.
MOLINE Ill.
MONACA Pa.
MONROE La.
MONSON Mass.
MUNCIE Ind.
NASHUA N.H.
NATICK Mass.
NEWARK N.J.
NEWTON Mass.
NORMAN Okla.
NUTLEY N.J.
OWOSSO Mich.
PALMER Mass.
PAWPAW Mich.
PAXTON Ill.
PAYSON Ut.
PEORIA Ill.
PIERRE* S.D.
PUTNAM Conn.
QUEENS N.Y.
QUINCY Mass.
RACINE Wis.
RAHWAY N.J.
RANGER Tex.
RENOVO Pa.
RENTON Wash.
REVERE Mass.
SALINA Kan.
SCOTIA N.Y.
SEGUIN Tex.
SENECA S.C.
SEWARD Alas., Neb.
SHARON Pa.
SHELBY N.C.
SIDNEY Ohio
SKOKIE Ill.
SLAYTON Tex.
SNYDER Tex.
SOLVAY N.Y.
SONORA Ariz., Cal.
SPARKS Nev.
STAMPS Ark.
STEGER Ill.
STPAUL* Minn.
STROUD Okla.
SUMTER S.C.

TACOMA Wash.
THROOP Pa.
TIFFIN Ohio
TIFTON Ga.
TIPTON Ind.
TOLEDO Ohio
TOPEKA* Kan.
TUCSON Ariz.
TULARE Cal.
TUPELO Miss.
UPLAND Cal.
URBANA Ill.
VERNAL Ut.
VERNON Tex.
VINITA Okla.
WALDEN N.Y.
WARREN Ohio
WAUSAU Wis.
WEISER Id.
WINONA Minn.
WOBURN Mass.
YAKIMA Wash.
YEADON Pa.

ABILENE Kan.
ALAMEDA Cal.
ALTOONA Pa.
AMHERST Mass.
ANDOVER Mass.
ANSONIA Conn.
ARDMORE Pa.
ASHLAND Ky.
ATLANTA* Ga.
ATTALLA Ala.
AUGUSTA Ga.
AUGUSTA* Me.
BASTROP La.
BAYCITY Mich.
BAYONNE N.J.
BEDFORD Ohio
BELMONT Mass.
BENICIA Cal.
BERKLEY Mich.
BETHANY Okla.
BEVERLY Mass.
BOONTON N.J.
BOULDER Col.
BOZEMAN Mont.
BRISTOL Conn.
BUFFALO N.Y.
CAMERON Tex.
CAMILLA Ga.
CHATHAM N.J.
CHELSEA Mass.
CHESTER Pa.
CHEVIOT Ohio
CHICAGO Ill.
CLAYTON Mo.
CLIFTON N.J.

CLINTON Ia.
CONCORD* N.H.
COOSBAY Ore.
CORDELE Ga.
CORINTH Miss.
CORNING N.Y.
COTULLA Tex.
CRAFTON Pa.
CROWLEY La.
CULLMAN Ala.
DECATUR Ill.
DECORAH Ia.
DELPHOS Ohio
DENISON Tex.
DETROIT Mich.
DICKSON Pa.
DORMONT Pa.
DOUGLAS Ariz.
DUBUQUE Ia.
DUNEDIN Fla.
DUNMORE Pa.
DURANGO Col.
ELKCITY Okla.
ELKHART Ind.
ENFIELD Conn.
EVERETT Mass.
FARRELL Pa.
FINDLAY Ohio
GADSDEN Ala.
GAFFNEY S.C.
GARDENA Cal.
GARRETT Ind.
GENESEO Ill.
GLENCOE Ill.
GRAFTON W.Va.
GREELEY Col.
GUTHRIE Okla.
HAMMOND Ind.
HAMPTON Va.
HIALEAH Fla.
HIBBING Minn.
HINGHAM Mass.
HOBOKEN N.J.
HOLYOKE Mass.
HORNELL N.Y.
HOUSTON Tex.
INKSTER Mich.
IRONTON Ohio
JACKSON* Miss.
KEARNEY N.J.
KENOSHA Wis.
KEWANEE Ill.
KEYWEST Fla.
KILGORE Tex.
KINSTON N.C.
KITTERY Me.
LACONIA N.H.
LANSING* Mich.
LAPORTE Ind.

LARAMIE Wyo.
LASALLE Ill.
LATROBE Pa.
LIBERAL Kan.
LINCOLN* Neb.
LIVONIA Mich.
LUBBOCK Tex.
LYNWOOD Cal.
MCALLEN Tex.
MADISON* Wis.
MANKATO Minn.
MATTOON Ill.
MAYWOOD Ill.
MEDFORD Mass.
MEMPHIS Tenn.
MENASHA Wis.
MILFORD Conn.
MINEOLA N.Y.
MOBERLY Mo.
MODESTO Cal.
MORENCI Ariz.
MULLINS S.C.
NATCHEZ Miss.
NEEDHAM Mass.
NEWPORT R.I.
NOGALES Ariz.
NORFOLK Va.
NORWALK Conn.
NORWOOD Ohio
OAKLAND Cal.
OAKPARK Ill.
OILCITY Pa.
OLDTOWN Me.
OLYMPIA* Wash.
ORLANDO Fla.
OSHKOSH Wis.
OTTUMWA Ia.
PADUCAH Ky.
PARAMUS N.J.
PARSONS Kan.
PASSAIC N.J.
PHOENIX* Ariz.
PULASKI Va.
QUITMAN Ga.
RALEIGH N.C.
RARITAN N.J.
READING Pa.
REDDING Cal.
ROANOKE Va.
ROSELLE N.J.
SAGINAW Mich.
SALINAS Cal.
SANFORD N.C.
SANJOSE Cal.
SANTAFE* N.M.
SAPULPA Okla.
SEATTLE Wash.
SEDALIA Mo.
SHAWNEE Okla.

SPENCER	Mass.
SPOKANE	Wash.
STURGIS	Mich.
SUFFOLK	Va.
SUNAPEE	N.H.
TARBORO	N.C.
TARRANT	Ala.
TEANECK	N.J.
TERRELL	Tex.
TRENTON*	N.J.
VALLEJO	Cal.
VANWERT	Ohio
VENTURA	Cal.
VISALIA	Cal.
WAREHAM	Mass.
WEBSTER	Mass.
WEIRTON	W.Va.
WESLACO	Tex.
WHEATON	Ill.
WICHITA	Kan.
WINDBER	Pa.
WINSTED	Conn.
WOOSTER	Ohio
YANKTON	S.D.
YONKERS	N.Y.

AMARILLO	Tex.
ANNARBOR	Mich.
ANNISTON	Ala.
BERKELEY	Cal.
BESSEMER	Ala.
BILLINGS	Mont.
BISMARCK*	N.D.
BOGALUSA	La.
BRAINERD	Minn.
BROCKTON	Mass.
BROOKLYN	N.Y.
BRYNMAWR	Pa.
CADILLAC	Mich.
CALDWELL	Id.
CALEXICO	Cal.
CARLISLE	Pa.
CARLSBAD	N.M.
CARTERET	N.J.
CHEYENNE*	Wyo.
COLUMBIA*	S.C.
COLUMBUS*	Ohio
CORTLAND	N.Y.
CRANSTON	R.I.
DANVILLE	Ill., Va.
DEARBORN	Mich.
DEERPARK	Ohio
EDINBURG	Tex.
EVANSTON	Ill.
FAIRMONT	W.Va.
FREDONIA	N.Y.
GASTONIA	N.C.
GLENDALE	Cal.
GREENBAY	Wis.
GULFPORT	Miss.
HANNIBAL	Mo.
HARTFORD*	Conn.
HASTINGS	Neb.
HAZLETON	Pa.
HONOLULU*	Haw.
KANKAKEE	Ill.
LACROSSE	Wis.
LAKEWOOD	N.J.
LASVEGAS	Nev.
LAWRENCE	Mass.
LEWISTON	Me.
LOCKPORT	N.Y.
MARIETTA	Ga.
MISSOULA	Mont.
MONTEREY	Cal.
MUSKEGON	Mich.
MUSKOGEE	Okla.
NEWBURGH	N.Y.
OAKRIDGE	Tenn.
OKMULGEE	Okla.
OSSINING	N.Y.
PALOALTO	Cal.
PASADENA	Cal.
PLYMOUTH	Mass.
PRESCOTT	Ariz.
RICHMOND*	Va.
ROCKFORD	Ill.
ROCKHILL	S.C.
SANDIEGO	Cal.
SANDUSKY	Ohio
SANMATEO	Cal.
SANTAANA	Cal.
SARASOTA	Fla.
SAVANNAH	Ga.
SCRANTON	Pa.
STAMFORD	Conn.
STAUNTON	Va.
STOCKTON	Cal.
SYRACUSE	N.Y.
TALLULAH	La.
TUSKEGEE	Ala.
VALDOSTA	Ga.
WATERLOO	Ia.
WAUKEGAN	Ill.
WAUKESHA	Wis.
WESTPORT	Conn.
WHEELING	W.Va.
WHITTIER	Cal.
WILMETTE	Ill.
WOODBURY	N.J.

ANNAPOLIS*	Md.
ARLINGTON	Va.
ASHEVILLE	N.C.
BALTIMORE	Md.
BARBERTON	Ohio
BELVEDERE	Cal.
BETHLEHEM	Pa.
BIDDEFORD	Me.
BRADENTON	Fla.
BRAINTREE	Mass.
BREMERTON	Wash.
BRUNSWICK	Ga.
CAMBRIDGE	Mass.
CHAMPAIGN	Ill.
CHARLOTTE	N.C.
CLEVELAND	Ohio
COVINGTON	Ky.
DESMOINES*	Ia.
ELIZABETH	N.J.
ENGLEWOOD	N.J.
FALLRIVER	Mass.
FLAGSTAFF	Ariz.
FONDULAC	Wis.
FORTDODGE	Ia.
FRANKFORT*	Ky.
HAMTRAMCK	Mich.
HOLLYWOOD	Cal.
JOHNSTOWN	Pa.
KALAMAZOO	Mich.
LANCASTER	Pa.
LEXINGTON	Ky.
MANHATTAN	N.Y.
MANHATTAN	Kan.
NASHVILLE*	Tenn.
PENSACOLA	Fla.
ROCHESTER	N.Y.
SALISBURY	N.C.
SANANGELO	Tex.
SOUTHBEND	Ind.
SOUTHGATE	Cal.
WATERBURY	Conn.
WESTALLIS	Wis.
WESTPOINT	N.Y.
WORCESTER	Mass.

FOREIGN CITIES

ABA	Nigeria
ABO	Finland
AIX	France
AUE	West Germany
AVA	Burma
BAM	Iran
BOR	Yugoslavia
DAX	France
DIR	Pakistan
EDE	Nigeria
EDO	Japan
EMS	West Germany

FES	Morocco
FEZ	Morocco
HOF	West Germany
HUE	South Vietnam
ICA	Peru
IRI	South Korea
ITA	Paraguay
IWO	Nigeria
KEM	USSR
KUM	Iran
LAE	Papua New Guinea
LEH	India
NIS	Yugoslavia
OYO	Nigeria
QUM	Iran
SAN	Mali
SPA	Belgium
TSU	Japan
UBE	Japan
UFA	USSR
ULM	West Germany
ACRE	Israel
ADEN	Yemen
ADUA	Ethiopia
AGAR	India
AGEN	France
AGRA	India
AIUD	Romania
ALBI	France
ALES	France
ALEY	Lebanon
AMOL	Iran
AMOY	China
AMUL	Iran
ANSI	China
APAM	Mexico
APIA	Western Samoa
APRA	Guam
ARAD	Romania
ASCH	Czechoslovakia
AYAN	USSR
BAGE	Brazil
BAJA	Hungary
BAKU	USSR
BALE	Switzerland
BARI	Italy
BATH	England
BERN	Switzerland
BIDA	Nigeria
BIEL	Switzerland
BISK	USSR
BLED	Yugoslavia
BONE	Algeria
BONN	West Germany
BRNO	Czechoslovakia
BUDA	Hungary
BUEA	Cameroon

BUGA	Colombia
BUNA	Papua New Guinea
BURG	East Germany
CAEN	France
CALI	Colombia
CEBU	Philippines
CHEB	Czechoslovakia
CHUR	Switzerland
CLUJ	Romania
COBH	Ireland
CORK	Ireland
CORO	Venezuela
DHAR	India
DILI	Indonesia
DOHA	Qatar
EGER	Hungary
ETAH	Greenland
FUYU	China
GAYA	India
GAZA	Israel
GENT	Belgium
GERA	East Germany
GIZA	Egypt
GRAZ	Austria
GYOR	Hungary
HAMM	West Germany
HILO	Hawaii
HOFU	Japan
HOKO	South Korea
HOMS	Libya; Syria
HULL	England
HUTT	New Zealand
IASI	Romania
IFNI	Morocco
IPIN	China
IPOH	Malaysia
IRUN	Spain
JAEN	Spain
JENA	East Germany
KANO	Nigeria
KHOI	Iran
KIEL	West Germany
KIEV	USSR
KOBE	Japan
KOFU	Japan
KURE	Japan
LABE	Guinea
LIDO	Italy
LIMA	Peru
LINZ	Austria
LODI	Italy
LODZ	Poland
LOME	Togo
LOTA	Chile
LVOV	USSR
LWOW	USSR
MALE	Maldive Islands
METZ	France

MITO	Japan
MOJI	Japan
MONS	Beglium
NAHA	Japan
NARA	Japan
NAWA	Syria
NICE	France
NISH	Yugoslavia
OBAN	Scotland
OITA	Japan
OMSK	USSR
ORAN	Algeria
OREL	USSR
ORLY	France
ORSK	USSR
OSLO	Norway
OTSU	Japan
OULU	Finland
PARA	Brazil
PEGU	Burma
PERM	USSR
PILA	Poland
PISA	Italy
POLA	Yugoslavia
PORI	Finland
PRAG	Czechoslovakia
PULA	Yugoslavia
PUNO	Peru
RIAD	Saudi Arabia
RIGA	Latvia
RIVA	Italy
ROME	Italy
SAIS	Egypt
SANA	Yemen
SENS	France
SETE	France
SIAN	China
STLO	France
SUEZ	Egypt
SUMY	USSR
SUSA	Iran
SUVA	Fiji
TARA	Ireland
TULA	USSR
URFA	Turkey
VIGO	Spain
VILA	Scotland
WIEN	Austria
WUHU	China
YAFA	Israel
ACCRA	Ghana
ADANA	Turkey
ADONI	India
ADOWA	Ethiopia
ADUWA	Ethiopia
AGANA	Guam
AHLEN	West Germany
AHWAZ	Iran

AIGUN China
AKITA Japan
AKOLA India
AKURE Nigeria
ALLOA Scotland
AMARA Iraq
AMBON Indonesia
AMBUR India
AMMAN Jordan
ANAPA USSR
ANCON Panama
ANCUD Chile
ANGOL Chile
ANGUL India
ANZIO Italy
APAPA Nigeria
ARCOT India
ARICA Chile
ARLES France
ARRAH India
ARRAS France
ASHIO Japan
ATAMI Japan
AVILA Spain
AVOLA Italy
BABUL Iran
BACAU Romania
BADEN Austria
BAHIA Brazil
BALLY India
BALTA USSR
BASEL Switzerland
BASRA Iraq
BATUM USSR
BAURU Brazil
BEIRA Portugal
BEKES Hungary
BELEM Brazil
BEPPU Japan
BERNE Switzerland
BIHAR India
BLOIS France
BOGOR Indonesia
BREST France
BULAN Philippines
BUNDI India
BURSA Turkey
BYTOV Poland
CADIZ Spain
CAIRO Egypt
CANEA Greece
CAPUA Italy
CAVAN Ireland
CEARA Brazil
CELLE West Germany
CEUTA Morocco
CHIBA Japan
CHITA USSR
CLEVE West Germany
COLON Panama
COWES England
DACCA Pakistan
DAKAR Senegal
DATIA India
DAVAO Philippines
DAVOS Switzerland
DEHLI India
DERNA Libya
DIJON France
DILLI Indonesia
DOORN Netherlands
DOUAI France
ELCHE Spain
EMDEN West Germany
ERLAU Hungary
ESSEN West Germany
FIUME Yugoslavia
FUSAN South Korea
GALLE Ceylon
GATUN Panama
GENOA Italy
GHENT Belgium
GIJON Spain
GOMEL USSR
GORKI USSR
GOTHA East Germany
GREIZ East Germany
HAGEN West Germany
HAIFA Israel
HALLE East Germany
HAMAR Norway
HANDA Japan
HANOI North Vietnam
HARAR Ethiopia
HERAT Afghanistan
HERNE West Germany
HORTA Portugal
HUBLI India
IJEBU Nigeria
ISCHL Austria
ITAMI Japan
IZMIR Turkey
IZMIT Turkey
JAFFA Israel
JEDDA Saudi Arabia
JEREZ Spain
JIDDA Saudia Arabia
KABUL Afghanistan
KANDY Ceylon
KASUR Pakistan
KAZAN USSR
KEIJO South Korea
KERCH USSR
KHIVA USSR
KIMPO South Korea
KIROV USSR
KIRYU Japan
KOCHI Japan
KONIA Turkey
KONYA Turkey
KOVNO Lithuania
KOWNO Lithuania
KYOTO Japan
LAGOS Nigeria
LAHTI Finland
LANUS Argentina
LAPAZ Bolivia
LEEDS England
LHASA China
LIEGE Belgium
LILLE France
LOMAS Argentina
LUTSK Poland
LYONS France
MAINZ West Germany
MALMO Sweden
MASAN North Korea
MECCA Saudi Arabia
MEDAN Indonesia
MEMEL Lithuania
MILAN Italy
MINSK USSR
MOSUL Iraq
NAMUR Belgium
NANCY France
NATAL Brazil
NIGEL South Africa
NIMES France
OGAKI Japan
OMURA Japan
OMUTA Japan
OPOLE Poland
ORURO Bolivia
OSAKA Japan
OSTIA Italy
OTARU Japan
PADUA Italy
PALMA Spain
PALOS Spain
PARIS France
PARMA Italy
PASAY Philippines
PATAN Nepal
PATNA India
PENKI China
PENZA USSR
PERAK Malaysia
PERTH Australia
PINSK USSR
PLZEN Czechoslovakia
PODOR Senegal
PONCE Puerto Rico
POONA Afghanistan
POSEN Poland
PRAHA Czechoslovakia
PUSAN South Korea
QUITO Ecuador

RABAT Morocco
RADOM Poland
REIMS France
RESHT Iran
REVAL Estonia
ROUEN France
SAGAR India
SAKAI Japan
SALTA Argentina
SEDAN France
SEOUL South Korea
SHASI China
SHOKA Rep. China
SIDON Lebanon
SIENA Italy
SIMLA India
SOFIA Bulgaria
SPLIT Yugoslavia
SUCRE Bolivia
SURAT India
SUWON South Korea
TAEGU South Korea
TANTA Egypt
TOKAY Hungary
TOKYO Japan
TOMSK USSR
TOURS France
TRANI Italy
TRENT Italy
TRIER West Germany
TUNIS Tunisia
TURIN Italy
TURKU Finland
VAASA Finland
VADUZ Liechtenstein
VARNA Bulgaria
VICHY France
VILNA Lithuania
VISBY Sweden
WILNA Lithuania
WORMS West Germany
WUHAN China
WUWEI China
YALTA USSR
YAREN Nauru
ZOMBA Malawi

AACHEN West Germany
AARHUS Denmark
ABADAN Iran
ABUKIR Egypt
AEGION Greece
AEGIUM Greece
AGADES Nigeria
AGADIR Morocco
AKASHI Japan
ALATYR USSR
ALBURY Australia
ALEPPO Syria
ALLADA Benin
ALTONA West Germany
ALTORF Switzerland
AMALFI Italy
AMBALA India
AMBATO Ecuador
AMIENS France
ANCONA Italy
ANGERS France
ANGKOR Cambodia
ANKARA Turkey
ANNECY France
ANSHAN China
AOMORI Japan
APATIN Yugoslavia
APOLDA East Germany
ARCOLE Italy
ARNHEM Netherlands
ASMARA Ethiopia
ASTARA USSR
ATHENS Greece
BAGUIO Philippines
BALBOA Panama
BAMAKO Mall
BANDRA India
BANGUI Central African Rep.
BANJUL Gambia
BARMEN West Germany
BARODA India
BASTIA France
BATUMI USSR
BEIRUT Lebanon
BEJAIA Algeria
BENONI South Africa
BERGEN Norway
BHOPAL India
BILBAO Spain
BINGEN West Germany
BOCHUM West Germany
BOGOTA Colombia
BOLTON England
BOMBAY India
BOUGIE Algeria
BRAILA Romania
BRASOV Romania
BREMEN West Germany
BRIONI Yugoslavia
BRUNEI Indonesia
BURGAS Bulgaria
CAGUAS Puerto Rico
CALAIS France
CALLAO Peru
CAMBAY India
CANNES France
CANTON China
CASSEL West Germany
CAVITE Philippines
CAXIAS Brazil
CEGLED Hungary
CHAPRA India
CHOLON South Vietnam
CHOSHI Japan
COLMAR France
CRACOW Poland
CUCUTA Colombia
DAIREN China
DANZIG Poland
DELPHI Greece
DODONA Greece
DUBLIN Ireland
DUMDUM India
DUNDEE Scotland
DURBAN South Africa
EDESSA Greece
ERFURT East Germany
ERIVAN USSR
EXETER England
FUSHUN China
GALATI Romania
GDYNIA Poland
GENEVA Switzerland
GONDAR Ethiopia
GOSLAR West Germany
GRASSE France
GRODNO USSR
GROZNY USSR
GUNTUR India
HAMELN West Germany
HANKOW China
HARARE Zimbabwe
HARBIN China
HARRAR Ethiopia
HAVANA Cuba
HIMEJI Japan
HOBART Australia
IBADAN Nigeria
ILOILO Philippines
ILORIN Nigeria
IMPHAL India
INCHON South Korea
INDORE India
JAIPUR India
JALAPA Mexico
JOHORE Malaysia
KALUGA USSR
KANPUR India
KAOLAN China
KASHAN Iran
KASSEL West Germany

KAUNAS	Lithuania
KAZVIN	Iran
KEDIRI	Indonesia
KIGALI	Rwanda
KUNSAN	South Korea
KUWAIT	Kuwait
LAHORE	Pakistan
LEIDEN	Netherlands
LEMANS	France
LERIDA	Spain
LEYDEN	Netherlands
LIDICE	Czechoslovakia
LISBON	Portugal
LONDON	England
LUANDA	Angola
LUBECK	West Germany
LUBLIN	USSR
LUGANO	Switzerland
LUSAKA	Zambia
MACEIO	Brazil
MADRAS	India
MADRID	Spain
MADURA	India
MALABO	Equatorial Guinea
MALAGA	Spain
MALANG	Indonesia
MANAMA	Bahrain
MANAUS	Brazil
MANTUA	Italy
MAPUTO	Mozambique
MASERU	Lesotho
MEDINA	Saudi Arabia
MENTON	France
MERIDA	Mexico
MESHED	Iran
MINDEN	West Germany
MINHOW	China
MODENA	Italy
MONACO	Monaco
MOSCOW	USSR
MUKDEN	China
MULTAN	Pakistan
MUNICH	West Germany
MURCIA	Spain
MUSCAT	Oman
MYSORE	India
NAGANO	Japan
NAGOYA	Japan
NAGPUR	India
NANTES	France
NAPLES	Italy
NARVIK	Norway
NIAMEY	Niger
NINGPO	China
NUMAZU	Greece
ODENSE	Denmark
ODESSA	USSR
OPORTO	Portugal
ORADEA	Romania
OREBRO	Sweden
ORENSE	Spain
OSTEND	Belgium
OTTAWA	Canada
OVIEDO	Spain
OXFORD	England
PADANG	Indonesia
PASSAU	West Germany
PATRAS	Greece
PEKING	China
PILSEN	Czechoslovakia
PLAUEN	East Germany
POTOSI	Bolivia
POZNAN	Poland
PRAGUE	Czechoslovakia
QUEBEC	Canada
QUETTA	Pakistan
RAGUSA	Yugoslavia
RAIPUR	India
RAMPUR	India
RECIFE	Brazil
RENNES	France
RIJEKA	Yugoslavia
RIMINI	Italy
RIYADH	Saudi Arabia
ROSTOV	USSR
SAIGON	South Vietnam
SANTOS	Brazil
SASEBO	Japan
SENDAI	Japan
SEVRES	France
SPARTA	Greece
STRESA	Italy
SUZUKA	Japan
SYDNEY	Australia
TABRIZ	Iran
TAIPEI	Rep. China
TALIEN	China
TEHRAN	Iran
TETUAN	Morocco
THEBES	Greece
TILSIT	USSR
TIRANA	Albania
TOBRUK	Libya
TOLEDO	Spain
TOULON	France
TOYAMA	Japan
TRALEE	Ireland
TSINAN	China
UPSALA	Sweden
VENICE	Italy
VERDUN	France
VERONA	Italy
VIENNA	Austria
VYBORG	USSR
WARSAW	Poland
YAHATA	Japan
YAWATA	Japan
YANGKU	China
ZAGREB	Yugoslavia
ZURICH	Switzerland

ABIDJAN	Ivory Coast
ALGIERS	Algeria
ALLEPPI	India
ANDORRA	France
ANTIBES	France
ANTIGUA	Guatemala
ANTWERP	Belgium
ARACAJU	Brazil
AVIGNON	France
BAGHDAD	Iraq
BANDUNG	Indonesia
BANGKOK	Thailand
BATAVIA	Indonesia
BEIJING	China
BELFAST	Ireland
BENARES	India
BENGASI	Libya
BERBERA	Somalia
BERGAMO	Italy
BIZERTE	Tunisia
BOLOGNA	Italy
BRESCIA	Italy
BRESLAU	Poland
BRISTOL	England
CALGARY	Canada
CALICUT	India
CARACAS	Venezuela
CARDIFF	Wales
CATANIA	Italy
CAYENNE	French Guiana
CHENGTU	China
COLOGNE	West Germany
COLOMBO	Ceylon
CONAKRY	Guinea
CORDOBA	Argentina
CORDOVA	Spain
CREMONA	Italy
DRESDEN	East Germany
DUNKIRK	France
FERRARA	Italy
GANGTOK	India
GLASGOW	Scotland
GRANADA	Spain
HAARLEM	Netherlands
HAMBURG	West Germany
HANOVER	West Germany
HANYANG	China

ISFAHAN	Iran
ISPAHAN	Iran
IVANOVO	USSR
JAKARTA	Indonesia
KALININ	USSR
KAMPALA	Uganda
KARACHI	Pakistan
KHARKOV	USSR
KOWLOON	China
LAPLATA	Argentina
LATAKIA	Syria
LEGHORN	Italy
LEHAVRE	France
LEIPZIG	East Germany
LIMOGES	France
LOCARNO	Switzerland
LUCERNE	Switzerland
MADEIRA	Portugal
MANAGUA	Nicaragua
MARSALA	Italy
MBABANE	Swaziland
MESSINA	Italy
NAIROBI	Kenya
NANKING	China
NICOSIA	Cyprus
NITEROI	Brazil
PALERMO	Italy
PAPEETE	Tahiti
POTSDAM	Germany
POLTAVA	USSR
PUNAKHA	Bhutan
RANGOON	Burma
RAPALLO	Italy
RAVENNA	Italy
ROSARIO	Argentina
ROSTOCK	East Germany
SALERNO	Italy
SANJOSE	Costa Rica
SANTAFE	Argentina
SAPPORO	Japan
SARATOV	USSR
SEVILLA	Spain
SEVILLE	Spain
SIALKOT	Pakistan
STALINO	USSR
STETTIN	Poland
TAMPICO	Mexico
TANGIER	Morocco
TARANTO	Italy
TBILISI	USSR
TEHERAN	Iran
TELAVIV	Israel
TILBURG	Netherlands
TORONTO	Canada
TORREON	Mexico
TRIESTE	Italy
TRIPOLI	Libya
TUCUMAN	Argentina
UTRECHT	Netherlands
VILNYUS	Lithuania
WINDSOR	Canada
WROCLAW	Poland
YAOUNDE	Cameroon

ABUDHABI	United Arab Emirates
ASUNCION	Paraguay
AUCKLAND	New Zealand
BATHURST	Gambia
BELMOPAN	Belize
BRASILIA	Brazil
BRUSSELS	Belgium
BUDAPEST	Hungary
CALCUTTA	India
CANBERRA	Australia
CAPETOWN	South Africa
DAMASCUS	Syria
DJAKARTA	Indonesia
DUISBURG	West Germany
FORTLAMY	Chad
FREETOWN	Sierra Leone
GABORONE	Botswana
GOTEBORG	Sweden
HANGCHOW	China
HELSINKI	Finland
KHARTOUM	Sudan
KINGSTON	Jamaica
LILONGWE	Malawi
MANNHEIM	West Germany
MONROVIA	Liberia
MONTREAL	Canada
NAGASAKI	Japan
NDJAMENA	Chad
NEWDELHI	India
PNOMPENH	Cambodia
PRETORIA	South Africa
SALONIKA	Greece
SANTIAGO	Chile
SARAJEVO	Yugoslavia
TASHKENT	USSR
VALLETTA	Malta
YOKOHAMA	Japan

AMSTERDAM	Netherlands
BUCHAREST	Romania
BUJUMBURA	Burundi
JERUSALEM	Israel
KATHMANDU	Nepal
MOGADISHU	Somalia
PHNOMPENH	Cambodia
PORTONOVO	Benin
PYONGYANG	North Korea
REYKJAVIK	Iceland
SANMARINO	San Marino
STOCKHOLM	Sweden
TASHICHHO	Bhutan
ULANBATOR	Mongolla
VIENTIANE	Laos

ISLANDS

RE	Atlantic
WE	Indonesia
ALS	North Sea
API	Pacific
ARU	Indonesia
CAT	Atlantic
COS	Greece
EPI	Pacific
FYN	North Sea
HOG	North America
HOY	Scotland
IKI	Japan
IOS	Greece
IZU	Japan
KAI	Indonesia
KEI	Indonesia
KOS	Greece
KRK	Yugoslavia
LAU	Pacific
MAN	England
OBI	Indonesia
OKI	Japan
PAG	Yugoslavia
RAB	Yugoslavia
REY	Panama
RUM	Scotland
SAL	Atlantic
UAP	Pacific
UEA	Pacific
VIS	Yugoslavia
WEH	Indonesia
YAP	Pacific
YEU	France
ZEA	Greece

ADAK	Bering
AERO	North Sea
AKUN	Bering
ALOR	Indian Ocean

ANAA Pacific
APEU Atlantic
ARAN Ireland
ARBE Yugoslavia
AROE Indonesia
ATIU Pacific
ATKA Bering
ATTU Bering
AVES Caribbean
BALI Indonesia
BATU Indonesia
BIAK Pacific
BUKA Pacific
BURU Indian Ocean
BUTE Atlantic
CEBU Philippines
COOK Pacific
CORN Caribbean
CRES Yugoslavia
CUBA Caribbean
CUYO Philippines
DALL Bering
EBON Pacific
EFAT Pacific
ELBA Mediterranean
FANO Denmark
FARO Baltic
FIJI Pacific
FOGO Atlantic
FOHR North Sea
GIZO Pacific
GOZO Mediterranean
GUAM Pacific
HERM England
HVAR Yugoslavia
IONA Scotland
JAVA Indian Ocean
JOLO Philippines
KAIS Iran
KEOS Greece
KURE Pacific
LAUT Indonesia
LEON Spain
LETI Indonesia
LIFU Pacific
MAHE Indian Ocean
MAUI Pacific
MILO Greece
MOEN Denmark
MONA Caribbean
MUHU Baltic
MULL Scotland
NIAS Indonesia
NIUE Pacific
OAHU Pacific
ORRS Caribbean
OSEL Estonia
OTEA New Zealand
PAGI Indonesia
PAXO Greece
PICO Atlantic
PLUM Pacific
QAIS Iran
RAPA Pacific
RODI Mediterranean
ROSS Indian Ocean, Pacific
ROTI Indonesia
SADO Japan
SARK England
SAVO Pacific
SAVU Indonesia
SCIO Greece
SKYE Scotland
SULA Indonesia
SULU Philippines
SYLT North Sea
SYRA Greece
TANA Pacific
TRUK Pacific
UIST Scotland
UNST Scotland
UVEA Pacific
VATE Pacific
WAKE Pacific

ABACO Caribbean
ALAND Baltic
ALOFI Pacific
ALSEN North Sea
AMAMI Japan
AMLIA Bering
AMMIN China
AMRUM North Sea
ARRAN Scotland
ARROE Indonesia
ARUBA Caribbean
BABAR Indonesia
BAKER North America
BALUT Pacific
BANDA Indian Ocean
BANKA Indian Ocean
BANKS Arctic
BATAN Philippines
BICOL Philippines
BOHOL Philippines
BONIN Pacific
BYLOT Arctic
CALDY Wales
CAPRI Italy (Mediterranean)
CERAM India Ocean, Pacific
CHEJU South Korea
CHIOS Greece
CIOVO Mediterranean
COATS Canada
COCOS Indian Ocean
CORFU Mediterranean
CRETE Mediterranean
DAMAR Indian Ocean
DELOS Greece
DEVON Arctic
DISKO Arctic
DOMEL Indian Ocean
DUCIE Pacific
EFATE Pacific
ELLIS Pacific
EXUMA Atlantic
FAYAL Atlantic
FOULA Atlantic
GOUGH Atlantic
HITRA North Sea
HONDO Japan
HOSTE Chile
ISLAY Scotland
IVIZA Mediterranean
KASOS Mediterranean
KAUAI Pacific
KISHM Iran
KISKA Bering
KUNIE Pacific
KURIL Pacific
LANAI Pacific
LEROS Greece
LETTI Indonesia
LEYTE Philippines
LOBOS Atlantic
LUZON Philippines
MACAO China
MAKIN Pacific
MALTA Mediterranean
MANUA Pacific
MELOS Greece
MISOL Pacific
NAURU Pacific
NAXOS Greece
NDENI Pacific
NEVIS Caribbean
OLAND Baltic
PAGAI Indonesia
PALAU Pacific
PANAY Philippines
PAPUA Pacific
PAROS Greece
PARRY Arctic
PAXOI Greece
PAXOS Greece
PELEE Canada
PELEW Pacific
PEMBA Indian Ocean
PSARA Greece
QUAIS Iran
QISHM Iran
RAOUL Pacific
ROCAS Brazil
RUGEN Baltic

SAMAR Philippines
SAMOA Pacific
SAMOS Greece
SANGI Indonesia
SOLTA Yugoslavia
SPICE Pacific
SUMBA Indian Ocean
SUNDA Indian Ocean
SYROS Greece
TANNA Pacific
TENOS Greece
THERA Greece
TIMOR Indonesia
UMNAK Bering
UPOLU Pacific
WAKDE Indian Ocean and Pacific
WHITE Arctic
WIGHT England
ZANTE Greece

AALAND Baltic
ACHILL Atlantic
AEGEAN Mediterranean
AEGINA Mediterranean
AGATTU Pacific
ALABAT Pacific
AMAGER Denmark
AMBRIM Pacific
AMELIA Atlantic
AMUKTA Bering
ANDROS Atlantic, Mediterranean
ANGAUR Pacific
AZORES Atlantic
BAFFIN Arctic
BAHAMA Atlantic
BINTAN Indonesia
BORNEO Indonesia
BOUVET Atlantic
BURIAS Philippines
CAMANO North America
CANARY Atlantic
CANDIA Mediterranean
CARMEN Atlantic, Mexico
CAYMAN Caribbean
CERIGO Mediterranean
CEYLON Indian Ocean
CHILOE Pacific
CYPRUS Mediterranean
EASTER Pacific, Chile
ELLICE Pacific
FLORES Atlantic, Indian Ocean
FUTUNA Pacific
GILLIS Arctic
GOMERA Atlantic

HAWAII Pacific
HONSHU Japan
INAGUA Atlantic
JERSEY Atlantic
KANAGA Bering
KOMODO Indonesia
KYOSAI South Korea
KYUSHU Japan
LABUAN Indonesia
LANTAR Siam
LEMNOS Greece
LESBOS Greece
LEUCAS Greece
LIPARI Italy
LOMBOK Indonesia
MACTAN Philippines
MADURA Indonesia
MALDEN Pacific
MARAJO Brazil
MIDWAY Pacific
NEGROS Philippines
ORKNEY Scotland
PARRIS North America
PENANG Indonesia
POMONA Scotland
PONAPE Pacific
RHODES Mediterranean, Greece
ROTUMA Atlantic
SAISHU South Korea
SANDAY Scotland
SAREMA Estonia
SAVAII Pacific
SCARBA Atlantic
SCILLY England
SHEMYA Bering
SIBUTU Philippines
SICILY Mediterranean, Italy
TAHITI Pacific
TAIWAN Pacific (Nationalist China)
TANAGA Bering
THASOS Greece
TINIAN Pacific
TOBAGO Caribbean
TORTUE Caribbean
TUBUAI Pacific
TULAGI Pacific
UNIMAK Bering
USEDOM Baltic
VIRGIN Caribbean

ACKLINS Atlantic
AGALEGA Indian Ocean
AMAKUSA Japan
ANDAMAN Indian Ocean

ANTIGUA Caribbean
AUSTRAL Pacific
BAHREIN Indian Ocean
BARANOF Pacific
BARENTS Arctic
BERMUDA Atlantic
CAYENNE South America
CELEBES Indonesia
CHATHAM Pacific
CORSICA Mediterranean
CURACAO Caribbean
DIOMEDE Bering
FAEROES Atlantic
FALSTER Denmark
FORMOSA Rep. China
GILBERT Pacific
IWOJIMA Pacific
JAMAICA Caribbean
KOLGUEV Arctic
LAALAND Denmark
LOFOTEN Arctic
LOLLAND Denmark
MADEIRA Atlantic
MAJORCA Mediterranean
MARIANA Pacific
MINDORO Philippines
MINORCA Mediterranean
MOLUCCA Pacific
NICOBAR Indian Ocean
OKINAWA Pacific
PALAWAN Philippines
REUNION Indian Ocean
SALAMIS Greece
SEMICHI Bering
TERNATE Indonesia
TORTOLA Caribbean
TORTUGA Caribbean

ALEUTIAN Bering
AMCHITKA Bering
ANTILLES Caribbean
BALEARES Mediterranean
BARBADOS Caribbean
BERMUDAS Atlantic
BORNHOLM Baltic
CAROLINE Pacific
CYCLADES Mediterranean
DOMINICA Caribbean
FALKLAND Atlantic
GOTTLAND Baltic
GUERNSEY England
HEBRIDES Scotland
HOKKAIDO Japan

MARIANAS Pacific
MARSHALL Pacific
MELVILLE Arctic
MINDANAO Philippines
MOLUCCAS Indonesia
SAKHALIN Pacific
SARDINIA Mediterranean, Italy
SHETLAND Scotland
SOMERSET Arctic
STHELENA Atlantic
TASMANIA Australia
TENERIFE Atlantic
TRINIDAD Caribbean
UNALASKA Bering
VICTORIA Arctic
ZANZIBAR Indian Ocean

BALEARICS Mediterranean
GALAPAGOS Pacific
GREENLAND Arctic

RIVERS OF THE UNITED STATES

DAN Va.
ELK Tenn., W.Va.
FOX Wisc.
NEW Va.
RED Okla.

EAST N.Y.
GILA N.M.
IOWA Ia.
KERN Cal.
LOUP Neb.
MILK Mont.
OHIO Midwest
ROCK Wis.

ALSEK Alas.
BLACK Mo., Ark.
BRONX N.Y.
CACHE Ark.
CEDAR Minn., Ia.
COOSA Ala., Ga.
FLINT Ga.
GRAND Mich., Mo., S.D.
GREEN Ky., Ill., Ind. Wyo., Col., Ut.
JAMES =DAKOTA
JAMES Va.
LLANO Tex.
MACON La.
MIAMI O.
NEUSE N.C.
OSAGE Kan., Mo.
PEARL Miss.
PECOS N.M., Tex.
ROGUE Ore.
SNAKE Northwest, Minn.
WHITE Ark., Col., Ut., S.D., Tex.
YAQUI N.M.
YAZOO Miss.
YUKON Alas.

BARREN Ky.
BEAVER Pa.
BRAZOS Tex.
CAHABA Ala.
CLINCH Tenn.
COPPER Alas.
DAKOTA N.D.
HUDSON N.Y.
KANSAS Kan.
MOHAWK N.Y.
NECHES Tex.
NEOSHO Kan., Okla.
NOATAK Alas.
NUECES Tex.
OCONEE Ga.
OWYHEE Id., Ore.
PEEDEE N.C., S.C.
PLATTE Ia., Mo., Neb.
POWDER Ore., Mont., Wyo.
SABINE Tex., La.
SALMON Id.
SANTEE S.C.
SCIOTO O.
TANANA Alas.
TONGUE Wyo., Mont.
WABASH Ind., Ill.

ALABAMA Ala.
BIGHORN Wyo., Mont.
CAHAWBA =CAHABA
DOLORES Col., Ut.
GENESEE Pa., N.Y.
HOLSTON Tenn.
JOHNDAY Ore.
KLAMATH Ore.
KOYUKUK Alas.
LARAMIE Col., Wyo.
LICKING Ky.
POTOMAC Mid-Atlantic
ROANOKE Va., N.C.
SANJUAN Southwest
STCROIX Wis., Minn.
STJOHNS Fla.
SUWANEE Ga., Fla.
TRINITY Cal., Tex.
WASHITA Okla., Tex.
WASHITA =OUACHITA

ALTAMAHA Ga.
ARKANSAS Southwest
BIGBLACK Miss.
CANADIAN Southwest
CAPEFEAR N.C.
CHEYENNE S.D.
CHIPPEWA Wisc.
CIMARRON N.M., Okla.
COLORADO Southwest
COLUMBIA Northwest
COLVILLE Alas.
DELAWARE Mid-atlantic
GUNNISON Col.
HUMBOLDT Nev.
ILLINOIS Ill.
KENNEBEC Me.
KENTUCKY Ky.
MISSOURI Central
NIOBRARA Wyo., Neb.
OUACHITA Ark., La.
RIOBRAVO =RIOGRANDE
RIOPECOS =PECOS
SAVANNAH Ga.

ALLEGHENY Pa.
DESCHUTES Ore.
DESMOINES Ia.
KUSKOKWIM Alas.
MERRIMACK N.H., Mass.
MINNESOTA Minn.
MUSKINGUM Ohio
PENOBSCOT Me.
PORCUPINE Alas.
RIOGRANDE Southwest
SMOKYHILL Col., Kan.
STFRANCIS Mo., Ark.
TENNESSEE South
TOMBIGBEE Ala., Miss.
WISCONSIN Wis.

CUMBERLAND Ky., Tenn.

FOREIGN RIVERS

AA	Algeria
BO	Chile
OB	USSR
OM	USSR
PO	Italy
SI	China
WU	China
AAR	Switzerland
AIN	France
APA	Paraguay
ARO	Venezuela
BOW	Canada
BUG	Poland
CAM	England
CHU	USSR
COI	China
DAL	Sweden
DEE	Scotland, Wales, England
DON	USSR
EMS	Germany
EXE	England
FLY	Papua New Guinea
HAB	Pakistan
HAN	China
ICA	Peru
ILI	USSR
ILL	Austria, France
INN	Germany
JIU	Romania
JUR	Egypt
KAN	China
KEM	USSR
LEE	Ireland
LOA	Chile
LOT	France
LYS	Belgium
MIN	China
MUN	Thailand
MUR	Austria
NAB	Germany
NAN	Thailand
OKA	USSR
OLT	Romania
OMO	Ethiopia
PEI	China
RUR	Germany
SAN	Poland
TAY	Scotland
TZU	China
UFA	USSR
UME	Sweden
UNA	Yugoslavia
URE	England
USK	Wales, England
VAH	Czechoslovakia

VAR	France
WEI	China
AARE	Switzerland
ABRA	Philippines
ADDA	Italy
AGNO	Philippines
AIRE	England, France
AKSU	Turkey
ALLE	Germany
ALMA	USSR
ALTA	Norway
AMGA	Iran
AMUR	Asia
ARAS	Turkey
ARDA	Bulgaria
ARNO	Italy
ARTA	Greece
ATHI	Kenya
AUBE	France
AUDE	France
AVON	England
AVRE	France
BANN	Ireland
BENI	Bolivia
BOBR	Poland
CHER	France
CLUJ	Romania
CRNA	Yugoslavia
DALY	Australia
DOCE	Brazil
DOON	Scotland
DRAU	Austria
DRIN	Albania
DUNA	USSR
EBRO	Spain
EDER	Germany
EGER	Czechoslovakia
ELBE	Germany
EMBA	USSR
EMME	Korea
ENNS	Austria
ERNE	Ireland
ESLA	Spain
EURE	France
GEBA	Africa
GERS	France
HRON	Czechoslovakia
HWAI	China
HWEI	China
IBAR	Gabon
ILEK	USSR
IPEL	Czechoslovakia
ISAR	Germany
ISER	Czechoslovakia
IVAI	Brazil

JARI	Brazil
JUBA	Africa
KAMA	USSR
KARA	USSR
KEMI	Finland
KLAR	Norway
KOSI	India
KUPA	Yugoslavia
KURA	USSR
KUSI	India
KWEI	China
LAHN	Germany
LENA	USSR
LIAO	China
LOIR	France
LULE	Sweden
LUNI	India
LWAN	China
MAAS	Netherlands
MALI	Burma
MAND	Iran
MAYA	USSR
MAYO	Mexico
META	Colombia
MONO	Togo
MSTA	USSR
MUSI	Indonesia
NAAB	Germany
NAPO	Ecuador
NASS	Canada
NERA	Italy
NEVA	USSR
NILE	Africa
NMAI	Burma
NORE	Ireland
NYSA	Poland
ODER	Poland
OHRE	Czechoslovakia
OISE	France
ONON	USSR
ORNE	France
OUSE	England
OXUS	USSR
PARA	Brazil
PARU	Brazil
PING	Thailand
PITE	Sweden
PRUT	Romania
RAAB	Austria
RABA	Austria
RAMU	Papua New Guinea
RAVI	India
REMS	Germany
RENO	Italy
RIET	South Africa

ROER Germany
RUHR Germany
SAAR France
SAMA Peru
SAVA Yugoslavia
SEIM USSR
SPEY Liechtenstein
STYR USSR
SULA USSR
SURA USSR
SWAN Australia
SWAT Pakistan
TAJO Spain
TANA Kenya, Norway
TARN France
TEJO Spain
TISA USSR
TOMO Colombia
TURA USSR
TYNE England
UELE Africa
URAL USSR
VAAL South Africa
VAKH USSR
WAAL Netherlands
YALU Korea
YANA USSR
YSER France
YUAN China

ABUNA Bolivia
ADIGE Italy
ADOUR France
AGOUT France
AGUAN Honduras
AISNE France
AKABA Mongolia
AKOBO Ethiopia
ALDAN USSR
ALLER Germany
ALLIA Italy
ALUTA Romania
AMECA Mexico
ANCRE France
ANGAT Philippines
ANNAN Scotland
ANYUI USSR
APURE Venezuela
AQABA Jordan
ARAKS Turkey
ARGES Romania
ARGOS Greece
ARGUN USSR
ATRAK Iran
ATREK Iran
ATUEL Argentina
BAKOY Sudan
BANAS India
BENIN Nigeria
BENUE Africa
BETWA India
BHIMA India
BOSNA Yugoslavia
BOYNE Ireland
BYTOM Poland
CAMPO Cameroon
CAUCA Colombia
CAURA Venezuela
CHARI Africa
CLYDE Scotland
CONGO Africa
CUITO Africa
DESNA USSR
DNEPR USSR
DOUBS France
DOURO Italy
DRAVA Yugoslavia
DRAVE Yugoslavia
DULCE Argentina
DVINA USSR
EIDER Germany
ETSCH Italy
ETSIN China
FARAH Afghanistan
FULDA Germany
GANGA India
GAUYA Latvia
GOGRA India
GUDEN Denmark
GUMAL Pakistan
HAVEL Germany
HWANG China
ILLER Germany
INDRE Colombia
INDUS Pakistan
INGUL USSR
IRIKI Brazil
ISERE France
ISHIM USSR
ISKER Bulgaria
JACUI Brazil
JUMNA India
JUTAI Brazil
KAFUE Africa
KAJAN Guatemala
KARUN Iran
KASAI Africa
KATUN USSR
KHETA USSR
KLONG Thailand
KOBDO Mongolia
KUBAN USSR
KURSK USSR
LAGAN Sweden
LALIN China
LEMPA El Salvador
LIARD Canada
LINDI Congo
LIPPE Germany
LOIRE France
LULUA Congo
MARNE France
MEUSE France
MEZEN USSR
MINHO Spain
MOSEL Germany
MUTAN China
NAMOI Australia
NEMAN USSR
NERIS Poland
NIGER Africa
NONNI China
NOTEC Poland
OGLIO Italy
OGOKI Canada
OGOWE Gabon
ORTON Peru
OSKOL USSR
PALAR India
PARDO Brazil
PATIA Colombia
PEACE Canada
PERAK Malaysia
PIAVE Italy
PIBOR Sudan
PIURA Peru
PURUS Peru
RAPTI Nepal
REGEN Germany
REUSS Switzerland
RHEIN Germany
RHINE Europe
RHONE France
ROPER Australia
SAALE Germany
SANGA Congo
SAONE France
SARRE France
SEINE France
SENNE Belgium
SHARI Africa
SHASI China
SIANG China
SIRET Romania
SOBAT Ethiopia
SOMES Hungary
SOSVA USSR
SPREE Germany
STOUR England
SURMA India
TAGUS Romania
TAPTI India
TEREK USSR
TIBER Italy
TIETE Brazil
TIGRE Ecuador
TIMIS Yugoslavia

TISTA India
TISZA USSR
TOBOL USSR
TORNE Finland
TRAUN Austria
TRENT England, Canada
VENTA USSR
VESLE France
VISLA Poland
WARTA Poland
WESER Germany
WISLA Poland
XINGU Brazil

ABAKAN USSR
AFRINE Turkey
AGUSAN Philippines
ALBANY Canada
AMAZON Brazil
ANGARA USSR
ARAGON Spain
ARAUCA Colombia
ARIEGE France
ATBARA Sudan
BAFING Sudan
BALIKH Turkey
BARCOO Australia
BARITO Indonesia
BEAVER Canada
BELAYA USSR
BIOBIO Chile
BRENTA Italy
CARONI Venezuela
CARROT Canada
CHUBUT Argentina
CHULYM USSR
DANUBE Europe
DAWSON Australia
DELICE Turkey
DNESTR USSR
DONETS USSR
ENISEI USSR
FRASER Canada
GALANA Kenya
GANDAK Nepal
GANGES India
GILGIT India
HAWASH Ethiopia
HINGOL Pakistan
IRTISH Asia
IRTYSH Asia
JAPURA Colombia
KHILOK USSR
KOLIMA USSR
KOMATI South Africa
KURUME Japan
LIMMAT Switzerland
LOANGE Congo
LOPORI Congo
MADIDI Bolivia
MAMORE Bolivia
MEKONG Asia
MODDER South Africa
MOISIE Canada
MOLDAU Czechoslovakia
MOLOGA USSR
MOSKVA USSR
MURGAB USSR
MURRAY Australia
NECKAR Germany
NEISSE Poland
NELSON Canada
OLDMAN Canada
OLENEK USSR
OMOLON USSR
ORANGE South Africa
ORKHON Mongolia
PAHANG Malaysia
PARANA Brazil
PATUCA Honduras
PENNER India
PINEGA USSR
PREGEL USSR
PRIPET USSR
RAJANG Indonesia
SALADO Argentina
SALWIN Burma
SAMARA USSR
SEVERN Wales, England
SONORA Mexico
SOURIS Canada
STRUMA Bulgaria
SUTLEJ India
THAMES England
THEISS USSR
TICINO Switzerland
TIGRIS Turkey
TUGELA South Africa
UAUPES Colombia
VIENNE France
VITAVA Czechoslovakia
YALUNG China
YAPURA Colombia
YELLOW China

ABITIBI Canada
ALBERGA Canada
BERMEJO South America
DARLING Australia
DNIEPER USSR
GARONNE France
GLENELG Australia
LIMPOPO Africa
MADEIRA Brazil
MARITSA Turkey
MOSELLE France
ORINOCO Venezuela
PECHORA USSR
SALWEEN Burma
SHANNON Ireland
SITTANG Burma
SUNGARI China
VISTULA Poland
YANGTZE China
YENISEI USSR
ZAMBESI Africa
ZAMBEZI Africa
AMUDARYA USSR
HAMILTON Canada
RIONEGRO Argentina
SYRDARYA USSR
ATHABASCA Canada
EUPHRATES Asia
IRRAWADDY India
MACKENZIE Canada
MAGDALENA Colombia
RIOGRANDE Mexico

CANADA AT A GLANCE

	Province	*Date**	*Abbr.*	*Capital*
1	Alberta	1905	Alta.	Edmonton
2	British Columbia	1871	B.C.	Victoria
3	Manitoba	1870	Man.	Winnipeg
4	New Brunswick	1867	N.B.	Fredericton
5	Newfoundland	1949	Nfld., Newf.	St. John's
6	Nova Scotia	1867	N.S.	Halifax

	Province	*Date**	*Abbr.*	*Capital*
7	Ontario[1]	1867	Ont.	Toronto
8	Prince Edward Island[2]	1873	P.E.I.	Charlottetown
9	Quebec[3]	1867	Que.	Quebec
10	Saskatchewan	1905	Sask.	Regina
	Territory		*Abbr.*	*Capital*
11	Yukon		Y.T.	Whitehorse
12	Northwest Territories		N.W.T.	Yellowknife

PRIME MINISTERS

Name	*Party*	*Term*	*Birthplace*	*Occupation*
MACDONALD, Sir John Alexander	Cons.	1867–73	Glasgow, Scotland	Lawyer
MACKENZIE, Alexander	Liberal	1873–78	Pertshire, Scotland	
(MACDONALD, Sir J.A.)		1878–91		
ABBOTT, Sir John Joseph Caldwell	Cons.	1891–92	St. Andrews, Que.	Lawyer
THOMPSON, Sir John Sparrow David	Cons.	1892–94	Halifax, N.S.	Lawyer
BOWELL, Sir Mackenzie	Cons.	1894–96	Rickinghall, England	Editor
TUPPER, Sir Charles	Cons.	1896	Amherst, N.S.	Doctor
LAURIER, Sir Wilfrid	Liberal	1896–1911	St. Lin, Que.	Lawyer
BORDEN, Sir Robert Laird	Cons.-Unionist	1911–20	Grand Pre, N.S.	Civil servant
MEIGHEN, Arthur	Cons.-Unionist	1920–21	Perth, Ont.	Lawyer
KING, William Lyon Mackenzie	Liberal	1921–26	Kitchener, Ont.	Civil servant
(MEIGHEN, Arthur)		1926		
(KING, W.L. Mackenzie)		1926–30		
BENNETT, Richard Bedford	Cons.	1930–35	Hopewell, N.B.	Lawyer
(KING, W.L. Mackenzie)		1935–48		
STLAURENT, Louis Stephen	Liberal	1948–57	Que.	Lawyer
DIEFENBAKER, John George	Prog. Cons.	1957–63	Grey Co., Ont.	Lawyer
PEARSON, Lester Bowles	Liberal	1963–68	Toronto, Ont.	Historian
TRUDEAU, Pierre Elliot	Liberal	1968–79	Montreal, Que.	Lawyer
CLARK, Joe	Prog. Cons.	1979–80	High River, Alta.	Lawyer
(TRUDEAU, Pierre Elliot)		1980–84		
TURNER John Napier	Liberal	1984	Richmond, England	Lawyer
MULRONEY, Martin Brian	Prog. Cons.	1984–	Baie Comeau, Que.	Lawyer

*Date of entry of province into Confederation
[1]Largest province in area
[2]Smallest province in area and population
[3]Largest province in population

THE UNITED STATES AT A GLANCE

State	*No.**	*Abbr.*	*Capitol*
1 ALABAMA	22	AL, Ala.	Montgomery
2 ALASKA[1]	49	AK, Alas.	Juneau
3 ARIZONA	48	AZ, Ariz.	Phoenix
4 ARKANSAS	25	AR, Ark.	Little Rock
5 CALIFORNIA[2]	31	CA. Cal(if).	Sacramento
6 COLORADO	38	CO, Col(o).	Denver
7 CONNECTICUT	5	CT, Conn.	Hartford
8 DELAWARE	1	DE, Del.	Dover
9 FLORIDA	27	FL, Fla.	Tallahassee
10 GEORGIA	4	GA, Ga.	Atlanta
11 HAWAII	50	HI, Haw.	Honolulu
12 IDAHO	43	ID, Id.	Boise
13 ILLINOIS	21	IL, Ill.	Springfield
14 INDIANA	19	IN, Ind.	Indianapolis
15 IOWA	29	IA, Ia.	Des Moines
16 KANSAS	34	KS, Kan(s).	Topeka
17 KENTUCKY	15	KY, Ky.	Frankfort
18 LOUISIANA	18	LA, La.	Baton Rouge
19 MAINE	23	ME, Me.	Augusta
20 MARYLAND	7	MD, Md.	Annapolis
21 MASSACHUSETTS	6	MA, Mass.	Boston
22 MICHIGAN	26	MI, Mich.	Lansing
23 MINNESOTA	32	MN, Minn.	St. Paul
24 MISSISSIPPI	20	MS, Miss.	Jackson
25 MISSOURI	24	MO, Mo.	Jefferson City
26 MONTANA	41	MT, Mont.	Helena
27 NEBRASKA	37	NE, Neb(r).	Lincoln
28 NEVADA	36	NV, Nev.	Carson City
29 NEW HAMPSHIRE	9	NH, N.H.	Concord
30 NEW JERSEY	3	NJ, N.J.	Trenton
31 NEW MEXICO	47	NM, N.M.	Sante Fe
32 NEW YORK	11	NY, N.Y.	Albany
33 NORTH CAROLINA	12	NC, N.C.	Raleigh
34 NORTH DAKOTA	39	ND, N.D.	Bismarck
35 OHIO	17	OH, O.	Columbus
36 OKLAHOMA	46	OK, Okla.	Oklahoma City
37 OREGON	33	OR, Ore.	Salem
38 PENNSYLVANIA	2	PA, Penn(a).	Harrisburg
39 RHODE ISLAND[3]	13	RI, R.I.	Providence
40 SOUTH CAROLINA	8	SC, S.C.	Columbia
41 SOUTH DAKOTA	40	SD, S.D.	Pierre
42 TENNESSEE	16	TN, Tenn.	Nashville
43 TEXAS	28	TX, Tex.	Austin
44 UTAH	45	UT, Ut.	Salt Lake City
45 VERMONT	14	VT, Vt.	Montpelier
46 VIRGINIA	10	VA, Va.	Richmond
47 WASHINGTON	42	WA, Wash.	Olympia
48 WEST VIRGINIA	35	WV, W.Va.	Charleston
49 WISCONSIN	30	WI, Wis(c).	Madison
50 WYOMING	44	WY, Wyo.	Cheyenne

*Order of admission into the Union; 1-13 Original States
[1]Largest in area, smallest in population
[2]Largest in population
[3]Smallest in area

	State Nickname	*State Motto*
1	Heart of Dixie, Cotton	We Dare Defend Our Rights
2	The Last Frontier	North to the Future
3	Grand Canyon, Sunset Land	Ditat Deus: God Enriches
4	Land of Opportunity, Wonder	Regnat Populus: Let the People Rule
5	Golden, Grape	Eureka: I Have Found It
6	Centennial, Rover	Nil Sine Numine: Nothing w/o Deity
7	Constitution, Nutmeg	He Who Transplanted, Sustains
8	First, Diamond	Liberty and Independence
9	Sunshine, Everglade	In God We Trust
10	Empire State of the South	Wisdom, Justice, Moderation
11	Aloha	The Life of the Land is Perpetuated In Righteousness
12	Gem, Gem of the Mountains	Esto Perpetua: Exist Forever
13	Prairie, Sucker	State Sovereignty, National Union
14	Hoosier, Carnation	Cross-roads of America
15	Hawkeye, Beautiful Land	Our Liberties We Prize, And Our Rights We Will Maintain
16	Sunflower, Jayhawk	Ad Astra Per Aspera: To The Stars Through Difficulties
17	Blue Grass	United We Stand, Divided We Fall
18	Pelican, Sugar, Creole	Union, Justice, Confidence
19	Pine Tree, Lumber	Dirigo: I Direct
20	Old Line, Free	Manly Deeds, Womanly Words
21	Bay, Old Colony	By the Sword We Seek Peace, but Peace Only Under Liberty
22	Wolverine, Lake	If You Seek a Pleasant Peninsula Look About You
23	North Star, Gopher	L'Etoile du Nord: Star of the North
24	Magnolia, Bayou	Virtute et Armis: By Virtue and Arms
25	Show Me, Bullion	The Welfare of the People Shall Be the Supreme Law
26	Treasure, Bonanza	Oro y Plata: Gold and Silver
27	Beef, Cornhusker	Equality Before the Law
28	Sagebrush, Silver, Battle-Born	All for Our Country
29	Granite, White Mountain	Live Free or Die
30	Garden	Liberty and Prosperity
31	Land of Enchantment, Sunshine	Crescit Eundo: It Grows as it Goes
32	Empire, Excelsior	Excelsior: Ever Upward
33	Tar Heel, Old North	To be Rather Than To Seem
34	Sioux, Flickertail	Liberty and Union, Now and Forever, One and Inseparable
35	Buckeye	With God All Things Are Possible
36	Sooner	Labor Conquers All Things
37	Beaver, Webfoot	The Union
38	Keystone, Quaker, Steel	Virtue, Liberty and Independence
39	Little Rhody, Gun Flint	Hope
40	Palmetto	Dum Spiro, Spero: While I Breathe, ^ I Hope
41	Coyote, Sunshine	Under God, The People Rule
42	Volunteer, Big Bend	Agriculture, Commerce
43	Lone Star, Beef	Friendship
44	Beehive, Mormon	Industry
45	Green Mountain	Freedom and Unity
46	Old Dominion, Cavalier	Sic Semper Tyrannis: Thus Always ^ to Tyrants
47	Evergreen, Chinook	Bye and Bye
48	Mountain, Panhandle	Mountaineers Always Free
49	Badger, Cheese	Forward
50	Equality	Equal Rights

	State Flower	*State Tree*	*State Bird*
1	Camelia	Southern pine	Yellowhammer
2	Forget-me-not	Sitka spruce	Willow ptarmigan
3	Saguaro cactus	Paloverde	Cactus wren
4	Apple blossom	Pine	Mockingbird
5	Golden poppy	Calif. redwood	Calif. valley quail
6	Columbine	Blue spruce	Lark bunting
7	Mountain laurel	White oak	American robin
8	Peach blossom	American holly	Blue hen chicken
9	Orange blossom	Sabal palmetto palm	Mockingbird
10	Cherokee rose	Live oak	Brown thrasher
11	Hibiscus	Candlenut	Hawaiian goose
12	Syringa	White pine	Mountain bluebird
13	Butterfly violet	White oak	Cardinal
14	Peony	Tulip poplar	Cardinal
15	Wild rose	Oak	Eastern goldfinch
16	Sunflower	Cottonwood	Western meadowlark
17	Goldenrod	Kentucky coffee tree	Cardinal
18	Magnolia	Cypress	Eastern brown pelican
19	Pine cone & tassel	Eastern white pine	Chickadee
20	Black-eyed susan	White oak	Baltimore oriole
21	Mayflower	American elm	Chickadee
22	Apple blossom	White pine	Robin
23	Lady's-slipper	Red pine	Common loon
24	Magnolia	Magnolia	Mockingbird
25	Hawthorn	Dogwood	Bluebird
26	Bitterroot	Ponderosa pine	Western meadowlark
27	Goldenrod	Cottonwood	Western meadowlark
28	Sagebrush	Single-leaf piñon	Mountain bluebird
29	Purple lilac	White birch	Purple finch
30	Purple violet	Red oak	Eastern goldfinch
31	Yucca	Piñon, pinyon	Roadrunner
32	Rose	Sugar maple	Bluebird
33	Dogwood	Dogwood	Cardinal
34	Wild prairie rose	American elm	Western meadowlark
35	Scarlet carnation	Buckeye	Cardinal
36	Mistletoe	Redbug	Scissortailed flycatcher
37	Oregon grape	Douglas fir	Western meadowlark
38	Mountain laurel	Hemlock	Ruffed grouse
39	Violet	Red maple	Rhode Island red
40	Carolina jessamine	Palmetto	Carolina wren
41	Pasque flower	Black Hills spruce	Ringnecked pheasant
42	Iris	Tulip poplar	Mockingbird
43	Bluebonnet	Pecan	Mockingbird
44	Sego lily	Blue spruce	Seagull
45	Red clover	Sugar maple	Hermit thrush
46	American dogwood	Dogwood	Cardinal
47	Western rhododendron	Western hemlock	Willow goldfinch
48	Big rhododendron	Sugar maple	Cardinal
49	Wood violet	Sugar maple	Robin
50	Indian paintbrush	Cottonwood	Meadowlark

N.B.: Refer to p. 308 for state numbers

HERALDRY

BEARINGS

CHARGE ORDINARY AND SUB-ORDINARY

*Indicates roundels

BAR	**CHIEF**	**CLOSET**	**CHEVRON**
BEND	**CROSS**	**COTISE**	**ENDORSE**
COST	**FESSE**	**FILLET**	**FLANCHE**
FESS	**FILET**	**GARTER**	**QUARTER**
FRET	**FUSIL**	**MASCLE**	**ROUNDEL***
GORE	**GEMEL**	**OGRESS***	**SALTIER**
GUZE*	**GOLPE**	**ORANGE***	**SALTIRE**
HURT*	**GYRON**	**PALLET**	**TORTEAU***
ORLE	**LABEL**	**PELLET***	**BARRULET**
PALE	**PLATE***	**RIBAND**	**DANCETTE**
PALL	**POMEY***	**RUSTRE**	**SALTOREL**
PILE	**SCARP**	**SCARPE**	**TRESSURE**
SYKE*	**BEZANT***	**VIROLE***	**CHEVRONEL**
BATON	**BILLET**	**ANNULET***	**SHAKEFORK**
BENDY	**CANTON**	**BORDURE**	

CROSS(LIKE)

CRUX	**ANCREE**	**POTENT**	**PATONCE**
PATY	**BOTONE**	**AVELLAN**	**SALTIRE**
URDE	**BOTONY**	**BOTONEE**	**CERCELEE**
URDY	**CLECHE**	**CERCELE**	**CRUSILEE**
FLORY	**FITCHE**	**CRUSILE**	**FOURCHEE**
POMME	**FLEURY**	**FITCHEE**	**SARCELLE**
URDEE	**MOLINE**	**FOURCHE**	

CREATURES

GRAY	badger	**TALBOT**	hound
LOUP	wolf	**WYVERN**	dragon
ALAND	mastiff	**ENFIELD**	fox-wolf
BROCK	badger	**GRIFFON**	lion-eagle
HARPY	woman-bird	**GRYPHON**	= **GRIFFON**
GRICE	young boar	**LIONCEL**	little lion
TYGER	tiger	**MARTLET**	bird
WYVER	dragon	**MUSIMON**	goat-ram
ALANDT	mastiff	**ALLERION**	eagle
BAGWYN	antelope-horse	**OPENICUS**	lion-dragon
CANNET	duck	**POPINJAY**	parrot
CHOUGH	raven	**SANGLIER**	wild boar

POSITIONS OF CREATURES

ASSIS	sitting	**VORANT**	eating
JACENT	lying over	**COURANT**	running
NATANT	swimming	**DORMANT**	lying down
SEJANT	sitting	**FLOTANT**	floating
VOLANT	flying	**FORCENE**	rearing

ISSUANT	partly visible	STATANT	standing
JESSANT	lying over	URINANT	diving
PASSANT	walking	COUCHANT	lying
RAMPANT	reared up	HAURIANT	diving
ROUSANT	rising	HAURIENT	diving
SALIENT	leaping	TRIPPANT	tripping

OBJECTS

VOL	two wings	TORSE	sheath
BREY	barnacle	GOUTTE	drop
SEAX	scimitar	MANCHE	sleeve
SYKE	fountain	MULLET	star
WEEL	fishtrap	TIRRET	manacle
BATON	staff	BOTEROL	sheath end
GERBE	sheaf	ESCROLL	scroll
LAVER	colter	ESTOILE	star
PHEON	arrowhead	LYMPHAD	boat

TINCTURES

OR	gold	TENNE	orange
VERT	green	ARGENT	silver
AZURE	blue	MURREY	dark red
GULES	red	PURPURE	purple
SABLE	black		

LINES OF PARTITION / FURS

LINES OF PARTITION			FURS
NOWY	NEBULY	DANCETTY	PEAN
ONDE	RAGULY	EMBATTLED	VAIR
UNDE	POTENTY	ENGRAILED	ERMINE
UNDY	INDENTED	RAYONNANT	POTENT
URDY	INVECTED	DOVETAILED	
WAVY			

CADENCY
LINE OF SUCCESSION

LABEL	heir	ANNULET	5th son
CRESCENT	2nd son	FLEURDELIS	6th son
MULLET	3rd son	ROSE	7th son
MARTLET	4th son	MOLINE	8th son

OTHER TERMS

AILE	winged	CHECKY	checkered
ENTE	grafted	COUPED	cut off
PALY	divided vertically	DEXTER	right side (of wearer)
SEME	sprinkled, strewn	GOBONY	divided into squares
VULN	to wound	GRINED	maned
BARRY	with horizontal bars	GUSSET	abatement
CLOUE	nail-studded	TIERCE	in 3 parts
GUTTE	semé of drops	TREFLE	three-lobed
GUTTY	= GUTTE	APPAUME	showing palm
NOWED	knotted	COMPONE	= GOBONY
ROMPU	broken	EMBOWED	bent
ACCOLE	side by side	ENFILED	passed through

FRACTED broken
IMBRUED blood-stained
MASCULY lozenged
UNGULED hoofed
ADDORSED back to back
AFFRONTE face to face
AVERSANT showing back
CABOSHED showing head
DEBRUISE cover partly
ENGOULED partly swallowed
SANGLANT bleeding
SINISTER left side (of wearer)

LITERATURE—FICTIONAL CHARACTERS

AMERICAN LITERATURE

EVA
JIM
RIP
TOM

AHAB
ANNA
BESS
BROM
BUDD
CORA
DICK
DRED
DUER
FINN
HIST
MOBY
OMOO
PREW
SLIM

APLEY

ARTIE
AUGIE
BRETT
CANTY
ELMER
GAMUT
HOLLY
HORNE
OHARA
PITTY
POLLY
PORGY
STARK
STUDS
TOPSY
TOZER
TRAUM
UNCAS

ASHLEY
AYLMER
BUMPPO

GANTRY
GATSBY
JESSUP
LAPHAM
LEGREE
LENNIE
MUNROE
PRYNNE
SAWYER
SHELBY
SNOPES
VENNER
WILKES
WINKLE

AGAPIDA
ANTONIA
BABBITT
DOREMUS
HAWKEYE
LONIGAN
MELANIE

PREWITT
REBECCA
SELLERS
WAPSHOT
ZENOBIA

HOLGRAVE
INJUNJOE
MCTEAGUE
QUEEQUEG
REDROVER
SCARLETT
STARBUCK
THATCHER
UNCLETOM

DODSWORTH
SNODGRASS
TOMSAWYER

ARROWSMITH

LITERATURE OF GREAT BRITAIN AND IRELAND

AGG
BHO
DAN
DHU
FAG
JIM
KIM
LEW
MEG
PEW
UMA
UNA
WAT

ABEL
AMAL
BECK
BEDE
CASS

COAN
COXE
ENID
EYRE
GANN
GARM
GUNN
HATT
HOOK
HYDE
IPPS
JANE
KULU
LAWS
LYON
MEON
MOLL
NIBS
RIMA

TUCK
WAGG

AISSA
AKELA
ARDEN
ARGAN
BALOO
BARDI
BLANE
BONEY
BRACY
BRECK
BULBO
DEANS
EDGAR
FOKER
GARTH
GLEGG

SHAWE
SILAS
SNOWE
SORTI
TESSA
TINTO
TORRE
TROIL
TRYAN
VINCY
WAMBA

ABDIEL
ARIOCH
ASHTON
ATOSSA
BEETLE
BESSEE
BINNIE

BOLTON
BOURKE
CRUSOE
DECOUD
DEEVER
DOBBIN
ESMOND
FLORAC
FRIDAY
GRAEME
HELDAR
JACQUE

JEKYLL
LARSEN
MAISIE
MARLOW
MARNER
MELEMA
MOWGLI
ROMOLA
ROWENA
SEYTON
ZEPHON

ADONAIS
ALASTOR
BELINDA
BLUDYER
CRAWLEY
DERONDA
DINMONT
FENELLA
GIZELLE
HARLETH
IVANHOE
LATIMER

LORDJIM
LYDGATE
MATILDA
RODRIGO
SHAFTON
SHANDON
SHIRLEY
SWEENEY
TRAVERS
URFRIED
WILLEMS
ZOPHIEL

LITERATURE OF CONTINENTAL EUROPE

ASE
BLY

ANNA
GOTZ
GYNT
NEMO
NORA
PEER
PERE
PONS

AOUDA
ARGAN
ATHOS
BAGOT
BRAND
BULBA
EYOLF
FAUST
HEDDA
HULAT
LELIE
MITYA
ORGON
SONIA
STIVA

TARAS
VANYA
WERLE

ALVING
ANITRA
ARAMIS
ARISTE
ASHLEY
BELINE
BUNGAY
CATHOS
COLLIN
DANTES
EGMONT
ESPARD
FEDORA
FROLLO
GABLER
GORIOT
HELMER
JAVERT
MARION
MARSAY
MIGNON
SHATOV

TRILBY

ALCESTE
ALOADIN
ALYOSHA
ANSELME
ARVALAN
CAMILLE
CLEANTE
COSETTE
DORANTE
GERONTE
GOBSECK
GRANDET
HERNANI
ISIDORE
KATUSHA
LEANDRE
MANDERS
MARTINE
MEISTER
MYSHKIN
POPINOT
PORTHOS
RESTAUD
SOLVEIG

VALJEAN
VAUTRIN
VRONSKI
WERTHER
WILHELM

ATHANAEL
BERGERET
CHRYSALE
DELORMES
FLORINDA
GORGIBUS
GRETCHEN
HARPAGON
KARENINA
LADURLAD
NASTASIA
RODERICK
SHIGALOV
TARTUFFE

CHICHIKOV
DARTAGNAN
ESMERALDA
KARAMAZOV
QUASIMODO

SHAKESPEARE

NYM
SAY

ADAM
CADE
DAVY
DION
HERO
IAGO
IDEN
IRAS
JAMY
JOHN
LEAR

LUCE
PETO
PUCK
ROSS
SNUG
VAUX

ANGUS
ARIEL
BAGOT
BIRON
BOYET
BUSHY
CAIUS

CELIA
CORIN
CURAN
CURIO
EGEUS
ELBOW
FESTE
FLUTE
FROTH
GOBBO
GOFFE
GOWER
HENRY
JULIA

LAFEU
LOVEL
LUCIO
MELUN
MOPSA
OSRIC
PHEBE
PINCH
REGAN
ROBIN
ROMEO
RUGBY
SNOUT
SOSIA

SPEED
TIMON
TITUS

ADRIAN
AEGEON
ALONSO
ANGELO
ANTONY
BANQUO
BIANCA
BOLEYN
BOTTOM
CAESAR
CAPHIS
CLOTEN
DORCAS
DROMIO
DUNCAN
FABIAN
FENTON
GREMIO
GRUMIO
HAMLET
JULIET
JULIUS
LAUNCE
LENNOX
MUTIUS
OBERON
ORSINO
PISTOL
POMPEY
PORTIA
RUMOUR
SCROOP
SEYTON
SILVIA
SIWARD
TALBOT
TAMORA
THAISA
THURIO
TRANIO
TYBALT
VERGES

WOLSEY

AEMILIA
ANTONIO
BEROWNE
BERTRAM
CALIBAN
CAMILLO
CAPULET
CLAUDIO
CONRADE
CRANMER
DUMAINE
ESCALUS
ESCANES
FLEANCE
GATESBY
GONERIL
GONZALO
GREGORY
HORATIO
HOTSPUR
IACHIMO
JESSICA
LARTIUS
LAVACHE
LAVINIA
LEONATO
LEONTES
LUCETTA
LUCIANA
MACBETH
MACDUFF
MALCOLM
MARCADE
MARSIUS
MIRANDA
MONTANO
MOWBRAY
NERISSA
OPHELIA
ORLANDO
OTHELLO
PAULINA
PERDITA
PHRYNIA

PISANIO
PROTEUS
PUBLIUS
RICHARD
SALANIO
SAMPSON
SHALLOW
SHYLOCK
SIMPCOX
SLENDER
SOLINUS
TEMPEST
THESEUS
TITANIA
TROILUS
TYRRELL
URSWICK
VALERIA
VARRIUS

ABHORSON
ANNEPAGE
AVIRAGUS
BAPTISTA
BARDOLPH
BASSANIO
BELARIUS
BENEDICK
BENVOLIO
BERNARDO
BORACHIO
CAMPEIUS
CAPUCIUS
CLAUDIUS
COMINIUS
CORDELIA
CRESSIDA
DOGBERRY
DONPEDRO
EGLAMOUR
FALSTAFF
FASTOLFE
FLUELLEN
GADSHILL
GARDINER
GARGRAVE

GRATIANO
HARCOURT
LAURENCE
LODOVICO
LYSANDER
MENTEITH
MERCUTIO
MONTAGUE
PANTHINO
PAROLLES
PERICLES
PHILOTUS
POLONIUS
PROSPERO
RATCLIFF
REIGNIER
RODERIGO
SALARINO
STEPHANO
TRINCULO
VIOLENTA
VIRGILIA
VOLUMNIA

APEMANTUS
BALTHASAR
BASSIANUS
BOURCHIER
BRABANTIO
CAITHNESS
CLEOPATRA
CORNELIUS
CYMBELINE
DESDEMONA
DONALBAIN
ERPINGHAM
GLENDOWER
GUIDERIUS
MARCELLUS
ROTHERHAM
SEBASTIAN
TOBYBELCH
VALENTINE
VINTIDIUS
VINCENTIO
VOLTINAND

DICKENS

AMY
BET
CLY
PIP
TOX

BAPS
BRAY
DORA
FANG
FIPS
FOGG
GAMP
HEEP
JOWL
KAGS
MELL
NELL
OMER
PEPS
POTT
PRIG
TIGG
VECK
WEGG

BALOO
BATES
BETSY
BEVAN
BRICK
CHOKE
CLARE
FAGIN
KROOK
MIGGS
NANCY
NOGGS
QUILP
RUDGE

SIKES	HARMON	JAGGERS	TINYTIM
SMIKE	JARLEY	JEDDLER	TROTTER
TWIST	LAMMLE	JELLYBY	
	MAYLIE	MANETTE	BAGSTOCK
BAILEY	MERDLE	MOWCHER	CRATCHIT
BARKIS	NIPPER	NADGETT	CRUMMLES
BOFFIN	OLIVER	NUBBLES	CRUNCHER
BUCKET	REDLAW	PIPCHIN	HAVISHAM
BUMBLE	SLEARY	PLUMMER	HORTENSE
BUZFUZ	TAPLEY	PODSNAP	LIRRIPER
CARKER	WARDLE	SCROOGE	MAGWITCH
CARTON		SLOWBOY	MICAWBER
DARNEY	BAILLIE	SLUMKEY	NICKLEBY
DARTLE	BLIMBER	SNAGSBY	PEGGOTTY
DODSON	BROWDIE	SNUBBIN	SKIMPOLE
DOMBEY	DEFARGE	SPENLOW	
DORRIT	ESTELLA	STRYVER	CHADBAND

MYTHOLOGY

GODS AND GODDESSES LISTED BY CULTURE

GREEK

GODS

PAN	fields, herds	PONTUS	sea
ZAN	= ZEUS	POTHOS	= EROS
ARES	war	TITANS	ancestors of gods; *see p. 317*
EROS	love	URANUS	heaven
ZEUS	chief	ALASTOR	avenger
CHAOS	first god	ANTEROS	Eros' foe
COMUS	joy, mirth	OCEANUS	waters
HADES	underworld	PHAETON	= HELIOS
HYMEN	marriage	PHOEBUS	= APOLLO
MOMUS	ridicule	PRIAPUS	life power
AEOLUS	winds	PROTEUS	sea
APOLLO	youth, sun	SILENUS	woods
BOREAS	north wind	DIONYSUS	wine, drama
CABIRI	earth gods	ENYALIUS	war
CRONUS	Titan: crops	HYPERION	sun
HELIOS	sun	MORPHEUS	sleep
HERMES	herds, science, herald	POSEIDON	sea
HYPNOS	sleep	THANATOS	death
KRONOS	= CRONUS	ASCLEPIUS	medicine
NEREUS	sea	HEPHAESTUS	fire

GODDESSES

GE	earth	CLIO	Muse: history
ARA	vengeance	DICE	= DIKE
ATE	discord, infatuation	DIKE	Hora: justice
EOS	dawn	ENYO	war
NOX	= NYX	ERIS	discord
NYX	night	GAEA	= GE

GAIA	= GE	HESTIA	hearth
HEBE	youth	HYGEIA	health
HERA	queen	MOIRAI	Fates
HORA	one of Horae	PALLAS	= ATHENA
IRIS	rainbow; messenger	PHOBOS	fear
KORE	= PERSEPHONE	SELENA	= SELENE
NIKE	victory	SELENE	moon
RHEA	gods' mother	SEMELE	earth
UPIS	childbirth	THALIA	Grace: bloom
ATTIS	vegetation	THEMIS	Titan: earth, law
BAUBO	sensuality	URANIA	Muse: astronomy
COTYS	vegetation	ANTHEIA	flowers
DIONE	Titan: earth	ARTEMIS	nature, moon
ERATO	Muse: poetry	ASTARTE	= ARTEMIS
HERSE	dew	ATROPOS	Fate: thread
HORAE	seasons	CHLORIS	flowers
HYGEA	health	COTYTTO	= COTYS
IRENE	Hora: peace	DEMETER	agriculture
MANES	dead spirits	EUNOMIA	Hora: law
MOIRA	fate	EUTERPE	Muse: music
MUSES	arts	NEMESIS	retribution
PARCA	Fate: birth	CALLIOPE	Muse: eloquence
TYCHE	fortune	LACHESIS	Fate: disposer of lots
AGLAIA	Grace: brilliance	POLYMNIA	Muse: sacred song
ATHENA	peace, arts	APHRODITE	love, beauty
BENDIS	= ARTEMIS	MELPOMENE	Muse: tragedy
CLOTHO	Fate: spinner	MNEMOSYNE	Titan: memory
CYBELE	nature, earth	AMPHITRITE	sea
EIRENE	= IRENE	EUPHROSYNE	Grace: joy
GRACES	gods' helpers	PERSEPHONE	queen of underworld
HECATE	moon, magic		

TITANS

Gods		*Goddesses*	
ZEUS	IAPETUS	LETO	PHOEBE
ATLAS	OCEANUS	MAIA	TETHYS
COEUS	HYPERION	RHEA	THEMIS
CREUS	EPIMETHEUS	DIONE	EURYNOME
CRONUS	PROMETHEUS	THEIA	MNEMOSYNE

WIVES AND LOVERS OF ZEUS

IO	AEGLE	EUROPA	ANTIOPE
HERA	DANAE	SEMELE	DEMETER
LEDA	DIONE	THEMIS	CALLISTO
LETO	METIS	ALCMENE	EURYNOME
MAIA	AEGINA		MNEMOSYNE

ROMAN

GODS

DIS	= Gk. PLUTO	JANUS	gates
SOL	= Gk. HELIOS	LARES	house gods
AMOR	= Gk. EROS	LIBER	= BACCHUS
JOVE	= Gk. ZEUS	ORCUS	= Gk. HADES
MARS	= Gk. ARES	PICUS	agriculture
MORS	= Gk. THANATOS	PLUTO	= Gk. HADES
CUPID	= Gk. EROS	CAELUS	sky

FAUNUS	= Gk. PAN	NEPTUNE	= Gk. POSEIDON
SATURN	= Gk. CRONUS	PENATES	household
SOMNUS	= Gk. HYPNOS	MULCIBER	= Gk. VULCAN
VULCAN	fire	QUIRINUS	war
BACCHUS	wine	SILVANUS	woods
JUPITER	= Gk. ZEUS	VERTUMNUS	season
MERCURY	= Gk. HERMES		

GODDESSES

OPS	= Gk. RHEA	VESTA	= Gk. HESTIA
PAX	= Gk. IRENE	AESTAS	summer
DIAN	= DIANA	ANNONA	crops
JUNO	= Gk. HERA	AURORA	= Gk. EOS
LUNA	moon	DECUMA	= Gk. LACHESIS
MAIA	Vulcan's mate	LUCINA	childbirth
NONA	= Gk. CLOTHO	MATUTA	dawn, birth
SPES	hope	PARCAE	Fates
CERES	= Gk. DEMETER	POMONA	fruit
DIANA	= Gk. ARTEMIS	TELLUS	earth
EPONA	horses	TRIVIA	= DIANA
FAUNA	fertility	VACUNA	hunting
FIDES	faith	BELLONA	war
FLORA	flowers	FERONIA	fountain
MORTA	= Gk. ATROPOS	FORTUNA	fortune
PALES	herds	MINERVA	= Gk. ATHENA
SALUS	= Gk. HYGEIA	JUVENTAS	= Gk. HEBE
TERRA	earth	LIBITINA	burials
VENUS	= Gk. APHRODITE	PROSERPINA	queen of underworld

EGYPTIAN
GODS

NU	chaos	APUAT	old chief god
RA	sun, first god (black bull)	HORUS	day (hawk head)
RE	= RA	KHNUM	builder (ram head)
SU	= SHU	MENTU	sun, war (falcon head)
BES	evil averter, pleasure	SEBEK	evil (crocodile head)
GEB	= KEB	SEKER	= SOKARI
KEB	earth	THOTH	wisdom, magic (ibis head)
MIN	procreation	ANUBIS	judge of dead (jackal head)
SEB	= KEB	DHOUTI	= THOTH
SET	war, evil	KHENSU	= KHONSU
SHU	atmosphere	KHNEMU	= KHNUM
TEM	sun, creator	KHONSU	Ra triad member
TUM	= TEM	MNEVIS	= RA
AMEN	gods' father	OSIRIS	underworld (judge of dead)
ATEN	solar disk	SOKARI	night, sun (falcon head)
ATMU	= TEM	HERSHEF	= OSIRIS
ATUM	= TEM	IMHOTEP	learning
HAPI	Nile	KHEPERA	morning sun, creator (beetle)
KHEM	= MIN		
MENT	= MENTU	KHEPERI	= KHEPERA
PTAH	world shaper	SERAPIS	= OSIRIS
SETH	= SET	SOKARIS	= SOKARI
SOKH	= SEBEK	HARMACHIS	rising sun
AMMON	= AMEN		

GODDESSES

MA	= MAAT	SATI	queen of gods
MUT	Ra triad member	AMENT	gods' mother
NUT	heavens	ATHOR	= HATHOR
ANTA	war	PACHT	= SEKHET
APET	maternity (hippo body)	HATHOR	love, joy (cow head)
BAST	"Lady of Life" (lion head)	SEKHET	sun heat (cat head)
BUTO	serpent	SESHAT	learning (lion head)
ISIS	fertility	SPHINX	wisdom
MAAT	truth, law	NEPHTHYS	dead ritual

ASSYRIAN, BABYLONIAN, PERSIAN, PHOENICIAN

GODS

EA	water, arts: triad member	GIRRU	fire
ZU	storm	MAZDA	= ORMAZD
ANU	heavens: triad member	NUSKU	fire, light
BEL	earth: triad member	SAMAS	= SHAMASH
EAR	= EA	SIRIS	liquor
HEA	= EA	AMESHA	= SPENTA
SIN	moon, wisdom	ANSHAR	gods' father
UTU	sun	ARIMAN	evil
ADAD	wind	BABBAR	sun
ADDA	= ADAD	ESHMUN	healing
ADDU	= ADAD	KISHAR	lower, world
APSU	chaos	MARDUK	chief, sun
ASUR	= ASHUR	MOLOCH	sacrifice
BAAL	fertility	NANNAR	= SIN
ENKI	= EA	NERGAL	sun; pest
ENZU	= SIN	OANNES	wisdom
IRRA	war	ORMAZD	creator, chief
NABU	wisdom	RAMMAN	= ADAD
NEBO	= NABU	RIMMON	= ADAD
UTUG	= UTU	SPENTA	Ormazd aid
AHURA	= ORMAZD	TAMMUZ	vegetation
ASHUR	chief, power	AHRIMAN	= ARIMAN
DAGAN	earth	MITHRAS	light, truth
DAGON	fish, fields	MINURTA	sun
ELLIL	= BEL	SHAMASH	sun, order
ENLIL	= BEL	NINGIRSU	war, fields

GODDESSES

ERUA	mother goddess	ALLATU	underworld
GULA	healing	BELILI	lower word
NAMA	= ARURU	INNINA	= ISHTAR
NINA	watery deep	ISHTAR	earth, war, love
ANATH	war	NINGAL	sun
ARURU	mother: earth	ANAHITA	earth
ISTAR	= ISHTAR	ASTARTE	love, moon
NANAI	earth	DAMKINA	earth
NINNI	= ISHTAR	ERESHKIGAL	= ALLATU
NINTU	= ARURU		

CELTIC, IRISH, BRITISH, WELSH, GAULISH

GODS

LER	sea	**LLUDD**	= **NUDD**
LUG	light, sun	**MIDER**	underworld
BELI	= **BELENUS**	**NUADA**	= **NUDD**
BRAN	the blessed	**NUADU**	= **NUDD**
BRES	god king	**PWYLL**	dead
ESUS	vegetation	**AENGUS**	an Angus
GWYN	underworld	**ELATHA**	a Fomorian
LLEU	= **LLEW**	**HAFGAN**	chief
LLEW	sun	**NODENS**	= **NODONS**
LLYR	sea	**NODONS**	sun
LUGH	= **LUG**	**OENGUS**	an Angus
NUDD	sun	**OGMIUS**	eloquence
ANGUS	love, beauty	**BELENUS**	sun
ARAWN	Annwn's lord	**CAMULUS**	war
BALOR	Fomorian giant	**GWYDION**	sky, arts, magic
DAGDA	chief	**PRYDERI**	underworld
DOMNU	a Fomorian	**DIANCECHT**	medicine
DYLAN	waves		

GODDESSES

ANA	mother goddess	**BRIGIT**	Mary of the Gael; fire
DON	= **DANA**	**BRANWEN**	sea
BADB	= **BODB**	**MORRIGU**	war
BODB	battle	**BELISAMA**	beauty
DANA	fertility; ancestress	**ARIANRHOD**	rivers
EPONA	horses, mules	**BRIGANTIA**	mother goddess

NORSE-TEUTONIC

GODS

AS	Aesir (singular)	**VILI**	world creator; Odin's brother
ER	= **TIU**	**AEGIR**	sea
TY	= **TIU**	**AESIR**	chief gods
VE	world creator, Odin's brother	**ALCIS**	twin gods
EAR	= **TIU**	**BALDR**	= **BALDUR**
LOK	= **LOKI**	**BRAGE**	= **BRAGI**
TIU	sky, war	**BRAGI**	poetry
TIW	= **TIU**	**DONAR**	thunder
TYR	= **TIU**	**HODER**	= **HOTH**
ULL	bow skill, beauty	**HOTHR**	= **HOTH**
ZIO	= **TIU**	**LODUR**	= **LOTHUR**
ASES	= **AESIR**	**NJORD**	fertility
BURI	father of gods	**VANIR**	early race of gods: crops, fertility
FREY	fertility		
HLER	= **AEGIR**	**WODAN**	= **ODIN**
HOTH	night; blind Balder slayer	**WODEN**	= **ODIN**
LOKE	= **LOKI**	**WOTAN**	= **ODIN**
LOKI	discord	**BALDER**	= **BALDUR**
ODIN	chief; war, wisdom; slays Ymir	**BALDUR**	peace
		HOENIR	creator of first human
THOR	thunder, serpent slayer	**LOTHUR**	weather, crops
VALI	Ragnarok survivor	**NJORTH**	= **NJORD**
VANS	= **VANIR**	**VITHAR**	Fenrir slayer

FORSETI	justice
VIDHARR	= **VITHAR**
HEIMDALL	Asgard guardian

GODDESSES

EIR	healing
HEL	dead; underworld
RAN	sea
SIF	home
URD	=**NORN**
ERDA	earth
FREA	= **FRIGG**
FRIA	= **FRIGG**
HELA	= **HEL**
NORN	fate; destiny
SAGA	sorcery
URTH	= **NORN**
FREYA	beauty, love
FRIGG	sky marriage; Friday source
SKULD	= **NORN**
GEFJON	= **FRIGG**
HERTHA	= **NERTHUS**
ASYNJUR	Aesirs' aid
NERTHUS	peace
VERTHANDI	= **NORN**

HINDU (VEDIC)

GODS

KA	unknown god
AGNI	fire
AKAL	Immortal one
CIVA	= **SIVA**
DEVA	= **DEWA**
DEWA	angel
KALI	"the black one"
KAMA	love (parrot)
RAMA	Vishnu avatar
SIVA	supreme; destroyer; arts; miracles
SOMA	ritual liquor
VASU	= **VISHNU**
VAYU	wind
YAMA	judge of dead
BHAGA	love, wealth
DYAUS	sky, dawn, fire
GAURI	"the brilliant"
INDRA	thunder
KALKI	Vishnu avatar
MARUT	storm
MITRA	sun
RUDRA	storm
SHIVA	= **SIVA**
SURYA	sun
ASVINS	dawn: twins
BRAHMA	creator
GANESA	wisdom
KALIKA	= **KALI**
KUBERA	wealth
PUSHAN	roads, cattle
SKANDA	war
VARUNA	cosmic order
VISHNU	supreme; preserver
GANESHA	= **GANESA**
HANUMAN	monkey king
PARVATI	"mountaineer"
SAVITAR	sun
BALARAMA	= **RAMA**
PARJANYA	rain
TRIMURTI	trinity
KARTIKEYA	= **SKANDA**

GODDESSES

SRI	beauty
UMA	splendor
VAC	speech
DEVI	mother goddess
SHRI	= **SRI**
USAS	= **USHAS**
VACH	= **VAC**
DURGA	"the inaccessible" (on tiger)
SHREE	= **SRI**
USHAS	dawn
BRAHMI	speech
CHANDI	"the fierce"
SHAKTI	mother goddess
BHAVANI	= **DEVI**
CHANDRA	moon
LAKSHMI	= **SRI**
ANNAPURNA	plenty
SARASVATI	= **SHAKTI**

MISCELLANEOUS

GODS

ATAU	god: Polynesian
CHAC	—*MOL*: rain
JOSS	home: Chinese
KANE	chief: Hawaiian
MAUI	chief culture hero: Polynesian
TANE	forests: Hawaiian

TIKI	man creator: Polynesian	HURAKAN	thunder: Quiche
ALLAH	supreme being	JUROJIN	happiness: Japanese
AMIDA	Jodo deity: Japanese	KANALOA	leading: Hawaiian
AMITA	= AMIDA	KWANNON	mercy: Chinese
EBISU	happiness: Japanese	MANITOU	great spirit
HOTEI	happiness: Japanese	MICTLAN	underworld: Aztec
TINIA	= Gk. ZEUS: Etruscan	BISHAMON	happiness: Japanese
WENTI	literature: Chinese	CENTEOTL	agriculture: Aztec
BENTEN	happiness: Japanese	KULULKAN	creator: Mayan
JUMULA	heavens: Finnish	MANABUSH	creator: Algonquian (Great Hare)
TAAROA	chief: Polynesian		
TLALOC	thunder: Aztec	TANGAROA	chief: Polynesian
DAIKOKU	happiness: Japanese	SVANTOVIT	chief: Slavic

GODDESSES

MAMA	fertility: Peruvian	SEDNA	culture: Eskimo
PELE	fire, volcano: Hawaiian	TANIT	moon: Carthage
TARI	earth: Khond	TANITH	= TANIT
ALLAT	mother goddess	PERCHTA	earth, spinning: German

GODS AND GODDESSES LISTED BY SPECIALTIES

*Indicates goddesses

CHIEF GODS, GODS' ANCESTORS, CREATORS, MOTHER GODDESSES

AS
EA
RA
RE
VE
ANA*
ANU
BEL
HEA
OPS*
ASES
ATMU
ATUM
BRES
BURI
CIVA
DEVI*
ENKI
ERUA*
HERA*
HLER
JOVE
JUNO*
KANE
MAUI
ODIN
PTAH
RAMA
RHEA*
SATI*
SIVA
VASU
VILI
ZEUS
AHURA
ALLAH
ALLAT*
AMENT*
APUAT
ARURU*
ASHUR
CHAOS
DAGDA
ELLIL
ENLIL
ISTAR*
MAZDA
NINNI*
NINTU*
VANIR
WODAN
WODEN
WOTAN
BRAHMA
HAFGAN
INNINA*
ISHTAR*
MARDUK
ORMAZD
SATURN
SHAKTI*
VISHNU
TAAROA
BHAVANI*
JUPITER
KANALOA
KUKULKAN
MANABUSH
TANGAROA

SUN, LIGHT, FIRE, SKY

ER
RA
RE
TY
ANU
EOS*
NUT*
SHU
SOL
TEM
TIU
TIW
TUM
TYR
UTU
AGNI
AMEN
AMON
ATEN
BELI
LLEU
LLEW
NUDD
PELE*
UTUG
DYAUS
FRIGG*
GIRRU

LLUDD
MITRA
NUADA
NUADU
NUSKU
SAMAS
SURYA
USHAS*
VESTA*
APOLLO
AURORA*
BABBAR
CAELUS
GEFJON*
HELIOS
HESTIA*
JUMALA
MARDUK
MATUTA*
NERGAL
NINGAL*
NODENS
SEKHET*
URANUS
VULCAN
BELENUS
KHEPERA
MITHRAS
NINURTA
PHAETON
PHOEBUS
SAVITAR
SHAMASH
SOKARIS
HYPERION
HARMACHIS

EARTH, FERTILITY, WOODS, HUNTING, FIELDS, NATURE

GE*
BEL
DON*
ERDA*
ESUS
FREY
GAEA*
GAIA*
ISIS*
MAMA*
NAMA*
TANE
TARI*
VANS
ATTIS*
GEB
KEB
MIN
ARURU*
CERES*
COTYS*
DAGON
DIANA*
DIONE*
FAUNA*
FLORA*
ISTAR*
NINTU*
NJORD
PALES*
OPS*
PAN
SEB
PICUS
TERRA*
VANIR
ANNONA*
BENDIS*
CABIRI
CRONUS
CYBELE*
ISHTAR*
LOTHUR
POMONA*
PUSHAN
BAAL
DANA*
DANU*
SATURN
SEMELE*
TELLUS*
VACUNA*
ANTHEIA*
ARTEMIS*
CHLORIS*
DEMETER*
PERCHTA*
SILENUS
SILVANUS
CENTEOTL

UNDERWORLD, DEATH, SLEEP, NIGHT, MAGIC, MOON

DIS
HEL*
NOX*
NYX*
SIN
ENZU
GWYN
HELA*
HOTH
KALI*
KORE*
LUNA*
MORS
SAGA*
YAMA
DIANA*
HADES
HODER
HOTHR
MANES
MIDER
ORCUS
PLUTO
PWYLL
SEKER
TANIT*
THOTH
ALLATU*
ANUBIS
BELILI*
BENDIS*
HECATE*
HYPNOS
KALIKA*
KISHAR
NANNAR
OSIRIS
SELENA*
SELENE*
SOKARI
SOMNUS
TANITH*
ARTEMIS*
ASTARTE*
CHANDRA
GWYDION
HERSHEF
MICTLAN
PRYDERI
SERAPIS
SOKARIS
LIBITINA*
MORPHEUS
NEPHTHYS*
THANATOS

FAITH, HOPE, FATE, HOME, HAPPINESS

URD*
JOSS
NONA*
NORN*
SPES*
URTH*
WYRD*
COMUS
EBISU
FIDES*
HOTEI
LARES
MOIRA*
MORTA*
TYCHE*
VESTA*
CLOTHO*
HATHOR*
HESTIA*
KUBERA
MOIRAI*
PARCAE*
ATROPOS*
DAIKOKU
FORTUNA*
JUROJIN
PENATES
BISHAMON
LACHESIS*
ANNAPURNA*

MEDICINE, HEALTH, ARTS, SCIENCE, WISDOM

EA
EIR*
HEA
SIN
VAC*
BELI
CIVA
ENKI
GULA*
NABU
NEBO
ODIN
SIVA
VACH*
BRAGE
BRAGI
HYGEA*
MUSES*
SALUS*
SEDNA*
SHIVA
THOTH
WENTI
ATHENA*
BRAHMI*
DHOUTI
ESHMUN
HERMES
HYGIEA*
GANESA
NANNAR
OGMIUS
SESHAT*
SPHINX*
BELENUS
GANESHA
IMHOTEP
MERCURY
MINERVA*
DIONYSUS
ASCLEPIUS
DIANCECHT

WAR, DISCORD, VENGEANCE, EVIL

ER
TY
ARA*
ATE*
EAR
MENT
ODIN
SETH
ANATH*
ANATU*
ISTAR*
TIU
TIW
TYR
ZIO
ANTA*
MENTU
SEBEK
WODAN
WODEN
WOTAN
ARIMAN
ARES
BADB*
BODB*
ENYO*
ERIS*
ISHTAR*
NERGAL
PHOBOS
SKANDA
ALASTOR
BELLONA*
FURY*
IRRA
LOKE
LOKI
MARS
CAMULUS
MORRIGU*
NEMESIS*
ENYALIUS
NINGIRSU
QUIRINUS

SEA, SEASON, WIND, WEATHER

EA
ZU
HEA
LER
RAN*
ADAD
ADDA
ADDU
ENKI
HAPI
IRIS*
LLYR
NINA*
THOR
VAYU
AEGIR
DONAR
DYLAN
EURUS
HERSE*
HORAE*
INDRA
MARUT
RUDRA
AEOLUS
AESTAS*
BOREAS
LOTHUR
NEREUS
PONTUS
RAMMAN
TLALOC
BRANWEN*
CHACMOL
HURAKAN
NEPTUNE
OCEANUS
PROTEUS
BELISAMA*
PARJANYA
POSEIDON
VERTUMNUS
AMPHITRITE

BEAUTY, LOVE, YOUTH, JOY, MARRIAGE, BIRTH

BES
SRI*
ULL
UMA*
AMOR
APET*
BAST*
EROS
HEBE*
KAMA
SHRI*
ULLR
UPIS*
ANGUS
BHAGA
COMUS
CUPID
FREYA*
FRIGG*
HYMEN
PARCA*
SHREE*
VENUS*
AENGUS
AGLAIA*
GEFJON*
GRACES*
HATHOR*
LUCINA*
MATUTA*
POTHOS
THALIA*
ASTARTE*
LAKSHMI*
JUVENTAS*
APHRODITE*
ARIANRHOD

JUSTICE, PEACE, LAW, TRUTH

PAX*
DICE*
DIKE*
MAAT*
BALDR
IRENE*
ATHENA*
BALDER
BALDUR
EIRENE*
HERTHA*
THEMIS*
FORSETI
MITHRAS
NERTHUS*

FAMILY RELATIONS

Father	*Offspring*
EA	Nina
RA	Shu, Maat
ANU	Nanai
BEL	Ninurta
GEB	Osiris, Set, Nephthys, Isis
SIF	Ull
SIN	Ishtar
AMEN	Khonsu
AMON	Bast
APSU	Mummu
ARES	Cycnus, Phobos, Alcippe
BANA	Usha
FINN	Ossian
ILUS	Laomedon
LLYR	Bran, Branwen, Manawyddan
LOKI	Hel, Fenris(wolf), Midgard (serpent)
MARS	Romulus, Remus
ODIN	Balder, Vali: Vale, Vithar
SIVA	Skanda, Ganesha
VAYU	Hanuman
WADE	Wayland
ZEUS	Ate, Ares, Eris, Hebe, Kore, Helen, Irene, Muses, Aeacus, Apollo, Athena, Graces, Hermes, Amphion, Artemis, Epaphus, Dionysus, Hercules, Sarpedon, Aphrodite, Persephone, Hephaestus
AESON	Jason
ATLAS	Hyades, Pleiades
BELUS	Ninus, Danaus
CHAOS	Nyx
COEUS	Leto
CREON	Jocasta, Haemon
CREUS	Pallas
DAGDA	Aengus, Brigit
HOGNI	Hild
INDRA	Arjuna
IPHIS	Evadne
LAIUS	Oedipus
LLUDD	Gwynn
MINOS	Ariadne, Phaedra
PRIAM	Paris, Hector, Helenus, Troilus, Polydorus, Polyxena, Deiphobus, Cassandra
ACHEUS	Telamon
AEACUS	Telamon, Peleus
AEETES	Medea
AEGEUS	Theseus
AGENOR	Cadmus, Europa
APOLLO	Asclepius, Ion, Hymen
ATREUS	Menelaus, Agamemnon

Father	*Offspring*
BALDER	Forseti
BOREAS	Calais
BRAHMA	Daksha
CADMUS	Ino, Semele
CRONUS	Zeus, Hades, Hestia, Poseidon, Hera, Demeter
DEVAKI	Krishna
ELATHA	Bres
EREBUS	Charon
HELIOS	Circe
HELLEN	Aeolus, Dorus
HERMES	Pan, Silenus
IASION	Plutus
NEREUS	Amphitrite, Nereids
NJORTH	Frey
OILEUS	Ajax
OSIRIS	Horus, Anubis
PALLAS	Nike
PELEUS	Achilles
PELIAS	Alcestis, Acastus
PELOPS	Atreus
PENEUS	Daphne
RUSTUM	Sohrab
SATURN	= CRONUS
SIGURD	Swanhild
URANUS	Rhea, Themis, Cronus
CECROPS	Herse
CEPHEUS	Andromeda
DELLING	Dag
EURYTUS	Iole
GWYDION	Dylan
HIMAVAT	Devi, Parvati, Shakti
IAPETUS	Atlas, Prometheus
ICARIUS	Penelope, Erigone
LAERTES	Ulysses
OCEANUS	Styx, Doris
OEDIPUS	Ismene
PANDION	Procne
PHORCYS	Gorgons, Graeae
SIGMUND	Sigurd
TELAMON	Ajax
THAUMUS	Harpies
THESEUS	Hippolytus
ULYSSES	Telemachus
ANCHISES	Aeneas
DAEDALUS	Icarus
HYPERION	Eos, Helios
LAOMEDON	Priam
POSEIDON	Otus, Zetes, Pelias, Triton, Antaeus, Aloeus
SISYPHUS	Glaucus
TANTALUS	Niobe, Pelops

Father	*Offspring*
TITHONUS	Laomedon, Memnon
TYNDAEUS	Diomed
AGAMEMNON	Electra, Orestes
DEUCALION	Hellen
SCAMANDAR	Teucer

Mother	*Offspring*
GE	Uranus, Titans
IO	Epaphus
EOS	Memnon
INO	Melicertes, Palaemon
NUT	Osiris, Set, Nephthys, Isis
NYX	Thanatos
OPS	= RHEA
CETO	Gorgons, Graeae
ENYO	Ares
GAEA	Erechtheus, Cronus, Pontus, Phoebe, Anteus, Themis
HERA	Ares, Hebe, Eris, Hephaestus
ISIS	Horus
LEDA	Helen, Castor, Pollux
LETO	Artemis, Apollo
MAIA	Hermes
NOTT	Dag
RHEA	Zeus, Hades, Hera, Poseidon, Hestia, Demeter
STYX	Nike
ADITI	Aditya
AEGLE	Graces
CERES	= DEMETER
DANAE	Perseus
DIONE	Aphrodite
DORIS	Nereids
FRIGG	Balder
METIS	Zeus
NIOBE	Argus
SIGYN	Hel
THEIA	Eos
VENUS	Cupid
AEGINA	Aeacus
AETHRA	Hyades
CANACE	Aloeus
CREUSA	Ion
CYBELE	Zeus
EUROPA	Minos, Sarpedon
HECUBA	Paris, Helenus, Hector, Troilus, Polydorus, Polyxena, Deiphobus, Cassandra
LATONA	= LETO
PHOEBE	Leto
SEMELE	Dionysus
TETHYS	Styx
THEMIS	Astraea, Irene, Prometheus

Mother	*Offspring*
THETIS	Achilles
URANIA	Hymen
ALCMENE	Hercules
ANTIOPE	Amphion
CLYMENE	Atlas
CORONIS	Asclepius
DEMETER	Persephone, Plotos
ELECTRA	Dardanus, Harpies
EURYBIA	Pallas
JOCASTA	Oedipus
PARVATI	Ganesha
PLEIONE	Pleiades
CALLIOPE	Orpheus
CALLISTO	Arcas
MNEMOSYNE	Muses
AMPHITRITE	Triton
RHEASYLVIA	Remus, Romulus
CLYTEMNESTRA	Electra, Orestes

Husband (Lover)	*Wife (Lover)*
EA	Damkina
ANA	Anatum
BEL	Belit
GEB	Nut
LER	Aoife
SET	Nephthys
SHU	Tefnut
AMEN	Mut
APSU	Tiamat
ATLI	Gudrun
BAAL	Baalat(h)
BRES	Brigit
CEYX	Halcyone
EROS	Psyche
FREY	Gerth (Gerd)
HLER	Ran
IDAS	Marpessa
LOKI	Sigyn
NUDD	Morrigu
ODIN	Frigg = Frea = Fria; Rind(r)
PTAH	Sekhet
RAMA	Sita
SIVA	Devi, Shakti, Parvati
THOR	Sif
ZEUS	*see page 317*
AEGIR	Ran
ATLAS	Pleione, Aethra
ATTIS	Cybele
BRAGE	Ithun(n) = Idun
DAGDA	Boann

Husband (Lover)	Wife (Lover)
CONOR	Deirdre, Medb
HADES	Kore = Cora
JASON	Creusa, Medea
KINGU	Tiamat
LAIUS	Jocasta
LYCUS	Dirce
MINOS	Pasiphae
NOISE	Deirdre
NINUS	Semiramis
ORION	Eos
PARIS	Oenone, Helen
PHAON	Sappho
PRIAM	Hecuba
PWYLL	Rhiannon

ADONIS	Aphrodite
AENEAS	Creusa, Dido, Lavinia
AILILL	Medb
APOLLO	Creusa, Urania, Cassandra
ATREUS	Aerope
BALDER	Nanna
BRAHMA	Brahmi, Sarasvati
CADMUS	Harmonia
CRONUS	Rhea
GUNNAR	Brunhild
HAEMON	Antigone
HECTOR	Andromache
MARDUK	Sarpanitu, Zirbanit, Erua
NEREUS	Doris
NERGAL	Allatu
NJORTH	Thjazi
OENEUS	Althaea
OSIRIS	Isis
PALLAS	Styx
PELOPS	Hippodamia
PONTUS	Gaea
RAVANA	Sita
SIGURD	Gudrun
TAMMUZ	Ishtar
TEREUS	Procne
URANUS	Gaea
VARUNA	Aditi
VISHNU	Lakshmi
VULCAN	Maia

Husband (Lover)	Wife (Lover)
ADMETUS	Alcestis
AMPHION	Niobe
ATHAMAS	Ino
ATHAMUS	Nephele
GUNTHER	Brunhild
GWYDION	Arianrhod
IAPETUS	Clymene
LEANDER	Hero
NINURTA	Gula
ORPHEUS	Eurydice
PERSEUS	Andromeda
PROCRIS	Cephalus
SHAMASH	Ai = Aya
THESEUS	Antiope, Ariadne, Phaedra
TROILUS	Cressida
ULYSSES	Penelope

ASTRAEUS	Eos
CEPANEUS	Evadne
CEPHALUS	Eos
DIARMEIT	Brainne
ENDYMION	Selene
HERCULES	Hebe, Auge, Deianira
HYPERION	Theia
MENELAUS	Helen
MELEAGER	Atalanta
MILANION	Atalanta
PHILEMON	Baucis
POSEIDON	Cancace, Amphitrite, Gaea
TITHONUS	Eos

DEIPHOBUS	Helen
DEUCALION	Pyrrha
NARCISSUS	Echo
SIEGFRIED	Kriemhild
TYNDAREUS	Leda

AMPHITRYON	Alcmene
EPIMETHEUS	Pandora
HEPHAESTUS	Charis
HIPPOMENES	Atalanta

TERMS AND NAMES

GREEK AND ROMAN

IO	became heifer
KER	doom spirit

AJAX	hero-suicide
ARGO	Jason ship
DIDO	Carthaga queen
FAUN	wood deity
IDAS	Castor slayer

ILUS	Troy founder
NUMA	—POMPILIUS, king
OTUS	giant

AEAEA	Circe's isle
AEGIS	Zeus' shield
ALTIS	sacred grove
ARGOS	sacred city
ARGUS	Io guard: monster

ARION	poet saved by fish; horse
ATLAS	heaven supporter
AULIS	Iphigenia saved
CIRCE	sorceress
DRYAD	wood nymph
GYGES	magic ring king
HARPY	bird-woman
HELEN	Troy war cause
HELLE	fell into sea
HYADS	nymphs
HYDRA	9-head monster
ILIUM	Troy
IXION	wheel-bound king
JASON	gets Golden Fleece
LAMIA	vampire
LINUS	poet: lacerated
MEDEA	sorceress; Jason aide
MIDAS	ass-eared king
MINOS	king-judge
MORMO	bugbear
NAIAD	sea nymph
NAPEA	wood nymph
NIOBE	became stone
OREAD	mountain nymph
ORION	hunter
PARIS	apple awarder; slew Achilles
PHAON	Lesbos boatman
PRIAM	Troy king
REMUS	Romulus' brother
SATYR	man-horse
SINON	deceived Troy
SIREN	bird-woman lure
SYBIL	seeress

AENEAS	Troy war hero
ANANKE	ultimate fate
ANCILE	sacred shield
AUGEAS	Elis king (stables)
BAUCIS	Zeus' host
CHARON	Styx boatman
CREUSA	slain by Medea
DANAUS	Lynceus foe
DAPHNE	became tree
DELPHI	oracle site
DODONA	oracle seat
EGERIA	well nymph
EREBUS	dark site
EUROPA	abducted by bull
GEMINI	Castor, Pollux
GORGON	monster
IOLAUS	Hercules' pal
MAENAD	Nymph; Dionysus attendant
MEDUSA	slain by Perseus
NAPAEA	wood nymph
NEREID	sea nymph
NESSUS	slain Centaur
PELIAS	Tolcus king
SPHINX	winged-lion woman slain by Oedipus
TRITON	sea demigod
TURNUS	Aeneas' rival
TYPHON	monster

ACTAEON	became stag
AGANICE	witch
ALOADAE	giants
ARACHNE	became spider
AVERNUS	inferno
BRISEIS	Achilles' captive
CALCHAS	Greek seer
CALYPSO	nymph (Ulysses)
CECROPS	Athens founder
CENTAUR	man-horse
CHIMERA	monster slain by Bellerophon
CYCLOPS	one-eyed giant
CYTHERA	Aphrodite isle
ELEUSIS	mysteries site
ERINYES	avenging spirits
GALATEA	Pygmalion statue
GLAUCUS	Argo helmsman
HELICON	sacred mountain
INACHUS	Argos king
LAOCOON	priest warner
LEMURES	night spirits
LYNCEUS	slew Danaus
MARSYAS	lost Apollo duel
OEDIPUS	Thebes king; slew father
OLYMPUS	sacred mountain
ORESTES	slew mother
PANDORA	box opener
PEGASUS	winged horse
ROMULUS	slew Remus
THESEUS	slew Minotaur
ULYSSES	Ithaca king

ACHILLES	Hector slayer; Patroclus pal
AGANIPPE	Muses' fountain
AMBROSIA	celestial food
ANTIGONE	buried alive
ATALANTA	huntress; picks golden apples
BRIAREUS	100-hand monster
CALLISTO	huntress; became boar
CERBERUS	Hades watchdog
DAEDALUS	maze-wing maker
GANYMEDE	gods' cupbearer
HELIADES	became trees
HERACLES	hero, strong
HERCULES	hero, man
MELAMPUS	seer
MINOTAUR	man-beast slain by Theseus
MYRMIDON	Achilles' ally
NAUSICAA	Ulysses' friend
PLEIADES	became stars

SISYPHUS	stone roller
TANTALUS	starving king
TIRESIAS	blind seer
TITHONUS	became butterfly
TIPHOEUS	100-head monster

HINDU AND VEDIC

AHI	sky serpent
ATMA	= **ATMAN**
BANA	100-arm giant
KALI	evil genius: Agni's tongue
KETU	Rahu's tail
MANU	wise ancestor
MERU	holy mountain
NAGA	semihuman serpent
RAHU	dragon: swallows sun
SURA	angel
YUGA	age of world
ASURA	evil spirit
ATMAN	universal ego
HANSA	Asvin's swan, goose
GANGA	holy river
KALPA	aeon
NANDI	Siva's bull
PITRI	semi-divine ancestor
PRANA	life breath
RISHI	holy sage
SESHA	= **SHESHA**
ARJUNA	gets Krishna revelation
AMRITA	life elixir
ANANTA	infinity
AVATAR	incarnation
BHRUGI	gods' messenger
DAITYA	evil spirit
DASYUS	evil-demons
GARUDA	man-bird Vishnu bearer
NARAKA	hell
PATALA	underworld series
RIBHUS	artisans of the gods
SHESHA	serpent king
SVARGA	Indra's paradise
VASUKI	Naga king
VRITRA	dragon slain by Indra
YADAVA	Krishna's race
APSARAS	nymph, dancer
NIRVANA	reunion with Brahma
PURUSHA	male principle
SRADDHA	ancestor rite
AIRAVATA	Indra's elephant
LOKAPALA	world guardian
MAHADEVA	Siva title
NATARAJA	Siva; cosmic dancer
RAKSHASA	goblins
RAMAYANA	sanskrit epic
TVASHTAR	divine artificer

NORSE

ASK	first man
DIS	female spirit
DAG	day; *see* **NATT**
LIF	human survivor
NIX	water sprite
ASKR	= **ASK**
ATLI	slain king
EGIL	"Tell story" hero; Voland brother
GARM	Hel's dog slays Tyr
GERI	Odin's wolf
GRAM	Sigurd sword
NATT	= **NOTT**: night
SURT	fire demon: Frey's slayer
WADE	= **WATE**: storm giant
YMIR	"rime cold giant"
EGILL	= **EGIL**
EMBLA	first woman
ETZEL	= **ATLI**
FREKI	Odin's wolf
GIMLE	home of blessed
GJOLL	Hel's icy river
HAGEN	Sigurd slayer; slain by Kriemhild
HOGNI	Hethin foe
HYMIR	sea giant
ITHUN	keeps golden apples of youth
JOTUN	giant
MIMIR	well-guarding giant
REGIN	Sigurd's evil tutor
SURTR	= **SURT**
TROLL	giant; dwarf
VOLVA	seeress
ALVISS	dwarf
ASGARD	god's abode
ITHUNN	= **ITHUN**
JOTUNN	= **JOTUN**
REGINN	= **REGIN**
SIGURD	Volsunga saga hero
VOLUND	inventive smith
ANDVARI	ring guardian
ALFHEIM	Frey's home
BIFROST	rainbow bridge
BALMUNG	Sigurd's sword
MIDGARD	man's abode: earth
NAGLFAR	giant's ship
NIFLHEL	Hel's region
VALHALL	Odin's hall of heroes
VINGOLF	Asgard hall
WAYLAND	= **VOLUND**
ALBERICH	Nibelung dwarf
BRUNHILD	strong queen

DRAUPNIR	Odin's ring	**RAGNAROK**	"twilight of gods"; Aesir giants fight
HRIMFAXI	Nott's horse	**SLEIPNER**	Odin's steed
IRMINSUL	sacred trees	**TARNHELM**	cap making invisible
MJOLLNIR	Thor's hammer	**VALKYRIE**	Odin's messenger
NIBELUNG	dwarf guarding treasure	**YGGDRASIL**	world tree
NIFLHEIM	Hel's region		

EGYPTIAN

AB	will, heart	**ATUM**	= **RA**
BA	soul (bird-man)	**BAST**	cat-goddess
KA	body	**BENU**	sacred heron
RA	sun-god	**DUAT**	underworld
AKH	spirit of man	**HAPI**	genius of Amenti
GEB	earth-god	**HATI**	= **AB**
NUN	chaos	**ISIS**	nature-goddess (cow-head)
NUT	sky-goddess	**PTAH**	thinker
SET	god of evil	**AMSET**	genius of Amenti
SHU	air-god	**APEPI**	great serpent
AANI	ape: dog-head	**HORUS**	solar deity (falcon-head)
AARU	abode of dead	**KHNUM**	ram-god
AMON	chief god	**TAURT**	hippo-head
ANKH	sacred cross	**THOTH**	ibis, patron of arts
APIS	sacred bull	**AMENTI**	abode of dead
ATOM	= **RA**	**OPHOIS**	war-god

BABYLONIAN

ROC	giant bird	**ALOROS**	king
AZHI	—**DAHAKA**: dragon	**ALULIM**	= **ALOROS**
DEVA	= **DEAVA**: demon	**ENGUDI**	wild man: Gilgamesh pal
YIMA	king of man	**ENUKKI**	gods' servants
ADAPA	first man	**RUSTAM**	= **RUSTUM**: hero
AHURA	benign genie	**SIMORG**	= **ROC**
ARALU	underworld	**FEROHER**	disk symbol
BELUS	king	**JAMSHID**	peri king
ETANA	eagle rider	**NAMTARU**	Hades messenger
HAOMA	sacred liquor	**SIMORGH**	= **ROC**
IGIGI	heavenly spirits	**FRAVASHI**	spiritual guardian
KINGU	slain by Marduk	**GILGAMESH**	epic hero
MUMMU	Apsu's agent		

CELTIC

LUD	king	**FIANNA**	Fenian heroes
MIL	= **MILEDH**	**LUGNAS**	harvest feast
CROM	—**DUBH'S SUNDAY**: feast	**MILEDH**	Irish ancestor
MEDB	Queen of Connault	**OSSIAN**	hero
SHEE	= **SIDHE**: fairy fort, folk	**TUATHA**	—**DE DANNAN**: gods
DRUID	sage, conjurer	**BANSHEE**	warning spirit
FOMOR	sea robber; evil power	**BELTANE**	Mayday rite
KELPY	water spirit	**MORGAIN**	fairy: sister of Arthur
POOKA	marsh goblin	**SAMHAIN**	feast of dead
AILILL	king	**FIRBOLGS**	Fomor foes
ANNWFN	= **ANNWN**: Eden	**TALIESIN**	bard
AVALON	Arthur abode	**LEPRECHAUN**	tricky old man

MONSTERS

OGRE	man-eater
ARGUS	100-eyed
HARPY	predatory, winged dragon
HYDRA	9-headed serpent
LAMIA	woman-serpent
SATYR	goat-man
BAGWYN	antelope-goat-horse
DRAGON	winged lizard
GERYON	3 bodies, winged
GORGON	snake-haired woman
KRAKEN	sea monster
SCYLLA	6-headed dog with 12 feet
SILENI	part man, part horse
SPHINX	winged lion-woman; riddle poser
TYPHON	flaming 100-headed
CENTAUR	half-man, half-horse
CHIMERA	lion-goat; flame-spewing
GRIFFIN	lion-eagle: gold guardian
LAMASSU	bull with human head
PEGASUS	winged horse
PISTRIX	sea monster
UNICORN	animal composite: 1 horn
BASILISK	dragon with fatal breath
MINOTAUR	youth-eating man-bull
BUCENTAUR	ox-man
CHARYBDIS	woman turned to whirlpool
MANTICORE	horned lion-man
SAGITTARY	Trojan ally

ROUND TABLE KNIGHTS AND RELATIONS

BORS	Lancelot's uncle
KAY	Arthur's foster brother
BORT	= **BOHORT:** Lancelot's nephew
BALAN	brother of Balin
BALIN	brother of Balan
ARTHUR	son of Uther, Igraine (Igerna)
ELAINE	Lancelot's love (Lily Maid)
GARETH	nephew of Arthur
GAWAIN	son of Morgain, Lancelot
ISOLDE	= **ISEULT,** beloved of Tristram; wife of Mark
MERLIN	magician
MODRED	Arthur's slayer slain by him
MORGAN	Arthur's sister
GERAINT	Enid's husband
GALAHAD	Sir —: son of Lancelot
MORDRED	= **MODRED**
MORGAIN	= **MORGAN**
PELLEAS	lover of Ettarre
TRISTAN	= **TRISTRAM**
BEDIVERE	took Arthur's body to Avalon
LANCELOT	son of Ban
PERCIVAL	= **PARSIFAL:** Grail seeker
TRISTRAM	Iseult's lover slain by Mark
GUINEVER	Arthur's wife
GUINEVERE	= **GUINEVER**

PREFIXES AND SUFFIXES (COMBINING FORMS)

PREFIXES

AB	away from
AC	= **AD**
AD	to(ward)
AF	= **AD**
AG	= **AD**
AL	= **AD**
AN	upward
AP	= **AD**
BE	all around; excessively
BI	two, twice
CO	joint action
DE	off; down; wholly
DI	two
EC	= **EX**
EO	early
EU	well
EX	out (of)
FY	become, make
NE	= **NEO**
OB	to(ward)
OO	egg
PY	pus
UN	not; back
ZO	animal
ANA	up; back; again
ANO	upward
APO	from; away
AZO	nitrogen
BIN	twice
BIO	life
BIS	twice

BLE able
CIS on this side
COM with; jointly
DIA through; apart
DIF = DIS
DIS not; apart
DYS poor condition
EPI on; over; among
EXO outside
GEO earth
GYN female
HEM blood
MAC son of
MAL bad
MIS bad; wrong; not
MYO muscle
NEO new
NON not
ORO mountain
OTO ear
OVI egg
OXA oxygen
OXY oxygen; sharp
PED feet
PRE before
PYO pus
PYR fire; heat
SYN with; at the same time
TOX poisonous
TRI three
URO tail
UNI one

ACRO high
ENDO within
EQUI equal
ESCE verb ending
GAMO union
GONO sex organs
GYNO female
HAEM blood
HEMI half
HEMO blood
HEXA six
HOLO whole
HOMO same
HYLO wood
IDEO re ideas
IDIO personal
INDO Indian
KATA down; away
KILO thousand
LEVO left
LIPO fat
LITE mineral; fossil
LOCO re a place
LOGO word; speech
LUNI moon

MEGA great
MESO middle
META along; after
MISO hate
MONO single
MUCO mucous
MYCO fungus
MYEL marrow; spine
NASO nose
NOSO disease
NUCI nut
NUDI bare
NYCT night
OCTA eight
OCTO eight
OLEO oil
OLIG few
OMNI all
PARA near; beyond; abnormal
PARI equal
PEDI foot
PEDO children
PHEN benzene deriv.
PHON sound; voice
PILI hair
POLY much
PRAE before
PYRO fire; heat
RENI kidney
RHEO flow
RHIN nose
SEMI half
SEPT seven
SINO Chinese
SOLI alone
TELE far off
THEO of God, gods
TOPO place
TOXO poisonous
VINI wine
XENO foreign
XERO wax
XYLO wood
ZYGO yoke; pair
ZYMO fermentation

ACETO acid
ADENO gland
AMPHI around
AMYLO starch
ANDRO man
ANEMO wind
ANGIO vessel
ANGLO English
ANISO unequal
ANTHO flower
ARCHI chief
ASTRO star

AVANT before
BRADY slow
BREVI short
CARDI heart
CARPO fruit
CENTI 1/100
CHIRO hand
CHOLO gall; bile
CHROM color
CHRON time
CIRRO curl
COENO recent
COSTO rib
CYANO blue
DENTI tooth
DERMO skin
DICHO in 2 parts
ETHNO race; people
GALLO Gallic
GRECO Greek
HAEMO blood
HAGIO sacred
HAPLO single
HECTO hundred
HELIO sun
HEPTA seven
HIERO sacred
HISTO tissue
HOMEO similar
HYALO glass
HYDRO water
HYGRO water
HYPER over; beyond
ICONO image-like
INFRA below
INTRA within
INTRO within
JUXTA near; together
KARYO cell nucleus
LACTO milk
LEPTO slender
LIGNO wood
LITHO stones
LUTEO yellow
MACRO large
MAGNI large
MANCY divination
MATRI mother
METRO measure
MEZZO intermediate
MICRO very small
MILLI 1/1000
MORPH form
MULTI many
MYRIA many
MYTHO myth
NEPHO cloud
NEPHR kidney
NEURO nerve

NOCTI	night
OCULO	eye
ODONT	tooth
OLIGO	few
ORTHO	straight
OSTEO	bone
PAEDO	child
PALEO	remote
PANTO	all
PATHO	disease
PATHY	suffering
PATRI	father
PENNI	feather
PETRO	stone
PHENO	benzene deriv.
PHILO	loving
PHONO	sound
PHREN	diaphragm
PHYCO	seaweed
PHYLL	leaf
PHYLO	tribe
PHYTO	plant
PICRO	bitter
PISCI	fish
PLANI	plane
PLATY	broad
PLURI	several
PROTO	first
PTERO	wing; feather
RECTI	straight
RETRO	behind
RHIZO	root

RHODO	rose; red
RUSSO	Russian
SACRO	holy
SAPRO	rotten
SARCO	flesh
SAURO	lizard
SPIRO	breath; spiral
SPORO	seed
STENO	little
TAUTO	same
TETRA	four
TRANS	across
TURBO	turbine-driven
TURCO	Turkish
UTERO	womb
VERMI	worm

ACTINO	of rays
ANTERO	front
ARTHRO	joint
AUSTRO	Austrian
CENTRI	central
CERATO	horn; cornea
CHALCO	copper; brass
CHRONO	time
CRYPTO	hidden
DENDRO	tree
DEXTRO	right
DODECA	twelve
ENTERO	intestine
FRANCO	French
HELICO	spiral

HETERO	other
KERATO	horn, horny
KINETO	moving
MEGALO	very large
MELANO	black
NEMATO	thread
OBTUSI	blunt
PHRENO	diaphragm
PHYSIO	nature
PLEURO	side
PNEUMO	lung
PRETER	beyond
PSUEDO	false
PSYCHO	of mind
RRHAGE	abnormal flow

SANGUI	blood
SCHIZO	split
SCLERO	hard
SESQUI	1½
SOMATO	body
SPHENO	wedge-shaped
SPLENO	spleen
STETHO	chest
SUBTER	underneath
TRICHO	hair
TROPHO	nutrition
VARICO	enlarged vein
VENTRO	belly
VESICO	bladder
XANTHO	yellow

SUFFIXES

AC	relating to
AL	like
CY	quality
ED	past tense
EL	diminutive
ER	doer
ET	diminutive
IC	adjective
IE	diminutive
IN	diminutive
LY	like
MO	numerical
OL	chem. derivative
RY	= ERY
TH	numerical
TY	quality; tens
YL	radical form

ACY	quality
ANE	relating to
ARD	one who is too
ARY	relating to
DOM	domain

ENT	adj. ending
ERY	condition; state
EST	superlative
ETH	numerical
FIC	adj. ending
FID	divided
GEN	producing agent
GON	geom. figures
IAL	adj. ending
ICS	activity area
IDE	chem. compound
INE	fem. noun
ING	noun-forming
ISE	cause to be
ISH	belonging to
ISM	doctrine
IST	believer
ITA	diminutive
ITE	native; product; believer; fossil; salt; rock
ITY	condition
IVE	tendency
IZE	treat; act on

Suffix	Meaning
KIN	diminutive
LET	diminutive
OCK	diminutive
OID	resembling
OLE	chem. compound
OMA	tumor
OPY	eye defect
ORY	pert. to
OSE	full of
OUS	full of; like
RIC	district
ULE	diminutive
URE	act, result of
ZOA	animal

Suffix	Meaning
ACEA	of the nature
ASIS	state; like
ATIC	of the kind
CENE	recent; new
CIDE	murder
CRAT	ruler
CRYO	cold, icy
CULE	diminutive
DERM	skin
EMIA	blood
ENCE	quality
ETTE	diminutive
FUGE	flight
GAMY	union
GENY	origin
GLOT	tongued
GONY	origin
GYNY	female
IBLE	able
ICAL	adj. ending
IOUS	adj. ending
ITIS	inflammation
KINS	diminutive
LING	diminutive
LITH	stone
LOGY	science
MENT	action
MONY	state
NOMY	study
ODUS	toothed
OPIA	eye defect
OSIS	process
OTIC	of ear
PEDE	feet
PHYL	leaf
PODA	feet
PODE	foot
RHEA	discharge
SAUR	lizard
SION	action; result
STAT	stationary
STER	occupation
TEEN	plus ten
TION	action; result

Suffix	Meaning
TOMY	cutting
TRIX	fem. agent
TUDE	noun ending
URET	chem. ending
URGY	working of
URIA	urine disease
VASO	blood vessel
VORE	eating
XION	action; result

Suffix	Meaning
AEMIA	blood
ALGIA	pain
ARCHY	ruling
ATION	result of being
ATIVE	relative to
ATORY	produced by
CIDAL	to kill
COELE	body cavity
CRACY	rule
EDRAL	faced
ESQUE	like
GENIC	of origin
HEMIA	blood
IASIS	morbid state
IATRY	treatment
ICIAN	practitioner
ILITY	noun ending
ISTIC	adj. ending
ITION	action; result
LATRY	worship
LETTE	diminutive
LYSIS	disintegration
METRY	measurement
OIDEA	class name
OLOGY	science
OPSIS	sight
OSITY	noun ending
PHAGE	eating
PHAGY	eating
PHANE	resembling
PHANY	appearance
PHASY	speech
PHILE	loving
PHOBE	fear
PHORE	bearer
PHYTE	plant
PLAST	structure
PLASY	formation
PLEGY	paralysis
PLOID	number form
POLIS	city
RRHEA	discharge
SCOPY	science; viewing
SOPHY	knowledge
TIOUS	adj. ending
TROPE	turning
TROPY	turning
ULENT	full of
ULOSE	marked by

ULOUS	full of
AGOGUE	leading
BILITY	ability
CARPAL	fruit
CHROIC	color
CRATIC	ruling
FEROUS	bearing; yielding
GAMOUS	uniting
GRAPHY	science
GYNOUS	female
ISTICS	science of
LITHIC	stone
MYCETE	fungus
ODYNIA	pain
OLATRY	worship of
PAROUS	giving birth
PATHIC	disease; feeling
PHAGIA	eating
PHASIA	speech
PHILIA	loving
PHOBIA	fear
PHONIA	voice
PLASIA	formation
PLEGIA	paralysis
PODIUM	leg
PODOUS	feet
THERMY	heat
VOROUS	eating

PRESIDENTIAL INFORMATION

	Name	*Year of Inaug.*	*Party*	*Vice-Pres.*
1	**WASHINGTON**, George	1789	Fed.	**ADAMS**
2	**ADAMS**, John	1797	Fed.	**JEFFERSON**
3	**JEFFERSON**, Thomas	1801	Dem.-Rep.	**BURR, CLINTON**
4	**MADISON**, James	1809	Dem.-Rep.	**CLINTON, GERRY**
5	**MONROE**, James	1817	Dem.-Rep.	**TOMPKINS**
6	**ADAMS**, John Quincy	1825	Ind.	**CALHOUN**
7	**JACKSON**, Andrew	1829	Dem.-Rep.	**CALHOUN, VAN BUREN**
8	**VAN BUREN**, Martin	1837	Dem.-Rep.	**JOHNSON**
9	**HARRISON**, William Henry	1841	Whig	**TYLER**
10	**TYLER**, John	1841	Whig	
11	**POLK**, James Knox	1845	Dem.	**DALLAS**
12	**TAYLOR**, Zachary	1849	Whig	**FILLMORE**
13	**FILLMORE**, Millard	1850	Whig	
14	**PIERCE**, Franklin	1853	Dem	**KING**
15	**BUCHANAN**, James	1857	Dem.	**BRECKENRIDGE**
16	**LINCOLN**, Abraham	1861	Rep.	**HAMLIN, JOHNSON**
17	**JOHNSON**, Andrew	1865	Dem.	
18	**GRANT**, Ulysses Simpson	1869	Rep.	**COLFAX, WILSON**
19	**HAYES**, Rutherford Birchard	1877	Rep.	**WHEELER**
20	**GARFIELD**, James Abram	1881	Rep.	**ARTHUR**
21	**ARTHUR**, Chester Alan	1881	Rep.	
22	**CLEVELAND**, Stephen Grover	1885	Dem.	**HENDRICKS**
23	**HARRISON**, Benjamin	1889	Rep.	**MORTON**
24	**CLEVELAND**, Stephen Grover	1893	Dem.	**STEVENSON**
25	**MC KINLEY**, William	1897	Rep.	**HOBART, ROOSEVELT**
26	**ROOSEVELT**, Theodore	1901	Rep.	**FAIRBANKS**
27	**TAFT**, William Howard	1909	Rep.	**SHERMAN**
28	**WILSON**, Thomas Woodrow	1913	Dem.	**MARSHALL**
29	**HARDING**, Warren Gamaliel	1921	Rep.	**COOLIDGE**
30	**COOLIDGE**, John Calvin	1923	Rep.	**DAWES**
31	**HOOVER**, Herbert Clark	1929	Rep.	**CURTIS**
32	**ROOSEVELT**, Franklin Delano	1933	Dem.	**GARNER, WALLACE, TRUMAN**
33	**TRUMAN**, Harry S	1945	Dem.	**BARKLEY**
34	**EISENHOWER**, Dwight David	1953	Rep.	**NIXON**
35	**KENNEDY**, John Fitzgerald	1961	Dem.	**JOHNSON**
36	**JOHNSON**, Lyndon Baines	1963	Dem.	**HUMPHREY**
37	**NIXON**, Richard Milhous	1969	Rep.	**AGNEW, FORD**
38	**FORD**, Gerald Rudolph	1974	Rep.	**ROCKEFELLER**
39	**CARTER**, James Earl, Jr.	1977	Dem.	**MONDALE**
40	**REAGAN**, Ronald Wilson	1981	Rep.	**BUSH**

PRESIDENTIAL INFORMATION

	Sec'y of State	*Def. Cand.*
1	Jefferson, Randolph, Pickering	
2	Pickering, Marshall	Jefferson
3	Madison	Burr, Pinckney
4	Smith, Monroe	Pinckney, Clinton
5	Adams	King, Adams
6	Clay	Jackson, Clay, Crawford
7	Van Buren, Livingston, McLane, Forsyth	Adams, Clay
8	Forsyth	Harrison
9	Webster	Van Buren
10	Webster, Upshur, Calhoun	
11	Calhoun, Buchanan	Clay
12	Buchanan, Clayton	Cass
13	Clayton, Webster, Everett	
14	Marcy	Scott
15	Marcy, Cass, Black	Fremont
16	Black, Seward	Douglas, Breckenridge, Bell, McClellan
17	Seward	
18	Washburne, Fish	Seymour, Greeley
19	Fish, Evarts	Tilden
20	Evarts, Blaine	Hancock
21	Blaine, Frelinghuysen	
22	Frelinghuysen, Bayard	Blaine
23	Bayard, Blaine, Foster	Cleveland
24	Gresham, Olney	Harrison, Weaver
25	Olney, Sherman, Day, Hay	Bryan
26	Hay, Root, Bacon	Parker
27	Bacon, Knox	Bryan
28	Knox, Bryan, Lansing, Colby	Roosevelt, Taft, Hughes
29	Hughes	Cox
30	Hughes, Kellogg	Davis, Lafollette
31	Kellogg, Stimson	Smith
32	Hull, Stettinius	Hoover, Landon, Willkie, Dewey
33	Stettinius, Byrnes, Marshall, Acheson	Dewey
34	Dulles, Herter	Stevenson
35	Rusk	Nixon
36	Rusk	Goldwater
37	Rogers, Kissinger	Humphrey, Wallace, McGovern
38	Kissinger	
39	Vance	Ford
40	Haig, Shultz	Carter, Mondale

PRESIDENTIAL INFORMATION

	Name	Birthplace	Age*	Profession
1	**WASHINGTON**	Wakefield, VA	57	Farmer
2	**ADAMS**	Braintree, MA	61	Lawyer
3	**JEFFERSON**	Shadwell, VA	57	Farmer
4	**MADISON**	Port Conway, VA	57	Lawyer
5	**MONROE**	Westmoreland County, VA	58	Lawyer
6	**ADAMS**	Braintree, MA	57	Lawyer
7	**JACKSON**	Waxhaw, SC	61	Lawyer
8	**VAN BUREN**	Kinderhook, NY	54	Lawyer
9	**HARRISON**	Berkeley, VA	68	Officer
10	**TYLER**	Greenway, VA	51	Lawyer
11	**POLK**	Mecklenburg County, NC	49	Lawyer
12	**TAYLOR**	Orange County, VA	64	Officer
13	**FILLMORE**	Cayuga County, NY	50	Wool carder, lawyer
14	**PIERCE**	Hillsboro, NH	48	Lawyer
15	**BUCHANAN**	Mercersburg, PA	64	Lawyer
16	**LINCOLN**	Hardin County, KY	52	Storekeeper, postmaster, lawyer
17	**JOHNSON**	Raleigh, NC	56	Tailor
18	**GRANT**	Point Pleasant, OH	46	Lawyer
19	**HAYES**	Delaware, OH	54	Officer
20	**GARFIELD**	Orange, OH	49	Bargeman, teacher
21	**ARTHUR**	Fairfield, VT	50	Teacher
22	**CLEVELAND**	Caldwell, NJ	47	Teacher, lawyer
23	**HARRISON**	North Bend, OH	55	Lawyer
24	**CLEVELAND**	Caldwell, NJ	55	Lawyer
25	**MCKINLEY**	Niles, OH	54	Lawyer
26	**ROOSEVELT**	New York, NY	42	Police head
27	**TAFT**	Cincinnati, OH	51	Lawyer
28	**WILSON**	Staunton, VA	56	Teacher
29	**HARDING**	Corsica, OH	55	Publisher
30	**COOLIDGE**	Plymouth, VT	51	Lawyer
31	**HOOVER**	West Branch, IA	54	Engineer
32	**ROOSEVELT**	Hyde Park, NY	51	Lawyer
33	**TRUMAN**	Lamar, MO	60	Storekeeper
34	**EISENHOWER**	Denison, TX	62	Officer
35	**KENNEDY**	Brookline, MA	43	Author
36	**JOHNSON**	Stonewall, TX	55	Teacher
37	**NIXON**	Yorba Linda, CA	56	Lawyer
38	**FORD**	Omaha, NB	61	Lawyer
39	**CARTER**	Plains, GA	52	Engineer
40	**REAGAN**	Tampico, IL	69	Actor

*at inauguration

PRESIDENTIAL INFORMATION

	Nickname	*Wife's Name*
1	Old fox	**CUSTIS**, Martha Dandridge
2	Duke of Baintree	**SMITH**, Abigail
3	Long Tom, Sage of Monticello	**SKELTON**, Martha Wayles
4		**TODD**, Dorothea (Dolley) Payne
5		**KORTWRIGHT**, Elizabeth
6	Accidental president	**JOHNSON**, Luisa Catherine
7	Old Hickory, Sharp Knife	**ROBARDS**, Rachel Donelson
8	Red Fox, Little Magician	**HOES**, Hannah
9	Hero of Tippecanoe	**SYMMES**, Anna
10		**CHRISTIAN**, Letitia (1) **GARDINER**, Julia (2)
11	Young Hickory	**CHILDRESS**, Sarah
12		**SMITH**, Margaret
13		**POWERS**, Abigail (1) **MCINTOSH**, Caroline Carmichael (2)
14		**APPLETON**, Jane Means
15	Old Buck, Ten-cent Jimmy	
16	Old Abe, Railsplitter	**TODD**, Mary
17	Sir Veto, King Andy	**MCCARDLE**, Eliza
18	Silent Man, Old Three-Stars	**DENT**, Julia
19.	Old Eight to Seven, President de facto	**WEBB**, Lucy Ware
20	Canal Boy, the Preacher	**RUDOLPH**, Lucretia
21		**HERNDON**, Ellen Lewis
22	Old Veto, Stuffed Prophet	**FOLSOM**, Frances
23	Little Ben	**SCOTT**, Caroline Lavinia (1) **DIMMICK**, Mary Scott Lord (2)
24	Perpetual Candidate	**FOLSOM**, Frances
25	Stocking-foot Orator	**SAXTON**, Ida
26	Bull Moose, Rough Rider	**LEE**, Alice Hathaway (1) **CAROW**, Edith Kermit (2)
27		**HERRON**, Helen
28	Woody	**AXSON**, Ellen Louise (1) **GALT**, Edith Bolling (2)
29		**DEWOLFE**, Florence Kling
30		**GOODHUE**, Grace Anne
31		**HENRY**, Lou
32	New Dealer	**ROOSEVELT**, Anna Eleanor
33		**WALLACE**, ELizabeth (Bess) Virginia
34	Ike	**DOUD**, Mamie Geneva
35		**BOUVIER**, Jacqueline Lee
36		**TAYLOR**, Claudia (Ladybird) Alta
37		**RYAN**, Thelma Catherine Patricia
38		**BLOOMER**, Elizabeth (Betty) Ann
39		**SMITH**, Rosalynn
40		**DAVIS**, Anne (Nancy) Frances Robbins

TIME DIVISIONS—CALENDARS

No. of Month	Jewish	Mohammedan	Hindu
1	TISHRI, ETHANIM	MUHARRAM	BAISAKH
2	HESHVAN, BUL	SAFAR	JETH
3	KISLEV	RABIA 1	ASARH
4	TEBET(H), TEVET	RABIA 2	SA(RA)WAN
5	SHEBAT, SHEVAT	JUMADA 1	BHADON
6	ADAR	JUMADA 2	ASIN, KUAR
7	NISAN, ABIB	RAJAB	KA(R)TIK
8	IYAR, ZIF	SHABAN	AGHAN
9	SIVAN	RAMADAN	PUS
10	TAMMUZ	SHAWWAL	MAGH
11	AB, AV	DULKAADA	PHA(L)GUN
12	ELUL	DULHEGGIA	CHAIT

No. of Month	French Revolutionary	Egyptian	Roman
1	VENDEMIAIRE (vintage)	THOTH	MARTIUS
2	BRUMAIRE (fog)	PAOPHI	APRILIS
3	FRIMAIRE (sleet)	HATHOR	MAIUS
4	NIVOSE (snow)	CHOIAK	JUNIUS
5	PLUVIOSE (rain)	TYBI	JULIUS; QUINCTILIS
6	VENTOSE (wind)	MECHIR	AUGUSTUS; SEXTILIS
7	GERMINAL (seed)	PHAMENOTH	SEPTEMBER
8	FLOREAL (blossom)	PHARMUTHI	OCTOBER
9	PRAIRIAL (pasture)	PACHONS	NOVEMBRIS; NOVEMBER
10	MESSIDOR (harvest)	PAYNI	DECEMBER
11	THERMIDOR (heat)	APAR	JANUARIUS
12	FRUCTIDOR (fruit)	MESORE	FEBRUARIUS

No. of Month	French	Spanish	German	Italian
1	JANVIER	ENERO	JANUAR	GENNAIO
2	FEVRIER	FEBRERO	FEBRUAR	FEBBRAIO
3	MARS	MARZO	MARZ	MARZO
4	AVRIL	ABRIL	APRIL	APRILE
5	MAI	MAYO	MAI	MAGGIO
6	JUIN	JUNIO	JUNI	GIUGNO
7	JUILLET	JULIO	JULI	LUGLIO
8	AOUT	AGOSTO	AUGUST	AUGUSTO
9	SEPTEMBRE	SEPTIEMBRE	SEPTEMBER	SETTEMBRE
10	OCTOBRE	OCTUBRE	OKTOBER	OTTOBRE
11	NOVEMBRE	NOVIEMBRE	NOVEMBER	NOVEMBRE
12	DECEMBRE	DICIEMBRE	DEZEMBER	DICEMBRE

SEASONS, DAYS, AND OTHER TERMS

English	*French*	*Spanish*	*German*	*Italian*
Spring	PRINTEMPS	PRIMAVERA	FRU(E)HLING	PRIMAVERA
Summer	ETE	VERANO	SOMMER	ESTATE
Fall	AUTOMNE	OTONO	HERBST	AUTUNNO
Winter	HIVER	INVIERNO	WINTER	INVERNO
Monday	LUNDI	LUNES	MONTAG	LUNEDI
Tuesday	MARDI	MARTES	DIENSTAG	MARTEDI
Wednesday	MERCREDI	MIERCOLES	MITTWOCH	MERCOLEDI
Thursday	JEUDI	JUEVES	DONNERSTAG	GIOVEDI
Friday	VENDREDI	VIERNES	FREITAG	VENERDI
Saturday	SAMEDI	SABADO	SONNABEND	SABATO
Sunday	DIMANCHE	DOMINGO	SONNTAG	DOMENICA
Year	ANNEE	ANO	JAHR	ANNO
Month	MOIS	MES	MONAT	MESE
Week	SEMAINE	SEMANA	WOCHE	SETTIMANA
Day	JOUR	DIA	TAG	GIORNO
Hour	HEURE	HORA	STUNDE	ORA
Time	TEMPS	TIEMPO	ZEIT	TEMPO

Latin

Time TEMPUS; pl. TEMPORA
Year ANNUS; ANNO
Month MENSIS
Day DIES; DIE
Hour HORA
First day of month, CALENDS; KALENDS, CALENDIS

7th day of March, May, July, October, 5th day of other months, NONES; NONAS; NONIS
15th day of March, May, July, October, 13th day of other months, IDIBUS, IDES, IDUS
Day before, PRIDIE

BIRTHSTONES

ONYX	July	AMETHYST	Feb.
OPAL	Oct.	ROZIRCON	Oct.
RUBY	July, Dec.	SAPPHIRE	April, Sept.
AGATE	May, June	SARDONYX	Aug.
BERYL	Oct.	CARNELIAN	Aug.
PEARL	June	MOONSTONE	June
TOPAZ	Nov.	TURQUOISE	July, Dec.
GARNET	Jan.	BLOODSTONE	March
JASPER	March	AQUAMARINE	March, Oct.
ZIRCON	Dec.	TOURMALINE	Oct.
DIAMOND	April	CHRYSOLITE	Sept.
EMERALD	May, June	ALEXANDRITE	June
PERIDOT	Aug.		

WEDDING ANNIVERSARIES

TIN	10	CHINA	9, 20	COTTON	2
GOLD	50	CORAL	35	SILVER	25
IRON	6	IVORY	14	CRYSTAL	15
LACE	13	LINEN	4	DIAMOND	60
RUBY	40	PAPER	1	EMERALD	55
SILK	4, 12	PEARL	30	LEATHER	3
WOOD	5	STEEL	11	POTTERY	9
WOOL	7	BRONZE	8	SAPPHIRE	45

TRIBES, PEOPLE, NATIVES

I. NORTH OF MEXICO

LO

AHT
AUK
FOX
HOH
ITA
KAW
OFO
OTO
REE
SAC
SIA
UTE
WEA

ADAI
ATKA
COOS
CREE
CROW
DENE
ERIE
HANO
HARE
HOHE
HOPI
HUPA
IONI
IOWA
KASO
LOUP
MOKI
MONO
NOZI
OTOE
PIMA
PIRO
POMO
SAUK
SERI
TAKU
TANO
TAOS
TATU
TEWA
TIOU
UTAH
WACO
YANA
YUIT
YUKI
YUMA
ZUNI

ACOMA
ALEUT
ATNAH
BANAK
BLOOD
BRULE
CADDO
CHAUI
COMOX
CONOY
CREEK
HAIDA
HURON
KANSA
KASKA
KERES
KIOWA
KOROA
KWAPA
LIPAN
MAIDU
MAKAH
MIAMI
MINGO
MODOC
MOQUI
NAMBE
OMAHA
OSAGE
OZARK
PECOS
PIUTE
PONCA
SARSI
SIOUX
SITKA
SKIDI
SOOKE
TETON
TIGUA
TINNE
TONTO
TWANA
UCHEE
UINTA
UNAMI
WAPPO
WASCO
WASHO
WIYAT
WIYOT
YAMEL
YAMIL
YAZOO
YUCHI
YUROK

ABNAKI
AGAWAM
AHTENA
APACHE
ATUAMI
BABINE
BILOXI
CAHITA
CALUSA
CAYUGA
CAYUSE
CHATOT
COCOPA
COOSUK
DAKOTA
DOGRIB
EYEISH
FARAON
HAIDAH
HAINAI
HAISLA
INNUIT
ISLETA
KOSIMO
KUCHIN
LENAPE
MANDAN
MAYEYE
MICMAC
MOHAVE
MOHAWK
MOLALA
NAHANE
NASHUA
NAVAHO
NAVAJO
NAUSET
NEVOME
NIPMUC
NIPMUK
NOOTKA
OGLALA
ONEIDA
OTTAWA
PAIUTE
PAKAWA
PAPAGO
PATWIN
PAWNEE
PEORIA
PEQUOT
PERICU
PIEGAN
PUEBLO
QUAPAW
SALINA
SALISH
SAMISH
SANTEE
SEKANE
SEKANI
SENECA
SLAVEY
SPOKAN
SUTAIO
TAGISH
TENINO
TOLOWA
TONGAS
TUNICA
TUTELO
UMPQUA
WALAPI
WIKENO
WINTUN
YAKIMA
YAMASI
YOKUTS

ALIBAMU
AMERIND
ANDARKO
ARAPAHO
ARIKARA
BANNOCK
BEOTHUK
CAHOKIA
CARRIZO
CATAWBA
CHEHALI
CHILCAT
CHINOOK

CHIWERE	OJIBWAY	YAVAPAI	KLIKITAT
CHOCTAW	PUJUNAN	YONKALA	KWAKIUTL
CHUMASH	SANETCH		MALECITE
CHUMAWI	SANPOIL	ALGONKIN	MASKEGON
CLALLAM	SANSARC	APALACHI	MENOMINI
CLATSOP	SERRANO	ARIKAREE	MIMDRENO
COLCINE	SHASTAN	ARIVAIPA	NESPELIM
DHEGIHA	SHAWNEE	ATFALATI	NEZPERCE
ESSELEN	SHUSWAP	CAHUILLA	NOTTOWAY
HELLELT	SIKSIKA	CHEROKEE	OKINAGAN
HIDATSA	STIKINE	CHEYENNE	ONONDAGA
HUCHNOM	TAHLTAN	CHIMAKUM	PANAMINT
KITAMAT	TAKELMA	CHIPPEWA	POWHATAN
KITLOPE	TEPEHUA	COLVILLE	QUERECHO
KLAMATH	TIMICUA	COMANCHE	QUILEUTE
KOASATI	TLINGIT	COWICHAN	SAHAPTIN
KOPRINO	TONKAWA	COWICHIN	SEMINOLE
KUTCHIN	TULALIP	COYOTERO	SHOSHONI
KUTENAI	TUTUTNI	DELAWARE	SIHASAPA
LLANERO	WAICURI	DIEGUENO	SISSETON
LUISENO	WAILAKI	FLATHEAD	SNONOWAS
MAHICAN	WALAPAI	HITCHITI	SOUHEGAN
MOHEGAN	WAMESIT	HUNKPAPA	TLAKLUIT
MOHICAN	WISHOSK	ILLINOIS	TUSKEGEE
MONACHI	WISHRAM	IROQUOIS	UMATILLA
MONTAUK	WYANDOT	KENIPSIM	UNALASKA
NANAIMO	YAKUTAT	KICKAPOO	WAHPETON
NATCHEZ	YAMHILL	KIKATSIK	YAMASSEE
NIANTIC	YANKTON	KLASKINO	YONKALLA
NIPMUCK			

II. MEXICO-CENTRAL AMERICA

MAM	HUAVE	DIRIAN	COTONAM
	KICHE	DORASK	GUALACA
BOTO	LENCA	EUDEVE	GUATUSO
CHOL	MOCOA	GUAYMI	HUASTEC
CUNA	NAHUA	GUETAC	HUATUSO
ITZA	OLIVE	KEKCHI	JICAQUE
JOVA	OPATA	LUCAYO	MAZAHUA
MAYA	OTOMI	MANGUE	MAZATEC
MAYO	PETEN	MIXTEC	MIXTECA
MIXE	PINTO	NEVOME	MIXTECO
PAME	PIPIL	OTOMAC	NAYARIT
PIMA	SMOOS	PAKAWA	NICARAO
RAMA	TAINO	PAPAGO	OTOMACA
SERI	XINCA	PERICU	OTOMACO
SUMO	YAQUI	SABUJA	PIRANDA
TECA	ZOQUE	SERIAN	POKOMAM
TECO		SUERRE	TARASCO
ULVA	AMUSGO	TARASC	TEPANEC
VOTO	ARAWAK	TOLTEC	TEPEHUA
WABI	BORUCA	WOOLWA	TIRRIBI
XOVA	BRIBRI		TZENTAL
	BRUNCA	AMISHGO	TZOTZIL
AZTEC	CAHITA	BAKAIRI	WAICURI
CARIB	CARIBI	CARIBEE	ZACATEC
CHUJE	CHOCHO	CHONTAL	ZAPATEC
CUEVA	DARIEN	CHUMULU	

CHANABAL
CHAPANEC
JACALTEC
MAZATECA
MAZATECO
MELCHORA
MOSQUITO
OROTINAN
POKONCHI
POPOLOCA
POPOLOCO
TLASCALA
TOTONACA
TZUTUHIL
ZACATECO
ZAPOTECA

III. SOUTH AMERICA

GES
ITE
ONA
URO
URU
YAO

AGAZ
ANDE
ANTA
ANTI
AUCA
BARE
BORO
CAME
CANE
CARA
CORA
DIAU
DUIT
GHES
INCA
INKA
IXIL
MAKU
MOJO
MOXO
MURO
MUSO
MUZO
PEBA
PIRO
PURU
TAMA
TAPA
TOBA
TRIO
TUPI
URAN
YNCA

ACROA
ARARA
ARAUA
ARUAC
AUCAN
BRAVO
BUGRE
CAITA
CAMPA
CHANE
CHIMU

CHOCO
CHOLO
COLAN
CUNZA
GESAN
GUANA
GUATO
HUARE
INERI
MBAYA
OYANA
PALTA
PAMPA
PASSE
PIOJE
PIOXE
QUITU
SAMBO
SENCI
SIUSI
UAUPE
VEJOZ
WAURA
YAGUA
YAMEO
YUNCA

AMORUA
APALAI
APIACA
APIBON
ARAUNA
ATORAI
AYMARA
BANIVA
BETOYA
BORORO
CANARI
CANCHI
CANELO
CARAHO
CARAJA
CARIRI
CAVINA
CAYAPA
CAYAPO
CHANCA
CHANGO
CHAYMA
CHORTI
COCAMA
COCOMA

COFANE
COROPO
COTOXO
GALIBI
GOYANA
HIBITO
IXIANA
JAPURA
JAVAHE
JAVAHI
JIVARO
JUCUNA
JUMANA
KECHUA
LAMANO
MACUSI
MIRANA
MUISCA
MUYACA
MUYSCA
NASCAN
NOCTEN
OMAGUA
OREJON
PIAROA
PURUHA
QUICHE
SALIVA
SAMUCU
SETIBO
SHUARA
SIPIBO
TACANA
TAHAMI
TAMOYO
TAPAJO
TAPUYA
TARUMA
TIMOTE
TOTORO
TUCANO
TUNEBO
VILELA
WARRAU
WITOTO
YAHGAN
YAHUNA
YARURO
YURUNA
ZAPARA
ZAPARO

ANDAQUI
APALAII
ARAUCAN
ARECUNA
AREKUNA
AYAHUCA
CABOCLO
CAINGUA
CAMACAN
CARANGA
CASHIBO
CHARRUA
CHATINO
CHIBCHA
CHIRINO
CHOROTE
CHOROTI
CHUNCHU
CHUROYA
CIBONEY
FUEGIAN
GOAJIRO
GUAHIBO
GUARANI
GUAYMIE
HUANUCO
HUANUCU
ITONAMA
JAVAHAI
LORENZO
MAIPURE
MAPUCHE
MARIANA
MIRANHA
MOLUCHE
PAMPEAN
PATAGON
PAUMARI
PAYAGUA
PUELCHE
PUINAVI
QUECHUA
SARIGUE
SATIENO
SINSIGA
TARIANA
TEHUECO
TERRABA
TIMBIRA
TOTONAC
UARAYCU
UGARONO

WOYAWAY
YUSTAGA

ALIKULUF
AMAHUACA
APOLISTA
ARAPAHOE
BARBACOA
BOTOCUDO
CADIUEIO
CAINGANG
CANAMARY
CARICUNA
CHAMBIOA
CHAVANTE
CHIQUITO
CHIRIANA
COCONUCO
CONCHULU
CORABECA
COVARECA
GUARAUNO
GUAYAQUI
JAVITERO
MAYORUNA
MOSETENA
PICUNCHE
PURUPURU
QUERENDI
TAMANACO
TOROMONA
TUMUPASA
YAMAMADI
YAUAPERY
YURUCARE
YURUCARI

IV. EUROPE

GEG Alb.
LAK Russ.
LAZ Russ.
VAN Russ.
VOD Finn
VOT Finn

AVAR Russ.
BALT Lith.
BOII Celt
CELT Brit., Fr.
CHAM Alb.
CHUD Finn
DANE
ESTH
FINN
FLEM Belg.
GAEL Celt.
GAUL Fr.
GEAT Swed.
GHEG Alb.
GOTH Ger.
IMER Russ.
JUTE Ger.
KAMI Russ.
KOMI Russ.
KURI Russ.
LAPP Scan.
LAZE Russ.
LAZI Russ.
LETT Lith.
MANX Celt.
PICT Brit.
POLE
REMI Belg.
RUSS
SCOT Celt
SERB Slav
SLAV
SORB Slav
SVAN Russ.
TOSK Alb.
UBII Ger.
VEND Slav
VEPS Finn
VOTE Finn
WEND Slav
ZIPS Ger.

AEQUI It.
ALANI
ALANS
ALMAN Ger.
ATTIC Greek
AVARS Russ.
BESSI Greek
BOIKO Russ.
CATTI Ger.
CROAT Slav
CYMRY Celt
CZECH Slav
DARGO Russ.
DIGOR Russ.
DUTCH
ELYMI It.
ERSAR Russ.
FRANK Ger.
GALGA Russ.
GREEK
GUZUL Russ.
GYPSY
IBERI Spain
ICENI Briton
IJORE Finn.
IRISH Celt
KAZAN Russ.
KUMAN Hung.
KUMYK Turk.
KYMRY Celt
LADIN Swiss
MARSI Ger., It.
MAZUR Pole
MORDV Russ.
NOGAI Russ.
NORSE Scan.
OSCAN It.
OSSET Russ.
PECHT Celt
PISAN It.
POLAB Slav
POMAK Bulg.
QUADI Ger.
ROMAN It.
SAXON Ger.
SCIOT Greek
SICEL It.
SUEVI Ger.
SVANE Russ.
SWISS
TAULI Russ.
USKOK Slav
VANNI Russ.
VENED Slav
VEPSE Finn.
VLACH Rum.
VOGUL Finn.
WELSH Celt
ZHMUD Lith.

ABKHAS Russ.
ADIGHE Russ.
ALEMAN Ger.
ALMAIN Ger.
ANGLES Ger.
BASQUE Sp. Fr.
BATAVI Ger.
BOSHAS Russ.
BRETON Fr.
BRITON
BULGAR
CARIAN Greek
CHATTI Ger.
DORIAN Greek
FRENCH
GASCON Fr.
GEATAS Swed.
GERMAN
GOIDEL Celt
HANSAS Ger.
HERULI Ger.
HRVATI Slav
IBERES Spain
INGUSH Russ.
IONIAN Greek
KABARD Russ.
KYURIN Russ.
LADINO Swiss
LITVAK Lith.
MAGYAR Hung.
MORDVA Russ.
MOSCHI Russ.

MOSCVA	Russ.
NEMEAN	Greek
NERVII	Celt
NORMAN	Fr., Scan.
PADUAN	It.
PICARD	Fr.
POLACK	Pole
ROMANY	Gypsy
RUTULI	It.
SABINE	It.
SAFINI	It.
SALIAN	Dutch
SAMIAN	Greek
SATRAE	Greek
SICANI	It.
SICULI	It.
TAGAUR	Russ.
TAVAST	Finn.
TEUTON	Ger.
THEBAN	Greek
TUSCAN	It.
UGRIAN	Finn.
VANDAL	Ger.
VANNAI	Russ.
VELIKA	Russ.
VENETI	It.
VOLCAE	Celt
VOLSKI	It.
VOTYAK	Finn
ZYRIAN	Russ.
AEOLIAN	Greek
AEQUIAN	It.
BASHKIR	Russ.
BELGIAN	
BOSNIAN	Slav
BRYTHON	Celt
BUKEYET	Russ.
CANDIOT	Greek
CATALAN	Spain
CHECHEN	Russ.
CHUVASH	Bulg.
CYPRIOT	Greek
DARDANI	Greek
DARGHIN	Russ.
FALISCI	It.
FAROESE	Dan.
FIRBOLG	Celt
FLEMING	Belg.
FRISIAN	Ger.
GADITAN	Spain
GALLEGO	Spain
GENOESE	It.
HELLENE	Greek
HESSIAN	Ger.
IBERIAN	Spain
ISTRIAN	It.
ITALIAN	
KARTHLI	Russ.
KARTVEL	Russ.
KASHUBE	Ger.
LATVIAN	Lith.
LEONESE	Spain
LESBIAN	Greek
LOMBARD	It.
MALTESE	
MANXMAN	Celt
MERCIAN	Eng.
MORDVIN	Russ.
OXONIAN	Eng.
PAPHIAN	Greek
PARMESE	It.
PATARIN	It.
PELASGI	Greek
PERMIAK	Finn
PERMIAN	Finn
RAURACI	Fr.
RAURICI	Fr.
RHODIAN	Greek
RUSSIAN	
RUTHENE	Russ.
SABELLI	It.
SAMNITE	It.
SENONES	Celt
SEQUANI	Celt
SERBIAN	Slav
SIENESE	It.
SILURES	Eng.
SLOVENE	Slav
SPARTAN	Greek
SUEVIAN	Ger.
SUIONES	Ger.
SULIOTE	Greek
SWABIAN	Ger.
TOLEDAN	Spain
UMBRIAN	It.
VAUDOIS	Swiss
VESTINI	It.
WALLOON	Belg.
ALBANIAN	
ANDORRAN	Spain
ARMENIAN	Russ.
ASTURIAN	Spain
AUSTRIAN	
BAVARIAN	Ger.
BISCAYAN	Spain
BOEOTIAN	Greek
BOHEMIAN	Slav
CHERUSCI	Ger.
CORSICAN	Fr.
CROATIAN	Slav
CYPRIOTE	Greek
ETRUSCAN	It.
FRIULIAN	It.
GALICIAN	Spain
GALLEGAN	Spain
ILLYRIAN	Alb.
KARELIAN	Russ.
KASUBIAN	Ger.
KHALDIAN	Finn
KONARIOT	Turk.
LEZGHIAN	Russ.
LIGURIAN	It.
LIVONIAN	Lith.
MAJORCAN	Spain
MAZOVIAN	Ger.
MEGARIAN	Greek
MILANESE	It.
MINORCAN	Spain
MORAVIAN	Slav
NORSEMAN	Scan.
NORTHMAN	Scan.
PANNONIC	Hung.
PARISIAN	Fr.
PARMESAN	It.
PATARINE	It.
PATAVIAN	It.
PELASGOI	Greek
PHYRGIAN	Greek
POLABIAN	Slav
POLANDER	Pole
PORTUGEE	
PRUSSIAN	Ger.
RHAETIAN	It.
RUMANIAN	
RUMELIAN	Bulg.
RUSSNIAK	Russ.
SALOPIAN	Eng.
SAVOYARD	Fr.
SEMNONES	Ger.
SICAMBRI	Ger.
SICILIAN	It.
SILESIAN	Ger.
SPANIARD	Spain
THRACIAN	Greek
TYROLESE	Aust.
ULTONIAN	Eng.
USIPETES	Ger.
VENETIAN	It.
VISIGOTH	Ger.
YUGOSLAV	Slav

V. AFRICA

GA
GI

ABO
ARO
EDO
EFE
EVE
EWE
FAN
FON
FUL
FUR
IBO
IJO
JUR
KRA
KRU
KUA
LUO
LVO
LWO
RUA
SAN
SUK
VAI
VEI
YAO

ABSI
AFAR
AKAN
AKIM
AKKA
AKRA
ALUR
ASHA
BARI
BAYA
BEJA
BENI
BERI
BINI
BOGO
BONI
BUBE
BUBI
DAGO
DAZA
DOKO
EBOE
EFIK
EGBA
EJAM
EKOI
FANG

FIOT
FONG
FULA
FUNG
FUNJ
GALA
GOGO
GOLO
GOMA
GUHA
HABE
HARB
HEHE
HIMA
HOVA
HUMA
IDJO
IDYO
IDZO
JAGA
KAFA
KORA
KROO
LUBA
LUOH
LURI
MABA
MADI
MARI
NAMA
NUBA
NUPE
QUNG
RAVI
RIFE
SAAN
SAHO
SARA
SERE
SHLU
SHOA
SOGA
SUKU
SUSU
SUTO
TEDA
TIBU
TOMA
VILI
VIRI
VITI
XOSA
YAKA
ZULU

AFIFI

AMADI
ATEBA
BALAO
BANDA
BANTU
BASSA
BATWA
BENIN
BONGO
BORAN
BRAVA
CHAGA
CONGO
DADJO
DINKA
DUALA
FANTI
FANWE
FULAH
FULBE
FUNJE
FUNJI
GABON
GALLA
GANDA
GIBBI
GREBO
HABAB
HABBE
HAUSA
IDDIO
IGARA
INKRA
JOLOF
KAFFA
KAMBA
KHUAI
KIOKO
KONDE
KONGO
KREPI
LANGO
LENDU
LUNDA
LUREM
MAKUA
MAKWA
MANDE
MARRI
MASAI
MAURI
MBUBA
MENDE
MENDI
MONGO
MOSGU

MOSSI
MUTER
NANDI
NEGRO
NILOT
NYORO
PONDO
PYGMY
RUNDI
SAKAI
SERER
SHLUH
SHONA
SONGO
SOTHO
SOTIK
SWAZI
TEMBU
TEMNE
TIBBU
TINNI
TONGA
VOLOF
WAASI
WARRI
WARUA
WAYAO
WOLOF
YOLOF
ZANDE

ABABUA
ABANTU
ABATOA
ABATUA
ABATWA
ABONGO
ACHIAS
AMHARA
ANTEVA
AZANDE
BAFIOT
BAHIMA
BAHUMA
BAHUTU
BAKELE
BAKUBA
BAKUTU
BALAWU
BALOLO
BALUBA
BANYAI
BASOGA
BASUTO
BATOKA
BEDUIN

BERBER
BERTAT
BORANA
BULLOM
CHAGGA
CHAWIA
DAMARA
DOROBO
FANTEE
FULANI
GABOON
GRIQUA
HAMITE
HARARI
HEIKUM
HERERO
IGBARA
IGBIRA
IKBERE
KABYLE
KAFFIR
KANURI
KIKUYU
KORANA
KPUESI
LATUKA
LIBYAN
LOBALE
LOTUKO
MAKARI
MARAVI
MBONDO
MBUNDA
MPONDO
MURREE
NUBIAN
NYAMBE
NZAMBI
OBONGA
OVAMPO
PANGWE
POKOMO
SENUSI
SESUTO
SHAGIA
SHILHA
SHUKRI
SOMALI
SONGOI
SUKUMA
SURHAI
THONGA
TIMNEH
TUAREG
WABENA

WABUMA
WAGOGO
WAGUHA
WAHABI
WAHEHE
WASOGA
WATUSI
WAVIRA
WOCHUA
YAKALA
YORUBA
ZARAMO
ZEHUGA
ZENAGA

ABABDEH
ACHANGO
AKWAPIM
AMAKOSA
AMAZULU
ANTAIVA
ASHANTI
BABONGO
BACONGO
BAGANDA
BAGARRA
BAGGARA
BAKALAI
BAKALEI
BAKONGO
BAKUNDA
BAKWIRI
BALANTA
BALANTE
BAMBARA
BAMBUBA
BAMBUTE
BANGALA
BANYORO
BARONGA
BAROTSE
BARUNDI
BASONGO
BATEKES
BATONGA
BATUSSI
BEDOUIN
BULANDA
BUNYORO
BUSHMAN
CABINDA
CUSHITE
DADSCHO
DAHOMAN
DANAGLA

DANAKIL
DANKALI
FALASHA
FALLATA
GAETULI
GETULAN
GUANCHE
GUHAYNA
HARATIN
IMOHAGH
KABINDA
KABONGA
KIRUNDI
KOLDAJI
KROOBOY
LOATUKO
LUGANDA
MACHOGO
MAIACCA
MAKONDE
MAREHAN
MASHONA
MOGRABI
MPANGWE
MUNANDI
NAMAQUA
NEGRITO
NEGROID
NILOTIC
PAHOUIN
SANDAWE
SANDAWI
SENOUSI
SHAIGIA
SHAMMAR
SHILLUH
SHILLUK
SHUKRIA
SONGHAI
SONGHAY
SONGHOI
SUKKIIM
SWAHILI
TUKULER
TURKANA
UGANDAN
WABUNGA
WACHAGA
WAGWENO
WAKAMBA
WAKWAFI
WAKWAVI
WAMBUBA
WAMBUGA

WANGONI
WANYASA
WASANGO
WASEGUA
WONGARA

ALGERIAN
AMATEMBU
ANDOROBO
ANGOLESE
ASHANTEE
AUXUMITE
BAGHIRMI
BAROLONG
BATETELA
BECHUANA
BISHARIN
CANGUELA
CONGOESE
EGYPTIAN
HADENDOA
HARRATIN
IMOSHAGH
KABABISH
KARAMOJO
KUKURUKU
LIBERIAN
MAGHRIBI
MAKARAKA
MALAGASY
MANDINGO
MATABELE
MOGREBEE
MOMBOTTU
MOROCCAN
NEGRILLO
NIAMNIAM
NIGERIAN
NYAMWEZI
RAHANVIN
SAKALAVA
SUDANESE
TUNISIAN
WAMBUTTI
WANGATTA
WAPOKOMO
WASAGARA

DANAGALEH
MANGBATTU
MATABELES
MAUGRABIN
OVAHERERO
WANDOROBO

VI. ASIA, AUSTRONESIA

CHINA, MONGOLIA, SIBERIA

HEH
HEI
YAO
CHUD
DAUR
GOLD
LOLO
MANS
MIAO
NOSU
SHIK
TOBA
USUN
UZUN
BURUT
CHUDE
DAURI
ELEUT
GOLDI
HAKKA
HOKLO
IGDYR
KALKA
KAZAK
LAMUT
MOGUL
OLCHA
OLCHI
SAGAI
SERES
SOYOT
TATAR
TURKI
UIGUR
USSUN
UZBEK
YAKUT
YURAK
ALTAIC
AMOYAN
BALKAR
BELTIR
BURIAT
DUNGAN
DURBAN
GILIAK
HAINAN
KALMUK
KALMYK
KASSAK
KHALKA
KOIBAL
KORIAK
MANCHU
MANTZU
MONGOL
OROKON
OSTYAK
SHARRA
TARTAR
TAVGHI
TELEUT
TUNGUS
UIGHUR
YAOMIN
ALTAIAN
AMOYESE
BOUROUT
BUKEYET
CHUKCHI
DZUNGAR
ITELMES
KALMUCK
KALMYCK
KAMASIN
KHALKHA
KIRGHIZ
OROCHON
SAMOYED
TURKMAN
YENISEI
YUKAGIR
TURKOMAN
YUKAGHIR

JAPAN, AUSTRALIA, PHILIPPINES

ATA
ATI
GOA
AETA
AINO
AINU
FIJI
KOKO
MORO
SULU
ARAWA
BATAK
BATAN
BICOL
BIKOL
DIERI
ILOCO
ILOKO
KIWAI
LANAO
LUCHU
MACRI
NIUAN
TAGAL
YAKAN
APAYAO
ARUNTA
BALUGA
BILAAN
BISAYA
BONTOK
GADDAN
IBANAG
IBILAO
IFUGAO
IGOROT
ITALON
ITAVES
KANAKA
KOIARI
MANOBO
MONTES
PAPUAN
SAMBAL
SAMOAN
TAGALA
TONGAN
VISAYA
YAMATO
ZAMBAL
BISAYAN
BISHMAN
CAGAYAN
DADAYAG
GADDANG
ILOCANO
ILOKANO
ILONGOT
ILPIRRA
JOLOANO
KALINGA
KOITAPU
LUCHUAN
MANGYAN
NABOLOT
NEGRITO
RINGATU
SANGGIL
SATSUMA
SUBANUM
TAGALOG
TIRURAI
VISAYAN
AWABAKAL
BUKIDNON
CHAMORRO
CHINHWAN
FORMOSAN
HAWAIIAN
IGORROTE
KANKANAI
MONTESCO
PAMPANGA
PAMPANGO
QUIANGAN
TAHITIAN
TINGGIAN

INDIA, PAKISTAN, TIBET, NEPAL

AO
HO
AKA
GOR
JAT
KHA
KOL
MEO
AHIR
AOUL
AWAN
BHAR
BHIL
DARD
GARO
GOND
KOCH
KOLI
KUKI
MAGH

MAGI
MARI
NAGA
NAIR
RAIS
REKI
TODA
TULU
TURI
ANGKA
BALTI
CHANG
COORG
DAFLA
DARDI
DOGRA
DRUPA
GADDI
ANGAMI
ARAINS
ARLENG
ARORAS
BADAGA
PANJAB
RAJPUT
RAMUSI
SANTAL
SAVARA
GUJAR
HINDI
HINDU
JUANG
KANDE
KHASI
KOERI
KONDH
KORWA
KOTAR
KUMNI
KUNBI
KURMI
LIMBU
MIKIR
MUNDA
MUREE
NEWAR
NURMI
ORAON
ORIYA
SAORA
SAURA
TAMIL
URIYA
VEDDA
WAKHI
AGHORI
BALUCH
BEHARI
BHOTIA
BHUMIJ
BHUTIA
BIHARI
CHAMAR
CHAMPA
DROKPA
DRUKPA
GURKHA
HINDOO
HOLEYA
JHURIA
KALWAR
KANWAR
KHARIA
KHASIA
KODAGU
KOMATI
KONYAK
KURUBA
LEPCHA
LOHANA
MADIGA
MANGAR
MISHMI
PAHARI
SHERPA
SINDHI
TANGUT
TELUGU
TIPURA
YERAVA
YUECHI
BALUCHI
BANGASH
BAZIGAR
BENGALI
BHOTIYA
BHUTANI
DRAVIDA
GUJRATI
KACHARI
KHARWAR
KHASIYA
KURUMBA
LAMBADI
MADRASI
MARATHA
MARWARI
ORAKZAI
PUNJABI
SHERANI
TAGHLIK
TIBETAN

MIDDLE EAST, AFGHANISTAN

AUS
LUR
ARAB
GHUZ
IBAD
KURD
SAFI
SEID
SLEB
TURK
FARSI
IHLAT
IRAKI
IRAQI
KAFIR
KAJAR
KHUZI
MAHRI
MUKRI
NEJDI
OMANI
SHIAH
SUNNI
TAJIK
TAULI
TEKKE
YEZDI
YURUK
ZIRAK
AFGHAN
AFSHAR
AUSHAR
BRAHUI
DEHWAR
DUNGAN
DURANI
GALCHA
GHEBER
GILAKI
HAZARA
HEJAZI
KAFFIR
MYSIAN
PAMIRI
PATHAN
SELJUK
SHIITE
SULABA
SULAIB
SUNNEE
SYRIAN
TUNGAN
YEMINI
YEZIDI
BELUCHI
BELUCKI
DURZADA
GHILZAI
HADJEMI
IRANIAN
ISRAELI
KHOKANI
OSMANLI
OTTOMAN
PAKHTUN
PUKHTUN
PERSIAN
SARACEN
SOGDIAN
SUNNITE
VIDDHAL
ACHAZKAI
BACTRIAN
LEBANESE

LAOS, CAMBODIA, VIETNAM, BURMA

WA	**THO**	**TSIN**	**YAOYIN**
KAW	**AHOM**	**KAREN**	**ANAMESE**
KHA	**AKHA**	**KHMER**	**BURMESE**
KUI	**CHIN**	**MUONG**	**LAOTIAN**
LAI	**KADU**	**BALAWA**	**MEITHEI**
LAO	**KUKI**	**BURMAN**	**PALAUNG**
MEO	**LOLO**	**KACHIN**	**SIAMESE**
MON	**SHAM**	**KHAMTI**	**ANNAMESE**
MRU	**SHAN**	**LUSHAI**	**TONKINESE**
TAI	**THAI**	**PEGUAN**	

INDONESIA, MALAYA

BUGI	**MALAY**	**SAMSAN**	**ACHINESE**
CHAM	**MURUT**	**SASSAK**	**BALINESE**
DYAK	**PUNAN**	**SELUNG**	**JAVANESE**
IBAN	**SAKAI**	**SEMANG**	**MACASSAR**
BAJAU	**SAMAL**	**TORAJA**	**MADURESE**
BATTA	**SASAK**	**BAKATAN**	**MAKASSAR**
BUKAT	**TZAAM**	**BORNEAN**	**SUDANESE**
CHIAM	**ALFURO**	**LAMPONG**	**SUMATRAN**
DAYAK	**BILAAN**	**MALAYAN**	**TAGBUANA**
DUSUN	**KALANG**	**NIASESE**	**TIMORESE**
JAKUN	**NESIOT**	**TORADJA**	
KAYAN	**REJANG**		

SECTION III
Word Locator

EXPLANATION OF USE

This section lists words in easy-to-read columns and gives definitions for them. This method eliminates the need for cross-references and makes it possible to find the word you want very quickly when you already have at least one letter of the word.

The alphabetization is based on letter-position in words. The two-letter word list is alphabetized starting with AA, giving all words with –A in the second position, then all words with –B in that position, and so on. Thus, if you are looking for a word ending in –B meaning "river," run your eye down the list of words ending in –B and you quickly find OB.

The three-letter word list is based on the same plan. First, all words ending in – –A are listed in alphabetical order from ABA to ZOA, then all words ending in – –B from ABB to ZAB, and so on. As soon as one end-letter is finished, the next letter begins. Then all words with –A– in the second position are listed (from BAA to TAZ), followed by –B– in the second position, and so on up to –Z–.

The four-letter words are listed first in a straight alphabetical group, from A– – – to Z– – –. This enables you to find a word if you have only the *first* letter. Then the positional lists begin. All words with –A– – as a second letter are now listed, from BAAL to ZAZA; then all words with –B– – as a second letter, and all the way to –Z– –. Next, all words with —A– as third letter, – –B– as third letter, and so on to – –Z–. Finally, all words with – – –A as fourth letter, – – –B as fourth letter, and so on.

The catchwords given in the upper left- and right-hand corners of each page direct you quickly to the letter position you want.

Note: Puzzle makers vary their definitions, but you should recognize most words despite this variation.

TWO-LETTER WORDS

AA rough lava (opp. to pahoehoe)
BA soul (bird with human head); bleat; Bachelor of Arts (degree)
DA ambari (hemp); yes: Russ.; prosecutor; — Gama
EA Eridu's chief god; river
FA syllable of scale (mi — sol); 4th tone
GA Gold Coast Negro
HA exclamation; have
IA Iowa
JA yes: Ger.
KA genius, double (Egypt); unknown Hindu god (Brahma, Prajapati)
LA syllable of scale (sol — ti); 6th tone; Louisiana; article: Sp., Fr., It.; — Paz; — Plata; — Crosse
MA mother; — Bellona (goddess); Ra's daughter; Master of Arts (degree); Maritime Administration
NA continent
PA papa; N.Z. fort, village
RA sun god; Nut's son; mus. note
SA continent
TA pagoda; article: Scot.; mus. note; weight
VA it proceeds (mus.); comment ça — (how are you?): Fr.; Virginia; Veterans Administration
WA Burmese native, language; measure
YA Arabic Y; diphthong
ZA Tartini's B-flat; prefix: very

AB immortal heart; 11th Jewish month; prefix: from
BB chess move; rifle shot size
FB fullback (football)
HB halfback (football)
KB chess move
OB objection; — and sol; prefix: to, before, against; river
QB quarterback (football); chess move
RB chess move

AC alternating current
BC time
CC 200
DC direct current; 600; Washington
EC prefix: from, house
IC suffix; integrated circuit
MC 1100; entertainer
OC yes; langue d'- (Fr. dialect)
XC 90

AD notice; toward: Lat.; — hoc; — lib; —infinitum
CD 400
DD Doctor of Divinity (degree)
ED verb ending; Jordan altar; nickname
ID fish; natural self; — est
MD Doctor of Medicine; Maryland
OD minced oath; alleged force
TD clay pipe

AE umlaut; Lat. plural; poet (G. W. Russell)
BE exist; subsist
CE Chemical, Civil Engineer; this: Fr.; n'est- pas?
DE prefix: from (Lat., Fr.); of, with: Sp.; — profundis
EE ye; eye: Scot.; Electrical Engineer
FE mus. syllable; Santa —
GE goddess; Gaea, Chaos's daughter, mother of Uranus, Titans; Tapuyan
HE man; anyone; Heb. letter, 5
IE screw pine (mat, basket); that is; diphthong
LE article: Fr.; mus. note; — Havre; — Bourget
ME pronoun; I; ego; mus. note; Maine
NE compass point; not
OE umlaut; whirlwind; islet
PE Heb. P, 80; weight; measure
RE regarding; syllable of scale (do — mi); Ra; Ile de —
SE compass point; mus. note; measure
TE right conduct (Tao — Ching); you: Sp.; thee: Fr.; mus. note; — Deum
UE umlaut
VE Odin's brother; Frigg's brother-in-law
WE pronoun; editorial, imperial I; Lindbergh book; island

YE you; yea

EF F; if
FF size of shot
IF provided; whether; condition; Chateau d'- (Monte Cristo's prison)
LF left field (baseball)
OF prep.; about
RF right field (baseball)

EG for example; that is
OG Bashan king; Whig poet Shadwell
UG feel fear, disgust

AH exclamation
CH digraph
EH exclamation
OH exclamation
PH digraph; Sorenson's symbol
RH digraph; — factor (blood substance)
SH digraph; hush!; quiet!
TH digraph; suffix
WH digraph

AI diphthong; exclamation; sloth; Shamash's wife; sweetfish; artificial intelligence
BI prefix: twice
CI 101
DI 501; gods: Lat.; prefix: away, twice, double; Diana
EI diphthong
FI mus. note; hi-
GI Liberian tribe; US Army enlisted man, woman (— Joe, — Jane)
HI salutation; -fi
II 2
LI 51; measure; weight; mus. note; propriety; — Tai-po (poet)
MI 1001; syllable of scale (re — fa)
OI diphthong; exclamation
PI Greek P, 80; math. ratio 3.1416; porcelain tokens; jumble(d type); mess
RI measure, note; Ir. king (ard-)
SI syllable of scale (sol la —); yes: Sp., It.; river
TI syllable of scale (si); palm
VI 6
WI with: Scot.
XI 11; Greek X, 60
YI Pu (emperor)

AK mudar; fiber shrub
BK chess move
IK Isaac
KK chess move
OK correct: approve
QK chess move
RK chess move

AL Indian mulberry; nickname; according to
CL 150
DL 550
EL God; Syrian deity; L; elevated train; the: Sp.; measure; :— Paso; — Capitan; — Alamein
IL the: It.; — Duce; prefix: not
ML 1050
OL suffix: alcohol, oil
XL 40

AM verb, part of "to be"; measure
CM 900
EM M; type measure; square; elec. unit; them; name; -cee
IM prefix: not; contraction
MM 2000
OM assent; mystic sound; mantra (Hinduism); med. suffix
UM exclamation; word of hesitation
AN anyone; article; and; prefix: not; -Najaf (Ali's shrine)
EN N; ½ em; chief priest; in: Fr.; — casserole; — passant; suffix: made of
IN among; at (home); nook; specially favored
ON cricket term; (proceeding) along; aware: Helliopolis
UN prefix: not; negative word; United Nations

AO Assam tribe; personification of light (opp. to po)
BO buddy; tramp; monk; chief; boo!; sacred tree (pipac); Song — (Papien river)
CO prefix: together
DO perform; syllable of scale (— re mi); Jap. district; stir; fare
EO prefix: dawn, early time
FO the Buddha
GO leave; move; energy; try; fashion; Jap. game
HO attend!; tally-; Kol dialect; tribe; measure; yo-
IO Inachus's daughter; Jupiter moon; hawk; butterfly; Iowa
JO sweetheart; nickname; measure; coin
KO Chin. porcelain, measure; knockout
LO behold!, Indian; St. —
MO book; instant; Mossi language; port; Missouri

NO denial; negative (vote); -gaku (drama); lake
OO bird; prefix: egg
PO realm of darkness (opp. to ao); river; P.I. title; Li Tai- (poet)
RO husband: Gypsy; Foster's language
SO king; thus; ever; if; very; sic!; mus. note
TO prep.; measure; takeout
UO diphthong; umlaut
WO falconer's cry; woo; woe
YO exclamation; -ho; Nan — (sacred mountain)
ZO zebra-yak hybrid; prefix: life

AP prefix: to; Associated Press
UP prep.; r(a)ise; United Press
XP monogram, symbol (Christ)

BQ chess move
IQ intelligence measure
KQ chess move
QQ chess move
RQ chess move

AR R; measure (100 sq. meters); critical point; city (Moab, Num)
BR chess move
ER stammering sound; he: Ger.; god; Judah's son
IR Benjamite
KR chess move
MR title
OR conjunction; alternative; tincture, gold: Her., Fr.; Côte d'-
QR chess move
RR chess move
UR Chaldean city (Abraham's home); primitive, original: Ger.

AS like; thus; since; qua; glacial ridge; coin; weight; city
ES weight; elec. unit; suffix; it: Ger.
IS verb, part of "to be"; Ville d'- (King Gradlon's capital); Iraq city (Hit)
OS bone; mouth; signal; glacial ridge
SS shortstop (baseball); Nazi police
TS digraph
US pronoun; America

AT prep.: by, in, near; coin
ET and: Lat., Fr.; diminutive; coin; — cetera; — alii
IT pronoun; charm; player
ST quiet!; saint; street
TT rifle shot size
UT Guido's note; Utah
VT Vermont
XT Christ

AU with the: Fr.; — gratin; gold symbol
BU Jap. coin; measure
DU thou: Ger.; — Barry
EU prefix: good, true
FU Chin. department
HU Northerner; Tatar; Mongol
IU diphthong
JU Chin. porcelain; diphthong
LU perused: Fr.; nickname
MU Greek M, 40; measure; electronic term
NU Greek N, 80; primeval chaos; naked: Fr.
OU oh!; where, or: Fr.; diphthong
PU coin; measure; Yi (emperor)
RU regret
SU Ra's son; known: Fr.
TU you: it; thou: Fr.
VU seen: Fr.; déjà — (paramnesia)
WU Chin. dialect; river
XU coin
YU jade stone
ZU storm god

CV 105
DV 505
IV 4; birth of Christ
LV 55
MV 1005
XV 15

AW exclamation
NW compass point
OW exclamation; diphthong
SW compass point

AX cutting tool; fell; destroy; ask
CX 110
DX 510
EX X; expense; prefix: without, from; former
IX 9
LX 60
MX 1010
OX bovine; draft animal
XX 20

AY ah; alas!; champagne; always; yes (vote)
BY goal; pass; beside; in; near; with
EY exclamation
HY prefix: arch
IY diphthong
KY Kentucky
LY measure; suffix; prefix: to loose
MY poss. pronoun; exclamation
OY grandchild: Scot.; exclamation

PY prefix: suppurative
SY scythe; diminutive suffix

TY suffix: tens, state; god (Tiu, Tyr)
WY Y

UZ Job's home; Shem's grandson

THREE-LETTER WORDS
– –A to – –Z

ABA camel hair; Arab. cloak; altazimuth
ADA fem. name; city; (Java) canvas
AEA (candlenut) bark cord
AGA bark; rope; title; Turk. officer; ruler
AHA exclamation
AIA Rizpah's father
AKA Assam tribesman, language; N.Z. vine
ALA Alabama; (army) wing; petal; after, according to; — mode; — carte
AMA chalice; (nurse) maid; American Medical Association; tree
ANA collection; prefix: up, back; Irish gods' mother; coin
APA Braz. tree; wallaba
ARA constellation; altar; macaw; textile screw pine; measure; goddess
ASA masc. name; healer; king of Judah; Norse god
ATA Mindanao tribe, language; flour; sweetsop
AVA anc. Burma capital; pepper; shrub; kava; liquor
AWA kava; tenpounder; milkfish
AYA Brahman title; Shamash's consort; Ai
BAA sheep's bleat
BOA constrictor; python; anaconda; (fur, feather) scarf
BRA underwaist
CHA rolled tea; -cha (V.I. white, dance)
CIA Central Intelligence Agency
DEA goddess: Lat.
DHA measure, weight
DIA through; prefix: apart; day: Sp.
DRA measure
ECA Economic Cooperation Administration
ELA highest note; bombast; extravagance
ERA epoch; geol. time division
ESA Economic Stability Administration
ETA Jap. outcasts; Greek E, 8; Negrito
EUA Tonga Isle
EVA Evangeline; Little — (Uncle Tom's Cabin)
FHA Federal Housing, Farmers' Home Administration
FLA Florida
FRA brother; monk; — Angelo, Diavolo (Michele Pezza); Angelico (painter)
GOA gazelle; mugger; crocodile; former Port. colony; Austral. native
GRA love(r); fondness
HEA Eridu's chief god
HIA hawk parrot
HOA hallo!
HUA Mao's successor
IBA P.I. fruit tree
ICA river; city
IDA Idaho; Crete mountain; Princess — (opera); Countess —, heiress (Thackeray)
ILA Bantu language
IMA — Hogg (heiress)
INA fem. name suffix; mother
IOA iwa; frigate bird
IRA Bib. ruler; Irish Republican Army; masc. name: watchful
ITA Negrito; Eskimo; labor union; city
IVA yellow bugle; herb eve; marsh elder
IWA frigate bird; -iwa: fern stalks
IYA (nurse)maid,

Koran verse; omen
KEA N.Z. parrot
KHA Nepalese; Laotian
KOA timber tree
KRA long-tailed ape
KUA Bantu tribe
LEA meadow; yarn measure; warp threads
LIA — Fail (crowning stone)
LOA worm; eye parasite; Lao; Mauna —
MAA sheep's cry; maw
MEA — culpa (my fault)
MFA Master of Fine Arts (degree)
MIA mine: It; missing in action
MNA mina (weight)
MOA flightless extinct bird
MYA long clam genus
NAA no
NEA National Education Association
NOA profane; common; no
NRA National Recovery Administration; FDR measure; Blue Eagle
OCA edible root; wood sorrel; oxalis
ODA harem room, inmate
OKA weight; oca; river
OLA palm leaf
OMA suffix: tumor
ONA measure; So. Amer. Indian
ORA Dan. money; mouths; — et labora (pray and work)
OVA eggs; Piman Indian
OXA prefix: oxygen
PEA seed; plant; marble; sweet —; — soup (fog); river
PIA arrowroot; — mater (brain part)
POA (blue)grass
PTA Parent-Teacher Association
PUA hemp; cordage fiber
PWA Public Works Administration
PYA coin
QUA in so far as; sine — non (necessity)
REA turmeric; Rhea; Cybele, mother of the gods
RIA narrow inlet; creek; estuary
RUA Congo Bantu
RYA Scand. rug
SAA measure
SEA water(s); wave; vast area; at — (lost); naval; — horse
SHA Shinto temple; urial; sheep
SIA Keresan Indian
SLA sloe
SNA snow: Scot.
SOA tub; milk pail; cowl
SPA mineral spring; resort
SUA hers: Lat.
SWA so
TAA Chin. pagoda
TEA beverage; collation; — green; — ball; — wagon
THA thee; thou
TIA aunt: Sp.
TOA brave warrior; beefwood; Casuarina
TRA Malay coin
TUA dyewood tree
TVA Tennessee Valley Administration
TWA two
UCA fiddler crab
UEA island
UFA river
ULA the gums; diminutive
UMA Devi (goddess of splendor); Wiltshire's wife (Stevenson)
UNA river; Dan's sister (Kipling); Red Cross Knight's wife: Truth personified in "Faerie Queene"
UTA lizard; Jap. song
UVA grape
VIA way, vessel: Lat.; through; — Dolorosa
WEA Algonquian
WOA stop!
WPA Works Progress Administration
YEA yes (vote); — and Nay (Richard I)
ZEA Indian corn; maize
ZIA Gad's descendant; N.M. pueblo
ZOA Blake's symbol(s); suffix: animals

ABB warp yarn; poorest fleece
ALB church vestment
BAB Babism founder
BBB rifle shot size
BIB sip; apron part; fish; nozzle
BKB chess move
BOB cheat; mock; weight; curtsy; Scot. dance; shilling; haircut; Robert; -sled; — up
BQB chess move
BUB small boy; liquor
CAB (ride in) taxi; engineer's place; measure; Civil Aeronautics Board
COB swan; horse; seagull; excel; strike
CUB young animal; boy (scout); — reporter; light

plane: grasshopper
DAB touch, tap; flounder; lizard; expert
DEB society girl; Deborah
DIB bob bait; dibble; dip
DOB dab; daub
DUB rub smooth; bestow title; play; do poorly; coin; add sound
EBB recede; delay; — tide; shallow
ELB jujube
FIB (tell white) lie; pummel
FOB pocket; cheat; trick; — chain
FUB plump child; cheat
GAB chatter; hook; notch; E.I. persimmon
GEB earth god; Osiris's father
GIB (tom)cat; salmon; prison; bearing plate; gut fish
GOB mouth(ful); mass; sailor; tar
HOB ferret; havoc; game pin; cut(ter); — and nob
HUB wheel center; nave; pipe; the — (Boston)
JAB punch; stab
JIB sail; mouth; crane arm; standstill
JOB (do odd) work; employment; OT book; patient sufferer; item
KAB measure
KEB earth god; Osiris's father
KOB Afr. antelope
KTB chess move
LAB rennet; study room
LIB castrate; ad —
LLB Bachelor of Laws (degree)
LOB go heavily; high curve (tennis); till; Puck
MAB fairy queen and midwife; Mabel
MIB marble
MOB crowd (about); masses; annoy; gang; cap
NAB lock keeper; arrest; river
NEB Nebraska; beak; mouth; kiss
NIB beak; pen(point); lint knot; scorer
NOB (blow on) head; knob(stick); hob and —
NUB knob; knot; gist
ORB disk; sphere; world; eye; encircle
PAB flax refuse (fuel)
POB porridge; post-office box
PUB inn; tavern
QKB chess move
QQB chess move
RAB teacher; mortar mixer; dog hero; Yugo. Isle
REB rebel
RIB costa; meat cut; wife; vein; part of sock, ship, umbrella; tease; purl
RKB chess move
ROB steal; mine coal; juice; — Roy (outlaw)
RQB chess move
RUB polish; vex; chafe; hindrance; gibe
SEB earth god; Osiris's father
SIB brother; sister; litter mate; kinsman; congenial
SOB weep; wail(ing); — story; — sister
SUB pinch hitter; under: Lat; — rosa
TAB flap; tag; account; Cambridge man; charges
TIB skip school
TOB anc. Syrian kingdom
TUB vessel; keg; wash
WEB gossamer; (en)mesh; membrane; network; rete
ZAB Great — (river)
ABC book; primer; rudiment
AEC Atomic Energy Commission
ARC curve part; light; rainbow
BAC ferryboat; cistern
BSC Bachelor of Chemical Science (degree)
CCC 300; Commodity Credit Corporation; Civilian Conservation Corps
CXC 190
DCC 700
DEC prefix: ten; December
DOC doctor; physician
DUC duke: Fr.
DXC 590
ETC and so on
FAC fact
FCC Federal Communi-cations Commission
HIC hiccuping sound; — et ubique
HOC card game; — anno; ad —
ICC Interstate Commerce Commission
IHC Jesus symbol
LAC varnish component; resin; milk (pharm.); 100,000 rupees

MAC son of: Ir., Scot.; Irishman; coat
MCC 1200
MDC 1600
MMC 2100
MXC 1090
ORC grampus; whale
PAC moccasin; half-boot
PIC measure; very small
ROC fabled bird; simurg; bomb
SAC cavity; pouch; Sauk; Indian; — and soc
SEC second; dry (wine); Securities & Exchange Commission
SIC thus!; — transit gloria; chase; incite
SOC A.S. jurisdiction district; sac and —
TAC prefix: touch
TEC detective
TIC twitch(ing); spasm; funny habit; correct (slang)
VAC speech goddess; Sarasvati
WAC Women's Army Corps
ZAC Caucasian ibex

ADD (sub)join; augment; annex; total, foot
AID help(er); succor; Agency for International Development
AND conjunction; plus
ARD suffix: excessive doer
BAD evil; poor; ill; severe; faulty; wrong; river; — Ems
BED base; bottom; matrix; lodge
BID reveal; offer; order; invite; — fair; — price
BOD clay plug
BUD develop; immature one; lad; in the —; — stick
CAD (act as) bounder
CID the —; Sp. hero, epic; Diaz de Vivar
COD fish; hoax; Cape —
CUD something ruminated; tobacco quid
DAD father
DID performed; acted
DOD clip off; metal plate; annular die
DUD garment; faulty bomb; failure
EED Moslem Easter
ELD old time; age
END limit; death; extreme; phase; remnant; aim; finish; — man; — use; open —
ERD earth; land; — shrew
FAD custom; craze; polish
FED nourished; fattened
FID mast support; pin; tobacco quid
FOD measure
GAD rod; rove(r); -fly; oath; Jacob's son; Israel tribe; Syrian god
GED oath (God)
GID sheep disease
GOD Jehovah; deity; deify; gallery occupant
HAD possessed; tricked
HID concealed
HOD brick tray; coal scuttle; — carrier
IND India (poet); Indiana
JOD yodh; Heb. Y, 10
KED sheep tick
KID young goat, child; fur; leather; tease
LAD boy; youth; stripling
LED guided; directed; diode
LID (eye) cover; curb; hat
LLD Doctor of Laws (degree)
LOD weight
LTD limited (company)
LUD oath; legendary king
MAD crazy; vain; angry; river
MID among; central; half-way
MMD 2500
MOD Scot. artist congress; fashion fad
MUD abusive charge; — lark; — Cat State (Miss.)
MVD Soviet Ministry of Interior Affairs
NED Edgar; Edmund; Edward
NID nest; pheasant brood
NOD drowse; (show) assent; Land of — ; East of Eden
ODD unpaired; queer; uneven; extra; fellow; — man wins
OID suffix: like
OLD stale; obsolete; passé; skilled; primeval; quondam; hoary; — hat
ORD mountain
PAD cushion; saddle; walk; tablet; robber; stuff; track; lodgings
PED basket; prefix: foot, boy, child
POD flock; socket; groove; bag; legume; suffix: foot
PUD paw; hand; weight
RAD afraid: Scot.; energy unit

RED color, dye; lurid; inflamed; golden; Communist; fowl; cent; river; sea; Jacket (Seneca chief)
RID free; clear; dispose
ROD stick; race; bar; gum; scepter; 5½ yards
RUD redness; fish
SAD gloomy; dull; poor; depressed; grievous; — sack
SED but: Lat.
SID Sydney
SOD soil; turf; sward
SUD soapy water; foam
TAD small child; Theodore
TED spread for drying; scatter; waste
TID girl; woman
TOD wool weight; (ivy) bush; death: Ger.
UND and: Ger.
URD bean; woolly pyrol; Norn; Wyrd; — Verthandi, Skuld
VOD Baltic Finn
WAD lump; plug; roll; money; black ocher
WED marry; unite(d)
YOD Heb. Y, 10
ZED Z
ABE Lincoln; the Great Emancipator
ACE one-spot; card; bit; hole in one; air hero; game point; expert; first-rate
ADE soft drink; humorist
AGE period; generation; era; ripen; mellow
AKE forever: Maori; N.Z. tree; hopbush
ALE beverage; malt liquor; festival
AME wooden form; soul: Fr.; — damnée
ANE ass; Fr.; chem. suffix
APE monkey; anthropoid; mimic; Hawaiian herb; apil
ARE measure; verb form
ASE enzyme; Peer Gynt's mother (Ibsen)
ATE goddess of infatuation, folly, discord (Zeus's daughter); consumed
AUE Polynesian exclamation
AVE — atque vale (hail and farewell!); rosary bead
AWE reverence; intimidate; mill bucket, sail
AXE tool; fell; destroy
AYE always; yes (vote)
BEE B; Apis; drone; contest; crazy idea
BLE grain: Fr.
BYE run (cricket), aside; secondary; inactive
CEE C; em- (master of ceremonies)
CHE shrub; Chin. flute
CIE abbr., company: Fr.
CLE diminutive suffix
COE sheep disease; Ia. college
CUE Q; signal; hint; hair twist; waiting line; billiard rod
DAE do: Scot.
DEE D; river; mathematician
DIE expire; long; vanish; stop; cube; chance; tool; shape
DOE female animal; biscuit color; John —
DUE owed; just; debt; — date
DYE color; stain
EAE classifying suffix
EDE Dutch commune; Afr. city
EKE piece out; augment
ELE aisle; eel
EME uncle; friend; gossip
ENE suffix; compass point
EPE Dutch commune
ERE before; sooner; — long
ESE suffix; compass point
ETE summer: Fr.
EVE twilight; time before; woman; mother of mankind
EWE sheep; Negro tribe
EXE Devon river
EYE vision; view; scan; loop; spot; brood; — bank
FAE foe: Scot.
FEE land grant; charge; tip; reward
FIE exclamation
FOE enemy; adversary
GEE G; horse command; evade; agree; oath; haw and —
GIE give: Scot.
GUE Shetland viol
HAE have: Scot.
HIE hasten; speed
HOE tool; dig; scrape; inventor
HUE color; shout; — and cry
HYE hedge; hie
ICE frost(ing); chill; dessert; diamonds
IDE fish; chem. suffix
IFE hemp; cordage

fiber
IKE Isaac; nickname (Eisenhower)
ILE isle: Fr.; suffix; -de-France; — de la Cité
INE suffix
IRE provoke; anger; choler; wrath
ISE suffix; fjord; bay (Atsuta)
ITE suffix: follower, resident; So. Amer. Indian
IVE contraction; suffix
IZE suffix
JOE coin; sweetheart; — Miller (joke); fat boy (Dickens)
KAE serve; oblige; jackdaw
LAE New Guinea port
LEE shelter; sediment; Annabel (Poe); Lorelei — (Loos); Francis Lightfoot —; Henry — (Light-Horse Harry)
LIE fib; mislead; be; extend; slope; golf term; Trygve (UN official)
LOE love: Scot.
LUE sift; bolt
LYE alkaline solution; lixivium
MAE — West (life preserver)
MME madame; My Lady
MOE masc. nickname
NAE no, not: Scot.
NEE born; by maiden name
NIE never: Ger.; eyes
NNE compass point
NYE pheasant brood; humorist
OBE Greek clan division; magic rite, fetish
ODE (Pindar) poem; song; canticle; hymn
OKE weight; measure
OLE palm leaf; old; Sp. victory cry
ONE single; unit(y); person; same; the absolute
OPE unlock (poet.)
ORE Oregon; seaweed; mineral; crude metal(lic rock); coin
OSE suffix: simple sugar
OTE suffix: resident
OVE egg-shaped ornament
OWE be obliged, indebted
OYE grandchild: Scot.
PEE P; turtle delicacy; calipee
PIE bird; mixed type; jumble; coin; tart
POE Edgar Allan — (Raven, Gold Bug); parson bird
PRE prefix: before
PUE pew
PYE poet; 1st engraver
QUE what, that: Fr.
RAE explorer; fem. name
REE sift; right; Arikara; fem. ruff; sandpiper
RHE fluidity unit
RIE grass, cereal
ROE deer; doe; fish eggs; streaks in wood
RUE herb; repent; regret; — de la Paix
RYE cereal; whisky; Gypsy; — and Indian (bread)
SAE so
SEE perceive; bishop's seat; curia; learn; call (bet); — red; — stars; astronomer
SHE woman; Haggard novel
SIE sye; you, she: Ger.
SOE tub; pail; cowl
SSE compass point
STE saint(e): Fr.
SUE urge; woo; plead; take court action
SYE scythe; drop; strain
TAE to; toe; take: Scot.
TEE T; game mark; golf term; top ornament; — beam, bar; to a —; -shirt
THE article
TIE bind; link; knot; duty; equal(ity); bond; beam; cravat, Ascot
TOE digit; drive aslant; golf club part; — the line; -hold
TRE prefix: town; three: It.
TSE Lao- (philosopher); Mao -tung
TUE parson bird
TYE mast chain
UBE P.I. yam
UKE ukulele; guitar
ULE caucho tree; rubber; diminutive suffix
UME Jap. apricot; river
UNE article, one: Fr.
URE suffix: chemist; river mist: Scot.
USE employ(ment); (ac)custom; treat(ment); gain; dupe; — and wont
UTE Shoshonean Indian; mountain
UVE P.I. yam
VAE alas!; — victis
VEE V; $5; neckline; refusal
VIE emulate; strive; compete; life: Fr.
VOE inlet; creek
WEE little; pig's squeak; Willie Winkle (Kipling)

WOE alas; sorrow(ful)
WYE Y; forked holder, track; river
YOE ewe
ZEE Z; zed

AEF American Expeditionary Force; WWI Amer. army; Pershing command
ALF Alfred; elf
AUF on, upon: Ger.
ELF fairy; sprite; dwarf
ERF ½-acre plot
HOF city
KAF myth. mountain, fabled bird abode; Arabic K
KEF hemp; languor
LIF — and Lifthrasir (myth. survivors)
LOF measure
NEF clock, vessel in form of ship; navicula; church nave
OAF elf's child; dolt; fool
OFF erring; away!; go; out; below par; — color; — stage
OLF bullfinch
ORF fish; yellow ide
OUF dog's bark; exclamation
QAF kaf
REF measure; referee
RIF measure
SIF Thor's wife; home guardian
VIF lively, animated: Fr.
ZIF Jewish month: Iyar

AGG carrier (Kipling)
BAG sac(k); measure; purse; seize; in the —
BEG ask; entreat; Turk. title; bey
BIG large; barley; — Bertha; — Ben; — Bend; — brother; — house; — Blue (river)
BOG mire; marsh; — down
BUG insect; defect; germ; fanatic; bulge (eyes); river
CAG offend; insult
CIG cigarette
COG cheat; (gear) tooth; (connect by) tenon; ship
DAG Nott and —, deities; antler; pistol; Hammarskjold, UN chief
DEG sprinkle; dampen
DIG (verbal) thrust; dwell
DOG Canis; gripper; andiron; crampon; track
DUG delved; excavated
EGG ovum; germ cell; coal; bomb; fellow; incite
ENG Chang's Siamese twin
ERG work unit; desert area
FAG cigarette; drudge; tire; Capt. Absolute's servant; liar
FIG fruit; fico; zero; rig
FOG vapor; daze; blue; blur
FUG reek
GAG pry open; choke; joke; closure; fish; illustrator
GEG No. Albanian
GIG fish spear, hook; boat; chaise, carriage; nap
GOG — and Magog (statues)
HAG harpy; witch; urge; copse; bog
HOG pig, boar; sheep; dime, shilling; glutton; monopolize
HUG embrace; keep close; bear —
ING suffix; A.S. peace god
JAG pendant; barb; slash; drunken spree
JIG dance; prank; drill
JOG jostle; remind; trot
JUG ewer; jail; stew; nest(le); bird sound
KEG cask; — of nails: 100 lb.
LAG linger; slacken; stave; jailbird
LEG meat cut; support; run; lap; — art: cheesecake
LOG cut timber; (ship) record
LUG ear; loop; drag; worm; sail; measure; god
MAG chatter; bird; Margaret; halfpenny (Brit.)
MEG Margaret; Princess —; Mag; Alcott heroine; horse (Burns); Merrilles (Scott)
MIG marble; duck; plane
MOG move slowly; depart
MUG cup; face; photograph; sheep; mungo; assault; overact; pose
NAG horse; annoy(ance); fret; snake; Nagaina's wife (Kipling)
NIG dress (stone); cut coin edge; revoke
NOG egg drink; peg; wood (block, fastener); pin
PAG island
PEG (cribbage) pin; support; pretext; leg; hit; plod; Margaret
PIG pork; litter;

glutton; cushion; ingot; — Iron; The — Baby (Carroll)
PUG dog; (mix) clay; boxer; — nose; footprint
RAG shred; scold; dance; slate; fog; — doll
REG desert region
RIG equip(ment); swindle; tackle; ardri
ROG shake; pull; stir
RUG mat; cozy
SAG droop; weaken; drift
SEG sedge; iris
SIG signature
SOG soak; drowse
TAG flap; tab; lock; cue; story moral; join; follow; game; label
TEG young sheep
TOG coat; dress up
TUG pull; lug; effort; towboat; — of war
TYG drinking vessel
VAG (arrest as) vagabond
VEG prank; wanderer
VOG weight
VUG lode cavity
WAG sway; gossip; joker
WIG hair(piece); peruke; judge
ZAG jaggged line angle
ZIG part of a zigzag
ZOG Albanian king
ZUG Swiss canton, lake

AKH spirit of man: Egypt
ASH tree; residue; burn; pallor; gray; — can: depth charge
AUH exclamation
BAH exclamation
BOH Burmese chief; boo; — da Thone (Kipling)
DAH Burmese knife
DOH do (note)
EDH A.S. letter: th
ETH A.S. letter: th; suffix; ordinal number
FOH exclamation
HAH exclamation
HEH Chin. tribe; Hei; Miao
HOH Quileute; Indian whaler
HSH hush; exclamation
HUH exclamation
ICH I, ego: Ger.; fish dermatitis
ISH adj. suffix
ITH Irish ancestor
JAH Jehovah; god
LEH Kashmir town
MAH moon angel
NTH any size; — degree; indefinite power
OCH alas!; oh!
PAH bah!; nasty; improper; N.Z. native fort
PEH river
POH bah!
RAH (cheer with) hurrah
REH salt mixture, alkali
SAH measure
SOH exclamation, gutta mixture
TCH exclamation
UGH assenting grunt
USH usher
VAH Danube tributary
WAH panda; measure
YAH yes; exclamation
ZOH zobo; yak; zebu hybrid

ABI Hezekiah's mother
ACI chem. prefix
AHI sky serpent; Vritra
AJI Capsicum plant
ALI Mohammed's son-in-law; Fatima's son; — Pasha: Lion of Janina
AMI friend: Fr.
ANI black bird; cuckoo
API prefix: bee
ATI P.I. Negrito
CCI 201
CDI 401
CHI Greek letter CH, 600; fem. Gypsy; Gold Coast language; Tshi
CII 102
CLI 151
CMI 901
COI river
CRI cry: Fr.; dernier —
CUI composer; engineer
CVI 106
CXI 111
DCI 601
DEI the gods: Lat.; agnus —
DII the gods; 502
DLI 551
DUI duets; twosomes
DVI 506
DXI 511
EHI Ahiram; Benjamin's son
ELI high priest; Samuel's teacher; Yale; — Whitney
EPI finial; grain, ear: Fr.; prefix: upon
ERI silkworm; bombyx; Gad's son
EVI Midianite king
FBI Federal Bureau of Investigation
FEI Yap stone money; banana
GHI buffalo butter; ghee
GOI non-Jew: Heb.
GRI horse: Gypsy
HAI Israelites defeat site
HEI cat's cradle; Miss — (Greene)
HOI yam; haw (as cattle)
HUI guild; partnership
ICI here: Fr.
IHI stitchbird; fish; halfbeak, skipper
III 3
IKI island
ILI river

IMI measure
INI suffix: order
IRI Bela's son; city
KAI N.Z. food; apple; island
KEI apple; island
KOI Jap. carp
KRI read(ing substitute)
KUI Asian group; Lolo; Kandh.
LAI medieval tale: Burmese
LEI wreath; coin
LII 52
LOI law: Fr.
LVI 56
LXI 61
MAI May: Ger.
MCI 1101
MDI 1501
MII 1002
MLI 1051
MMI 2001
MOI I: Fr.; Asian tribes
MUI — tsai: girl slave(ry)
MVI 1006
MXI 1011
NEI Eastern flute
OBI girdle; sash
OII N.Z. muttonbird
OKI evil spirit; archipelago
OMI sacred mountain
ONI any: Scot.
ORI prefix: mouth; limit
OVI prefix: egg
PAI money; weight
PEI river
PHI Greek letter PH, 500
POI Hawaiian food (taro)
PPI radarscope
QUI who, that: Fr.; — vive (watchword)
RAI measure
REI coin; David's friend
RII small streams; Venice canals
ROI fern rootstock; king: Fr.; vive le —
SAI Capuchin monkey; Cebus
SHI weight
SKI glide(r); runner; sport; — lift
SRI glorious; holy; Lakshmi (goddess)
SUI Chin. dynasty; — generis
TAI porgy; Laos; Shan; Siamese; Li -po (poet); — Shan (sacred mountain)
TJI river: Java; weight
TOI you, thou: Fr.
TRI prefix: three
TUI dyewood tree; parson bird
TWI prefix: double; Tshi
UBI where: Lat; white yam
UDI N. Caucasian language
UJI silkworm disease
UNI plainly woven; goddess (Juno); prefix: single
UPI news, wire service; United Press International
URI Swiss canton
UVI — yam (white yam)
VAI Liberian Negro
VEI Liberian Negro
VII 7
WEI Chin. dynasty, state; river
XCI 91
XII 12
XLI 41
XVI 16
XXI 21
YOI hunting cry

GAJ coin
GUJ Moti—: elephant (Kipling)
HAJ pilgrimage to Mecca
RAJ reign, rule: India
SAJ teak tree
TAJ (dervish) cap; — Mahal

ACK -ack (antiaircraft)
AIK oak: Scot
ALK — gum (turpentine)
ARK Arkansas; refuge; broadhorn; flatboat; wanigan; — of the covenant
ASK question; seek; need; invite; beg
AUK sea bird; Tlingit Indian
BIK poison; aconite
BOK Amer. editor
DAK India mail
ELK deer, wapiti; sambar; leather; color lama; river; city
HAK legal claim; share
HUK P.I. guerrilla
ICK fish dermatitis
ILK family; class; same
INK sepia; cuttlefish; fluid; black; sign
IRK abhor; annoy; bore
KRK island
KTK chess move
LAK grouse's wooing strut
LEK gather(ing); coin; river
LOK god of discord; Balder slayer
NAK stigmatic point; mango
OAK Quercus; Casuarina; encina; — brown; poison —; — Park; — Ridge
OCK weight
ORK whale
OUK week: Scot.
PIK measure
ROK Korean soldier
SAK white cotton
SOK measure
SUK Nilotic Negro
TSK exclamation
USK river
YAK Tibet ox; beast of burden
YOK A.S. G; Middle English Y

ZAK measure
AAL Indian mulberry; red dye; morindin
AFL American Federation of Labor
AIL be ill
ALL whole; each; only; very; universe; according to; — out; — hands; — hours; — clear; — in one
AWL shoemaker's tool
BAL mine; ball: Fr.
BEL fruit, tree; Bengal quince; golden apple; power ratio; earth god; Marduk; — Affris (Shaw)
BUL Canaanite's 8th month; Heshvan
CAL California; wolframite
CCL 250
CDL 450
CML 950
COL Colorado; mountain pass
CUL -de-sac; blind alley
CXL 140
DAL split pea; pigeon pea; Swedish river
DCL 650
DEL Delaware
DXL 540
EEL teleost fish: conger; moray; elver; lamprey; vinegar worm
ELL cloth measure; aune; building annex
FUL Hamitic Sudanese
GAL girl; speed unit
GEL jellify; harden; set
GOL God (euphemistic form)
GUL rose: Persian
HAL Henry, Harry; Prince — (Henry V); Bluff King — (Henry VIII)
HEL Loki's daughter; Niflheim goddess
HOL prefix: complete
HUL Shem's descendant
HYL prefix: wood
IAL adj. suffix
ILL Illinois; sick; bad(ly); evil; river
KEL caul; net; film
KIL Ir. church; monk's cell
KOL Dravidian native; Munda, Larka
KYL Himalayan ibex
LIL book, paper, letter: Gypsy; little; — Abner
MAL — de mer (sea sickness); Sudra caste Hindu; prefix: evil; measure
MCL 1150
MEL honey; prefix: limb, black
MIL 1/1000 inch (wire measure); coin; Ir. eponymous ancestor
MML 2050
MOL gram molecule
MUL measure
MXL 1040
NIL nothing; Indigo dye; ipomoea; nilgal
NUL no, nothing (law)
OIL painting; fuel; grease; flatter(y); bribe
OWL bird (of prey); night-
PAL partner; (to) chum
PEL prefix: mud, clay
PIL prefix: hair
POL degree without honors
PUL Tiglathpileser (king); coin; OT people
REL electric unit
SAL salt; — tree; tamarisk; rock; Sarah
SEL salt: Fr.; self: Scot.
SIL yellow ocher
SOL sun (god); tone G; coin; fluid
TAL palm fiber; hand clapping; cymbals
TEL prefix: distant, end
TIL tree; sesame; mark
TOL Sanskrit school
ULL chief god; Sif's son: Thor's stepson
VOL wings (Her.); battery iron block
ZAL Rustam's father
ZEL Oriental cymbal

AAM liquid measure
AHM liquid measure
AIM direct(ion), design; scheme; end
ARM branch; sleeve; bay; power; fortify
AUM measure
BAM hoax; Iranian town
BEM Pol. general; pasha
BIM Barbados man
BOM So. Amer. serpent
BUM sponge upon; tramp; inferior; Levant ship
CAM awry; gear; rotating, sliding part; Ouse tributary
COM prefix: together, with
CUM summa — laude (with highest praise)
CWM cirque (geol. process)
DAM obstruct(ion); wall; weir; coin; female parent; Nobel biochemist

DEM Democrat: opp. to Rep(ublican)
DIM dark(en); dull; obscure; — view
DOM monastic title; church; low caste Hindu
DUM doom palm; gingerbread tree
EAM uncle; gossip
ELM tree; Ulmus; — City (New Haven)
FAM hand (slang)
FUM feng-huang; myth. bird
GAM whale school; visit; botanical suffix
GEM muffin; — State (Idaho); prize piece; jewel
GIM neat; spruce
GUM adhesive; exudate; resin; jaw tissue; overshoe; humbug
GYM sports hall
HAM Noah's son; Shem's brother; amateur radio; actor
HEM (cloth) edge; confine; surround; hesitate; haw
HIM pronoun; male
HUM buzz; sing; murmur; melody; hoax
ISM doctrine; system
JAM tight place; crush; interfere; preserve; native chief; — pack; — session
JEM James
JIM James; — Crow; -dandy; Lord — (Conrad); Finn's friend (Twain)
JUM cultivation method
KAM crooked
KEM river; port
KIM — O'Hara: waif (Kipling)
KUM Shiite pilgrim site; river
LAM beat; escape; loom lever
LIM blue pine; toon
LUM chimney; sink; pond
MAM Mayan Indian
MCM 1900; fin de siècle; Boxer Rebellion
MEM Heb. letter M, 40
MIM (act) affectedly shy
MMM 3000
MOM mama
MUM chrysanthemum; hush; beer; mask; madam
NAM distrain(t)
NIM steal; margosa tree
NOM name: Fr.; — de plume (pseudonym); — de guerre
NYM Falstaff follower
OHM electric unit; -'s law
OLM amphibian
OOM Paul Kruger (Boer president)
PAM card game
POM Pomeranian (dog)
QUM Shiite pilgrim site
RAM sheep; batter(ing —); weight; ship beak; pump; stuff; constellation: Aries
RIM border; edge; margin; wheel part
ROM Gypsy husband
RUM liquor; odd; tough; fine; dye
SAM unite; curdle; Uncle —
SEM Noah's son; Ham's brother
SIM Simeon; Simon
SUM total; amount; all; epitomize; in —; — up
TAM Scot. cap
TEM sun god; Atmu, (A)tum
TIM Tiny —: cripple (Dickens)
TOM male; Thomas; Ob tributary; — Thumb ("General" Charles Sherwood Stratton); — o' Bedlam (madman); — Alibi (Scott); — Canty (Twain); Aunt Chloe's husband
TUM sun god; Atmu; card (wool); banjo sound; The Rum — Tugger (Eliot)
ULM Danube city
VIM force; energy; spirit
VUM vow; swear
WEM spot; stain (in wood)
YAM sweet potato; batata; edible root; tuber; posthouse
YOM day: Heb.; — Kippur (Atonement Day); river

AIN well; spring; 16th Heb. letter, 70; Rhone tributary
ALN measure
ANN stipend; fem. name; Nancy; Nina; Rutledge (Lincoln's fiancee)
ARN alder tree
AWN (remove grain) beard
BAN edict; forbid; curse; title; muslin; coin; kokumin (Jap. reserve); Lancelot's father
BEN son; Moringa seed, oil; Phaseolus; wild hog; — Lomond

(mountain)
BIN box; crib; pungi (flute); Vina
BON good, bond: Fr.; bean; grass; Jap. festival (of lanterns); Tibet religion; Cape—
BUN bread; roll; hair knot; boat; tipsiness
CAN vessel; preserve; tin; dismiss; jail; weight
CON learn; against; deceive; — game; — man; — amore
DAN title; Daniel; buoy; Jacob's (Bilhah's) son; tribe; from — to Beersheba; river; Una's brother (Kipling)
DEN retreat; lair; haunt; scout unit (pack part)
DIN noise; uproar; resound; Gunga —
DON Sir; tutor; put on; goddess; mother of Gwydion, Arianrhod; river
DUN urge payment; dingy (brown); May fly; cure fish
EAN bring forth; to lamb
EEN Ir. suffix; even (poet.)
EIN one, article: Ger.
EON time period; age; eternity
ERN sea eagle
FAN cool(er); vane; winnow; spread; stimulate; devotee; African; Pangwe; Pahouin; — dance
FEN marsh; weight; forbid; — Ho (river)
FIN (fish) appendage; part of keel, aircraft; kite
FON Dahomey Negro (Ewe)
FUN amusement; joke; weight
FYN island
GAN Roland's destroyer
GEN suffix: heredity factor
GIN liquor; snare; female (kangaroo); cotton — ; — fizz; — rummy; — mill
GON measure; prefix: knee; suffix: angled figure
GUN firearm; pump; hunt; mug; — dog; speed up
GYN prefix: woman
HAN Chin. dynasty; Japanese barony; Yangtze tributary
HEN female bird, fish; fowl; coward; measure; — party
HIN measure
HUA Mao's successor
HUN vandal; invader; Boche
IAN John; Fleming (James Bond author)
IBN — Saud (king)
INN ho(s)tel; lodge; river
ION charged particle; molecule; son of Apollo, Creusa
JAN — of Leiden, fanatic; Hus, reformer
JIN Oriental demon(s)
KAN Kansas; measure; river
KEN insight; Japanese measure, prefecture, games
KIN relative(s); zither; koto; Tatar dynasty
KON weight
KUN Bela —, (revolutionary)
LAE New Guinea port
LAN name prefix; measure; Swed. district
LIN linen; flax; linden; — Yutang (author); river
LON Alonso
LYN waterfall
MAN individual; homo; male; anyone; valet; game piece; fortify; tame; to a —; — of war; isle of —
MEN crew; hands; people; troops; lunar god
MIN chief deity; ruler; river
MON my: Fr.; family badge; Pegu Burmese; prefix: one; — Dieu!
MUN must; mouth; roisterer; river
NAN fem. name; river
NEN river
NON not: Lat; no: Fr.; prefix; sine qua —
NUN Niger mouth; convent woman; pigeon, smew; Heb. N, 50; Joshua's father; chaos
OON final syllable
OWN acknowledge; have
PAN tub; dish; ape; wash; result; betel leaf; sir; god: Faunus, Inuus (part goat); face; son of Hermes; prefix: all; Peter (Barrie); dead-
PEN confine; jail; feather; style; write(r); fem. swan
PIN fasten(er); peg; badge; skittle; dowel; -curl; -up

PON pagoda; gold coin
PUN play on words; paranomasia
RAN twine hank; sea deity; Aegir's wife; sped
RIN Jap. coin, measure
RON King Arthur's lance
RUN hurry; operate; stretch; contest; flee; series; brook; trail
RYA Scand. rug
SAN Greek letter, 900; Bushmen; hemp
SEN coin; measure; Sun Yat- (Chin. leader)
SIN (do) wrong; vice; err; Heb. S, 300; moon god; Enzu
SMU Dallas college
SON male descendant; scion; — of Man; river
SUN star; shine; Apollo; Helios; Phoebus; Yat-sen (Chin. leader)
SYN prefix: with
TAN make leather; brown; beat; Gypsy camp
TEN bill; card; X; many; denary; deca; big casino
TIN metal; element; stannium; can; preserve; inferior; 10th anniversary
TON weight; style: Fr.; bon —; suffix: town
TUN vat; cask; measure; guzzle; Mayan year
URN vessel; grave; bury
VAN (fore)front; lead; car; Urartu: Armenia; Turk. lake, town
VIN wine: Fr.; — blanc; — rouge
VON by noble birth: Ger.
WAN (grow) pale; dark; dim
WEN cyst; growth; coin; wyn
WIN gain; earn; persuade
WON obtained; conquered
WUN Burmese governor
WYN Old Eng. rune W
YEN desire; urge; Jap. money
YIN Shang dynasty; weight; female principle (opp. to yang)
YON at a distance; thither
YUN Laos tribesman
ZAN Zeus; Olympia statue
ZEN Buddhist sect, belief
ZIN Bib. wilderness

ABO Finn seaport; Turku
ADO do; trouble; fuss; stir
AGO past; since
AHO exclamation
AKO measure
AMO I love: Lat.
ANO blackbird; prefix: up
APO prefix: away; P.I. volcano; mil. address; Mount — (P.I.)
ARO Nigerian
ASO Jap. volcano
AZO nitrogenous
BOO ostrich tail; hoot; jeer; scary cry
CHO measure
CIO Congress of Industrial Organizations
COO dove cry; amorous talk
CRO -Magnon; homo sapiens; murder fine
DAO P.I. tree (fruit, fiber)
DIO Cassius (historian)
DJO measure; Niger Negro
DSO Distinguished Service Order (Brit.)
DUO two; dust; pair
EBO tree; — oil; Niger Negro
ECO prefix: environment
EDO Nigerian; Ibo
EGO I; whole man; alter —; self(ishness)
ESO prefix: within
ETO European Theater of Operations (WW II)
EXO prefix: outside
FLO Florence; Flora; arrow
FOO Chin. prefecture
FRO from; away; to and —
GAO river
GEO Georgia; prefix: earth, soil
GOO sticky substance
HAO Chin. dynasty
IAO honey eater bird; manuao
IBO Niger Negro
IDO artificial language: de Couturat, Jespersen
ILO International Labor Organization
INO Cadmus's daughter; Athamas's wife
ISO prefix: equal
ITO Zionist (Zangwill's) group; Jap. admiral, statesman
IWO — Jima, island; Afr. city
IYO Afr. bass; palm fiber; P.I. vine
KIO ngaio; N.Z. fruit tree
KOO Chin. statesman

LAO Tai native, language: -tzu, -tse (philosopher)
LEO constellation; Lion; composer; emperor; pope; — Tolstoy
LJO Niger delta Negro
LOO card game: halloo
LUO White Nile Negro
LWO White Nile Negro
MAO peacock; — Tse-tung (Chin. leader)
MEO Indian farmer caste
MHO unit of conductance
MIO my: Sp., It.; dio —
MOO cow's cry; low; weight
NEO advocate of new; prefix: recent
NOO now; new; prefix: mind
ODO William the Conqueror's half brother; Eudes; Count of Paris
OFO Siouan language
OHO exclamation
OJO grassy spring; oasis
OMO prefix: shoulder; river
ORO gold: Sp.; Tahiti god; mouth; prefix: mountain
OTO Siouan; prefix: ear
OVO ab — (from the egg, start)
OYO Nigerian town
PHO exclamation
POO Nanki —: Yum-Yum's husband
PRO for; expert; yes vote(r); quid — quo
QUO measure; quid pro —; status —
REO old car
RHO Greek R, 100
RIO coffee; river; canal: It.; — Grande
ROO kangaroo
SAO measure; — Paulo (city)
SHO pshaw!; sure; measure
SOO murmur; sow
SRO box office sign
TAO man: P.I.; Chin. road, cosmic order, truth; — Te Ching: Lao-tse's work
THO Tonkin peasant
TIO uncle: Sp.
TKO boxing term
TOO also; excessively
TWO card; pair; in —: in half; little casino; — bits; -faced; -time
UDO Japanese herb; edible shoot
UFO flying saucer
ULO prefix: gums; shell money
UNO one: It., Sp.
URO So. Amer. Indian; Puqina
WHO rel. pronoun
WOO make love; court; sue
WRO angle; passage; nook
WYO Wyoming
YAO Chin. aborigines, emperor; Bantu; Indian
YEO officer; bodyguard
ZIO sky, war god; Tyr
ZOO animal collection; menagerie

ALP mountain; renegade (Byron)
AMP elec. unit of intensity; ampere
ASP adder; viper; uraeus: symbol; Cleo's snake
BAP bread loaf, roll
BOP bravura jazz
CAP top; cover; match; crown, explosive; detonator; paper size; capital; tread renewal
COP (wind) yarn; catch; thicket; policeman
CUP vessel; ½ pint; portion; prize; golf hole; crater; bloodletting —
CYP princewood tree
DAP dibble; drop bait; dip; rebound; skip
DIP immerse; lower; ladle; candle; pickpocket; hat; downturn
DOP diamond cup; — brandy
ESP 6th sense; extrasensory perception; especially
FIP coin (four-, sixpence); picayune
FOP dandy; coxcomb; dude
GAP opening; breach; pass; hiatus; ravine
GIP gut fish
GOP Republican party
GUP gossip
GYP steal; swindle(r); bitch; college servant
HAP chance; befall; wrap
HEP wise to; informed; exclamation; -cat
HIP cheer; haunch; rose's false fruit (pseudocarp); bump
HOP leap; dance; limp; air trip; vine; bryony; opium; drug; stimulate
HUP command to horses
HYP make melancholy
IMP petty demon;

urchin; rascal; mock
JAP Nipponese
JIP dog (Dickens)
KEP catch; haul
KIP undressed hide; gym feat; sleeping place; weight
KOP hill; measure
KUP measure
LAP fold; wrap; cut; polish; circuit; drink; ripple; take eagerly
LIP (saucy) speech; edge; spout; kiss; — service
LOP choppy sea; cut off; droop; act lazily
MAP chart; survey; image; Mercator; plan
MOP wipe(r); swab; hair; pout; — up
NAP doze; siesta; hairy surface; pile; game; seize
NEP catnip; cotton fiber knot; Soviet policy
NIP pinch; check; bite; sip; dram; Japanese
OLP blight; bullfinch
OOP up; bind; join: Scot.
ORP fret; weep: Scot.
PAP soft food; paste; dad; simple discourse
PEP energy; stimulate
PIP radar sign; disease; seed; chirp; break shell; spot on card; great!
POP sound; burst; sho(o)t; plant; protrude; ask; drink
PUP young dog, seal; bad security; silly fop
RAP coin; least bit; strike; knock; criticize; jail
sentence
REP fabric; lewd one; Republican: opp. to Dem(ocrat)
RIP tear; (move full) speed; split; hay; basket; van Winkle (Irving); — tide
SAP juice; vigor; money; fool; drain; trench; weaken
SIP drink; taste
SOP dip in; soak; ooze; wet food; bribe
SUP drink; eat; entertain; mouthful
TAP rap; signal; half sole; dance; spigot; liquor; ask money; draw
TIP tilt; upset; dump; apex; (apply) end; touch; hint; fee; bestow
TOP head; acme; best; cut off; cover; outdo; toy; upset; foremost; — secret
TUP ram; mallet; butt
UMP (act as) referee
VIP big shot (very important person)
WAP blow; wrap; truss
YAP yelp; gab; hoodlum; island
YEP yes
YIP yelp; squeal; outcry
ZEP zeppelin; airship
ZIP bullet sound; (move with) vim; energy
KTQ chess move
SUQ Moslem booth, market
AAR (underground) river
AER prefix: gas, air; chalice veil
AFR Africa
AIR ether; gas; breath; breeze; veil; tune; expose; manner; dismissal; — express; — lift
AYR Scot. county, port
BAR obstruct(ion); rod; gate; strip(e); counter; court; except; fish; maigre; mus. measure; son of; sandbank; rifle; Cocheba (Heb. rebel)
BER jujube; elb
BKR chess move
BOR neighbor; Yugo. mine town
BQR chess move
BUR burr; seed coat; whirr; cut(ter)
CAR lift cage; chariot; for: Fr.; fish box; balloon basket; — Nicobar (island)
COR heart; main star; prefix: pupil
CUR mongrel dog; cad
DAR abode; gateway; tree; patriotic group
DER prefix: neck; the: Ger.
DIR to you: Ger.; Pakistan state
DOR beetle; bumblebee; Bongo; Sundanese; Le Coq —: opera; Côte — (Fr. dept.)
DUR major (mus.)
EAR sense; attention; grain spike; handle; front page box; god; Tiwaz; Tiu
EER ever (poet.); suffix
EIR healing goddess
EUR Europe

FAR greatly; widely; long; distant; advanced
FER iron: Fr.; chemin de — (railroad, baccarat)
FIR (ever)green; balsam; Douglas —; — Domnann (Ir. people)
FOR to; because; namely; pro; fur
FUR pelt; coat(ing); Negro
GAR needlefish
GER resident (Hebr. law); Judaism convert
GOR Indus tribesman
GRR exclamation; growl
GUR raw sugar; massecuite
HAR chill fog: Scot.
HER pronoun; female
HIR her
HOR Edom mountain
HUR Ben —: hero (Wallace); Thamar's son; Tirzah's brother
IER noun suffix
IHR you: Ger.
IOR (comparative) ending
ITR attar; rose perfume
JAR grate; snake; drill; clash; shock; vessel; preserve
JUR Nile Negro; Luo; river
KER evil spirit; fate
KIR Bib. Syrian exile
KOR measure; homer
KTR chess move
LAR gibbon; house god; ancestral spirit
LER Brythonic god; Celtic Neptune; children of — (swans)
LUR Persian tribesman; trumpet
MAR spoil; mutilate; — Ignatius (patriarch of Antioch)
MER sea: Fr.; mal de —
MIR chief; Eastern title; Russian communist; to me: Ger.; peace: Russ.
MOR forest humus
MUR wall: Fr.; Yugo. river
NAR near(ly): Scot.
NER Abner's father; Saul's uncle
NOR conjunction: and not
ORR Nobel physiologist
PAR value; equality; average; standard golf score; by: Fr.
PER through; via; for each
PIR Moslem saint, tomb
POR push; kick; poke(r)
PUR sound (cat, motor)
PYR prefix: fire, heat, fever; light unit
QKR chess move
QQR chess move
RKR chess move
RQR chess move
RUR Rhine tributary; Capek play
SAR sixty sixties: 3,600 (Babylonian number)
SER It. title; weight; exist: Sp.; prefix: serum
SIR knight; address
SUR upon (law); prefix: over; south: Sp.; Tyre (Lebanon city)
TAR pitch; coal — (saccharine source); sailor; lute; telegram; river
TER prefix: thrice
TIR shooting (match)
TOR hill; peak; fool: Ger.
TUR pigeon pea; aurochs; urus; ibex; wild goat
TYR god; Aesir, Riu (Tuesday), Odin's son slain by Garm
VER worm: Fr.
VIR man: Lat.; vigor: Scot.
VOR before: Ger.
WAR strife; battle; fight; — bride; — cabinet
WER who: Ger.; murder fine
WIR we: Ger.
XER prefix: dry
YAR growl; maneuverable
YER suffix: your
ZAR measure
ZER measure; weight
ABS Bedouin tribesman
AES Roman bronze; money
ALS when, than: Ger.
ANS Liège commune
ARS art: Lat.; — Amandi (Ovid); — longa, vita brevis
ASS Equus; donkey; kiang; weight; dolt
AUS out of, finished: Ger.; Arab tribesman
BAS low, stocking: Fr.; à — (down!); — relief; roulette bet
BES pleasure god
BIS twice; encore; replica
BOS cow: Lat.; genus
BUS vehicle; enough; — boy
CAS en tout —: Fr.; vanity bag; umbrella
CES these: Fr.
CIS prefix: on this side
COS lettuce; romaine;

trigonometric function
DAS cony; badger: Dutch; the: Ger.; — Kapital
DDS Doctor of Dental Surgery (degree)
DES of the: Ger., Fr.; from, since: Fr.; — Moines
DIS Valkyrie; Norn; Freya; — pater (Pluto, Hades); prefix: apart
DOS dowry; back: Fr. -a-dos; — Passos
EES eyes: Scot.
EIS ice: Ger.
EMS Bad — (spa); river
ENS being; essence, entity
EOS goddess; dawn; Aurora; Tithonus's wife
ERS bitter vetch
ESS S; fem. suffix; worm; curve
FAS divine law: Roman
FES sacred city
GAS fuel; anesthetic; chatter; boast; tear —, poison —, natural —, coal —
GBS playwright: George Bernard Shaw
GES Tapuyan Indian
GIS soldiers: servicemen
GOS goshawk bird: Scot.
GUS Augustus; Gustavus
HAS possesses; -been
HES men; males
HIS poss. pronoun
HMS — Pinafore (G & S opera)
HUS Jan (reformer)
ICS science suffix
IHS symbol (Jesus)
ILS they: Fr.
INS International News Service
IOS Hawaiian hawks
IRS Internal Revenue Service
ITS poss. pronoun
IUS right, law: Lat.
JHS symbol (Jesus)
JUS law(s): Lat.; legal power; gravy, juice: Fr.
KAS cupboard, wardrobe: Dutch
KOS island
LAS alas; the: Sp.; — Vegas
LES the: Fr.; — Misérables
LIS (fairy) fort; lily: Fr.; fleur-de-
LOS the: Sp.; — Alamos; — Islands; — Negros (Admiralty I.)
LYS prefix: loosening; fleur-de-lis; river
MAS master; suffix: festival
MES my: Fr.; prefix: middling, intermediate
MIS prefix: wrong, evil
MOS custom; folkway; mores (sing.)
MRS title; address; — Grundy
MUS mouse, rodent genus
NAS has not, was not
NIS goblin; kobold; Constantine's birthplace; Yugo. city
NOS we: Lat.; our: Fr.; prefix: disease
OAS Organization of American States
ODS minced oath
OES Os
ONS cricket field parts; weight
OPS goddess; Consus; Rhea; Saturn's wife; Ceres' mother
OSS Office of Strategic Services
OUS suffix: abounding
PAS dance step; — de deux; n'est-ce — ?
PES foot(like part)
PPS additional postscript
PUS suppuration; Hindu month
RAS fabric; prince; cape; Fascist leader
RES thing: Lat.; legal matter; in medias —
RIS — de veau (sweetbread)
RLS novelist: Robert Louis Stevenson
ROS prefix: Cornish names; rulers; Varangians
RUS rulers; Ros
SES his, her: Fr.
SIS girl; sweetheart; relative; Cecilia
SOS distress signal
SSS Selective Service System
SUS swine genus
TES your: Fr.
TIS contraction: it is
UNS us: Ger.
VAS pledge; surety; duct, vessel (anat.)
VIS force: Lat.; weight; -a-vis; Yugo. isle
WAS existed; the past
WIS Wisconsin; suppose; think
YES affirmative (vote)

ABT — system (mountain railroads); composer
ACT deed; decree; feign; do; play part; prayer; — of God, — of faith
AET of the age: Lat.
AFT astern; back; behind
AHT Wakashan Indian
AIT (river) islet
ALT high in pitch (octave); old: Ger.
AMT county: Dan.; public office: Ger.
ANT insect; formic

acid source; emmet; pismire

APT fit; likely; ready

ART skill; science; trade; craft; wile; where — thou?; leg —: cheesecake

ATT coin

AUT prefix: self, same

BAT club; hit; brick; blow; flying mammal; wink; gray; bomb

BET stake; wager; Betsy (Dickens)

BIT part of bridle, key; blade; check; drill; mite; morsel; 12½ cents

BKT chess move

BOT botfly larva

BUT conjunction: except, unless, yet, only

CAT feline; whip; shrew; fish; tripod; game; island; ship (tackle); jazz fan

CET that: Fr.

CIT townsman; civilian

COT hut; coop; small bed

CUT sever; carve; lower; cross; shorten; gash; slight; sarcasm

DDT insecticide

DIT poem, surnamed: Fr.; on —

DOT dowry; speck; point; scatter; mus. sign; — and dash (Morse)

EAT consume; gnaw; erode; rust; waste

ECT prefix: outside, without

EFT lizard; newt

ELT knead

ENT suffix; prefix: inner

ERT urge on: Scot.

EST suffix; is: Fr.; id —; n' -ce pas?; Eastern Standard Time

FAT oil(y); rich; gross; obese; stout; useful

FET measure

FIT suit(able); proper; ready; adjust- (ment); attack; mood; spell

FOT measure

FUT measure

GAT channel; gun

GET obtain; reach; hit; persuade; divorce bill

GIT get; mold channel

GOT past tense of get

GUT intestine; eviscerate; destroy; good: Ger.

HAT headwear; cardinal's office; has: Ger.

HIT strike; reach; agree; impact; success

HOT torrid; burning; eager; violent; fresh; urgent; biting; exciting; stolen; contraband; — seat; — dog; -shot; -rod

HRT boiler

HUT hovel; cabin; hat: Ger.

INT anoint

IST adherent; practitioner; fanatic; is: Ger.

JAT Punjab Hindu

JET gush; spurt; gist; black; — set; — plane

JOT point; iota; tittle; brief note; — down

JUT project; extend

KAT weight; narcotic shrub

KET kat; rubbish: Scot.; Ob tributary

KIT violin; toolbox; young feline; Catherine; -cat (London club); — (Christopher) Carson

KUT -al-Imara (Brit. defeat)

LAT coin; Buddhist pillar

LET obstacle; allow(ed) to pass, be used; rent; tennis term

LIT coin; drunk; ignited; bed: Fr.; wagon-

LOT fate; share; plot, parcel of land; great deal; river

LST landing ship tank

LUT weight

MAT fabric; door —; entangle; dull (finish); matrix; picture border; matador nickname

MET came upon; convened; opera co.

MIT with: Ger.; therewith; glove

MOT pithy saying; quoits mark

MUT cur; dolt; Amen's wife; courage: Ger.

NAT Siam nature spirit; hornless; Blake (Alcott)

NET mesh; snare; web; pure; chain; line system; capture; profit; — income

NIT parasitic egg

NOT negation; hornless; smooth

NUT crank; fastener; kernel; head; guy; show investment; goddess; Geb's wife

OAT grain; Avena; feed; straw pipe

OCT prefix: eight

OFT frequently (poet.)

OLT Aluta; Danube tributary

OOT out: Scot.

OPT choose (citizenship)
ORT morsel; leftover; weight; place: Ger.
OST prefix: bone; oven; East(ern): Ger.
OUT absent; nook; game term; (at) odd(s); begone!; known; passe; wrong; on strike
PAT tap; flatten; stroke; jute; Irishman; foot; aptly
PET fondle(d); cosset; pet lamb, darling; favorite; sulk(iness)
PIT stone; hole; vat; hell; pocket; (rain) sound; floor of exchange, theater; river
POT drink; fish trap; sho(o)t; stake; much money; win; preserve; pepper —: soup
PST call for attention; quiet!
PUT lay; set; attach; throw; rustic; urge; golf shot; game; stay; — and call; -in-Bay (Perry's victory site)
QKT chess move
RAT rodent; Mus; bandicoot; deserter; scab; hair pad; yellow; adviser: Ger.; -race
RET soak flax; macerate
RIT scratch; cut; pierce
RKT chess move
ROT ret; decay; die; nonsense; disease
RUT routine; groove; habit; oxcart; heat
SAT measure; Brahman bliss; conferred; Saturday
SET seat; fix(ed); established; direct; adjust; intent; series; group; rigid; descent; habit; harden; brood; scenery; young of plant, oyster; Osiris' evil brother
SIT rest; squat; fit; roost; press; confer; pose; -down
SOT guzzle(r); befool; waste; fixed; obstinate
SUT coal dust; smudge
TAT Indian(s); make lace; deed: Ger.; die; Hindu absolute
TIT horse; bird; return blow; twit
TNT explosive, toluene
TOT add; child; dead: Ger.
TST hissed sound; quiet!
TUT mild rebuke; rounders; game; staccato
TYT quickly promptly
UIT out: Dutch
UST used to
VAT tub; measure; — dyes; salt pit; temple
VET (treat as) animal doctor; veterinarian
VOT Finn in Ingria
WAT temple; monument; Walter; hare; — the Devil (Scott)
WET moist(ure); rainy; not dried; fish; tipsy; soak; crazy; anti-prohibitionist; — nurse
WIT know-how; to —; mind power; humor(ist); wag
YAT opening; that
YET but; though; besides; still; further; too
YOT measure
ZAT slate trimming tool

ABU battle cry; deity; Ninurta; father; — Hassan; Mount — (Jain temples)
ACU prefix: needle
AHU gazelle; way-mark; burial place
AKU victorfish
ANU sky god; triad (—, Bel, Ea); Irish gods' mother; Danu
ARU indeed; really
AWU volcano
AYU sweetfish
CHU river
COU neck: Fr.
CRU tract of land; vineyard
DHU black; Roderick —, outlaw (Scott)
EAU water: Fr.; — de vie; — de Cologne; — Claire (river, city)
ECU shield; coin
EMU ostrichlike bird; Austral. tree, apple, millet
FEU fee; tenure, grant; fire: Fr.; pot au —
FLU grippe; 1918–19 pandemic
FOU full bushel: Scot.; fool(ish): Fr.
GAU Ger. region
GNU antelope; goat; takin
GRU practice: Scot.
HAU majagua; fiber tree
HEU alas!; hay: Ger.

HOU measure
IMU baking pit
IOU debt confirmation; note; I owe you
IRU Caleb's eldest son
ITU city
IZU peninsula
JAU city
JEU game: Fr.; — de mots (word play); — d'esprit (wit)
JIU river
KHU transfigured soul: Ka
KOU Hawaiian tree
KRU Liberian (language)
LAU islands
LEU Rumanian coin
LOU nickname
MAU measure; — Mau (Afr. rebels)
MEU spicknel herb; Meum
MOU measure
MRU Indo-Chinese native
NGU measure
NIU measure
PAU finished; measure; resort (Henry IV born); Edomite city
PEU little: Fr.; — à peu
PHU Cretan spikenard
PIU more: It.
REU Peleg's son
ROU Rollo
SHU deity; Ra's, Hathor's son; Geb's, Nut's father; Tefnut's husband
SMU Dallas college
SOU small coin
SSU Chin. weight
TAU Greek T, 300; ankh; St. Anthony's cross
TEU strive; fuss; worry
TIU sky god; Tiwaz, Tyr (Tuesday source)
TOU measure
TSU Jap. seaport
TZU river
ULU Eskimo woman's knife
UMU Polynesian earth oven
URU Bolivian Indian
UTU sun god; Shamash; Babbar; Maori compensation; hoot
VAU Heb. letter, 6; digamma
YOU pronoun; — bet
ZIU Tiu, Tyr
CCV 205
CDV 405
CIV 104
CLV 155
CMV 905
CXV 115
DCV 605
DEV deity, angel, demon
DIV to do: Scot; dev; 504
DLV 555
DXV 515
GAV village: Gypsy
LEV Bulgarian coin
LIV Finn(ic language); 54
LXV 65
MCV 1105
MDV 1505
MIV 1004
MLV 1055
MMV 2005
MXV 1015
NEV Nevada
REV step up motor
SOV gold coin: Br. slang; sovereign
TAV Heb. T, TH, 400
VAV Heb. letter, 6; digamma
XCV 95
XIV 14; death of Augustus
XLV 45
XXV 25

BAW exclamation: bah!
BOW weapon; archer; 6 feet; fiddlestick; Apollo's instrument; nod; yield; bend; prow; river
CAW crow's cry
COW bovine; Bos; tree raft; bogy; daunt; dolt
DAW bird; Corvus; grackle; eye color
DEW moist(ure); bloom; dawn liquor
DOW befit; Arab. sailboat; Burmese knife; Neal (prohibitionist)
FAW fall: Scot.
FEW not many; quite a —
GAW drain, trench: Scot.
HAW tree; berry; command to horse; 3rd eyelid; hem and —; N.C. river
HEW chop; fell; stroke
HOW why; what; method; know-; Indian salute
JAW mandible; maxilla; scold(ing talk)
JEW Hebrew; Semite; Wandering —
JOW measure
KAW Burma tribe; Siouan
KEW London suburb
KOW bogy; goblin
LAW (body of) rules; code; ordinance; canon; jus; legal statute; decree; commandment; — officer; act
LEW shelter; coin; nickname; "Piggy": drummer boy (Kipling)
LOW moo; weak; inferior; plain; coarse; cheap(ly); soft(ly); cartoonist; Girl Scouts founder
MAW stomach; craw's gullet; seed of

opium poppy
MEW gull; shed; molt; cage; conceal; cat's cry; spicknel
MOW cut down; (stack) hay
NAW know; no
NEW novel; (a)fresh; late; different; — look; — Deal; — Frontier
NNW compass point
NOW at this time; present(ly); admonition
PAW foot; hand(le fondly, clumsily); make fuss
PEW bench; rostrum; chirp; fishing prong
POW sound of blow; prisoner of war
RAW not cooked, spun, diluted; crude; sore; cold
REW series; pity
ROW brawl; propel; series; line; tier; file; Rotten —: Hyde Park; Skid —
SAW tool; cut; blade; disk; slice; fiddle; maxim; viewed
SEW stitch; close; — up; balk; swindle; cinch
SOW fem. swine; mold; scatter; seed; — dragons teeth
SSW compass point
TAW marble; prepare with alum (tan); Heb. T, TH, 400
TEW fishing tackle
TIW sky god; Tiwaz; Tyr; Tiu (Tuesday source)
TOW draw; tug(boat); rope; flax fibers; spun yarn
VOW promise; dedicate
WAW Arab. W
WNW compass point
WOW sensational success; excite audience; sound distortion
WSW compass point
YAW deviate; steer widely; yes
YEW evergreen; Taxus; grief symbol; — green
YOW yelp; howl; miaow
ZIW Iyar; Heb. month
AEX (mandarin) duck genus
AIX aex; -les-Bains (spa); -la-Chapelle: Aachen
ARX citadel
AUX according to, a la: Fr.; — armes (to arms!)
BOX fight; spar; tree (topiary, Eucalyptus); mix paint; stow; gift; baseball term; Cox and —; -spring; — camera; — seat
CCX 210
CDX 410; 1st sack of Rome
CIX 109
CLX 160
CMX 910
COX steersman; — and Box; painter; reformer; politician (Pres. nominee)
CXX 120
DAX Fr. spa
DCX 610
DIX pinochle score; ten: Fr.; Dorothy (Elizabeth Meriwether Gilmer); 509
DLX 560
DUX fugue theme; leader
DXX 520
FAX hair; suffix: maker
FIX fasten; set(tle); mend; arrange; determine; dilemma; limit; bribe; narcotic shot
FOX Vulpes; vixen; trick(ster); discolor; rope yarn; brown; river; orator; Quaker; educator; — Islands
HEX bewitch; jinx
HOX hamstring; pester
LAX loose; slack; salmon; remiss; vague
LEX law, statute: Lat.
LIX 59
LOX (smoked) salmon; — and bagels
LUX light unit
LXX 70; Septuagint; Temple at Jerusalem destroyed
MAX Maximillian; Maximus; Becky Sharp's love (Thackeray)
MCX 1100
MDX 1510
MIX mingle; cross; blend; prepared ingredients; 1009
MLX 1060
MMX 2010
MUX mess; botch
MXX 1020
NIX sprite; no(thing); undeliverable mail
NOX night goddess
NYX night goddess; Chaos's daughter; mother of day and night
PAX peace goddess; Irene; — Britannica; — vobiscum
PIX box; Eucharist case; ciborium; photos
POX infectious disease
PYX box: Eucharist case; ciborium
REX king: Lat; Reginald; rabbit

RIX rush; reed
RUX worry; play; sport
SAX cutting tool; sword; wind instrument
SEX gender; — appeal; weaker —
SIX card; die face; boat; — Hundred (Light Brigade)
TAX assess; censure; duty; charge; octroi
TEX Texas
TOX intoxicate
TUX men's evening dress
VEX afflict; annoy; harass
VOX voice: Lat.; — populi, — dei; — angelica
WAX grow; bee secretion; yellow; polish; rage; defeat
XIX 19
XXX 30; Crucifixion of Christ
YEX hiccup; cough
YOX hiccup; cough
ZAX slate trimmer

ABY endure; last; continue
ACY suffix: quality, state
ADY measure
AGY aged; old
ALY like malt drink
AMY female name; prochein — (nearest friend: law); (Little) — Dorrit: Dickens
ANY some; one; at all
ARY any; suffix: pert. to, engaged in
BAY inlet; compartment; dam; window; laurel; bark(ing); brown; horse; — State (Mass.); — City (Mich.); bomb —
BEY Tunis ruler; title
BLY Chief — (Saroyan); Nellie —, newspaperwoman
BOY youth; servant; act, treat as lad; office —; — orator: W. J. Bryan; Blue — (Gainsborough)
BUY (good) purchase; bribe; redeem
CAY key; islet
CLY seize; steal; servant (Dickens)
COY demure; bashful; shy; entice; hoax
CRY call; wail; weep; beg; summon; slogan; — wolf
DAY date; lifetime; solar, sidereal, lunar —; distance; — in court; educator; 1st printer
DEY Afr. ruler; (maid)servant
DRY hard; shrewd; arid; plain; dull; vapid; evaporate; — Tortugas (isles); dwindle(d); drought; — goods; — cell; — run; simulated
ELY cathedral city; mountain; island; Bishop of —
ERY suffix: conduct, art, place
FAY unite closely; fit; elf; cleanse; white man; name
FEY elfin; visionary
FLY leap; soar; vanish; pilot; tent canvas; printer's devil; keen; on the —; river
FOY feast; gift
FRY young brood; pancook; vex(ation); prison reformer
GAY merry; glad; John — (Beggar's Opera)
GEY considerable; very
GOY non-Jew: Heb.
GRY horse: Gypsy
GUY rope; chain; effigy; fellow; chaff; Fawkes; Octavius (Collins)
HAY fencer's cry; fodder; timothy; yellow; river; statesman, Lincoln's secretary
HEY call for attention
HOY barge; exclamation; Orkney Isle
ICY frosty; chilling
IVY vine; arbutus; crepper; overgrow
JAY J; (chatter)bird; blue; stupid one; Gatsby (Fitzgerald); 1st chief justice
JOY happiness; bliss; gaiety; exult; name
KAY K; islet; Catherine; Sir —; King Arthur's brother
KEY islet; bolt; clue; solution; pitch; style; fasten; attune; Francis Scott (Star-Spangled Banner)
KUY Siamese; Shan group; Kandh language
LAY reclined; song; secular; unprofessional; superimpose; apply; bet; attach; plan; still; price; — of the land
LEY tax; Rumanian coin
LOY post-hole spade; a slick; name
MAY can; prime;

heydey; hawthorn; spiraea; fem. name; Mary; month; Cape —
MUY very, greatly: Sp.
NAY no (vote); denial; refuse; Moslem flute
NEY Napoleonic marshal
ONY any
ORY like ore, seaweed; suffix: of
OXY of an ox; sharp; acute; prefix: oxygen
PAY tar vessel; wages; remit; reward(ing); punish(ment); satisfy
PLY fold; bend; strand (thickness); wield; practice; urge; paper web
POY boat pole
PRY lever(age); peep(er); gaze; Paul — (meddler)
PUY volcanic hill
RAY fish; torpedo; skate; sting —; father of natural history; particle; shine; radiance; vision; Raymond; Philip —: Annie Arden's husband (Tennyson)
REY king: Sp.
ROY name; Rob (outlaw, Scott hero), cocktail
SAY tell; state; suggest; opinion, influence
SEY pollack; coalfish
SHY timid; wary; bashful; shrink; avoid; fling; trial
SKY heaven; firmament; blue; climate; raise
SLY shrewd; foxy; roguish; secretive; on the —; tinker (Shaks.)
SMY sprat
SNY abound; swarm; bend; curved plank
SOY bean; sauce
SPY watch(er); discover; search(ing); secret agent
STY pig enclosure; eyelid swelling
TAY river; Firth of —
THY poss. pronoun
TOY (diversionary) trifle; trinket; play(thing)
TRY attempt, test; prove; strain; annoy; essay; render fat; conduct court procedure
VLY low-land; marsh; creek; temporary lake
WAY route; means; distance; style; journey; point; scope; momentum; — out
WEY weight unit (40 bushels)
WHY reason; problem; enigma; for which; exclamation
WRY deflect; twist(ed); disgusted; askew
YOY yes

ADZ cutting tool
BIZ business (slang); show —
BOZ Dickens pseudonym
BUZ son of Nahor, Mileah
COZ cousin
FEZ red tasseled cap; tarboosh; Morocco city
FIZ hiss(ing sound); fuss; champagne
GAZ coin; guz
GEZ guz
GIZ dialect; Ethiopic
GOZ coin
GUZ measure; zar; arshin
HUZ Abraham's nephew
LAZ Caucasian tribesman
LIZ Elizabeth
LUZ Bib. site; Bethel
NEZ nose: Fr.; — Perce (Shahaptian Indian); pince-
ODZ minced oath
PAZ peace: Sp.; La —: Bolivia
POZ positive(ly)
RIZ rice: Fr.
SUZ exclamation
TAZ river; — Bay
TEZ pungent; violent
VIZ namely
WIZ magician; genius
YEZ you

THREE-LETTER WORDS -A- to -Z-

BAA sheep's bleat
MAA sheep's cry; maw
NAA no
SAA measure
TAA Chin. pagoda
BAB Babism founder
CAB (ride in) taxi; engineer's place; measure; Civil Aeronautics Board

DAB touch; tap; flounder; lizard; expert
GAB chatter; hook; notch; E.I. persimmon
JAB punch; stab
KAB measure
LAB rennet; study room
MAB fairy queen and midwife; Mabel
NAB lock keeper; arrest; river
PAB flax refuse (fuel)
RAB teacher; mortar mixer; dog hero; Yugo. isle
TAB flap; tag; account; Cambridge man; charges
ZAB Great — (river)
BAC ferryboat; cistern
FAC fact
LAC varnish component; resin; milk (pharm.); 100,000 rupees
MAC son of: Ir., Scot.; Irishman; coat
PAC moccasin; half-boot
SAC cavity; pouch; Sauk; Indian; — and soc
TAC prefix: touch
VAC speech goddess; Sarasvati
WAC Women's Army Corps
ZAC Caucasian ibex
BAD evil; poor; ill; severe; faulty; wrong; river; — Ems
CAD (act as) bounder
DAD father
FAD custom; craze; polish
GAD rod; rove(r); -fly; oath; Jacob's son; Israel tribe; Syrian god
HAD possessed; tricked
LAD boy; youth; stripling
MAD crazy; vain; angry; river
PAD cushion; saddle; walk; tablet; robber; stuff; track; lodgings
RAD afraid: Scot.; energy unit
SAD gloomy; dull; poor; depressed; grievous; — sack
TAD small child; Theodore
WAD lump; plug; roll; money; black ocher
DAE do: Scot.
EAE classifying suffix
FAE foe: Scot.
HAE have: Scot.
KAE serve; oblige; jackdaw
LAE New Guinea port
MAE — West (life preserver)
NAE no, not: Scot.
RAE explorer; fem. name
SAE so
TAE to; toe; take; Scot.
VAE alas!; — victis
KAF myth. mountain, fabled bird abode; Arabic K
OAF elf's child; dolt; fool
QAF kaf
BAG sac(k); measure; purse; seize; in the —
CAG offend; insult
DAG Nott and —, deities; antler; pistol; Hammarskjold, UN chief
FAG cigarette; drudge; tire; Capt. Absolute's servant; liar
GAG pry open; choke; joke; closure; fish; illustrator
HAG harpy; witch; urge; copse; bog
JAG pendant; barb; slash; drunken spree
LAG linger; slacken; stave; jailbird
MAG chatter; bird; Margaret; half-penny (Brit.)
NAG horse; annoy(ance); fret; snake; Nagaine's wife (Kipling)
PAG island
RAG shred; scold; dance; slate; fog; — doll
SAG droop; weaken; drift
TAG flap; tab; lock; cue; story moral; join; follow; game; label
VAG (arrest as) vagabond
WAG sway; gossip; joker
ZAG jagged line angle
BAH exclamation
DAH Burmese knife
HAH exclamation
JAH Jehovah; god
MAH moon angel
PAH bah!; nasty; improper; N.Z. native fort
RAH (cheer with) hurrah
SAH measure
VAH Danube tributary
WAH panda; measure
YAH yes; exclamation
HAI Israelites defeat site
KAI N.Z. food; apple; island
LAI medieval tale: Burmese
MAI May: Ger.
PAI money; weight
RAI measure
SAI Capuchin monkey; Cebus
TAI porgy; Laos; Shan; Siamese; Li -po (poet); — Shan (sacred mountain)
VAI Liberian Negro
GAJ coin
HAJ pilgrimage to Mecca
RAJ reign, rule: India
SAJ teak tree

TAJ (dervish) cap; — Mahal
DAK India mall
HAK legal claim; share
LAK grouse's wooing strut
NAK stigmatic point; mango
OAK Quercus; Casuarina; encina; — brown; poison —; — Park; — Ridge
SAK white cotton
YAK Tibet ox; beast of burden
ZAK measure
AAL Indian mulberry; red dye; morindin
BAL mine; ball: Fr.
CAL California; wolframite
DAL split pea; pigeon pea; Swedish river
GAL girl; speed unit
HAL Henry, Harry; Prince — (Henry V); Bluff King — (Henry VIII)
IAL adj. suffix
MAL — de mer (sea sickness); Sudra caste Hindu; prefix: evil; measure
PAL partner; (to) chum
SAL salt; — tree; tamarisk; rock; Sarah
TAL palm fiber; hand clapping; cymbals
ZAL Rustam's father
AAM liquid measure
BAM hoax; Iranian town
CAM awry; gear; rotating, sliding part; Ouse tributary
DAM obstruct(ion); wall; weir; coin; female parent; Nobel biochemist
EAM uncle; gossip
FAM hand (slang)
GAM whale school; visit; botanical suffix
HAM Noah's son; Shem's brother; amateur radio; actor
JAM tight place; crush; interfere; preserve; native chief; — pack; — session
KAM crooked
LAM beat; escape; loom lever
MAM Mayan Indian
NAM distrain(t)
PAM card game
RAM sheep; batter(ing —); weight; ship beak; pump; stuff; constellation: Aries
SAM unite; curdle; Uncle —
TAM Scot. cap
YAM sweet potato; batta; edible root; tuber; posthouse
BAN edict; forbid; curse; title; muslin; coin; kokumin (Jap. reserve); Lancelot's father
CAN vessel; preserve; tin; dismiss; jail; weight
DAN title; Daniel; buoy; Jacob's (Bilhah's) son; tribe; from — to Beersheba; river; Una's brother (Kipling)
EAN bring forth; to lamb
FAN cool(er), vane; winnow; spread; stimulate; devotee; African; Pangwe; Pahouin; — dance
GAN Roland's destroyer
HAN Chin. dynasty; Japanese barony; Yangtze tributary
IAN John; Fleming (James Bond author)
JAN — of Leiden, fanatic; — Hus, reformer
KAN Kansas; measure; river
LAN name prefix; measure; Swed. district
MAN individual; homo; male; anyone; valet; game piece; fortify; tame; to a —; — of war; Isle of —
NAN fem. name; river
PAN tub; dish; ape; wash; result; betel leaf; sir; god: Faunus, Inuus (part goat); face; son of Hermes; prefix: all; Peter — (Barrie); deadpan
RAN twine hank; sea deity; Aegir's wife; sped
SAN Greek letter, 900; Bushmen; hemp
TAN make leather; brown; beat; Gypsy camp
VAN (fore)front; lead; car; Urartu: Armenia; Turk. lake, town
WAN (grow) pale; dark; dim
ZAN Zeus; Olympia statue
DAO P.I. tree (fruit, fiber)
GAO river
HAO Chin. dynasty
IAO honey eater bird; manuao
LAO Tal native, language; -tzu, -tse (philosopher)
MAO peacock; — Tse-

tung (Chin. leader)
SAO measure; — Paulo (city)
TAO man: P.I.; Chin. road, cosmic order, truth; — Te Ching: Lao-tse's work
YAO Chin. aborigines, emperor; Bantu; Indian
BAP bread loaf, roll
CAP top; cover; match; crown; explosive; detonator; paper size; capital; tread renewal
DAP dibble; drop bait; dip; rebound; skip
GAP opening; breach; pass; hiatus; ravine
HAP chance; befall; wrap
JAP Nipponese
LAP fold; wrap; cut; polish; circuit; drink; ripple; take eagerly
MAP chart; survey, image; Mercator; plan
NAP doze; siesta; hairy surface; pile; game; seize
PAP soft food; paste; dad; simple discourse
RAP coin; least bit; strike; knock; criticize; jail sentence
SAP juice; vigor; money; fool; drain; trench; weaken
TAP rap; signal; half sole; dance; spigot; liquor; ask money; draw
WAP blow; wrap; truss
YAP yelp; gab; hoodlum; island
AAR (underground) river
BAR obstruct(ion); rod; gate; strip(e); counter; court; except; fish; maigre; mus. measure; son of; sandbank; rifle; — Cocheba (Heb. rebel)
CAR lift cage; chariot; for: Fr.; fish box; balloon basket; — Nicobar (Island)
DAR abode; gateway; tree; patriotic group
EAR sense; attention; grain spike; handle; front page box; god; Tiwaz; Tiu
FAR greatly; widely; long; distant; advanced
GAR needlefish
HAR chill fog: Scot.
JAR grate; shake; drill; clash; shock; vessel; preserve
LAR gibbon; house god; ancestral spirit
MAR spoil; mutilate; Ignatius (patriarch of Antioch)
NAR near(ly): Scot.
PAR value; equality; average; standard golf score; by: Fr.
SAR sixty sixties: 3,600 (Babylonian number)
TAR pitch; coal — (saccharine source); sailor; lute; telegram; river
WAR strife; battle; fight; — bride; — cabinet
YAR growl;
ZAR maneuverable measure
BAS low, stocking: Fr.; à — (down!); — relief; roulette bet
CAS en tout —: Fr.; vanity bag; umbrella
DAS cony; badger: Dutch; the: Ger.; — Kapital
FAS divine law: Roman
GAS fuel; anesthetic; chatter; boast; tear —, poison —, natural —, coal —
HAS possesses; -been
KAS cupboard, wardrobe: Dutch
LAS alas; the: Sp.; — Vegas
MAS master; suffix: festival
NAS has not, was not
OAS Organization of American States
PAS dance step; — de deux; n'est-ce ?
RAS fabric; prince; cape; Fascist leader
VAS pledge; surety; duct, vessel (anat.)
WAS existed; the past
BAT club; hit; brick; blow; flying mammal; wink; gray; bomb
CAT feline; whip; shrew; fish; tripod; game; Island; ship (tackle); jazz fan
EAT consume; gnaw; erode; rust; waste
FAT oil(y); rich; gross; obese; stout; useful
GAT channel; gun
HAT headwear; cardinal's office; has: Ger.
JAT Punjab Hindu
KAT weight; narcotic shrub
LAT coin; Buddhist pillar
MAT fabric; door —;

entangle; dull (finish); matrix; picture border; matador nickname

NAT Siam nature spirit; hornless; Blake (Alcott)

OAT grain; Avena; feed; straw pipe

PAT tap; flatten; stroke; jute; Irishman; foot; aptly

RAT rodent; Mus; bandicoot; deserter; scab; hair pad; yellow; adviser: Ger.; -race

SAT measure; Brahman bliss; conferred; Saturday

TAT Indian(s); make lace; deed: Ger.; die; Hindu absolute

VAT tub; measure; — dyes; salt pit; temple

WAT temple; monument; Walter; hare; — the Devil (Scott)

YAT opening; that

ZAT slate trimming tool

EAU water: Fr.; — de vie; — de Cologne; — Claire (river, city)

GAU Ger. region

HAU majagua; fiber tree

JAU city

LAU islands

MAU measure; — Mau (Afr. rebels)

PAU finished; measure; resort (Henry IV born); Edomite city

TAU Greek T, 300; ankh; St. Anthony's cross

VAU Heb. letter, 6; digamma

GAV village; Gypsy

TAV Heb. T, TH, 400

VAV Heb. letter, 6; digamma

BAW exclamation: bah!

CAW crow's cry

DAW bird; Corvus; grackle; eye color

FAW fall: Scot.

GAW drain, trench: Scot.

HAW tree; berry; command to horse; 3rd eyelid; hem and —; N.C. river

JAW mandible; maxilla; scold(ing talk)

KAW Burma tribe; Siouan

LAW (body of) rules; code; ordinance; canon; jus; legal statute; decree; commandment; — officer; act

MAW stomach; craw's gullet; seed of opium poppy

NAW know; no

PAW foot; hand(le fondly, clumsily); make fuss

RAW not cooked, spun, diluted; crude; sore; cold

SAW tool; cut; blade; disk; slice; fiddle; maxim; viewed

TAW marble; prepare with alum (tan); Heb. T, TH, 400

WAW Arab. W

YAW deviate; steer widely; yes

DAX Fr. spa

FAX hair; suffix: maker

LAX loose; slack; salmon; remiss; vague

MAX Maximillian; Maximus; Becky Sharp's love (Thackeray)

PAX peace goddess; Irene; — Britannica; — vobiscum

SAX cutting tool; sword; wind instrument

TAX assess; censure; duty; charge; octroi

WAX grow; bee secretion; yellow; polish; rage; defeat

ZAX slate trimmer

BAY inlet; compartment; dam; window; laurel; bark(ing); brown; horse; — State (Mass.); — City (Mich.); bomb —

CAY key; islet

DAY date; lifetime; solar, sidereal, lunar —; distance; — in court; educator; 1st printer

FAY unite closely; fit; elf; cleanse; white man; name

GAY merry; glad; John (Beggar's Opera)

HAY fencer's cry; fodder; timothy; yellow; river; statesman, Lincoln's secretary

JAY J; (chatter)bird; blue; stupid one; Gatsby (Fitzgerald); 1st chief justice

KAY K; islet; Catherine; Sir —; King Arthur's brother

LAY reclined; song; secular; unprofessional; superimpose; apply; bet; attach; plan; still; price; — of

the land
MAY can; prime; heydey; hawthorn; spiraea; fem. name; Mary; month; Cape —
NAY no (vote); denial; refuse; Moslem flute
PAY tar vessel; wages; remit; reward(ing); punish(ment); satisfy
RAY fish; torpedo; skate; sting —; father of natural history; particle; shine; radiance; vision; Raymond; Philip —: Annie Arden's husband (Tennyson)
SAY tell; state; suggest; opinion, influence
TAY river; Firth of —
WAY route; means; distance; style; journey; point; scope; momentum; — out
GAZ coin; guz
LAZ Caucasian tribesman
PAZ peace: Sp.; La —: Bolivia
TAZ river; — Bay

ABA camel hair; Arab. cloak; altazimuth
IBA P.I. fruit tree
ABB warp yarn; poorest fleece
BBB rifle shot size
EBB recede; delay; — tide; shallow
ABC book; primer; rudiment
ABE Lincoln; the Great Emancipator
OBE Greek clan division; magic rite; fetish
UBE P.I. yam
ABI Hezekiah's mother
FBI Federal Bureau of Investigation
OBI girdle; sash
UBI where: Lat; white yam
IBN — Saud (king)
ABO Finn seaport; Turku
EBO tree; — oil; Niger Negro
IBO Niger Negro
ABS Bedouin tribesman
GBS playwright: George Bernard Shaw
ABT — system (mountain railroads); composer
ABU battle cry; deity: Ninurta; father; — Hassan; Mount — (Jain temples)
ABY endure; last; continue

ECA Economic Cooperation Administration
ICA river; city
OCA edible root; wood sorrel; oxalis
UCA fiddler crab
CCC 300; Commodity Credit Corporation; Civilian Conservation Corps
DCC 700
FCC Federal Communications Commission
ICC Interstate Commerce Commission
MCC 1200
ACE one-spot; card; bit; hole in one; air hero; game point; expert; first-rate
ICE frost(ing); chili; dessert; diamonds
ACH alas; Indian mulberry
ICH I, ego: Ger.; fish dermatitis
OCH alas!; oh!
TCH exclamation
ACI chem. prefix
CCI 201
DCI 601
ICI here: Fr.
MCI 1101
XCI 91
ACK -ack (antiaircraft)
ICK fish dermatitis
OCK weight
CCL 250
DCL 650
MCL 1150
MCM 1900; fin de siècle; Boxer Rebellion
ECO prefix: environment
ICS science suffix
ACT deed; decree; feign; do; play part; prayer; — of God, — of faith
ECT prefix: outside, without
OCT prefix: eight
ACU prefix: needle
ECU shield; coin
CCV 205
DCV 605
MCV 1105
XCV 95
CCX 210
DCX 610
MCX 1110
ACY suffix: quality, state
ICY frosty; chilling

ADA fem. name; city; (Java) canvas
IDA Idaho; Crete mountain; Princess — (opera); Countess —, heiress (Thackeray)
ODA harem room, inmate
MDC 1600
ADD (sub)join; augment; annex; total, foot
ODD unpaired; queer; uneven; extra; fellow; — man

wins
ADE soft drink; humorist
EDE Dutch commune; Afr. city
IDE fish; chem. suffix
ODE (Pindar) poem; song; canticle; hymn
EDH A.S. letter: th
CDI 401
MDI 1501
UDI N. Caucasian language
CDL 450
ADO do; trouble; fuss; stir
EDO Nigerian: Ibo
IDO artificial language; de Couturat, Jesperson
ODO William the Conqueror's half brother; Eudes; Count of Paris
UDO Japanese herb; edible shoot
DDS Doctor of Dental Surgery (degree)
ODS minced oath
DDT insecticide
CDV 405
MDV 1505
CDX 410; 1st sack of Rome
MDX 1510
ADY measure
ADZ cutting tool
ODZ minced oath

AEA (candlenut) bark cord
DEA goddess: Lat.
HEA Eridu's chief god
KEA N.Z. parrot
LEA meadow; yarn measure; warp threads
MEA — culpa (my fault)
NEA National Education Association
PEA seed; plant; marble; sweet —; — soup (fog); river
REA turmeric; Rhea; Cybele, mother of the gods
SEA water(s); wave; vast area; at — (lost); naval; — horse
TEA beverage; collation; — green; — ball; — wagon
UEA island
WEA Algonquian
YEA yes (vote); — and Nay (Richard I)
ZEA Indian corn; maize
DEB society girl; Deborah
GEB earth god; Osiris's father
KEB earth god; Osiris's father
NEB Nebraska; beak; mouth; kiss
REB rebel
SEB earth god; Osiris's father
WEB gossamer; (en)mesh; membrane; network; rete
AEC Atomic Energy Commission
DEC prefix: ten; December
SEC second; dry (wine); Securities & Exchange Commission
TEC detective
BED base; bottom; matrix; lodge
EED Moslem Easter
FED nourished; fattened
GED oath (God)
KED sheep tick
LED guided; directed; diode
NED Edgar; Edmund; Edward
PED basket; prefix: foot, boy, child
RED color, dye; lurid; inflamed; golden; Communist; fowl; cent; river; sea; Jacket (Seneca chief)
SED but: Lat.
TED spread for drying; scatter; waste
WED marry; unite(d)
ZED Z
BEE B; Apis; drone; contest; crazy idea
CEE C; em- (master of ceremonies)
DEE D; river; mathematician
FEE land grant; charge; tip; reward
GEE G; horse command; evade; agree; oath; haw and —
LEE shelter; sediment; Annabel (Poe); Lorelei (Loos); Francis Lightfoot; Henry (Light-Horse Harry)
NEE born; by maiden name
PEE P; turtle delicacy; calipee
REE sift; right; Arikara; fem. ruff; sandpiper
SEE perceive; bishop's seat; curia; learn; call (bet); — red; — stars; astronomer
TEE T; game mark; golf term; top ornament; — beam, bar; to a —; shirt
VEE V; $5; neckline; refusal
WEE little; pig's squeak; Willie Winkle (Kipling)
ZEE Z; zed
AEF American Expeditionary Force; WWI Amer. army; Pershing command
KEF hemp; languor
NEF clock, vessel in form of ship;

navicula; church nave
REF measure; referee
BEG ask; entreat; Turk. title; bey
DEG sprinkle; dampen
GEG No. Albanian
KEG cask; — of nails: 100 lb.
LEG meat cut; support; run; lap; — art: cheese-cake
MEG Margaret; Princess —; Mag; Alcott heroine; horse (Burns); Merrilies (Scott)
PEG (cribbage) pin; support; pretext; leg; hit; plod; Margaret
REG desert region
SEG sedge; iris
TEG young sheep
VEG prank; wanderer
HEH Chin. tribe; Hei; Miao
LEH Kashmir town
PEH river
REH salt mixture; alkali
DEI the gods: Lat.; agnus —
FEI Yap stone money; banana
HEI cat's cradle; Miss — (Greene)
KEI apple; island
LEI wreath; coin
NEI Eastern flute
PEI river
REI coin; David's friend
VEI Liberian Negro
WEI Chin. dynasty, state; river
LEK gather(ing); coin; river
BEL fruit, tree; Bengal quince; golden apple; power ratio; earth god; Marduk; — Affris (Shaw)
DEL Delaware
EEL teleost fish: conger; moray; elver; lamprey; vinegar worm
GEL jellify; harden; set
HEL Loki's daughter; Niflheim goddess
KEL caul; net; film
MEL honey; prefix: limb, black
PEL prefix: mud, clay
REL electric unit
SEL salt: Fr.; self: Scot.
TEL prefix: distant, end
ZEL Oriental cymbal
BEM Pol. general; pasha
DEM Democrat: opp. to Rep(ublican)
GEM muffin; — State (Idaho); prize piece; jewel
HEM (cloth) edge; confine; surround; hesitate; haw
JEM James
KEM river; port
MEM Heb. letter M, 40
SEM Noah's son; Ham's brother
TEM sun god; Atmu, (A)tum
WEM spot; stain (in wood)
DEN retreat; lair; haunt; scout unit (pack part)
EEN Ir. suffix; even (poet.)
FEN marsh; weight; forbid; — Ho (river)
GEN suffix: heredity factor
HEN female bird, fish; fowl; coward; measure; — party
KEN insight; Japanese measure, prefecture, games
MEN crew; hands; people; troops; lunar god
NEN river
PEN confine; jail; feather; style; write(r), fem. swan
SEN coin; measure; Sun Yat (Chin. leader)
TEN bill; card; X; many; denary; deca; big casino
WEN cyst; growth; coin; wyn
YEN desire; urge; Jap. money
ZEN Buddhist sect, belief
GEO Georgia; prefix: earth, soil
LEO constellation; Lion; composer; emperor; pope; Tolstoy
MEO Indian farmer caste
NEO advocate of new; prefix: recent
REO old car
YEO officer; bodyguard
HEP wise to; informed; exclamation; -cat
KEP catch; haul
NEP catnip; cotton fiber knot; Soviet policy
PEP energy; stimulate
REP fabric; lewd one; Republican: opp. to Dem(ocrat)
YEP yes
ZEP zeppelin: airship
AER prefix: gas, air; chalice veil
BER jujube; elb
DER prefix: neck; the: Ger.
EER ever (poet.); suffix
FER iron: Fr.; chemin de — (railroad, baccarat)
GER resident (Heb. law); Judaism convert
HER pronoun; female
IER noun suffix
KER evil spirit; fate
LER Brythonic god;

Celtic Neptune; children of — (swans)
MER sea: Fr.; mal de —
NER Abner's father; Saul's uncle
PER through; via; for each
SER It. title; weight; exist: Sp.; prefix: serum
TER prefix: thrice
VER worm: Fr.
WER who: Ger.; murder fine
XER prefix: dry
YER suffix: your
ZER measure; weight
AES Roman bronze; money
BES pleasure god
CES these: Fr.
DES of the: Ger., Fr.; from, since: Fr.; — Moines
EES eyes: Scot.
FES sacred city
GES Tapuyan Indian
HES men; males
LES the: Fr.; — Misérables
MES my: Fr.; prefix: middling, intermediate
OES Os
PES foot(like part)
RES thing: Lat.; legal matter; in medias —
SES his, her: Fr.
TES your: Fr.
YES affirmative (vote)
AET of the age: Lat.
BET stake; wager; Betsy (Dickens)
CET that: Fr.
FET measure
GET obtain; reach; hit; persuade; divorce bill
JET gush; spurt; gist; black; — set; — plane
KET kat; rubbish: Scot.; Ob tributary
LET obstacle; allow(ed) to pass, be used; rent; tennis term
MET came upon; convened
NET mesh; snare; web; pure; chain; line system; capture; profit; — income
PET fondle(d); cosset; pet lamb; darling; favorite; sulk(iness)
RET soak flax; macerate
SET seat; fix(ed); established; direct; adjust; intent; series; group; rigid; descent; habit; harden; brood; scenery; young of plant, oyster; Osiris' evil brother
VET (treat as) animal doctor; veterinarian
WET moist(ure); rainy; not dried; fish; tipsy; soak; crazy; antiprohibitionist; — nurse
YET but; though; besides; still; further; too
FEU fee; tenure; grant; fire: Fr.; pot au —
HEU alas!; hay: Ger.
JEU game: Fr.; — de mots (word play); — d'esprit (wit)
LEU Rumanian coin
MEU spicknel herb; Meum
PEU little: Fr.; — à peu
REU Peleg's son
TEU strive; fuss; worry
DEV deity, angel, demon
LEV Bulgarian coin
NEV Nevada
REV step up motor
DEW moist(ure); bloom; dawn liquor
FEW not many; quite a —
HEW chop; fell; stroke
JEW Hebrew; Semite; Wandering —
KEW London suburb
LEW shelter; coin; nickname; "Piggy": drummer boy (Kipling)
MEW gull; shed; molt; cage; conceal; cat's cry; spicknel
NEW novel; (a)fresh; late; different; — look; — Deal; — Frontier
PEW bench; rostrum; chirp; fishing prong
REW series; pity
SEW stitch; close; — up; balk; swindle; cinch
TEW fishing tackle
YEW evergreen; Taxus; grief symbol; — green
AEX (mandarin) duck genus
HEX bewitch; jinx
LEX law, statute: Lat.
REX king: Lat.; Reginald; rabbit
SEX gender; — appeal; weaker
TEX Texas
VEX afflict; annoy; harass
YEX hiccup; cough
BEY Tunis ruler; title
DEY Afr. ruler; (maid)servant
FEY elfin; visionary
GEY considerable; very
HEY call for attention
KEY islet; bolt; clue; solution; pitch; style; fasten; attune; Francis Scott — (Star-Spangled Banner)

LEY tax; Rumanian coin
NEY Napoleonic marshal
REY king: Sp.
SEY — pollack; coalfish
WEY weight unit (40 bushels)
FEZ red tasseled cap; tarboosh; Morocco city
GEZ guz
NEZ nose: Fr.; — Perce (Shahaptian Indian); pince-
TEZ pungent; violent
YEZ you

MFA Master of Fine Arts (degree)
UFA river
IFE hemp; cordage fiber
OFF erring; away!; go; out; below par; — color; — stage
AFL American Federation of Labor
OFO Siouan language
UFO flying saucer
AFR Africa
AFT astern; back; behind
EFT lizard; newt
OFT frequently (poet.)
AGA bark; rope; title; Turk. officer; ruler
AGE period; generation; era; ripen; mellow
AGG carrier (Kipling)
EGG ovum; germ cell; coal; bomb; fellow; incite
UGH assenting grunt
AGO past; since
EGO I; whole man; alter —; self-(ishness)
NGU measure
AGY aged; old

AHA exclamation
CHA rolled tea; -cha (V.I. white, dance)
DHA measure, weight
FHA Federal Housing, Farmers' Home Administration
KHA Nepalese; Laotian
SHA Shinto temple; urial; sheep
THA thee; thou
IHC Jesus symbol
CHE shrub; Chin. flute
RHE fluidity unit
SHE woman; Haggard novel
THE article
AHI sky serpent; Vritra
CHI Greek letter CH, 600; fem. Gypsy; Gold Coast language; Tshi
EHI Ahiram; Benjamin's son
GHI buffalo butter; ghee
IHI stitchbird; fish; halfbeak; skipper
PHI Greek letter PH, 500
SHI weight
AHM liquid measure
OHM electric unit; -'s law
AHO exclamation
CHO measure
MHO unit of conductance
OHO exclamation
PHO exclamation
RHO Greek R, 100
SHO pshaw!; sure; measure
THO Tonkin peasant
WHO rel. pronoun
IHR you: Ger.
IHS symbol (Jesus)
JHS symbol (Jesus)
AHT Wakashan Indian
AHU gazelle; waymark; burial place
CHU river
DHU black; Roderick —, outlaw (Scott)
KHU transfigured soul: Ka
PHU Cretan spikenard
SHU deity; Ra's, Hathor's son; Geb's, Nut's father; Tefnut's husband
SHY timid; wary; bashful; shrink; avoid; fling; trial
THY poss. pronoun
WHY reason; problem; enigma; for which; exclamation

AIA Rizpah's father
CIA Central Intelligence Agency
DIA through; prefix: apart; day: Sp.
HIA hawk parrot
LIA — Fail (crowning stone)
MIA mine: It; missing in action
PIA arrowroot; — mater (brain part)
RIA narrow inlet; creek; estuary
SIA Keresan Indian
TIA aunt: Sp.
VIA way, vessel: Lat.; through; — Dolorosa
ZIA Gad's descendant; N.M. pueblo
BIB sip; apron part; fish; nozzle
DIB bob bait; dibble; dip
FIB (tell white) lie; pummel
GIB (tom)cat; salmon; prison; bearing plate: gut fish
JIB sail; mouth; crane arm; standstill
LIB castrate; ad —
MIB marble
NIB beak; pen(point); lint knot; scorer
RIB costa; meat cut; wife; vein; part of sock, ship, umbrella; tease; purl

SIB brother; sister; litter mate; kinsman; congenial
TIB skip school
HIC hiccuping sound; — et ubique
PIC measure; very small
SIC thus!; — transit gloria; chase; incite
TIC twitch(ing); spasm; funny habit; correct (slang)
AID help(er); succor; Agency for International Development
BID reveal; offer; order; invite; — fair; — price
CID the —; Sp. hero, epic; Diaz de Vivar
DID performed; acted
FID mast support; pin; tobacco quid
GID sheep disease
HID concealed
KID young goat; child; fur; leather; tease
LID (eye) cover; curb; hat
MID among; central; half-way
NID nest; pheasant brood
OID suffix: like
RID free; clear; dispose
SID Sydney
TID girl; woman
CIE abbr., company: Fr.
DIE expire; long; vanish; stop; cube; chance; tool; shape
FIE exclamation
GIE give: Scot.
HIE hasten; speed
LIE fib; mislead; be; extend; slope; golf term; Trygve (UN official)
NIE never: Ger.; eyes
PIE bird; mixed type; jumble; coin; tart
RIE grass, cereal
SIE sye; you, she: Ger.
TIE bind; link; knot; duty; equal(ity); bond; beam; cravat, Ascot
VIE emulate; strive; compete; life: Fr.
LIF — and Lifthrasir (myth. survivors)
RIF measure
SIF Thor's wife; home guardian
VIF lively, animated: Fr.
ZIF Jewish month: Iyar
BIG large; barley; — Bertha; — Ben; — Bend; — brother; — house — Blue (river)
CIG cigarette
DIG (verbal) thrust; dwell
FIG fruit; fico; zero; rig
GIG fish spear, hook; boat; chaise, carriage; nap
JIG dance; prank; drill
MIG marble; duck; plane
NIG dress (stone); cut coin edge; revoke
PIG pork; litter; glutton; cushion; ingot; — iron; The — Baby (Carroll)
RIG equip(ment); swindle; tackle; ardri
SIG signature
WIG hair(piece); peruke; judge
ZIG part of a zigzag
CII 102
DII the gods; 502
III 3
LII 52
MII 1002
OII N.Z. muttonbird
RII small streams; Venice canals
VII 7
XII 12
AIK oak: Scot
BIK poison; aconite
PIK measure
AIL be ill
KIL Ir. church; monk's cell
LIL book, paper, letter: Gypsy; little; — Abner
MIL 1/1000 inch (wire measure); coin; Ir. eponymous ancestor
NIL nothing; indigo dye; ipomoea; nilgal
OIL painting: fuel; grease; flatter(y); bribe
PIL prefix: hair
SIL yellow ocher
TIL tree; sesame; mark
AIM direct(ion), design; scheme; end
BIM Barbados man
DIM dark(en); dull; obscure; — view
GIM neat; spruce
HIM pronoun; male
JIM James; — Crow; -dandy; Lord — (Conrad); friend (Twain)
KIM — O'Hara: waif (Kipling)
LIM blue pine; toon
MIM (act) affectedly shy
NIM steal; margosa tree
RIM border; edge; margin; wheel part
SIM Simeon; Simon
TIM Tiny —: cripple (Dickens)
VIM force; energy; spirit
AIN well; spring; 16th Heb. letter,

70; Rhone tributary
BIN box; crib; pungi (flute); Vina
DIN noise; uproar; resound; Gunga —
EIN one, article: Ger.
FIN (fish) appendage; part of keel, aircraft; kite
GIN liquor; snare; female (kangaroo); cotton —; — fizz; — rummy; — mill
HIN measure
JIN Oriental demon(s)
KIN relative(s); zither; koto; Tatar dynasty
LIN linen; flax; linden; — Yutang (author); river
MIN chief deity; ruler; river
PIN fasten(er); peg; badge; skittle; dowel; -curl; -up
RIN Jap. coin, measure
SIN (do) wrong; vice; err; Heb. S, 300; moon god; Enzu
TIN metal; element; stannium; can; preserve; inferior; 10th anniversary
VIN wine: Fr.; — blanc; — rouge
WIN gain; earn; persuade
YIN Shang dynasty; weight; female principle (opp. to yang)
ZIN Bib. wilderness
CIO Congress of Industrial Organizations
DIO Cassius — (historian)
KIO ngaio; N.Z. fruit tree
MIO my: Sp., It.; dio —
RIO coffee; river; canal: It.; — Grande
TIO uncle: Sp.
ZIO sky, war god; Tyr
DIP immerse; lower; ladle; candle; pickpocket; hat; downturn
FIP coin (four-, sixpence); picayune
GIP gut fish
HIP cheer; haunch; rose's false fruit (pseudocarp); bump
JIP dog (Dickens)
KIP undressed hide; gym feat; sleeping place; weight
LIP (saucy) speech; edge; spout; kiss; — service
NIP pinch; check; bite; sip; dram; Japanese
PIP radar sign; disease; seed; chirp; break shell; spot on card; great!
RIP tear; (move full) speed; split; hay; basket; van Winkle (Irving); — tide
SIP drink; taste
TIP tilt; upset; dump; apex; (apply) end; touch; hint; fee; bestow
VIP big shot (very important person)
YIP yelp; squeal; outcry
ZIP bullet sound; (move with) vim; energy
AIR ether; gas; breath; breeze; veil; tune; expose; manner; dismissal; — express; — lift
DIR to you: Ger.; Pakistan state
EIR healing goddess
FIR (ever)green; balsam; Douglas —; — Domnann (Ir. people)
HIR her
KIR Bib. Syrian exile
MIR chief; Eastern title; Russian communist; to me: Ger.; peace: Russ.
PIR Moslem saint, tomb
SIR knight; address
TIR shooting (match)
VIR man: Lat.; vigor: Scot.
WIR we: Ger.
BIS twice; encore; replica
CIS prefix: on this side
DIS Valkyrie; Norn; Freya; — pater (Pluto, Hades); prefix; apart
EIS ice: Ger.
GIS soldiers; servicemen
HIS poss. pronoun
LIS (fairy) fort; lily: Fr.; fleur-de-
MIS prefix: wrong, evil
NIS goblin; kobold; Constantine's birthplace; Yugo. city
RIS — de veau (sweetbread)
SIS girl; sweetheart; relative; Cecilia
TIS contraction: it is
VIS force: Lat.; weight; -a-vis; Yugo. isle
WIS Wisconsin; suppose; think
AIT (river) islet
BIT part of bridle, key; blade; check; drill; mite; morsel; 12½ cents
CIT townsmen; civilian
DIT poem, surnamed:

Fr.; on —
FIT suit(able); proper; ready; adjust-(ment); attack; mood; spell
GIT get; mold channel
HIT strike; reach; agree; impact; success
KIT violin; toolbox; young feline; Catherine; -cat (London club); — (Christopher) Carson
LIT coin; drunk; ignited; bed: Fr.; wagon-
MIT with: Ger.; therewith; glove
NIT parasitic egg
PIT stone; hole; vat; hell; pocket; (rain) sound; floor of exchange, theater; river
RIT scratch; cut; pierce
SIT rest; squat; fit; roost; press; confer; pose; -down
TIT horse; bird; return blow; twit
UIT out: Dutch
WIT know-how; to —; mind power; humor(ist); wag
JIU river
NIU measure
PIU more: It.
TIU sky god: Tiwaz, Tyr (Tuesday source)
ZIU Tiu, Tyr
CIV 104
DIV to do: Scot; dev; 504
LIV Finn(ic language); 54
MIV 1004
XIV 14; death of Augustus
TIW sky god; Tiwaz; Tyr; Tiu (Tuesday source)
ZIW Iyar; Heb. month
AIX aex; -les-Bains (spa); -la-Chapelle: Aachen
CIX 109
DIX pinochle score; ten: Fr.; Dorothy — (Elizabeth Meriwether Gilmer); 509
FIX fasten; set(tle); mend; arrange; determine; dilemma; limit; bribe; narcotic shot
LIX 59
MIX mingle; cross; blend; prepared ingredients; 1009
NIX sprite; no(thing); undeliverable mail
PIX box; Eucharist case; ciborium; photos
RIX rush; reed
SIX card; die face; boat; — Hundred (Light Brigade)
XIX 19
BIZ business (slang); show —
FIZ hiss(ing sound); fuss; champagne
GIZ dialect; Ethiopic
LIZ Elizabeth
RIZ rice: Fr.
VIZ namely
WIZ magician; genius

AJI Capsicum plant
TJI river: Java; weight
UJI silkworm disease
DJO measure; Niger Negro
LJO Niger delta Negro
OJO grassy spring; oasis

AKA Assam tribesman, language; N.Z. vine
OKA weight; oca; river
BKB chess move
QKB chess move
RKB chess move
AKE forever: Maori; N.Z. tree; hopbush
EKE piece out; augment
IKE Isaac; nickname (Eisenhower)
OKE weight; measure
UKE ukelele; guitar
AKH spirit of man: Egypt
IKI island
OKI evil spirit; archipelago
SKI glide(r); runner; sport; — lift
AKO measure
TKO boxing term
BKR chess move
QKR chess move
RKR chess move
BKT chess move
QKT chess move
RKT chess move
AKU victorfish
SKY heaven; firmament; blue; climate; raise

ALA Alabama; (army) wing; petal; after, according to; — mode; — carte
ELA highest note; bombast; extravagance
FLA Florida
ILA Bantu language
OLA palm leaf
SLA sloe
ULA the gums; diminutive
ALB church vestment
ELB jujube
LLB Bachelor of Laws (degree)
ELD old time; age
LLD Doctor of Laws (degree)
OLD state; obsolete; passé; skilled; primeval; quondam; hoary; — hat

ALE beverage; malt liquor; festival
BLE grain: Fr.
CLE diminutive suffix
ELE aisle; eel
ILE isle: Fr.; suffix; -de-France; — de la Cité
OLE palm leaf; old; Sp. victory cry
ULE caucho tree; rubber; diminutive suffix
ALF Alfred; elf
ELF fairy; sprite; dwarf
OLF bullfinch
ALI Mohammed's son-in-law; Fatima's son; — Pasha: Lion of Janina
CLI 151
DLI 551
ELI high priest; Samuel's teacher; Yale; — Whitney
ILI river
MLI 1051
XLI 41
ALK — gum (turpentine)
ELK deer; wapiti; sambar; leather; color lama; river; city
ILK family; class; same
ALL whole; each; only; very; universe; according to; — out; — hands; — hours; — clear; — in one
ELL cloth measure; aune; building annex
ILL Illinois; sick; bad(ly); evil; river
ULL chief god: Sif's son; Thor's stepson
ELM tree; Ulmus; — City (New Haven)
OLM amphibian
ULM Danube city
ALN measure
FLO Florence; Flora; arrow
ILO International Labor Organization
ULO prefix: gums; shell money
ALP mountain; renegade (Byron)
OLP blight; bullfinch
ALS when, than: Ger.
ILS they: Fr.
RLS novelist: Robert Louis Stevenson
ALT high in pitch (octave); old: Ger.
ELT knead
OLT Aluta; Danube tributary
FLU grippe; 1918–19 pandemic
ULU Eskimo woman's knife
CLV 155
DLV 555
MLV 1055
XLV 45
CLX 160
DLX 560
MLX 1060
ALY like malt drink
BLY Chief — (Saroyan); Nellie, newspaperwoman
CLY seize; steal; servant (Dickens)
ELY cathedral city; mountain; island; Bishop of —
FLY leap; soar; vanish; pilot; tent canvas; printer's devil; keen; on the —; river
PLY fold; bend; strand (thickness); wield; practice; urge; paper web
SLY shrewd; foxy; roguish; secretive; on the —; tinker (Shaks.)
VLY low-land; marsh; creek; temporary lake
AMA chalice; (nurse) maid; American Medical Association; tree
IMA — Hogg (heiress)
OMA suffix: tumor
UMA Devi (goddess of splendor); Wiltshire's wife (Stevenson)
MMC 2100
MMD 2500
AME wooden form; soul: Fr.; — damnée
EME uncle; friend; gossip
MME madame; My Lady
UME Jap. apricot; river
AMI friend: Fr.
CMI 901
IMI measure
MMI 2001
OMI sacred mountain
CML 950
MML 2050
MMM 3000
AMO I love: Lat.
OMO prefix: shoulder; river
AMP elec. unit of intensity; ampere
IMP pretty demon; urchin, rascal; mock
UMP (act as) referee
EMS Bad — (spa); river
HMS — Pinafore (G & S opera)
AMT county: Dan.; public office: Ger.
EMU ostrichlike bird; Austral. tree, apple, millet
IMU baking pit
SMU Dallas College
UMU Polynesian earth oven
CMV 905
MMV 2005
CMX 910
MMX 2010

AMY female name; prochein — (nearest friend: law); (Little) — Dorrit: Dickens
SMY sprat
ANA collection; prefix: up, back; Irish gods' mother; coin
INA fem. name, suffix; mother
MNA mina (weight)
ONA measure; So. Amer. Indian
SNA snow: Scot.
UNA river; Dan's sister (Kipling); Red Cross Knight's wife: Truth personified in "Faerie Queene"
AND conjunction; plus
END limit; death; extreme; phase; remnant; aim; finish; — man; — use; open —
IND India (poet.); Indiana
UND and: Ger.
ANE ass: Fr.; chem. suffix
ENE suffix; compass point
INE suffix
NNE compass point
ONE single; unit(y); person; same; the absolute
UNE article, one: Fr.
ENG Chang's Siamese twin
ING suffix; A.S. peace god
ANI black bird; cuckoo
INI suffix: order
ONI any: Scot.
UNI plainly woven; goddess (Juno); prefix: single
INK sepia; cuttlefish fluid; black; sign
ANN stipend; fem. name; Nancy; Nina; Rutledge (Lincoln's fiancee)
INN ho(s)tel; lodge; river
ANO blackbird; prefix: up
INO Cadmus's daughter; Athamas's wife
UNO one: It., Sp.
ANS Liège commune
ENS being; essence, entity
INS International News Service
ONS cricket field parts; weight
UNS us: Ger.
ANT insect; formic acid source; emmet; pismire
ENT suffix; prefix: inner
INT anoint
TNT explosive; toluene
ANU sky god; triad (—, Bel, Ea); Irish gods' mother; Danu
GNU antelope; goat; takin
NNW compass point
WNW compass point
ANY some; one; at all
ONY any
SNY abound; swarm; bend; curved plank
BOA constrictor; python; anaconda; (fur, feather) scarf
GOA gazelle; mugger; crocodile; former Port. colony; Austral. native
HOA hallo!
IOA Iwa; frigate bird
KOA timber tree
LOA worm; eye parasite; Lao; Mauna — (volcano)
MOA flightless extinct bird
NOA profane; common; no
POA (blue)grass
SOA tub; milk pail; cowl
TOA brave warrior; beefwood; Casuarina
WOA stop!
ZOA Blake's symbol(s); suffix: animals
BOB cheat; mock; weight; curtsy; Scot. dance; shilling; haircut; Robert; -sled; — up
COB swan; horse; seagull; excel; strike
DOB dab; daub
FOB pocket; cheat, trick; — chain
GOB mouth(ful); mass; sailor; tar
HOB ferret; havoc; game pin; cut(ter); — and nob
JOB (do odd) work; employment; OT book; patient sufferer; item
KOB Afr. antelope
LOB go heavily; high curve (tennis); till; Puck
MOB crowd (about); masses; annoy; gang; cap
NOB (blow on) head; knob(stick); hob and —
POB porridge; post-office box
ROB steal; mine coal; juice: — Roy (outlaw)
SOB weep; wail(ing); — story; — sister
TOB anc. Syrian kingdom
DOC doctor; physician
HOC card game; — anno; ad —

ROC fabled bird; simurg; bomb
SOC A.S. jurisdiction district; sac and —
BOD clay plug
COD fish; hoax; Cape —
DOD clip off; metal plate; annular die
FOD measure
GOD Jehovah; deity; deify; gallery occupant
HOD brick tray; coal scuttle; — carrier
JOD yodh; Heb. Y, 10
LOD weight
MOD Scot. artist congress; fashion fad
NOD drowse; (show) assent; Land of —; East of Eden
POD flock; socket; groove; bag; legume; suffix: foot
ROD stick; race; bar; gun; scepter; 5½ yards
SOD soil; turf; sward
TOD wool weight; (ivy) bush; death: Ger.
VOD Baltic Finn
YOD Heb. Y, 10
COE sheep disease; Ia. college
DOE female animal; biscuit color; John —
FOE enemy; adversary
HOE tool; dig; scrape; inventor
JOE coin; sweetheart; — Miller (joke); fat boy (Dickens)
LOE love: Scot.
MOE masc. nickname
POE Edgar Allan — (Raven, Gold Bug); parson bird
ROE deer; doe; fish eggs; streaks in wood
SOE tub; pail; cowl
TOE digit; drive aslant; golf club part; — the line; -hold
VOE inlet; creek
WOE alas; sorrow(ful)
YOE ewe
HOF city
LOF measure
BOG mire; marsh; — down
COG cheat; (gear) tooth; (connect by) tenon; ship
DOG Canis; gripper; andiron; crampon; track
FOG vapor; daze; blue; blur
GOG — and Magog (statues)
HOG pig, boar; sheep; dime, shilling; glutton; monopolize
JOG jostle; remind; trot
LOG cut timber; (ship) record
MOG move slowly; depart
NOG egg drink; peg; wood (block, fastener); pin
ROG shake; pull; stir
SOG soak; drowse
TOG coat; dress up
VOG weight
ZOG Albanian king
BOH Burmese chief; boo; da Thone (Kipling)
DOH do (note)
FOH exclamation
HOH Quileute; Indian whaler
POH bah!
SOH exclamation; gutta mixture
ZOH zobo; yak; zebu hybrid
COI river
GOI non-Jew: Heb.
HOI yam; haw (as cattle)
KOI Jap. carp
LOI law: Fr.
MOI I: Fr.; Asian tribes
POI Hawaiian food (taro)
ROI fern rootstock; king; Fr.; vive le —
TOI you, thou: Fr.
YOI hunting cry
BOK Amer. editor
LOK god of discord; Balder slayer
ROK Korean soldier
SOK measure
YOK A.S. G; Middle English Y
COL Colorado; mountain pass
GOL God (euphemistic form)
HOL prefix: complete
KOL Dravidian native; Munda, Larka
MOL gram molecule
POL degree without honors
SOL sun (god); tone G; coin; fluid
TOL Sanskrit school
VOL wings (Her.); battery iron block
BOM So. Amer. serpent
COM prefix: together, with
DOM monastic title; church; low caste Hindu
MOM mamma
NOM name: Fr.; — de plume (pseudonym); — de guerre
OOM — Paul Kruger (Boer president)
POM Pomeranian (dog)
ROM Gypsy husband
TOM male; Thomas; Ob tributary; — Thumb ("General" Charles Sherwood Stratton); — o' Bedlam (madman); — Alibi (Scott); — Canty (Twain); Aunt Chloe's

husband
YOM day: Heb.; — Kippur (Atonement Day); river
BON good, bond: Fr.; bean; grass; Jap. festival (of lanterns); Tibet religion: Cape —
CON learn; against; deceive; — game; — man; — amore
DON Sir; tutor; put on; goddess; mother of Gwydion, Arianrhod; river
EON time period; age; eternity
FON Dahomey Negro (Ewe)
GON measure; prefix: knee; suffix: angled figure
ION charged particle; molecule; son of Apollo, Creusa
KON weight
LON Alonso
MON my: Fr.; family badge; Pegu Burmese; prefix: one; — Dieu!
NON not: Lat.; no: Fr.; prefix; sine qua —
OON final syllable
PON pagoda; gold coin
RON King Arthur's lance
SON male descendant; scion; — of Man; river
TON weight; style: Fr.; bon —; suffix: town
VON by noble birth: Ger.
WON obtained; conquered
YON at a distance; thither
BOO ostrich tail; hoot; jeer; scary cry
COO dove cry; amorous talk
FOO Chin. prefecture
GOO sticky substance
KOO Chin. statesman
LOO card game; halloo
MOO cow's cry; low; weight
NOO now; new; prefix: mind
POO Nanki —: Yum-Yum's husband
ROO kangaroo
SOO murmur; sow
TOO also; excessively
WOO make love; court; sue
ZOO animal collection; menagerie
BOP bravura jazz
COP (wind) yarn; catch; thicket; policeman
DOP diamond cup; — brandy
FOP dandy; coxcomb; dude
GOP Republican party
HOP leap; dance; limp; air trip; vine; bryony; opium; drug; stimulate
KOP hill; measure
LOP choppy sea; cut off; droop; act lazily
MOP wipe(r); swab; hair; pout; — up
OOP up; bind; join: Scot.
POP sound; burst; sho(o)t; plant; protrude; ask; drink
SOP dip in; soak; ooze; wet food; bribe
TOP head; acme; best; cut off; cover; outdo; toy; upset; foremost; — secret
BOR neighbor; Yugo. mine town
COR heart; main star; prefix: pupil
DOR beetle; bumblebee; Bongo; Sudanese; Le Coq —: opera; Côte — (Fr. dept.)
FOR to; because; namely; pro; fur
GOR Indus tribesman
HOR Edom mountain
IOR (comparative) ending
KOR measure; homer
MOR forest humus
NOR conjunction: and not
POR push; kick; poke(r)
TOR hill; peak; fool: Ger.
VOR before: Ger.
BOS cow: Lat.; genus
COS lettuce; romaine; trigonometric function
DOS dowry; back: Fr. -a-dos; — Passos
EOS goddess; dawn; Aurora; Tithonus's wife
GOS goshawk bird: Scot.
IOS Hawaiian hawks
KOS island
LOS the: Sp.; — Alamos; — Islands; — Negros (Admiralty I.)
MOS custom; folkway; mores (sing.)
NOS we: Lat.; our: Fr.; prefix: disease
ROS prefix: Cornish names; rulers; Varangians
SOS distress signal
BOT botfly larva
COT hut; coop; small bed
DOT dowry; speck; point; scatter; mus. sign; — and dash (Morse)
FOT measure
GOT past tense of get
HOT torrid; burning; eager; violent;

fresh; urgent; biting; exciting; stolen; contraband; — seat; — dog; -shot; -rod
JOT point; iota; title; brief note; — down
LOT fate; share; plot, parcel of land; great deal; river
MOT pithy saying; quoits mark
NOT negation; hornless; smooth
OOT out: Scot.
POT drink; fish trap; sho(o)t; stake; much money; win; preserve; pepper —: soup
ROT ret; decay; die; nonsense; disease
SOT guzzle(r); befool; waste; fixed; obstinate
TOT add; child; dead: Ger.
VOT Finn in Ingria
YOT measure
COU neck: Fr.
FOU full bushel: Scot.; fool(ish): Fr.
HOU measure
IOU debt confirmation; note; I owe you
KOU Hawaiian tree
LOU nickname
MOU measure
ROU Rollo
SOU small coin
TOU measure
YOU pronoun; — bet
SOV gold coin: Br. slang; sovereign
BOW weapon; archer; 6 feet; fiddlestick; Apollo's instrument; nod; yield; bend; prow; river
COW bovine; Bos; tree raft; bogy; daunt; dolt
DOW befit; Arab. sailboat; Burmese knife: Neal — (prohibitionist)
HOW why; what; method; know-; Indian salute
JOW measure
KOW bogy; goblin
LOW moo; weak; inferior; plain; coarse; cheap(ly): soft(ly); cartoonist; Girl Scouts founder
MOW cut down; (stack) hay
NOW at this time; present(ly); admonition
POW sound of blow; prisoner of war
ROW brawl; propel; series; line; tier; file; Rotten —: Hyde Park; skid —
SOW fem. swine; mold; scatter; seed; — dragons teeth
TOW draw; tug(boat); rope; flax fibers; spun yarn
VOW promise; dedicate
WOW sensational success; excite audience; sound distortion
YOW yelp; howl; miaow
BOX fight; spar; tree (topiary, Eucalyptus); mix paint; stow; gift; baseball term; Cox and —; -spring; — camera; — seat
COX steersman: — and Box; painter; reformer; politican (Pres. nominee)
FOX Vulpes; vixen; trick(ster); discolor; rope yarn; brown; river; orator; Quaker; educator; — islands
HOX hamstring; pester
LOX (smoked) salmon; — and bagels
NOX night goddess
POX infectious disease
TOX intoxicate
VOX voice: Lat.; — populi, — Dei; — angelica
YOX hiccup; cough
BOY youth; servant; act, treat as lad; office —; — orator: W. J. Bryan; Blue — (Gainsborough)
COY demure, bashful; shy; entice; hoax
FOY feast; gift
GOY non-Jew: Heb.
HOY barge; exclamation; Orkney Isle
JOY happiness; bliss; gaiety; exult; name
LOY post-hole spade; a slick; name
POY boat pole
ROY name; Rob — (outlaw, Scott hero, cocktail)
SOY bean; sauce
TOY (diversionary) trifle; trinket; play(thing)
YOY yes
BOZ Dickens pseudonym
COZ cousin
GOZ coin
POZ positive(ly)
APA Braz. tree; wallaba
SPA mineral spring; resort
WPA Works Progress Administration
APE monkey, anthropoid; mimic. Hawaiian herb; apii
EPE Dutch commune
OPE unlock (poet.)
API prefix: bee
EPI finial; grain, ear: Fr.; prefix: upon
PPI radarscope
UPI news, wire

service; United Press International
APO prefix: away; P.I. volcano; mil. address; Mount — (P.I.)
OPS goddess; Consus; Rhea; Saturn's wife; Ceres' mother
PPS additional postscript
APT fit; likely; ready
OPT choose (citizenship)
SPY watch(er); discover; search(ing); secret agent

BQB chess move
QQB chess move
RQB chess move
BQR chess move
QQR chess move
RQR chess move

ARA constellation; altar; macaw; textile screw pine; measure; goddess
BRA underwaist
DRA measure
ERA epoch; geol. time division
FRA brother; monk; — Angelo, Diavolo (Michele Pezza); Angelico (painter)
GRA love(r); fondness
IRA Bib. ruler; Irish Republican Army; masc. name: watchful
KRA long-tailed ape
NRA National Recovery Administration: FDR measure; Blue Eagle
ORA Dan. money; mouths; — et labora (pray and work)
TRA Malay coin
ORB disk; sphere; world; eye; encircle
ARC curve part; light; rainbow
ORC grampus (whale)
ARD suffix: excessive doer
ERD earth; land; -shrew
ORD mountain (Ariz.)
URD bean; woolly pyrol; Norn; Wyrd; — Verthandi, Skuld
ARE measure; verb form
ERE before; sooner; — long
IRE provoke; anger; choler; wrath
ORE Oregon; seaweed; mineral; crude metal(lic rock); coin
PRE prefix: before
TRE prefix: town; three: It.
URE suffix: chemist; river mist: Scot.
ERF ½-acre plot
ORF fish; yellow ide
ERG work unit; desert area
CRI cry: Fr.; dernier —
ERI silkworm; bombyx; Gad's son
GRI horse: Gypsy
IRI Bela's son; city
KRI read(ing substitute)
ORI prefix: mouth; limit
SRI glorious; holy; Lakshmi (goddess)
TRI prefix: three
URI Swiss canton
ARK Arkansas; refuge; broadhorn; flatboat; wanigan; — of the covenant
IRK abhor; annoy; bore
KRK island
ORK whale
ARM branch; sleeve; bay; power; fortify
ARN alder tree
ERN sea eagle
URN vessel; grave; bury
ARO Nigerian
CRO -Magnon; homo sapiens; murder fine
FRO from; away; to and —
ORO gold: Sp.; Tahiti god; mouth; prefix: mountain
PRO for; expert; yes vote(r); quid — quo
SRO box office sign
URO So. Amer. Indian; Puqina
WRO angle; passage; nook
ORP fret; weep: Scot.
GRR exclamation; growl
ORR Nobel physiologist
ARS art: Lat.; — Amandi (Ovid); — longa, vita brevis
ERS bitter vetch
IRS Internal Revenue Service
MRS title; address; — Grundy
ART skill; science; trade; craft; wile; where — thou?; leg — : cheesecake
ERT urge on: Scot.
HRT boiler
ORT morsel; leftover; weight; place: Ger.
ARU indeed; really
CRU tract of land; vineyard
GRU practice: Scot.
IRU Caleb's eldest son
KRU Liberian (language)
MRU Indo-Chinese native
URU Bolivian Indian
ARX citadel
ARY any; suffix: pert.

to, engaged in
CRY call; wail; weep; beg; summon; slogan; — wolf
DRY hard; shrewd; arid; plain; dull; vapid; evaporate; — Tortugas (Isles); dwindle(d); drought; — goods; — cell; — run; simulated
ERY suffix: conduct, art, place
FRY young brood; pancook; vex(ation); prison reformer
GRY horse: Gypsy
ORY like ore, seaweed; suffix: of
PRY lever(age); peep(er); gaze; Paul — (meddler)
TRY attempt; test; prove; strain; annoy; essay; render fat; conduct court procedure
WRY deflect; twist(ed); disgusted; askew

ASA masc. name; healer; king of Judah; Norse god
ESA Economic Stability Administration
BSC Bachelor of Chemical Science (degree)
ASE enzyme; Peer Gynt's mother (Ibsen)
ESE suffix; compass point
ISE suffix; fjord; bay (Atsuta)
OSE suffix: simple sugar
SSE compass point
TSE Lao- (philosopher); Mao -tung
USE employ(ment); (ac)custom; treat(ment); gain; dupe; — and wont
ASH tree; residue; burn; pallor; gray; — can: depth charge
HSH hush; exclamation
ISH adj. suffix
USH to usher
PSI Greek letter PS, 700
ASK question; seek; need; invite; beg
TSK exclamation
USK river
ISM doctrine; system
ASO Jap. volcano
DSO Distinguished Service Order (Brit.)
ESO prefix: within
ISO prefix: equal
ASP adder; viper; uraeus: symbol; Cleo's snake
ESP 6th sense; extrasensory perception; especially
ASS Equus; donkey; kiang; weight; dolt
ESS S; fem. suffix; worm; curve
OSS Office of Strategic Services
SSS Selective Service System
EST suffix; is: Fr.; id —; n' -ce pas?; Eastern Standard Time
IST adherent; practitioner; fanatic; is: Ger.
LST landing ship tank
OST prefix: bone; oven; East(ern): Ger.
PST call for attention; quiet!
TST hissed sound; quiet!
UST used to
SSU Chin. weight
TSU Jap. seaport
WSW compass point
SSW compass point
ATA Mindanao tribe, language; flour; sweetsop
ETA Jap. outcasts; Greek E, 8; Negrito
ITA Negrito; Eskimo; labor union; city
PTA Parent-Teacher Association
UTA lizard; Jap. song
KTB chess move
ETC and so on
LTD limited (company)
ATE goddess of infatuation, folly, discord (Zeus's daughter); consumed
ETE summer: Fr.
ITE suffix: follower, resident; So. Amer. Indian
OTE suffix: resident
STE saint(e): Fr.
UTE Shoshonean Indian; mountain
ETH A.S. letter: th; suffix: ordinal number
ITH Irish ancestor
NTH any size; — degree; indefinite power
ATI P.I. Negrito
KTK chess move
ETO European Theater of Operations (WW II)
ITO Zionist (Zangwill's) group; Jap. admiral, statesman
OTO Siouan; prefix: ear
KTQ chess move
ITR attar; rose perfume
KTR chess move
ITS poss. pronoun
ATT coin
ITU city
UTU sun god; Shamash; Babbar; Maori compen-

sation; hoot
STY pig enclosure; eyelid swelling
EUA Tonga isle
HUA Mao's succesor
KUA Bantu tribe
PUA hemp; cordage fiber
QUA in so far as; sine — non (necessity)
RUA Congo Bantu
SUA hers: Lat.
TUA dyewood tree
BUB small boy; liquor
CUB young animal; boy (scout); — reporter; light plane: grass-hopper
DUB rub smooth; bestow title; play; do poorly; coin; add sound
FUB plump child; cheat
HUB wheel center; nave; pipe; the — (Boston)
NUB knob; knot; gist
PUB inn; tavern
RUB polish; vex; chafe; hindrance; gibe
SUB pinch hitter; under: Lat.; — rosa
TUB vessel; keg; wash
DUC duke: Fr.
BUD develop; im-mature one; lad; in the —; — stick
CUD something ruminated; tobacco quid
DUD garment; faulty bomb; failure
LUD oath; legendary king
MUD abusive charge; — lark; — Cat State (Miss.)
PUD paw; hand; weight
RUD redness; fish
SUD soapy water; foam
AUE Polynesian exclamation
CUE Q; signal; hint; hair twist; waiting line; billiard rod
DUE owed; just; debt; — date
GUE Shetland viol
HUE color; shout; — and cry
LUE sift; bolt
PUE pew
QUE what, that: Fr.
RUE herb; repent; regret; — de la Paix
SUE urge; woo; plead; take court action
TUE parson bird
AUF on, upon: Ger.
OUF dog's bark; exclamation
BUG insect; defect; germ; fanatic; bulge (eyes); river
DUG delved; excavated
FUG reek
HUG embrace; keep close; bear —
JUG ewer; jail; stew; nest(le); bird sound
LUG ear; loop; drag; worm; sail; measure; god
MUG cup; face; photograph; sheep; mungo; assault; overact; pose
PUG dog; (mix) clay; boxer; — nose; footprint
RUG mat; cozy
TUG pull; lug; effort; towboat; — of war
VUG lode cavity
ZUG Swiss canton, lake
AUH exclamation
HUH exclamation
CUI composer; engineer
DUI duets; twosomes
HUI guild; partnership
KUI Asian group; Lolo; Kandh
MUI — tsai: girl slave(ry)
QUI who, that: Fr.; — vive (watchword)
SUI Chin. dynasty; — generis
TUI dyewood tree; parson bird
GUJ Moti —: elephant (Kipling)
AUK sea bird; Tlingit Indian
HUK P.I. guerrilla
OUK week: Scot.
SUK Nilotic Negro
BUL Canaanite's 8th month; Heshvan
CUL -de-sac; blind alley
FUL Hamitic Sudanese
GUL rose: Persian
HUL Shem's descen-dant
MUL measure
NUL no, nothing (law)
PUL Tiglathpileser (king); coin; OT people
AUM measure
BUM sponge upon; tramp; inferior; Levant ship
CUM summa — laude (with highest praise)
DUM doom palm; gingerbread tree
FUM feng-huang; myth. bird
GUM adhesive; exu-date; resin; jaw tissue; overshoe; humbug
HUM buzz; sing; murmur; melody; hoax
JUM cultivation method
KUM Shiite pilgrim site; river
LUM chimney; sink; pond
MUM chrysanthemum; hush; beer;

mask; madam
QUM Shiite pilgrim site
RUM liquor; odd; tough; fine; dye
SUM total; amount; all; epitomize; in —; — up
TUM sun god: Atmu; card (wool); banjo sound; The Rum — Tugger (Eliot)
VUM vow; swear
BUN bread; roll; hair knot; boat; tipsiness
DUN urge payment; dingy (brown); May fly; cure fish
FUN amusement; joke; weight
GUN firearm; pump; hunt; mug; — dog; speed up
HUN vandal; invader; Boche
KUN Bela —, (revolutionary)
MUN must; mouth; roisterer; river
NUN Niger mouth; convent woman; pigeon, smew; Heb. N, 50; Joshua's father; chaos
PUN play on words; paronomasia
RUN hurry; operate; stretch; contest; flee; series; brook; trail
SUN star; shine; Apollo; Helios; Phoebus; — Yat-sen (Chin. leader)
TUN vat; cask; measure; guzzle; Mayan year
WUN Burmese governor
YUN Laos tribesman
DUO two; duet, pair
LUO White Nile Negro
QUO measure; quid pro —; status —
CUP vessel; ½ pint; portion; prize; golf hole; crater; bloodletting —
GUP gossip
HUP command to horses
KUP measure
PUP young dog, seal; bad security; silly fop
SUP drink; eat; entertain; mouthful
TUP ram; mallet; butt
SUQ Moslem booth, market
BUR burr; seed coat; whirr; cut(ter)
CUR mongrel dog; cad
DUR major (mus.)
EUR Europe
FUR pelt; coat(ing); Negro
GUR raw sugar; massecuite
HUR Ben —: hero (Wallace); Thamar's son; Tirzah's brother
JUR Nile Negro; Luo; river
LUR Persian tribesman; trumpet
MUR wall: Fr.; Yugo. river
PUR sound (cat, motor)
RUR Rhine tributary; Capek play
SUR upon (law); prefix: over; south: Sp.; Tyre (Lebanon city)
TUR pigeon pea; aurochs; urus; ibex; wild goat
AUS out of, finished: Ger.; Arab tribesman
BUS vehicle; enough; — boy
GUS Augustus; Gustavus
HUS Jan — (reformer)
IUS right, law: Lat.
JUS law(s): Lat.; legal power; gravy, juice: Fr.
MUS mouse, rodent genus
OUS suffix: abounding
PUS suppuration; Hindu month
RUS rulers; Ros
SUS swine genus
AUT prefix: self, same
BUT conjunction: except, unless, yet, only
CUT sever; carve; lower; cross; shorten; gash; slight; sarcasm
FUT measure
GUT intestine; eviscerate; destroy; good: Ger.
HUT hovel; cabin; hat: Ger.
JUT project; extend
KUT -al-Imara (Brit. defeat)
LUT weight
MUT cur; dolt; Amen's wife; courage: Ger.
NUT crank; fastener; kernel; head; guy; show investment; goddess, Geb's wife
OUT absent; nook; game term; (at) odd(s); begone!; known; passé; wrong; on strike
PUT lay; set; attach; throw; rustic; urge; golf shot; game; stay —; — and call; -in-Bay (Perry's victory site)
RUT routine; groove; habit; oxcart; heat
SUT coal dust; smudge
TUT mild rebuke; rounders; game; staccato
AUX according to, a la: Fr.; — armes

(to arms!)
DUX fugue theme; leader
LUX light unit
MUX mess; botch
RUX worry; play; sport
TUX men's evening dress
BUY (good) purchase; bribe; redeem
GUY rope; chain; effigy; fellow; chaff; Fawkes; Octavius (Collins)
KUY Siamese; Shan group; Kandh language
MUY very, greatly: Sp.
PUY volcanic hill
BUZ son of Nahor, Mileah
GUZ measure; zar; arshin
HUZ Abraham's nephew
LUZ Bib. site; Bethel
SUZ exclamation
AVA anc. Burma capital; pepper; shrub; kava; liquor
EVA Evangeline; Little — (Uncle Tom's Cabin)
IVA yellow bugle; herb eve; marsh elder
OVA eggs; Piman Indian
TVA Tennessee Valley Administration
UVA grape
MVD Soviet Ministry of Interior Affairs
AVE — atque vale (hail and farewell); rosary bead
EVE twilight; time before; woman; mother of mankind
IVE contraction; suffix
OVE egg-shaped ornament
UVE P.I. yam
CVI 106
DVI 506
EVI Midianite king
LVI 56
MVI 1006
OVI prefix: egg
UVI — yam (white yam)
XVI 16
OVO ab — (from the egg, start)
IVY vine; arbutus; creeper; overgrow
AWA kava; ten-pounder; milkfish
IWA frigate bird; -iwa: fern stalks
PWA Public Works Administration
SWA so
TWA two
AWE reverence; intimidate; mill bucket; sail
EWE sheep; Negro tribe
OWE be obliged, indebted
TWI prefix: double; Tshi
AWL shoemaker's tool
OWL bird (of prey); night-
CWM cirque (geol. process)
AWN (remove grain) beard
OWN acknowledge; have
IWO — Jima, island; Afr. city
LWO White Nile Negro
TWO card; pair; in —; in half; little casino; — bits; -faced; -time
AWU volcano
OXA prefix: oxygen
CXC 190
DXC 590
MXC 1090
AXE tool; fell; destroy
EXE Devon river
CXI 111
DXI 511
LXI 61
MXI 1011
XXI 21
CXL 140
DXL 540
MXL 1040
EXO prefix: outside
CXV 115
DXV 515
LXV 65
MXV 1015
XXV 25
CXX 120
DXX 520
LXX 70; Septuagint; Temple at Jerusalem destroyed
MXX 1020
XXX 30; Crucifixion of Christ
OXY of an ox; sharp; ocute; prefix: oxygen
AYA Brahman title; Shamash's consort; Ai
IYA (nurse)maid; Koran verse; omen
MYA long clam genus
PYA coin
RYA Scand. rug
AYE always; yes (vote)
BYE run (cricket); aside; secondary; inactive
DYE color; stain
EYE vision; view; scan; loop; spot; brood; — bank
HYE hedge; hie
LYE alkaline solution; lixivium
NYE pheasant brood; humorist
OYE grandchild: Scot.
PYE poet; 1st engraver
RYE cereal; whisky; Gypsy; — and Indian (bread)
SYE scythe; drop; strain
TYE mast chain

WYE Y; forked holder; tract; river
TYG drinking vessel
HYL prefix: wood
KYL Himalayan ibex
GYM sports hall
NYM Falstaff follower
FYN island
GYN prefix: woman
LYN waterfall
SYN prefix: with
WYN Old Eng. rune W
IYO Afr. bass; palm fiber; P. I. vine
OYO Nigerian town
WYO Wyoming

CYP princewood tree
GYP steal; swindle(r); bitch; college servant
HYP make melancholy
AYR Scot. county, port
PYR prefix: fire, heat, fever; light unit
TYR god; Aesir, Riu (Tuesday), Odin's son slain by Garm
LYS prefix: loosening; fleur-de-lis; river

TYT quickly; promptly
AYU sweetfish
NYX night goddess; Chaos's daughter; mother of day and night
PYX box; Eucharist case; ciborium
IZE suffix
AZO nitrogenous
IZU peninsula
TZU river

FOUR-LETTER WORDS
AA– – to ZY– –

AALI pasha
AALU Hades; heaven
AANI ape
AARE river
AARU Hades; heaven
ABAC calculator
ABAS down: Fr.
ABBA father; title
ABBE priest; title; Amer. meteorologist
ABBY Abigail
ABCS first principles, alphabet
ABED in bed; bedridden
ABEL Adam's son; Cain's brother; Magwitch (Dickens); letter A; monkey
ABET aid; incite
ABEY waive
ABIA Samuel's son
ABIB month
ABIE 's Irish Rose; name
ABIR red powder
ABLE fit; adept; suffix; -bodied
ABLY deftly
ABOO war cry
ABOT Mishnah

ABOU father; deity
ABOX braced
ABRA narrow pass; river
ABRI shelter
ABSI tribe
ABUT touch
ACCA fabric
ACER tree
ACHE pain; yearn
ACHT eight: Ger.
ACHY painful
ACID sour; biting
ACIS river; (Galatea's) lover
ACLE tree
ACME peak; crisis
ACNE disease
ACON boat
ACOR acidity
ACRE field; measure; city
ACTA deeds; records
ACTH hormone medicine
ACTO action: Sp.
ACTS NT book
ACTU act: Lat.
ACUS pin
ACYL acid part
ADAD fiber; god
ADAH wife of Lamech, Esau; fem. name

ADAI tribe
ADAK Aleut. island
ADAM first man; sin; composer; architect
ADAN prayer call
ADAR month
ADAT law
ADAY atomic attack date
ADDA god; river; skink
ADDU skink; fiber; god
ADDY Adeline
ADEN comb. form: gland; city; gulf; region
ADER Benjamite
ADES Hades
ADIB star
ADIN name
ADIT entrance
ADMI gazelle
ADRY thirsty
ADZE tool
AEON age
AERA age; era
AERI prefix: air
AERO go by aircraft
AERY ethereal; nest
AETA Negrito; native
AFAR far away; tribe
AFFA from off

AFFY join
AFRA name; union
AFRO hairstyle
AGAG king
AGAL cord
AGAO language
AGAR wood
AGAU language
AGAZ Indian
AGED old; oxygian
AGEE awry; Shammah's father; James (novelist)
AGER apparatus; field
AGHA officer; title
AGIB dervish
AGIO fee; commission
AGIS king
AGLA acrostic
AGNI god; lambs
AGNO Luzon river
AGOG eager
AGON contest; argument
AGRA comb. form; carpet; city (Taj Mahal site)
AGRI fields
AGRO prefix: soil
AGUA water; toad
AGUE fever
AHAB king; captain; prophet
AHAZ king
AHEM interjection
AHER Benjamite
AHET season (of inundation)
AHEY ho
AHIO Ark driver
AHIR caste
AHOM Assam native
AHOY call; ship —
AHUM humming
AIAH Edomite, Rizpah's father
AICH alloy
AIDA opera; Rad-ames' lover
AIDE help; -de-camp; — mémoire
AIEA town
AIEL writ of —
AILE winged
AINE elder
AINO Jap. aboriginal
AINT contraction
AINU Jap. aboriginal
AIPI cassava
AIRA grass
AIRE nobleman; river
AIRS pretensions; side
AIRT guide; turn
AIRY breezy; light
AITU god; demon
AJAR opened
AJAX hero (Telamon's son)
AJEE awry
AJOG jogging
AKAL deity
AKAN Negro
AKEE tree
AKEY weight
AKHA tribe; Burmese; Kaw
AKIA shrub (fish poison)
AKIM Negro; Tamiroff
AKIN related
AKKA Pygmy
AKOV measure
AKRA Negrito; vetch
AKTI peninsula
AKUA deity
AKUT ape man (Burroughs)
ALAE wings
ALAI regiment; mountain; jai —
ALAN dog; name
ALAR winglike; axillary
ALAS sad cry
ALAY marble
ALBA garb; poem; brain matter; duke
ALBE album
ALBI flagellants
ALBO prefix: white
ALCA auk
ALCO dog
ALDA soprano; hamlet: Sp.
ALEA Athena (war goddess)
ALEC fish; sauce; nickname
ALEE to shelter
ALEF letter
ALEM fruit
ALEN measure
ALEP city
ALES city
ALEY city
ALFA grass
ALGA plant
ALGY Algernon; suffix: pain
ALIA other: Lat.
ALIF letter
ALII royalty (Hawaiian)
ALIM teacher
ALIN measure
ALIT descended
ALIX fem. name
ALKY alcohol
ALLA by: It.
ALLE bird; all: Ger.
ALLO prefix: other, dissimilar
ALLY unite, confederate
ALMA girl; silk; river; city
ALME dancer
ALMS charity
ALOD estate
ALOE plant; tonic
ALOP lopsided
ALOR island
ALOW below
ALPH river (Coleridge: Kubla Khan)
ALPS mountains
ALSO besides
ALTA tall: Sp.
ALTE old: Ger.; Adenauer
ALTO hill: Sp.; voice
ALUM emetic; astringent; styptic
ALUR Negro
ALVA duke; city; Thomas — Edison
ALYA star
ALYS name: Alice
AMAH nurse
AMAN Ahasuerus's minister
AMAR measures
AMBA mountain
AMBI about; prefix: both
AMBO pulpit
AMEN assent; verily;

deity; — Ra
AMER bitter
AMES author; Ia. city, college
AMEX Amer. Expeditionary Force
AMGA Siberian river
AMIA fish
AMIC amidic
AMID among
AMIE friend: Fr.
AMIL plant; remedy
AMIN agent
AMIR prince
AMIS friends: Fr.
AMIT headdress
AMLA tree
AMLI tree
AMMA abbess; god
AMMI herb
AMMO ammunition; prefix: sand
AMMU ammunition
AMOI mine: Fr.
AMOK frenzy
AMON deity; King of Judah
AMOR love; Cupid; — patriae
AMOS prophet
AMOY island
AMOZ Isaiah's father
AMRA plum
AMUN deity
AMUR river
AMYL starch; alcohol
ANAI termite
ANAK giant race
ANAL pert. to anus
ANAM tree; Vietnam region
ANAN tree; interjection
ANAS duck
ANAT sky god; med. term
ANAX Castor, Pollux (Dioscuri)
ANAY fruit
ANBA title
ANCE suffix; — errand
ANCY suffix
ANDA tree
ANDE tribe
ANDI language
ANDY Andrew
ANEM prefix: wind; city
ANER city
ANES once
ANET dill
ANEW over again
ANGE angel: Fr.
ANGO herb; dye
ANIL shrub, indigo
ANIS fennel; birds
ANKH cross
ANNA coin; bird; name; — Christie (O'Neill); — Karenina (Tolstoi)
ANNE queen; Boleyn; Henry VIII wife; Elizabeth's mother; Shakespeare's wife; Dombey's maid (Dickens); Queen — style; Queen —'s lace
ANNI years: Lat.
ANNO — Domini (year of Our Lord)
ANOA ox
ANON again; now; soon; author unknown
ANSA handle; loop
ANSE handle: Fr.
ANSU Korean apricot
ANTA porch; nut; tapir; goddess; pier; theater group
ANTE stake; pay; before; -bellum
ANTI opposed; prefix: against; Indian
ANTU rat poison
ANUS end of alimentary canal
ANZU apricot
AONE first-rate
AOUL Nepalese
APAP month
APAR armadillo
APER imitator; boar
APET goddess
APEX summit; crisis
APIA port (Samoa)
APII plant
APIO celery: Sp.
APIS sacred bull (Ptah); bee; bull (Kipling)
APOD footless
APSE recess; throne
APSU primordial chaos
APUS bird; constellation
AQUA water; green-blue
ARAB Semite; horse; nomad; urchin
ARAD plant; city
ARAH exclamation
ARAK palm; spirit
ARAL lake
ARAM country (Syria); Eugene (murderer)
ARAN Seir's descendant; island
ARAR tree
ARAS river
ARBA cart
ARCA box; dish; shell
ARCH support; curve; chief; fingerprint; triumphal —
ARDU slave
AREA zone, region; scope; tract
AREG deserts
AREO prefix: Mars
ARES war; Mars; Zeus's, Hera's son; Eris' brother
ARGH timid
ARGO ship; therefore; constellation
ARGY argue
ARIA tune; city (Herat)
ARID dry; barren
ARIL seed covering
ARIS molding edge
ARME weapon: Fr.; — blanche (saber)
ARMS mil. science; ensigns; weapons; branches; limbs
ARMY multitude; force
ARNA buffalo

ARND theologian
ARNE composer; region
ARNI buffalo
ARNO river; cartoonist
ARNT contraction
AROA Venezuela copper center
AROD son of Gad
AROE Islands, New Guinea
AROO indeed
AROW in a line
ARPA harp: It.
ARRA oath
ARRY cockney worker
ARTA Ionian gulf
ARTO prefix: bread
ARTS skills; sciences; fine — ; — and crafts
ARTY artistic
ARUI sheep
ARUM herb; starch
ARYA Caucasian
ASAK tree
ASAR glacial ridges; eskers
ASCH Scholem (author)
ASCI spore sacs
ASEA at sea
ASEM alloy
ASER Jacob's son
ASHA tribe
ASHY gray, pale
ASIA continent; Orient; East
ASIN month
ASIR Arab. principate
ASKR — and Embia: Norse Adam and Eve
ASNO donkey: Sp.
ASOK tree
ASOP sopping
ASOR lyre
ASSE caama; fox
ASSI holly
ASTA measure; dog
ASTI city; — spumante
ASUR war god
ATAP palm
ATAR perfume; essence
ATEF crown (Osiris)
ATEN solar disk
ATEO Polynesian god
ATES sweetsop
ATHI Kenya river
ATIK star
ATIP expectant
ATIS monkshood; fruit
ATIU one of Cook Islands
ATKA fish; Aleut. island
ATLE tree
ATLI Gudrun's husband-king
ATMA soul
ATMO prefix: steam
ATMU sun god
ATOM whit; particle; nuclear complex
ATON solar disk
ATOP at the peak
ATRI It. town
ATRY lay to (naut.)
ATTA soul; native; flour; fruit; ant
ATTU Aleut. island
ATUA demon
ATUM sun god (Tem)
ATWO asunder
ATYS god (Cybele's lover)
AUCA Indian
AUDE Fr. dept.; river
AUER violinist
AUGE priestess
AULA hall; tree; brain part
AULD old; — lang syne
AULU tree
AUNE measure
AUNT parent's sister; tia: Sp.; tante: Fr., Ger.
AURA wind; emanation; bird
AURI prefix: gold, ear
AUSA Vich (Sp. commune)
AUSU tree
AUTE tree
AUTO prefix: same, self; drama: Sp.; (ride in) car
AUZU tree
AVAL grandparental
AVAR Caucasian language
AVEC with: Fr.
AVER assert; asseverate
AVES birds: Lat.
AVID eager; greedy
AVIS bird: Lat.
AVON river; Shakespeare home (Stratford)
AVOW declare; justify; confess
AVUS grandfather: Lat.
AWAG wagging
AWAN tribe
AWAY onward; hence; far; off; absent
AWNY bearded
AWOL absent without leave
AWRY distorted; perverse(ly)
AXAL around an axis
AXIL leaf angle
AXIS center line; spine; stem; deer; power alliance; partnership
AXLE spindle
AXON axis; cell process
AYAH nurse; sign
AYAN spruce
AYES yes votes
AYIN Heb. 16th letter, 70
AZAM sir: Persian
AZAN prayer call
AZEL Saul's descendant
AZHA star
AZID compound
AZIN chem. compound
AZOF town; sea
AZON bomb
AZOV town; sea
AZUL blue: Sp.
AZUN Hananiah's father
AZUR Côte d'— (Riviera); Hananiah's father

BAAL deity
BAAR weight
BAAS master
BABA nurse; title; cake
BABE baby; — Ruth; girl
BABI sect
BABU Hindu gentleman
BABY doll; indulge
BACH live alone; composer
BACK help; tub; past; retreat; kick-; dorsal; posterior; spine
BADB goddess
BADE waited; asked; invited; commanded
BAEL thorny (fruit) tree
BAER prizefighter, actor
BAEZ singer
BAFF strike; stroke
BAFT astern; cotton
BAGA turnip
BAGG heiress (Thackeray)
BAGO shrub
BAHI fortune
BAHO prayer stick
BAHR sea; — El Azrak
BAHT coin
BAIA state; city; resort; bay
BAIL bond; security; set free; dip out; hoop
BAIN bath: Fr.
BAIS caste
BAIT lure; harass; pest poison
BAJU jacket
BAKA devil
BAKE dry; roast; biscuit
BAKU hat; tree; rug; city; oil field
BALA geol. epoch
BALD naked; — eagle
BALE woe; bundle
BALI demon; monkey; offering; island
BALK thwart; signal
BALL game; confuse; dance; — bearing; good time; point; Amer. sculptor
BALM plant; soothe; — in Gilead
BALT Lithuanian; Esth; Latvian, Lett
BALU wildcat
BANA Titan
BANC (judge's) bench
BAND strip; group; orchestra; range; tie; sash
BANE woe; curse; poison
BANG beat; thump; hair; sardine; interjection
BANI coins
BANK mound; bench; deposit; bird flock; Left, Right —; blood —; eye —
BANS marriage notice
BANT diet
BAPS dancing master (Dickens)
BARA measure
BARB sharp point; fish; dog; mow; pigeon
BARD armor; poet; — of Avon (Shakespeare)
BARE expose(d); mere; Indian
BARI hut; Negro; city
BARK peel; tan; cough
BARM yeast
BARN storehouse; stable
BARO big; prefix: weight
BARR elephant's cry
BART man's name
BARU tree
BASE bottom; source; home; headquarters; found; diamond corner; ignoble
BASH smash; bruise
BASK luxuriate; warm
BASS fish; fiber; lowest part; singer; clef (F); musical instrument, viol
BAST (woody) fiber; goddess; phloem
BATA child; servant
BATE diminish; tanner's bath; restrain
BATH tub; measure; spa; order
BATT matted mass
BATZ coin
BAUD speed unit
BAUL mendicant
BAUM Vicki (novelist); Oz creator; tree: Ger.; — marten
BAUR joke
BAVE double silk thread
BAWD procuress
BAWL cry; howl; — out (chide)
BAWN mud enclosure; white
BAYA weaverbird; Bantu
BEAD globule; ball; drop; aim
BEAK bill; nose; judge
BEAL river mouth
BEAM bar; timber; breadth; ray; smile; on the —; broadcast
BEAN plant; trifle; head; strike
BEAR carry; yield; endure; relate; animal; Ursa; short-seller; pessimist
BEAS Punjab river
BEAT strike; defeat; mystify; throb; scoop; field; sphere; — the Dutch
BEAU dandy; lover; — Brummell, — Nash
BECK nod; bidding;

dyeing vat; Pol., Ger. officer, statesman
BEDE Adam (Eliot); the Venerable (monk)
BEEF ox, steer, cow, bos; brawn; rage; complain(t)
BEEN charmer's clarinet; participle
BEEP radio sound
BEER beverage; ale; mead
BEES yeast
BEET vegetable; root; sugar —; — top
BEGA measure
BEHN herb; tree
BEID star
BEIN good; fine
BEJA Nile nomad
BEKA weight
BELA jasmine; Benjamin's 1st son; Hungarian king
BELI myth. Brit. king
BELL ringing cup; gong; time period; flower shape; helmet; Brontë pseudonym; — the cat; diving —
BELT strap; zone; beat
BEMA platform; altar; measure
BENA grass (vetiver)
BEND turn; curve; flex; bow
BENE wild hog; well: It. & Lat.
BENG devil (Gypsy)
BENI Bolivian river; sesame
BENJ hemp; narcotic
BENN seed
BENO alcoholic palm sap
BENT crooked; inclination; grass
BENU holy bird
(Ra-Osiris)
BERA king of Sodom
BERG iceberg; mountain
BERI Sudanese (Fulah); -beri (disease)
BERM (l)edge; road shoulder
BERN Swiss capital
BERT nickname
BESA coin
BESS nickname; Mrs. Truman
BEST most (good); defeat
BETA Greek B, 2; star; ray
BETE beast; silly: Fr.; — noire
BETH Heb. B, 2; Alcott heroine (Little Women)
BEVY company; flock
BHAR Kolarian native
BHAT minstrel; scholar
BHEL thorny (fruit) tree
BHIL low-caste Indian
BHOY gang member; rowdy
BHUT Dravidian ghost
BIAS diagonal (incline); prejudice
BIBB mast's timber piece
BIBI title: Lady, Mrs. (India)
BICE blue, green pigment
BIDE wait; tarry; dwell
BIEN good, fine: Fr.; — aimée (well beloved)
BIER litter; coffin
BIFF (deal a) blow
BIGA two-horse chariot
BIGG barley
BIJA kino tree
BIKE bicycle
BIKH aconite; poison
BILE liver secretion; choler
BILK defraud
BILL beak; weapon; law; poster; invoice; debt; nickname: William; — and coo; Sikes (Dickens)
BILO Balkan karst area
BIMI orangutan (Kipling)
BINA Hindu guitar
BIND tie; protect; sew; cohere
BINE (hop) stem
BING bed roll; sharp sound
BINH weight
BINI Nigerian
BINN box; frame; crib
BINO alcoholic palm sap
BINT daughter; woman
BIOD animal life force
BION physiological individual (morphon)
BIOS life: animal, plant
BIRD avian; flyer; fowl; shuttlecock; person; Blue —
BIRI cheap cigarette
BIRL revolve; spin
BIRN clarinet socket
BIRR wind force; sound
BISA antelope
BISE cold wind; winter
BISH aconite; poison
BISK soup; ice cream; red-yellow
BITE cut; pierce; grip; eat (into); sting; respond; snack
BITI blackwood
BITO tree; poison; oil
BITT naut. fastener
BIUR Heb. com-

mentary
BIWA loquat
BIXA tree genus; achiote
BIZE cold wind; winter
BIZZ buzz
BKKT chess move
BLAA bunk
BLAB tattle
BLAE bleak
BLAH nonsense
BLAS Gil (Le Sage novel)
BLAT sheep's cry
BLAY bleak
BLEA bleak; livid
BLEB blister; bubble
BLED emitted or drew blood, sap; extorted
BLET fruit decay
BLEU blue, rookie: Fr.
BLEW stormed; puffed; sounded
BLIP radar screen sign
BLOB drop; daub; sound; fish; zero score
BLOC political unit; casting
BLOT stain; mar; dry
BLOW move (air); puff, pant; brag; expend; stroke; calamity; disappointment; — up (enlarge)
BLUB swell; puff out
BLUE color; ocean; sky; sailor; sad; -blood; puritanical
BLUP air bubble sound
BLUR obscure; stain
BLUT blood: Ger.
BNAI B'rith (Jewish society)
BOAR (wild) hog; male
BOAS Franz (anthropologist)
BOAT (go by) ship; gravy-
BOAZ Ruth's husband
BOBA chicken snake
BOBO owala tree; mullet
BOCA harbor mouth: Sp.
BOCE colored fish
BOCK beer; leather
BODB goddess
BODE presage; augur; omen
BODO Indo-Chin. language
BODY structure; anatomy; bulk; corpse; group
BOER So. Afr. Dutch
BOGA basslike fish
BOGO Eritrean Hamite
BOGY specter; bugbear
BOHO grass; weep; shout
BOHR Nils (Nobel physicist)
BOID of boas, anacondas
BOII Celtic tribe
BOIL heat; bubble; agitation, abscess
BOIS wood: Fr.; wine (cognac); — de Boulogne
BOJO grass
BOKO evil spirit (Haiti)
BOLA missile; majagua (tree)
BOLD valiant; brazen; strong, heavy (type)
BOLE trunk; clay; brown
BOLL (strip) plant pod
BOLO knife; Rafflesia (plant); pacifist
BOLT sift; refine; shaft; lightning; bar; plant; rifle part; flight; refusal
BOMA Afr. stockade; post
BOMB explosive; dispenser; A-, H-; lead-lined container; buzz —
BONA good: Lat.; — fide
BOND adhesion; tie; covenant; paper; captivity; certificate
BONE study hard; plug; os
BONG bell sound
BONI African; Boschneger
BONK bar money (Dutch E.I.)
BONN city; Ger. capital
BONO Johnny (Briton); cui —
BONY skeletal; osseous; Napoleon
BOOB simpleton
BOOF stare; peach brandy
BOOH exclamation
BOOK tome; volume; Bible; libretto; (bet) record; register; throw the —
BOOL curved handle
BOOM hum; grow, push; beam
BOON benefit; convivial
BOOR rustic; lout; Boer
BOOT shoe; wader; sheath; torture; recruit; compartment; tube; kick; to — (in addition)
BORA north wind; rite
BORD -and-pillar (mining)
BORE pierce; hole; tire; dullard; tidal flow
BORG borough: Dan.
BORI Lucrezia (singer)
BORN given birth to; née; quantum physicist
BORO spring rice;

Indian (Mirhana); — Budur (temple)
BORS king (Lancelot's uncle); Bohort (finder of Holy Grail)
BORT finder of Holy Grail; impure diamond
BOSA Arab. drink
BOSC best pear
BOSE test ground by sound
BOSH furnace part; nonsense (nothing: Turk.)
BOSK thicket
BOSS knob; pad; stud; master, employer
BOTA measure
BOTE house repair; amends
BOTH the two
BOTO Indian; Voto
BOTT clay plug; fly larva
BOUD malt weevil
BOUT contest; attack
BOUW measure
BOWK steep; soak in lime
BOWL basin; dish; (roll) ball
BOXY boxlike; squarish
BOZA Arab. drink
BOZO fellow
BQKT chess move
BRAB palm
BRAD nail
BRAE slope
BRAG boast; game
BRAJ basha
BRAM Abraham
BRAN god-king; seed coat; chaff
BRAS arm: Fr.
BRAT apron; child
BRAW handsome; fine
BRAY (donkey's) cry; grind; Mrs. Nickleby (Dickens)
BREA resin; tree; asphalt
BRED procreated; brought up
BREE (eye)brow
BREI soft tissue
BREN (machine) gun
BRER Rabbit (Harris: Uncle Remus)
BRES Elatha's beautiful son (Fomorian)
BREW beverage; plot; concoct
BREY barnacle
BRIE cheese
BRIG sailing ship; prison
BRIM rim; edge; swell
BRIN fan plate; silk thread
BRIO con — (with spirit)
BRIT young herring
BRIX scale (hydrometer)
BROB support spike
BROH macaque; monkey
BROM Bones (Ichabod's rival)
BROT bread: Ger.
BROW forehead; high-, low-
BROZ Josip (Tito)
BRUH pig-tailed macaque
BRUT dry: Fr.; Brit. king (New Troy, London)
BUAL wine
BUBA tropical sore
BUBE boy, jack: Ger.; Fernando Po Bantu
BUBI Fernando Po Bantu
BUBO horned —; eagle owl
BUCK deer; fop; butt; male; Pearl (novelist); pass the —
BUDA It. millet
BUDD Lanny (Sinclair)
BUDE light; burner
BUFF leather; coat; tan; ward off; polish; wheel; bare skin; enthusiast
BUFO toad genus; agua
BUGI Celebes Malay
BUHL inlaid decoration
BUHR whetstone
BUKA dried leaves
BUKH prate; talk
BUKK prate; talk
BULB bud; tuber; corm; lamp; swell
BULK mass, volume; loom; -head (stall)
BULL (bovine) male; stud; papal letter; optimist; Taurus; policeman; blunder; glib talk; -fight
BULT hill; ridge
BUMP coincide; hit; swelling; — off (kill)
BUNA synthetic rubber
BUND embankment; league
BUNG stop(per); throw
BUNK case; bed; nonsense
BUNN cake
BUNT sag (net, sail); (fungus) disease; butt (ball)
BUOY float; sustain; life-; channel marker
BURA steppe blizzard
BURD noble lady
BURE brown red-yellow
BURG (fortified) town
BURH (fortified) town
BURI palm (fiber); talipot
BURL (pick) knot; Ives (actor)
BURN (be on) fire; yearn; waste; speed; brand
BURP belch; — gun
BURR (prickly) nut, knob; reamer; banyan tree;

Aaron (statesman)
BURT butt; gore; dent
BURY hide; inter; lose
BUSH shrub; thicket; tall
BUSK stir about; hasten; corset bone; Indian New Year
BUSS ship; kiss; calf
BUST bosom; statue; failure; break
BUSY (keep) active; in use
BUTE island; Scot. county; parson (Thackeray)
BUTO serpent goddess; Leto
BUTT cask; mound; target; ram; hinge; jut; halibut
BUXY paymaster
BUYO betel leaf; nut
BUZI Ezekel's father
BUZZ hum; fly low (over); — bomb (V1, V2)
BYEE measure
BYGO pass by
BYKE nest of bees
BYON clayey earth
BYRD explorer; Va. statesman
BYRE cow house
BYTE computer word

CAAM loom; heddles
CABA measure
CABO Yubi
CACA goddess
CACO bandit
CADE cask; tree; pet; rebel
CADI judge
CADY golf boy
CAEN city
CAFE restaurant; coffee; -au-lait; society
CAGE confine; enclosure; elevator car; nor iron bars a —
CAGN mantis; deity
CAGY shrewd
CAID alcaide
CAIN tribute; (Abel's) slayer; mark of —
CAJA box; bank
CAJI snapper
CAJU fruit; mahagony
CAKE bar; dough; harden
CAKY crusty
CALE Gypsy; cabbage
CALF bovine, etc., young; fur; leather; skin; lower leg
CALI Colombian city
CALK tighten; stop; sleep; tool; copy
CALL summon; visit; cry; telephone; — girl; — money
CALM quiet; mold
CALO Gypsy
CALP limestone
CALX residue; heel: Lat.
CAME arrived; lead rod; Indian
CAMP tent(s); town; stay; boot —
CANA Indian
CANE stem; rattan; stick; walking —; sugar —; candy —
CANG wooden collar
CANO canal: Sp.
CANT angle; change course; log; tilt; whine; jargon; be unable
CAPA cloak: Sp.
CAPE cloak; promontory; — Cod, — Horn, — Good Hope
CAPH star, letter
CAPO head: It.; crime boss
CAPP Al (cartoonist: Abner, Dogpatch)
CARA dear (one): It.; Indian
CARD comb; pasteboard; menu; playing —; calling —
CARE grief; heed; responsibility; anxiety; foster; relief organization
CARF slit; notch
CARK trouble
CARL rustic; villain; Charles
CARN stone heap
CARO dear (one): It.; Caroline
CARP fish; complain
CARR pool
CART wagon; transport
CASA house, building: Sp., It.
CASE event; fact; record, problem (medical, etc.); legal action; argument; grammar form; container, chest, box; queer phenomenon; inspect
CASH money; exchange; hemlock
CASK barrel; measure
CASO Dodecanese Island
CASS treasure; Timberlane (Lewis); Squire (Eliot)
CAST throw; project; shed; deposit; form; found; actors; (assign) roles
CASY ex-preacher (Steinbeck)
CATA down; prefix: away
CATE delicacy
CATO the Censor (Roman statesman); foe of Carthage
CATS — cradle

CAUK (secure by a) tenon
CAUL basket; covering membrane
CAUP tribute: Scot.
CAVA pepper shrub, root; gum resin; vein
CAVE cavern; — in (collapse); — canem (beware of dog)
CAVY rodent; guinea pig; stray animal(s)
CAWK bird's cry; mineral
CAWL basket
CAXI snapper (fish)
CAYO island, reef: Sp.
CAZA Turkish district
CAZI Moslem judge
CAZY Moslem judge
CCIV 204; Septimus Severus reign
CCIX 209; Septimus Severus reign
CEBA tree; kapok source
CEBU Visayan Island
CECH Czech
CEDE yield; grant; transfer
CEIL overlay, line, ceiling
CELA that: Fr.
CELL cubicle; group; elec. jar; organism
CELT Irish, Scot, Welsh, Breton; chisel
CENA (Last) supper
CENE suffix: recent
CENS payment due
CENT coin; penny; game
CEPA onion
CEPE boletus (edible fungus)
CERA prefix: horn, wax
CERE wax; (wrap in a) waxed cloth; beak part
CERN decide
CERO mackerel
CESS tax; luck
CEST girdle; belt (Venus)
CETE marine mammals
CETO prefix: whale
CEYX Halcyone's husband
CHAA tea
CHAB bird
CHAC -Mool (god); -chac (instr.)
CHAD lake; nation
CHAI person
CHAL man
CHAM tribe; title; bite
CHAN resthouse; lord; title
CHAO measure
CHAP fellow; crack; jaw
CHAR trout; burn; sandbank; -woman
CHAT talk; bird; spike
CHAW masticate
CHAY red dye plant
CHEE weight
CHEF head (cook); — d'oeuvre
CHEK Chin. foot (measure)
CHEN snow goose
CHER dear: Fr.
CHEW masticate; ruminate; — the cud; — the rag
CHEZ at home of, with: Fr.
CHIA salvia beverage, oil
CHIB tongue; language
CHIC stylish(ness)
CHIH Chin. foot (measure)
CHIL cheer pine; kite (Kipling)
CHIN lower jaw; chatter; weight; dynasty; Burmese
CHIP fragment; cut; hew
CHIR pheasant; pine
CHIT child; sprout; memo; voucher; mind
CHIV knife
CHOB grain spike
CHOL desolate plain; Mayan
CHOP cut; crack; eat; barter; jaw
CHOR thief; steal (Gypsy)
CHOU cabbage, darling: Fr.; Chin. dynasty; En Lai (statesman)
CHOW food; dog
CHOY red dye root
CHUB fallfish; dace; chevin
CHUD Mongols; Vepse; Vote; Tavastian
CHUG pull; fish; (move with) vibration
CHUM friend, scrap fish
CHUN Chin. pottery
CHUR Swiss canton
CHUT nonsense!
CIEL ceiling; sky: Fr.
CIII 103; Trajan reign
CIMA mountain peak: It.
CINE movie: Sp.
CINQ five: Fr.
CION plant shoot
CIPO liana
CIRC circle; recess; corrie
CIRL bunting; bird
CISE dice term: six
CIST chest; roofed pit
CITE summon; quote
CITS citizens; mufti
CITY urban place
CIVA Hindu deity
CIVE chive garlic
CIXO Ecuador Indian
CLAD dressed; plated
CLAM mollusk; hush
CLAN clique; family; group
CLAP rap; applaud; flatten
CLAT mess; chatter

CLAW nail; ungula; chela; scratch; hammer
CLAY earth; ceramic; pipe; — pigeon; color; Henry (statesman)
CLEE redshank; bird
CLEF musical sign; roman à —; key
CLEM riot; suffer hunger; nickname
CLEO queen (Cleopatra)
CLEW yarn ball; sail loop; cocoon; hint
CLII 152; Hadrian reign
CLIM — of the Clough (archer outlaw)
CLIO history Muse; mollusk
CLIP clasp; cut(ting); gait
CLIV 154; Antoninus Pius reign
CLIX 159; Antoninus Pius reign
CLOD lump; soil; dolt
CLOE fem. name
CLOG block; sandal; stop; impede; choke
CLOP limp; hobble
CLOT mass; coagulate
CLOW sluice; floodgate
CLOY glut; surfeit
CLUB bat; beat; society; suit (cards)
CLUE hint; guide; thread
CLUM clutch roughly
CLYM — of the Clough (archer outlaw)
CMIV 904
CMIX 909
CNUT king; son of Magnus
COAD cushion
COAG dowel
COAK tenon
COAL ember; fuel
COAN pert. to Cos Island
COAT fur; skin; cover; — of arms
COAX flatterer; cajole
COBB Irvin S. (writer); Tyrus R. (baseball)
COBH Irish port
COCA cocaine source; shrub; leaf to chew; flavor
COCK male fowl; vane; leader; tap; tee; hay pile; cog
COCO palm; nut; grass
CODA finale; mark
CODE body of law (Julian, Justinian, Napoleonic); signal system; cipher; — duello
CODO measure
CODY William (Buffalo Bill)
COED girl student
COEL cuckoo
COEN Jan (empire builder)
COHO silver salmon
COIF defensive skullcap; make up (hair)
COIL curl; wind; twist
COIN money; mint; invent; corner
COIR coconut fiber
COIX grass; Job's-tears
COJA title; teacher
COKE coal residue; fuel
COKY grimed; drug addict
COLA tree; nut; drink
COLD chill; frigid; indifferent; common —; coryza; — blood; — chisel
COLE brassica genus; Porter (composer)
COLI intestinal bacterium
COLL embrace; hug; Vincent (gangster: "mad dog")
COLP pasture; Irish acre
COLT young horse; pistol; — .45
COLY long-tailed bird
COMA torpor; blur; tuft
COMB crest; rake; scrape
COME arrive; chance; fare
COMO lake, resort (Italy)
COND direct helmsman
CONE geometric solid; pine fruit; strobile; peak; ice cream —; nose —
CONI It. commune
CONK nose; head; decay; fail; hit
CONN direct helmsman
CONY rabbit; daman; pika
COOK chef; concoct; falsify; James (explorer)
COOL chill; calm; unmoved
COOM coal dust; refuse
COON animal; fur; sly man
COOP pen; jail; confine; cooperative
COOS Bay (laurel); Indian
COOT rail; surf duck; dolt
COPA tree; yaya; landmark
COPE vestment; cover; bend; contend
COPT Egypt. Christian

COPY duplicate; mimic; follow; text
CORA gazelle; Indian; name; Persephone; Demeter's daughter
CORD string; twine; ribbed fabric; measure (wood)
CORE heart; nucleus; gist
CORI Carl, Gerty (Nobel winners)
CORK tree; bark; stop(per); brown; Irish city (Lee)
CORM bulblike stem (crocus)
CORN grain; ear, kernel; callus; whiskey; preserve; granulate(d); clavus; banality; red-yellow
COSE (friendly) chat
COSH snug; happy; math. term
COSO open space: Sp.
COSS measure
COSY snug; teapot cover
COTA P.I. fort
COTE birdhouse; sheep shed; coast: Fr. (d'Or; d'Azur)
COTO bark; stomachic
COTY Fr. statesman; cosmetics
COUE psychotherapist ("Day by day . . .")
COUP blow; master stroke
COUS cowlike
COVE bay; recess; pass; chap; Gypsy
COWL hood; auto body front
COXA hip (joint)
COXE Capt. (Scott)
COYN corner(stone)
COYO avocado; chinin
COZE (friendly) chat
COZY snug; teapot cover
CRAB crustacean; apple; sign; anger
CRAG cliff; neck
CRAL hut; village
CRAM press; stuff; study
CRAN bird; measure
CRAP dregs; money; dice cast (craps)
CRAW gullet; stomach
CRAX curassow (bird)
CREA linen, cotton fabric
CREE Indian
CREW company; gang; -cut
CREX corn crake (bird)
CRIB manger; hut; bin; box; steal; "pony," "trot"
CRIC lamp condensing ring
CRIG blow
CRIN heavy silk
CRIS dagger; stab
CROC harquebus support; crocodile
CROM Cruaich (Irish idol)
CROP craw; harvest; trim
CROW raven; corvine bird; bar; black; Indian; Jim —; -bar
CRUS leglike part; shank
CRUX (Southern) Cross; crucial point
CUBA W.I. island; Pearl of Antilles; measure
CUBE square solid; 3rd power; die; plant poison
CUBI measure
CUCA cocaine source
CUFF slap; manacle; sleeve end; miser; on the —
CUIR leather; dorado
CUKE cucumber
CULE diminutive suffix
CULL pick out; assort
CULM grass stem; coal dust; shoal water deposit
CULT sect; worship system
CUNA Panama Indian
CUON wild dog (dhole)
CURA parish priest: Sp.
CURB restrain(t); sidewalk edge; market
CURD coagulated milk
CURE heal; remedy; preserve; priest: Fr.
CURL coil; twist; hair lock
CURR to murmur (as owlet)
CURT short; concise
CUSH sorghum; cow; money; Ham's son; country
CUSK fish; burbot; eel
CUSP (crescent) point; tooth edge
CUSS curse; person
CUTE clever; attractive
CUVY sea girdles; kelp
CUYA hardwood tree
CVII 107; Trajan reign
CXII 112; Trajan reign
CXIV 114; Trajan reign
CXIX 119; Hadrian reign
CYAN green-blue
CYKE cyclorama
CYLE brewing; beer; wort

CYMA cornice molding
CYME inflorescence
CYON wild dog (dhole)
CYST box; abnormal sac
CYTE prefix: hollow vessel
CZAR emperor; dictator
DACE fish
DADA father; cult
DADE support
DADO wall part; groove
DADU saint
DAER re borrowed stock
DAEZ daze
DAFF put aside
DAFT foolish; giddy
DAGG pistol
DAGH hill
DAGO tribe
DAIL legislature; — Eireann
DAIN Patusan chief (Conrad); Curse (Hammett); measure
DAIS platform
DALE valley; share; trough
DALI tree; offering; Salvador —
DALL sheep
DAMA gazelle
DAME woman; title; — aux Camélias
DAMN curse; — the torpedoes
DAMP moist(ure); depress
DANA goddess; editor; author; lake
DANE Scandinavian; great — (dog); Hamlet
DANG curse (damn)
DANK moist; rank
DANS in: Fr.
DANU goddess
DARD language group
DARE venture; defy; fish; Virginia (1st Amer. child)
DARI grain sorghum; carpet
DARK unlighted; wicked; dismal
DARN mend; interjection
DARR bird
DART missile; fish; seam; run
DASH sprint; smash; small portion
DASI concubine
DASS Durga, Ram (twins, Kipling)
DATA facts
DATE fruit; tree; brown; (make) appointment
DATO tribal chief
DATU tribal chief
DAUB plaster; besmear
DAUD dad
DAUK relay post
DAUN — stage (geol. period)
DAUR Manchu
DAUW zebra
DAVE David
DAVY David; lamp; affidavit; Jones' locker
DAWK relay transport; mai
DAWM coin
DAWN daybreak; Eos; Aurora; red
DAYE printer (Bay Psalm Book)
DAYS by day
DAZA Negro-Berber
DAZE stupefy; mica
DAZY confused
DDAY operation start
DEAD deceased; entire; absolute(ly); — reckoning
DEAF unhearing; inattentive; — and dumb; — mute
DEAL bargain; transaction; unfinished wood; apportion(ment); policy: New —, Fair —
DEAN clergyman; educator; oldest member, doyen
DEAR costly; loved; loved one
DEBS Eugene (socialist)
DEBT fault; liability; obligation
DECA prefix: ten
DECI prefix: tenth
DECK ship floor; pack, cards; array; adorn
DEDO measure
DEED act; property transfer
DEEM consider; judge
DEEP profound; extensive; ocean
DEER ruminant; cervine; — Park (Buddha site)
DEFI challenge; defiance
DEFT skillful; trim
DEFY challenge; dare
DEGU rodent (Octodon)
DEHA body (theosophy)
DEIL devil; -'s-bit (plant)
DEIN your(s): Ger.
DEJA already: Fr.
DELE omit; erase
DELF quarry; pottery; blue
DELI delicatessen
DELL valley; dingle; wench
DEME Greek commune
DEMI prefix: half
DEMO prefix; populace
DEMY coin; scholar; paper size
DENE measure; dune; Indian
DENS tooth: Lat.
DENT depress(ion); notch
DENY refuse; contradict
DEPA measure

DERA suffix: neck types
DERE — Mable (Streeter book)
DERM prefix, suffix: skin layer
DESI jute; Arnaz
DESK table; lectern; department
DEUL Hindu temple
DEUM Te — (hymn)
DEUS god: Lat.; — ex machina
DEUX two: Fr.
DEVA deity (Indra); demon
DEVI goddess; Siva's wife (Shakti); title: Mrs., Lady
DEWA deity (Indra); demon
DEWY moist; refreshing
DHAI midwife
DHAK tree
DHAL split pea, lentil
DHAN wealth; loan
DHAO knife (Burma)
DHAR state; town (India)
DHAW billhook
DHER mound; land share
DHOW Arab. sailboat
DIAD pair
DIAL plate; face; call; sun-
DIAN reveille
DIAU Indian
DIAZ Bartholomeu (Port. navigator)
DIBS juice: grape, date
DICE (cut into) cubes; gamble; gaming implements
DICH you: Ger.
DICK Richard; whip; lad; detective; Whittington (London mayor)
DIDO trick; caper; Carthage queen, Aeneas' beloved
DIEB jackal
DIEM day: Lat.; per —
DIER one moribund
DIES day(s): Lat.; — irae; Cong. committee
DIET fare; food regimen; parliament
DIEU god: Fr.; mon —!
DIKA bread; fat; oil
DIKE levee; ditch; dig; goddess (Horae)
DILL flavoring herb; pickle
DILO poon tree
DIME coin; — novel
DINE eat; have dinner
DING thump; sound; urge
DINK small boat; cut out
DINO prefix: terrible
DINT blow; force; notch
DIOL chem. compound; suffix
DION lord in Winter's Tale
DIOS God: Sp.
DIRE evil; fatal; extreme
DIRK dagger; Theodoric
DIRT muck; earth; gossip; do one —; — cheap
DISA showiest orchid
DISC disk; record; — jockey
DISH receptacle; serve
DISK plate; harrow; puck
DISS reed grass
DITA tree; bark; upas
DITE mite; indict
DITT close up; obstruct
DIVA prima donna; blue
DIVE plunge; duck; low resort; — bomb(er)
DIVI divine ones
DIXI I have spoken: Lat.
DIXY camp pot
DOAB tract
DOAT drivel; be silly, overfond; wood rot
DOBE brick (house)
DOBY brick (house)
DOCE Brazil river
DOCK weed; rumex; (cur)tail; pier
DODD cut off (wool)
DODE nickname: Theodore
DODO extinct bird; reactionary
DOEG Saul's herdsman; poet's nickname; Indian
DOER performer; agent
DOES performs
DOFF put off; remove
DOGE Venice, Genoa ruler
DOGS scaup duck
DOGY calf; duck
DOIT coin; whit; bit
DOKO Afr. pygmy
DOLA weight
DOLE ration; (relief) alms; deal (out)
DOLI weights
DOLL plaything; puppet; dress up; girl
DOLT dunce; ignoramus
DOME edifice; cupola; roof
DOMN Rumanian ruler; lord
DOMY domelike
DONA lady; sapek (coin)
DONE agreed; exhausted
DONG sound; weight; ding-; money
DONI fishing boat
DONT contraction; prohibition
DOOB Bermuda grass
DOOK wooden brick; demon
DOOM (last) judgment;

fate; condemn
DOON tree (varnish resin)
DOOR portal; entrance; open — policy
DOPA chemical (pigment test) crystalline
DOPE drug; information; guess; nitwit
DOPP diamond cup
DOPY sluggish
DORA Mrs. David Copperfield
DORE bullion; gold; pike; Paul Gustave (Fr. artist)
DORM dormitory; sleep
DORN thornback ray
DORP hamlet; city (So. Afr.)
DORR Rebellion (R.I.)
DORY John (fish); boat
DOSA sheik's ritual ride; hatred
DOSE portion; (give) medicine
DOSS bed; sleep; — house
DOST (you) do: archaic
DOTE love to excess; drivel; timber rot
DOTH does
DOTO sea slug genus
DOTY discolored by rot
DOUB Bermuda grass
DOUC variegated monkey
DOUM palm
DOUP weaver's thread
DOUR sullen; gloomy
DOVE pigeon; — blue, gray; Columba; plunged
DOWD slovenly woman
DOWL feathery down
DOWN to below; reduce; defeat; feathers; eider-; dejected
DOXA religious stanzas
DOXY doctrine; hussy
DOZE drowse; timber rot
DOZY drowsy; decayed; doty
DRAA measure
DRAB dull; box; wench; cloth; drug
DRAG haul; harrow; obstacle; puff; auto race
DRAH measure
DRAM measure; drink
DRAP cloth
DRAT oath
DRAW drag; attract; gain; infer; extract; sketch; undecided contest
DRAY cart; squirrel's nest; — horse
DRED Scott (slave)
DREE endure; tedious
DREG lees; residue
DREI three: Ger.
DREW sketched; pulled
DREY squirrel's nest
DRIB drop; a little
DRIN Balkan river
DRIP let fall
DROP globule; fall; discard; minim; trap door; die; pendant
DRUB (beat with) stick
DRUG medicine; dope; — on the market; — addict
DRUM spool; instrument: tympanum; beat
DRUN road (Gypsy)
DUAB tract
DUAD pair
DUAL double
DUAN canto; poem
DUAR mountain pass
DUAT Hades
DUBB Syrian bear; lizard
DUCE chief: It.; Mussolini
DUCK bird; webfoot; wild fowl; canvas; pet; plunge; evade; -soup; vehicle
DUCO pyroxylin lacquer
DUCT tube; vessel; pipe
DUDE dandy; fop; city fellow; — ranch
DUDS clothes; failures
DUEL combat; meeting
DUET music for two
DUFF pudding; cheat
DUFY Raoul (Fr. artist)
DUHR star
DUIM measure
DUIN demons
DUIT Chibchan Indian; coin
DUKE prince; cherry
DUKU lanseh tree fruit
DULL blunt(ed); dismal; inert, tedious; Shaks. character
DULY properly; timely
DUMA Russ. parliament
DUMB mute; stupid; — waiter, deaf and —
DUMP unload; junkyard; thud; mean place; holey dollar
DUNE sandhill; twine color
DUNG excrement; fertilize(r); weight
DUNK dip into; immerse
DUNS dull; stupid
DUNT split (ceramics)
DUNY having many dunes
DUOS duets
DUPE trick(ed one); copy
DURA — mater

(spinal membrane)
DURN gatepost
DURO Sp. peso; dollar
DURR grain sorghum
DUSE Incubus; Eleanora (actress)
DUSK twilight; gloom
DUST powdered matter; rubbish; clean; dust to —; gold —
DUTY obligation; task; tax
DYAD pair
DYAK Bornean
DYAS Permian (geol. period)
DYCE thus!: naut. command
DYCK Anthony Van (painter)
DYER tinter; Mary (Quaker martyr)
DYKE levee; checkers opening
DYNA prefix: power
DYNE unit of force

EABA measure
EACH every(one)
EADS engineer; bridge
EARL nobleman; count; name
EARN gain; win; deserve
EASE repose; comfort; moderate; facilitate
EAST direction; Asia; Orient
EASY simple; calm; soft; — Street
EATS food; consumes
EAUX waters: Fr.
EAVE roof edge
EBAL Mount (Joshua's altar)
EBED Gaal's father
EBEN Ebenezer
EBER Hebrew ancestor
EBOE tree; oil; Negrito
EBON ebony; black
EBRO Sp. river
EBUR ivory: Lat.
ECAD modified organism
ECCA geol. period (Karroo)
ECCE lo: Lat.; — homo
ECHO Narcissus's nymph; repeat; response; fruit tree (gingko)
ECHT genuine: Ger.
ECRU beige; unbleached
ECTO prefix: outside
EDAM city; cheese
EDAR Bib. site
EDDA Norse epic
EDDO taro root
EDDY whirlpool; Mary Morse Baker (Christian Science)
EDEA reproduction organs
EDEL noble: Ger.
EDEN paradise; West of Nod
EDER river
EDGE brink; sharpness; goad; advantage; — on
EDGY sharp; snappish
EDIT correct; redact; blue-pencil
EDNA female name; Ferber (novelist)
EDOM Esau's country; Idumaea
EELY wriggling; slippery
EENY —, meeny, miny, mo
EERY weird; uncanny; timid
EFIK Negro
EFOD priestly garb; image
EGAD oath
EGAL equal: Fr.
EGAN horse (Kipling)
EGBA Negro; Yoruba
EGBO secret society (Ogboni)
EGER river
EGGS ova; — and bacon, ham; — and butter (flowers)
EGGY egg-stained; yolky
EGIL Volund's (Wayland's) brother
EGIS protection; patronage; shield (symbol of Zeus, Athena)
EGMA enigma
EGOL antiseptic
EHEU alas
EHUD judge of Israel
EIDE ideas; forms
EINE one: Ger.
EILD barren; milkless
EIRE Ireland; Erin
EJAM Bantu
EJOO palm; fiber
EKER water cress
EKKA carriage
EKOI Bantu
ELAH king
ELAM kingdom
ELAN dash; ardor
ELBA Napoleon's exile isle
ELBE river
ELEF letter
ELEN biblical jurist
ELIA Charles Lamb (essayist)
ELIM Bib. oasis
ELIS Greek city-state
ELLA Eleanor; she: Sp.; fem. suffix
ELLE measure; she: Fr.
ELMY rich in elms
ELOD alleged force
ELOI Eli; God
ELON Esau's father-in-law; college (N.C.)
ELSA — of Brabant (Lohengrin's bride)
ELSE other(wise); besides
ELUL month
EMER Cuchulainn's wife (ideal womanhood)

EMEU bird (ostrich-like)
EMIL man's name
EMIM Moabites; giants
EMIR ruler; title
EMIT eject; issue; voice
EMMA letter M; name; Austen novel; Bovary (Flaubert)
EMMY TV award; nickname
EMOL rock salt
EMPT empty
EMYD terrapin
EMYS tortoise
ENAM gift; land grant
ENAN Prince of Naphtali
ENCE suffix
ENDO prefix: within
ENID fem. name; Geraint's wife; city
ENIF star
ENIN blue grape pigment
ENKI Babylonian god
ENNA Sicilian resort
ENNE prefix: nine; fem. suffix
ENNS river
ENOL chem. suffix
ENON Paris's wife (nymph); John the Baptist site
ENOS Seth's son, Adam's grandson (905 years old); taken by God
ENOW enough
ENSE suffix
ENTE grafted (Her.); being: Sp.
ENTO prefix: inner
ENVY covet; grudge; 7th deadly sin
ENYO war goddess
ENZU moon god (Sin)
EOAN pert. to east; dawn
EOIN John; Sean
EPEE fencing sword
EPHA Heb. dry measure
EPHI measure
EPIC heroic poem
EPOS epic poetry; events
EPPY Euphemia
EQUI prefix: equal, same
ERAL epochal
ERAN Ephraim's grandson
ERAT was: Lat.; quod — demonstrandum (Q.E.D.)
ERDA earth goddess; Wagner role
ERER sooner
ERGO hence; prefix: work
ERIA silk(worm)
ERIC male name; Viking; the Red
ERIE Iroquoian; lake; city
ERIN Eire; Ireland
ERIS goddess of discord, Ares' sister
ERMA Ermengarde
ERNE sea eagle
EROS (god of) love; Cupid; asteroid; Antony's friend
ERRA — Pater (almanac)
ERSE Irish; Gaelic
ERST former; first
ERUA mother goddess
ERUC cordage fiber
ERYX sand snake
ESAU Isaac's, Rebecca's son; Jacob's twin; hairy; red; Edom
ESAY Isaiah
ESCA apoplexy (plant disease)
ESCE suffix: begin to be
ESEK Isaac's well
ESER weight
ESNE slave
ESOP fable writer
ESOX fish (pike, pickerel, muskellunge)
ESPY behold; detect; meteorologist
ESSE existence; to be: Lat.
ESTA this: Sp.
ESTE It. family; this: Sp.
ESTH Balt; Estonian (Tallinn man)
ESUS Gaulish god (Mars)
ETAH Eskimo settlement; town
ETAL and others: Lat.
ETAT state: Fr.; L' — c'est moi!
ETCH eat into; engrave
ETES (you) are: Fr.
ETNA stove; volcano
ETON school, college; collar, jacket; playing field of —
ETRE exist; be: Fr.; raison d'—
ETTA Henrietta; Harriet
ETTE suffix: fem.
ETUI (vanity) case; box
ETYM Moabites, giants; abbr.: word sources
EUER your(s): Ger.
EUGE bravo!
EVAN name (Welsh)
EVAT eft
EVEA madder (tree); ipecac
EVEN evening; level; fair(ly); equal(ly); moderate; just; not odd; flush
EVER always; at anytime
EVET eft; newt
EVIL bad; sinful; injury; disease
EVOE bacchanals' wild cry; Punch editor
EWAN name (Welsh)
EWER pitcher; udder
EWRY linen storeroom
EXAM interrogation; test

EXES letters; expenses
EXIT depart(ure); die
EXON Exeter man
EYAH nurse; sign
EYAS nestling
EYED looked at; ogled
EYER needle maker
EYEY having holes
EYOT islet
EYRA wild cat
EYRE Jane (Brontë heroine); circuit (court)
EYRY bird's nest
EZAN prayer call
EZBA measure
EZEL juniper tree
EZRA prophet; OT book

FAAM tea; leaves
FABA bean; vetch
FACE surface; oppose; line
FACT deed; reality
FACY fresh
FADE weaken; flat; dissolve
FADO tune
FADY weakening
FAEX dregs
FAIL fall short; err
FAIN glad; eager
FAIR pleasing; ample; just; ar; — and square; — deal
FAIT fact; — accompli
FAKE loop; cheat; sham
FAKY spurious
FALA refrain; dog
FALL descend; ruin; autumn; — of Man
FALX weapon; — cerebri (brain fold)
FAMA rumor
FAME reputation
FAMN measure
FANA Sufistic concept
FANE temple
FANG tooth; measure; Dickens character
FANO cloth; cape
FAON fawn color
FARD face paint; date
FARE passenger; price; happen; food; travel
FARL cake (part)
FARM till; land; — out; club
FARO card game; Pharaoh
FASH rough edges; vex
FASS measure
FAST not eat; fixed(ly); quick(ly); wild; — and loose
FATA — Morgana (fairy, mirage)
FATE destiny (goddess); end; kismet
FAUN deity; satyr
FAUT comme il — (proper): Fr.
FAVI tiles; flagstones
FAVN measure
FAWN deer; cringe; toady; brown
FAZE disturb
FEAK twitch; wipe
FEAL conceal
FEAR fright; doubt
FEAT deed; accomplishment
FECK amount
FEED nourish; gratify; graze; fodder
FEEL sense; test; suffer
FEES charges; tips
FEET measure
FEIL comfortable; neat
FEIS convention; — of Tara
FEKE trick device
FELD field: Ger.
FELL skin; cut, hew (down); savage
FELS Eastern coin
FELT pressed fibers; hat; sensed
FEME wife; tribunal
FEND keep off; parry
FENT slit; cleft
FEOD feudal estate
FERK measure
FERN seedless plant
FERU bast fiber
FESS broad band (Her.); confess
FEST festive gathering
FETE festival; regale
FEUD strife; vendetta; fee
FIAT sanction; edict; money; automobile (It.)
FICO trifle
FIDE entrust; — et amore
FIDO fog evaporation; dog's name
FIEF feudal estate
FIFE flute; checkers opening
FIFO inventory method
FIJI Islands (Lau, Yasawa)
FILE tool; rasp; smooth; march; column; folder; arrange
FILI learned poet
FILL pack; complete; glut; — the bill
FILM skin; coating; haze; photograph; picture
FILO silk thread
FILS son: Fr.; Dumas (Camille); Iraq coin
FIND discover(y); (re)gain
FINE end; superior; thin; keen; well; (set) penalty; gell —, derb — (Irish clans)
FINK finch; derb; informer; strikebreaker
FINN man of Finland, Helsinki; Ugric; Mickey (KO drops); Huckle-

berry (Twain novel)
FIOT Congo tribe
FIPS Martin Chuzzlewit
FIRE combustion; ardor; discharge
FIRM fixed; solid; company
FIRN granular snow(field)
FISC exchequer
FISH piscine; angle; probe; search; tin — (torpedo)
FISK exchequer; Jim (speculator); tire
FIST grasp; effort; tightwad
FIVE number; basketball team; card
FIXE prix —
FIZZ hissing sound; drink
FLAG flower; standard; stone; signal; limp; reduce, dwindle
FLAK antiaircraft
FLAM trick; drum beat
FLAN tart; disk; net
FLAP slap; leaf; sway; -jack
FLAT level; (make) insipid; dull; wholly; — tire
FLAW crack; defect; wind
FLAX plant; fiber; thrash
FLAY (strip off) skin
FLEA insect; puce; — market
FLED ran away: shunned
FLEE run away; shun
FLEM Fleming; Belgian
FLEW aviated; winged
FLEX bend
FLEY fright(en)
FLIP toss; tap; drink; hop
FLIT flutter; move
FLIX down; fur; flax
FLOB move clumsily
FLOC flock(y mass); shreds
FLOE floating ice
FLOG whip
FLOP slump down; flap; change; fail(ure); bed; sleep
FLOT lateral ore deposit
FLOW gush; stream; flux; roll; ebb and —
FLUB blunder; botch
FLUE net; lint; barb; air passage; pipe
FLUX flow; change; melt
FOAL colt; equine young
FOAM froth; rage; rubber
FOCH Ferdinand (Fr. marshal; WW I commander)
FOCI center points
FOGG Phileas (Verne)
FOGO stench
FOGY dull, bigoted man
FOHN warm dry wind
FOIE liver: Fr.; — gras (pâté)
FOIL balk; defeat; sword; leaf; sheet
FOLD plait; envelope; fail; quit; flock
FOLK people; — ways, laws, song, dance
FOND basis; fount; loving
FONG Ewe-speaking Negro
FONO Samoan council
FONT basin; spring; stoup; type
FONS fount; source
FOOD nutriment; victuals
FOOL dolt; jester; trick
FOOT pedal part; base; dance; trip; skip; pay; add
FORA meeting places; courts
FORB non-grassy herb
FORD crossing shallow; Henry (automobile); Shaks. character
FORE front; prior; golf cry
FORK implement (pronged); tuner; place of divergence
FORM shape; mold; fashion; school grade
FORT stronghold; trading post; dun
FOSS canal; ditch; moat
FOUD district magistrate
FOUL rotten; poor; illegal; invalid
FOUR number; card; boat
FOWL poultry; cock; hen
FOXY wily; brown; rank; sour
FRAB worry
FRAM spear
FRAP tighten
FRAT fraternity
FRAU Mrs., wife, Mme., woman: Ger.
FRAY contest; tumult; wear off
FREA Frigg; Odin's wife; goddess
FRED nickname
FREE independent; immune; rid; exempt; — and easy; — lance, port, trade, style
FRET gnaw; vex; worry; embroider; ridge; ornament
FREY god (Njorth's son, Gerth's

husband)
FRIA Frigg (Odin's wife)
FRIB dirty short wool
FRIM juicy; soluble
FRIT fuse; partly; fried: Fr.; waste
FRIZ curl; crisp; wig
FROE cleaver; steel wedge
FROG amphibian; hoarseness; loop; rail device
FROM out of
FROT rub; chafe
FROW Dutch woman; cleaver
FRUG dance
FUAD Arab king
FUCI rockweeds; algae
FUEL combustible matter
FUGA fugue: It.
FUGU poisonous fish
FUJI wisteria; cherry; volcano
FULA Sudanese
FULK unfair shove (marbles)
FULL filled; replete; quite; — dress; — house
FUME smoke; fit; rage
FUMY vaporous; smoky
FUND supply; finance; money; sinking —
FUNG Sennar Negroid
FUNJ Sennar Negroid
FUNK fear; coward; Casimir (vitamins); Isaac (lexicographer); — & Wagnalls
FUNT weight; Allen (TV)
FURL roll up (sail, flag)
FURY rage; avenging spirit; Erinys, Fate, Parca

(Atropos)
FUSC dusky; somber
FUSE detonator; melt; unite
FUSS tumult; bustle; -budget
FUST pilaster; smell stale
FUTE Eskimo curlew
FUYE Jap. flute
FUZE detonator; melt; unite
FUZZ fine fibers; police
FYKE fish bag net
FYRD old English army

GAAL brewing
GABE taro
GABI taro
GABY fool
GADE fish; composer
GADS -hill (Dickens)
GAEA goddess; Titans' mother
GAEL Celt; Irishman
GAFF spear; ordeal; hoax
GAGE pledge; fruit; gauge; general; governor
GAGL sweet gale
GAIA goddess
GAIL Abigail; brewing
GAIN reach; earn; profit; notch
GAIT walk; pace
GAJO non-Gypsy
GALA festival; tribe
GALE storm, wind
GALI abuse
GALL bile; venom; wound; chafe; swelling; impudence
GALT clay bed
GAMA Vasco da (navigator); grass
GAMB leg
GAME amusement; quarry; resolute; lame
GAMP umbrella; Sairey (nurse: Dickens)
GANE yawn
GANG crew; associate; rock
GANO Count (Roland's destroyer)
GANT yawn; gaunt; gannet; Eugene (Wolfe character)
GANZ all, totally: Ger.
GAOL prison
GAON Jewish title
GAPA guided missile
GAPE yawn; stare; gap
GAPO (inundated) forest
GAPY yawning
GARA coin
GARB apparel; array
GARE wool; station, beware: Fr.
GARM Hel's dog
GARN yarn; go on
GARO Assam native
GARY city, steel center
GASH (make) incision
GASP pant (eagerly)
GATA nurse shark
GATE entrance; pass; judgment; money
GATH Philistine city
GAUB persimmon (astringent)
GAUD ornament; bead
GAUE German regions
GAUL Celt, Frenchman; France
GAUM attention
GAUP gape
GAUR wild cattle
GAUS region: Ger.
GAUT range; pass; river bank stairs
GAVE donated
GAWD ornament; bead
GAWK lout; stare
GAWN gallon; tub
GAWP gape; simpleton
GAZA Israel (Philistine) seaport; Mozambique

district; eyeless in — (Samson)
GAZE stare; wonder
GAZI warrior; title
GAZY gaping
GEAL pert. to earth
GEAN cherry
GEAR notched wheel; equipment; adjust; harmonize
GEAT channel in mold; Scandinavian (Beowulf)
GEBA Jonathan's victory site
GEEK carnival wild man
GEEZ Version (Ethiopic Bible)
GEIN glucoside (Geum urbanum)
GELD castrate; prune; tax
GELT money
GENA cheek; beak part
GENE hereditary factor; chromosome part; nickname
GENS clan: Lat.; people: Fr.
GENT gentleman; Belg. city
GENU knee: Lat.
GEON paradise river; Jerusalem spring
GERA city
GERB sheaf; firework
GERD Frey's wife
GERE Odin's wolf
GERI Odin's wolf
GERM bud; seed; microbe
GEST deed; romance tale, adventure
GESU Jesus: It.
GETA Jap. wooden clogs
GETT bill of divorce
GEUM plant (astringent)
GHAT range; bank; river bank stairs
GHEE butter
GHEG Albanian
GHES Tapuyan Indian
GHOR Dead Sea valley
GHOS Chin. dynasty
GHUZ Turkish invader
GIAN -Carlo (Menotti)
GIBE scoff; jeer; agree
GIDE André (author)
GIER eagle (vulture)
GIFT donation; talent
GIGA medieval fiddle
GILA — monster; lizard; Ariz. river
GILD lay gold on; adorn; — the lily; trade society
GILL measure; brook; breathing organ; wattle; coin; lass
GILO woody vine (tonic)
GILT gold; sow
GIMP silk fabric; vim
GINK eccentric one
GIRD encircle; clothe; brace
GIRL young female; maid; Gibson —; — Friday; — of the Golden West; chorus —
GIRO tour; round; credit system; aircraft (auto-)
GIRT encircled; prepared
GISH Moroccan public land; Lillian, Dorothy (actresses)
GIST main point; pith
GITA Bhagavad —; Indian scriptures (yoga)
GITE shelter: Fr.; mad
GIVE bestow; yield; grant
GIZA site: pyramids, Sphinx
GJOA ship (Northwest Passage: Amundsen)
GLAD pleased
GLED kite; buzzard
GLEN rival
GLIA neuroglia (nerve tissue)
GLIB flippant, smooth(ly)
GLIM light; eye
GLIS dormouse genus
GLOM watch; steal
GLOP look wildly; stare
GLOW shine; incandesce; flush; ardor; wax
GLUB make gulping sound
GLUE adhesive; stick
GLUG sound of liquids
GLUM moody; sullen
GLUT sate; surfeit; oversupply; wedge
GMAN U.S. police agent
GNAR growl
GNAT (biting) fly
GNAW bite; corrode
GOAD rod; decoy; urge
GOAF grain; rick
GOAI shrub
GOAL purpose, objective; score
GOAN pert. to Goa
GOAT ruminant; scape-; brown
GOBI Mongolian desert
GOBO burdock; okra; camera; mike shield
GOBY fish; passing
GOEL reclaimer; avenger
GOER runner
GOES walks; proceeds
GOFF clown; fool

GOGH Vincent van (painter)
GOGO vine; bark soap; beetle; bugaboo; Bantu; dancer
GOLA storeroom; caste; cyma
GOLD metal; element; — dust, medal
GOLF game; blood-red; — links
GOLI musket ball; pill
GOLL Irish hero (Fenian)
GOLO Nilotic Sudanese
GOLP roundel purpure (Her.)
GOMA Bantu (Wagoma)
GONA New Guinea victory
GOND Dravidian Indian
GONE departed; enamored; lost; germ cell
GONG bell; tom-tom
GONY albatross
GOOD able; brave; sound; profit; happiness; welfare; benefit
GOOF dolt; blunder
GOOK trash; ooze; native
GOOM cultivation method
GOON thug; strikebreaker
GOOP nonsense creature
GOOR sugar; massecuite
GORA musical instrument
GORE stab; blood; triangular insert
GORY bloody; murderous
GOSH oath; -awful
GOTH Teuton (Theodoric, Alaric); barbarian; Ostro-, Visi-
GOUL monster; grave robber
GOUR cattle; koulan (onager)
GOUT drop; disease (arthritis); taste: Fr.
GOWK simpleton; fool
GOWL gad; defile; howl; monster
GOWN dress; toga; robe
GOYA Sp. painter; — red
GRAB grasp; capture; game
GRAD centesimal unit
GRAF nobleman: Ger.; — Spee (Zeppelin)
GRAM sword; plant; weight; —'s method; grandma
GRAN weight; grandma
GRAO weight
GRAS horse; foie — (pâté)
GRAY dull; dismal; hoary; Dorian (Wilde); Asa (botanist); Elisha (inventor)
GRAZ Austrian city (Mur)
GRES stoneware: Fr.
GREW increased
GREY color; neutral; dull; Zane (writer); Vivian (Disraeli novel)
GRID grating
GRIG dwarf; cricket; fowl
GRIM ruthless; ghastly
GRIN smile
GRIP grasp; power; valise; Barnaby's raven (Dickens)
GRIS gray: Fr.
GRIT sand(stone); bravery; grate
GROG liquor (with water)
GROS coin; fabric; weight
GROT cave; Bremen coin
GROW expand; sprout; wax; develop
GRUB larva; food; dig(ger)
GRUE shiver; shudder
GRUM morose; guttural
GRUS constellation (Crane)
GUAD tree
GUAM Mariana island
GUAN bird
GUAO tree
GUAR legume; cluster bean
GUEG Albanian
GUFA round boat
GUFF humbug; chaff
GUGU P.I. soldier; insurrecto
GUHA Bantu
GUHR earthy deposit
GUIB harnessed antelope
GULA upper throat; goddess (Ninurta's consort)
GULE of August (Lamma's Day)
GULF bay; chasm; eddy
GULL bird; cheat; dupe
GULO wolverine genus
GULP swallow; catch breath
GUMI shrub, flower, fruit
GUMP silly, stupid one; Andy, Chester, Min (cartoon family)
GUNA Sankhya term
GUNJ granary; market
GUNL gunwale
GUNK jilt; hoax
GUNN castaway (Stevenson)
GURU teacher
GUSH flow; spout; be effusive
GUST outburst of wind
GUTI Sumer settler;

Kurd
GUZE red roundel (Her.)
GWYN Llud's son; deity
GYBE jibe; scoff; agree
GYLE brewing; wort; vat
GYNE prefix: female
GYPS gypsum
GYRE turn; ring; vortex
GYRI brain ridges
GYRO prefix: ring, spiral
GYVE fetter; shackle

HAAB year
HAAF fishing grounds
HAAK fish; wander
HAAR fog
HABA bean
HABE tribe
HABU pit viper
HACK chop; writer; horse
HADE angle; strip
HADJ pilgrimage
HAEC this one (fem.): Lat.
HAEM prefix: blood
HAFF lagoon
HAFT handle
HAGG demoness; hack; wood
HAGI clover; prefix: saint
HAHA laugh; fence
HAHN Otto (Nobel physicist)
HAIG soldier (Douglas)
HAIK garment; frame
HAIL ice pieces; salute; — fellow
HAIR filament; cilium, seta; fabric; -trigger
HAJE cobra
HAJI pilgrim
HAJJ pilgrimage
HAKA dance
HAKE fish; pester; frame
HAKH claim(er); legal claim; share
HAKO rite
HAKU fish
HALA pine tree
HALE healthy; Nathan (patriot)
HALF moiety; -breed, -caste, -nelson, -shell
HALI prefix: sea, salt
HALL building; room; town —; guild-; astronomer; -Mills
HALM plant stems
HALO circle; glow; nimbus; prefix: sea, salt
HALS Frans (painter)
HALT stop; lame
HAMI hooked processes
HAND control; aid; worker; measure; pass; player; cards; penmanship
HANG suspend; plan; bit; die on gallows
HANK coil; Morgan (Twain)
HANO Indian
HANS John; Johannes; Castorp (Mann)
HANT ghost
HAPH weight
HAPI bull; Nile (god)
HAPU clan
HARA Jap. statesman
HARB Bedouin
HARD solid; firm; close; severe; difficult
HARE leporid; rabbit; run
HARI river; Mata (spy)
HARK listen
HARL barb; filament
HARM hurt; evil; injury
HARP coin; seal; Lyra; constellation; Irishman; nag
HARR hinge
HART stag; deer
HARZ German mountains
HASH chop up; mixture; mess
HASP clasp
HASS throat; embrace
HAST contraction: havest
HATE detest; aversion
HATH contraction: haveth
HATI heart
HATT measure
HAUL drag; shift; loot
HAUT high: Fr.; — monde
HAVE possess; aux. verb; must; deceive
HAWK bird; predator; peddle; mortarboard
HAWM loiter
HAYA arrow poison
HAYZ zodiacal situation
HAZE mist; drizzle; harass
HAZY dim; obscure
HEAD skull; top; brain; chief; crux; source
HEAF pasture
HEAL cure; restore
HEAP pile; crowd; car
HEAR listen; perceive by ear
HEAT warmth; rage; height; dead —; pressure; strain
HEBE cupbearer of gods; Zeus's daughter, Hercules' wife; color
HECK (weaving) frame; cough; oath
HEED notice; attention
HEEL back part; end; slant; follow; scoundrel
HEEP Uriah (Dickens villain)
HEER Mr., Sir: Dutch
HEFT weight; bulk;

notebook: Ger.
HEGH exclamation; hey!
HEHE Bantu tribe
HEII Hawaiian fern
HEIL hail: Ger.
HEIN surprise!: Fr.
HEIR inherit(or); — apparent, presumptive
HELA goddess; Loki's daughter
HELD kept; retained
HELI prefix: sun, spiral
HELL Hades; state of misery; -bent
HELM steer (wheel); tiller
HELO squeamish
HELP relieve; avoid; wait on, aid(e); servants
HEMA prefix: blood
HEME reduced hematin
HEMI prefix: half
HEMO prefix: blood
HEMP herb; hashish; cannabis; rope (fiber)
HENS fowl; -foot (herb)
HERA Zeus's sister, wife
HERB plant; nick-name
HERD crowd; feed together
HERE vicinity; pre-sent
HERL (feather) barb
HERO protagonist; demigod; — and Leander; Beatrice's cousin
HERR lord, Mister, Sir: Ger.
HERS fem., poss. pronoun
HEST command; precept
HETH son of Canaan; Hittite ancestor
HETT Hittite ancestor
HEVI apple (tree)
HEWN felled; squared
HICK hiccup; rube; jake
HIDE land measure; skin; conceal; shelter; — and hair
HIEL Jericho's rebuilder
HIEN Chin. govern-ment seat
HIER here: Ger.; yesterday: Fr.
HIFI faithful sound rendition
HIGH lofty; elevated; noble; expen-sive; shrill; tainted; tipsy
HIKE toss; tramp; raise
HIKU scabbard fish
HILA 'eyes' of bean
HILD Hethin's victim princess
HILL mound; Jenny (Shaw char-acter); -billy
HILO grass; city (Hawaii)
HILT sword
HIMA Hamitic Negro
HIND fish; grouper; deer; posterior
HING asafetida (gum resin; antispas-modic)
HINO timber tree; dye
HINT suggestion; imply
HIPE wrestler's throw
HIRE engage; rent; wage
HIRO measure
HISH hiss; swish
HISS sibilant (of disapproval); goose; serpent; steam sound; Alger (Com-munist)
HIST call to attention; Indian girl (Cooper)
HIVE bees' swarm, house
HLER sea god (wife: Ran)
HOAR frost; gray; -hound
HOAX deceive; trick
HOBB havoc; fireplace ledge; pin; peg
HOBO vagrant worker
HOCH high: Ger.
HOCK leg joint; hamstring; wine; faro card; pawn
HOEK stream bend; van Holland (Dutch cape, city)
HOEN weight
HOER scraper
HOEY partnership (Hawaii)
HOGA hill pasture
HOGG unshorn sheep
HOGO taint; stench
HOHE Siouan tribe
HOJA title; teacher
HOJU Jap. army reserve
HOLA fish poison; herb; hello
HOLD grasp; have; retain; believe; keep; bear; lair; prison
HOLE pit; cavity; flaw; — in one; — card; ace in the —
HOLI spring festival
HOLL ditch
HOLM holly; oak; islet
HOLT willow planta-tion; hill; lair; Eliot hero; actor
HOLY sacred; pious; — City; — Alliance; — Roller
HOMA sacred drink
HOME habitat; asy-lum; plate; natural
HOMO man; — sapiens; prefix: same
HOMY homey; inti-mate
HONE sharpen(er)
HONG Chin. trade

guild
HONI — soit qui mal y pense; shamed
HONK goose cry; toot; ooga
HOOD cowl; cloak; seal; gangster; Thomas (poet)
HOOF ungula; foot; beast; walk; dance
HOOK trap; curve; catch; steal; — and eye; pirate (Peter Pan: Barrie)
HOON coin; gold pagoda
HOOP circle(t); wicket; — skirt
HOOT derisive (owl's) cry
HOPE trust, expect(ation); wish; -chest
HOPI French beige; Moqui Indian
HOPS beer
HORA book of hours; Israeli dance
HORN prong; antenna; trumpet; brass wind; cup; Cape —
HORS out of: Fr.; — d'oeuvre
HOSE stockings; pipe; drench
HOSS house; One — Shay (Holmes)
HOST army; throng; bread as Christ's body; innkeeper; person having guests
HOTH blind god (Balder slayer)
HOTI cause; reason
HOUR time unit; H- or zero —
HOVA Madagascar native; Malagasy
HOVE ground ivy; raised
HOWE hollow; empty; Elias (inventor); Julia Ward (Battle Hymn); Brit. general, admiral
HOWL (distress) cry; wail
HOYA honey plant (milkweed)
HSIA 1st Chin. dynasty
HUBB pipe end
HUCH Danube fish
HUCK towel fabric
HUED colored; tinged
HUEY Long (La. governor)
HUFF inflate; bully; anger
HUGE enormous; immense
HUGH name; saint (of Cluny)
HUGO name; Victor (novelist)
HUIA bird (starling)
HUIT eight: Fr.
HUKE hooded cape
HULA Hawaiian dance
HULE caucho source
HULK ship body; bulky thing
HULL husk; ship body; Cordell (statesman)
HULU o-o's feather tuft
HUMA Uganda Negro
HUME philosopher
HUMP protuberance; mound; crisis; Himalayan peaks; -back
HUND dog: Ger.
HUNG suspended; undecided (jury)
HUNH exclamation
HUNK pierce; lump; OK
HUNT seek; chase; Leigh (writer)
HUON pine; timber tree
HUPA Athapascan Indian
HUPP call to horse
HURA bishop's cap; sandbox tree; possumwood
HURE head of boar, wolf
HURI Abihail's father
HURL throw; pitch; rush
HURR to snarl
HURT harm(ed); pain
HUSE beluga; whale; huchen
HUSH quiet; silence; -hush; -puppy; — money
HUSI fine P. I. fiber
HUSK covering (of seed, corn); shell
HUSO beluga; whale; huchen
HUSS dogfish; John (religious leader)
HUZZ buzz; murmur
HYDE — Park; Dr. Jekyll and Mr. —; measure
HYKE cry to urge dogs
HYLA frog; toad
HYLE matter (philos.); demon
HYMN song (of praise)
HYPE wrestler's throw; ad
HYPO photo solution; needle; injection
HYPS hypochondria
IAGO villain (Othello)
IALU Hades; heaven
IAMB verse foot
IBAD Hira Arab
IBAN dyak (Borneo)
IBEX wild goat; bouquetin
IBID P.I. lizard (tidbit); the same: abbr.
IBIS (sacred) wading bird
IBIT P.I. lizard (tidbit)
ICAL compound suffix
ICED frozen; chilled
ICER freezer; mixer
ICHO fruit tree

(gingko)
ICHU valuable grass
ICON image; statue
IDAS Marpessa's lover; Castor's slayer
IDEA conception; fancy; key meaning; opinion
IDEE — fixe: Fr.
IDEM same: Lat.; semper —
IDEN Henry VI figure
IDEO prefix: idea
IDES Roman date; — of March (fateful day)
IDIC pert. to ids
IDIO prefix: one's own
IDJO Niger delta Negro
IDLE not working; empty; lazy; waste
IDLY vainly; lazily
IDOL god, deity; image; adored one
IDUN Bragi's wife (Norse)
IDYL pastoral poem
IDYO Niger delta Negro
IDZO Niger delta Negro
IFFY contingent
IFIL tree (brown dye)
IGAL Moses' spy
IGLU Eskimo hut; seal hole
IGOR Prince (opera)
IHVH God; Tetragrammaton
IISM egoism
IIWI bird (mamo)
IJMA Moslem principle (Sunna)
IKAT shrub; weight
IKMO betel palm, pepper
IKON image; statue
IKRA superior caviar
ILAI David's man
ILEX holm oak; holly
ILIA (hip)bones
ILLE that one: Lat.
ILLS troubles
ILLY badly; ill
ILOG river (Tagalog)
ILOT islet; ait; eyot
ILUS son of Tros; Priam's grandfather
IMAM priest; title
IMBE cordage fiber plant
IMER Caucasian
IMID chem. compound
IMLA Micalah's father
IMMI measure
IMNA Asherites' chief
IMPI armed Kaffirs
IMPY impish
INBE be within
INCA Quechuan Indian (ruler)
INCH measure; move slowly
INDE blue (indigo)
INDY — pink (carnation)
INEE arrow poison
INEZ Don Juan's mother
INGA timber tree; mimosa
INGE prelate ("Gloomy Dean"); playwright (Bus Stop)
INIA Amazon cetacean
INKA Inca
INKY black; stained
INLY within; heartily
INRE concerning; actually
INRO Jap. receptacle
INTI Incas' deified sun; sun god
INTO penetrating; toward
IODO prefix: iodine
IOLA Kansas town
IOLE Eurytus' daughter (Hercules' captive)
IONA Scot. isle; Celt church; college
IONE Pompeii heroine (Bulwer-Lytton)
IONI Hainai; Chaddo Indian
IOTA Greek I, 10; jot
IOUS promissory notes; suffix
IOWA state; Indian
IPIL tree (brown dye)
IPSE himself: Lat.; — dixit
IPSO — jure, — facto
IRAD Enoch's son
IRAE Dies — (Day of Wrath)
IRAK country
IRAN Persia
IRAQ country
IRAS Cleopatra's maid
IRBM ballistics missile
IRID iris; crocus
IRIS rainbow; goddess; eye part; plant (flag); spirit (Shaks.); red-blue; March (Arien)
IRMA name
IROK gomuti (palm)
IRON metal; element; weapon; instrument; club; shackle; press; strong; Age
IRRA war god
IRUS Odyssey beggar
ISAR river (Munich)
ISBA log hut
ISER river
ISHA Upanishad
ISIS goddess; Osiris's wife, sister; Horus's mother
ISLE ait; eyot; insulate; key
ISMY doctrinaire
ISUI Asher's son
ITCH skin irritation; desire

ITEA shrub; Virginia willow
ITEM also; article; bit; entry
ITEN So. Amer. Indian
ITER road; passage (brain)
ITIS suffix: inflammation, mania; Tereus' son
ITMO betel pepper
ITOL suffix: alcohol(ic)
ITYS Tereus' son
ITZA Mayan Indian
IUNO Jupiter's wife
IVAH Bib. city
IVAN John; — the Terrible
IVER ever
IVES inventor (photo-engr.)
IWIS certainly
IXIA corn lily; bulb
IXIL Mayan Indian
IXLE cordage fiber
IYAR month
IYNX wryneck (woodpecker)
IZAR Moslem garment; star

JAAL goat
JACA tree
JACK flag; tool; card; fruit; raise
JACU bird
JADE gem; horse; exhaust
JADU magic
JADY gemlike
JAEL Sisera's killer; Heber's wife
JAGA Bantu
JAGG pendant; tooth; slash
JAIL prison; gaol
JAIN sect (Indian)
JAKE Jacob; rube; money; satisfactory; ginger
JAKO parrot
JAMA tunic
JAMB leg armor; pillar; door part
JAMI mosque
JANE woman; false hair; cloth; — Eyre; Lady — Grey
JANN genii
JAOB measure
JAPE deride
JARA palm
JARL Norse chief; earl
JASS card game; jack
JATI caste
JATO jet-assisted takeoff
JAUN palanquin
JAVA coffee; hood; (Indonesian) Sunda Isles; — man (Pithecanthropus)
JAVE Jehovah
JAWY talkative
JAZZ dance; music; banter
JEAN name; cotton cloth
JEEL pool; marsh
JEEP vehicle; automobile
JEER scoff; taunt
JEFE chief; leader
JEFF rope; nickname; Mutt and —
JEHU (chariot) driver; prophet, King (Israel)
JELL solidify; mature
JENA Ger. city (optical; Napoleonic victory); glass
JERK grab; twist; spasm; soda man; dullard; beef
JERL boat joint
JERM Levantine boat
JESS strap on hawk leg
JEST joke
JESU name: Jesus
JETE ballet jump
JETH Hindu month
JEUX cards, hands, games: Fr.
JEUZ chief Benjamite
JEWS -harp
JHOW tamarisk shrub
JHUM cultivation method
JHVH Jehovah; God; Tetragrammaton
JHWH Jahweh; God; Tetragrammaton
JIBE sneer; agree; coincide; shift course
JIBI extinct bird
JIFF instant
JILL girl; sweetheart; Jack and —
JILT betray in love
JINK prank
JINN demon; spirit
JINX hoodoo; bad luck
JITI Rajmahal creeper
JIVA life energy
JIVE dialect (dance, jazz)
JOAB (David's) captain
JOAD philosopher; Tom (Grapes of Wrath: Steinbeck)
JOAH record keeper
JOAN lass; cap; of Arc (the Maid, la Pucelle)
JOAR durra; millet
JOBO hog plum; gumbo limbo
JOCH yoke, measure: Ger.
JOCK John; jockey; hobo
JOCU dog snapper
JODO Buddhist paradise (Gokaruku)
JOEL prophet, OT book
JOEY coin; clown; odd-job man; young kangaroo; Pal (O'Hara character)
JOGI yogi; ascetic
JOHN name; saint, evangelist; cop; man; Bull

(England); Long — Silver (Stevenson)
JOIE — de vivre (zest for life)
JOIN mix; unite; coalesce
JOKE jest; laughing stock
JOKY jocular
JOLE jowl; cheek
JOLI pretty, nice: Fr.
JOLL move clumsily; knock
JOLT shake; hard blow
JOMS Vikings Norse colony
JONK jonquil
JOOK perch; slumber
JOOM cultivation method
JORD Odin's wife; Thor's mother
JOSE Carmen lover
JOSH make fun; banter
JOSS Chin. deity
JOSY nickname
JOTA Sp. peasant dance
JOTI astrologer; astronomer
JOUG iron collar; pillory
JOUR day: Fr.
JOVA Opata; Pimian Indian
JOVE god; Jupiter; Zeus
JOWL jaw; cheek; wattle; gambler (Dickens)
JOZY Josepha; Josephine
JUAN John; Don —, Don Giovanni
JUAR durra; millet
JUBA ghost; dance; mane; river
JUBE chancel screen; lozenge
JUCA cassava; manioc
JUCK partridge call
JUDA James' brother
JUDE name; NT book, author; Jew: Ger.; — the Obscure (Hardy)
JUDO self-defense art
JUDY name; Punch and —; Judith; Kipling character
JUEZ judge, juror: Sp.
JUGA carrot ridges; yokes
JUGE judge: Fr.
JUJU Afr. magic, charm
JUKE partridge call; — box; sociological name (with Kallikak)
JULA suspension bridge
JULE name: Julian, Julius
JULY (5th Roman) month
JUMP leap; bounce; move; headstart; — the gun
JUNE month; beetle; — moon, bride
JUNG young: Ger.; Carl Gustave (psychologist)
JUNK ship; trash; scrap
JUNO goddess; Jupiter's wife, Hera; stately woman; missile
JUPE skirt
JURA rights; mountain range
JURE de — (by law)
JURY (court) panel; committee; grand; petit —; hung —
JUSI fine P.I. fiber
JUST fair; virtuous; exact(ly)
JUTE fiber plant; Corchorus; Low German
JUZA star
JYNX wryneck; charm
KAAN inn; title
KAAT shrub; weight
KADA measure
KADE tick
KADI judge
KADU tribe
KAFA Ethiopian
KAGO conveyance
KAGS convict (Dickens)
KAGU bird
KAHA proboscis monkey
KAHN banker; test
KAHU harrier; bird
KAID chief; alcaide
KAIF languor; hemp
KAIK village
KAIL tree; ibex; kale
KAIN tribute
KAIO fruit
KAIR fiber
KAIS island
KAKA parrot
KAKI bird; tree
KALA bird
KALB de — (general)
KALE cabbage
KALI glasswort; carpet; evil genius; Agni's tongue; Siva's wife
KALO taro root
KAMA love god; desire; river
KAME hill
KAMI language; deity
KANA Japanese writing
KANE god
KANG — Hsi (Chinese emperor)
KANO painting school
KANT change course; Immanuel (philosopher)
KAON particle
KAPA cloth(es)
KAPH letter
KAPP measure
KAPU forbidden; taboo
KARA river
KARI gum tree
KARL Charles; — Marx

KARN stone heap
KARO plant
KASA grass
KASI tile work
KASM measure
KATE bird; Shaks. shrew; Greenaway
KATH astringent
KATI weight
KATY Catherine; -did
KAUN resthouse; lord; title
KAVA pepper shrub, root; gum resin; vein
KAVI Java language
KAWA pepper shrub, root; gum resin; vein
KAWI Java language
KAWN resthouse; lord; title
KAYO knock out
KAZI Moslem judge
KAZY Moslem judge
KEAL cabbage
KECK vomit; show disgust
KEEF hemp; languor
KEEK fashion spy
KEEL ship bottom; navigate; ocher; guinea fowl
KEEN sharp; acute; bewail
KEEP tend; retain; preserve; last
KEET guinea fowl
KEID star
KEIF hemp; languor
KEIR bleaching vat
KELA measures
KELD spring; fountain
KELE weight
KELK fish roe
KELL Gaul; net; film
KELP seaweed, iodine source
KELT Celt; cloth; trout
KEMP fur refuse
KENO lotto (game); prefix: empty
KENT Eng. county, duchy; Lear's follower
KEPI military cap
KEPT retained; lasted
KERB gutter part
KERE read(ing substitute)
KERF cut; notch
KERI read(ing substitute)
KERN soldier; peasant; grain; type part; Jerome (composer)
KERR physicist
KERS cress
KETA dog salmon
KETU eclipse demon (Rahu)
KEUP measure
KEYS House of (Isle of Man legislature); cays: Florida —
KHAN resthouse; lord; title; Agha —
KHAR weight
KHAS special; noble
KHAT measure
KHEM chief god (Min)
KHET mortal body; measure
KHOR watercourse; gorge
KHOT farmer; contractor
KIAK canoe
KIBE chilblain crack
KIBO Afr. peak (Kilimanjaro)
KICK hit; die; object(ion); excitement; -back
KIDD William (privateer)
KIDS star (Auriga)
KIEF hemp; languor
KIEL ocher; ruddle; seaport; — Canal
KIER bleaching vat
KIEV Ukranian city
KIFF languor
KIHO peacock butterfly
KIKI castor oil plant
KIKU chrysanthemum
KILE measure; weight
KILL slay; veto; creek
KILN (burn in) oven
KILO measure; -gram, -meter; prefix: 1000
KILT Scot's skirt
KINA quinine
KIND sort; species; gentle
KINE cattle
KING monarch; ruler; chief; chessman; card
KINK twist; loop; cramp
KINO gum (catechu); prefix: moving
KIPE basket
KIPP peak (Glacier National Park); gymnastic feat
KIRI paulownia tree; knobkerrie (missile)
KIRK church
KIRN harvest feast
KISH powder; basket; measure; Saul's father
KISS touch gently; caress; sweetmeat
KIST chest; installment; measure
KITE hawk; rogue; flying toy; banking fraud
KITH acquaintance; — and kin
KIVA ceremonial chamber
KIVE brewer's vat
KIVU tsetse fly
KIWI flightless bird; apteryx; nonflyer
KIYI herring; cisco; yelp
KLAM weight
KLAN Ku Klux —
KLEE Paul (painter)
KLIP rock; cliff
KLOM weight
KLOP hard sound
KMET Slav; tenant; mayor

KNAB nibble
KNAG spur; knot
KNAP summit; rap; talk; bite; button
KNAR knot; burr
KNEE joint; bend(ing)
KNEW understood; was aware
KNEZ Slavic prince
KNIP bite; crop; rap
KNIT looped, tie(d); unite; contract
KNOB lump; hill; antler; handle
KNOP button; finial; stud
KNOR knot (wood); gnarl
KNOT tie; loop; hitch; sandpiper; problem; blemish; stud; Gordian —
KNOW understand; recognize; -how; -nothing (party)
KNUB waste silk
KNUR gnarl; knot; wood ball
KNUT king; son of Magnus
KOAE red-tailed bird
KOBA antelope
KOBE Honshu port
KOBI Japanese reserve duty (term)
KOBU seaweed food (kelp)
KOCH cook: Ger.; Robert (bacteriologist)
KOEL cuckoo
KOFF Dutch sailboat
KOHL eye shadow; horse
KOIL cuckoo
KOJI Jap. yeast cake
KOKO bird; palm; tribe; executioner (Mikado)
KOKU measure
KOLA caffeine nut; jackal; river; city; bay (Murmansk)
KOLI low-caste tribesman
KOLO folk dance
KOME Greenland geol. division
KOMI Soviet republic; Zyrians
KONA Hawaiian storm; weight
KONK conk
KOOP purchase; bargain
KOPH Heb. K, Q, 100
KOPI N.Z. tree (karaka)
KOPT Copt
KORA water cock; Hottentot dialect; instrument
KORE Persephone; Demeter's daughter; chaos (Maori myth.)
KORI bustard; low weaver
KOSO tree; cusso; Panamint Indian
KOSS measure
KOTA P.I. fort; Dravidian language
KOTO Jap. zither
KOZO paper mulberry
KRAG rifle
KRAL hut; village
KRAN coin
KRAS tahr (goat)
KRIS dagger; stab
KROO Liberian Negro
KTKB chess move
KTKR chess move
KTKT chess move
KTQB chess move
KTQR chess move
KUAN pottery; official
KUAR month
KUBA carpet; measure
KUDU Afr. antelope
KUEI disembodied spirit
KUFA round boat
KUGE Jap. courtier
KUHL eyelid cosmetic
KUKI Burma Mongol
KUKU N.Z. fruit pigeon; kukupa
KULA measure; gift exchange
KULI low-cast Indian
KULM crane; heron
KULU old woman (Kipling)
KUNG public
KUNK measure
KURD Sunnite Mohammedan; Iranian
KURE Jap. city; Hawaiian isle
KURI Lezhgian tribesman
KURK church: Scot.
KURU disease
KUSA ceremonial grass
KUSH Ham's son; country
KVAS sour beer, cider (Russian)
KWAN coin; weight
KWEI disembodied spirit
KYAH partridge
KYAK canoe
KYAR coconut fiber
KYAT weight; Burmese money
KYKE fashion spy
KYLE sore; ulcer; farmer
LAAP secretion; insect
LABE city
LACE cord; flavor; netting
LACK need
LACT prefix: milk
LACY netlike
LADE load; dip
LADY title; bird
LAEL Gershonite's father
LAET freedman
LAGO lake
LAHN river
LAHR Bert (comedian)
LAIC secular
LAID put down; calmed
LAIN reclined
LAIR resting place
LAIS hetaera
LAIT milk: Fr.; café-au-
LAKE sea; pool; red

(cochineal)
LAKH 100,000; coin
LAKY red
LALO composer
LAMA priest; llama; brown; Dalai, Panchen, Tashi —
LAMB amateur speculator; Charles (Elia: essayist)
LAME cripple(d); halt; plate; fabric
LAMP light; bulb
LANA wood; flannel
LAND ground; debark; state: Ger.
LANE (fixed) route; throat
LANG auld — syne; Fritz
LANK thin; lean(ness)
LANX platter
LAON Fr. city
LAOS country
LAPP N. Scandinavian
LARA Byron poem
LARD fat; stuff
LARE Mid. Eng. lore
LARI money; sea birds
LARK bird; frolic; yellow
LARP secretion; insect
LARS Porsena (conqueror)
LASH (whip) stroke; tie; eye part
LASI tribe
LASS girl; sweetheart
LAST block: final(ly); endure; measure
LATA jumping disease
LATE dead; tardy
LATH strip; slat
LATU gold coins
LAUD praise
LAUK exclamation
LAUN ceramic sieve
LAVA fluid rock; obsidian's source; red
LAVE pour; bathe
LAWK surprise!
LAWN fabric; grass
plot; bishopric
LAWS rules; principles
LAZE idle(ness); tribesman
LAZI tribesman
LAZO lasso
LAZY idle
LEAD metal; element; plummet; bullets; color; guide; command
LEAF plant part; sheet; tea
LEAH fem. name; Leban's daughter; Jacob's wife
LEAK loss; ooze; crack
LEAL loyal: Scot.
LEAN be supported; incline; thin
LEAP jump, skip; — year
LEAR learning: Scot.; king; father of Goneril, Regan, Cordelia
LECH slab; capstone; river
LEDA mollusk; mother of Castor, Pollux, Helen, Clytemnestra; wooed by Zeus as swan
LEEK plant (onion; liliaceous); — green (Wales emblem)
LEER sly gaze; oven; loin
LEES dregs
LEET court; list
LEFT departed; blow; — of center (Liberals)
LEHI prophet
LEHR oven; Lew (comedian)
LEIF Ericson (explorer)
LEIL faithful, loyal (Land of the —)
LEIR sea god (Lear)
LELY Dutch painter
LENA firewood: Sp.; river; Conrad heroine
LEND make loan, grant; — an ear
LENE smooth; consonant
LENO (cotton, silk) fabric
LENS eye part; glass (optical); herb
LENT fasting period; slow; made loan
LEON country, city; Ponce de (explorer)
LERO Dodecanese isle
LERP secretion; insect
LESE — majesty (disrespect)
LESS shorter; fewer; inferior; minus
LEST for fear that
LETE quadrille set
LETI island off Timor
LETO mother of Apollo, Artemis
LETT Latvian, Balt (Riga man)
LEUD feudal tenant
LEVI Jacob's, Leah's son; tribe
LEVO prefix: left
LEVY assess; seize; tax
LEWD lecherous; obscene
LIAM O'Flaherty: "Informer"
LIAO Manchuria river
LIAR prevaricator; plant
LIAS geol. period
LICE insects (louse)
LICK tongue; stroke; whip; conquer; bit
LIDA Alida
LIDE March (month)
LIDO Venice beach
LIED fibbed; song: Ger.

LIEF gladly; freely
LIEN claim; attachment; garnishment
LIER rester; layer
LIEU place; stead
LIFE existence; vivacity; biography
LIFO inventory method
LIFT exalt; steal; elevator
LIII 53; Claudius reign
LIIN measure
LIJA unicorn fish
LIKE as; similar(ly); love; prefer; probable
LILA deity manifestation
LILE little
LILL small pin; loll; Lillian
LILT (sing) lively tune
LILY flowers; Turk's-cap; pure; white
LIMA city; bean, yam; mollusk
LIMB leg; arm; member
LIME calcium oxide (mortar); snare; caustic; linden (tree); amber; citrus fruit
LIMN portray; delineate
LIMP halt; flaccid; loose
LIMU edible seaweed
LIMY viscous
LINA measure; Caroline
LIND Jenny (singer, Swedish Nightingale)
LINE thin mark; cable; cord; wire; piping; row; direction; cover; align; track; flax
LING fish; burbot; hake
LINK (chain) loop; connect; join; torch; measure
LINN waterfall; linden
LINO measure
LINT raveling, fiber (of linen); netting
LINY streaky
LINZ Austrian city
LION cat; king of beasts; celebrity
LIPA fat
LIRA money; lyre; hairlike ridge
LIRE coins; read: Fr.
LISA fem. name; nickname
LISK flank; loin
LISP speech defect
LISS (fairy) fort; release; peace; fleur-de-lis
LIST strip(e); roll; register; enter; inclination; careen
LITE suffix: mineral, rock
LITH prefix, suffix: stone
LITI medieval peasants
LITZ braided wire
LIVE exist; continue; vital; alert
LIVY Roman historian; Titus Livius
LLEW Celt deity (Gwydion's son)
LLYN lake; pool
LOAD burden; measure
LOAF bread; idle
LOAM clay; soil
LOAN lend
LOBB go heavily; tennis stroke; till
LOBE projection; ear part
LOBO timber wolf
LOCH lake, bay: Scot.
LOCI places; sites
LOCK gate (canal, dam); tuft; wool; fasten(ing); grapple; tie up; -out (labor)
LOCO (render) mad; weed
LODE ore deposit; vein; load
LODI city; Napoleon victory
LODZ Polish city
LOFT attic; warehouse floor; golf stroke
LOGE theater box
LOGY heavy; dull
LOIN body part; hips; meat cut
LOIR dormouse; river
LOIS name; Timothy's grandmother
LOJA bark (quinine)
LOKA sphere universe
LOKE Loki; surprise!
LOKI god of discord; Aesir; Balder slayer
LOLA fem. name
LOLL droop; lounge; sprawl
LOLO Caucasian Chinese
LOMA fringe; lap; hill
LOME Togo seaport
LONE single; — Star
LONG lengthy; extended, yearn; John Silver (Stevenson); Huey (La. politician); — time no see
LONK black-faced sheep
LOOD weight
LOOF luff; sponge gourd
LOOK observe; appear(ance); eye (wink); care
LOOM auk; appear(ance); weaver's frame
LOON diving bird; lout
LOOP noose; catch;

aerial stunt; Chicago area
LOOS Anita (writer: Gentlemen Prefer Blondes)
LOOT plunder; booty
LOPE go; move; gait
LORA thong; strap
LORD ruler; Jehovah; Jesus; duck; planet
LORE history; learning
LORI lemur; Afr. Negro
LORN forsaken; bereft
LORO monk parrot; fish
LORS exclamation: lord!
LORY parrot; touraco
LOSE miss; forfeit; fall; forget
LOSH wash leather
LOSS forfeiture; bereavement; waste; defeat; — leader
LOST not won; misplaced; confused; ruined; — cause
LOTA water pot; burbot genus
LOTE lotus (poetic); weights
LOTH averse; reluctant
LOTI Pierre (writer: Viaud)
LOTO pot; game
LOTS tracts; quantities, very much; chances
LOUD noisy; showy; vulgar
LOUN loon; lout
LOUP half mask; Skidi Indian; river; fish
LOUR frown; lower; scowl
LOUT boor; bumpkin; dolt
LOVE affection; like; Cupid; Eros; zero
LOWA bush quail
LOWN calm; quiet; doit
LOWY banlieue; suburb
LOXA pale bark: quinine
LUAU feast; cook-out
LUBA Bantu; Bashilange
LUBE machine oil
LUBS of Lubeck (city)
LUCE fish, pike; Adriana's servant; Henry (editor); Clare Boothe (writer, stateswoman)
LUCK chance; event; fortune
LUCY fleur-de-lis; fem. name; camera lucida; Lemonade (Mrs. Hayes); Stone (suffragist)
LUDI Roman public games
LUDO game; pachisi
LUES syphilis
LUFF sail nearer wind
LUFT air: Ger.; -waffe
LUGE lodge; small sled
LUGH Celtic light god
LUIF loof
LUKE name; evangelist; Paul's companion; author Acts; -warm
LULA name; Louisa
LULL (temporary) quiet
LULU barn owl; name; Louisa
LUMP mass; swelling; barge; like it or — it
LUNA moon goddess; silver
LUNE crescent; hawk leash
LUNG air bladder; iron —
LUNN Sally (teacake)
LUNT light; smoke; Alfred (actor)
LUNY crazy (man)
LUOH White Nile Negro
LUPE Samoan fruit pigeon; Velez (actress)
LURA brain opening
LURE entice; decoy; trumpet
LURG marine worm
LURI Lake Albert Negro
LURK lie in wait; skulk
LUSH luxurious; drunkard
LUSK lazy (fellow)
LUST sensual desire
LUTE cement; bricklayer's tool; Apollo's musical instrument; jar ring
LUXE elegance; de —
LVII 57; Nero reign
LWOW Polish city
LXII 62; Nero reign
LXIV 64; Nero reign
LYAM bloodhound
LYAS geol. period
LYME bloodhound
LYNX wildcat; fur; constellation
LYON Fr. city; bean
LYRA glockenspiel; constellation
LYRE harp; constellation
LYSE undergo lysis
MAAL measure
MAAM madam
MAAN city
MAAS river
MAAT goddess
MAAZ Judah's descendant
MABA Negro; tree
MABI tree
MACE staff; spice; weight; coin

MACK coat
MACO cotton
MADE successful; created; constructed
MADI Negro
MADO fish
MAFU stable boy
MAGE magician
MAGG bird; chatter
MAGH month
MAGI caste; priests; wise men, kings of Orient: Melchior, Gaspar, Balthazar
MAHA monkey; deer
MAHE island
MAHI river
MAHR marriage settlement
MAIA goddess; crab; star
MAID servant; — of Orleans
MAIL coin; tax; armor; post
MAIM disgfigure; mutilate
MAIN conduit; first; river; Spanish —
MAIS but, corn: Fr.
MAJA crab
MAJO dandy; shrub
MAKE produce, create; cause; reach; type; identify
MAKI lemur
MAKO shark
MAKU Indian
MALA evil(s), wrong(s): Lat.; jaw
MALE man(ly); tribe
MALI caste; nation; river
MALL mallet; game; bird; assembly (place)
MALM limestone
MALO loincloth
MALT barley; beer
MAMA mother; goddess
MAMO bird
MANA magic power; Chinese letter
MAND grass
MANE hair; in the morning: Lat.
MANG bat (Kipling)
MANI peanut; prefix: hand
MANN man: Ger.; Horace (educator); Thomas (writer)
MANO grindstone; hand: It.
MANS Chinese aborigine; Le — (city; auto race)
MANU prefix: hand; Laws (Hindu code book)
MANX pert. to Isle of Man; cat
MANY numerous
MAON Nabal's home
MAPO goby (fish)
MARA demon; aborigine; Naomi
MARC residue; name; weight
MARD spoil
MARE blues; sea; moon area; horse; shanks' —
MARI prefix: sea; husband: Fr.; native
MARK sign; alm; stamp; money; observe; evangelist; easy —; — time
MARL clayey soil; fertilizer; fiber
MARM ma'am; school-
MARO ship name: Jap.
MARS war god; planet
MART market; nickname
MARU ship name: Jap.
MARX Karl (economist)
MARY female name; queen; sister of Lazarus, Martha; Virgin; Lady
MASA corn meal
MASH crush; brew; mixture; hammer; flirt
MASK disguise; screen; domino
MASS rite, service; bulk; mob; populace; assemble
MAST pole; brown; nuts
MASU salmon
MATA Hari (spy)
MATE companion; match; tea; check-
MATH mowing; monastery; school course
MATT lusterless
MATY (assistant) servant
MAUD plaid; rug; name; Muller; Whittier; Tennyson heroine
MAUI Polynesian hero
MAUL hammer; bruise; mangle
MAUN must
MAWK maggot
MAYA weaverbird; (Mexican) Indian; magic; Buddha's mother
MAYO Indian; physicians; clinic (Rochester)
MAZE labyrinth; daze; perplex
MAZO de la Roche (novelist: Jaina)
MAZY perplexing
MCII 1102
MCIV 1104; First Crusade, conquest of Acre
MCIX 1109
MEAD drink; meadow; lake; Margaret (anthropolo-

gist)
MEAH wall tower
MEAL grain; pulverize; repast
MEAN intend; denote; base; unkind; middle
MEAT flesh; kernel; food
MEDA secret Indian sect
MEDB Conchobor's wife; goddess; Queen Mab
MEDE ancient Asia
MEDI prefix: middle
MEED reward
MEEK mild; submissive
MEER sea: Ger.
MEET encounter; face; combat; fulfill; fit
MEGA prefix: great
MEIN Chinese noodles; chow —
MEIO measure
MELA festival; prefix: black
MELD announce (score); merge
MELE Hawaiian poem; chant
MELL (beat with) hammer; teacher (Dickens)
MELT liquefy
MEMO note; statement
MEND repair; improve
MENE — tekel upharsin (handwriting on the wall)
MENG mix
MENO prefix: month
MENS mind: Lat.
MENT falcon-headed god
MENU bill of fare
MEOU cat's cry; measure
MEOW cat's cry; measure
MERE fen; lake; boundary; war club; bare; only; simple; mother: Fr.
MERL blackbird
MERO grouper (fish)
MERU fabled mountain
MESA flat hill; oakwood color
MESE Greek mus. term
MESH net; netting; entangle
MESS banquet; meal; muddle; disorder; botch
META goal post; river
METE measure; allot
METZ city, former fort
MEUM carrotlike herb, spicknel; mine: Lat.
MEWL whimper; miaou
MEWS (royal) stables
MIAM hut
MIAN sir; title
MIAO Chinese aborigine
MIAS orangutan
MICA isinglass (silicate)
MICE rodents (mouse)
MICH me; Ger.
MICK Irishman
MICO marmoset
MIDE Ojibway secret order
MIDI south(ern France)
MIEN manner; bearing; air
MIFF quarrel; offend
MIGG marble (duck)
MIII 1003
MIKE Michael; Mick; microphone
MILA measure
MILD calm(ly); soft; tame
MILE measure; distance
MILK nutritious fluid; sap; white; exploit; drain
MILL grind(er); quern; box; John Stuart (economist)
MILO name; grain; sorghum; Venus (Melos)
MILT spleen; fish gland; nickname
MIMA woman actor
MIME drama; act; actor; clown; smith (Nibelungs)
MIMI nickname; opera heroine
MINA weight; money; myna; watchman
MIND intellect; brain; memory; wish; mood; plan; tend; dislike
MINE possessive pronoun; dig; pit; rich source; explosive
MING Chin. dynasty
MINK weasel-like animal
MINO Jap. straw coat
MINT herb; menthol; bonanza; coin; — Julep
MINX pert girl
MINY of a mine
MIRA star
MIRE bog; (stick in) mud
MIRK dark(ness)
MIRO tree; wood robin
MIRY boggy; filthy
MISE levy; stake; tax; — en scène
MISS fail(ure); omit; want; girl; maiden
MIST dim; haze; gray
MITE arachnid; parasite; small (coin)
MITT glove; hand
MITU curassow; bird
MITY parasite-infested
MIXE Mexican Indian
MIXY confusedly mixed

MLII 1052
MLIV 1054; Catholic Church schism
MLIX 1059
MMIV 2004
MMIX 2009
MOAB kingdom; language; Lot's son
MOAN lament
MOAT trench
MOBY — Dick (whale: Melville)
MOCK jeer; taunt; sham; — apple, turtle
MODE manner; fashion; drab; à la —
MOED festivals (Mishnah)
MOFF Caucasian silk
MOGO stone hatchet
MOHA millet; delusion
MOHO bird; honey eater
MOHR gazelle; bezoar
MOIL toil; trouble; spot
MOIO measure
MOJI Jap. seaport
MOJO tree; majagua; voodoo charm; Indian
MOKE donkey; dolt
MOKI N.Z. raft
MOKO Maori tattoo; -moko (lizard)
MOLA sunfish genus
MOLD fungus; humus; die, matrix; shape; mix
MOLE nevus; birthmark; pier; burrow(ing animal); Mossi language
MOLL Mary; girl; Flanders (Defoe); minor (mus.)
MOLT shed (hair)
MOLY magic herb (Homer)
MOME buffoon; -rath
MOMO owl
MONA monkey; Lisa (La Gioconda: da Vinci)
MONG among; barter
MONK ascetic; friar; bird; fish; spot; ferret
MONO monkey; Indian; prefix: single, one
MONS mountain: Lat.; city (Belgium: WW I battle)
MONT mountain: Fr.; — Blanc (peak, Alps)
MOOD humor; temper; verb form
MOON satellite; crescent; month; Diana; Cynthia; languish
MOOR heath; anchor; Moslem; Moroccan; blacka-
MOOT arguable; ring gauge
MOPE be dull, listless (person)
MORA default; short syllable; Spartan army; stool
MORE greater; additional; St. Thomas (Utopia)
MORG measure
MORN A.M., dawn; East
MORO finch; P.I. Moslem tribe
MORS deity; death
MORT nickname; woman; salmon; the kill; dead: Fr.
MOSE Moses
MOSK Moslem temple; Masjid
MOSS bryophyte; lichen; green; rose; Hart (writer)
MOST greatest; almost
MOSY moldy; rotten
MOTA Moslem marriage
MOTE speck; particle
MOTH lepidopterous insect; -ball; -eaten; gypsy —; page (Shaks.)
MOTI elephant (Kipling)
MOTO movement: It.; con —
MOTT clump of trees; James, Lucretia (abolitionists)
MOUE pout; grimace: Fr.
MOVE impel; shift; excite; act; depart(ure); play
MOWN cut down; trimmed
MOXA cautery wormwood
MOXO Arawakan Indian
MOYO measure
MOZA manservant
MOZO manservant: Sp.
MUAV geol. epoch
MUCH great (deal); far; — Ado (Shaks.)
MUCK (rid of) manure; mess
MUDD measure; doctor of Booth (Lincoln assassin)
MUFF handwarmer; bungle
MUGA silk; moth
MUID measure
MUIR moor (Scot.)
MULE equine hybrid; spinning jenny; slipper
MULK freehold land
MULL muslin; ointment; ponder, humus
MUMM mask; disguise
MUMP beg; mumble; cheat
MUND protection right
MUNG grass
MUNJ tough grass; twine

MUNT sash bar
MUON particle
MURA Brazil Indian
MURE thrust against wall
MURK (make) gloomy
MUSA banana genus
MUSE meditate; goddess
MUSH meal; hasty pudding; flattery; proceed!
MUSK odor; aromatic secretion (of deer, ox, etc.)
MUSO Chibchan Indian
MUSS mess; rumple; row
MUST be obliged to; necessity; new wine; stum; staleness; frenzy
MUTA mus. change; Moslem marriage
MUTE silent; dumb; muffle
MUTH measure
MUTT cur; stupid one; — and Jeff
MVII 1007
MXII 1012
MXIV 1014; Brian Boru defeats Danes
MXIX 1019
MYAL cultic
MYNA talking bird: grackle
MYRA name; ancient city
MYSA buffalo (Kipling)
MYST Greek priest
MYTH (religious) legend; fiction
MYXA plum (geiger) tree; sebesten
MYXO slime mold

NAAB river
NAAM distrain
NABK shrub
NABO shrub
NABU god; mountain
NACH after: Ger.
NAEL weight
NAGA snake
NAGY Hungarian premier
NAHA city
NAHE river; near: Ger.
NAIA cobra
NAID worm
NAIF naive; of true luster
NAIK leader
NAIL fasten(er); claw; seize; expose
NAIO tree
NAIR native
NAIS nymph
NAJA cobra
NALA hero
NAMA Hottentot; herb
NAME title; reputation; clan; cite
NANA nurse; Aztec hero's wife; Zola novel; dog (Peter Pan: Barrie)
NANE own; none
NAOS star
NAPA leather; wine region; city; river
NAPE neck back
NAPU ruminant
NARD plant; ointment
NARE Loki's son
NARK informer; tease
NARY not one
NASA space-travel agency
NASE promontory; nose: Ger.
NASH soft; humorist
NASI prince; patriarch
NAST cartoonist
NATA Nana's hero
NATE born
NATH star
NATO International (Western) alliance; treaty organization
NATR weight
NAUT sea mile
NAVE hub; church part
NAVY fleet; blue; tobacco; — yard
NAZE promontory
NAZI fascist; Hitlerite
NEAL male name; novelist
NEAP wagon pole; tide
NEAR close(ly); approach
NEAT tidy; trim; straight
NEBO wisdom god; Moab mountain (Moses died)
NECK body part; violin part; isthmus; pet
NEED compulsion; lack; want
NEEM tree; Margosa
NEEP turnip
NEER never; kidney
NEIF serf; native; fist
NEIL male name
NEIN no: Ger.
NEIR kidney
NEJD kingdom
NELL Ellen; Helen; Little (Dickens girl)
NEMA eelworm; prefix: thread
NEMO nobody: Lat.; prefix: glade; Captain (Verne hero)
NENE Hawaiian goose
NEON gas(eous) element; lamp
NEPA water scorpion; needle bug
NERA Tiber tributary
NERI Blacks: It.
NERO emperor; fiddler; Agrippine's son; Wolfe (Stout)
NESH soft; juicy; dainty
NESS cape; promon-

tory; suffix
NEST (make a) home
NETE Greek mus. term
NETI eulalia (thatch grass)
NETT undeductible
NEUE new
NEUF nine, new: Fr.
NEVA river (Leningrad)
NEVE snow; firn
NEWS intelligence; tidings
NEWT salamander; eft
NEXT nearest; following
NGAI spiritual power
NGAN measure
NIAS Ind. Ocean island(er)
NIBS personage (VIP); in Peter Pan (Barrie)
NICE good; kind; pleasing; delicate; dainty; quimper color; Riviera port
NICK notch; moment; cheat; cut; Old (devil); Carter (detective)
NIDE pheasant's nest
NIDI breeding places
NIEL alloy
NIFE earth's core
NIGH near(ly); direct
NIKE victory goddess (Samothrace); missile
NILE river; green, blue
NILL refuse; negate
NILS Bohr (physicist)
NIMB nimbus; halo
NINA goddess (Ea's daughter); ship (Pinta, —, Santa Maria); girl: Sp.
NINE number (of Muses); baseball team
NINO boy: Sp.
NIOG coconut palm
NIOU measure
NIPA palm; juice; mat; atap
NISH Yugo. city
NISI unless: Lat.
NITO climbing fern
NIUE Savage Island language
NIXY undeliverable mail
NIZY fool
NKVD Soviet secret police
NOAH patriarch (Ark builder)
NOAP bullfinch
NOBS knave, jack (card, cribbage)
NOCK notch (in bow)
NODE knob; knot; orbit point; joint
NODI knots; difficulties
NOEL Christmas; carol; — Coward
NOGG egg drink
NOIL combing (wool fiber)
NOIO noddy tern
NOIR black: Fr.; bet
NOIX edible gland
NOLA fem. name; time
NOLI — me tangere
NOLL Oliver (Cromwell); head; noddle
NOLO — contendere
NOME city (Alaska)
NONA fate goddess; prefix: ninth
NONE not one; 9th hour
NONO ninth: It.
NOOK corner; retreat
NOON midday; meal; acme
NORA Helmer (Ibsen heroine)
NORE Thames estuary
NORI seaweed food
NORM type; standard; integer
NORN demigoddess (Urth, Skuld, Verthandi)
NOSE proboscis; smeller; scent; search; front; touch; — out (defeat); -dive
NOSU Lolo; Chin. Caucasian
NOSY fragrant; prying
NOTA insect backs; — bene (N.B.)
NOTE sign; tone; fame; heed; memo; IOU; record; see
NOTT Norse night (Dag)
NOUN speech part; name; substantive
NOUP steep promontory
NOUS mind; reason; wit; we: Fr.
NOVA star: new, temporary
NOVE nine: It.
NOWT neat cattle; dolt
NOWY having curvature
NOXA harmful thing
NOYL fiber knot
NOZI of Yanan tribe
NUBA Nubian; Berberi language
NUBK shrub
NUCI prefix: nut
NUDA ctenophore; Berolda
NUDD Brythonic god, king
NUDE naked; art work; color
NUIT night: Fr.
NULL nil; void; code filler
NUMA Pompilius (Roman king)
NUMB deaden(ed); helpless
NUNS sisters; veiling, fabric
NUPE Nigeria Negro
NURL wood knot; to mill
NUSS nurse
NUZO Chibchan Indian

OAHU (Hawaiian) island

OAKS horse race; trees
OAKY oaklike
OARY oarlike
OAST kiln
OATH appeal; pledge; vow; curse
OATY full of oats
OBAN coin
OBED David's grandfather
OBEX brain matter
OBEY submit; comply
OBIA Ashanti religion
OBIE Off-Broadway award
OBIT death notice
OBOE woodwind; chanter
OBOL 1/16 drachma (coin)
OBRA works: Sp.
OBUS howitzer shell
OCHA weight
OCHS Adolph (publisher)
OCRA vegetable; gumbo
OCTA prefix: eight
OCTO prefix: eight
ODAL land; vine
ODAX rock whiting (fish)
ODDS inequality; advantage; at —; -on
ODEA theaters; halls; galleries
ODED prophet or his father
ODEL vine; land ownership
ODER river
ODIC pert. to ode, od
ODIN one-eyed Norse god: Frigg's husband, Thor's father
ODIO hatred: It.
ODOR smell; repute
ODUM tree (iroko)
ODYL alleged force
OEIL eye: Fr.; — de boeuf
OENO prefix: wine
OESE bacteriologist's wire
OEUF egg: Fr.
OFFA Angles' hero (Beowulf)
OFFS cricket-field sides
OGAM Irish alphabet
OGEE arch; molding
OGLE gaze (amorously)
OGOR early Turkic man
OGPU Soviet police body
OGRE giant; monster
OGUM Irish alphabet
OHAD Simeon's son
OHEL Zerubabbel's son
OHIA timber tree; apple
OHIO Buckeye state
OHNE without: Ger.
OHOY ahoy; call
OILY unctuous; bland; suave
OIME alas
OINT apply oil
OISE Fr. river
OKAY approve; all right
OKEE evil spirit
OKEH all right; O.K.
OKET ounce
OKIA Moroccan money
OKIE migratory worker
OKRA vegetable; gumbo
OKRO plant; stew; soup; gumbo
OLAF (Vi)king
OLAM infinity; — haba (life after death)
OLAN Wang Lung's wife (Pearl Buck: The Good Earth)
OLAX tree
OLAY palm
OLEA shrub; olive
OLEO margarine
OLGA fem. name
OLIC chem. suffix
OLID smelly; fetid
OLIO medley; olla-podrida
OLLA jar; meat dish; -podrida (medley)
OLOR swan genus; Cygnus
OLPE oil flask; pitcher
OLPH bullfinch
OMAN Arabian state; sultanate; Muscat
OMAO thrush
OMAR Khayyam; tentmaker; caliph
OMEI Buddhist mountain
OMEN presage; portent; sign
OMER measure; sheaf; undertake (Dickens)
OMIT leave out; neglect
OMNI prefix: all
OMRI king of Israel
OMSK Siberian city
ONAN Indian; Judah's son
ONCA ounce
ONCE one time; if ever; former(ly)
ONDE wave: Fr.: wavy (Her.)
ONDY wavy (Her.)
ONER ace; blow; individual
ONES individuals
ONLY alone; but; single; exclusively
ONTO upon; wise to
ONUS burden; duty
ONYM technical name (biol.)
ONYX cameo stone; quartz; gem
ONZA Sp. ounce (1/16 libra); coin
OOAA Hawaiian bird
OOFY rich (Eng. slang)
OOID egg-shaped
OONS mild oath
OONT camel; mole
OORD coin (double dolt, 1/4 stiver)
OOZE exude; slime; liquor
OOZY muddy; slimy
OPAH fish
OPAL birthstone

(Oct.); girasol
OPEN undefended; plain; frank; -end; uncertain; bare; start; unfold; public; — sesame
OPIE Eng. painter
OPUS work
ORAD mouthward
ORAL spoken; of the mouth
ORAN seaport
ORAS Danish money
ORBY revolving
ORCA killer whale
ORDO order: Lat.; feast list
ORDU Turk. military district, army corps
OREB Midianite defeated by Gideon
OREL Russian city
OREN Judah's descendant
ORFE fish; yellow ide
ORGY carousal; Saturnalia, Bacchanalia
ORLE shield border; fillet
ORLO smooth surface; plinth
ORLY Paris airport
ORNA measure
ORNE measure; river (Caen)
ORRA oddly; laborer
ORYX antelope, gemsbok
ORZO pasta
OSAR glacial ridges; eskers
OSER dare: Fr.
OSID suffix: sugar
OSLO city (Norway); Christiania
OSSA bones; Mt. (Olympus)
OSTE prefix: bone
OTEA Great Barrier Island
OTHO Roman emperor
OTIC of the ear; auditory
OTIS bustard genus; general; inventor (elevator)
OTOE Sioux Indian
OTRA other: Sp.
OTRO other, another: Sp.
OTTO name; palindrome; perfume; Ger. ruler
OTUS giant slain by Apollo
OUCH exclamation
OUGH exclamation
OURS possessive pronoun
OUSE Great — (river)
OUST eject; discharge
OVAL egg-shaped; elliptic; arena
OVEN (bake in) stove; kiln
OVER above; across; beyond; again; surplus; ended; Roger and —
OVID poet (Metamorphoses); P.O.N.; Naso
OVIS sheep genus
OVUM germ cell; egg
OWEN (Welsh) name; socialist; zoologist
OWER debtor
OWSE tan liquor
OXAN gas
OXEA sponge spicule
OXEN bovines; draft animals
OXER hedge (fox hunting)
OXID oxygen compound
OXIM chem. compound
OXYL oxygen radical
OYER hearing (law); — and terminer
OYES court crier's cry
OYEZ court crier's cry
OZEM David's brother
OZNI Gad's son
PAAL measure
PAAN town
PAAR sand
PAAS Easter
PABA vitamin
PACA rodent
PACE step; speed; peace: It.
PACK bundle; cosmetic paste; cards; crowd; animal(s)
PACO alpaca
PACT agreement
PADI rice
PAGA rice
PAGE young attendant; call, summon; leaf
PAGO -Pago (city)
PAHA hill
PAHI ship
PAHO prayer stick
PAID recompensed; discharged; satisfied
PAIL bucket
PAIN ache; trouble; forfeit
PAIR couple; brace
PAIS country
PAJO prayer stick
PALA weight; antelope; vine; rice
PALE wan; pallid; ashy; picket; stake; beyond the —
PALI slope; coral parts; Buddhist language
PALL cloak; covering; cloy
PALM tree; measure; hand part; paddle; conceal; grease the —
PALO pole, wood: Sp.
PALP appendage; feeler
PALY wan; heraldic design
PANA city
PANE glass; panel
PANG agony
PANI madam: Polish
PANK weight
PANT gasp; yearn
PAON peacock blue

PAPA father; Pope; potato: Sp.; baboon; clay
PAPE bunting (bird)
PARA coin; weight; river; city (Belem)
PARC park; oyster farm: Fr.
PARD chum; leopard
PARE cut off; peel
PARI weight; prefix: equal (common)
PARK grounds; green; deposit; Hyde, Central, etc.
PARR young fish; skegger; Catherine (Henry VII wife)
PARS part: Lat.
PART portion; duty; role; separate; split; go
PASA raisin
PASH hurl; smash
PASI low-caste Hindu
PASO measure
PASS opening; go through; by; license; abstention; condition; amatory gesture
PAST tense; ago; after
PATA painting; turban; sword
PATE head; paste
PATH track; route
PATO Muscovy duck
PATT stalemate(d)
PATU weapon
PAUL click; detent; Apostle; Bunyan; Revere; pope
PAUN betel leaf
PAUP walk idly
PAVE cover firmly; — the way; jewel setting
PAVO peacock; constellation
PAVY peach
PAWA weight
PAWL click; detent; tent
PAWN chessman; pledge
PEAG money
PEAI medicine man
PEAK point; top; summit
PEAL ring; loud sound; fish
PEAN panegyric; praise; fur
PEAR fruit, tree
PEAT darling; turf; fuel
PEAU skin: Fr.
PEAY medicine man
PEBA armadillo; Indian
PECA coin
PECK measure; nip; bite; kiss
PECO black tea
PEDA pastoral staffs
PEDI prefix: foot
PEDO child
PEEK sly glance; pry; chirp
PEEL pare; tower; spade
PEEN hammer head
PEEP chirp; bird; peer slyly; Bo —; jeep
PEER gaze; equal; nobleman
PEET darling; turf; fuel
PEGA remora fish
PEGU Burmese language, city
PEHO morepork (bird)
PEKE (Pekinese) dog
PELA wax(-secreting insect)
PELE fire goddess
PELF booty; riches
PELO hair: It.
PELT skin; hurl; strike
PELU hardwood tree
PEND hang; be delayed
PENE (hammer) head
PENK minnow
PENN William (Pa. founder)
PENT confined; -house
PEON laborer
PEOR Bib. mountain
PEPO pumpkin; squash; melon; cucumber
PERA Istanbul district
PERE father, priest: Fr.; — Goriot (Balzac)
PERI fairy; elf; beauty
PERK lift up; preen; cocky; percolate
PERM elec. unit; hair wave
PERN honey buzzard
PERO but: Sp.
PERT bold; lively; sandpiper
PERU country
PESA coin
PESO coin; Sp. money
PESS hassock
PEST plague; insect; nuisance
PETE stongbox; Peter
PETO wahoo (fish); Henry IV figure
PEUL Fulah (Sudanese)
PEUR fear: Fr.
PEVA Peru Indian
PEVY lumberman's hook
PFUI exclamation
PHAD star
PHAG comb. form: eating
PHAN measure
PHAO wolf (Kipling)
PHEW exclamation
PHIL nickname; Philip; prefix: loving
PHIT bullet sound
PHIZ physiognomy; face
PHON loudness measure
PHOO disgusting!
PHOS phosphorus
PHOT light unit
PHUD bullet sound; exclamation
PHUT (bullet) sound;

OT people
PIAN tumor
PIAT magpie; anti-tank gun
PIAY medicine man
PICA type size; magpies
PICE coin; weight
PICI birds (woodpeckers)
PICK tool; scratch; choose; rob; eat; best
PICO peak; game; weight
PICT British aborigine
PIED variegated; Piper; -à-terre
PIEN arris (sharp edge)
PIER mole; dock; pillar
PIET magpie
PIFF bullet sound; exclamation
PIKA little chief hare
PIKE fish; weapon; pierce, highway; farmer gamble; Zebulon (explorer; peak)
PIKI maize bread; pik
PIKY full of fish
PILE hair; heap (up); awn; atomic —
PILI nut; grass; hairs
PILL medicine tablet
PILY pilelike
PIMA Ariz. Indian; cotton
PIMP procurer; bawd; maquereau
PINA pineapple; silver cone
PINE tree; conifer; evergreen; yearn; mourn
PING (bullet, striking) sound
PINK color (red); ship; cut; hunter's coat; carnation; in the — (healthy)
PINO pine tree
PINT measure
PINY pinelike; peony
PION dig; excavate
PIOT magpie
PIPA toad; measure
PIPE tube; flute; cask (measure); -dream; — down
PIPI astringent; mollusk
PIPY tubular; weepy
PIRN reed; bobbin; nose ring
PIRO Tanoan Indian
PIRR wind gust; whiz; gull
PISA city (leaning tower)
PISE building material
PISH reject; nonsense!
PISK nighthawk
PISO weight
PIST attention; track
PITA fiber; flax; hemp; brocket (deer)
PITH marrow; kernel; gist
PITO fiber; flax; hemp; brocket (deer)
PITT statesman (Commoner, Chatham); diamond
PITY sympathy; mercy
PIUS Pope: X (St., Sarto); XI (Ratti); XII (Pacelli)
PIXY impish sprite
PLAN design; scheme
PLAP fall loudly
PLAT plait; map; plot; fish
PLAY frolic; act; drama; contend; sport; game
PLEA excuse; prayer; request; pretext; allegation
PLEB freshman cadet; common man
PLED pleaded
PLET three-lash whip
PLEW beaver skin
PLEX form a network
PLIM swell; swollen
PLOD trudge; drudge
PLOP sound of fall
PLOT tract; ground; press (soap); scheme; intrigue
PLOW implement; till; cut; stars
PLOY make column; frolic; coup
PLUG stop(per); plod; shoot; spark —; horse; praise
PLUM fruit (damson; greengage); tree; raisin; choice job
PLUP sound of (soft) fall
PLUS and; more; extra; — fours
PNYX Greek voting site
POBS porridge; pap
POCK pustule
POCO slightly; old-clothes man
PODA suffix: foot
PODE suffix: foot
POEM verse creation
POET writer of verse; artist
POGO springy stick
POGY menhaden; trout
POHA gooseberry (jelly)
POIL raw silk thread
POKE thrust; prod; pry; sack; potter; herb
POKU antelope
POKY shabby; dull; bonnet
POLA Yugo. city (Pula)

POLE rod; tail; terminal: axis, battery; — Star; Polish, Polack
POLK Cossack regiment; James Knox (President)
POLL head; register; survey; cut off; Mary; parrot; vote
POLO game; Marco —
POLT knock; trump; club
POLY herb; Teucrium; prefix: many
POMA rosa (rose apple)
POME fruit; ball; globe
POMO California Indian
POMP pageant(ry); splendor
POND lake; pool; weight
PONE corn bread; writ
PONG sound; improvise
PONS bridge: Lat.; — asinorum; Lily (singer)
PONT ferry(boat); bridge: Fr.
PONY small equine (Shetland, polo); glass (1 oz.); translation
POOA pua hemp
POOD weight
POOF exclamation
POOH pshaw!; Bah (Mikado); Winnie (bear: Milne)
POOK hobgoblin; disk
POOL pond; puddle; game; stake; fund; Thames
POON tree (mastwood)
POOP deck; cabin; dickey; exhaust; tire
POOR indigent; scanty; feeble; lowgrade; lean; ill; hapless; cod (fish)
POOT disgusting!
POPE pontiff; Holy Father; — Joan (game); Alexander (poet); bird
PORE gaze; ponder; opening
PORK meat; swine; — barrel
PORO Sierra Leone secret society
PORR push; poke; kick
PORT harbor; haven; wine; blue-red; left side; tune; demeanor
PORY porous; permeable
POSE posture; affectation; baffle; propound
POSH slush; elegant
POST pillar; advertise; mil. station; mail; inform; record
POSY flower; nosegay; poem
POTE poker; stick
POTT paper size; editor (Dickens)
POUF puff; ottoman; bang!
POUL Russ. coin
POUR (make) flow; for: Fr.; emit; — le mérite
POUS measure
POUT sulk(iness); fish
POWE weight
PRAD horse
PRAH canoe
PRAM carriage
PRAO canoe
PRAT buttock
PRAU swift canoe
PRAY ask; beseech; please
PREP prepare; student
PRES near: Fr.
PRET measure
PREX (college) president
PREY victim; pillage; booty
PRIG precisian; steal; thief; fop
PRIX price: Fr.; — fixe (table d'hôte)
PROA Malay outrigger
PROD reminder; goad; horse; prodigy
PROG (steal) food; forage
PROM dance, ball (college)
PROO slow up! (horse call)
PROP support; shore; theater equipment
PROW ship's bow; stem; beak
PRUT exclamation; river
PSHA exclamation
PTAH god
PUAN latex
PUCA goblin; specter
PUCE flea: Fr.; eureka red
PUCK sprite; Robin Goodfellow; Shaks. character; hockey disk
PUDU Chilean deer
PUFF blow; pastry; distend; hair roll; adder; powder —
PUGH pshaw!; fish prong
PUJA worship; festival
PUKA rare N.Z. tree
PUKE cloth; vomit
PUKU Afr. antelope
PUKY nauseated
PULA Yugo. city
PULE cheep; whimper
PULI coins
PULK (Cossack) regiment
PULL drag; influence
PULP pith; tissue; paper; magazine

PULU tree fern
PULY whining; complaining
PUMA cougar; catamount
PUME Yarura(n language)
PUMP force; draw out; slipper
PUNA high Andes; wind; sickness (soroche)
PUND weight
PUNG (drive) box sleigh; mah jongg term
PUNK touchwood; tinder; conch; tramp; bad
PUNO Pacific trade wind; city (Peru)
PUNT (propel) flatboat; kick; bet
PUNY weak; slight
PUPA chrysalis; snail; instar
PURE unmixed; chaste; sheer; free; Simon —
PURI Indian yellow
PURL knitting stitch; beer; murmur; spin; swirl
PURR cat's sound
PURU of Arawakan
PUSH shove; thrust; strive; -button
PUSS cat; lip; face
PUTT golf stroke
PUUD weight
PUXY ill-tempered
PUYA pineapple genus
PYAL veranda
PYAT magpie
PYET magpie
PYIC purulent
PYLA brain opening
PYLE Ernie (journalist); Howard (artist)
PYOT piebald; chatty
PYRE funeral pile, fire
PYRO prefix: fire, fever

QAID alcaide
QAIS island
QERE read(ing substitute)
QERI read(ing substitute)
QKKT chess move
QOPH Heb. K, Q, 100
QQKT chess move
QUAB fish
QUAD type; four; -rangle, -ruplet, etc.
QUAE — vide (which see)
QUAG morass
QUAI pier
QUAN money
QUAR fill; choke
QUAS sour beer, cider (Russian)
QUAT squat
QUAY pier
QUEI measure
QUID cud; essence; pound; — pro quo
QUIP witty sally; jest
QUIT abandon; yield; stop; free
QUIZ test; odd one; hoax
QUNG So. Afr. Bushman
QUOD prison; — erat demonstrandum (Q.E.D.)

RAAB river
RAAD assembly; fish
RABA river
RABI crop; physicist
RACA reproach; fool
RACE run; contest; people; speed; Cape —; rat-
RACK framework; clouds; gait; torture
RACY smart
RADA legislature
RADE elated
RAFF Raphael
RAFT collection; float
RAGA state of nirvana
RAGE fury; storm; fad
RAGI grass
RAHU demon
RAIA ottoman; fish
RAID attack; foray
RAIK weight; measure
RAIL bird; scold; paling
RAIN shower; scratch; — check
RAIP rope
RAIS chief (Nepalese)
RAJA prince; fish
RAKE incline; tool; collect; roué; —'s Progress
RAKH hayfield
RAKI spirits
RAKU -ware
RALE rattling sound
RALO measure
RAMA Indian; Vishnu incarnation; bull (Kipling)
RAME branch
RAMI branches
RAMP inclined way; rear
RANA frog; prince; Aegir's wife
RAND border; ridge; strip; So. Afr. gold mine
RANG sounded
RANI princess; wife
RANK luxuriant; gross; fetid; grade; array
RANN verse; stanza; kite (Kipling)
RANT scold; rave; frolic
RANZ — des vaches (Alpine melodies)
RAPE herb; ravish
RAPT engrossed; rapture
RARA — avis (rare bird)
RARE underdone; thin; uncommon
RASA essence; tabula —
RASE rub; demolish
RASH hasty; careless

RASP grate; file
RATA tree; chestnut; rate; pro —
RATE censure; ratio; charge; estimate; rank; tax
RATH chariot; fort; temple; early; mome-
RATI weight
RATS bah!
RAVE rant, rage; enthusiasm; rod
RAVI tribesman
RAYA broadbill
RAZE scrape; demolish
RAZZ chaff; ridicule
READ interpret; learn; study; understand
REAL coin; true; genuine; very
REAM 500 (paper) quantity; bevel; enlarge
REAP cut; harvest
REAR back; raise; — admiral
REBA weight
RECK heed; concern
RECT element (philos.)
REDD make tidy; free of; scold
REDE interpet; counsel
REDO make over
REED woody grass; pipe; mouthpiece; Walter (doctor, hospital)
REEF shoal; lode; reduce sail
REEK cloud; exude; smell
REEL wind(er); dance; waver; sway
REEM ox; unicorn
REFT cleft; rift; deprived
REIM oxhide strap
REIN strap; check; direct; kidney
REIS money; (boat) captain; effendi (state officer)
REJA screen, grille: Sp.
REKE rick; pile
REKI Baluchistan nomad
RELY trust; depend
REMI Gaul people; prefix: oar
REMS river
RENA rockfish
REND tear; rupture; bark trees
RENI It. painter; prefix: kidney
RENO Nev. city ("biggest little"; divorce, gambling)
RENT torn; schism; let, lease; payment, income
REPP silk or wool fabric
RESE shake; rush
RESH Heb. 20th letter, 200; plant
REST pause; stop; peace; prop; stay; rely; mus. sign; remainder; set; found
RETE network
REUS defendant: Lat.
REVE (muse in) dream: Fr.
REVS rotations per minute
RHEA Cybele, mother of the gods; Gaea's daughter; Cronos's wife; ostrich; satellite; grass
RHIA China grass
RHIN Rhine: Fr.
RHOB juice; jelly
RHUM alcoholic drink
RHUS sumac genus
RIAL coin
RICE cereal; use ricer; Elmer (playwright)
RICH wealthy; vivid; full; fragrant; fat
RICK pile (up); haystack
RIDD Lorna Doone's rescuer
RIDE be borne; float; endure; manage; mount; journey
RIEL Canadian (Indian) rebel
RIEM oxhide strap
RIEN nothing: Fr.; — ne va plus
RIER oil cask (whaling)
RIFE abundant; prevalent
RIFF Berber; Kabyle; ripple
RIFI Riffs
RIFT split; divide; cleft
RIGA Latvian city, gulf
RIGI Swiss mountain
RIIS Jacob (journalist)
RIKK tambourine
RILE irritate; vex
RILL (run in a) brook
RILY turbid; irritated
RIMA fissure; breadfruit; child heroine (Hudson)
RIME frost; (make) rhymes; chink; rung
RIMU red pine; imou pine
RIMY frosty; rhyming
RIND bark; peel; Vali's mother, Odin's wife
RINE hemp; ditch
RING gird; arena; prizefighting; gang; atomic order; sound (bell); Vienna landmark; Nibelungen cycle (Wagner)
RINK skating arena
RIOT tumult; success; — act, squad

RIPA river bank
RIPE mature; fit; tipsy
RIRE to laugh: Fr.
RISE climb; grow(th); begin; emerge(nce); thrive; retort
RISK peril; hazard; subject of insurance
RISP metal bar
RISS glaciation stage
RIST engrave; scratch
RITA cosmic order (Vedic); Rio —; fem. name
RITE ceremony; liturgy
RIVA shore: It.
RIVE tear; split; — droite (right bank), — gauche (left bank)
RIVO stream: It.
RKKT chess move
ROAD (rail)way; track; anchorage
ROAM wander
ROAN horse; yellow-red
ROAR loud sound; laugh
ROBE gown; mantle; Douglas novel
ROCH Saint (14th cent.)
ROCK stone; Gibraltar; cliff; staunch support; diamond; candy; sway, lull; — the boat
RODA Nile island
RODD crossbow
RODE anchor rope; measure; was borne; cross
RODI Medit. island
ROED filled with roe
ROER hunting gun
ROEY of mottled grain
ROIL disturb; muddy; vex
ROJO redskin: Sp.
ROKA mafura (tree)
ROKE vapor; smoke
ROKY misty; hoarse
ROLE actor's part
ROLL wrap; trill; drumbeat; rotate; list; bank-
ROMA Rome: It.
ROME city (Eternal); Church; beauty (apple)
ROMI Gypsy wife
ROMP girl; gambol, frolic
RONE brushwood
RONG · Sikkimese language
ROOD crucifix; measure
ROOF cover; house; top
ROOK bird; cheat; dupe; chessman (tower)
ROOL crumple; ruffle
ROOM space; apartment; lodge; — and board
ROON treasure; darling
ROOS Ger. painter
ROOT underlying source; rhizome; base; dig; applaud; plant; eradicate
ROPE cord; cable; noose; bind; chain
ROPY viscous; stringy
RORI Bantu tribe
RORY O'More (Irish novel)
ROSA shrub genus; name; sub —; Bonheur (artist)
ROSE stood up; got up; flower; tree; wood; red; pink; window; Abie's Irish —; Eng. emblem
ROSS rough bark; seal; island; navigator; Harold (editor)
ROSY blushing; optimistic
ROTA roster; curia tribunal; a round; hurdy-gurdy
ROTE surf noise; routine
ROTI roasted: Fr.
ROTL Afr. weight
ROTO ragged: Sp.; printing
ROUB measure
ROUD fish
ROUE dissolute man; rake
ROUP a cold; hoarseness
ROUT defeat; tumult; mob; the brant; snare
ROUX (soup, sauce) thickener; physician
ROVE wander; ramble; draw through an eye
ROWY streaked
ROXY name: Roxana; Rothafel (impresario); theater
RYOT Indian peasant
RQKT chess move
RSVP please reply: Fr.
RUAY weight
RUBE Reuben; rustic; yokel
RUBY gem; corundum; bird; name; Oswald killer
RUCK crowd; rake; wrinkle
RUDD carplike fish
RUDE rough; boorish; vulgar
RUER repenter
RUFF collar; bird; fish; plait; trump
RUGA stomach membrane
RUGG pull
RUHR Ger. industrial area
RUIN destroy;

destruction; violate
RUKH fabled bird; jungle
RULE law; guide; reign; method; control; — Britannia; ruler; line
RULL to wheel; trundle
RUMB compass point
RUMP sirloin part; remnant; — Parliament
RUNE Teutonic sign; magic
RUNG wheel spoke; hooped
RUNT small animal, man
RUPA body form (Buddhism)
RURU N.Z. morepork
RUSA deer; sambar; grass; oil
RUSE trick; deceit; slip
RUSH haste(n); attack; red (mace); cattail
RUSK bread; biscuit; Dean (statesman)
RUSS Russian; Slav
RUST oxidize; corrode; inaction; reddish-brown
RUTA herb genus; rue
RUTE measure
RUTH pity; grief; name; OT book, heroine (Moabitess); wife of Boaz
RYAL coin
RYAN peak (Idaho)
RYAZ coin
RYEL coin
RYME water surface
RYND millstone support
RYPE ptarmigan
SAAH measure
SAAL hall: Ger.
SAAN Bushmen
SAAR river; region
SABA fiber; kingdom; island
SABE know
SACK dismiss; plunder; wine; bag; gown; sad —
SACO weight; river
SADD dam; waste matter
SADE letter; Marquis
SADH holy man
SADI poet
SADO carriage; island; river
SADR tree
SAER tenant
SAFE secure; box
SAFI Afghan
SAGA legend; story; goddess; weight
SAGE herb; wise; Russell (financier)
SAGO palm; starch
SAGY wise
SAHA measure
SAHH measure
SAHO language
SAHU spiritual body
SAIC Near East ketch
SAID before-mentioned; Port — (city); name
SAIL canvas; rigging; journey; travel
SAIM grease
SAIN consecrate; tree
SAIR savor
SAIS groom; city; know: Fr.
SAKA era; Scythians
SAKE purpose; beer
SAKI monkey; Munro
SALA dining room: Sp.
SALE bargain; auction; willow; salted: Fr.
SALM star
SALP marine animal
SALT sodium chloride, NaCl; sailor; season; — away; — Lake City; — Sea
SAMA fish; trance-inducing music
SAME identical
SAMH bread plant
SAMP maize
SANA Yemen's capital; fiber
SAND grit; silica; polish; smooth; red-yellow; George (novelist: Dudevant)
SANE rational
SANG Hindu group; herb; weight; did sing
SANK descended
SANS without: Fr.; — culotte (radical); — gêne
SAPA grape juice
SAPH giant (Philistine)
SAPO soap; toadfish
SARA native
SARD carnelian; gem; Sardinian
SARG Toni (puppeteer)
SARI Hindu garment
SARK Channel island
SART Iranian Turk
SARY sorry
SASA fencer's cry
SASH casement; scarf; belt
SASS sauce
SATE gratify; glut
SATI queen of the gods
SAUD Ibn (king)
SAUF except, safe: Fr.; — conduit
SAUK Indian; Mont. river
SAUL tree; king (son of Kish); — of Tarsus (Paul)
SAUM weight
SAUR prefix, suffix: lizard
SAVA Yugo. river
SAVE rescue; avoid; lay by; but; — face
SAWK measure
SAWN sawed; cut

SAXE Saxony; blue
SAYA outer skirt
SCAB crust; strike-breaker
SCAD fish; large amount
SCAN examine; measure poetry
SCAP skull
SCAR rock; cicatrix; mar(k); fish
SCAT buffet; scatter; begone!; tax; skat
SCAW promontory
SCIO prefix: sky
SCOB fabric defect
SCON teacake
SCOP bard; poet
SCOT Celt; Highlander; taxi; — free
SCOW flat-bottomed boat
SCUD run fast; wind-driven clouds; skim; flea
SCUG squirrel: Brit.
SCUM dross; refuse; rabble
SCUP pan fish; porgy
SCUR horn tissue
SCUT rabbit's tail; fur
SEAH measure
SEAL otarian; pinniped; fur; fasten; brown; ratify; stamp
SEAM fold; crevice; join; ornament; measure
SEAN John
SEAR burn; dried up; gun-lock catch
SEAT chair; fundament; site; membership; install; hot —
SEBA Bib. country; Ham's grandson
SEBI prefix: tallow
SECH such
SECK unprofitable (rent)
SECT group; denomination
SEED fertile germ; progeny; decay; plant; extract
SEEK ask; try; hunt
SEEL shut eyes of; blind
SEEM look; appear
SEEN observed
SEEP ooze; small spring
SEER prophet
SEGO herb; bulb; lily; Utah state flower
SEHR very: Ger.
SEID tribe; lord; chief; Mohammed's descendant
SEIK Hindu sectarian
SEIL rope: Ger.
SEIM Polish assembly
SEIN poss. pronoun, be, being: Ger.
SEIP seep; ooze
SEIR Bib. mountain (Hor), Edom (Esau's home)
SEIS six: Sp.
SEIT measure
SEJM Polish assembly
SELA Dead Sea town
SELF identity; ego; one
SELL vend; betray; persuade; hoax; — short
SEME (sprinkling) pattern
SEMI half
SEMO Sancus (deity); Dius Fidius
SEND transmit; dispatch; propel; swing; enthrall
SENN Swiss herdsman
SEPS snake; lizard
SEPT social unit; screen; seven: Fr.
SERA antitoxins; blood parts; whey; evening: It.
SERB Servian; Yugo(slav)
SERE wither(ed); Negroid
SERF slave; peasant
SERI betel; Indian
SERO prefix: thin; late pupil
SERT Sp. painter
SESI black-fin snapper
SESS soap frame bar
SETA caterpillar's hair; spine
SETH banker; Adam's son; Osiris' evil brother
SETI river; pharaoh
SETT tool; paving stone
SEVE wine delicacy: Fr.
SEWN stitched
SEXT canonical hour (noon); organ stop; sixth
SEXY sexually appealing
SHAB paltry guy
SHAD fish
SHAG hair; tobacco; bird; rascal; dance step
SHAH ruler
SHAM deceit; fake
SHAN Thai
SHAP silk yarn
SHAT saline lake
SHAW thicket; pshaw; George Bernard (playwright)
SHAY chaise; carriage
SHEA tree; butter
SHED cast off; abandon; drop; hut; shelter
SHEE Irish fairyfolk
SHEM Noah's son; Semite
SHEN Christian God (China)
SHER tiger
SHEW show: Brit.; -bread
SHIH weight; measure
SHIK Arabian Turkoman
SHIM leveling slip; shingle; knife

SHIN leg, calf front; run; climb
SHIP vessel; send; — of state
SHIR cook; gathers; tiger
SHIV bit of husk; fluff; blade
SHLU Moroccan Berber
SHOA Abyssinian
SHOD wearing shoes
SHOE foot covering; crakow; wheel drag; tire
SHOG shake; jog
SHOO scare away; begone!
SHOP store; buy; buying place; talk —; window-
SHOQ tree (tanning); chogak
SHOR salt lake; Tatar tribe
SHOT missile; pellet; guess; range; marksman; film record; long —; big —
SHOU Tibetan deer
SHOW exhibit(ion); reveal; appear(ance); 3rd place; no — (airline term)
SHRI glorious; holy; Lakshmi (goddess)
SHUA Abraham's son
SHUE Tibetan deer
SHUL synagogue
SHUN avoid; abstain (from)
SHUT close; refine
SIAK latex
SIAL earth's outer part
SIAM Thailand; Anna's king (The King and I)
SICE number 6 on die
SICK urge (dog); ill; weak
SIDA herb; shrub; hemp
SIDE region; part(y); oblique; aspect; support; lateral
SIDI Moslem title; Negro
SIDY pretentious
SIEG victory: Ger.
SIER pintado (fish)
SIFT screen; separate; bolt
SIGH lament(ing sound)
SIGN symbol; signal; subscribe; ratify; hire
SIKA Jap. deer
SIKH Hindu soldier
SILK fiber; thread; -worm
SILL beam (door, window)
SILO fodder pit; ensile
SILT sediment; scum; drift
SIMA igneous rock
SIME monkey
SIMI Dodecanese isle
SIMP simpleton
SINA drug; mountain (Moses)
SIND river; Pakistan province; are: Ger.
SINE math. ratio; without: Lat.; — qua non; — die
SING vocalize; warble; tell
SINH math. term
SINK fall; droop; conceal; basin
SINN — Fein (Irish society)
SINO prefix: Chinese
SIOL great Irish clan
SION purple seaweed; Zion
SIPO liana
SIRE father; beget; king
SIRI betel
SIRS gentlemen
SISE six (dice)
SISH slushy ice
SISI porkfish
SISS hiss; shamel; girl
SIST stay; delay; summon
SITA Ramachandra's wife (Sanskrit Ramayana)
SITE location; scene
SITO prefix: grain
SIUM water parsnip
SIVA Hindu deity; cosmic dancer (Nataraja)
SIVE sickle; knife
SIZE bulk; quality; glue; filler; — up
SIZY viscous
SIZZ hiss(ing sound)
SKAG boat; keel part
SKAL health toast
SKAT card game; star
SKEE ski
SKEG keel part; plum; tear
SKEN squint
SKEO fisherman's hut
SKEP basket; measure; beehive
SKEW twist; swerve; distort(ed); slant(ing)
SKEY yoke bar
SKID clog; slide; — Road, Row
SKIL candlefish; beshow
SKIM scoop off; scud; brush
SKIN hide; pelt; peel; fleece; — and bones
SKIP jump; escape; mess; captain; -tracer
SKIR fly; scurry; skim
SKIT comedy sketch; jest
SKIV sovereign (coin)
SKUA bird; great —; jaeger
SKUN skinned
SKYE Isle; dog, terrier
SKYR sour curdled milk

SKYT move fast; dart; slip
SLAB slice; road
SLAG dross; lava
SLAM bang; criticize; grand —
SLAP strike; — bang
SLAT lath; slab; sheep's hide; flap
SLAV Eastern European
SLAW cabbage
SLAY kill; overwhelm
SLEB nomadic Arab
SLED vehicle, snow or ice
SLEE sly
SLEW killed; twist; swamp; large number
SLEY weaver's reed
SLID glided; slipped
SLIM slight; scanty; sly; slenderize
SLIP slide; err(or); escape; pier; leash; garment; memo; cut
SLIT cut; slash; opening
SLOB slovenly one
SLOE blackthorn; plum; blue-black
SLOG hit (hard); slug; slam
SLOO swamp
SLOP slush; gush; mash
SLOT (cut) opening; bolt; deer; track; — machine
SLOW dilatory; tardy; inert; boring; hinder
SLUB twisted wool roll
SLUE swamp; twist; lot
SLUG snail; idle; metal spacer; small drink; bullet; strike
SLUM dilapidated district
SLUR pass over; mumble; defame; stigma; glide (mark)
SLUT slattern; harlot
SMEE pintail duck; widgeon; Peter Pan pirate
SMEW merganser; duck
SMIT struck; destroyed
SMOG fog and smoke; haze
SMUG tidy; neat; priggish
SMUR mist; cloud
SMUT soot; coal dust; plant disease; obscenity
SNAB hill part; girl
SNAG stump; cut; obstacle; tangle
SNAP seize; break; click; shut; photo; vigor; easy task; — out
SNED lop; prune
SNEE cut; snick(er) —
SNIB escape logging work
SNIG chop off; drag; pilfer
SNIP cut; shred; slip
SNOB social climber; game
SNOD trim; snug; plausible
SNOT wick end; blow nose
SNOW ice crystals; white hair; cocaine; — goose; TV spots
SNUB rebuke; slight; stumpy
SNUG cozy; trim; Shaks. character
SNUP snap up cheaply
SNUR snort
SOAK absorb; sot
SOAP cleanser; detergent; money; soft —; -box; — opera
SOAR fly high; glide
SOBK evil deity
SOCK beat; wind cone; stocking
SOCO heron; bittern
SODA carbonated water; Vichy; drink; sodium compound (bicarbonate)
SODI Gaddiel's father (spy)
SOFA couch; divan
SOFT giving way; easy; light(ly); mild; tractable
SOGA grass rope: Sp.; Bantu
SOHO exclamation; London district
SOIA food plant
SOIE silk
SOIL earth, ground; land; stain; pollute
SOIR evening: Fr.
SOJA bean; glycine
SOKA drought blight
SOKE jurisdiction
SOLA herb (topee source); alone; holla!
SOLD vended; persuaded; cheated
SOLE pelma (bottom); flatfish; single; only
SOLI single performances; prefix: sun, alone
SOLO song; (fly) alone
SOMA vine; sacred drink; body
SOME various; any; somewhat; part
SONE loudness unit
SONG poem (music); pittance
SOOK Moslem market; hog call
SOOL pull, tousle about
SOON promptly;

willingly
SOOT powdery carbon smudge
SOPH 2nd year student
SOPT Dog Star; Isis
SORA bird; rail
SORB wild apple; Slav
SORE painful; vexed; sensitive; deer
SORI clusters; spores
SORS lot: Lat.; divination
SORT type; kind; quality; classify
SORY vitriolic earth
SOSH jag; drunk; dash
SOSO middling; passably
SOSS hog call for food
SOTO Hernando de (explorer)
SOTS yeast
SOUD pay
SOUF sigh
SOUK Moslem market
SOUL spirit; inspirer; force; psyche; person
SOUP broth; stew; — and fish; duck —; step (up); explosive; fog
SOUR acid(ify); tart; disagreeable
SOUS coins; under: Fr.
SOWN scattered; seeded
SOYA bean; dill; fennel
SPAD nail
SPAE prophecy
SPAN stretch; team; measure; dog
SPAR mineral; mast; gaff; box
SPAT mollusk; gaiter; snap; tiff
SPAY deer; castrate
SPEC speculation
SPED hastened
SPEE Graf — (ship, admiral)
SPES (goddess of) hope
SPET spit; barracuda
SPEW eject; scatter; gush
SPEX spectacles
SPEY river
SPIN whirl; twist; aerial stunt; — a yarn
SPIR prefix: coiled
SPIT land point; rod; impale; expectorate; — and image
SPIV slacker: Brit.
SPOT stain; point, place; fish; small amount; espy
SPRY nimble; brisk; smart
SPUD scrape(r); potato; dig
SPUN twisted; whirled
SPUR point; good; kick; otter track; ridge
SPUT boiler plate
STAB pierce; trial
STAD town
STAG deer; men's party; warn
STAR sun; heavenly body; asterisk; hummingbird; excel
STAT photocopy
STAY rope; fasten; prop; endure; wait; remain; stop(ping); — put
STEM shaft; trunk; stock; axis; dam; check; derive; turn skis
STEN weight; gun
STEP pace; foot rest; rank; act; dance; crush; — on it
STER suffix: agent
STET let it stand!
STEV stanza
STEW boil; steep; hash; worry; study; oyster bed
STIB sandpiper (dunlin)
STIR agitate; rouse; ado; jail
STLO WW II battle site
STOA portico; poikile (Zeno)
STOD Danish speech
STOF measure
STOG stall in mud
STOL short takeoff and landing
STOM prefix: mouth
STOP halt; discontinue; arrest; close; instrument part; period
STOT stumble; stutter
STOW pack; hide; hold; skiing resort
STUB stump; penpoint; short, stocky; extirpate; ticket part; bump
STUD breeding stock; knob; stump; dot; poker
STUM grape juice; must; renew wine
STUN stupefy; daze
STYX Hades river; nymph: daughter of Oceanus, Tethys
STUT horsefly
STYE eyelid swelling
SUAN — pan: Chin. abacus
SUCH of this kind; same
SUCK draw in; bleed; drink
SUDD Nile waste matter; dam
SUDS lather; froth; beer
SUER prosecutor; suitor
SUET hard fat
SUEZ canal; seaport
SUFI mystic ascetic
SUGI Jap. cedar

SUIT costume; card set; legal action; please; (out)fit
SUJI wheat; semolina
SUKE Susan; teakettle
SUKU Bantu
SUKY Susan; teakettle
SULA genus; booby; gannet
SULD measure
SULK mope; be sullen
SULU Moro
SUMO Ulvan
SUMP dig pit; tank; cistern
SUNG chanted; Chin. dynasty
SUNK immersed; overcome
SUNN hemp: fiber plant
SUNT babul: gum tree; pod; are: Lat.
SUPA P.I. tree; lamp oil
SUPE stage extra; supercharge
SURA Koran section; deva
SURD irrational; mute
SURE safe; firm; certain
SURF swell of sea; foam
SURT Frey's slayer
SUSA Elam city (Esther story)
SUSI fine cotton
SUSU blind dolphin; Congo
SUSY name: Susan; Susanna
SUUM hum; — cuique
SUZY name: Susanna
SVAN Caucasian
SWAB mop; lout
SWAD mass; soldier
SWAG bag; booty; sway; sag
SWAM floated
SWAN constellation; dive; — song
SWAP barter; exchange
SWAT hit (hard); river, state (Pakistan); sultan of — (Ruth)
SWAY oscillate; veer; rule
SWIG gulp; hoist; tackle
SWIM move in water; float; teem
SWIZ swindle
SWOB sponge; wipe; mop
SWOP trade
SWOT hard work; grind; hit
SWOW I — (oath)
SWUM swim participle
SYCE groom
SYED Moslem chief
SYKE fountain (Her.)
SYNC synchronize
SYPE ooze
SYRA Aegean island
SYRT quicksand
SYUD Moslem prince; title
TAAL lake; volcano; language
TAAR tambourine
TABI sock
TABU forbidden
TACE steel splint
TACK hook; rope; course; attach
TACT diplomacy; perception
TAEL weight; coin
TAEN taken
TAFT President; Republican; rower's seat; -Hartley Act
TAHA bird
TAHR goat
TAIL end; cue; follow; highplate
TAIN plate
TAIR goat
TAIT marsupial
TAJO trench
TAKE acquire, seize; scene part; receipts
TAKT beat(s); tempo
TAKU Indian
TAKY taking
TALA tree; basin; ruin
TALC soapy mineral
TALE story; — of Two Cities; count
TALI gold piece; weight
TALK speak; converse; conference; empty words; dialect; — turkey
TALL high; incredible
TAMA Indian
TAME gentle; subdue
TAMP fill up; pound down; tool
TANA shrew; rabbi; police station; lake (Blue Nile)
TANE Polynesian god
TANG spur; flavor; sound; seaweed; dynasty
TANH math. term
TANK basin; store; war vehicle; panzer
TANO Indian
TAOS Indian
TAPA bark; cloth
TAPE band; tie; Indian; record; red—; ticker—
TAPS lights-out signal; bugle call
TAPU taboo
TARA fern; goddess; palm
TARE vetch; allowance (weight)
TARI coin; goddess
TARN lake
TARO rootstock; pol; elephant's ear
TARP canvas; sailor; hat
TARR tease
TART sour; pastry; harlot
TASH fabric
TASK labor; assignment; take to

— (censure)
TASS Soviet News Agency
TASU measure
TATE wool; hair lock
TATH dung
TATT knot lace
TATU Indian; armadillo; tattoo
TAUN measure
TAUR Taurus (bull)
TAUT snug; tense
TAVE Octavia
TAVY Octavia
TAWA tree
TAWN tawny
TAXI (ride a) cab; prefix: arrangement
TAXO prefix: arrangement
TCHA (rolled) tea
TCHE fruit tree; Chin. flute
TCHI measure
TCHU exclamation
TEAK tree; dark
TEAL duck (blue)
TEAM group; yoke
TEAN tone: Scot.
TEAP ram
TEAR drop; weep; rip; glass defect
TEAT nipple
TEBJ Negro Berber
TECA teak; Indian
TECH technical school
TECK readymade tie
TECO Indian
TEDA Negro Berber
TEEL sesame
TEEM abound
TEEN 13–19; injury; pain
TEER golfer; mix colors
TEES river (North Sea)
TEFF grain plant
TEGG sheep in 2nd year
TEHR wild goat
TEIG Teague; Thaddeus; Timothy; dough: Ger.
TEIL linden tree; lime
TEJU lizard
TELA tissue; web; banana port
TELE prefix: far, complete
TELI low (merchant) caste
TELL inform; discern; chat; William (Swiss hero)
TEMA musical theme; Arab
TEMS sieve; sift
TEND serve; incline
TENE suffix: ribbon
TENG measure
TENT cloth shelter; pup —; wine; frame
TEOS Ionian city
TERA Buddhist monastery
TERM phrases; word; condition; time, period
TERN gull; threefold; ship
TERP prehistoric mound
TESA Indian buzzard
TESS Theresa, Hardy heroine
TEST shell; cupel; examination; try
TETE head: Fr.; — à tête; hairdo
TETH Heb. J, 9
TEWA N. M. Indian
TEXT (literary) substance; topic; Scripture passage; type
TEYL linden; lime tree
THAI Siamese
THAN in comparison with; conjunction
THAR goat
THAT so; which; pronoun; connective; that's —
THAW melt; unbend
THEA tea source; name
THEB measure
THEE you
THEM pronoun
THEN at a time; therefore
THEO prefix: god
THEW muscle; sinew
THEY pronoun; people; men
THIN lean; dim; rare; dilute; — ice
THIO prefix: brimstone
THIS pronoun, demonstrative
THOB rationalize
THOR thunder god (Thursday); Midgard slayer; Odin's son; missile
THOS jackal genus
THOU 2nd pers. pronoun
THUD dull sound; blow
THUG assassin; hoodlum
THUS in this way; hence
TIAM language
TIAO Chinese money
TIAR crown; shrub
TIBS — eve (never-never)
TIBU Negro-Berber
TICE lure; yorker (bowled ball)
TICK parasite; mattress; count; tic
TIDE ocean's rise, fall; season; drift; endure; current; help
TIDY (make) neat
TIED bound; knotted; drawn
TIEN sky: Chin.; Chu (Lord of Heaven); your(s): Fr.
TIER row; layer; pinafore
TIFF (petty) quarrel
TIGE rifle steel pin; dog
TIGG swindler (Dickens)

TIKE child
TIKI god; first man; image
TILE ceramic slab; drain pipe; domino; tessera; slate
TILL until; plow; cultivate; tray, cash box
TILT cover; incline; tip; joust; sport
TIME period; moment; credit term; speed rate; meter, rhythm; Father —; space —
TINA fem. nickname
TIND kindle
TINE tooth; prong; pain; grass
TING sound; Chin. pottery
TINO Sambal language
TINT color; shade; tinge
TINY small; -tim (herb); Tim (Dickens)
TION suffix
TIOU Indian (Tonikan)
TIPE rabbit trap
TIPI wigwam
TIRE fatigue; bore; wheel covering; rubber; shoe
TIRO amateur; novice
TITI monkey; tree; petrel
TITO Yugo. leader (Broz)
TIVY huntsman's cry
TIZA ulexite mineral
TLAC coin
TMAN U.S. Treasury agent
TMEN U.S. Treasury agents
TOAD amphibian; anuran; fawn
TOAG Indian
TOAT plane handle
TOBA Tatar; Chaco Indian
TOBE cotton cloth; future
TOBY cigar; mug; dog; rob
TOCK hornbill
TOCO toucan
TODA Ceylon aborigine
TODE (haul with) sled
TODO bustle; stir; ado
TODY green — (bird)
TOED stepped (gingerly)
TOFF dandy
TOFT — and croft (house)
TOGA Roman garb; gown; senatorship
TOGO Afr. republic; Jap. admiral and statesman
TOGS clothes
TOGT trading enterprise
TOHO halt! (to dogs)
TOHU -bohu (confusion)
TOIL work; drudge(ry); snare
TOKO Chin. store; flogging
TOLA weight
TOLD narrated; counted
TOLE entice; told; tinware
TOLL tax; lure; sound
TOLT writ; isolated peak
TOLU balsam (rose odor)
TOMA Liberian Negro
TOMB grave; monument; bury
TOME book; papal letter
TONE pitch; accent; Wolfe (Ir. rebel)
TONG secret society
TONK (cow bell) clang; honky-; game
TONY nickname (Anthony); stylish
TOOA hero; beefwood
TOOK seized; caught; endured; supposed
TOOL instrument; polish; dupe
TOON tree (dye); mahogany
TOOP measure
TOOT sound horn; carousal
TOPE drink; shark; stupa; orchard
TOPH drum; porous rock
TOPI antelope; pith hat
TOPO prefix: place
TOPS most superior
TORA hartebeest; law (of Moses); Pentateuch
TORE ripped; geom. surface
TORI moldings
TORN ripped; damaged
TORO N.Z. tree
TORP croft; Swed. small farm
TORT wrongful act
TORU N.Z. tree
TORY conservative
TOSH bath(tub)
TOSK Albanian
TOSS throw; fling; change
TOTA grivet monkey
TOTE carry; haul; total
TOTO baby (animal); all
TOTY low-caste worker
TOUG horsetail standard
TOUP Malay lugger
TOUR trip; circuit; — de force
TOUT tip(ster); praise; all: Fr.; — à fait; — de suite
TOWN city; Hamlet; — hall; man about —

TOWY like flax fibers
TOXA sponge spicule
TRAM trolley; gauge
TRAP snare; mouth; net; catch; clothe; basalt; — shooting
TRAY salver; platter;
TREE wood, plant; family —; boot; shoe —
TREF homestead
TREK migrate; journey
TRES very: Fr.; three: Sp.
TRET weight allowance
TREY three(spot)
TRIG trim; sound; prim; math. course
TRIM shear; adjust; adorn; rebuke; defeat; neat
TRIN one of triplets
TRIO set of 3; So. Amer. Indian
TRIP move; slip; journey; (mis)step
TRIS prefix: thrice
TRIT prefix: third
TRIX fem. suffix
TROD walked; track
TROP too much: Fr.
TROT jog; gait; race; translation; fishing line
TROW believe; fishing boat
TROY weight system; Ilium, Ilion (Troas); city
TRUE factual; loyal; align
TRUK islands (Carolines)
TRYP parasite in blood (sleeping sickness, nagana, surra)
TSAO Chinese state
TSAR emperor; dictator
TSHI Gold Coast language
TSIA tea
TSIN Chin. dynasty
TSUN measure (1/10 ch'ih)
TUAN measure; sir; title
TUBA saxhorn; tree; nut; fish poison; palm sap
TUBE cylinder; tunnel; subway; radio, TV part; Audion (DeForest)
TUCK draw up; fold (in); eat; Friar (Robin Hood)
TUEL furnace
TUFA porous rock
TUFF volcanic rock
TUFT crest; clump; tassle
TUKE fabric; canvas
TULA metal; niello; city; Toltec ruins
TULE bulrush; cattail
TULU Dravidian Indian
TUMP drag slain deer
TUNA fish; pear; opuntia
TUND pound; bruise
TUNE song; pitch; harmony
TUNG tree; oil
TUNK rap; thump; game
TUNO rubber tree; gum
TUNU rubber tree; gum
TUNY melodious
TUPI Amazon Indian
TUPY Amazon Indian
TURB crowd; clump
TURF sod; grassy ground; peat; racing
TURI Pathan tribesman
TURK Mongoloid; Seijuk; Ottoman; Osmanli; horse
TURM troop; company
TURN bending; corner; revolve; reverse; change; shape; act; movement
TURP turpentine
TUSH tooth; Georgian; pshaw!
TUSK long tooth
TUTE to tutor
TUTU N.Z. shrub; poison; ballet skirt
TUUM thin: Lat.
TUWI P.I. dyewood tree
TUZA pocket gopher
TWEE bird's cry
TWIG discover; branch; beat
TWIN double; match; — Cities
TWIT taunt; yarn snarl
TYBI 1st Egypt. spring month
TYEE chief
TYER binder
TYKE dog; child
TYLO dog (Maeterlinck)
TYMP blast furance stone
TYNE Eng. river
TYPE kind, sort; class(ify); printer's letter; use typewriter, produce copy
TYPO printing error
TYPP yarn count unit
TYPY typical
TYRE Phoenician city; Sur
TYRO beginner; novice
TYRR Odin's son; war god
TYTO barn owl; Strix; Aluco
TYTY farmer of God's Little Acre
TZAR emperor; dictator
UANG beetle
UBER over: Ger.
UBII Teutonic tribe
UDAD sheep
UDAL land
UDIC Caucasian

language
UEBA measure
UFER fir pole; shore: Ger.
UGLY badlooking; unpleasant; plug-
ULAM Gilead's descendant
ULAN lancer; — Bator
ULEX spine shrub (furze)
ULLA grass; paper pulp
ULLO Indian shell money
ULLR chief god: Sif's son; Thor's stepson
ULME elm
ULMO muermo; hardwood
ULNA elbow bone; ell
ULUA cavalla; fish; caranx
ULVA sea lettuce; laver
UMBO shield boss; shell beak
UMPH grunt
UNAL land
UNAU sloth
UNBE cease to be
UNCA 8th note
UNCI hooks; claws
UNCO strange; very: Scot.
UNDE waving, wavy (Her.)
UNDO untie; unfasten; ruin
UNDY waving, wavy (Her.)
UNIE unicorn fish
UNIO mussel
UNIS Etats — (USA): Fr.
UNIT single thing; basic amount; one; monad
UNTO to; for; toward
UNTZ weight
UNUK star; — al Hay
UNZE weight
UPAS tree (juice); arrow poison
UPDO upswept hair
UPGO ascend
UPIS Artemis, Nemesis
UPLA cow dung; fuel
UPON prep: above, against
UPSY -daisy
URAL -Altaic; mountains; hypnotic
URAN lizard; Indian
URAO trona (mineral)
URBS (capital) city
URDE key-shaped (Her.)
URDU Hindustani language
URDY key-shaped (Her.)
UREA chemical compound
UREY Nobel physicist
URFA Turkish city (Edessa)
URGA Outer Mongolia
URGE prod; impel; impulse
URIA Bathsheba's husband; auk
URIM — and Thummim (sacred instruments)
URIS Leon (author)
URNA measure
URSA bear; stars: — Major, Minor; Great, Little Bear (Dipper)
URTH Norn; Wyrd (with Verthandi, Skuld); Weird Sister
URUS wild ox
URVA mongoose
USAR salt; grass
USAS dawn goddess
USED accustomed; secondhand
USEE future user
USER employer
USES law of — (beneficiary)
USHA Bana's daughter; sorceress
USUN ancient North Chinese
USUS user, use: Lat.
UTAH state; Indian; Deseret (Mormon)
UTAI noh songs (yo-kyoku)
UTAS 8 day feast; Jap. songs
UTCH "I"
UTIA rodent
UTOR to use: Lat.
UTUG horsetail standard
UTUM small owl
UVAL grapelike
UVEA iris layer
UVIC grapelike; acid
UVID moist; wet
UZAI Palal's father
UZAL Shem's descendant
UZAN weight
UZUN ancient North Chinese

VAAL river
VACH goddess
VADE leave; — mecum
VADY vade mecum; summons
VAGI nerves
VAIL inventor
VAIN empty, idle; futile; proud
VAIR fur
VALE valley; — of tears; farewell: Lat.
VALI Odin's son; viceroy
VALL valley
VAMP sock; shoe part; fireman; ghost; flirt
VANE weathercock; feather; blade
VANG rope
VANS race of gods
VARA measure
VARE weasel
VARI lemur; prefix: diverse
VARY alter; differ
VASA ducts; Swedish dynasty
VASE vessel
VASO vase: It; prefix: blood vessel
VAST huge (space)

VASU deity (Vishnu); nephew
VAUX village; fort (Verdun battle)
VAYU wind god
VEAL calf; meat
VEAU veal, calf: Fr.
VEDA sacred Hindu books
VEEP vice-president
VEER shift (course); waver
VEGA meadow
VEHM medieval tribunal
VEIL screen; facial garment; cloistered life
VEIN channel; streak; blood vessel
VELA membranes; soft palates; the Sails (Argo constellation)
VELD So. Afr. grassland
VELO speed unit
VELT measure
VENA vein: Lat.
VEND Slav; sell; sale
VENI prefix: vein; —, vidi, vici (I came, I saw, I conquered)
VENO prefix: vein
VENT hole; let out; issue
VEPS Finnish tribe (Chud); Dog Star (Isis): Horus
VERA tree; measure; name
VERB action word
VERD green(leafed)
VERI centipede
VERT green (Her.); veer; convert
VERY true; same; extremely; light signals; flare
VEST waistcoat; clothe; empower
VETA mountain sickness
VETO prohibit(ion); no

VIAL vessel
VIBO gulf (Italy)
VICA Pota (goddess)
VICE sin; fault; vise; proxy; — versa
VIDA feminine of David
VIDE see: Lat.; for example; quae —
VIER striver; four: Ger.
VIEW sight; see; aim; opinion; scene
VIGA rafter; log
VIII 8; Augustus reign
VILA fairy; New Hebrides
VILE base; evil; odious
VILI brother of Odin; Ve
VILL village; township
VILY fairies
VINA harp; guitar; wines
VINE creeping plant
VINO palm liquor
VINT card game
VINY entwining
VIOL string instrument
VIRA Bantu
VIRE feathered arrow
VISA endorse(ment); -vis
VISE tool; clamp; endorse
VISS weight
VITA life: Lat.
VITE quick, lively: Fr.
VITI East African
VIVA salute (long live); — voce (spoken aloud)
VIVE — le roi!; long live!: Fr.
VIVO spirited
VLEI marsh; lake; creek
VLEY marsh; swamp; creek
VOCE voice: It.; sotto, viva —

VOET measure
VOGT medieval official
VOID empty; vacuum; cancel
VOIR see: Fr.
VOLA palm (hand, foot)
VOLE rodent; slam (cards)
VOLK people: Ger.; workmen (So. Afr.)
VOLT sideways gait; fencing leap; elec. unit
VONE robot bomb
VOOG lode cavity
VOTA Roman festivals
VOTE ballot; suffrage; voice; enact; propose; Ingrian Finn
VOTH Ingrian Finn
VOTO So. Amer. Indian
VTOL vertical takeoff and landing
VTWO robot bomb
VUGG lode cavity
VUGH lode cavity
VULN wound (Her.)
WAAC fem. soldier
WAAG monkey
WABE tree
WABI Indian; tree
WACO city
WADD mineral
WADE pass; demon; Hampton
WADI valley; river; oasis
WADY valley; river; oasis
WAEG bird; kittiwake
WAER dam
WAFD Egyptian
WAFF flapping; paltry
WAFT float; flag; whiff
WAGE carry on; -earner; pay, salary
WAGH interjection
WAHA lake trout
WAHR true: Ger.
WAIF stray

WAIL lament
WAIN wagon; Charles's —
WAIT attend; defer; serenader; lie in —
WAKA canoe
WAKE track; arouse; vigil; island
WAKF trust fund
WAKY alert
WALE streak; texture; ridge; welt
WALI prefect
WALK go on foot; path; pass, base on balls; — the plank
WALL barrier; fence; enclose; knot; Berlin —
WALT Whitman
WAMP elder
WAND rod; staff; magic —
WANE ebb; lessen
WANG weight; meadow; prince
WANT lack; desire
WANY diminished
WAPP rope guide
WAQF trust fund
WARD (safe)guard; parry; district; charge; Artemus (Browne)
WARE merchandise; beware
WARF warp
WARM hot; genial; newly made; heat; — Springs
WARN caution; give notice
WARP threads; twist; falsify
WART protuberance; -hog
WARY watchful
WASH bathe; laundry; tint
WASP yellow jacket; hornet; fem. flyer: WW II
WAST were
WATE sea demon
WATT inventor, elec. unit (volt-ampere); hare
WAUK wake: Scot.
WAUL wail
WAVE billow; swell; undulation, flutter; signal; — length; navy woman
WAVY fluctuating; undulating
WAWA gibbon
WAXY viscid; pliable
WAYS wise; — and means
WEAK feeble; pliable; light
WEAL body politic; stripe
WEAN withdraw; alienate
WEAR be clothed in; impair; endure; deteriorate
WEBB Beatrice Potter (writer)
WEED plant; tobacco; remove
WEEK time unit; sennight; squeak
WEEL fish basket, trap; pool
WEEP cry; bend; leak
WEET bird; cry of bird
WEFT yarn; mist; (weave) web
WEGA star
WEGG Silas (ballad seller: Dickens)
WEIN wine: Ger.
WEIR dam; fish trap
WEKA flightless bird
WEKI fern
WELD unite; junction
WELF ducal family
WELK (gather) snail; Lawrence (musician)
WELL (water) pit; shaft; eddy; flow; rightly; very; sound; healthy
WELS sheatfish
WELT ridge; wale; strip; sew; beat; universe; Ger.
WEND Slav; go; travel
WENT departed
WEPT cried; Jesus —
WERE verb form; prefix: metamorphosed human
WERF farmyard
WERI aweto (caterpillar)
WERT were: archaic, poetic
WESE we shall
WEST wind; painter, author; occident; go —; Mae —
WETA wingless locust
WEVE contraction
WHAM exclamation
WHAT interrogative; pronoun; what's —
WHAU why; tree
WHEE whistle sound
WHEN whereas; how soon
WHET sharpen; excite; edge
WHEW whistle; exclamation
WHEY milk serum; thin; pale; curds and —
WHIG U.S., Brit. party
WHIM fancy; caprice
WHIN gorse; restharrow; rock; winch
WHIP lash; urge; defeat
WHIR fly; hurry; buzz
WHIT bit; jot; dull sound
WHIZ hum; bargain; corker
WHOA stop!; opp. of giddap
WHOO exclamation
WHOM pronoun
WHOP dash; beat; bump
WHUN gorse; restharrow
WHYO gangster; footpad
WICK part of candle, lamp

WIDE broad; far; lax; astray
WIDU Moslem ablution
WIEL whirlpool
WIES Ys
WIFE spouse; marry
WIGG peruke; long hair
WIGS — on the green (fray)
WILD rough; savage; mad; eager; unruly; wilderness
WILE trick; guile; lure
WILK (gather) snail
WILL volition; choice; decree; bequeath; testament
WILT droop; lose spirit
WILY artful; subtle
WIND turn; coil; blowing air; mere talk
WINE fermented juice
WING alar appendage; faction; annex; fly
WINK blink; signal
WINY vinous; drunken
WIPE rub off; beat
WIRE cable; snare
WIRY tough; sinewy
WISE sage; learned
WISH desire; request
WISP torch; shred; flock; brush; ignis fatuus
WIST know; knew; measure
WITH prep.: including, and
WIVE marry; act as wife
WOAD herb
WOKE stirred; roused
WOLD upland plain
WOLF canid (dog); Lupus; larva; devour; dissonance; cry —; flirtatious man
WONG field; meadow
WONT custom; contraction
WOOD timber; forest; Grant (painter); Leonard (general)
WOOF crossthreads; texture; weft; bark
WOOL (sheep) fleece; down
WOON Burmese governor
WORD term; news; promise; order; phrase
WORE had on (clothes); tired
WORK labor; mental product; act; operate; function; needlework
WORM crawler; maggot; screw; insinuate
WORN used (as clothing); shabby; tired
WORT plant; (pot)herb
WOTE Ingrian Finn
WOVE entwined; spun
WRAC women's army corp
WRAF air force; aviatrix
WRAP cloak; blanket; coat
WREN bird; navy woman; architect
WRIG wriggle
WRIT legal order; Holy —
WROX rot
WUDU Moslem ablution
WUFF gruff bark sound
WUKF trust fund
WURD Norn; Urth
WURM glacial period
WUZU Moslem ablution
WYCH -hazel; — elm
WYND alley; small court
WYNN timber truck; Ed (actor: Perfect Fool)
WYRD Norn; Urth

XEMA artic gull
XENO guest; prefix: foreign
XERO prefix: dry
XIII 13; Augustus reign
XINA nickname: Christina
XIPE -totec (Aztec god)
XMAS Christmas
XOSA Kaffir
XOVA Opata; Pimian Indian
XXIV 24; Tiberius reign

YABA bark; cabbage tree
YABU Afghan pony
YAGE plant
YAGI antenna
YAHO tribesman
YAJE plant
YAKA Bantu
YAKI cayman
YALE university; lock; Eli, Elihu —; myth. antelope
YALI mansion
YALU river (Korean War)
YAMA first mortal (Judge of Dead)
YAMP herb; tuber
YANA tribe
YANG honk; male or positive principle (opp. to yin)
YANK jerk; New Englander; Union soldier; American
YAPA leaf mat
YAPP (bookbinding) style
YARD 3 feet; grounds; enclosure; spar
YARE prompt; ready
YARK yerk
YARL Norse chief; earl

YARM scream; wail
YARN spun wool; story
YARR growl; snarl; herb
YARU Hades; heaven
YATE eucalyptus
YATI ascetic; devotee
YAUP yap; yawn
YAVA weight
YAWL (sail)boat
YAWN open wide; gape; chasm
YAWP yap; yawn
YAWS skin disease
YAYA copa, lancewood (tree)
YEAH yes
YEAN to lamb
YEAR time period; twelve month; leap —; calendar, fiscal —
YEAS yes votes
YEDO Tokyo
YEGG safecracker; tramp
YELD barren; milkless
YELK yolk
YELL cry; cheer
YELP shrill bark
YELT gilt (sow)
YENI So. Amer. tanager
YERK wrench; kick; trump
YESO plaster of Paris; gypsum
YETA Jap. outcast
YETI abominable snowman
YGUN antisub gun
YHVH God, Yahveh, Tetragrammaton
YHWH God, Yahweh, Tetragrammaton
YIMA Avestan demigod
YIPE howl; cry
YIRM fret; whine: Scot., Ir.
YIRN whine; grimace; smirk: Scot., Ir.
YIRR growl; snarl; Scot.
YITE bird (yellowhammer)
YMCA welfare organization
YMER myth. giant
YMIR rime-cold giant
YNCA Quechuan Indian (ruler); Inca
YOBI Jap. military service
YODH Hebrew Y, 10
YOGA mental discipline
YOGH Mid. Eng. G, Y
YOGI ascetic; yoga disciple
YOKE join; link; slavery
YOKY coupled
YOLK egg yellow; essence
YOND past; beyond
YOOP sobbing sound
YORE ancient (times); long ago
YORK city; archbishopric; imperial (apple); Sgt. Alvin (WWI)
YOUP yelp; scream; yawn
YOUR possessive pronoun
YOWL howl(ing); yell
YPIL tree (brown dye)
YSER river
YUAN dynasty; money
YUCA cassava; manioc
YUFT Russ. leather
YUGA Hindu age cycle
YUIT Asian Eskimo
YUKI Ca. Indian
YULE Christmas
YUMA Indian (Ca.); city
YUNX woodpecker genus
YURT Kirghiz tent
YUTU Peru tinamou; bird
YWCA welfare organization
ZACH name
ZAIN horse
ZAMA Hannibal's defeat
ZANT fish
ZANY clown(ish)
ZARA city; Judah's son
ZARF holder for cup
ZARP policeman
ZATI bonnet monkey
ZAZA opera (Leoncavallo)
ZEAL ardor; enthusiasm
ZEBU ox; Brahman bull
ZEIN protein
ZEKE Ezekiel
ZEME (abode of) spirit; fetish
ZEMI (abode of) spirit; fetish
ZEND — Avesta (holy text)
ZENO philosopher (Stoic, Cynic); emperor
ZENU Afr. sheep
ZERO nothing; cipher; nullity; — hour; Jap. plane
ZEST orange peel; relish; gusto
ZETA Greek Z, 7
ZEUS chief god; Jupiter; Hera's husband; son of Cronus, Rhea
ZIMB Ethiopian fly
ZINC metal; element; color
ZING sharp thrill; vim
ZION Israelites; heaven
ZIPA Chibcha chief
ZIPS Czech
ZIRA measure
ZITA Austrian empress
ZIZA Rehoboam's son
ZIZZ whirring sound
ZOAR town; Bela; city of Lot

ZOAS symbolic figures (Blake)
ZOBO mongrel yak
ZOEA crab larva
ZOGO sacred object
ZOIC pert. to animals
ZOID organic body cell
ZOLA author: Emile (J'accuse, Dreyfus case; Nana)
ZOLL measure
ZONA girdle; shingles
ZONE area; band; partition
ZOOM buzz; climb; approach suddenly
ZOON developed compound animal
ZOOT — suit: extreme style
ZORI sandal
ZULU Bantu; Kaffir; ship; artificial fly
ZUNI Indian; reservation
ZUPA Yugo. district
ZUPH Samuel's ancestor
ZUZA weight
ZWEI two: Ger.
ZYGA rowers' benches; brain fissures
ZYME ferment

FOUR-LETTER WORDS -AA- to -ZU-

BAAL deity
BAAR weight
BAAS master
CAAM loom; heddies
FAAM tea; leaves
GAAL brewing
HAAB year
HAAF fishing grounds
HAAK fish; wander
HAAR fog
JAAL goat
KAAN inn; title
KAAT shrub; weight
LAAP secretion; insect
MAAL measure
MAAM madam
MAAN city
MAAS river
MAAT goddess
MAAZ Judah's descendant
NAAB river
NAAM distrain
PAAL measure
PAAN town
PAAR sand
PAAS Easter
RAAB river
RAAD assembly; fish
SAAH measure
SAAL hall: Ger.
SAAN Bushmen
SAAR river; region
TAAL lake; volcano; language
TAAR tambourine
VAAL river
WAAC fem. soldier
WAAG monkey
BABA nurse; title; cake
BABE baby; — Ruth; girl
BABI sect
BABU Hindu gentleman
BABY doll; indulge
CABA measure
CABO Yubi
EABA measure
FABA bean; vetch
GABE taro
GABI taro
GABY fool
HABA bean
HABE tribe
HABU pit viper
LABE city
MABA Negro; tree
MABI tree
NABK shrub
NABO shrub
NABU god; mountain
PABA vitamin
RABA river
RABI crop; physicist
SABA fiber; kingdom; island
SABE know
TABI sock
TABU forbidden
WABE tree
WABI Indian; tree
YABA bark; cabbage tree
YABU Afghan pony
BACH live alone; composer
BACK help; tub; past; retreat; kick-; dorsal, posterior; spine
CACA goddess
CACO bandit
DACE fish
EACH every(one)
FACE surface; oppose; line
FACT deed; reality
FACY fresh
HACK chop; writer; horse
JACA tree
JACK flag; tool; card; fruit; raise
JACU bird
LACE cord; flavor; netting
LACK need
LACT prefix: milk
LACY netlike
MACE staff; spice; weight; coin
MACK coat
MACO cotton
NACH after: Ger.
PACA rodent

PACE step; speed; peace: It.
PACK bundle; cosmetic paste; cards; crowd; animal(s)
PACO alpaca
PACT agreement
RACA reproach; fool
RACE run; contest; people; speed; Cape —; rat-
RACK framework; clouds; gait; torture
RACY smart
SACK dismiss; plunder; wine; bag; gown; sad —
SACO weight; river
TACE steel splint
TACK hook; rope; course; attach
TACT diplomacy; perception
VACH goddess
WACO city
ZACH name
BADB goddess
BADE waited; asked; invited; commanded
CADE cask; tree; pet; rebel
CADI judge
CADY golf boy
DADA father; cult
DADE support
DADO wall part; groove
DADU saint
EADS engineer; bridge
FADE weaken; flat; dissolve
FADO tune
FADY weakening
GADE fish; composer
GADS -hill (Dickens)
HADE angle; strip
HADJ pilgrimage
JADE gem; horse; exhaust
JADU magic
JADY gemlike
KADA measure
KADE tick
KADI judge
KADU tribe
LADE load; dip
LADY title; bird
MADE successful; created; constructed
MADI Negro
MADO fish
PADI rice
RADA legislature
RADE elated
SADD dam; waste matter
SADE letter; Marquis
SADH holy man
SADI poet
SADO carriage; island; river
SADR tree
VADE leave; — mecum
VADY vade mecum; summons
WADD mineral
WADE pass; demon; Hampton
WADI valley; river; oasis
WADY valley; river; oasis
BAEL thorny (fruit) tree
BAER prizefighter, actor
BAEZ singer
CAEN city
DAER re borrowed stock
DAEZ daze
FAEX dregs
GAEA goddess; Titans' mother
GAEL Celt; Irishman
HAEC this one (fem.): Lat.
HAEM prefix: blood
JAEL Sisera's killer; Heber's wife
LAEL Gershonite's father
LAET freedman
NAEL weight
SAER tenant
TAEL weight; coin
TAEN taken
WAEG bird; kittiwake
WAER dam
BAFF strike; stroke
BAFT astern; cotton
CAFE restaurant; coffee; -au-lait; society
DAFF put aside
DAFT foolish; giddy
GAFF spear; ordeal; hoax
HAFF lagoon
HAFT handle
KAFA Ethiopian
MAFU stable boy
RAFF Raphael
SAFI collection; float
RAFT secure; box
SAFE Afghan
TAFT President; Republican; rower's seat; -Hartley Act
WAFD Egyptian
WAFF flapping; paltry
WAFT float; flag; whiff
BAGA turnip
BAGG heiress (Thackeray)
BAGO shrub
CAGE confine; enclosure; elevator car; nor iron bars a —
CAGN mantis; deity
CAGY shrewd
DAGG pistol
DAGH hill
DAGO tribe
GAGE pledge; fruit; gauge; general; governor
GAGL sweet gale
HAGG demoness; hack; wood
HAGI clover; prefix: saint
IAGO villain (Othello)
JAGA Bantu
JAGG pendant; tooth; slash
KAGO conveyance
KAGS convict (Dickens)
KAGU bird
LAGO lake
MAGE magician
MAGG bird; chatter
MAGH month
MAGI caste; priests; wise men,

kings of Orient: Melchior, Gaspar, Balthazar
NAGA snake
NAGY Hungarian premier
PAGA rice
PAGE young attendant; call, summon; leaf
PAGO -Pago (city)
RAGA state of nirvana
RAGE fury; storm; fad
RAGI grass
SAGA legend; story; goddess; weight
SAGE herb; wise; Russell (financier)
SAGO palm; starch
SAGY wise
VAGI nerves
WAGE carry on; -earner; pay; salary
WAGH interjection
YAGE plant
YAGI antenna
BAHI fortune
BAHO prayer stick
BAHR sea; — El Azrak
BAHT coin
HAHA laugh; fence
HAHN Otto (Nobel physicist)
KAHA proboscis monkey
KAHN banker; test
KAHU harrier; bird
LAHN river
LAHR Bert (comedian)
MAHA monkey; deer
MAHE island
MAHI river
MAHR marriage settlement
NAHA city
NAHE river; near: Ger.
OAHU (Hawaiian) island
PAHA hill
PAHI ship
PAHO prayer stick
RAHU demon
SAHA measure
SAHH measure
SAHO language
SAHU spiritual body
TAHA bird
TAHR goat
WAHA lake trout
WAHR true: Ger.
YAHO tribesman
BAIA state; city; resort; bay
BAIL security; bond; set free; dip out; hoop
BAIN bath: Fr.
BAIS caste
BAIT lure; harass; pest poison
CAID alcaide
CAIN tribute; (Abel's) slayer; mark of —
DAIL legislature; — Eireann
DAIN Patusan chief (Conrad); Curse (Hammett); measure
DAIS platform
FAIL fall short; err
FAIN glad; eager
FAIR pleasing; ample; just; bazaar; — and square; — deal
FAIT fact; — accompli
GAIA goddess
GAIL Abigail; brewing
GAIN reach; earn; profit; notch
GAIT walk; pace
HAIG soldier (Douglas)
HAIK garment; frame
HAIL ice pieces; salute; — fellow
HAIR filament; cilium, seta; fabric; -trigger
JAIL prison; gaol
JAIN sect (Indian)
KAID chief; alcaide
KAIF languor; hemp
KAIK village
KAIL tree; ibex; kale
KAIN tribute
KAIO fruit
KAIR fiber
KAIS island
LAIC secular
LAID put down; calmed
LAIN reclined
LAIR resting place
LAIS hetaera
LAIT milk: Fr.; café-au-
MAIA goddess; crab; star
MAID servant; — of Orleans
MAIL coin; tax; armor; post
MAIM disfigure; mutilate
MAIN conduit; first; river; Spanish —
MAIS but, corn: Fr.
NAIA cobra
NAID worm
NAIF native; of true luster
NAIK leader
NAIL fasten(er); claw; seize; expose
NAIO tree
NAIR native
NAIS nymph
PAID recompensed; discharged; satisfied
PAIL bucket
PAIN ache; trouble; forfeit
PAIR couple; brace
PAIS country
QAIS island
QAID alcaide
RAIA ottoman; fish
RAID attack; foray
RAIK weight; measure
RAIL bird; scold; paling
RAIN shower; scratch; — check
RAIP rope
RAIS chief (Nepalese)
SAIC Near East ketch
SAID before-men-

tioned; Port — (city); name
SAIL canvas; rigging; journey, travel
SAIM grease
SAIN consecrate; tree
SAIR savor
SAIS groom; city; know: Fr.
TAIL end; cue; follow; high-
TAIN plate
TAIR goat
TAIT marsupial
VAIL inventor
VAIN empty, idle; futile; proud
VAIR fur
WAIF stray
WAIL lament
WAIN wagon; Charles's —
WAIT attend; defer; serenader; lie in —
ZAIN horse
BAJU jacket
CAJA box; bank
CAJI snapper
CAJU fruit; mahogany
GAJO non-Gypsy
HAJE cobra
HAJI pilgrim
HAJJ pilgrimage
MAJA crab
MAJO dandy; shrub
NAJA cobra
PAJO prayer stick
RAJA prince; fish
TAJO trench
YAJE plant
BAKA devil
BAKE dry; roast; biscuit
BAKU hat; tree; rug; city; oil field
CAKE bar; dough; harden
CAKY crusty
FAKE loop; cheat; sham
FAKY spurious
HAKA dance
HAKE fish; pester; frame
HAKH claim(er); legal claim; share
HAKO rite
HAKU fish
JAKE Jacob; rube; money; satisfactory; ginger
JAKO parrot
KAKA parrot
KAKI bird; tree
LAKE sea; pool; red (cochineal)
LAKH 100,000; coin
LAKY red
MAKE produce; create; cause; reach; type; identify
MAKI lemur
MAKO shark
MAKU Indian
OAKS horse race; trees
OAKY oaklike
RAKE incline; tool; collect; roué; —'s Progress
RAKH hayfield
RAKI spirits
RAKU -ware
SAKA era; Scythians
SAKE purpose; beer
SAKI monkey; Munro
TAKE acquire; seize; scene part; receipts
TAKT beat(s); tempo
TAKU Indian
TAKY taking
WAKA canoe
WAKE track; arouse; vigil; island
WAKF trust fund
WAKY alert
YAKA Bantu
YAKI cayman
AALI pasha
AALU Hades; heaven
BALA geol. epoch
BALD naked; — eagle
BALE woe; bundle
BALI demon; monkey; offering; island
BALK thwart; signal
BALL game; confuse; dance; — bearing; good time; -point; Amer. sculptor
BALM plant; soothe; — in Gilead
BALT Lithuanian, Esth; Latvian; Lett
BALU wildcat
CALE Gypsy; cabbage
CALF bovine, etc., young; fur; leather; skin; lower leg
CALI Colombian city
CALK tighten; stop; sleep; tool; copy
CALL summon; visit; cry; telephone; — girl; — money
CALM quiet; mold
CALO Gypsy
CALP limestone
CALX residue; heel: Lat.
DALE valley; share; trough
DALI tree; offering; Salvador —
DALL sheep
FALA refrain; dog
FALL descend; ruin; autumn; — of Man
FALX weapon; — cerebri (brain fold)
GALA festival; tribe
GALE storm, wind
GALI abuse
GALL bile; venom; wound; chafe; swelling; impudence
GALT clay bed
HALA pine tree
HALE healthy; Nathan (patriot)
HALF moiety; -breed, -caste, -nelson, -shell
HALI prefix: sea, salt
HALL building; room; town —; guild-; astronomer; -Mills
HALM plant stems
HALO circle; glow; nimbus; prefix:

sea, salt

HALS Frans (painter)

HALT stop; lame

IALU Hades; heaven

KALA bird

KALB de — (general)

KALE cabbage

KALI glasswort; carpet; evil genius; Agni's tongue; Siva's wife

KALO taro root

LALO composer

MALA evil(s), wrong(s): Lat.; jaw

MALE man(ly); tribe

MALI caste; nation; river

MALL mallet; game; bird; assembly (place)

MALM limestone

MALO loincloth

MALT barley; beer

NALA hero

PALA weight; antelope; vine; rice

PALE wan; pallid; ashy; picket; stake; beyond the —

PALI slope; coral parts; Buddhist language

PALL cloak; covering; cloy

PALM tree; measure; hand part; paddle; conceal; grease the —

PALO pole, wood: Sp.

PALP appendage; feeler

PALY wan; heraldic design

RALE rattling sound

RALO measure

SALA dining room: Sp.

SALE bargain; auction; willow; salted: Fr.

SALM star

SALP marine animal

SALT sodium chloride, NaCl; sailor; season; — away; — Lake City; — Sea

TALA tree; basin; ruin

TALC soapy mineral

TALE story; — of Two Cities; count

TALI gold piece; weight

TALK speak, converse; conference; empty words; dialect; — turkey

TALL high; incredible

VALE valley; — of tears; farewell: Lat.

VALI Odin's son; viceroy

VALL valley

WALE streak; texture; ridge; welt

WALI prefect

WALK go on foot; path; pass, base on balls; — the plank

WALL barrier; fence; enclose; knot; Berlin —

WALT Whitman

YALE university; lock; Eli, Elihu —; myth. antelope

YALI mansion

YALU river (Korean War)

CAME arrived; lead rod; Indian

CAMP tent(s); town; stay; boot —

DAMA gazelle

DAME woman; title; — aux Camelias

DAMN curse; — the torpedoes

DAMP moist(ure); depress

FAMA rumor

FAME reputation

FAMN measure

GAMA Vasco da (navigator); grass

GAMB leg

GAME amusement; quarry; resolute; lame

GAMP umbrella; Sairey (nurse: Dickens)

HAMI hooked processes

IAMB verse foot

JAMA tunic

JAMB leg armor; pillar; door part

JAMI mosque

KAMA love god; desire; river

KAME hill

KAMI language; deity

LAMA priest; llama; brown; Dalai, Panchen, Tashi —

LAMB amateur speculator; Charles (Elia: essayist)

LAME cripple(d); halt; plate; fabric

LAMP light; bulb

MAMA mother; goddess

MAMO bird

NAMA Hottentot; herb

NAME title; reputation; clan; cite

RAMA Indian; Vishnu incarnation; bull (Kipling)

RAME branch

RAMI branches

RAMP inclined way; rear

SAMA fish; trance-inducing music

SAME identical

SAMH bread plant

SAMP maize

TAMA Indian

TAME gentle; subdue

TAMP fill up; pound down; tool

VAMP sock; shoe part; fireman; ghost; flirt

WAMP eider

YAMA first mortal

(Judge of Dead)
YAMP herb; tuber
ZAMA Hannibal's defeat
AANI ape
BANA Titan
BANC (judge's) bench
BAND strip; group; orchestra; range; tie; sash
BANE woe; curse; poison
BANG beat; thump;. hair; sardine; interjection
BANI coins
BANK mound; bench; deposit; bird flock; Left, Right —; blood —; eye —
BANS marriage notice
BANT diet
CANA Indian
CANE stem; rattan; stick; walking —; sugar —; candy —
CANG wooden collar
CANO canal: Sp.
CANT angle; change course; log; tilt; whine; jargon; be unable
DANA goddess; editor; author; lake
DANE Scandinavian; great — (dog); Hamlet
DANG curse (damn)
DANK moist; rank
DANS in: Fr.
DANU goddess
FANA Sufistic concept
FANE temple
FANG tooth; measure; Dickens character
FANO cloth; cape
GANE yawn
GANG crew; associate; rock
GANO Count (Roland's destroyer)
GANT yawn; gaunt; gannet; Eugene (Wolfe character)
GANZ all, totally: Ger.
HAND control; aid; worker; measure; pass; player; cards; penmanship
HANG suspend; plan; bit; die on gallows
HANK coil; Morgan (Twain)
HANO Indian
HANS John; Johannes; Castorp (Mann)
HANT ghost
JANE woman; false hair; cloth; — Eyre; Lady — Grey
JANN genii
KANA Japanese writing
KANE god
KANG — Hsi (Chinese emperor)
KANO painting school
KANT change course; Immanuel (philosopher)
LANA wood; flannel
LAND ground; debark; state: Ger.
LANE (fixed) route; throat
LANG auld — syne; Fritz
LANK thin; lean(ness)
LANX platter
MANA magic power; Chinese letter
MAND grass
MANE hair; in the morning: Lat.
MANG bat (Kipling)
MANI peanut; prefix: hand
MANN man: Ger.; Horace (educator); Thomas (writer)
MANO grindstone; hand: It.
MANS Chinese aborigine; Le — (city; auto race)
MANU prefix: hand; Laws (Hindu code book)
MANX pert. to the Isle of Man; cat
MANY numerous
NANA nurse; Aztec hero's wife; Zola novel; dog (Peter Pan: Barrie)
NANE own; none
PANA city
PANE glass; panel
PANG agony
PANI madam: Polish
PANK weight
PANT gasp; yearn
RANA frog; prince; Aegir's wife
RAND border; ridge; strip; So. Afr. gold mine
RANG sounded
RANI princess; wife
RANK luxuriant; gross; fetid; grade; array
RANN verse; stanza; kite (Kipling)
RANT scold; rave; frolic
RANZ — des vaches (Alpine melodies)
SANA Yemen's capital; fiber
SAND grit; silica; polish, smooth; red-yellow; George (novelist: Dudevant)
SANE rational
SANG Hindu group; herb; weight; did sing
SANK descended
SANS without: Fr.; — culotte (radical); — gêne
TANA shrew; rabbi; police station; lake (Blue Nile)
TANE Polynesian god
TANG spur; flavor; sound; seaweed; dynasty

TANH math. term
TANK basin; store; war vehicle; panzer
TANO Indian
UANG beetle
VANE weathercock; feather; blade
VANG rope
VANS race of gods
WAND rod; staff; magic —
WANE ebb; lessen
WANG weight; meadow; prince
WANT lack; desire
WANY diminished
YANA tribe
YANG honk; male or positive principle (opp. to yin)
YANK jerk; New Englander; Union soldier; American
ZANT fish
ZANY clown(ish)
FAON fawn color
GAOL prison
GAON Jewish title
JAOB measure
KAON particle
LAON Fr. city
LAOS country
MAON Nabal's home
NAOS star
PAON peacock blue
TAOS Indian
BAPS dancing master (Dickens)
CAPA cloak; Sp.
CAPE cloak; promontory; — Cod, — Horn, — Good Hope
CAPH star, letter
CAPO head: It.; crime boss
CAPP Al (cartoonist: Abner, Dogpatch)
GAPA guided missile
GAPE yawn; stare; gap
GAPO (inundated) forest
GAPY yawning
HAPH weight
HAPI bull; Nile (god)
HAPU clan
JAPE deride
KAPA cloth(es)
KAPH letter
KAPP measure
KAPU forbidden; taboo
LAPP N. Scandinavian
MAPO goby (fish)
NAPA leather; wine region; city; river
NAPE neck back
NAPU ruminant
PAPA father; Pope; potato: Sp.; baboon; clay
PAPE bunting (bird)
RAPE herb; ravish
RAPT engrossed; rapture
SAPA grape juice
SAPH giant (Philistine)
SAPO soap; toadfish
TAPA bark; cloth
TAPE band; tie; Indian; record; red —; ticker —
TAPS lights-out signal; bugle call
TAPU taboo
WAPP rope guide
YAPA leaf mat
YAPP (bookbinding) style
WAQF trust fund
AARE river
AARU Hades; heaven
BARA measure
BARB sharp point; fish; dog; mow; pigeon
BARD armor; poet; — of Avon (Shakespeare)
BARE expose(d); mere; Indian
BARI hut; Negro; city
BARK peel; tan; cough
BARM yeast
BARN storehouse; stable
BARO big; prefix: weight
BARR elephant's cry
BART man's name
BARU tree
CARA dear (one): It.; Indian
CARD comb; pasteboard; menu; playing —; calling —
CARE grief; heed; responsibility; anxiety; foster; relief organization
CARF slit; notch
CARK trouble
CARL rustic; villain; Charles
CARN stone heap
CARO dear (one): It.; Caroline
CARP fish; complain
CARR pool
CART wagon; transport
DARD language group
DARE venture; defy; fish; Virginia (1st Amer. child)
DARI grain sorghum; carpet
DARK unlighted; wicked; dismal
DARN mend; interjection
DARR bird
DART missile; fish; seam; run
EARL nobleman; count; name
EARN gain; win; deserve
FARD face paint; date
FARE passenger; price; happen; food; travel
FARL cake (part)
FARM till; land; — out; club
FARO card game; Pharaoh
GARA coin
GARB apparel; array
GARE wool; station, beware: Fr.

GARM Hel's dog
GARN yarn; go on
GARO Assam native
GARY city, steel center
HARA Jap. statesman
HARB Bedouin
HARD solid; firm; close; severe; difficult
HARE leporid; rabbit; run
HARI river; Mata (spy)
HARK listen
HARL barb; filament
HARM hurt; evil; injury
HARP coin; seal; Lyra; constellation; Irishman; nag
HARR hinge
HART stag; deer
HARZ German mountains
JARA palm
JARL Norse chief; earl
KARA river
KARI gum tree
KARL Charles; — Marx
KARN stone heap
KARO plant
LARA Byron poem
LARD fat; stuff
LARE Mid. Eng. lore
LARI money; sea birds
LARK bird; frolic; yellow
LARP secretion; insect
LARS Porsena (conqueror)
MARA demon; aborigine; Naomi
MARC residue; name; weight
MARD spoil
MARE blues; sea; moon area; horse; shanks' —
MARI prefix: sea; husband: Fr.; native
MARK sign; aim; stamp; money; observe; evangelist; easy —; — time
MARL clayey soil; fertilizer; fiber
MARM ma'am; school-
MARO ship name: Jap.
MARS war god, planet
MART market; nickname
MARU ship name: Jap.
MARX Karl (economist)
MARY female name; queen; sister of Lazarus, Martha; Virgin; Lady
NARD plant; ointment
NARE Loki's son
NARK informer; tease
NARY not one
OARY oarlike
PARA coin; weight; river; city (Belem)
PARC park; oyster farm: Fr.
PARD chum; leopard
PARE cut off; peel
PARI weight; prefix: equal
PARK (common) grounds; green; deposit; Hyde, Central, etc.
PARR young fish; skegger; Catherine (Henry VIII wife)
PARS part: Lat.
PART portion; duty; role; separate; split; go
RARA — avis (rare bird)
RARE underdone; thin; uncommon
SARA native
SARD carnelian; gem; Sardinian
SARG Toni (puppeteer)
SARI Hindu garment
SARK Channel island
SART Iranian Turk
SARY sorry
TARA fern; goddess; palm
TARE vetch; allowance (weight)
TARI coin; goddess
TARN lake
TARO rootstock; poi; elephant's ear
TARP canvas; sailor; hat
TARR tease
TART sour; pastry; harlot
VARA measure
VARE weasel
VARI lemur; prefix: diverse
VARY alter; differ
WARD (safe)guard; parry; district; charge; Artemus (Browne)
WARE merchandise; beware
WARF warp
WARM hot; genial; newly made; neat; — Springs
WARN caution; give notice
WARP threads; twist; falsify
WART protuberance; -hog
WARY watchful
YARD 3 feet; grounds; enclosure; spar
YARE prompt; ready
YARK yerk
YARL Norse chief; earl
YARM scream; wall
YARN spun wool; story
YARR growl; snarl; herb
YARU Hades; heaven
ZARA city; Judah's son
ZARF holder for cup
ZARP policeman
BASE bottom; source;

home; headquarters; found; diamond corner; ignoble
BASH smash; bruise
BASK luxuriate; warm oneself
BASS fish; fiber; lowest part; singer; musical instrument
BAST (woody) fiber; goddess, phloem
CASA house, building: Sp., It.
CASE event; fact; record, problem (medical, etc.); legal action; argument; grammar form; container, chest, box; queer phenomenon; inspect
CASH money; exchange; hemlock
CASK barrel; measure
CASO Dodecanese island
CASS treasure; Timberlane (Lewis); Squire (Eliot)
CAST throw; project; shed; deposit; form; found; actors; (assign) roles
CASY ex-preacher (Steinbeck)
DASH sprint; smash; small portion
DASI concubine
DASS Durga, Ram (twins, Kipling)
EASE repose; comfort; moderate; facilitate
EAST direction; Asia; Orient
EASY simple; calm; soft; — Street
FASH rough edges; vex
FASS measure
FAST not eat; fixed(ly); quick(ly); wild; — and loose
GASH (make) incision
GASP pant (eagerly)
HASH chop up; mixture; mess
HASP clasp
HASS throat; embrace
HAST contraction; havest
JASS card game
KASA grass
KASI tile work
KASM measure
LASH (whip) stroke; tie; eye part
LASI tribe
LASS girl; sweetheart
LAST block, final(ly); endure; measure
MASA corn meal
MASH brew; mixture; hammer; flirt
MASK disguise; screen; domino
MASS rite; bulk; populace; assemble
MAST pole; brown; nuts
MASU salmon
NASA space-travel agency
NASE promontory; nose: Ger.
NASH soft; humorist
NASI prince; patriarch
NAST cartoonist
OAST kiln
PASA raisin
PASH hurl; smash
PASI low-caste Hindu
PASO measure
PASS opening; go through; by; license; condition; amatory gesture
PAST tense; ago; after
RASA essence; tabula
RASE rub; demolish
RASH hasty; careless
RASP grate; file
SASA fencer's cry
SASH casement; scarf; belt
SASS sauce
TASH fabric
TASK labor; assignment; take to — (censure)
TASS Soviet News Agency
TASU measure
VASA ducts; Swedish dynasty
VASE vessel
VASO vase: It.; prefix: blood vessel
VAST huge (space)
VASU deity (Vishnu); nephew
WASH bathe; laundry; tint
WASP yellow jacket; hornet; fem. flyer: WW II
WAST were
BATA child; servant
BATE diminish; tanner's bath; restrain
BATH tub; measure; spa; order
BATT matted mass
BATZ coin
CATA down; prefix: away
CATE delicacy
CATO the Censor (Roman statesman); foe of Carthage
CATS — cradle
DATA facts
DATE fruit; tree; brown; (make) appointment
DATO tribal chief
DATU tribal chief
EATS food; consumes
FATA — Morgana (fairy, mirage)
FATE destiny (goddess); end; kismet
GATA nurse shark
GATE entrance; pass; judgment; money
GATH Philistine city

HATE detest; aversion
HATH contraction: haveth
HATI heart
HATT measure
JATI caste
JATO jet-assisted takeoff
KATE bird; Shaks. shrew; Greenaway
KATH astringent
KATI weight
KATY Catherine; -did
LATA jumping disease
LATE dead; tardy
LATH strip; slat
LATU gold coins
MATA Hari (spy)
MATE companion; match; tea; check-
MATH mowing; monastery; school course
MATT lusterless
MATY (assistant) servant
NATA Nana's hero
NATE born
NATH star
NATO international (Western) alliance; treaty organization
NATR weight
OATH appeal; pledge; vow; curse
OATY full of oats
PATA painting; turban; sword
PATE head; paste
PATH track; route
PATO Muscovy duck
PATT stalemate(d)
PATU weapon
RATA tree; chestnut; rate; pro —
RATE censure; ratio; charge; estimate; rank; tax
RATH chariot; fort; temple; early; mome-
RATI weight
RATS bah!
SATE gratify; glut
SATI queen of the gods
TATE wool; hair lock
TATH dung
TATT knot lace
TATU Indian; armadillo; tattoo
WATE sea demon
WATT inventor, elec. unit (volt-ampere); hare
YATE eucalyptus
YATI ascetic; devotee
ZATI bonnet monkey
BAUD speed unit
BAUL mendicant
BAUM Vicki (novelist); Oz creator; tree: Ger.; — marten
BAUR joke
CAUK (secure by a) tenon
CAUL basket; covering membrane
CAUP tribute: Scot.
DAUB plaster; besmear
DAUD dad
DAUK relay post
DAUN — stage (geol. period)
DAUR Manchu
DAUW zebra
EAUX waters: Fr.
FAUN deity; satyr
FAUT comme il — (proper): Fr.
GAUB persimmon (astringent)
GAUD ornament; bead
GAUE German regions
GAUL Celt, Frenchman; France
GAUM attention
GAUP gape
GAUR wild cattle
GAUS region: Ger.
GAUT range; pass; river bank stairs
HAUL drag; shift; loot
HAUT high: Fr.; — monde
JAUN palanquin
KAUN resthouse; lord; title
LAUD praise
LAUK exclamation
LAUN ceramic sieve
MAUD plaid; rug; name; Muller; Whittier; Tennyson heroine
MAUI Polynesian hero
MAUL hammer; bruise; mangle
MAUN must
NAUT sea mile
PAUL click; detent; Apostle; Bunyan; Revere; pope
PAUN betel leaf
PAUP walk idly
SAUD Ibn (king)
SAUF except, safe: Fr.; — conduit
SAUK Indian, Mont. river
SAUL tree; king (son of Kish) — of Tarsus (Paul)
SAUM weight
SAUR prefix, suffix: lizard
TAUN measure
TAUR Taurus (bull)
TAUT snug; tense
VAUX village, fort (Verdun battle)
WAUK wake: Scot.
WAUL wail
YAUP yap; yawn
BAVE double silk thread
CAVA pepper shrub, root; gum resin; vein
CAVE cavern; — in (collapse); — canem (beware of dog)
CAVY rodent; guinea pig; stray animal(s)
DAVE David
DAVY David; lamp; affidavit; Jones' locker
EAVE roof edge

FAVI tiles; flagstones
FAVN measure
GAVE donated
HAVE possess; aux. verb; must; deceive
JAVA coffee; hood; (Indonesian) Sunda Isles; — man (Pithecanthropus)
JAVE Jehovah
KAVA pepper shrub, root; gum resin; vein
KAVI Java language
LAVA fluid rock; obsidian's source; red
LAVE pour; bathe
NAVE hub; church part
NAVY fleet; blue; tobacco; — yard
PAVE cover firmly; — the way; jewel setting
PAVO peacock; constellation
PAVY peach
RAVE rant, rage; enthusiasm; rod
RAVI tribesman
SAVA Yugo. river
SAVE rescue; avoid; lay by; but; — face
TAVE Octavia
TAVY Octavia
WAVE billow, swell; undulation flutter; signal; — length; Navy woman
WAVY fluctuating; undulating
YAVA weight
BAWD procuress
BAWL cry; howl; — out (chide)
BAWN mud enclosure; white
CAWK bird's cry; mineral
CAWL basket
DAWK relay transport; mall
DAWM coin
DAWN daybreak, Eos; Aurora; red
FAWN deer, cringe; toady; brown
GAWD ornament, bead
GAWK lout; stare
GAWN gallon; tub
GAWP gape; simpleton
HAWK bird; predator; peddle; mortarboard
HAWM loiter
JAWY talkative
KAWA pepper shrub, root; gum resin; vein
KAWI Java language
KAWN resthouse; lord; title
LAWK surprise!
LAWN fabric; grass plot; bishopric
LAWS rules; principles
MAWK maggot
PAWA weight
PAWL click; detent; tent
PAWN chessman; pledge
SAWK measure
SAWN sawed; cut
TAWA tree
TAWN tawny
WAWA gibbon
YAWL (sail)boat
YAWN open wide; gape; chasm
YAWP yap; yawn
YAWS skin disease
CAXI snapper (fish)
SAXE Saxony; blue
TAXI (ride a) cab; prefix: arrangement
TAXO prefix: arrangement
WAXY viscid; pliable
BAYA weaverbird; Bantu
CAYO island; reef: Sp.
DAYE printer (Bay Psalm Book)
DAYS by day
HAYA arrow poison
HAYZ zodiacal situation
KAYO knock out
MAYA weaverbird; (Mexican) Indian; magic; Buddha's mother
MAYO Indian; physicians, clinic (Rochester)
RAYA broadbill
SAYA outer skirt
VAYU wind god
WAYS wise; — and means
YAYA copa, lancewood (tree)
CAZA Turkish district
CAZI Moslem judge
CAZY Moslem judge
DAZA Negro-Berber
DAZE stupefy; mica
DAZY confused
FAZE disturb
GAZA Israel (Philistine) seaport; Mozambique district; eyeless in — (Samson)
GAZE stare; wonder
GAZI warrior; title
GAZY gaping
HAZE mist; drizzle; harass
HAZY dim; obscure
JAZZ dance; music; banter
KAZI Moslem judge
KAZY Moslem judge
LAZE idle(ness); tribesman
LAZI tribesman
LAZO lasso
LAZY idle
MAZE labyrinth; daze; perplex
MAZO de la Roche (novelist: Jaina)
MAZY perplexing
NAZE promontory
NAZI fascist; Hitlerite
RAZE scrape; demolish
RAZZ chaff; ridicule
ZAZA opera (Leoncavallo)
ABAC calculator

ABAS down: Fr.
EBAL Mount (Joshua's altar)
IBAD Hira Arab
IBAN dyak (Borneo)
OBAN coin
ABBA father; title
ABBE priest; title; Amer. meteorologist
ABBY Abigail
ABCS first principles; alphabet
ABED in bed; bedridden
ABEL Adam's son; Cain's brother; Magwitch (Dickens); letter A; monkey
ABET aid; incite
ABEY waive
EBED Gaal's father
EBEN Ebenezer
EBER Hebrew ancestor
IBEX wild goat; bouquetin
OBED David's grandfather
OBEX brain matter
OBEY submit; comply
UBER over: Ger.
ABIA Samuel's son
ABIB month
ABIE 's Irish Rose; name
ABIR red powder
IBID P.I. lizard (tidbit); the same: abbr.
IBIS (sacred) wading bird
IBIT P.I. lizard (tidbit)
OBIA Ashanti religion
OBIE Off-Broadway award
OBIT death notice
UBII Teutonic tribe
ABLE fit; adept; suffix; -bodied
ABLY deftly
ABOO war cry
ABOT Mishnah
ABOU father; deity
ABOX braced
EBOE tree; oil; Negrito
EBON ebony; black
OBOE woodwind; chanter
OBOL 1/16 drachma (coin)
ABRA narrow pass; river
ABRI shelter
EBRO Sp. river
OBRA works: Sp.
ABSI tribe
ABUT touch
EBUR ivory: Lat.
OBUS howitzer shell
ECAD modified organism
ICAL compound suffix
SCAB crust; strikebreaker
SCAD fish; large amount
SCAN examine; measure poetry
SCAP skull
SCAR rock; cicatrix; mar(k); fish
SCAT buffet; scatter; begone!; tax; skat
SCAW promontory
ACCA fabric
ECCA geol. period (Karroo)
ECCE lo: Lat.; — homo
ACER tree
ICED frozen; chilled
ICER freezer; mixer
ACHE pain; yearn
ACHT eight: Ger.
ACHY painful
ECHO Narcissus's nymph; repeat; response; fruit tree (ginko)
ECHT genuine: Ger.
ICHO fruit tree (ginko)
ICHU valuable grass
OCHA weight
OCHS Adolph (publisher)
TCHA (rolled) tea
TCHE fruit tree; Chin. flute
TCHI measure
TCHU exclamation
ACID sour; biting
ACIS river; (Galatea's) lover
CCIV 204; Septimus Severus reign
CCIX 209; Septimus Severus reign
MCII 1102
MCIV 1104; First Crusade, conquest of Acre
MCIX 1109
SCIO prefix: sky
ACLE tree
ACME peak; crisis
ACNE disease
ACON boat
ACOR acidity
ICON image; statue
SCOB fabric defect
SCON teacake
SCOP bard; poet
SCOT Celt; Highlander; tax; — free
SCOW flat-bottomed boat
ACRE field; measure; city
ECRU beige; unbleached
OCRA vegetable; gumbo
ACTA deeds; records
ACTH hormone medicine
ACTO action: Sp.
ACTS NT book
ACTU act: Lat.
ECTO prefix: outside
OCTA prefix: eight
OCTO prefix: eight
ACUS pin
SCUD run fast; wind-driven clouds; skim; flea
SCUG squirrel: Brit.
SCUM dross; refuse; rabble
SCUP pan fish; porgy
SCUR horn tissue
SCUT rabbit's tail; fur
ACYL acid part

ADAD fiber; god
ADAH wife of Lamech, Esau; fem. name
ADAI tribe
ADAK Aleut. island
ADAM first man; sin; composer; architect
ADAN prayer call
ADAR month
ADAT law
ADAY date atomic attack
DDAY operation start
EDAM city; cheese
EDAR Bib. site
IDAS Marpessa's lover; Castor's slayer
ODAL land; vine
ODAX rock whiting (fish)
UDAD sheep
UDAL land
ADDA god; river; skink
ADDU skink; fiber; god
ADDY Adeline
EDDA Norse epic
EDDO taro root
EDDY whirlpool; Mary Morse Baker (Christian Science)
ODDS inequality; advantage; at —; -on
ADEN comb. form: gland; city; gulf; region
ADER Benjamite
ADES Hades
EDEA reproduction organs
EDEL noble: Ger.
EDEN paradise; West of Nod
EDER river
IDEA conception; fancy; key meaning; opinion
IDEE — fixe: Fr.
IDEM same: Lat.; semper —
IDEN Henry VI figure
IDEO prefix: idea
IDES Roman date; — of March (fateful day)
ODEA theaters; halls; galleries
ODED prophet or his father
ODEL vine; land ownership
ODER river
EDGE brink; sharpness; goad; advantage; — on
EDGY sharp; snappish
ADIB star
ADIN name
ADIT entrance
EDIT correct; redact; blue-pencil
IDIC pert. to ids
IDIO prefix: one's own
ODIC pert. to ode, od
ODIN one-eyed Norse god: Frigg's husband, Thor's father
ODIO hatred: It.
UDIC Caucasian language
IDJO Niger delta Negro
IDLE not working; empty; lazy; waste
IDLY vainly; lazily
ADMI gazelle
EDNA female name; Ferber (novelist)
EDOM Esau's country; Idumaea
IDOL god, deity; image; adored one
ODOR smell; repute
ADRY thirsty
IDUN Bragi's wife (Norse)
ODUM tree (iroko)
IDYL pastoral poem
IDYO Niger delta Negro
ODYL alleged force
ADZE tool
IDZO Niger delta Negro
BEAD globule; ball; drop; aim
BEAK bill; nose; judge
BEAL river mouth
BEAM bar; timber; breadth; ray; smile; on the —; broadcast
BEAN plant; trifle; head; strike
BEAR carry; yield; endure; relate; animal; Ursa; short-seller; pessimist
BEAS Punjab river
BEAT strike; defeat; mystify; throb; scoop; field; sphere; — the Dutch
BEAU dandy; lover; — Brummell, — Nash
DEAD deceased; entire; absolute(ly); — reckoning
DEAF unhearing; inattentive; — and dumb; — mute
DEAL bargain; transaction; unfinished wood; apportion(ment); policy; New —, Fair —
DEAN clergyman; educator; oldest member; doyen
DEAR costly; loved; loved one
FEAK twitch; wipe
FEAL conceal
FEAR fright; doubt
FEAT deed; accomplishment
GEAL pert. to earth
GEAN cherry
GEAR notched wheel; equipment; adjust; harmonize
GEAT channel in

mold; Scandinavian (Beowulf)
HEAD skull; top; brain; chief; crux; source
HEAF pasture
HEAL cure; restore
HEAP pile; crowd; car
HEAR listen; perceive by ear
HEAT warmth; rage; height; dead —; pressure; strain
JEAN name; cotton cloth
KEAL cabbage
LEAD metal; element; plummet; bullets; color; guide; command
LEAF plant part; sheet; tea
LEAH fem. name; Laban's daughter; Jacob's wife
LEAK loss; ooze; crack
LEAL loyal: Scot.
LEAN be supported; incline; thin
LEAP jump, skip; — year
LEAR learning: Scot.; king; father of Goneril, Regan, Cordelia
MEAD drink; meadow; lake; Margaret (anthropologist)
MEAH wall tower
MEAL grain; pulverize; repast
MEAN intend; denote; base; unkind; middle
MEAT flesh; kernel; food
NEAL male name; novelist
NEAP wagon pole; tide
NEAR close(ly); approach
NEAT tidy; trim; straight
PEAG money
PEAI medicine man
PEAK point; top; summit
PEAL ring; loud sound; fish
PEAN panegyric; praise; fur
PEAR fruit, tree
PEAT darling; turf; fuel
PEAU skin: Fr.
PEAY medicine man
READ interpret; learn; study; understand
REAL coin; true; genuine; very
REAM 500 (paper) quantity; bevel; enlarge
REAP cut; harvest
REAR back; raise; — admiral
SEAH measure
SEAL otarian; pinniped; fur; fasten; brown; ratify; stamp
SEAM fold; crevice; join; ornament; measure
SEAN John
SEAR burn; dried up; gun-lock catch
SEAT chair; fundament; site; membership; install; hot —
TEAK tree; dark
TEAL duck (blue)
TEAM group; yoke
TEAN tone: Scot.
TEAP ram
TEAR drop; weep; rip; glass defect
TEAT nipple
VEAL calf; meat
VEAU veal, calf: Fr.
WEAK feeble; pliable; light
WEAL body politic; stripe
WEAN withdraw; alienate
WEAR be clothed in; impair; endure; deteriorate
YEAH yes
YEAN to lamb
YEAR time period; twelve month; leap —; calendar, fiscal —
YEAS yes votes
ZEAL ardor; enthusiasm
CEBA tree; kapok source
CEBU Visayan island
DEBS Eugene (socialist)
DEBT fault; liability; obligation
GEBA Jonathan's victory site
HEBE cupbearer of gods; Zeus's daughter, Hercules' wife; color
NEBO wisdom god; Moab mountain (Moses died)
PEBA armadillo; Indian
REBA weight
SEBA Bib. country; Ham's grandson
SEBI prefix; tallow
TEBJ Negro Berber
UEBA measure
WEBB Beatrice Potter (writer)
ZEBU ox; Brahman bull
BECK nod; bidding; dyeing vat; Pol., Ger. officer, statesman
CECH Czech
DECA prefix: ten
DECI prefix: tenth
DECK ship floor; pack, cards; array, adorn
FECK amount
HECK (weaving) frame; cough; oath
KECK vomit; show

disgust
LECH slab; capstone; river
NECK body part; violin part; isthmus; pet
PECA coin
PECK measure; nip; bite; kiss
PECO black tea
RECK heed; concern
RECT element (philos.)
SECH such
SECK unprofitable (rent)
SECT group; denomination
TECA teak; Indian
TECH technical school
TECK readymade tie
TECO Indian
BEDE Adam (Eliot); the Venerable (monk)
CEDE yield; grant; transfer
DEDO measure
LEDA mollusk; mother of Castor, Pollux, Helen, Clytemnestra; wooed by Zeus as swan
MEDA secret Indian sect
MEDB Conchobor's wife; goddess; Queen Mab
MEDE ancient Asian
MEDI prefix: middle
PEDA pastoral staffs
PEDI prefix: foot
PEDO child
REDD make tidy; free of; scold
REDE interpret; counsel
REDO make over
TEDA Negro Berber
VEDA sacred Hindu books
YEDO Tokyo
BEEF ox, steer, cow, bos; brawn; rage; complain(t)
BEEN charmer's clarinet; participle
BEEP radio sound
BEER beverage; ale; mead
BEES yeast
BEET vegetable; root; sugar —; — top
DEED act; property transfer
DEEM consider; judge
DEEP profound; extensive; ocean
DEER ruminant; cervine; — Park (Buddha site)
FEED nourish; gratify; graze; fodder
FEEL sense; test; suffer
FEES charges; tips
FEET measure
GEEK carnival wild man
GEEZ Version (Ethiopic Bible)
HEED notice; attention
HEEL back part; end; slant; follow; scoundrel
HEEP Uriah (Dickens villain)
HEER Mr., Sir: Dutch
JEEL pool; marsh
JEEP vehicle; automobile
JEER scoff; taunt
KEEF hemp; languor
KEEK fashion spy
KEEL ship bottom; navigate; ocher; guinea fowl
KEEN sharp; acute; bewail
KEEP tend; retain; preserve; last
KEET guinea fowl
LEEK plant (onion, illiaceous); — green (Wales emblem)
LEER sly gaze; oven; loin
LEES dregs
LEET court; list
MEED reward
MEEK mild; submissive
MEER sea: Ger.
MEET encounter; face; combat; fulfill; fit
NEED compulsion; lack; want
NEEM tree; Margosa
NEEP turnip
NEER never; kidney
PEEK sly glance; pry; chirp
PEEL pare; tower; spade
PEEN hammer head
PEEP chirp; bird; peer slyly; Bo —; jeep
PEER gaze; equal; nobleman
PEET darling; turf; fuel
REED woody grass; pipe; mouthpiece; Walter (doctor, hospital)
REEF shoal; lode; reduce sail
REEK cloud; exude; smell
REEL wind(er); dance; waver; sway
REEM ox; unicorn
SEED fertile germ; progeny; decay; plant; extract
SEEK ask; try; hunt
SEEL shut eyes of; blind
SEEM look; appear
SEEN observed
SEEP ooze; small spring
SEER prophet
TEEL sesame
TEEM abound
TEEN 13–19; injury; pain
TEER golfer; mix colors
TEES river (North Sea)

VEEP vice-president
VEER shift (course); waver
WEED plant; tobacco; remove
WEEK time unit; sennight; squeak
WEEL fish basket, trap; pool
WEEP cry; bend; leak
WEET bird; cry of bird
DEFI challenge; defiance
DEFT skillful; trim
DEFY challenge; dare
HEFT weight; bulk; notebook: Ger.
JEFE chief; leader
JEFF rope; nickname; Mutt and —
LEFT departed; blow; — of center (Liberals)
REFT cleft; rift; deprived
TEFF grain plant
WEFT yarn; mist; (weave) web
BEGA measure
DEGU rodent (Octodon)
HEGH exclamation; hey!
MEGA prefix: great
PEGA remora fish
PEGU Burmese language, city
SEGO herb; bulb; lily; Utah state flower
TEGG sheep in 2nd year
VEGA meadow
WEGA star
WEGG Silas (ballad seller: Dickens)
YEGG safecracker; tramp
BEHN herb; tree
DEHA body (theosophy)
HEHE Bantu tribe
JEHU (chariot) driver; prophet, king (Israel)
LEHI prophet
LEHR oven; Lew (comedian)
PEHO morepork (bird)
SEHR very: Ger.
TEHR wild goat
VEHM medieval tribunal
BEID star
BEIN good; fine
CEIL overlay; line; ceiling
DEIL devil's-bit (plant)
DEIN your(s): Ger.
FEIL comfortable; neat
FEIS convention; — of Tara
GEIN glucoside (Geum urbanum)
HEII Hawaiian fern
HEIL hail: Ger.
HEIN surprise!: Fr.
HEIR inherit(or); — apparent, presumptive
KEID star
KEIF hemp; languor
KEIR bleaching vat
LEIF Ericson (explorer)
LEIL faithful, loyal (Land of the —)
LEIR sea god (Lear)
MEIN Chinese noodles; chow —
MEIO measure
NEIF serf; native; fist
NEIL male name
NEIN no: Ger.
NEIR kidney
OEIL eye: Fr.; — de boeuf
REIM oxhide strap
REIN strap; check; direct; kidney
REIS money; (boat) captain; effendi (state officer)
SEID tribe; lord; chief; Mohammed's descendant
SEIK Hindu sectarian
SEIL rope: Ger.
SEIM Polish assembly
SEIN poss. pronoun, be, being: Ger.
SEIP seep; ooze
SEIR Bib. mountain (Hor), Edom (Esau's home)
SEIS six: Sp.
SEIT measure
TEIG Teague; Thaddeus; Timothy; dough: Ger.
TEIL linden tree; lime
VEIL screen; facial garment; cloistered life
VEIN channel; streak; blood vessel
WEIN wine: Ger.
WEIR dam; fish trap
ZEIN protein
BEJA Nile nomad
DEJA already: Fr.
NEJD kingdom
REJA screen, grille: Sp.
SEJM Polish assembly
TEJU lizard
BEKA weight
FEKE trick device
PEKE (Pekinese) dog
REKE rick; pile
REKI Baluchistan nomad
WEKA flightless bird
WEKI fern
ZEKE Ezekiel
BELA jasmine; Benjamin's 1st son; Hungarian king
BELI myth. Brit. king
BELL ringing cup; gong; time period; flower shape; helmet; Brontë pseudonym; — the cat; diving —
BELT strap; zone; beat
CELA that: Fr.
CELL cubicle; group;

elec. jar; organism
CELT Irish, Scot, Welsh, Breton; chisel
DELE omit; erase
DELF quarry; pottery; blue
DELI delicatessen
DELL valley; dingle; wench
EELY wriggling; slippery
FELD field: Ger.
FELL skin; cut, hew (down); savage
FELS Eastern coin
FELT pressed fibers; hat; sensed
GELD castrate; prune; tax
GELT money
HELA goddess; Loki's daughter
HELD kept; retained
HELI prefix: sun, spiral
HELL Hades; state of misery; -bent
HELM steer (wheel); tiller
HELL squeamish
HELP relieve; avoid; wait on, aid(e); servants
JELL solidify; mature
KELA measures
KELD spring; fountain
KELE weight
KELK fish roe
KELL Gaul; net; film
KELP seaweed, iodine source
KELT Celt; cloth; trout
LELY Dutch painter
MELA festival; prefix: black
MELD announce (score); merge
MELE Hawaiian poem; chant
MELL (beat with) hammer; teacher (Dickens)
MELT liquefy
NELL Ellen; Helen; Little (Dickens girl)
PELA wax (secreting insect)
PELE fire goddess
PELF booty; riches
PELO hair: It.
PELT skin; hurl; strike
PELU hardwood tree
RELY trust; depend
SELA Dead Sea town
SELF identity; ego; one
SELL vend; betray; persuade; hoax; — short
TELA tissue; web; banana port
TELE prefix: far, complete
TELI low (merchant) caste
TELL inform; discern; chat; William (Swiss hero)
VELA membranes; soft palates; the Sails (Argo constellation)
VELD So. Afr. grassland
VELT measure
VELO speed unit
WELD unite; junction
WELF ducal family
WELK (gather) snail; Lawrence (musician)
WELL (water) pit; shaft; eddy; flow; rightly; very; sound; healthy
WELS sheatfish
WELT ridge; wale; strip; sew; beat; universe: Ger.
YELD barren; milkless
YELK yolk
YELL cry; cheer
YELP shrill bark
YELT gilt (sow)
BEMA platform; altar; measure
DEME Greek commune
DEMI prefix: half
DEMO prefix: populace
DEMY coin; scholar; paper size
FEME wife; tribunal
HEMA prefix: blood
HEME reduce hematin
HEMI prefix: half
HEMO prefix: blood
HEMP herb; hashish; cannabis; rope (fiber)
KEMP fur refuse
MEMO note; statement
NEMA eelworm; prefix: thread
NEMO nobody: Lat.; prefix: glade; Captain (Verne hero)
REMI Gaul people; prefix: oar
REMS river
SEME (sprinkling) pattern
SEMI half
SEMO Sancus (deity); Dius Fidius
TEMA musical theme; Arab
TEMS sieve; sift
XEMA arctic gull
ZEME (abode of) spirit; fetish
ZEMI (abode of) spirit; fetish
BENA grass (vetiver)
BEND turn; curve; flex; bow
BENE wild hog; well: It. & Lat.
BENG devil (Gypsy)
BENI Bolivian river; sesame
BENJ hemp; narcotic
BENN seed
BENO alcoholic palm sap
BENT crooked; inclination; grass
BENU holy bird (Ra-Osiris)
CENA (Last) supper
CENE suffix: recent
CENS payment due
CENT coin; penny; game
DENE measure; dune; Indian

DENS tooth: Lat.
DENT depress(ion); notch
DENY refuse; contradict
EENY —, meeny, miny, mo
FEND keep off; parry
FENT slit; cleft
GENA cheek; beak part
GENE hereditary factor; chromosome part; nickname
GENS clan: Lat.; people: Fr.
GENT gentleman; Belg. city
GENU knee: Lat.
HENS fowl; -foot (herb)
JENA Ger. city (optical; Napoleonic victory); glass
KENO lotto (game); prefix: empty
KENT Eng. county duchy; Lear's follower
LENA firewood: Sp.; river; Conrad heroine
LEND make loan, grant; — an ear
LENE smooth; consonant
LENO (cotton, silk) fabric
LENS eye part; glass (optical); herb
LENT fasting period; slow; made loan
MEND repair; improve
MENE — tekel upharsin (handwriting on the wall)
MENG mix
MENO prefix: month
MENS mind: Lat.
MENT falcon-headed god
MENU bill of fare
NENE Hawaiian goose
OENO prefix: wine
PEND hang; be delayed
PENE (hammer) head
PENK minnow
PENN William (Pa. founder)
PENT confined; -house
RENA rockfish
REND tear; rupture; bark trees
RENI It. painter; prefix: kidney
RENO Nev. city ("biggest little"; divorce, gambling)
RENT torn; schism; let, lease; payment, income
SEND transmit; dispatch; propel; swing; enthrall
SENN Swiss herdsman
TEND serve; incline
TENE suffix: ribbon
TENG measure
TENT cloth; shelter; pup —; wine; frame
VENA vein: Lat.
VEND Slav; sell; sale
VENI prefix: vein; —, vidi, vici (I came, I saw, I conquered)
VENO prefix: vein
VENT hole; let out; issue
WEND Slav; go; travel
WENT departed
XENO guest; prefix: foreign
YENI So. Amer. tanager
ZEND — Avesta (holy text)
ZENO philosopher (Stoic, Cynic); emperor
ZENU Afr. sheep
AEON age
FEOD feudal estate
GEON paradise river; Jerusalem spring
LEON country, city; Ponce de (explorer)
MEOU cat's cry; measure
MEOW cat's cry; measure
NEON gas(eous) element; lamp
PEON laborer
PEOR Bib. mountain
TEOS Ionian city
CEPA onion
CEPE boletus (edible fungus)
DEPA measure
KEPI military cap
KEPT retained; lasted
NEPA water scorpion; needle bug
PEPO pumpkin; squash; melon; cucumber
REPP silk or wool fabric
SEPS snake; lizard
SEPT social unit; screen; seven: Fr.
VEPS Finnish tribe (Chud); Dog Star (Isis); Horus
WEPT cried; Jesus —
AERA age; era
AERI prefix: air
AERO go by aircraft
AERY ethereal; nest
BERA king of Sodom
BERG iceberg; mountain
BERI Sudanese (Fulah); -beri (disease)
BERM (l)edge; road shoulder
BERN Swiss capital
BERT nickname
CERA prefix: horn, wax
CERE wax; (wrap in a) waxed cloth; beak part
CERN decide
CERO mackerel
DERA suffix: neck types

DERE — Mable (Streeter book)
DERM prefix, suffix: skin layer
KERY weird; uncanny; timid
FERK measure
FERN seedless plant
FERU bast fiber
GERA city
GERB sheaf; firework
GERD Frey's wife
GERE Odin's wolf
GERI Odin's wolf
GERM bud; seed; microbe
HERA Zeus's sister, wife
HERB plant; nickname
HERD crowd; feed together
HERE vicinity; present
HERL (feather) barb
HERO protagonist; demigod; — and Leander; Beatrice's cousin
HERR lord, Mister, Sir: Ger.
HERS fem., poss. pronoun
JERK grab; twist; spasm; soda man; dullard; beef
JERL boat joint
JERM Levantine boat
KERB gutter part
KERE read(ing substitute)
KERF cut; notch
KERI read(ing substitute)
KERN soldier; peasant; grain; type part; Jerome (composer)
KERR physicist
KERS cress
LERO Dodecanese Isle
LERP secretion; insect
MERE fen; lake; boundary; war club; bare; only; simple; mother: Fr.
MERL blackbird
MERO grouper (fish)
MERU fabled mountain
NERA Tiber tributary
NERI Blacks: It.
NERO emperor; fiddler; Agrippina's son; Wolfe (Stout)
PERA Istanbul district
PERE father, priest: Fr.; — Goriot (Balzac)
PERI fairy; elf; beauty
PERK lift up; preen; cocky; percolate
PERM elec. unit; hair wave
PERN honey buzzard
PERO but: Sp.
PERT bold; lively; sandpiper
PERU country
QERE read(ing substitute)
QERI read(ing substitute)
SERA antitoxins; blood parts; whey; evening: It.
SERB Servian; Yugo(slav)
SERE wither(ed); Negroid
SERF slave; peasant
SERI betel; Indian
SERO prefix: thin; late pupil
SERT Sp. painter
TERA Buddhist monastery
TERM phrase; word; condition; time; period
TERN gull; threefold; ship
TERP prehistoric mound
VERA tree; measure; name
VERB action word
VERD green(leafed)
VERI centipede
VERT green (Her.); veer; convert
VERY true; same; extremely; light signals; flare
WERE verb form; prefix: metamorphosed human
WERF farmyard
WERI aweto (caterpillar)
WERT were: archaic, poetic
XERO prefix: dry
YERK wrench; kick; trump
ZERO nothing; cipher; nullity; — hour; Jap. plane
BESA coin
BESS nickname; Mrs. Truman
BEST most (good); defeat
CESS tax; luck
CEST girdle; belt (Venus)
DESI jute; Arnaz
DESK table; lectern; department
FESS broad band (Her.); confess
FEST festive gathering
GEST deed; romance tale, adventure
GESU Jesus: It.
HEST command; precept
JESS strap on hawk leg
JEST joke
JESU name: Jesus
LESE — majesty (disrespect)
LESS shorter; fewer; inferior; minus
LEST for fear that
MESA flat hill; oakwood color
MESE Greek mus. term
MESH net; netting; entangle
MESS banquet; meal; muddle; dis-

order; botch
NESH soft; juicy; dainty
NESS cape; promontory; suffix
NEST (make a) home
OESE bacteriologist's wire
PESA coin
PESO coin; Sp. money
PESS hassock
PEST plague; insect; nuisance
RESE shake; rush
RESH Heb. 20th letter, 200; plant
REST pause; stop; peace; prop; stay; rely; mus. sign; remainder; set; found
SESI black-fin snapper
SESS soap frame bar
TESA Indian buzzard
TESS Theresa; Hardy heroine
TEST shell; cupel; examination; try
VEST waistcoat; clothe; empower
WESE we shall
WEST wind; painter; author; occident; go —; Mae —
YESO plaster of Paris; gypsum
ZEST orange peel; relish; gusto
AETA Negrito; native
BETA Greek B, 2; star; ray
BETE beast, silly: Fr.; — noire
BETH Heb. B, 2; Alcott heroine (Little Women)
CETE marine mammals
CETO prefix: whale
FETE festival; regale
GETA Jap. wooden clogs
GETT bill of divorce
HETH son of Canaan; Hittite ancestor
HETT Hittite ancestor
JETE ballet jump
JETH Hindu month
KETA dog salmon
KETU eclipse demon (Rahu)
LETE quadrille set
LETI island off Timor
LETO mother of Apollo, Artemis
LETT Latvian, Balt (Riga man)
META goal post; river
METE measure; allot
METZ city, former fort
NETE Greek mus. term
NETI eulalia (thatch grass)
NETT undeductible
PETE strongbox; Peter
PETO wahoo (fish); Henry IV figure
RETE network
SETA caterpillar's hair; spine
SETH banker; Adam's son; Osiris' evil brother
SETI river; pharaoh
SETT tool; paving stone
TETE head; Fr.; — à tête; hairdo
TETH Heb. J, 9
VETA mountain sickness
VETO prohibit(ion); no
WETA wingless locust
YETA Jap. outcast
YETI abominable snowman
ZETA Greek Z, 7
DEUL Hindu temple
DEUM Te — (hymn)
DEUS god: Lat.; — ex machina
DEUX two: Fr.
FEUD strife; vendetta; fee
GEUM plant (astringent)
JEUX cards, hands, games: Fr.
JEUZ chief Benjamite
KEUP measure
LEUD feudal tenant
MEUM carrotlike herb, spicknel; mine: Lat.
NEUE new
NEUF nine, new: Fr.
OEUF egg: Fr.
PEUL Fulah (Sudanese)
PEUR fear: Fr.
REUS defendant: Lat.
ZEUS chief god; Jupiter; Hera's husband; son of Cronus, Rhea
BEVY company; flock
DEVA deity (Indra); demon
DEVI goddess; Siva's wife (Shakti); title: Mrs., Lady
HEVI apple (tree)
LEVI Jacob's, Leah's son; tribe
LEVO prefix: left
LEVY assess; seize; tax
NEVA river (Leningrad)
NEVE snow; firn
PEVA Peru Indian
PEVY lumberman's hook
REVE (muse in) dream: Fr.
REVS rotations per minute
SEVE wine delicacy: Fr.
WEVE contraction
DEWA deity (Indra); demon
DEWY moist; refreshing
HEWN felled; squared
JEWS -harp
LEWD lecherous; obscene
MEWL whimper; miaou

MEWS	(royal) stables
NEWS	intelligence; tidings
NEWT	salamander; eft
SEWN	stitched
TEWA	N.M. Indian
NEXT	nearest; following
SEXT	canonical hour (noon); organ stop; sixth
SEXY	sexually appealing
TEXT	(literary) substance; topic; Scripture passage; type
CEYX	Halcyone's husband
KEYS	House of (Isle of Man legislature); cays; Florida —
TEYL	linden; lime tree
AFAR	far away; tribe
UFER	fir pole; shore: Ger.
AFFA	from off
AFFY	join
IFFY	contingent
OFFA	Angles' hero (Beowulf)
OFFS	cricket-field sides
EFIK	Negro
IFIL	tree (brown dye)
EFOD	priestly garb; image
AFRA	name; union
AFRO	hairstyle
PFUI	exclamation
AGAG	king
AGAL	cord
AGAO	language
AGAR	wood
AGAU	language
AGAZ	Indian
EGAD	oath
EGAL	equal: Fr.
EGAN	horse (Kipling)
IGAL	Moses' spy
NGAI	spiritual power
NGAN	measure
OGAM	Irish alphabet
EGBA	Negro; Yoruba
EGBO	secret society (Ogboni)
AGED	old; oxygian
AGEE	awry; Shammah's father; James (novelist)
AGER	apparatus; field
EGER	river
OGEE	arch; molding
EGGS	ova; — and bacon, ham; — and butter (flowers)
EGGY	egg-stained; yolky
AGHA	officer; title
AGIB	dervish
AGIO	fee; commission
AGIS	king
EGIL	Volund's (Wayland's) brother
EGIS	protection; patronage; shield (symbol of Zeus, Athena)
AGLA	acrostic
IGLU	Eskimo; hut; seal hole
OGLE	gaze (amorously)
UGLY	badlooking; unpleasant; plug-
EGMA	enigma
AGNI	god; lambs
AGNO	Luzon river
AGOG	eager
AGON	contest; argument
EGOL	antiseptic
IGOR	Prince (opera)
OGOR	early Turkic man
OGPU	Soviet police body
AGRA	comb. form; carpet; city (Taj Mahal site)
AGRI	fields
AGRO	prefix: soil
OGRE	giant; monster
AGUA	water; toad
AGUE	fever
OGUM	Irish alphabet
YGUN	antisub gun
AHAB	king; captain; prophet
AHAZ	king
BHAR	Kolarian native
DHAT	minstrel; scholar
CHAA	tea
CHAB	bird
CHAC	-Mool (god); -chac (instr.)
CHAD	lake; nation
CHAI	person
CHAL	man
CHAM	tribe; title; bite
CHAN	resthouse; lord; title
CHAO	measure
CHAP	fellow; crack; jaw
CHAR	trout; burn; sandbank; -woman
CHAT	talk; bird; spike
CHAW	masticate
CHAY	red dye root
DHAI	midwife
DHAK	tree
DHAL	split pea, lentil
DHAN	wealth; loan
DHAO	knife (Burma)
DHAR	state; town (India)
DHAW	billhook
GHAT	range; bank; river bank stairs
KHAN	resthouse; lord; title; Agha —
KHAR	weight
KHAS	special; noble
KHAT	measure
OHAD	Simeon's son
PHAD	star
PHAG	comb. form: eating
PHAN	measure
PHAO	wolf (Kipling)
SHAB	paltry guy
SHAD	fish
SHAG	hair; tobacco; bird, rascal; dance step
SHAH	ruler

SHAM deceit; fake
SHAN Thai
SHAP silk yarn
SHAT saline lake
SHAW thicket; pshaw; George Bernard (playwright)
SHAY chaise; carriage
THAI Siamese
THAN in comparison with; conjunction
THAR goat
THAT so; which; pronoun; connective; that's —
THAW melt; unbend
WHAM exclamation
WHAT interrogative; pronoun; what's —
WHAU why; tree
AHEM interjection
AHER Benjamite
AHET season (of inundation)
AHEY ho
BHEL thorny (fruit) tree
CHEE weight
CHEF head (cook); — d'oeuvre
CHEK Chin. foot (measure)
CHEN snow goose
CHER dear: Fr.
CHEW masticate; ruminate; — the cud; — the rag
CHEZ at home of, with: Fr.
DHER mound; land share
EHEU alas
GHEE butter
GHEG Albanian
GHES Tapuyan Indian
KHEM chief god (Min)
KHET mortal body; measure
OHEL Zerubabbel's son
PHEW exclamation
RHEA Cybele, mother of the gods; Gaea's daughter; Cronos's wife; ostrich; satellite; grass
SHEA tree; butter
SHED cast off; abandon; drop; hut; shelter
SHEE Irish fairyfolk
SHEM Noah's son; Semite
SHEN Christian God (China)
SHER tiger
SHEW show: Brit.; -bread
THEA tea source; name
THEB measure
THEE you
THEM pronoun
THEN at a time; therefore
THEO prefix: god
THEW muscle; sinew
THEY pronoun; people; men
WHEE whistle sound
WHEN whereas; how soon
WHET sharpen; excite; edge
WHEW whistle; exclamation
WHEY milk serum; thin; pale; curds and —
AHIO Ark driver
AHIR caste
BHIL low-caste Indian
CHIA salvia beverage, oil
CHIB tongue; language
CHIC stylish(ness)
CHIH Chin. foot (measure)
CHIL cheer pine; kite (Kipling)
CHIN lower jaw; chatter; weight; dynasty; Burmese
CHIP fragment; cut; hew
CHIR pheasant; pine
CHIT child; sprout; memo; voucher; mind
CHIV knife
OHIA timber tree; apple
OHIO Buckeye state
PHIL nickname; Philip; prefix: loving
PHIT bullet sound
PHIZ physiognomy; face
RHIA China grass
RHIN Rhine: Fr.
SHIH weight; measure
SHIK Arabian Turkoman
SHIM leveling slip; shingle; knife
SHIN leg, calf front; run; climb
SHIP vessel; send; — of state
SHIR cook; gathers; tiger
SHIV bit of husk; fluff; blade
THIN lean; dim; rare; dilute; — ice
THIO prefix: brimstone
THIS pronoun, demonstrative
WHIG U.S., Brit. party
WHIM fancy; caprice
WHIN gorse; rest-harrow; rock; winch
WHIP lash; urge; defeat
WHIR fly; hurry; buzz
WHIT bit; jot; dull sound
WHIZ hum; bargain; corker
SHLU Moroccan Berber
OHNE without: Ger.
AHOM Assam native
AHOY call; ship —
BHOY gang member; rowdy
CHOB grain spike
CHOL desolate plain; Mayan
CHOP cut; crack; eat; barter; jaw
CHOR thief; steal

(Gypsy)
CHOU cabbage; darling: Fr.; Chin. dynasty; En Lai (statesman)
CHOW food; dog
CHOY red dye root
DHOW Arab. sailboat
GHOR Dead Sea valley
GHOS Chin. dynasty
JHOW tamarisk shrub
KHOR watercourse; gorge
KHOT farmer; contractor
OHOY ahoy; call
PHON loudness measure
PHOO disgusting!
PHOS phosphorus
PHOT light unit
RHOB juice; jelly
SHOA Abyssinian
SHOD wearing shoes
SHOE foot covering; crackow; wheel drag; tire
SHOG shake; jog
SHOO scare away; begone!
SHOP store; buy; buying place; talk —; window-
SHOQ tree (tanning); chogak
SHOR salt lake; Tatar tribe
SHOT missile; pellet; guess; range; marksman; film record; long —; big —
SHOU Tibetan deer
SHOW exhibit(ion); reveal; appear(ance); 3rd place; no — (airline term)
THOB rationalize
THOR thunder god (Thursday); Midgard slayer; Odin's son; missile
THOS jackal genus
THOU 2nd pers. pronoun
WHOA stop!; opp. of giddap
WHOM pronoun
WHOO exclamation
WHOP dash; beat; bump
SHRI glorious; holy; Lakshmi (goddess)
AHUM humming
BHUT Dravidian ghost
CHUB fallfish; dace; chevin
CHUD Mongols; Vepse; Vote; Tavastian
CHUG pull; fish; (move with) vibration
CHUM friend; scrap fish
CHUN Chin. pottery
CHUR Swiss canton
CHUT nonsense!
EHUD judge of Israel
GHUZ Turkish invader
JHUM cultivation method
PHUD bullet sound; exclamation
PHUT (bullet) sound; OT people
RHUM alcoholic drink
RHUS sumac genus
SHUA Abraham's son
SHUE Tibetan deer
SHUL synagogue
SHUN avoid; abstain
SHUT close; refine
THUD dull sound; blow
THUG assassin; hoodlum
THUS in this way; hence
WHUN gorse; rest-harrow
IHVH God; Tetragrammaton
JHVH Jehova; God; Tetragrammaton
YHVH God; Yahveh; Tetragrammaton
JHWH Jahweh; God; Tetragrammaton
YHWH God; Yahweh; Tetragrammaton
WHYO gangster; footpad
AIAH Edomite, Rizpah's father
BIAS diagonal (incline); prejudice
DIAD pair
DIAL plate; face; call; sunreveille
DIAN reveille
DIAU Indian
DIAZ Bartholomeu (Port. navigator)
FIAT sanction; edict; money; automobile (It.)
GIAN — Carlo (Menotti)
KIAK canoe
LIAM O'Flaherty; "Informer"
LIAO Manchuria river
LIAR prevaricator; plant
LIAS geol. period
MIAM hut
MIAN sir; title
MIAO Chinese aborigine
MIAS orangutan
NIAS Ind. Ocean island(er)
PIAN tumor
PIAT magpie; antitank gun
PIAY medicine man
RIAL coin
SIAK latex
SIAL earth's outer part
SIAM Thailand; Anna's king (The King and I)
TIAM language
TIAO Chinese money
TIAR crown; shrub
VIAL vessel
BIBB mast's timber

piece

BIBI title: Lady, Mrs. (India)

DIBS juice: grape, date

GIBE scoff; jeer; agree

JIBE sneer; agree; coincide; shift course

JIBI extinct bird

KIBE chilblain crack

KIBO Afr. peak (Kilimanjaro)

NIBS personage (VIP); Peter Pan (Barrie)

TIBS — eve (never-never)

TIBU Negro-Berber

VIBO gulf (Italy)

AICH alloy

BICE blue, green pigment

DICE (cut into) cubes; gamble; gaming implements

DICH you: Ger.

DICK Richard; whip; lad; detective; Whittington (London mayor)

FICO trifle

HICK hiccup; rube; jake

KICK hit; die; object(ion); excitement; -back

LICE insects (louse)

LICK tongue; stroke; whip; conquer; bit

MICA isinglass (silicate)

MICE rodents (mouse)

MICH me: Ger.

MICK Irishman

MICO marmoset

NICE good; kind; pleasing; delicate; dainty; quimper color; Riviera port

NICK notch; moment; cheat; cut; Old — (devil); Carter (detective)

PICA type size; magpies

PICE coin; weight

PICI birds (woodpeckers)

PICK tool; scratch; choose; rob; eat; best

PICO peak; game; weight

PICT British aborigine

RICE cereal; use ricer; Elmer (playwright)

RICH wealthy; vivid; full; fragrant; fat

RICK pile (up); haystack

SICE number 6 on die

SICK urge (dog); ill; weak

TICE lure; yorker (bowled ball)

TICK parasite; mattress; count; tic

VICA Pota (goddess)

VICE sin; fault; vise; proxy; — versa

WICK part of candle, lamp

AIDA opera; Radames' lover

AIDE help; de-camp; — mémoire

BIDE wait; tarry; dwell

DIDO trick; caper; Carthage queen, Aeneas' beloved

EIDE ideas; forms

FIDE entrust; — et amore

FIDO fog evaporation; dog's name

GIDE André (author)

HIDE land measure; skin; conceal; shelter; — and hair

KIDD William (privateer)

KIDS star (Auriga)

LIDA Alida

LIDE March (month)

LIDO Venice beach

MIDE Ojibway secret order

MIDI south(ern France)

NIDE pheasant's nest

NIDI breeding places

RIDD Lorna Doone's rescuer

RIDE be borne; float; endure; manage; mount; journey

SIDA herb; shrub; hemp

SIDE region, part(y); oblique; aspect; support; lateral

SIDI Moslem title; Negro

SIDY pretentious

TIDE ocean's rise, fall; season; drift; endure; current; help

TIDY (make) neat

VIDA feminine of David

VIDE see: Lat.; for example; quae —

WIDE broad; far; lax; astray

WIDU Moslem ablution

AIEA town

AIEL writ of —

BIEN good, fine: Fr.; — aimée (well beloved)

BIER litter; coffin

CIEL ceiling; sky: Fr.

DIEB jackal

DIEM day: Lat.; per —

DIER one moribund

DIES day(s): Lat.; — irae; Cong. committee

DIET fare; food regimen; parliament

DIEU god: Fr.; mon —!

FIEF feudal estate

GIER eagle (vulture)
HIEL Jericho's rebuilder
HIEN Chin. government seat
HIER here: Ger.; yesterday: Fr.
KIEF hemp; languor
KIEL ocher; ruddle; seaport; — Canal
KIER bleaching vat
KIEV Ukrainian city
LIED fibbed; song: Ger.
LIEF gladly; freely
LIEN claim; attachment; garnishment
LIER rester; layer
LIEU place; stead
MIEN manner; bearing; air
NIEL alloy
PIED variegated; Piper; -à-terre
PIEN arris (sharp edge)
PIER mole; dock; pillar
PIET magpie
RIEL Canadian (Indian) rebel
RIEM oxhide strap
RIEN nothing: Fr.; — ne va plus
RIER oil cask (whaling)
SIEG victory: Ger.
SIER pintado (fish)
TIED bound; knotted; drawn
TIEN sky: Chin.; Chu (Lord of Heaven); your(s): Fr.
TIER row; layer; pinafore
VIER striver; four: Ger.
VIEW sight; see; aim; opinion; scene
WIEL whirlpool
WIES Ys
BIFF (deal a) blow
FIFE flute; checkers opening
FIFO inventory method
GIFT donation; talent
HIFI faithful sound rendition
JIFF instant
KIFF languor
LIFE existence; vivacity; biography
LIFO inventory method
LIFT r(a)ise; exalt; steal; elevator
MIFF quarrel; offend
NIFE earth's core
PIFF bullet sound; exclamation
RIFE abundant; prevalent
RIFF Berber; Kabyle; ripple
RIFI Riffs
RIFT split; divide; cleft
SIFT screen; separate; bolt
TIFF (petty) quarrel
WIFE spouse; marry
BIGA two-horse chariot
BIGG barley
GIGA medieval fiddle
HIGH lofty: elevated; noble; expensive; shrill; tainted; tipsy
MIGG marble (duck)
NIGH near(ly); direct
RIGA Latvian city, gulf
RIGI Swiss mountain
SIGH lament(ing sound)
SIGN symbol; signal; subscribe; ratify; hire
TIGE rifle steel pin; dog
TIGG swindler (Dickens)
VIGA rafter; log
WIGG peruke; long hair
WIGS — on the green (fray)
KIHO peacock butterfly
CIII 103; Trajan reign
LIII 53; Claudius reign
LIIN measure
MIII 1003
RIIS Jacob (journalist)
VIII 8; Augustus reign
XIII 13; Augustus reign
BIJA kino tree
FIJI islands (Lau, Yasawa)
LIJA unicorn fish
BIKE bicycle
BIKH aconite; poison
DIKA bread; fat; oil
DIKE levee; ditch; dig; goddess (Horae)
HIKE toss; tramp; raise
HIKU scabbard fish
KIKI castor oil plant
KIKU chrysanthemum
LIKE as; similar(ly); love; prefer; probable
MIKE Michael; Mick; microphone
NIKE victory goddess (Samothrace); missile
PIKA little chief hare
PIKE fish; weapon; pierce; highway; farmer; gamble; Zebulon (explorer; peak)
PIKI maize bread; pik
PIKY full of fish
RIKK tambourine
SIKA Jap. deer
SIKH Hindu soldier
TIKE child
TIKI god; first man; image
AILE winged
BILE liver secretion; choler
BILK defraud

BILL beak; weapon; law; poster; invoice; debt; nickname: William; — and coo; Sikes (Dickens)
BILO Balkan karst area
DILL flavoring herb; pickle
DILO poon tree
EILD barren; milkless
FILE tool; rasp; smooth; march; column; folder; arrange
FILI learned poet
FILL pack; complete; glut; — the bill
FILM skin; coating; haze; photograph; picture
FILO silk thread
FILS son: Fr.; Dumas (Camille); Iraq coin
GILA — monster; lizard; Ariz. river
GILD lay gold on; adorn; — the lily; trade society
GILL measure; brook; breathing organ; wattle; coin; lass
GILO woody vine (tonic)
GILT gold; sow
HILA 'eyes' of bean
HILD Hethin's victim princess
HILL mound; Jenny (Shaw character); -billy
HILO grass; city (Hawaii)
HILT sword
JILL girl; sweetheart; Jack and —
JILT betray in love
KILE measure; weight
KILL slay; veto; creek
KILN (burn in) oven
KILO measure; -gram, -meter; prefix: 1000
KILT Scot's skirt
LILA deity manifestation
LILE little
LILL small pin; loll; Lillian
LILT (sing) lively tune
LILY flower; Turk's-cap; pure; white
MILA measure
MILD calm(ly); soft; tame
MILE measure; distance
MILK nutritious fluid; sap; white; exploit; drain
MILL grind(er); quern; box; John Stuart (economist)
MILO name; grain; sorghum; Venus (Melos)
MILT spleen; fish gland; nickname
NILE river; green, blue
NILL refuse; negate
NILS Bohr (physicist)
OILY unctuous; bland; suave
PILE hair; heap (up); awn; atomic —
PILI nut; grass; hairs
PILL medicine tablet
PILY pilelike
RILE irritate; vex
RILL (run in a) brook
RILY turbid; irritated
SILK fiber; thread; -worm
SILL beam (door, window)
SILO fodder pit; ensile
SILT sediment; scum; drift
TILE ceramic slab; drain pipe; domino; tessera; slate
TILL until; plow; cultivate; tray; cash box
TILT cover; incline; tip; joust; sport
VILA fairy; New Hebrides
VILE base; evil; odious
VILI brother of Odin; Ve
VILL village; township
VILY fairies
WILD rough; savage; mad; eager; unruly; wilderness
WILE trick; guile; lure
WILK (gather) snail
WILL volition; choice; decree; bequeath; testament
WILT droop; lose spirit
WILY artful; subtle
BIMI orangutan (Kipling)
CIMA mountain peak: It.
DIME coin; — novel
GIMP silk fabric; vim
HIMA Hamitic Negro
LIMA city; bean; yam; mollusk
LIMB leg; arm; member
LIME calcium oxide (mortar); snare; caustic; linden (tree); amber; citrus fruit
LIMN portray; delineate
LIMP halt; flaccid; loose
LIMU edible seaweed

LIMY viscous
MIMA woman actor
MIME drama; act; actor; clown; smith (Nibelungs)
MIMI nickname; opera heroine
NIMB nimbus; halo
OIME alas
PIMA Ariz. Indian; cotton
PIMP procurer; bawd; maquereau
RIMA fissure; breadfruit; child heroine (Hudson)
RIME frost; (make) rhymes; chink; rung
RIMU red pine; Imou pine
RIMY frosty; rhyming
SIMA igneous rock
SIME monkey
SIMI Dodecanese isle
SIMP simpleton
TIME period; moment; credit term; speed rate; meter, rhythm; Father —; space-
YIMA Avestan demigod
ZIMB Ethiopian fly
AINE elder
AINO Jap. aborigine
AINT contraction
AINU Jap. aborigine
BINA Hindu guitar
BIND tie; protect; sew; cohere
BINE (hop) stem
BING bed roll; sharp sound
BINH weight
BINI Nigerian
BINN box; frame; crib
BINO alcoholic palm sap
BINT daughter; woman
CINE movie: Sp.
CINQ five: Fr.
DINE eat; have dinner
DING thump; sound; urge
DINK small boat; cut out
DINO prefix: terrible
DINT blow; force; notch
EINE one: Ger.
FIND discover(y); (re)gain
FINE end; superior; thin; keen; well; (set) penalty; geil —, derb — (Irish clans)
FINK finch; derb; informer; strikebreaker
FINN man of Finland; Helsinki; Ugric; Mickey (KO drops); Huckleberry (Twain novel)
GINK eccentric one
HIND fish; grouper; deer; posterior
HING asafetida (gum resin; antispasmodic)
HINO timber tree; dye
HINT suggestion; imply
JINK prank
JINN demon; spirit
JINX hoodoo; bad luck
KINA quinine
KIND sort; species; gentle
KINE cattle
KING monarch; ruler; chief; chessman; card
KINK twist; loop; cramp
KINO gum (catechu); prefix: moving
LINA measure; Caroline
LIND Jenny (singer, Swedish Nightingale)
LINE thin mark; cable; cord; wire; piping; row; direction; cover; align; track; flax
LING fish; burbot; hake
LINK (chain) loop; connect; join; torch; measure
LINN waterfall; linden
LINO measure
LINT raveling, fiber (of linen); netting
LINY streaky
LINZ Austrian city
MINA weight; money; myna; watchman
MIND intellect; brain; memory; wish; mood; plan; tend; dislike
MINE possessive pronoun; dig; pit; rich source; explosive
MING Chin. dynasty
MINK weasel-like animal
MINO Jap. straw coat
MINT herb; menthol; bonanza; coin; — julep
MINX pert girl
MINY of a mine
NINA goddess (Ea's daughter); ship (Pinta, —, Santa Maria); girl: Sp.
NINE number (of Muses); baseball team
NINO boy: Sp.
OINT apply oil
PINA pineapple; silver; cone
PINE tree; conifer; evergreen; yearn; mourn
PING (bullet, striking) sound
PINK color (red); ship; cut; hunter's coat;

carnation; in the — (healthy)
PINO pine tree
PINT measure
PINY pinelike; peony
RIND bark; peel; Vali's mother, Odin's wife
RINE hemp; ditch
RING gird; arena; prizefighting; gang; atomic order; sound (bell); Vienna landmark; Nibelungen cycle (Wagner)
RINK skating arena
SINA drug; mountain (Moses)
SIND river; Pakistan province; are: Ger.
SINE math. ratio; without: Lat.; — qua non; — die
SING vocalize; warble; tell
SINH math. term
SINK fall; droop; conceal; basin
SINN — Fein (Irish society)
SINO prefix: Chinese
TINA fem. nickname
TIND kindle
TINE tooth; prong; pain; grass
TING sound; Chin. pottery
TINO Sambal language
TINT color; shade; tinge
TINY small; -tim (herb); Tim (Dickens)
VINA harp; guitar; wines
VINE creeping plant
VINO palm liquor
VINT card game
VINY entwining
WIND turn; coil; blowing air; mere talk
WINE fermented juice
WING alar appendage; faction; annex; fly
WINK blink; signal
WINY vinous; drunken
XINA nickname: Christina
ZINC metal; element; color
ZING sharp thrill; vim
BIOD animal life force
BION physiological individual (morphon)
BIOS life: animal, plant
CION plant shoot
DIOL chem. compound; suffix
DION lord in Winter's Tale
DIOS God: Sp.
FIOT Congo tribe
LION cat; king of beasts; celebrity
NIOG coconut palm
NIOU measure
PION dig; excavate
PIOT magpie
RIOT tumult; success; — act, squad
SIOL great Irish clan
SION purple seaweed; Zion
TION suffix
TIOU Indian (Tonikan)
VIOL string instrument
ZION Israelites; heaven
AIPI cassava
CIPO liana
FIPS Martin Chuzzlewit
HIPE wrestler's throw
KIPE basket
KIPP peak (Glacier National Park); gymnastic feat
LIPA fat
NIPA palm; juice; mat; atap
PIPA toad; measure
PIPE tube; flute; cask (measure); — dream; — down
PIPI astringent; mollusk
PIPY tubular; weepy
RIPA river bank
RIPE mature; fit; tipsy
SIPO liana
TIPE rabbit trap
TIPI wigwam
WIPE rub off; beat
XIPE -totec (Aztec god)
YIPE howl; cry
ZIPA Chibcha chief
ZIPS Czech
AIRA grass
AIRE nobleman; river
AIRS pretensions; side
AIRT guide; turn
AIRY breezy; light
BIRD avian; flyer; fowl; shuttlecock; person; Blue —
BIRI cheap cigarette
BIRL revolve; spin
BIRN clarinet socket
BIRR wind force; sound
CIRC circle; recess; corrie
CIRL bunting; bird
DIRE evil; fatal; extreme
DIRK dagger; Theodoric
DIRT muck; earth; gossip; do one —; — cheap
EIRE Ireland; Erin
FIRE combustion; ardor; discharge
FIRM fix; solid; company
FIRN granular snow(field)
GIRD encircle; clothe; brace
GIRL young female; maid; Gibson —; — of the

Golden West; chorus —; — Friday
GIRO tour; round; credit system; aircraft (auto-)
GIRT encircled; prepared
HIRE engage; rent; wage
HIRO measure
KIRI paulownia tree; knob-kerrie (missile)
KIRK church
KIRN harvest feast
LIRA money; lyre; hairlike ridge
LIRE coins; read: Fr.
MIRA star
MIRE bog; (stick in) mud
MIRK dark(ness)
MIRO tree; wood robin
MIRY boggy; filthy
PIRN reed; bobbin; nose ring
PIRO Tanoan Indian
PIRR wind gust; whiz; gull
RIRE to laugh: Fr.
SIRE father; beget; king
SIRI betel
SIRS gentlemen
TIRE fatigue; bore; wheel covering; rubber; shoe
TIRO amateur; novice
VIRA Bantu
VIRE feathered arrow
WIRE cable; snare
WIRY tough; sinewy
YIRM fret; whine: Scot., Ir.
YIRN whine; grimace; smirk: Scot., Ir.
YIRR growl; snarl: Scot.
ZIRA measure
BISA antelope
BISE cold wind; winter
BISH aconite; poison
BISK soup; ice cream; red-yellow
CISE dice term: six
CIST chest; roofed pit
DISA showiest orchid
DISC disk; record; — jockey
DISH receptacle; serve
DISK plate; harrow; puck
DISS reed grass
FISC exchequer
FISH piscine: angle; probe; search; tin — (torpedo)
FISK exchequer; Jim (speculator); tire
FIST grasp; effort; tightwad
GISH Moroccan public land; Lillian, Dorothy (actresses)
GIST main point; pith
HISH hiss; swish
HISS sibilant (of disapproval); goose; serpent; steam sound; Alger (Communist)
HIST call to attention; Indian girl (Cooper)
IISM egoism
KISH powder; basket; measure; Saul's father
KISS touch gently; caress; sweetmeat
KIST chest; installment; measure
LISA fem. name; nickname
LISK flank; loin
LISP speech defect
LISS (fairy) fort; release; peace; fleur-de-lis
LIST strip(e); roll; register; enter; inclination; careen
MISE levy; stake; tax; — en scène
MISS fail(ure); omit; want; girl; maiden
MIST dim; haze; gray
NISH Yugo. city
NISI unless; Lat.
OISE Fr. river
PISA city (leaning tower)
PISE building material
PISH reject; nonsense!
PISK nighthawk
PISO weight
PIST attention!; track
RISE climb; grow(th); begin; emerge(nce); thrive; retort
RISK peril; hazard; subject of insurance
RISP metal bar
RISS glaciation stage
RIST engrave; stretch
SISE six (dice)
SISH slushy ice
SISI porkfish
SISS hiss; shame!; girl
SIST stay; delay; summon
VISA endorse(ment); — vis
VISE tool; clamp; endorse
VISS weight
WISE sage; learned
WISH desire; request
WISP torch; shred; flock; brush; ignis fatuus
WIST know; knew; measure
AITU god; demon
BITE cut; pierce; grip; eat (into); sting; respond; snack
BITI blackwood

BITO tree; poison; oil
BITT naut. fastener
CITE summon; quote
CITS citizens; mufti
CITY urban place
DITA tree; bark; upas
DITE mite; indict
DITT close up; obstruct
GITA Bhagavad —; Indian scriptures (yoga)
GITE shelter: Fr.; mad
JITI Rajmahal creeper
KITE hawk; rogue; flying toy; banking fraud
KITH acquaintance; — and kin
LITE suffix: mineral, rock
LITH prefix; suffix: stone
LITI medieval peasants
LITZ braided wire
MITE arachnid; parasite; small (coin)
MITT glove; hand
MITU curassow; bird
MITY parasite-infested
NITO climbing fern
PITA fiber; flax; hemp; brocket (deer)
PITH marrow; kernel; gist
PITO fiber; flax; hemp; brocket (deer)
PITT statesman (Commoner, Chatham); diamond
PITY sympathy; mercy
RITA cosmic order (Vedic); Rio —; fem. name
RITE ceremony; liturgy
SITA Ramachandra's wife (Sanskrit Ramayana)
SITE location; scene
SITO prefix: grain
TITI monkey; tree; petrel
TITO Yugo. leader (Broz)
VITA life: Lat.
VITE quick, lively: Fr.
VITI East African
WITH prep.: including, and
YITE bird (yellow-hammer)
ZITA Austrian empress
BIUR Heb. commentary
NIUE Savage Island language
PIUS Pope: X (St.; Sarto); XI (Ratti); XII (Pacelli)
SIUM water parsnip
CIVA Hindu deity
CIVE chive garlic
DIVA prima donna; blue
DIVE plunge; duck; low resort; — bomb(er)
DIVI divine ones
FIVE number; basketball team; card
GIVE bestow; yield; grant
HIVE bees' swarm, house
JIVA life energy
JIVE dialect (dance, jazz)
KIVA ceremonial chamber
KIVE brewer's vat
KIVU tsetse fly
LIVE exist; continue; vital; alert
LIVY Roman historian; Titus Livius
RIVA shore: It.
RIVE tear; split; — droite (right bank), — gauche (left bank)
RIVO stream: It.
SIVA Hindu deity; cosmic dancer (Nataraja)
SIVE sickle; knife
TIVY huntsman's cry
VIVA salute (long live); — voce (spoken aloud)
VIVE — le roi!; long live!: Fr.
VIVO spirited
WIVE marry; act as wife
BIWA loquat
IIWI bird (mamo)
KIWI flightless bird; apteryx; non-flyer
BIXA tree genus; achiote
CIXO Ecuador Indian
DIXI I have spoken: Lat.
DIXY camp pot
FIXE prix —
MIXE Mexican Indian
MIXY confusedly mixed
NIXY undeliverable mail
PIXY impish sprite
KIYI herring; cisco; yelp
BIZE cold wind; winter
BIZZ buzz
FIZZ hissing sound; drink
GIZA site; pyramids, Sphinx
NIZY fool
SIZE bulk; quality; glue; filler; — up
SIZY viscous
SIZZ hiss(ing sound)
TIZA ulexite mineral
ZIZA Rehoboam's son
ZIZZ whirring sound
AJAR opened
AJAX hero (Telamon's son)
EJAM Bantu
AJEE awry
IJMA Moslem prin-

ciple (Sunna)
AJOG jogging
EJOO palm; fiber
GJOA ship (Northwest Passage: Amundsen)
AKAL deity
AKAN Negro
IKAT shrub; weight
OKAY approve; all right
SKAG boat; keel part
SKAL health toast
SKAT card game; star
AKEE tree
AKEY weight
EKER water cress
OKEE evil spirit
OKEH all right; O.K.
OKET ounce
SKEE ski
SKEG keel part; plum; tear
SKEN squint
SKEO fisherman's hut
SKEP basket; measure; beehive
SKEW twist; swerve; distort(ed); slant(ing)
SKEY yoke bar
AKHA tribe; Burmese; Kaw
AKIA shrub (fish poison)
AKIM Negro; Tamiroff
AKIN related
OKIA Moroccan money
OKIE migratory worker
SKID clog; slide; — Road, Row
SKIL candlefish; beshow
SKIM scoop off; scud; brush
SKIN hide; pelt; peel; fleece; — and bones
SKIP jump; escape; mess; captain; -tracer
SKIR fly; scurry; skim
SKIT comedy sketch; jest
SKIV sovereign (coin)
AKKA Pygmy
BKKT chess move
EKKA carriage
QKKT chess move
RKKT chess move
IKMO betel palm, pepper
AKOV measure
EKOI Bantu
IKON image; statue
AKRA Negrito; vetch
IKRA superior caviar
OKRA vegetable; gumbo
OKRO plant; stew; soup; gumbo
AKTI peninsula
AKUA deity
AKUT ape man (Burroughs)
SKUA bird; great —; jaeger
SKUN skinned
NKVD Soviet secret police
SKYE Isle; dog, terrier
SKYR sour curdled milk
SKYT move fast; dart; slip
ALAE wings
ALAI regiment; mountain; jai —
ALAR winglike; axillary
ALAN dog; name
ALAS sad cry
ALAY marble
BLAA bunk
BLAB tattle
BLAE bleak
BLAH nonsense
BLAS Gil (Le Sage novel)
BLAT sheep's cry
BLAY bleak
CLAD dressed; plated
CLAM mollusk; hush
CLAN clique; family; group
CLAP rap; applaud; flatten
CLAT mess; chatter
CLAW nail; ungula; chela; scratch; hammer
CLAY earth; ceramic; pipe; — pigeon; color; Henry (statesman)
ELAH king
ELAM kingdom
ELAN dash; ardor
FLAG flower; standard; stone; signal; limp; reduce, dwindle
FLAK antiaircraft
FLAM trick; drum beat
FLAN tart; disk; net
FLAP slap; leaf; sway; -jack
FLAT level; (make) insipid, dull; wholly; — tire
FLAW crack; defect; wind
FLAX plant; fiber; thrash
FLAY (strip off) skin
GLAD pleased
ILAI David's man
KLAM weight
KLAN Ku Klux —
OLAF (Vi)king
OLAM infinity; — haba (life after death)
OLAN Wang Lung's wife (Pearl Buck: The Good Earth)
OLAX tree
OLAY palm
PLAN design; scheme
PLAP fall loudly
PLAT plait; map; plot; fish
PLAY frolic; act; drama; contend; sport; game
SLAB slice; road
SLAG dross; lava
SLAM bang; criticize; grand —
SLAP strike; — bang
SLAT lath; slab; sheep's hide; flap
SLAV Eastern Euro-

pean
SLAW cabbage
SLAY kill; overwhelm
TLAC coin
ULAM Gilead's descendant
ULAN lancer; — Bator
ALBA garb; poem; brain matter; duke
ALBE album
ALBI flagellants
ALBO prefix: white
ELBA Napoleon's exile isle
ELBE river
ALCA auk
ALCO dog
ALDA soprano; hamlet: Sp.
ALEA Athena (war goddess)
ALEC fish; sauce; nickname
ALEE to shelter
ALEF letter
ALEM fruit
ALEN measure
ALEP city
ALES city
ALEY city
BLEA bleak; livid
BLEB blister; bubble
BLED emitted or drew blood, sap; extorted
BLET fruit decay
BLEU blue, rookie: Fr.
BLEW stormed; puffed; sounded
CLEE redshank; bird
CLEF musical sign; roman à —; key
CLEM riot; suffer hunger; nickname
CLEO queen (Cleopatra)
CLEW yarn ball; sail loop; cocoon; hint
ELEF letter
ELEN biblical jurist
FLEA insect; puce; — market
FLED ran away; shunned
FLEE run away; shun
FLEM Fleming; Belgian
FLEW aviated; winged
FLEX bend
FLEY fright(en)
GLED kite; buzzard
GLEN rival
HLER sea god (wife: Ran)
ILEX holm oak; holly
KLEE Paul (painter)
LLEW Celt deity (Gwydion's son)
OLEA shrub; olive
OLEO margarine
PLEA excuse; prayer; request; pretext; allegation
PLEB freshman cadet; common man
PLED pleaded
PLET three-lash whip
PLEW beaver skin
PLEX form a network
SLEB nomadic Arab
SLED vehicle, snow or ice
SLEE sly
SLEW killed; twist; swamp; large number
SLEY weaver's reed
ULEX spine shrub (furze)
VLEI marsh; lake; creek
VLEY marsh; swamp; creek
ALFA grass
ALGA plant
ALGY Algernon; suffix: pain
OLGA fem. name
ALIA other: Lat.
ALIF letter
ALII royalty (Hawaiian)
ALIM teacher
ALIN measure
ALIT descended
ALIX fem. name
BLIP radar screen sign
CLII 152; Hadrian reign
CLIM — of the Clough (archer outlaw)
CLIO history Muse; mollusk
CLIP clasp; cut(ting); gait
CLIV 154; Antoninus Pius reign
CLIX 159; Antoninus Pius reign
ELIA Charles Lamb (essayist)
ELIM Bib. oasis
ELIS Greek city-state
FLIP toss; tap; drink; hop
FLIT flutter; move
FLIX down; fur; flax
GLIA neuroglia (nerve tissue)
GLIB flippant, smooth(ly)
GLIM light; eye
GLIS dormouse genus
ILIA (hip)bones
KLIP rock; cliff
MLII 1052
MLIV 1054; Catholic Church schism
MLIX 1059
OLIC chem. suffix
OLID smelly; fetid
OLIO medley; olla-podrida
PLIM swell; swollen
SLID glided; slipped
SLIM slight; scanty; sly; slenderize
SLIP slide; err(or); escape; pier; leash; garment; memo; cut
SLIT cut; slash; opening
ALKY alcohol
ALLA by: It.
ALLE bird; all: Ger.
ALLO prefix: other, dissimilar
ALLY unite, confederate

ELLA Eleanor; she: Sp.; fem. suffix
ELLE measure; she: Fr.
ILLE that one: Lat.
ILLS troubles
ILLY badly; ill
OLLA jar; meat dish; -podrida (medley)
ULLA grass; paper pulp
ULLO Indian shell money
ULLR chief god; Sif's son; Thor's stepson
ALMA girl; silk; river; city
ALME dancer
ALMS charity
ELMY rich in elms
ULME elm
ULMO muermo; hardwood
ULNA elbow bone; ell
ALOD estate
ALOE plant; tonic
ALOP lopsided
ALOR island
ALOW below
BLOB drop; daub; sound; fish; zero score
BLOC political unit; casting
BLOT stain; mar; dry
BLOW move (air); puff, pant; brag; expend; stroke; calamity; disappointment; — up (enlarge)
CLOD lump; soil; dolt
CLOE fem. name
CLOG block; sandal; stop; impede; choke
CLOP limp; hobble
CLOT mass; coagulate
CLOW sluice; floodgate
CLOY glut; surfeit
ELOD alleged force
ELOI Eli; God
ELON Esau's father-in-law; college (N.C.)
FLOB move clumsily
FLOC flock(y mass); shreds
FLOE floating ice
FLOG whip
FLOP slump down; flap; change; fail(ure); bed; sleep
FLOT lateral ore deposit
FLOW gush; stream; flux; roll; ebb and —
GLOM watch; steal
GLOP look wildly; stare
GLOW shine; incandesce; flush; ardor; wax
ILOG river (Tagalog)
ILOT islet; ait; eyot
KLOM weight
KLOP hard sound
OLOR swan genus; Cygnus
PLOD trudge; drudge
PLOP sound of fall
PLOT tract; ground; press (soap); scheme; intrigue
PLOW implement; till; cut; stars
PLOY make column; frolic; coup
SLOB slovenly one
SLOE blackthorn; plum; blue-black
SLOG hit (hard); slug; slam
SLOO swamp
SLOP slush; gush; mash
SLOT (cut) opening; bolt; deer; track; — machine
SLOW dilatory; tardy; inert; boring; hinder
ALPH river (Coleridge: Kubla Khan)
ALPS mountains
OLPE oil flask; pitcher
OLPH bullfinch
ALSO besides
ELSA — of Brabant (Lohengrin's bride)
ELSE other(wise); besides
ALTA tall: Sp.
ALTE old: Ger.; Adenauer
ALTO hill: Sp.; voice
ALUM emetic; astringent; styptic
ALUR Negro
BLUB swell; puff out
BLUE color; ocean; sky; sailor; sad; -blood; puritanical
BLUP air bubble sound
BLUR obscure; stain
BLUT blood: Ger.
CLUB bat; beat; society; suit (cards)
CLUE hint; guide; thread
CLUM clutch roughly
ELUL month
FLUB blunder; botch
FLUE net; lint; barb; air passage; pipe
FLUX flow; change; melt
GLUB make gulping sound
GLUE adhesive; stick
GLUG sound of liquids
GLUM moody; sullen
GLUT sate; surfeit; oversupply; wedge
ILUS son of Tros; Priam's grandfather
PLUG stop(per); plod; shoot; spark —; horse; praise
PLUM fruit (damson; greengage); tree; raisin; choice job
PLUP sound of (soft) fall

PLUS and; more; extra; — fours
SLUB twisted wool roll
SLUE swamp; twist; lot
SLUG snail; idle; metal spacer; small drink; bullet; strike
SLUM dilapidated district
SLUR pass over; mumble; defame; stigma; glide (mark)
SLUT slattern; harlot
ULUA cavalla; fish; caranx
ALVA duke; city; Thomas — Edison
ULVA sea lettuce; laver
ALYA star
ALYS name: Alice
CLYM — of the Clough (archer outlaw)
LLYN lake; pool
AMAH nurse
AMAN Ahasuerus's minister
AMAR measures
GMAN U.S. police agent
IMAM priest; title
OMAN Arabian state; sultanate; Muscat
OMAO thrush
OMAR Khayyam; tentmaker; caliph
TMAN U.S. Treasury agent
XMAS Christmas
AMBA mountain
AMBI about; prefix: both
AMBO pulpit
IMBE cordage fiber plant
UMBO shield boss; shell beak
YMCA welfare organization

AMEN assent; verily; deity; — Ra
AMER bitter
AMES author; Ia. city, college
AMEX Amer. Expeditionary Force
EMER Cuchulainn's wife (ideal womanhood)
EMEU bird (ostrich-like)
IMER Caucasian
KMET Slav; tenant; mayor
OMEI Buddhist mountain
OMEN presage; portent; sign
OMER measure; sheaf; undertaker (Dickens)
SMEE pintail duck; widgeon; Peter Pan pirate
SMEW merganser; duck
TMEN U.S. Treasury agents
YMER myth. giant
AMGA Siberian river
AMIA fish
AMIC amidic
AMID among
AMIE friend: Fr.
AMIL plant; remedy
AMIN agent
AMIR prince
AMIS friends: Fr.
AMIT headdress
CMIV 904
CMIX 909
EMIL man's name
EMIM Moabites; giants
EMIR ruler; title
EMIT eject; issue; voice
IMID chem. compound
MMIV 2004
MMIX 2009
OMIT leave out; neglect
SMIT struck; destroyed
YMIR rime-cold giant
AMLA tree
AMLI tree

IMLA Micaiah's father
AMMA abbess; god
AMMI herb
AMMO ammunition; prefix: sand
AMMU ammunition
EMMA letter M; name; Austen novel; Bovary (Flaubert)
EMMY TV award; nickname
IMMI measure
IMNA Asherites' chief
OMNI prefix: all
AMOI mine: Fr.
AMOK frenzy
AMON deity; King of Judah
AMOR love; Cupid; — patriae
AMOS prophet
AMOY island
AMOZ Isaiah's father
EMOL rock salt
SMOG fog and smoke; haze
EMPT empty
IMPI armed Kaffirs
IMPY impish
UMPH grunt
AMRA plum
OMRI king of Israel
OMSK Siberian city
AMUN deity
AMUR river
SMUG tidy; neat; priggish
SMUR mist; cloud
SMUT soot; coal dust; plant disease; obscenity
AMYL starch; alcohol
EMYD terrapin
EMYS tortoise

ANAI termite
ANAK giant race
ANAL pert. to anus
ANAM tree; Vietnam region
ANAN tree; interjection
ANAS duck
ANAT sky god; med. term

ANAX Castor, Pollux (Dioscuri)
ANAY fruit
BNAI B'rith (Jewish society)
ENAM gift; land grant
ENAN Prince of Naphtali
GNAR growl
GNAT (biting) fly
GNAW bite; corrode
KNAB nibble
KNAG spur; knot
KNAP summit; rap; talk; bite; button
KNAR knot; burr
ONAN Indian; Judah's son
SNAB hill part; girl
SNAG stump; cut; obstacle; tangle
SNAP seize; break; click; shut; photo; vigor; easy task; — out
UNAL land
UNAU sloth
ANBA title
INBE be within
UNBE cease to be
ANCE suffix; — errand
ANCY suffix
ENCE suffix
INCA Quechuan Indian (ruler)
INCH measure; move slowly
ONCA ounce
ONCE one time; if ever; former(ly)
UNCA 8th note
UNCI hooks; claws
UNCO strange; very: Scot.
YNCA Quechuan Indian (ruler); Inca
ANDA tree
ANDE tribe
ANDI language
ANDY Andrew
ENDO prefix: within
INDE blue (indigo)
INDY — pink (carnation)
ONDE wave: Fr.; wavy (Her.)
ONDY wavy (Her.)
UNDE waving, wavy (Her.)
UNDO untie; unfasten; ruin
UNDY waving, wavy (Her.)
ANEM prefix: wind; city
ANER city
ANES once
ANET dill
ANEW over again
INEE arrow poison
INEZ Don Juan's mother
KNEE joint; bend(ing)
KNEW understood; was aware
KNEZ Slavic prince
ONER ace; blow; individual
ONES individuals
SNED lop; prune
SNEE cut; snick(er) —
ANGE angel: Fr.
ANGO herb; dye
INGA timber tree; mimosa
INGE prelate ("Gloomy Dean"); playwright (Bus Stop)
ANIL shrub, indigo
ANIS fennel; birds
ENID fem. name; Geraint's wife; city
ENIF star
ENIN blue grape pigment
INIA Amazon cetacean
KNIP bite; crop; rap
KNIT looped, tie(d); unite; contract
SNIB escape logging work
SNIG chop off; drag; pilfer
SNIP cut; shred; slip
UNIE unicorn fish
UNIO mussel
UNIS Etats — (USA): Fr.
UNIT single thing; basic amount; one; monad
ANKH cross
ENKI Babylonian god
INKA Inca
INKY black; stained
INLY within; heartily
ONLY alone; but; single; exclusively
ANNA coin; bird; name; — Christie (O'Neill); — Karenina (Tolstoi)
ANNE Queen; Boleyn; Henry VIII wife; Elizabeth's mother; Shakespeare's wife; Dombey's maid (Dickens); Queen — style; Queen —'s lace
ANNI years: Lat.
ANNO — Domini (Year of our Lord)
ENNA Sicilian resort
ENNE prefix: nine; fem. suffix
ENNS river
ANOA ox
ANON again; now; soon; author unknown
ENOL chem. suffix
ENON Paris's wife (nymph); John the Baptist site
ENOS Seth's son, Adam's grandson (905 years old); taken by God
ENOW enough
KNOB lump; hill; antler; handle
KNOP button; finial; stud
KNOR knot (wood); gnarl
KNOT tie; loop; hitch; sandpiper; problem;

	blemish; stud; Gordian —
KNOW	understand; recognize; -how; -nothing (party)
SNOB	social climber; game
SNOD	trim; snug; plausible
SNOT	wick end; blow nose
SNOW	ice crystals; white hair; cocaine; — goose; TV spots
INRE	concerning; actually
INRO	Jap. receptacle
ANSA	handle; loop
ANSE	handle: Fr.
ANSU	Korean apricot
ANTA	porch; nut; tapir; goddess; pier; theater group
ANTE	stake; pay; before; -bellum
ANTI	opposed; prefix: against; Indian
ANTU	rat poison
ENSE	suffix
ENTE	grafted (Her.); being: Sp.
ENTO	prefix: inner
INTI	Incas' deified sun; sun god
INTO	penetrating; toward
ONTO	upon; wise to
UNTO	to; for; toward
UNTZ	weight
ANUS	end of alimentary canal
CNUT	king; son of Magnus
KNUB	waste silk
KNUR	gnarl; knot; wood ball
KNUT	king; son of Magnus
ONUS	burden; duty
SNUB	rebuke; slight; stumpy
SNUG	cozy; trim; Shaks. character
SNUP	snap up cheaply
SNUR	snort
UNUK	star; — al Hay
ENVY	covet; grudge; 7th deadly sin
ENYO	war goddess
ONYM	technical name (biol.)
ONYX	cameo stone; quartz; gem
PNYX	Greek voting site
ANZU	apricot
ENZU	moon god (Sin)
ONZA	Sp. ounce (1/16 libra); coin
UNZE	weight
BOAR	(wild) hog; male
BOAS	Franz (anthropologist)
BOAT	(go by) ship; gravy-
BOAZ	Ruth's husband
COAD	cushion
COAG	dowel
COAK	tenon
COAL	ember; fuel
COAN	pert. to Cos Island
COAT	fur; skin; cover; — of arms
COAX	flatter; cajole
DOAB	tract
DOAT	drivel; be silly, overfond; wood rot
EOAN	pert. to east; dawn
FOAL	colt; equine young
FOAM	froth; rage; rubber
GOAD	rod; decoy; urge
GOAF	grain; rick
GOAI	shrub
GOAL	purpose, objective; score
GOAN	pert. to Goa
GOAT	ruminant; scape-; brown
HOAR	frost; gray; -hound
HOAX	deceive; trick
JOAB	(David's) captain
JOAD	philosopher; Tom (Grapes of Wrath: Steinbeck)
JOAH	record keeper
JOAN	lass; cap; of Arc (the Maid, la Pucelle)
JOAR	durra; millet
KOAE	red-tailed bird
LOAD	burden; measure
LOAF	bread; idle
LOAM	clay; soil
LOAN	lend
MOAB	kingdom; language; Lot's son
MOAN	lament
MOAT	trench
NOAH	patriarch (Ark builder)
NOAP	bullfinch
OOAA	Hawaiian bird
ROAD	(rail)way; track; anchorage
ROAM	wander
ROAN	horse; yellow-red
ROAR	loud sound; laugh
SOAK	absorb; sot
SOAP	cleanser; detergent; money; soft —; -box; — opera
SOAR	fly high; glide
TOAD	amphibian; anuran; fawn
TOAG	Indian
TOAT	plane handle
WOAD	herb
ZOAR	town; Bela; city of Lot
ZOAS	symbolic figures (Blake)
BOBA	chicken snake
BOBO	owala tree; mullet
COBB	Irvin S. (writer); Tyrus R. (baseball)
COBH	Irish port
DOBE	brick (house)
DOBY	brick (house)

GOBI Mongolian desert
GOBO burdock; okra; camera; mike shield
GOBY fish; passing
HOBB havoc; fireplace ledge; pin; peg
HOBO vagrant worker
JOBO hog plum; gumbo limbo
KOBA antelope
KOBE Honshu port
KOBI Japanese reserve duty (term)
KOBU seaweed food (kelp)
LOBB go heavily; tennis stroke; till
LOBE projection; ear part
LOBO timber wolf
MOBY — Dick (whale: Melville)
NOBS knave, jack (card, cribbage)
POBS porridge; pap
ROBE gown; mantle; Douglas novel
SOBK evil deity
TOBA Tatar; Chaco Indian
TOBE cotton cloth; future
TOBY cigar; mug; dog; rob
YOBI Jap. military service
ZOBO mongrel yak
BOCA harbor mouth: Sp.
BOCE colored fish
BOCK beer; leather
COCA cocaine source; shrub; leaf to chew; flavor
COCK male fowl; vane; leader; tap; tee; hay pile; cog
COCO palm; nut; grass
DOCE Brazil river
DOCK weed; rumex; (cur)tail; pier
FOCH Ferdinand (Fr. marshal; WW I commander)
FOCI center points
HOCH high: Ger.
HOCK leg joint; hamstring; wine; faro card; pawn
JOCH yoke, measure: Ger.
JOCK John; jockey; hobo
JOCU dog snapper
KOCH cook: Ger.; Robert (bateriologist)
LOCH lake, bay: Scot.
LOCI places; sites
LOCK gate (canal, dam); tuft; wool; fasten(ing); grapple; tie up; -out (labor)
LOCO (render) mad; weed
MOCK jeer; taunt; sham; — apple, turtle
NOCK notch (in bow)
POCK pustule
POCO slightly; old-clothes man
ROCH Saint (14th cent.)
ROCK stone; Gibraltar; cliff; staunch support; diamond; candy; sway, lull; — the boat
SOCK beat; wind cone; stocking
SOCO heron; bittern
TOCK hornbill
TOCO toucan
VOCE voice: It.; sotto, viva —
BODB goddess
BODE presage; augur; omen
BODO Indo-Chin. language
BODY structure; anatomy; bulk; corpse;
group
CODA finale; mark
CODE body of law (Julian, Justinian, Napoleonic); signal system; cipher; — duello
CODO measure
CODY William (Buffalo Bill)
DODD cut off (wool)
DODE nickname; Theodore
DODO extinct bird; reactionary
IODO prefix: iodine
JODO Buddhist paradise (Gokaruku)
LODE ore deposit; vein; load
LODI city; Napoleon victory
LODZ Polish city
MODE manner; fashion; drab; à la —
NODE knob; knot; orbit; point; joint
NODI knots; difficulties
PODA suffix: foot
PODE suffix: foot
RODA Nile island
RODD crossbow
RODE anchor rope; measure; was borne; cross
RODI Medit. island
SODA carbonated water; Vichy; drink; sodium compound (bicarbonate)
SODI Gaddiel's father (spy)
TODA Ceylon aborigine
TODE (haul with) sled
TODO bustle; stir; ado
TODY green — (bird)
YODH Hebrew Y, 10
BOER So. Afr. Dutch
COED girl student
COEL cuckoo

COEN Jan (empire builder)
DOEG Saul's herdsman; poet's nickname; Indian
DOER performer; agent
DOES performs
GOEL reclaimer; avenger
GOER runner
GOES walks; proceeds
HOEK stream bend; van Holland (Dutch cape, city)
HOEN weight
HOER scraper
HOEY partnership (Hawaii)
JOEL prophet, OT book
JOEY coin; clown; odd-job man; young kangaroo; Pal (O'Hara character)
KOEL cuckoo
MOED festivals (Mishnah)
NOEL Christmas; carol; — Coward
POEM verse creation
POET writer of verse; artist
ROED filled with roe
ROER hunting gun
ROEY of mottled grain
TOED stepped (gingerly)
VOET measure
ZOEA crab larva
DOFF put off; remove
GOFF clown; fool
KOFF Dutch sailboat
LOFT attic; warehouse floor; golf stroke
MOFF Caucasian silk
OOFY rich (Eng. slang)
SOFA couch; divan
SOFT giving way; easy; light(ly); mild; tractable
TOFF dandy
TOFT — and croft (house)
BOGA basslike fish
BOGO Eritrean Hamite
BOGY specter; bugbear
DOGE Venice, Genoa ruler
DOGS scaup duck
DOGY calf; duck
FOGG Phileas (Verne)
FOGO stench
FOGY dull, bigoted man
GOGH Vincent van (painter)
GOGO vine; bark soap; beetle; bugaboo; Bantu; dancer
HOGA hill pasture
HOGG unshorn sheep
HOGO taint; stench
JOGI yogi; ascetic
LOGE theater box
LOGY heavy; dull
MOGO stone hatchet
NOGG egg drink
POGO springy stick
POGY menhaden; trout
SOGA grass rope: Sp.; Bantu
TOGA Roman garb; gown; senatorship
TOGO Afr. republic; Jap. admiral and statesman
TOGS clothes
TOGT trading enterprise
VOGT medieval official
YOGA mental discipline
YOGH Mid. Eng. G, Y
YOGI ascetic; yoga disciple
ZOGO sacred object
BOHO grass; weep; shout
BOHR Nils (Nobel physicist)
COHO silver salmon
FOHN warm dry wind
HOHE Siouan tribe
JOHN name; saint, evangelist; cop; man; Bull (England); Long — Silver (Stevenson)
KOHL eye shadow; horse
MOHA millet; delusion
MOHO bird; honey eater
MOHR gazelle; bezoar
POHA gooseberry (jelly)
SOHO exclamation; London district
TOHO halt! (to dogs)
TOHU -bohu (confusion)
BOID of boas, anacondas
BOII Celtic tribe
BOIL heat; bubble; agitation; abscess
BOIS wood: Fr.; wine (cognac); — de Boulogne
COIF defensive skullcap; make up (hair)
COIL curl; wind; twist
COIN money; mint; invent; corner
COIR coconut fiber
COIX grass; Job's-tears
DOIT coin; whit; bit
EOIN John; Sean
FOIE liver: Fr.; — gras (pâté)
FOIL balk; defeat; sword; leaf; sheet
JOIE — de vivre (zest for life)
JOIN mix; unite; coalesce
KOIL cuckoo
LOIN body part; hips; meat cut
LOIR dormouse; river
LOIS name; Timothy's grand-

mother
MOIL toil; trouble; spot
MOIO measure
NOIL combing (wool fiber)
NOIO noddy tern
NOIR black: Fr.; bet
NOIX edible gland
OOID egg-shaped
POIL raw silk thread
ROIL disturb; muddy; vex
SOIA food plant
SOIE silk
SOIL earth, ground; land; stain; pollute
SOIR evening: Fr.
TOIL work; drudge(ry); snare
VOID empty; vacuum; cancel
VOIR see: Fr.
ZOIC pert. to animals
ZOID organic body cell
BOJO grass
COJA title; teacher
HOJA title; teacher
HOJU Jap. army reserve
KOJI Jap. yeast cake
LOJA bark (quinine)
MOJI Jap. seaport
MOJO tree; majagua; voodoo charm; Indian
ROJO redskin: Sp.
SOJA bean; glycine
BOKO evil spirit (Haiti)
COKE coal residue; fuel
COKY grimed; drug addict
DOKO Afr. pygmy
JOKE jest; laughing stock
JOKY jocular
KOKO bird; palm; tribe; executioner (Mikado)
KOKU measure
LOKA sphere; universe
LOKE Loki; surprise!
LOKI god of discord; Aesir; Balder slayer
MOKE donkey; dolt
MOKI N.Z. raft
MOKO Maori tattoo; -moko (lizard)
POKE thrust; prod; pry; sack; potter; herb
POKU antelope
POKY shabby; dull; bonnet
ROKA mafura (tree)
ROKE vapor; smoke
ROKY misty; hoarse
SOKA drought blight
SOKE jurisdiction
TOKO Chin. store; flogging
WOKE stirred; roused
YOKE join; link; slavery
YOKY coupled
BOLA missile; majagua (tree)
BOLD valiant; brazen; strong, heavy (type)
BOLE trunk; clay; brown
BOLL (strip) plant pod
BOLO knife; Rafflesia (plant); pacifist
BOLT sift; refine; shaft; lightning; bar; plant; rifle part; flight; refusal
COLA tree; nut; drink
COLD chill; frigid; indifferent; common —; coryza; — blood; — chisel
COLE brassica genus; Porter (composer)
COLI intestinal bacterium
COLL embrace; hug; Vincent (gangster: "mad dog")
COLP pasture; Irish acre
COLT young horse; pistol; — .45
COLY long-tailed bird
DOLA weight
DOLE ration; (relief) alms; deal (out)
DOLI weights
DOLL plaything; puppet; dress up; girl
DOLT dunce; ignoramus
FOLD plait; envelop; fail; quit; flock
FOLK people; — ways, laws, song, dance
GOLA storeroom; caste; cyma
GOLD metal; element; — dust, medal
GOLF game; blood-red; — links
GOLI musket ball; pill
GOLL Irish hero (Fenian)
GOLO Nilotic Sudanese
GOLP roundel purpure (Her.)
HOLA fish poison; herb; hello
HOLD grasp; have; retain; believe; keep; bear; lair; prison
HOLE pit; cavity; flaw; — in one; — card; ace in the —
HOLI spring festival
HOLL ditch
HOLM holly; oak; islet
HOLT willow plantation; hill; lair; Eliot hero; actor
HOLY sacred; pious; — City; — Alliance; — Roller
IOLA Kansas town
IOLE Eurytus'

daughter (Hercules' captive)
JOLE jowl; cheek
JOLI pretty, nice: Fr.
JOLL move clumsily; knock
JOLT shake; hard blow
KOLA caffeine nut; jackal; river; city; bay (Murmansk)
KOLI low-caste tribesman
KOLO folk dance
LOLA fem. name
LOLL droop; lounge; sprawl
LOLO Caucasian Chinese
MOLA sunfish genus
MOLD fungus; humus; die, matrix; shape; mix
MOLE nevus; birthmark; pier; burrow(ing animal); Mossi language
MOLL Mary; girl; Flanders (Defoe); minor (mus.)
MOLT shed (hair)
MOLY magic herb (Homer)
NOLA fem. name; time
NOLI — me tangere
NOLL Oliver (Cromwell); head; noddle
NOLO — contendere
POLA Yugo. city (Pula)
POLE rod; tail; terminal: axis, battery; — Star; Polish, Polack
POLK Cossack regiment; James Knox (President)
POLL head; register; survey; cut off; Mary; parrot; vote
POLO game; Marco —
POLT knock; trump; club
POLY herb; Teucrium; prefix: many
ROLE actor's part
ROLL wrap; trill; drumbeat; rotate; list; bank-
SOLA herb (topee source); alone; holla!
SOLD vended; persuaded; cheated
SOLE pelma (bottom); flatfish; single; only
SOLI single performances; prefix: sun, alone
SOLO song; (fly) alone
TOLA weight
TOLD narrated; counted
TOLE entice; told; tinware
TOLL tax; lure; sound
TOLT writ; isolated peak
TOLU balsam (rose odor)
VOLA palm (hand, foot)
VOLE rodent; slam (cards)
VOLK people: Ger.; workmen (So. Afr.)
VOLT sideways gait; fencing leap; elec. unit
WOLD upland plain
WOLF canid (dog); Lupus; larva; devour; dissonance; cry —; flirtatious man
YOLK egg yellow; essence
ZOLA Emile (author: J'accuse, Dreyfus case; Nana)
ZOLL measure
BOMA Afr. stockade; post
BOMB explosive; dispenser; A-, H-; lead-lined container; buzz —
COMA torpor; blur; tuft
COMB crest; rake; scrape
COME arrive; chance; fare
COMO lake, resort (Italy)
DOME edifice; cupola; roof
DOMN Rumanian ruler; lord
DOMY domelike
GOMA Bantu (Wagoma)
HOMA sacred drink
HOME habitat; asylum; plate; natural
HOMO man; — sapiens; prefix: same
HOMY homey; intimate
JOMS Vikings Norse colony
KOME Greenland geol. division
KOMI Soviet republic; Zyrians
LOMA fringe; lap; hill
LOME Togo seaport
MOME buffoon; -rath
MOMO owl
NOME city (Alaska)
POMA rosa (rose apple)
POME fruit; ball; globe
POMO California Indian
POMP pageant(ry); splendor
ROMA Rome: It.
ROME city (Eternal); Church; beauty (apple)
ROMI Gypsy wife
ROMP girl; gambol, frolic
SOMA vine; sacred

drink; body
SOME various; any; somewhat; part
TOMA Liberian Negro
TOMB grave; monument; bury
TOME book; papal letter
AONE first-rate
BONA good: Lat.; — fide
BOND adhesion; tie; convenant; paper; captivity; certificate
BONE study hard; plug; os
BONG bell sound
BONI African; Boschneger
BONK bar money (Dutch E.I.)
BONN city; Ger. capital (Beethoven born)
BONO Johnny (Briton); cui —
BONY skeletal; osseous; Napoleon
COND direct helmsman
CONE geometric solid; pine fruit, strobile; peak; ice cream —; nose —
CONI It. commune
CONK nose; head; decay; fail; hit
CONN direct helmsman
CONY rabbit; daman; pika
DONA lady; sapek (coin)
DONE agreed; exhausted
DONG sound; weight; ding-; money
DONI fishing boat
DONT contraction; prohibition
FOND basis; fount; loving
FONG Ewe-speaking Negro
FONO Samoan council
FONS fount; source
FONT basin; spring; stoup; type
GONA New Guinea victory
GOND Dravidian Indian
GONE departed; enamored; lost; germ cell
GONG bell; tom-tom
GONY albatross
HONE sharpen(er)
HONG Chin. trade guild
HONI — soit qui mal y pense; shamed
HONK goose cry; toot; ooga
IONA Scot. isle; Celt church; college
IONE Pompeii heroine (Bulwer Lytton)
IONI Hainal; Chaddo Indian
JONK jonquil
KONA Hawaiian storm; weight
KONK conk
LONE single; — Star
LONG lengthy; extended; yearn; John Silver (Stevenson); Huey (La. politician); — time no see
LONK black-faced sheep
MONA monkey; Lisa (La Gioconda: da Vinci)
MONG among; barter
MONK ascetic; friar; bird; fish; spot; ferret
MONO monkey; Indian; prefix: single, one
MONS mountain: Lat.; city (Belgium: WW I battle)
MONT mountain: Fr.; — Blanc (peak, Alps)
NONA fate goddess; prefix: ninth
NONE not one; 9th hour
NONO ninth: It.
OONS mild oath
OONT camel; mole
POND lake; pool; weight
PONE corn bread; writ
PONG sound; improvise
PONS bridge: Lat.; — asinorum; Lily (singer)
PONT ferry(boat); bridge: Fr.
PONY small equine (Shetland, polo); glass (1 oz.); translation
RONE brushwood
RONG Sikkimese language
SONE loudness unit
SONG poem (music); pittance
TONE pitch; accent; Wolfe (Ir. rebel)
TONG secret society
TONK (cow bell) clang; honky-; game
TONY nickname (Anthony); stylish
VONE robot bomb
WONG field; meadow
WONT custom; contraction
YOND past; beyond
ZONA girdle; shingles
ZONE area; band; partition
BOOB simpleton
BOOF stare; peach brandy
BOOH exclamation
BOOK tome; volume; Bible; libretto; (bet) record; register; throw the —
BOOL curved handle
BOOM hum; grow,

push; beam
BOON benefit; convivial
BOOR rustic; lout; Boer
BOOT shoe; wader; sheath; torture; recruit; compartment; tube; kick; to — (in addition)
COOK chef; concoct; falsify; James (explorer)
COOL chill; calm; unmoved
COOM coal dust; refuse
COON animal; fur; sly man
COOP pen; jail; confine; coöperative
COOS Bay (laurel); Indian
COOT rail; surf duck; dolt
DOOB Bermuda grass
DOOK wooden brick; demon
DOOM (last) judgment; fate; condemn
DOON tree (varnish resin)
DOOR portal; entrance; open — policy
FOOD nutriment; victuals
FOOL dolt; jester; trick
FOOT pedal part; base; dance; trip; skip; pay; add
GOOD able; brave; sound; profit; happiness; welfare; benefit
GOOF dolt; blunder
GOOK trash; ooze; native
GOOM cultivation method
GOON thug; strikebreaker
GOOP nonsense creature
GOOR sugar; massecuite
HOOD cowl; cloak; seal; gangster; Thomas (poet)
HOOF ungula; foot; beast; walk; dance
HOOK trap; curve; catch; steal; — and eye; pirate (Peter Pan: Barrie)
HOON coin; gold pagoda
HOOP circle(t); wicket; — skirt
HOOT derisive (owl's) cry
JOOK perch; slumber
JOOM cultivation method
KOOP purchase; bargain
LOOD weight
LOOF luff; sponge gourd
LOOK observe; appear(ance); eye(wink); care
LOOM auk; appear(ance); weaver's frame
LOON diving bird; lout
LOOP noose; catch; aerial stunt; Chicago area
LOOS Anita (writer: Gentlemen Prefer Blondes)
LOOT plunder; booty
MOOD humor; temper; verb form
MOON satellite; crescent; month; Diana; Cynthia; languish
MOOR heath; anchor; Moslem; Moroccan; blackamoor
MOOT arguable; ring gauge
NOOK corner; retreat
NOON midday; meal; acme
POOA pua hemp
POOD weight
POOF exclamation
POOH pshaw!; -Bah (Mikado); Winnie (bear: Milne)
POOK hobgoblin; disk
POOL pond; puddle; game; stake; fund; Thames
POON tree (mastwood)
POOP deck; cabin; dickey; exhaust; tire
POOR indigent; scanty; feeble; lowgrade; lean; ill; hapless; cod (fish)
POOT disgusting!
ROOD crucifix; measure
ROOF cover; house; top
ROOK bird; cheat; dupe; chessman (tower)
ROOL crumple; ruffle
ROOM space; apartment; lodge; — and board
ROON treasure; darling
ROOS Ger. painter
ROOT underlying source; rhizome; base; dig; applaud; plant; eradicate
SOOK Moslem market; hog call
SOOL pull, tousle about
SOON promptly; willingly
SOOT powdery carbon smudge
TOOA hero; beefwood
TOOK seized; caught; endured; supposed
TOOL instrument; polish; dupe
TOON tree (dye); mahogany
TOOP measure

TOOT sound horn; carousal
VOOG lode cavity
WOOD timber; forest; Grant (painter); Leonard (general)
WOOF crossthreads; texture; weft; bark
WOOL (sheep) fleece; down
WOON Burmese governor
YOOP sobbing sound
ZOOM buzz; climb; approach suddenly
ZOON developed compound animal
ZOOT — suit: extreme style
COPA tree; yaya; landmark
COPE vestment; cover; bend; contend
COPT Egypt. Christian
COPY duplicate; mimic; follow; text
DOPA chemical (pigment test) crystalline
DOPE drug; information; guess; nitwit
DOPP diamond cup
DOPY sluggish
HOPE trust, expect(ation); wish; -chest
HOPI French beige; Moqui Indian
HOPS beer
KOPH Heb. K, Q, 100
KOPI N.Z. tree (karaka)
KOPT Copt
LOPE go; move; gait
MOPE be dull, listless (person)
POPE pontiff; Holy Father; — Joan (game); Alexander (poet); bird
QOPH Heb. K, Q, 100
ROPE cord; cable; noose; bind; chain
ROPY viscous; stringy
SOPH 2nd year student
SOPT Dog Star; Isis
TOPE drink; shark; stupa; orchard
TOPH drum; porous rock
TOPI antelope; pith hat
TOPO prefix: place
TOPS most superior
BORA north wind; rite
BORD -and-pillar (mining)
BORE pierce; hole; tire; dullard; tidal flow
BORG borough: Dan.
BORI Lucrezia (singer)
BORN given birth to; née; quantum physicist
BORO spring rice; Indian (Mirhana); — Budur (temple)
BORS king (Lancelot's uncle); Bohort (finder of Holy Grail)
BORT finder of Holy Grail; impure diamond
CORA gazelle; Indian; name; Persephone; Demeter's daughter
CORD string; twine; ribbed fabric; measure (wood)
CORE heart; nucleus; gist
CORI Carl, Gerty (Nobel winners)
CORK tree; bark; stop(per); brown; Irish city (Lee)
CORM bulblike stem (crocus)
CORN grain; ear, kernel; callus; whisky; preserve; granulate(d); clavus; banality; red-yellow
DORA Mrs. David Copperfield
DORE bullion; gold; pike; Paul Gustave (Fr. artist)
DORM dormitory; sleep
DORN thornback ray
DORP hamlet; city (So. Afr.)
DORR Rebellion (R.I.)
DORY John (fish); boat
FORA meeting places; courts
FORB non-grassy herb
FORD crossing shallow; Henry (automobile); Shaks. character
FORE front; prior; golf cry
FORK implement (pronged); tuner; place of divergence
FORM shape; mold; fashion; school grade
FORT stronghold; trading post; dun
GORA musical instrument
GORE stab; blood; triangular insert
GORY bloody; murderous
HORA book of hours; Israeli dance
HORN prong; antenna; trumpet; brass wind; cup; Cape —
HORS out of: Fr.; — d'oeuvre
JORD Odin's wife; Thor's mother
KORA water cock;

Hottentot dialect; instrument
KORE Persephone; Demeter's daughter; chaos (Maori myth.)
KORI bustard; low weaver
LORA thong; strap
LORD ruler; Jehovah; Jesus; duck; planet
LORE history; learning
LORI lemur; Afr. Negro
LORN forsaken; bereft
LORO monk parrot; fish
LORS exclamation: lord!
LORY parrot; touraco
MORA default; short syllable; Spartan army; stool
MORE greater; additional; St. Thomas (Utopia)
MORG measure
MORN A.M.; dawn: East
MORO finch; P.I. Moslem tribe
MORS deity; death
MORT nickname; woman; salmon; the kill; dead: Fr.
NORA Helmer (Ibsen heroine)
NORE Thames estuary
NORI seaweed food
NORM type; standard; integer
NORN demigoddess (Urth, Skuld, Verthandi)
OORD coin (double doit, 1/4 stiver)
PORE gaze; ponder; opening
PORK meat; swine; — barrel
PORO Sierra Leone secret society
PORR push; poke; kick
PORT harbor; haven; wine; blue-red; left side; tune; demeanor
PORY porous; permeable
RORI Bantu tribe
RORY O'More (Irish novel)
SORA bird; rail
SORB wild apple; Slav
SORE painful; vexed; sensitive; deer
SORI clusters; spores
SORS lot: Lat.; divination
SORT type; kind; quantity; classify
SORY vitriolic earth
TORA hartebeest; law (of Moses); Pentateuch
TORE ripped; geom. surface
TORI moldings
TORN ripped; damaged
TORO N.Z. tree
TORP croft; Swed. small farm
TORT wrongful act
TORU N.Z. tree
TORY conservative
WORD term; news; promise; order; phrase
WORE had on (clothes); tired
WORK labor; mental product; act; operate; function; needlework
WORM crawler; maggot; screw; insinuate
WORN used (as clothing); shabby; tired
WORT plant; (pot)herb
YORE ancient (times); long ago
YORK city; archbishopric; imperial (apple); Sgt. Alvin (WWI)
ZORI sandal
BOSA Arab. drink
BOSC best pear
BOSE test ground by sound
BOSH furnace part; nonsense (nothing: Turk.)
BOSK thicket
BOSS knob; pad; stud; master, employer
COSE (friendly) chat
COSH snug; happy; math. term
COSO open space: Sp.
COSS measure
COSY snug; teapot cover
DOSA sheik's ritual ride; hatred
DOSE portion; (give) medicine
DOSS bed; sleep; — house
DOST (you) do: archaic
FOSS canal; ditch; moat
GOSH oath; -awful
HOSE stockings; pipe; drench
HOSS house; One — Shay (Holmes)
HOST army; throng; bread as Christ's body; innkeeper; person having guests
JOSE Carmen lover
JOSH make fun; banter
JOSS Chin. deity
JOSY nickname
KOSO tree; cusso; Panamint Indian
KOSS measure
LOSE miss; forfeit; fail; forget
LOSH wash leather
LOSS forfeiture; bereavement; waste; defeat;

— leader
LOST not won; misplaced; confused; ruined; — cause
MOSE Moses
MOSK Moslem temple; Masjid
MOSS bryophyte; lichen; green; rose; Hart (writer)
MOST greatest; almost
MOSY moldy; rotten
NOSE proboscis; smeller; scent; search; front; touch; — out (defeat); -dive
NOSU Lolo; Chin. Caucasian
NOSY fragrant; prying
POSE posture; affectation; baffle; propound
POSH slush; elegant
POST pillar; advertise; mil. station; mail; inform; record
POSY flower; nosegay; poem
ROSA shrub genus; name; sub —; Bonheur (artist)
ROSE stood up; got up; flower; tree; wood; red; pink; window; Abie's Irish —; Eng. emblem
ROSS rough bark; seal; island; navigator; Harold (editor)
ROSY blushing; optimistic
SOSH jag; drunk; dash
SOSO middling; passably
SOSS hog call for food
TOSH bath(tub)
TOSK Albanian
TOSS throw; fling; change
XOSA Kaffir
BOTA measure
BOTE house repair; amends
BOTH the two
BOTO Indian; Voto
BOTT clay plug; fly larva
COTA P.I. fort
COTE birdhouse; sheep shed; coast: Fr. (d'Or; d'Azur)
COTO bark; stomachic
COTY Fr. statesman; cosmetics
DOTE love to excess; drivel; timber rot
DOTH does
DOTO sea slug genus
DOTY discolored by rot
GOTH Teuton (Theodoric, Alaric); barbarian; Ostro-, Visi-
HOTH blind god (Balder slayer)
HOTI cause; reason
IOTA Greek 1, 10; jot
JOTA Sp. peasant dance
JOTI astrologer; astronomer
KOTA P.I. fort; Dravidian language
KOTO Jap. zither
LOTA water pot; burbot genus
LOTE lotus (poetic); weights
LOTH averse; reluctant
LOTI Pierre (writer: Viaud)
LOTO pot; game
LOTS tracts; quantities; very much; chances
MOTA Moslem marriage
MOTE speck; particle
MOTH lepidopterous insect; -ball; -eaten; gypsy —; page (Shaks.)
MOTI elephant (Kipling)
MOTO movement: It.; con —
MOTT clump of trees; James, Lucretia (abolitionists)
NOTA insect backs; — bene (N.B.)
NOTE sign; tone; fame; heed; memo; IOU; record; see
NOTT Norse night (Dag)
POTE poker; stick
POTT paper size; editor (Dickens)
ROTA roster; curia tribunal; a round; hurdy-gurdy
ROTE surf noise; routine
ROTI roasted: Fr.
ROTL Afr. weight
ROTO ragged: Sp.; printing
SOTO Hernando de (explorer)
SOTS yeast
TOTA grivet monkey
TOTE carry, haul; total
TOTO baby (animal); all
TOTY low-caste worker
VOTA Roman festivals
VOTE ballot; suffrage; voice; enact; propose; Ingrian Finn
VOTH Ingrian Finn
VOTO So. Amer. Indian
WOTE Ingrian Finn
AOUL Nepalese
BOUD malt weevil
BOUT contest; attack
BOUW measure
COUE psychotherapist ("Day by day . . .")
COUP blow; master stroke

COUS cowlike
DOUB Bermuda grass
DOUC variegated monkey
DOUM palm
DOUP weaver's thread
DOUR sullen; gloomy
FOUD district magistrate
FOUL rotten; poor; illegal; invalid
FOUR number; card; boat
GOUL monster; grave robber
GOUR cattle; koulan (onager)
GOUT drop; disease (arthritis); taste: Fr.
HOUR time unit; H-or zero —
IOUS promissory notes; suffix
JOUG iron collar; pillory
JOUR day: Fr.
LOUD noisy; showy; vulgar
LOUN loon; lout
LOUP half mask; Skidi Indian; river; fish
LOUR frown; lower; scowl
LOUT boor; bumpkin; dolt
MOUE pout; grimace: Fr.
NOUN speech part; name; substantive
NOUP steep promontory
NOUS mind; reason; wit; we: Fr.
POUF puff; ottoman; bang!
POUL Russ. coin
POUR (make) flow; for: Fr.; emit; — le mérite
POUS measure
POUT sulk(iness); fish
ROUB measure
ROUD fish
ROUE dissolute man; rake
ROUP a cold; hoarseness
ROUT defeat; tumult; mob; the brant; snare
ROUX (soup, sauce) thickener; physician
SOUD pay
SOUF sigh
SOUK Moslem market
SOUL spirit; inspirer; force; psyche; person
SOUP broth; stew; — and fish; duck —; step (up); explosive; fog
SOUR acid(ify); tart; disagreeable
SOUS coins; under: Fr.
TOUG horsetail standard
TOUP Malay lugger
TOUR trip; circuit; — de force
TOUT tip(ster); praise; all: Fr.; — à fait; — de suite
YOUP yelp; scream; yawn
YOUR possessive pronoun
COVE bay; recess; pass; chap; Gypsy
DOVE pigeon; blue, gray; Columba; plunged
HOVA Madagascar native; Malagasy
HOVE ground ivy; raised
JOVA Opata; Pimian Indian
JOVE god; Jupiter; Zeus
LOVE affection; like; Cupid; Eros; zero
MOVE impel; shift; excite; act; depart(ure); play
NOVA star; new, temporary
NOVE nine: It.
ROVE wander; ramble; draw through an eye
WOVE entwined; spun
XOVA Opata; Pimian Indian
BOWK steep; soak in lime
BOWL basin; dish; (roll) ball
COWL hood; auto body front
DOWD slovenly woman
DOWL feathery down
DOWN to below; reduce; defeat; feathers; eider-; dejected
FOWL poultry; cock; hen
GOWK simpleton; fool
GOWL gad; defile; howl; monster
GOWN dress; toga; robe
HOWE hollow; empty; Elias (inventor); Julia Ward (Battle Hymn); Brit. general, admiral
HOWL (distress) cry; wail
IOWA state; Indian
JOWL jaw; cheek; wattle; gambler (Dickens)
LOWA bush quail
LOWN calm; quiet; dolt
LOWY banlieue; suburb
MOWN cut down; trimmed
NOWT neat cattle; dolt
NOWY having curvature
POWE weight
ROWY streaked
SOWN scattered; seeded
TOWN city; hamlet; — hall; man about —

TOWY like flax fibers
YOWL howl(ing); yell
BOXY boxlike; squarish
COXA hip (joint)
COXE Capt. (Scott)
DOXA religious stanzas
DOXY doctrine; hussy
FOXY wily; brown; rank; sour
LOXA pale bark: quinine
MOXA cautery wormwood
MOXO Arawakan Indian
NOXA harmful thing
ROXY name: Roxana; Rothafel (impresario); theater
TOXA sponge spicule
COYN corner(stone)
COYO avocado; chinin
GOYA Sp. painter; — red
HOYA honey plant (milkweed)
MOYO measure
NOYL fiber knot
SOYA bean; dill; fennel
BOZA Arab. drink
BOZO fellow
COZE (friendly) chat
COZY snug; teapot cover
DOZE drowse; timber rot
DOZY drowsy; decayed; doty
JOZY Josepha; Josephine
KOZO paper mulberry
MOZA manservant
MOZO manservant: Sp.
NOZI of Yanan tribe
OOZE exude; slime; liquor
OOZY muddy; slimy
APAP month
APAR armadillo
OPAH fish
OPAL birthstone (Oct.); girasol

SPAD nail
SPAE prophecy
SPAN stretch; team; measure; dog
SPAR mineral; mast; gaff; box
SPAT mollusk; gaiter; snap; tiff
SPAY deer; castrate
UPAS tree (juice); arrow poison
UPDO upswept hair
APER imitator; boar
APET goddess
APEX summit; crisis
EPEE fencing sword
OPEN undefended; plain; frank; — end; uncertain; bare; start; unfold; public; — sesame
SPEC speculation
SPED hastened
SPEE Graf — (ship, admiral)
SPES (goddess of) hope
SPET spit; barracuda
SPEW eject; scatter; gush
SPEX spectacles
SPEY river
UPGO ascend
EPHA Heb. dry measure
EPHI measure
APIA port (Samoa)
APII plant
APIO celery: Sp.
APIS sacred bull (Ptah); bee; bull (Kipling)
EPIC heroic poem
IPIL tree (brown dye)
OPIE Eng. painter
SPIN whirl; twist; aerial stunt; — a yarn
SPIR prefix: coiled
SPIT land point; rod; impale; expectorate; — and image
SPIV slacker: Brit.
UPIS Artemis, Nemesis
YPIL tree (brown dye)

UPLA cow dung; fuel
APOD footless
EPOS epic poetry; events
SPOT stain; point, place; fish; small amount; espy
UPON prep.: above, against
EPPY Euphemia
SPRY nimble; brisk; smart
APSE recess; throne
APSU primordial chaos
IPSE himself: Lat.; — dixit
IPSO — jure, — facto
UPSY -daisy
APUS bird; constellation
OPUS work
SPUD scrape(r); potato; dig
SPUN twisted; whirled
SPUR point; good; kick; otter track; ridge
SPUT boiler plate
BQKT chess move
QQKT chess move
RQKT chess move
AQUA water; green-blue
EQUI prefix: equal, same
ARAB Semite; horse; nomad; urchin
ARAD plant; city
ARAH exclamation
ARAK palm; spirit
ARAL lake
ARAM country (Syria); Eugene (murderer)
ARAN Seir's descendant; island
ARAR tree
ARAS river
BRAB palm
BRAD nail
BRAE slope
BRAG boast; game
BRAJ basha

BRAM Abraham
BRAN god-king; seed coat; chaff
BRAS arm: Fr.
BRAT apron; child
BRAW handsome; fine
BRAY (donkey's) cry; grind; Mrs. Nickleby (Dickens)
CRAB crustacean; apple; sign; anger
CRAG cliff; neck
CRAL hut; village
CRAM press; stuff; study
CRAN bird; measure
CRAP dregs; money; dice cast (craps)
CRAW gullet; stomach
CRAX curassow (bird)
DRAA measure
DRAB dull; box; wench; cloth; drug
DRAG haul; harrow; obstacle; puff; auto race
DRAH measure
DRAM measure; drink
DRAP cloth
DRAT oath
DRAW drag; attract; gain; infer; extract; sketch; undecided contest
DRAY cart; squirrel's nest; — horse
ERAL epochal
ERAN Ephraim's grandson
ERAT was: Lat; quod — demonstrandum (Q.E.D.)
FRAB worry
FRAM spear
FRAP tighten
FRAT fraternity
FRAU Mrs., wife, Mme., woman: Ger.
FRAY contest; tumult; wear off
GRAB grasp; capture; game
GRAD centesimal unit
GRAF nobleman: Ger.; — Spee (Zeppelin)
GRAM sword; plant; weight; —'s method; grandma
GRAN weight; grandma
GRAO weight
GRAS horse; foie — (pâté)
GRAY dull; dismal; hoary; Dorian (Wilde); Asa (botanist); Elisha (inventor)
GRAZ Austrian city (Mur)
IRAD Enoch's son
IRAE Dies — (Day of Wrath)
IRAK country
IRAN Persia
IRAQ country
IRAS Cleopatra's maid
KRAG rifle
KRAL hut; village
KRAN coin
KRAS tahr (goat)
ORAD mouthward
ORAL spoken; of the mouth
ORAN seaport
ORAS Danish money
PRAD horse
PRAH canoe
PRAM carriage
PRAO canoe
PRAT buttock
PRAU swift canoe
PRAY ask; beseech; please
TRAM trolley; gauge
TRAP snare; mouth; net; catch; clothe; basalt; — shooting
TRAY salver; platter; old dog
URAL -Altaic; mountains; hypnotic
URAO trona (mineral)
WRAC women's army corp
WRAF air force; aviatrix
WRAP cloak; blanket; coat
ARBA cart
IRBM ballistics missile
ORBY revolving
URBS (capital) city
ARCA box; dish; shell
ARCH support; curve; chief; fingerprint; triumphal —
ORCA killer whale
ARDU slave
ERDA earth goddess; Wagner role
ORDO order: Lat.; feast list
ORDU Turk. military district, army corps
URDE key-shaped (Her.)
URDU Hindustani language
URDY key-shaped (Her.)
AREA zone, region; scope; tract
AREG deserts
AREO prefix: Mars
ARES war; Mars; Zeus's, Hera's son; Eris' brother
BREA resin; tree; asphalt
BRED procreated; brought up
BREE (eye)brow
BREI soft tissue
BREN (machine) gun
BRER Rabbit (Harris: Uncle Remus)
BRES Elatha's beautiful son (Fomorian)
BREW beverage; plot; concoct
BREY barnacle
CREA linen, cotton fabric
CREE Indian
CREW company; gang; -cut
CREX corn crake

(bird)
DRED Scott (slave)
DREE endure; tedious
DREG lees; residue
DREI three: Ger.
DREW sketched; pulled
DREY squirrel's nest
ERER sooner
FREA Frigg; Odin's wife; goddess
FRED nickname
FREE independent; immune; rid; exempt; — and easy; — lance, port, trade, style
FRET gnaw; vex; worry; embroider; ridge; ornament
FREY god (Njorth's son, Gerth's husband)
GRES stoneware: Fr.
GREW increased
GREY color; neutral; dull; Zane (writer); Vivian (Disraeli novel)
OREB Midianite defeated by Gideon
OREL Russian city
OREN Judah's descendant
PREP prepare; student
PRES near: Fr.
PRET measure
PREX (college) president
PREY victim; pillage; booty
TREE wood, plant; family —; boot, shoe —
TREF homestead
TREK migrate; journey
TRES very: Fr.; three: Sp.
TRET weight allowance
TREY three(spot)
UREA chemical compound
UREY Nobel physicist
WREN bird; navy woman; architect
ORFE fish; yellow ide
URFA Turkish city (Edessa)
ARGH timid
ARGO ship; therefore; constellation
ARGY argue
ERGO hence; prefix: work
ORGY carousal; Saturnalia, Bacchanalia
URGA Outer Mongolia
URGE prod; impel; impulse
ARIA tune; city (Herat)
ARID dry; barren
ARIL seed covering
ARIS molding edge
BRIE cheese
BRIG sailing ship; prison
BRIM rim; edge; swell
BRIN fan plate; silk thread
BRIO con — (with spirit)
BRIT young herring
BRIX scale (hydrometer)
CRIB manger; hut; bin; box; steal; "pony," "trot"
CRIC lamp condensing ring
CRIG blow
CRIN heavy silk
CRIS dagger; stab
DRIB drop; a little
DRIN Balkan river
DRIP let fall
ERIA silk(worm)
ERIC male name; Viking; the Red
ERIE Iroquoian; lake; city
ERIN Eire; Ireland
ERIS goddess of discord, Ares' sister
FRIA Frigg (Odin's wife)
FRIB dirty short wool
FRIM juicy; soluble
FRIT fuse; partly; fried: Fr.; waste
FRIZ curl; crisp; wig
GRID grating
GRIG dwarf; cricket; fowl
GRIM ruthless; ghastly
GRIN smile
GRIP grasp; power; valise; Barnaby's raven (Dickens)
GRIS gray: Fr.
GRIT sand(stone); bravery; grate
IRID iris; crocus
IRIS rainbow; goddess; eye part; plant (flag); spirit (Shaks.); red-blue; March (Arlen)
KRIS dagger; stab
PRIG precisian; steal; thief; fop
PRIX price: Fr.; — fixe (table d'hôte)
TRIG trim; sound; prim; math. course
TRIM shear; adjust; adorn; rebuke; defeat; neat
TRIN one of triplets
TRIO set of 3; So. Amer. Indian
TRIP move; slip; journey; (mis)step
TRIS prefix: thrice
TRIT prefix: third
TRIX fem. suffix
URIA Bathsheba's husband; auk
URIM — and Thummim (sacred instruments)
URIS Leon (author)
WRIG wriggle
WRIT legal order;

Holy —
ORLE shield border; fillet
ORLO smooth surface; plinth
ORLY Paris airport
ARME weapon: Fr.; — blanche (saber)
ARMS mil. science; ensigns; weapons; branches; limbs
ARMY multitude; force
ERMA Ermengarde
IRMA name
ARNA buffalo
ARND theologian
ARNE composer; region
ARNI buffalo
ARNO river; cartoonist
ARNT contraction
ERNE sea eagle
ORNA measure
ORNE measure; river (Caen)
URNA measure
AROA Venezuela copper center
AROD son of Gad
AROE islands, New Guinea
AROO indeed
AROW in a line
BROB support spike
BROH macaque; monkey
BROM Bones (Ichabod's rival)
BROT bread: Ger.
BROW forehead; high-, low-
BROZ Josip (Tito)
CROC harquebus support; crocodile
CROM Cruaich (Irish idol)
CROP craw; harvest; trim
CROW raven; corvine bird; bar; black; Indian; Jim —; -bar
DROP globule; fall; discard; minim; trap door; die; pendant
EROS (god of) love; Cupid; asteroid; Antony's friend
FROE cleaver; steel wedge
FROG amphibian; hoarseness; loop; rail device
FROM out of
FROT rub; chafe
FROW Dutch woman; cleaver
GROG liquor (with water)
GROS coin; fabric; weight
GROT cave; Bremen coin
GROW expand; sprout; wax; develop
IROK gomuti (palm)
IRON metal; element; weapon; instrument; club; shackle; press; strong; Age
KROO Liberian Negro
PROA Malay outrigger
PROD reminder; goad; horse; prodigy
PROG (steal) food; forage
PROM dance, ball (college)
PROO slow up! (horse call)
PROP support; shore; theater equipment
PROW ship's bow; stem; beak
TROD walked; footstep; track
TROP too much: Fr.
TROT jog; gait; race; translation; fishing line
TROW believe; fishing boat
TROY weight system; Ilium, Ilion (Troas); city
WROX rot
ARPA harp: It.
ARRA oath
ARRY cockney worker
ERRA — Pater (almanac)
IRRA war god
ORRA oddly; laborer
ERSE Irish; Gaelic
ERST former; first
URSA bear; stars: — Major, Minor; Great, Little Bear (Dipper)
ARTA Ionian gulf
ARTO prefix: bread
ARTS skills; sciences; fine —; — and crafts
ARTY artistic
URTH Norn; Wyrd (with Verthandi, Skuld); Weird Sister
ARUI sheep
ARUM herb; starch
BRUH pig-tailed macaque
BRUT dry: Fr.; Brit. king (New Troy, London)
CRUS leglike part; shank
CRUX (Southern) Cross; crucial point
DRUB (beat with) stick
DRUG medicine; dope; — on the market; — addict
DRUM spool; instrument: tympanum; beat
DRUN road (Gypsy)
ERUA mother goddess
ERUC cordage fiber
FRUG dance
GRUB larva; food; dig(ger)
GRUE shiver; shudder
GRUM morose; guttural
GRUS constellation (Crane)
IRUS Odyssey beggar
PRUT exclamation; river
TRUE factual; loyal; align

TRUK islands (Carolines)
URUS wild ox
URVA mongoose
ARYA Caucasian
ERYX sand snake
ORYX antelope, gemsbok
TRYP parasite in blood (sleeping sickness, nagana, surra)
ORZO pasta

ASAK tree
ASAR glacial ridges; eskers
ESAU Isaac's, Rebecca's son; Jacob's twin; hairy; red; Edom
ESAY Isaiah
ISAR river (Munich)
OSAR glacial ridges; eskers
TSAO Chinese state
TSAR emperor; dictator
USAR salt; grass
USAS dawn goddess
ISBA log hut
ASCH Scholem (author)
ASCI spore sacs
ESCA apoplexy (plant disease)
ESCE suffix: begin to be
ASEA at sea
ASEM alloy
ASER Jacob's son
ESEK Isaac's well
ESER weight
ISER river
OSER dare: Fr.
USED accustomed; secondhand
USEE future user
USER employer
USES law of — (beneficiary)
YSER river
ASHA tribe
ASHY gray, pale
ISHA Upanishad
PSHA exclamation
TSHI Gold Coast language

USHA Bana's daughter; sorceress
ASIA continent; Orient; East
ASIN month
ASIR Arab. principate
HSIA 1st Chin. dynasty
ISIS goddess; Osiris's wife, sister; Horus's mother
OSID suffix: sugar
TSIA tea
TSIN Chin. dynasty
ASKR — and Embla: Norse Adam and Eve
ISLE ait; eyot; insulate; key
OSLO city (Norway); Christiania
ISMY doctrinaire
ASNO donkey: Sp.
ESNE slave
ASOK tree
ASOP sopping
ASOR lyre
ESOP fable writer
ESOX fish (pike, pickerel, muskel-lunge)
ESPY behold; detect; meteorologist
ASSE caama; fox
ASSI holly
ESSE existence; to be: Lat.
OSSA bones; Mt. (Olympus)
ASTA measure; dog
ASTI city; — spumante
ESTA this: Sp.
ESTE It. family; this: Sp.
ESTH Balt; Estonian (Tallinn man)
OSTE prefix: bone
ASUR war god
ESUS Gaulish god (Mars)
ISUI Asher's son
TSUN measure (1/10 ch'ih)
USUN ancient North Chinese
USUS user, use: Lat.

RSVP please reply: Fr.
ATAP palm
ATAR perfume; essence
ETAH Eskimo settlement; town
ETAL and others: Lat.
ETAT state: Fr.; L' — c'est moi!
PTAH god
STAB pierce; trial
STAD town
STAG deer; men's party; warn
STAR sun; heavenly body; asterisk; hummingbird; excel
STAT photocopy
STAY rope; fasten; prop, endure; wait; remain; stop(ping); — put
UTAH state; Indian; Deseret (Mormon)
UTAI no songs (yo-kyoku)
UTAS 8 day feast; Jap. songs
ETCH eat into; engrave
ITCH skin irritation; desire
UTCH "I"
ATEF crown (Osiris)
ATEN solar disk
ATEO Polynesian god
ATES sweetsop
ETES (you) are: Fr.
ITEA shrub; Virginia willow
ITEM also; article; bit; entry
ITEN So. Amer. Indian
ITER road; passage (brain)
OTEA Great Barrier island
STEM shaft; trunk; stock; axis; dam; check; derive; turn skis

STEN weight; gun
STEP pace; foot rest; rank; act; dance; crush; — on it
STER suffix: agent
STET let it stand!
STEV stanza
STEW boil; steep; hash; worry; study; oyster bed
ATHI Kenya river
OTHO Roman emperor
ATIK star
ATIP expectant
ATIS monkshood; fruit
ATIU one of Cook Islands
ITIS suffix: inflammation, mania; Tereus' son
OTIC of the ear; auditory
OTIS bustard genus; general; inventor (elevator)
STIB sandpiper (dunlin)
STIR agitate; rouse; ado; jail
UTIA rodent
ATKA fish; Aleut. island
KTKB chess move
KTKR chess move
KTKT chess move
ATLE tree
ATLI Gudrun's husband-king
STLO WW II battle site
ATMA soul
ATMO prefix: steam
ATMU sun god
ITMO betel pepper
ETNA stove; volcano
ATOM whit; particle; nuclear complex
ATON solar disk
ATOP at the peak
ETON school, college; collar; jacket; playing field of —
ITOL suffix: alcohol(ic)
OTOE Sioux Indian
STOA portico; poikile (Zeno)
STOD Danish speech
STOF measure
STOG stall in mud
STOL short takeoff and landing
STOM prefix: mouth
STOP halt; discontinue; arrest; close; instrument part; period
STOT stumble; stutter
STOW pack; hide; hold; skiing resort
UTOR to use: Lat.
VTOL vertical takeoff and landing
KTQB chess move
KTQR chess move
ATRI It. town
ATRY lay to (naut.)
ETRE exist, be: Fr.; raison d'—
OTRA other: Sp.
OTRO other, another: Sp.
ATTA soul; native; flour; fruit; ant
ATTU Aleut. island
ETTA Henrietta; Harriet
ETTE suffix: fem.
OTTO name; palindrome; perfume; Ger. ruler
ATUA demon
ATUM sun god (Tem)
ETUI (vanity) case; box
OTUS giant slain by Apollo
STUB stump; penpoint; short, stocky; extirpate; ticket part; bump
STUD breeding stock; knob; stump; dot; poker
STUM grape juice; must; renew wine
STUN stupefy; daze
STUT horsefly
UTUG horsetail standard
UTUM small owl
ATWO asunder
VTWO robot bomb
ATYS god (Cybele's lover)
ETYM Moabites, giants; abbr.: word sources
ITYS Tereus' son
STYE eyelid swelling
STYX Hades river; nymph: daughter of Oceanus, Tethys
ITZA Mayan Indian
BUAL wine
DUAB tract
DUAD pair
DUAL double
DUAN canto; poem
DUAR mountain pass
DUAT Hades
FUAD Arab king
GUAD tree
GUAM Mariana island
GUAN bird
GUAO tree
GUAR legume; cluster bean
JUAN John; Don —; Don Giovanni
JUAR durra; millet
KUAN pottery; official
KUAR month
LUAU feast; cook-out
MUAV geol. epoch
PUAN latex
QUAB fish
QUAD type; four; -rangle, -ruplet, etc.
QUAE — vide (which see)
QUAG morass
QUAI pier
QUAN money
QUAR fill; choke
QUAS sour beer, cider (Russian)
QUAT squat
QUAY pier
RUAY weight
SUAN — pan: Chin. abacus

TUAN measure; sir; title
YUAN dynasty; money
BUBA tropical sore
BUBE boy; jack: Ger.; Fernando Po Bantu
BUBI Fernando Po Bantu
BUBO horned —; eagle owl
CUBA W.I. island; Pearl of Antilles; measure
CUBE square solid; 3rd power; die; plant poison
CUBI measure
DUBB Syrian bear; lizard
HUBB pipe end
JUBA ghost; dance; mane; river
JUBE chancel screen; lozenge
KUBA carpet; measure
LUBA Bantu; Bashilange
LUBE machine oil
LUBS of Lubeck (city)
NUBA Nubian; Berberi language
NUBK shrub
RUBE Reuben; rustic; yokel
RUBY gem; corundum; bird; name; Oswald killer
TUBA saxhorn; tree; nut; fish poison; palm sap
TUBE cylinder; tunnel; subway; radio, TV part; Audion (DeForest)
AUCA Indian
BUCK deer; fop; butt; male; Pearl (novelist); pass the —
CUCA cocaine source
DUCE chief: It.; Mussolini
DUCK bird; webfoot; wild fowl; canvas; pet; plunge; evade; — soup; vehicle
DUCO pyroxylin lacquer
DUCT tube; vessel; pipe
FUCI rockweeds; algae
HUCH Danube fish
HUCK towel fabric
JUCA cassava; manioc
JUCK partridge call
LUCE fish, pike; Adriana's servant; Henry (editor); Clare Boothe (writer, stateswoman)
LUCK chance; event; fortune
LUCY fleur-de-lis; fem. name; camera lucida; Lemonade (Mrs. Hayes); Stone (suffragist)
MUCH great (deal); far; — Ado (Shaks.)
MUCK (rid of) manure; mess
NUCI prefix: nut
OUCH exclamation
PUCA goblin; specter
PUCE flea: Fr.; eureka red
PUCK sprite; Robin Goodfellow; Shaks. character; hockey disk
RUCK crowd; rake; wrinkle
SUCH of this kind; same
SUCK draw in; bleed; drink
TUCK draw up; fold (in); eat; Friar (Robin Hood)
YUCA cassava; manioc
AUDE Fr. dept.; river
BUDA It. millet
BUDD Lanny (Sinclair)
BUDE light; burner
DUDE dandy; fop; city fellow; — ranch
DUDS clothes; failures
JUDA James' brother
JUDE name; NT book, author; Jew: Ger.; — the Obscure (Hardy)
JUDO self-defense art
JUDY name; Punch and —; Judith; Kipling character
KUDU Afr. antelope
LUDI Roman public games
LUDO game; pachisi
MUDD measure; doctor of Booth (Lincoln assassin)
NUDA ctenophore; Beroida
NUDD Brythonic god, king
NUDE naked; art work; color
PUDU Chilean deer
RUDD carplike fish
RUDE rough; boorish; vulgar
SUDD Nile waste matter; dam
SUDS lather; froth; beer
WUDU Moslem ablution
AUER violinist
DUEL combat; meeting
DUET music for two
EUER your(s): Ger.
FUEL combustible matter
GUEG Albanian
HUED colored; tinged
HUEY Long (La. governor)
JUEZ judge, juror: Sp.
KUEI disembodied spirit
LUES syphilis
QUEI measure

RUER repenter
SUER prosecutor; suitor
SUET hard fat
SUEZ canal; seaport
TUEL furnace
BUFF leather; coat; tan; ward off; polish; wheel; bare skin; enthusiast
BUFO toad genus; agua
CUFF slap; manacle; sleeve end; miser; on the —
DUFF pudding; cheat
DUFY Raoul (Fr. artist)
GUFA round boat
GUFF humbug; chaff
HUFF inflate; bully; anger
KUFA round boat
LUFF sail nearer wind
LUFT air: Ger.; -waffe
MUFF handwarmer; bungle
PUFF blow; pastry; distend; hair roll; adder; powder —
RUFF collar; bird; fish; plait; trump
SUFI mystic ascetic
TUFA porous rock
TUFF volcanic rock
TUFT crest; clump; tassle
WUFF gruff bark sound
YUFT Russ. leather
AUGE priestess
BUGI Celebes Malay
EUGE bravo!
FUGA fugue: It.
FUGU poisonous fish
GUGU P.I. soldier; insurrecto
HUGE enormous; immense
HUGH name; saint (of Cluny)
HUGO name; Victor (novelist)
JUGA carrot ridges; yokes
JUGE judge: Fr.
KUGE Jap. courtier
LUGE lodge; small sled
LUGH Celtic light god
MUGA silk; moth
OUGH exclamation
PUGH pshaw!; fish prong
RUGA stomach membrane
RUGG pull
SUGI Jap. cedar
VUGG lode cavity
VUGH lode cavity
YUGA Hindu age cycle
BUHL inlaid decoration
BUHR whetstone
DUHR star
GUHA Bantu
GUHR earthy deposit
KUHL eyelid cosmetic
RUHR Ger. industrial area
CUIR leather; dorado
DUIM measure
DUIN demons
DUIT Chibchan Indian; coin
GUIB harnessed antelope
HUIA bird (starling)
HUIT eight: Fr.
LUIF loof
MUID measure
MUIR moor (Scot.)
NUIT night: Fr.
QUID cud; essence; pound; — pro quo
QUIP witty sally; jest
QUIT abandon; yield; stop; free
QUIZ test; odd one; hoax
RUIN destroy; destruction; violate
SUIT costume; card set, legal action; please; (out)fit
YUIT Asian Eskimo
FUJI wisteria; cherry; volcano
JUJU Afr. magic, charm
PUJA worship; festival
SUJI wheat; semolina
BUKA dried leaves
BUKH prate; talk
BUKK prate; talk
CUKE cucumber
DUKE prince; cherry
DUKU lanseh tree fruit
HUKE hooded cap
JUKE partridge call; — box; sociological name (with Kallikak)
KUKI Burma Mongol
KUKU N.Z. fruit pigeon; kukupa
LUKE name; evangelist; Paul's companion; author Acts; -warm
PUKA rare N.Z. tree
PUKE cloth; vomit
PUKU Afr. antelope
PUKY nauseated
RUKH fabled bird; jungle
SUKE Susan; teakettle
SUKU Bantu
SUKY Susan; teakettle
TUKE fabric; canvas
WUKF trust fund
YUKI Cal. Indian
AULA hall; tree; brain part
AULD old; — lang syne
AULU tree
BULB bud; tuber; corm; lamp; swell
BULK mass, volume; loom; -head (stall)
BULL (bovine) male; stud; papal letter; optimist; Taurus; policeman; blunder; glib talk; -fight

BULT hill; ridge
CULE diminutive suffix
CULL pick out; assort
CULM grass stem; coal dust; shoal water deposit
CULT sect; worship system
DULL blunt(ed); dismal; inert; tedious; Shaks. character
DULY properly; timely
FULA Sudanese
FULK unfair shove (marbles)
FULL filled; replete; quite; — dress; — house
GULA upper throat; goddess (Ninurta's consort)
GULE of August (Lamma's Day)
GULF bay; chasm; eddy
GULL bird; cheat; dupe
GULO wolverine genus
GULP swallow; catch breath
HULA Hawaiian dance
HULE caucho source
HULK ship body; bulky thing
HULL husk; ship body; Cordell (statesman)
HULU o-o's feather tuft
JULA suspension bridge
JULE name: Julian; Julius
JULY (5th Roman) month
KULA measure; gift exchange
KULI low-caste Indian
KULM crane; heron
KULU old woman (Kipling)
LULA name; Louisa
LULL (temporary) quiet
LULU barn owl; name; Louisa
MULE equine hybrid; spinning jenny; slipper
MULK freehold land
MULL muslin; ointment; ponder; humus
NULL nil; void; code filler
PULA Yugo. city
PULE cheep; whimper
PULI coins
PULK (Cossack) regiment
PULL drag; influence
PULP pith; tissue; paper; magazine
PULU tree fern
PULY whining; complaining
RULE law; guide; reign method; control; — Britannia; ruler; line
RULL to wheel; trundle
SULA genus; booby; gannet
SULD measure
SULK mope; be sullen
SULU Moro
TULA metal; niello; city; Toltec ruins
TULE bulrush; cattail
TULU Dravidian Indian
VULN wound (Her.)
YULE Christmas
ZULU Bantu; Kaffir; ship; artificial fly
BUMP coincide; hit; swelling; — off (kill)
DUMA Russ. parliament
DUMB mute; stupid; — waiter; deaf and —
DUMP unload; junkyard; thud; mean place; holey dollar
FUME smoke; fit; rage
FUMY vaporous; smoky
GUMI shrub, flower, fruit
GUMP silly, stupid one; Andy, Chester, Min (cartoon family)
HUMA Uganda Negro
HUME philosopher
HUMP protuberance; mound; crisis; Himalayan peaks; -back
JUMP leap; bounce; move; headstart; — the gun
LUMP mass; swelling; barge; like it or — it
MUMM mask; disguise
MUMP beg; mumble; cheat
NUMA Pompilius (Roman king)
NUMB deaden(ed); helpless
PUMA cougar; catamount
PUME Yarura(n language)
PUMP force; draw out; slipper
RUMB compass point
RUMP sirloin part; remnant; — Parliament
SUMO Ulvan
SUMP dig pit; tank; cistern
TUMP drag slain deer
YUMA Indian (Cal.); city
AUNE measure
AUNT parent's sister; tia: Sp.; tante: Fr., Ger.
BUNA synthetic rubber
BUND embankment; league

BUNG stop(per); throw
BUNK case; bed; nonsense
BUNN cake
BUNT sag (net, sail); (fungus) disease; butt (ball)
CUNA Panama Indian
DUNE sandhill; twine color
DUNG excrement; fertilize(r); weight
DUNK dip into; immerse
DUNS dull; stupid
DUNT split (ceramics)
DUNY having many dunes
FUND supply; finance; money; sinking —
FUNG Sennar Negroid
FUNJ Sennar Negroid
FUNK fear; coward; Casimir (vitamins); Isaac (lexicographer); — & Wagnalls
FUNT weight; Allen (TV)
GUNA Sankhya term
GUNJ granary; market
GUNK jilt; hoax
GUNL gunwale
GUNN castaway (Stevenson)
HUND dog: Ger.
HUNG suspended; undecided (jury)
HUNH exclamation
HUNK pierce; lump; OK
HUNT seek; chase; Leigh (writer)
IUNO Jupiter's wife
JUNE month; beetle; — moon, bride
JUNG young: Ger.; Carl Gustave (psychologist)
JUNK ship; trash; scrap
JUNO goddess; Jupiter's wife; Hera; stately woman; missile
KUNG public
KUNK measure
LUNA moon goddess; silver
LUNE crescent; hawk leash
LUNG air bladder; iron —
LUNN Sally (teacake)
LUNT light; smoke; Alfred (actor)
LUNY crazy (man)
MUND protection right
MUNG grass
MUNJ tough grass; twine
MUNT sash bar
NUNS sisters; veiling, fabric
PUNA high Andes; wind; sickness (soroche)
PUND weight
PUNG (drive) box sleigh; mah jongg term
PUNK touchwood; tinder; conch; tramp; bad
PUNO Pacific trade wind; city (Peru)
PUNT propel) flatboat; kick; bet
PUNY weak; slight
QUNG So. Afr. Bushman
RUNE Teutonic sign; magic
RUNG wheel spoke; hooped
RUNT small animal, man
SUNG chanted; Chin. dynasty
SUNK immersed; overcome
SUNN hemp: fiber plant
SUNT babul: gum tree; pod; are: Lat.
TUNA fish; pear: opuntia
TUND pound; bruise
TUNE song; pitch; harmony
TUNG tree; oil
TUNK rap; thump; game
TUNO rubber tree; gum
TUNU rubber tree; gum
TUNY melodious
YUNX woodpecker genus
ZUNI Indian; reservation
BUOY float; sustain; life-; channel marker
CUON wild dog (dhole)
DUOS duets
HUON pine; timber tree
LUOH White Nile Negro
QUOD prison; — erat demonstrandum (Q.E.D.)
DUPE trick(ed one); copy
HUPA Athapascan Indian
HUPP call to horse
JUPE skirt
LUPE Samoan fruit pigeon; Velez (actress)
NUPE Nigeria Negro
PUPA chrysalis; snail; instar
RUPA body form (Buddhism)
SUPA P.I. tree; lamp oil
SUPE stage extra; supercharge
TUPI Amazon Indian
TUPY Amazon Indian
ZUPA Yugo district
ZUPH Samuel's ancestor
AURA wind; emanation; bird
AURI prefix: gold, ear
BURA steppe blizzard
BURD noble lady

BURE brown red-yellow
BURG (fortified) town
BURH (fortified) town
BURI palm (fiber); talipot
BURL (pick) knot; Ives (actor)
BURN (be on) fire; yearn; waste; speed; brand
BURP belch; — gun
BURR (prickly) nut, knob; reamer; banyan tree; Aaron (statesman)
BURT butt; gore; dent
BURY hide; inter; lose
CURA parish priest: Sp.
CURB restrain(t); sidewalk edge; market
CURD coagulated milk
CURE heal; remedy; preserve; priest: Fr.
CURL coil; twist; hair lock
CURR to murmur (as owlet)
CURT short; concise
DURA — mater (spinal membrane)
DURN gatepost
DURO Sp. peso; dollar
DURR grain sorghum
FURL roll up (sail, flag)
FURY rage; avenging spirit; Erinys, Fate, Parca (Atropos)
GURU teacher
HURA bishop's cap; sandbox tree; possumwood
HURE head of boar, wolf
HURI Abihail's father
HURL throw; pitch; rush
HURR to snarl
HURT harm(ed); pain
JURA rights; mountain range
JURE de — (by law)
JURY (court) panel; committee; grand, petit —; hung —
KURD Sunnite Mohammedan; Iranian
KURE Jap. city; Hawaiian isle
KURI Lezhgian tribesman
KURK church: Scot.
KURU disease
LURA brain opening
LURE entice; decoy; trumpet
LURG marine worm
LURI Lake Albert Negro
LURK lie in wait; skulk
MURA Brazil Indian
MURE thrust against wall
MURK (make) gloomy
NURL wood knot; to mill
OURS possessive pronoun
PURE unmixed; chaste; sheer; free; Simon —
PURI Indian yellow
PURL knitting stitch; beer; murmur; spin; swirl
PURR cat's sound
PURU of Arawakan
RURU N.Z. morepork
SURA Koran section; deva
SURD irrational; mute
SURE safe; firm; certain
SURF swell of sea; foam
SURT Frey's slayer
TURB crowd; clump
TURF sod; grassy ground; peat; racing
TURI Pathan tribesman
TURK Mongoloid; Seijuk; Ottoman; Osmanil; horse
TURM troop; company
TURN bending; corner; revolve; reverse; change shape; act; movement
TURP turpentine
WURD Norn; Urth
WURM glacial period
YURT Kirghiz tent
AUSA Vich (Sp. commune)
AUSU tree
BUSH shrub; thicket; tail
BUSK stir about; hasten; corset bone; Indian New Year
BUSS ship; kiss; calf
BUST bosom; statue; failure; break
BUSY (keep) active; in use
CUSH sorghum; cow; money; Ham's son; country
CUSK fish; burbot; eel
CUSP (crescent) point; tooth edge
CUSS curse; person
DUSE incubus; Eleanora (actress)
DUSK twilight; gloom
DUST powdered matter; rubbish; clean; dust to —; gold —
FUSC dusky; somber
FUSE detonator; melt; unite
FUSS tumult; bustle; -budget
FUST pilaster; smell stale
GUSH flow; spout; be effusive
GUST outburst of wind
HUSE beluga; whale; huchen
HUSH quiet; silence; -hush; -puppy; — money

HUSI fine P.I. fiber
HUSK covering (of seed, corn); shell
HUSO beluga; whale; huchen
HUSS dogfish; John (religious leader)
JUSI fine P.I. fiber
JUST fair; virtuous; exact(ly)
KUSA ceremonial grass
KUSH Ham's son; country
LUSH luxurious; drunkard
LUSK lazy (fellow)
LUST sensual desire
MUSA banana genus
MUSE meditate; goddess
MUSH meal; hasty pudding; flattery; proceed!
MUSK odor; aromatic secretion (of deer, ox, etc.)
MUSO Chibchan Indian
MUSS mess; rumple; row
MUST be obliged to; necessity; new wine; stum; staleness; frenzy
NUSS nurse
OUSE Great — (river)
OUST eject; discharge
PUSH shove; thrust; strive; -button
PUSS cat; lip; face
RUSA deer; sambar; grass; oil
RUSE trick; deceit; slip
RUSH haste(n); attack; red (mace); cattail
RUSK bread; biscuit; Dean (statesman)
RUSS Russian; Slav
RUST oxydize; corrode; inaction; reddish-brown
SUSA Elam city (Esther story)
SUSI fine cotton
SUSU blind dolphin; Congo
SUSY name: Susan; Susanna
TUSH tooth; Georgian; pshaw!
TUSK long tooth
AUTE tree
AUTO prefix: same, self; drama: Sp.; (ride in) car
BUTE island; Scot. county; parson (Thackeray)
BUTO serpent goddess; Leto
BUTT cask; mound; target; ram; hinge; jut; halibut
CUTE clever; attractive
DUTY obligation; task; tax
FUTE Eskimo curlew
GUTI Sumer settler; Kurd
JUTE fiber plant; Corchorus; Low German
LUTE cement; bricklayer's tool; Apollo's musical instrument; jar ring
MUTA mus. change; Moslem marriage
MUTE silent; dumb; muffle
MUTH measure
MUTT cur; stupid one; — and Jeff
PUTT golf stroke
RUTA herb genus; rue
RUTE measure
RUTH pity; grief; name; OT book, heroine (Moabitess); wife of Boaz
TUTE to tutor
TUTU N.Z. shrub; poison; ballet skirt
YUTU Peru tinamou; bird
PUUD weight
SUUM hum; — cuique
TUUM thin: Lat.
CUVY sea girdles; kelp
TUWI P.I. dyewood tree
BUXY paymaster
LUXE elegance; de —
PUXY ill-tempered
BUYO betel leaf; nut
CUYA hardwood tree
FUYE Jap. flute
PUYA pineapple genus
AUZU tree
BUZI Ezekiel's father
BUZZ hum; fly low (over); — bomb (V1, V2)
FUZE detonator; melt; unite
FUZZ fine fibers; police
GUZE red roundel (Her.)
HUZZ buzz; murmur
JUZA star
NUZO Chibchan Indian
SUZY name: Susanna
TUZA pocket gopher
WUZU Moslem ablution
ZUZA weight
AVAL grandparental
AVAR Caucasian language
EVAN name (Welsh)
EVAT eft
IVAH Bib. city
IVAN John; — the Terrible
KVAS sour beer, cider
OVAL egg-shaped; elliptic; arena
SVAN Caucasian
UVAL grapelike
AVEC with: Fr.
AVER assert; asseverate
AVES birds: Lat.
EVEA madder (tree);

ipecac
EVEN evening; level; fair(ly); equal(ly), moderate; just; not odd; flush
EVER always; at anytime
EVET eft; newt
IVER ever
IVES inventor (photo -engr.)
OVEN (bake in) stove; kiln
OVER above; across; beyond; again; surplus; ended; Roger and —
UVEA iris layer
AVID eager; greedy
AVIS bird: Lat.
CVII 107; Trajan reign
EVIL bad; sinful; injury; disease
LVII 57; Nero reign
MVII 1007
OVID poet (Metamorphoses); P.O.N.; Naso
OVIS sheep genus
UVIC grapelike; acid
UVID moist; wet
AVON river; Shakespeare home (Stratford)
AVOW declare; justify; confess
EVOE bacchanals' wild cry; Punch editor
AVUS grandfather: Lat.
OVUM germ cell; egg

AWAG wagging
AWAN tribe
AWAY onward; hence; far; off; absent
EWAN name (Welsh)
KWAN coin; weight
SWAB mop; lout
SWAD mass; soldier
SWAG bag; booty; sway; sag
SWAM floated
SWAN constellation; dive; — song
SWAP barter; exchange
SWAT hit (hard); river, state (Pakistan); Sultan of — (Ruth)
SWAY oscillate; veer; rule
YWCA welfare organization
EWER pitcher; udder
KWEI disembodied spirit
OWEN (Welsh) name; socialist; zoölogist
OWER debtor
TWEE bird's cry
ZWEI two: Ger.
IWIS certainly
SWIG gulp; hoist; tackle
SWIM move in water; float; teem
SWIZ swindle
TWIG discover; branch; beat
TWIN double; match; — Cities
TWIT taunt; yarn snarl
AWNY bearded
AWOL absent without leave
LWOW Polish city
SWOB sponge; wipe; mop
SWOP trade
SWOT hard work; grind; hit
SWOW I — (oath)
AWRY distorted; perverse(ly)
EWRY linen storeroom
OWSE tan liquor
SWUM swim participle
GWYN Liud's son; diety

AXAL around an axis
EXAM interrogation; test
OXAN gas
EXES letters; expenses
OXEA sponge spicule
OXEN bovines; draft animals
OXER hedge (fox hunting)
AXIL leaf angle
AXIS center line; spine; stem; deer; power alliance; partnership
CXII 112; Trajan reign
CXIV 114; Trajan reign
CXIX 119; Hadrian reign
EXIT depart(ure); die
IXIA corn lily; bulb
IXIL Mayan Indian
LXII 62; Nero reign
LXIV 64; Nero reign
MXII 1012
MXIV 1014; Brian Boru defeats Danes
MXIX 1019
OXID oxygen compound
OXIM chem. compound
XXIV 24; Tiberius reign
AXLE spindle
IXLE cordage fiber
AXON axis; cell process
EXON Exeter man
OXYL oxygen radical

AYAH nurse; sign
AYAN spruce
CYAN green-blue
DYAD pair
DYAK Bornean
DYAS Permian (geol. period)
EYAH nurse; sign
EYAS nestling
IYAR month
KYAH partridge
KYAK canoe
KYAR coconut fiber
KYAT weight; Burmese money
LYAM bloodhound
LYAS geol. period
MYAL cultic
PYAL veranda
PYAT magpie
RYAL coin

RYAN peak (Idaho)
RYAZ coin
GYBE jibe; scoff; agree
TYBI 1st Egypt. spring month
DYCE thus!: naut. command
DYCK Anthony Van (painter)
SYCE groom
WYCH -hazel; — elm
HYDE — Park; Dr. Jekyll and Mr. —; measure
AYES yes votes
BYEE measure
DYER tinter; Mary (Quaker martyr).
EYED looked at; ogled
EYER needle maker
EYEY having holes
OYER hearing (law); — and terminer
OYES court crier's cry
OYEZ court crier's cry
PYET magpie
RYEL coin
SYED Moslem chief
TYEE chief
TYER binder
BYGO pass by
ZYGA rowers' benches; brain fissures
AYIN Heb. 16th letter, 70
PYIC purulent
BYKE nest of bees
CYKE cyclorama
DYKE levee; checkers opening
FYKE fish bag net
HYKE cry to urge dogs
KYKE fashion spy
SYKE fountain (Her.)
TYKE dog, child
CYLE brewing; beer; wort
GYLE brewing; wort; vat
HYLA frog; toad
HYLE matter (philos.); demon
KYLE sore; ulcer; farmer
PYLA brain opening
PYLE Ernie (journalist); Howard (artist)
TYLO dog (Maeterlinck)
CYMA cornice molding
CYME inflorescence
HYMN song (of praise)
LYME bloodhound
RYME water surface
TYMP blast furnace stone
ZYME ferment
DYNA prefix: power
DYNE unit of force
GYNE prefix: female
IYNX wryneck (woodpecker)
JYNX wryneck; charm
LYNX wildcat; fur; constellation
MYNA talking bird; grackle
RYND millstone support
SYNC synchronize
TYNE Eng. river
WYND alley; small court
WYNN timber truck; Ed (actor: Perfect Fool)
BYON clayey earth
CYON wild dog (dhole)
EYOT islet
LYON Fr. city; bean
PYOT piebald; chatty
RYOT Indian peasant
GYPS gypsum
HYPE wrestler's throw; ad
HYPO photo solution; needle; injection
HYPS hypochondria
RYPE ptarmigan
SYPE ooze
TYPE kind, sort; class(ify); printer's letter; use typewriter, produce copy
TYPO printing error
TYPP yarn count unit
TYPY typical
BYRD explorer; Va. statesman
BYRE cow house
EYRA wild cat
EYRE Jane (Brontë heroine); circuit (court)
EYRY bird's nest
FYRD old English army
GYRE turn; ring; vortex
GYRI brain ridges
GYRO prefix: ring, spiral
LYRA glockenspiel; constellation
LYRE harp; constellation
MYRA name; ancient city
PYRE funeral pile, fire
PYRO prefix: fire, fever
SYRA Aegean island
SYRT quicksand
TYRE Phoenician city; Sur
TYRO beginner; novice
TYRR Odin's son; war god
WYRD Norn; Urth
CYST box; abnormal sac
LYSE undergo lysis
MYSA buffalo (Kipling)
MYST Greek priest
BYTE computer word
CYTE prefix: hollow vessel
MYTH (religious) legend; fiction
TYTO barn owl; Strix; Aluco
TYTY farmer of God's Little Acre
SYUD Moslem prince; title
GYVE fetter; shackle
MYXA plum (geiger) tree; sebesten

MYXO slime mold

AZAM sir: Persian
AZAN prayer call
CZAR emperor; dictator
EZAN prayer call
IZAR Moslem garment; star
TZAR emperor; dictator
UZAI Palal's father
UZAL Shem's descendant
UZAN weight
EZBA measure
AZEL Saul's descendant
EZEL juniper tree
OZEM David's brother
AZHA star
AZID compound
AZIN chem. compound
OZNI Gad's son
AZOF town; sea
AZON bomb
AZOV town; sea
EZRA prophet; OT book
AZUL blue: Sp.
AZUN Hananiah's father
AZUR Côte d'— (Riviera); Hananiah's father
UZUN ancient North Chinese

FOUR-LETTER WORDS
--AA to --ZZ

BLAA bunk
CHAA tea
DRAA measure
OOAA Hawaiian bird
AHAB king; captain; prophet
ARAB Semite; horse; nomad; urchin
BLAB tattle
BRAB palm
CHAB bird
CRAB crustacean; apple; sign; anger
DOAB tract
DRAB dull; box; wench; cloth; drug
DUAB tract
FRAB worry
GRAB grasp; capture; game
HAAB year
JOAB (David's) captain
KNAB nibble
MOAB kingdom; language; Lot's son
NAAB river
QUAB fish
RAAB river
SCAB crust; strikebreaker
SHAB paltry guy
SLAB slice; road
SNAB hill part; girl
STAB pierce; trial
SWAB mop; lout
ABAC calculator
CHAC -Mool (god); -chac (instr.)
TLAC coin
WAAC fem. soldier
WRAC women's army corps
ADAD fiber; god
ARAD plant; city
BEAD globule; ball; drop; aim
BRAD nail
CHAD lake; nation
CLAD dressed; plated
COAD cushion
DEAD deceased; entire; absolute(ly); — reckoning
DIAD pair
DUAD pair
DYAD pair
ECAD modified organism
EGAD oath
FUAD Arab king
GLAD pleased
GOAD rod; decoy; urge
GRAD centesimal unit
GUAD tree
HEAD skull; top; brain; chief; crux; source
IBAD Hira Arab
IRAD Enoch's son
JOAD philosopher; Tom (Grapes of Wrath: Steinbeck)
LEAD metal; element; plummet; bullets; color; guide; command
LOAD burden; measure
MEAD drink; meadow; lake; Margaret (anthropologist)
OHAD Simeon's son
ORAD mouthward
PHAD star
PRAD horse
QUAD type; four; -rangle, -ruplet, etc.
RAAD assembly; fish
READ interpret; learn; study; understand
ROAD (rail)way; track; anchorage
SCAD fish; large amount
SHAD fish
SPAD nail
STAD town

SWAD mass; soldier
TOAD amphibian; anuran; fawn
UDAD sheep
WOAD herb
ALAE wings
BLAE bleak
BRAE slope
IRAE Dies — (Day of Wrath)
KOAE red-tailed bird
QUAE — vide (which see)
SPAE prophecy
DEAF unhearing; inattentive; — and dumb; — mute
GOAF grain; rick
GRAF nobleman: Ger.; — Spee (Zeppelin)
HAAF fishing grounds
HEAF pasture
LEAF plant part; sheet; tea
LOAF bread; idle
OLAF (Vi)king
WRAF air force; aviatrix
AGAG king
AWAG wagging
BRAG boast; game
COAG dowel
CRAG cliff; neck
DRAG haul; harrow; obstacle; puff; auto race
FLAG flower; standard; stone; signal; limp; reduce, dwindle
KNAG spur; knot
KRAG rifle
PEAG money
PHAG comb. form: eating
QUAG morass
SHAG hair; tobacco; bird; rascal; dance step
SKAG boat; keel part
SLAG dross; lava
SNAG stump; cut; obstacle; tangle
STAG deer; men's party; warn
SWAG bag; booty; sway; sag
TOAG Indian
WAAG monkey
ADAH wife of Lamech, Esau; fem. name
AIAH Edomite, Rizpah's father
AMAH nurse
ARAH exclamation
AYAH nurse; sign
BLAH nonsense
DRAH measure
ELAH king
ETAH Eskimo settlement; town
EYAH nurse; sign
IVAH Bib. city
JOAH record keeper
KYAH partridge
LEAH fem. name; Laban's daughter; Jacob's wife
MEAH wall tower
NOAH patriarch (Ark builder)
OPAH fish
PRAH canoe
PTAH god
SAAH measure
SEAH measure
SHAH ruler
UTAH state; Indian; Deseret (Mormon)
YEAH yes
ADAI tribe
ALAI regiment; mountain; jai —
ANAI termite
BNAI B'rith (Jewish Society)
CHAI person
DHAI midwife
GOAI shrub
ILAI David's man
NGAI spiritual power
PEAI medicine man
QUAI pier
THAI Siamese
UTAI noh songs (yo-kyoku)
UZAI Palal's father
BRAJ basha
ADAK Aleut. island
ANAK giant race
ARAK palm; spirit
ASAK tree
BEAK bill; nose; judge
COAK tenon
DHAK tree
DYAK Bornean
FEAK twitch; wipe
FLAK antiaircraft
HAAK fish; wander
IRAK country
KIAK canoe
KYAK canoe
LEAK loss; ooze; crack
PEAK point; top; summit
SIAK latex
SOAK absorb; sot
TEAK tree; dark
WEAK feeble; pliable; light
AGAL cord
AKAL deity
ANAL pert. to anus
ARAL lake
AVAL grandparental
AXAL around an axis
BAAL diety
BEAL river mouth
BUAL wine
CHAL man
COAL ember; fuel
CRAL hut; village
DEAL bargain; transaction; unfinished wood; apportion(ment); policy: New—, Fair —
DHAL split pea, lentil
DIAL plate; face; call; sun-
DUAL double
EBAL Mount (Josuha's altar)
EGAL equal: Fr.
ERAL epochal
ETAL and others: Lat.
FEAL conceal
FOAL colt; equine young
GAAL brewing
GEAL pert. to earth
GOAL purpose; objective; score
HEAL cure; restore
ICAL compound suffix
IGAL Moses' spy

JAAL	goat
KEAL	cabbage
KRAL	hut; village
LEAL	loyal: Scot.
MAAL	measure
MEAL	grain; pulverize; repast
MYAL	cultic
NEAL	male name; novelist
ODAL	land; vine
OPAL	birthstone (Oct.); girasol
ORAL	spoken; of the mouth
OVAL	egg-shaped; elliptic; arena
PAAL	measure
PEAL	ring; loud sound; fish
PYAL	veranda
REAL	coin; true; genuine; very
RIAL	coin
RYAL	coin
SAAL	hall: Ger.
SEAL	otarian; pinniped; fur; fasten; brown; ratify; stamp
SIAL	earth's outer part
SKAL	health toast
TAAL	lake; volcano; language
TEAL	duck (blue)
UDAL	land
UNAL	land
URAL	-Altaic; mountains; hypnotic
UVAL	grapelike
UZAL	Shem's descendant
VAAL	river
VEAL	calf; meat
VIAL	vessel
WEAL	body politic; stripe
ZEAL	ardor; enthusiasm
ADAM	first man; sin; composer; architect
ANAM	tree; Vietnam region
ARAM	country (Syria); Eugene (murderer)
AZAM	sir: Persian
BEAM	bar; timber; breadth; ray; smile; on the —; broadcast
BRAM	Abraham
CAAM	loom; heddles
CHAM	tribe; title; bite
CLAM	mollusk; hush
CRAM	press; stuff; study
DRAM	measure; drink
EDAM	city; cheese
EJAM	Bantu
ELAM	kingdom
ENAM	gift; land grant
EXAM	interrogation; test
FAAM	tea; leaves
FLAM	trick; drum beat
FOAM	froth; rage; rubber
FRAM	spear
GRAM	sword; plant; weight; —'s method; grandma
GUAM	Mariana island
IMAM	priest; title
KLAM	weight
LIAM	O'Flaherty: "Informer"
LOAM	clay; soil
LYAM	bloodhound
MAAM	madam
MIAM	hut
NAAM	distrain
OGAM	Irish alphabet
OLAM	infinity; — haba (life after death)
PRAM	carriage
REAM	500 (paper) quantity; bevel; enlarge
ROAM	wander
SEAM	fold; crevice; join; ornament; measure
SHAM	deceit; fake
SIAM	Thailand; Anna's king (The King and I)
SLAM	bang; criticize; grand —
SWAM	floated
TEAM	group; yoke
TIAM	language
TRAM	trolley; gauge
ULAM	Gilead's descendant
WHAM	exclamation
ADAN	prayer call
AKAN	Negro
ALAN	dog; name
AMAN	Ahasuerus's minister
ANAN	tree; interjection
ARAN	Seir's descendant; island
AWAN	tribe
AYAN	spruce
AZAN	prayer call
BEAN	plant; trifle; head; strike
BRAN	god-king; seed coat; chaff
CHAN	resthouse; lord; title
CLAN	clique; family; group
COAN	pert. to Cos island
CRAN	bird; measure
CYAN	green-blue
DEAN	clergyman; educator; oldest member, doyen
DHAN	wealth; loan
DIAN	reveille
DUAN	canto; poem
EGAN	horse (Kipling)
ELAN	dash; ardor
ENAN	Prince of Naphtali
EOAN	pert. to east; dawn
ERAN	Ephraim's grandson
EVAN	name (Welsh)
EWAN	name (Welsh)
EZAN	prayer call
FLAN	tart; disk; net
GEAN	cherry
GIAN	-Carlo (Menotti)
GMAN	U.S. police agent
GOAN	pert. to Goa
GRAN	weight; grandma
GUAN	bird
IBAN	dyak (Borneo)
IRAN	Persia

IVAN John; — the Terrible
JEAN name; cotton cloth
JOAN lass; cap; of Arc (the Maid, la Pucelle)
JUAN John; Don —; Don Giovanni
KAAN inn; title
KHAN resthouse; lord; title; Agha —
KLAN Ku Klux —
KRAN coin
KUAN pottery; official
KWAN coin; weight
LEAN be supported; incline; thin
LOAN lend
MAAN city
MEAN intend; denote; base; unkind; middle
MIAN sir; title
MOAN lament
NGAN measure
OBAN coin
OLAN Wang Lung's wife (Pearl Buck: The Good Earth)
OMAN Arabian state; sultanate; Muscat
ONAN Indian; Judah's son
ORAN seaport
OXAN gas
PAAN town
PEAN panegyric; praise; fur
PHAN measure
PIAN tumor
PLAN design; scheme
PUAN latex
QUAN money
ROAN horse; yellow-red
RYAN peak (Idaho)
SAAN Bushmen
SCAN examine; measure poetry
SEAN John
SHAN Thai
SPAN stretch; team; measure; dog
SUAN — pan: Chin. abacus

SVAN Caucasian
SWAN constellation; dive; — song
TEAN tone: Scot.
THAN in comparison with; conjunction
TMAN U.S. Treasury agent
TUAN measure; sir; title
ULAN lancer; — Bator
URAN lizard; Indian
UZAN weight
WEAN withdraw; alienate
YEAN to lamb
YUAN dynasty; money
AGAO language
CHAO measure
DHAO knife (Burma)
GRAO weight
GUAO tree
LIAO Manchuria river
MIAO Chinese aborigine
OMAO thrush
PHAO wolf (Kipling)
PRAO canoe
TIAO Chinese money
TSAO Chinese state
URAO trona (mineral)
APAP month
ATAP palm
CHAP fellow; crack; jaw
CLAP rap; applaud; flatten
CRAP dregs; money; dice cast (craps)
DRAP cloth
FLAP slap; leaf; sway; -jack
FRAP tighten
HEAP pile; crowd; car
KNAP summit; rap; talk; bite; button
LAAP secretion; insect
LEAP jump, skip; — year
NEAP wagon pole; tide

NOAP bullfinch
PLAP fall loudly
REAP cut; harvest
SCAP skull
SHAP silk yarn
SLAP strike; — bang
SNAP seize; break; click; shut; photo; vigor; easy task; — out
SOAP cleanser; detergent; money; soft —; -box; — opera
SWAP barter; exchange
TEAP ram
TRAP snare; mouth; net; catch; clothe; basalt; — shooting
WRAP cloak; blanket; coat
IRAQ country
ADAR month
AFAR far away; tribe
AGAR wood
AJAR opened
ALAR winglike; axillary
AMAR measures
APAR armadillo
ARAR tree
ASAR glacial ridges; eskers
ATAR perfume; essence
AVAR Caucasian language
BAAR weight
BEAR carry; yield; endure; relate; animal; Ursa; short-seller; pessimist
BHAR Kolarian native
BOAR (wild) hog; male
CHAR trout; burn; sandbank; -woman
CZAR emperor; dictator
DEAR costly; loved; loved one
DHAR state; town (India)

DUAR mountain pass
EDAR Bib. site
FEAR fright; doubt
GEAR notched wheel; equipment; adjust; harmonize
GNAR growl
GUAR legume; cluster bean
HAAR fog
HEAR listen; perceive by ear
HOAR frost; gray; -hound
ISAR river (Munich)
IYAR month
IZAR Moslem garment; star
JOAR durra; millet
JUAR durra; millet
KHAR weight
KNAR knot; burr
KUAR month
KYAR coconut fiber
LEAR learning: Scot.; king; father of Goneril, Regan, Cordelia
LIAR prevaricator; plant
NEAR close(ly); approach
OMAR Khayyam; tentmaker; caliph
OSAR glacial ridges; eskers
PAAR sand
PEAR fruit, tree
QUAR fill; choke
REAR back; raise; — admiral
ROAR loud sound; laugh
SAAR river; region
SCAR rock; cicatrix; mar(k); fish
SEAR burn; dried up; gun-lock catch
SOAR fly high; glide
SPAR mineral; mast; gaff; box
STAR sun; heavenly body; asterisk; hummingbird; excel
TAAR tambourine
TEAR drop; weep; rip; glass defect
THAR goat
TIAR crown; shrub
TSAR emperor; dictator
TZAR emperor; dictator
USAR salt; grass
WEAR be clothed in; impair; endure; deteriorate
YEAR time period; twelve month; leap —; calendar, fiscal —
ZOAR town; Bela; city of Lot
ABAS down: Fr.
ALAS sad cry
ANAS duck
ARAS river
BAAS master
BEAS Punjab river
BIAS diagonal (incline); prejudice
BLAS Gil (Le Sage novel)
BOAS Franz (anthropologist)
BRAS arm: Fr.
DYAS Permian (geol. period)
EYAS nestling
GRAS horse; foie — (pâté)
IDAS Marpessa's lover; Castor's slayer
IRAS Cleopatra's maid
KHAS special; noble
KRAS tahr (goat)
KVAS sour beer, cider (Russian)
LIAS geol. period
LYAS geol. period
MAAS river
MIAS orangutan
NIAS Ind. Ocean island(er)
ORAS Danish money
PAAS Easter
QUAS sour beer, cider (Russian)
UPAS tree (juice); arrow poison
USAS dawn goddess
UTAS 8 day feast; Jap. songs
XMAS Christmas
YEAS yes votes
ZOAS symbolic figures (Blake)
ADAT law
ANAT sky god; med. term
BEAT strike; defeat; mystify; throb; scoop; field; sphere; — the Dutch
BHAT minstrel; scholar
BLAT sheep's cry
BOAT (go by) ship; gravy-
BRAT apron; child
CHAT talk; bird; spike
CLAT mess; chatter
COAT fur; skin; cover; — of arms
DOAT drivel; be silly, overfond; wood rot
DRAT oath
DUAT Hades
ERAT was: Lat.; quod — demonstrandum (Q.E.D.)
ETAT state: Fr.; L', — c'est moi!
EVAT eft
FEAT deed; accomplishment
FIAT sanction; edict; money; automobile (It.)
FLAT level; (make) insipid, dull; wholly; — tire
FRAT fraternity
GEAT channel in mold; Scandinavian (Beowulf)
GHAT range; bank; river bank stairs
GNAT (biting) fly
GOAT ruminant; scape-; brown
HEAT warmth; rage; height; dead

—; pressure, strain
IKAT shrub; weight
KAAT shrub; weight
KHAT measure
KYAT weight; Burmese money
MAAT goddess
MEAT flesh; kernel; food
MOAT trench
NEAT tidy; trim; straight
PEAT darling; turf; fuel
PIAT magpie; anti-tank gun
PLAT plait; map; plot; fish
PRAT buttock
PYAT magpie
QUAT squat
SCAT buffet; scatter; begone!; tax; skat
SEAT chair; fundament; site; membership; install; hot —
SHAT saline lake
SKAT card game; star
SLAT lath; slab; sheep's hide; flap
SPAT mollusk; gaiter; snap; tiff
STAT photocopy
SWAT hit (hard); river, state (Pakistan); Sultan of — (Ruth)
TEAT nipple
THAT so; which; pronoun; connective; that's —
TOAT plane handle
WHAT interrogative; pronoun; what's —
AGAU language
BEAU dandy; lover; — Brummell; — Nash
DIAU Indian
ESAU Isaac's, Rebecca's son; Jacob's twin; hairy; red; Edom
FRAU Mrs., wife, Mme., woman: Ger.
LUAU feast; cook-out
PEAU skin: Fr.
PRAU swift canoe
UNAU sloth
VEAU veal, calf: Fr.
WHAU why; tree
MUAV geol. epoch
SLAV Eastern European
BRAW handsome; fine
CHAW masticate
CLAW nail; ungula; chela; scratch; hammer
CRAW gullet; stomach
DHAW billhook
DRAW drag; attract; gain; infer; extract; sketch; undecided contest
FLAW crack; defect; wind
GNAW bite; corrode
SCAW promontory
SHAW thicket; pshaw; George Bernard (playwright)
SLAW cabbage
THAW melt; unbend
AJAX hero (Telamon's son)
ANAX Castor, Pollux (Dioscuri)
COAX flatter; cajole
CRAX curassow (bird)
FLAX plant; fiber; thrash
HOAX deceive; trick
ODAX rock whiting (fish)
OLAX tree
ADAY atomic attack date
ALAY marble
ANAY fruit
AWAY onward; hence; far; off; absent
BLAY bleak
BRAY (donkey's) cry; grind; Mrs. Nickleby (Dickens)
CHAY red dye root
CLAY earth; ceramic; pipe; — pigeon; color; Henry (statesman)
DDAY operation start
DRAY cart; squirrel's nest; — horse
ESAY Isaiah
FLAY (strip off) skin
FRAY contest; tumult; wear off
GRAY dull; dismal; hoary; Dorian (Wilde); Asa (botanist); Elisha (inventor)
OKAY approve; all right
OLAY palm
PEAY medicine man
PIAY medicine man
PLAY frolic; act; drama; contend; sport; game
PRAY ask; beseech; please
QUAY pier
RUAY weight
SHAY chaise; carriage
SLAY kill; overwhelm
SPAY deer; castrate
STAY rope; fasten; prop, endure; wait; remain; stop(ping); — put
SWAY oscillate; veer; rule
TRAY salver; platter; old dog
AGAZ Indian
AHAZ king
BOAZ Ruth's husband
DIAZ Bartholomeu (Port. navigator)
GRAZ Austrian city (Mur)
MAAZ Judah's descendant
RYAZ coin
ABBA father; title

ALBA garb; poem; brain matter; duke
AMBA mountain
ANBA title
ARBA cart
BABA nurse; title; cake
BOBA chicken snake
BUBA tropical sore
CABA measure
CEBA tree; kapok source
CUBA W.I. island; Pearl of Antilles; measure
EABA measure
EGBA Negro; Yoruba
ELBA Napoleon's exile isle
EZBA measure
FABA bean; vetch
GEBA Jonathan's victory site
HABA bean
ISBA log hut
JUBA ghost; dance; mane; river
KOBA antelope
KUBA carpet; measure
LUBA Bantu; Bashilange
MABA Negro; tree
NUBA Nubian; Berberi language
PABA vitamin
PEBA armadillo; Indian
RABA river
REBA weight
SABA fiber; kingdom; island
SEBA Bib. country; Ham's grandson
TOBA Tatar; Chaco Indian
TUBA saxhorn; tree; nut; fish poison; palm sap
UEBA measure
YABA bark; cabbage tree
BIBB mast's timber piece
COBB Irvin S. (writer); Tyrus R. (baseball)
DUBB Syrian bear; lizard
HOBB havoc; fireplace ledge; pin; pig
HUBB pipe end
LOBB go heavily; tennis stroke; till
WEBB Beatrice Potter (writer)
ABBE priest; title; Amer. meteorologist
ALBE album
BABE baby; — Ruth; girl
BUBE boy, jack: Ger.; Fernando Po Bantu
CUBE square solid; 3rd power; die; plant poison
DOBE brick (house)
ELBE river
GABE taro
GIBE scoff; jeer; agree
GYBE jibe; scoff; agree
HABE tribe
HEBE cupbearer of gods; Zeus's daughter, Hercules' wife; color
IMBE cordage fiber plant
INBE be within
JIBE sneer; agree; coincide; shift course
JUBE chancel screen; lozenge
KIBE chilblain crack
KOBE Honshu port
LABE city
LOBE projection; ear part
LUBE machine oil
ROBE gown; mantle; Douglas novel
RUBE Reuben; rustic; yokel
SABE know
TOBE cotton cloth; future
TUBE cylinder; tunnel; subway; radio, TV part; Audion (DeForest)
UNBE cease to be
WABE tree
COBH Irish port
ALBI flagellants
AMBI about; prefix: both
BABI sect
BIBI title: Lady, Mrs. (India)
BUBI Fernando Po Bantu
CUBI measure
GABI taro
GOBI Mongolian desert
JIBI extinct bird
KOBI Japanese reserve duty (term)
MABI tree
RABI crop; physicist
SEBI prefix: tallow
TABI sock
TYBI 1st Egypt. spring month
WABI Indian; tree
YOBI Jap. military service
TEBJ Negro Berber
NABK shrub
NUBK shrub
SOBK evil deity
IRBM ballistic missile
ALBO prefix: white
AMBO pulpit
BOBO owala tree; mullet
BUBO horned —; eagle owl
CABO Yubi
EGBO secret society (Ogboni)
GOBO burdock; okra; camera; mike shield
HOBO vagrant worker
JOBO hog plum; gumbo limbo
KIBO Afr. peak (Kilimanjaro)
LOBO timber wolf
NABO shrub
NEBO wisdom god; Moab mountain (Moses died)

UMBO shield boss; shell beak
VIBO gulf (Italy)
ZOBO mongrel yak
DEBS Eugene (socialist)
DIBS juice: grape, date
LUBS of Lubeck (city)
NIBS personage (VIP); Peter Pan (Barrie)
NOBS knave, jack (card, cribbage)
POBS porridge; pap
TIBS — eve (never-never)
URBS (capital) city
DEBT fault; liability; obligation
BABU Hindu gentleman
CEBU Visayan island
HABU pit viper
KOBU seaweed food (kelp)
NABU god; mountain
TABU forbidden
TIBU Negro-Berber
YABU Afghan pony
ZEBU ox; Brahman bull
ABBY Abigail
BABY doll; indulge
DOBY brick (house)
GABY fool
GOBY fish; passing
MOBY — Dick (whale: Melville)
ORBY revolving
RUBY gem; corundum; bird; name; Oswald killer
TOBY cigar; mug; dog; rob

ACCA fabric
ALCA auk
ARCA box; dish; shell
AUCA Indian
BOCA harbor mouth: Sp.
CACA goddess
COCA cocaine source; shrub; leaf to chew; flavor
CUCA cocaine source
DECA prefix: ten
ECCA geol. period (Karroo)
ESCA apoplexy (plant disease)
INCA Quechuan Indian (ruler)
JACA tree
JUCA cassava; manioc
MICA isinglass (silicate)
ONCA ounce
ORCA killer whale
PACA rodent
PECA coin
PICA type size; magpies
PUCA goblin; specter
RACA reproach; fool
TECA teak; Indian
UNCA 8th note
VICA Pota (goddess)
YMCA welfare organization
YNCA Quechuan Indian (ruler); Inca
YUCA cassava; manioc
YWCA welfare organization
ANCE suffix; — errand
BICE blue, green pigment
BOCE colored fish
DACE fish
DICE (cut into) cubes; gamble; gaming implements
DOCE Brazil river
DUCE chief: It.; Mussolini
DYCE thus!: naut. command
ECCE lo: Lat.; — homo
ENCE suffix
ESCE suffix: begin to be
FACE surface; oppose; line
LACE cord; flavor; netting
LICE insects (louse)
LUCE fish, pike; Adriana's servant; Henry (editor); Clare Boothe (writer, stateswoman)
MACE staff; spice; weight; coin
MICE rodents (mouse)
NICE good; kind; pleasing; delicate; dainty; quimper color; Riviera port
ONCE one time; if ever; former(ly)
PACE step; speed; peace: It.
PICE coin; weight
PUCE flea: Fr.; eureka red
RACE run; contest; people; speed; Cape —; rat-
RICE cereal; use ricer; Elmer (playwright)
SICE number 6 on die
SYCE groom
TACE steel splint
TICE lure; yorker (bowled ball)
VICE sin; fault; vise; proxy; — versa
VOCE voice: It.; sotto, viva —
AICH alloy
ARCH support; curve; chief; fingerprint; triumphal —
ASCH Scholem — (author)
BACH live alone; composer
CECH Czech
DICH you: Ger.
EACH every(one)
ETCH eat into; engrave
FOCH Ferdinand (Fr. marshal; WW I commander)
HOCH high: Ger.
HUCH Danube fish
INCH measure; move slowly

ITCH skin irritation; desire
JOCH yoke, measure: Ger.
KOCH cook: Ger.; Robert (bacteriologist)
LECH slab; capstone; river
LOCH lake, bay: Scot.
MICH me: Ger.
MUCH great (deal); far; — Ado (Shaks.)
NACH after: Ger.
OUCH exclamation
RICH wealthy; vivid; full; fragrant; fat
ROCH Saint (14th cent.)
SECH such
SUCH of this kind; same
TECH technical school
UTCH "I"
VACH goddess
WYCH -hazel; — elm
ZACH name
ASCI spore sacs
DECI prefix: tenth
FOCI center points
FUCI rockweeds; algae
LOCI places; sites
NUCI prefix: nut
PICI birds (woodpeckers)
UNCI hooks; claws
BACK help; tub; past; retreat; kick-; dorsal, posterior; spine
BECK nod; bidding; dyeing vat; Pol., Ger. officer, statesman
BOCK beer; leather
BUCK deer; fop; butt; male; Pearl (novelist); pass the —
COCK male fowl; vanes; leader; tap; tee; hay pile, cog
DECK ship floor; pack, cards; array; adorn
DICK Richard; whip; lad; detective; Whittington (London mayor)
DOCK weed; rumex; (cur)tail; pier
DUCK bird; webfoot; wild fowl; canvas; pet; plunge; evade; — soup; vehicle
DYCK Anthony Van (painter)
FECK amount
HACK chop; writer; horse
HECK (weaving) frame; cough; oath
HICK hiccup; rube; jake
HOCK leg joint; hamstring; wine; faro card; pawn
HUCK towel fabric
JACK flag; tool; card; fruit; raise
JOCK John; jockey; hobo
JUCK partridge call
KECK vomit; show disgust
KICK hit; die; object(ion); excitement; -back
LACK need
LICK tongue; stroke; whip; conquer; bit
LOCK gate (canal, dam); tuft; wool; fasten(ing), grapple; tie up; -out (labor)
LUCK chance; event; fortune
MACK coat
MICK Irishman
MOCK jeer; taunt; sham; — apple, turtle
MUCK (rid of) manure; mess
NECK body part; violin part; isthmus; pet
NICK notch; moment; cheat; cut; Old — (devil); Carter (detective)
NOCK notch (in bow)
PACK bundle; cosmetic; cards; crowd; animal(s)
PECK measure; nip; bite; kiss
PICK tool; scratch; choose; rob; eat; best
POCK pustule
PUCK sprite; Robin Goodfellow; Shaks. character; hockey disk
RACK framework; clouds; gait; torture
RECK heed; concern
RICK pile (up); haystack
ROCK stone; Gibraltar; cliff; staunch support; diamond; candy; sway, lull; — the boat
RUCK crowd; rake; wrinkle
SACK dismiss; plunder; wine; bag; gown; sad —
SECK unprofitable (rent)
SICK urge (dog); ill; weak
SOCK beat; wind cone; stocking
SUCK draw in; bleed; drink
TACK hook; rope; course; attach
TECK readymade tie
TICK parasite; mattress; count; tic
TOCK hornbill
TUCK draw up; fold (in); eat; Friar (Robin Hood)

WICK part of candle, lamp
ALCO dog
CACO bandit
COCO palm; nut; grass
DUCO pyroxylin lacquer
FICO trifle
LOCO (render) mad; weed
MACO cotton
MICO marmoset
PACO alpaca
PECO black tea
PICO peak; game; weight
POCO slightly; old-clothes man
SACO weight; river
SOCO heron; bittern
TECO Indian
TOCO toucan
UNCO strange; very: Scot.
WACO city
ABCS first principles; alphabet
DUCT tube; vessel; pipe
FACT deed; reality
LACT prefix: milk
PACT agreement
PICT British aborigine
RECT element (philos.)
SECT group; denomination
TACT diplomacy; perception
JACU bird
JOCU dog snapper
ANCY suffix
FACY fresh
LACY netlike
LUCY fleur-de-lis; fem. name; camera lucida; Lemonade (Mrs. Hayes); Stone (suffragist)
RACY smart

ADDA god; river; skink
AIDA opera; Radames' lover
ALDA soprano; hamlet: Sp.
ANDA tree
BUDA It. millet
CODA finale; mark
DADA father; cult
EDDA Norse epic
ERDA earth goddess; Wagner role
JUDA James' brother
KADA measure
LEDA mollusk; mother of Castor, Pollux, Helen, Clytemnestra; wooed by Zeus as swan
LIDA Alida
MEDA secret Indian sect
NUDA ctenophore; Beroida
PEDA pastoral staffs
PODA suffix: foot
RADA legislature
RODA Nile island
SIDA herb; shrub; hemp
SODA carbonated water; Vichy; drink; sodium compound (bicarbonate)
TEDA Negro Berber
TODA Ceylon aborigine
VEDA sacred Hindu books
VIDA feminine of David
BADB goddess
BODB goddess
MEDB Conchobor's wife; goddess; Queen Mab
BUDD Lanny (Sinclair)
DODD cut off (wool)
KIDD William (privateer)
MUDD measure; doctor of Booth (Lincoln assassin)
NUDD Brythonic god, king
REDD make tidy; free of; scold
RIDD Lorna Doone's rescuer
RODD crossbow
RUDD carplike fish
SADD dam; waste matter
SUDD Nile waste; dam
WADD mineral
AIDE help; -de-camp; — mémoire
ANDE tribe
AUDE Fr. dept; river
BADE waited; asked; invited; commanded
BEDE Adam (Eliot); the Venerable (monk)
BIDE wait; tarry; dwell
BODE presage; augur; omen
BUDE light; burner
CADE cask; tree; pet; rebel
CEDE yield; grant; transfer
CODE body of law (Julian, Justinian, Napoleonic); signal system; cipher; — duello
DADE support
DODE nickname: Theodore
DUDE dandy; fop; city fellow; — ranch
EIDE ideas; forms
FADE weaken; flat; dissolve
FIDE entrust; — et amore
GADE fish; composer
GIDE André (author)
HADE angle; strip
HIDE land measure; skin; conceal; shelter; — and hair
HYDE — Park; Dr. Jekyll and Mr. —; measure
INDE blue (indigo)
JADE gem; horse; exhaust

JUDE	name; NT book, author; Jew: Ger.; — the Obscure (Hardy)	**WADE**	pass; demon; Hampton	**PEDO**	child
KADE	tick	**WIDE**	broad; far; lax; astray	**REDO**	make over
LADE	load; dip	**SADH**	holy man	**SADO**	carriage; island; river
LIDE	March (month)	**YODH**	Hebrew Y, 10	**TODO**	bustle; stir; ado
LODE	ore deposit; vein; load	**ANDI**	language	**UNDO**	untie; unfasten; ruin
MADE	successful; created; constructed	**CADI**	judge	**UPDO**	upswept hair
MEDE	ancient Asian	**KADI**	judge	**YEDO**	Tokyo
MIDE	Ojibway secret order	**LODI**	city; Napoleon victory	**SADR**	tree
MODE	manner; fashion; drab; à la —	**LUDI**	Roman public games	**DUDS**	clothes; failures
NIDE	pheasant's nest	**MADI**	Negro	**EADS**	engineer; bridge
NODE	knob; knot; orbit point; joint	**MEDI**	prefix: middle	**GADS**	-hill (Dickens)
NUDE	naked; art work; color	**MIDI**	south(ern France)	**KIDS**	star (Auriga)
ONDE	wave: Fr.; wavy (Her.)	**NIDI**	breeding places	**ODDS**	inequality; advantage; at —; -on
PODE	suffix; foot	**NODI**	knots; difficulties	**SUDS**	lather; froth; bear
RADE	elated	**PADI**	rice	**ADDU**	skink; fiber; god
REDE	interpret; counsel	**PEDI**	prefix: foot	**ARDU**	slave
RIDE	be borne; float; endure; manage; mount; journey	**RODI**	Medit. island	**DADU**	saint
RODE	anchor rope; measure; was borne; cross	**SADI**	poet	**JADU**	magic
RUDE	rough; boorish; vulgar	**SIDI**	Moslem title; Negro	**KADU**	tribe
SADE	letter; Marquis	**SODI**	Gaddiel's father (spy)	**KUDU**	Afr. antelope
SIDE	region; part(y); oblique; aspect; support; lateral	**WADI**	valley; river; oasis	**ORDU**	Turk. military district, army corps
TIDE	ocean's rise, fall; season; drift; endure; current; help	**HADJ**	pilgrimage	**PUDU**	Chilean deer
TODE	(haul with) sled	**BODO**	Indo-Chin. language	**URDU**	Hindustani language
UNDE	waving, wavy (Her.)	**CODO**	measure	**WIDU**	Moslem ablution
URDE	key-shaped (Her.)	**DADO**	wall part; groove	**WUDU**	Moslem ablution
VADE	leave; — mecum	**DEDO**	measure	**ADDY**	Adeline
VIDE	see: Lat.; for example; quae —	**DIDO**	trick; caper; Carthage queen, Aeneas' beloved	**ANDY**	Andrew
		DODO	extinct bird; reactionary	**BODY**	structure; anatomy; bulk; corpse; group
		EDDO	taro root	**CADY**	golf boy
		ENDO	prefix: within	**CODY**	William (Buffalo Bill)
		FADO	tune	**EDDY**	whirlpool; Mary Morse [Baker] (Christian Science)
		FIDO	fog evaporation; dog's name	**FADY**	weakening
		IODO	prefix: iodine	**INDY**	— pink (carnation)
		JODO	Buddhist paradise (Gokaruku)	**JADY**	gemlike
		JUDO	self-defense art	**JUDY**	name; Punch and —; Judith; Kipling character
		LIDO	Venice beach		
		LUDO	game; pachisi		
		MADO	fish		
		ORDO	order: Lat.; feast list		

LADY title; -bird
ONDY wavy (Her.)
SIDY pretentious
TIDY (make) neat
TODY green — (bird)
UNDY waving, wavy (Her.)
URDY key-shaped (Her.)
VADY vade mecum; summons
WADY valley; river; oasis
LODZ Polish city
AIEA town
ALEA Athena (war goddess)
AREA zone, region; scope; tract
ASEA at sea
BLEA bleak; livid
BREA resin; tree; asphalt
CREA linen, cotton fabric
EDEA reproduction organs
EVEA madder (tree); ipecac
FLEA insect; puce; — market
FREA Frigg; Odin's wife; goddess
GAEA goddess; Titans' mother
IDEA conception; fancy; key meaning; opinion
ITEA shrub; Virginia willow
ODEA theaters; halls; galleries
OLEA shrub; olive
OTEA Great Barrier Island
OXEA sponge spicule
PLEA excuse; prayer; request; pretext; allegation
RHEA Cybele; mother of the gods; Gaea's daughter; Cronos's wife; ostrich; satellite; grass
SHEA tree; butter
THEA tea source; name
UREA chemical compound
UVEA iris layer
ZOEA crab larva
BLEB blister; bubble
DIEB jackal
OREB Midianite defeated by Gideon
PLEB freshman cadet; common man
SLEB nomadic Arab
THEB measure
ALEC fish; sauce; nickname
AVEC with: Fr.
HAEC this one (fem.): Lat.
SPEC speculation
ABED in bed; bedridden
AGED old; oxygian
BLED emitted or drew blood, sap; extorted
BRED procreated; brought up
COED girl student
DEED act; property transfer
DRED Scott (slave)
EBED Gaal's father
EYED looked at; ogled
FEED nourish; gratify; graze; fodder
FLED ran away; shunned
FRED nickname
GLED kite; buzzard
HEED notice; attention
HUED colored; tinged
ICED frozen; chilled
LIED fibbed; song: Ger.
MEED reward
MOED festivals (Mishnah)
NEED compulsion; lack; want
OBED David's grandfather
ODED prophet or his father
PIED variegated; Piper; -à-terre
PLED pleaded
REED woody grass; pipe; mouthpiece; Walter (doctor, hospital)
ROED filled with roe
SEED fertile germ; progeny; decay; plant; extract
SHED cast off; abandon; drop; hut; shelter
SLED vehicle, snow or ice
SNED lop; prune
SPED hastened
SYED Moslem chief
TIED bound; knotted; drawn
TOED stepped (gingerly)
USED accustomed; secondhand
WEED plant; tobacco; remove
AGEE awry; Shammah's father; James (novelist)
AJEE awry
AKEE tree
ALEE to shelter
BREE (eye)brow
BYEE measure
CHEE weight
CLEE redshank; bird
CREE Indian
DREE endure; tedious
EPEE fencing sword
FLEE run away; shun
FREE independent; immune; rid; exempt; — and easy; — lance, port, trade, style
GHEE butter
IDEE — fixe: Fr.
INEE arrow poison
KLEE Paul (painter)
KNEE joint; bend(ing)
OGEE arch; molding
OKEE evil spirit
SHEE Irish fairyfolk
SKEE ski
SLEE sly
SMEE pintail duck; widgeon; Peter

Pan pirate
SNEE cut; snick(er) —
SPEE Graf — (ship, admiral)
THEE you
TREE wood, plant; family —; boot, shoe —
TWEE bird's cry
TYEE chief
USEE future user
WHEE whistle sound
ALEF letter
ATEF crown (Osiris)
BEEF ox, steer, cow, bos; brawn; rage; complain(t)
CHEF head (cook); — d'oeuvre
CLEF musical sign; roman à —; key
ELEF letter
FIEF feudal estate
KEEF hemp; languor
KIEF hemp; languor
LIEF gladly; freely
REEF shoal; lode; reduce sail
TREF homestead
AREG deserts
DOEG Saul's herdsman; poet's nickname; Indian
DREG lees; residue
GHEG Albanian
GUEG Albanian
SIEG victory: Ger.
SKEG keel part; plum; tear
WAEG bird; kittiwake
OKEH all right, O.K.
BREI soft tissue
DREI three: Ger.
KUEI disembodied spirit
KWEI disembodied spirit
OMEI Buddhist mountain
QUEI measure
VLEI marsh; lake; creek
ZWEI two: Ger.
CHEK Chin. foot (measure)
ESEK Isaac's well
GEEK carnival wild man
HOEK stream bend; van Holland (Dutch cape, city)
KEEK fashion spy
LEEK plant (onion; illiaceous); — green (Wales emblem)
MEEK mild; submissive
PEEK sly glance; pry; chirp
REEK cloud; exude; smell
SEEK ask; try; hunt
TREK migrate; journey
WEEK time unit; sennight; squeak
ABEL Adam's son; Cain's brother; Magwitch (Dickens); letter A; monkey
AIEL writ of —
AZEL Saul's descendant
BAEL thorny (fruit) tree
BHEL thorny (fruit) tree
CIEL ceiling; sky: Fr.
COEL cuckoo
DUEL combat; meeting
EDEL noble: Ger.
EZEL juniper tree
FEEL sense; test; suffer
FUEL combustible matter
GAEL Celt; Irishman
GOEL reclaimer; avenger
HEEL back part; end; slant; follow; scoundrel
HIEL Jericho's rebuilder
JAEL Sisera's killer; Heber's wife
JEEL pool; marsh
JOEL prophet, OT book
KEEL ship bottom; navigate; ocher; guinea fowl
KIEL ocher; ruddle; seaport; — Canal
KOEL cuckoo
LAEL Gershonite's father
NAEL weight
NIEL alloy
NOEL Christmas; carol; — Coward
ODEL vine; land ownership
OHEL Zerubabbel's son
OREL Russian city
PEEL pare; tower; spade
REEL wind(er); dance; waver; sway
RIEL Canadian (Indian) rebel
RYEL coin
SEEL shut eyes of; blind
TAEL weight; coin
TEEL sesame
TUEL furnace
WEEL fish basket, trap; pool
WIEL whirlpool
AHEM interjection
ALEM fruit
ANEM prefix: wind; city
ASEM alloy
CLEM riot; suffer hunger; nickname
DEEM consider; judge
DIEM day: Lat.; per —
FLEM Fleming; Belgian
HAEM prefix: blood
IDEM same: Lat.; semper —
ITEM also; article; bit; entry
KHEM chief god (Min)
NEEM tree; Margosa
OZEM David's brother

POEM verse creation
REEM ox; unicorn
RIEM oxhide strap
SEEM look; appear
SHEM Noah's son; Semite
STEM shaft; trunk; stock; axis; dam; check; derive; turn skis
TEEM abound
THEM pronoun
ADEN comb. form: gland; city; gulf; region
ALEN measure
AMEN assent; verily; deity; — Ra
ATEN solar disk
BEEN charmer's clarinet; participle
BIEN good, fine: Fr.; — aimée (well beloved)
BREN (machine) gun
CAEN city
CHEN snow goose
COEN Jan (empire builder)
EBEN Ebenezer
EDEN paradise; West of Nod
ELEN biblical jurist
EVEN evening; level; fair(ly); equal(ly); moderate; just; not odd; flush
GLEN rival
HIEN Chin. government seat
HOEN weight
IDEN Henry VI figure
ITEN So. Amer. Indian
KEEN sharp; acute; bewail
LIEN claim; attachment; garnishment
MIEN manner; bearing; air
OMEN presage; portent; sign
OPEN plain; frank; undefended; uncertain; bare; start; unfold; public; — sesame
OREN Judah's descendant
OVEN (bake in) stove; kiln
OWEN (Welsh) name; socialist; zoölogist
OXEN bovines; draft animals
PEEN hammer head
PIEN arris (sharp edge)
RIEN nothing: Fr.; — ne va plus
SEEN observed
SHEN Christian God (China)
SKEN squint
STEN weight; gun
TAEN taken
TEEN 13–19; injury; pain
THEN at a time; therefore
TIEN sky: Chin.; Chu (Lord of Heaven); your(s): Fr.
TMEN U.S. Treasury agents
WHEN whereas; how soon
WREN bird; navy woman; architect
AREO prefix: Mars
ATEO Polynesian god
CLEO queen (Cleopatra)
IDEO prefix: idea
OLEO margarine
SKEO fisherman's hut
THEO prefix: god
ALEP city
BEEP radio sound
DEEP profound; extensive; ocean
HEEP Uriah (Dickens villain)
JEEP vehicle; automobile
KEEP tend; retain; preserve; last
NEEP turnip
PEEP chirp; bird; peer slyly; Bo —; jeep
PREP prepare; student
SEEP ooze; small spring
SKEP basket; measure; beehive
STEP pace; foot rest; rank; act; dance; crush; — on it
VEEP vice-president
WEEP cry; bend; leak
ACER tree
ADER Benjamite
AGER apparatus; field
AHER Benjamite
AMER bitter
ANER city
APER imitator; boar
ASER Jacob's son
AUER violinist
AVER assert; asserverate
BAER prizefighter, actor
BEER beverage; ale; mead
BIER litter; coffin
BOER S. Afr. Dutch
BRER Rabbit (Harris: Uncle Remus)
CHER dear: Fr.
DAER reborrowed stock
DEER ruminant; cervine; — Park (Buddha site)
DHER mound; land share
DIER one moribund
DOER performer; agent
DYER tinter; Mary (Quaker martyr)
EBER Hebrew ancestor
EDER river
EGER river
EKER water cress
EMER Cuchulainn's wife (ideal womanhood)

ERER sooner
ESER weight
EUER your(s): Ger.
EVER always; at any time
EWER pitcher; udder
EYER needle maker
GIER eagle (vulture)
GOER runner
HEER Mr., Sir: Dutch
HIER here: Ger.; yesterday: Fr.
HLER sea god (wife: Ran)
HOER scraper
ICER freezer; mixer
IMER Caucasian
ISER river
ITER road; passage (brain)
IVER ever
JEER scoff; taunt
KIER bleaching vat
LEER sly gaze; oven; loin
LIER rester; layer
MEER sea: Ger.
NEER never; kidney
ODER river
OMER measure; sheaf; undertaker (Dickens)
ONER ace; blow; individual
OSER dare: Fr.
OVER above; across; beyond; again; surplus; ended; Roger and —
OWER debtor
OXER hedge (fox hunting)
OYER hearing (law); — and terminer
PEER gaze; equal; nobleman
PIER mole; dock; pillar
RIER oil cask (whaling)
ROER hunting gun
RUER repenter
SAER tenant
SEER prophet
SHER tiger
SIER pintado (fish)
STER suffix: agent
SUER prosecutor; suitor
TEER golfer; mix colors
TIER row; layer; pinafore
TYER binder
UBER over: Ger.
UFER fir pole; shore: Ger.
USER employer
VEER shift (course); waver
VIER striver; four: Ger.
WAER dam
YMER myth, giant
YSER river
ADES Hades
ALES city
AMES author; Ia. city, college
ANES once
ARES war; Mars; Zeus's, Hera's son; Eris' brother
ATES sweetsop
AVES birds: Lat.
AYES yes votes
BEES yeast
BRES Elatha's beautiful son (Formorian)
DIES day(s): Lat; — Irae; Cong. committee
DOES performs
ETES (you) are: Fr.
EXES letters; expenses
FEES charges; tips
GHES Tapuyan Indian
GOES walks; proceeds
GRES stoneware: Fr.
IDES Roman date; — of March (fateful day)
IVES inventor (photo-engr.)
LEES dregs
LUES syphilis
ONES individuals
OYES court crier's cry
PRES near: Fr.
SPES (goddess of) hope
TEES river (North Sea)
TRES very: Fr.; three: Sp.
USES law of — (beneficiary)
WIES Ys
ABET aid; incite
AHET season (of inundation)
ANET dill
APET goddess
BEET vegetable; root; sugar — — top
BLET fruit decay
DIET fare; food regimen; parliament
DUET music for two
EVET eft; newt
FEET measure
FRET gnaw; vex; worry; embroider; ridge; ornament
KEET guinea fowl
KHET mortal body; measure
KMET Slav; tenant; mayor
LAET freedman
LEET court; list
MEET encounter; face; combat; fulfill; fit
OKET ounce
PEET darling; turf; fuel
PIET magpie
PLET three-lash whip
POET writer of verse; artist
PRET measure
PYET magpie
SPET spit; barracuda
STET let it stand!
SUET hard fat
TRET weight allowance
VOET measure
WEET bird; cry of bird
WHET sharpen; excite; edge
BLEU blue, rookie: Fr.
DIEU god: Fr.; mon —!

EHEU alas
EMEU bird (ostrichlike)
LIEU place; stead
KIEV Ukrainian city
STEV stanza
ANEW over again
BLEW stormed; puffed; sounded
BREW beverage; plot; concoct
CHEW masticate; ruminate; — the cud; — — the rag
CLEW yarn ball; sail loop; cocoon; hint
CREW company; gang; cut
DREW sketched; pulled
FLEW aviated; winged
GREW increased
KNEW understood; was aware
LLEW Celt deity (Gwydion's son)
PHEW exclamation
PLEW beaver skin
SHEW show: Brit.; bread
SKEW twist; swerve; distort(ed); slant(ing)
SLEW killed; twist; swamp; large number
SMEW merganser; duck
SPEW eject; scatter; gush
STEW boil; steep; hash; worry; study; oyster bed
THEW muscle; sinew
VIEW sight; see; aim; opinion; scene
WHEW whistle; exclamation
AMEX Amer. Expeditionary Force
APEX summit; crisis
CREX corn crake (bird)
FAEX dregs
FLEX bend
IBEX wild goat; bouquetin
ILEX holm oak; holly
OBEX brain matter
PLEX form a network
PREX (college) president
SPEX spectacles
ULEX spine shrub (furze)
ABEY waive
AHEY ho
AKEY weight
ALEY city
BREY barnacle
DREY squirrel's nest
EYEY having holes
FLEY fright(en)
FREY god (Njorth's son, Gerth's husband)
GREY color; neutral; dull; Zane (writer); Vivian (Disraeli novel)
HOEY partnership (Hawaii)
HUEY Long (La. governor)
JOEY coin; clown; odd-job man; young kangaroo; Pal (O'Hara character)
OBEY submit; comply
PREY victim; pillage; booty
ROEY of mottled grain
SKEY yoke bar
SLEY weaver's reed
SPEY river
THEY pronoun; people; men
TREY three(spot)
UREY Nobel physicist
VLEY marsh; swamp; creek
WHEY milk serum; thin; pale; curds and —
BAEZ singer
CHEZ at home of, with: Fr.
DAEZ daze
GEEZ Version (Ethiopic Bible)
INEZ Don Juan's mother
JEUZ chief Benjamite
JUEZ judge, juror: Sp.
KNEZ Slavic prince
OYEZ court crier's cry
SUEZ canal; seaport
AFFA from off
ALFA grass
GUFA round boat
KAFA Ethiopian
KUFA round boat
OFFA Angles' hero (Beowulf)
SOFA couch; divan
TUFA porous rock
URFA Turkish city (Edessa)
WAFD Egyptian
CAFE restaurant; coffee; — -au-lait; society
FIFE flute; checkers opening
JEFE chief; leader
LIFE existence; vivacity; biography
NIFE earth's core
ORFE fish; yellow ide
RIFE abundant; prevalent
SAFE secure; box
WIFE spouse; marry
BAFF strike; stroke
BIFF (deal a) blow
BUFF leather; coat; tan; ward off; polish; wheel; bare skin; enthusiast
CUFF slap; manacle; sleeve end; miser; on the —
DAFF put aside
DOFF put off; remove
DUFF pudding; cheat
GAFF spear; ordeal; hoax
GOFF clown; fool
GUFF humbug; chaff

HAFF lagoon
HUFF inflate; bully; anger
JEFF rope; nickname; Mutt and —
JIFF instant
KIFF languor
KOFF Dutch sailboat
LUFF sail nearer wind
MIFF quarrel; offend
MOFF Caucasian silk
MUFF handwarmer; bungle
PIFF bullet sound; exclamation
PUFF blow; pastry; distend; hair roll; adder; powder —
RAFF Raphael
RIFF Berber; Kabyle; ripple
RUFF collar; bird; fish; plait; trump
TEFF grain plant
TIFF (petty) quarrel
TOFF dandy
TUFF volcanic rock
WAFF flapping; paltry
WUFF gruff bark sound
DEFI challenge; defiance
FUFI wisteria; cherry; volcano
HIFI faithful sound rendition
RIFI Riffs
SAFI Afghan
SUFI mystic ascetic
BUFO toad genus; agua
FIFO inventory method
LIFO inventory method
OFFS cricket-field sides
BAFT astern; cotton
DAFT foolish; giddy
DEFT skillful; trim
GIFT donation; talent
HAFT handle
HEFT weight; bulk; notebook: Ger.
LEFT departed; blow; — of center (Liberals)
LIFT r(a)ise; exalt; steal; elevator
LOFT attic; warehouse floor; golf stroke
LUFT air: Ger.; -waffe
RAFT collection; float
REFT cleft; rift; deprived
RIFT split; divide; cleft
SIFT screen; separate; bolt
SOFT giving way; easy; light(ly); mild; tractable
TAFT President; Republican; rower's seat; -Hartley Act
TOFT — and croft (house)
TUFT crest; clump; tassle
WAFT float; flag; whiff
WEFT yarn; mist; (weave) web
YUFT Russ. leather
MAFU stable boy
AFFY join
DEFY challenge; dare
DUFY Raoul (Fr. artist)
IFFY contingent
OOFY rich (Eng. slang)

ALGA plant
AMGA Siberian river
BAGA turnip
BEGA measure
BIGA two-horse chariot
BOGA basslike fish
FUGA fugue: It.
GIGA medieval fiddle
HOGA hill pasture
INGA timber tree; mimosa
JAGA Bantu
JUGA carrot ridges; yokes
MEGA prefix: great
MUGA silk; moth
NAGA snake
OLGA fem. name
PAGA rice
PEGA remora fish
RAGA state of nirvana
RIGA Latvian city, gulf
RUGA stomach membrane
SAGA legend; story; goddess; weight
SOGA grass rope: Sp.; Bantu
TOGA Roman garb; gown; senatorship
URGA Outer Mongolia
VEGA meadow
VIGA rafter; log
WEGA star
YOGA mental discipline
YUGA Hindu age cycle
ZYGA rowers' benches; brain fissures
ANGE angel: Fr.
AUGE priestess
CAGE confine; enclosure; elevator car; nor iron bars a —
DOGE Venice, Genoa ruler
EDGE brink; sharpness; goad; advantage; — on
EUGE bravo!
GAGE pledge; fruit; gauge; general
HUGE enormous; immense
INGE prelate ("Gloomy Dean"); playwright (Bus Stop)
JUGE judge: Fr.
KUGE Jap. courtier
LOGE theater box
LUGE lodge; small sled
MAGE magician
PAGE young atten-

dant; call, summon; leaf
RAGE fury; storm; fad
SAGE herb; wise; Russell (financier)
TIGE rifle steel pin; dog
URGE prod; impel; impulse
WAGE carry on; -earner; pay, salary
YAGE plant
BAGG heiress (Thackeray)
BIGG barley
DAGG pistol
FOGG Phileas (Verne)
HAGG demoness; hack; wood
HOGG unshorn sheep
JAGG pendant; tooth; slash
MAGG bird; chatter
MIGG marble (duck)
NOGG egg drink
RUGG pull
TEGG sheep in 2nd year
TIGG swindler (Dickens)
VUGG lode cavity
WEGG Silas (ballad seller: Dickens)
WIGG peruke; long hair
YEGG safecracker; tramp
ARGH timid
DAGH hill
GOGH Vincent van (painter)
HEGH exclamation; hey!
HIGH lofty; elevated; noble; expensive; shrill; tainted; tipsy
HUGH name; saint (of Cluny)
LUGH Celtic light god
MAGH month
NIGH near(ly); direct
OUGH exclamation
PUGH pshaw!; fish prong
SIGH lament(ing sound)
VUGH lode cavity
WAGH interjection
YOGH Mid. Eng. G, Y
BUGI Celebes Malay
HAGI clover; prefix: saint
JOGI yogi; ascetic
MAGI caste; priests; wise men; kings of Orient: Melchior, Gaspar, Balthazar
RAGI grass
RIGI Swiss mountain
SUGI Jap. cedar
VAGI nerves
YAGI antenna
YOGI ascetic; yoga disciple
GAGL sweet gale
CAGN mantis; deity
SIGN symbol; signal; subscribe; ratify; hire
ANGO herb; dye
ARGO ship; therefore; constellation
BAGO shrub
BOGO Eritrean Hamite
BYGO pass by
DAGO tribe
ERGO hence; prefix: work
FOGO stench
GOGO vine; bark soap; beetle; bugaboo; Bantu; dancer
HOGO taint; stench
HUGO name; Victor
IAGO (villain (Othello)
KAGO conveynance
LAGO lake
MOGO stone hatchet
PAGO -Pago (city)
POGO springy stick
SAGO palm; starch
SEGO herb; bulb; lily; Utah state flower
TOGO Afr. republic; Jap. admiral and statesman
UPGO ascend
ZOGO sacred object
DOGS scaup duck
EGGS ova; — and bacon, ham; — and butter (flowers)
KAGS convict (Dickens)
TOGS clothes
WIGS — on the green (fray)
TOGT trading enterprise
VOGT medieval official
DEGU rodent (Octodon)
FUGU poisonous fish
GUGU P.I. soldier; insurrecto
KAGU bird
PEGU Burmese language; city
ALGY Algernon; suffix: pain
ARGY argue
BOGY specter; bugbear
CAGY shrewd
DOGY calf; duck
EDGY sharp; snappish
EGGY egg-stained; yolky
FOGY dull, bigoted man
LOGY heavy; dull
NAGY Hungarian premier
ORGY carousal; Saturnalia, Bacchanalia
POGY menhaden; trout
SAGY wise
AGHA officer; title
AKHA tribe; Burmese; kaw
ASHA tribe
AZHA star
DEHA body (theosophy)
EPHA Heb. dry measure
GUHA Bantu
HAHA laugh; fence
ISHA Upanishad
KAHA proboscis monkey

MAHA monkey; deer
MOHA millet; delusion
NAHA city
OCHA weight
PAHA hill
POHA gooseberry (jelly)
PSHA exclamation
SAHA measure
TAHA bird
TCHA (rolled) tea
USHA Bana's daughter; sorceress
WAHA lake trout
ACHE pain; yearn
HEHE Bantu tribe
HOHE Siouan tribe
MAHE island
NAHE river; near: Ger.
TCHE fruit tree; Chin. flute
SAHH measure
ATHI Kenya river
BAHI fortune
EPHI measure
LEHI prophet
MAHI river
PAHI ship
TCHI measure
TSHI Gold Coast language
BUHL inlaid decoration
KOHL eye shadow; horse
KUHL eyelid cosmetic
VEHM medieval tribunal
BEHN herb; tree
FOHN warm dry wind
HAHN Otto (Nobel physicist)
JOHN name; saint, evangelist; cop; man; Bull (England); Long — Silver (Stevenson)
KAHN banker; test
LAHN river
BAHO prayer stick
BOHO grass; weep; shout
COHO silver salmon
ECHO Narcissus's nymph; repeat; response; fruit tree (gingko)
ICHO fruit tree (gingko)
KIHO peacock butterfly
MOHO bird; honey eater
OTHO Roman emperor
PAHO prayer stick
PEHO morepork (bird)
SAHO language
SOHO exclamation; London district
TOHO halt! (to dogs)
YAHO tribesman
BAHR see; — El Azrak
BOHR Nils (Nobel physicist)
BUHR whetstone
DUHR star
GUHR earthy deposit
LAHR Bert (comedian)
LEHR oven; Lew (comedian)
MAHR marriage settlement
MOHR gazelle; bezoar
RUHR Ger. industrial area
SEHR very: Ger.
TAHR goat
TEHR wild goat
WAHR true: Ger.
OCSH Adolph (publisher)
ACHT eight: Ger.
BAHT coin
ECHT genuine: Ger.
ICHU valuable grass
JEHU (chariot) driver; prophet, king (Israel)
KAHU harrier; bird
OAHU (Hawaiian) island
RAHU demon
SAHU spiritual body
TCHU exclamation
TOHU -bohu (confusion)
ACHY painful
ASHY gray, pale
ABIA Samuel's son
AKIA shrub (fish poison)
ALIA other: Lat.
AMIA fish
APIA port (Samoa)
ARIA tune; city (Herat)
ASIA continent; Orient; East
BAIA state; city; resort; bay
CHIA salvia beverage, oil
ELIA Charles Lamb (essayist)
ERIA silk(worm)
FRIA Frigg (Odin's wife)
GAIA goddess
GLIA neuroglia (nerve tissue)
HSIA 1st Chin. dynasty
HUIA bird (starling)
ILIA (hip) bones
INIA Amazon cetacean
IXIA corn lily; bulb
MAIA goddess; crab; star
NAIA cobra
OBIA Ashanti religion
OHIA timber tree; apple
OKIA Moroccan money
RAIA ottoman; fish
RHIA China grass
SOIA food plant
TSIA tea
URIA Bathsheba's husband; auk
UTIA rodent
ABIB month
ADIB star
AGIB dervish
CHIB tongue; language
CRIB manger; hut; bin; box; steal; "pony," "trot"
DRIB drop; a little
FRIB dirty short wool
GLIB flippant, smooth(ly)
GUIB harnessed antelope
SNIB escape logging work

STIB sandpiper (dunlin)
AMIC amidic
CHIC stylish(ness)
CRIC lamp condensing ring
EPIC heroic poem
ERIC male name; Viking; the Red
IDIC pert. to ids
LAIC secular
ODIC pert. to ode, od
OLIC chem. suffix
OTIC of the ear; auditory
PYIC purulent
SAIC Near East ketch
UDIC Caucasian language
UVIC grapelike; acid
ZOIC pert. to animals
ACID sour; biting
AMID among
ARID dry; barren
AVID eager; greedy
AZID compound
BEID star
BOID of boas, anacondas
CAID alcaide
ENID fem. name; Geraint's wife; city
GRID grating
IBID P.I. lizard (tidbit); the same: abbr.
IMID chem. compound
IRID iris; crocus
KAID chief; alcaide
KEID star
LAID put down; calmed
MAID servant; — of Orleans
MUID measure
NAID worm
OLID smelly; fetid
OOID egg-shaped
OSID suffix: sugar
OVID poet (Metamorphoses); P.O.N.; Naso
OXID oxygen compound
PAID recompensed; discharged; satisfied
QAID alcaide
QUID cud; essence; pound; — pro quo
RAID attack; foray
SAID before-mentioned; Port — (city); name
SEID tribe; lord; chief; Mohammed's descendant
SKID clog; slide; — Road, Row
SLID glided; slipped
UVID moist; wet
VOID empty; vacuum; cancel
ZOID organic body cell
ABIE 's Irish Rose; name
AMIE friend: Fr.
BRIE cheese
ERIE Iroquoian; lake; city
FOIE liver: Fr.; — gras (pâté)
JOIE — de vivre (zest for life)
OKIE migratory worker
OBIE Off-Broadway award
OPIE Eng. painter
SOIE silk
UNIE unicorn fish
ALIF letter
COIF defensive skullcap; make up (hair)
ENIF star
KAIF languor; hemp
KEIF hemp; languor
LEIF Ericson (explorer)
LUIF loof
NAIF naive; of true luster
NEIF serf; native; fist
WAIF stray
BRIG sailing ship; prison
CRIG blow
GRIG dwarf; cricket; fowl
HAIG soldier (Douglas)
PRIG precisian; steal; thief; fop
SNIG chop off; drag; pilfer
SWIG gulp; hoist; tackle
TEIG Teague; Thaddeus; Timothy
TRIG trim; sound; prim; math. course
TWIG discover; branch; beat
WHIG U.S., Brit. party
WRIG wriggle
CHIH Chin. foot (measure)
SHIH weight; measure
ALII royalty (Hawaiian)
APII plant
BOII Celtic tribe
CIII 103; Trajan reign
CLII 152; Hadrian reign
CVII 107; Trajan reign
CXII 112; Trajan reign
HEII Hawaiian fern
LIII 53; Claudius reign
LVII 57; Nero reign
LXII 62; Nero reign
MCII 1102
MIII 1003
MLII 1052
MVII 1007
MXII 1012
UBII Teutonic tribe
VIII 8; Augustus reign
XIII 13; Augustus reign
ATIK star
EFIK Negro
HAIK garment; frame
KAIK village
NAIK leader
RAIK weight; measure

SEIK Hindu sectarian
SHIK Arabian Turkoman
AMIL plant; remedy
ANIL shrub; indigo
ARIL seed covering
AXIL leaf angle
BAIL security; bond; set free; dip out; -hoop
BHIL low-caste Indian
BOIL heat; bubble; agitation; abscess
CEIL overlay; line; ceiling
CHIL cheer pine; kite (Kipling)
COIL curl; wind; twist
DAIL legislature; — Eireann
DEIL devil; -'s-bit (plant)
EGIL Volund's (Wayland's) brother
EMIL man's name
EVIL bad; sinful; injury; disease
FAIL fall short; err
FEIL comfortable; neat
FOIL balk; defeat; sword; leaf; sheet
GAIL Abigail; brewing
HAIL ice pieces; salute; — fellow
HEIL hail: Ger.
IFIL tree (brown dye)
IPIL tree (brown dye)
IXIL Mayan Indian
JAIL prison; gaol
KAIL tree; ibex; kale
KOIL cuckoo
LEIL faithful, loyal (Land of the —)
MAIL coin; tax; armor; post
MOIL toil; trouble; spot
NAIL fasten(er); claw; seize; expose
NEIL male name
NOIL combing (wool fiber)
OEIL eye: Fr.; — de boeuf
PAIL bucket
PHIL nickname; prefix: loving
POIL raw silk thread
RAIL bird; scold; paling
ROIL disturb; muddy; vex
SAIL canvas; rigging; journey; travel
SEIL rope: Ger.
SKIL candlefish; beshow
SOIL earth, ground; land; stain; pollute
TAIL end; cue; follow; high-
TEIL linden tree; lime
TOIL work; drudge(ry); snare
VAIL inventor
VEIL screen; facial garment; cloistered life
WAIL lament
YPIL tree (brown dye)
AKIM Negro; — Tamiroff
ALIM teacher
BRIM rim; edge; swell
CLIM — of the Clough (archer outlaw)
DUIM measure
ELIM Bib. oasis
EMIM Moabites; giants
FRIM juicy; soluble
GLIM light; eye
GRIM ruthless; ghastly
MAIM disfigure; mutilate
OXIM chem. compound
PLIM swell; swollen
REIM oxhide strap
SAIM grease
SEIM Polish assembly
SHIM leveling slip; shingle; knife
SKIM scoop off; scud; brush
SLIM slight; scanty; sly; slender
SWIM move in water; float; teem
TRIM shear; adjust; adorn; rebuke; defeat; neat
URIM — and Thummim (sacred instruments)
WHIM fancy; caprice
ADIN name
AKIN related
ALIN measure
AMIN agent
ASIN month
AYIN Heb. 16th letter; 70
AZIN chem. compound
BAIN bath: Fr.
BEIN good; fine
BRIN fan plate; silk thread
CAIN tribute; (Abel's) slayer; mark of —
CHIN lower jaw; chatter; weight; dynasty; Burmese
COIN money; mint; invent; corner
CRIN heavy silk
DAIN Patusan chief (Conrad); Curse (Hammett); measure
DEIN your(s): Ger.
DRIN Balkan river
DUIN demons
ENIN blue grape pigment
EOIN John; Sean
ERIN Eire; Ireland
FAIN glad; eager
GAIN reach; earn; profit; notch
GEIN glucoside (Geum urbanum)

GRIN smile
HEIN surprise!: Fr.
JAIN sect (Indian)
JOIN mix; unite; coalesce
KAIN tribute
LAIN reclined
LIIN measure
LOIN body part; hips; meat cut
MAIN conduit; first;, river; Spanish —
MEIN Chinese noodles; chow —
NEIN no: Ger.
ODIN one-eyed Norse god: Frigg's husband, Thor's father
PAIN ache; trouble; forfeit
RAIN shower; scratch; — check
REIN strap; check; direct; kidney
RHIN Rhine: Fr.
RUIN destroy; destruction; violate
SAIN consecrate; tree
SEIN poss. pronoun, be, being: Ger.
SHIN leg, calf front; run; climb
SKIN hide; pelt; peel; fleece; — and bones
SPIN whirl; twist; aerial stunt; — a yarn
TAIN plate
THIN lean; dim; rare; dilute; — ice
TRIN one of triplets
TSIN Chin. dynasty
TWIN double; match; — Cities
VAIN empty, idle; futile; proud
VEIN channel; streak; blood vessel
WAIN wagon; Charles's —
WEIN wine: Ger.
WHIN gorse; rest-harrow; rock; winch
ZAIN horse
ZEIN protein
AGIO fee; commission
AHIO Ark driver
APIO celery: Sp.
BRIO con — (with spirit)
CLIO history Muse; mollusk
IDIO prefix: one's own
KAIO fruit
MEIO measure
MOIO measure
NAIO tree
NOIO noddy tern
ODIO hatred: It.
OHIO Buckeye state
OLIO medley; olla-podrida
SCIO prefix: sky
THIO prefix: brimstone
TRIO set of 3; So. Amer. Indian
UNIO mussel
ATIP expectant
BLIP radar screen sign
CHIP fragment; cut; hew
CLIP clasp; cut(ting); gait
DRIP let fall
FLIP toss; tap; drink; hop
GRIP grasp; power; valise; Barnaby's raven (Dickens)
KLIP rock; cliff
KNIP bite; crop; rap
QUIP witty sally; jest
RAIP rope
SEIP seep; ooze
SHIP vessel; send; — of state
SKIP jump; escape; mess; captain; -tracer
SLIP slide; err(or); escape; pier; leash; garment; memo; cut
SNIP cut; shred; slip
TRIP move; slip; journey; (mis)step
WHIP lash; urge; defeat
ABIR red powder
AHIR caste
AMIR prince
ASIR Arab. principate
CHIR pheasant; pine
COIR coconut fiber
CUIR leather; dorado
EMIR ruler; title
FAIR pleasing; ample; just; bazaar; — and square; — deal
HAIR filament; cilium, seta; fabric; -trigger
HEIR inherit(or); — apparent, presumptive
KAIR fiber
KEIR bleaching vat
LAIR resting place
LEIR sea god (Lear)
LOIR dormouse; river
MUIR moor (Scot.)
NAIR native
NEIR kidney
NOIR black: Fr.; bet
PAIR couple; brace
SAIR savor
SEIR Bib. mountain (Hor.), Edom (Esau's home)
SHIR cook; gather; tiger
SKIR fly; scurry; skim
SOIR evening: Fr.
SPIR prefix: coiled
STIR agitate; rouse; ado; jail
TAIR goat
VAIR fur
VOIR see: Fr.
WEIR dam; fish trap
WHIR fly; hurry; buzz
YMIR rime-cold giant
ACIS river; (Galatea's) lover
AGIS king
AMIS friends: Fr.

ANIS fennel; birds
APIS sacred bull (Ptah); bee; bull (Kipling)
ARIS molding edge
ATIS monkshood; fruit
AVIS bird: Lat.
AXIS center line; spine; stem; deer; power alliance; partnership
BAIS caste
BOIS wood: Fr.; wine (cognac); — de Boulogne
CRIS dagger; stab
DAIS platform
EGIS protection; patronage; shield (symbol of Zeus, Athena)
ELIS Greek city-state
ERIS goddess of discord, Ares' sister
FEIS convention; — of Tara
GLIS dormouse genus
GRIS gray: Fr.
IBIS (sacred) wading bird
IRIS rainbow; goddess; eye part; plant (flag); spirit (Shaks.); red-blue; March (Arien)
ISIS goddess; Osiris's wife, sister; Horus's mother
ITIS suffix: inflammation, mania; Tereus' son
IWIS certainly
KAIS island
KRIS dagger; stab
LAIS hetaera
LOIS name; Timothy's grandmother
MAIS but, corn: Fr.
NAIS nymph
OTIS bustard genus; general; inventor (elevator)
OVIS sheep genus
PAIS country
QAIS island
RAIS chief (Nepalese)
REIS money; (boat) captain; effendi (state officer)
RIIS Jacob (journalist)
SAIS groom; city; know: Fr.
SEIS six: Sp.
THIS pronoun, demonstrative
TRIS prefix: thrice
UNIS Etats — (USA): Fr.
UPIS Artemis, Nemesis
URIS Leon (author)
ADIT entrance
ALIT descended
AMIT headdress
BAIT lure; harass; pest poison
BRIT young herring
CHIT child; sprout; memo; voucher; mind
DOIT coin; whit; bit
DUIT Chibchan Indian; coin
EDIT correct; redact; blue-pencil
EMIT eject; issue; voice
EXIT depart(ure); die
FAIT fact; — accompli
FLIT flutter; move
FRIT fuse; fried: Fr.; waste
GAIT walk; pace
GRIT sand(stone); bravery; grate
HUIT eight: Fr.
IBIT P.I. lizard (tidbit)
KNIT looped, tie(d); unite; contract
LAIT milk: Fr.; café-au-
NUIT night: Fr.
OBIT death notice
OMIT leave out; neglect
PHIT bullet sound
QUIT abandon; yield; stop; free
SEIT measure
SKIT comedy sketch; jest
SLIT cut; slash; opening
SMIT struck; destroyed
SPIT land point; rod; impale; expectorate; — and image
SUIT costume; card set; legal action; please; (out)fit
TAIT marsupial
TRIT prefix: third
TWIT taunt; yarn snarl
UNIT single thing; basic amount; one; monad
WAIT attend; defer; serenader; lie in —
WHIT bit; jot; dull sound
WRIT legal order; Holy —
YUIT Asian Eskimo
ATIU one of Cook Islands
CCIV 204; Septimus Severus reign
CHIV knife
CLIV 154; Antoninus Pius reign
CMIV 904
CXIV 114; Trajan reign
LXIV 64; Nero reign
MCIV 1104; First Crusade, conquest of Acre
MLIV 1054; Catholic church schism
MMIV 2004
MXIV 1014; Brian Boru defeats Danes
SHIV bit of husk; fluff; blade
SKIV sovereign (coin)
SPIV slacker: Brit.

XXIV 24; Tiberius reign
ALIX fem. name
BRIX scale (hydrometer)
CCIX 209; Septimus Severus reign
CLIX 159; Antoninus Pius reign
CMIX 909
COIX grass; Job's-tears
CXIX 119; Hadrian reign
FLIX down; fur; flax
MCIX 1109
MLIX 1059
MMIX 2009
MXIX 1019
NOIX edible gland
PRIX price: Fr.; — fixe (table d'hôte)
TRIX fem. suffix
FRIZ curl; crisp; wig
PHIZ physiognomy; face
QUIZ test; odd one; hoax
SWIZ swindle
WHIZ hum; bargain; corker

BEJA Nile nomad
BIJA kino tree
CAJA box; bank
COJA title; teacher
DEJA already: Fr.
HOJA title; teacher
LIJA unicorn fish
LOJA bark (quinine)
MAJA crab
NAJA cobra
PUJA worship; festival
RAJA prince; fish
REJA screen; grille: Sp.
SOJA bean; glycine
NEJD kingdom
HAJE cobra
YAJE plant
CAJI snapper
FIJI islands (Lau, Yasawa)
FUJI wisteria; cherry; volcano
HAJI pilgrim
KOJI Jap. yeast cake
MOJI Jap. seaport
SUJI wheat; semolina
HAJJ pilgrimage
SEJM Polish assembly
BOJO grass
GAJO non-Gypsy
IDJO Niger delta Negro
MAJO dandy; shrub
MOJO tree; majagua; voodoo charm; Indian
PAJO prayer stick
ROJO redskin: Sp.
TAJO trench
BAJU jacket
CAJU fruit; mahogany
HOJU Jap. army reserve
JUJU Afr. magic, charm
TEJU lizard

AKKA Pygmy
ATKA fish; Aleut. Island
BAKA devil
BEKA weight
BUKA dried leaves
DIKA bread; fat; oil
EKKA carriage
HAKA dance
KAKA parrot
LOKA sphere; universe
PIKA little chief hare
PUKA rare N.Z. tree
ROKA mafura (tree)
SAKA era; Scythians
SIKA Jap. deer
SOKA drought blight
WAKA canoe
WEKA flightless bird
YAKA Bantu
KTKB chess move
BAKE dry; roast; biscuit
BIKE bicycle
BYKE nest of bees
CAKE bar; dough; harden
COKE coal residue; fuel
CUKE cucumber
CYKE cyclorama
DIKE levee; ditch; dig; goddess (Horae)
DUKE prince; cherry
DYKE levee; checkers opening
FAKE loop; cheat; sham
FEKE trick device
FYKE fish bag net
HAKE fish; pester; frame
HIKE toss; tramp; raise
HUKE hooked cape
HYKE cry to urge dogs
JAKE Jacob; rube; money; satisfactory; ginger
JOKE jest; laughing stock
JUKE partridge call; — box; sociological name (with Kallikak)
KYKE fashion spy
LAKE sea; pool; red (cochineal)
LIKE as; similar(ly); love; prefer; probable
LOKE Loki; surprise!
LUKE name; evangelist; Paul's companion; author Acts; -warm
MAKE produce, create; cause; reach; type; identify
MIKE Michael; Mick; microphone
MOKE donkey; dolt
NIKE victory goddess (Samothrace); missile
PEKE (Pekinese) dog
PIKE fish; weapon; pierce; highway; farmer; gamble; Zebulon (explorer; peak)
POKE thrust; prod; pry; sack; potter; herb

PUKE cloth; vomit
RAKE incline; tool; collect; roué; —'s Progress
REKE rick; pile
ROKE vapor; smoke
SAKE purpose; beer
SOKE jurisdiction
SUKE Susan; tea-kettle
SYKE fountain (Her.)
TAKE acquire; seize; scene part; receipts
TIKE child
TUKE fabric; canvas
TYKE dog, child
WAKE track; arouse; vigil; island
WOKE stirred; roused
YOKE join; link; slavery
ZEKE Ezekiel
WAKF trust fund
WUKF trust fund
ANKH cross
BIKH aconite; poison
BUKH prate; talk
HAKH claim(er); legal claim; share
LAKH 100,000; coin
RAKH hayfield
RUKH fabled bird; jungle
SIKH Hindu soldier
ENKI Babylonian god
KAKI bird; tree
KIKI castor oil plant
KUKI Burma Mongol
LOKI god of discord; Aesir; Balder slayer
MAKI lemur
MOKI N.Z. raft
PIKI maize bread; pik
RAKI spirits
REKI Baluchistan nomad
SAKI monkey; Munro
TIKI god; first man; image
WEKI fern
YAKI cayman
YUKI Cal. Indian
BUKK prate; talk
RIKK tambourine
BOKO evil spirit (Haiti)
DOKO Afr. pygmy
HAKO rite
JAKO parrot
KOKO bird; palm; tribe; executioner (Mikado)
MAKO shark
MOKO Maori tattoo; -moko (lizard)
TOKO Chin. store; flogging
ASKR — and Embla: Norse Adam and Eve
KTKR chess move
OAKS horse race; trees
BKKT chess move
BQKT chess move
KTKT chess move
QKKT chess move
QQKT chess move
RKKT chess move
RQKT chess move
TAKT beat(s); tempo
BAKU hat; tree; rug; city; oil field
DUKU lanseh tree fruit
HAKU fish
HIKU scabbard fish
KIKU chrysanthemum
KUKU N.Z. fruit pigeon; kukupa
MAKU Indian
POKU antelope
PUKU Afr. antelope
RAKU -ware
SUKU Bantu
TAKU Indian
ALKY alcohol
CAKY crusty
COKY grimed; drug addict
FAKY spurious
INKY black; stained
JOKY jocular
LAKY red
OAKY oaklike
PIKY full of fish
POKY shabby; dull; bonnet
PUKY nauseated
ROKY misty; hoarse
SUKY Susan; tea-kettle
TAKY taking
WAKY alert
YOKY coupled

AGLA acrostic
ALLA by: It.
AMLA tree
AULA hall; tree; brain part
BALA geol. epoch
BELA jasmine; Benjamin's 1st son; Hungarian king
BOLA missile; majagua (tree)
CELA that: Fr.
COLA tree; nut; drink
DOLA weight
ELLA Eleanor; she: Sp.; fem. suffix
FALA refrain; dog
FULA Sudanese
GALA festival; tribe
GILA — monster; lizard; Ariz. river
GOLA storeroom; caste; cyma
GULA upper throat; goddess (Ninurta's consort)
HALA pine tree
HELA goddess; Loki's daughter
HILA 'eyes' of bean
HOLA fish poison; herb; hello
HULA Hawaiian dance
HYLA frog; toad
IMLA Micaiah's father
IOLA Kansas town
JULA suspension bridge
KALA bird
KELA measures
KOLA caffeine nut; jackal; river; city; bay (Murmansk)
KULA measure; gift exchange
LILA deity manifestation
LOLA fem. name
LULA name; Louisa
MALA evil(s);

wrong(s): Lat.; jaw

MELA festival; prefix: black

MILA measure

MOLA sunfish genus

NALA hero

NOLA fem. name; tune

OLLA jar; meat dish; -podrida (medley)

PALA weight; antelope; vine; rice

PELA wax (secreting insect)

POLA Yugo. city (Pula)

PULA Yugo. city

PYLA brain opening

SALA dining room: Sp.

SELA Dead Sea town

SOLA herb (topee source); alone; holla!

SULA genus; booby; gannet

TALA tree; basin; ruin

TELA tissue; web; banana port

TOLA weight

TULA metal; niello; city; Toltec ruins

ULLA grass; paper pulp

UPLA cow dung; fuel

VELA membranes; soft palates; the Sails (Argo constellation)

VILA fairy; New Hebrides

VOLA palm (hand, foot)

ZOLA Emile (author: J'accuse, Dreyfus case; Nana)

BULB bud; tuber; corm; lamp; swell

KALB de — (general)

TALC soapy mineral

AULD old; — lang syne

BALD naked; — eagle

BOLD valiant; brazen; strong, heavy (type)

COLD chill; frigid; indifferent; common —; coryza; — blood; — chisel

EILD barren; milkless

FELD field: Ger.

FOLD plait; envelop; fail; quit; flock

GELD castrate; prune; tax

GILD lay gold on; adorn; — the lily; trade society

GOLD metal; element; — dust, medal

HELD kept; retained

HILD Hethin's victim princess

HOLD grasp; have; retain; believe; keep; bear; lair; prison

KELD spring; fountain

MELD announce (score); merge

MILD calm(ly); soft; tame

MOLD fungus; humus; die, matrix; shape; mix

SOLD vended; persuaded; cheated

SULD measure

TOLD narrated; counted

VELD So. Afr. grassland

WELD unite; junction

WILD rough; savage; mad; eager; unruly; wilderness

WOLD upland plain

YELD barren; milkless

ABLE fit; adept; suffix; -bodied

ACLE tree

AILE winged

ALLE bird; all: Ger.

ATLE tree

AXLE spindle

BALE woe; bundle

BILE liver secretion; choler

BOLE trunk; clay; brown

CALE Gypsy; cabbage

COLE brassica genus; Porter (composer)

CULE diminutive suffix

CYLE brewing; beer; wort

DALE valley; share; trough

DELE omit; erase

DOLE ration; (relief) alms; deal out

ELLE measure; she: Fr.

FILE tool; rasp; smooth; march; column; folder; arrange

GALE storm, wind

GULE of August (Lamma's Day)

GYLE brewing; wort; vat

HALE healthy; Nathan (patriot)

HOLE pit; cavity; flaw; — in one; — card; ace in the —

HULE caucho source

HYLE matter (philos.); demon

IDLE not working; empty; lazy; waste

ILLE that one: Lat.

IOLE Eurytus' daughter (Hercules' captive)

ISLE ait; eyot; insulate; key

IXLE cordage fiber

JOLE jowl; cheek

JULE name: Julian; Julius

KALE cabbage

KELE weight

KILE measure; weight

KYLE sore; ulcer; farmer

LILE little
MALE man(ly); tribe
MELE Hawaiian poem; chant
MILE measure; distance
MOLE nevus; birthmark; pier; burrow(ing animal); Mossi language
MULE equine hybrid; spinning jenny; slipper
NILE river; green, blue
OGLE gaze (amorously)
ORLE shield border; fillet
PALE wan; pallid; ashy; picket; stake; beyond the —
PELE fire goddess
PILE hair; heap (up); awn; atomic —
POLE rod; tail; terminal: axis, battery; — Star; Polish, Polack
PULE cheep; whimper
PYLE Ernie (journalist); Howard (artist)
RALE rattling sound
RILE irritate; vex
ROLE actor's part
RULE law; guide; reign method; control; — Britannia; ruler; line
SALE bargain; auction; willow; salted: Fr.
SOLE pelma (bottom); flatfish; single; only
TALE story; — of Two Cities; count
TELE prefix: far, complete
TILE ceramic slab; drain pipe; domino; tessera; slate
TOLE entice; told; tinware
TULE bulrush; cattail
VALE valley; — of tears; farewell: Lat.
VILE base; evil; odious
VOLE rodent; slam (cards)
WALE streak; texture; ridge; welt
WILE trick; guile; lure
YALE university; lock; Eli, Elihu —; myth. antelope
YULE Christmas
CALF bovine, etc., young; fur; leather; skin; lower leg
DELF quarry; pottery; blue
GOLF game; blood-red; — links
GULF bay; chasm; eddy
HALF moiety; -breed -caste, -nelson, -shell
PELF booty; riches
SELF identity; ego; one
WELF ducal family
WOLF canid (dog); Lupus; larva; devour; dissonance; cry —; flirtatious man
AALI pasha
AMLI tree
ATLI Gudrun's husband-king
BALI demon; monkey; offering; island
BELI myth. Brit. king
CALI Colombian city
COLI intestinal bacterium
DALI tree; offering; Salvador —
DELI delicatessen
DOLI weights
FILI learned poet
GALI abuse
GOLI musket ball; pill
HALI prefix: sea, salt
HELI prefix: sun, spiral
HOLI spring festival
JOLI pretty, nice: Fr.
KALI glasswort; carpet; evil genius; Agni's tongue; Siva's wife
KOLI low-caste tribesman
KULI low-caste Indian
MALI caste; nation; river
NOLI — me tangere
PALI slope; coral parts; Buddhist language
PILI nut; grass; hairs
PULI coins
SOLI single performances; prefix: sun, alone
TALI gold piece; weight
TELI low (merchant) caste
VALI Odin's son; viceroy
VILI brother of Odin; Ve
WALI prefect
YALI mansion
BALK thwart; signal
BILK defraud
BULK mass, volume; loom; -head (stall)
CALK tighten; stop; sleep; tool; copy
FOLK people; — ways, laws, song, dance
FULK unfair shove (marbles)
HULK ship body; bulky thing
KELK fish roe
MILK nutritious

fluid; sap; white; exploit; drain
MULK freehold land
POLK Cossack regiment; James Knox (President)
PULK (Cossack) regiment
SILK fiber; thread; -worm
SULK mope; be sullen
TALK speak; converse; conference; empty words; dialect; — turkey
VOLK people: Ger.; workmen (So. Afr.)
WALK go on foot; path; pass, base on balls; — the plank
WELK (gather) snail; Lawrence (musician)
WILK (gather) snail
YELK yolk
YOLK egg yellow; essence
BALL game; confuse; dance; — bearing; good time; -point; Amer. sculptor
BELL ringing cup; gong; time period; flower shape; helmet; Brontë pseudonym; — the cat; diving —
BILL beak; weapon; law; poster; invoice; debt; nickname: William; — and coo; Sikes (Dickens)
BOLL (strip) plant pod
BULL (bovine) male; stud; papal letter; optimist; Taurus; policeman; blunder; glib talk; -fight
CALL summon; visit; cry; telephone; — girl; — money
CELL cubicle; group; elec. jar; organism
COLL embrace; hug; Vincent (gangster: "mad dog")
CULL pick out; assort
DALL sheep
DELL valley; dingle; wench
DILL flavoring herb; pickle
DOLL plaything; puppet; dress up; girl
DULL blunt(ed); dismal; inert; tedious; Shaks. character
FALL descend; ruin; autumn; — of Man
FELL skin; cut, hew (down); savage
FILL pack; complete; glut; — the bill
FULL filled; replete; quite; — dress; — house
GALL bite; venom; wound; chafe; swelling; impudence
GILL measure; brook; breathing organ; wattle; coin; lass
GOLL Irish hero (Fenian)
GULL bird; cheat; dupe
HALL building; room; town —; guild-; astronomer; -Mills
HELL Hades; state of misery; -bent
HILL mound; Jenny (Shaw character); -billy
HOLL ditch
HULL husk; ship body; Cordell (statesman)
JELL solidify; mature
JILL girl; sweetheart; Jack and —
JOLL move clumsily; knock
KELL Gaul; net; film
KILL slay; veto; creek
LILL small pin; loll; Lillian
LOLL droop; lounge; sprawl
LULL (temporary) quiet
MALL mallet; game; bird; assembly (place)
MELL (beat with) hammer; teacher (Dickens)
MILL grind(er); quern; box; John Stuart (economist)
MOLL Mary, girl; Flanders (Defoe); minor (mus.)
MULL muslin; ointment; ponder; humus
NELL Ellen; Helen; Little — (Dickens girl)
NILL refuse; negate
NOLL Oliver (Cromwell); head; noddle
NULL nil; void; code filler
PALL cloak; covering; cloy
PILL medicine tablet
POLL head; register, survey; cut off; Mary; parrot; vote
PULL drag; influence
RILL (run in a) brook
ROLL wrap; trill;

drumbeat; rotate; list; bank-

RULL to wheel; trundle

SELL vend; betray; persuade; hoax; — short

SILL beam (door, window)

TALL high; incredible

TELL inform; discern; chat; William (Swiss hero)

TILL until; plow; cultivate; tray, cash box

TOLL tax; lure; sound

VALL valley

VILL village; township

WALL barrier; fence; enclose; knot; Berlin —

WELL (water) pit; shaft; eddy; flow; rightly; very; sound, healthy

WILL volition; choice; decree; bequeath; testament

YELL cry; cheer

ZOLL measure

BALM plant; soothe; — in Gilead

CALM quiet; mold

CULM grass stem; coal dust; shoal water deposit

FILM skin; coating; haze; photograph; picture

HALM plant stems

HELM steer (wheel); tiller

HOLM holly; oak; islet

KULM crane; heron

MALM limestone

PALM tree; measure; hand part; paddle; conceal; grease the —

SALM star

KILN (burn in) oven

VULN wound (Her.)

ALLO prefix: other, dissimilar

BILO Balkan karst area

BOLO knife; Rafflesia (plant); pacifist

CALO Gypsy

DILO poon tree

FILO silk thread

GILO woody vine (tonic)

GOLO Nilotic Sudanese

GULO wolverine genus

HALO circle; glow; nimbus; prefix: sea, salt

HELO squeamish

HILO grass; city (Hawaii)

KALO taro root

KILO measure; -gram, -meter; prefix: 1000

KOLO folk dance

LALO composer

LOLO Caucasian Chinese

MALO loincloth

MILO name; grain; sorghum; Venus (Melos)

NOLO — contendere

ORLO smooth surface; plinth

OSLO city (Norway); Christiania

PALO pole, wood: Sp.

PELO hair: It.

POLO game; Marco —

RALO measure

SILO fodder pit; ensile

SOLO song; (fly) alone

STLO WW II battle site

TYLO dog (Maeterlinck)

ULLO Indian shell money

VELO speed unit

CALP limestone

COLP pasture; Irish acre

GOLP roundel purpure (Her.)

GULP swallow; catch breath

HELP relieve; avoid; wait on, aid(e); servants

KELP seaweed, iodine source

PALP appendage; feeler

PULP pith; tissue; paper; magazine

SALP marine animal

YELP shrill bark

ULLR chief god; Sif's son; Thor's stepson

FELS Eastern coin

FILS son: Fr.; Dumas (Camille); Iraq coin

HALS Frans (painter)

ILLS troubles

NILS Bohr (physicist)

WELS sheatfish

BALT Lithuanian; Esth; Latvian; Lett

BELT strap; zone; beat

BOLT sift; refine; shaft; lightning; bar; plant; rifle part; flight; refusal

BULT hill; ridge

CELT Irish, Scot, Welsh, Breton; chisel

COLT young horse; pistol; — .45

CULT sect; worship system

DOLT dunce; ignoramus

FELT pressed fibers; hat; sensed

GALT clay bed

GELT money

GILT gold; sow

HALT stop; lame

HILT sword

HOLT willow plantation; hill; lair; Eliot

hero; actor
JILT betray in love
JOLT shake; hard blow
KELT Celt; cloth; trout
KILT Scot's skirt
LILT (sing) lively tune
MALT barley; beer
MELT liquefy
MILT spleen; fish gland; nickname
MOLT shed (hair)
PELT skin; hurl; strike
POLT knock; trump; club
SALT sodium chloride, NaCl; sailor; season; — away; — Lake City; — Sea
SILT sediment; scum; drift
TILT cover; incline; tip; joust; sport
TOLT writ; isolated peak
VELT measure
VOLT sideways gait; fencing leap; elec. unit
WALT Whitman
WELT ridge; wale; strip; sew; beat; universe: Ger.
WILT droop; lost spirit
YELT gilt (sow)
AALU Hades; heaven
AULU tree
BALU wildcat
HULU o-o's feather tuft
IALU Hades; heaven
IGLU Eskimo hut; seal hole
KULU old woman (Kipling)
LULU barn owl; name; Louisa
PELU hardwood tree
PULU tree fern
SHLU Moroccan Berber
SULU Moro
TOLU balsam (rose odor)
TULU Dravidian Indian
YALU river (Korean War)
ZULU Bantu Kaffir; ship; artificial fly
CALX residue; heel: Lat.
FALX weapon; — cerebri (brain fold)
ABLY deftly
ALLY unite, confederate
COLY long-tailed; bird
DULY properly; timely
EELY wriggling; slippery
HOLY sacred; pious; — City; — Alliance; — Roller
IDLY vainly; lazily
ILLY badly; ill
INLY within; heartily
JULY (5th Roman) month
LELY Dutch painter
LILY flower; Turk's-cap; pure; white
MOLY magic herb (Homer)
OILY unctuous; bland; suave
ONLY alone; but; single; exclusively
ORLY Paris airport
PALY wan; heraldic design
PILY pilelike
POLY herb; Teucrium; prefix: many
PULY whining; complaining
RELY trust, depend
RILY turbid; irritated
UGLY badlooking, unpleasant; plug-
VILY fairies
WILY artful; subtle
ALMA girl; silk; river; city
AMMA abbess; god
ATMA soul
BEMA platform; altar; measure
BOMA Afr. stockade; post
CIMA mountain peak: It.
COMA torpor; blur, tuft
CYMA cornice; molding
DAMA gazelle
DUMA Russ. parliament
EGMA enigma
EMMA letter M; name; Austen novel; Bovary (Flaubert)
ERMA Ermengarde
FAMA rumor
GAMA Vasco da (navigator); grass
GOMA Bantu (Wagoma)
HEMA prefix: blood
HIMA Hamitic Negro
HOMA sacred drink
HUMA Uganda Negro
IJMA Moslem principle (Sunna)
IRMA name
JAMA tunic
KAMA love god; desire; river
LAMA priest; llama; brown; Dalai, Panchen, Tashi —
LIMA city; bean; yam; mollusk
LOMA fringe; lap; hill
MAMA mother; goddess
MIMA woman actor
NAMA Hottentot; herb
NEMA eelworm; prefix: thread
NUMA Pompilius (Roman king)
PIMA Ariz. Indian;

cotton
POMA rosa (rose apple)
PUMA cougar; catamount
RAMA Indian; Vishnu incarnation; bull (Kipling)
RIMA fissure; breadfruit; child heroine (Hudson)
ROMA Rome: It.
SAMA fish; trance-inducing music
SIMA igneous rock
SOMA vine; drink; body
TAMA Indian
TEMA musical theme; Arab
TOMA Liberian Negro
XEMA arctic gull
YAMA first mortal (Judge of Dead)
YIMA Avestan demigod
YUMA Indian (Cal.); city
ZAMA Hannibal's defeat
BOMB explosive; dispenser; A-, H-; lead-lined container; buzz —
COMB crest; rake; scrape
DUMB mute; stupid; — waiter; deaf and —
GAMB leg
IAMB verse foot
JAMB leg armor; pillar; door part
LAMB amateur speculator; Charles (Elia: essayist)
LIMB leg; arm; member
NIMB nimbus; halo
NUMB deaden(ed); helpless
RUMB compass point
TOMB grave; monument; bury
ZIMB Ethiopian fly
ACME peak; crisis
ALME dancer
ARME weapon: Fr.; — blanche (saber)
CAME arrived; lead rod; Indian
COME arrive; chance; fare
CYME inflorescence
DAME woman; title; — aux Camélias
DEME Greek commune
DIME coin; — novel
DOME edifice; cupola; roof
FAME reputation
FEME wife; tribunal
FUME smoke; fit; rage
GAME amusement; quarry; resolute; lame
HEME reduced hematin
HOME habitat; asylum; plate; natural
HUME philosopher
KAME hill
KOME Greenland division
LAME cripple(d); halt; plate; fabric
LIME calcium oxide (mortar); snare; caustic; linden (tree); amber; citrus fruit
LOME Togo seaport
LYME bloodhound
MIME drama; act; actor; clown; smith (Nibelungs)
MOME buffoon; -rath
NAME title; reputation; clan; cite
NOME city (Alaska)
OIME alas
POME fruit; ball; globe
PUME Yarura(n language)
RAME branch
RIME frost; (make) rhymes; chink;
rung
ROME city (Eternal); Church; beauty (apple)
RYME water surface
SAME identical
SEME (sprinkling) pattern
SIME monkey
SOME various; any; somewhat; part
TAME gentle; subdue
TIME period; moment; credit term; speed rate; meter, rhythm; Father —; space —
TOME book; papal letter
ULME elm
ZEME (abode of) spirit; fetish
ZYME ferment
SAMH bread plant
ADMI gazelle
AMMI herb
BIMI orangutan (Kipling)
DEMI prefix: half
GUMI shrub, flower, fruit
HAMI hooked processes
HEMI prefix: half
IMMI measure
JAMI mosque
KAMI language; deity
KOMI Soviet republic; Zyrians
MIMI nickname; opera heroine
RAMI branches
REMI Gaul people; prefix: oar
ROMI Gypsy wife
SEMI half
SIMI Dodecanese isle
ZEMI (abode of) spirit; fetish
MUMM mask; disguise
DAMN curse; — the torpedoes
DOMN Rumanian lord
FAMN measure
HYMN song (of praise)
LIMN portray; delineate

AMMO ammunition; prefix: sand
ATMO prefix: steam
COMO lake, resort (Italy)
DEMO prefix: populace
HEMO prefix: blood
HOMO man; — sapiens; prefix: same
IKMO betel palm, pepper
ITMO betel pepper
MAMO bird
MEMO note; statement
MOMO owl
NEMO nobody: Lat.; prefix: glade; Captain (Verne hero)
POMO California Indian
SEMO Sancus (deity); Dius Fidius
SUMO Ulvan
ULMO muermo; hardwood
BUMP coincide; hit; swelling; — off (kill)
CAMP tent(s); town; stay; boot —
DAMP moist(ure); depress
DUMP unload; junkyard; thud; mean place; holey dollar
GAMP umbrella; Sairey (nurse: Dickens)
GIMP silk fabric; vim
GUMP silly, stupid one; Andy, Chester, Min (cartoon family)
HEMP herb; hashish; cannabis; rope (fiber)
HUMP protuberance; mound; crisis; Himalayan peaks; -back
JUMP leap; bounce; move; headstart; — the gun
KEMP fur refuse
LAMP light; bulb
LIMP halt; flaccid; loose
LUMP mass; swelling; barge; like it or — it
MUMP beg; mumble; cheat
PIMP procurer; bawd; maquereau
POMP pageant(ry); splendor
PUMP force; draw out; slipper
RAMP inclined way; rear
ROMP girl; gambol; frolic
RUMP sirloin part; remnants; — Parliament
SAMP maize
SIMP simpleton
SUMP dig pit; tank; cistern
TAMP fill up; pound down; tool
TUMP drag slain deer
TYMP blast furnace stone
VAMP sock; shoe part; fireman; ghost; flirt
WAMP elder
YAMP herb; tuber
ALMS charity
ARMS mil. science; ensigns; weapons; branches; limbs
JOMS Viking; Norse colony
REMS river
TEMS sieve; sift
AMMU ammunition
ATMU sun god
LIMU edible seaweed
RIMU red pine; imou pine
ARMY multitude; force
DEMY coin; scholar; paper size
DOMY domelike
ELMY rich in elms
EMMY TV award; nickname
FUMY vaporous; smoky
HOMY homey; intimate
ISMY doctrinaire
LIMY viscous
RIMY frosty; rhyming
ANNA coin; bird; name; — Christie (O'Neill); — Karenina (Tolstoi)
ARNA buffalo
BANA Titan
BENA grass (vetiver)
BINA Hindu guitar
BONA good: Lat.; — fide
BUNA synthetic rubber
CANA Indian
CENA (Last) supper
CUNA Panama Indian
DANA goddess; author; editor; lake
DONA lady; sapek (coin)
DYNA prefix: power
EDNA female name; Ferber (novelist)
ENNA Sicilian resort
ETNA stove; volcano
FANA Sufistic concept
GENA cheek; beak part
GONA New Guinea victory
GUNA Sankhya term
IMNA Asherites' chief
IONA Scot. isle; Celt church; college
JENA Ger. city (optical, Napoleonic victory); glass
KANA Japanese writing
KINA quinine
KONA Hawaiian storm; weight
LANA wood; flannel
LENA firewood: Sp.; river; Conrad heroine
LINA measure;

Caroline
LUNA moon goddess; silver
MANA magic power; Chinese letter
MINA weight; money; myna; watchman
MONA monkey; Lisa (La Gioconda: da Vinci)
MYNA talking bird: grackle
NANA nurse; Aztec hero's wife; Zola novel; dog (Peter Pan: Barrie)
NINA goddess (Ea's daughter); ship (Pinta, —, Santa Maria); girl: Sp.
NONA fate goddess; prefix: ninth
ORNA measure
PANA city
PINA pineapple; silver cone
PUNA high Andes; wind; sickness (soroche)
RANA frog; prince; Aegir's wife
RENA rockfish
SANA Yemen's capital; fiber
SINA drug; mountain (Moses)
TANA shrew; rabbi; police station; lake (Blue Nile)
TINA fem. nickname
TUNA fish; pear: opuntia
ULNA elbow bone; ell
URNA measure
VENA vein: Lat.
VINA harp; guitar; wines
XINA nickname: Christina
YANA tribe
ZONA girdle; shingles
BANC (judge's) bench
SYNC synchronize
ZINC metal; element; color
ARND theologian
BAND strip; group; orchestra; range; tie; sash
BEND turn; curve; flex; bow
BIND tie; protect; sew; cohere
BOND adhesion; tie; covenant; paper; captivity; certificate
BUND embankment; league
COND direct helmsman
FEND keep off; parry
FIND discover(y); (re)gain
FOND basis; fount; loving
FUND supply; finance; money; sinking —
GOND Dravidian Indian
HAND control; aid; worker; measure; pass; player; cards; penmanship
HIND fish; grouper; deer; posterior
HUND dog: Ger.
KIND sort; species; gentle
LAND ground; debark; state: Ger.
LEND make loan; grant; — an ear
LIND Jenny (singer, Swedish Nightingale)
MAND grass
MEND repair; improve
MIND intellect; brain; memory; wish; mood; plan; tend; dislike
MUND protection right
PEND hang; be delayed
POND lake; pool; weight
PUND weight
RAND border; ridge; strip; So. Afr. gold mine
REND tear; rupture; bark trees
RIND bark; peel; Vali's mother, Odin's wife
RYND millstone support
SAND grit; silica; polish, smooth; red-yellow; George (novelist; Dudevant)
SEND transmit; dispatch; propel; swing; enthrall
SIND river; Pakistan province; are: Ger.
TEND serve; incline
TIND kindle
TUND pound; bruise
VEND Slav; sell; sale
WAND rod; staff; magic —
WEND Slav; go; travel
WIND turn; coil; blowing air; mere talk
WYND alley; small court
YOND past; beyond
ZEND — Avesta (holy text)
ACNE disease
AINE elder
ANNE queen; Boleyn; Henry VIII wife; Elizabeth's mother; Shakespeare's wife; Dombey's maid (Dickens); Queen — style; Queen —'s lace
AONE first-rate
ARNE composer; region
AUNE measure
BANE woe; curse; poison
BENE wild hog; well: It. & Lat.
BINE (hop) stem
BONE study hard;

plug; os
CANE stem; rattan; stick; walking —; sugar —; candy —
CENE suffix: recent
CINE movie: Sp.
CONE geometric solid; pine fruit, strobile; peak; ice cream —; nose —
DANE Scandinavian; great — (dog); Hamlet
DENE measure; dune; Indian
DINE eat; have dinner
DONE agreed; exhausted
DUNE sandhill; twine color
DYNE unit of force
EINE one: Ger.
ENNE prefix: nine; fem. suffix
ERNE sea eagle
ESNE slave
FANE temple
FINE end; superior; thin; keen; well; (set) penalty; geil —, derb — (Irish clans)
GANE yawn
GENE hereditary factor; chromosome part; nickname
GONE departed; enamored; lost; germ cell
GYNE prefix: female
HONE sharpen(er)
IONE Pompeii heroine (Bulwer-Lytton)
JANE woman; false hair; cloth; — Eyre; Lady — Grey
JUNE month; beetle; — moon, bride
KANE god
KINE cattle
LANE (fixed) route; throat
LENE smooth; consonant
LINE thin mark; cable; cord; wire; piping; row; direction; cover; align; track; flax
LONE single; — Star
LUNE crescent; hawk leash
MANE hair; in the morning: Lat.
MENE — tekel upharsin (handwriting on the wall)
MINE possessive pronoun; dig; pit; rich source; explosive
NANE own; none
NENE Hawaiian goose
NINE number (of Muses); baseball team
NONE not one; 9th hour
OHNE without: Ger.
ORNE measure; river (Caen)
PANE glass; panel
PENE (hammer) head
PINE tree; conifer; evergreen; yearn; mourn
PONE corn bread; writ
RINE hemp; ditch
RONE brushwood
RUNE Teutonic sign; magic
SANE rational
SINE math. ratio; without: Lat.; — qua non; — die
SONE loudness unit
TANE Polynesian god
TENE suffix: ribbon
TINE tooth; prong; pain; grass
TONE pitch; accent; Wolfe (Ir. rebel)
TUNE song; pitch; harmony
TYNE Eng. river
VANE weathercock; feather; blade
VINE creeping plant
VONE robot bomb
WANE ebb; lessen
WINE fermented juice
ZONE area; band; partition
BANG beat; thump; hair; sardine; interjection
BENG devil (Gypsy)
BING bed roll; sharp sound
BONG bell sound
BUNG stop(per); throw
CANG wooden collar
DANG curse (damn)
DING thump; sound; urge
DONG sound; weight; ding-; money
DUNG excrement; fertilize(r); weight
FANG tooth; measure; Dickens character
FONG Ewe-speaking Negro
FUNG Sennar Negroid
GANG crew; associate; rock
GONG bell; tom-tom
HANG suspend; plan; bit; die on gallows
HING asefetida (gum resin; antispasmodic)
HONG Chin. trade guild
HUNG suspended; undecided (jury)
JUNG young: Ger.; Carl Gustave (psychologist)
KANG — Hsi (Chinese emperor)
KING monarch; ruler; chief; chessman; card
KUNG public

LANG auld — syne; Fritz
LING fish; burbot; hake
LONG lengthy; extended; yearn; John Silver (Stevenson); Huey; (La. politician); — time no see
LUNG air bladder; iron-
MANG bat (Kipling)
MENG mix
MING Chin. dynasty
MONG among; barter
MUNG grass
PANG agony
PING (bullet, striking) sound
PONG sound; improvise
PUNG (drive) box sleigh; mah jongg term
QUNG So. Afr. Bushman
RANG sounded
RING gird; arena; prizefighting; gang; atomic order; sound (bell); Vienna landmark; Nibelungen cycle (Wagner)
RONG Sikkimese language
RUNG wheel spoke; hooped
SANG Hindu group; herb; weight; did sing
SING vocalize; warble; tell
SONG poem (music); pittance
SUNG chanted; Chin. dynasty
TANG spur; flavor; sound; seaweed; dynasty
TENG measure
TING sound; Chin. pottery
TONG secret society
TUNG tree; oil
UANG beetle
VANG rope
WANG weight; meadow; prince
WING alar appendage; faction; annex; fly
WONG field; meadow
YANG honk; male or positive principle (opp. to yin)
ZING sharp thrill; vim
BINH weight
HUNH exclamation
SINH math. term
TANH math. term
AANI ape
AGNI god; lambs
ANNI years: Lat.
ARNI buffalo
BANI coins
BENI Bolivian river; sesame
BINI Nigerian
BONI African; Boschneger
CONI It. commune
DONI fishing boat
HONI — soit qui mal y pense; shamed
IONI Hainai; Chaddo Indian
MANI peanut; prefix: hand
OMNI prefix: all
OZNI Gad's son
PANI madam: Polish
RANI princess; wife
RENI It. painter; prefix: kidney
VENI prefix: vein; —, vidi, vici (I came, I saw, I conquered)
YENI So. Amer. tanager
ZUNI Indian; reservation
BENJ hemp; narcotic
FUNJ Sennar Negroid
GUNJ granary; market
MUNJ tough grass; twine
BANK mound; bench; deposit; bird flock; Left, Right —; blood —; eye —
BONK bar money (Dutch E.I.)
BUNK case; bed; nonsense
CONK nose; head; decay; fail; hit
DANK moist; rank
DINK small boat; cut out
DUNK dip into; immerse
FINK finch; derb; informer; strikebreaker
FUNK fear; coward; Casimir (vitamins); Isaac (lexicographer); — & Wagnalls
GINK eccentric one
GUNK jilt; hoax
HANK coil; Morgan (Twain)
HONK goose cry; toot; ooga
HUNK piece; lump; OK
JINK prank
JONK jonquil
JUNK ship; trash; scrap
KINK twist; loop; cramp
KONK conk
KUNK measure
LANK thin; lean(ness)
LINK (chain) loop; connect; join; torch; measure
LONK black-faced sheep
MINK weasel-like animal
MONK ascetic; friar; bird; fish; spot; ferret
PANK weight
PENK minnow
PINK color (red); ship; cut; hunter's coat; carnation; in the — (healthy)
PUNK touchwood; tinder; conch;

tramp; bad
RANK luxuriant; gross; fetid; grade; array
RINK skating arena
SANK descended
SINK fall; droop; conceal; basin
SUNK immersed; overcome
TANK basin; store; war vehicle; panzer
TONK (cow bell) clang; honky-; game
TUNK rap; thump; game
WINK blink; signal
YANK jerk; New Englander; Union soldier; American
GUNL gunwale
BENN seed
BINN box; frame; crib
BONN city; Ger. capital (Beethoven born)
BUNN cake
CONN direct helmsman
FINN man of Finland, Helsinki; Ugric; Mickey (KO drops); Huckleberry (Twain novel)
GUNN castaway (Stevenson)
JANN genii
JINN demon; spirit
LINN waterfall; linden
LUNN Sally (teacake)
MANN man; Ger.; Horace (educator); Thomas (writer)
PENN William (Pa. founder)
RANN verse, stanza; kite (Kipling)
SENN Swiss herdsman
SINN — Fein (Irish society)
SUNN hemp: fiber plant
WYNN timber truck; Ed (actor: Perfect Fool)
AGNO Luzon river
AINO Jap. aborigine
ANNO — Domini (year of our Lord)
ARNO river; cartoonist
ASNO donkey: Sp.
BENO alcoholic palm sap
BINO alcoholic palm sap
BONO Johnny (Briton); cui —
CANO canal: Sp.
DINO prefix: terrible
FANO cloth; cape
FONO Samoan council
GANO Count (Roland's destroyer)
HANO Indian
HINO timber tree; dye
IUNO Jupiter's wife
JUNO goddess; Jupiter's wife, Hera; stately woman; missile
KANO painting school
KENO lotto (game); prefix: empty
KINO gum (catechu); prefix: moving
LENO (cotton, silk) fabric
LINO measure
MANO grindstone; hand: It.
MENO prefix: month
MINO Jap. straw coat
MONO monkey; Indian; prefix: single, one
NINO boy: Sp.
NONO ninth: It.
OENO prefix: wine
PINO pine tree
PUNO Pacific trade wind; city (Peru)
RENO Nev. city ("biggest little"; divorce, gambling)
SINO prefix: Chinese
TANO Indian
TINO Sambal language
TUNO rubber tree; gum
VENO prefix: vein
VINO palm liquor
XENO guest; prefix: foreign
ZENO philosopher (Stoic, Cynic); emperor
CINQ five: Fr.
BANS marriage notice
CENS payment due
DANS in: Fr.
DENS tooth: Lat.
DUNS dull; stupid
ENNS river
FONS fount; source
GENS clan: Lat.; people: Fr.
HANS John; Johannes; Castorp (Mann)
HENS fowl; -foot (herb)
LENS eye part; glass (optical); herb
MANS Chinese aborigine; Le — (city; auto race)
MENS mind: Lat.
MONS mountain: Lat.; city (Belgium: WW I battle)
NUNS sisters; veiling, fabric
OONS mild oath
PONS bridge: Lat.; — asinorum; Lily (singer)
SANS without: Fr.; — culotte (radical); -gêne
VANS race of gods
AINT contraction
ARNT contraction
AUNT parent's sister; tia: Sp.; tante: Fr., Ger.
BANT diet
BENT crooked; inclination; grass

BINT	daughter; woman
BUNT	sag (net, sail); (fungus) disease; butt (ball)
CANT	angle; change course; log; tilt; whine; jargon; be unable
CENT	coin; penny; game
DENT	depress(ion); notch
DINT	blow; force; notch
DONT	contraction; prohibition
DUNT	split (ceramics)
FENT	slit; cleft
FONT	basin; spring; stoup; type
FUNT	weight; Allen (TV)
GANT	yawn; gaunt; gannet; Eugene (Wolfe character)
GENT	gentleman; Belg. city
HANT	ghost
HINT	suggestion; imply
HUNT	seek; chase; Leigh (writer)
KANT	change course; Immanuel (philosopher)
KENT	Eng. county, duchy; Lear's follower
LENT	fasting period; slow; made loan
LINT	raveling, fiber (of linen); netting
LUNT	light; smoke; Alfred (actor)
MENT	falcon-headed god
MINT	herb; menthol; bonanza; coin; — julep
MONT	mountain: Fr.; — Blanc (peak, Alps)
MUNT	sash bar
OINT	apply oil
OONT	camel; mole
PANT	gasp; yearn
PENT	confined; -house
PINT	measure
PONT	ferry(boat); bridge: Fr.
PUNT	(propel) flatboat; kick; bet
RANT	scold; rave; frolic
RENT	torn; schism; let, lease; payment, income
RUNT	small animal, man
SUNT	babul: gum tree; pod; are: Lat.
TENT	cloth shelter; pup —; wine; frame
TINT	color; shade; tinge
VENT	hole; let out; issue
VINT	card game
WANT	lack; desire
WENT	departed
WONT	custom; contraction
ZANT	fish
AINU	Jap. aboriginal
BENU	holy bird (Ra-Osiris)
DANU	goddess
GENU	knee: Lat.
MANU	prefix: hand; Laws (Hindu code book)
MENU	bill of fare
TUNU	rubber tree; gum
ZENU	Afr. sheep
IYNX	wryneck (woodpecker)
JINX	hoodoo; bad luck
JYNX	wryneck; charm
LANX	platter
LYNX	wildcat; fur; constellation
MANX	pert. to Isle of Man; cat
MINX	pert girl
YUNX	woodpecker
	genus
AWNY	bearded
BONY	skeletal; osseous; Napoleon
CONY	rabbit; daman; pika
DENY	refuse; contradict
DUNY	having many dunes
EENY	—, meeny, miny, mo
GONY	albatross
LINY	streaky
LUNY	crazy (man)
MANY	numerous
MINY	of a mine
PINY	pinelike; peony
PONY	small equine (Shetland, polo); glass (1 oz.); translation
PUNY	weak; slight
TINY	small; -tim (herb); Tim (Dickens)
TONY	nickname (Anthony); stylish
TUNY	melodious
VINY	entwining
WANY	diminished
WINY	vinous; drunken
ZANY	clown(ish)
GANZ	all, totally: Ger.
LINZ	Austrian city
RANZ	— des vaches
ANOA	ox
AROA	Venezuela copper center
GJOA	ship (Northwest Passage: Amundsen)
POOA	pua hemp
PROA	Malay outrigger
SHOA	Abyssinian
STOA	portico; poikile (Zeno)
TOOA	hero; beefwood
WHOA	stop!; opp. of giddap
BLOB	drop; daub; sound; fish; zero score
BOOB	simpleton

BROB support spike
CHOB grain spike
DOOB Bermuda grass
FLOB move clumsily
JAOB measure
KNOB lump; hill; antler; handle
RHOB juice; jelly
SCOB fabric defect
SLOB slovenly one
SNOB social climber; game
SWOB sponge; wipe; mop
THOB rationalize
BLOC political unit; casting
CROC harquebus support; crocodile
FLOC flock(y mass); shreds
ALOD estate
APOD footless
AROD son of Gad
BIOD animal life force
CLOD lump; soil; dolt
EFOD priestly garb; image
ELOD alleged force
FEOD feudal estate
FOOD nutriment; victuals
GOOD able; brave; sound; profit; happiness; welfare; benefit
HOOD cowl; cloak; seal; gangster; Thomas (poet)
LOOD weight
MOOD humor; temper; verb form
PLOD trudge; drudge
POOD weight
PROD reminder; goad; horse; prodigy
QUOD prison; — erat demonstrandum (Q.E.D.)
ROOD crucifix; measure
SHOD wearing shoes
SNOD trim; snug; plausible
STOD Danish speech
TROD walked; track
WOOD timber; forest; Grant (painter); Leonard (general)
ALOE plant; tonic
AROE islands, New Guinea
CLOE fem. name
EBOE tree, oil; Negrito
EVOE bacchanal's wild cry; Punch editor
FLOE floating ice
FROE cleaver; steel wedge
OBOE woodwind; chanter
OTOE Sioux Indian
SHOE foot covering; crakow; wheel drag; tire
SLOE blackthorn; plum; blue-black
AZOF town; sea
BOOF stare; peach brandy
GOOF dolt; blunder
HOOF ungula; foot; beast; walk; dance
LOOF luff; sponge gourd
POOF exclamation
ROOF cover; house; top
STOF measure
WOOF crossthreads; texture; weft; bark
AGOG eager
AJOG jogging
CLOG block; sandal; stop; impede; choke
FLOG whip
FROG amphibian; hoarseness; loop; rail device
GROG liquor (with water)
ILOG river (Tagalog)
NIOG coconut palm
PROG (steal) food; forage
SHOG shake; jog
SLOG hit (hard); slug; slam
SMOG fog and smoke; haze
STOG stall in mud
VOOG lode cavity
BOOH exclamation
BROH macaque; monkey
LUOH White Nile Negro
POOH pshaw!; Bah (Mikado); Winnie (bear: Milne)
AMOI mine: Fr.
EKOI Bantu
ELOI Eli; God
AMOK frenzy
ASOK tree
BOOK tome; volume; Bible; libretto, (bet) record; register; throw the —
COOK chef; concoct; falsify; James (explorer)
DOOK wooden brick; demon
GOOK trash; ooze; native
HOOK trap; curve; catch; steal; — and eye; pirate (Peter Pan: Barrie)
IROK gomuti (palm)
JOOK perch; slumber
LOOK observe; appear(ance); eye(wink); care
NOOK corner; retreat
POOK hobgoblin; disk
ROOK bird; cheat; dupe; chessman (tower)
SOOK Moslem market; hog call
TOOK seized; caught; endured; supposed
AWOL absent without leave
BOOL curved handle
CHOL desolate plain; Mayan

COOL chill; calm; unmoved
DIOL chem. compound; suffix
EGOL antiseptic
EMOL rock salt
ENOL chem. suffix
FOOL dolt; jester; trick
GAOL prison
IDOL god, deity; image; adored one
ITOL suffix: alcohol(ic)
OBOL 1/16 drachma (coin)
POOL pond; puddle; game; stake; fund; Thames
ROOL crumple; ruffle
SIOL great Irish clan
SOOL pull, tousle about
STOL short takeoff and landing
TOOL instrument; polish; dupe
VIOL string instrument
VTOL vertical takeoff and landing
WOOL (sheep) fleece; down
AHOM Assam native
ATOM whit; particle; nuclear complex
BOOM hum; grow, push; beam
BROM Bones (Ichabod's rival)
COOM coal dust; refuse
CROM Cruaich (Irish idol)
DOOM (last) judgment; fate; condemn
EDOM Esau's country; Idumaea
FROM out of
GLOM watch; steal
GOOM cultivation method
JOOM cultivation method
KLOM weight
LOOM auk; appear(ance); weaver's frame
PROM dance, ball (college)
ROOM space; apartment; lodge; — and board
STOM prefix: mouth
WHOM pronoun
ZOOM buzz; climb; approach suddenly
ACON boat
AEON age
AGON contest; argument
AMON deity; King of Judah
ANON again; now; soon; author unknown
ATON solar disk
AVON river; Shakespeare home (Stratford)
AXON axis; cell process
AZON bomb
BION physiological individual (morphon)
BOON benefit; convivial
BYON clayey earth
CION plant shoot
COON animal; fur; sly man
CUON wild dog (dhole)
CYON wild dog (dhole)
DION lord in Winter's Tale
DOON tree (varnish resin)
EBON ebony; black
ELON Esau's father-in-law; college (N.C.)
ENON Paris's wife (nymph); John the Baptist site
ETON school, college; collar, jacket; playing fields of —
EXON Exeter man
FAON fawn color
GAON Jewish title
GEON paradise river; Jerusalem spring
GOON thug; strikebreaker
HOON coin; gold pagoda
HUON pine; timber tree
ICON image; statue
IKON image; statue
IRON metal; element; weapon; instrument; club; shackle; press; strong; Age
KAON particle
LAON Fr. city
LEON country, city; Ponce de (explorer)
LION cat; king of beasts; celebrity
LOON diving bird; lout
LYON Fr. city; bean
MAON Nabal's home
MOON satellite; crescent; month; Diana; Cynthia; languish
NEON gas(eous) element; lamp
NOON midday; meal; acme
PAON peacock blue
PEON laborer
PHON loudness measure
PION dig; excavate
POON tree (mastwood)
ROON treasure; darling
SCON teacake
SION purple seaweed; Zion
SOON promptly; willingly
TION suffix
TOON tree (dye); mahogany
UPON prep.: above, against
WOON Burmese governor
ZION Israelites;

heaven
ZOON developed compound animal
ABOO war cry
AROO indeed
EJOO palm; fiber
KROO Liberian Negro
PHOO disgusting!
PROO slow up! (horse call)
SHOO scare away; begone!
SLOO swamp
WHOO exclamation
ALOP lopsided
ASOP sopping
ATOP at the peak
CHOP cut; crack; eat; barter; jaw
CLOP limp; hobble
COOP pen; jail; confine; co-operative
CROP craw; harvest; trim
DROP globule; fall; discard; minim; trap door; die; pendant
ESOP fable writer
FLOP slump down; flap; change; fail(ure); bed; sleep
GLOP look wildly; stare
GOOP nonsense creature
HOOP circle(t); wicket; — skirt
KLOP hard sound
KNOP button; finial; stud
KOOP purchase; bargain
LOOP noose; catch; aerial stunt; Chicago area
PLOP sound of fall
POOP deck; cabin; dickey; exhaust; tire
PROP support; shore; theater equipment
SCOP bard; poet
SHOP store; buy; buying place; talk —; window-
SLOP slush; gush; mash
STOP halt; discontinue; arrest; close; instrument part; period
SWOP trade
TOOP measure
TROP too much: Fr.
WHOP dash; beat; bump
YOOP sobbing sound
SHOQ tree (tanning); chogak
ACOR acidity
ALOR island
AMOR love; Cupid; — patriae
ASOR lyre
BOOR rustic; lout; Boer
CHOR thief; steal (Gypsy)
DOOR portal; entrance; Open — policy
GHOR Dead Sea valley
GOOR sugar; massecuite
IGOR Prince (opera)
KHOR watercourse; gorge
KNOR knot (wood); gnarl
MOOR heath; anchor; Moslem; Moroccan; blacka-
ODOR smell; repute
OGOR early Turkic man
OLOR swan genus; Cygnus
PEOR Bib. mountain
POOR indigent; scanty; feeble; lowgrade; lean; ill; hapless; cod (fish)
SHOR salt lake; Tatar tribe
THOR thunder god (Thursday); Midgard slayer; Odin's son; missile
UTOR to use: Lat.
AMOS prophet
BIOS life: animal, plant
COOS Bay (laurel); Indian
DIOS God: Sp.
DUOS duets
ENOS Seth's son, Adam's grandson (905 years old); taken by God
EPOS epic poetry; events
EROS (god of) love; Cupid; asteroid; Antony's friend
GHOS Chin. dynasty
GROS coin; fabric; weight
LAOS country
LOOS Anita (writer: Gentlemen Prefer Blondes)
NAOS star
PHOS phosphorus
ROOS Ger. painter
TAOS Indian
TEOS Ionian city
THOS jackal genus
ABOT Mishnah
BLOT stain; mar; dry
BOOT shoe; wader; sheath; torture; recruit; compartment; tube; kick; to — (in addition)
BROT bread: Ger.
CLOT mass; coagulate
COOT rail; surf duck; dolt
EYOT islet
FIOT Congo tribe
FLOT lateral ore deposit
FOOT pedal part; base; dance; trip; skip; pay; add
FROT rub; chafe
GROT cave; Bremen coin
HOOT derisive (owl's) cry

ILOT islet; ait; eyot
KHOT farmer; contractor
KNOT tie; loop; hitch; sandpiper; problem; blemish; stud; Gordian —
LOOT plunder; booty
MOOT arguable; ring gauge
PHOT light unit
PIOT magpie
PLOT tract; ground; press (soap); scheme; intrigue
POOT disgusting!
PYOT piebald; chatty
RIOT tumult; success; act, squad
ROOT underlying source; rhizome; base; dig; applaud; plant; eradicate
RYOT Indian peasant
SCOT Celt; Highlander; tax; — free
SHOT missile; pellet; guess; range; marksman; film record; long —; big —
SLOT (cut) opening; bolt; deer; track; — machine
SNOT wick end; blow nose
SOOT powdery carbon smudge
SPOT stain; point, place; fish; small amount; espy
STOT stumble; stutter
SWOT hard work; grind; hit
TOOT sound horn; carousal
TROT jog; gait; race; translation; fishing line
ZOOT — suit; extreme style
ABOU father; deity
CHOU cabbage, darling: Fr.; Chin. dynasty; En Lai (statesman)
MEOU cat's cry; measure
NIOU measure
SHOU Tibetan deer
THOU 2nd pers. pronoun
TIOU Indian (Tonikan)
AKOV measure
AZOV town; sea
ALOW below
AROW in a line
AVOW declare; justify; confess
BLOW move (air); puff, pant; brag; expend; stroke; calamity; disappointment; — up (enlarge)
BROW forehead; high-, low-
CHOW food; dog
CLOW sluice; floodgate
CROW raven; corvine; black; Indian; Jim —; -bar
DHOW Arab. sailboat
ENOW enough
FLOW gush; stream; flux; roll; ebb and —
FROW Dutch woman; cleaver
GLOW shine; incandesce; flush; ardor; wax
GROW expand; sprout; wax; develop
JHOW tamarisk shrub
KNOW understand; recognize; -how; -nothing (party)
LWOW Polish city
MEOW cat's cry; measure
PLOW implement; till; cut; stars
PROW ship's bow; stem; beak
SCOW flat-bottomed boat
SHOW exhibit(ion); reveal; appear(ance); 3rd place; no — (airline term)
SLOW dilatory; tardy; inert; boring; hinder
SNOW ice crystals; white hair; cocaine; — goose; TV spots
STOW pack; hide; hold; skiing resort
SWOW I — (oath)
TROW believe; fishing boat
ABOX braced
ESOX fish (pike, pickerel, muskellunge)
WROX rot
AHOY call; ship —
AMOY island
BHOY gang member; rowdy
BUOY float; sustain; life-; channel marker
CHOY red dye root
CLOY glut; surfeit
OHOY ahoy; call
PLOY make column; frolic; coup
TROY weight system; Ilium, Ilion (Troas); city
AMOZ Isaiah's father
BROZ Josip (Tito)
ARPA harp: It.
CAPA cloak: Sp.
CEPA onion
COPA tree; yaya; landmark
DEPA measure
DOPA chemical (pigment test)
GAPA guided missile
HUPA Athapascan Indian
KAPA cloth(es)
LIPA fat
NAPA leather; wine

region; city; river
NEPA water scorpion; needle bug
NIPA palm; juice; mat; atap
PAPA father; Pope; potato: Sp.; baboon; clay
PIPA toad; measure
PUPA chrysalis; snail; instar
RIPA river bank
RUPA body form (Buddhism)
SAPA grape juice
SUPA P.I. tree; lamp oil
TAPA bark; cloth
YAPA leaf mat
ZIPA Chibcha chief
ZUPA Yugo. district
CAPE cloak; promontory; — Cod, — Horn, — Good Hope
CEPE boletus (edible fungus)
COPE vestment; cover; bend; contend
DOPE drug; information; guess; nitwit
DUPE trick(ed one); copy
GAPE yawn; stare; gap
HIPE wrestler's throw
HOPE trust; expect(ation); wish; -chest
HYPE wrestler's throw; ad
JAPE deride
JUPE skirt
KIPE basket
LOPE go; move; gait
LUPE Samoan fruit pigeon; Velez (actress)
MOPE be dull, listless (person)
NAPE neck back
NUPE Nigeria Negro
OLPE oil flask; pitcher
PAPE bunting (bird)
PIPE tube; flute; cask (measure); -dream; — down
POPE pontiff; Holy Father; — Joan (game); Alexander (poet); bird
RAPE herb; ravish
RIPE mature; fit; tipsy
ROPE cord; cable; noose; bind; chain
RYPE ptarmigan
SUPE stage extra; supercharge
SYPE ooze
TAPE band; tie; Indian; record; red —; ticker —
TIPE rabbit trap
TOPE drink; shark; stupa; orchard
TYPE kind, sort; classi(fy); printer's letter; use typewriter, produce copy
WIPE rub off; beat
XIPE -totec (Aztec god)
YIPE howl; cry
ALPH river (Coleridge: Kubla Khan)
CAPH star, letter
HAPH weight
KAPH letter
KOPH Heb. K, Q, 100
OLPH bullfinch
QOPH Heb. K, Q, 100
SAPH giant (Philistine)
SOPH 2nd-year student
TOPH drum; porous rock
UMPH grunt
ZUPH Samuel's ancestor
AIPI cassava
HAPI bull; Nile (god)
HOPI French beige; Moqui Indian
IMPI armed Kaffirs
KEPI military cap
KOPI N. Z. tree (karaka)
PIPI astringent; mollusk
TIPI wigwam
TOPI antelope; pith hat
TUPI Amazon Indian
CAPO head: It.; crime boss
CIPO liana
GAPO (inundated) forest
HYPO photo solution; needle; injection
MAPO goby (fish)
PEPO pumpkin; squash; melon; cucumber
SAPO soap; toadfish
SIPO liana
TOPO prefix: place
TYPO printing error
CAPP Al (cartoonist, Abner: Dogpatch)
DOPP diamond cup
HUPP call to horse
KAPP measure
KIPP peak (Glacier National Park); gymnastic feat
LAPP N. Scandinavian
REPP silk or wool fabric
TYPP yarn count unit
WAPP rope guide
YAPP (bookbinding) style
ALPS mountains
BAPS dancing master (Dickens)
FIPS Martin Chuzzlewit
GYPS gypsum
HOPS beer
HYPS hypochondria
SEPS snake; lizard
TAPS lights-out signal; bugle call
TOPS most superior
VEPS Finnish tribe (Chud); Dog Star (Isis); Horus
ZIPS Czech

COPT Egypt, Christian
EMPT empty
KEPT retained; lasted
KOPT Copt
RAPT engrossed; rapture
SEPT social unit; screen; seven: Fr.
SOPT Dog Star; Isis
WEPT cried; Jesus —
HAPU clan
KAPU forbidden; taboo
NAPU ruminant
OGPU Soviet police body
TAPU taboo
COPY duplicate; mimic; follow; text
DOPY sluggish
EPPY Euphemia
ESPY behold; detect; meteorologist
GAPY yawning
IMPY impish
PIPY tubular; weepy
ROPY viscous; stringy
TUPY Amazon Indian
TYPY typical

KTQB chess move
WAQF trust fund
KTQR chess move

ABRA narrow pass; river
AERA age; era
AFRA name; union
AGRA comb. form; carpet; city (Taj Mahal site)
AIRA grass
AKRA Negrito; vetch
AMRA plum
ARRA oath
AURA wind; emanation; bird
BARA measure
BERA king of Sodom
BORA north wind; rite
BURA steppe blizzard
CARA dear (one): It.; Indian
CERA prefix: horn, wax
CORA gazelle; Indian; name; Persephone; Demeter's daughter
CURA parish priest: Sp.
DERA suffix: neck types
DORA Mrs. David Copperfield
DURA — mater (spinal membrane)
ERRA — Pater (almanac)
EYRA wild cat
EZRA prophet; OT book
FORA meeting places; courts
GARA coin
GERA city
GORA musical instrument
HARA Jap. statesman
HERA Zeus's sister, wife
HORA book of hours; Israeli dance
HURA bishop's cap; sandbox tree; possumwood
IKRA superior caviar
IRRA war god
JARA palm
JURA rights; mountain range
KARA river
KORA water cock; Hottentot dialect; instrument
LARA Byron poem
LIRA money; lyre; hairlike ridge
LORA thong; strap
LURA brain opening
LYRA glockenspiel; constellation
MARA demon; aborigine; Naomi
MIRA star
MORA default; short syllable; Spartan army; stool
MURA Brazil Indian
MYRA name; ancient city
NERA Tiber tributary
NORA Helmer (Ibsen heroine)
OBRA works: Sp.
OCRA vegetable; gumbo
OKRA vegetable; gumbo
ORRA oddly; laborer
OTRA other: Sp.
PARA coin; weight; river; city (Belem)
PERA Istanbul district
RARA — avis (rare bird)
SARA native
SERA antitoxins; blood parts; whey; evening: It.
SORA bird; rail
SURA Koran section; deva
SYRA Aegean island
TARA fern; goddess; palm
TERA Buddhist monastery
TORA hartebeest; law (of Moses); Pentateuch
VARA measure
VERA tree; measure; name
VIRA Bantu
ZARA city; Judah's son
ZIRA measure
BARB sharp point; fish; dog; mow; pigeon
CURB restrain(t); sidewalk edge; market
FORB non-grassy herb
GARB apparel; array
GERB sheaf; firework
HARB Bedouin
HERB plant; nickname
KERB gutter part
SERB Servian; Yugo(slav)
SORB wild apple; Slav
TURB crowd; clump

VERB action word
CIRC circle; recess; corrie
MARC residue; name; weight
PARC park; oyster farm: Fr.
BARD armor; poet; — of Avon (Shakespeare)
BIRD avian; flyer; fowl; shuttlecock; person; Blue —
BORD -and-pillar (mining)
BURD noble lady
BYRD explorer; Va. statesman
CARD comb; pasteboard; menu; playing —; calling —
CORD string; twine; ribbed fabric; measure (wood)
CURD coagulated milk
DARD language group
FARD face paint; date
FORD crossing shallow; Henry (automobile): Shaks. character
FYRD old English army
GERD Frey's wife
GIRD encircle; clothe; brace
HARD solid; firm; close; severe; difficult
HERD crowd; feed together
JORD Odin's wife; Thor's mother
KURD Sunnite Mohammedan; Iranian
LARD fat; stuff
LORD ruler; Jehovah; Jesus; duck; planet
MARD spoil
NARD plant; ointment
OORD coin (double doit, ¼ stiver)
PARD chum; leopard
SARD carnelian; gem; Sardinian
SURD irrational; mute
VERD green(-leafed)
WARD (safe)guard; parry; district; charge; Artemus (Browne)
WORD term; news; promise; order; phrase
WURD Norn; Urth
WYRD Norn; Urth
YARD 3 feet; grounds; enclosure; spar
AARE river
ACRE field; measure; city
AIRE nobleman; river
BARE expose(d); mere; Indian
BORE pierce; hole; tire; dullard; tidal flow
BURE brown redyellow
BYRE cow house
CARE grief; heed; responsibility; anxiety; foster; relief organization
CERE wax; (wrap in a) waxed cloth; beak part
CORE heart; nucleus; gist
CURE heal; remedy; preserve; priest: Fr.
DARE venture; defy; fish; Virginia (1st Amer. child)
DERE — Mable (Streeter book)
DIRE evil; fatal; extreme
DORE bullion; gold; pike; Paul Gustave (Fr. artist)
EIRE Ireland; Erin
ETRE exist; be: Fr.; raison d'—
EYRE Jane (Brontë heroine); circuit (court)
FARE passenger; price; happen; food; travel
FIRE combustion; ardor; discharge
FORE front; prior; golf cry
GARE wool; station; beware: Fr.
GERE Odin's wolf
GORE stab; blood; triangular insert
GYRE turn; ring; vortex
HARE leporid; rabbit; run
HERE vicinity; present
HIRE engage; rent; wage
HURE head of boar, wolf
INRE concerning; actually
JURE de — (by law)
KERE read(ing substitute)
KORE Persephone; Demeter's daughter; chaos (Maori myth.)
KURE Jap. city; Hawaiian isle
LARE Mid. Eng. lore
LIRE coins; read: Fr.
LORE history; learning
LURE entice; decoy; trumpet
LYRE harp; constellation
MARE blues; sea; moon area; horse; shanks' —
MERE fen; lake; boundary; war club; bare; only; simple; mother: Fr.
MIRE bog; (stick in) mud
MORE greater; additional; St. Thomas

(Utopian)
MURE thrust against wall
NARE Loki's son
NORE Thames estuary
OGRE giant; monster
PARE cut off; peel
PERE father, priest: Fr.; — Goriot (Balzac)
PORE gaze; ponder; opening
PURE unmixed; chaste; sheer; free; Simon —
PYRE funeral pile, fire
QERE read(ing substitute)
RARE underdone; thin; uncommon
RIRE to laugh: Fr.
SERE wither(ed); Negroid
SIRE father; beget; king
SORE painful; vexed; sensitive; deer
SURE safe; firm; certain
TARE vetch; allowance (weight)
TIRE fatigue; bore; wheel covering; rubber; shoe
TORE ripped; geom. surface
TYRE Phoenician city; Sur
VARE weasel
VIRE feathered arrow
WARE merchandise; beware
WERE verb form; prefix: metamorphosed human
WIRE cable; snare
WORE had on (clothes); tired
YARE prompt; ready
YORE ancient (times); long ago
CARF slit; notch
KERF cut; notch
SERF slave; peasant
SURF swell of sea; foam
TURF sod; grassy ground; peat; racing
WARF warp
WERF farmyard
ZARF holder for cup
BERG iceberg; mountain
BORG borough: Dan.
BURG (fortified) town
LURG marine worm
MORG measure
SARG Toni (puppeteer)
BURH (fortified) town
ABRI shelter
AERI prefix: air
AGRI fields
ATRI It. town
AURI prefix: gold, ear
BARI hut; Negro; city
BERI Sudanese (Fulah); -beri (disease)
BIRI cheap cigarette
BORI Lucrezia (singer)
BURI palm (fiber); talipot
CORI Carl, Gerty (Nobel winners)
DARI grain sorghum; carpet
GERI Odin's wolf
GYRI brain ridges
HARI river; Mata (spy)
HURI Abihail's father
KARI gum tree
KERI read(ing substitute)
KIRI paulownia tree; knobkerrie (missile)
KORI bustard; low weaver
KURI Lezhgian tribesman
LARI money; sea birds
LORI lemur; Afr. Negro
LURI Lake Albert Negro
MARI prefix: sea; husband: Fr.; native
NERI Blacks: It.
NORI seaweed food
OMRI king of Israel
PARI weight; prefix: equal
PERI fairy; elf; beauty
PURI Indian yellow
QERI read(ing substitute)
RORI Bantu tribe
SARI Hindu garment
SERI betel; Indian
SHRI glorious; holy; Lakshmi (goddess)
SIRI betel
SORI clusters; spores
TARI coin; goddess
TORI moldings
TURI Pathan tribesman
VARI lemur; prefix: diverse
WERI aweto (caterpillar)
ZORI sandal
BARK peel; tan; cough
CARK trouble
CORK tree; bark; stop(per); brown; Irish city (Lee)
DARK unlighted; wicked; dismal
DIRK dagger; Theodoric
FERK measure
FORK implement (pronged); tuner; place of divergence
HARK listen
JERK grab; twist; spasm; soda man; dullard; beef
KIRK church
KURK church: Scot.
LARK bird; frolic; yellow
LURK lie in wait; skulk
MARK sign; aim; stamp; money;

observe; evangelist; easy —; — time
MIRK dark(ness)
MURK (make) gloomy
NARK informer; tease
PARK (common) grounds; green; deposit; Hyde, Central, etc.
PERK lift up; preen; cocky; percolate
PORK meat; swine; — barrel
SARK Channel island
TURK Mongoloid; Seljuk; Ottoman; Osmanil; horse
WORK labor; mental product; act; operate; function; needlework
YARK yerk
YERK wrench; kick; trump
YORK city; archbishopric; imperial (apple); Sgt. Alvin (WW I)
BIRL revolve; spin
BURL (pick) knot; Ives (actor)
CARL rustic; villain; Charles
CIRL bunting; bird
CURL coil; twist; hair lock
EARL nobleman; count; name
FARL cake (part)
FURL roll up (sail, flag)
GIRL young female; maid; Gibson —; — Friday; — of the Golden West; chorus —
HARL barb; filament
HERL (feather) barb
HURL throw; pitch; rush
JARL Norse chief; earl
JERL boat joint
KARL Charles; — Marx
MARL clayey soil; fertilizer; fiber
MERL blackbird
NURL wood knot; to mill
PURL knitting stitch; beer; murmur; spin; swirl
YARL Norse chief; earl
BARM yeast
BERM (l)edge; road shoulder
CORM bulblike stem (crocus)
DERM prefix, suffix: skin layer
DORM dormitory; sleep
FARM till; land; — out; club
FIRM fixed; solid; company
FORM shape; mold; fashion; school grade
GARM Hel's dog
GERM bud; seed; microbe
HARM hurt; evil; injury
JERM Levantine boat
MARM ma'am; school-
NORM type; standard; integer
PERM elec. unit; hair wave
TERM phrase; word; condition; time, period
TURM troop; company
WARM hot; genial; newly made; heat; — Springs
WORM crawler; maggot; screw; insinuate
WURM glacial period
YARM scream; wail
YIRM fret; whine: Scot., Ir.
BARN storehouse; stable
BERN Swiss capital
BIRN clarinet socket
BORN given birth to; née; quantum physicist
BURN (be on) fire; yearn; waste; speed; brand
CARN stone heap
CERN decide
CORN grain; ear, kernel; callus; whisky; preserve; granulate(d); clavus; banality; red-yellow
DARN mend; interjection
DORN thornback ray
DURN gatepost
EARN gain; win; deserve
FERN seedless plant
FIRN granular snow(field)
GARN yarn; go on
HORN prong; antenna; trumpet; brass wind; cup; Cape —
KARN stone heap
KERN soldier; peasant; grain; type part; Jerome (composer)
KIRN harvest feast
LORN forsaken; bereft
MORN A.M.; dawn; East
NORN demigoddess (Urth, Skuld, Verthandi)
PERN honey buzzard
PIRN reed; bobbin; nose ring
TARN lake
TERN gull; threefold; ship
TORN ripped; damaged
TURN bending; corner; revolve; reverse; change; shape; act; movement
WARN caution; give notice
WORN used (as clothing);

shabby; tired
YARN spun wool; story
YIRN whine; grimace; smirk: Scot., Ir.
AERO go by aircraft
AFRO hairstyle
AGRO prefix: soil
BARO big; prefix: weight
BORO spring rice; Indian (Mirhana); — Budur (temple)
CARO dear (one): It.; Caroline
CERO mackerel
DURO Sp. peso; dollar
EBRO Sp. river
FARO card game; Pharaoh
GARO Assam native
GIRO tour; round; credit system; aircraft (auto-)
GYRO prefix: ring, spiral
HERO protagonist; demigod; — and Leander; Beatrice's cousin
HIRO measure
INRO Jap. receptacle
KARO plant
LERO Dodecanese isle
LORO monk parrot; fish
MARO ship name: Jap.
MERO grouper (fish)
MIRO tree; wood robin
MORO finch; P.I. Moslem tribe
NERO emperor; fiddler; Agrippina's son; Wolfe (Stout)
OKRO plant; stew; soup; gumbo
OTRO other, another: Sp.
PERO but: Sp.
PIRO Tanoan Indian
PORO Sierra Leone secret society
PYRO prefix: fire, fever
SERO prefix: thin; late pupil
TARO rootstock; poi; elephant's ear
TIRO amateur; novice
TORO N.Z. tree
TYRO beginner; novice
XERO prefix: dry
ZERO nothing; cipher; nullity; — hour; Jap. plane
BURP belch; — gun
CARP fish; complain
DORP hamlet; city (So. Afr.)
HARP coin; seal; Lyra; constellation; Irishman; nag
LARP secretion; insect
LERP secretion; insect
TARP canvas; sailor; hat
TERP prehistoric mound
TORP croft; Swed. small farm
TURP turpentine
WARP threads; twist; falsify
ZARP policeman
BARR elephant's cry
BIRR wind force; sound
BURR (prickly) nut, knob; reamer; banyan tree; Aaron (statesman)
CARR pool
CURR to murmur (as owlet)
DARR bird
DORR Rebellion (R.I.)
DURR grain sorghum
HARR hinge
HERR lord, Mister, Sir: Ger.
HURR to snarl
KERR physicist
PARR young fish; skegger; Catherine (Henry VIII wife)
PIRR wind gust; whiz; gull
PORR push; poke; kick
PURR cat's sound
TARR tease
TYRR Odin's son; war god
YARR growl; snarl; herb
YIRR growl; snarl: Scot.
AIRS pretensions; side
BORS king (Lancelot's uncle); Bohort (finder of Holy Grail)
HERS fem., poss. pronoun
HORS out of: Fr.; — d'oeuvres
KERS cress
LARS Porsena (conqueror)
LORS exclamation: lord!
MARS war god; planet
MORS deity; death
OURS possessive pronoun
PARS part: Lat.
SIRS gentlemen
SORS lot: Lat.; divination
AIRT guide; turn
BART man's name
BERT nickname
BORT finder of Holy Grail; impure diamond
BURT butt; gore; dent
CART wagon; transport
CURT short; concise
DART missile; fish; seam; run
DIRT muck; earth; gossip; do one —; — cheap
FORT stronghold; trading post; dun
GIRT encircled;

prepared
HART stag; deer
HURT harm(ed); pain
MART market; nickname
MORT nickname; woman; salmon; the kill; dead: Fr.
PART portion; duty; role; separate; split; go
PERT bold; lively; sandpiper
PORT harbor; haven; wine; blue-red; left side; tune; demeanor
SART Iranian Turk
SERT Sp. painter
SORT type; kind; quantity; classify
SURT Frey's slayer
SYRT quicksand
TART sour; pastry; harlot
TORT wrongful act
VERT green (Her.); veer; convert
WART protuberance; -hog
WERT were; archaic, poetic
WORT plant; (pot)herb
YURT Kirghiz tent
AARU Hades; heaven
BARU tree
ECRU beige; unbleached
FERU bast fiber
GURU teacher
KURU disease
MARU ship name: Jap.
MERU fabled mountain
PERU country
PURU of Arawakan
RURU N.Z. morepork
TORU N.Z. tree
YARU Hades; heaven
MARX Karl (economist)
ADRY thirsty
AERY ethereal; nest
AIRY breezy; light
ARRY cockney worker
ATRY lay to (naut.)
AWRY distorted; perverse(ly)
BURY hide; inter; lose
DORY John (fish); boat
EERY weird; uncanny; timid
EWRY linen storeroom
EYRY bird's nest
FURY rage; avenging spirit; Erinys, Fate, Parca (Atropos)
GARY city, steel center
GORY bloody; murderous
JURY (court) panel; committee; grand, petit —; hung —
LORY parrot; touraco
MARY female name; queen; sister of Lazarus, Martha; Virgin; Lady
MIRY boggy; filthy
NARY not one
OARY oarlike
PORY porous; permeable
RORY O'More (Irish novel)
SARY sorry
SORY vitriolic earth
SPRY nimble; brisk; smart
TORY conservative
VARY alter; differ
VERY true; same; extremely; light signals; flare
WARY watchful
WIRY tough; sinewy
HARZ Ger. mountains
ANSA handle; loop
AUSA Vich (Sp. commune)
BESA coin
BISA antelope
BOSA Arab. drink
CASA house, building: Sp., It.
DISA showiest orchid
DOSA sheik's ritual ride; hatred
ELSA — of Brabant (Lohengrin's bride)
KASA grass
KUSA ceremonial grass
LISA fem. name; nickname
MASA corn meal
MESA flat hill; oakwood color
MUSA banana genus
MYSA buffalo (Kipling)
NASA space-travel agency
OSSA bones; Mt. (Olympus)
PASA raisin
PESA coin
PISA city (leaning tower)
RASA essence; tabula —
ROSA shrub genus; name; sub —; Bonheur (artist)
RUSA deer; sambar; grass; oil
SASA fencer's cry
SUSA Elam city (Esther story)
TESA Indian buzzard
URSA bear; stars: — Major, Minor; Great, Little Bear (Dipper)
VASA ducts; Swedish dynasty
VISA endorse(ment); -vis
XOSA Kaffir
BOSC best pear
DISC disk; record; — jockey
FISC exchequer
FUSC dusky; somber
ANSE handle: Fr.
APSE recess; throne
ASSE caama; fox
BASE bottom; source; home; headquarters; found; diamond corner; ignoble
BISE cold wind;

winter
BOSE test ground by sound
CASE event; fact; record, problem (medical, etc.); legal action; argument; grammar form; container, chest, box; queer phenomenon; inspect
CISE dice term: six
COSE (friendly) chat
DOSE portion; (give) medicine
DUSE incubus; Eleanora (actress)
EASE repose; comfort; moderate; facilitate
ELSE other(wise); besides
ENSE suffix
ERSE Irish; Gaelic
ESSE existence; to be: Lat.
FUSE detonator; melt; unite
HOSE stockings; pipe; drench
HUSE beluga; whale; huchen
IPSE himself: Lat.; — dixit
JOSE Carmen lover
LESE — majesty (disrespect)
LOSE miss; forfeit; fall; forget
LYSE undergo lysis
MESE Greek mus. term
MISE levy; stake; tax; — en scène
MOSE Moses
MUSE meditate; goddess
NASE promontory; nose: Ger.
NOSE proboscis; smeller; scent; search; front; touch; — out (defeat); -dive
OESE bacteriologist's wire
OISE Fr. river.
DUSE Great — (river)
OWSE tan liquor
PISE building material
POSE posture; affectation; baffle; propound
RASE rub; demolish
RESE shake; rush
RISE climb; grow(th); begin; emerge(nce); thrive; retort
ROSE stood up; got up; flower; tree; wood; red; pink; window; Abie's Irish —; Eng. emblem
RUSE trick; deceit; slip
SISE six (dice)
VASE vessel
VISE tool; clamp; endorse
WESE we shall
WISE sage; learned
BASH smash; bruise
BISH aconite; poison
BOSH furnace part; nonsense (nothing: Turk.)
BUSH shrub; thicket; tail
CASH money; exchange; hemlock
COSH snug; happy; math. term
CUSH sorghum; cow; money; Ham's son; country
DASH sprint; smash; small portion
DISH receptacle; serve
FASH rough edges; vex
FISH piscine; angle; probe; search; tin — (torpedo)
GASH (make) incision
GISH Moroccan public land; Lillian, Dorothy (actresses)
GOSH oath; -awful
GUSH flow; spout; be effusive
HASH chop up; mixture; mess
HISH hiss; swish
HUSH quiet; silence; -hush; -puppy; — money
JOSH make fun; banter
KISH powder; basket; measure; Saul's father
KUSH Ham's son; country
LASH (whip) stroke; tie; eye part
LOSH wash leather
LUSH luxurious; drunkard
MASH crush; brew; mixture; hammer; flirt
MESH net; netting; entangle
MUSH meal; hasty pudding; flattery; proceed!
NASH soft; humorist
NESH soft; juicy; dainty
NISH Yugo. city
PASH hurl; smash
PISH reject; nonsense!
POSH slush; elegant
PUSH shove; thrust; strive; button
RASH hasty; careless
RESH Heb. letter, 200; plant
RUSH haste(n); attack; red (mace); cattail
SASH casement; scarf; belt
SISH slushy ice
SOSH jag; drunk; dash
TASH fabric
TOSH bath(tub)
TUSH tooth; Georgian; pshaw!
WASH bathe; laundry; tint
WISH desire; request

ABSI tribe
ASSI holly
DASI concubine
DESI jute; Arnaz
HUSI fine P.I. fiber
JUSI fine P.I. fiber
KASI tile work
LASI tribe
NASI prince; patriarch
NISI unless: Lat.
PASI low-caste Hindu
SESI black-fin snapper
SISI porkfish
SUSI fine cotton
BASK luxuriate; warm
BISK soup; ice cream; red-yellow
BOSK thicket
BUSK stir about; hasten; corset bone; Indian New Year
CASK barrel; measure
CUSK fish; burbot; eel
DESK table; lectern; department
DISK plate; harrow; puck
DUSK twilight; gloom
FISK exchequer; Jim (speculator); tire
HUSK covering (of seed, corn); shell
LISK flank; loin
LUSK lazy (fellow)
MASK disguise; screen; domino
MOSK Moslem temple; Masjid
MUSK odor; aromatic secretion (of deer, ox, etc.)
OMSK Siberian city
PISK nighthawk
RISK peril; hazard; subject of insurance
RUSK bread; biscuit; Dean (statesman)
TASK labor; assignment; take to — (censure)
TOSK Albanian
TUSK long tooth
IISM egoism
KASM measure
ALSO besides
CASO Dodecanese island
COSO open space: Sp.
HUSO beluga; whale; huchen
IPSO — jure, — facto
KOSO tree; cusso; Panamint Indian
MUSO Chibchan Indian
PASO measure
PESO coin; Sp. money
PISO weight
SOSO middling; passably
VASO vase: It.; prefix: blood vessel
YESO plaster of Paris; gypsum
CUSP (crescent) point; tooth edge
GASP pant (eagerly)
HASP clasp
LISP speech defect
RASP grate; file
RISP metal bar
WASP yellow jacket; hornet; fem. flyer: WW II
WISP torch; shred; flock; brush; ignis fatuus
BASS fish; fiber; lowest part; singer; clef (F); musical instrument, viol
BESS nickname; Mrs. Truman
BOSS knob; pad; stud; master; employer
BUSS ship; kiss; calf
CASS treasure; Timberlane (Lewis); Squire (Eliot)
CESS tax; luck
COSS measure
CUSS curse; person
DASS Durga, Ram (twins, Kipling)
DISS reed grass
DOSS bed; sleep; — house
FASS measure
FESS broad band (Her.); confess
FOSS canal; ditch; moat
FUSS tumult; bustle; -budget
HASS throat; embrace
HISS sibilant (of disapproval); goose; serpent; steam sound; Alger (Communist)
HOSS horse; One — Shay (Holmes)
HUSS dogfish; John (religious leader)
JASS card game; Jack
JESS strap on hawk leg
JOSS Chin. deity
KISS touch gently; caress; sweetmeat
KOSS measure
LASS girl; sweetheart
LESS shorter; fewer; inferior; minus
LISS (fairy) fort; release; peace; fleur-de-lis
LOSS forfeiture; bereavement; waste; defeat; — leader
MASS rite, service; bulk; mob, populace; assemble
MESS banquet; meal; muddle; disorder; botch
MISS fail(ure); omit; want; girl; maiden
MOSS bryophyte; lichen; green; rose; Hart (writer)

MUSS mess; rumple; row
NESS cape; promontory; suffix
NUSS nurse
PASS opening; go through; by; license; abstention; condition; amatory gesture
PESS hassock
PUSS cat; lip; face
RISS glaciation stage
ROSS rough bark; seal; island; navigator; Harold (editor)
RUSS Russian; Slav
SASS sauce
SESS soap frame bar
SISS hiss, shame!; girl
SOSS hog call for food
TASS Soviet News Agency
TESS Theresa; Hardy heroine
TOSS throw; fling; change
VISS weight
BAST (woody) fiber; goddess, phloem
BEST most (good); defeat
BUST bosom; statue; failure; break
CAST throw; project; shed; deposit; form; found; actors; (assign) roles
CEST girdle; belt (Venus)
CIST chest; roofed pit
CYST box; abnormal sac
DOST (you) do: archaic
DUST powdered matter; rubbish; clean; dust to —; gold —
EAST direction; Asia; Orient
ERST former; first
FAST not eat; fixed(ly); quick(ly); wild; — and loose
FEST festive gathering
FIST grasp; effort; tightwad
FUST pilaster; smell stale
GEST deed; romance tale, adventure
GIST main point; pith
GUST outburst of wind
HAST contraction: havest
HEST command; precept
HIST call to attention; Indian girl (Cooper)
HOST army; throng; bread as Christ's body; innkeeper; person having guests
JEST joke
JUST fair; virtuous; exact(ly)
KIST chest; installment; measure
LAST block; final(ly); endure; measure
LEST for fear that
LIST strip(e); roll; register; enter; inclination; careen
LOST not won; misplaced; confused; ruined; — cause
LUST sensual desire
MAST pole; brown; nuts
MIST dim; haze; gray
MOST greatest; almost
MUST be obliged to; necessity; new wine; stum; staleness; frenzy
MYST Greek priest
NAST cartoonist
NEST (make a) home
OAST kiln
OUST eject; discharge
PAST tense; ago; after
PEST plague; insect; nuisance
PIST attention!; track
POST pillar; advertise; mil. station; mail; inform; record
REST pause; stop; peace; prop; stay; rely; mus. sign; remainder; set; found
RIST engrave; scratch
RUST oxidize; corrode; inaction; reddish-brown
SIST stay; delay; summon
TEST shell; cupel; examination; try
VAST huge (space)
VEST waistcoat; clothe; empower
WAST were
WEST wind; painter, author; occident; go —; Mae —
WIST know; knew; measure
ZEST orange peel; relish; gusto
ANSU Korean apricot
APSU primordial chaos
AUSU tree
GESU Jesus: It.
JESU name: Jesus
MASU salmon
NOSU Lolo; Chin. Caucasian
SUSU blind dolphin; Congo
TASU measure

VASU deity (Vishnu); nephew
BUSY (keep) active; in use
CASY ex-preacher (Steinbeck)
COSY snug; teapot cover
EASY simple; calm; soft; — Street
JOSY nickname
MOSY moldy; rotten
NOSY fragment; prying
POSY flower; nosegay; poem
ROSY blushing; optimistic
SUSY name: Susan; Susanna
UPSY -daisy

ACTA deeds; records
AETA Negrito; native
ALTA tall: Sp.
ANTA porch; nut; tapir; goddess; pier; theater group
ARTA Ionian gulf
ASTA measure; dog
ATTA soul; native; flour; fruit; ant
BATA child; servant
BETA Greek B, 2; star; ray
BOTA measure
CATA down; prefix: away
COTA P.I. fort
DATA facts
DITA tree; bark; upas
ESTA this: Sp.
ETTA Henrietta; Harriet
FATA — Morgana (fairy, mirage)
GATA nurse shark
GETA Jap. wooden clogs
GITA Bhagavad —; Indian scriptures (yoga)
IOTA Greek I, 10; jot
JOTA Sp. peasant dance
KETA dog salmon
KOTA P. I. fort; Dravidian language
LATA jumping disease
LOTA water pot; burbot genus
MATA Hari (spy)
META goal post; river
MOTA Moslem marriage
MUTA change; Moslem marriage
NATA Nana's hero
NOTA insect backs; — bene (N.B.)
OCTA prefix: eight
PATA painting; turban; sword
PITA fiber; flax; hemp; brocket (deer)
RATA tree; chestnut; rate; pro —
RITA cosmic order (Vedic); Rio —; fem. name
ROTA roster; curia tribunal; round; hurdy-gurdy
RUTA herb genus; rue
SETA caterpillar's hair; spine
SITA Ramachandra's wife (Sanskrit Ramayana)
TOTA grivet monkey
VETA mountain sickness
VITA life: Lat.
VOTA Roman festivals
WETA wingless locust
YETA Jap. outcast
ZETA Greek Z, 7
ZITA Austrian empress

ALTE old: Ger.; Adenauer
ANTE stake; pay; before; -bellum
AUTE tree
BATE diminish; tanner's bath; restrain
BETE beast, silly: Fr.; — noire
BITE cut; pierce; grip; eat (into); sting; respond; snack
BOTE house repair; amends
BUTE island; Scot. county; parson (Thackeray)
CATE delicacy
CETE marine mammals
CITE summon; quote
COTE birdhouse; sheep shed; coast: Fr. (d'Or; d'Azur)
CUTE clever; attractive
CYTE prefix: hollow vessel
DATE fruit; tree; brown; (make) appointment
DITE mite; indict
DOTE love to excess; drivel; timber rot
ENTE grafted (Her.); being: Sp.
ESTE It. family; this: Sp.
ETTE suffix: fem.
FATE destiny (goddess); end; kismet
FETE festival; regale
FUTE Eskimo curlew
GATE entrance; pass; judgment; money
GITE shelter: Fr.; mad
HATE detest; aversion
JETE ballet jump
JUTE fiber plant; Corchorus; Low German
KATE bird; Shaks. shrew; Greenaway
KITE hawk; rogue; flying toy; banking fraud
LATE dead; tardy
LETE quadrille set
LITE suffix: mineral, rock
LOTE lotus (poetic);

weights
LUTE cement; bricklayer's tool; Apollo's musical instrument; jar ring
MATE companion; match; tea; check-
METE measure; allot
MITE arachnid; parasite; small (coin)
MOTE speck; particle
MUTE silent; dumb; muffle
NATE born
NETE Greek mus. term
NOTE sign; tone; fame; head; memo; IOU; record; see
OSTE prefix: bone
PATE head; paste
PETE strongbox; Peter
POTE poker; stick
RATE censure; ratio; charge; estimate; rank; tax
RETE network
RITE ceremony; liturgy
ROTE surf noise; routine
RUTE measure
SATE gratify; glut
SITE location; scene
TATE wool; hair lock
TETE head: Fr.; — à tête; hairdo
TOTE carry; haul; total
TUTE tutor
VITE quick, lively: Fr.
VOTE ballot; suffrage; voice; enact; propose; Ingrian Finn
WATE sea demon
WOTE Ingrian Finn
YATE eucalyptus
YITE bird (yellowhammer)
ACTH hormone medicine
BATH tub; measure; spa; order
BETH Heb. B, 2; Alcott heroine (Little Women)
BOTH the two
DOTH does
ESTH Balt; Estonian (Tallinn man)
GATH Philistine city
GOTH Teuton (Theodoric, Alaric); barbarian; Ostro-; Visi-
HATH contraction: haveth
HETH son of Canaan; Hittite ancestor
HOTH blind god (Balder slayer)
JETH Hindu month
KATH astringent
KITH acquaintance; — and kin
LATH strip; slat
LITH prefix, suffix: stone
LOTH averse; reluctant
MATH mowing; monastery; school course
MOTH lepidopterous insect; -ball; -eaten; gypsy —; page (Shaks.)
MUTH measure
MYTH (religious) legend; fiction
NATH star
OATH appeal; pledge; vow; curse
PATH track; route
PITH marrow; kernel; gist
RATH chariot; fort; temple; early; mome-
RUTH pity; grief; name; OT book, heroine (Moabitess); wife of Boaz
SETH banker; Adam's son; Osiris' evil brother
TATH dung
TETH Heb. T, 9
URTH Norn; Wyrd (with Verthandi, Skuld); Weird Sister
VOTH Ingrian Finn
WITH prep.: including, and
AKTI peninsula
ANTI opposed; prefix: against; Indian
ASTI city; — spumante
BITI blackwood
GUTI Sumer settler; Kurd
HATI heart
HOTI cause; reason
INTI Incas' deified sun; sun god
JATI caste
JITI Rajmahal creeper
JOTI astrologer; astronomer
KATI weight
LETI island off Timor
LITI medieval peasants
LOTI Pierre (writer: Viaud)
MOTI elephant (Kipling)
NETI eulalia (thatch grass)
RATI weight
ROTI roasted: Fr.
SATI queen of the gods
SETI river; pharaoh
TITI monkey; tree; petrel
VITI East African
YATI ascetic; devotee
YETI abominable snowman
ZATI bonnet monkey
ROTL Afr. weight
ACTO action: Sp.
ALTO hill: Sp.; voice
ARTO prefix: bread
AUTO prefix: same, self; drama: Sp.; (ride in) car
BITO tree; poison; oil
BOTO Indian; Voto
BUTO serpent god-

dess; Leto
CATO the Censor (Roman statesman); foe of Carthage
CETO prefix: whale
COTO bark; stomachic
DATO tribal chief
DOTO sea slug genus
ECTO prefix: outside
ENTO prefix: inner
INTO penetrating; toward
JATO jet-assisted take-off
KOTO Jap. zither
LETO mother of Apollo, Artemis
LOTO pot; game
MOTO movement: It.; con —
NATO international (Western) alliance; treaty organization
NITO climbing fern
OCTO prefix: eight
ONTO upon; wise to
OTTO name; palindrome; perfume; Ger. ruler
PATO Muscovy duck
PETO wahoo (fish); Henry IV figure
PITO fiber; flax; hemp; brocket (deer)
ROTO ragged: Sp.; printing
SITO prefix: grain
SOTO Hernando de (explorer)
TITO Yugo. leader (Broz)
TOTO baby (animal); all
TYTO barn owl; Strix; Aluco
UNTO to; for; toward
VETO prohibit(ion); no
VOTO So. Amer. Indian
NATR weight
ACTS NT book
ARTS skills; sciences; fine —; — and crafts
CATS — cradle
CITS citizens; mufti
EATS food; consumes
LOTS tracts; quantities; very much; chances
RATS bah!
SOTS yeast
BATT matted mass
BITT naut. fastener
BOTT clay plug; fly larva
BUTT cask; mound; target; ram; hinge; jut; halibut
DITT close up; obstruct
GETT bill of divorce
HATT measure
HETT Hittite ancestor
LETT Latvian, Balt (Riga man)
MATT lusterless
MITT glove, hand
MOTT clump of trees; James, Lucretia (abolitionists)
MUTT cur; stupid one; — and Jeff
NETT undeductible
NOTT Norse night (Dag)
PATT stalemate(d)
PITT statesman (Commoner, Chatham); diamond
POTT paper size; editor (Dickens)
PUTT golf stroke
SETT tool; paving stone
TATT knot lace
WATT inventor, elec. unit (volt-ampere); hare
ACTU act: Lat.
AITU god; demon
ANTU rat poison
ATTU Aleut. Island
DATU tribal chief
DETU eclipse demon (Rahu)
LATU gold coins
MITU curassow; bird
PATU weapon
TATU Indian; armadillo; tattoo
TUTU N.Z. shrub; poison; ballet skirt
YUTU Peru tinamou; bird
ARTY artistic
CITY urban place
COTY Fr. statesman; cosmetics
DOTY discolored by rot
DUTY obligation; task; tax
KATY Catherine; -did
MATY (assistant) servant
MITY parasite-infested
OATY full of oats
PITY sympathy; mercy
TOTY low-caste worker
TYTY farmer of God's Little Acre
BATZ coin
LITZ braided wire
METZ city, former fort
UNTZ weight
AGUA water; toad
AKUA deity
AQUA water; green-blue
ATUA demon
ERUA mother goddess
SHUA Abraham's son
SKUA bird; great —; jaeger
ULUA cavalla; fish; caranx
BLUB swell; puff out
CHUB fallfish; dace; chevin
CLUB bat; beat; society; suit (cards)
DAUB plaster; besmear
DOUB Bermuda grass
DRUB (beat with) stick

FLUB blunder; botch
GAUB persimmon (astringent)
GLUB make gulping sound
GRUB larva; food; dig(ger)
KNUB waste silk
ROUB measure
SLUB twisted wool roll
SNUB rebuke; slight; stumpy
STUB stump; pen-point; short, stocky; extirpate; ticket part; bump
DOUC variegated monkey
ERUC cordage fiber
BAUD speed unit
BOUD malt weevil
CHUD Mongols; Vepse; Vote; Tavastian
DAUD dad
EHUD judge of Israel
FEUD strife; vendetta; fee
FOUD district magistrate
GAUD ornament; bead
LAUD praise
LEUD feudal tenant
LOUD noisy; showy; vulgar
MAUD plaid; rug; name; Muller; Whittier, Tennyson heroine
PHUD bullet sound; exclamation
PUUD weight
ROUD fish
SAUD Ibn (king)
SCUD run fast; wind-driven clouds; skim; flea
SOUD pay
SPUD scrape(r); potato; dig
STUD breeding stock; knob; stump; dot; poker
SYUD Moslem prince; title
THUD dull sound; blow
AGUE fever
BLUE color; ocean; sky; sailor; sad; -blood; puritanical
CLUE hint; guide; thread
COUE psychotherapist ("Day by day . . .")
FLUE net; lint; barb; air passage; pipe
GAUE German regions
GLUE adhesive; stick
GRUE shiver; shudder
MOUE pout; grimace: Fr.
NEUE new
NIUE Savage Island language
ROUE dissolute man; rake
SHUE Tibetan deer
SLUE swamp; twist; lot
TRUE factual; loyal; align
NEUF nine, new: Fr.
OEUF egg: Fr.
POUF puff; ottoman; bang!
SAUF except, safe: Fr.; — conduit
SOUF sigh
CHUG pull; fish; (move with) vibration
DRUG medicine; dope; — on the market; — addict
FRUG dance
GLUG sound of liquids
JOUG iron collar; pillory
PLUG stop(per); plod; shoot; spark —; horse; praise
SCUG squirrel: Brit.
SLUG snail; idle; metal spacer; small drink; bullet; strike
SMUG tidy; neat; priggish
SNUG cozy; trim; Shaks. character
THUG assassin; hoodlum
TOUG horsetail standard
UTUG horsetail standard
BRUH pig-tailed macaque
ARUI sheep
EQUI prefix: equal, same
ETUI (vanity) case; box
ISUI Asher's son
MAUI Polynesian hero
PFUI exclamation
CAUK (secure by a) tenon
DAUK relay post
LAUK exclamation
SAUK Indian; Mont. river
SOUK Moslem market
TRUK islands (Carolines)
UNUK star; — al Hay
WAUK wake: Scot.
AOUL Nepalese
AZUL blue: Sp.
BAUL mendicant
CAUL basket; covering membrane
DEUL Hindu temple
ELUL month
FOUL rotten; poor; illegal; invalid
GAUL Celt, Frenchman; France
GOUL monster; grave robber
HAUL drag; shift; loot
MAUL hammer; bruise; mangle
PAUL click; detent; Apostle; Bunyan; Revere; pope
PEUL Fulah (Sudanese)
POUL Russ. coin

SAUL tree; king (son of Kish); — of Tarsus (Paul)
SHUL synagogue
SOUL spirit; inspirer; forces; psyche; person
WAUL wail
AHUM humming
ALUM emetic; astringent; styptic
ARUM herb; starch
ATUM sun god (Tem)
BAUM Vicki (novelist); Oz creator; tree: Ger.; — marten
CHUM friend; scrap fish
CLUM clutch roughly
DEUM Te — (hymn)
DOUM palm
DRUM spool; instrument: tympanum; beat
GAUM attention
GEUM plant (astringent)
GLUM moody; sullen
GRUM morose; guttural
JHUM cultivation method
MEUM carrotlike herb, spicknel; mine: Lat.
ODUM tree (iroko)
OGUM Irish alphabet
OVUM germ cell; egg
PLUM fruit (damson; greengage); tree; raisin; choice job
RHUM alcoholic drink
SAUM weight
SCUM dross; refuse; rabble
SIUM water parsnip
SLUM dilapidated district
STUM grape juice, must; renew wine
SUUM hum; — cuique
SWUM swim participle
TUUM thine: Lat.
UTUM small owl
AMUN deity
AZUN Hananiah's father
CHUN Chin. pottery
DAUN stage (geol. period)
DRUN road (Gypsy)
FAUN deity; satyr
IDUN Bragl's wife (Norse)
JAUN palanquin
KAUN resthouse; lord; title
LAUN ceramic sieve
LOUN loon; lout
MAUN must
NOUN speech part; name; substantive
PAUN betel leaf
SHUN avoid; abstain (from)
SKUN skinned
SPUN twisted; whirled
STUN stupefy; daze
TAUN measure
TSUN measure (1/10 ch'ih)
USUN ancient North Chinese
UZUN ancient North Chinese
WHUN gorse; restharrow
YGUN antisub gun
BLUP air bubble sound
CAUP tribute: Scot.
COUP blow; master stroke
DOUP weaver's thread
GAUP gape
KEUP measure
LOUP half mask; Skidi Indian; river; fish
NOUP steep promontory
PAUP walk idly
PLUP sound of (soft) fall
ROUP a cold; hoarseness
SCUP pan fish; porgy
SNUP snap up cheaply
SOUP broth; stew; — and fish; duck —; step (up); explosive; fog
TOUP Malay lugger
YAUP yap; yawn
YOUP yelp; scream; yawn
ALUR Negro
AMUR river
ASUR war god
AZUR Côte d'— (Riviera); Hananiah's father
BAUR joke
BIUR Heb. commentary
BLUR obscure; stain
CHUR Swiss canton
DAUR Manchu
DOUR sullen, gloomy
EBUR ivory: Lat.
FOUR number; card; boat
GAUR wild cattle
GOUR cattle; koulan (onager)
HOUR time unit; H- or zero —
JOUR day: Fr.
KNUR gnarl; knot; wood ball
LOUR frown; lower; scowl
PEUR fear: Fr.
POUR (make) flow; for: Fr.; emit; — le mérite
SAUR prefix, suffix: lizard
SCUR horn tissue
SLUR pass over; mumble; defame; stigma; glide (mark)
SMUR mist; cloud
SNUR snort
SOUR acid(ify); tart; disagreeable
SPUR point; good; kick; otter track; ridge
TAUR Taurus (bull)
TOUR trip; circuit; — de force
YOUR poss. pronoun
ACUS pin
ANUS end of alimentary canal
APUS bird; constel-

lation
AVUS grandfather: Lat.
COUS cowlike
CRUS leglike part; shank
DEUS god: Lat.; — ex machina
ESUS Gaulish god (Mars)
GAUS region: Ger.
GRUS constellation (Crane)
ILUS son of Tros; Priam's grandfather
IOUS promissory notes; suffix
IRUS Odyssey beggar
NOUS mind; reason; wit; we: Fr.
OBUS howitzer shell
ONUS burden; duty
OPUS work
OTUS giant slain by Apollo
PIUS Pope: X (St.; Sarto); XI (Ratti); XII (Pacelli)
PLUS and; more; extra; — fours
POUS measure
REUS defendant: Lat.
RHUS sumac genus
SOUS coins; under: Fr.
THUS In this way; hence
URUS wild ox
USUS user, use: Lat.
ZEUS chief god; Jupiter; Hera's husband; son of Cronus, Rhea
ABUT touch
AKUT ape man (Burroughs)
BHUT Dravidian ghost
BLUT blood: Ger.
BOUT contest; attack
BRUT dry: Fr.; Brit. king (New Troy, London)
CHUT nonsense!
CNUT king; son of Magnus
FAUT comme il — (proper): Fr.
GAUT range; pass; river bank stairs
GLUT safe; surfeit; oversupply; wedge
GOUT drop; disease (arthritis); taste: Fr.
HAUT high: Fr.; — monde
KNUT king; son of Magnus
LOUT boor; bumpkin; dolt
NAUT sea mile
PHUT (bullet) sound; OT people
POUT sulk(iness); fish
PRUT exclamation; river
ROUT defeat; tumult; mob; the brant; snare
SCUT rabbit's tail; fur
SHUT close; refine
SLUT slattern; harlot
SMUT soot; coal dust; plant disease; obscenity
SPUT boiler plate
STUT horsefly
TAUT snug; tense
TOUT tip(ster); praise; all: Fr.; — à fait; — de suite
BOUW measure
DAUW zebra
CRUX (Southern) Cross; crucial point
DEUX two: Fr.
EAUX waters: Fr.
FLUX flow; change; melt
JEUX cards, hands, games: Fr.
ROUX (soup, sauce) thickener; physician
VAUX village; fort (Verdun battle)
GHUZ Turkish invader
JEUZ chief Benjamite
ALVA duke; city; Thomas — Edison
CAVA pepper shrub, root; gum resin; vein
CIVA Hindu deity
DEVA deity (Indra); demon
DIVA prima donna; blue
HOVA Madagascar native; Malagasy
JAVA coffee; hood; (Indonesian) Sunda isles; — man (Pithecanthropus)
JIVA life energy
JOVA Opata; Pimian Indian
KAVA pepper shrub, root; gum resin; vein
KIVA ceremonial chamber
LAVA fluid rock; obsidian's source; red
NEVA river (Leningrad)
NOVA star: new, temporary
PEVA Peru Indian
RIVA shore: It.
SAVA Yugo. river
SIVA Hindu deity; cosmic dancer (Nataraja)
ULVA sea lettuce; laver
URVA mongoose
VIVA salute (long live); — voce (spoken aloud)
XOVA Opata; Pimian Indian
YAVA weight
NKVD Soviet secret police
BAVE double silk thread
CAVE cavern; — in (collapse); — canem (beware

of dog)
CIVE chive garlic
COVE bay; recess; pass; chap; Gypsy
DAVE David
DIVE plunge; duck; low resort; — bomb(er)
DOVE pigeon; blue, gray; Columba; plunged
EAVE roof edge
FIVE number; basketball team; card
GAVE donated
GIVE bestow; yield; grant
GYVE fetter; shackle
HAVE possess; aux. verb; must; deceive
HIVE bees' swarm, house
HOVE ground ivy; raised
JAVE Jehovah
JIVE dialect (dance, jazz)
JOVE god; Jupiter; Zeus
KIVE brewer's vat
LAVE pour; bathe
LIVE exist; continue; vital; alert
LOVE affection; like; Cupid; Eros; zero
MOVE impel; shift; excite; act; depart(ure); play
NAVE hub; church part
NEVE snow; firn
NOVE nine: It.
PAVE cover firmly; — the way; jewel setting
RAVE rant, rage; enthusiasm; rod
REVE (muse in) dream: Fr.
RIVE tear; split; — droite (right bank), — gauche (left bank)
ROVE wander; ramble; draw through an eye
SAVE rescue; avoid; lay by; but; — face
SEVE wine delicacy: Fr.
SIVE sickle; knife
TAVE Octavia
VIVE — le roi!; long live!: Fr.
WAVE billow; swell; undulation, flutter; signal; — length; navy woman
WEVE contraction
WIVE marry; act as wife
WOVE entwined; spun
IHVH God; Tetragrammaton
JHVH Jehovah; God; Tetragrammaton
YHVH God; Yahveh; Tetragrammaton
DEVI goddess, Siva's wife (Shakti); title: Mrs., Lady
DIVI divine ones
FAVI titles; flagstones
HEVI apple (tree)
KAVI Java language
LEVI Jacob's, Leah's son; tribe
RAVI tribesman
FAVN measure
LEVO prefix: left
PAVO peacock; constellation
RIVO stream: It.
VIVO spirited
RSVP please reply: Fr.
REVS rotations per minute
KIVU tsetse fly
BEVY company; flock
CAVY rodent; guinea pig; stray animal(s)
CUVY sea girdles; kelp
DAVY David; lamp; affidavit; Jones' locker
ENVY covet; grudge; 7th deadly sin
LEVY assess; seize; tax
LIVY Roman historian; Titus Livius
NAVY fleet; blue; tobacco; — yard
PAVY peach
PEVY lumberman's hook
TAVY Octavia
TIVY huntsman's cry
WAVY fluctuating; undulating
BIWA loquat
DEWA deity (Indra); demon
IOWA state; Indian
KAWA pepper shrub, root; gum resin; vein
LOWA bush quail
PAWA weight
TAWA tree
TEWA N.M. Indian
WAWA gibbon
BAWD procuress
DOWD slovenly woman
GAWD ornament; bead
LEWD lecherous; obscene
HOWE hollow; empty; Elias (inventor); Julia Ward (Battle Hymn); Brit. general, admiral
POWE weigh
JHWH Jahweh; God; Tetragrammaton
YHWH God; Yahweh; Tetragrammaton
IIWI bird (mamo)
KAWI Java language
KIWI flightless bird; apteryx; non-

flyer
TUWI P.I. dyewood tree
BOWK steep; soak in lime
CAWK bird's cry; mineral
DAWK relay transport; mail
GAWK lout; stare
GOWK simpleton; fool
HAWK bird; predator; peddle; mortar-board
LAWK surprise!
MAWK maggot
SAWK measure
BAWL cry; howl; — out (chide)
BOWL basin; dish; (roll) ball
CAWL basket
COWL hood; auto body front
DOWL feathery down
FOWL poultry; cock; hen
GOWL gad; defile; howl; monster
HOWL (distress) cry; wail
JOWL jaw; cheek; wattle; gambler (Dickens)
MEWL whimper; miaou
PAWL click; detent; tent
YAWL (sail)boat
YOWL howl(ing); yell
DAWM coin
HAWM loiter
BAWN mud enclosure; white
DAWN daybreak; Eos; Aurora; red
DOWN to below; reduce; defeat; feathers; eider-; dejected
FAWN deer; cringe; toady; brown
GAWN gallon; tub
GOWN dress; toga; robe
HEWN felled; squared
KAWN resthouse; lord; title
LAWN fabric; grass

plot; bishopric
LOWN calm; quiet; dolt
MOWN cut down; trimmed
PAWN chessman; pledge
SAWN sawed; cut
SEWN stitched
SOWN scattered; seeded
TAWN tawny
TOWN city; hamlet; — hall; man about —
YAWN open wide; gape; chasm
ATWO asunder
VTWO robot bomb
GAWP gape; simpleton
YAWP yap; yawn
JEWS -harp
LAWS rules; principles
MEWS (royal) stables
NEWS intelligence; tidings
YAWS skin disease
NEWT salamander; eft
NOWT neat cattle; dolt
DEWY moist; refreshing
JAWY talkative
LOWY banlieue; suburb
NOWY having curvature
ROWY streaked
TOWY like flax fibers

BIXA tree genus; achiote
COXA hip (joint)
DOXA religious stanzas
LOXA pale bark: quinine
MOXA cautery wormwood
MYXA plum (geiger) tree; sebesten
NOXA harmful thing
TOXA sponge spicule
COXE Capt. (Scott)
FIXE prix —
LUXE elegance; de —

MIXE Mexican Indian
SAXE Saxony; blue
CAXI snapper (fish)
DIXI I have spoken: Lat.
TAXI (ride a) cab; prefix: arrangement
CIXO Ecuador Indian
MOXO Arawakan Indian
MYXO slime mold
TAXO prefix: arrangement
NEXT nearest; following
SEXT canonical hour (noon); organ stop; sixth
TEXT (literary) substance; topic; Scripture passage; type
BOXY boxlike; squarish
BUXY paymaster
DIXY camp pot
DOXY doctrine; hussy
FOXY wily; brown; rank; sour
MIXY confusedly mixed
NIXY undeliverable mail
PIXY impish sprite
PUXY ill-tempered
ROXY name: Roxana; Rothafel (impresario); theater
SEXY sexually appealing
WAXY viscid; pliable

ALYA star
ARYA Caucasian
BAYA weaverbird; Bantu
CUYA hardwood tree
GOYA Sp. painter; — red
HAYA arrow poison
HOYA honey plant (milkweed)
MAYA weaverbird; (Mexican) Indian; magic; Buddha's mother

PUYA pineapple genus
RAYA broadbill
SAYA outer skirt
SOYA bean; dill; fennel
YAYA copa, lance-wood (tree)
DAYE printer (Bay Psalm Book)
EMYD terrapin
FUYE Jap. flute
SKYE Isle; dog, terrier
STYE eyelid swelling
KIYI herring; cisco; yelp
ACYL acid part
AMYL starch; alcohol
IDYL pastoral poem
NOYL fiber knot
ODYL alleged force
OXYL oxygen radical
TEYL linden; lime tree
CLYM — of the Clough (archer outlaw)
ETYM Moabites; giants; abbr.: word sources
ONYM technical name (biol.)
COYN corner(stone)
GWYN Llud's son; deity
LLYN lake; pool
BUYO betel leaf; nut
CAYO island, reef: Sp.
COYO avocado; chinin
ENYO war goddess
IDYO Niger delta Negro
KAYO knock out
MAYO Indian; physicians, clinic (Rochester)
MOYO measure
WHYO gangster; footpad
TRYP parasite in blood (sleeping sickness, nagana, surra)
SKYR sour curdled milk
ALYS name: Alice
ATYS god; Cybele's lover
DAYS by day
EMYS tortoise
ITYS Tereus' son
KEYS House of — (Isle of Man legislature); cays: Florida —
WAYS wise; — and means
SKYT move fast; dart; slip
VAYU wind god
CEYX Halcyone's husband
ERYX sand snake
ONYX cameo stone; quartz; gem
ORYX antelope; gemsbok
PNYX Greek voting site
STYX Hades river; nymph: daughter of Oceanus, Tethys
HAYZ zodiacal situation
BOZA Arab. drink
CAZA Turkish district
DAZA Negro-Berber
GAZA Israel (Philistine) seaport; Mozambique district; eyeless in — (Samson)
GIZA site: pyramids, Sphinx
ITZA Mayan Indian
JUZA star
MOZA manservant
ONZA Sp. ounce (1/16 libra); coin
TIZA ulexite mineral
TUZA pocket gopher
ZAZA opera (Leoncavallo)
ZIZA Rehoboam's son
ZUZA weight
ADZE tool
BIZE cold wind; winter
COZE (friendly) chat
DAZE stupefy; mica
DOZE drowse; timber rot
FAZE disturb
FUZE detonator; melt; unite
GAZE stare; wonder
GUZE red roundel (Her.)
HAZE mist; drizzle; harass
LAZE idle(ness); tribesman
MAZE labyrinth; daze; perplex
NAZE promontory
OOZE exude; slime; liquor
RAZE scrape; demolish
SIZE bulk; quality; glue; filler; — up
WNZE weight
BUZI Ezekiel's father
CAZI Moslem judge
GAZI warrior; title
KAZI Moslem judge
LAZI tribesman
NAZI fascist; Hitlerite
NOZI of Yanan tribe
BOZO fellow
IDZO Niger delta Negro
KOZO paper mulberry
LAZO lasso
MAZO de la Roche (novelist: Jaina)
MOZO manservant: Sp.
NUZO Chibchan Indian
ORZO pasta
ANZU apricot
ANZU tree
ENZU moon god (Sin)
WUZU Moslem ablution
CAZY Moslem judge
COZY snug; teapot cover
DAZY confused
DOZY drowsy; decayed; doty
GAZY gaping
HAZY dim; obscure
JOZY Josepha; Josephine
KAZY Moslem judge
LAZY idle
MAZY perplexing

NIZY fool
OOZY muddy; slimy
SIZY viscous
SUZY name: Susanna
BIZZ buzz
BUZZ hum; fly low
(over); — bomb (V1, V2)
FIZZ hissing sound; drink
FUZZ fine fibers; police
HUZZ buzz; murmur
JAZZ dance; music; banter
RAZZ chaff; ridicule
SIZZ hiss(ing sound)
ZIZZ whirring sound

FOUR-LETTER WORDS A--A to Z--Z

ABBA father; title
ABIA Samuel's son
ABRA narrow pass; river
ACCA fabric
ACTA deeds; records
ADDA god; river; skink
AERA age; era
AETA Negrito; native
AFFA from off
AFRA name; union
AGHA officer; title
AGLA acrostic
AGRA comb. form; carpet; city (Taj Mahal site)
AGUA water; toad
AIDA opera; Radames' lover
AIEA town
AIRA grass
AKHA tribe; Burmese; Kaw
AKIA shrub (fish poison)
AKKA Pygmy
AKRA Negrito; vetch
AKUA deity
ALBA garb; poem; brain matter; duke
ALCA auk
ALDA soprano; hamlet; Sp.
ALEA Athena (war goddess)
ALFA grass
ALGA plant
ALIA other: Lat.
ALLA by: It.
ALMA girl; silk; river; city
ALTA tall: Sp.
ALVA duke; city; Thomas — Edison
ALYA star
AMBA mountain
AMGA Siberian river
AMIA fish
AMLA tree
AMMA abbess; god
AMRA plum
ANBA title
ANDA tree
ANNA coin; bird; name; — Christie (O'Neill); — Karenina (Tolstoi)
ANOA ox
ANSA handle; loop
ANTA porch; nut; tapir; goddess; pier; theater group
APIA port (Samoa)
AQUA water; green-blue
ARBA cart
ARCA box; dish; shell
AREA zone, region; scope; tract
ARIA tune; city (Herat)
ARNA buffalo
AROA Venezuela copper center
ARPA harp: It.
ARRA oath
ARTA Ionian gulf
ARYA Caucasian
ASEA at sea
ASHA tribe
ASIA continent; Orient; East
ASTA measure; dog
ATKA fish; Aleut. Island
ATMA soul
ATTA soul; native; flour; fruit; ant
ATUA demon
AUCA Indian
AULA hall; tree; brain part
AURA wind; emanation; bird
AUSA Vich (Sp. commune)
AZHA star
BABA nurse; title; cake
BAGA turnip
BAIA state; city; resort; bay
BAKA devil
BALA geol. epoch
BANA Titan
BARA measure
BATA child; servant
BAYA weaverbird; Bantu
BEGA measure
BEJA Nile nomad
BEKA weight
BELA jasmine; Benjamin's 1st son; Hungarian king
BEMA platform; altar; measure
BENA grass (vetiver)
BERA king of Sodom
BESA coin
BETA Greek B, 2; star; ray

BIGA two-horse chariot
BIJA kino tree
BINA Hindu guitar
BISA antelope
BIWA loquat
BIXA tree genus; achiote
BLAA bunk
BLEA bleak; livid
BOBA chicken snake
BOCA harbor mouth: Sp.
BOGA basslike fish
BOLA missile; majagua (tree)
BOMA Afr. stockade; post
BONA good: Lat.; — fide
BORA north wind; rite
BOSA Arab. drink
BOTA measure
BOZA Arab. drink
BREA resin; tree; asphalt
BUBA tropical sore
BUDA It. millet
BUKA dried leaves
BUNA synthetic rubber
BURA steppe blizzard

CABA measure
CACA goddess
CAJA box; bank
CANA Indian
CAPA cloak: Sp.
CARA dear (one): It.; Indian
CASA house, building: Sp., It.
CATA down; prefix: away
CAVA pepper shrub, root; gum resin; vein
CAZA Turkish district
CEBA tree; kapok source
CELA that: Fr.
CENA (Last) supper
CEPA onion
CERA prefix: horn, wax
CHAA tea
CHIA salvia beverage, oil
CIMA mountain peak: It.
CIVA Hindu deity
COCA cocaine source; shrub; leaf to chew; flavor
CODA finale; mark
COJA title; teacher
COLA tree; nut; drink
COMA torpor; blur; tuft
COPA tree; yaya; landmark
CORA gazelle; Indian; name; Persephone; Demeter's daughter
COTA P.I. fort
COXA hip (joint)
CREA linen, cotton fabric
CUBA W.I. island; Pearl of Antilles; measure
CUCA cocaine source
CUNA Panama Indian
CURA parish priest: Sp.
CUYA hardwood tree
CYMA cornice molding

DADA father; cult
DAMA gazelle
DANA goddess; author; editor; lake
DATA facts
DAZA Negro-Berber
DECA prefix: ten
DEHA body (theosophy)
DEJA already: Fr.
DEPA measure
DERA suffix; neck types
DEVA deity (Indra); demon
DEWA deity (Indra); demon
DIKA bread; fat; oil
DISA showiest orchid
DITA tree; bark; upas
DIVA prima donna; blue
DOLA weight
DONA lady; sapek (coin)
DOPA chemical (pigment test)
DORA Mrs. David Copperfield
DOSA sheik's ritual ride; hatred
DOXA religious stanzas
DRAA measure
DUMA Russ. parliament
DURA — mater (spinal membrane)
DYNA prefix: power

EABA measure
ECCA geol. period (Karroo)
EDDA Norse epic
EDEA reproduction organs
EDNA female name; Ferber (novelist)
EGBA Negro; Yoruba
EGMA enigma
EKKA carriage
ELBA Napoleon's exile isle
ELIA Charles Lamb (essayist)
ELLA Eleanor; she: Sp.; fem. suffix
ELSA — of Brabant (Lohengrin's bride)
EMMA letter M; name; Austen novel; Bovary (Flaubert)
ENNA Sicilian resort
EPHA Heb. dry measure
ERDA earth goddess; Wagner role
ERIA silk(worm)
ERMA Ermengarde
ERRA — Pater (almanac)
ERUA mother goddess
ESCA apoplexy (plant disease)
ESTA this: Sp.
ETNA stove; volcano
ETTA Henrietta;

Harriet
EVEA madder (tree); ipecac
EYRA wild cat
EZBA measure
EZRA prophet; OT book
FABA bean; vetch
FALA refrain; dog
FAMA rumor
FANA Sufistic concept
FATA — Morgana (fairy, mirage)
FLEA insect; puce; — market
FORA meeting places; courts
FREA Frigg; Odin's wife; goddess
FRIA Frigg (Odin's wife)
FUGA fugue: It.
FULA Sudanese
GAEA goddess; Titans' mother
GAIA goddess
GALA festival; tribe
GAMA Vasco da (navigator); grass
GAPA guided missile
GARA coin
GATA nurse shark
GAZA Israel (Philistine) seaport; Mozambique district; eyeless in — (Samson)
GEBA Jonathan's victory site
GENA cheek; beak part
GERA city
GETA Jap. wooden clogs
GIGA medieval fiddle
GILA — monster; lizard; Ariz. river
GITA Bhagavad —; Indian scriptures (yoga)
GIZA site: pyramids, Sphinx
GJOA ship (Northwest Passage: Amundsen)
GLIA neuroglia (nerve tissue)
GOLA storeroom; caste; cyma
GOMA Bantu (Wagoma)
GONA New Guinea victory
GORA musical instrument
GOYA Sp. painter; — red
GUFA round boat
GUHA Bantu
GULA upper throat; goddess (Ninurta's consort)
GUNA Sankhya term
HABA bean
HAHA laugh; fence
HAKA dance
HALA pine tree
HARA Jap. statesman
HAYA arrow poison
HELA goddess; Loki's daughter
HEMA prefix: blood
HERA Zeus's sister, wife
HILA 'eyes' of bean
HIMA Hamitic Negro
HOGA hill pasture
HOJA title; teacher
HOLA fish poison; herb; hello
HOMA sacred drink
HORA book of hours; Israeli dance
HOVA Madagascar native; Malagasy
HOYA honey plant (milkweed)
HSIA 1st Chin. dynasty
HUIA bird (starling)
HULA Hawaiian dance
HUMA Uganda Negro
HUPA Athapascan Indian
HURA bishop's cap; sandbox tree; possumwood
HYLA frog; toad
IDEA conception; fancy; key meaning; opening
IJMA Moslem principle (Sunna)
IKRA superior caviar
ILIA (hip) bones
IMLA Micaiah's father
IMNA Asherites chief
INCA Quechuan Indian (ruler)
INGA timber tree; mimosa
INIA Amazon cetacean
INKA Inca
IOLA Kansas town
IONA Scot. isle; Celt church; college
IOTA Greek I, 10; jot
IOWA state, Indian
IRMA name
IRRA war god
ISBA log hut
ISHA Upanishad
ITEA shrub; Virginia willow
ITZA Mayan Indian
IXIA corn lily; bulb
JACA tree
JAGA Bantu
JAMA tunic
JARA palm
JAVA coffee; hood; (Indonesian) Sunda isles; — man (Pithecanthropus)
JENA Ger. city (optical; Napoleonic victory); glass
JIVA life energy
JOTA Sp. peasant dance
JOVA Opata; Pimian Indian
JUBA ghost; dance; mane; river
JUCA cassava; manioc
JUDA James' brother
JUGA carrot ridges; yokes
JULA suspension bridge
JURA rights; mountain range
JUZA star

KADA measure
KAFA Ethiopian
KAHA proboscis monkey
KAKA parrot
KALA bird
KAMA love god; desire; river
KANA Japanese writing
KAPA cloth(es)
KARA river
KASA grass
KAVA pepper shrub, root; gum resin; vein
KAWA pepper shrub, root; gum resin; vein
KELA measures
KETA dog salmon
KINA quinine
KIVA ceremonial chamber
KOBA antelope
KOLA caffeine nut; jackal; river; city; bay (Murmansk)
KONA Hawaiian storm; weight
KORA water cock; Hottentot dialect; instrument
KOTA P.I. fort; Dravidian language
KUBA carpet; measure
KUFA round boat
KULA measure; gift exchange
KUSA ceremonial grass
LAMA priest; llama; brown; Dalai, Panchen, Tashi —
LANA wood; flannel
LARA Byron poem
LATA jumping disease
LAVA fluid rock; obsidian's source; red
LEDA mollusk; mother of Castor, Pollux, Helen, Clytemnestra; wooed by Zeus as swan
LENA firewood: Sp.; river; Conrad heroine
LIDA Alida
LIJA unicorn fish
LILA deity manifestation
LIMA city; bean, yam; mollusk
LINA measure; Caroline
LIPA fat
LIRA money; lyre; hairlike ridge
LISA fem. name; nickname
LOJA bark (quinine)
LOKA sphere; universe
LOLA fem. name
LOMA fringe; lap; hill
LORA thong; strap
LOTA water pot; burbot genus
LOWA bush quail
LOXA pale bark: quinine
LUBA Bantu; Bashilange
LULA name; Louisa
LUNA moon goddess; silver
LURA brain opening
LYRA glockenspiel; constellation
MABA Negro; tree
MAHA monkey; deer
MAIA goddess; crab; star
MAJA crab
MALA evil(s), wrong(s): Lat.; jaw
MAMA mother; goddess
MANA magic power; Chin. letter
MARA demon; aborigine; Naomi
MASA corn meal
MATA Hari (spy)
MAYA weaverbird; (Mexican) Indian; magic; Buddha's mother
MEDA secret Indian sect
MEGA prefix: great
MELA festival; prefix: black
MESA flat hill; oakwood color
META goal post; river
MICA isinglass (silicate)
MILA measure
MIMA woman actor
MINA weight; money; myna; watchman
MIRA star
MOHA millet; delusion
MOLA sunfish genus
MONA monkey; Lisa (La Gioconda: da Vinci)
MORA default; short syllable; Spartan army; stool
MOTA Moslem marriage
MOXA cautery wormwood
MOZA manservant
MUGA silk; moth
MURA Brazil Indian
MUSA banana genus
MUTA change; Moslem marriage
MYNA talking bird: grackle
MYRA name; ancient city
MYSA buffalo (Kipling)
MYXA plum (geiger) tree; sebesten
NAGA snake
NAHA city
NAIA cobra
NAJA cobra
NALA hero
NAMA Hottentot; herb
NANA nurse; Aztec hero's wife; Zola novel; dog (Peter Pan: Barrie)
NAPA leather; wine

region; city; river
NASA space-travel agency
NATA Nana's hero
NEMA eelworm; prefix: thread
NEPA water scorpion; needle bug
NERA Tiber tributary
NEVA river (Leningrad)
NINA goddess (Ea's daughter); ship (Pinta, —, Santa Maria); girl: Sp.
NIPA palm; juice; mat; atap
NOLA fem. name; tune
NONA fate goddess; prefix: ninth
NORA Helmer (Ibsen heroine)
NOTA insect backs; — bene (N.B.)
NOVA star: new, temporary
NOXA harmful thing
NUBA Nubian; Berberi language
NUDA ctenophore; Berolda
NUMA Pompilius (Roman king)
OBIA Ashanti religion
OBRA works: Sp.
OCHA weight
OCRA vegetable; gumbo
OCTA prefix: eight
ODEA theaters; halls; galleries
OFFA Angles' hero (Beowulf)
OHIA timber tree; apple
OKIA Moroccan money
OKRA vegetable; gumbo
OLEA shrub; olive
OLGA fem. name
OLLA jar; meat dish; -podrida (medley)
ONCA ounce
ONZA Sp. ounce (1/16 libra); coin
OOAA Hawaiian bird
ORCA killer whale
ORNA measure
ORRA oddly; laborer
OSSA bones; Mt. (Olympus)
OTEA Great Barrier Island
OTRA other: Sp.
OXEA sponge spicule
PABA vitamin
PACA rodent
PAGA rice
PAHA hill
PALA weight; antelope; vine; rice
PANA city
PAPA father; Pope; potato: Sp.; baboon; clay
PARA coin; weight; river; city (Belem)
PASA raisin
PATA painting; turban; sword
PAWA weight
PEBA armadillo; Indian
PECA coin
PEDA pastoral staffs
PEGA remora fish
PELA wax (secreting insect)
PERA Istanbul district
PESA coin
PEVA Peru Indian
PICA type size; magpies
PIKA little chief hare
PIMA Ariz. Indian; cotton
PINA pineapple; silver cone
PIPA toad; measure
PISA city (leaning tower)
PITA fiber; flax; hemp; brocket (deer)
PLEA excuse; prayer; request; pretext; allegation
PODA suffix: foot
POHA gooseberry (jelly)
POLA Yugo. city (Pula)
POMA rosa (rose apple)
POOA pua hemp
PROA Malay outrigger
PSHA exclamation
PUCA goblin; specter
PUJA worship; festival
PUKA rare N.Z. tree
PULA Yugo. city
PUMA cougar; catamount
PUNA high Andes; wind; sickness (soroche)
PUPA chrysalis; snail; instar
PUYA pineapple genus
PYLA brain opening
RABA river
RACA reproach; fool
RADA legislature
RAGA state of nirvana
RAIA ottoman; fish
RAJA prince; fish
RAMA Indian; Vishnu incarnation; bull (Kipling)
RANA frog; prince; Aegir's wife
RARA — avis (rare bird)
RASA essence; tabula —
RATA tree; chestnut; rate; pro —
RAYA broadbill
REBA weight
REJA screen; grille: Sp.
RENA rockfish
RHEA Cybele; mother of the gods; Gaea's daughter; Cronus's wife; ostrich; satellite; grass
RHIA China grass
RIGA Latvian city, gulf
RIMA fissure; breadfruit; child heroine (Hudson)

RIPA river bank
RITA cosmic order (Vedic); Rio —; fem. name
RIVA shore: It.
RODA Nile island
ROKA mafura (tree)
ROMA Rome: It.
ROSA shrub genus; name; sub —; Bonheur (artist)
ROTA roster; curia tribunal; round; hurdy-gurdy
RUGA stomach membrane
RUPA body form (Buddhism)
RUSA deer; sambar; grass; oil
RUTA herb genus; rue
SABA fiber; kingdom; island
SAGA legend; story; goddess; weight
SAHA measure
SAKA era; Scythians
SALA dining room: Sp.
SAMA fish; trance-inducing music
SANA Yemen's capital; fiber
SAPA grape juice
SARA native
SASA fencer's cry
SAVA Yugo. river
SAYA outer skirt
SEBA Bib. country; Ham's grandson
SELA Dead Sea town
SERA antitoxins; blood parts; whey; evening: It.
SETA caterpillar's hair; spine
SHEA tree; butter
SHOA Abyssinian
SHUA Abraham's son
SIDA herb; shrub; hemp
SIKA Jap. deer
SIMA igneous rock
SINA drug; mountain (Moses)
SITA Ramachandra's wife (Sanskrit Ramayana)
SIVA Hindu deity; cosmic dancer (Nataraja)
SKUA bird; great —; jaeger
SODA carbonated water; Vichy; drink; sodium compound (bicarbonate)
SOFA couch; divan
SOGA grass rope: Sp.; Bantu
SOIA food plant
SOJA bean; glycine
SOKA drought blight
SOLA herb (topee source); alone; holla!
SOMA vine; drink; body
SORA bird; rail
SOYA bean; dill; fennel
STOA portico; poikile (Zeno)
SULA genus; booby; gannet
SUPA P.I. tree; lamp oil
SURA Koran section; deva
SUSA Elam city (Esther story)
SYRA Aegean island
TAHA bird
TALA tree; basin; ruin
TAMA Indian
TANA shrew; rabbi; police station; lake (Blue Nile)
TAPA bark; cloth
TARA fern; goddess; palm
TAWA tree
TCHA (rolled) tea
TECA teak; Indian
TEDA Negro Berber
TELA tissue; web; banana port
TEMA musical theme; Arab
TERA Buddhist monastery
TESA Indian buzzard
TEWA N.M. Indian
THEA tea source; name
TINA fem. nickname
TIZA ulexite mineral
TOBA Tatar; Chaco Indian
TODA Ceylon aborigine
TOGA Roman garb; gown; senatorship
TOLA weight
TOMA Liberian Negro
TOOA hero; beefwood
TORA hartebeest; law (of Moses); Pentateuch
TOTA grivet monkey
TOXA sponge spicule
TSIA tea
TUBA saxhorn; tree; nut; fish poison; palm sap
TUFA porous rock
TULA metal; niello; city; Toltec ruins
TUNA fish; pear; opuntia
TUZA pocket gopher
UEBA measure
ULLA grass; paper pulp
ULNA elbow bone; ell
ULUA cavalla; fish; caranx
ULVA sea lettuce; laver
UNCA 8th note
UPLA cow dung; fuel
UREA chemical compound
URFA Turkish city (Edessa)
URGA Outer Mongolia
URIA Bathsheba's husband; auk
URNA measure
URSA bear; stars: — Major, Minor; Great, Little Bear (Dipper)
URVA mongoose
USHA Bana's daughter; sorceress

UTIA rodent
UVEA Iris layer
VARA measure
VASA ducts; Swedish dynasty
VEDA sacred Hindu books
VEGA meadow
VELA membranes; soft palates; the Sails (Argo constellation)
VENA vein: Lat.
VERA tree; measure; name
VETA mountain sickness
VICA Pota (goddess)
VIDA feminine of David
VIGA rafter; log
VILA fairy; New Hebrides
VINA harp; guitar; wines
VIRA Bantu
VISA endorse(ment); -vis
VITA life: Lat.
VIVA salute (long live); — voce (spoken aloud)
VOLA palm (hand, foot)
VOTA Roman festivals
WAHA lake trout
WAKA canoe
WAWA gibbon
WEGA star
WEKA flightless bird
WETA wingless locust
WHOA stop!; opp. of giddap
XEMA arctic gull
XINA nickname: Christina
XOSA Kaffir
XOVA Opata; Pimian Indian
YABA bark; cabbage tree
YAKA Bantu
YAMA first mortal (Judge of Dead)
YANA tribe
YAPA leaf mat
YAVA weight
YAYA copa, lancewood (tree)
YETA Jap. outcast
YIMA Avestan demigod
YMCA welfare organization
YNCA Quechuan Indian (ruler); Inca
YOGA mental discipline
YUCA cassava; manioc
YUGA Hindu age cycle
YUMA Indian (Cal.); city
YWCA welfare organization
ZAMA Hannibal's defeat
ZARA city; Judah's son
ZAZA opera (Leoncavallo)
ZETA Greek Z, 7
ZIPA Chibcha chief
ZIRA measure
ZITA Austrian empress
ZIZA Rehoboam's son
ZOEA crab larva
ZOLA Emile (author: J'accuse, Dreyfus case; Nana)
ZONA girdle; shingles
ZUPA Yugo. district
ZUZA weight
ZYGA rower's benches; brain fissures

ABIB month
ADIB star
AGIB dervish
AHAB king; captain; prophet
ARAB Semite; horse; nomad; urchin
BADB goddess
BARB sharp point; fish; dog; mow; pigeon
BIBB mast's timber piece
BLAB tattle
BLEB blister; bubble
BLOB drop; daub; sound; fish; zero score
BLUB swell; puff out
BODB goddess
BOMB explosive; dispenser; A-, H-; lead-lined container; buzz —
BOOB simpleton
BRAB palm
BROB support spike
BULB bud; tuber; corm; lamp; swell
CHAB bird
CHIB tongue; language
CHOB grain spike
CHUB fallfish; dace; chevin
CLUB bat; beat; society; suit (cards)
COBB Irvin S. (writer); Tyrus R. (baseball)
COMB crest; rake; scrape
CRAB crustacean; apple; sign; anger
CRIB manger; hut; bin; box; steal; "pony," "trot"
CURB restrain(t); sidewalk edge; market
DAUB plaster; besmear
DIEB jackal
DOAB tract
DOOB Bermuda grass
DOUB Bermuda grass
DRAB dull; box; wench; cloth; drug
DRIB drop; a little
DRUB (beat with) stick
DUAB tract
DUBB Syrian bear; lizard
DUMB mute; stupid; — waiter; deaf and —
FLOB move clumsily
FLUB blunder; botch

FORB non-grassy herb
FRAB worry
FRIB dirty short wool
GAMB leg
GARB apparel; array
GAUB persimmon (astringent)
GERB sheaf; firework
GLIB flippant, smooth(ly)
GLUB make gulping sound
GRAB grasp; capture; game
GRUB larva; food; dig(ger)
GUIB harnessed antelope
HAAB year
HARB Bedouin
HERB plant; nickname
HOBB havoc; fireplace ledge; pin; peg
HUBB pipe end
IAMB verse foot
JAMB leg armor; pillar; door part
JAOB measure
JOAB (David's) captain
KALB de — (general)
KERB gutter part
KNAB nibble
KNOB lump; hill; antler; handle
KNUB waste silk
KTKB chess move
KTQB chess move
LAMB amateur speculator; Charles (Elia: essayist)
LIMB leg; arm; member
LOBB go heavily; tennis stroke; till
MEDB Conchobor's wife; goddess; Queen Mab
MOAB kingdom; language; Lot's son
NAAB river
NIMB nimbus; halo
NUMB deaden(ed); helpless
OREB Medianite defeated by Gideon
PLEB freshman cadet; common man
QUAB fish
RAAB river
RHOB juice; jelly
ROUB measure
RUMB compass point
SCAB crust; strikebreaker
SCOB fabric defect
SERB Servian Yugo(slav)
SHAB paltry guy
SLAB slice; road
SLEB nomadic Arab
SLOB slovenly one
SLUB twisted wool roll
SNAB hill part; girl
SNIB escape logging work
SNOB social climber; game
SNUB rebuke; slight; stumpy
SORB wild apple; Slav
STAB pierce; trial
STIB sandpiper (dunlin)
STUB stump; penpoint; short, stocky; extirpate; ticket part; bump
SWAB mop; lout
SWOB sponge; wipe; mop
THEB measure
THOB rationalize
TOMB grave; monument; bury
TURB crowd; clump
VERB action word
WEBB Beatrice Potter (writer)
ZIMB Ethiopian fly

ABAC calculator
ALEC fish; sauce; nickname
AMIC amidic
AVEC with: Fr.
BANC (judge's) bench
BLOC political unit; casting
BOSC best pear
CHAC -Mool (god); -chac (instr.)
CHIC stylish(ness)
CIRC circle; recess; corrie
CRIC lamp condensing ring
CROC harquebus support; crocodile
DISC disk; record; — jockey
DOUC variegated monkey
EPIC heroic poem
ERIC male name; Viking; the Red
ERUC cordage fiber
FISC exchequer
FLOC flock(y mass); shreds
FUSC dusky; somber
HAEC this one (fem.): Lat.
IDIC pert to ids
LAIC secular
MARC residue; name; weight
ODIC pert. to ode, od
OLIC chem. suffix
OTIC of the ear; auditory
PARC park; oyster farm: Fr.
PYIC purulent
SAIC Near East ketch
SPEC speculation
SYNC synchronize
TALC soapy mineral
TLAC coin
UDIC Caucasian language
UVIC grapelike; acid
WAAC fem. soldier
WRAC women's army corp
ZINC metal; element; color
ZOIC pert. to animals

ABED in bed; bedridden

ACID sour; biting
ADAD fiber; god
AGED old; oxygian
ALOD estate
AMID among
APOD footless
ARAD plant; city
ARID dry; barren
ARND theologian
AROD son of Gad
AULD old; — lang syne
AVID eager; greedy
AZID compound
BALD naked; — eagle
BAND strip; group; orchestra; range; tie; sash
BARD armor; poet; — of Avon (Shakespeare)
BAUD speed unit
BAWD procuress
BEAD globule; ball; drop; aim
BEID star
BEND turn; curve; flex; bow
BIND tie; protect; sew; cohere
BIOD animal life force
BIRD avian; flyer; fowl; shuttlecock; person; Blue —
BLED emitted or drew blood, sap; extorted
BOID of boas, anacondas
BOLD valiant; brazen; strong, heavy (type)
BOND adhesion; tie; covenant; paper; captivity; certificate
BORD -and-pillar (mining)
BOUD malt weevil
BRAD nail
BRED procreated; brought up
BUDD Lanny (Sinclair)
BUND embankment; league
BURD noble lady
BYRD explorer; Va.

statesman
CAID alcaide
CARD comb; pasteboard; menu; playing —; calling —
CHAD lake; nation
CHUD Mongols; Vepse; Vote; Tavastian
CLAD dressed; plated
CLOD lump; soil; dolt
COAD cushion
COED girl student
COLD chill; frigid; indifferent; common —; coryza; — blood; — chisel
COND direct helmsman
CORD string; twine; ribbed fabric; measure (wood)
CURD coagulated milk
DARD language group
DAUD dad
DEAD deceased; entire; absolute(ly); — reckoning
DEED act; property transfer
DIAD pair
DODD cut off (wool)
DOWD slovenly woman
DRED Scott (slave)
DUAD pair
DYAD pair
EBED Gaal's father
ECAD modified organism
EFOD priestly garb; image
EGAD oath
EHUD judge of Israel
EILD barren; milkless
ELOD alleged force
EMYD terrapin
ENID fem. name; Geraint's wife; city
EYED looked at; ogled

FARD face paint; date
FEED nourish; gratify; graze; fodder
FELD field: Ger.
FEND keep off; parry
FEOD feudal estate
FEUD strife; vendetta; fee
FIND discover(y); (re)gain
FLED ran away; shunned
FOLD plait; envelop; fall; quit; flock
FOND basis; fount; loving
FOOD nutriment; victuals
FORD crossing shallow; Henry (automobile); Shaks. character
FOUD district magistrate
FRED nickname
FUAD Arab king
FUND supply; finance; money; sinking —
FYRD old English army
GAUD ornament; bead
GAWD ornament; bead
GELD castrate; prune; tax
GERD Frey's wife
GILD lay gold on; adorn; — the lily; trade society
GIRD encircle; clothe; brace
GLAD pleased
GLED kite; buzzard
GOAD rod; decoy; urge
GOLD metal; element; — dust, medal
GOND Dravidian Indian
GOOD able; brave; sound; profit; happiness;

welfare; benefit
GRAD centesimal unit
GRID grating
GUAD tree
HAND control; aid; worker; measure; pass; player; cards; penmanship
HARD solid; firm; close; severe; difficult
HEAD skull; top; brain, chief; crux; source
HEED notice; attention
HELD kept; retained
HERD crowd; feed together
HILD Hethin's victim princess
HIND fish; grouper; deer; posterior
HOLD grasp; have; retain; believe; keep; bear; lair; prison
HOOD cowl; cloak; seal; gangster; Thomas (poet)
HUED colored; tinged
HUND dog: Ger.
IBAD Hira Arab
IBID P.I. lizard (tidbit), the same: abbr.
ICED frozen; chilled
IMID chem. compound
IRAD Enoch's son
IRID iris; crocus
JOAD philosopher; Tom (Grapes of Wrath: Steinbeck)
JORD Odin's wife; Thor's mother
KAID chief; alcaide
KEID star
KELD spring; fountain
KIDD William (privateer)
KIND sort; species; gentle
KURD Sunnite Mohammedan; Iranian
LAID put down; calmed
LAND ground; debark; state: Ger.
LARD fat; stuff
LAUD praise
LEAD metal; element; plummet; bullets; color; guide; command
LEND make loan; grant; — an ear
LEUD feudal tenant
LEWD lecherous; obscene
LIED fibbed; song: Ger.
LIND Jenny (singer, Swedish Nightingale)
LOAD burden; measure
LOOD weight
LORD ruler; Jehovah; Jesus; duck; planet
LOUD noisy; showy; vulgar
MAID servant; — of Orleans
MAND grass
MARD spoil
MAUD plaid; rug; name; Muller; Whittier, Tennyson heroine
MEAD drink; meadow; lake; Margaret (anthropologist)
MEED reward
MELD announce (score); merge
MEND repair; improve
MILD calm(ly); soft; tame
MIND intellect; brain; memory; wish; mood; plan; tend; dislike
MOED festivals (Mishnah)
MOLD fungus; humus; die, matrix; shape; mix
MOOD humor; temper; verb form
MUDD measure; doctor of Booth (Lincoln assassin)
MUID measure
MUND protection right
NAID worm
NARD plant; ointment
NEED compulsion; lack; want
NEJD kingdom
NKVD Soviet secret police
NUDD Brythonic god, king
OBED David's grandfather
ODED prophet or his father
OHAD Simeon's son
OLID smelly; fetid
OOID egg-shaped
OORD coin (double doit, ¼ stiver)
ORAD mouthward
OSID suffix; sugar
OVID poet (Metamorphoses); P.O.N.; Naso
OXID oxygen compound
PAID recompensed; discharged; satisfied
PARD chum; leopard
PEND hang; be delayed
PHAD star
PHUD bullet sound; exclamation
PIED variegated; Piper; -à-terre
PLED pleaded
PLOD trudge; drudge
POND lake; pool; weight
POOD weight
PRAD horse
PROD reminder; goad; horse; prodigy
PUND weight
PUUD weight
QAID alcaide
QUAD type; four; -rangle, -ruplet, etc.

QUID cud; essence; pound; — pro quo
QUOD prison; — erat demonstrandum (Q.E.D.)
RAAD assembly; fish
RAID attack; foray
RAND border; ridge; strip; So. Afr. gold mine
READ interpret; learn; study; understand
REDD make tidy; free of; scold
REED woody grass; pipe; mouthpiece; Walter (doctor, hospital)
REND tear; rupture; bark trees
RIDD Lorna Doone's rescuer
RIND bark; peel; Vali's mother, Odin's wife
ROAD (rail)way; track; anchorage
RODD crossbow
ROED filled with roe
ROOD crucifix; measure
ROUD fish
RUDD carplike fish
RYND millstone support
SADD dam; waste matter
SAID before-mentioned; Port — (city); name
SAND grit; silica; polish, smooth; red-yellow; George (novelist: Dudevant)
SARD carnelian; gem; Sardinian
SAUD Ibn (king)
SCAD fish; large amount
SCUD run fast; wind-driven clouds; skim; flea
SEED fertile germ; progeny decay; plant; extract
SEID tribe; lord; chief; Mohammed's descendant
SEND transmit; dispatch; propel; swing; enthrall
SHAD fish
SHED cast off; abandon; drop; hut; shelter
SHOD wearing shoes
SIND river; Pakistan province; are: Ger.
SKID clog; slide; — Road, Row
SLED vehicle, snow or ice
SLID glided; slipped
SNED lop; prune
SNOD trim; snug; plausible
SOLD vended; persuaded; cheated
SOUD pay
SPAD nail
SPED hastened
SPUD scrape(r); potato; dig
STAD town
STOD Danish speech
STUD breeding stock; knob; stump; dot; poker
SUDD Nile waste; dam
SULD measure
SURD irrational; mute
SWAD mass; soldier
SYED Moslem chief
SYUD Moslem prince; title
TEND serve; incline
THUD dull sound; blow
TIED bound; knotted; drawn
TIND kindle
TOAD amphibian; anuran; fawn
TOED stepped (gingerly)
TOLD narrated; counted
TROD walked; track
TUND pound; bruise
UDAD sheep
USED accustomed; secondhand
UVID moist; wet
VELD So. Afr. grassland
VEND Slav; sell; sale
VERD green(-leafed)
VOID empty; vacuum; cancel
WADD mineral
WAFD Egyptian
WAND rod; staff; magic —
WARD (safe)guard; parry; district; charge; Artemus (Browne)
WEED plant; tobacco; remove
WELD unite; junction
WEND Slav; go; travel
WILD rough; savage; mad; eager; unruly; wilderness
WIND turn; coil; flowing air; mere talk
WOAD herb
WOLD upland plain
WOOD timber; forest; Grant (painter); Leonard (general)
WORD term; news; promise; order; phrase
WURD Norn; Urth
WYND alley; small court
WYRD Norn; Urth
YARD 3 feet; grounds; enclosure; spar
YELD barren; milkless
YOND past; beyond
ZEND — Avesta (holy text)
ZOID organic body cell

AARE river
ABBE priest; title; Amer. meteorologist

ABIE 's Irish Rose; name
ABLE fit; adept; suffix; -bodied
ACHE pain; yearn
ACLE tree
ACME peak; crisis
ACNE disease
ACRE field; measure; city
ADZE tool
AGEE awry; Shammah's father; James (novelist)
AGUE fever
AIDE help; -de-camp; — mémoire
AILE winged
AINE elder
AIRE nobleman; river
AJEE awry
AKEE tree
ALAE wings
ALBE album
ALEE to shelter
ALLE bird; all: Ger.
ALME dancer
ALOE plant; tonic
ALTE old: Ger.; Adenauer
AMIE friend: Fr.
ANCE suffix; — errand
ANDE tribe
ANGE angel: Fr.
ANNE queen; Boleyn; Henry VIII wife; Elizabeth's mother; Shakespeare's wife; Domby's maid (Dickens); Queen — style; Queen —'s lace
ANSE handle: Fr.
ANTE stake; pay; before; -bellum
AONE first-rate
APSE recess; throne
ARME weapon: Fr.; — blanche (saber)
ARNE composer; region
AROE islands, New Guinea
ASSE caama; fox
ATLE tree
AUDE Fr. dept.; river
AUGE priestess
AUNE measure
AUTE tree
AXLE spindle
BABE baby; — Ruth; girl
BADE waited; asked; invited; commanded
BAKE dry; roast; biscuit
BALE woe; bundle
BANE woe; curse; poison
BARE expose(d); mere; Indian
BASE bottom; source; home; headquarters; found; diamond corner; ignoble
BATE diminish; tanner's bath; restrain
BAVE double silk thread
BEDE Adam (Eliot); the Venerable (monk)
BENE wild hog; well: It. & Lat.
BETE beast, silly: Fr.; — noire
BICE blue, green pigment
BIDE wait; tarry; dwell
BIKE bicycle
BILE liver secretion; choler
BINE (hop) stem
BISE cold wind; winter
BITE cut; pierce; grip; eat (into); sting; respond; snack
BIZE cold wind; winter
BLAE bleak
BLUE color; ocean; sky; sailor; sad; -blood; puritanical
BOCE colored fish
BODE presage; augur; omen
BOLE trunk; clay; brown
BONE study hard; plug; os
BORE pierce; hole; tire; dullard; tidal flow
BOSE test ground by sound
BOTE house repair; amends
BRAE slope
BREE (eye)brow
BRIE cheese
BUBE boy, jack: Ger.; Fernando Po Bantu
BUDE light; burner
BURE brown red-yellow
BUTE island; Scot. county; parson (Thackeray)
BYEE measure
BYKE nest of bees
BYRE cow house
BYTE computer word
CADE cask; tree; pet; rebel
CAFE restaurant; coffee; -au-lait; society
CAGE confine; enclosure; elevator car; nor iron bars a —
CAKE bar; dough; harden
CALE Gypsy; cabbage
CAME arrived; lead rod; indian
CANE stem; rattan; stick; walking —; sugar —; candy —
CAPE cloak; promontory; — Cod, — Horn, — Good Hope
CARE grief; heed; responsibility; anxiety; foster; relief organization
CASE event; fact; record, problem (medical, etc.); legal action; argument; grammar form;

container, chest, box; queer phenomenon; inspect
CATE delicacy
CAVE cavern; — in (collapse); — canem (beware of dog)
CEDE yield; grant; transfer
CENE suffix: recent
CEPE boletus (edible fungus)
CERE wax; (wrap in a) waxed cloth; beak part
CETE marine mammals
CHEE weight
CINE movie: Sp.
CISE dice term: six
CITE summon; quote
CIVE chive garlic
CLEE redshank; bird
CLOE fem. name
CLUE hint; guide; thread
CODE body of law (Julian, Justinian; Napoleonic); signal system; cipher; — duello
COKE coal residue; fuel
COLE brassica genus; Porter (composer)
COME arrive; chance; fare
CONE geometric solid; pine fruit, strobile; peak; ice cream —; nose —
COPE vestment; cover; bend; contend
CORE heart; nucleus; gist
COSE (friendly) chat
COTE birdhouse; sheep shed; coast: Fr. (d'Or; d'Azur)
COUE psychotherapist ("Day by day . . .")
COVE bay; recess; pass; chap; Gypsy
COXE Capt. (Scott)
COZE (friendly) chat
CREE Indian
CUBE square solid; 3rd power; die; plant poison
CUKE cucumber
CULE diminutive suffix
CURE heal; remedy; preserve; priest: Fr.
CUTE clever; attractive
CYKE cyclorama
CYLE brewing; beer; wort
CYME inflorescence
CYTE prefix: hollow vessel
DACE fish
DADE support
DALE valley; share; trough
DAME woman; title; — aux Camélias
DANE Scandinavian; great — (dog); Hamlet
DARE venture; defy; fish; Virginia (1st Amer. child)
DATE fruit; tree; brown; (make) appointment
DAVE David
DAYE printer (Bay Psalm Book)
DAZE stupefy; mica
DELE omit; erase
DEME Greek commune
DENE measure; dune; Indian
DERE — Mable (Streeter book)
DICE (cut into) cubes; gamble; gaming implements
DIKE levee; ditch; dig; goddess (Horae)
DIME coin; — novel
DINE eat; have dinner
DIRE evil; fatal; extreme
DITE mite; indict
DIVE plunge; duck; low resort; — bomb(er)
DOBE brick (house)
DOCE Brazil river
DODE nickname: Theodore
DOGE Venice, Genoa ruler
DOLE ration; (relief) alms; deal (out)
DOME edifice; cupola; roof
DONE agreed; exhausted
DOPE drug; information; guess; nitwit
DORE bullion; gold; pike; Paul Gustave (Fr. artist)
DOSE portion; (give) medicine
DOTE love to excess; drivel; timber rot
DOVE pigeon; blue, gray; Columba; plunged
DOZE drowse; timber rot
DREE endure; tedious
DUCE chief: It.; Mussolini
DUDE dandy; fop; city fellow; — ranch
DUNE sandhill; twine color
DUPE trick(ed one); copy
DUSE incubus; Eleanora (actress)
DYCE thus!: naut. command
DYKE levee; checkers opening
DYNE unit of force
EASE repose; comfort; moderate;

facilitate
EAVE roof edge
EBOE tree; oil; Negrito
ECCE lo: Lat.; — homo
EDGE brink; sharpness; goad; advantage; — on
EIDE ideas; forms
EINE one: Ger.
EIRE Ireland; Erin
ELBE river
ELLE measure; she: Fr.
ELSE other(wise); besides
ENCE suffix
ENNE prefix: nine; fem. suffix
ENSE suffix
ENTE grafted (Her.); being: Sp.
EPEE fencing sword
ERIE Iroquoian; lake; city
ERNE sea eagle
ERSE Irish; Gaelic
ESCE suffix: begin to be
ESNE slave
ESSE existence; to be: Lat.
ESTE It. family; this: Sp.
ETRE exist; be: Fr.; raison d'—
ETTE suffix: fem.
EUGE bravo!
EVOE bacchanals' wild cry; Punch editor
EYRE Jane (Brontë heroine); circuit (court)
FACE surface; oppose; line
FADE weaken; flat; dissolve
FAKE loop; cheat; sham
FAME reputation
FANE temple
FARE passenger; price; happen; food; travel
FATE destiny (goddess); end; kismet
FAZE disturb
FEKE trick device
FEME wife; tribunal
FETE festival; regale
FIDE entrust; — et amore
FIFE flute; checkers opening
FILE tool; rasp; smooth; march; column; folder; arrange
FINE end; superior; thin; keen; well; (set) penalty; geil —, derb — (Irish clans)
FIRE combustion; ardor; discharge
FIVE number; basketball team; card
FIXE prix —
FLEE run away; shun
FLOE floating ice
FLUE net; lint; barb; air passage; pipe
FOIE liver: Fr.; — gras (pâté)
FORE front; prior; golf cry
FREE independent; immune; rid; exempt; — and easy; — lance, port, trade, style
FROE cleaver; steel wedge
FUME smoke; fit; rage
FUSE detonator; melt; unite
FUTE Eskimo curlew
FUYE Jap. flute
FUZE detonator; melt; unite
FYKE fish bag net
GABE taro
GADE fish; composer
GAGE pledge; fruit; gauge; general; governor
GALE storm, wind
GAME amusement; quarry; resolute; lame
GANE yawn
GAPE yawn; stare; gap
GARE wool; station, beware: Fr.
GATE entrance; pass; judgement; money
GAUE German regions
GAVE donated
GAZE stare; wonder
GENE hereditary factor; chromosome part; nickname
GERE Odin's wolf
GHEE butter
GIBE scoff; jeer; agree
GIDE André (author)
GITE shelter: Fr.; mad
GIVE bestow; yield; grant
GLUE adhesive; stick
GONE departed; enamored; lost; germ cell
GORE stab; blood; triangular insert
GRUE shiver; shudder
GULE of August (Lamma's Day)
GUZE red roundel (Her.)
GYBE jibe; scoff; agree
GYLE brewing; wort; vat
GYNE prefix: female
GYRE turn; ring; vortex
GYVE fetter; shackle
HABE tribe
HADE angle; strip
HAJE cobra
HAKE fish; pester; frame
HALE healthy; Nathan (patriot)
HARE leporid; rabbit; run
HATE detest; aversion
HAVE possess; aux.

verb; must; deceive
HAZE mist; drizzle; harass
HEBE cupbearer of gods; Zeus's daughter, Hercules' wife; color
HEHE Bantu tribe
HEME reduced hematin
HERE vicinity; present
HIDE land measure; skin; conceal; shelter; — and hair
HIKE toss; tramp; raise
HIPE wrestler's throw
HIRE engage; rent; wage
HIVE bees' swarm, house
HOHE Siouan tribe
HOLE pit; cavity; flaw; — in one; — card; ace in the —
HOME habitat; asylum; plate; natural
HONE sharpen(er)
HOPE trust, expect(ation); wish; — chest
HOSE stockings; pipe; drench
HOVE ground ivy; raised
HOWE hollow; empty; Elias (inventor); Julia Ward (Battle Hymn); Brit. general, admiral
HUGE enormous; immense
HUKE hooked cape
HULE caucho source
HUME philosopher
HURE head of boar, wolf
HUSE beluga; whale; huchen
HYDE — Park; Dr. Jekyll and Mr. —; measure
HYKE cry to urge on dogs
HYLE matter (philos.): demon
HYPE wrestler's throw; ad
IDEE — fixe: Fr.
IDLE not working; empty; lazy; waste
ILLE that one: Lat.
IMBE cordage fiber plant
INBE be within
INDE blue (Indigo)
INEE arrow poison
INGE prelate ("Gloomy Dean"); playwright (Bus Stop)
INRE concerning; actually
IOLE Eurytus' daughter (Hercules captive)
IONE Pompeii heroine (Bulwer-Lytton)
IPSE himself: Lat.; — dixit
IRAE Dies — (Day of Wrath)
ISLE ait; eyot; insulate; key
IXLE cordage fiber
JADE gem; horse; exhaust
JAKE Jacob; rube; money; satisfactory; ginger
JANE woman; false hair; cloth; — Eyre; Lady — Grey
JAPE deride
JAVE Jehovah
JEFE chief; leader
JETE ballet jump
JIBE sneer; agree; coincide; shift course
JIVE dialect (dance, jazz)
JOIE — de vivre (zest for life)
JOKE jest; laughing stock
JOLE jowl; cheek
JOSE Carmen lover
JOVE god; Jupiter; Zeus
JUBE chancel screen; lozenge
JUDE name: NT book, author; Jew: Ger.; — the Obscure (Hardy)
JUGE judge: Fr.
JUKE partridge call; — box; sociological name (with Kallikak)
JULE name: Julian; Julius
JUNE month; beetle; — moon, bride
JUPE skirt
JURE de — (by law)
JUTE fiber plant; Corchorus; Low Ger.
KADE tick
KALE cabbage
KAME hill
KANE god
KATE bird; Shaks. shrew; Greenaway
KELE weight
KERE read(ing substitute)
KIBE chilblain crack
KILE measure; weight
KINE cattle
KIPE basket
KITE hawk; rogue; flying toy; banking fraud
KIVE brewer's vat
KLEE Paul (painter)
KNEE joint; bend(ing)
KOAE red-tailed bird
KOBE Honshu port
KOME Greenland division
KORE Persephone; Demeter's daughter; chaos (Maori myth.)
KUGE Jap. courtier

KUKE prince; cherry
KURE Jap. city; Hawaiian isle
KYKE fashion spy
KYLE sore; ulcer; farmer
LABE city
LACE cord; flavor; netting
LADE load; dip
LAKE sea; pool; red (cochineal)
LAME cripple(d); halt; plate; fabric
LANE (fixed) route; throat
LARE Mid. Eng. lore
LATE dead; tardy
LAVE pour; bathe
LAZE idle(ness); tribesman
LENE smooth; consonant
LESE — majesty (disrespect)
LETE quadrille set
LICE insects (louse)
LIDE March (month)
LIFE existence; vivacity; biography
LIKE as; similar(ly); love; prefer; probable
LILE little
LIME calcium oxide (mortar); snare; caustic; linden (tree); amber; citrus fruit
LINE thin mark; cable; cord; wire; piping; row; direction; cover; align; track; flax
LIRE coins; read: Fr.
LITE suffix: mineral, rock
LIVE exist; continue; vital; alert
LOBE projection; ear part
LODE ore deposit; vein; load
LOGE theater box
LOKE Loki; surprise!
LOME Togo seaport
LONE single; — Star
LOPE go; move; gait
LORE history; learning
LOSE miss; forfeit; fall; forget
LOTE lotus (poetic); weights
LOVE affection; like; Cupid: Eros; zero
LUBE machine oil
LUCE fish, pike; Adriana's servant; Henry (editor); Clare Boothe (writer, stateswoman)
LUGE lodge; small sled
LUKE name; evangelist; Paul's companion; author Acts; -warm
LUNE crescent; hawk leash
LUPE Samoan fruit pigeon; Velez (actress)
LURE entice; decoy; trumpet
LUTE cement; bricklayer's tool; Apollo's musical instrument; jar ring
LUXE elegance; de —
LYME bloodhound
LYRE harp; constellation
LYSE undergo lysis
MACE staff; spice; weight; coin
MADE successful; created; constructed
MAGE magician
MAHE island
MAKE produce; create; cause; reach; type; identify
MALE man(ly); tribe
MANE hair; in the morning: Lat.
MARE blues; sea; moon area; horse; shanks' —
MATE companion; match; tea; check-
MAZE labyrinth; daze; perplex
MEDE ancient Asian
MELE Hawaiian poem; chant
MENE — tekel upharsin (handwriting on the wall)
MERE fen; lake; boundary; war club; bare; only; simple; mother: Fr.
MESE Greek mus. term
METE measure; allot
MICE rodents (mouse)
MIDE Ojibway secret order
MIKE Michael; Mick; microphone
MILE measure; distance
MIME drama; act; actor; clown; smith (Nibelungs)
MINE possessive pronoun; dig; pit; rich source; explosive
MIRE bog; (stick in) mud
MISE levy; stake; tax; — en scène
MITE arachnid; parasite; small (coin)
MIXE Mexican Indian
MODE manner; fashion; drab; à la —
MOKE donkey; dolt
MOLE nevus; birthmark; pier; burrow(ing animal); Mossi language
MOME buffoon; -rath
MOPE be dull, listless (person)
MORE greater; additional; St.

Thomas (Utopia)
MOSE Moses
MOTE speck; particle
MOUE pout; grimace: Fr.
MOVE impel; shift; excite; act; depart(ure); play
MULE equine hybrid; spinning jenny; slipper
MURE thrust against wall
MUSE meditate; goddess
MUTE silent; dumb; muffle
NAHE river; near: Ger.
NAME title; reputation; clan; cite
NANE own; none
NAPE neck back
NARE Loki's son
NASE promontory; nose: Ger.
NATE born
NAVE hub; church part
NAZE promontory
NENE Hawaiian goose
NETE Greek mus. term
NEUE new
NEVE snow; firn
NICE good; kind; pleasing; delicate, dainty; quimper color; Riviera port
NIDE pheasant's nest
NIFE earth's core
NIKE victory goddess (Samothrace); missile
NILE river; green, blue
NINE number (of Muses); baseball team
NIUE Savage island language
NODE knob; knot; orbit point; joint
NOME city (Alaska)
NONE not one; 9th hour
NORE Thames estuary
NOSE proboscis; smeller; scent; search; front; touch; — out (defeat); -dive
NOTE sign; tone; fame; heed; memo; IOU; record; see
NOVE nine: It.
NUDE naked; art work; color
NUPE Nigeria Negro
OBIE Off-Broadway award
OBOE woodwind; chanter
OESE bacteriologist's wire
OGEE arch; molding
OGLE gaze (amorously)
OGRE giant; monster
OHNE without: Ger.
OIME alas
OISE Fr. river
OKEE evil spirit
OKIE migratory worker
OLPE oil flask; pitcher
ONCE one time; if ever; former(ly)
ONDE wave: Fr.; wavy (Her.)
OOZE exude; slime; liquor
OPIE Eng. painter
ORFE fish; yellow ide
ORLE shield border; fillet
ORNE measure; river (Caen)
OSTE prefix: bone
OTOE Sioux Indian
OUSE Great — (river)
OWSE tan liquor
PACE step; speed; peace: It.
PAGE young attendant; call, summon; leaf
PALE wan; pallid; ashy; picket; stake; beyond the —
PANE glass; panel
PAPE bunting (bird)
PARE cut off; peel
PATE head; paste
PAVE cover firmly; — the way; jewel setting
PEKE (Pekinese) dog
PELE fire goddess
PENE (hammer) head
PERE father, priest: Fr.; — Goriot (Balzac)
PETE strongbox; Peter
PICE coin; weight
PIKE fish; weapon; pierce; highway; farmer; gamble; Zebulon (explorer; peak)
PILE hair; heap (up); awn; atomic —
PINE tree; conifer; evergreen; yearn; mourn
PIPE tube; flute; cask (measure); -dream; — down
PISE building material
PODE suffix: foot
POKE thrust; prod; pry; sack; potter; herb
POLE rod; tail; terminal: axis; battery; — Star; Polish; Polack
POME fruit; ball; globe
PONE corn bread; writ
POPE pontiff; Holy Father; — Joan (game); Alexander (poet); bird
PORE gaze; ponder; opening
POSE posture; affec-

tation; baffle; propound
POTE poker; stick
POWE weight
PUCE flea: Fr.; eureka red
PUKE cloth; vomit
PULE cheep; whimper
PUME Yarura(n language)
PURE unmixed; chaste; sheer; free; Simon —
PYLE Ernie (journalist); Howard (artist)
PYRE funeral pile, fire
QERE read(ing substitute)
QUAE — vide (which see)
RACE run; contest; people; speed; Cape —; rat-
RADE elated
RAGE fury; storm; fad
RAKE incline; tool; collect; roué; —'s Progress
RALE rattling sound
RAME branch
RAPE herb; ravish
RARE underdone; thin; uncommon
RASE rub; demolish
RATE censure; ratio; charge; estimate; rank; tax
RAVE rant; rage; enthusiasm; rod
RAZE scrape; demolish
REDE interpret; counsel
REKE rick; pile
RESE shake; rush
RETE network
REVE (muse in) dream: Fr.
RICE cereal; use ricer; Elmer (playwright)
RIDE be borne; float; endure; manage; mount; journey
RIFE abundant; prevalent
RILE irritate; vex
RIME frost; (make) rhymes; chink; rung
RINE hemp; ditch
RIPE mature; fit; tipsy
RIRE to laugh: Fr.
RISE climb; grow(th); begin; emerge(nce); thrive; retort
RITE ceremony; liturgy
RIVE tear; split; — droite (right bank), — gauche (left bank)
ROBE gown; mantle; Douglas novel
RODE anchor rope; measure; was borne; cross
ROKE vapor; smoke
ROLE actor's part
ROME city (Eternal); Church; beauty (apple)
RONE brushwood
ROPE cord; cable; noose; bind; chain
ROSE stood up; got up; flower; tree; wood; red; pink; window; Abie's Irish —; Eng. emblem
ROTE surf noise; routine
ROUE dissolute man; rake
ROVE wander; ramble; draw through an eye
RUBE Reuben; rustic; yokel
RUDE rough; boorish; vulgar
RULE law; guide; reign; method; control; — Britannia; ruler; line
RUNE Teutonic sign; magic
RUSE trick; deceit; slip
RUTE measure
RYME water surface
RYPE ptarmigan
SABE know
SADE letter; Marquis
SAFE secure; box
SAGE herb; wise; Russell (financier)
SAKE purpose; beer
SALE bargain; auction; willow; salted: Fr.
SAME identical
SANE rational
SATE gratify; glut
SAVE rescue; avoid; lay by; but; — face
SAXE Saxony; blue
SEME (sprinkling) pattern
SERE wither(ed); Negroid
SEVE wine delicacy: Fr.
SHEE Irish fairyfolk
SHOE foot covering; crakow; wheel drag; tire
SHUE Tibetan deer
SICE number 6 on die
SIDE region; part(y); oblique; aspect; support; lateral
SIME monkey
SINE math. ratio; without: Lat.; — qua non; — die
SIRE father; beget; king
SISE six (dice)
SITE location; scene
SIVE sickle; knife
SIZE bulk; quality; glue; filler; — up
SKEE ski
SKYE Isle; dog, terrier
SLEE sly

SLOE blackthorn; plum; blue-black
SLUE swamp; twist; lot
SMEE pintail duck; widgeon; Peter Pan pirate
SNEE cut; snick(er) —
SOIE silk
SOKE jurisdiction
SOLE pelma (bottom); flatfish; single; only
SOME various; any; somewhat; part
SONE loudness unit
SORE painful; vexed; sensitive; deer
SPAE prophecy
SPEE Graf — (ship, admiral)
STYE eyelid swelling
SUKE Susan; tea-kettle
SUPE stage extra; supercharge
SURE safe; firm; certain
SYCE groom
SYKE fountain (Her.)
SYPE ooze
TACE steel splint
TAKE acquire, seize; scene part; receipts
TALE story; — of Two Cities; count
TAME gentle; subdue
TANE Polynesian god
TAPE band; tie; Indian; record; red —; ticker —
TARE vetch; allowance (weight)
TATE wool; hair lock
TAVE Octavia
TCHE fruit tree; Chin. flute
TELE prefix: far, complete
TENE suffix: ribbon
TETE head: Fr.; — à tête; hairdo
THEE you
TICE lure; yorker (bowled ball)
TIDE ocean's rise, fall; season; drift; endure; current; help
TIGE rifle steel pin; dog
TIKE child
TILE ceramic slab; drain pipe; domino; tessera; slate
TIME period; moment; credit term; speed rate; meter, rhythm; Father —; space —
TINE tooth; prong; pain; grass
TIPE rabbit trap
TIRE fatigue; bore; wheel covering; rubber; shoe
TOBE cotton cloth; future
TODE (haul with) sled
TOLE entice; told; tinware
TOME book; papal letter
TONE pitch; accent; Wolfe (Ir. rebel)
TOPE drink; shark; stupa; orchard
TORE ripped; geom. surface
TOTE carry; haul; total
TREE wood, plant; family —; boot, shoe —
TRUE factual; loyal; align
TUBE cylinder; tunnel; subway; radio, TV part; Audion (DeForest)
TUKE fabric; canvas
TULE bulrush; cattail
TUNE song; pitch; harmony
TUTE tutor
TWEE bird's cry
TYEE chief
TYKE dog, child
TYNE Eng. river
TYPE kind, sort; class(ify); printer's letter; use typewriter, produce copy
TYRE Phoenician city; Sur
ULME elm
UNBE cease to be
UNDE waving, wavy (Her.)
UNIE unicorn fish
URDE key-shaped (Her.)
URGE prod; impel; impulse
USEE future user
VADE leave; — mecum
VALE valley; — of tears; farewell: Lat.
VANE weathercock; feather; blade
VARE weasel
VASE vessel
VICE sin; fault; vise; proxy; — versa
VIDE see: Lat.; for example; quae —
VILE base; evil; odious
VINE creeping plant
VIRE feathered arrow
VISE tool; clamp; endorse
VITE quick, lively: Fr.
VIVE — le roi; long live!: Fr.
VOCE voice: It.; sotto, viva —
VOLE rodent; slam (cards)
VONE robot bomb
VOTE ballot; suffrage; voice; enact; propose; Ingrian Finn
WABE tree
WADE pass; demon; Hampton
WAGE carry on; -earner; pay,

salary
WAKE track; arouse; vigil; island
WALE streak; texture; ridge; welt
WANE ebb; lessen
WARE merchandise; beware
WATE sea demon
WAVE billow; swell; undulation, flutter; signal; — length; navy woman
WERE verb form; prefix: metamorphosed human
WESE we shall
WEVE contraction
WHEE whistle sound
WIDE broad; far; lax; astray
WIFE spouse; marry
WILE trick; guile; lure
WINE fermented juice
WIPE rub off; beat
WIRE cable; snare
WISE sage; learned
WIVE marry; act as wife
WNZE weight
WOKE stirred; roused
WORE had on (clothes); tired
WOTE Ingrian Finn
WOVE entwined; spun
XIPE -totec (Aztec god)
YAGE plant
YAJE plant
YALE university; lock; Eli, Elihu —; myth. antelope
YARE prompt; ready
YATE eucalyptus
YIPE howl; cry
YITE bird (yellowhammer)
YOKE join; link; slavery
YORE ancient (times); long ago
YULE Christmas
ZEKE Ezekiel
ZEME (abode of) spirit; fetish
ZONE area; band; partition
ZYME ferment

ALEF letter
ALIF letter
ATEF crown (Osiris)
AZOF town; sea
BAFF strike; stroke
BEEF ox, steer, cow, boss; brawn; rage; complain(t)
BIFF (deal a) blow
BOOF stare; peach brandy
BUFF leather; coat; tan; ward off; polish; wheel; bare skin; enthusiast
CALF bovine, etc., young; fur; leather; skin; lower leg
CARF slit; notch
CHEF head (cook); — d'oeuvre
CLEF musical sign; roman à —; key
COIF defensive skullcap; make up (hair)
CUFF slap; manacle; sleeve end; miser; on the —
DAFF put aside
DEAF unhearing; inattentive; — and dumb; — mute
DELF quarry; pottery; blue
DOFF put off; remove
DUFF pudding; cheat
ELEF letter
ENIF star
FIEF feudal state
GAFF spear; ordeal; hoax
GOAF grain; rick
GOFF clown; fool
GOLF game; blood-red; — links
GOOF dolt; blunder
GRAF nobleman: Ger.; — Spee (Zeppelin)
GUFF humbug; chaff
GULF bay; chasm; eddy
HAAF fishing grounds
HAFF lagoon
HALF moiety; -breed, -caste, -nelson, -shell
HEAF pasture
HOOF ungula; foot; beast; walk; dance
HUFF inflate; bully; anger
JEFF rope; nickname; Mutt and —
JIFF instant
KAIF languor; hemp
KEEF hemp; languor
KEIF hemp; languor
KERF cut; notch
KIEF hemp; languor
KIFF languor
KOFF Dutch sailboat
LEAF plant part; sheet; tea
LEIF Ericson (explorer)
LIEF gladly; freely
LOAF bread; idle
LOOF luff; sponge gourd
LUFF sail nearer wind
LUIF loof
MIFF quarrel; offend
MOFF Caucasian silk
MUFF handwarmer; bungle
NAIF naive; of true luster
NEIF serf; native; fist
NEUF nine, new: Fr.
OEUF egg: Fr.
OLAF (Vi)king
PELF booty; riches
PIFF bullet sound; exclamation
POOF exclamation
POUF puff; ottoman; bang!
PUFF blow; pastry; distend; hair roll; adder;

powder —
RAFF Raphael
REEF shoal; lode; reduce sail
RIFF Berber; Kabyle; ripple
ROOF cover; house; top
RUFF collar; bird; fish; plait; trump
SAUF except, safe: Fr.; — conduit
SELF identity; ego; one
SERF slave; peasant
SOUF sigh
STOF measure
SURF swell of sea; foam
TEFF grain plant
TIFF (petty) quarrel
TOFF dandy
TREF homestead
TUFF volcanic rock
TURF sod; grassy ground; peat; racing
WAFF flapping; paltry
WAIF stray
WAKF trust fund
WAQF trust fund
WARF warp
WELF ducal family
WERF farmyard
WOLF canid (dog); Lupus; larva; devour; dissonance; cry —; flirtatious man
WOOF crossthreads; texture; weft; bark
WRAF air force; aviatrix
WUFF gruff bark sound
WUKF trust fund
ZARF holder for cup

AGAG king
AGOG eager
AJOG jogging
AREG deserts
AWAG wagging
BAGG heiress (Thackeray)
BANG beat; thump; hair; sardine; interjection
BENG devil (Gypsy)
BERG iceberg; mountain
BIGG barley
BING bed roll; sharp sound
BONG bell sound
BORG borough: Dan.
BRAG boast; game
BRIG sailing ship; prison
BUNG stop(per); throw
BURG (fortified) town
CANG wooden collar
CHUG pull; fish; (move with) vibration
CLOG block; sandal; stop; impede; choke
COAG dowel
CRAG cliff; neck
CRIG blow
DAGG pistol
DANG curse (damn)
DING thump; sound; urge
DOEG Saul's herdsman; poet's nickname; Indian
DONG sound; weight; ding-; money
DRAG haul; harrow; obstacle; puff; auto race
DREG lees; residue
DRUG medicine; dope; — on the market; — addict
DUNG excrement; fertilize(r); weight
FANG tooth; measure; Dickens character
FLAG flower; standard; stone; signal; limp; reduce, dwindle
FLOG whip
FOGG Phileas (Verne)
FONG Ewe-speaking Negro
FROG amphibian; hoarseness; loop; rail device
FRUG dance
FUNG Sennar Negroid
GANG crew; associate; rock
GHEG Albanian
GLUG sound of liquids
GONG bell; tom-tom
GRIG dwarf; cricket; fowl
GROG liquor (with water)
GUEG Albanian
HAGG demoness; hack; wood
HAIG soldier (Douglas)
HANG suspend; plan; bit; die on gallows
HING asafetida (gum resin; antispasmodic)
HOGG unshorn sheep
HONG Chin. trade guild
HUNG suspended; undecided (jury)
ILOG river (Tagalog)
JAGG pendant; tooth; slash
JOUG iron collar; pillory
JUNG young: Ger.; Carl Gustave (psychologist)
KANG — Hsi (Chinese emperor)
KING monarch; ruler; chief; chessman; card
KNAG spur; knot
KRAG rifle
KUNG public
LANG auld — syne; Fritz
LING fish; burbot; hake
LONG lengthy; extended; yearn; John Silver (Stevenson);

Huey (La. politician); — time no see
LUNG air bladder; Iron —
LURG marine worm
MAGG bird; chatter
MANG bat (Kipling)
MENG mix
MIGG marble (duck)
MING Chin. dynasty
MONG among; barter
MORG measure
MUNG grass
NIOG coconut palm
NOGG egg drink
PANG agony
PEAG money
PHAG comb. form: eating
PING (bullet, striking) sound
PLUG stop(per); plod; shoot; spark —; horse; praise
PONG sound; improvise
PRIG precisian; steal; thief; fop
PROG (steal) food; forage
PUNG (drive) box sleigh; mah jongg term
QUAG morass
QUNG So. Afr. Bushman
RANG sounded
RING gird; arena; prizefighting; gang; atomic order; sound (bell); Vienna landmark; Nibelungen cycle (Wagner)
RONG Sikkimese language
RUGG pull
RUNG wheel spoke; hooped
SANG Hindu group; herb; weight; did sing
SARG Toni (puppeteer)
SCUG squirrel: Brit.
SHAG hair; tobacco; bird; rascal; dance step
SHOG shake; jog
SIEG victory: Ger.
SING vocalize; warble; tell
SKAG boat; keel part
SKEG keel part; plum; tear
SLAG dross; lava
SLOG hit (hard); slug; slam
SLUG snail; idle; metal spacer; small drink; bullet; strike
SMOG fog and smoke; haze
SMUG tidy; neat; priggish
SNAG stump; cut; obstacle; tangle
SNIG chop off; drag; pilfer
SNUG cozy; trim; Shaks. character
SONG poem (music); pittance
STAG deer; men's party; warn
STOG stall in mud
SUNG chanted; Chin. dynasty
SWAG bag; booty; sway; sag
SWIG gulp; hoist; tackle
TANG spur; flavor; sound; seaweed; dynasty
TEGG sheep in 2nd year
TEIG Teague; Thaddeus; Timothy
TENG measure
THUG assassin; hoodlum
TIGG swindler (Dickens)
TING sound; Chin. pottery
TOAG Indian
TONG secret society
TOUG horsetail standard
TRIG trim; sound; prim; math. course
TUNG tree; oil
TWIG discover; branch; beat
UANG beetle
UTUG horsetail standard
VANG rope
VOOG lode cavity
VUGG lode cavity
WAAG monkey
WAEG bird; kittiwake
WANG weight; meadow; prince
WEGG Silas (ballad seller: Dickens)
WHIG U.S., Brit. party
WIGG peruke; long hair
WING alar appendage; faction; annex; fly
WONG field; meadow
WRIG wriggle
YANG honk; male or positive principle (opp. to yin)
YEGG safecracker; tramp
ZING sharp thrill; vim

ACTH hormone medicine
ADAH wife of Lamech, Esau; fem. name
AIAH Edomite, Rizpah's father
AICH alloy
ALPH river (Coleridge: Kubla Khan)
AMAH nurse
ANKH cross
ARAH exclamation
ARCH support; curve; chief; fingerprint; triumphal —
ARGH timid
ASCH Scholem (author)
AYAH nurse; sign
BACH live alone; composer
BASH smash; bruise
BATH tub; measure;

spa; order
BETH Hebrew B, 2; Alcott heroine (Little Women)
BIKH aconite; poison
BINH weight
BISH aconite; poison
BLAH nonsense
BOOH exclamation
BOSH furnace part; nonsense (nothing: Turk.)
BOTH the two
BROH macaque monkey
BRUH pig-tailed macaque
BUKH prate; talk
BURH (fortified) town
BUSH shrub; thicket; tall
CAPH star; letter
CASH money; exchange; hemlock
CECH Czech.
CHIH Chin. foot (measure)
COBH Irish port
COSH snug; happy; math. term
CUSH sorghum; cow; money; Ham's son; country
DAGH hill
DASH sprint; smash; small portion
DICH you: Ger.
DISH receptacle; serve
DOTH does
DRAH measure
EACH every(one)
ELAH king
ESTH Balt; Estonian (Tallinn man)
ETAH Eskimo settlement; town
ETCH eat into; engrave
EYAH nurse; sign
FASH rough edges; vex
FISH piscine; angle; probe; search; tin — (torpedo)
FOCH Ferdinand (Fr. marshal; WW I commander)
GASH (make) incision
GATH Philistine city
GISH Moroccan public land; Lillian, Dorothy (actresses)
GOGH Vincent van (painter)
GOSH oath; -awful
GOTH Teuton (Theodoric, Alaric); barbarian; Ostro-; Visi-
GUSH flow; spout; be effusive
HAKH claim(er); legal claim; share
HAPH weight
HASH chop up; mixture; mess
HATH contraction: haveth
HEGH exclamation; hey!
HETH son of Canaan; Hittite ancestor
HIGH lofty; elevated; noble; expensive; shrill; tainted; tipsy
HISH hiss; swish
HOCH high: Ger.
HOTH blind god (Balder slayer)
HUCH Danube fish
HUGH name; saint (of Cluny)
HUNH exclamation
HUSH quiet; silence; -hush; -puppy; — money
IHVH God; Tetragrammaton
INCH measure; move slowly
ITCH skin irritation; desire
IVAH Bib. city
JETH Hindu month
JHVH Jahweh; God; Tetragrammaton
JHWH Jahweh; God; Tetragrammaton
JOAH record keeper
JOCH yoke, measure: Ger.
JOSH make fun; banter
KAPH letter
KATH astringent
KISH powder; basket; measure; Saul's father
KITH acquaintance; — and kin
KOCH cook: Ger.; Robert (bacteriologist)
KOPH Heb. K, Q, 100
KUSH Ham's son; country
KYAH partridge
LAKH 100,000; coin
LASH (whip) stroke; tie; eye part
LATH strip; slat
LEAH fem. name; Laban's daughter; Jacob's wife
LECH slab; capstone; river
LITH prefix, suffix: stone
LOCH lake, bay; Scot.
LOSH wash leather
LOTH averse; reluctant
LUGH Celtic light god
LUOH White Nile Negro
LUSH luxurious; drunkard
MAGH month
MASH crush; brew; mixture; hammer; flirt
MATH mowing; monastery; school course
MEAH wall tower
MESH net; netting; entangle
MICH me: Ger.
MOTH lepidopterous insect; -ball; -eaten; gypsy —; page (Shaks.)
MUCH great (deal); far; —Ado (Shaks.)
MUSH meal; hasty pudding;

flattery; proceed!
MUTH measure
MYTH (religious) legend; fiction
NACH after: Ger.
NASH soft; humorist
NATH star
NESH soft; juicy; dainty
NIGH near(ly); direct
NISH Yugo. city
NOAH patriarch (Ark builder)
OATH appeal; pledge; vow; curse
OKEH all right, O.K.
OLPH bullfinch
OPAH fish
OUCH exclamation
OUGH exclamation
PASH hurl; smash
PATH track; route
PISH reject; nonsense!
PITH marrow; kernel; gist
POOH pshaw!; Bah (Mikado); Winnie (bear: Milne)
POSH slush; elegant
PRAH canoe
PTAH god
PUGH pshaw!; fish prong
PUSH shove; thrust; strive; -button
QOPH Heb. K, Q, 100
RAKH hayfield
RASH hasty; careless
RATH chariot; fort; temple; early; mome-
RESH Heb. letter, 200; plant
RICH wealthy; vivid; full; fragrant; fat
ROCH Saint (14th cent.)
RUKH fabled bird; jungle
RUSH haste(n); attack; red (mace); cattail
RUTH pity; grief; name; OT book, heroine
(Moabitess); wife of Boaz
SAAH measure
SADH holy man
SAHH measure
SAMH bread plant
SAPH giant (Philistine)
SASH casement; scarf; belt
SEAH measure
SECH such
SETH banker; Adam's son; Osiris' evil brother
SHAH ruler
SHIH weight; measure
SIGH lament(ing sound)
SIKH Hindu soldier
SINH math. term
SISH slushy ice
SOPH 2nd-year student
SOSH jag; drunk; dash
SUCH of this kind; same
TANH math. term
TASH fabric
TATH dung
TECH technical school
TETH Heb. T, 9
TOPH drum; porous rock
TOSH bath(tub)
TUSH tooth; Georgian; pshaw!
UMPH grunt
URTH Norn; Wyrd (with Verthandi, Skuld), Weird Sister
UTAH state; Indian; Deseret (Mormon)
UTCH "I"
VACH goddess
VOTH Ingrian Finn
VUGH lode cavity
WAGH interjection
WASH bathe; laundry; tint
WISH desire; request
WITH prep.: including, and
WYCH -hazel; — elm
YEAH yes
YHVH God, Yahveh, Tetragrammaton
YHWH God, Yahweh, Tetragrammaton
YODH Hebrew Y, 10
YOGH Mid. Eng. G, Y
ZACH name
ZUPH Samuel's ancestor

AALI pasha
AANI ape
ABRI shelter
ABSI tribe
ADAI tribe
ADMI gazelle
AERI prefix: air
AGNI god; lambs
AGRI fields
AIPI cassava
AKTI peninsula
ALAI regiment; mountain; jai —
ALBI flagellants
ALII royalty (Hawaiian)
AMBI about; prefix: both
AMLI tree
AMMI herb
AMOI mine: Fr.
ANAI termite
ANDI language
ANNI years: Lat.
ANTI opposed; prefix: against; Indian
APII plant
ARNI buffalo
ARUI sheep
ASCI spore sacs
ASSI holly
ASTI city; — spumante
ATHI Kenya river
ATLI Gudrun's husband-king
ATRI It. town
AURI prefix: gold, ear
BABI sect
BAHI fortune
BALI demon; monkey; offering; Island
BANI coins

BARI hut; Negro; city
BELI myth. Brit. king
BENI Bolivian river; sesame
BERI Sudanese (Fulah); -beri (disease)
BIBI title: Lady, Mrs. (India)
BIMI orangutan (Kipling)
BINI Nigerian
BIRI cheap cigarette
BITI blackwood
BNAI B'rith (Jewish Society)
BOII Celtic tribe
BONI African; Boschneger
BORI Lucrezia (singer)
BREI soft tissue
BUBI Fernando Po Bantu
BUGI Celebes Malay
BURI palm (fiber); talipot
BUZI Ezekiel's father
CADI judge
CAJI snapper
CALI Colombian city
CAXI snapper (fish)
CAZI Moslem Judge
CHAI person
CIII 103; Trajan reign
CLII 152; Hadrian reign
COLI intestinal bacterium
CORI It. commune
CONI Carl, Gerty (Nobel winners)
CUBI measure
CVII 107; Trajan reign
CXII 112; Trajan reign
DALI tree; offering; Salvador —
DARI grain sorghum; carpet
DASI concubine
DECI prefix: tenth
DEFI challenge; defiance
DELI delicatessen
DEMI prefix: half
DESI jute; Arnaz
DEVI goddess; Siva's wife (Shakti); title: Mrs., Lady
DHAI midwife
DIVI divine ones
DIXI I have spoken: Lat.
DOLI weights
DONI fishing boat
DREI three: Ger.
EKOI Bantu
ELOI Eli: God
ENKI Babylonian god
EPHI measure
EQUI prefix: equal, same
ETUI (vanity) case; box
FAVI tiles; flagstones
FIJI Islands (Lau, Yasawa)
FILI learned poet
FOCI center points
FUCI rockweeds; algae
FUJI wisteria; cherry; volcano
GABI taro
GALI abuse
GAZI warrior; title
GERI Odin's wolf
GOAI shrub
GOBI Mongolian desert
GOLI musket ball; pill
GUMI shrub, flower, fruit
GUTI Sumer settler; Kurd
GYRI brain ridges
HAGI clover; prefix: saint
HAJI pilgrim
HALI prefix: sea, salt
HAMI hooked processes
HAPI bull; Nile (god)
HARI river; Mata (spy)
HATI heart
HEII Hawaiian fern
HELI prefix: sun, spiral
HEMI prefix: half
HEVI apple (tree)
HIFI faithful sound rendition
HOLI spring festival
HONI — soit qui mal y pense; shamed
HOPI French beige; Moqul Indian
HOTI cause; reason
HURI Abihail's father
HUSI fine P.I. fiber
IIWI bird (mamo)
ILAI David's man
IMMI measure
IMPI armed Kaffirs
INTI Incas' deified sun, sun god
IONI Hainai; Chaddo Indian
ISUI Asher's son
JAMI mosque
JATI caste
JIBI extinct bird
JITI Rajmahal creeper
JOGI yogi; ascetic
JOLI pretty, nice: Fr.
JOTI astrologer; astronomer
JUSI fine P.I. fiber
KADI judge
KAKI bird; tree
KALI glasswort; carpet; evil genius; Agni's tongue; Siva's wife
KAMI language; deity
KARI gum tree
KASI tile work
KATI weight
KAVI Java language
KAWI Java language
KAZI Moslem judge
KEPI military cap
KERI read(ing substitute)
KIKI castor oil plant
KIRI paulownia tree; knobkerrie (missile)
KIWI flightless bird; apteryx; nonflyer; fruit

KIYI herring; cisco; yelp
KOBI Japanese reserve duty (term)
KOJI Jap. yeast cake
KOLI low-caste tribesman
KOMI Soviet republic; Zyrians
KOPI N.Z. tree (karaka)
KORI bustard; low weaver
KUEI disembodied spirit
KUKI Burma Mongol
KULI low-caste Indian
KURI Lezhgian tribesman
KWEI disembodied spirit
LARI money; sea birds
LASI tribe
LAZI tribesman
LEHI prophet
LETI island off Timor
LEVI Jacob's, Leah's son; tribe
LIII 53; Claudius reign
LITI medieval peasants
LOCI places; sites
LODI city; Napoleon victory
LOKI god of discord; Aesir; Balder slayer
LORI lemur; Afr. Negro
LOTI Pierre (writer: Viaud)
LUDI Roman public games
LURI Lake Albert Negro
LVII 57; Nero reign
LXII 62; Nero reign
MABI tree
MADI Negro
MAGI caste; priests; wise men, kings of Orient: Melchior, Gaspar, Balthazar
MAHI river
MAKI lemur
MALI caste; nation; river
MANI peanut; prefix: hand
MARI prefix: sea; husband: Fr.; native
MAUI Polynesian hero
MCII 1102
MEDI prefix: middle
MIDI south(ern France)
MIII 1003
MIMI nickname; opera heroine
MLII 1052
MOJI Jap. seaport
MOKI N.Z. raft
MOTI elephant (Kipling)
MVII 1007
MXII 1012
NASI prince; patriarch
NAZI fascist; Hitlerite
NERI Blacks: It.
NETI eulalia (thatch grass)
NGAI spiritual power
NIDI breeding places
NISI unless: Lat.
NODI knots; difficulties
NOLI — me tangere
NORI seaweed food
NOZI of Yanan tribe
NUCI prefix: nut
OMEI Buddhist mountain
OMNI prefix: all
OMRI king of Israel
OZNI Gad's son
PADI rice
PAHI ship
PALI slope; coral parts; Buddhist language
PANI madam: Polish
PASI low-caste Hindu
PARI weight; prefix: equal
PEAI medicine man
PEDI prefix: foot
PERI fairy; elf; beauty
PFUI exclamation
PICI birds (woodpeckers)
PIKI maize bread; pik
PILI nut; grass; hairs
PIPI astringent; mollusk
PULI coins
PURI Indian yellow
QERI read(ing substitute)
QUAI pier
QUEI measure
RABI crop; physicist
RAGI grass
RAKI spirits
RAMI branches
RANI princess; wife
RATI weight
RAVI tribesman
REKI Baluchistan nomad
REMI Gaul people; prefix: oar
RENI It. painter; prefix: kidney
RIFI Riffs
RIGI Swiss mountain
RODI Medit. island
ROMI Gypsy wife
RORI Bantu tribe
ROTI roasted: Fr.
SADI poet
SAFI Afghan
SAKI monkey; Munro
SARI Hindu garment
SATI queen of the gods
SEBI prefix: tallow
SEMI half
SERI betel; indian
SESI black-fin snapper
SETI river; pharaoh
SHRI glorious; holy; Lakshmi (goddess)
SIDI Moslem title; Negro
SIMI Dodecanese isle
SIRI betel

SISI	porkfish
SODI	Gaddiel's father (spy)
SOLI	single performances; prefix: sun, alone
SORI	clusters; spores
SUFI	mystic ascetic
SUGI	Jap. cedar
SUJI	wheat; semolina
SUSI	fine cotton
TABI	sock
TALI	gold piece; weight
TARI	coin; goddess
TAXI	(ride a) cab; prefix: arrangement
TCHI	measure
TELI	low (merchant) caste
THAI	Siamese
TIKI	god; first man; image
TIPI	wigwam
TITI	monkey; tree; petrel
TOPI	antelope; pith hat
TORI	moldings
TSHI	Gold Coast language
TUPI	Amazon Indian
TURI	Pathan tribesman
TUWI	P.I. dyewood tree
TYBI	1st Egypt. spring month
UBII	Teutonic tribe
UNCI	hooks; claws
UTAI	noh songs (yo-kyoku)
UZAI	Palal's father
VAGI	nerves
VALI	Odin's son; viceroy
VARI	lemur; prefix: diverse
VENI	prefix: vein; —, vidi, vici (I came, I saw, I conquered)
VERI	centipede
VIII	8 (Augustus reign)
VILI	brother of Odin; Ve
VITI	East African
VLEI	marsh; lake; creek
WABI	Indian; tree
WADI	valley; river; oasis
WALI	prefect
WEKI	fern
WERI	aweto (caterpillar)
XIII	13; Augustus reign
YAGI	antenna
YAKI	cayman
YALI	mansion
YATI	ascetic; devotee
YETI	abominable snowman
YENI	So. Amer. tanager
YOBI	Jap. military service
YOGI	ascetic; yoga disciple
YUKI	Cal. Indian
ZATI	bonnet monkey
ZEMI	(abode of) spirit; fetish
ZORI	sandal
ZUNI	Indian; reservation
ZWEI	two: Ger.
BENJ	hemp; narcotic
BRAJ	basha
FUNJ	Sennar Negroid
GUNJ	granary; market
HADJ	pilgrimage
HAJJ	pilgrimage
MUNJ	tough grass; twine
TEBJ	Negro Berber
ADAK	Aleut. island
AMOK	frenzy
ANAK	giant race
ARAK	palm; spirit
ASAK	tree
ASOK	tree
ATIK	star
BACK	help; tub; past; retreat; kick-; dorsal, posterior; spine
BALK	thwart; signal
BANK	mound; bench; deposit; bird flock; Left, Right —; blood —; eye —
BARK	peel; tan; cough
BASK	luxuriate; warm
BEAK	bill; nose; judge
BECK	nod; bidding; dyeing vat; Pol., Ger. officer, statesman
BILK	defraud
BISK	soup; ice cream; red-yellow
BOCK	beer; leather
BONK	bar money (Dutch E.I.)
BOOK	tome; volume; Bible; libretto; (bet) record; register; throw the —
BOSK	thicket
BOWK	steep; soak in lime
BUCK	deer; fop; butt; male; Pearl (novelist); pass the —
BUKK	prate; talk
BULK	mass, volume; loom; -head (stall)
BUNK	case; bed; nonsense
BUSK	stir about; hasten; corset bone; Indian New Year
CALK	tighten; stop; sleep; tool; copy
CARK	trouble
CASK	barrel; measure
CAUK	(secure by a) tenon
CAWK	bird's cry; mineral
CHEK	Chin. foot (measure)
COAK	tenon
COCK	male fowl; vane; leader; tap; tee; hay pile; cog

CONK nose; head; decay; fall; hit

COOK chef; concoct; falsify; James (explorer)

CORK tree; bark; stop(per); brown; Irish city (Lee)

CUSK fish; burbot; eel

DANK moist; rank

DARK unlighted; wicked; dismal

DAUK relay post

DAWK relay transport; mall

DECK ship floor; pack, cards; array; adorn

DESK table; lectern; department

DHAK tree

DICK Richard; whip; lad; detective; Whittington (London mayor)

DINK small boat; cut out

DIRK dagger; Theodoric

DISK plate; harrow; puck

DOCK weed; rumex; (cur)tail; pier

DOOK wooden brick; demon

DUCK bird; webfoot; wild fowl; canvas; pet; plunge; evade; — soup; vehicle

DUNK dip into; immerse

DUSK twilight; gloom

DYAK Bornean

DYCK Anthony Van (painter)

EFIK Negro

ESEK Isaac's well

FEAK twitch; wipe

FECK amount

FERK measure

FINK finch; derb; informer; strikebreaker

FISK exchequer; Jim (speculator); tire

FLAK antiaircraft

FOLK people; — ways, laws, song, dance

FORK implement (pronged); tuner; place of divergence

FULK unfair shove (marbles)

FUNK fear; coward; Casimir (vitamins); Issac (lexicographer); — & Wagnalls

GAWK lout; stare

GEEK carnival wild man

GINK eccentric one

GOOK trash; ooze; native

GOWK simpleton; fool

GUNK jilt; hoax

HAAK fish; wander

HACK chop; writer; horse

HAIK garment; frame

HANK coil; Morgan (Twain)

HARK listen

HAWK bird; predator; peddle; mortarboard

HECK (weaving) frame; cough; oath

HICK hiccup; rube; jake

HOCK leg joint; hamstring; wine; faro card; pawn

HOEK stream bend; van Holland (Dutch cape, city)

HONK goose cry; toot; ooga

HOOK trap; curve; catch; steal; — and eye; pirate (Peter Pan; Barrie)

HUCK towel fabric

HULK ship body; bulky thing

HUNK piece; lump; OK

HUSK covering (of seed, corn); shell

IRAK country

IROK gomuti (palm)

JACK flag; tool; card; fruit; raise

JERK grab; twist; spasm; soda man; dullard; beef

JINK prank

JOCK John; jockey; hobo

JONK jonquil

JOOK perch; slumber

JUCK partridge call

JUNK ship; trash; scrap

KAIK village

KECK vomit; show disgust

KEEK fashion spy

KELK fish roe

KIAK canoe

KICK hit; die; object(ion); excitement; -back

KINK twist; loop; cramp

KIRK church

KONK conk

KUNK measure

KURK church: Scot.

KYAK canoe

LACK need

LANK thin; lean(ness)

LARK bird; frolic; yellow

LAUK exclamation

LAWK surprise!

LEAK loss; ooze; crack

LEEK plant (onion, liliaceous); — green (Wales emblem)

LICK tongue; stroke; whip; conquer; bit

LINK (chain) loop; connect; join; torch; measure

LISK flank; loin

LOCK gate (canal, dam); tuft; wool; fasten(ing), grapple;

tie up; -out (labor)
LONK black-faced sheep
LOOK observe; appear(ance); eye(wink); care
LUCK chance; event; fortune
LURK lie in wait; skulk
LUSK lazy (fellow)
MACK coat
MARK sign; aim; stamp; money; observe; evangelist; easy —; — time
MASK disguise; screen; domino
MAWK maggot
MEEK mild; submissive
MICK Irishman
MILK nutritious fluid; sap; white; exploit; drain
MINK weasel-like animal
MIRK dark(ness)
MOCK jeer; taunt; sham; — apple, turtle
MONK ascetic; friar; bird; fish; spot; ferret
MOSK Moslem temple; Masjid
MUCK (rid of) manure; mess
MULK freehold land
MURK (make) gloomy
MUSK odor; aromatic secretion (of deer, ox, etc.)
NABK shrub
NAIK leader
NARK informer; tease
NECK body part; violin part; isthmus; pet
NICK notch; moment; cheat; cut; Old (devil); Carter (detective)
NOCK notch (in bow)
NOOK corner; retreat
NUBK shrub
OMSK Siberian city
PACK bundle; cosmetic paste; cards; crowd; animal(s)
PANK weight
PARK (common) grounds; green; deposit; Hyde, Central, etc.
PEAK point; top; summit
PECK measure; nip; bite; kiss
PEEK sly glance; pry; chirp
PENK minnow
PERK lift up; preen; cocky; percolate
PICK tool; scratch; choose; rob; eat; best
PINK color (red); ship; cut; hunter's coat; carnation; in the — (healthy)
PISK nighthawk
POCK postule
POLK Cossack regiment; James Knox (President)
POOK hobgoblin; disk
PORK meat; swine; — barrel
PUCK sprite; Robin Goodfellow; Shaks. character; hockey disk
PULK (Cossack) regiment
PUNK touchwood; tinder; conch; tramp; bad
RACK framework; clouds; gait; torture
RAIK weight; measure
RANK luxuriant; gross; fetid; grade; array
RECK heed; concern
REEK cloud; excude; smell
RICK pile (up); haystack
RIKK tambourine
RINK skating arena
RISK peril; hazard; subject of insurance
ROCK stone; Gibraltar; cliff; staunch support; diamond; candy; sway, lull; — the boat
ROOK bird; cheat; dupe; chessman (tower)
RUCK crowd; rake; wrinkle
RUSK bread; biscuit; Dean (statesman)
SACK dismiss; plunder; wine; bag; gown; sad —
SANK descended
SARK Channel island
SAUK Indian; Mont. river
SAWK measure
SECK unprofitable (rent)
SEEK ask; try; hunt
SEIK Hindu sectarian
SHIK Arab. Turkoman
SIAK latex
SICK urge (dog); ill; weak
SILK fiber; thread; -worm
SINK fall; droop; conceal; basin
SOAK absorb; sot
SOBK evil deity
SOCK beat; wind cone; stocking
SOOK Moslem market; hog call
SOUK Moslem market
SUCK draw in; bleed; drink
SULK mope; be

sullen
SUNK immersed; overcome
TACK hook; rope; course; attach
TALK speak; converse; conference; empty words; dialect; — turkey
TANK basin; store; war vehicle; panzer
TASK labor; assignment; take to — (censure)
TEAK tree; dark
TECK readymade tie
TICK parasite; mattress; count; tic
TOCK hornbill
TONK (cow bell) clang; honky-; game
TOOK seized; caught; endured; supposed
TOSK Albanian
TREK migrate; journey
TRUK islands (Carolines)
TUCK draw up; fold (in); eat; Friar (Robin Hood)
TUNK rap; thump; game
TURK Mongoloid; Seljuk; Ottoman; Osmanil; horse
TUSK long tooth
UNUK star; — al Hay
VOLK people: Ger.; workmen (So. Afr.)
WALK go on foot; path; pass, base on balls; — the plank
WAUK wake: Scot.
WEAK feeble; pliable; light
WEEK time unit; sennight; squeak
WELK (gather) snail; Lawrence

(musician)
WICK part of candle, lamp
WILK (gather) snail
WINK blink; signal
labor; mental
WORK product; act; operate; function; needlework
YANK jerk; New Englander; Union soldier; American
YARK yerk
YELK yolk
YERK wrench; kick; trump
YOLK egg yellow; essence
YORK city; archbishopric; imperial (apple); Sgt. Alvin (WW I)

ABEL Adam's son; Cain's brother; Magwitch (Dickens); letter A; monkey
ACYL acid part
AGAL cord
AIEL writ of —
AKAL deity
AMIL plant; remedy
AMYL starch; alcohol
ANAL pert. to anus
ANIL shrub, indigo
AOUL Nepalese
ARAL lake
ARIL seed covering
AVAL grandparental
AWOL absent without leave
AXAL around an axis
AXIL leaf angle
AZEL Saul's descendant
AZUL blue: Sp.
BAAL deity
BAEL thorny (fruit) tree
BAIL security; bond; set free; dip out; hoop
BALL game; confuse; dance; —

bearing; good time; -point; Amer. sculptor
BAUL mendicant
BAWL cry; howl; — out (chide)
BEAL river mouth
BELL ringing cup; gong; time period; flower shape; helmet; Brontë pseudonym; — the cat; diving —
BHEL thorny (fruit) tree
BHIL low-caste Indian
BILL beak; weapon; law; poster; invoice; debt; nickname: William; — and coo; Sikes (Dickens)
BIRL revolve; spin
BOIL heat; bubble; agitation; abscess
BOLL (strip) plant pod
BOOL curved handle
BOWL basin; dish; (roll) ball
BUAL wine
BUHL inlaid decoration
BULL (bovine) male; stud; papal letter; optimist; Taurus; policeman; blunder; glib talk; -fight
BURL (pick) knot; Ives (actor)
CALL summon; visit; cry; telephone; — girl; — money
CARL rustic; villain; Charles
CAUL basket; covering membrane
CAWL basket
CEIL overlay; line; ceiling
CELL cubicle; group; elec. jar; organism

CHAL man
CHIL cheer pine; kite (Kipling)
CHOL desolate plain; Mayan
CIEL ceiling; sky: Fr.
CIRL bunting; bird
COAL ember; fuel
COEL cuckoo
COIL curl; wind; twist
COLL embrace; hug; Vincent (gangster: "mad dog")
COOL chill; calm; unmoved
COWL hood; auto body front
CRAL hut; village
CULL pick out; assort
CURL coil; twist; hair lock
DAIL legislature; — Eireann
DALL sheep
DEAL bargain; transaction; unfinished wood; apportion(ment); policy: New —, Fair —
DEIL devil; -'s-bit (plant)
DELL valley; dingle; wench
DEUL Hindu temple
DHAL split pea, lentil
DIAL plate; face; call; sun-
DILL flavoring herb; pickle
DIOL chem. compound; suffix
DOLL plaything; puppet; dress up; girl
DOWL feathery down
DUAL double
DUEL combat; meeting
DULL blunt(ed); dismal; inert; tedious; Shaks.
character
EARL nobleman; court; name
EBAL Mount (Joshua's altar)
EDEL noble: Ger.
EGAL equal: Fr.
EGIL Volund's (Wayland's) brother
EGOL antiseptic
ELUL month
EMIL man's name
EMOL rock salt
ENOL chem. suffix
ERAL epochal
ETAL and others: Lat.
EVIL bad; sinful; injury; disease
EZEL juniper tree
FAIL fall short; err
FALL descend; ruin; autumn; — of Man
FARL cake (part)
FEAL conceal
FEEL sense; test; suffer
FEIL comfortable; neat
FELL skin; cut, hew (down); savage
FILL pack; complete; glut; — the bill
FOAL colt; equine young
FOIL balk; defeat; sword; leaf; sheet
FOOL dolt; jester; trick
FOUL rotten; poor; illegal; invalid
FOWL poultry; cock; hen
FUEL combustible matter
FULL filled; replete; quite; — dress; — house
FURL roll up (sail, flag)
GAAL brewing
GAEL Celt; Irishman
GAGL sweet gale
GAIL Abigail; brewing
GALL bile; venom; wound; chafe; swelling; impudence
GAOL prison
GAUL Celt, Frenchman; France
GEAL pert. to earth
GILL measure; brook; breathing organ; wattle; coin; lass
GIRL young female; maid; Gibson —; — Friday; — of the Golden West; chorus —
GOAL purpose; objective; score
GOEL reclaimer; avenger
GOLL Irish hero (Fenian)
GOUL monster; grave robber
GOWL gad; defile; howl; monster
GULL bird; cheat; dupe
GUNL gunwale
HAIL ice pieces; salute; — fellow
HALL building; room; town —; guild-; astronomer; Mills
HARL barb; filament
HAUL drag; shift; loot
HEAL cure; restore
HEEL back part; end; slant; follow; scoundrel
HEIL hail: Ger.
HELL Hades; state of misery; -bent
HERL (feather) barb
HIEL Jericho's rebuilder
HILL mound; Jenny (Shaw character); -billy
HOLL ditch
HOWL (distress) cry; wail
HULL husk; ship

body; Cordell (statesman)
HURL throw; pitch; rush
ICAL compound suffix
IDOL god, deity; image adored one
IDYL pastoral poem
IFIL tree (brown dye)
IGAL Moses' spy
IPIL tree (brown dye)
ITOL suffix; alcohol(ic)
IXIL Mayan Indian
JAAL goat
JAEL Sisera's killer; Heber's wife
JAIL prison; gaol
JARL Norse chief; earl
JEEL pool; marsh
JELL solidify; mature
JERL boat joint
JILL girl; sweetheart; Jack and —
JOEL prophet, OT book
JOLL move clumsily; knock
JOWL jaw; cheek; wattle; gambler (Dickens)
KAIL tree; ibex; kale
KARL Charles; — Marx
KEAL cabbage
KEEL ship bottom; navigate; ocher; guinea fowl
KELL Gaul; net; film
KIEL ocher; ruddle; seaport; — Canal
KILL slay; veto; creek
KOEL cuckoo
KOHL eye shadow; horse
KOIL cuckoo
KRAL hut; village
KUHL eyelid cosmetic
LAEL Gershonite's father
LEAL loyal: Scot.
LEIL faithful, loyal (Land of the —)
LILL small pin; loll; Lillian
LOLL droop; lounge; sprawl
LULL (temporary) quiet
MAAL measure
MAIL coin; tax; armor; post
MALL mallet; game; bird; assembly (place)
MARL clayey soil; fertilizer; fiber
MAUL hammer; bruise; mangle
MEAL grain; pulverize; repast
MELL (beat with) hammer; teacher (Dickens)
MERL blackbird
MEWL whimper; miaou
MILL grind(er); quern; box; John Stuart (economist)
MOIL toil; trouble; spot
MOLL Mary; girl; Flanders (Defoe); minor (mus.)
MULL muslin; ointment; ponder; humus
MYAL cultic
NAEL weight
NAIL fasten(er); claw; seize; expose
NEAL male name; novelist
NEIL male name
NELL Ellen; Helen; Little — (Dickens girl)
NIEL alloy
NILL refuse; negate
NOEL Christmas; carol; — Coward
NOIL combing (wool fiber)
NOLL Oliver (Cromwell); head; noddle
NOYL fiber knot
NULL nil; void; code filler
NURL wood knot; to mill
OBOL 1/16 drachma (coin)
ODAL land; vine
ODEL vine; land ownership
ODYL alleged force
OEIL eye: Fr.; — de boeuf
OHEL Zerubabbel's son
OPAL birthstone (Oct.); girasol
ORAL spoken; of the mouth
OREL Russian city
OVAL egg-shaped; elliptic; arena
OXYL oxygen radical
PAAL measure
PAIL bucket
PALL cloak; covering; cloy
PAUL click; detent; Apostle; Bunyan; Revere; pope
PAWL click; detent; tent
PEAL ring; loud sound; fish
PEEL pare; tower; spade
PEUL Fulah (Sudanese)
PHIL nickname; prefix: loving
PILL medicine tablet
POIL raw silk thread
POLL head; register; survey; cut off; Mary; parrot; vote
POOL pond; puddle; game; stake; fund; Thames
POUL Russ. coin
PULL drag; influence
PURL knitting stitch; beer; murmur; spin; swirl
PYAL veranda

RAIL bird; scold; paling
REAL coin; true; genuine; very
REEL wind(er); dance; waver; sway
RIAL coin
RILL (run in a) brook
RIEL Canadian (Indian) rebel
ROIL disturb; muddy; vex
ROLL wrap; trill; drumbeat; rotate; list; bank-
ROOL crumple; ruffle
ROTL Afr. weight
RULL to wheel; trundle
RYAL coin
RYEL coin
SAAL hall: Ger.
SAIL canvas; rigging; journey; travel
SAUL tree; king (son of Kish; — of Tarsus (Paul)
SEAL otarian; pinniped; fur; fasten; brown; ratify; stamp
SEEL shut eyes of; blind
SEIL rope: Ger.
SELL vend; betray; persuade; hoax; — short
SHUL synagogue
SIAL earth's outer part
SILL beam (door, window)
SIOL great Irish clan
SKAL health toast
SKIL candlefish; beshow
SOIL earth; ground; land; stain; pollute
SOOL pull, tousle about
SOUL spirit; inspirer; force; psyche; person
STOL short takeoff and landing
TAAL lake; volcano; language
TAEL weight; coin
TAIL end; cue; fellow; high-
TALL high; incredible
TEAL duck (blue)
TEEL sesame
TEIL linden tree; lime
TELL inform; discern; chat; William (Swiss hero)
TEYL linden; lime tree
TILL until; plow; cultivate; tray, cash box
TOIL work; drudge(ry); snare
TOLL tax; lure; sound
TOOL instrument; polish; dupe
TUEL furnace
UDAL land
UNAL land
URAL -Altaic; mountains; hypnotic
UVAL grapelike
UZAL Shem's descendant
VAAL river
VAIL inventor
VALL valley
VEAL calf; meat
VEIL screen; facial garment; cloistered life
VIAL vessel
VILL village; township
VIOL string instrument
VTOL vertical takeoff and landing
WAIL lament
WALL barrier; fence; enclose; knot; Berlin —
WAUL wall
WEAL body politic; stripe
WEEL fish basket; trap; pool
WELL (water) pit; shaft; eddy; flow; rightly; very; sound, healthy
WIEL whirlpool
WILL volition; choice; decree; bequeath; testament
WOOL (sheep) fleece; down
YARL Norse chief; earl
YAWL (sail)boat
YELL cry; cheer
YOWL howl(ing); yell
YPIL tree (brown dye)
ZEAL ardor; enthusiasm
ZOLL measure

ADAM first man; sin; composer; architect
AHEM interjection
AHOM Assam native
AHUM humming
AKIM Negro; Tamiroff
ALEM fruit
ALIM teacher
ALUM emetic; astringent; styptic
ANAM tree; Vietnam region
ANEM prefix; wind; city
ARAM country (Syria); Eugene (murderer)
ARUM herb; starch
ASEM alloy
ATOM whit; particle; nuclear complex
ATUM sun god (Tem)
AZAM sir: Persian
BALM plant; soothe; — in Gilead
BARM yeast
BAUM Vicki (novelist); Oz creator; tree: Ger.; — marten
BEAM bar; timber; breadth; ray; smile; on the —; broadcast
BERM (l)edge; road shoulder
BOOM hum; grow,

push; beam
BRAM Abraham
BRIM rim; edge; swell
BROM Bones (Ichabod's rival)
CAAM loom; heddies
CALM quiet; mold
CHAM tribe; title; bite
CHUM friend; scrap fish
CLAM mollusk; hush
CLEM riot; suffer hunger; nickname
CLIM — of the Clough (archer outlaw)
CLUM clutch roughly
CLYM — of the Clough (archer outlaw)
COOM coal dust; refuse
CORM bulblike stem (crocus)
CRAM press; stuff; study
CROM Cruaich (Irish idol)
CULM grass stem; coal dust; shoal water deposit
DAWM coin
DEEM consider; judge
DERM prefix, suffix: skin layer
DEUM Te — (hymn)
DIEM day: Lat.; per —
DOOM (last) judgment; fate; condemn
DORM dormitory; sleep
DOUM palm
DRAM measure; drink
DRUM spool; instrument: tympanum; beat
DUIM measure
EDAM city; cheese
EDOM Esau's country; Idumaea
EJAM Bantu
ELAM kingdom
ELIM Bib. oasis
EMIM Moabites; giants
ENAM gift; land grant
ETYM Moabites, giants; abbr.: word sources
EXAM interrogation; test
FAAM tea; leaves
FARM till; land; — out; club
FILM skin; coating; haze; photograph; picture
FIRM fixed; solid; company
FLAM trick; drum beat
FLEM Fleming; Belgian
FOAM froth; rage; rubber
FORM shape; mold; fashion; school grade
FRAM spear
FRIM juicy; soluble
FROM out of
GARM Hel's dog
GAUM attention
GERM bud; seed; microbe
GEUM plant (astringent)
GLIM light; eye
GLOM watch; steal
GLUM moody; sullen
GOOM cultivation method
GRAM sword; plant; weight; —'s method; grandma
GRIM ruthless; ghastly
GRUM morose; guttural
GUAM Mariana island
HAEM prefix: blood
HALM plant stems
HARM hurt; evil; injury
HAWM loiter
HELM steer (wheel); tiller
HOLM holly; oak; islet
IDEM same: Lat.; semper —
IISM egoism
IMAM priest; title
IRBM ballistic missile
ITEM also; article; bit; entry
JERM Levantine boat
JHUM cultivation method
JOOM cultivation method
KASM measure
KHEM chief god (Min)
KLAM weight
KLOM weight
KULM crane; heron
LIAM O'Flaherty: "informer"
LOAM clay; soil
LOOM auk; appear(ance); weaver's frame
LYAM bloodhound
MAAM madam
MAIM disgfigure; mutilate
MALM limestone
MARM ma'am; school-
MEUM carrotlike herb; spicknel; mine: Lat.
MIAM hut
MUMM mask; disguise
NAAM distrain
NEEM tree; Margosa
NORM type; standard; integer
ODUM tree (Iroko)
OGAM Irish alphabet
OGUM Irish alphabet
OLAM infinity; — haba (life after death)
ONYM technical name (biol.)
OVUM germ cell; egg
OXIM chem. compound
OZEM David's brother
PALM tree; measure; hand part; paddle; conceal; grease the —
PERM elec. unit; hair wave
PLIM swell; swollen
PLUM fruit (damson; greengage); tree; raisin; choice job

POEM verse creation
PRAM carriage
PROM (college) dance, ball
REAM 500 (paper) quantity; bevel; enlarge
REEM ox; unicorn
REIM oxhide; strap
RHUM alcoholic drink
RIEM oxhide strap
ROAM wander
ROOM space; apartment; lodge; — and board
SAIM grease
SALM star
SAUM weight
SCUM dross; refuse; rabble
SEAM fold; crevice; join; ornament; measure
SEEM look; appear
SEIM Polish assembly
SEJM Polish assembly
SHAM deceit; fake
SHEM Noah's son; Semite
SHIM leveling slip; shingle; knife
SIAM Thailand; Anna's king (The King and I)
SIUM water parsnip
SKIM scoop off; scud; brush
SLAM bang; criticize; grand —
SLIM slight; scanty; sly; slender
SLUM dilapidated district
STEM shaft; trunk; stock; axis; dam; check; derive; turn skis
STOM prefix: mouth
STUM grape juice; must; renew wine
SUUM hum; — cuique
SWAM floated
SWIM move in water; float; teem
SWUM swim participle
TEAM group; yoke
TEEM abound
TERM phrase; word; condition; time, period
THEM pronoun
TIAM language
TRAM trolley; gauge
TRIM shear; adjust; adorn; rebuke; defeat; neat
TURM troop; company
TUUM thin: Lat.
ULAM Gilead's descendant
URIM — and Thummim (sacred instruments)
UTUM small owl
VEHM medieval tribunal
WARM hot; genial; newly made; heat; — Springs
WHAM exclamation
WHIM fancy; caprice
WHOM pronoun
WORM crawler; maggot; screw; insinuate
WURM glacial period
YARM scream; wail
YIRM fret; whine: Scot., Ir.
ZOOM buzz; climb; approach suddenly

ACON boat
ADAN prayer call
ADEN comb. form: gland; city; gulf; region
ADIN name
AEON age
AGON contest; argument
AKAN Negro
AKIN related
ALAN dog; name
ALEN measure
ALIN meaure
AMAN Ahasuerus's minister
AMEN assent; verily; deity; — Ra
AMIN agent
AMON deity; King of Judah
AMUN deity
ANAN tree; interjection
ANON again; now; soon; author unknown
ARAN Seir's descendant; island
ASIN month
ATEN solar disk
ATON solar disk
AVON river; Shakespeare home; (Stratford)
AWAN tribe
AXON axis; cell process
AYAN spruce
AYIN Heb. 16th letter, 70
AZAN prayer call
AZIN chem. compound
AZON bomb
AZUN Hananiah's father
BAIN bath: Fr.
BARN storehouse; stable
BAWN mud enclosure; white
BEAN plant; trifle; head; strike
BEEN charmer's clarinet; participle
BEHN herb; tree
BEIN good; fine
BENN seed
BERN Swiss capital
BIEN good, fine: Fr.; — aimée (well beloved)
BINN box; frame; crib
BION physiological individual (morphon)
BIRN clarinet socket
BONN city; Ger. capital (Beethoven born)
BOON benefit; convivial

BORN given birth to; née; quantum physicist
BRAN god-king; seed coat; chaff
BREN (machine) gun
BRIN fan plate; silk thread
BUNN cake
BURN (be on) fire; yearn; waste; speed; brand
BYON clayey earth
CAEN city
CAGN mantis; deity
CAIN tribute; (Abel's) slayer; mark of —
CARN stone heap
CERN decide
CHAN resthouse; lord; title
CHEN snow goose
CHIN lower jaw; chatter; weight; dynasty; Burmese
CHUN Chin. pottery
CION plant shoot
CLAN clique; family; group
COAN pert. to Cos island
COEN Jan (empire builder)
COIN money; mint; invent; corner
CONN direct helmsman
COON animal; fur; sly man
CORN grain; ear, kernel; callus; whisky; preserve; granulate(d); clavus; banality; red-yellow
COYN corner(stone)
CRAN bird; measure
CRIN heavy silk
CUON wild dog (dhole)
CYAN green-blue
CYON wild dog (dhole)
DAIN Patusan chief (Conrad); Curse (Hammett); measure
DAMN curse; — the torpedoes
DARN mend; interjection
DAUN stage (geol. period)
DAWN daybreak; Eos; Aurora; red
DEAN clergyman; educator; oldest member, doyen
DEIN your(s): Ger.
DHAN wealth; loan
DIAN reveille
DION lord in Winter's Tale
DOMN Rumanian lord
DOON tree (varnish resin)
DORN thornback ray
DOWN to below; reduce; defeat; feathers; elder-; dejected
DRIN Balkan river
DRUN road (Gypsy)
DUAN canto; poem
DUIN demons
DURN gatepost
EARN gain; win; deserve
EBEN Ebenezer
EBON ebony; black
EDEN paradise; West of Nod
EGAN horse (Kipling)
ELAN dash; ardor
ELEN biblical jurist
ELON Esau's father-in-law; college (N.C.)
ENAN Prince of Naphtall
ENIN blue grape pigment
ENON Paris's wife (nymph); John the Baptist site
EOAN pert. to east; dawn
EOIN John; Sean
ERAN Ephraim's grandson
ERIN Eire; Ireland
ETON school, college; collar; jacket; playing fields of —
EVAN name (Welsh)
EVEN evening; level; fair(ly); equal(ly), moderate; just; not odd; flush
EWAN name (Welsh)
EXON Exeter man
EZAN prayer call
FAIN glad; eager
FAMN measure
FAON fawn color
FAUN deity; satyr
FAVN measure
FAWN deer; cringe; toady; brown
FERN seedless plant
FINN man of Finland, Helsinki; Ugric; Mickey (KO drops); Huckleberry (Twain novel)
FIRN granular snow(field)
FLAN tart; disk; net
FOHN warm dry wind
GAIN reach; earn; profit; notch
GAON Jewish title
GARN yarn; go on
GAWN gallon; tub
GEAN cherry
GEIN glucoside (Geum urbanum)
GEON paradise river; Jerusalem spring
GIAN -Carlo (Menotti)
GLEN rival
GMAN U.S. police agent
GOAN pert. to Goa
GOON thug; strikebreaker
GOWN dress; toga; robe
GRAN weight; grandma
GRIN smile
GUAN bird
GUNN castaway (Stevenson)

GWYN Llud's son; deity
HAHN Otto (Nobel physicist)
HEIN surprise!: Fr.
HEWN felled; squared
HIEN Chin. government seat
HOEN weight
HOON coin; gold pagoda
HORN prong; antenna; trumpet; brass wind; cup; Cape —
HUON pine; timber tree
HYMN song (of praise)
IBAN dyak (Borneo)
ICON image; statue
IDEN Henry VI figure
IDUN Bragi's wife (Norse)
IKON image; statue
IRAN Persia
IRON metal; element; weapon; instrument; club; shackle; press; strong; Age
ITEN So. Amer. Indian
IVAN John; — the Terrible
JAIN sect (Indian)
JANN genii
JAUN palanquin
JEAN name; cotton cloth
JINN demon; spirit
JOAN lass; cap; of Arc (the Maid, la Pucelle)
JOHN name; saint, evangelist, cop; man; Bull (England); Long — Silver (Stevenson)
JOIN mix; unite; coalesce
JUAN John; Don —; Don Giovanni
KAAN inn, title
KAHN banker; test
KAIN tribute
KAON particle
KARN stone heap
KAUN resthouse; lord; title
KAWN resthouse; lord; title
KEEN sharp; acute; bewail
KERN soldier; peasant; grain; type part; Jerome (composer)
KHAN resthouse; lord; title; Agha —
KILN (burn in) oven
KIRN harvest feast
KLAN Ku Klux —
KRAN coin
KUAN pottery; official
KWAN coin; weight
LAHN river
LAIN reclined
LAON Fr. city
LAUN ceramic sieve
LAWN fabric; grass plot; bishopric
LEAN be supported; incline; thin
LEON country, city; Ponce de (explorer)
LIEN claim; attachment; garnishment
LIIN measure
LIMN portray; delineate
LINN waterfall; linden
LION cat, king of beasts; celebrity
LLYN lake; pool
LOAN lend
LOIN body part; hips; meat cut
LOON diving bird; lout
LORN forsaken; bereft
LOUN loon; lout
LOWN calm; quiet; dolt
LUNN Sally (teacake)
LYON Fr. city; bean
MAAN city
MAIN conduit; first; river; Spanish —
MANN man: Ger.; Horace (educator); Thomas (writer)
MAON Nabal's home
MAUN must
MEAN intend; denote; base; unkind; middle
MEIN Chin. noodles; chow —
MIAN sir; title
MIEN manner; bearing; air
MOAN lament
MOON satellite; crescent; month; Diana; Cynthia; languish
MORN A.M.; dawn; East
MOWN cut down; trimmed
MUON particle
NEIN no: Ger.
NEON gas(eous) element; lamp
NGAN measure
NOON midday; meal; acme
NORN demigoddess (Urth, Skuld, Verthandi)
NOUN speech part; name; substantive
OBAN coin
ODIN one-eyed Norse god: Frigg's husband, Thor's father
OLAN Wang Lung's wife (Pearl Buck: The Good Earth)
OMAN Arab. state; sultanate; Muscat
OMEN presage; portent; sign
ONAN Indian; Judah's son
OPEN plain; frank; undefended; uncertain; bare; start;

unfold; public; — sesame
ORAN seaport
OREN Judah's descendant
OVEN (bake in) stove; kiln
OWEN (Welsh) name; socialist; zoologist
OXAN gas
OXEN bovines; draft animals
PAAN town
PAIN ache; trouble; forfeit
PAON peacock blue
PAUN betel leaf
PAWN chessman; pledge
PEAN panegyric; praise; fur
PEEN hammer head
PENN William (Pa. founder)
PEON laborer
PERN honey buzzard
PHAN measure
PHON loudness measure
PIAN tumor
PIEN arris (sharp edge)
PION dig; excavate
PIRN reed; bobbin; nose ring
PLAN design; scheme
POON tree (mastwood)
PUAN latex
QUAN money
RAIN shower; scratch; — check
RANN verse, stanza; kite (Kipling)
REIN strap; check; direct; kidney
RHIN Rhine: Fr.
RIEN nothing: Fr.; — ne va plus
ROAN horse; yellow-red
ROON treasure; darling
RUIN destroy; destruction; violate
RYAN peak (Idaho)
SAAN Bushmen
SAIN consecrate; tree
SAWN sawed; cut
SCAN examine; measure poetry
SCON teacake
SEAN John
SEEN observed
SEIN poss. pronoun, be, being: Ger.
SENN Swiss herdsman
SEWN stitched
SHAN Thai
SHEN Christian God (China)
SHIN leg, calf front; run; climb
SHUN avoid; abstain (from)
SIGN symbol; signal; subscribe; ratify; hire
SINN — Fein (Irish society)
SION purple seaweed; Zion
SKEN squint
SKIN hide; pelt; peel; fleece; — and bones
SKUN skinned
SOON promptly; willingly
SOWN scattered; seeded
SPAN stretch; team; measure; dog
SPIN whirl; twist; aerial stunt; — a yarn
SPUN twisted; whirled
STEN weight; gun
STUN stupefy; daze
SUAN — pan: Chin. abacus
SUNN hemp: fiber plant
SVAN Caucasian
SWAN constellation; dive; — song
TAEN taken
TAIN plate
TARN lake
TAUN measure
TAWN tawny
TEAN tone: Scot.
TEEN 13–19; injury; pain
TERN gull; threefold; ship
THAN in comparison with; conjunction
THEN at a time; therefore
THIN lean; dim; rare; dilute; — ice
TIEN sky: Chin.; Chu (Lord of Heaven); your(s): Fr.
TION suffix
TMAN U.S. Treasury agent
TMEN U.S. Treasury agents
TOON tree (dye); mahogany
TORN ripped; damaged
TOWN city; hamlet; — hall; man about —
TRIN one of triplets
TSIN Chin. dynasty
TSUN measure (1/10 ch'ih)
TUAN measure; sir; title
TURN bending; corner; revolve; reverse; change; shape; act; movement
TWIN double; match; — Cities
ULAN lancer; — Bator
UPON prep.: above, against
URAN lizard; Indian
USUN ancient North Chin.
UZAN weight
UZUN ancient North Chin.
VAIN empty, idle; futile; proud
VEIN channel; streak; blood vessel
VULN wound (Her.)
WAIN wagon; Charles's —

WARN caution; give notice
WEAN withdraw; alienate
WEIN wine: Ger.
WHEN whereas; how soon
WHIN gorse; rest-harrow; rock; winch
WHUN gorse; rest-harrow
WOON Burmese governor
WORN used (as clothing); shabby; tired
WREN bird; navy woman; architect
WYNN timber truck; Ed (actor, Perfect Fool)
YARN spun wool; story
YAWN openwide; gape; chasm
YEAN to lamb
YGUN antisub gun
YIRN whine; grimace; smirk: Scot., Ir.
YUAN dynasty; money
ZAIN horse
ZEIN protein
ZION Israelites; heaven
ZOON developed; compound animal

ABOO war cry
ACTO action: Sp.
AERO go by aircraft
AFRO hairstyle
AGAO language
AGIO fee; commission
AGNO Luzon river
AGRO prefix: soil
AHIO Ark driver
AINO Jap. aborigine
ALBO prefix: white
ALCO dog
ALLO prefix: other, dissimilar
ALSO besides
ALTO hill: Sp.; voice
AMBO pulpit
AMMO ammunition; prefix: sand
ANGO herb; dye
ANNO — Domini (year of our Lord)
APIO celery: Sp.
AREO prefix: Mars
ARGO ship; therefore: constellation
ARNO river; cartoonist
AROO indeed
ARTO prefix: bread
ASNO donkey: Sp.
ATEO Polynesian god
ATMO prefix: steam
ATWO asunder
AUTO prefix: same, self; drama: Sp.; (ride in) car
BAGO shrub
BAHO prayer stick
BARO big; prefix: weight
BENO alcoholic palm sap
BILO Balkan karst area
BINO alcoholic palm sap
BITO tree; poison; oil
BOBO owala tree; mullet
BODO Indo-Chin. language
BOGO Eritrean Hamite
BOHO grass; weep; shout
BOJO grass
BOKO evil spirit (Haiti)
BOLO knife; Rafflesia (plant); pacifist
BONO Johnny (Briton); cui —
BORO spring rice; Indian (Mirhana); — Budur (temple)
BOTO Indian; Voto
BOZO fellow
BRIO con — (with spirit)
BUBO horned —; eagle owl
BUFO toad genus; agua
BUTO serpent goddess; Leto
BUYO betel leaf; nut
BYGO pass by
CABO Yubi
CACO bandit
CALO Gypsy
CANO canal: Sp.
CAPO head: It.; crime boss
CARO dear (one): It.; Caroline
CASO Dodecanese island
CATO the Censor (Roman statesman); foe of Carthage
CAYO island, reef: Sp.
CERO mackerel
CETO prefix: whale
CHAO measure
CIPO liana
CIXO Ecuador Indian
CLEO queen (Cleopatra)
CLIO history Muse; mollusk
COCO palm; nut; grass
CODO measure
COHO silver salmon
COMO lake, resort (Italy)
COSO open space: Sp.
COTO bark; stomachic
COYO avocado; chinin
DADO wall part; groove
DAGO tribe
DATO tribal chief
DEDO measure
DEMO prefix: populace
DHAO knife (Burma)
DIDO trick; caper; Carthage queen, Aeneas' beloved
DILO poon tree
DINO prefix: terrible
DODO extinct bird; reactionary
DOKO Afr. pygmy
DOTO sea slug genus

DUCO pyroxylin lacquer
DURO Sp. peso; dollar
EBRO Sp. river
ECHO Narcissus's nymph; repeat; response; fruit tree (gingko)
ECTO prefix: outside
EDDO taro root
EGBO secret society (Ogboni)
EJOO palm; fiber
ENDO prefix: within
ENTO prefix: inner
ENYO war goddess
ERGO hence; prefix: work
FADO tune
FANO cloth; cape
FARO card game; Pharaoh
FICO trifle
FIDO fog evaporation; dog's name
FIFO inventory method
FILO silk thread
FOGO stench
FONO Samoan council
GAJO non-Gypsy
GANO Count (Roland's destroyer)
GAPO (inundated) forest
GARO Assam native
GILO woody vine (tonic)
GIRO tour; round; credit system; aircraft (auto-)
GOBO burdock; okra; camera; mike shield
GOGO vine; bark soap; beetle; bugaboo; Bantu; dancer
GOLO Nilotic Sudanese
GRAO weight
GUAO tree
GULO wolverine genus
GYRO prefix: ring, spiral
HAKO rite
HALO circle; glow; nimbus; prefix: sea, salt
HANO Indian
HELO squeamish
HEMO prefix: blood
HERO protagonist; demigod; — and Leander; Beatrice's cousin
HILO grass; city (Hawaii)
HINO timber tree; dye
HIRO measure
HOBO vagrant worker
HOGO taint; stench
HOMO man; — sapiens; prefix: same
HUGO name; Victor (novelist)
HUSO beluga; whale; huchen
HYPO photo solution; needle; injection
IAGO villain (Othello)
ICHO fruit tree (gingko)
IDEO prefix: idea
IDIO prefix: one's own
IDJO Niger delta Negro
IDYO Niger delta Negro
IDZO Niger delta Negro
IKMO betel palm; pepper
INRO Jap. receptacle
INTO penetrating; toward
IODO prefix: iodine
IPSO — jure, — facto
ITMO betel pepper
IUNO Jupiter's wife
JAKO parrot
JATO jet-assisted take off
JOBO hog plum; gumbo limbo
JODO Buddhist paradise (Gokaruku)
JUDO self-defense art
JUNO goddess; Jupiter's wife, Hera; stately woman; missile
KAGO conveyance
KAIO fruit
KALO taro root
KANO painting school
KARO plant
KAYO knock out
KENO lotto (game); prefix: empty
KIBO Afr. peak (Kilimanjaro)
KIHO peacock butterfly
KILO measure; -gram, -meter; prefix: 1000
KINO gum (catechu); prefix: moving
KOKO bird; palm; tribe; executioner (Mikado)
KOLO folk dance
KOSO tree; cusso; Panamint Indian
KOTO Jap. zither
KOZO paper mulberry
KROO Liberian Negro
LAGO lake
LALO composer
LAZO lasso
LENO (cotton, silk) fabric
LERO Dodecanese isle
LETO mother of Apollo, Artemis
LEVO prefix: left
LIAO Manchuria river
LIDO Venice beach
LIFO inventory method
LINO measure
LOBO timber wolf
LOCO (render) mad; weed
LOLO Caucasian Chinese

LORO monk parrot; fish
LOTO pot; game
LUDO game; pachisi
MACO cotton
MADO fish
MAJO dandy; shrub
MAKO shark
MALO loincloth
MAMO bird
MANO grindstone; hand: It.
MAPO goby (fish)
MARO ship name: Jap.
MAYO Indian; physicians, clinic (Rochester)
MAZO de la Roche (novelist: Jaina)
MEIO measure
MEMO note; statement
MENO prefix: month
MERO grouper (fish)
MIAO Chinese aborigine
MICO marmoset
MILO name; grain; sorghum; Venus (Melos)
MINO Jap. straw coat
MIRO tree; wood robin
MOGO stone hatchet
MOHO bird; honey eater
MOIO measure
MOJO tree; majagua; voodoo charm; Indian
MOKO Maori tattoo; -moko (lizard)
MOMO owl
MONO monkey; Indian; prefix: single, one
MORO finch; P.I. Moslem tribe
MOTO movement: It.; con —
MOXO Arawakan Indian
MOYO measure
MOZO manservant: Sp.
MUSO Chibchan Indian
MYXO slime mold
NABO shrub
NAIO tree
NATO international (Western) alliance; treaty organization
NEBO wisdom god; Moab mountain (Moses died)
NEMO nobody: Lat.; prefix; glade; Captain (Verne hero)
NERO emperor; fiddler; Agrippina's son; — Wolfe (Stout)
NINO boy: Sp.
NITO climbing fern
NOIO noddy tern
NOLO — contendere
NONO ninth: It.
NUZO Chibchan Indian
OCTO prefix: eight
ODIO hatred; It.
OENO prefix: wine
OHIO Buckeye state
OKRO plant; stew; soup; gumbo
OLEO margarine
OLIO medley; olla-podrida
OMAO thrush
ONTO upon; wise to
ORDO order: Lat.; feast list
ORLO smooth surface; plinth
ORZO pasta
OSLO city (Norway); Christiania
OTHO Roman emperor
OTRO other, another: Sp.
OTTO name; palindrome; perfume; Ger. ruler
PACO alpaca
PAGO -Pago (city)
PAHO prayer stick
PAJO prayer stick
PALO pole, wood: Sp.
PASO measure
PATO Muscovy duck
PAVO peacock; constellation
PECO black tea
PEDO child
PEHO morepork (bird)
PELO hair: It.
PEPO pumpkin; squash; melon; cucumber
PERO but: Sp.
PESO coin; Sp. dollar
PETO wahoo (fish); Henry IV figure
PHAO wolf (Kipling)
PHOO disgusting!
PICO peak; game; weight
PINO pine tree
PIRO Tanoan Indian
PISO weight
PITO fiber; flax; hemp; brocket (deer)
POCO slightly; old-clothes man
POGO springy stick
POLO game; Marco —
POMO California Indian
PORO Sierra Leone secret society
PRAO canoe
PROO slow up! (horse call)
PUNO Pacific trade wind; city (Peru)
PYRO prefix: fire, fever
RALO measure
REDO make over
RENO Nev. city ("biggest little"; divorce, gambling)
RIVO stream: It.
ROJO redskin: Sp.
ROTO ragged: Sp.; printing
SACO weight; river
SADO carriage; island; river
SAGO palm; starch
SAHO language
SAPO soap; toadfish
SCIO prefix: sky

SEGO	herb; bulb; lily; Utah state flower
SEMO	Sancus (deity); Dius Fidius
SERO	prefix: thin; late pupil
SHOO	scare away; begone!
SILO	fodder pit; ensile
SINO	prefix: Chin.
SIPO	liana
SITO	prefix: grain
SKEO	fisherman's hut
SLOO	swamp
SOCO	heron; bittern
SOHO	exclamation; London district
SOLO	song; (fly) alone
SOSO	middling; passably
SOTO	Hernando de (explorer)
STLO	WW II battle site
SUMO	Ulvan
TAJO	trench
TANO	Indian
TARO	rootstock; poi; elephant's ear
TAXO	prefix: arrangement
TECO	Indian
THEO	prefix: god
THIO	prefix: brimstone
TIAO	Chin. money
TINO	Sambal language
TIRO	amateur; novice
TITO	Yugo. leader (Broz)
TOCO	toucan
TODO	bustle; stir; ado
TOGO	Afr. republic; Jap. admiral and statesman
TOHO	halt! (to dogs)
TOKO	Chin. store; flogging
TOPO	prefix: place
TORO	N.Z. tree
TOTO	baby (animal); all
TRIO	set of 3; So. Amer. Indian
TSAO	Chin. state
TUNO	rubber tree; gum
TYLO	dog (Maeterlinck)
TYPO	printing error
TYRO	beginner; novice
TYTO	barn owl; Strix; Aluco
ULLO	Indian shell money
ULMO	muermo; hardwood
UMBO	shield boss; shell beak
UNCO	strange; very: Scot.
UNDO	untie; unfasten; ruin
UNIO	mussel
UNTO	to; for; toward
UPDO	upswept hair
UPGO	ascend
URAO	trona (mineral)
VASO	vase: It.; prefix: blood vessel
VELO	speed unit
VENO	prefix: vein
VETO	prohibit(ion); no
VIBO	gulf (Italy)
VINO	palm liquor
VIVO	spirited
VOTO	So. Amer. Indian
VTWO	robot bomb
WACO	city
WHOO	exclamation
WHYO	gangster; footpad
XENO	guest; prefix: foreign
XERO	prefix: dry
YAHO	tribesman
YEDO	Tokyo
YESO	plaster of Paris; gypsum
ZENO	philosopher (Stoic, Cynic); emperor
ZERO	nothing; cipher; nullity; — hour; Jap. plane
ZOBO	mongrel yak
ZOGO	sacred object
ALEP	city
ALOP	lopsided
APAP	month
ASOP	sopping
ATAP	palm
ATIP	expectant
ATOP	at the peak
BEEP	radio sound
BLIP	radar screen sign
BLUP	air bubble sound
BUMP	coincide; hit; swelling; — off (kill)
BURP	belch; — gun
CALP	limestone
CAMP	tent(s); town; stay; boot —
CAPP	Al (cartoonist: Abner, Dogpatch)
CARP	fish; complain
CAUP	tribute: Scot.
CHAP	fellow; crack; jaw
CHIP	fragment; cut; hew
CHOP	cut; crack; eat; barter; jaw
CLAP	rap; applaud; flatten
CLIP	clasp; cut(ting); gait
CLOP	limp; hobble
COLP	pasture; Irish acre
COOP	pen; jail; confine; cooperative
COUP	blow; master stroke
CRAP	dregs; money; dice cast (craps)
CROP	craw; harvest; trim
CUSP	(crescent) point; tooth edge
DAMP	moist(ure); depress
DEEP	profound; extensive; ocean
DOPP	diamond cup

DORP hamlet; city (So. Afr.)
DOUP weaver's thread
DRAP cloth
DRIP let fall
DROP globule; fall; discard; minim; trap door; die; pendant
DUMP unload; junkyard; thud; mean place; holey dollar
ESOP fable writer
FLAP slap; leaf; sway; -jack
FLIP toss; tap; drink; hop
FLOP slump down; flap; change; fail(ure); bed; sleep
FRAP tighten
GAMP umbrella; Sairey (nurse: Dickens)
GASP pant (eagerly)
GAUP gape
GAWP gape; simpleton
GIMP silk fabric; vim
GLOP look wildly; stare
GOLP roundel purpure (Her.)
GOOP nonsense creature
GRIP grasp; power; valise; Barnaby's raven (Dickens)
GULP swallow; catch breath
GUMP silly, stupid one; Andy, Chester, Min (cartoon family)
HARP coin; seal; Lyra; constellation; Irishman; nag
HASP clasp
HEAP pile; crowd; car
HEEP Uriah (Dickens villain)
HELP relieve; avoid; wait on, aid(e); servants
HEMP herb; hashish; cannabis; rope (fiber)
HOOP circle(t); wicket; — skirt
HUMP protuberance; mound; crisis; Himalayan peaks; -back
HUPP call to horse
JEEP vehicle; automobile
JUMP leap; bounce; move; headstart; — the gun
KAPP measure
KEEP tend; retain; preserve; last
KELP seaweed, iodine source
KEMP fur refuse
KEUP measure
KIPP peak (Glacier National Park); gymnastic feat
KLIP rock; cliff
KLOP hard sound
KNAP summit; rap; talk; bite; button
KNIP bite; crop; rap
KNOP button; finial; stud
KOOP purchase; bargain
LAAP secretion; insect
LAMP light; bulb
LAPP N. Scandinavian
LARP secretion; insect
LEAP jump, skip; — year
LERP secretion; insect
LIMP halt; flaccid; loose
LISP speech defect
LOOP noose; catch; aerial stunt; Chicago area
LOUP half mask; Skidi Indian; river; fish
LUMP mass; swelling; barge; like it or — it
MUMP beg; mumble; chest
NAIP native
NEAP wagon pole; tide
NEEP turnip
NOAP bullfinch
NOUP steep promontory
PALP appendage; feeler
PAUP walk idly
PEEP chirp; bird; peer slyly; Bo —; jeep
PIMP procurer; bawd; maquereau
PLAP fall loudly
PLOP sound of fall
PLUP sound of (soft) fall
POMP pageant(ry); splendor
POOP deck; cabin; dickey; exhaust; tire
PREP prepare; student
PROP support; shore; theater equipment
PULP pith; tissue; paper; magazine
PUMP force; draw out; slipper
QUIP witty sally; jest
RAIP rope
RAMP inclined way; rear
RASP grate; file
REAP cut; harvest
REPP silk or wool fabric
RISP metal bar
ROMP girl; gambol, frolic
ROUP a cold; hoarseness
RSVP please reply: Fr.
RUMP sirloin part; remnant; — Parliament
SALP marine animal
SAMP maize

SCAP	skull
SCOP	bard; poet
SCUP	pan fish; porgy
SEEP	ooze; small spring
SEIP	seep; ooze
SHAP	silk yarn
SHIP	vessel; send; — of state
SHOP	store; buy; buying place; talk —; window-
SIMP	simpleton
SKEP	basket; measure; beehive
SKIP	jump; escape; mess; captain; -tracer
SLAP	strike; — bang
SLIP	slide; err(or); escape; pier; leash; garment; memo; cut
SLOP	slush; gush; mash
SNAP	seize; break; click; shut; photo; vigor; easy task; — out
SNIP	cut; shred; slip
SNUP	snap up cheaply
SOAP	cleanser; detergent; money; soft —; -box; — opera
SOUP	broth; stew; — and fish; duck —; step (up); explosive; fog
STEP	pace; foot rest; rank; act; dance; crush; — on it
STOP	halt; discontinue; arrest; close; instrument part; period
SUMP	dig pit; tank; cistern
SWAP	barter; exchange
SWOP	trade
TAMP	fill up; pound down; tool
TARP	canvas; sailor; hat
TEAP	ram
TERP	prehistoric mound
TOOP	measure
TORP	croft; Swed. small farm
TOUP	Malay lugger
TRAP	snare; mouth; net; catch; clothe; basalt; — shooting
TRIP	move; slip; journey; (mis)-step
TROP	too much; Fr.
TROT	jog; gait; race; translation; fishing line
TRYP	parasite in blood (sleeping sickness, nagana, surra)
TUMP	drag slain deer
TURP	turpentine
TYMP	blast furnace stone
TYPP	yarn count unit
VAMP	sock; shoe part; fireman; ghost; flirt
VEEP	vice-president
WAMP	elder
WAPP	rope guide
WARP	threads; twist; falsify
WASP	yellow jacket; hornet; fem. flyer; WW II
WEEP	cry; bend; leak
WHIP	lash; urge; defeat
WHOP	dash; beat; bump
WISP	torch; shred; flock; brush; ignis fatuus
WRAP	cloak; blanket; coat
YAMP	herb; tuber
YAPP	(bookbinding) style
YAUP	yap; yawn
YAWP	yap; yawn
YELP	shrill bark
YOOP	sobbing sound
YOUP	yelp; scream; yawn
ZARP	policeman
CINQ	five: Fr.
IRAQ	country
SHOQ	tree (tanning); chogak
ABIR	red powder
ACER	tree
ACOR	acidity
ADAR	month
ADER	Benjamite
AFAR	far away; tribe
AGAR	wood
AGER	apparatus; field
AHER	Benjamite
AHIR	caste
AJAR	opened
ALAR	winglike; axillary
ALOR	island
ALUR	Negro
AMAR	measures
AMER	bitter
AMIR	prince
AMOR	love; Cupid; — patriae
AMUR	river
ANER	city
APAR	armadillo
APER	imitator; boar
ARAR	tree
ASAR	glacial ridges; eskers
ASER	Jacob's son
ASIR	Arab. principate
ASKR	— and Embla: Norse Adam and Eve
ASOR	lyre
ASUR	war god
ATAR	perfume; essence
AUER	violinist
AVAR	Caucasian language
AVER	assert; asseverate
AZUR	Côte d' — (Riviera); Hananiah's father
BAAR	weight
BAER	prizefighter; actor
BAHR	sea; — El

Azrak
BARR elephant's cry
BAUR joke
BEAR carry; yield; endure; relate; animal; Ursa; short-seller; pessimist
BEER beverage; ale; mead
BHAR Kolarian native
BIER litter; coffin
BIRR wind force; sound
BIUR Heb. commentary
BLUR obscure; stain
BOAR (wild) hog; male
BOER So. Afr. Dutch
BOHR Nils (Nobel physicist)
BOOR rustic; lout; Boer
BRER Rabbit (Harris: Uncle Remus)
BUHR whetstone
BURR (prickly) nut, knob; reamer; banyan tree; Aaron (statesman)
CARR pool
CHAR trout; burn; sandbank; -woman
CHER dear: Fr.
CHIR pheasant; pine
CHOR thief; steal (Gypsy)
CHUR Swiss canton
COIR coconut fiber
CUIR leather; dorado
CURR to murmur (as owlet)
CZAR emperor; dictator
DAER re borrowed stock
DARR bird
DAUR Manchu
DEAR costly; loved; loved one
DEER ruminant; cervine; — Park (Buddha site)
DHAR state; town (India)
DHER mound; land share
DIER one moribund
DOER performer; agent
DOOR portal; entrance; Open — policy
DORR Rebellion (R.I.)
DOUR sullen; gloomy
DUAR mountain pass
DUHR star
DURR grain sorghum
DYER tinter; Mary (Quaker martyr)
EBER Hebrew ancestor
EBUR ivory: Lat.
EDAR Bib. site
EDER river
EGER river
EKER water cress
EMER Cuchulainn's wife (ideal womanhood)
EMIR ruler; title
ERER sooner
ESER weight
EUER your(s): Ger.
EVER always; at any time
EWER pitcher; udder
EYER needle maker
FAIR pleasing; ample; just; bazaar; — and square; — deal
FEAR fright; doubt
FOUR number; card; boat
GAUR wild cattle
GEAR notched wheel; equipment; adjust; harmonize
GHOR Dead Sea valley
GIER eagle (vulture)
GNAR growl
GOER runner
GOOR sugar; massecuite
GOUR cattle; koulan (onager)
GUAR legume; cluster bean
GUHR earthy deposit
HAAR fog
HAIR filament; cilium, seta; fabric; -trigger
HARR hinge
HEAR listen; perceive by ear
HEER Mr., Sir: Dutch
HEIR inherit(or); — apparent, presumptive
HEER lord, Mister, Sir: Ger.
HIER here: Ger.; yesterday: Fr.
HLER sea god (wife: Ran)
HOAR frost; gray; -hound
HOER scraper
HOUR time unit; H- or zero —
HURR to snarl
ICER freezer, mixer
IGOR Prince (opera)
IMER Caucasian
ISAR river (Munich)
ISER river
ITER road; passage (brain)
IVER ever
IYAR month
IZAR Moslem garment; star
JEER scoff; taunt
JOAR durra; millet
JOUR day: Fr.
JUAR durra; millet
KAIR fiber
KEIR bleaching vat
KERR physicist
KHAR weight
KHOR watercourse; gorge
KIER bleaching vat
KNAR knot; burr
KNOR knot (wood); gnarl
KNUR gnarl; knot; wood ball
KTKR chess move
KTQR chess move
KUAR month
KYAR coconut fiber
LAHR Bert (comedian)
LAIR resting place
LEAR learning: Scot.; king; father of Goneril, Regan,

Cordelia
LEER sly gaze; oven; loin
LEHR oven; Lew (comedian)
LEIR sea god (Lear)
LIAR prevaricator; plant
LIER rester; layer
LOIR dormouse; river
LOUR frown; lower; scowl
MAHR marriage settlement
MEER sea: Ger.
MOHR gazelle; bezoar
MOOR heath; anchor; Moslem; Moroccan; blacka-
MUIR moor (Scot.)
NATR weight
NEAR close(ly); approach
NEER never; kidney
NEIR kidney
NOIR black: Fr.; bet
ODER river
ODOR smell; repute
OGOR early Turkic man
OLOR swan genus; Cygnus
OMAR Khayyam; tentmaker; caliph
OMER measure; sheaf; undertaker (Dickens)
ONER ace; blow; individual
OSAR glacial ridges; eskers
OSER dare: Fr.
OVER above; across; beyond; again; surplus; ended; Roger and —
OWER debtor
OXER hedge (fox hunting)
OYER hearing (law); — and terminer
PAAR sand
PAIR couple; brace
PARR young fish; skegger; Catherine (Henry VIII wife)
PEAR fruit, tree
PEER gaze; equal; nobleman
PEOR Bib. mountain
PEUR fear: Fr.
PIER mole; dock; pillar
PIRR wind gust; whiz; gull
POOR indigent; scanty; feeble; lowgrade; lean; ill; hapless; cod (fish)
PORR push; poke; kick
POUR (make) flow; for: Fr.; emit; — le mérite
PURR cat's sound
QUAR fill; choke
REAR back; raise; — admiral
RIER oil cask (whaling)
ROAR loud sound; laugh
ROER hunting gun
RUER repenter
RUHR Ger. industrial area
SAAR river; region
SADR tree
SAER tenant
SAIR savor
SAUR prefix, suffix: lizard
SCAR rock; cicatrix; mar(k); fish
SCUR horn tissue
SEAR burn; dried up; gun-lock catch
SEER prophet
SEHR very: Ger.
SEIR Bib. mountain (Hor), Edom (Esau's home)
SHER tiger
SHIR cook; gather; tiger
SHOR salt lake; Tatar tribe
SIER pintado (fish)
SKIR fly; scurry; skim
SKYR sour curdled milk
SLUR pass over; mumble; defame; stigma; glide (mark)
SMUR mist; cloud
SNUR snort
SOAR fly high; glide
SOIR evening: Fr.
SOUR acid(ify); tart; disagreeable
SPAR mineral; mast; gaff; box
SPIR prefix: coiled
SPUR point; goad; kick; otter track; ridge
STAR sun; heavenly body; asterisk; hummingbird; excel
STER suffix: agent
STIR agitate; rouse; ado; jail
SUER prosecutor; suitor
TAAR tambourine
TAHR goat
TAIR goat
TARR tease
TAUR Taurus (bull)
TEAR drop; weep, rip; glass defect
TEER golfer; mix colors
TEHR wild goat
THAR goat
THOR thunder god (Thursday); Midgard slayer; Odin's son; missile
TIAR crown; shrub
TIER row; layer; pinafore
TOUR trip; circuit; — de force
TSAR emperor; dictator
TYER binder
TYRR Odin's son; war god
TZAR emperor; dictator
UBER over: Ger.
UFER fir pole; shore: Ger.
ULLR chief god;

Sif's son; Thor's stepson
USAR salt; grass
USER employer
UTOR to use: Lat.
VAIR fur
VEER shift (course); waver
VIER striver; four: Ger.
VOIR see: Fr.
WAER dam
WAHR true: Ger.
WEAR be clothed in; impair; endure; deteriorate
WEIR dam; fish trap
WHIR fly; hurry; buzz
YARR growl; snarl: herb
YEAR time period; twelve month; leap —; calendar, fiscal —
YIRR growl; snarl: Scot.
YMER myth giant
YMIR rime-cold giant
YOUR poss. pronoun
YSER river
ZOAR town; Bela; city of Lot

ABAS down: Fr.
ABCS first principles; alphabet
ACIS river; (Galatea's) lover
ACTS NT book
ACUS pin
ADES Hades
AGIS king
AIRS pretensions; side
ALAS sad cry
ALES city
ALMS charity
ALPS mountains
ALYS name: Alice
AMES author; Ia. city, college
AMIS friends: Fr.
AMOS prophet
ANAS duck
ANES once
ANIS fennel; birds
ANUS end of alimentary canal
APIS sacred bull (Ptah); bee; bull (Kipling)
APUS bird; constellation
ARAS river
ARES war; Mars; Zeus's, Hera's son; Eris' brother
ARIS molding edge
ARMS mil. science; ensigns; weapons; branches; limbs
ARTS skills; sciences; fine —; — and crafts
ATES sweetsop
ATIS monkshood; fruit
ATYS god (Cybele's lover)
AVES birds: Lat.
AVIS bird: Lat.
AVUS grandfather: Lat.
AXIS center line; spine; stem; deer; power alliance; partnership
AYES yes votes
BAAS master
BAIS caste
BANS marriage notice
BAPS dancing master (Dickens)
BASS fish; fiber; lowest part; singer; clef (F), musical instrument, — viol
BEAS Punjab river
BEES yeast
BESS nickname: Mrs. Truman
BIAS diagonal (incline); prejudice
BIOS life: animal, plant
BLAS Gil (Le Sage novel)
BOAS Franz (anthropologist)
BOIS wood: Fr.; wine (cognac); — de Boulogne
BORS king (Lancelot's uncle); Bohort (finder of Holy Grail)
BOSS knob; pad; stud; master; employer
BRAS arm: Fr.
BRES Elatha's beautiful son (Fomorian)
BUSS ship; kiss; calf
CASS treasure; Timberlane (Lewis); Squire (Eliot)
CATS — cradle
CENS payment due
CESS tax; luck
CITS citizens; mufti
COOS Bay (laurel); Indian
COSS measure
COUS cowlike
CRIS dagger; stab
CRUS leglike part; shank
CUSS curse; person
DAIS platform
DANS in: Fr.
DASS Durga, Ram (twins, Kipling)
DAYS by day
DEBS Eugene (socialist)
DENS tooth: Lat.
DEUS god: Lat.; — ex machina
DIBS juice: grape, date
DIES day(s): Lat.; — irae; Cong. committee
DIOS God: Sp.
DISS reed grass
DOES performs
DOGS scaup duck
DOSS bed; sleep; — house
DUDS clothes; failures
DUNS dull; stupid
DUOS duets
DYAS Permian (geol. period)
EADS engineer; bridge
EATS food; consumes

EGGS ova; — and bacon, ham; — and butter (flowers)
EGIS protection; patronage; shield (symbol of Zeus, Athena)
ELIS Greek city-state
EMYS tortoise
ENNS river
ENOS Seth's son, Adam's grandson (905 years old); taken by God
EPOS epic poetry; events
ERIS goddess of discord, Ares' sister
EROS (god of) love; Cupid; asteroid; Antony's friend
ESUS Gaulish god (Mars)
ETES (you) are: Fr.
EXES letters; expenses
EYAS nestling
FASS measure
FEES charges; tips
FEIS convention; — of Tara
FELS Eastern coin
FESS broad band (Her.); confess
FILS son: Fr.; Dumas (Camille); Iraq coin
FIPS Martin Chuzzlewit
FONS fount; source
FOSS canal; ditch; moat
FUSS tumult; bustle; -budget
GADS -hill (Dickens)
GAUS region: Ger.
GENS clan: Lat.; people: Fr.
GHES Tapuyan Indian
GHOS Chin. dynasty
GLIS dormouse genus
GOES walks; proceeds
GRAS horse; foie — (pâté)
GRES stoneware: Fr.
GRIS gray: Fr.
GROS coin; fabric; weight
GRUS constellation (Crane)
GYPS gypsum
HALS Frans (painter)
HANS John; Johannes; Castorp (Mann)
HASS throat; embrace
HENS fowl; -foot (herb)
HERS fem., poss. pronoun
HISS sibilant (of disapproval); goose; serpent; steam sound; Alger (Communist)
HOPS beer
HORS out of: Fr.; — d'oeuvres
HOSS horse; One — Shay (Holmes)
HUSS dogfish; John (religious leader)
HYPS hypochondria
IBIS (sacred) wading bird
IDAS Marpessa's lover; Castor's slayer
IDES Roman date; — of March (fateful day)
ILLS troubles
ILUS son of Tros; Priam's grandfather
IOUS promissory notes; suffix
IRAS Cleopatra's maid
IRIS rainbow; goddess; eye part; plant (flag); spirit (Shaks.); red-blue; March (Arlen)
IRUS Odyssey beggar
ISIS goddess; Osiris's wife, sister; Horus's mother
ITIS suffix: inflammation, mania; Tereus' son
ITYS Tereus' son
IVES inventor (photo-engr.)
IWIS certainly
JASS card game; jack
JESS strap on hawk leg
JEWS -harp
JOMS Vikings; Norse colony
JOSS Chin. deity
KAGS convict (Dickens)
KAIS island
KERS cress
KEYS House of (Isle of Man legislature); cays; Florida —
KHAS special; noble
KIDS star (Auriga)
KISS touch gently; caress; sweetmeat
KOSS measure
KRAS tahr (goat)
KRIS dagger; stab
KVAS sour beer, cider (Russ.)
LAIS hetaera
LAOS country
LARS Porsena (conqueror)
LASS girl; sweetheart
LAWS rules; principles
LEES dregs
LENS eye part; glass (optical); herb
LESS shorter; fewer; inferior; minus
LIAS geol. period
LISS (fairy) fort; release; peace; fleur-de-lis
LOIS name; Timothy's grandmother
LOOS Anita (writer: Gentlemen Prefer Blondes)

LORS exclamation: lord!
LOSS forfeiture; bereavement; waste; defeat; — leader
LOTS tracts; quantities, very much; chances
LUBS of Lubeck (city)
LUES syphilis
LYAS geol. period
MAAS river
MAIS but, corn: Fr.
MANS Chinese aborigine; Le — (city; auto race)
MARS war god; planet
MASS rite; service; bulk; populace; mob, assemble
MENS mind: Lat.
MESS banquet; meal; muddle; disorder; botch
MEWS (royal) stables
MIAS orangutan
MISS fail(ure); omit; want; girl; maiden
MONS mountain: Lat.; city (Belgium: WW I battle)
MORS deity; death
MOSS bryophyte; lichen; green; rose; Hart (writer)
MUSS mess; rumple; row
NAIS nymph
NAOS star
NESS cape; promontory; suffix
NEWS intelligence; tidings
NIAS Ind. Ocean island(er)
NIBS personage (VIP); in Peter Pan (Barrie)
NILS Bohr (physicist)
NOBS knave, jack (card, cribbage)
NOUS mind; reason; wit; we: Fr.
NUNS sisters; veiling, fabric
NUSS nurse
OAKS horse race; trees
OBUS howitzer shell
OCHS Adolph (publisher)
ODDS inequality; advantage; at —; -on
OFFS cricket-field sides
ONES individuals
ONUS burden; duty
OONS mild oath
OPUS work
ORAS Danish money
OTIS bustard genus; general; inventor (elevator)
OTUS giant slain by Apollo
OURS possessive pronoun
OVIS sheep genus
OYES court crier's cry
PAAS Easter
PAIS country: Fr.
PARS part: Lat.
PASS opening; go through; by; license; abstention; condition; amatory gesture
PESS hassock
PHOS phosphorous
PIUS Pope: X (St., Sarto); XI (Ratti); XII (Pacelli)
PLUS and; more; extra; — fours
POBS porridge; pap
PONS bridge: Lat.; — asinorum; Lily (singer)
POUS measure
PRES near: Fr.
PUSS cat; lip; face
QAIS island
QUAS sour beer, cider (Russian)
RAIS chief (Nepalese)
RATS bah!
REIS money; (boat) captain; effendi (state officer)
REMS river
REUS defendant: Lat.
REVS rotations per minute
RHUS sumac genus
RIIS Jacob (journalist)
RISS glaciation stage
ROOS Ger. painter
ROSS rough bark; seal; island; navigator; Harold (editor)
RUSS Russian; Slav
SAIS groom; city; know: Fr.
SANS without: Fr.; — culotte (radical); — gêne
SASS sauce
SEIS six: Sp.
SEPS snake; lizard
SESS soap frame bar
SIRS gentlemen
SISS hiss; shame!; girl
SORS lot: Lat.; divination
SOSS hog call for food
SOTS yeast
SOUS coins; under: Fr.
SPES (goddess of) hope
SUDS lather; froth; beer
TAOS Indian
TAPS lights-out signal; bugle call
TASS Soviet News Agency
TEES river (North sea)
TEMS sieve; sift
TEOS Ionian city
TESS Theresa; Hardy heroine
THIS pronoun, demonstrative
THOS jackal genus
THUS in this way; hence

TIBS — eve (never-never)
TOGS clothes
TOPS most superior
TOSS throw; fling; change
TRES very: Fr.; three: Sp.
TRIS prefix: thrice
UNIS Etats — (USA): Fr.
UPAS tree (juice); arrow poison
UPIS Artemis, Nemesis
URBS (capital) city
URIS Leon (author)
URUS wild ox
USAS dawn goddess
USES law of — (beneficiary)
USUS user, use: Lat.
UTAS 8 day feast; Jap. songs
VANS race of gods
VEPS Finnish tribe (Chud); Dog Star (Isis); Horus
VISS weight
WAYS wise; — and means
WELS sheatfish
WIES Ys
WIGS — on the green (fray)
XMAS Christmas
YAWS skin disease
YEAS yes votes
ZIPS Czech.
ZOAS symbolic figures (Blake)
ZEUS chief god; Jupiter; Hera's husband; son of Cronus, Rhea

ABET aid; incite
ABOT Mishnah
ABUT touch
ACHT eight: Ger.
ADAT law
ADIT entrance
AHET season (of inundation)
AINT contraction
AIRT guide; turn
AKUT ape man (Burroughs)
ALIT descended
AMIT headdress
ANAT sky god; med. term
ANET dill
APET goddess
ARNT contraction
AUNT parent's sister; tia: Sp.; tante: Fr., Ger.
BAFT astern; cotton
BAHT coin
BAIT lure; harass; pest poison
BALT Lithuanian; Esth; Latvian, Lett
BANT diet
BART man's name
BAST (woody) fiber; goddess; phloem
BATT matted mass
BEAT strike; defeat; mystify; throb; scoop; field; sphere; — the Dutch
BEET vegetable; root; sugar —; — top
BELT strap; zone; beat
BENT crooked; inclination; grass
BERT nickname
BEST most (good); defeat
BHAT minstrel; scholar
BHUT Dravidian ghost
BINT daughter; woman
BITT naut. fastener
BKKT chess move
BLAT sheep's cry
BLET fruit decay
BLOT stain; mar; dry
BLUT blood: Ger.
BOAT (go by) ship; gravy-
BOLT sift; refine; shaft; lightning; bar; plant; rifle part; flight; refusal
BOOT shoe; wader; sheath; torture; recruit; compartment; tube; kick; to — (in addition)
BORT finder of Holy Grail; impure diamond
BOTT clay plug; fly larva
BOUT contest; attack
BQKT chess move
BRAT apron; child
BRIT young herring
BROT bread: Ger.
BRUT dry: Fr.; Brit. king (New Troy, London)
BULT hill; ridge
BUNT sag (net, sail); (fungus) disease; butt (ball)
BURT butt; gore; dent
BUST bosom; statue; failure; break
BUTT cask; mound; target; ram; hinge; jut; halibut
CANT angle; change course; log; tilt; whine; jargon; be unable
CART wagon; transport
CAST throw; project; shed; deposit; form; found; actors; (assign) roles
CELT Irish, Scot, Welsh, Breton; chisel
CENT coin; penny; game
CEST girdle; belt (Venus)
CHAT talk; bird; spike
CHIT child; sprout; memo; voucher; mind
CHUT nonsense!
CIST chest; roofed pit
CLAT mess; chatter
CLOT mass; coagulate
CNUT king; son of

Magnus
COAT fur; skin; cover; — of arms
COLT young horse; pistol; — .45
COOT rail; surf duck; dolt
COPT Egypt. Christian
CULT sect; worship system
CURT short; concise
CYST box; abnormal sac
DAFT foolish; giddy
DART missile; fish; seam; run
DEBT fault; liability; obligation
DEFT skillful; trim
DENT depress(ion); notch
DIET fare; food regimen; parliament
DINT blow; force; notch
DIRT muck; earth; gossip; do one—; — cheap
DITT close up; obstruct
DOAT drivel; be silly, overfond; wood rot
DOIT coin; whit; bit
DOLT dunce; ignoramus
DONT contraction; prohibition
DOST (you) do: archaic
DRAT oath
DUAT Hades
DUCT tube; vessel; pipe
DUET music for two
DUIT Chibchan Indian; coin
DUNT split (ceramics)
DUST powdered matter; rubbish; clean; dust to —; gold —
EAST direction; Asia; Orient
ECHT genuine: Ger.
EDIT correct; redact; blue-pencil
EMIT eject; issue; voice
EMPT empty
ERAT was: Lat.; quod — demonstrandum (Q.E.D.)
ERST former; first
ETAT state: Fr.; L'— c'est moi!
EVAT eft
EVET eft; newt
EXIT depart(ure); die
EYOT islet
FACT deed; reality
FAIT fact; — accompli
FAST not eat; fixed(ly); quick(ly); wild; — and loose
FAUT comme il — (proper): Fr.
FEAT deed; accomplishment
FEET measures
FELT pressed fibers; hat; sensed
FENT slit; cleft
FEST festive gathering
FIAT sanction; edict; money; automobile (It.)
FIOT Congo tribe
FIST grasp; effort; tightwad
FLAT level; (make) insipid, dull; wholly; — tire
FLIT flutter; move
FLOT lateral ore deposit
FONT basin; spring; stoup; type
FOOT pedal part; base; dance; trip; skip; pay; add
FORT stronghold; trading post; dun
FRAT fraternity
FRET gnaw; vex; worry; embroider; ridge; ornament
FRIT fuse; fried: Fr.; waste
FROT rub; chafe
FUNT weight; Allen (TV)
FUST pilaster; smell stale
GAIT walk; pace
GALT clay bed
GANT yawn; gaunt; gannet; Eugene (Wolfe character)
GAUT range; pass; river bank stairs
GEAT channel in mold; Scandinavian (Beowulf)
GELT money
GENT gentleman; Belg. city
GEST deed; romance tale, adventure
GETT bill of divorce
GHAT range; bank; river bank stairs
GIFT donation; talent
GILT gold; sow
GIRT encircled; prepared
GIST main point; pith
GLUT sate; surfeit; oversupply; wedge
GNAT (biting) fly
GOAT ruminant; scape-; brown
GOUT drop; disease (arthritis); taste: Fr.
GRIT sand(stone); bravery; grate
GROT cave; Bremen coin
GUST outburst of wind
HAFT handle
HALT stop; lame
HANT ghost
HART stag; deer
HAST contraction; havest
HATT measure
HAUT high: Fr.; —

monde
HEAT warmth; rage; height; dead —; pressure, strain
HEFT weight; bulk; notebook: Ger.
HEST command; precept
HETT Hittite ancestor
HILT sword
HINT suggestion; imply
HIST call to attention; Indian girl (Cooper)
HOLT willow plantation; hill; lair; Eliot hero; actor
HOOT derisive (owl's) cry
HOST army; throng; bread as Christ's body; innkeeper; person having guests
HUIT eight: Fr.
HUNT seek; chase; Leigh (writer)
HURT harm(ed); pain
IBIT P.I. lizard (tidbit)
IKAT shrub; weight
ILOT islet; ait; eyot
JEST joke
JILT betray in love
JOLT shake; hard blow
JUST fair; virtuous; exact(ly)
KAAT shrub; weight
KANT change course; Immanuel (philosopher)
KEET guinea fowl
KELT Celt; cloth; trout
KENT Eng. county, duchy; Lear's follower
KEPT retained; lasted
KHAT measure
KHET mortal body; measure
KHOT farmer; contractor
KILT Scot's skirt
KIST chest; installment; measure
KMET Slav; tenant; mayor
KNIT looped, tie(d); unite; contract
KNOT tie; loop; hitch; sandpiper; problem; blemish; stud; Gordian —
KNUT king; son of Magnus
KOPT Copt
KTKT chess move
KYAT weight; Burmese money
LACT prefix: milk
LAET freedman
LAIT milk: Fr.; café-au-
LAST block; final(ly); endure; measure
LEET court; list
LEFT departed; blow; — of center (Liberals)
LENT fasting period; slow; made loan
LEST for fear that
LETT Latvian, Balt (Riga man)
LIFT r(a)ise; exalt; steal; elevator
LILT (sing) lively tune
LINT raveling, fiber (of linen); netting
LIST strip(e); roll; register; enter; inclination; careen
LOFT attic; warehouse floor; golf stroke
LOOT plunder; booty
LOST not won; misplaced; confused; ruined; — cause
LOUT boor; bumpkin; dolt
LUFT air: Ger.; -waffe
LUNT light; smoke; Alfred (actor)
LUST sensual desire
MAAT goddess
MALT barley; beer
MART market; nickname
MAST pole; brown; nuts
MATT lusterless
MEAT flesh; kernel; food
MEET encounter; face; combat; fulfill; fit
MELT liquefy
MENT falcon-headed god
MILT spleen; fish gland; nickname
MINT herb; menthol; bonanza; coin; — julep
MIST dim; haze; gray
MITT glove; hand
MOAT trench
MOLT shed (hair)
MONT mountain: Fr.; — Blanc (peak, Alps)
MOOT arguable; ring gauge
MORT nickname; woman; salmon; the kill; dead: Fr.
MOST greatest; almost
MOTT clump of trees; James, Lucretia (abolitionists)
MUNT sash bar
MUST be obliged to; necessity; new wine; stum; staleness; frenzy
MUTT cur; stupid one; — and Jeff
MYST Greek priest
NAST cartoonist
NAUT sea mile
NEAT tidy; trim; straight
NEST (make a) home
NETT undeductible
NEWT salamander;

eft
NEXT nearest; following
NOTT Norse night (Dag)
NOWT neat cattle; dolt
NUIT night: Fr.
OAST kiln
OBIT death notice
OINT apply oil
OKET ounce
OMIT leave out; neglect
OONT camel; mole
OUST eject; discharge
PACT agreement
PANT gasp; yearn
PART portion; duty; separate; role; split; go
PAST tense; ago; after
PATT stalemate(d)
PEAT darling; turf; fuel
PEET darling; turf; fuel
PELT skin; hurl; strike
PENT confined; -house
PERT bold; lively; sandpiper
PEST plague; insect; nuisance
PHIT bullet sound
PHOT light unit
PHUT (bullet) sound; OT people
PIAT magpie; anti-tank gun
PICT British aborigine
PIET magpie
PINT measure
PIOT magpie
PIST attention; track
PITT statesman (Commoner, Chatham); diamond
PLAT plait; map; plot; fish
PLET three-lash whip
PLOT tract; ground; press (soap); scheme; intrigue
POET writer of verse, artist
POLT knock; trump; club
PONT ferry(boat); bridge: Fr.
POOT disgusting!
PORT harbor; haven; wine; blue-red; left side; tune; demeanor
POST pillar; advertise; mil. station; mail; inform; record
POTT paper size; editor (Dickens)
POUT sulk(iness); fish
PRAT buttock
PRET measure
PRUT exclamation; river
PUNT (propel) flatboat; kick; bet
PUTT golf stroke
PYAT magpie
PYET magpie
PYOT piebald; chatty
QKKT chess move
QQKT chess move
QUAT squat
QUIT abandon; yield; stop; free
RAFT collection; float
RANT scold; rave; frolic
RAPT engrossed; rapture
RECT element (philos.)
REFT cleft; rift; deprived
RENT torn; schism; let, lease; payment; income
REST pause; stop; peace; prop; stay; rely; mus. sign; remainder; set; found
RIFT split; divide; cleft
RIOT tumult; success; act, squad
RIST engrave; scratch
RKKT chess move
ROOT underlying source; rhizome; base; dig; applaud; plant; eradicate
ROUT defeat; tumult; mob; the brant; snare
RQKT chess move
RUNT small animal, man
RUST oxidize; corrode; inaction; reddish-brown
RYOT Indian peasant
SALT sodium chloride, NaCl; sailor; season; — away; — Lake City; — Sea
SART Iranian Turk
SCAT buffet; scatter; begone!; tax; skat
SCOT Celt; Highlander; tax; — free
SCUT rabbit's tail; fur
SEAT chair; fundament; site; membership; install, hot —
SECT group; denomination
SEIT measure
SEPT social unit; screen; seven: Fr.
SERT Sp. painter
SETT tool; paving stone
SEXT canonical hour (noon); organ stop; sixth
SHAT saline lake
SHOT missile; pellet; guess; range; marksman; film record; long —; big —
SHUT close; refine
SIFT screen; separate; bolt

SILT sediment; scum; drift
SIST stay; delay; summon
SKAT card game; star
SKIT comedy sketch; jest
SKYT move fast; dart; slip
SLAT lath; slab; sheep's hide; flap
SLIT cut; slash; opening
SLOT (cut) opening; bolt; deer; track; — machine
SLUT slattern; harlot
SMIT struck; destroyed
SMUT soot; coal dust; plant disease; obscenity
SNOT wick end; blow nose
SOFT giving way; easy; light(ly); mild; tractable
SOOT powdery carbon smudge
SOPT Dog Star; Isis
SORT type; kind; quantity; classify
SPAT mollusk; gaiter; snap; tiff
SPET spit; barracuda
SPIT land point; rod; impale; expectorate; — and image
SPOT stain; point, place; fish; small amount; espy
SPUT boiler plate
STAT photocopy
STET let it stand!
STOT stumble; stutter
STUT horsefly
SUET hard fat
SUIT costume; card set; legal action; please; (out)fit
SUNT babul: gum tree; pod; are: Lat.
SURT Frey's slayer
SWAT hit (hard); river, state (Pakistan); Sultan of — (Ruth)
SWOT hard work; grind; hit
SYRT quicksand
TACT diplomacy; perception
TAFT President; Republican; rower's seat; -Hartley Act
TAIT marsupial
TAKT beat(s); tempo
TART sour; pastry; harlot
TATT knot lace
TAUT snug; tense
TEAT nipple
TENT cloth shelter; pup —; wine; frame
TEST shell; cupel; examination; try
TEXT (literary) substance; topic; Scripture passage; type
THAT so; which; pronoun; connective; that's —
TILT cover; incline; tip; joust; sport
TINT color; shade; tinge
TOAT plane handle
TOFT — and croft (house)
TOGT trading enterprise
TOLT writ; isolated peak
TOOT sound horn; carousal
TORT wrongful act
TOUT tip(ster); praise; all: Fr.; — à fait; — de suite
TRET weight allowance
TRIT prefix: third
TUFT crest; clump; tassle
TWIT taunt; yarn snarl
UNIT single thing; basic amount; one; monad
VAST huge (space)
VELT measure
VENT hole; let out; issue
VERT green (Her.); veer; convert
VEST waistcoat; clothe; empower
VINT card game
VOET measure
VOGT medieval official
VOLT sideways gait; fencing leap; elec. unit
WAFT float; flag; whiff
WAIT attend; defer; serenader; lie in —
WALT Whitman
WANT lack; desire
WART protuberance; -hog
WAST were
WATT inventor, elec. unit (volt-ampere); hare
WEET bird; cry of bird
WEFT yarn; mist; (weave) web
WELT ridge; wale; strip; sew; beat; universe: Ger.
WENT departed
WEPT cried; Jesus —
WERT were: archaic, poetic
WEST wind; painter, author; occident; go —; Mae —
WHAT interrogative; pronoun; what's —
WHET sharpen; excite; edge
WHIT bit; jot; dull

sound
WILT droop; lose spirit
WIST know; knew; measure
WONT custom; contraction
WORT plant; (pot)herb
WRIT legal order; Holy —
YELT gilt (sow)
YUFT Russ. leather
YUIT Asian Eskimo
YURT Kirghiz tent
ZANT fish
ZEST orange peel; relish; gusto
ZOOT — suit: extreme style

AALU Hades; heaven
AARU Hades; heaven
ABOU father; deity
ACTU act: Lat.
ADDU skink; fiber; god
AGAU language
AINU Jap. aborigine
AITU god; demon
AMMU ammunition
ANSU Korean apricot
ANTU rat poison
ANZU apricot
APSU primordial chaos
ARDU slave
ATIU one of Cook Islands
ATMU sun god
ATTU Aleut. island
AULU tree
AUSU tree
AUZU tree
BABU Hindu gentleman
BAJU jacket
BAKU hat; tree; rug; city; oil field
BALU wildcat
BARU tree
BEAU dandy; lover; — Brummell; — Nash
BENU holy bird (Ra-Osiris)
BLEU blue, rookie: Fr.
CAJU fruit; mahogany
CEBU Visayan island
CHOU cabbage, darling: Fr.; Chin. dynasty; En Lai (statesman)
DADU saint
DANU goddess
DATU tribal chief
DEGU rodent (Octodon)
DETU eclipse demon (Rahu)
DIAU Indian
DIEU god: Fr.; mon —
DUKU lanseh tree fruit
ECRU beige; unbleached
EHEU alas
EMEU bird (ostrich-like)
ENZU moon god (Sin)
ESAU Isaac's, Rebecca's son; Jacob's twin; hairy; red; Edom
FERU bast fiber
FRAU Mrs., wife, Mme., woman: Ger.
FUGU poisonous fish
GENU knee: Lat.
GESU Jesus: It.
GUGU P.I. soldier; insurrecto
GURU teacher
HABU pit viper
HAKU fish
HAPU clan
HIKU scabbard fish
HOJU Jap. army reserve
HULU o-o's feather tuft
IALU Hades; heaven
ICHU valuable grass
IGLU Eskimo hut; seal hole
JACU bird
JADU magic
JEHU (chariot) driver; prophet, king (Israel)
JESU name: Jesus
JOCU dog snapper
JUJU Afr. magic, charm
KADU tribe
KAGU bird
KAHU harrier; bird
KAPU forbidden; taboo
KIKU chrysanthemum
KIVU tsetse fly
KOBU seaweed food (kelp)
KUDU Afr. antelope
KUKU N.Z. fruit pigeon; kukupa
KULU old woman (Kipling)
KURU disease
LATU gold coins
LIEU place; stead
LIMU edible seaweed
LUAU feast; cook-out
LULU barn owl; name; Louisa
MAFU stable boy
MAKU Indian
MANU prefix: hand; Laws (Hindu code book)
MARU ship name: Jap.
MASU salmon
MENU bill of fare
MEOU cat's cry; measure
MERU fabled mountain
MITU curassow; bird
NABU god; mountain
NAPU ruminent
NIOU measure
NOSU Lolo; Chin. Caucasian
OAHU (Hawaiian) island
OGPU Soviet police body
ORDU Turk. military district, army corps
PATU weapon
PEAU skin: Fr.
PEGU Burmese language; city
PELU hardwood tree
PERU country
POKU antelope
PRAU swift canoe
PUDU Chilean deer
PUKU Afr. antelope
PULU tree fern

PURU of Arawakan
RAHU demon
RAKU -ware
RIMU red pine; imou pine
RURU N.Z. morepork
SAHU spiritual body
SHLU Moroccan Berber
SHOU Tibetan deer
SUKU Bantu
SULU Moro
SUSU blind dolphin; Congo
TABU forbidden
TAKU Indian
TAPU taboo
TASU measure
TATU Indian; armadillo; tattoo
TCHU exclamation
TEJU lizard
THOU 2nd pers. pronoun
TIBU Negro-Berber
TIOU Indian (Tonikan)
TOHU -bohu (confusion)
TOLU balsam (rose odor)
TORU N.Z. tree
TULU Dravidian Indian
TUNU rubber tree; gum
TUTU N.Z. shrub; poison; ballet skirt
UNAU sloth
URDU Hindustani language
VASU deity (Vishnu); nephew
VAYU wind god
VEAU veal, calf: Fr.
WHAU why; tree
WIDU Moslem ablution
WUDU Moslem ablution
WUZU Moslem ablution
YABU Afghan pony
YALU river (Korean War)
YARU Hades; heaven
YUTU Peru tinamou; bird
ZEBU ox; Brahman bull
ZENU Afr. sheep
ZULU Bantu; Kaffir; ship; artificial fly

AKOV measure
AZOV town; sea
CCIV 204; Septimus Severus reign
CHIV knife
CLIV 154; Antoninus Pius reign
CMIV 904
CXIV 114; Trajan reign
KIEV Ukranian city
LXIV 64; Nero reign
MCIV 1104; First Crusade, conquest of Acre
MLIV 1054; Catholic Church schism
MMIV 2004
MUAV geol. epoch
MXIV 1014; Brian Boru defeats Danes
SHIV bit of husk; fluff; blade
SKIV sovereign (coin)
SLAV Eastern European
SPIV slacker: Brit.
STEV stanza
XXIV 24; Tiberius reign

ALOW below
ANEW over again
AROW in a line
AVOW declare; justify; confess
BLEW stormed; puffed; sounded
BLOW move (air); puff, pant; brag; expend; stroke; calamity; disappointment; — up (enlarge)
BOUW measure
BRAW handsome; fine
BREW beverage; plot; concoct
BROW forehead; high-, low-
CHAW masticate
CHEW masticate; ruminate; — the cud; — the rag
CHOW food; dog
CLAW nail; ungula; chela; scratch; hammer
CLEW yarn ball; sail loop; cocoon; hint
CLOW sluice; floodgate
CRAW gullet; stomach
CREW company; gang; -cut
CROW raven; corvine; black; Indian; Jim —; -bar
DAUW zebra
DHAW billhook
DHOW Arab. sailboat
DRAW drag; attract; gain; infer; extract; sketch; undecided contest
DREW sketched; pulled
ENOW enough
FLAW crack; defect; wind
FLEW aviated; winged
FLOW gush; stream; flux; roll; ebb and —
FROW Dutch woman; cleaver
GLOW shine; incandesce; flush; ardor; wax
GNAW bite; corrode
GREW increased
GROW expand; sprout; wax; develop
JHOW tamarisk shrub
KNEW understood; was aware
KNOW understand; recognize; -how; -nothing (party)
LLEW Celt deity (Gwydion's son)

LWOW Polish city
MEOW cat's cry; measure
PHEW exclamation
PLEW beaver skin
PLOW implement; till; cut; stars
PROW ship's bow; stem; beak
SCAW promontory
SCOW flat-bottomed boat
SHAW thicket; pshaw; George Bernard (playwright)
SHEW show: Brit.; -bread
SHOW exhibit(ion); reveal; appear(ance); 3rd place; no — (airline term)
SKEW twist; swerve; distort(ed); slant(ing)
SLAW cabbage
SLEW killed; twist; swamp; large number
SLOW dilatory; tardy; inert; boring; hinder
SMEW merganser; duck
SNOW ice crystals; white hair; cocaine; — goose; TV spots
SPEW eject; scatter; gush
STEW boil; steep; hash; worry; study; oyster bed
STOW pack; hide; hold; skiing resort
SWOW I — (oath)
THAW melt; unbend
THEW muscle; sinew
TROW believe; fishing boat
VIEW sight; see; aim; opinion; scene
WHEW whistle; exclamation

ABOX braced
AJAX hero (Telamon's son)
ALIX fem. name
AMEX Amer. Expeditionary Force
ANAX Castor, Pollux (Dioscuri)
APEX summit; crisis
BRIX scale (hydrometer)
CALX residue; heel: Lat.
CCIX 209; Septimus Severus reign
CEYX Halcyone's husband
CLIX 159; Antoninus Pius reign
CMIX 909
COAX flatter; cajole
COIX grass; Job's-tears
CRAX curassow (bird)
CREX corn crake (bird)
CRUX (Southern) Cross; crucial point
CXIX 119; Hadrian reign
DEUX two: Fr.
EAUX waters: Fr.
ERYX sand snake
ESOX fish (pike, pickerel, muskellunge)
FAEX dregs
FALX weapon; — cerebri (brain fold)
FLAX plant; fiber; thrash
FLEX bend
FLIX down; fur; flax
FLUX flow; change; melt
HOAX deceive; trick
IBEX wild goat; bouquetin
ILEX holm oak; holly
IYNX wryneck (woodpecker)
JEUX cards, hands, games: Fr.
JINX hoodoo; bad luck
JYNX wryneck; charm
LANX platter
LYNX wildcat; fur; constellation
MANX pert. to Isle of Man; cat
MARX Karl (economist)
MCIX 1109
MINX pert girl
MLIX 1059
MMIX 2009
MXIX 1019
NOIX edible gland
OBEX brain matter
ODAX rock whiting (fish)
OLAX tree
ONYX cameo stone; quartz; gem
ORYX antelope; gemsbok
PLEX form a network
PNYX Greek voting site
PREX (college) president
PRIX price: Fr.; — fixe (table d'hôte)
ROUX (soup, sauce) thickener; physician
SPEX spectacles
STYX Hades river; nymph: daughter of Oceanus, Tethys
TRIX fem. suffix
ULEX spine shrub (furze)
VAUX village; fort (Verdun battle)
WROX rot
YUNX woodpecker genus

ABBY Abigail
ABEY waive
ABLY deftly
ACHY painful
ADAY atomic attack date
ADDY Adeline
ADRY thirsty

AERY	ethereal; nest
AFFY	join
AHEY	ho
AHOY	call; ship —
AIRY	breezy; light
AKEY	weight
ALAY	marble
ALEY	city
ALGY	Algernon; suffix: pain
ALKY	alcohol
ALLY	unite, confederate
AMOY	island
ANAY	fruit
ANCY	suffix
ANDY	Andrew
ARGY	argue
ARMY	multitude; force
ARRY	cockney worker
ARTY	artistic
ASHY	gray, pale
ATRY	lay to (naut.)
AWAY	onward; hence; far; off; absent
AWNY	bearded
AWRY	distorted; perverse(ly)
BABY	doll; indulge
BEVY	company; flock
BHOY	gang member; rowdy
BLAY	bleak
BODY	structure; anatomy; bulk; corpse; group
BOGY	specter; bugbear
BONY	skeletal; osseous; Napoleon
BOXY	boxlike; squarish
BRAY	(donkey's) cry; grind; Mrs. Nickleby (Dickens)
BREY	barnacle
BUOY	float; sustain; life-; channel marker
BURY	hide; inter; lose
BUSY	(keep) active; in use

BUXY	paymaster
CADY	golf boy
CAGY	shrewd
CAKY	crusty
CASY	ex-preacher (Steinbeck)
CAVY	rodent; guinea pig; stray animal(s)
CAZY	Moslem judge
CHAY	red dye root
CHOY	red dye root
CITY	urban place
CLAY	earth; ceramic; pipe; — pigeon; color; Henry (statesman)
CLOY	glut; surfeit
CODY	William (Buffalo Bill)
COKY	grimed; drug addict
COLY	long-tailed bird
CONY	rabbit; daman; pika
COPY	duplicate; mimic; follow; test
COSY	snug; teapot cover
COTY	Fr. statesman; cosmetics
COZY	snug; teapot cover
CUVY	sea girdles; kelp
DAVY	David; lamp; affidavit; Jones' locker
DAZY	confused
DDAY	operation start
DEFY	challenge; dare
DEMY	coin; scholar; paper size
DENY	refuse; contradict
DEWY	moist; refreshing
DIXY	camp pot
DOBY	brick (house)
DOGY	calf; duck
DOMY	domelike
DOPY	sluggish
DORY	John (fish); boat
DOTY	discolored by rot
DOXY	doctrine; hussy

DOZY	drowsy; decayed; doty
DRAY	cart; squirrel's nest; horse
DREY	squirrel's nest
DUFY	Raoul (Fr. artist)
DULY	properly; timely
DUNY	having many dunes
DUTY	obligation; task; tax
EASY	simple; calm; soft; — Street
EDDY	whirlpool; Mary Morse Baker (Christian Science)
EDGY	sharp; snappish
EELY	wriggling; slippery
EENY	—, meeny, miny, mo
EERY	weird; uncanny; timid
EGGY	egg-stained; yolky
ELMY	rich in elms
EMMY	TV award; nickname
ENVY	covet; grudge; 7th deadly sin
EPPY	Euphemia
ESAY	Isaiah
ESPY	behold; detect; meteorologist
EWRY	linen storeroom
EYEY	having holes
EYRY	bird's nest
FACY	fresh
FADY	weakening
FAKY	spurious
FLAY	(strip off) skin
FLEY	fright(en)
FOGY	dull, bigoted man
FOXY	wily; brown; rank; sour
FRAY	contest; tumult; wear off
FREY	god (Njorth's son, Gerth's husband)
FUMY	vaporous; smoky
FURY	rage; avenging

spirit; Erinys, Fate, Parca (Atropos)
GABY fool
GAPY yawning
GARY city, steel center
GAZY gaping
GOBY fish; passing
GONY albatross
GORY bloody; murderous
GRAY dull; dismal; hoary; Dorian (Wilde); Asa (botanist); Elisha (inventor)
GREY color; neutral; dull; Zane (writer); Vivian (Disraeli novel)
HAZY dim; obscure
HOEY partnership (Hawaii)
HOLY sacred; pious; — City; — Alliance; — Roller
HOMY homey; intimate
HUEY Long (La. governor)
IDLY vainly; lazily
IFFY contingent
ILLY badly; ill
IMPY impish
INDY — pink (carnation)
INKY black; stained
INLY within; heartily
ISMY doctrinaire
JADY gemlike
JAWY talkative
JOEY coin; clown; odd-job man; young kangaroo; Pal (O'Hara character)
JOKY jocular
JOSY nickname
JOZY Josepha; Josephine
JUDY name; Punch and —; Judith; Kipling character
JULY (5th Roman) month
JURY (court) panel; committee; grand, petit —; hung —
KATY Catherine; -did
KAZY Moslem judge
LACY netlike
LADY title; bird
LAKY red
LAZY idle
LELY Dutch painter
LEVY assess; seize; tax
LILY flower; Turk's-cap; pure; white
LIMY viscous
LINY streaky
LIVY Roman historian; Titus Livius
LOGY heavy; dull
LORY parrot; touraco
LOWY banlieue; suburb
LUCY fleur-de-lis; fem. name; camera lucida; Lemonade (Mrs. Hayes); Stone (suffragist)
LUNY crazy (man)
MANY numerous
MARY female name; queen; sister of Lazarus, Martha; Virgin; Lady
MATY (assistant) servant
MAZY perplexing
MINY of a mine
MIRY boggy; filthy
MITY parasite-infested
MIXY confusedly mixed
MOBY — Dick (whale: Melville)
MOLY magic herb (Homer)
MOSY moldy; rotten
NAGY Hungarian premier
NARY not one
NAVY fleet; blue; tobacco; — yard
NIXY undeliverable mail
NIZY fool
NOSY fragrant; prying
NOWY having curvature
OAKY oaklike
OARY oarlike
OATY full of oats
OBEY submit; comply
OHOY ahoy; call
OILY unctuous; bland; suave
OKAY approve; all right
OLAY palm
ONDY wavy (Her.)
ONLY alone; but; single; exclusively
OOFY rich (Eng. slang)
OOZY muddy; slimy
ORBY revolving
ORGY carousal; Saturnalia, Bacchanallia
ORLY Paris airport
PALY wan; heraldic design
PAVY peach
PEAY medicine man
PEVY lumberman's hook
PIAY medicine man
PIKY full of fish
PILY pilelike
PINY pinelike; peony
PIPY tubular; weepy
PITY sympathy; mercy
PIXY impish sprite
PLAY frolic; act; drama; contend; sport; game
PLOY make column; frolic; coup
POGY menhaden; trout
POKY shabby; dull; bonnet
POLY herb; Teucrium; prefix: many
PONY small equine (Shetland,

polo); glass (1 oz.); translation
PORY porous; permeable
POSY flower; nosegay; poem
PRAY ask; beseech; please
PREY victim; pillage; booty
PUKY nauseated
PULY whining; complaining
PUNY weak; slight
PUXY ill-tempered
QUAY pier
RACY smart
RELY trust; depend
RILY turbid; irritated
RIMY frosty; rhyming
ROEY of mottled grain
ROKY misty; hoarse
ROPY viscous; stringy
RORY O'More (Irish novel)
ROSY blushing; optimistic
ROWY streaked
ROXY name: Roxana; Rothafel (impresario); theater
RUAY weight
RUBY gem; corundum; bird; name; Oswald killer
SAGY wise
SARY sorry
SEXY sexually appealing
SHAY chaise; carriage
SIDY pretentious
SIZY viscous
SKEY yoke bar
SLAY kill; overwhelm
SLEY weaver's reed
SORY vitriolic earth
SPAY deer; castrate
SPEY river
SPRY nimble; brisk; smart
STAY rope; fasten; prop, endure; wait; remain; stop(ping); — put
SUKY Susan; teakettle
SUSY name: Susan; Susanna
SUZY name: Susanna
SWAY oscillate; veer; rule
TAKY taking
TAVY Octavia
THEY pronoun; people; men
TIDY (make) neat
TINY small; -tim (herb); Tim (Dickens)
TIVY huntsman's cry
TOBY cigar; mug; dog; rob
TODY green — (bird)
TONY nickname (Anthony); stylish
TORY conservative
TOTY low-caste worker
TOWY like flax fibers
TRAY salver; platter; old dog
TREY three(spot)
TROY weight system; Ilium, Ilion (Troas); city
TUNY melodious
TUPY Amazon Indian
TYPY typical
TYTY farmer of God's Little Acre
UGLY badlooking; unpleasant; plug-
UNDY waving, wavy (Her.)
UPSY -daisy
URDY key-shaped (Her.)
UREY Nobel physicist
VADY vade mecum; summons
VARY alter; differ
VERY true; same; extremely; light signals; flare
VILY fairies
VINY entwining
VLEY marsh; swamp; creek
WADY valley; river; oasis
WAKY alert
WANY diminished
WARY watchful
WAVY fluctuating; undulating
WAXY viscid; pliable
WHEY milk serum; thin; pale; curds and —
WILY artful; subtle
WINY vinous; drunken
WIRY tough; sinewy
YOKY coupled
ZANY clown(ish)

AGAZ Indian
AHAZ king
AMOZ Isaiah's father
BAEZ singer
BATZ coin
BIZZ buzz
BOAZ Ruth's husband
BROZ Josip (Tito)
BUZZ hum; fly low (over); — bomb (V1, V2)
CHEZ at home of, with: Fr.
DAEZ daze
DIAZ Bartholomeu (Port. navigator)
FIZZ hissing sound; drink
FRIZ curl; crisp; wig
FUZZ fine fibers; police
GANZ all, totally: Ger.
GEEZ Version (Ethiopic Bible)
GHUZ Turkish invader
GRAZ Austrian city (Mur)
HARZ Ger. mountains
HAYZ zodiacal situation
HUZZ buzz; murmur
INEZ Don Juan's mother
JAZZ dance; music; banter
JEUZ chief Benjamite
JUEZ judge, juror: Sp.
KNEZ Slavic prince
LINZ Austrian city

LITZ	braided wire	**PHIZ**	physiognomy; face	**RYAZ**	coin
LODZ	Polish city	**QUIZ**	test; odd one; hoax	**SIZZ**	hiss(ing sound)
MAAZ	Judah's descendant	**RANZ**	— des vaches (Alpine melodies)	**SUEZ**	canal; seaport
METZ	city, former fort	**RAZZ**	chaff; ridicule	**SWIZ**	swindle
OYEZ	court crier's cry			**UNTZ**	weight
				WHIZ	hum; bargain; corker
				ZIZZ	whirring sound

SOLVING "CRYTPIC" CROSSWORD PUZZLES

The hidden-clues puzzle originated in England in the early 1920s. The originator was Powys Mathers, whose pseudonym was "Torquemada." The pseudonym became internationally famous; the name Mathers, because he so long concealed his connection with the puzzles, remained little known to crossword-puzzle solvers.

Torquemada's first puzzles had a considerable vogue and spread all over England where, in fact, the cryptic puzzle virtually replaced the conventional crossword puzzle as it is published in American newspapers, magazines, and books today. Unlike American-style crosswords, the English puzzles leave many of the letters unkeyed, and their definitions frequently content themselves with stating the clues, these having no connection with the defined term. Most American cryptic definitions contain both a clue and a straight definition, as described below.

Cryptic puzzles may appear under a variety of names, such as "Puns and Anagrams," "Doubletalk," or simply "cryptic." Any puzzles reprinted from English sources are likely to be cryptic, whether so titled or not. The essential difference between cryptic puzzles and conventional crossword puzzles is that the difficulty in solving lies in the definitions, which must be deciphered, rather than in the obscurity of the answer word. In cryptic puzzles the answers are almost always common words. Since the definition both defines and clues the answer word, the solver can always tell if the answer he has found is the right one.

We will describe here briefly the most frequently used methods of constructing cryptic definitions. Sometimes definitions provide only a clue as to the deciphering of the answer. More often in American and Canadian cryptic puzzles the definition, in addition to containing a clue to finding the answer word, also contains a straight definition of it. Often the definition is divided, one half (roughly) defining the answer, the other containing the answer disguised in some manner or telling how to obtain it. Punctuation and captilization are designed to confuse and should be ignored (exception: See no. 6, below).

1. ANAGRAM. This is the most common type of definition. The answer word is contained in the definition, but its letters are rearranged to form a new word or words. For example,

"A mixed diet is correct." *Ans.:* edit.

("diet" is an anagram for "edit"; mixed tells us that the letters are rearranged. "Correct" is a definition of "edit")

"Mad liar? Must be Yamamoto." *Ans.:* admiral.

("mad liar" is an anagram for "admiral")

Hint: Look for some word, or for some connected combination of words, which has the same number of letters as the word you need. Try rearranging the letters and see if suddenly the whole definition makes sense.

2. CHARADES. The syllables of a word are dealt with sequentially, as in charades. For example:

"It follows Ed is correct." *Ans.:* edit.

("it" follows "ed" = put "it" after "ed": ed-it)

"Exclude Edward—he's been exposed." *Ans.:* bared.

("exclude" = "bar", "Edward" = "Ed": bar-ed)

3. SPLIT WORDS. Syllables are interlocked in a way described in the definition. For example:

"It's correct that ET embraced a princess." *Ans.:* edit.

(the letters "E" and "T" "embrace" princess "Di": "e-di-t")

"A bloke in a bar." *Ans.:* beggar.

("bloke" = "egg," placed in "bar": b-egg-ar)

4. HIDDEN WORDS. The word is spelled out but is hidden among other words. Often this type of definition contains a hint that the word is hidden, through use of the word "hidden," "hiding," concealed," etc. For example:

"To refine is within the grasp of all educat*ed It*alians." *Ans.:* edit.

("within the grasp" suggests a hidden word clue)

"The Nazis marched into Yugoslavi*a, then s*outhward through Greece." *Ans.:* Athens.

5. BACKWARD SPELLINGS. The answer word is found in the definition—or in a word suggested by the definition—but reversed (backward or upside down). The definition always tells the solver in some way that a reversal is involved. For example:

"It's correct that the tide has turned." *Ans.:* edit.
("tide" "turned" around is "edit")
"Take your pay from the right drawer." *Ans.:* reward.
("drawer" read from the right is "reward")

6. PUNS. The sound of words is used, usually suggested in the definition by a word such as "we hear," "orally," etc., or by the presence of an exclamation point (!) or a question mark (?). For example:

"I heard that the score was even! The reverse is correct." *Ans.:* edit.
("score was even" = "tied"; sounds like "tide", which reversed makes "edit")
"I take a whiskey but not straight!" *Ans.:* awry.
("a whisky" is "a rye"; sounds like "awry", a definition of which is "not straight")

7. DOUBLE DEFINITIONS. The simplest kind of definition, in which the second clue is also a definition. Example:

"Amend copyreader's work." *Ans.:* edit.
(both "amend" and "copyreader's work" define "edit")
"Assist your subordinate." *Ans.:* second.
(both "assist" and "subordinate" define "second")

8. PIECES OF WORDS. Clues may indicate part of a word: "head" indicates the first letter; "tail" the last; "heart" the middle. Half of a word may be used, or part of a word may be removed. There are in addition some standard abbreviations: right = R; left = L; love = O; time, temperature, etc. = T; loud = F; soft = P; thousand = G; and Roman numerals are commonly used. Examples:

"Revise edict by cutting the chapter head." *Ans.:* edit.
("chapter head" = "c", which when cut from "edict" leaves "edit")
"Redemption lost import here." *Ans:* Eden.
(take the letters of "import" out of "redemption", what's left is "Eden")

"Initially Em's daughter in Toledo was correct." *Ans.:* edit.

(first letters of "Em's daughter in Toledo": "edit")

"Revise New York's summer time by one." *Ans.:* edit.

(one = I, added to EDT—Eastern Daylight Time, New York's summer time—makes "edit")

"Is it correct that ET was around 501?" *Ans.:* edit.

(501 = "DI" in Roman numerals; surrounded by E and T: edit)

THE NEW AMERICAN CROSSWORD PUZZLE DICTIONARY AND CRYPTIC PUZZLES

While the deceptive nature of the cryptic clue makes use of a dictionary more difficult, the solver will find this book most helpful in the following circumstances:

1. When the definition part of the clue has been determined, the dictionary can be used to find possible answers, which can then be checked by solving the cryptic part of the clue.
2. The Word Locator (Section III of the dictionary) can be very useful in finding problem words of 2, 3, or 4 letters for which some letters have been determined.